# Dictionary of Information Science and Technology

## Volume I
## A–J

Mehdi Khosrow-Pour
*Information Resources Management Association, USA*

**IDEA GROUP REFERENCE**

Hershey · London · Melbourne · Singapore

| | |
|---|---|
| Acquisitions Editor: | Kristin Klinger |
| Development Editor: | Kristin Roth |
| Senior Managing Editor: | Jennifer Neidig |
| Managing Editor: | Sara Reed |
| Copy Editor: | Maria Boyer |
| Typesetter: | Diane Huskinson |
| Cover Design: | Lisa Tosheff |
| Printed at: | Yurchak Printing Inc. |

Published in the United States of America by
Idea Group Reference (an imprint of Idea Group Inc.)
701 E. Chocolate Avenue, Suite 200
Hershey PA 17033
Tel: 717-533-8845
Fax: 717-533-8661
E-mail: cust@idea-group.com
Web site: http://www.idea-group-ref.com

and in the United Kingdom by
Idea Group Reference (an imprint of Idea Group Inc.)
3 Henrietta Street
Covent Garden
London WC2E 8LU
Tel: 44 20 7240 0856
Fax: 44 20 7379 0609
Web site: http://www.eurospanonline.com

Library of Congress Cataloging-in-Publication Data

Dictionary of information science and technology / Mehdi Khosrow-Pour, editor.
        p. cm.
  Summary: "This book is the premier comprehensive reference source for the latest terms, acronyms and definitions related to all aspects of information science and technology. It provides the most current information to researchers on every level"--Provided by publisher.
  Includes bibliographical references and index.
  ISBN 1-59904-385-8 (hardcover) -- ISBN 1-59904-386-6 (ebook)
  1. Information science--Dictionaries. 2. Information technology--Dictionaries. I. Khosrowpour, Mehdi, 1951-
  T58.5.D499 2006
  020.03--dc22
                                          2006030015

British Cataloguing in Publication Data
A Cataloguing in Publication record for this book is available from the British Library.

All work contributed to this handbook is new, previously-unpublished material. The views expressed in this handbook are those of the authors, but not necessarily of the publisher.

495—
2 vol
set

# Contents

## Volume I

## Volume II

# Preface

During the past few decades, considerable advancements of computer technologies, combined with innovations achieved in telecommunication technologies, have served as fuel for the formation of a new discipline, known today as information science and technology (IST). Since its inception, IST has grown to encompass many other specific areas within the field itself, allowing the IST domain of studies to expand exponentially. Moreover, the primary focus of IST as a discipline is broadening the science of information processing, management, and dissemination. This newly developed scientific paradigm is comprised of many resources and components, including: (1) type of information; (2) computer hardware technologies; (3) computer software technologies; (4) telecommunication technologies; (5) technology applications; (6) information processing systems structures; (7) systems personnel and management; (8) end users; and (9) management skills and programs (Khosrow-Pour & Yaverbaum, 1990). In recent years, the IST revolution has globally impacted all aspects of life at the individual, organizational, and societal level. In many ways, IST has been the principal driving force behind the second industrial revolution, known as the digital revolution.

The expansion of IST as a science, like other scientific fields, such as medicine, has created a new language filled with terminologies, key words, and acronyms unique to IST and its specific disciplines. Furthermore, the sheer volume of ongoing discoveries of new technologies and applications, as well as transpiring research findings, continue to expand the list of terminology associated with the field of IST. Because of these incessant advancements, it is nearly impossible to maintain an understanding of the jargon related to IST and its peripheral domains of study without comprehending its emerging technological vernacular.

To provide the most comprehensive coverage of IST language, the idea of a new *Dictionary of Information Science and Technology* was formed to provide the most in-depth and complete introduction to all terms, acronyms, and definitions related to some of most commonly studied areas of IST, such as accounting information systems; database management and technologies; data warehousing and mining; decision support systems technologies; distance education technologies; e-collaboration; electronic commerce technologies management; end user computing; enterprise resource planning, expert systems; geographical information systems; global IT management; human computer interaction; human side of IT; information resources management; information security management; information systems research; information technology education; IT evaluation methods and management; IT management in libraries; IT management in health care; IT in small business; IT personnel; professional IT association; intelligent information systems; knowledge management; minorities in information technology; mobile computing and commerce; multimedia information management; objected oriented technologies; open source technologies and systems; social responsibility in the information age; software engineering; strategic IT management; telecommunications and networking technologies; unified modeling languages and unified process; and virtual communities and IT.

Perhaps the most challenging task related to the compilation of a dictionary for such a young field of science, is the fact that there is no single or standard definition in existence for each element of the vocabulary. Instead, individual researchers have formed distinctive descriptions of the terminology, providing a much more meaningful and broader understanding of each term. To achieve this goal, all attempts were made to supply the user of this dictionary with the most inclusive definition used to describe every term, and not just a singular definition designated by the editor. An exhibition of numerous language contributions from different researchers have been listed for each of the terms, allowing the user to be exposed to different angles of each definition in hopes that the user will form a much broader understanding of the vocabulary that is specific to IST.

This dictionary is divided into two sections. The first section lists all terms and acronyms in alphabetical order. Each term may consist of multiple definitions, numbered in sequential order, and ends with the source/reference from which the definition was derived. The second section includes the complete reference information, also organized in alphabetical order and formatted to comply with American Psychological Association (APA) recommended style guidelines. Although one might notice a wide range of definitions for various terms, it is our opinion that it is much more helpful to provide an expansive list of definitions rather than limit the meaning to a singular description. Furthermore, to defuse any inaccuracy in the definitions obtained from different sources, it was decided to provide the most complete meaning as possible, allowing for any confusion that may result from the descriptions to be dealt with in light of other explanations.

The two-volume *Dictionary of Information Science and Technology* is the premier comprehensive resource composed of the latest terms and definitions related to all aspects of the information science and technology field. This complete and timely reference collection of over 13,000 definitions for more than 11,000 terms and acronyms will provide researchers, practitioners, educators and students with the most accurate and current knowledge available of prevalent key words in the ever-expanding world of IST. Terms and definitions included in this important reference publication were contributed by over 2,500 noted researchers from over 40 countries. The *Dictionary of Information Science and Technology* will prove to be a valuable and essential reference publication for libraries and individuals worldwide.

To make sure that the *Dictionary of Information Science and Technology* and its coverage stays up-to-date, access to the dictionary's online database, which provides complete search capabilities, will be offered to all libraries at a discount of 50% off the subscription price upon purchase of the print copy. This database will be updated on a regular basis with new terms, acronyms, and their definitions, and will provide coverage of all new and emerging terminologies and their definitions as they materialize.

The comprehensive coverage of thousands of terms and acronyms provided in this two-volume resource will contribute to a better understanding of the technical and managerial language available and its applications for the field of information science and technology. Furthermore, the definitions included in this dictionary will be instrumental in the body of knowledge expanding in this vast field. The coverage of this two-volume dictionary provides strength to this source of reference for both information science and technology researchers in obtaining a greater comprehension of the language of IST. It is my sincere hope that this reference publication and its immeasurable amount of valuable information will assist my research colleagues, all faculty, their students, and practitioners in enhancing their understanding of this discipline. Perhaps this publication will even inspire additional breakthroughs in this gigantic field and elevate it to a much higher level within the world of scientific discoveries.

*Mehdi Khosrow-Pour, D.B.A.*
*Information Resources Management Association, USA*

## Reference

Khosrow-Pour, M., & Yaverbaum, G.J. (1990). *Information technology resources utilization and management: Issues and trends*. Hershey, PA: Idea Group Publishing.

# Acknowledgments

Putting together a comprehensive publication of this magnitude requires tremendous involvement and assistance from many individuals. The most important goal of editing this dictionary was to compile a comprehensive list of terms, acronyms and their definitions in the field of information science and technology. This goal could not have been achieved without the valuable contributions of more than 2,500 researchers in the field of IST, and I am very thankful for their contributions to this publication.

In terms of editorial assistance, I would like to convey my deep appreciation and gratitude to my editorial staff at Idea Group Reference (IGR), including Ms. Michelle Potter, former acquisitions and development editor, for her immeasurable assistance during the development process for this publication. I would also like to express my many thanks to Ms. Kristin Roth, development editor, Ms. Lynley Lapp, former assistant development editor, Ms. Kristin Klinger, acquisitions editor, Ms. Lauren Kenes, former editorial assistant, Ms. Sara Reed, managing editor, Ms. Jennifer Neidig, senior managing editor, Ms. Diane Huskinson, assistant managing editor, Ms. Lisa Tosheff, graphic artist, and Ms. Maria Boyer, copy editor for their involvement and assistance with this publication. My warmest thanks also go to my wife, Beth Peiffer, for her support, wisdom, encouragement, understanding, patience, and love. My heart also goes to my two young girls, Basha and Anar, for the joys that they have brought to my life. Finally, much gratitude goes to all those who have taught me immeasurable amounts during the past three decades.

*Mehdi Khosrow-Pour, D.B.A.*
*Information Resources Management Association, USA*

# About the Editor

**Mehdi Khosrow-Pour**, DBA is currently the executive director of the Information Resources Management Association (IRMA), USA, and senior academic editor for Idea Group Reference. Previously, he served on the faculty of the Pennsylvania State University as an associate professor of information systems for 20 years. He has written or edited over 30 books in information technology management, and he is also the editor of the *Information Resources Management Journal*, *Journal of Electronic Commerce in Organizations*, *Journal of Cases on Information Technology*, and *International Journal of Cases on Electronic Commerce*.

# A

**Aad:** See *Attitude Toward the Ad.*

**AAR:** See *After-Action Review.*

## Abduction
**1:** Abduction is the process by which a new concept is formed on the basis of an existing concept that is perceived as having something in common with it. Therefore abduction focuses on associations. (Nobre, 2006a) **2:** The explanatory process of inferring certain facts and/or hypotheses that explain or discover some phenomenon or observation. (Magnani & Bardone, 2006)

## Abductive Mode
This mode permits programs to explore "how did this happen?" or provides for diagnostic programming features. (Murthy & Krishnamurthy, 2005c)

## Ability Grouping
The practice of forming learning groups of students of similar abilities, for example, putting students who read on a third-grade level with other students who read on a third-grade level. (Trammell, 2005)

## Abort
Cancels all modifications of a transaction. (Meixner, 2005)

**ABS:** See *Australian Bureau of Statistics.*

## Absolute Difference
A measure that represents the difference between an association and a conditional association based on a given measure. The condition provides a plausible explanation. (Yao & Zhao, 2005)

## Absorptive Capacity
**1:** An organization's ability to absorb new knowledge; often based on the prior experience and knowledge base of its employees. The greater the absorptive capacity of an organization, the greater its ability to learn and adapt to changing market forces. (Jones & Gupta, 2005) **2:** Reflects the receiving employee's ability to absorb the knowledge sent by the giving employee. (Chen, Duan, et al., 2006) **3:** The ability of a firm to recognize the value of new, external information; assimilate it; and apply it to commercial ends. (Priestley, 2006; Yaniv & Schwartz, 2006; Lertwongsatien & Wongpinunwatana, 2005)

## Abstract Dimension
Describes the soft issues of a relationship. (Leonard, 2005)

## Abstract Windows Toolkit (AWT)
Library of classes for writing window interfaces. (Lucas, 2005)

## Abstraction Levels
A model is an abstraction, and as such it may represent an aspect of reality with some level of detail. Different models can represent the same aspect, each with a different abstraction level. The abstraction level is directly related to the amount of detail represented in the model. (Tobar et al., 2006)

## Academic Accountability
The emphasis from society, government, and academia that education should lead to beneficial outcomes and learning that can be measured. (Lindsay, Williams, et al., 2005)

## Academic Administration
Administration procedures or formalities linked with university education, such as registrations for semesters or examinations, progress reviews and monitoring, eligibility formalities, student history records or progress archiving, promotions to levels or years, academic timetables, and so forth. (Fernando, 2005)

### Acceptable Use Policy (AUP)

**1:** A policy created in an organization to outline the permitted and restricted uses of the company's networks and computer systems. (Urbaczewski, 2005) **2:** A written policy document that defines what activities are appropriate and inappropriate for a user of a particular resource. A document indicating the understanding and acceptance of an AUP is often required to be formally signed by a user before he or she gains access to the resource. (Knight & Labruyere, 2005)

### Access

**1:** One of the three preconditions for citizen participation in e-democracy (access–competence–motivation). Access to communication involves existence of technical and logical access point, communications device, and permission to access. (Keskinen & Kuosa, 2005) **2:** Citizens have access to the technology they need. Access is both physical (ICT is located at a physically appropriate place, such as in the home, community center, library, or school) and economic (it is affordable). (Williamson, 2005) **3:** Refers to the ability to get into, and use, an online system. Access to the Internet through commercial online services requires an account, an access telephone number, a password, and special software designed for that service. (Magagula, 2005) **4:** The ability to find or to exchange information via online media. (St.Amant, 2005d) **5:** The ability to physically or electronically obtain data or information. (Buche & Vician, 2005) **6:** The ability, the opportunity, or the right to enter or use technology and all that it has to offer in today's society. (Reilly, 2005) **7:** The quality principle that is the fundamental motivation for online learning, access means that people who are qualified and motivated can obtain affordable, quality education in the discipline of choice. (Moore, Bourne, et al., 2005)

### Access Board Standards

Technical and functional performance criteria developed by the Architectural and Transformation Barriers Compliance Board (the "Access Board"), a U.S. government agency, under Section 508. Only electronic and information technology conforming to these standards is considered accessible. (Schmetzke, 2005)

### Access Control

**1:** Methods used to determine if requests to use a system, network, application, or resource should be granted or denied. (Knight & Labruyere, 2005) **2:** Restriction of access to some resource through the application of a mechanism which grants, denies, or revokes permissions. (Mundy & Otenko, 2005) **3:** Software control of the use of a computer. (N.C. Rowe, 2006c)

### Access Control List (ACL)

A list of people or other entities permitted to access a computer resource. (Mattord & Whitman, 2005)

### Access History

Navigation path taken by a user as he/she surfs a Wireless Application Protocol (WAP). (Quah & Seet, 2006)

### Access Latency

The delay time when a data item or object is accessed. (Tse, 2006)

### Access Link

Web page address used for navigation purposes. (Quah & Seet, 2006)

### Access Method

**1:** A data structure that enables fast access over the records of a database file. Careful tuning or selection of the appropriate access method is very important in database performance. (Tzouramanis, 2005) **2:** In the database domain, indexes are designed to access data that are stored in a specific structure. The type of data and the type of the structure used determine the procedures followed by the index to access these data, which is referred to as the access method. (Gaffar, 2005) **3:** A technique of organizing data that allows the efficient retrieval of data according to a set of search criteria. R-trees and Quadtrees are two well-known families of such techniques. (Vassilakopoulos & Corral, 2005)

**Access Network:** See *Local Network.*

### Access Point (AP)

**1:** A device that "connects" wireless communication devices to create a wireless network. A wireless access point acts as the network's arbitrator, negotiating when each nearby client device can transmit. Many access points can be connected together to create a larger network that allows "roaming," where a person using the network can infrastructure a network. In contrast, a network where the client devices manage themselves is called an ad-hoc network. (Kao & Rerrer, 2006) **2:** Equivalent to a cellular base station, this Wi-Fi component provides Wi-Fi stations with access to each other and to the Internet. (Efstathiou &

Polyzos, 2006) **3:** Typically, infrastructure-based wireless networks provide access to the wired backbone network via an AP. The AP may act as a repeater, bridge, router, or even as a gateway to regenerate, forward, filter, or translate messages. All communication between mobile devices has to take place via the AP. (Sarkar, 2005)

## Access Point Device

The device that bridges wireless networking components and a wired network. It forwards traffic from the wired side to the wireless side and from the wireless side to the wired side, as needed. (Lawson-Body, 2005)

## Access Rights Management

The process of assigning digital rights to users which can then be used in conjunction with an access control system to obtain access to some resource. The management infrastructure covers for example the allocation, renewal, and revocation of users' rights. (Mundy & Otenko, 2005)

## Access Table

A table listing the transactions to be implemented with an application. For each transaction, it shows the classes from the Class Diagram it needs to visit, including the number and types of accesses (Read, Write) in order to collect the data necessary for composing the final result. (Polese et al. 2005)

## Accessibility

**1:** A characteristic of information technology that allows it to be used by people with different abilities. In more general terms, accessibility refers to the ability of people with disabilities to access public and private spaces. (Keates et al., 2006) **2:** An individual's perception that he/she can contact or reach his/her leader when so desired. (Connaughton, 2005) **3:** Accessibility is achieved when individuals with disabilities can access and use information technology in ways comparable to those available to people without disabilities. A narrower, operational definition conceptualizes accessibility in terms of conformance to certain accessibility criteria. (Schmetzke, 2005) **4:** Just as computers vary by operating system, processor speed, screen size, memory, and networking abilities, users vary in ways both expected and unexpected. Some differences more commonly thought of are language, gender, age, cultures, preferences, and interests. However, some of the differences that need to be paid more attention to by the software and Web development community are skills, ability levels, and constraints under which users may be

operating. Designing for diversity not only increases the number of people able to access software or a Web site, but also increases their level of involvement with it. (Singh, 2005b) **5:** Problems encountered by Internet users with perceptual and cognitive challenges, physical conditions, or other factors such as geographical location; sociocultural, political, and economic issues; language; and so forth, which influence their use of the Web. (Campbell, 2005) **6:** The ability to easily navigate and move about in the environment. Usually thought of in terms of the architecture of buildings, but since the recent advent of the Web Accessibility Initiative (WAI), has been expanded to include the architecture of the World Wide Web and all electronic and information technology. (Proctor, 2005) **7:** The measure of whether a person can perform an interaction, access information, or do anything else. It does not measure how well he or she can do it, though. (Polovina & Pearson, 2006) **8:** The relative ease by which the locations of activities, such as work, school, shopping, and health care, can be reached from a given location. (Wang & Lou, 2005) **9:** The sum of the space and time between an individual and an activity. (Kenyon, 2005)

## Accessibility Data Quality

An aspect of data quality that refers to the ease with which one can get to data. (Borchers, 2005)

## Accessibility Legal Issues

Many governments around the globe issued laws and regulations demanding accessibility for public organizations' sites, usually starting from W3C WAI technical recommendations. (Costagliola, Di Martino, Ferrucci, & Gravino, 2006)

## Accessibility Toolkit

Refers to software tools and resources, provided by operating system manufacturers, that help in the developing accessibility software (e.g., screen readers). (Lahiri & Basu, 2005)

## Accessible

Describes a product, information, or environment that is fully usable by a person, with or without assistive technology. (Burgstahler, 2005b)

## Accessible Technology

Products, devices, or equipment that can be used, with or without assistive technology, by individuals with disabilities. (Keates et al., 2006)

**A**

## Accessible Web Design

Also sometimes referred to as "barrier-free Web design." Web design that strives to accommodate the needs of people with disabilities, including those using assistive technology, to access the Web environment. (Schmetzke, 2005)

## Accommodation

**1:** A mental process individuals use to create new schemata or to modify old schemata as the result of interaction with new environmental stimulus. Both of these actions result in cognitive development. (Gillani, 2005a) **2:** Modification or adjustment to a task or an environment that allows a person with a disability an equal opportunity to complete a task or to access an environment. Not all persons with disabilities, or kinds of disability, require accommodations. Environmental accommodations include, but are not limited to, ramps, curb cuts, handicapped-accessible bathrooms, accessible computer stations, touch screens, and light switches. Education accommodations include, but are not limited to, tape recorders, screen readers, oral tests, extra time to complete related course work, materials printed in Braille, and note takers and interpreters provided to students with disabilities. (Proctor, 2005; Burgstahler, 2005a) **3:** Provisions made in how a student accesses and/or demonstrates learning. The term focuses on changes in the instruction, or how students are expected to learn, along with changes in methods of assessment that demonstrate or document what has been learned. The use of an accommodation does not change the educational goals, standards, or objectives, the instructional level, or the content, and provides the student with equal access and equal opportunity to demonstrate his or her skills and knowledge. (T. Cavanaugh, 2005)

## Accommodation Management Systems

Integrated software (desktop, network, or Web-based) to assist a variety of functions for accommodation establishments. This may include reservations, room maintenance, banquet booking, finance, and customer relationship management. (Carson, 2005)

## Accountability

**1:** A responsibility to account for and/or explain actions undertaken; obligation of government, public services, or funding agencies in compliance with agreed rules and standards. (Park, 2006) **2:** Accountability of parties means holding to account, scrutinizing, and being required to give an account; especially in white-collar crime, accountability is often associated with governance. (Mitrakas, 2006) **3:** Being called to account or held responsible for discharging higher education mission and goals, generally understood in terms of higher education's responsibility to ensure student learning at a reasonable cost. (Keinath, 2005) **4:** Responsibility of member behavior for their actions among the community. Such notion is strictly related to identity management in a virtual community. (Bertino et al., 2006) **5:** Transparency of responsibility for performance, the management of performance, and resulting implications for the deployment of future resources. (Wright & Taylor, 2005)

## Accountable Identification

A way to identify a person in an electronic interaction and to give legal status to electronic documents. Different technologies have been tried out, for example, chip cards and digital signatures. (Jaeger, 2005)

## Accounting Performance Measures

Evaluation of the impact of information systems investments including typical accounting rations such as return on assets and return on equity. (Dykman, 2005)

## Accreditation

**1:** An external quality-review process used by higher education to evaluate colleges, universities, and educational programs or courses to ensure and improve quality. (Kung-Ming, 2005) **2:** Endorsement of quality performance by an outside agency. (C. Cavanaugh, 2005) **3:** Recognition by a certifying organization or agency that a college meets certain acceptable standards in its education programs, services, and facilities. Regional accreditation applies to a college as a whole and not to any particular program or course of study. (Riffee & Sessums, 2005) **4:** The primary means by which colleges and universities and other higher learning programs assure academic quality to students and to the public. (Garten & Thompson, 2005) **5:** The process of certifying whether a program meets the standards and expectations of any association to which it belongs. (Howell & Wilcken, 2005) **6:** The seal of approval granted by an accrediting agency to an academic institution indicating that certain quality standards are met. (Kostopoulos, 2005)

## Accreditation Mills

Associations that claim to extend academic accreditation, while they themselves do not have any officials or otherwise recognized capacity. (Kostopoulos, 2005)

## Accrediting Agency

An organization that grants seals of approval to academic institutions for having met a certain level of quality standards. Normally authorized by a cognizant government entity. (Kostopoulos, 2005)

## Accrediting Commissions

In the United States there are both regional and professional accreditation systems that serve as the gatekeepers for quality in higher education. The six geographic regions of the U.S. each have their own commissions (some have two) that are made up of individuals from the member institutions served by the region. These regional accrediting commissions also serve a role in determining institutional eligibility to administer federal financial aid for students. (S.M. Johnstone, 2005)

## Accrual

The concept that all revenues and costs that are accrued and matched within the same economic year. (Tahinakis et al., 2006)

## Acculturation

The process by which a person adopts and assimilates characteristics of another culture into one's own culture. (Petter et al., 2005)

## Accuracy

**1:** The agreement between the real measurement and some objective standard taken as the "ground truth." In a given measurement experimentation, the high accuracy could be achieved using correct sample design and measurement methods. An accurate measurement is also called an unbiased measurement. (Y.-J. Zhang, 2005c) **2:** The measure of how well a pattern can generalize. In classification it is usually defined as the percentage of examples that are correctly classified. (Zhou, 2005)

**ACF:** See *Amplitude Change Function.*

## ACID Properties

**1:** Properties of transactions: atomicity, an operation is either completely performed or not at all; consistency, an operation transfers the database from one consistent state to another consistent state; isolation, intermediate states of a transaction are not visible to the outside; durability, changes made to a database are persistent. (Meixner, 2005) **2:** The properties imply that a transaction is atomic, transforms the database from one consistent state to another consistent state, is executed as if it were isolated from other concurrent transactions, and is durable after it has been committed. (Frank, 2005b) **3:** Conventional online transaction processing (OLTP) requires the following properties called "ACID properties": Atomicity (A): All changes are totally done (committed) or totally undone (rolled back); Consistency (C): The effect of a transaction preserves the invariant properties of the system; Isolation (I): Intermediate results are not visible to other transactions. Transactions have the effect of executing serially, although they act concurrently; Durability (D): The effects of a transaction are persistent; changes are not lost except under catastrophic failure. (Murthy & Krishnamurthy, 2005c)

**ACL:** See *Access Control List.*

## ACML

The XML encoding of the Agent Communication Language defined by the Foundation for Intelligent Physical Agent (FIPA). (De Meo, Quattrone, et al., 2005)

## Acoustic Metadata

Metadata obtained from an analysis of the audio signal. (Pachet, 2006)

## Acquisition-of-Expertise Hypothesis

States that people will perform better in dynamic tasks, if they acquire the requisite expertise. (Qudrat-Ullah, 2006)

**ACS:** See *American Community Survey.*

## Actants

A general term used to refer to both human and non-human artifacts that can be acted on or move the action onto some other. Actants are heterogeneous entities that form a network. (Wenn, 2006b)

## Action

**1:** A sequence of goal-directed steps or operations. (Daneshgar, 2005; Ale & Espil, 2005) **2:** Part of a trigger that is executed when the condition in the trigger is evaluated and found true. This is the most open-ended part of a trigger, because different database vendors have allowed different functionality in their implementations. At a minimum, data manipulation operations (e.g., insert, delete, update) are allowed. (Badia, 2005b)

## Action Learning

**1:** A collaborative but challenging group process of cyclic inquiry that facilitates insight in an individual group

member facing an important real-life problem such that (s)he may take reasoned action to resolve her/his problem, and the individual and other group members learn through the overall process. (Smith, 2006a) **2:** A practical and structured process focused on real organizational problems and the development of a case study describing the problem, including team-based research within an online environment. Action learning includes a continuous renewal process of reflective observation, abstract conceptualization, active experimentation, and concrete experience. (Baskin et al., 2005)

## Action or Capacity Learning

In verb form, gaining capacity for effective action; in noun form, capacity for effective action. (Lick & Kaufman, 2005)

## Action Plan

A portfolio of complementary activities which aim to have an effective and the desired effect on the organization when implemented. (Shaw, Baker, et al., 2006)

## Action Research (AR)

**1:** A research approach operationalized by constant cycles of planning, acting, observing, and reflecting, which encourages the participation of local subjects as active agents in the research process, and which works hand in hand with people-centered research methodologies. (Foth, 2005) **2:** Action research, labeled as such, has its origins in British social science research at the end of World War II. There are many types and manifestations of action research, each having in common the goal of researchers engaged in social problem solving. In essence, action research is a value-driven mode of research. Types of action research that are particularly relevant for Internet research and communication practice are educational action research, technical action research, and hermeneutic action research. Educational action research consists of applied learning in a social context, with a focus on solving community problems. Technical action research involves particular persons who, because of greater experience and qualifications (for example, in Web design and multimedia), may be regarded by collaborators as technical experts. In this case, technical knowledge is put to the service of solving a community problem that hinges on communication and public visibility. Hermeneutic action research involves mutual analysis and collaborative documentary research conducted between partners, designed to draw out greater self-understanding

and facilitate the articulation of self-definitions for a wider audience. In each case, action research involves the identification of a "problem," an understanding of for whom the research is being conducted, and a notion of some "disadvantage" that is to be addressed or solved through research. (Forte, 2005) **3:** Research that is designed not simply to establish the facts about a situation, but which is designed to facilitate the goals of the organization being researched. (David, 2005) **4:** Type of research approach in which the researcher attempts to improve the research client, which can be an organization, while at the same time generating relevant academic knowledge. (Kock, 2005) **5:** An action-oriented methodology or intervention process that is collaborative in nature. It aims to work with stakeholders. (Braun, 2005a)

## Action Theory

Perspective on action facilitation that makes a distinction between acts, actions, and operations in performing a task. A basic principle of the theory is that the tools used should provide sufficient feedback to allow for adaptation of task execution. (Verburg et al., 2005)

## Action-Mediating Web

Services and actions are enabled by the Web including learning actions. This complements the traditional idea of the Semantic Web as knowledge representation structure. (Liu & Koppelaar, 2005)

## Action-Oriented Formal Specification Language

Time can be considered in the specification. There are several ways of doing this: considering time as linear or branching, synchronous, asynchronous, and so forth. (Dasso & Funes, 2005)

## Actionability

Actionability of a pattern indicates its usefulness. Essentially, a pattern is actionable if a user can act on it to his or her advantage. Though it has a great practical orientation, actionability is difficult to operationalize due to the inherent difficulty in mapping patterns to useful actions. (Natarajan & Shekar, 2006)

## Actionable Information

Information that can be used as the basis for a decision, or for taking action, usually to change something. (Holstein & Crnkovic, 2005)

## Actionable Rule

A rule is actionable if the user can do an action to his/her advantage based on this rule. (Ras, Tzacheva, et al., 2005)

## Actionscript

A full object-oriented scripting language developed by Macromedia to work within the Flash™ environment that allows developers to add more complex interactivity to their movies. It is capable of handling the complex mathematical formulations normally associated with more conventional programming languages. (Burrage & Pelton, 2005)

## Activation-Emotion Space

A 2D representation of the emotion space, with the two axes representing the magnitude and the hue of a specific emotion. (Karpouzis et al., 2005)

## Activation Function

Transforms the net input of a neural network into an output signal, which is transmitted to other neurons. (Yeo, 2005)

## Active Audience

Uses and gratifications theory presumes media users are actively involved in selection and use of media, and are not passive recipients. This implies the need to specifically target media offerings to perceived user needs. (Stafford, 2005)

## Active Database

A database with the capability for reacting to stimula. (Ale & Espil, 2005)

## Active Design

Also called agent environment co-design. The main idea is to split the work of building the intelligence into a load belonging to the agents and a load belonging to the environment. (Liu & Koppelaar, 2005)

## Active Disk

A disk whose controller runs application code, which can process data on disk. (Thomasian, 2005a)

## Active Integrity Constraint

A formula of the first order predicate calculus of the form: $r = (X) [\Phi \supset \psi]$ where $\Phi$ is a range restricted conjunction of literals, and $\psi$ is a disjunction of update atoms. (Flesca, Greco, & Zumpano, 2005b)

## Active Interface

An interface that monitors and tracks its interaction with the user. (Soh, 2006)

## Active Learning

**1:** A key concept within the constructivist perspective on learning that perceives learners as mentally active in seeking to make meaning. (Torrisi-Steele, 2005) **2:** A learning philosophy derived from the theories of Piaget, Bruner, Vygotsky, and so forth, emphasizing that improved learning occurs with learner-centered activities requiring more mental processing on the part of the learner. In active learning, lectures often are replaced with a variety of learning resources that move students from a passive, note-taking role to an active, learning role. (Twigg, 2005) **3:** As a group, earners read, write, discuss, or are otherwise engaged in solving problems. Students engage in such higher-order thinking tasks as analysis, synthesis, and evaluation. (Jennings et al., 2005) **4:** Detecting and asking the user to label only the most informative examples in the domain (rather than randomly chosen examples). (Muslea, 2005) **5:** A form of learning that directly engages the student in his or her learning process. It can be contrasted with passive learning, whereby the student is passively taking in information, for example, from a lecture. (Sala, 2005b) **6:** Learning by playing or solving problems, instead of just memorizing. This way, students have ample opportunities to clarify, question, apply, and consolidate new knowledge. There are a number of teaching strategies that can be employed to actively engage students in the learning process, including group discussions, problem solving, case studies, role plays, journal writing, and structured learning groups. Information and communication technology makes the use of such strategies easy. (Pedreira et al., 2005) **7:** Learning modules that support active learning select the best examples for class labeling and training without depending on a teacher's decision or random sampling. (H.-J. Kim, 2005) **8:** Learning where students perform tasks, that is, post notes on a discussion board, to help in the learning process. (Benrud, 2005) **9:** The three-pronged process of selecting, organizing, and integrating information. The basic idea is that when active learning is optimized, then meaningful outcomes can be more effectively reached. (M. Mitchell, 2005c)

## Active Learning Techniques

Techniques where students do more than simply listen to a lecture. Students are doing something, including discovering, processing, and applying information. Active learning derives from two basic assumptions: (1) learning is by nature an active endeavor, and (2) different people learn in different ways. (Beck & Schornack, 2005)

## Active Mechanism

A system responsible for detecting events and reacting automatically to such events according to predefined active rules or ECA rules. Traditionally, active mechanisms are embedded within Active Database Management Systems (ADBMSs). Unbundled active mechanisms have been proposed for federated database systems and for component database systems. (Vargas-Solar, 2005)

## Active Modality

Modality voluntarily and consciously used by users to issue a command to the computer; for example, a voice command or a pen gesture. (Bourguet, 2006)

## Active Participation

Citizens are actively engaged in the policy-making process. The government acknowledges citizens as partners; citizens participate proposing policy options and shaping the policy dialogue. (Kaufman, 2005)

## Active/Passive Community Participants

Active participants regularly contribute to the community in a variety of ways (e.g., posting messages, acting as moderators, responding to queries). Passive participants, by contrast, only read material within the community and rarely make a contribution (similar to "lurkers"). (Waterson, 2006)

## Active Processing Assumption

Asserts that intentional and significant mental processing of information must occur for enduring and meaningful learning to take place. (Boechler, 2006b)

## Active Replica

The replica that directly processes a given transaction, generating the updates that later will be transmitted to the other, passive replicas. The active status of a replica functionally depends on the given transaction. (Muñoz-Escoí et al., 2005)

## Active RFID Tags

Tags containing their own power source (batteries). (Loebbecke, 2006)

## Active Rule

This is represented by an ECA structure, meaning when an event is produced, if the condition is verified, execute an action. The event part represents a situation that triggers the rule, the condition part represents the state of a system execution or of a database, and the action part denotes a set of operations or a program. (Vargas-Solar, 2005)

## Active Server Page (ASP) Scripting

A simple server-side scripting approach where script code (usually VBScript or Jscript) is mixed with HTML code on a Web page. The script code is processed by a script engine before the page is rendered by the server. This can be used to create dynamic Web pages and to share data within or between Web sessions. This is a predecessor of ASP.NET technology. (Westin, 2005)

## Active Tag

An active tag is powered by its own battery, and it can transmit its ID and related information continuously. (Owens et al., 2005)

## ActiveX Control

A Microsoft™ software module that enables another program to add functionality by calling ready-made components that blend in and appear as normal parts of the program. (Friedman, 2005)

## Activities

Single tasks or chains of tasks that form business processes and allow a firm to differentiate itself in the marketplace. (Hanebeck, 2005)

## Activities-Based Costing

A costing method that assesses a given activity in terms of component costs for all persons and resources involved in the activity; the alternative is parsing costs of an activity by looking at aggregate cost data for only those key institutions or units directly responsible for that activity. (Fisher, 2005)

## Activity

**1:** A logically connected set of actions that are carried out as a unit in some order. It is associated with a state (called action state) in which the system remains while the activity is performed. (Rittgen, 2005) **2:** Sometimes used as shorthand to refer to opportunities, services, social networks, and other goods, as well as to people, communities, and other locations. (Kenyon, 2005)

## Activity Diagram

A UML diagram showing operations and triggers between operations; a diagram which shows system dynamics via cause and effect relationships. An activity diagram is a state diagram in which most of the states are action states, and most of the transitions are triggered by the completion of these action states. (D. Brandon, Jr., 2005a)

## Activity Level

A measure of the number of participant-initiated actions that take place during a time interval. (Kushnir, 2006)

## Activity List

A prose description of a task or subtask divided into lines to represent separate task behaviors; it usually has only one main agent and one action per line. (Diaper, 2006)

## Activity Logging

Electronic recordkeeping of such system or network actions as applications accessed, commands executed, files accessed, and traffic generated from a system. (Knight & Labruyere, 2005)

## Activity Recorder

Software that monitors important user activities within the virtual environment and records this information into a database for later perusal. (Lepouras & Vassilakis, 2006)

## Actor

**1:** A person or (computer) system that can perform an activity. The actor does not refer to a particular individual but rather to a role (e.g., teacher). (Rittgen, 2005) **2:** An actor plays one or more roles in relation to a set of use cases. An actor could correspond to a job title (e.g., purchasing agent, sales clerk) or can be non-human (e.g., another system or database). Each actor in a use case must be directly involved at some point and is not merely a stakeholder (someone or something that is affected by the success or failure of a particular transaction). (Dobing & Parsons, 2005) **3:** An entity that can make its presence individually felt by other actors. Actors can be human or non-human, non-human actors including such things as computer programs, portals, companies, and other entities that cannot be seen as individual people. An actor can be seen as an association of heterogeneous elements that constitute a network. This is especially important with non-human actors, as there are always some human aspects within the network. (Tatnall, 2005a) **4:** Someone that initiates an action by signaling an event. An actor is outside a system and can be either another system or a human being. (Hvannberg et al., 2006)

## Actor-Network Theory (ANT)

An approach to research in which network associations and interactions between actors (both human and non-human) are the basis for investigation. (Tatnall, 2005a)

## Actual Level of Awareness

The awareness that a role actually possesses within the ERP process. Actual awareness is represented by an integer number ranging from zero to four, representing various levels of awareness. Actual awareness is a property of an actor who performs one or more roles within the ERP process. (Daneshgar, 2005)

## Actuary

A statistician who practices the collection and interpretation of numerical data; especially someone who uses statistics to calculate insurance premiums. (Kitchens, 2005)

## Ad Hoc

A class of wireless networking architectures in which there is no fixed infrastructure or wireless access points. In ad hoc networks, each mobile station acts as a router to communicate with other stations. Such a network can exist on a temporary basis to share some resources among the mobile stations. (Sarkar, 2005)

## Ad Hoc Network

Peer-to-peer 802.11 network formed automatically when several computers come together without an access point. Such computers can exchange data within the network, but cannot access the Internet. (Houser & Thornton, 2005)

**ADA:** See *Americans with Disabilities Act.*

**AdaBoost:** See *Adaptive Boosting.*

## Adaptability

**1:** One says this of a system that can perform adaptation based on configurations set by the user before or during the execution of the system. (Tobar et al., 2006) **2:** The ease with which software satisfies differing system constraints and user needs. (Guan, 2006b)

## Adaptable Personalization Systems

Systems that can be customized by the user in an explicit manner; that is, the user can change the content, layout,

**A**

appearance, and so forth to his or her needs. (Anke & Sundaram, 2006)

## Adaptable Systems

Systems that offer personalization—that is, pre-defined before the execution of the system and which may be modified by users. (Gaudioso & Montero, 2006)

## Adaptation

A system characteristic concerned with the capacity of adjusting its behavior according to one or a combination of targets: the user, the human computer interaction process, or the computational platform. (Tobar et al., 2006)

## Adaptation Engineering

The process of constructing the automatic adjustment of an application to the user; often in adaptation engineering, models are created for the domain, the user, and the adaptation. (Houben, Aroyo, & Dicheva, 2006)

## Adaptation Model

Representation of the way in which both the selection and presentation of content are adapted to the user. (Houben et al., 2006)

## Adapter

Intermediate software that understands proprietary back-end application interfaces and provides easy access interfaces for EAI technology integration. (Bussler, 2005b)

## Adaptive Algorithm

Method used to modify the filter coefficients, online, in order to minimize the power of an adaptive filter output error. (Perez-Meana & Nakano-Miyatake, 2005)

## Adaptive Boosting (AdaBoost)

An iterative bootstrap replication of the sample units of the training sample such that at any iteration, misclassified/worse predicted cases have higher probability to be included in the current bootstrap sample, and the final decision rule is obtained by majority voting. (Siciliano & Conversano, 2005)

## Adaptive Cognition

A cognitive style that prefers to think sequentially and work within current paradigms. (Kaluzniacky, 2006)

## Adaptive Collaboration Support in CSCL

Using models of different learners to form a matching group of learners for different kinds of collaboration. (Devedžić, 2006)

## Adaptive Feedback

Immediate feedback in the form of an explanation or discussion that is tailored to the qualities of the student's answer. (Owen & Aworuwa, 2005)

## Adaptive Filter

Linear system that modifies its parameters, minimizing some given criterion of the difference between its output and a given reference signal. Widely used in echo and noise canceling, equalization of communication channels, antenna arrays, and so forth. (Perez-Meana & Nakano-Miyatake, 2005)

## Adaptive Hypermedia System (AHS)

**1:** An adaptive concept-based system that is based on applying adaptation to a hypermedia application; characteristic is the (virtual) construction of a hyperdocument. (Houben et al., 2006) **2:** A hypertext and hypermedia system that can adapt various visible aspects of the system in order to reflect users' features. (Wu & Chen, 2005) **3:** Focuses on adaptive presentation and adaptive navigation support; uses knowledge about its users and can incorporate domain knowledge to adapt various visible aspects of the system to the user. (Esmahi, 2005)

## Adaptive Interfaces

Interfaces that allow for some user customization and personalization. (Zaphiris & Kurniawan, 2005)

## Adaptive Learning

An algorithm that can learn a hidden concept from interactive feedback provided by a user or the underlying environment. (Meng & Chen, 2005)

## Adaptive Personalization System

A system that changes the presentation implicitly by using secondary data. This data can be obtained from a variety of sources, for example, from the user's actions, from the behavior of other users on that site, or based on the currently displayed content. (Anke & Sundaram, 2006)

## Adaptive Services

In order to support personalized application, a system provides special content, presentation, and interaction adaptively to individual users according to their needs, abilities, and experiences. (Liu & Koppelaar, 2005)

## Adaptive Synchronization Framework (ASF)

A framework that adopts a mechanism to re-compute the synchronization relations that are destroyed by unexpected events (e.g., window resizing or font size change), so as to restore a presentation system to synchronization. (Liu & Chen, 2005)

## Adaptive System

**1:** A system adapting its behavior on the basis of the environment it is operating in. (De Meo, Quattrone, et al., 2005) **2:** A system that offers personalization that is dynamically built and automatically performed based on what these systems learn about the users. (Gaudioso & Montero, 2006)

## Adaptive Task-Based System

An adaptive concept-based system that is based on organizing the conceptual structures and the adaptation on the basis of the tasks and goals of the user; characteristic is the explicit representation of tasks. (Houben et al., 2006)

## Adaptive User Interfaces

An interface that uses a user model to change its behavior or appearance to increase user satisfaction with time. These interfaces are used extensively in assistive devices. (Abhishek & Basu, 2006)

## Adaptive Virtual Learning Environment (AVLE)

An e-learning environment that provides adaptive components to personalize learning instruction, to match with each learner's individual cognitive capability in order for knowledge construction to occur. In AVLEs, individual learners can be uniquely identified, with content that is specifically presented for him or her, and learning progress that can be individually monitored, tailored, and accessed. (Xu & Wang, 2006)

## Adaptive VR-Mall System

An e-commerce site that offers an immersive or semi-immersive environment for e-shoppers to navigate in, and tailors the content delivered taking into account the individual e-shopper preferences and interests. (Lepouras & Vassilakis, 2006)

## Adaptive Web Site

A Web site that semi-automatically improves its organization and presentation by learning from user access patterns. Web usage mining techniques are employed to determine the adaptation of the site. (Y. Fu, 2005)

## Adaptive Web-Based Information System

An adaptive concept-based system that is based on the principle of using hypermedia to present output from a structured repository or database, and that performs the adaptation on the hypermedia presentation and the content retrieval; characteristic is the role of navigation. (Houben et al., 2006)

## Adaptivity

**1:** Allows the content and the display of the content to be altered according to the characteristics of any individual user. Provides a dynamic adaptation of the content and appearance based on each individual user. (Shareef & Kinshuk, 2005) **2:** One says this of a system that can perform adaptation automatically. Generally, the system acquires and analyzes external data in order to make inferences and execute adaptation actions. (Tobar et al., 2006)

## Added Social Value

A positive social effect (main or subsidiary impact on social relations) resulting from goal-seeking activity of social actors. (Pazyuk, 2005)

## Added Value

Traditional usage is as an indication that the particular packaging, delivery method, or combination of services in a product brings extra benefits than one would otherwise receive. Applied to educational technology, it communicates that the use of technology brings added value to the teaching or learning processes when it makes possible something that otherwise would be impossible or less viable to do. (Dexter, 2005)

**ADDIE:** See *Analysis, Design, Development, Implementation, and Evaluation Model.*

## Adding Value

This is giving something that was not anticipated, such as selling a customer a product, and then giving additional information about gaining maximum benefit from it, or giving advice about safety issues relating to the product. (Mitchell, 2005b)

**A**

**Addressable Unit**
A specific unit within a particular digital asset such as a digital video movie. (Subramanian, 2005)

**ADF:** See *Automatically Defined Function.*

**Ad-Hoc Communication**
A connection method for wireless LANs that requires no base station. Devices discover others within range to form a network for those computers. They may search for target nodes that are out of range by flooding the network with broadcasts that are forwarded by each node. (Kao & Rerrer, 2006)

**Ad-Hoc Network**
**1:** A local area network or other small network, especially one with wireless or temporary plug-in connections, in which some of the network devices (sometimes mobile) are part of the network only for the duration of a communication session or because some of the devices are in some close proximity, so a communication session can take place. (Maamar, 2005) **2:** A special type of computer network where communication does not require any fixed computer network infrastructure (e.g., it does not need a router); the nodes communicate directly with each other without access points. In host-multicast, mobile peering hosts a construct ad-hoc network. (Hosszú, 2005b) **3:** A self-configuring mobile network of routers (and hosts), connected wirelessly, in which the nodes may move freely and randomly, resulting in a rapid and unpredictable change in the network's wireless topology. See also Mobile Ad hoc Network (MANET). (Akhtar, 2005)

**ADISSA:** See *Architectural Design of Information Systems Based on Structured Analysis.*

**Adjacency Matrix**
A matrix representing a graph with n vertex. It is an n-by-n array of Boolean values with the entry in row u and column v defined to be 1 if there is an edge connecting vertex u and v in the graph, and to be 0 otherwise. (Li, 2005)

**ADL/SCORM ADLNet:** See *Advanced Distributed Learning Network.*

**Administrative and Institutional Support**
All the benefits students enjoy when they are on campus, but in a format that is available via the Internet or the Web, beyond the access to e-learning courses and interactions

with the professor. These include e-registration, e-financial aid, e-library, e-bookstore, e-advisors, e-student organizations, and virtual communities. (Levy & Ramim, 2005a)

**Administrative Tasks**
The tasks that support educational tasks (such as enrollment, recording results, and so forth). (Darbyshire & Burgess, 2005)

**Admission Control**
The algorithms used by the system to accept or refuse new radio links (e.g., new users) in the system. (Iossifides et al., 2005)

**Adoption**
**1:** Changes in employee attitudes, perceptions, and actions that lead them to try new practices, activities, or innovations that are different from their normal routines or behaviors. (Jones & Gupta, 2005) **2:** Result of an innovation decision process. Decision to use an innovation. (Voeth & Liehr, 2005) **3:** The decision to accept or invest in a technology. (Signoret, 2006b) **4:** The decision to implement an innovation. (Klobas & Renzi, 2005a) **5:** The stage of technology diffusion in which an individual or organization decides to select a technology for use. (Green, Day, et al., 2005)

**Adoption Factors**
The major factors that encourage (or discourage) an organization to adopt an innovation. These include the following keywords. (Cragg & Mills, 2005)

**ADSL:** See *Asymmetric Digital Subscriber Line; Asymmetric DSL; Asynchronous Digital Subscriber Line; Digital Subscriber Line.*

**Adult Education**
This term is used to show awareness of the reality that many adults come to formal educational programs with different orientations to study, motivations, and prior experiences from younger learners. These differences need to be accommodated in the learning designs used. (Ching et al., 2005)

**Adult Learner**
A student typically 25 years of age or older who is self-directed, motivated, and an active participant in his or her learning process. (Ordonez, 2005)

**A**

## Advance Organizer

**1:** A general statement at the beginning of the information or lesson to activate existing cognitive structure or to provide the appropriate cognitive structure to learn the details in the information or the lesson. (Ally, 2005c) **2:** Any presentation of information that displays and represents the content and structure of a hypertext or text. (Shapiro, 2006)

## Advanced Authentication Measures

Techniques beyond passwords that can be used to identify the end user to determine if they are who they say they are. (Medlin et al., 2006)

## Advanced Distributed Learning Network (ADL/SCORM ADLNet)

An initiative sponsored by the U.S. federal government to "accelerate large-scale development of dynamic and cost-effective learning software and to stimulate an efficient market for these products in order to meet the education and training needs of the military and the nation's workforce of the future." As part of this objective, ADL produces SCORM (Sharable Content Object Reference Model), a specification for reusable learning content. Outside the defense sector, SCORM is being adopted by a number of training and education vendors as a useful standard for learning content. (Sánchez-Segura et al., 2005)

## Advanced Information Technology Structure

The rules and resources offered by systems such as computer-aided software engineering tools, enterprise resource planning systems, and database management systems that support the intended purposes and utilization of those systems. (LeRouge & Webb, 2005)

## Advanced Internet Applications

The set of more complex Internet technologies based around design activities, back-end data management activities, and remote access to Internet services. (Griffin, 2005)

## Advanced Methods of Software-Facilitated Communication

Communication that includes features such as interactive chat rooms, whiteboards (live interactive chats), group teleconferences, customized course calendars, interactive simulations, and virtual project labs. (Gold, 2005)

## Advanced Mobile Phone System (AMPS)

Obsolete cellular phone standard. (Gilbert, 2005c)

## Advanced Research Projects Agency Network (ARPAnet)

**1:** Network in which the Internet has roots; developed by the Department of Defense. (Inoue & Bell, 2005) **2:** The first multi-site, packet-switched network, ARPAnet was designed to support the Advanced Research Projects Agency (ARPA) for the transferring of files and resource sharing. (Kontolemakis et al., 2005)

## Adverse Effect

Any untoward medical occurrence that may be life threatening and requires in-patient hospitalization. (Kusiak & Shah, 2005)

## Advertising Fee

A payment received from an advertiser for including an advertisement on a Web site. (Shan et al., 2006b)

## Advertising Waste

Advertising that reaches an audience that is outside of its target market or intended audience. (Owen, 2006a)

## Advisory Agent

Intelligent agent that provides intelligent advice and decision support autonomously. These agents decide what information is needed, seek it out, and use it to make recommendations. (Gates & Nissen, 2005a)

## Advisory System

Front-end software system that guides customers according to their profiles and preferences through a personalized consulting process resulting in the generation of product configurations that better fulfill customers' needs. In opposition to the commonly used product-oriented interfaces in configurators, advisory systems are customer oriented and do not assume any specific technical knowledge of the product. (Blecker, 2006b)

## AEM: See *Agent-Based E-Marketplace.*

## Aerophones

The category of musical instruments, called wind instruments, producing sound by the vibration of air. Woodwinds and brass (lip-vibrated) instruments belong to this category, including single reed woodwinds (e.g.,

**A**

clarinet), double reeds (oboe), flutes, and brass (trumpet). (Wieczorkowska, 2005)

## Aesthetic Integrity
A principle that advocates that a design should be visually appealing and should follow common principles of visual design—consistency, a clear identity, a clear visual hierarchy, good alignment, contrast, and proportions. (Singh, 2005b)

## Aesthetics of Use
The behavioral aspects of an artifact, system, or device that precipitate an aesthetic experience based on temporal as well as spatial elements. (Kettley, 2006a)

**AF:** See *Assured Forwarding.*

## Affect
An umbrella term used to refer to mood, emotion, and other processes, which address related phenomena. At times, the term "affective reaction" is more specifically used to distinguish an individual's initial, spontaneous, undifferentiated, and largely physiologically driven response to an event, person, or object from the more cognitively differentiated "emotion." (Hassenzahl, 2006)

## Affective
Domain of learning concerned with inward disposition, feeling, intent, intention, earnest, reality; contrasted with merely cognitive development and/or external manifestation. (Rogers & Howell, 2005)

## Affective Complexity
How much communication is sensitive to attitudes or changes in disposition toward the communication partner or subject matter. (Willis, 2005)

## Affective Computing
**1:** A domain of computer science research combining fields such as Artificial Intelligence and Human-Computer Interaction in the endeavor to develop computers that can recognize, express, and have emotions. (Byl & Toleman, 2005) **2:** A recent theory that recognizes that emotions play an essential role in perception and learning by shaping the mechanisms of rational thinking. In order to enhance the process of interaction, we should design systems with the ability to recognize, to understand, and even to have and express emotions. (Karpouzis et al., 2005) **3:** The research

area concerned with computing that relates to, arises from, or deliberately influences emotion. Affective computing expands HCI by including emotional communication, together with the appropriate means of handling affective information. (Pantic, 2005a)

## Affective Learning
The attitude of the student toward the educational experience. (Woods & Baker, 2005)

## Affective Learning Outcomes
Learning that is associated with feelings rather than knowledge or skills, such as learning to accept an idea or concept, or learning to appreciate a point of view. (Aworuwa & Owen, 2005)

## Affective Trust
Interpersonal bonds among individuals and institutions, including perceptions of a person's motivation, intentions, ethics, and citizenship. (Sonnenwald, 2005)

## Affiliate Marketing
When companies use third parties to provide services on their behalf. The affiliates may deliver customer lists or customers to the main company in return for a commission payment or cross-selling opportunity. (Brindley, 2006)

## Affiliate Referral Fees
Payment to a Web site for steering customers to another "affiliate" site. The company is entitled to a referral fee or is offered a commission for each purchase the customer makes at the affiliate site. (Shan et al., 2006b)

## Affinity Communities
Communities that are based on profession, common interest, cause, demographic, or marketer-generated phenomenon. (Roy, A., 2005)

## Affinity Network
Groups of people who are drawn together based on one or more shared personal attributes. Their activities are highly relationship oriented and typically include networking, mentoring, and representing a collective voice in both organizational and external community affairs. (Archer, 2006)

## Affinity Portal
A special type of vertical portal that targets specific segments of the market and is designed to appeal to

people's emotions, values, and belief systems. (Vrazalic & Hyland, 2005)

## Affordance

**1:** Can be viewed as a property of an object that supports certain kinds of actions rather than others. (Magnani & Bardone, 2006) **2:** A features of an environment or artifact that "affords" or permits certain behaviors. (Graham, Allen, et al., 2005) **3:** The actual or perceived properties of an object that determine how the object could be used. (Yong, 2005)

**AFIS:** See *Automated Fingerprint Identification System.*

## African Networking Renaissance

Used to describe business organizations finding innovative ways of doing business by harnessing information and communication technologies (ICTs), cultural strengths, and inspiration to meet the challenges of its local needs and global competition. (Averweg, 2006)

**AFTA:** See *Australian Federation of Travel Agents.*

## After-Action Review (AAR)

The AAR process, developed mainly in the U.S. Army, is a central building block of KM in the military, conducted immediately (or as soon as possible) after every mission, training exercise, or project. It is a non-hierarchical knowledge event that allows debriefing, understanding, and realizing the value of tacit knowledge on the local level. (Ariely, 2006b)

**AFX:** See *Animation Framework eXtension.*

## Agenda Setting

Recognition of a problem that may be solved through innovation. (Klobas & Renzi, 2005a)

## Agent

**1:** A complex system constituting elements that are individual performers, which can be described by their interrelationships, knowledge/skill, performance and constraints factors. (Plekhanova, 2005a) **2:** A component of software and/or hardware that is capable of acting in order to accomplish tasks on behalf of its user. Software agents are agents in the form of programs (code) that operate in computer environments. (Cardoso & Freire, 2005) **3:** A computational entity capable of both perceiving dynamic changes in the environment it is operating in and autonomously performing user-delegated tasks, possibly by communicating and cooperating with other similar entities. (De Meo, Quattrone, et al., 2005) **4:** A computational entity which acts on behalf of other entities. (Karoui, 2005) **5:** A convenient metaphor for building software to interact with the range and diversity of online resources is that of an agent. An agent is a program that performs some task on your behalf. You expect an agent to act even if all the details are not specified or if the situation changes. You expect an agent to communicate effectively with other agents. Using agents adds a layer of abstraction that localizes decisions about dealing with local peculiarities of format, knowledge conventions, and so forth, and thus helps to understand and manage complexity. (Hamdi, 2005b) **6:** A module that is able to sense its environment, receive stimuli from the environment, make autonomous decisions, and actuate the decisions, which in turn change the environment. (Soh, 2006) **7:** A piece of software that autonomously performs a given task using information collected from its environment to act in a suitable manner so as to complete the task successfully. This software should be able to adapt itself based on changes occurring in its environment, so that a change in circumstances will still yield the intended result. (Camarinha-Matos & Ferrada, 2006) **8:** A program designed to provide specialized and well-defined services. An agent can be static—executing on the computer where it was installed, or mobile—executing on computer nodes in a network. (Raisinghani, Klassen, & Schkade, 2005) **9:** A software agent is a piece of autonomous or semi-autonomous, proactive and reactive computer software. Many individual communicative software agents may form a multi-agent system. (Guan, 2006f) **10:** A software agent is a programmable artifact capable of intelligent autonomous action toward an objective. (Nabuco et al., 2006) **11:** A system that is capable of perceiving events in its environment, or representing information about the current state of affairs and of acting in its environment guided by perceptions and stored information (current definition by AOIS, agent-oriented information system community). (Murthy & Krishnamurthy, 2005a) **12:** A virtual representation of real or imaginary human beings in software systems. (Arya, 2005) **13:** An agent is an encapsulated computer system that is situated in some environment and that is capable of flexible, autonomous action in that environment in order to meet its design objectives. Agents normally exhibit autonomous, reactive, proactive, and social behaviors. (Kefalas et al., 2005)

## Agent and Autonomous Agent

Software that carries out specialized tasks for a user. Agents operate on behalf of their owners in the absence of full or constant supervision. Autonomous agents have a greater degree of decision-making control invested in them by their owners. (Duchastel, 2006)

## Agent Attributes

An agent can be classified using some of its characteristics called attributes. An agent has three basic attributes: mobility, intelligence, and interaction. (Karoui, 2005)

## Agent Framework

A program or code library that provides a comprehensive set of capabilities that are used to develop and support software agents. (Zwitserloot & Pantic, 2005)

## Agent Ontology

A description (like a formal specification of a program) of the concepts and relationships that can exist for an agent or a community of agents. (De Meo, Quattrone, et al., 2005)

## Agent Orientation

The next step in the evolution of computational modeling, programming methodologies, and software engineering paradigms. Aspects of agent orientation include both cooperative and competitive interactions, knowledge, economic and logical rationality, and learning, all of which are useful for designing distributed computations in open dynamic environments. (Ghenniwa & Huhns, 2005)

## Agent's Compatibility

A capability of an agent to work with other agents without adaptation, adjustment, or modification. (Plekhanova, 2005a)

## Agent-Based Approach to ASP

This approach to ASP is well equipped to address the challenges of multi-market package to e-procurement. Service agents within the ASP model are the system's gateway to external sources of goods and services. Service agents are not only able to determine which requests it can service, but also proactively read these requests and try to find an acceptable solution. (Guah & Currie, 2005)

## Agent-Based E-Marketplace

A distributed multi-agent system formed by stationary and mobile agents that provide e-commerce services to end users within a business context. (Fortino, Garro, et al., 2006)

## Agent-Based Simulation

Simulation of organizations as interacting autonomous entities with their own interests, goals, and discrete processes. (Janssen, 2005)

## Agent-Mediated E-Commerce (AMEC)

Concerned with providing agent-based solutions that support different stages of the trading processes in e-commerce, including needs identification, product brokering, merchant brokering, contract negotiation and agreement, payment and delivery, and service and evaluation. (Fortino, Garro, et al., 2006)

## Agglomeration Economies

Refers to the spatial concentration of economic activities. For example, a firm that is located in close proximity to other firms in the same industry can take advantage of localization economies. These intra-industry benefits include access to specialized know-how (i.e., knowledge diffusion), the presence of buyer-supplier networks, and opportunities for efficient subcontracting. Employees with industry-specific skills will be attracted to such clusters, giving firms access to a larger specialized labor pool. Another case of agglomeration economies external to the firm relates to benefits that accrue from being located in close proximity to firms in other industries— that is, urbanization economies. These inter-industry benefits include easier access to complementary services (publishing, advertising, banking), availability of a large labor pool with multiple specialization, inter-industry information transfers, and the availability of less costly general infrastructure. (Moodley, 2005)

## Aggregate Conceptual Direction

Describes the trend in the data along which most of the variance occurs, taking the missing data into account. (H. Wang & S. Wang, 2005)

## Aggregate Function

A function that is used to aggregate a set of values to get a single value. (Deshpande & Ramasamy, 2005)

## Aggregate Materialized View

A materialized view in which the results of a query containing aggregations (like count, sum, average, etc.) are stored. (Tininini, 2005b)

## Aggregate Range Query

Selects a range of values in each dimension (dimensions not specified in the query are by default completely selected) and computes an aggregate (e.g., SUM, MAX, or COUNT) over the measure values of all data cube cells whose coordinates fall into the selected range. A typical aggregate range query is: "Compute the total sales of cameras in California for the first half of January 1999." (Riedewald et al., 2005)

## Aggregate Similarity Search

The search operation in 3D structures that matches the structures point-to-point in their entirety. (X. Wang, 2005)

## Aggregation

**1:** A relationship in which a composite object ("whole") consists of other component objects ("parts"). (Taniar, Pardede, & Rahayu, 2005) **2:** Also commonly called a summary, an aggregation is the calculation of a value from a bag or (multi)set of entities. Typical aggregations are sum, count, and average. (Perlich & Provost, 2005) **3:** Metaphorical boundaries that indicate a community network's zones of inclusion and exclusion, and structures of content, activity, and functionality within the site. (Gibbs et al., 2005)

## Aggregation Process

The process that allows one to obtain multi-dimensional aggregate data from disaggregate data. (Rafanelli, 2005)

## Aggregation Queries

Common queries executed by decision support systems that aggregate and group large amounts of data, where aggregation operators are typically SUM, COUNT, AVG, and so forth. (Das, 2005)

## Agile

Being agile means to be proficient at change, which allows an organization to do anything it wants, whenever it wants. Since virtual enterprises do not own significant capital resources of their own, it helps if they are agile, so they can be formed and changed very rapidly. (Wong, 2005)

## Agile Development Methodologies

An approach used in building non-critical computer systems. (Singh, 2005)

## Aging and Dejuvenization of the Working Population

The increasing proportion of older people coupled with decreasing proportions of young people in the labor force. (Scholarios et al., 2005)

## Aging Effect

Software artifacts evolve over time due to the changes in domain requirements, platform, and even language. After their release, software needs to be modified regularly. These modifications introduce errors to the software and reduce its overall quality over time, which is often called the aging effect. (Gaffar, 2005)

## Aging-Related Declines

Age-related differences in cognitive, motor, and perceptual abilities. (Zaphiris & Kurniawan, 2005)

## Aglets

Platforms for mobile agents to operate on and on which to perform transactions. (Quah, Leow, & Ong, 2006)

**A-GPS:** See *Assisted Global Positioning System.*

**AHIMA:** See *American Health Information Management Association.*

**AHS:** See *Adaptive Hypermedia Systems.*

**AI:** See *Artificial Intelligence.*

**AIC:** See *Akaike Information Criterion and Schwartz Bayesian Criterion.*

## AIC Criterion

The AIC criterion is defined by the following equation:

$$AIC = -2 \log L(\hat{\vartheta}; x_1, ..., x_n) + 2q$$

where $\log L(\hat{\vartheta}; x_1, ..., x_n)$ is the logarithm of the likelihood function calculated in the maximum likelihood parameter estimate and q is the number of parameters of the model. (Giudici, 2005)

**A**

**AICC:** See *Aviation Industry CBT (Computer-Based Training) Committee.*

**AICC (Aviation Industry CBT [Computer-Based Training] Committee)**
An international association that develops guidelines for the aviation industry in the development, delivery, and evaluation of CBT and related training technologies. The objectives of the AICC are to:

- Assist airplane operators in development of guidelines which promote the economic and effective implementation of computer-based training (CBT).
- Develop guidelines to enable interoperability.
- Provide an open forum for the discussion of CBT (and other) training technologies.

(Sánchez-Segura et al., 2005)

**Aides Memoires**
Aids to the memory or mental artifacts that indicate the sources of information rather than the information itself. (Atkinson & Burstein 2006)

**AIML:** See *Artificial Intelligence Markup Language.*

**AIP:** See *Application Infrastructure Provider.*

**Air Traffic Control (ATC)**
Refers to both the activities and the systems involved in the management of flights by air traffic controllers. The air traffic controllers' main task is to ensure flight safety with an efficient, secure, and ordered air traffic flow. ATC systems are dedicated to the support of these tasks. (Bastide et al., 2006)

**AIT:** See *Analytical Information Technology.*

**Akaike Information Criterion (AIC) and Schwartz Bayesian Criterion (SBC)**
The two most commonly used model selection criteria. They trade off fitness of a model for the complexity of the model. If the AIC (or SBC) of model A is smaller than that of model B, it is said that model A is better than model B. (Cho, 2005)

**Akruti ™**
A brand name of Indian language software. (Literal meaning of Akruti is *figure.*) (Shaligram, 2005)

**AL Set**
The name given to an AL group. (Smith, 2006a)

**ALC:** See *Alternative Learning Center.*

**Algebraic Function**
An aggregate function F is algebraic if F of an n-dimensional cuboid can be computed by using a constant number of aggregates of the (n+1)-dimensional cuboid. (Abdulghani, 2005a)

**Algebraic Specification**
A technique whereby an object is specified in terms of the relationships between the operations that act on that object. A specification is presented in four parts: the Introduction, where the sort of the entity being specified is introduced and the name of any other specifications that are required are set out; the Informal Description of the sort and its operations; the Signature, where the names of the operations on that object and the sorts of their parameters are defined; and the Axioms, where the relationships between the sort operations are defined. (Felice & Riesco, 2005)

**Algorithm**
A step-by-step procedure for solving a problem, in this case that of determining completion and retention rates. No national, standardized algorithm exists yet for calculating these rates. (Lindsay, Howell, et al., 2005)

**Algorithm Animation**
Visualization of a piece of software illustrating the main ideas or steps (i.e., its algorithmic behavior), but without a close relationship to the source code. (Pareja-Flores & Iturbide, 2005)

**Algorithmic Information Theory**
"Absolute information theory" based on Kolmogorov complexity theory. (T. Y. Lin, 2005)

**ALife:** See *Artificial Life.*

**Alignment**
**1:** A dynamic process that requires close, continual assessment (because the goals keep on moving) and cooperation between achieving competitive advantage and surviving. (Lubbe, 2005) **2:** An orientation based on a series of ongoing processes based on the will to achieve a common goal. Alignment is distinguished from the more static concept of fit, and is conceptualized as an outcome

with determinant factors that affect the degree to which one set of objectives are mutually consistent and supportive of the other. (Dery & Samson, 2005) **3:** Explicit mapping of characters of a sequence to characters of one or more other sequence(s). (Tsunoda et al., 2005) **4:** Means the alignment of the strategic vision for information technology with the organization's strategic vision, ensuring the strategic vision for information technology supports the organization's strategic vision. (Brabston, 2005) **5:** The arrangement or position of different separate elements (strategies) in relation to each other. (Johnston, 2005)

## Alignment Map

A representation on a surface to clearly show the arrangement or positioning of relative items on a straight line or a group of parallel lines. (Alkhalifa, 2006)

## All Rules Search

An algorithm that finds all rules of a defined format that satisfy a defined set of constraints. (Richards & de la Iglesia, 2005)

## Alliance Management

Allows two different organizations to effectively work together and combine resources, which is expected to bring benefits to both organizations. (Mandal et al., 2005)

## Allied Model of IPFS

A model that describes the provision of integrated personal financial services through inter-organizational alliances. (Gordon & Mulligan, 2005)

## Alliterate

A person who has the ability to read, yet chooses not to use it. (Trammell, 2005)

**ALM:** See *Application-Layer Multicast.*

## ALM Routing Protocol

The members of the hosts construct a delivery tree using similar algorithms as the IP-multicast routing protocols do. (Hosszú, 2006)

**ALN:** See *Asynchronous Learning Network.*

## Alpha-Helix

A helical conformation of a polypeptide chain, once of the most common secondary structures in proteins. (Tsunoda et al., 2005)

## Alt String

An HTML tag for attaching text to a media object. (N.C. Rowe, 2005b)

## Alternative Assessment

Activities developed by an instructor to assist the student in identifying the processes and products of learning beyond the "one right answer" approach, and where the scoring or rating criteria are distributed at the same time as the assignment directions. (B.L. MacGregor, 2005)

## Alternative Document Model

A conceptual rule for grouping together Web pages into larger units, such as sites and domains, for more effective data mining, particularly useful in Web-structure mining. (Thelwall, 2005)

## Alternative Hypothesis

The hypothesis that an object is relevant. In general terms, the alternative hypothesis refers to the set of events that is the complement of the null hypothesis. (Mukherjee, 2005)

## Alternative Learning Center (ALC)

A program that provides educational options to students who are at risk of experiencing failure or already have been unsuccessful in a traditional school setting. (Dorniden, 2005)

## Alternative Staffing

Support systems for student learning that consist of various kinds of instructional personnel, often replacing expensive personnel with relatively inexpensive personnel as appropriate. (Twigg, 2005)

## Alternative Storage

An array of storage media that consists of two forms of storage: near-line storage and/or second storage. (Yao, Liu, et al., 2005)

## ALT-Text

Stands for alternative text, primarily used to render graphics when the image is not being displayed or cannot be viewed due to visual impairments or blindness. (Yu, 2005b)

## Ambient Intelligence

**1:** Represents a vision of the future where people will be surrounded by electronic environments that are sensitive and responsive to people. (Hua et al., 2006) **2:** The merging of mobile communications and sensing technologies with the aim of enabling a pervasive and unobtrusive intelligence in the surrounding environment supporting the activities and interactions of the users. Technologies like face-based interfaces and affective computing are inherent ambient-intelligence technologies. (Pantic, 2005b)

## Ambiguity

Something difficult to interpret, difficult to understand, unclear. A situational factor proposed to contribute to the occurrence of Limited-Perspective Bias. (Moore & Burke, 2005)

## Ambiguous Definition of Distance Education

There are many differing definitions for distance education, spanning from videotape exchange through simple video supported to completely asynchronous (different time/different place) environments. (Martz & Shepherd, 2005)

## Ambulatory Measurement Device

A data-gathering instrument that can be worn during everyday experiences. The device gathers biophysical data for later transmission or reading. (Molinari, Dupler, et al., 2005a)

**AMEC:** See *Agent-Mediated E-Commerce.*

## America Online® (AOL)

A U.S. online service provider based in Vienna, Virginia, AOL claims to be the largest and fastest growing provider of online services in the world, with the most active subscriber base. AOL offers its three million subscribers electronic mail, interactive newspapers and magazines, conferencing, software libraries, computing support, and online classes, among other services. (Kontolemakis et al., 2005)

## American Community Survey (ACS)

An ongoing survey conducted by the U.S. Census Bureau that collects detailed demographic and socioeconomic information on a sample of the population. (Garb & Wait, 2005a)

## American Health Information Management Association (AHIMA)

A professional association that represents more than 50,000 specially educated health information management professionals who work throughout the health care industry. (Zender, 2006)

## American Society for Training & Development (ASTD)

Beginning in 1944, a leading association of workplace learning and performance professionals, 70,000 members from more than 100 countries—multi-national corporations, medium-sized and small businesses, government, and academia. (Rhoten, 2006b)

## American Standard Code for Information Interchange (ASCII)

**1:** A code for information exchange between computers made by different companies; a string of seven binary digits represents each character; used in most microcomputers. (Rhoten, 2006a) **2.** A standard method of encoding upper and lower case text and other symbols with a 7-bit code. (Kieler & West, 2005) **3:** Serves a code for representing English characters as numbers with each letter assigned a number from 0 to 127. (Pang, 2005a) **4:** System used to convert simple text to computer readable form. (McCarthy, 2005a)

## Americans with Disabilities Act (ADA)

**1:** U.S. public law enacted in 1990 ensuring rights for people with disabilities. This legislation mandates reasonable accommodation and effective communication. (Yu, 2005a) **2:** Section 508 of the federal Rehabilitation Act requires that all Web sites developed with federal dollars meet certain accessibility requirements so that those with physical or mental impairments can access Web-based information. This is sometimes referred to as ADA compliance. (Glick, 2005a) **3:** U.S. civil rights legislation passed in 1990 that prohibits discrimination against people with disabilities in the areas of employment, transportation, telecommunications, and public accommodation. (Schmetzke, 2005)

## Amortize-Scans

Amortizing disk reads by computing as many group-bys as possible, simultaneously in memory. (Tan, 2005a)

## Amplitude Change Function (ACF)

A polynomial relationship of the form H0(w)= P[H(w)] between the amplitude responses of the overall and the prototype filters, H0(w) and H(w), respectively. (Jovanovic-Dolecek & Díaz-Carmona, 2005)

**AMPS:** See *Advanced Mobile Phone System.*

## Analog

Encoding a physical phenomenon by a direct, perceptually continuous variation of a physical property such as electromagnetic intensity (recording tape), mechanical displacement (vinyl disk), or opaqueness (photographic film). (Kieler & West, 2005)

## Analysis

**1:** The stage of the intelligence cycle in which the strategic significance of environmental data is determined. In this stage, the intelligence is produced. During analysis, intelligence professionals may use different models and techniques to interpret and value environmental data (e.g., SWOT analysis, growth-share matrix, or scenario analysis). (Achterbergh, 2005a) **2:** The word 'analysis' can have different meanings in different contexts. Within the natural computing domain, analysis corresponds to the investigation of a given phenomenon in order to obtain some information from it or to derive simplified computational systems (or theoretical models) that somewhat mimic the behavior of the natural system being analyzed. (de Castro, 2005)

## Analysis Filter Bank

Decomposes the input signal into a set of sub-band signals, with each sub-band signal occupying a portion of the original frequency band. (Jovanovic-Dolecek, 2005b)

## Analysis Model

A model developed to learn all aspects of a problem domain to determine the best way to solve a specific set of user needs. (Krogstie, 2005a)

## Analysis, Design, Development, Implementation, and Evaluation (ADDIE) Model

**1:** An Instructional System Design model on which almost all other ISD models are based. (Aisami, 2005) **2:** The five phases of most instructional design models: analyze, design, develop, implement, and evaluate. Some models follow the phases in a linear fashion, while others may approach the phases in a holistic or phenomenologic manner. (Rogers, 2005a)

## Analyst

A user who collaborates with designers as a domain expert analyzing constraints and trade-offs in existing and envisioned work practices is called an analyst. This is the second stage in the developmental theory of participatory-design relationships between users and designers. (Carroll, 2005)

## Analytic Method

Method in which a system is evaluated based on its interface design attributes (typically by a usability expert). (Danielson, 2006b)

## Analytical Data

All data that are obtained from optimization, forecasting, and decision support models. (Mathieu & Levary, 2005)

## Analytical Information Technology (AIT)

An information technology that facilitates tasks like predictive modeling, data assimilation, planning, or decision making through automated data-driven methods, numerical solutions of physical or dynamical systems, human-computer interaction, or a combination. AIT includes DMT, DSS, BI, OLAP, GIS, and other supporting tools and technologies. (Ganguly et al., 2005)

## Analytical Query

A query on a data warehouse for identifying business intelligence. These queries often have complex expressions, access many kinds of data, and involve statistical functions. (Lu, 2005)

## Analyzing the Market

Identification of possible markets based upon Market Stratification data on educational materials that are available. This is when entrepreneurial considerations are put to the litmus test in terms of the chance for success or failure. (Robinson, 2005)

## Anchor Domain

The area that provides (drives, catalyzes, or enables) the change forces applied to the pivot domain. (Abou-Zeid, 2005a)

## Anchored Instruction

Learning is anchored in a real-world context. Within this context, learners engage in different activities to solve a problem, such as math calculations or geographic coordinates to travel across a continent or sale a ship. (Jennings et al., 2005)

## Anchored Learning Instructions

High learning efficiency with easier transferability of mental models and the facilitation of strategic problem-solving skills in ill-structured domains emerge if instructions are anchored on a particular problem or set of problems. (Kwok Lai-yin & Tan Yew-Gee, 2005)

**A**

## Anchoring

An evaluator bias in analytic methods in which a system is evaluated with respect to users too similar to the evaluator to be representative of the user population. (Danielson, 2006a)

## Andragogy

**1:** The art and science of helping adults learn. (Whitfield, 2005) **2:** The study of adult education. The term andragogy was coined by Malcolm Knowles, a leading researcher in the study of adult learners. (Ordonez, 2005) **3:** This concept was first developed by Knowles in the late 1960s as a science of teaching adults; its key assumptions, based on the characteristics of adult learners, are: (1) self-directedness and independence increases as a person matures; (2) adult experience constitutes a resource for learning; (3) readiness to learn is related to needs, which in turn are related to the different developmental tasks, phases, and roles of adult life; (4) as a person matures, his or her orientation to learn is more directed toward the immediacy of application and to one of problem centeredness; and (5) in the adult, learning motivation is intrinsic. (Correia & Sarmento, 2005)

## Anecdote

A naturally occurring story or the recounting of an experience in conversation or when prompted. Anecdotes are in effect a response to some form of stimulus and recount real or imagined experience. (Snowden, 2006)

## Angle of Arrival (AOA)

**1:** A positioning technology in which the mobile network sends directional antenna beams to locate a mobile device at the intersection of the directions of maximum signal strength. (Giaglis, 2005) **2:** A positioning technique that determines a mobile user's location by the angle of an incoming signal. AOA covers only the arc of a circle instead of the whole cell. (Fraunholz et al., 2005) **3:** The angle-of-arrival method measures the angle of a signal arriving at the antenna of a base station. The intersection of the projection of two calculated angles (from the antennas of two base stations) on the two-dimensional space reveals the location of the mobile phone. (Ververidis & Polyzos, 2006)

## Animated Pedagogical Agents

Animated figures operating in a learning environment and aiming at supporting learners in their learning process, and capable of adapting their support to the learners' paths. (Clarebout et al., 2005a)

## Animation

**1:** A graphical representation of a simulation process. The major popularity of animation is its ability to communicate the essence of the model to managers and other key project personnel, greatly increasing the model's credibility. It is also used as a debugging and training tool. (Al-Hanbali & Sadoun, 2006) **2:** A synthetic apparent motion created through artificial means. (Yong & Choo, 2005) **3:** Technique of imparting motion and activity in graphic images of such objects as products and cartoons to create a condition of being alive, active, or spirited. (Gao, 2005b)

## Animation Framework eXtension (AFX)

Standard conducted by the Synthetic and Natural Hybrid Coding group within MPEG; its goal is to specify compression schemes for 3D animation data and tools, such as body animation, image-based rendering, texture-mapping, and so forth. (Di Giacomo et al., 2005)

## Animation Model

A graphical representation of a problem situation that can consist of a visualization of the time-ordered dynamics of objects, a static background, an overview of performance indicators, and a user interface. (Janssen, 2005)

**ANN:** See *Artificial Neural Network.*

## Annotation

**1:** A technique for content adaptation. Special tags are added to the HTML page to allow browsers to operate in a pre-defined function. (Goh & Kinshuk, 2005) **2:** Also referred to as "metadata"; a document containing knowledge about another document—hence the "meta" prefix. According to the specification language used, one distinguishes informal annotations (interpreted by humans) and formal annotations (intended to be interpreted by machines). Concerning the content of these annotations, knowledge can relate either to the contents of an annotated document (e.g., by means of a collection of concepts expressed in the document) or to a document's overall properties (e.g., author, publication date, language used, etc). (Fortier & Kassel, 2006) **3:** Descriptive text attached to multimedia objects. (Hurson & Yang, 2005) **4:** Information about a multimedia object. This information may directly describe the semantic content of an object (e.g., this photo shows a cityscape) or describe its relations to other external objects (e.g., this photo was made in the year 1999). (Windhouwer & Kersten, 2005) **5:** Comments, typographical corrections, hypotheses, or ratings given by a reader playing the role of an author, which makes a statement about the document or some part of it at a certain time. (Qayyum, 2005)

## Annotation Extraction Algorithm

An algorithm that automatically extracts a (set of) annotations that describe the content of a media object. The input of such an algorithm can consist of the media object itself combined with previously extracted annotations or other additional information. (Windhouwer & Kersten, 2005)

## Annotation Extraction Process

The semi-automatic extraction of annotations aimed at describing the content of a digital media object. In this process, annotation extraction algorithms are called in the correct order, so their out- and input dependencies are met. (Windhouwer & Kersten, 2005)

## Annotation Maintenance

When the annotation extraction algorithms or the media objects change, the already extracted annotations must be revalidated. If a dependency description for the extraction algorithms is available, an incremental extraction process can be started where only the affected annotations are (re)produced. (Windhouwer & Kersten, 2005)

## Annotation Pipeline

A media object (and its growing collection of annotations) is pushed or pulled through a sequence of annotation extraction algorithms. (Windhouwer & Kersten, 2005)

## Annotation Pool

Annotations of digital media are stored in a data pool. Annotation extraction algorithms populate this pool when their input is available. (Windhouwer & Kersten, 2005)

## Anomaly

**1:** An unwanted consequence of inadequate database design. Data can be unintentionally lost or be more difficult to add or modify than the designer intended. (Schultz, 2005) **2:** A value or observation that deviates from the rule or analogy. A potentially incorrect value. (Morantz, 2005)

## Anomaly Detection

Analysis strategy that identifies intrusions as unusual behavior that differs from the normal behavior of the monitored system. (Lazarevic, 2005)

## Anonymity

**1:** A feature of an ARS that can protect the identity of a participant. (Banks, 2005) **2:** Ability to conceal one's identity. (N.C. Rowe, 2006c) **3:** A distinct characteristic of peer-to-peer networks, derived from the peer-to-peer philosophy. The identity and usage records of a peer are hidden from others to prevent piracy violation and censorship. (Kwok, Cheung, et al., 2006) **4:** The lack of the identity due to the eliminated social cues (e.g., visual or verbal indication of a communication partner's presence in the social interaction circumstance). Anonymity may encourage people to be more open to sharing their feelings and opinions, freeing them from social pressure to follow norms of groups in which they are involved. (Kang et al., 2006) **5:** The degree to which a software system or component allows for or supports anonymous transactions. (Guan, 2005a)

## Anonymity in GSS

**1:** The situation when participants' names are not made public in a GSS environment. (Limayem, 2005) **2:** Communicators do not know owners of expressed ideas in group interaction processes. (Chuang et al., 2005)

## Analysis of Variance (ANOVA)

A powerful statistical method for studying the relationship between a response or criterion variable and a set of one or more predictor or independent variable(s). (Morantz, 2005)

**ANOVA:** See *Analysis of Variance.*

## ANSI C++®

Complete set of standards provided by the American National Standards Institute in collaboration with ISO standardization committee to define an industrial standard for the C++ programming language. (Gaffar, 2005)

**ANT:** See *Actor Network Theory.*

## Antenna

The part of a transmitting or receiving device that radiates or receives electromagnetic radiation (electromagnetic waves). (Statica & Deek, 2006)

## Anthropomorphic

An attribution of human characteristic or behavior to natural phenomena or inanimate objects—that is, the embodiment of a graphic user interface agent can be anthropomorphic since the representation may take on human attributes or qualities. Anthropomorphism is an attempt to design technologies to be user friendly. (Faiola, 2006)

## Anthropomorphism
To ascribe human characteristics to things not human. Some authors argue that, unlike a human being, an organization can have no memory. It has been argued that the idea of organizational memory raises problems of anthropomorphism. (Jasimuddin et al., 2006)

## Anthropopathy
Attribution of human feelings to non-humans (animals, objects, or virtual entities). (Analide et al., 2006)

## Antimonicity Constraint
The antimonicity constraint states that any supergraph of an infrequent graph must be infrequent itself (Fischer & Meinl, 2005)

## Antimonotonic
A property of some pattern-finding problems stating that patterns of size k can only exist if certain patterns with sizes smaller than k exist in the same dataset. This property is used in level-wise algorithms, such as the a priori algorithm used for association rule mining or some algorithms for inclusion dependency mining. (Koeller, 2005)

## Antinoise
Estimated replica of acoustic noise generated by an active noise canceller system, which is used to cancel an environmental noise. (Perez-Meana & Nakano-Miyatake, 2005)

## Antivirus Software
A class of programs that searches networks, hard drives, floppy disks, and other data access devices, such as CD-ROM/DVD-ROMs and zip drives, for any known or potential viruses. The market for this kind of program has expanded because of Internet growth and the increasing use of the Internet by businesses concerned about protecting their computer assets. (Luo & Warkentin, 2005)

## Any Time, Any Place (ATAP) Learning
A basic characteristic of Web-based education courses in that they are available to the student on a 24/7 basis. (Marold, 2005)

## Anycast
Introduced in IPv6, associates an address with multiple nodes. Packets sent to an anycast address are routed to the nearest node having that address, depending on the distance of the routing path. Anycast can be used to provide high availability (automatic failover) and load balancing for stateless services, for example, access to replicated data. (Papagiannidis et al., 2005)

## Anytime, Anywhere Work
Describes a situation where people can do tasks wherever they want and without any consideration for time—that is, their work can be done anytime, anywhere. (Wiberg, 2005)

**AOA:** See *Angle of Arrival.*

**AOL:** See *America Online®.*

**AP:** See *Access Point.*

## APA
Association for Project Management. (D. Brandon, 2005b)

**Apache™:** See *Apache Software Foundation.*

## Apache™ Software Foundation
**1:** Provides support for the Apache community of open source software projects. The Apache projects are characterized by a collaborative, consensus-based development process, an open and pragmatic software license, and a desire to create high-quality software that leads the way in its field. Most famous projects among them are: http (the well-known Web server), XML (an instrument for the development of Web pages based on XML—Extended Markup Language), and Jakarta (Java server). (Cartelli, 2005b) **2:** An open source HTTP server for operating systems, including UNIX and Windows NT. A project supported by the Apache Software Foundation. (Goh & Kinshuk, 2005) **3:** An open source Web server. Web servers use http to enable a computer user to connect to the Internet. (Boateng & Boateng, 2006a)

**APDIP:** See *Asia Pacific Development Information Program.*

**API:** See *Application Programming Interface.*

**APICS®:** See *American Production and Inventory Control Society.*

**APON:** See *APON or Broadband PON.*

## APON or Broadband PON (APON/BPON)

APON is defined by the ITU-T G.983 series of recommendations. It features a passive optical network for fiber-to-the-home service that uses ATM as its transmission protocol. BPON is an alternate name for this technology. (Kelic, 2005)

## Apparent Distance

The perceived proximity of faculty and students in a distance education environment. Close apparent distance is the term used to describe a relationship that is perceived as positive, supporting, in regular communication—a relationship in which the student and faculty are well known to each other and where communications flow easily. (Sales, 2005)

## Applet

A computer program that is portable between operating systems and requires only minimal memory to run, often written in the Java programming language. (Fagan, 2005)

## Application 1

**1:** An application is a program, script, or other collection of instructions that direct the operation of a processor. This is a wide definition of "application." It does not distinguish Web-based software from stand-alone software. Nor does this definition distinguish system software from goal-specific software. (Maris, 2005) **2:** Knowledge integration to create organizational capability through directives, organizational routines, and self-contained task teams. (Lindsey, 2006)

## Application Aware vs. Application Transparent

In application-aware fault tolerance, the application programmer writes code for fault tolerance methods that perform specific operations. In application-transparent fault tolerance, the fault tolerance middleware performs those operations automatically, using standard operating system functions and the technique of library interpositioning. (Zhao, Moser, et al., 2005)

## Application Domain

That part of the assumed real world that is changed by a work system to achieve the work system's goals. (Diaper, 2006)

## Application Infrastructure Provider (AIP)

A type of ASP that usually originates from telecommunication operators that run their own networks and Internet data centers. The AIP focuses on server hosting and network infrastructure management for other ASPs and corporate clients, and provides value-added services based on its technology leadership, for example, online security and e-payment services. (D. Kim, 2005)

## Application Integration

The process of bringing data or a function from one application program together with that of another application program. (Karakostas, 2005)

## Application Layer

Layer 7 of the OSI model. This layer determines the interface of the system with the user. (Ngoh & Shankar, 2005)

## Application Program Interface (API)

**1:** Part of the run-time environment described in SCORM. It provides a standardized way for content to communicate with the learning management system. (Stavredes, 2005b) **2:** A set of programming tools that provide developers with a simple, consistent mechanism for extending the functionality of an application and for accessing existing computing systems. (Yow & Moertiyoso, 2005) **3:** A description of the way one piece of software asks another program to perform a service. A standard API for data mining enables different data-mining algorithms from various vendors to be easily plugged into application programs. (Zendulka, 2005a)

## Application Service Provider (ASP)

**1:** A company that hosts an application on its servers so the client does not need to worry about the technical issues. The client then accesses the content and software via the Internet. (Kapp, 2005) **2:** A service company that can support and relieve a firm from the daunting challenges of finding, hiring, inspiring, and training technical personnel to manage an application in-house. An ASP provides software applications on a pay-per-use or service basis via the Internet and leased lines. (Archer,

2005) **3:** A company that manages and hosts a software program on behalf of a client. (Baker & Schihl, 2005) **4:** A service company offering outsourcing solutions that supply, develop, and manage application-specific software and hardware so that customers' internal information technology resources can be freed up. (Zhu, 2005) **5:** The provisioning to individuals and companies of software applications and ICT-related services, via the Internet or other data networks, that are to be paid on a rental/usage base. (Iacob et al., 2005) **6:** A provider of application services over the Internet or an intranet. (Feuerlicht & Vorisek, 2006) **7:** A specialized operator that offers a bundle of customized software applications from a remote position through the Internet, in exchange for a periodic fee. (Morabito & Provera, 2005) **8:** A third-party service firm that deploys, manages, and remotely hosts software applications through centrally located services in a rental or lease agreement. Such application deliveries are done to multiple entities from data centers across a wide area network (WAN) as a service rather than a product, priced according to a license fee and maintenance contract set by the vendor. An ASP is considered by many to be the new form of IT outsourcing, usually referred to as application outsourcing. (Guah & Currie, 2005) **9:** An HTML page that includes one or more scripts that are processed on a Microsoft™ Web server before the page is sent to the user. An ASP is somewhat similar to a server-side or a common gateway interface (CGI) application in that all involve programs that run on the server, usually tailoring a page for the user. (Lee, Suh, et al., 2005)

## Application Solution Providers

Third-party vendors who provide data center, telecommunications, and application options for major companies. (DeLorenzo, 2005)

## Application State

Current snapshot of the application itself and all of the resources it addresses. (Trossen & Molenaar, 2005)

## Application Synchronization

A specific type of wireless application whereby the data on the wireless device is synchronized with that on the main server. (K. J. MacGregor, 2005)

## Application-Layer Multicast (ALM)

This does not require any additional protocol in the network routers, since it uses the traditional unicast IP-transmission. Its other names are host-multicast or end-host multicast. (Hosszú, 2006)

## Application-Sharing Space

A groupware tool that produces multiple distributed remote views of a particular space. Any single-user application put under the control of the particular space can be viewed remotely and controlled by the group members that have access to this space. Therefore, the application-sharing space transforms any single-user application put under its control into a multi-user shared application. (Villemur & Drira, 2006)

## Application-Specific Ontology

An engineering object defining the model of knowledge in a specific application case. (Cristani & Cuel, 2006)

## Applicative-Oriented Formal Specification Language

Does not allow the use of variables. (Dasso & Funes, 2005)

## Applied Behavior Analysis

Experimental analysis of behavior in which the three-term contingency, antecedent conditions, response, and consequent events are analyzed to explain behavior. (Lazarus, 2005a)

## Applied Ethics

**1:** The branch of ethics that emphasizes not theories of morality but ways of analyzing and resolving issues and conflicts in daily life, the professions, and public affairs. (Goodman, 2005) **2:** The study of a morally controversial practice, whereby the practice is described and analyzed, and moral principles and judgments are applied, resulting in a set of recommendations. (Cook, 2005)

## Appreciative Settings

A body of linked connotations of personal or collective interest, discrimination, and valuation which we bring to the exercise of judgment and which tacitly determine what we shall notice, how we shall discriminate situations of concern from the general confusion of an ongoing event, and how we shall regard them. (Vat, 2005a)

## Appreciative Systems

Developed by Vickers in the 1960s, the concepts of appreciative systems and of appreciative inquiry go beyond the paradigm of goal seeking to explain the processes of social activity, including decision making and action. Vickers criticized the reductionism of the perspective of focusing exclusively on goals, which he thought would be adequate to explain the 'behavior of rats in mazes'.

In order to describe and to explain the processes that characterize social systems, it is necessary to capture the establishing and modifying of relationships through time. Vickers also rejects the cybernetic paradigm where the course to be steered is available from outside the system, whereas systems of human activity themselves generate and regulate multiple and sometimes mutually inconsistent courses. Vickers' model is cyclical and starts with previous experiences which have created certain tacit patterns, standards, values, or norms; these lead to a readiness to notice certain features which determine which facts are relevant; the facts noticed are evaluated against the norms, leading both to regulatory action and to the modification of the norms so that future experiences may be evaluated differently. The organization of this process is the appreciative system which creates an individual and a social appreciative world. The appreciative settings condition new experience but are also modified by the new experience. Since the state of an appreciative system is the function of its own history, this implies that they are learning systems, and for Vickers, learning is the most central and basic social process. Soft systems methodology and complex systems thinking have extended the use and notion of appreciative systems. (Nobre, 2006b)

## Appropriation

The idea that active exploration enables people—while creating their own texts—to appropriate the knowledge that will help them read other texts. (Pryor, 2005)

## Appropriation and Delivery Structure

The rules and resources that determine the choices made by educators regarding strategies for integrating the learning model(s) and supporting technologies within a selected instructional design. (LeRouge & Webb, 2005)

## Approved

Term used to describe an educational institution or program that has the explicit recognition of an accrediting agency. (Kostopoulos, 2005)

## Approximate Searching

Searching that permits some differences between the pattern specification and its text occurrences. (Navarro, 2005)

## Approximation Set

An alternative (and more technically correct) name for a rough set, which is defined by two sets, the lower

approximation and the upper approximation. (Voges, 2005)

## Apriori Algorithm

**1:** An efficient association rule mining algorithm developed by Agrawal in 1993. Apriori employs a breadth-first search and uses a hash tree structure to count candidate item sets efficiently. The algorithm generates candidate item sets of length k from k–1 length item sets. Then, the patterns that have an infrequent subpattern are pruned. Following that, the whole transaction database is scanned to determine frequent item sets among the candidates. For determining frequent items in a fast manner, the algorithm uses a hash tree to store candidate item sets. (Huang, 2005) **2:** A classic algorithm that popularized association rule mining. It pioneered a method to generate candidate itemsets by using only frequent itemsets in the previous pass. The idea rests on the fact that any subset of a frequent itemset must be frequent as well. This idea is also known as the 'downward closure' property. (Woon et al., 2005) **3:** A level-wise algorithm for finding association rules. Apriori uses the support of an itemset to prune the search space of all itemsets. It then uses the confidence metric to find association rules. (Imberman & Tansel, 2006) **4:** Association rule mining algorithm that uses the fact that the support of a non-empty subset of an item set cannot be smaller than the support of the item set itself. (Denton & Besemann, 2005) **5:** The method of generating candidates before testing them during a scan over the database, insuring that if a candidate may be frequent, then it will be generated. See also Generating-Pruning. (Masseglia et al., 2005) **6:** Analysis and description of the media content at the time of insertion in the database. The gained information is stored in a database and enables content-based retrieval of the corresponding media object without actually accessing the latter. (Geisler & Kao, 2005)

## APS-Based Virtual Enterprise

A net of distributed APSs with those same objectives of traditional virtual enterprises, but with higher flexibility managing partners' core competences domain. (Pires et al., 2006)

**AR:** See *Action Research.*

## Arabization

The transformation of software applications into the Arabic language, in terms of usage as well as interface, to be able to cater for a community that stands in 2003 at around 300 million people. (Kamel, 2005a)

**A**

## Arbitrage

The simultaneous purchase of an undervalued security and sale of an overvalued but equivalent security to obtain a riskless profit on the price differential. Taking advantage of a market efficiency in a riskless manner. (Roofe, 2005)

## Arbitration

A private form of conflict resolution. The litigating parties may voluntarily submit a dispute to one or more independent, neutral experts (arbitrators) who decide upon the case similarly to a court, generally in a shorter period of time. Arbitrations are usually regulated by law. (Cevenini, 2005)

## Archetype

A naturally occurring constituent and output of a story tradition in which characters emerge from a body of anecdotes and stories that over time become more extreme until each archetype represents one aspect of that society. In a true archetype, all members of a community would recognize some aspect of themselves in each archetype. Archetypes are often associated with the work of Jung and Campbell who, in different contexts, argue for the existence of universal archetypes. This is not the only interpretation; many authors (including this one) argue from experience that archetypes across cultures may appear similar, but are in fact very different. For example, the trickster archetype of Norse legend is Loki, whose primary purpose if any seems at times destructive, whereas in many Native American stories the trickster is the coyote, whose function is to teach and advance humans to greater understanding. (Snowden, 2006)

## Architectural Design of Information Systems based on Structured Analysis (ADISSA)

An analysis and design methodology. In the analysis stage it utilizes hierarchical DFDs; in the design stage the DFDs are used to design the various components of the system. These include: (1) top-level descriptions of the transactions which eventually become detailed descriptions of the applications programs; (2) the user interfaces (menus); (3) the input and output screens and reports; and (4) the database schema in the form of normalized relations, and SQL commands for retrieving and updating the database. (Shoval & Kabeli, 2005)

## Architecture

**1:** A tailored interactive communications and information structure that leads to online transactions including curriculum content, networked relationships, various applications, and outcomes. (Baskin et al., 2005) **2:** The configuration of the network of neurons into layers of neurons is referred to as the neural architecture. To specify, the architecture involves declaring the number of input variables, hidden layers, hidden neurons, and output neurons. (Smith, 2005) **3:** The fundamental organization of a system, embodied in its components, their relationships to each other and the environment, and the principles governing its design and evolution (ANSI/IEEE Standard 1471-2000). (Stojanovic & Dahanayake, 2005) **4:** The organization of components of a system that enables their interacting with one another to achieve the objectives of the system. (Fulton, 2005) **5:** Used to describe the basic building blocks, functions, interfaces, and relationships of complex systems on an abstract level of detail. It is also used as a blueprint or reference model for implementing information systems, for example, enterprise architectures, information-system architectures, or software architectures. (Maier & Hädrich, 2006)

## Architecture of Integrated Information Systems (ARIS)

A modeling and design tool for business processes. (Sundaram & Portougal, 2005a)

## Architecture Viewpoint

An abstraction of a set of concerns on a system derived by using a set of concepts and rules of structure (RM-ODP). (Stojanovic & Dahanayake, 2005)

## Area of Black Pixels

The total number of black pixels in the binary image. (Chakravarty et al., 2005a)

## Area of Interest

An analysis method used in eye tracking. Researchers define areas of interest over certain parts of a display or interface under evaluation and analyze only the eye movements that fall within such areas. (Poole & Ball, 2006)

## Area of the Search Space

Set of specific ranges or values of the input variables that constitute a subset of the search space. (Rabuñal Dopico et al., 2005)

**Areal Interpolation**
A method of estimating counts or quantities for one configuration of geographic units (target zones) based on known counts from a different configuration of the same geographic space (source zones). (Garb & Wait, 2005a)

**ARIS:** See *Architecture of Integrated Information Systems.*

**Arity**
The number of roles in a fact type (unary = 1, binary = 2, ternary = 3, etc.). In ORM, fact types may be of arity 1 or more. In UML, fact types (associations) may be of arity 2 or more. (Halpin, 2005)

**ARL:** See *Association of Research Libraries.*

**Around-the-Clock Development**
A software development style in which software teams that are geographically distributed make use of time zones to develop software. (Lui & Chan, 2005)

**Around-the-Sun Development:** See *Around-the-Clock Development.*

**ARPAnet:** See *Advanced Research Projects Agency Network.*

**Array**
An item of this information category consists of a nonempty set of (point,value) pairs where the points have n-D integer coordinates and together completely cover an n-D interval, the so-called spatial domain of the array. (Baumann, 2005)

**ARS:** See *Audience Response System.*

**Artefact**
In the context of CoPs, indicates objects, articles, and "things" that have been created by the CoP to assist the members in their work and may have some of the community's knowledge embedded in them. Artefacts do not have to be concrete—a process or procedure may be an artefact. (Kimble & Hildreth, 2005)

**Articulated Object**
Structure composed of two or more rigid bodies interconnected by means of joints. The degrees of freedom associated with each joint define the different structure configurations. (Sappa et al., 2005)

**Articulation**
**1:** One of four knowledge transmission mechanisms according to Nonaka. Articulation is about explicit or codified knowledge being transferred to become explicit knowledge elsewhere by recombining two or more sets of coded knowledge. (Brock & Zhou, 2006) **2:** The process by which sounds are formed; the manner in which notes are struck, sustained, and released. Examples: staccato (shortening and detaching of notes), legato (smooth), pizzicato (plucking strings), vibrato (varying the pitch of a note up and down), muted (stringed instruments, by sliding a block of rubber or similar material onto the bridge), brass (by inserting a conical device into the bell). (Wieczorkowska, 2005)

**Artifact**
**1:** Any object produced or consumed by an activity of a business process. (De Lucia et al., 2006) **2:** Evidence in a portfolio; a product that demonstrates an aspect of performance or a professional work that has been selected by the creator of a portfolio. (Wieseman, 2005a) **3:** Actual examples of lesson plans, philosophies, and correspondence that show evidence of teacher competency in standards. (Shaw & Slick, 2005) **4:** Any human-made object. It can be physical (e.g., paper, application) or conceptual (e.g., norm, convention, habit). (Munkvold, 2006)

**Artifact Sharing**
A natural part of everyday work among community members where documents, charts, and images are shared for the purposes of planning, reflection, discussion, and solving problems. (Chua, 2006)

**Artificial Intelligence (AI)**
**1:** A research discipline whose aim is to make computers able to simulate human abilities, especially the ability to learn. AI is separated as neural net theory, expert systems, robotics, fuzzy control systems, game theory, and so forth. (R., 2005) **2:** Refers to the capability of a machine, and more specifically a computer or computer program, to perform functions that are normally associated with human intelligence, such as reasoning and optimization through experience. AI is the branch of computer science that attempts to approximate the results of human reasoning by organizing and manipulating factual and heuristic knowledge. (Hamdi, 2005b) **3:** A field of information technology that studies how to imbue computers with human characteristics and thought. Expert systems, natural language, and neural networks fall under the AI research area.(Athappilly & Rea, 2005) **4:** A set of computer

**A**

systems that feature automated human-intelligent, rational behavior and employ knowledge representation and reasoning methods. (Heucke et al., 2005) **5:** The branch of computer science concerned with making computers behave like humans. John McCarthy coined the term in 1956 while at the Massachusetts Institute of Technology. It refers to the science that provides computers with the ability to solve problems not easily solved through algorithmic models. (Becerra-Fernandez & Sabherwal, 2006) **6:** The field of science that studies how to make computers "intelligent." It consists mainly of the fields of machine learning (neuronal networks and decision trees) and expert systems. The principal problem is how to represent knowledge. (Rodríguez-Tastets, 2005b) **7:** The study of the principles of intelligence (scientific objective), and the design and build of intelligent machines like robots (engineering objective). (Gelepithis, 2005) **8:** The use of computer systems, software, and models to imitate human thought and reasoning when completing a task. (Ally, 2005b)

## Artificial Intelligence Markup Language (AIML)

An XML specification for programming chat agents like ALICE. The free ALICE AIML includes a knowledge base of approximately 41,000 categories. (Sourin, 2006)

## Artificial Life (ALife)

**1:** The synthetic or virtual approach to the study of life-like patterns (forms), behaviors, systems, and organisms, independently of the matter used for synthesis. (de Castro, 2005) **2:** The reproduction in digital models of certain aspects of organic life, particularly the ability of evolving adaptation through mutations that provide a better fit to the environment. In information sciences, artificial life is not concerned with the physico-chemical recreation of life. (Duchastel, 2006)

## Artificial Neural Network (ANN)

**1:** A network of nodes modeled after a neuron or neural circuit. The neural network mimics the processing of the human brain. (Garrity et al., 2005) **2:** Commonly referred to as "neural network" or "neural net," a computer architecture implemented in either hardware or software, modeled after biological neural networks. Nodes are connected in a manner suggestive of connections between the biological neurons they represent. The resulting network "learns" through directed trial and error. Most neural networks have some sort of "training" algorithm to adjust the weights of connections between nodes on the basis of

patterns found in sample or historical data. (Kitchens, 2005) **3:** Biologically inspired statistical tools modeled after the structure of the human brain. Neural networks are composed of interconnected units or nodes (similar to neurons) with associated weights and activation values. Training or learning rules are incorporated into the network to accomplish forecasting or classification tasks based on the pattern of interconnection throughout the network. (Fuller & Wilson, 2006) **4:** Parallel distributed processor formed by single processing units that has a natural capacity of storing experimental knowledge and making it available for use. Artificial neural networks are designed to model complex problems such as time series forecasting, pattern recognition, and so forth. (Castro & Braga, 2006) **5:** A network of many simple processors ("units" or "neurons") that imitates a biological neural network. The units are connected by unidirectional communication channels, which carry numeric data. Neural networks can be trained to find nonlinear relationships in data, and are used in applications such as robotics, speech recognition, signal processing, or medical diagnosis. (Rabuñal Dopico et al., 2005) **6:** A system composed of many simple processing elements operating in parallel whose function is determined by network structure, connection strengths, and the processing performed at computing elements or units. (Zhou, 2005) **7:** Approach based on the neural structure of the brain with the capability to identify and learn patterns from different situations as well as to predict new situations. (Hentea, 2005b) **8:** A nonlinear predictive model that learns through training and resembles biological neural networks in structure. (Hamdi, 2005a) **9:** Type of machine learning paradigm that simulates the densely interconnected, parallel structure of the mammalian brain. ANNs have been shown to be powerful tools for function approximation. (Wen, Hong, et al., 2005)

## Artificially Intelligent Systems

Information systems that help users manage data and models by delivering virtual expertise and other forms of artificial intelligence in support of these tasks. (Forgionne, 2005)

**AS:** See *Autonomous System.*

## ASAP System

The abbreviation of a synchronous approach for photo sharing across devices to facilitate photo viewing across multiple devices, which can simultaneously present similar photos across multiple devices at the same time for comparative viewing or searching. (Hua et al., 2006)

**ASCII:** See *American Standard Code for Information Interchange.*

**ASEAN**

Association of Southeast Asian Countries. (Sanzogni & Arthur-Gray, 2005)

**ASF:** See *Adaptive Synchronization Framework.*

**Asia Pacific Development Information Program (APDIP)**

The regional ICT program of UNDP. (Hutchinson, 2005)

**Asia-Pacific Telecommunity**

A 32-member body established in 1979 through joint initiatives of the United Nations Economic and Social Commission for Asia & the Pacific and the International Telecommunication Union. Members of the APT include governments, telecom service providers, manufactures of communication equipment, and research and development organizations. (Hassall, 2005)

**ASP:** See *Application Service Provider; Active Server Page Scripting.*

**ASP Aggregator**

The ASP aggregator model is based on the premise that the rapid proliferation of firms offering ASP services has created an overly complex market for medium-sized enterprises to deal with when investigating application outsourcing options. (Guah & Currie, 2005)

**Aspect**

Defines a set of related node properties, attributable to nodes with the same value for an aspect descriptor. For a given node, aspects can be added and removed at runtime by manipulating the values for its aspect descriptors. (Lemahieu, 2005)

**Aspect Descriptor**

Attribute for which each possible value defines an aspect of a node. (Lemahieu, 2005)

**Assertion**

**1:** A statement (entity definition, attribute value, constraint, rule, function, and the like) assumed to be true and therefore supporting the theory of the ontology. Example: Gravity is an attracting force in nature. (Buchholz, 2006) **2:** Authoritatively convincing others of a project's potential benefits so they dedicate their efforts to the project. (Sipior, 2005) **3:** Expression in a relational database system that allows stating a condition involving several attributes and several tables. Assertions are first-class database entities, such as tables. (Badia, 2005b)

**Assertion Between Knowledge Patterns**

A particular interschema property. It indicates either a subsumption or an equivalence between knowledge patterns. Roughly speaking, knowledge patterns can be seen as views on involved information sources. (De Meo, Terracina, et al., 2005)

**Assertion of Copyright**

Retention of the protection right of copyright by an individual, and hence the ability to collect any royalties that may be apportioned. (Fleming, 2005b)

**Assertional Reasoning**

A description logic knowledge base is made up of two parts, a terminological part (the terminology or Tbox) and an assertional part (the Abox), each part consisting of a set of axioms. The AbBox contains extensional knowledge that is specific to the individuals of the domain of discourse. There has been a great deal of work on the development of reasoning algorithms for expressive DLs, but in most cases these only consider Tbox reasoning. Reasoning mechanisms for the Abox (i.e., instance checking) are called assertional reasoning. Assertional reasoning is important for real Semantic Web applications. (Roldán-García et al., 2005)

**Assessment**

**1:** A process by which learning is measured, often through content-related assignments such as papers, projects, or tests. (Hawkins & Baker, 2005) **2:** A process of assisting an individual with a disability in the selection of appropriate assistive technology devices and/or configurations of standard information technology devices. (Trewin & Keates, 2006) **3:** Determining how much someone has learned or how well someone understands a particular subject. (Bieber et al., 2005) **4:** Process by which learning gains or performance chance are measured and labelled according to a consistent scoring criterion. (Collis & Moonen, 2005a) **5:** Systematic evaluation of student work and learning based on scoring criteria and leading to a mark or grade. (Collis & Moonen, 2005b) **6:** The evaluation of the amount, value, quality, or importance of something. (Kung-Ming, 2005) **7:** The process of comparing the actual measurements of the characteristics of interest with

**A**

the specifications of those characteristics. (Leung, 2005) **8:** The process of gathering, describing, or quantifying information about performance. (Brace & Berge, 2006)

## Assessment of Learning Outcomes

The process of examining the achievement of intended learning outcomes by students. (Naidu, 2005a)

## Assessment Tools

Methods used to obtain information about student learning to guide a variety of educational strategies and decisions. (Beck & Schornack, 2005)

## Asset Creator

Anyone who creates an asset, which could be in any digital format, and provides the asset and its associated information to the asset manager. (Subramanian, 2005)

## Asset Manager

The asset manager converts the information associated with the asset into an XML metadata format, builds the appropriate data type definitions, and passes the information and the asset to the metadata manager. (Subramanian, 2005)

## Assignment

A repartition in which we allocate the available resources to achieve the different tasks. (Kacem, 2005)

## Assisted Global Positioning System (A-GPS)

**1.** A variation of the global positioning system (GPS) in which the mobile network or a third-party service provider assists the mobile handset in determining its geographical position (either by directing it to look for specific satellites or by collecting data from the handset to perform location identification calculations that the handset itself may be unable to perform due to limited processing power). (Giaglis, 2005) **2:** A system that uses measurements from fixed GPS receivers scattered throughout the mobile network in order to assist a mobile phone in locating the available satellites and calculating its location. (Ververidis & Polyzos, 2006)

## Assistive and Augmentative Communication

A multidisciplinary field that seeks to design devices and methods to alleviate the problems faced by physically challenged people running programs they do not know and/or trust. (Abhishek & Basu, 2006)

## Assistive Technology

**1:** A set of solutions, both hardware and software, aimed at supporting people with disabilities in interacting with digital content. (Costagliola, Di Martino, Ferrucci, & Gravino, 2006) **2:** Examples of assistive technology include wheelchairs, hand controls for automobiles, prostheses, communication aids, hand splints, hearing aids, and alternatives to computer keyboards (also called Technology-Related Assistance). (Burgstahler, 2005b) **3:** Any item, piece of equipment, or system that is commonly used to increase, maintain, or improve functional capabilities of individuals with disabilities. Examples include screen readers, teletypewriters (TTYs), and Braille keyboards. (Bursa, Justice, & Kessler, 2005) **4:** Products, devices, or equipment, whether acquired commercially, modified, or customized, that are used to maintain, increase, or improve the functional capabilities of individuals with disabilities. (Keates et al., 2006) **5:** Specialized software or hardware, such as screen readers, magnification software, and a modified keyboard, used by some people with disabilities to interact with the computer. (Schmetzke, 2005) **6:** Technologies designed to support disabled individuals in the conduct of their daily tasks. (Roldan, 2005)

## Association

**1:** A relationship between two statistical variables. Unlike a correlation, an association does not yield a quantitative result, but is contingent upon the ranking of the bivariate data values only. (Mullany, 2005) **2:** A technique in data mining that attempts to identify similarities across a set of records, such as purchases that occur together across a number of transactions. (Amaravadi, 2005) **3:** The degree to which participation in global communication confers on participants some of the prestige associated with more glamorous lifestyles. (Pryor, 2005)

## Association (Undirected Association Rule)

A subtuple of a bag relation whose support is greater than a given threshold. (T. Y. Lin, 2005)

## Association Analysis

Use of statistics criteria to measure the proximity of two distinct objects or texts using some of their properties or attributes. A method for identifying correlation or dependencies among elements or attributes, using statistical techniques. (Antonio do Prado et al., 2005)

## Association of Research Libraries (ARL)

An organization that unites the 123 leading research libraries in North America. (McCarthy, 2005b)

## Association Rule

**1:** A kind of rule in the form $X \rightarrow I_j$, where X is a set of some items and Ij is a single item not in X. (Wong & Fu, 2005) **2:** A pair of frequent itemsets (A, B), where the ratio between the support of $A \cup B$ and A itemsets is greater than a predefined threshold, denoted minconf. (Dumitriu, 2005) **3:** A relation between the occurrences of a set of items with another set of items in a large data set. (Jha & Sural, 2005) **4:** A rule in the form of "if this, then that." It states a statistical correlation between the occurrence of certain attributes in a database. (Huang, 2005) **5:** A rule of the form $A \rightarrow B$, meaning "if the set of items A is present in a transaction, the set of items B is likely to be present too." A typical example constitutes associations between items purchased at a supermarket. (Denton & Besemann, 2005) **6:** A rule relating two itemsets—the antecedent and the consequent. The rule indicates that the presence of the antecedent implies that the consequent is more probable in the data. Written as (Butler & Webb, 2005) **7:** A rule showing the association between two or more nominal attributes. Associations can be directed or undirected. For instance, a rule of the form, If the customer buys French fries and hamburgers she or he buys ketchup, is a directed association rule. The techniques for learning association rules are specific, and many of them, such as the Apriori Algorithm, are based on the idea of finding frequent item sets in the data. (Hernandez-Orallo, 2005b) **8:** A statement A => B, which states that if A is true, then we can expect B to be true with a certain degree of confidence. A and B are sets of items, and the $\Rightarrow$ operator is interpreted as "implies." (Ale & Rossi, 2005) **9:** An association between two sets of items co-occurring frequently in groups of data. (Meo & Psaila, 2005) **10:** An association has the form $I_1 \rightarrow I_2$, where $I_1$ and $I_2$ are two itemsets. The support of an association rule is the support of the itemset $I_1 \cup I_2$, and the confidence of a rule is the ratio of support of $I_1 \cup I_2$ and the support of $I_1$. (Zhou & Wang, 2005) **11:** An implication rule $XY$ that shows the conditions of co-occurrence of disjoint itemsets (attribute value sets) $X$ and $Y$ in a given database. (Shen, 2005) **12:** Given a set $I = \{ i_1, i_2, i_3, \dots i_n \}$ of items, any subset of I is called an itemset. Let X and Y be subsets of I such that $X \cap Y = \phi$. An association rule is a probabilistic implication $X \Rightarrow Y$. (Imberman & Tansel, 2006) **13:** Implication of the form $X \Rightarrow Y$, meaning that database tuples satisfying the conditions of X are also likely to satisfy the conditions of Y. (Chung & Mangamuri, 2005) **14:** The implication of connections for variables that are explored in databases, having a form of A→B, where A and B are disjoint subsets of a dataset of binary attributes. (Wu & Lee, 2005) **15:** An implication of the form A $\Rightarrow$ B, where A and B are database itemsets. Association rules must satisfy the pre-set minimum support (minsup) and minimum confidence (minconf) constraints. (Daly & Taniar, 2005a) **16:** An implication rule between two itemsets with statistical measures of range (support) and precision (confidence). (Pasquier, 2005) **17:** An implication rule that brings out hidden relationships among attributes on the basis of co-occurrence of attributes. In the market-basket context, it informs about items that are likely to be purchased together, thereby providing an insight into customer purchasing behavior. Formally, an association rule is an implication of the form A $\Rightarrow$ B, where A and B can be single items or sets of items, with no commonality between sets A and B, e.g., {Bread} $\Rightarrow$ {Butter}, {Bread, Jam} $\Rightarrow$ {Butter}, and so forth. An association rule is characterized by two measures, support (a statement of generality) and confidence (a statement of predictive ability). These rules are very general, having a simple interpretation with minimal restrictions on their structure. {Bread} $\Rightarrow$ {Butter} with support =20% and confidence = 60% means that 60% of the transactions that contain Bread also contain Butter, and they are purchased together in 20% of the transactions. (Natarajan & Shekar, 2006) **18:** Let X1, .., Xp be a collection of random variables. In general, a pattern for such variables identifies a subset of all possible observations over them. A rule is a logical statement between two patterns, say α and β, written as α→β. (Giudici & Cerchiello, 2005) **19:** Predicts the occurrence of an event based on the occurrences of another event. (Yeo, 2005) **20:** Uncovering interesting trends, patterns, and rules in large data sets with support s and confidence c. (Swierzowicz, 2005) **21:** Used to associate items in a database sharing some relationship (e.g., co-purchase information). Often takes the form "if this, then that," such as, "If the customer buys a handheld videogame, then the customer is likely to purchase batteries." (Schafer, 2005)

## Association Rule Discovery

**1:** A rule in the form of "if this, then that" which associates events in a database. Association rule discovery can be used to find unordered correlations between items found in a set of database transactions, such as the association between purchased items at a department (Hu, Yang, Lee, et al., 2005) **2:** Implication of the form X ⇒ Y, where X and Y are sets of items; implies that if the condition X is verified, the prediction Y is valid. (Jourdan et al., 2005)

## Association Rule Mining

**1:** The process of examining the data for "if this then that" rules is called association rule mining. (Ramasamy & Deshpande, 2005) **2:** The data-mining task of finding all association rules existing in a database, having support and confidence greater than a minimum support value and a minimum confidence value. (Ale & Rossi, 2005) **3:** The process of finding interesting association or correlation relationships among a large set of data items. (Perrizo, Ding, Ding, et al., 2005)

## Assurance

Statement, indication, or presumption that inspires confidence while excluding doubt. Assurance is an aspect of trust. Given the fact that trust cannot be quantified precisely, assurance provides a basis for quantitatively or qualitatively specifying the level of trust towards a system. (Oermann & Dittmann, 2006)

## Assured Forwarding (AF)

A per-hop behavior defined in DiffServ. AF provides different levels of forwarding assurances depending on available resources, the current number of flows in that AF class, and the drop precedence associated with the IP datagram. (DaSilva, 2005)

**Ast:** See *Attitude Toward the Site.*

**ASTD:** See *American Society for Training & Development.*

## Asymmetric Communication

A process in which both communicating parties are at different levels of economic and social development. (Targowski & Metwalli, 2005)

## Asymmetric Cryptography

A data encryption system that uses two separate but related encryption keys. The private key is known only to its owner, while the public key is made available in a key repository or as part of a digital certificate. Asymmetric cryptography is the basis of digital signature systems. (Richter & Roth, 2006)

**Asymmetric Digital Subscriber Line (ADSL):** See *Digital Subscriber Line.*

## Asymmetric DSL (ADSL)

A DSL technology that allows the use of a copper line to send a large quantity of data from the network to the end user (downstream data rates up to 8 Mbit/s), and a small quantity of data from the end user to the network (upstream data rates up to 1 Mbit/s). It can be used for fast Internet applications and video-on-demand. (Chochliouros, Spiliopoulou-Chochliourou, & Lalopoulos, 2005c)

## Asymmetric Threat

An adversarial situation characterized by the inequality in resources between the contenders, which usually results in one of them resorting to covert and terrorist activities to continue the conflict. (Badia, 2006)

## Asymmetry

Used in IT to mean that parties are heterogeneous and possess diverse knowledge bases. Asymmetry manifests also in corporate culture and management. (Blomqvist, 2005)

## Asynchronous

**1:** A form of online discussion among students, workers, or instructors. Participants post comments, opinions, reflections, or questions to a type of online discussion board. Participants can read and respond to others' postings. Participants can access or post at any time. (Iannarelli, 2005) **2:** Communication between parties in which the interaction does not take place simultaneously. (Danenberg & Chen, 2005) **3:** Communication occurring via a time delay, such as posts to an electronic bulletin board. (Hawkins & Baker, 2005) **4:** Communication that allows for the sharing of ideas over a period of time, such as through discussion boards, e-mail, or a newsroom. (Etter & Byrnes, 2005) **5:** Communications between the student and teacher which do not take place simultaneously. (T. Cavanaugh, 2005) **6:** Denotes a communication method which participants use to interact in a time-delayed context, that is, without everyone gathering at a particular time. (Al-Saggaf & Weckert, 2005) **7:** Occurring at different times. In the context of communications technologies, asynchronous technologies allow communicators to interact with the conversation at different times—for example, e-mail or threaded discussions. (Newberry, 2005) **8:** Occurring at different times; typically used to refer to technologies such as a discussion board or e-mail that may be utilized at the user's convenience. (Ordonez, 2005) **9:** Online, asynchronous refers to communication that occurs at different times. Common examples of asynchronous communications are e-mail, ListProc (listserv), or the WebCT discussions tool. (Paoletti, 2005) **10:** Out of synchronicity. Conversations with time lags, as in e-mail. (Coakes, 2006b) **11:** Refers to the ability of learners to complete required tasks at different times. Discussion tools (i.e., bulletin boards) are examples of asynchronous tools used in the Web-based environment. (Morphew, 2005) **12:** The 24-hour classroom discussion is always open; plenty of time for reflection, analysis, and composition; encourages thinking, retrospective analysis; the whole transcript discussion is there for review; class discussion is open ended, not limited to the end of a period. (Nandavadekar, 2005) **13:** Time-delayed interaction that does not require participants to be online simultaneously; individuals send or post messages, and the recipients read them at a later time. (Woods & Baker, 2005)

## Asynchronous Collaboration

Collaborative interactions, for example, over the Internet that are not synchronized in real time such as e-mail exchanges, browser-based shared editing (wikis), and postings to newsgroups. (Carroll et al., 2005)

## Asynchronous Communication

**1:** A delayed time communication, typically in text format, between the learner and instructor or among learners. (Gold, 2005) **2:** An electronically transmitted exchange of ideas that allows participation to occur at discontinuous points in time. (Baugher et al., 2005) **3:** Communication between parties that does not require the parties to be available for communication all at the same time. (Lam et al., 2006) **4:** Communication that does not occur in real time. There can be a delay between sending information and retrieving it. Responses to messages may be delayed, with each message waiting until the recipient is ready to read and/or reply. Asynchronous communication utilizes such tools as e-mail and discussion groups. (Erlich, 2005) **5:** Communication that does not occur in real time (e.g., e-mail, letters, and telegrams). (Dell, 2005) **6:** Communication that does not require both the sender and receiver to be present/logged in at the same time. Common asynchronous forms of computer-mediated communication are e-mail and newsgroups. (Roberts, Smith, & Pollock, 2006b) **7:** Communication where the message is not sent and received simultaneously (e.g., e-mail, discussion forums, listservs). (Stodel et al., 2005) **8:** Computer-based communication tool in which interaction between parties does not take place simultaneously. (Ketelhut et al., 2005) **9:** Information exchanges sent and received at different times,

often taking place in geographically dispersed locations and time zones. (Wong-MingJi, 2005) **10:** Information sharing and interaction between individuals taking place at different times, as in the sending of e-mails where messages are sent and then read at a later time. (Ally, 2005d) **11:** The sharing of messages with delayed feedback. (Han & Hill, 2006) **12:** When participants decide when to retrieve and respond to others in the online environment through tools such as discussion boards and e-mail. (S.-K. Wang, 2005) **13:** Communications that occur between two or more people in which the method of communication of one or more individuals does not occur at the same time as the others involved (Day, 2005) **14:** When messages are exchanged during different time intervals (Burke et al., 2005)

## Asynchronous Communication Channels

Communication channels that support communication that usually requires a period of time to pass between communicative transactions. These channels include e-mail, discussion boards, fax, and so forth. (Pauleen, 2005)

## Asynchronous Communication Opportunity

The provision of the choice between immediate interaction and asynchronous interaction in terms of the timing of interaction engagement (e.g., response) without physical constraints such as geographical distance and physical time to deliver the information (e.g., such constraints in conventional mailing system). (Kang et al., 2006)

## Asynchronous Communication Tool

**1:** Communication does not occur in real time. Communication can be received "any time." E-mail is an example of an asynchronous tool, as an electronic mail message waits for the recipient to open it. (Schoenfeld & Berge, 2005) **2:** A tool that facilitates communication at different times. The best example is postal mail (or "snail" mail). The receiver can read the message at any time he/she wants. (Karoulis & Pombortsis, 2005b)

## Asynchronous Computer-Mediated Communication

A set of techniques allowing participants to contribute from different locations and, more importantly, at different times. Tools available include e-mail, listservs, and discussion groups. (Salter, 2005a)

**Asynchronous Cooperation**

Members are not present in the same time within the cooperation group (no co-presence). They communicate with asynchronous media (e.g., e-mail messages) on top of extended and improved message systems. (Villemur & Drira, 2006)

**Asynchronous Delivery Mode**

Material to be delivered is made available by the instructor through technology, and students are able to access the material based upon their own schedules. (Hunter & Carr, 2005)

**Asynchronous Digital Subscriber Line (ADSL)**

A digital switched technology that provides very high data transmission speeds over telephone system wires. The speed of the transmission is asynchronous, meaning that the transmission speeds for uploading and downloading data are different. For example, upstream transmissions may vary from 16 Kbps to 640 Kbps, and downstream rates may vary from 1.5Mbps to 9Mbps. Within a given implementation, the upstream and downstream speeds remain constant. (Raisinghani & Ghanem, 2005)

**Asynchronous Discussion**

**1:** Discussion that occurs irrespective of time and location. Asynchronous discussion allows readers (e.g., from different time zones and/or at different times) to create and respond to learners who are typically not online at the same time. (Bedard-Voorhees, 2005) **2:** Online discussions that occur independent of time and space. Participants do not have to be online simultaneously, and can read and contribute to the conversation on their own schedules. (Ingram, 2005) **3:** The exchange of information that occurs over a period of time. This discussion method allows for reflection and considered opinions. (Ingram & Hathorn, 2005b)

**Asynchronous Discussion Forum**

This is at the heart of many computer-based courses. It is the place where student-student and student-faculty interaction occurs and learning takes place. The participants in the discussion need not be present in the learning environment at the same time, and they make contributions to selected threads as needed. (Shaw, 2005)

**Asynchronous Distance Delivery**

An anytime, anywhere experience where all participants work independently at times convenient to them and that includes methods such as online discussion boards, e-mail, and video programming, and the implicit absence of immediate interaction with the teacher or other students. (C. Wright, 2005)

**Asynchronous Distance Learning**

The mode of distance learning where provider and recipient are communicating off-line—that is, leaving messages for each other or viewing each other's pre-recordings while geographically apart. (Kostopoulos, 2005)

**Asynchronous Group Communication Technology**

Allows participants to send and respond to messages without being online simultaneously. (Alavi et al., 2005)

**Asynchronous Instructional Dyad**

Material placed on electronic media for access by students as needed; an example is a detailed instruction sheet that supplements explanations given during regular class sessions. (Lerch et al., 2005)

**Asynchronous Interaction**

**1:** Communication that takes place over a network at different times. Examples of asynchronous interaction include communication via group support systems, e-mail, and electronic bulletin boards. The opposite of asynchronous interaction is synchronous interaction, which occurs when participants interact over a network simultaneously (i.e., in real time). (Klein, 2005) **2:** Interactions that do not take place simultaneously for the involved participants (e.g., email communication). (Taylor et al., 2005)

**Asynchronous Learning**

**1:** A type of learning that is both time and location independent; the learner can be located anywhere and contribute anytime. Also called delayed learning as opposed to real-time learning. (Bonk et al., 2005) **2:** Learners use a computer and communications technologies to work with remote learning resources, without the requirement to be online at the same time or in the same location. Participation in online discussion boards is an example of asynchronous learning. (Chapman, 2005a) **3:** Learning in which interaction between instructors and students occurs intermittently with a time delay. Examples are self-paced courses taken via the Internet or CD-ROM, Q&A mentoring, online discussion groups, and e-mail. (Torres-Coronas, 2005) **4:** Learning that occurs at the place and time of the students' choosing, not the instructor's.

(Novitzki, 2005) **5:** Online courses that allow students to participate at anytime from any location with Internet access. (Lazarus, 2005b)

### Asynchronous Learning Network (ALN)

**1:** Technology-enabled networks for communications and learning communities. (Moore et al., 2005) **2:** Anytime, anywhere education using computer and communication technologies without the requirement for learners to be online at the same time. (Rovai & Gallien, 2006) **3:** Communication between people that does not occur simultaneously. (Brown, 2006)

### Asynchronous Learning Tool

Software package designed to support education at any location and at any time. (Novitzki, 2005)

### Asynchronous Media

Delayed delivery of media (e.g., video, e-mail). (Whateley et al., 2005)

### Asynchronous Mode

A non-real-time education where students and teachers interact with each other, but not at same time, e.g., by using a bulletin board or e-mail. (Lammintakanen & Rissanen, 2005a)

### Asynchronous Online Distance Education

Courses that use software that contains course content and pedagogy that allow students to participate when and where they want. (Novitzki, 2005)

### Asynchronous Replication

Lazy replication—that is, all updates of a transaction (if any) are transmitted to passive replicas once the transaction is committed, but never ahead of commit time. (Muñoz-Escoí et al., 2005)

### Asynchronous System

Allows students to participate at a time and place convenient to them. In an asynchronous system, interaction between the student and the faculty takes place intermittently through e-mail, HTML (Hypertext Markup Language) content, and/or news or discussion groups. The interaction does not require participation at the same time. (Sivakumar, 2006)

### Asynchronous Technology

**1:** Technology that creates a delay in communication, such as e-mail or a discussion board. (Wei & Wang, 2006) **2:**

Technology that does not require real-time, simultaneous participation, and that does not support anytime, anyplace communication. (Wild, 2005)

### Asynchronous Transfer Mode (ATM)

**1:** A high-speed transmission protocol in which data blocks are broken into cells that are transmitted individually and possibly via different routes in a manner similar to packet-switching technology. (Raisinghani & Ghanem, 2005) **2:** A network technology based on transferring data in cells or packets of a fixed size. The small, constant cell size allows ATM equipment to transmit video, audio, and computer data over the same network, and assure that no single type of data hogs the line. (Wong, 2006) **3:** A high-speed, low-delay, multiplexing and switching technology that allows voice, image, data, and video to be transmitted simultaneously rather than through traffic-specific networks. (Hin & Subramaniam, 2005c) **4:** A transmission technique that transmits combined information in small, fixed-size packets called ATM cells. (Louvros, Karaboulas, et al., 2005)

### Asynchrony

A condition whereby events occur that are not coordinated in time. In online education, asynchrony makes it possible to perform course tasks at the most convenient time, not tied to a schedule. (Rollier & Niederman, 2005)

**ATAP:** See *Any Time, Any Place Learning.*

**ATC:** See *Air Traffic Control.*

### Ateleology

In the context of IS development, refers to the development of an IS which does not aim at the attainment of a specific set of goals only, expressed in the form of user requirements as they have been articulated at a specific point of time, but rather refers to developing an IS that addresses a range of issues within a specific problem domain and, at the same time, is flexible enough to accommodate changes and extensions of the IS behavior while it is being operated. (Stamoulis et al., 2005)

**ATM:** See *Asynchronous Transfer Mode; Automatic Teller Machine System.*

### Atoma

The most abstract level of representation of a real-world entity, encompassing only the most basic data and functionality for representing and manipulating the entity. (Lepouras et al., 2006)

## Atomic Broadcast

Requires that each correct process deliver all messages in the same order—that is, a reliable broadcast with total order. (Muñoz-Escoí et al., 2005)

## Atomic Transaction

A transaction whose updates are either all executed or removed (the "A" in the ACID properties). The atomicity property makes it easier to complete database recovery. (Frank, 2005b)

## At-Risk Learners

Typically individuals who struggle with the structure and/or content of formal education. (Crichton, 2005)

## Attachment

An extra file, in any file format, that is linked to a e-mail message. The e-mail message itself must structurally conform to messaging protocols. (Horiuchi, 2005b)

## Attacks

Any processing that circumvents the intended purpose of the watermarking technique for a given application. An attack potentially breaks the robustness of the watermark. (Sattar & Yu, 2006)

## Attack Signature

Patterns observed in previously known attacks that are used to distinguish malicious packets from normal traffic. (Syed, Nur, et al., 2005)

## Attack vs. Intrusion

A subtle difference, intrusions are the attacks that succeed. Therefore, the term 'attack' represents both successful and attempted intrusions. (Kayacik et al., 2005)

## Attention

**1:** An internal cognitive process by which one actively selects which part of the environmental information surrounds them and focuses on that part or maintains interest while ignoring distractions. (Alkhalifa, 2006) **2:** Mental processing that consumes our conscious thinking. Through a variety of mechanisms, there is a limit to the amount of processing that can take place in our consciousness. (Owen, 2006b) **3:** Associated with a variety of more specific constructs such as mental effort, mental focus, mental elaboration, and such. Processes associated with the attention-related constructs are what we presume to be detecting in dual-task studies. (Owen, 2006c)

## Attention Object

An information carrier that delivers the author's intention and catches part of the user's attention as a whole. An attention object often represents a semantic object, such as a human face, a flower, a mobile car, a text sentence, and so forth. (Hua et al., 2006)

## Attention-Based IT Infrastructure

An IT infrastructure that is able to sort through volumes of data and produce the right information at the right time for the right persons to consume. (Chen, Zhang, et al., 2005b)

## Attention-Deficit Principle

Recognizes that organizations have limited attention capacity, and attention should be treated as a resource that needs to be managed. (Yaniv & Schwartz, 2006)

## Attentional Capacity

Cognitive capacity divided and allocated to perform cognitive task. (Seta, 2006)

## Attentive User Interfaces

AUIs are based on the idea that modeling the deployment of user attention and task preferences is the key for minimizing the disruptive effects of interruptions. By monitoring the user's physical proximity, body orientation, eye fixations, and the like, AUIs can determine what device, person, or task the user is attending to. Knowing the focus of attention makes it possible in some situations to avoid interrupting the users in tasks that are more important or time-critical than the interrupting one. (Oulasvirta & Salovaara, 2006)

## Attenuation

Loss of signal strength and power as a signal passes through the optical fiber medium. (Littman, 2006)

## Attitude Toward the Ad (Aad)

A mediator of advertising response that influences brand attitude and purchase intentions. (Gao et al., 2006)

## Attitude Toward the Site (Ast)

A Web user's predisposition to respond either favorably or unfavorably to a Web site in a natural exposure situation. (Gao, 2005b)

## Attribute

**1:** A substantial feature of a whole that is perceived by an observer with the potential to produce or cause a product or effect. (Gelman et al., 2005) **2:** A property of an object/class. The class Car, for example, can have an attribute Color, its value for the object MyCar: Car might be blue. (Rittgen, 2005) **3:** Column of a dataset. (Gehrke, 2005) **4:** Pieces of information contained in a GIS database that describe or detail a spatially referenced element. (Crossland, 2005)

## Attribute Dependency

Introduces when it falls within a dimension caused by attribute hierarchies. (Tan, 2005a)

## Attribute Discretization

The process of converting a (continuous) attribute value range to a set of discrete intervals and representing all the values in each interval with a single (interval) label. (Shen & Horiguchi, 2005)

## Attribute Fuzzification

A process that converts numeric attribute values into membership values of fuzzy sets. (Shen & Horiguchi, 2005)

## Attribute Realism

An ontological position that the properties of entities exist in the world independent of their being perceived by the modeler. (Artz, 2005c)

## Attribute-Tolerant Transactions

These transactions can be permitted to be locally relaxed in terms of certain constraints on attributes, but globally consistent eventually. (Murthy & Krishnamurthy, 2005c)

## Attributed Graph

A graph whose vertices and edges have attributes typically defined by vectors and matrices, respectively. (Caelli, 2005)

## Attribution

Source code published under this license may be used freely, provided that the original author is attributed. (Fleming, 2005b)

## Attrition

The falling off or stoppage of coursework and degree progression that results in a decrease in the number of learners or students engaged in some course of study. (Adkins & Nitsch, 2005)

## Auction

A type of market in which sellers post an initial price for the item being offered and a deadline by which the item needs to be sold. Buyers make bids on the offered item. The auction mechanism determines the dynamics of the prices bid by the buyers, the winner-determination strategy, and the bid-disclosure strategy. Common auction mechanisms include the English auction, Dutch auction, and Vickrey auction. (Dasgupta et al., 2006)

## Auction-Based Market

A form of centralized facility or clearinghouse by which consumers and suppliers execute trades in an open and competitive bidding process. (Ghenniwa & Huhns, 2005)

## Audience Class

Group of target visitors of a Web site with the same requirements. (De Troyer, 2005)

## Audience Response System (ARS)

An electronic system designed to support and enhance face-to-face group interaction by means of individual handheld communication devices. (Banks, 2005)

## Audience Track

Part of a Web site that provides information and services specifically tailored to an audience class. (De Troyer, 2005)

## Audience-Driven Web Design

The different audiences and their requirements are taken as the starting point for the design of the Web site. The information and services in the Web site are organized around the different audience classes. (De Troyer, 2005)

## Audio Browser

Also referred to as "talking browser." Software that interprets the HTML code of Web pages and provides speech output for text-based components, along with information provided by the HTML markup tags. Typically, it also enables users to navigate the Web page through alternative keystrokes. (Schmetzke, 2005)

**A**

**Audio File**
A computer file that contains audio instruction or explanation. It might also contain graphic images that correlate with the audio. (Cooper, 2005)

**Audio Memo**
A recorded audio message of speech. Speech is digitally recorded via a built-in or attached microphone and stored as a digital audio file on the storage media of the PDA. (Garrett, 2006b)

**Audio Packet**
Packet encoding an audio sample in digital form. Each audio packet has a timestamp and a sequence number as additional information. Timestamps are used to measure the end-to-end delay (jitter) experienced during the communication, and sequence numbers are used to detect packet losses. Typically, during an audio communication, audio packets are transmitted over the network, received in a playout buffer, decoded in sequential order, and finally, played out by the audio device. (Roccetti & Ferretti, 2005)

**Audio Sample**
The amplitude of a waveform is measured (sampled) at regular time intervals and converted into an integer value. Each of these instantaneous measurements is an audio sample. (Roccetti & Ferretti, 2005)

**Audiographic Communication**
A multimedia approach with simultaneous resources for listening, viewing, and interacting with materials. (C. Wright, 2005)

**Audiographic Teleconferencing**
Voice communication supplemented with the transmission of still images. (Lateh & Raman, 2005)

**Audio-Lingual Method**
The method of studying a foreign language that stresses hearing the language spoken by native speakers, and then imitating the patterns of pronunciation and grammar heard in the example. (Switala, 2005)

**Audioteleconferencing**
Voice-only communication via ordinary phone lines. Audio systems include telephone conference calls, as well as more sophisticated systems that connect multiple locations. (C. Wright, 2005)

**Audit**
The review and monitor of the performance of a system. (Sarkis & Sundarraj, 2005)

**Audit Analysis**
The review of the Internal Audit data to determine what material can be easily re-purposed, as well as the possible market potential for those materials. (Robinson, 2005)

**Auditing**
A systematic process of objectively obtaining and evaluating evidence of assertions about economic actions and events to ascertain the correspondence between those assertions and established criteria, and to communicate the results to interested parties. (Garrity et al., 2005)

**Auditory Icon**
Icons that use everyday sounds to represent application objects or activities. (Lumsden, 2005)

**Augmented Reality**
Intermixing a physical reality and a virtual reality. (Terashima, 2005)

**AUP:** See *Acceptable Use Policy.*

**Authentic Activities**
Activities that reflect the ways in which knowledge and skills are used in real-world practice. These are usually simplified in a formal learning environment rather than being identical to the activities a practitioner might perform. (Bennett, 2005)

**Authentic Learning**
Learning that uses real-world problems and projects, and that allows students to explore and discuss these problems in ways that are relevant to them. (Bieber et al., 2005)

**Authentication**
1: A signaling procedure in cellular networks to identify the subscribers when access to certain services are demanded. (Louvros et al., 2006) 2: Determines a user's identity, as well as determining what a user is authorized to access. (Medlin et al., 2006) 3: Guarantees that an individual or organization involved in a transaction is who they say they are. (Lowry, Stephens, et al., 2005) 4: The process by which a system can provably verify the identity of a resource such as an individual, a system, an application, and

so on. (Mundy & Otenko, 2005) **5:** Method of assuring the identities of entities engaged in electronic communication. (Calzonetti & deChambeau, 2006) **6:** A set of procedures employed to verify the identity of an entity. (Buche & Vician, 2005) **7:** Technique by which a process verifies that its communication partner is who it is supposed to be and is not an imposter. It makes sure that the parties engaging in business are who they claim to be. Integrity allows the system to verify whether modifications have occurred; it does not ensure that information was not altered. (Pierre, 2006b) **8:** The action of verifying information such as identity, ownership, or authorization. (Vatsa et al., 2005) **9:** The process by which a contemporary biometric sample is acquired from an individual and is used to compare against a historically enrolled sample. If the samples match, the user is authenticated. Depending on the type of system, the authentication may be prompted by some additional information—a key to the identity of the user or the pseudonym against which the enrolled data was registered. (Fleming, 2005a) **10:** The process of determining whether someone or something is who or what they declare to be. In private or public computer networks, authentication is commonly done through the use of logon passwords or digital certificates. (Butcher-Powell, 2005) **11:** The process of ensuring that an individual is who he or she claims to be. (Guan, 2006h) **12:** Verification that one is who they say they are. (Lawson-Body et al., 2005) **13:** Biometric identifiers operate either in verification (authentication) mode or in a recognition (identification) mode. A verification system authenticates a person's identity by comparing the captured biometric characteristic with the person's own biometric "original." In a recognition system, the system establishes a subject's identity by searching the entire template for a match, without the subject initially claiming an identity. (Scott et al., 2006)

## Authentication System

System used to verify the identity of an entity (user, application, host, system, device) that is attempting to participate in a computing environment. (Knight & Labruyere, 2005)

## Authenticity

**1:** Divided in two sections: Data origin authenticity and entity authenticity. Data origin authenticity is the proof of the data's origin, genuineness, originality, truth, and realness. Entity authenticity is the proof that a person or other agent has been correctly identified, or that a message is stored and received as transmitted. (Oermann & Dittmann, 2006) **2:** The agentive participation in meaning making,

as opposed to passive reception. This is the only way in which an individual can relate incoming information to the context of his or her own lifeworld, without which meaning does not exist for that person. We often sense the lack of authenticity in interaction without necessarily understanding our own misgivings. (Kettley, 2006b) **3:** Undisputed credibility of being genuine, honest with oneself as well as others; an absence of hypocrisy or self-deception. (Park, 2006)

## Author

Much of the philosophy extended in analyses of technology stems from literary theory. Author has connotations synonymous with artist and designer, and may be useful in future discussions regarding terminology across more or less user-centered processes. (Kettley, 2006a)

## Author Cocitation Analysis

The analysis of how authors are cited together. (Chen & Liu, 2005)

## Authoring

The creation and organization of multimedia or hypermedia content. (Lemahieu, 2005)

## Authoring Language

A program designed for use by a non-computer expert to create e-learning products. An authoring system does not require programming knowledge to operate. It allows the placement of graphics, text, and other multimedia elements into an e-learning program. It functions like word processing software. (Kapp, 2005)

## Authoring Program

Software used to develop multimedia applications. (Berg, 2005e)

## Authoring Shell

Internet-based template that consists of various electronic tools and functions with which a user can create a customized Web environment. (Ketelhut et al., 2005)

## Authoring Tool

**1:** A software application or program used by trainers and instructional designers to create e-learning courseware. Types of authoring tools include instructionally focused authoring tools, Web authoring and programming tools, template-focused authoring tools, knowledge capture systems, and text and file creation tools. (Sánchez-Segura et al., 2005) **2:** A software program with standard user interface elements, such as books or flow charts. (Brown, 2006)

## Authority

**1:** A Web site that provides the best source of information on a specific topic. (Hu, Yang, Yeh, et al., 2005) **2:** An established power to enforce moral or legal decisions. Organizational authority is accountable for its actions. Authority is a right to demand and instruct subordinates. Authority may also be delegated or be derived from delegated control. The organization may mandate power to a role, position a group or individual in authority, or power may be assigned or sanctioned by consensus. (Zyngier, 2006) **3:** Link analysis considers Web pages of high quality to be authorities for their topic. That means these pages contain the best, most convincing, most comprehensive, and objective information for that topic. (Mandl, 2006) **4:** The power, right, or control to give orders or to make decisions. (Park, 2006)

## Authority Page

The page that contains the most definitive, central, and useful information in the context of query topics. (Lee-Post & Jin, 2005a)

## Authorization

**1:** Granting of rights; includes granting of access based on access rights or privileges, and implies the rights to perform some operation and that those rights or privileges have been granted to some process, entity, or human agent. (Karnouskos & Vilmos, 2006) **2:** One or many access rights assigned to an entity by a certification authority (CA). Authorization does not make sure that messages received really do come from a given counterpart. (Pierre, 2006b) **3:** Privileges afforded to an entity to access equipment and/or information. (Buche & Vician, 2005) **4:** The process of determining if a requesting party has sufficient rights to access a resource. (Mundy & Otenko, 2005)

## Authorization for Informationbase

Regulates access to informationbase—that is, what chapters and entries are available to a particular person or authority to initiate informationbase updating and to change informationbase structure. (Dragan, 2005)

## Auto ID Technology

A precursor to the RFID technology that led to the definitions of RFID technology, including electronic product code. (Owens et al., 2005)

## Auto-Personalization

Self-adaptive features of WAP applications. (Quah & Seet, 2006)

## Autobiographical Memory

The aspect of memory systems that allows the perception of the historic order in which experiential remembrances are stored in long-term memory. (Atkinson & Burstein 2006)

## Autocorrelation

Measures the correlation between observations of a time series and the same values at a fixed time offset interval. (Cho, 2005)

## Automated Approaches

The industrialization of the teaching process using technology. (Laws, Howell, & Lindsay, 2005)

## Automated Delivery

A system whereby information or course content is delivered in a pre-programmed manner without the need for any action on the part of the teacher. This could include non-interactive methods, such as a course delivered via cable TV, but could also include highly interactive methods, such as automatic tutoring via a computer. (Aworuwa & Owen, 2005)

## Automated Fingerprint Identification System (AFIS)

A system that provides computerized fingerprint identification of arrestees, applicants for licensing and employment, and crime scene fingerprints of potential suspects. (Holland, 2005)

## Automated Planning

An area of artificial intelligence concerned with solving the problem of finding a sequence of actions that transforms a specified initial state into a specified goal state. (Babaian, 2005)

## Automated Port Scan

An intruder sending a request to a host name or a range of IP addresses followed by a port number to see if any services, including file transfer protocol (FTP), TELNET, and hypertext transfer protocol (HTTP), are listening on that port. Automated port scans typically are carried out by hackers trying to gain large amounts of information about a particular network so that an attack can be planned. (Butcher-Powell, 2005)

## Automated Theorem Prover

A software tool that (semi-)automatically performs mathematical proofs. Available theorem provers range from fully interactive tools to provers that, given a proof, check if the proof is correct with no further interaction from the user. (Campos & Harrison, 2006)

## Automatic Classification

The process by which a classificatory system processes information in order to classify data accurately; also the result of such process. (Wieczorkowska, 2005)

## Automatic Documentation

Allows for a structured view of the application and generates books of HTML documentation. Knowledge mining's automatic documentation focuses on the ability to save diagrams and reports in various formats. (Raisinghani, 2005)

## Automatic Facial Expression Analysis

A process of locating the face in an input image, extracting facial features from the detected face region, and classifying these data into some facial-expression-interpretative categories such as facial muscle action categories, emotion (affect), attitude, and so forth. (Pantic, 2005b)

## Automatic Indexing

A process that algorithmically examines information items to build a data structure that can be quickly searched. (Hu, Yang, Yeh, et al., 2005)

## Automatic Teller Machine (ATM) System

A system installed by a bank in different locations in order to enable customers to access their bank accounts and withdraw cash from them. (Al-Hanbali & Sadoun, 2006)

## Automatic Thesaurus Construction

The process of using a computer to automatically extract thesauri from texts. (Kulyukin & Nicholson, 2005)

## Automatic Transcription

The process of extracting the musical content from an audio signal and representing it in standard music notation. (Dixon, 2005)

## Automatic Tutoring

Programmed-machine methods that interact with the learner in a way that mimics a human teacher by adjusting new content on the basis of the learner's response to content presented by the machine. (Aworuwa & Owen, 2005)

## Automatic Tutoring Device

A device that uses programmed branching and adaptive feedback. Learning results from cognitive reasoning. (Owen & Aworuwa, 2005)

## Automatically Defined Function (ADF)

Parametric functions that are learned and assigned names for reuse as subroutines. ADFs are related to the concept of macro-operators or macros in speedup learning. (Hsu, 2005b)

## Automation

The technique, method, or system of operating or controlling a process by highly automatic means, as by electronic devices, reducing human intervention to a minimum. When applied to education, automation means increasing teacher/student ratio, reducing teacher/student contact, and reducing qualified staff with automated teaching methods and tutorials. (Reilly, 2005)

## Automatism

An attention mechanism established through practice whereby the performance of a task apparently no longer interferes with the concurrent performance of other tasks. (Owen, 2006b)

## Autonomous Agent

**1:** A system situated within an environment and a part of an environment that senses that environment and acts on it, over time, in pursuit of its own agenda, so as to affect what it senses in the future. (Raisinghani et al., 2005) **2:** Software components capable of working for the performance of tasks to the benefit of its users. An agent is anything that can be viewed as perceiving its environment through sensors and acting upon that environment through actuators. (Castro & Braga, 2006)

## Autonomous Information System

Information system existing as an independent entity. (Ras & Dardzinska, 2005)

## Autonomous Learning

The student is engaged in the learning environment independent of instructor guidance/supervision and peer interaction/communication. S/he takes primary responsibility for her/his learning needs and goals, as well as for self-assessment of work completed. (McCracken, 2005)

## Autonomous Production System

Part of a company directly exposed to the market which is able to become part of a virtual enterprise when an adequate business opportunity arises. (Pires et al., 2006)

## Autonomous Robot

A robot that is capable of existing independent of human control. (Hall & Woods, 2006)

## Autonomous Software Agent

An agent with the ability to anticipate changes in the environment so that the agent will change its behavior to improve the chance that it can continue performing its intended function. (Zwitserloot & Pantic, 2005)

## Autonomous (Sub)System

A system that decides about its own information input and output requirements. (Szczerbicki, 2005)

## Autonomous System (AS)

**1:** A network where the main routers are in common administration. The Internet is composed of peering ASs. (Hosszu, 2005a) **2:** A basic building element of the Internet. Each AS is independent from the others. (Hosszú, 2006)

## Autopoietic System

A self-making or self-organizing system. (Murphy, 2005a)

## Autoregressive

Uses historical data to predict future results. (Kushnir, 2006)

## Auxiliary View

A view materialized in the DW exclusively for reducing the view maintenance cost. (Theodoratos & Simitsis, 2005)

## AV Encoder

An encoder used to encode the input audio/video signal to specific digital format. (Liu & Chen, 2005)

## Availability

**1:** Indicates the assurance that resources, like information, services, or equipment, are working adequately and available at a specified time to authorized entities. An available system has to be safe and secure from attacks.

(Oermann & Dittmann, 2006) **2:** Availability of data is the degree to which a system is operable and in a committable state at the start of an assignment. (Mitrakas, 2006) **3:** Prevention of unauthorized withholding of information or resources. (Tong & Wong, 2005a)

## Availability of Data

The probability of having access to the data. Replication will normally increase data availability. (Frank, 2005a)

## Avatar

**1:** A computer-generated representation almost always graphical in nature, and sometimes a three-dimensional construct that represents the user/operator in the virtual world. (Ajiferuke & Markus, 2005) **2:** A graphical representation of a user or a character controlled by a user. (Champion, 2006b) **3:** A virtual representation generated by computers. It can be, for example, a copy of a user's body to try on virtual clothes. (Volino et al., 2005) **4:** An image representing a user in a multi-user virtual reality space. (Yong & Choo, 2005) **5:** Personification of a user in a graphic virtual reality. An avatar can be an icon, an image, or a character, and it interacts with other avatars in the shared virtual reality. The term is drawn from the Hindu culture, where it refers to the incarnation of a deity. (Pace, 2005) **6:** The computer-simulated graphic of the human body in which specific physical and mental attributes are embodied. (Park & Lepawsky, 2006) **7:** The word comes from Indian culture and means "reincarnation." On the Internet, the word is used to describe the "object" representing the user in forms of two- or three-dimensional photo, design, picture, or animation. (Pöysä & Lowyck, 2005) **8:** Computer-generated personas that are adopted by users to interface with other humans and agents involved in a social interaction, particularly in interacting in online virtual reality worlds. (Duchastel, 2006) **9:** Synthetic representation of a human body able to be animated. Avatars are often used in games for representing players or in virtual environments when the presence of the user must be visible. (Prêteux & Preda, 2005)

## Average Cost

The averaged cost of all of the learning experiences in an enterprise. (Norris, 2005)

## Average Precision (P_Avg)

A well-known measure of retrieval performance, it is the average of the precision scores calculated every time a new relevant document is found, normalized by the total number of relevant documents in the collection. (Fan & Pathak, 2005)

**AVLE:** See *Adaptive Virtual Learning Environment.*

## Awareness

**1:** A specialized knowledge about the objects that leads an actor to an understanding of various aspects of the ERP collaborative process. It is defined and measured in terms of the semantic concepts (task, role, process resource, and collaborative resource) used in the map. (Daneshgar, 2005) **2:** A stage in the knowledge management cycle in which a decision maker is made aware of the potential application of organizational memory to a current issue. (Yaniv & Schwartz, 2006) **3:** Conscious knowledge about a communicative situation in a computer-supported environment including all the persons involved. (Beuschel et al., 2005)

## Awareness Model

A model that represents various levels of awareness. Level-0 awareness consists of the concepts that lead an actor to knowledge about all the tasks that an actor performs within the process. A role's level-3 awareness is its level-2 awareness, plus awareness about all the interactions (represented by the process resources used/shared) that occur between any two roles within the process. And finally, level-4 awareness is the highest level of awareness that a role can have in any ERP process. It is defined as the knowledge about how everything fits together to form the ERP process. (Daneshgar, 2005)

**AWT:** See *Abstract Windows Toolkit.*

## Axiom

**1:** A rule or maxim accepted as a truth in the ontology. Axioms provide the inferencing or logical power of the ontology. Example: "If and only if a wine is red, then it is derived from a grape that is red." (Buchholz, 2006) **2:** A generally accepted proposition or principle sanctioned by experience; a universally established principle or law that is not necessarily true. (Polgar, 2005b)

## Axiomatic Semantics

The meaning is given in terms of conditions, pre and post. (Dasso & Funes, 2005)

## Axiomatic Theory

Consists of a language and a set of statements of the language called axioms. The language allows one to express statements about a certain collection of objects, and the axioms express properties that the objects of the language are assumed to possess. An axiomatic theory represents a collection of mathematical models—namely, those models that have the same objects as the language of the theory and that satisfy the axioms of the theory. (Farmer, 2006)

**A**

**B**

# B

**BA:** See *Behavior Aggregate.*

## Ba
A physical, virtual, or mental context that enables effective knowledge creation; based on the Japanese idea of "place." (Medeni, 2006a)

## Back Propagation
A training method used to calculate the weight in a neural net from the data. (Kumar, 2005)

## Back-Channel
The standard use of e-mail, person to person, without routing through the community's available channels. (Patrick et al., 2006)

## Back-End Application System
A software system that manages business domain-specific data for businesses, e.g., enterprise resource planning (ERP) systems. (Bussler, 2005a)

## Back-End Interoperability
Business-process-centric integration approach that interconnects different application systems in order to enable the execution of cross-organizational business processes. (Werth, 2005)

## Back-End Processing
Dealing with the raw data, which is stored in either tables (ROLAP) or arrays (MOLAP). (Tan, 2005b)

## Back-End System
The support components of a computer system. Typically refers to the database management system (DBMS), which is the storehouse for the data. (Mockler et al., 2006)

## Back-Testing
Testing a mathematical model for its performance over past intervals. Back-testing often uses out-of-sample data that was not used to optimize model parameters. (Kushnir, 2006)

## Backbone Network
Long-haul networks such as CA*net 4 and GÉANT 2, Long-Haul that interconnect network segments in WAN configurations to facilitate resource sharing and e-collaborative information exchange. (Littman, 2006)

## Backpropagation
**1:** A learning algorithm for modifying a feed-forward neural network which minimizes a continuous "error function" or "objective function." Back-propagation is a "gradient descent" method of training in that it uses gradient information to modify the network weights to decrease the value of the error function on subsequent tests of the inputs. Other gradient-based methods from numerical analysis can be used to train networks more efficiently. (Kitchens, 2005) **2:** A neural network training algorithm for feed-forward networks where the errors at the output layer are propagated back to the previous layer to update connection weights in learning. If the previous layer is not the input layer, then the errors at this hidden layer are propagated back to the layer before. (An, 2005) **3:** Method for computing the error gradient for a feed-forward neural network. (Yeo, 2005) **4:** The name of the most common learning algorithm for MFNNs. It involves modifying the weights of the MFNN in such a way that the error (difference between the MFNN output and the training data desired output) is minimized over time. The error at the hidden neurons is approximated by propagating the output error backwards, hence the name backpropagation. (Smith, 2005)

## Backpropagation Algorithm
Learning algorithm of artificial neural networks based on minimizing the error obtained from the comparison between the outputs that the network gives after the application of a set of network inputs and the outputs it

should give (the desired outputs). (Rabuñal Dopico et al., 2005)

## Backpropagation, Feed-Forward Neural Network

A type of neural network popular for use in classification data mining. The neurons in a feed-forward network are organized into an input layer and enable the network to represent the knowledge present in the data. (Fuller & Wilson, 2006)

## Backsourcing

Taking work that had been outsourced back in-house. (Beaumont, 2005)

## Bag Relation

A relation that permits repetition of tuples. (T.Y. Lin, 2005)

## Bagging (Bootstrap Aggregating)

A bootstrap replication of the sample units of the training sample, each having the same probability to be included in the bootstrap sample to generate single prediction/ classification rules that being aggregated provides a final decision rule consisting in either the average (for regression problems) or the modal class (for classification problems) among the single estimates. (Siciliano & Conversano, 2005)

## Balanced Score Card (BSC)

**1:** A management framework for translating strategy into tactics through identification of metrics for aligning processes with visions. Initiatives needed to meet the objectives of the business are identified. (Dykman, 2005) **2:** A strategic management system and performance measurement. (Lee & Pai, 2005) **3:** A tool for developing "measures," "objectives," "targets," and "initiatives" for "financial," "customer," "internal process," and "learning and growth" categories derived from the overall company vision statement. (Clegg & Tan, 2006) **4:** A selected collection of measures (both financial and non-financial) derived from an organization's strategies. Usually, balanced scorecard is considered to be the most prevalent form of performance measurement system. (Saha, 2005). **5:** A valuation methodology, here applied to IT, that assigns metrics to non-financial value contributions for the organization, including customer service, innovation, and others. (Mendonca, 2005)

## Balanced Scorecard Collaborative

A strategic management system that measures—by means of quantitative relations of different selected variables—the behavior of the organization, taking into account the settled aims established in different perspectives (e.g., increase, internal processes, customers, finances). The analysis is based on the cause-effect relations between the variables and ratios that represent them. (Xodo & Nigro, 2005)

## Balancing (Counteracting) Feedback

A systemic pattern that is responsible for stability, balance, and control. It represents adjusting, correcting, and counteracting processes that resist, slow down, or impede change and growth. (Maani, 2005)

## Bandwidth

**1:** A measure of how much information or data path times frequency. For example, the ISA bus has a data path of 16 bits (it can send 16 bits at a time) and typically operates at 8.33MHz, so it has a bandwidth of 133.28 megabits per second. It is the speed of a connection between computers. The range of frequencies (size of the "pipe") available for carrying information, and the total amount of data or information that can be transmitted via a given communications channel (e.g., between a hard drive and the host PC) in a given unit of time. (Magagula, 2005) **2:** A measure of the data transmission capacity of a communications link. (Ruppel & Ruppel, 2005) **3:** The amount of data that can be transferred in a fixed amount of time using a specified communications channel/pathway in a computer network. The term is often used as a synonym for data transfer rate. (Pease et al., 2005) **4:** Colloquially, the amount of network capacity available for a connection. (Urbaczewski, 2005) **5:** Defining the capacity of a communication channel, it refers to the amount of data that can be transmitted in a fixed time over the channel; it is commonly expressed in bits per second. (Hin & Subramaniam, 2005a) **6:** Determines the rate at which information can be sent through a channel. (Singh, 2006a) **7:** In networks, bandwidth is often used as a synonym for data transfer rate: the amount of data that can be carried from one point to another in a given time period (usually a second). This kind of bandwidth is usually expressed in bits (of data) per second (bps). (Olla, 2005a) **8:** Maximum data transfer capacity of a communication channel. (Arya, 2005) **9:** Range of frequencies within a communication channel or capacity to carry data. (Lawson-Body et al., 2005) **10:** Refers to the range of frequencies available for a specific broadcast, for example, radio/television channels,

**B**

mobile phones, and so on. In computer networks, bandwidth refers to the amount of data that can be transferred in a given period of time. (Papagiannidis et al., 2005) **11:** Term used to denote the capacity of a communication channel for information: a narrow bandwidth implies slow or limited communication. It describes the carrying capacity of the user's connection or the server connection. It is commonly measured in bits or bytes per second. (Boersma & Kingma, 2006) **12:** The amount of data per second that can be delivered to your computer. A 56K modem has a bandwidth of 56 kilobits/second. The term bandwidth is also used in conjunction with data rate when discussing video. (Cosemans, 2005a)

## Bandwidth Management

Determines the information capacity of a network per unit of time. Wireless networks deliver lower bandwidth than wired networks. The choice of appropriate bandwidth for efficient and cost-effective transmission of voice, data, and pictures is called bandwidth management. (Murthy & Krishnamurthy, 2005d)

## Bandwidth of Communication Channel

Actual speed of communication medium available at the time of transmission. Limitations of bandwidth can substantially affect quality of interaction and efficiency of learning. (Rugelj, 2005)

## Banner

A typically rectangular advertisement placed on a Web site either above, below, or on the sides of the main content and linked to the advertiser's own Web site. In the early days of the Internet, banners were advertisements with text and graphic images. Today, with technologies such as Flash™, banners have gotten much more complex and can be advertisements with text, animated graphics, and sound. (Lalopoulos, Chochliouros, & Spiliopoulou-Chochliourou, 2005b)

## Bar Codes

Simple form of optical character recognition where information is encoded in printed bars of relative thickness and spacing. RFID combines this technology with radio frequency. (Kotzab, 2005)

## Barriers to Human-Computer Interaction

Anything that poses as a challenge to a human interacting with technology. Examples include poor organization of a Web site and language conversion issues. (Carstens, 2005)

## Barriers to Knowledge Sharing

Characteristics of the knowledge-sharing environment that may limit or preclude the knowledge-sharing transaction. The evaluation of barriers to knowledge sharing should actually be measured in terms of knowledge workers' perceptions of barriers to knowledge sharing since knowledge workers may not be able to elucidate the actual barriers. (Lindsey, 2006)

## Base Class

User-defined class; a collection of objects that have the same behavior and state definition. (Alhajj & Polat, 2005b)

## Base Station Controller (BSC)

The intelligent element of the Base Station Subsystem. It has complex functions in radio resource and traffic management. (Hackbarth et al., 2005)

## Base Station Transceiver (BST)

The first element that contacts the mobile terminal in the connection, and the first element of the fixed part of the mobile network. (Hackbarth et al., 2005)

## Baseband

In radio communications systems, the range of frequencies starting at 0 Hz (DC) and extending up to an upper frequency as required to carry information in an electronic form, such as a bitstream before it is modulated onto a carrier in transmission or after it is demodulated from a carrier in reception. In cable communications, such as those of a local area network (LAN), it is a method whereby signals are transmitted without prior frequency conversion. (Chochliouros et al., 2005b)

## Baseline Data

The data in a study captured before an intervention or innovation is introduced in an experimental setting, in order to describe the situation before the experimental intervention or innovation is effected. (Fisher, 2005)

## Basic Methods of Computer-Mediated Communication

Includes such tools as threaded discussions, gradebooks, class announcements, and lecture notes. (Gold, 2005)

## Basic Navigation Support

Basic WCDSS navigation structures such as the categories of offerings that provide browsing aids for searching. (F. Wang, 2006)

## Basic Residential Register Network

A network to confirm the being of a person or a subject. Its use is common throughout Japan and jointly operated by local authorities. (Kitagaki, 2005)

## Basic Service Set (BSS)

A WLAN architecture consisting of dedicated station computers and a dedicated wireless access point. (Pulkkis, Grahn, & Karlsson, 2005)

## Basis for Association Rules

A set of association rules that is minimal with respect to some criteria, and from which all association rules can be deduced with support and confidence. (Pasquier, 2005)

**BAT:** see *Beam Analysis Tool.*

## Batch Learning

Learning by using an algorithm that views the entire dataset at once, and can access any part of the dataset at any time and as many times as desired. (Oza, 2005)

## Baud

The unit in which the information-carrying capacity or signaling rate of a communication channel is measured. One baud is one symbol (state transition or level transition) per second. (Vician & Buche, 2005)

## Baudot

A 5-bit standard encoding method for upper-case letters. (Kieler & West, 2005)

## Bayes Factor

Ratio between the probability of the observed data under one hypothesis divided by its probability under an alternative hypothesis. (Ramoni & Sebastiani, 2005)

## Bayes' Rule

**1:** Mathematical equation relating prior and posterior probabilities. (Rippon & Mengersen, 2005) **2:** Shows how probabilities can be updated in the light of evidence. Derives from a simple reordering of terms in the product rule and by subsequently applying the law of total probability. (Lauría, 2005)

## Bayes' Theorem

Result in probability theory that states the conditional probability of a variable A, given B, in terms of the conditional probability of variable B, given A, and the marginal probability of A alone. (Bashir et al., 2005)

## Bayesian Behavior Network

**1:** In this network, the agents are organized into agencies, where each agency activates one or more component behavior depending on the inference in the underlying Bayesian behavior network. (Potgieter et al., 2005) **2:** A specialized Bayesian network used by Bayesian agents to collectively mine and model relationships between emergent behaviors and the interactions that caused them to emerge, in order to adapt the behavior of the system. (Potgieter et al., 2005)

## Bayesian Hyperstructure

A Bayesian Behavior Network is a Bayesian hyperstructure that in turn constitutes the internal model of the complex adaptive system. (Potgieter et al., 2005)

## Bayesian Information Criterion

An approximation to the Bayes factor which can be used to estimate the Bayesian posterior probability of a specified model. (Burr, 2005b)

## Bayesian Learning

Learning algorithm based on Bayes' rule. (Rippon & Mengersen, 2005)

## Bayesian Method

Means of quantifying uncertainty based on the probability theory. The method defines a rule for refining a hypothesis by factoring in additional evidence and background information. It uses results of previous events to predict results of future events. (Polgar, 2005a)

## Bayesian Network

**1:** A directed acyclic graph (DAG) that encodes the probabilistic dependencies between the variables within a domain and is consistent with a joint probability distribution (JPD) for that domain. For example, a domain with variables {A,B,C,D}, in which the variables B and C depend on A and the variable D depends on C and D, would have the following JPD: P(A,B,C,D) = p(A)p(B|A)p(C|A)p(D|C,D) and the following graph (Vargas, 2005):

**2:** A directed acyclic graph where the nodes represent random variables and arcs represent the relationships between them. Their strength is represented by means of conditional probability distributions stored in the nodes. (de Campos, Fernández-Luna, & Huete, 2005) **3:** A graphical model that encodes the probability distribution of a set of random variables by specifying a set of conditional independence assumptions, together with a set of relationships among these variables and their related joint probabilities. (Lauría, 2005) **4:** A graphical model defining the dependencies between random variables. (Caelli, 2005)

## Bayesian Neural Network (BNN)

A neural network where a Bayesian approach is used to calculate the posterior distribution for the weights. Rather than selecting the single most likely set of weights, model averaging is used to predict outputs. (Rippon & Mengersen, 2005)

**BBA:** See *Bone-Based Animation.*

**BBS:** See *Bulletin Board System.*

**BDHM:** See *Block Data Hiding Method.*

## Beam Analysis Tool (BAT)

A nonlinear-capable online software developed using the Macromedia Flash™ programming environment and which focuses on beam deflection problems using the moment-area method. (Burrage & Pelton, 2005)

## Beat Tracking

The process of finding the times of musical beats in an audio signal, including following tempo changes, similar to the way that people tap their feet in time to music. (Dixon, 2005)

## Behavior Aggregate (BA)

A set of packets going in one direction of a link that exhibit similar QoS characteristics. (Gutiérrez & Ting, 2005)

## Behavioral Biometric

A biometric characterized by a behavioral trait learned and acquired over time. (Vatsa et al., 2005)

## Behavioral/Value Information

Information that represents how large-scale, complex systems, including social systems, interact under different environmental conditions and in conjunction with different stimuli. (McIntosh & Siau, 2005)

## Belief

A positive function that represents the confidence that a proposition lies in a focal element or any subset of it. (Beynon, 2005a)

## Belief Revision

The process of changing beliefs to reflect the acquisition of new information. A fundamental issue in belief revision is how to decide information to retract in order to maintain consistency, when the addition of a new belief to a theory would make it inconsistent. (Colucci et al., 2006)

## Below-View

Elements of experience that are not available to direct inspection without applying some semiotic tool such as linguistic analysis. (Zappavigna-Lee & Patrick, 2005)

## Benchmark

**1:** A standard program that runs on different systems to provide an accurate measure of their performance. (Darmont, 2005) **2:** A standard, usually from outside sources and usually representing the best or better-than-average performance against which an activity's metric is compared. For example, world-class competitors have 35 defects per unit within the first six months; we have 85. (Holstein & Crnkovic, 2005)

## Benchmark Audiovisual Affect Database

A readily accessible centralized repository for retrieval and exchange of audio and/or visual training and testing material, and for maintaining various test results obtained for a reference audio/visual data set in the research on automatic human affect analysis. (Pantic, 2005a)

## Benchmark Toolkit

A tool that has been proposed for fair comparisons of different implementation alternatives, mostly of access methods. Its main components are: a synthetic data generator and/or some sets of real data, a query processor, and a set of access methods whose behavior has to be investigated. The output of a benchmark is a set of values describing the performance of each access method for a given data set and a set of queries that were executed iteratively by the query processor. Often these values describe separately the input/output time and CPU time needed for the index construction and for the computation of the queries. (Tzouramanis, 2005)

## Benchmarking

**1:** To identify the "best in class" of business processes, which might then be implemented or adapted for use by other businesses. (Troutt & Long, 2005) **2:** An improvement process in which a company measures its performance against that of "best in class" companies, determines how those companies achieved their performance levels, and uses the information to improve its own performance. The subjects that can be benchmarked include strategies, operations, processes, and procedures. (Archer, 2006) **3:** Procedure to compare and improve manufacturing quality and services based on the comparison of operations, methods, procedures, and processes inside and outside the organization. (Xodo, 2005)

## Benchmarking E-Government

The continuous process of measuring products, services, and practices against successful governments, and making comparisons with them and then learning the lessons that those comparisons throw up. (Yigitcanlar & Baum, 2006a)

## Benchmarking/Best Practices

The continuous process of measuring products, services, and practices against others. Mostly used to identify processes, services, and so forth generally considered to be superior in approach, and results in other methods internal or external to the enterprise. (Ribière & Román, 2006)

## Benefit Function

Theoretical algebraic functions depicting the user satisfaction for a multimedia service in correlation with the allocated resources. (Koumaras et al., 2005)

## Benefits Management

A managed and controlled process of checking, implementing, and adjusting expected results and continuously adjusting the path leading from investments to expected business benefits. (Lin & Pervan, 2005)

**Benefits Realization:** See *Benefits Management.*

## Benevolence

**1:** An act intending or showing goodwill and kindness. (Wong, 2005) **2:** The belief that the other party cares about the trustor. (Paravastu & Gefen, 2006)

## Best Practice

**1:** A superior method or innovative practice that contributes to the improved performance of an organization, usually recognized as "best" by other peer organizations. (Pemberton & Stalker, 2006) **2:** An explicit recognition of the fact that 'optimization' techniques and the goal of obtaining specific objective function maximization or minimization is inapplicable in the context. Best practice in the end is determined by the stakeholders and the producers, and may involve many subjective criteria. (Nicholls, 2006) **3:** Industry-agreed best way of doing a process. (Brady, 2005) **4:** Superior performance within a function independent of industry, leadership, management, or operational methods or approaches that lead to exceptional performance; best practice is a relative term and usually indicates innovative or interesting business practices that have been identified as contributing to improved performance at leading companies. Best practice exercises routinely employ a variety of strategies to facilitate knowledge sharing and the creation of knowledge content in pursuit of enhanced customer service and ultimately customer loyalty. (Archer, 2006) **5:** Generic business processes that are programmed into ERP software. They are based on cumulative knowledge about widely accepted practices that have been seen to work effectively across organizations in generic industries. (Tarafdar, 2005) **6:** Process procedures of recognized excellence, usually obtained from companies' experience and/or process optimization analysis. (Framinan, 2005)

## Better-Faster-Cheaper

A shorthand label for processes that contribute value through better quality, less costly products and services, at a faster production pace. (Mendonca, 2005)

## Betweenness Centrality

A measurement of centrality indicating how powerful an actor is in terms of controlling information flow in a network. The idea here is that actors are central if they lie between other actors on the shortest paths connecting these actors. (Assimakopoulos & Yan, 2006)

**BHR:** See *Byte Hit Rate.*

**BI:** See *Bibliographic Instruction; Business Intelligence.*

## Biased Marketplace

Electronic marketplace owned and operated by one or more organizations primarily for the purpose of conducting electronic commerce with trading partners. (Turner, 2006)

**B**

## Biased Sampling

A random sample of k tuples of a database, where the probability of a tuple belonging to the sample varies across tuples. (Das, 2005)

## Bibliographic Instruction (BI)

Teaching and presenting information on library and information resources in a systematic way to library users/patrons. How to access, use, analyze, and critique information are all parts of BI. (Buchanan, 2005)

## Bibliometrics

**1:** The study of the relationship among scientific publications. The most important application is the calculation of impact factors for publications. During this process, a large number of references is considered to be an indicator for high scientific quality. Other analyses include the structure and the development of scientific communities. (Mandl, 2006) **2:** The study of regularities in citations, authorship, subjects, and other extractable facets from scientific communication using quantitative and visualization techniques. This allows researchers to understand patterns in the creation and documented use of scholarly publishing. (Nicholson & Stanton, 2005)

## Bibliomining

**1:** Data mining applied to digital libraries to discover patterns in large collections. (Cunningham & Hu, 2005) **2:** The application of statistical and pattern-recognition tools to large amounts of data associated with library systems in order to aid decision making or justify services. The term "bibliomining" comes from the combination of bibliometrics and data mining, which are the two main toolsets used for analysis. (Nicholson & Stanton, 2005)

**BIFS:** see *Binary Format for Scenes.*

## Big-Bang Approach

Implementing all modules of an ERP system in all locations or plants of the company simultaneously. (de Souza & Zwicker, 2005)

## Big-Bang ERP Implementation

ERP implementation strategy consisting of implementing all required modules and features at once. (Framinan, 2005)

## Big Deal

Online aggregation of journals offered by publishers. Big Deal can oblige libraries to subscribe to marginal journals to have access to must-have journals. (Rennard, 2006)

## Bilingual Learning Environments

Learning contexts where two languages are needed. Often this is because the course content is in English but the learners are not fluent in English; discussion and exploration of meaning occurs in a language other than English. Translation is needed before questions can be asked of any International Instructor involved in the teaching. (Ching et al., 2005)

## Bilingual Learning Facilitator

A tutor or local instructor whose first language is the same as the learners, but who is reasonably fluent in English as well and also familiar with the content domain. Such facilitators have a major role in bridging the gap between the international instructors and the local learners. (Ching et al., 2005)

## Bill of Materials (BOM)

A hierarchical product structure showing the sub-components and interdependencies of any given finished good. Akin to a recipe, it is the underlying link between end product demand and material requirements. It also facilitates production costing, as each component in the hierarchy can be costed. (Carton & Adam, 2005)

## Bill of Materials and Movements

Includes in a traditional bill of materials the necessary movement of materials between virtual enterprise members. (Pires et al., 2006)

## Billing

A signaling procedure in cellular networks to transfer call-related data to the billing center for charging the subscribers. (Louvros et al., 2006)

## Binarization

The process of deriving a binary representation for numerical and/or categorical attributes. (Boros et al., 2005)

## Binary Coding

A basic coding in which a solution of some problems can be represented in a list of zeros and ones. (Kacem, 2005)

## Binary Image

An image made up of black and white pixels with values of 0s or 1s. (Chen, Chen, & Cheng, 2005)

## Binary Format for Scenes (BIFS)

Based on VRML97, BIFS is extended with commands that can update, delete, or replace objects in the scene. For streaming scenarios, BIFS also offers an integrated binary compression scheme, media mixing, and audio composition. (Di Giacomo et al., 2005)

## Binary Large Object (BLOB)

A usually large (i.e., MB to GB) byte string stored in the database; the DBMS does not have any knowledge about the semantics of the byte string; hence, it cannot offer semantically adequate functionality and query optimization. (Baumann, 2005)

## Binding Propagation

Optimization technique based on the exploitation of binding propagation techniques, which reduce the size of the data relevant to answer the query, and consequently minimize both the complexity of computing a single model and the number of models to be considered. (Greco & Zumpano, 2005b)

## Biographical Analysis

An interpretive research approach to understand how individuals take part in social contexts and make sense of them. The analysis of the interviews helps to reveal the structures of personal and social processes of action. Usually, at the beginning of the interview, there is nothing that would be recognized as "relevant categories"; these should emerge from the analysis of data. (Correia & Sarmento, 2005)

## Bioinformatics

**1:** All aspects of information processing on biological data, in particular genomic data. The rise of bioinformatics is driven by the genomic projects. (L.M. Fu, 2005) **2:** An integration of mathematical, statistical, and computational methods to organize and analyze biological data. (Chen & Liu, 2005) **3:** Data mining applied to medical digital libraries. (Cunningham & Hu, 2005) **4:** Field of science in which biology, computer science, and information technology merge into a single discipline. (Jourdan et al., 2005) **5:** The analysis of biological information using computers and statistical techniques; the science of developing and utilizing computer databases and algorithms to accelerate and enhance biological research (Ge & Liu, 2005) **6:** The development and application of computational and mathematical methods for organizing, analyzing, and interpreting biological data. (Liu, 2005)

**7:** The processing of the huge amount of information pertaining to biology. (Liberati, 2005)

## Biological Model

A construct developed from the observation of biophysical processes of living things. (Atkinson & Burstein, 2006)

## Biological Neural Network

A network of neurons that function together to perform some function in the body such as thought, decision making, reflex, sensation, reaction, interpretation, behavior, and so forth. (Kitchens, 2005)

## Biomedical

Relating to biomedicine, the application of natural sciences—especially biology and physiology—to clinical medicine. (Knight, Whittington, Ford, & Jenkins, 2005)

## Biometric

**1:** A measurable, physical characteristic or personal behavioral trait used to recognize the identity or verify the claimed identity of an enrollee. A biometric identification system identifies a human from a measurement of a physical feature or repeatable action of the individual (for example, hand geometry, retinal scan, iris scan, fingerprint patterns, facial characteristics, DNA sequence characteristics, voice prints, and handwritten signature). (Lovell & Chen, 2005) **2:** A physiological or behavioral characteristic used to recognize the claimed identity of any user. The technique used for measuring the characteristic and comparing it is known as biometrics. (Vatsa et al., 2005) **3:** Some measurement of the biological characteristics of a human subject. A useful biometric is one that is easily acquired and digitized, and where historical samples can be readily compared with contemporary ones. (Fleming, 2005a) **4:** The application of computational methods to biological features, especially with regard to the study of unique biological characteristics of humans. (Scott et al., 2006) **5:** The automated technique of measuring a physical characteristic or personal trait of an individual and comparing that characteristic to a comprehensive database for purposes of identification. (Vatsa et al., 2005) **6:** The science of automatically identifying people or verifying people's identity based on unique human physiological or behavioral characteristics such as face, fingerprint, iris retina, voice, and so forth. (Li, 2006) **7:** The science of measuring, analyzing, and matching human biological data such as fingerprints, irises, and voice/facial patterns. In information system security,

**B**

these measures are increasingly being introduced for authentication purposes and will play a critical role in the future of digital security. (Tassabehji, 2005a) **8:** The use of computational methods to evaluate the unique biological and behavioral traits of people. (Lowry et al., 2005b) **9:** The use of technological devices to identify people through scans of their faces, hands, fingers, eyes, or voice. (Szewczak, 2005) **10:** Using one or more physical characteristics of a person for identification. Fingerprints, retina scans, hand profiles, voice recognition, face recognition, and many others may be used. (Strauss, 2005) **11:** Usually refers to technologies for measuring and analyzing human physiological characteristics such as fingerprints, eye retinas and irises, voice patterns, facial patterns, and hand measurements, especially for authentication purposes. In a typical IT biometric system, a person registers with the system when one or more of his physiological characteristics are obtained, processed by a numerical algorithm, and entered into a database. Ideally, when he logs in, all of his features match 100%; then when someone else tries to log in, she does not fully match, so the system will not allow her to log in. (Wong, 2006) **12:** Generally, biometrics refers to the study of measurable biological characteristics. In computer security, biometric technologies are defined as automated methods of identifying or authenticating the identity of a living person based on his or her physiological (e.g., fingerprint, hand, ear, face, eye—iris/retina) or behavioral (e.g., signature, voice, keystroke) characteristic. This method of identification is preferred over current methods involving passwords and pin numbers, as the person to be identified is required to be physically present at the point of identification, so the person or user is identified, not the device, as in case of PIN and password. (Mezgár, 2006b)

## Biometric Authentication

The identification of individuals using their physiological and behavioral characteristics. (Chakravarty et al., 2005a)

## Biometric Encryption

A technique whereby the biometric data is used as a personal or private key to be used in some cryptographic process. (Fleming, 2005a)

## Biometric Identifier

The use of biometric data to enable the reliable identification of an individual from the measurement of a physiological property which provides the ability to control and protect the integrity of sensitive data stored in information systems. (Scott et al., 2006)

## Biometric Sample

The unprocessed image or physical or behavioral characteristic captured to generate the biometric template. (Vatsa et al., 2005)

## Biometric Template

The mathematical representation of the biometric sample which is finally used for matching. The size of a template varies from 9 bytes for hand geometry to 256 bytes for iris recognition to thousands of bytes for face. (Vatsa et al., 2005)

## Biophysical Variables

Objective physical data collected during experiments such as pulse, blood pressure, hormone levels, electroencephalograms, and electrocardiograms. (Molinari, Anderberg, et al., 2005)

**B-ISDN:** See *Broadband Integrated-Services Data Network*.

## Bit Depth

The number of bits used for color resolution when viewing a movie. (Vitolo et al., 2005)

## Bit Rate

**1:** A data rate expressed in bits per second. In video encoding, the bit rate can be constant, which means that it retains a specific value for the whole encoding process, or it can be variable, which means that it fluctuates around a specific value according to the content of the video signal. (Koumaras et al., 2005) **2:** In a bit stream, the number of bits occurring per unit time, usually expressed in bits per second. Usually, it measures the rate of transmission of information. (Ragazzi, 2005)

## Bit Stream

The actual data stream, which is the transmission of characters at a fixed rate of speed. No stop and start elements are used, and there are no pauses between bits of data in the stream. (Knight & Angelides, 2005)

## Bit-Parallelism

A technique to store several values in a single computer word so as to process them all at once. (Navarro, 2005)

## Bit-Slice Signature File

A file in which one bit per signature for all the signatures is stored. For a set of signatures of length F, F bit-slice files will be generated. (Chen & Shi, 2005)

## Bitmap Index

**1:** An index containing a series of bitmaps such that for attribute A on relation R, each bitmap tells us if a given record in R has a certain value for A. Bitmap indices are often used in decision support environments, since used in conjunction with other bitmap or regular indices, they can cut down on disk accesses for selections, thereby improving query response time. (Badia, 2005a) **2:** Consists of a collection of bitmap vectors, each of which is created to represent each distinct value of the indexed column. A bit i in a bitmap vector, representing value x, is set to 1, if the record i in the indexed table contains x. (Bellatreche & Mohania, 2005)

## Bi-Temporal Database

This database supports both types of time that are necessary for storing and querying time-varying data. It aids significantly in knowledge discovery, because only the bi-temporal database is able to fully support the time dimension on three levels: the DBMS level with transaction time, the data level with valid time, and the user-level with user-defined time. (Raisinghani & Klassen, 2005)

## Bi-Temporal Query

Refers to a query that involves both valid and transaction time points or intervals. (Rodríguez-Tastets, 2005b)

## Black Boxing

A technique used for simplification. Multiple actors can be put into a black box so that it is not necessary to look at them in detail. The portal could be considered as a black box containing the ISP, portal software, data storage devices, modems, telephone devices, and so on. Black-boxing is done for convenience, as it means that an entity can then be seen as just another actor, and it saves looking at the detail until necessary. The black box can later be reopened to investigate its contents. (Tatnall, 2005a)

## Blackboard®

An e-learning software platform that is utilized to deliver and manage instructional activities online. (Aisami, 2005)

## Blackboard Metaphor

A metaphor used in query languages, its philosophy is to let users draw the sketch of their query. (Ferri & Rafanelli, 2005)

## Black-Scholes Option Pricing Model

A model that is used to calculate the value of an option by taking into account the stock price, strike price and expiration date, the risk-free return, and the standard deviation of the stock's return. (Li, 2005b)

## Blank Node

A node in the RDF graph that does not correspond to a Web resource. Blank nodes are normally used to refer to a set of resources or an entire statement. With respect to querying, they can be used to represent a variable in an RDF query. (Stuckenschmidt, 2005)

## blaxxun™

A server-based platform for creating and deploying interactive, Web-based, rich-media applications. (Sourin, 2006)

## Blend

A judicious mixture of face-to-face and computer-mediated interactions to facilitate collaboration. (Córdoba & Robson, 2006)

## Blended Course

A course that utilizes a combination of different delivery modalities, combining face-to-face interaction with online delivery as appropriate. (Shaw, 2006)

## Blended Learning

**1:** Defined broadly, the integration of classroom face-to-face learning with online or technology-supported learning, including a range of pedagogical approaches and delivery systems. Strategic applications of blended learning have shown achievement of learning gains while tackling other problems faced by our universities, most notably the pressures of increasing class sizes, and limitations in funding, classroom space, and learning support. (Campbell, 2005) **2:** E-learning used in conjunction with other teaching and learning methods. (Dixon et al., 2005) **3:** Learning design that combines various activities such as face-to-face meetings, Internet-based learning modules, and virtual learning communities. (Link & Wagner, 2006) **4:** Learning that results from using mixed methods of instructional

**B**

delivery (i.e., face to face and Internet.) (Chapman, 2005b). See *Mixed-Mode Learning.*

## Blended Learning Environment
A learning environment that combines face-to-face and computer-mediated instruction. (Graham et al., 2005)

## Blended Learning Model (BLM): See *Blended Model.*

## Blended Model
**1:** A learning model utilizing traditional lecture-/classroom-style teaching with computer-aided models to aid in independent learning based on a student's learning-styles assessment requirements. (Rhoten, 2006b) **2:** An instructional model or instruction that combines two or more instructional models. (Askar et al., 2005) **3:** A face-to-face instructor-delivered instruction in a brick-and-mortar location supplemented by a variety of online resources. (Aworuwa & Owen, 2005)

**BLOB:** See *Binary Large Object.*

## Block Data Hiding Method (BDHM)
In BDHM, an image will be partitioned into blocks and sub-blocks. Then based on the characteristic values of these sub-blocks, the most suitable sub-block will be chosen for hiding. Data hidden in the block will not be visually easy to detect and must not modify the original characteristic value of the block. (Chen, Chen, & Cheng, 2005)

## Block Scheduling
A daily schedule for middle schools and high schools that involves fewer class periods, but each one is longer than traditional 40- to 55-minute periods. Advocates claim that block scheduling allows for a wider variety of instructional techniques, increased ability for teachers and students to focus on complex tasks, and makes for a calmer school environment. (Glick, 2005b)

## Blocking
**1:** A means of disallowing access to Internet content and services by restricting access at the corporate gateway. (Urbaczewski, 2005) **2:** Allows an IM user to control the ability of his or her online status. When you block someone, that person will not be able to send messages to you until you remove that person from your block list. (Hwang & Stewart, 2005)

## Blocklisting
Set up as an approach for blocking unsolicited or junk e-mail. blocklists provide lists of URLs or Web addresses from which spammers operate. The blocklists therefore provide a way of ameliorating or preventing spam from reaching the intended destination. (de Freitas & Levene, 2006a)

## Blog
**1:** A personal diary and a collaborative space. A breaking-news outlet, a collection of links, your own private thoughts. In simple terms, a blog is a Web site where you write material on an ongoing basis. New entries show up at the top, so your visitors can read what is new. Then they comment on it or link to it, or they e-mail you. (Robinson, 2006) **2:** A Web log that allows for a diary-style forum for posting one's personal thoughts and experiences. (Cannoy & Iyer, 2006) **3:** An online diary in which a Netizen or Cybercitizen records thoughts and opinions on a theme or topic of interest to its creator. (Goldsmith, 2006) **4:** A type of Web page that serves as a publicly accessible personal journal, typically updated frequently. Blog software usually has archives of old blogs and is searchable. (Paoletti, 2005) **5:** A form of Web-based communication that has increased in popularity in the last several years. Blogs facilitate easy publishing and sharing of ideas between individuals. (Graham & Misanchuk, 2005) **6:** Usually a personal journal on the Web, it could be of opinions, social issues, or reflections. People that blog are often identified as bloggers. (Boateng & Boateng, 2006b) **7:** Typically, an individual's journal entries presented in last-in-first-out format. Some blogs also allow for user commentary in response to these entries, creating a type of interactive community. (Isaak, 2006) **8:** Personal, online journals and one of the fastest growing trends on the Internet. Blogs are now considered one of the tools to maintain knowledge communities. (Yamazaki, 2006)

## Blogger
One who maintains a blog—an online journal, diary, or record. (Baim, 2006b)

## Bloom's Taxonomy of Learning
A scale that represents an organization of learning levels (five levels) that are characterized by the student's immersion into the theory and application of principles of course content. (Marold, 2005)

## Bluetooth

**1:** A short-range radio technology aimed at simplifying communications among Internet devices, and between devices and the Internet. It also aims to simplify data synchronization between Internet devices and other computers. (Lalopoulos et al., 2005a) **2:** A short-range wireless radio standard aimed at enabling communications between digital devices. The technology supports data transfer at up to 2Mbps in the 2.45GHz band over a 10m range. It is used primarily for connecting PDAs, cell phones, PCs, and peripherals over short distances. (Garrett, 2006a) **3:** A specification for personal radio networks, named after the nickname of the Danish king Harald who united Norway and Denmark in the 10th century. (Kaspar & Hagenhoff, 2005) **4:** A wireless technology developed by Ericsson, Intel, Nokia, and Toshiba that specifies how mobile phones, computers, and PDAs interconnect with each other, with computers, and with office or home phones. The technology enables data connections between electronic devices in the 2.4 GHz range. Bluetooth can replace cable or infrared connections for such devices. (Bose et al., 2005) **5:** A wireless networking protocol designed to replace cable network technology for devices within 30 feet. Like IEEE 802.11b, Bluetooth also operates in unlicensed 2.4GHz spectrum, but it only supports data rates up to 1 Mbp. (Akhtar, 2005) **6:** Low-power radio communication technology similar to cordless phones, used to connect up to eight peripherals with a computer over distances of a few meters. Typically used in cordless keyboards, or to connect laptops or PDAs with cell-phone modems. Competes with IR and 802.11. (Houser & Thornton, 2005) **7:** Short-range wireless technology limited to less than 30 feet. (Lawson-Body et al., 2005) **8:** A low-power wireless-network standard that allows computers, peripherals, and consumer electronic devices to talk to each other at distances of up to 30 feet. (Galanxhi-Janaqi & Nah, 2005) **9:** A wireless telecommunications system that provides a way to connect and exchange information between devices like personal digital assistants or mobile phones. (Flavián & Guinalíu, 2006)

**BM_VEARM:** See *BM_Virtual Enterprise Architecture Reference Model.*

## BM_Virtual Enterprise

A virtual enterprise in total or partial conformance with the BM_Virtual Enterprise Architecture Reference Model (BM_VEARM). (Cunha & Putnik, 2005)

## BM_Virtual Enterprise Architecture Reference Model (BM_VEARM)

A virtual enterprise (VE) reference model conceived to enable the highest organizational/structural/reconfiguration and operational interenterprise dynamics of virtual enterprise or agile/virtual enterprise, employing three main mechanisms for VE dynamic creation, reconfiguration, and operation: Market of Resources, Broker, and Virtuality. Additionally, BM_VEARM implies the highest level of integration and (geographic) distribution of VE elements (partners in the VE network). (Cunha & Putnik, 2005)

**BNN:** See *Bayesian Neural Network.*

## Bobby

A Web page accessibility validation service provided by the Center for Applied Special Technologies (CAST); uses the W3C's Web Content Accessibility Guidelines, and evaluates Web pages for possible errors and ranks them in order of priority. (Yu, 2005a)

**BOM:** See *Bill of Materials.*

## Bone-Based Animation (BBA)

**1:** A part of MPEG-4 specifications dealing with the definition and the animation at very low bit rate of a generic articulated model based on a seamless representation of the skin and a hierarchical structure of bones and muscles. (Prêteux & Preda, 2005) **2:** An AFX tool allowing for the compression of virtual human animation, including skin deformations, and also for generic hierarchical animation. (Di Giacomo et al., 2005)

## Bookshelf

The combination of text, graphics, audio, and video with tools that allow the user to navigate, interact, create, and communicate the content or his or her own ideas, but which lack the links to connect the information. (Bradley et al., 2005)

## Boolean Function

**1:** A binary function that maps binary strings (with fixed length) into a binary value. Every Boolean function can be written as an expression containing only AND, OR, and NOT operations. (Muselli, 2005) **2:** A function from $\{0,1\}n$ to $\{0,1\}$. A function from a subset of $\{0,1\}n$ to $\{0,1\}$ is called a partially defined Boolean function (pdBf). A pdBf is defined by a pair of datasets (T, F), where T (resp.,

F) denotes a set of data vectors belonging to positive (resp., negative) class. (Boros et al., 2005)

## Boolean Query

A query that uses Boolean operators (AND, OR, and NOT) to formulate a complex condition. A Boolean query example can be "university" OR "college." (Wei & Li, 2005)

## Boolean Reasoning

Based on construction for a given problem P of a corresponding Boolean function fP with the following property: The solutions for the problem P can be decoded from prime implicants of the Boolean function fP. (Pawlak et al., 2005)

## Boosting

**1:** Assigning and updating weights on data points according to a particular formula in the process of refining classification models. (B. Zhang, 2005) **2:** Creation of an ensemble of hypotheses to convert a weak learner to strong one by modifying expected instance distribution. (Lenič et al., 2005) **3:** Generates multiple models or classifiers (for prediction or classification), and to derive weights to combine the predictions from those models into a single prediction or predicted classification. (Yeo, 2005) **4:** One of the most effective types of learners for text categorization. A classifier built by boosting methods is actually a committee (or ensemble) of classifiers, and the classification decision is made by combining the decisions of all the members of the committee. The members are generated sequentially by the learner, who attempts to specialize each member by correctly classifying the training documents the previously generated members have misclassified most often. (Sebastiani, 2005)

## Bootstrap

**1:** A resampling scheme in which surrogate data is generated by resampling the original data or sampling from a model that was fit to the original data. (Burr, 2005a) **2:** A European method for software process assessment and improvement. It enhanced and refined the Capability Maturity Model developed at the Software Engineering Institute for software process assessment, and adapted it to the European software industry. (Leung, 2005) **3:** Generating artificial patterns from the given original patterns. (This does not mean that the artificial set is larger in size than the original set; also, artificial patterns need not be distinct from the original patterns.) (Viswanath et al., 2005)

## Border Meetings

Brings together some of the members of two or more communities of practice in order to foster an interchange of practices and to trigger thinking processes into the community itself or in the "border practices." (Falivene & Kaufman, 2006)

## Bot

Short for robot. Any type of autonomous software that operates as an agent for a user or program, or simulates a human activity. (Sourin, 2006)

## Bottom-Up Approach

**1:** Proceeding from the bottom of a hierarchy or process upwards. This approach involves the community at the start of the project. (Gnaniah, Yeo, et al., 2005) **2:** Development approach founded upon the principle that communities are better placed to coordinate and integrate efforts at the local level. (Thompson, 2005)

## Bottom-Up Cube Computation

Cube construction that starts by computing from the bottom of the cube lattice and then working up toward the cells with a greater number of dimensions. (Abdulghani, 2005a)

## Bounce Rate

A ratio of the number of Web page visitors who enter and then back out (leave) without linking from anything on the page (e.g., viewing other pages on the site) vs. the total number of visitors (total pageviews), expressed as a percentage. (Owen, 2006a)

## Boundary

**1:** A social construction that defines knowledge and people to be included (or to benefit) from a decision. (Córdoba, 2006a) **2:** A systems concept whereby all systems are held to have a boundary, and often judgments at the boundary will yield insightful results. (Green & Hurley, 2006)

## Boundary Crossing

**1:** The crossing of one's own professional, disciplinary, or expertise boundaries (i.e., knowledge zones), and venturing into others. This is required when people work in situations that require multi-faceted input, where no one possesses all the different types of knowledge necessary (e.g., a medical doctor working with a structural engineer on an artificial limb project). (Fong, 2006a) **2:** Virtual teams are often characterized by their boundary spanning attributes; that is, they usually cross time and distance, and often include different national (ethnic), organizational, and functional cultures. (Pauleen, 2005)

## Boundary Element Method
Numerical method to solve the differential equations with boundary/initial conditions over the surface of a domain. (Kanapady & Lazarevic, 2005)

## Boundary Encounters
The ways in which different communities of practice may meet to exchange knowledge. (Wenn, 2006a)

## Boundary Object
**1:** An element that enables community members to participate together and communicate outside of the community. (Córdoba, 2006b) **2:** As knowledge crosses three forms of boundaries (syntactic, semantic, and pragmatic), certain objects assist this knowledge flow. They can be repositories, standard forms, objects and models, and maps of boundaries. They are both concrete and abstract objects. (Paquette, 2006a) **3:** Describes an actant that is able to bring a degree of commensurability to the knowledge practices of different communities for some shared purpose. It takes knowledge from one community and presents it to another in such a way that it makes sense to that community. (Wenn, 2006a)

## Boundary Paradox
In the knowledge transfer process, the giving and receiving organizations' borders must be open to flows of information and knowledge from the networks and markets in which they operate, but at the same time, the organization must protect and nurture its own knowledge base and intellectual capital. (Chen, Duan, et al., 2006)

## Boundary Region
Those objects that may or may not be in the approximation set. It is the difference between the upper approximation and the lower approximation. If the boundary region is empty, the set is said to be crisp. If the boundary region is not empty, the set is rough. (Voges, 2005)

## Boundary Representation (B-Rep)
In boundary representation, complex geometrical forms are described using their boundary surfaces. In this process, the surface of an object is broken down into smaller polygons, mainly triangles. This therefore makes this type of modeling particularly suitable for irregularly shaped surfaces. Most animation programs use this method. (Cruz et al., 2005)

## Bounded Rationality
A theory of individual decision making that contends decisions are not made in a purely rational manner, due to limited cognitive capabilities and incomplete information. (Moore & Burke, 2005)

## Box-Jenkins Approach
A very versatile linear approach that can model trend, seasonal, and other behaviors by using moving averages, autoregression, and difference equations. (G.P. Zhang, 2005)

**BPA:** See *Business-Process Analysis.*

**BPEL4WS:** See *Business Process Execution Language for Web Services.*

## B+-Tree
A particular form of search tree in which the keys used to access data are stored in the leaves. Particularly efficient for key-access to data stored in slow memory devices (e.g., disks). (Tininini, 2005b)

**BPON:** See *APON or Broadband PON; Broadband Passive Optical Network.*

**BPR:** See *Business Process Reengineering.*

## Braille Embosser
Analogous to a regular computer printer, this embosser outputs Braille text on special Braille paper. It produces dots on the thick Braille paper by mechanically striking it with a set of styluses. These dots follow the Braille code and can be read by touch. (Lahiri & Basu, 2005)

## Brain Drain
The emigration of highly educated workers from developing countries to developed countries. (Negash, 2005)

## Branch
A single path down a decision tree, from root to a leaf node, denoting a single if-then rule. (Beynon, 2005b)

## Branching
A subgraph of a directed graph in which there are no cycles and the indegree of each node is 1 or 0. (Chen, 2005a)

**Branching Digital Skills**
The ability of learners to form knowledge in a nonlinear way as they work in hypermedia digital environments. (Eshet, 2005)

**Brand**
**1:** A name, term, sign, symbol, or design—or a combination of them—intended to identify the goods and services of one seller or a group of sellers, and to differentiate them from those of competition. (Roberts & Schwaab, 2006) **2:** The promise that a Web site, company, product, or service makes to its customers. (T.S. Chan, 2005)

**Brand Equity**
The value of a brand, measured in financial terms. (Roberts & Schwaab, 2006)

**Branding**
"Campusversities" use "branding" (e.g., McGill sweaters, Concordia backpacks) as marketing tactics. A large part of what most students hope for is to take on some of the prestigious institutional identity of their university. Any community is partly a matter of symbolic identification. (Boyd & Zhang, 2005)

**Brand Presence**
The presence of a product offering that is distinguished from its competitors through the use of a symbol, design, or characteristic, or a combination of these. (Brindley, 2006)

**Breadth-First**
The method of growing the intermediate result by adding items both at the beginning and the end of the sequences. (Masseglia et al., 2005)

**B-Rep:** See *Boundary Representation.*

**Brick and Mortar**
**1:** The direct physical (non-virtual) channel for conducting business or exchanging value, typically requiring a specific location. (Bahn, 2006) **2:** Operations that take place in conventional off-line settings as opposed to those that take place online. For example, offering items for sale at a conventional store as opposed to selling them online. (Aigbedo, 2005)

**Brick-and-Mortar Organization**
An organization located or serving customers in a physical facility, as opposed to a virtual organization. (Zhao, 2005)

**Bricks and Mortar School**
**1:** Traditional schools where students attend a physical school building. (Russell, 2005b) **2:** Conventional schools used for face-to-face classes. (Russell, 2005a)

**Broadband**
**1:** Refers to a telecommunication service in which a "wide band" of frequencies is available to transmit information. When a wide band of frequencies is available to subscribers, information can be multiplexed and sent on many different frequencies or channels within the band concurrently. This means more information can be transmitted in a given amount of time, just as more lanes on a highway allow more cars to travel on it at the same time. As a general rule, the greater the bandwidth, the faster the service. (De Weaver, 2005) **2:** A class of communication channels capable of supporting a wide range of frequencies, typically from audio up to video frequencies. A broadband channel can carry multiple signals by dividing the total capacity into multiple, independent bandwidth channels, where each channel operates only on a specific range of frequencies. The term has come to be used for any kind of Internet connection with a download speed of more than 56K baud. (Vician & Buche, 2005) **3:** A digital delivery system using fiber optics to establish an interactive infrastructure that carries large quantities of interactive information. (Weber & Lim, 2005) **4:** A network capable of delivering high bandwidth. Broadband networks are used by Internet and cable television providers. For cable, they range from 550 MHz to 1GHz. A single TV regular broadcast channel requires 6MHz, for example. In the Internet domain, bandwidth is measured in bits-per-second (BPS). (Pagani, 2005a) **5:** A service or connection allowing a considerable amount of information to be conveyed, such as video. It is generally defined as a bandwidth of over 2 Mbit/s. (Chochliouros et al., 2005c) **6:** A transmission facility having a bandwidth sufficient to carry multiple voice, video, or data channels simultaneously. (Singh, 2006b) **7:** A type of data transmission in which a single medium (such as fiber optic wire) can carry several channels at once. Cable TV, for example, uses broadband transmission. (Braun, 2005c) **8:** A new way of connecting to the

Internet that will ensure rapid access, faster download times, and better overall performance such as high-resolution, graphics, and CD-quality sound. Broadband connections are sometimes also called "fat pipes" due to the substantial amounts of data they can carry compared to more traditional "narrowband" connections, such as a modem which delivers variable service quality with slow download speeds. A broadband connection can be delivered in several different ways: cable, DSL, fixed wireless, and satellite. (Cosemans, 2005a) **9:** High-speed transmission services such as xDSLs and CATV lines which allow users to access the Internet at significantly higher speeds than dial-up modems or narrowband. (Park & Lepawsky, 2006) **10:** In data communications, generally refers to systems that provide user data rates of greater than 2 Mbps and up to 100s of Mbps. (Ngoh & Shankar, 2005) **11:** Internet connection with a download speed of more than 56k band. (Msiska, 2005) **12:** Transmission facility having a bandwidth sufficient to carry multiple voice, video, or data channels simultaneously, often greater than 512 Mbit/sec. Each channel occupies (is modulated to) a different frequency bandwidth on the transmission medium and is demodulated to its original frequency at the receiving end. (Negash, 2005)

## Broadband Access

**1:** A form of Internet access that provides information and communication services to end users with high-bandwidth capabilities. (Hentea, 2005a) **2:** The process of using ADSL, fiber cable, or other technologies to transmit large amounts of data at rapid rates. (Hin & Subramaniam, 2005a)

## Broadband Digital Services

These allow very high data transmission rates, and are the most popular and widely used kinds of digital services. These services include DSL, ADSL, and cable modem services. (Pease et al., 2005)

## Broadband Integrated-Services Data Network (B-ISDN)

An ISDN that supports a wider range of voice and non-voice applications. (Louvros et al., 2005b)

## Broadband Network

**1:** A telecommunications network that can transmit information well above the normal rate (56K) on ordinary phone lines. (Hin & Subramaniam, 2005c) **2:** A telecommunications network that leverages on various

technologies to vastly speed up rates of information transfer between communication devices such as computers. (Hin & Subramaniam, 2005b) **3:** A telecommunications network that allows for rapid transmission of voluminous amounts of information. (Hin & Subramaniam, 2006) **4:** A network that operates at a wide band of frequencies. In these communications networks, the bandwidth can be divided and shared by multiple simultaneous signals (for voice or data or video). (Barolli & Koyama, 2005a)

## Broadband Passive Optical Network (BPON)

Features point-to-multipoint architecture for provisioning access to high-speed broadband applications such as video-on-demand over the first-mile. (Littman, 2006)

## Broadband Transmission

A form of data transmission in which data are carried on high-frequency carrier waves; the carrying capacity medium is divided into a number of subchannels for data such as video, low-speed data, high-speed data, and voice, allowing the medium to satisfy several communication needs. (Hentea, 2005a)

## Broadband Wireless Access

A form of access using wireless technologies. (Hentea, 2005a)

## Broadcast

A transmission to multiple unspecified recipients. (Prata, 2005)

## Broadcast Channel

Unidirectional wireless channel to disseminate a set of database items periodically to multiple numbers of mobile users. (Waluyo et al., 2005)

## Broadcast Cycle

A complete broadcast file. (Waluyo et al., 2005)

## Broadcast Database

A mobile database whose contents are being broadcast, fully or partially, to a population of mobile clients. (Leong, 2005a)

## Broadcast Disk

Distributes data according to a predefined schedule so that interested clients can pick up the data from the schedule. (Fiege, 2005)

## Broadcast TV Service

A television service that provides a continuous flow of information distributed from a central source to a large number of users. (Hulicki, 2005)

## Broker

**1:** A manager of a virtual enterprise. A broker acts as an intermediary with the buyer of goods or services. A broker may also manage and control the ICT and provide educational services to small and medium enterprises, SMEs, or micro-companies. (Richards et al., 2005) **2:** Also called organization configuration, structure, organization, or architecture manager, a broker is the main agent of agility and virtuality in an agile/virtual enterprise (A/VE), acting either between two operations of the A/VE (off-line reconfigurability, providing agility only) or online with the operation of the A/VE (online reconfigurability, providing virtuality and a higher level of agility). (Cunha & Putnik, 2005) **3:** Generically, a certified entity authorized to link two different layers. (Pires et al., 2006)

## Brokerage

The activity of connecting two or more unconnected nodes in a network. (Dekker & Hendriks, 2006)

## Browse

To view formatted documents. For example, one looks at Web pages with a Web browser. "Browse" is often used in the same sense as "surf." (Singh, 2005a)

## Browser

**1:** An application that interprets the computer language and presents it in its final Web page format. (Falk & Sockel, 2005) **2:** A client software program used for searching and viewing various kinds of resources such as information on a Web site or on an intranet. (Vaast, 2005) **3:** A computer software program that requests Web pages and other associated applications over the Internet, and that can display these files using the right format. (Dasgupta & Chandrashekaran, 2005) **4:** A software program running on a client computer that allows a person to read hypertext. The browser permits viewing the contents of pages and navigating from one page to another. Netscape Navigator, Microsoft Internet Explorer™, and Lynx are common browser examples. (Vician & Buche, 2005)

## Browser Caching

A Web browser keeps a local copy of server pages in an area called a "cache" on client's computer. This is to avoid repeated requests to the server. However, this also makes server logs incomplete because some requests are served by the cache. A related issue is the management of the cache to improve its hit rate. (Y. Fu, 2005)

## Browser Log

A computer file (program) running on the client's browser that lists all requests for individual files and ads. (Dasgupta & Chandrashekaran, 2005)

## Browsewrap Agreement

Generally pertains to accessing information on a Web page. A notice is placed on the Web site informing the user that continued use of (browsing) the Web site constitutes acceptance of a license agreement (the terms of which are usually made available by the user selecting a link on the Web site). (Sprague, 2005)

**BSC:** See *Balanced Score Card; Base Station Controller.*

**BSP:** See *Business System Planning.*

**BSS:** See *Basic Service Set.*

**BST:** See *Base Station Transceiver.*

## BS7799-2:2002

Part 2 is an information security management system (ISMS) that adopts a systematic approach to managing sensitive company information that encompasses people, processes, and IT systems. (Tassabehji, 2005b)

**B2A:** See *Business-to-Administration.*

**B2B:** See *Business-to-Business.*

**B2B E-Commerce:** See *Business-to-Business Electronic Commerce.*

**B2B Integration Technology:** See *Business-to-Business Integration Technology.*

**B2C:** See *Business-to-Consumer.*

**B2E:** See *Business-to-Employee.*

## Bucket

An element obtained by partitioning the domain of an attribute X of a relation into non-overlapping intervals. Each bucket consists of a tuple <inf, sup, val>, where val is an aggregate information (i.e., sum, average, count, etc.) about tuples with that value of X belonging to the interval (inf, sup). (Buccafurri & Lax, 2005)

## Bucket-Based Histogram

A type of histogram whose construction is driven by the search of a suitable partition of the attribute domain into buckets. (Buccafurri & Lax, 2005)

## Buddy List

Presence awareness technology that allows users to monitor the online status of others. A buddy list window shows whether buddies are online or off-line. Users double-click on a screen name of an active friend, and a message is automatically initiated. (Hwang & Stewart, 2005)

## Buffer Query

This spatial query involves two spatial datasets and a distance threshold d. The answer is a set of pairs of spatial objects from the two input datasets that are within distance d from each other. (Corral & Vassilakopoulos, 2005)

## Buffet Model of Course Redesign

This model moves instruction away from a fixed menu of activities and resources to a "buffet" of choices for learners, offering a large variety of offerings that can be customized to fit the needs of the individual learner. (Twigg, 2005)

## Building Block

**1:** A basic element or part of something. (Askar & Kocak-Usluel, 2005) **2:** Reflects one of the many the critical success factors of the information technology industry that include: hardware, software, human resources "humanware," networking, and information. (Kamel, 2005a)

## Bulkload

Adding a (large) set of data to a database rather than individual tuples. (Schmidt et al., 2005)

## Bulletin Board

**1:** A discussion forum, similar to that of Usenet newsgroups, in which questions and responses are connected in a "thread," resembling a conversation. (Teigland & Wasko, 2005) **2:** An electronic message database where people can log in and leave messages. (Coakes & Willis, 2005)

## Bulletin Board System (BBS)

**1:** An electronic message center where one can read and respond to comments made by other users. Also a term used for early local Internet service providers, since their message board function was a key service. (Paoletti, 2005) **2:** A computerized meeting and announcement system that allows people to carry on discussions, upload and download files, and make announcements without people being connected to the computer at the same time. In the early 1990s, there were millions of BBSs around the world, most very small, running on a single IBM clone PC with one or two phone lines. Some are very large, and the line between a BBS and a system like CompuServe gets crossed at some point, but it is not clearly drawn. (Chim, 2006)

## Bullwhip Effect

**1:** A situation in which ineffective network effects occur because each successive node in the supply chain orders more supplies than the previous one based on wrong assumptions, a lack of communication, and flawed planning processes. (Hanebeck, 2005) **2:** Demand amplification from its source across the supply chain. This is largely caused by information asymmetry among the entities in the supply chain. (Aigbedo, 2005)

## Burst

In OBS networks, IP packets (datagrams) are assembled into a very large-sized data packet called a burst. (Rodrigues, Freire, Monteiro, & Lorenz, 2005)

## Burst Assembly

The process of aggregating and assembling packets into bursts at the ingress edge node of an OBS network. (Rodrigues et al. 2005)

## Burst Detection

The identification of sharp changes in a time series of values. Examples of bursts include the increasing use of certain words in association with given events. (Chen, Toprani, et al., 2006)

**Burst Header Packet:** See *Control Packet.*

## Burst Offset

The interval of time at the source node between the processing of the first bit of the setup message and the transmission of the first bit of the data burst. (Rodrigues et al., 2005)

## Business Alignment

Actions to be undertaken by an organization, to answer a market opportunity with the provision of the required product, with the required specifications, at the required time, with the lowest cost, and with the best possible return. (Cunha & Putnik, 2005)

## Business and IT Executive

A senior person at a business organization, such as the chief information officer (CIO), chief technology officer (CTO), or chief executive officer (CEO). (Henry, 2006)

## Business and Scientific Applications

End-user modules that are capable of utilizing Analytical Information Technology along with domain-specific knowledge (e.g., business insights or constraints, process physics, engineering know-how). Applications can be custom built or pre-packaged and are often distinguished from other information technologies by their cognizance of the specific domains for which they are designed. This can entail the incorporation of domain-specific insights or models, as well as pre-defined information and process flows. (Ganguly et al., 2005)

## Business Complexity

Degree of difficulty associated with supplier- and customer-facing processes. It incorporates diversity and volatility aspects. (Setzekorn et al., 2005)

## Business Ecosystem

A system in which companies work cooperatively and competitively to support new products, satisfy customers, and create the next round of innovation in key market segments. (Lee et al., 2006)

## Business Engineering

The integral design of both organizational structures and information systems. (Janssen, 2005)

## Business Games

Computer-based simulations designed to teach business-related concepts. (Proserpio & Magni, 2005)

## Business Incubators

Property-based organizations with identifiable administrative centers focused on the mission of business acceleration through knowledge agglomeration and resource sharing. The main role of the incubator is to assist entrepreneurs with business start-ups and development. (Moodley, 2005)

## Business Intelligence (BI)

**1:** A popularized umbrella term introduced by Howard Dresner of the Gartner Group in 1989 to describe a set of concepts and methods to improve business decision making by using fact-based support systems. The decision support purpose is to provide managers with information or business intelligence. The term is sometimes used interchangeably with briefing books and executive information systems. A business intelligence system is a data-driven DSS. (Power, 2005) **2:** A broad set of tools and technologies that facilitate management of business knowledge, performance, and strategy through automated analytics or human-computer interaction. (Ganguly et al., 2005) **3:** Software and a set of tools that allow end users to view and analyze data and business knowledge through automated analytics or human-computer interaction. (Khan et al., 2006) **4:** Business information systems have transitioned from function-oriented to knowledge-oriented systems. Business intelligence is a study of business rules that are the best in practice. Intelligence is the execution of knowledge. Business intelligence is related to the knowledge acquisition, repository, sharing, and application in the activities of an organization. Business intelligence is becoming a necessity to most business organizations to be carried out in their business procedures and functions. Business intelligence has now emerged as a sharable commodity embodied in commercial software and is no longer something that could only be possessed by a small bunch of experts. (Li, 2005a) **5:** Deployment of (usually artificial intelligence-based) techniques such as On-Line Analytical Processing and data mining to analyze information in the operational data sources. (Trcek, 2005) **6:** Information that enables high-level business managers and executives to make strategic and long-term business decisions. (Athappilly & Rea, 2005) **7:** The process of gathering information in the field of business. The goal is to gain competitive advantage. The information gathered usually refers to customers (their needs, their decision-making processes), the market (competitors, conditions in the industry), and general factors that may affect the market (the economy at large, technology, culture). (Badia, 2006) **8:** The type of detailed information that business managers need for analyzing sales trends, customers' purchasing habits, and other key performance metrics in the company.(Zhu, 2005) **9:** A term used in two ways: (1) as a synonym for competitive intelligence, and (2) to indicate a specific set of ICT tools to support managerial decision making. This set of tools often consists of a data warehouse and the tools to store, retrieve, and present the information it contains (e.g., data-mining software). (Vriens, 2005a)

## Business Mission

A basic role or function that a firm performs in a specific environment. (Cepeda-Carrión, 2006)

## Business Model

**1:** A specific arrangement of organizational strategies, goals, processes, resources (technologies, finances, people, etc.), structures, products, and services that enable a firm to successfully compete in the marketplace. Many EC researchers have taken a narrower view, based on organizations involved (i.e., B2B, B2C, B2G, etc.) or specific framework used (i.e., hierarchy, hub, or intermediary for e-markets). While there is not yet a consensus about what makes up a business model, the trend is away from a narrower view. (Craig, 2005) **2:** Architecture for products, services, and information flows, including descriptions of the various business actors and their roles, the potential benefits, and the sources of revenue. (Shan et al., 2006b) **3:** Means by which a new venture will attract and serve customers, in order to generate revenue and profit. (Craig, 2006b) **4:** The method of doing business by which a company can generate revenue to sustain itself. (Lee et al., 2006) **5:** With regard to business models, we must verify which cooperation partner is responsible for which partial tasks. We can either assign services that have been provided by the public sector to the private sector (privatization), or both cooperation partners can invest resources to accomplish these tasks (partnership). Outsourcing is an example of privatization, while franchising is an example of partnership. (Knust & Hagenhoff, 2005)

## Business Opportunity

Perfect time interval to efficiently match a specific market need to a core competence and available capacity. (Pires et al., 2006)

## Business Performance

Reflects an organization's overall results and is often measured using a number of financial measures; for example, annual sales revenue, sales growth, annual profit, and profit growth. Rather than seek empirical data, some studies ask managers for their perceptions, for example, their perception of sales growth compared to competitors. (Cragg & Todorova, 2005)

## Business Process

**1:** A collection of interrelated work tasks initiated in response to an event that achieves a specific result for the customer of the process. (Sundaram & Portougal, 2005a) **2:** A collection of business activities which take several inputs and creates one or more outputs. (Johnston, 2005) **3:** A process at the business layer of an organization. Since the 1990s, the focus of any business reengineering project and one of the central inputs for IT design. It is sometimes also used as a synonym for workflow. (Heucke et al., 2005) **4:** A series of related activities performed by staff in a business organization to achieve a specific output (for example: loan processing). (Henry, 2006) **5:** A set of interrelated activities performed in an organization with the goal of generating value in connection with a product or service. (Kock, 2006) **6:** A set of one or more linked activities which collectively realize a business objective or goal, normally within the context of an organizational structure. (Cardoso, 2006) **7:** A set of organized work-related tasks and resources to pursue a specific organizational objective influencing learning experiences by defining two specific relationships: process-based roles (between business process and people) and learning tasks (between business process and information systems). (Rentroia-Bonito & Jorge, 2005) **8:** A term widely used in business to indicate anything from a single activity, such as printing a report, to a set of activities, such as an entire transaction cycle. Sometimes used as a synonym of transaction cycle. (Dunn & Grabski, 2005) **9:** The sequence of activities, the people, and the technology involved in carrying out some business or achieving some desired results in an organization. (Galatescu, 2005) **10:** Business transactions that realize a business objective. (Johannesson, 2005) **11:** The interaction, coordination, communication, and decision choices made by organizations in order to transform inputs (resources)—personnel, equipment, technology, information, energy, capital, and so forth—into products or services of added value to the customer/citizen. (Joia, 2006) **12:** The specific processes into which each primary activity of the value chain can be decomposed. (Scupola, 2005)

## Business Process Execution Language for Web Services (BPEL4WS)

Provides a language for the formal specification of business processes; extends the Web services model and enables it to support business transactions. (Cardoso, 2006)

**B**

## Business Process (of a Virtual Enterprise)

A set of linked activities that are distributed at member enterprises of the virtual enterprise and collectively realize its common business goal. (Protogeros, 2006)

## Business Process Outsourcing

Service recipients hand over the responsibility for the execution of complete business processes to service providers. Most of the business processes in business process outsourcing are IT-related processes. (Beulen, 2005)

## Business Process Reengineering (BPR)

**1:** Any radical change in the way in which an organization performs its business activities; BPR involves a fundamental re-think of the business processes followed by a redesign of business activities to enhance all or most of its critical measures—costs, quality of service, staff dynamics, and so forth. (Colmenares & Otieno, 2005) **2:** Analysis and redesign of workflow within and between enterprises. (Sarmento, 2005) **3:** The analysis and redesign of processes within and between organizations. Usually differentiated from process improvement, which is less transformational. (Mendonca, 2005) **4:** The fundamental rethinking and radical redesign of business processes to achieve significant improvements of the performances, such as cost, quality, service, and speed. (Aversano et al., 2005) **5:** Related to the alignment between business processes and the ERP business model and related best practices. This process will allow the improvement of the software functionality according to current and future organization needs. Managers must decide if they do business process reengineering before, during, or after ERP implementation. (Esteves & Pastor, 2005) **6:** Redesign of business processes with the purpose of a dramatic improvement in business performances and productivity. (Peterson & Kim, 2005)

## Business Q&A Exchange

One of the most popular knowledge exchanges in knowledge communities. The most refined software structure is called Q&A community. (Yamazaki, 2006)

## Business Rule

**1:** A constraint or derivation rule that applies to the business domain. A static constraint restricts the possible states of the business, and a dynamic constraint restricts the possible transitions between states. A derivation rule declares how a fact may be derived from existing facts, or how an object is defined in terms of existing objects. (Halpin, 2005) **2:** Originally, a statement that defines or constrains the evolution of data pertaining to an enterprise's business. Business rules usually are implemented by integrity constraints or triggers, or stored procedures. (Decker, 2005) **3:** Statement that defines or constrains business objects, their behavior, and relationships. Usually expressed in a semiformal language, using a vocabulary of business terms and verbs such as have to, should, and must. (Badia, 2005b) **4:** Statements that model the reaction to events that occur in the real world, having tangible side effects on the database content. They respond to application needs. (Rivero, 2005) **5:** Precise statements that describe, constrain, and control the structure, operations, and strategy of a business. They may be thought of as small pieces of knowledge about a business domain. (Cilia, 2005)

## Business Rule Extraction

Enables concise business rules to be extracted from within legacy programs and across entire legacy systems. (Raisinghani, 2005)

## Business Strategy

**1:** A description of the plans, actions, or steps an organization intends to take in order to strengthen and grow itself. (Johnston, 2005) **2:** The main way the organization chooses to compete; for example, via cost leadership, differentiation, niche, and so forth. (Cragg & Todorova, 2005)

## Business System Planning (BSP)

IBM®'s developed methodology of investing in information technology. An example of a system approach methodology of developing an information system. (Janczewski & Portougal, 2005)

## Business Term

Word or expression denoting a concept that has a particular meaning in the context of an enterprise. (Badia, 2005b)

## Business Value

The overall value that an investment brings to a corporation. Examples of performance measures of the business value of electronic commerce can be: (1) profitability—that is, whether electronic commerce contributes to an increase in the profitability of the corporation; or (2) competitive advantage that could be measured as an increase in market share, shareholder value, or customer satisfaction. (Scupola, 2005)

## Business-Continuity Planning

The objective of business-continuity planning is to counteract interruptions to business activities and critical business processes from the effects of major failures or disasters. (Tong & Wong, 2005a)

## Business-Episode Concept

The approach to classify and cluster public services by repeating specific situations that often occur during the life of a citizen resp. the different periods of an enterprise. Typical examples are marriage for a citizen and VAT declaration for a company. (Werth, 2005)

## Business-Process Analysis (BPA)

A set of technologies that provide support for obtaining relevant properties of business-process models in order to reason about them, detect functional errors, or improve their performance. (Fisteus & Kloos, 2006)

## Business-to-Administration (B2A)

Data interchange between commercial organizations and government bodies using e-technologies such as EDI or an Internet Web site. A component of e-government. (Whiteley, 2006)

## Business-to-Business (B2B)

**1:** Business made electronically (mainly by Internet) between companies by the selling or purchasing of goods or services. Includes data interchange. (de Medeiros et al., 2006) **2:** A business that provides some kind of services or sells some product to other businesses. (Youn & McLeod, 2006) **3:** Interactions between two businesses, such as transfers of information, purchases and so forth, are said to follow a B2B format. (Baim, 2006a) **4:** Business-to-business trading involves the sale of goods or services by one business to another business. (Braun, 2005c) **5:** E-procurement systems improve the efficiency of the procurement process by automating and decentralizing the procurement process. The traditional methods of sending Request for Quotes (RFQ) documents and obtaining invoices are carried out over the Web through purchasing mechanisms such as auctions or other electronic marketplace functions, including catalogs. (Møller, 2005) **6:** A business selling goods and/or services online to another business. (Toland, 2006) **7:** Commercial transactions between commercial trading partners using e-technologies such as EDI or an Internet e-shop. (Whiteley, 2006) **8:** Automated processes between trading partners. (Shih & Fang, 2006) **9:** Used to describe an e-business solution that caters to other businesses. It offers integrated business applications and services that allow small and mid-sized organizations and divisions of large enterprises to connect employees, customers, and suppliers for improved efficiency. (Passi et al., 2005)

## Business-to-Business Electronic Commerce (B2B E-Commerce)

**1:** A transaction that occurs between and among firms that are related to the procurements of goods and/or services through electronic medium. The typical medium of transaction is the Internet and World Wide Web. (Aigbedo, 2005) **2:** The process for conducting transactions involving the exchange of valued goods, information, or services for monetary or non-monetary compensation between two or more business organizations. (Turner, 2006) **3:** Focuses on direct transactions between businesses and end consumers. Consumers are able to purchase goods and services such as books, computer products, or music, at any time that is convenient to the consumer. (Peszynski, 2005) **4:** Any business transaction conducted between two business entities. An example is where a manufacturer buys raw material from a supplier over the Internet. (Gangopadhyay & Huang, 2005) **5:** The sale of products or services, or an information exchange, among two or more businesses through electronic technology, usually involving the Internet, through a public or private exchange. (Mockler et al., 2006)

## Business-to-Business Integration Technology (B2B Integration Technology)

A software system that provides business-to-business integration functionality by sending and receiving messages, and retrieving and storing them in back-end application systems. (Bussler, 2005a)

## Business-to-Business Model

Provision of education content to another institution, which then enters the teaching and learning agreements with the learner. (Robinson, 2005)

## Business-To-Business Transaction

Electronic commercial transaction from business to business. (Pierre, 2006a)

## Business-to-Consumer (B2C)

**1:** Retail selling via the Internet. (de Medeiros et al., 2006) **2:** Interactions between a business and its customers are said to follow a B2C format. In common usage of the term B2C, the distinction between customers (purchasers of a product/service) and consumers (end users of a product/service) is not rigorously made. (Baim, 2006a) **3:** Involves the sale of goods or services by a business directly to individual customers. (Braun, 2005a) **4:** A form of e-commerce applications in which the seller is a business organization and the buyer is consumer. A typical example is Amazon.com. (Hwang & Stewart, 2006) **5:** A business selling goods and/or services online to private customers. (Toland, 2006) **6:** An e-commerce business model that facilitates transactions between a company and a consumer, as opposed to a transaction between companies (called B2B) or a transaction between consumers (C2C). (O'Buyonge & Chen, 2006) **7:** Commercial transactions between commercial organizations and members of the public, typically using an Internet e-shop. (Whiteley, 2006) **8:** In this method, products or services are sold from a firm to a consumer. (Shih & Fang, 2006) **9:** Any business transaction conducted through the Internet between a business and a consumer. An example includes a commercial Web site that sells products to individual customers. (Gangopadhyay & Huang, 2005)

### Business-to-Consumer Model

Provision of educational content directly to the learner. (Robinson, 2005)

### Business-to-Consumer Transaction

Electronic commercial transaction from business to consumer. (Pierre, 2006a)

### Business-to-Employee (B2E)

Intranets or knowledge management systems provide the employee with an updated personalized portal to the enterprise on his desktop. The perspectives of the intranet and knowledge management systems increase in the context of the ERP II concept. (Møller, 2005)

### Busy Hour

The hour at which a mobile telephone network handles the maximum call traffic in a 24-hour period. It is that hour during the day or night when the product of the average number of incoming calls and average call duration is at its maximum. (Mani et al., 2005)

### Buy-and-Hold Strategy

An investment strategy for buying portfolios of stocks or mutual funds with solid, long-term growth potential. The underlying value and stability of the investments are important, rather than the short- or medium-term volatility of the market. (Hou, Sheng, et al., 2005)

### Buyer-Driven Value Chain

The customer states what he or she wants and sets out the terms and conditions that the supplier should meet. (Jeffcoate, 2005)

### Buyer's Reservation Price

The maximum unit price that the buyer is willing to pay for an item. The buyer's reservation price is typically drawn from a uniform or normal distribution. (Dasgupta et al., 2006)

### Buying Process

In B2B settings, buying raw materials, maintenance, repairs, and operating supplies is a necessary business activity involving multiple decision makers and formal vendor selection and evaluation procedures. (Bridges et al., 2006)

### Buzz

**1:** A buzzword referring to word-of-mouth off-line or on the Internet. (Goldsmith, 2006) **2:** Word of mouth or social communication—consumers talking to consumers, spreading influence and information. (Waterson, 2006)

### Byte Hit Rate (BHR)

The ratio of bytes served by the cache over the total number of bytes requested by the clients. BHR can be significantly different from HR in a case where only a few large files are being served by the cache. (Danalis, 2005)

### Byte-Code

This machine-independent code is translated into the machine language of the computer on which it is running. (Lucas, 2005)

# C

**CA:** See *Certificate (or Certification) Authority; Conditional Access Service.*

**CAAT:** See *Computerized Assisted Auditing Technique.*

## Cable Access
A form of broadband access using a cable modem attached to a cable TV line to transfer data. (Hentea, 2005a)

## Cache
**1:** A region of a computer's memory which stores recently or frequently accessed data so that the time of repeated access to the same data can decrease. (Lin et al., 2005) **2:** Disk space used to store the documents loaded from the server for future use. (Kacimi et al., 2005) **3:** A storage area on the user computer's hard disk where recently viewed Web pages are stored. (Dasgupta & Chandrashekaran, 2005) **4:** Memory that mirrors often-used parts of a slower but larger memory. The term cache mainly refers to the function, not to the memory technology. Cache can be standard random access memory that is used to speed up disk access, but it also can be very specialized high-speed memory that is used to speed up processor access to main memory. (Meixner, 2005)

## Cache Invalidation
The procedure of validating whether the cached data is consistent with the master copy at the server. (Xu, 2006)

## Cache Memory
A technology developed to reduce file download time and maximize network performance. (Szewczak, 2005)

## Cache Replacement
The procedure of finding the victim data item(s) to be dropped from the cache in order to allocate sufficient cache space for an incoming data item. (Xu, 2006)

## Cache Replacement Policy
The policy to choose a data item or object to be deleted from the cache when a new data item or object is stored to a full cache. (Tse, 2006)

## Cache Result
The Result of a group-by is obtained from other group-by computation (in memory). (Tan, 2005a)

## Caching
**1:** A replication method where access to frequently used data is optimized. In remote caching, a primary copy of the frequently used data is normally stored on a very fast medium to optimize access to data. In local caching, an often inconsistent secondary copy of the frequently used data is stored in or close to the location of some users to optimize their access to the data. (Frank, 2005a) **2:** The technique of copying data from a server machine (the central storage place) to a client machine's local disk or memory; users then access the copy locally. Caching reduces network load because the data does not have to be fetched across the network more than once (unless the central copy changes). (Bose et al., 2005) **3:** Using a buffer within your own computer's fast memory to hold recently accessed data. Designed to speed up access to the same data later. (Cosemans, 2005b)

## Caching Proxy
A caching proxy or proxy server or proxy is a server that acts as an intermediary between a client and a content server. It intercepts the requests of the client and checks whether it can serve the client from its own cache, and if not, it forwards the requests to the content server. (Katsaros & Manolopoulos, 2005a)

**CAD:** See *Computer-Aided Design.*

**CAFS:** See *Content-Addressable File Store.*

**CAGR:** See *Cumulative Annual Growth Rate.*

**C**

**CAI:** See *Computer-Assisted Instruction.*

**Calculative Trust**
Trust based on the weights of the costs and benefits of certain actions, and on a view of man as a rational actor. (Huotari & Iivonen, 2005)

**Calculative-Based Trust**
Trust based on the calculation that it is not in the best interest of the trusted party to cheat or take advantage of the situation, regardless of his or her trustworthiness. (Paravastu & Gefen, 2006)

**Calculus-Based Trust (CBT)**
Trust that is grounded in both the fear of punishment and the rewards for preserving the trusting relationship. (Wang & Gwebu, 2006)

**Calibration**
Correspondence between accuracy and confidence. Calibration exists when there is correspondence. (Goldsmith & Pillai, 2006)

**CAL:** See *Computer-Aided Learning.*

**CALL:** See *Computer-Assisted Language Learning; Computer-Aided Language Learning.*

**Call-Back Locking (CBL)**
An avoidance-based protocol that supports inter-transactional page caching. Transactions executing under an avoidance-based scheme must obey the read-once write-all (ROWA) replica management approach, which guarantees the correctness of data from the client cache by enforcing that all existing copies of an updated object have the same value when an updating transaction commits. (Parker & Chen, 2005)

**CALT:** See *Computer-Assisted Language Testing.*

**CAM:** See *Computer-Aided Manufacturing.*

**Camera Calibration**
A process of setting digital imaging components to standardized settings that will produce accurate and predictable results in the output. (Ozer et al., 2005)

**Cancelable Biometrics**
A technique that allows the user to choose non-invertible transformation functions to be operated on his/her original biometric sample in order to generate multiple variants to represent the same person. (Li, 2006)

**Candidate Generation**
Creating new subgraphs out of smaller ones; then it checks to see how often this new subgraph appears in the analyzed graph database. (Fischer & Meinl, 2005)

**Candidate Key**
Minimum set of attributes that uniquely identify each tuple of a given relation. One candidate key is selected as the primary key. (Alhajj & Polat, 2005a)

**CAP:** See *Carrierless Amplitude-Phase.*

**Capability**
Any method, tool, or piece of knowledge that supports the achievement of a goal. (Berztiss, 2006a)

**Capability Differential**
Resource and competence configuration, that is to say, a configuration to reach competitive advantage sources. (Cepeda-Carrión, 2006)

**Capability Maturity Model (CMM)**
**1:** A framework to achieve maturity in project activities in the software field which presents five maturity levels, each corresponding to a set of structural requirements for key process areas. (Monteiro de Carvalho et al., 2005) **2:** A methodology used to evaluate an organization's software development process. The model describes a five-level evolutionary path of increasingly organized and systematically more mature processes. (Hawk & Kaiser, 2005) **3:** A model used to assess the capability and the maturity of a software process. The CMM levels range from 1 (initial, ad hoc) to 5 (optimizing, process improvement). (Gaffar & Seffah, 2005) **4:** A model containing the essential elements of effective processes for one or more disciplines. Also describes an evolutionary improvement path from ad hoc, immature processes to disciplined, mature processes with improved quality and effectiveness. (Gibson, 2005) **5:** Developed at the Software Engineering Institute of Carnegie-Mellon University and also known as CMM-SW, this model helps a software development organization to identify its strengths and weaknesses, and provides a well-defined plan for improvement. (Berztiss, 2006a) **6:** A five-level framework laying out a generic path to process improvement for software development in organizations. (Brewer, 2005) **7:** A suite of models that update and upgrade the CMM. (Berztiss, 2006a)

**8:** An integration of best practices from proven process improvement models, including the SW-CMM, EIA731, and the Integrated Product Management CMM. Included are tools that help organizations improve their ability to develop and maintain quality products and services. (Leung, 2005)

## Capability Table

A list that specifies data items or physical devices (for example, printers) that users are authorized to access. (Mattord & Whitman, 2005)

## Capability Transformation Model

Traditional logistics, transport, and warehousing capabilities are based on the ability to provide physical resources to assist the customer. These appear to be transforming, with the inclusion of knowledge-based skills and service additions. For example, an e-fulfillment provider may extend traditional supplier-pickup services (which is a physical outcome) to an offer to manage a complete supplier relationship (which is based on knowledge of contracts and supplier environment). Note that the mere inclusion of an information system (for example, a track-and-trace system in a transport operation) does not imply a knowledge capability, but rather is a means to improve a physical capability. Such a model can be used to assess each of a provider's capabilities for the balance between physical and knowledge-based outcomes, and arrive at an index representing the overall degree of knowledge-based outcomes offered by the company. (Alexander & Burn, 2006)

## Capacity

The amount of stimuli that can be noticed and processed in a given time period, or the number of concurrent issues that can be processed by a decision maker. (Yaniv & Schwartz, 2006)

## Capacity Building

Building the skills, commitment, and confidence of community members to develop networks to influence what happens around them in their environment, and give them the capability to contribute to shaping and planning their community's future. (Sutcliffe, 2005)

## Capacity Building Program

A strategy for training targeted individuals in an organization, sector, or discipline to develop specific skills and knowledge base that can then be leveraged for achieving other, more broad goals. (M. Mitchell, 2005b)

## Capacity Miss

This miss occurs because the cache cannot accommodate all requested objects. (Katsaros & Manolopoulos, 2005a)

## Capacity Provisioning Network (CPN)

A network of cache servers owned, operated, and coordinated through capacity trading by different Internet service providers. Unlike a Content Distribution Network (CDN) with the purpose of replicating content from specifically contracted content providers, the CPN's goal is to cache whatever content users access from around the world of content servers. Qualitatively, a CDN services the supply side of content distribution; a CPN services the demand side. (Katsaros & Manolopoulos, 2005a)

**CAPE:** See *Computer-Aided Production Engineering.*

## Caption

**1:** A short textual description used to summarize a picture, table, or other non-text information. (Fagan, 2005) **2:** Text describing a media object. (N.C. Rowe, 2005b)

## Cardinality Constraints

One constraint established in a relationship. It limits the number of entity occurrences that are associated in a relationship. (Cuadra et al., 2005)

## Career Management Account (CMA)

A federal Department of Labor initiative under the Clinton Administration that was intended to provided a Web-based "lock-box" for career and education-related information. (Wasko, 2005)

## Career Trajectory

Describes the positions, roles, and experience that individuals have accumulated, up to and including the position they currently hold. (Ali & Warne, 2005)

## CareerOneStop

The federal Department of Labor's Web-based gateway to job listings, résumés, and career information nationwide. (Langer, 2005)

## Carrier

A transmitted signal that can carry information, usually in the form of modulation. (Chochliouros et al., 2005b)

**C**

## Carrier Sensing

Determination that the medium is not being used by a neighboring transmitter before accessing the channel. (Erbas, 2005)

## Carrier-Neutral Collocation Facility

A facility, especially in a city, built by a company to allow the interconnection of networks between competing service providers and for the hosting of Web servers, storage devices, and so forth. These are rapidly becoming the obvious location for terminating customer-owned dark fiber. (Such facilities, also called carrier-neutral hotels, feature diesel-power backup systems and the most stringent security systems. They are open to carriers, Web-hosting firms and application service firms, Internet service providers, and so forth. Most of them feature a "meet-me" room where fiber cables can be cross-connected to any service provider within the building. With a simple change in the optical patch panel in the collocation facility, the customer can quickly and easily change service providers on very short notice.) (Chochliouros et al., 2005a)

## Carrier-Sense Multiple Access (CSMA)

A Media-Access Control (MAC) protocol in which a node verifies the absence of other traffic before transmitting on a shared physical medium, such as an electrical bus or a band of electromagnetic spectrum. Carrier sense describes the fact that a transmitter listens for a carrier wave before trying to send. That is, it tries to detect the presence of an encoded signal from another station before attempting to transmit. Multiple access describes the fact that multiple nodes may concurrently send and receive on the medium. (Dhar, 2005)

## Carrierless Amplitude-Phase (CAP)

A modulation technique in which the entire frequency range of a communications line is treated as a single channel and data is transmitted optimally. (Hin & Subramaniam, 2005a)

**CART:** See *Classification and Regression Tree.*

## Cartography

The art, science, and engineering of mapmaking. (Sadoun, 2006)

**CAS:** See *Course Applicability System.*

**CASE:** See *Computer-Aided Software Engineering.*

## Case Grammar

A linguistic theory of the ways in which an action can be associated with other concepts. (N.C. Rowe, 2006d)

## Case History

Specialized historical research focusing on failure incidents. Case histories emphasize the background and context that can help in untangling relationships and causes. (Dalcher, 2005)

## Case Mix Information System (CMIS)

An information system, fed with data from an array of hospital subsystems, for the principal purpose of clinical and financial audit of patient cases. Further developments to CMIS have seen other functionality added, such as contract planning, quality assurance, waiting lists, and clinical support. (Barnes, 2005)

## Case Study

**1:** A detailed analysis of a person or group from a social, psychological, or medical point of view. A careful study of some social unit (a corporation or a division within a corporation) that attempts to determine what factors led to its success or failure. (Sarmento, 2005) **2:** A scenario used to illustrate the application of a learning concept. May be either factual or hypothetical. (Sánchez-Segura et al., 2005) **3:** A systematic way of looking at what is happening, collecting data, analyzing information, and reporting the results. (M. Mitchell, 2005b) **4:** An examination of a phenomenon in its natural setting using fixed boundaries such as time. (Trauth, 2005b) **5:** An instruction tool containing a detailed description of a real-world situation. (Pendegraft, 2005) **6:** Investigation of phenomena in a naturalistic setting, conducted to enable in-depth analysis of that phenomena. (Dalcher, 2005) **7:** Research conducted to assess a single instance of a phenomenon. (Schifter, 2005) **8:** The intensive examination of a single instance of a phenomenon or where one or just a few cases are intensively examined using a variety of data-gathering techniques. (Thompson, 2005)

## Case Study Research

An in-depth investigation that attempts to capture lessons learned through studying the environment, procedures, results, achievements, and failures of a particular project or set of circumstances. (McPherson, 2005)

## CASE Tool

A software tool that helps software designers and developers specify, generate, and maintain some or all software components of an application. Most CASE tools provide functions to allow developers to draw database schemas and to generate the corresponding DDL code. (Hainaut et al., 2005)

## Case-Based Expert System
An expert system that uses modeled representations of previous cases and decisions to make inferences about new cases. (Svensson, 2005)

## Case-Based Learning (CBL)
Stemming from case-based reasoning, the process of determining and storing cases of new problem-solution scenarios in a casebase. (Soh, 2006)

## Case-Based Reasoning (CBR)
**1:** A reasoning process that derives a solution to the current problem based on adapting a known solution to a previously encountered, similar problem to the current one. (Soh, 2006) **2:** An Artificial Intelligence approach that solves new problems using the solutions of past cases. (Lorenzi & Ricci, 2005)

## Casebase
A collection of cases with each case containing a problem description and its corresponding solution approach. (Soh, 2006)

## Catalog
The collection of records used to describe and locate the items contained in a library. (Hänisch, 2005)

## Categorical Attribute
An attribute that takes values from a discrete domain. (Gehrke, 2005)

## Categorical Data
Fits into a small number of distinct categories of a discrete nature, in contrast to continuous data; may be ordered (ordinal), for example, high, medium, or low temperatures, or non-ordered (nominal), for example, gender or city. (Zhu, 2005)

## Categorical Models Power
As a rule, formal mathematical constructs appear within consistent systems of concepts rather than discretely. Such systems normally explicate some integral non-trivial intuition, partially embedded in each of the constructs that the system consists of. This way the intuition behind

a mathematical construct (like the roots of a tree) can go much wider and deeper than can be seen in the construct as such. The result is that in mathematical modeling, an apt formal counterpart F of a real-world phenomenon/artifact W can give much more than initially expected from stating the correspondence "F models W." The history of applying mathematics to science and engineering is full of examples of when formalisms turned out to be surprisingly clever in their modeling and predictive capabilities. (Gaffar & Seffah, 2005)

## Categorization
**1:** The process of deducing, from the content of an artifact, the potentially multiple ways in which the artifact can be classified for the purpose of later retrieval from a database, library, collection, or physical storage system. (Heucke et al., 2005) **2:** A cognitive process based on similarity of mental schemes and concepts in which subjects establish conditions that are both necessary and sufficient (properties) to capture meaning and/or the hierarchy inclusion (as part of a set) by family resemblances shared by their members. Every category has a prototypical internal structure, depending on the context. (Amoretti, 2005)

## Category
**1:** A collection of objects or entities that is a subset of the union of different entity types; entities offering a similar role are grouped into a category. (Bagui, 2005) **2:** Special type of entity that represents the union of two or more different entity types. (Mani & Badia, 2005) **3:** A set of levels of observed actions or choices made by an individual. (Medlin et al., 2006)

## Category Attribute
The variable that describes the summary data of an aggregate data structure. (Rafanelli, 2005)

## Category 5 Ethernet (Cat5)
The most common form of cable used for networking containing (four) twisted pairs of copper wire, supporting data transmission speeds of 100 Mbps. (D. Stern, 2005)

## Category Theory (CT)
A branch of modern algebra, providing a language and machinery for defining and manipulating mathematical structures in an abstract and generic way. The method of CT is to present the universe of discourse as a collection of objects (nodes) and morphisms (arrows) between them. The latter can be composed, and so the universe is presented

as a category: directed graph with composable arrows. For example, models of a given sort (meta-model) and mappings between them form a category in a very natural way. If one wants to work with a heterogeneous universe of models (that is, models of different meta-models), one should use fibrations described in "Math-II." The philosophy of CT is that everything one wants to say about objects, one must say in terms of arrows between objects. Correspondingly, an object's structure is a structure over its arrow interface. This way of defining structures and manipulations with them is often called arrow thinking. (Diskin, 2005)

**Cat5:** See *Category 5 Ethernet.*

## Cathedral and Bazaar

Paper by Eric Raymond (most recent version in 2001) that contrasts the "Cathedral" software development approach of a closed hierarchy (e.g., for proprietary software and most open source software such as the earlier GNU Project) with the "Bazaar" approach of loose collaboration with light centralized moderation (as was the used for the Linux and Fetchmail open source projects). (Carillo & Okoli, 2006)

## Causal Ambiguity

**1:** Refers to uncertainty, by competitors, regarding the causes of efficiency and effectiveness of a company, when it is unclear which resource combinations are enabling specific competitive capabilities that are earning the company profits. (Potgieter et al., 2005) **2:** The "knowability" (the extent to which something can be known) and "knowness" (the extent to which something is known) of two sets of elements: the organizational inputs, and the causal factors that are used in combination to generate outcomes. (Priestley, 2006)

## Causal Chain

A sequence of instances of causal relations such that the effect of each instance except the last one is the cause of the next one in sequence. (Kontos & Malagardi, 2006)

## Causal Link

**1:** An arrow on a group map which represents a causal relationship between the two issues represented by the contributions it links. (Shaw, 2006) **2:** An arrow that denotes the cause-effect relationships between two variables in a system dynamics model. (Casado, 2005)

## Causal Loop Diagram (CLD)

**1:** A tool that captures the causal interrelationships among a set of variables. CLDs reveal systemic patterns underlying complex relationships, and highlight hidden causes and unintended consequences. (Maani, 2005) **2:** A diagram of two or more variables connected by links, which usually take the form of arrows. These diagrams depict three major components: feedback loops, cause-effect relationships, and delays. (Saha, 2005)

**CBIR:** See *Content-Based Image Retrieval.*

**CBIS:** See *Computer-Based Information System.*

**CBL:** See *Case-Based Learning; Call-Back Locking.*

**CBR:** See *Case-Based Reasoning.*

**CBT:** See *Calculus-Based Trust; Computer-Based Training.*

**CCH:** See *Computerized Criminal History.*

**CCR:** See *Customer Conversion Rate.*

**CCNA:** See *Cisco-Certified Network Associate.*

**ccTLD:** See *Country Code Top-Level Domain.*

**CDI:** See *Customer Data Integration.*

**CDM:** See *Common Data Model.*

**CDMA:** See *Code Division Multiple Access.*

## CDMA-2000

Sometimes also known as IS-136 and IMT-CDMA multi-carrier (1X/3X), CDMA-2000 is an evolution of narrowband radio transmission technology known as CDMA-ONE (also called CDMA or IS-95) to third generation. 1X refers to the use of 1.25 Mhz channel while 3X refers to 5 Mhz channel. (Akhtar, 2005)

**CDN:** See *Content Distribution Network; Content Delivery Network.*

**CDPD:** See *Cellular Digital Packet Data.*

**CDR:** See *Charging Data Record.*

**CD-ROM:** See *Compact Disc Read-Only Memory.*

## CD-ROM Program
Standard computer disk-operated software that runs on a stand-alone computer or on multiple computers through a file server. (Switala, 2005)

## CD-Web Hybrid System
A system combining CD-ROM and Internet technology to deliver distance education to students. A system that looks into achieving the best of both worlds using the speed of CD-ROMs and the currency of the Internet. This can also be seen as a two-layered model where the CD-ROM is one layer and the Internet is the other, with each carrying out a different function of the system. (Shareef & Kinshuk, 2005)

**CE:** See *Computer Engineering.*

## Cell
A point in the multi-dimensional data space. For a d-dimensional data cube, it is defined by a d-tuple of dimension values. A cell contains the values of the measure attributes of the data item that falls into that cell. If there is no such data item, then the cell is empty. (Riedewald et al., 2005)

## Cell Global Identity (CGI)
Each base station in a cellular network has a unique ID that the mobile phone receives when entering the area of the base station. Cell global identity uses this unique ID in order to pinpoint the base station's area of coverage in which the mobile phone is located. (Ververidis & Polyzos, 2006)

## Cell Global Identity with Timing Advance (CGI-TA)
A positioning method that uses the time needed for a signal to travel from the mobile phone to the base station to compute the distance between the phone and the mobile station. Along with the base station's ID, this method provides a rough estimation of the position of the phone in the base station's area of coverage. (Ververidis & Polyzos, 2006)

## Cell Identification (Cell-ID)
The Cell-ID method is the basic technique to provide location services and applications in second-generation mobile communication networks. The method relies on the fact that mobile networks can identify the approximate position of a mobile handset by knowing which cell site the device is using at a given time. (Giaglis, 2005)

**Cell Phone:** See *Mobile Phone.*

**Cell-ID:** See *Cell Identification.*

## Cellular Communication
Wireless communication between mobile devices (e.g., cell phones, PDAs, and PCs) and fixed base stations. The base stations serve relatively small areas of a few square miles (called cells) and are interconnected by a fixed telecommunication infrastructure that provides connection with other telecommunication systems. As a mobile device passes from one cell to another, one base station hands off the communication with the device to another without disrupting communication. (Melliar-Smith & Moser, 2005)

## Cellular Digital Packet Data (CDPD)
A wireless standard providing two-way data transmission at 19.2 kbps over existing cellular phone systems. (Akhtar, 2005)

## Cellular Network
**1:** A wireless communications network in which fixed antennas are arranged in a hexagonal pattern, and mobile stations communicate through nearby fixed antennas. (Ngoh & Shankar, 2005) **2:** A network consisting of several cells served by a fixed, pre-established infrastructure to cover a geographic area, for example GSM, IS-95, UMTS. (Erbas, 2005)

## Cellular Telephony
A mobile telephone service employing a network of cell sites distributed over a wide area. Each cell site contains a radio transceiver and a base station controller that manages, sends, and receives traffic from the mobiles in its geographical area to a cellular telephone switch. It also employs a tower and antennas, and provides a link to the distant cellular switch called a mobile telecommunications switching office (MTSO). The MTSO places calls from land-based telephones to wireless customers, switches calls between cells as mobiles travel across cell boundaries, and authenticates wireless customers before they make calls. (Latchem, 2005)

**C**

## Cellular Value-Added Service Categories

Can be categorized as message-based service, entertainment service, financial service, and information service. (Lee & Pai, 2005)

## Censored

Censored cases are those in which the survival times are unknown. (Chen, Oppenheim, et al., 2005)

## Census II X-11

A method that systematically decomposes a time series into trend, cyclical, seasonal, and error components. It was developed by the Bureau of the Census of the Department of Commerce and is widely used in deseasonalizing economic data. (G.P. Zhang, 2005)

## Center-Based Clustering

Similarity among the data points is defined through a set of centers. The distance from each data point to a center determined the data points association with that center. The clusters are represented by the centers. (B. Zhang, 2005)

## Center of Gravity

The center of gravity of the image is calculated as per the following equation:

$$X = \sum_{y=1}^{m} (y \cdot P_h [y]) / \sum_{y=1}^{m} P_h [y]$$

and

$$Y = \sum_{x=1}^{n} (x \cdot P_v [x]) / \sum_{x=1}^{n} P_v [x]$$

where X and Y are the x and y coordinates of the center of gravity of the image, and $P_h$ and $P_v$ are the horizontal and vertical projections respectively. (Chakravarty et al., 2005a)

## Centrality

1: An index used to indicate how critical an actor is in a network. Degree is the most popular way to measure centrality.; see also Betweenness Centrality; Closeness Centrality. (Assimakopoulos & Yan, 2006) 2: The extent to which ties give an individual or subgroup a central position in a network. (Dekker, & Hendriks, 2006)

## Centralization

An index at group level, measuring how variable or heterogeneous the actor centralities are. It records the extent to which a single actor has high centrality, and the other, low centrality. (Assimakopoulos & Yan, 2006)

## Centralized Model

The concentration of decision making in a single point in the organization in which a single decision applies. (Peterson, 2005)

## Centralized Representation Repository

A single database in which all real-world entity representation models are stored, and any information system willing to access a model that retrieves it from there. This approach keeps the models consistent, but shifts the maintenance issues to the client information systems. (Lepouras et al., 2006)

## Centralized Static Virtual Enterprise

Refers to a dominant business domain (also called business integrator) that coordinates the business relationships among network members. (Tahinakis et al., 2006)

## Centralized Strategy

1: A managerial approach through which support for information technology use for all constituencies is provided by a single on-campus structure. (Poda & Brescia, 2005) 2: In contrast with decentralization, the centralized structure is sometimes referred to as vertical, bureaucratic, mechanistic, rigid, or inflexible. (Wang, Chen, et al., 2006)

## Central Limit Theorem

When an infinite number of successive random samples is taken from a population, the distribution of sample means calculated for each sample will become approximately normally distributed with mean $\mu$ and standard deviation $\sigma/\sqrt{N}$ ($\sim N(\mu, \sigma/\sqrt{N})$). (Fernández & Layos, 2005)

## Central Route to Persuasion

A term used in the elaboration likelihood model involving intense thought and analysis concerning a persuasive message. The central route to persuasion involves high degrees of message-related thinking or careful scrutiny about an argument and its merits in order to arrive at an evaluation of the advocated message. When the central route to persuasion is taken, attitudes are thought to be more accessible, persistent, resistant to change, and better predictors of behavior than when the peripheral route is taken. (Duthler, 2005)

## Certification

**1:** A procedure by which a third party gives written assurance that a product, process, or service conforms to specified characteristics. Certification involves assessment. (Leung, 2005) **2:** The confirmation that external professional requirements have been met. (D.B. Johnstone, 2005)

## Certificate (or Certification) Authority (CA)

**1:** A trusted third party whose purpose is to sign certificates for network entities that it has authenticated using secure means. Other network entities can check the signature to verify that a CA has authenticated the bearer of a certificate. (Pulkkis et al., 2005b) **2:** An authority that manages the allocation of digital identity certificates to users. The CA exists as part of a PKI. The CA in conjunction with a Registration Authority (RA) initially checks to ensure the identity of a user. Once identity has been confirmed, the CA issues digital identity certificates that electronically assure the identity of a user based on the CA's digital signature. (Mundy & Otenko, 2005) **3:** An entity (typically a company) that issues digital certificates to other entities (organizations or individuals) to allow them to prove their identity to others. (Fortino, 2005) **4:** An authority such as GlobalSign that issues, suspends, or revokes a digital certificate. (Mitrakas, 2005) **5:** An authority trusted by one or more users to create and assign public key certificates. (Trcek, 2005) **6:** A trusted third party in a network that issues, signs, and manages certificates for network entities. Technically, a CA provides a set of digital certificate management services, including verification. (Xu & Korba, 2005)

## Certification Practice Statement

A statement of the practices of a certificate authority and the conditions of issuance, suspension, revocation, and so forth of a certificate. (Mitrakas, 2005)

**CFF:** See *Critical Failure Factor.*

## C4ISR

Command, control, communications, computers, intelligence, surveillance, and reconnaissance—a military application framework that makes extensive use of GIS technologies. (Morris-Jones & Carter, 2005)

**CG:** See *Computer Graphic.*

**CGI:** See *Cell Global Identity; Common Gateway Interface.*

**CGI Program:** See *Common Gateway Interface Program.*

**CGI-TA:** See *Cell Global Identity with Timing Advance.*

**CHAID:** See *Chi-Square Automatic Interaction Detection.*

## Chain Graphical Model

A graph that contains both undirected and directed links. Such models can show both symmetric and asymmetric relationships; they give rise to graphical chain models. (Giudici & Cerchiello, 2005)

## Chain of Sustainability

An evolving, dynamic, and matched mix between company resources (arranged in value-generating combinations) and the changing marketplace that gives the company a competitive edge. (Potgieter et al., 2005)

## Challenge and Response

A cryptographic technique used to identify a client to a server. Server and client share a common secret key. The server sends bit strings (challenges) to the client who encrypts these strings and resends them to the server (response). The server may then check the correctness by applying the secret key and comparing the result to the original bit string. (Stickel, 2005)

## Challenged Project

A completed and approved project that is over budget, late, and has fewer features and functions than originally specified. (Dalcher, 2005)

## Change Advocate

A person or group who supports a change but does not have the authority to sanction the change effort. (Lick & Kaufman, 2005)

## Change Agent

A person or group who is responsible for implementing the desired change. (Lick & Kaufman, 2005)

**C**

**Change Creation**

The process whereby an institution and its people invite, accept, and welcome change as a vital component in defining and achieving future success; define the future they want to design and deliver; and develop and implement a change plan that capably transitions its people, processes, and circumstances, and especially its culture, from the existing paradigm to the new, desired one. (Lick & Kaufman, 2005)

**Change Culture**

Recognizes the multi-dimensional nature of complex change and actively works to create conditions where it can thrive. These conditions include but are not limited to understanding the nature of complex change, providing research-based support for making complex change, and allowing sufficient time for complex change to occur. A fundamental assumption of a change culture is that its members must think conditionally about their current knowledge structures, behaviors, and values. Thinking conditionally requires individuals consistently to seek new information that prompts the emergence or enhancement of cognitive structures that enable rethinking of prior ideas and actions. (Johnson, 2005)

**Change Management**

1: A formal process for planning for and managing change in an organization. Involves navigation, expeditionary development, leadership, enablement, and engagement. (Norris, 2005) 2: An organized application of knowledge, tools, and resources that helps organizations to achieve their business strategy. (Partow-Navid & Slusky, 2005) 3: The process of assisting individuals and organizations in passing from an old way of doing things to a new way of doing things. (Häyrinen & Saranto, 2005) 4: Successfully implementing a new position, course, or direction for individuals, processes, or products. (Hanson et al., 2005) 5: The application of many different ideas from the engineering, business, and psychology fields that focus on observable, measurable business elements. These elements, which can be changed or improved, include business strategy, processes, systems, organizational structures, and job roles. (Hanson, 2005) 6: The coordination and action by management required to lead the change of organizational systems and structures in order to support a new business activity or effort. (Ash & Burn, 2006) 7: The procedure that controls the evolution of public services to keep them consistent with their governing legislation, user needs, technological developments, and so forth. (Vassilakis & Lepouras, 2006)

**Change Process**

The process where an individual or group of individuals works over time and with continual adjustments in attitudes, skills, and resources to do something significant differently. In general for the process to be successful, it must address a priority need, the essential features of the change must be defined and practical, and the plan for making the change must be based on a realistic assessment of what is needed to accomplish it. (Johnson, 2005)

**Change Readiness**

An organizational mindset that welcomes challenges to established structures and processes and administrative orthodoxies. (Wright & Taylor, 2005)

**Change Sponsor**

A person or group who authorizes and legitimizes a change. (Lick & Kaufman, 2005)

**Change Target**

A person or group who must change as a result of the change effort. (Lick & Kaufman, 2005)

**Change-Based CQs**

The CQs that are fired when new data arrives at a source. (Khan, 2005)

**Changes to XML**

Given two XML document, the set of edit operations that transform one document to another. (Zhao & Bhowmick, 2005)

**Channel**

1: A chat "room" on Internet Relay Chat (IRC). The /LIST command can be used to list all public channels, with the channel topic and number of occupants for each channel. (Roberts et al., 2006a) 2: A course or pathway through which information is transmitted or business is transacted. (Bahn, 2006)

**Channel Availability**

A feature of any communication medium. A communication medium's channel can be contextual, audio, visual, or any combination of the three. For example, telephone is an audio-only communication medium, while videoconferencing is an audio-visual communication medium. (Y.D. Wang, 2005)

## Channel Capacity

**1:** The maximum possible information rate through a channel subject to the constraints of that channel. (Statica & Deek, 2006) **2:** The potential to transmit a high variety of cues and languages. (Willis, 2005)

## Channel Conflict

Situation in which an e-channel creates a conflict with existing channels because of real or perceived damage from inter-channel competition. (I. Lee, 2005)

## Channel Expansion

A theory that posits that as communication participants acquire experience with the communication (channel, topic, context, co-participants), they increase the richness of their message encoding and message decoding. Technology leads to increasingly rich communication as users increase their ability to communicate effectively using the given technology. In addition, when individual decision makers have a shared knowledge base, they obtain richer results with leaner media. The channel-expansion theory helps to support the notion that decision makers, especially remote decision makers, may use a knowledge network for solving equivocal tasks and for sharing tacit knowledge. (Croasdell & Wang, 2006)

## Channel Expansion Effect

Communication over computer-mediated communication channels such as the Internet can increase in richness and social presence over time, while keeping its nominal channel capacity. This effect occurs as user experience with the medium, the topic, the communication partner, and the communication context accumulates. (Brock & Zhou, 2006)

## Channel Flexibility

The convenience and availability of distribution channels other than the Internet which contributes to increased profit and customer retention. (Wang & Forgionne, 2006)

## Channel Symmetry

A feature of any communication medium. A communication medium affords symmetry if the recipient of a message can respond with the same type of message. For example, telephone and e-mail tools are symmetric (two-way) communication media, while television and Web sites are asymmetric (one-way) communication media. (Y.D. Wang, 2005)

## Chaos Theory

**1:** A theory that deals with complex and dynamic arrangements of connections between elements forming a unified whole, the behavior of which is simultaneously both unpredictable (chaotic) and patterned (orderly). (Smith, 2006b) **2:** A theory that describes systems that are apparently disordered or uncertain, but which may have an underlying order. An underlying tenet is that a small change in the initial conditions can drastically change the long-term behavior of a system. (Burrage & Pelton, 2005)

## Characteristic

Abstraction of a property of a set of objects. For example, "Dan has blue-gray eyes" means "blue-gray eyes" is the property of Dan associated with the characteristic "eye color" of people. The term property is misused in the ISO/IEC 11179 standard. There, it means the same thing as characteristic. (Gillman, 2006)

## Characteristics of a Virtual Community

A virtual community is characterized by its level of cohesion, effectiveness, helpfulness of members, quality of the relationships, language, and self-regulatory mechanisms. (A. Roy, 2005)

## Characterizing Function

A mathematical description of a fuzzy number. (Viertl, 2005)

## Character Segmentation

The technique that partitions images of lines or words into individual characters. (Chan, Ho, et al., 2005)

## Character Set

The set of symbols used to represent a language (alphabet, numerals, special symbols). (D. Brandon, Jr., 2005b)

## Charging Data Record (CDR)

A specific file format that contains call-related data readable from the billing center server. (Louvros et al., 2006)

## Charter School

**1:** An independent public school created by teachers, parents, and others with approval of the governing state to create an alternative choice for students seeking a program that matches their educational interests and/or needs. (Dorniden, 2005) **2:** A governance model where the school exists independent from a larger school district, and is run primarily by teachers and parents. (Glick, 2005a) **3:** A public school operated independently of the local school board, often with a curriculum and educational philosophy different from the other schools in the system. (Schrum, 2005)

## Chase

A kind of a recursive strategy applied to a database V, based on functional dependencies or rules extracted from V, by which a null value or an incomplete value in V is replaced by a new, more complete value. (Ras & Dardzinska, 2005)

## Chat

**1:** A technology that provides the capability of instant, textual conversation with another individual through a computer session. (Panton, 2005) **2:** A computer-mediated real-time written conversation. It has the characteristics of a casual conversation and is usually not stored. A chat can be Web based or software based. The first means that it can be accessed from any computer with a Web connection, the latter that certain software needs to be installed on the computer. There are open chat forums that anyone can visit to chat, to find new acquaintances or information. Just as often, people prefer to chat with friends, using chat tools that require authentication before allowed chatting. Examples of software chat tools are Irc and Mirc. (Dunkels, 2005) **3:** A real-time conferencing capability that uses text by typing on the keyboard, not speaking. Generally between two or more users on a local area network (LAN), on the Internet, or via a Bulletin Board Service (BBS). (Burke et al., 2005) **4:** A software system that enables real-time communication among users through the exchange of textual messages.(Loh et al., 2005) **5:** An interactive communication between two or more people who can enter text by typing on the keyboard, and have the entered text appear in real-time on the other user's monitor. Internet Relay Chat (IRC) is an early example. (O'Hagan, 2005) **6:** In combination with asynchronous conferencing, chat allows people to gather and interact with a small group at a very low cost. It is very effective for small group meetings where decisions can be made and details arranged. (Kardaras & Karakostas, 2006) **7:** One-to-one synchronous communication in which two persons exchange messages in real time. (Erlich, 2005) See Instant Messaging.

## Chat Room

**1:** A Web site, or part of a Web site, that allows individuals to communicate in real time. (Whitty, 2005) **2:** An area where synchronous, text-based, online conversation can take place. Sometimes conversations can be conducted ad hoc, or they can be scheduled for a specific time and topic. (Coakes, 2006b) **3:** Interactive "conversation" involving several people (via typing on a computer terminal or PC) usually centered on a single topic utilizing the Internet. Occasionally members of the chat room break off to form a smaller, more intimate conversation, to the exclusion of all others, thus invoking privacy privileges. (Friedman, 2005) **4:** Many-to-many synchronous communication that provides communities of users with a common interest of the opportunity to communicate in real time. Users register and log into a particular "room," and chat by typing messages that are instantly visible in the communal message area (room). Synonym: Group Chat. (Erlich, 2005) **5:** In online chat meetings, people come together, in real time over long distances, by typing on their computers. All comments are recorded on screen so that participants can view what has been discussed. (Gillani, 2005b) **6:** Online spaces where virtual users can "converse" in real time about issues of specific interest. Users can engage in both public and private chats with other users. (Boateng & Boateng, 2006b) **7:** A real-time online interactive discussion group. (Hwang & Stewart, 2005)

## Chat Session

A live discussion online with a variable number of participants in a Web-based class. Can be formal and led by the instructor, or can be leaderless informal conversations. A chat session is synchronous. (Marold, 2005)

## Chat Tool

A Web-based tool that enables text-based synchronous communication among individuals in a learning community. (Morphew, 2005)

## Chatiquette

Standard rules of courtesy and correct behavior for online chat. (Link & Wagner, 2006)

**CHEA:** See *Council for Higher Education Agency.*

## Check

Expression in a relational database system that allows stating a condition involving an attribute in a table; used with CREATE DOMAIN or CREATE TABLE statements. (Badia, 2005b)

## Checkpointing (Full, Incremental)
In full checkpointing, all of the state of the process is captured. In incremental checkpointing, only that part of the state that has changed since the last checkpoint in captured. (Zhao et al., 2005)

## Chemoinformatics
Storage, analysis, and drawing inferences from chemical information (obtained from chemical data) by using computational methods for drug discovery. (Lodhi, 2005)

## Chen Approach
One way to calculate cardinality constraints. It limits the participation of a combination of the other entity(ies) with an entity in the relationship. (Cuadra et al., 2005)

## Chief Information Officer (CIO)
The head of the IS department in an organization. (Johnston, 2005)

## Chief Information Security Officer
Employee of an organization who is the top authority in relation to information security issues. (Janczewski & Portougal, 2005)

## Chief Knowledge Officer (CKO)
A senior-level executive responsible for managing a firm's knowledge management initiative. (Herschel, 2005)

## Chi-Square Automatic Interaction Detection (CHAID)
A decision tree technique used for classification of a data set. CHAID provides a set of rules that can be applied to a new (unclassified) data set to predict which records will have a given outcome. CHAID segments a data set by using chi square tests to create multi-way splits. (Yeo, 2005)

## Choiceboard
An interactive, Web-based tool that lets customers design their own products and services by choosing from a menu of options. (Roberts & Schwaab, 2006)

## Chordophones
The category of musical instruments producing sound by means of a vibrating string; stringed instruments.

Examples: guitar, violin, piano, harp, lyre, musical bow. (Wieczorkowska, 2005)

## Choreography
The message exchange behavior that a business exposes in order to participate in a business relationship based on electronic message exchange. (Bussler, 2005a)

## Choropleth Map
A color-coded map, also called a "thematic" map, in which geographic areas are portrayed in different hues or intensities according to their values on some quantities. (Garb & Wait, 2005b)

## Chromatic Dispersion
Spreading of light pulses as they transit an optical fiber. Results from variations in the density of the optic fiber medium and culminates in signal distortion. (Littman, 2006)

**CIF:** See *Common Interface Format; Corporate Information Factory.*

**CIM:** See *Common Information Model.*

**CIO:** See *Chief Information Officer.*

## Circuit Switched
A type of network in which a physical path is obtained for and dedicated to a single connection between two endpoints in the network for the duration of the connection. Ordinary voice phone service is circuit switched. The telephone company reserves a specific physical path to the number you are calling for the duration of your call. During that time, no one else can use the physical lines involved. (Olla, 2005a)

## Circuit Switching
**1:** A type of communication in which a dedicated channel (or circuit) is established for the duration of a transmission. (Lee & Warkentin, 2006) **2:** A circuit-switched network establishes a permanent physical connection between communicating devices. For the time of the communication, this connection can be used exclusively by the communicating devices. (Kaspar & Hagenhoff, 2005)

## Circulation Database
The information of material usages that are stored in a database, including user identifier, material identifier,

**C**

date the material is borrowed and returned, and so forth. (Wu & Lee, 2005)

**CIS:** See *Computer Information System.*

## Cisco-Certified Network Associate (CCNA)

A data communications industry certification. (Dixon et al., 2005)

## Citation Indexing

The indexing mechanism invented by Eugene Garfield in which cited work, rather than subject terms, is used as part of the indexing vocabulary. (Chen & Lobo, 2006)

## Citizen Engagement

A two-way process through which a government or agency can develop an understanding of citizens' concerns and needs and respond to them, conversely enabling citizens to develop an appreciation of how they can positively contribute to and influence the future of their community and region. (Sutcliffe, 2005)

## Citizen Rights

Those rights that an individual has by virtue of being a member of a government unit (country, state, province, etc.). They vary from government unit to government unit. (Gilbert, 2005)

## Citizen Satisfaction

Term coined to describe the overall approval rating of services received by citizens within their communities. A 100% rating indicates total satisfaction with services received. Ratings may be taken "per service" or represent satisfaction with an entire government structure. (Baim, 2005)

## Citizens' Jury

A group of people selected for preparation of public opinion. The jury is typically selected using stratified sampling in order to match a profile of a given population. The participants (usually a group of 12 to 20) spend two to three days deliberating on a "charge" under the guidance of an impartial moderator. Participants have opportunities to question experts and to discuss the complexities of the issue, and are asked to work toward a consensus response. (Keskinen & Kuosa, 2005)

## Citizen-Centered Approach to E-Government

A way to study e-government that emphasizes the social and political nature of the relationships between citizens and government, and conceptualizes citizens as the most important stakeholder of e-government initiatives. (Almazán & Gil-García, 2006)

## Citizen-Centric

A new approach to organization of government information and dissemination of government services that focuses on citizen needs and desires instead of traditional bureaucratic functions. For example, a citizen-centric Web site may combine various services, provided by different departments or agencies, under a common heading based on life events. (Schelin, 2005)

## Citizen-Led E-Democracy

Bottom-up, transformative process. Citizens create and sustain ICT applications, including e-mail lists, discussion boards, chat, and Web sites, that accurately capture and reflect the discourse of citizen. Such fora can be vertical (subject) or horizontal (geographic). Such an entity must be able to influence government actions either directly (through shared involvement) or indirectly (through public, media, or political influence). Citizen-led e-democracy involves governments "working with," rather than "delivering to" citizens. (Williamson, 2005)

## Citizen-Oriented Model

A model in which citizens are considered to be decision makers with equal opportunities to reach representative decision makers. In this model, the citizens set the agenda, not the politicians, or this process is interactive and based on win-win strategies. However, there has to be a procedure to coordinate this process and avoid the continuous need for voter input. The citizens should be able to take part in strategic decision making, while "conventional" decision makers take the role of executive decision makers. (Keskinen & Kuosa, 2005)

## Citizenship

A complex part of collective identity, refers to the relationship between the individual and the community and between the individuals within a community/state. (Kozeluh, 2005)

## City and Regional Planning/Engineering

The field that deals with the methods, designs, issues, and models used to have successful plans and designs for cities, towns, and regions. (Al-Hanbali & Sadoun, 2006)

## Civic Engagement

Describes the level of citizens' participation in all those activities that concern fostering democratic values and public virtues such as trustworthiness, freedom of speech, and honesty. (Magnani et al., 2006)

## Civil Infrastructure System

The physical infrastructure that enables basic services such as transportation (railroads, roads, airports), water supply, sewage disposal, electric power generation and supply, telecommunications services, and so forth. (Jeong et al., 2006)

## Civil Law

The legal tradition that has its origin in Roman law and was subsequently developed in Continental Europe. It is highly systematized and structured, and relies on declarations of broad, general principles, often ignoring the details. (Zeleznikow, 2006)

## Civil Society

**1:** Refers to the sphere of associative activity between the individual and the state. Analysts differ between those who include the economy and those who do not. (Smith & Smythe, 2005) **2:** There are many definitions of the term "civil society," none of which receives universal acquiescence. There are many ways one could classify the different organizations of civil society—by sector, focus, origins, scale, level of formality, values base, and different theoretical perspectives. As with definitions, there is no universally accepted schema, and the details of each typology should always be adapted to reflect the needs of particular tasks. (Finquelievich, 2005)

## Civil Society Organization

A civic organization, association, or network that occupies the "social space" between the family and the state who come together to advocate their common interests through collective action. Includes volunteer and charity groups, parent/teacher associations, senior citizen groups, sports clubs, arts and culture groups, faith-based groups, workers' clubs and trade unions, non-profit think-tanks, and "issue-based" activist groups. (Arkhypska et al., 2005)

**CKO:** See *Chief Knowledge Officer.*

## Clan

An organized gaming team that enters leagues and tournaments. (Griffiths et al., 2006)

## Class

**1:** A blueprint or prototype that defines the variables and the methods common to all objects of a certain kind. **2:** A collection of objects sharing certain characteristics (such as producer, customer, product, company, etc.). Individual objects are called instances of the class. The classes of an ontology describe the important concepts of a particular domain being modeled. (Antoniou et al., 2005) **3:** A collection of objects that have the same behavior and state definition. (Alhajj & Polat, 2005a) **4:** A program construct representing a type of thing (abstract data type) which includes a definition of both form (information or data) and functionality (methods); the implementation of the design concept of "object type." (D. Brandon, Jr., 2005a) **5:** A template for similar objects defining attributes and operations. (Rittgen, 2005)

## Class Algebra

This fuzzy Boolean algebra can be used either to state necessary conditions (declarations) or sufficient conditions (queries). Because of the decidability of the containment of one class algebra expression by another, any set of class algebra expressions forms an IS-A hierarchy. (Buehrer, 2005)

## Class Diagram

**1:** A diagram that shows a set of classes and their relationships (association, dependency, generalization/specialization, realization); class diagrams address the static design view of a system. (Favre et al., 2005) **2:** Shows the classes of the system, their interrelationships, and the collaboration between those classes. (Riesco et al., 2005)

## Class Hierarchy

**1:** A Directed Acyclic Graph (DAG) that describes the subclass/superclass relationships among classes. Each node represents a class, the children of a node represent the direct subclasses of a class, and the parents of a node represent the direct superclasses of a class. (Alhajj & Polat, 2005b) **2:** Classes are usually organized in a conceptual space along a generalization/specialization axis. A class A is more general (superclass) than a class B when each instance of B is also an instance of A. (Antoniou et al., 2005)

## Class-Conditional Independence

Property of a multivariate distribution with a categorical class variable c and a set of other variables (e.g., x and y).

**C**

The probability of observing a combination of variable values given the class label is equal to the product of the probabilities of each variable value given the class: $P(x,y|c) = P(x|c)*P(y|c)$. (Perlich & Provost, 2005)

## Classification

**1:** A method of categorizing or assigning class labels to a pattern set under the supervision. (Oh et al., 2005) **2:** A process of predicting the classes of unseen instances based on patterns learned from available instances with predefined classes. (Liu & Yu, 2005) **3:** A systematic arrangement of objects (texts) or groups according to (pre) established criteria, or the process of allocating elements in predefined classes. The classification needs a predefined taxonomy in contrast with the clustering technique that works without previous knowledge. Sometimes it is also associated with the process of identifying classes, that is, discovering attributes that characterize one class and that distinguish this from others. (Antonio do Prado et al., 2005) **4:** A technique dividing a dataset into mutually exclusive groups. Unlike clustering, classification relies on predefined classes. (Chen, Tsai, et al., 2005) **5:** A technique in data mining that attempts to group data according to pre-specified categories, such as "loyal customers" vs. "customers likely to switch." (Amaravadi, 2005) **6:** Also known as a recognition problem; the identification of the class to which a given object belongs. (Martí, 2005) **7:** Given a set of training examples in which each example is labeled by a class, build a model, called a classifier, to predict the class label of new examples that follow the same class distribution as training examples. A classifier is accurate if the predicted class label is the same as the actual class label. (Zhou & Wang, 2005) **8:** The process of distributing things into classes or categories of the same type by a learnt mapping function. (Fung & Ng, 2005) **9:** Mapping a data item into one of several pre-defined categories. Stored data are used to locate data in predetermined groups. For example, a retail store chain could use customer purchase data to determine when customers visit and what they typically buy. (Lauría, 2005) **10:** The central problem in (supervised) data mining. Given a training data set, classification algorithms provide predictions for new data based on predictive rules and other types of models. (Muruzábal, 2005) **11:** The distribution of things into classes or categories of the same type, or the prediction of the category of data by building a model based on some predictor variables. (Zhu, 2005) **12:** The process of dividing a dataset into mutually exclusive groups such that the members of each group are as close as possible to one another, and different groups are as far as possible from one another, where distance is measured with respect to specific variables one is trying to predict. For example, a typical classification problem is to divide a database of companies into groups that are as homogeneous as possible with respect to a creditworthiness variable with values good and bad. Supervised classification is when we know the class labels and the number of classes. (Hamdi, 2005a) **13:** The process of predicting the classes of unseen instances based on patterns learned from available instances with predefined classes. (Yu & Liu, 2005) **14:** The task of inferring concepts from observations. It is a mapping from a measurement space into the space of possible meanings, viewed as finite and discrete target points (class labels). It makes use of training data. (Domeniconi & Gunopulos, 2005)

## Classification and Regression Tree (CART)

A tool for data mining that uses decision trees. CART provides a set of rules that can be applied to a new dataset for predicting outcomes. CART segments data records by creating binary splits. (Wilson, et al., 2006a)

## Classification Error

**1:** Error produced by incorrect classifications which consists of two types: correct negative (wrongly classify an item belonging to one class into another class) and false positive (wrongly classify an item from other classes into the current class). (Y.-J. Zhang, 2005b) **2:** Number of elements that are classified in the wrong class by a classification rule. In two class problems, the classification error is divided into the so-called false positive and false negative. (Felici & Truemper, 2005)

## Classification Level

A security level that represents both the confidentiality degree of the information and its category. (Gabillon, 2005)

## Classification Model

A pattern or set of patterns that allows a new instance to be mapped to one or more classes. Classification models (also known as classifiers) are learned from data in which a special attribute is selected as the "class." For instance, a model that classifies customers between likely to sign a mortgage and customers unlikely to do so is a classification model. Classification models can be learned by many different techniques: decision trees, neural networks, support vector machines, linear and nonlinear discriminants, nearest neighbors, logistic models, Bayesian, fuzzy, genetic techniques, and so forth. (Hernandez-Orallo, 2005b)

## Classification Rule

The association that occurs in classification data between an antecedent containing a set of predicates expressing the values of particular attributes or features and a consequent expressing a class label. Classification rules represent concise descriptions of the target class. (Richards & de la Iglesia, 2005)

## Classification Rule Mining

A technique/procedure aiming to discover a small set of rules in the database to form an accurate classifier for classification. (Y.-J. Zhang, 2005b)

## Classification Tree

**1:** A decision tree that places categorical variables into classes. (Kumar, 2005) **2:** A decision tree where the dependent attribute is categorical. (Gehrke, 2005) **3:** An oriented tree structure obtained by a recursive partitioning of a sample of cases on the basis of a sequential partitioning of the predictor space such to obtain internally homogenous groups and externally heterogeneous groups of cases with respect to a categorical variable. (Siciliano & Conversano, 2005) **4:** Type of decision tree that is used to predict categorical variables, whereas regression trees are decision trees used to predict continuous variables. (Hirji, 2005)

## Classifier

**1:** A decision-supporting system that, given an unseen input object, yields a prediction (e.g., it classifies the given object to a certain class). (Bruha, 2005) **2:** An algorithm that, given as input two or more classes (or labels), automatically decides to which class or classes a given document belongs, based on an analysis of the contents of the document. A single-label classifier is one that picks one class for each document. When the classes among which a single-label classifier must choose are just two, it is called a binary classifier. A multi-label classifier is one that may pick zero, one, or many classes for each document. (Sebastiani, 2005)

## Classifier System

A rich class of evolutionary computation algorithms building on the idea of evolving a population of predictive (or behavioral) rules under the enforcement of certain competition and cooperation processes. Note that classifier systems can also be understood as systems capable of performing classification. Not all CSs qualify as classifier systems in the broader sense, but a variety of CS algorithms concerned with classification do. (Muruzábal, 2005)

## Class Label

A label identifying the concept or class of an instance. (Maloof, 2005)

## Classroom Community

Sense of community in a classroom setting. (Rovai & Gallien, 2006)

## Classroom Interaction

The interaction that can only be achieved face to face in a classroom. (W.B. Martz, Jr. & V.K. Reddy, 2005)

**CLC:** See *Conversation Learning Community.*

**CLD:** See *Causal Loop Diagram.*

## CLDS

The facetiously named system development life cycle (SDLC) for analytical, DSS systems. CLDS is so named because in fact it is the reverse of the classical SDLC. (Yao et al., 2005)

## Cleansing

To filter the irrelevant entries in the Web log, such as graphics files. The HTTP protocol is stateless, which requires a separate connection for each file that is requested from the Web server. Therefore, several log entries may result from a request to view a single page, since the files for the graphics embedded in the page are automatically downloaded from the Web server. Such filtering can be done by checking the suffixes of the URI name such as jpg and gif. (Yao & Xiao, 2005)

## Clear Case

A case that experts agree can be solved in an acceptable manner by simply applying the existing legal rules to it. (Svensson, 2005)

## Clear Direction

Goals that facilitate creativity are clear, negotiated, attainable, shared, and valued. (Torres-Coronas & Gascó-Hernández, 2005)

**C**

**Clearance Level**
A security level that represents both the trust level of the user and his or her need to know. (Gabillon, 2005)

**Clementine**
Data-mining software developed by SPSS Corporation that is used to create predictive models to solve business challenges. (Athappilly & Rea, 2005)

**CLF:** See *Common Log Format.*

**Click Fraud**
Clicking on an online advertisement link for the premeditated purpose of causing a PPC advertiser to pay for the click without the intent to take any other actions (such as buy a product). (Owen, 2006a)

**Click-and-Mortar**
1: A firm that operates both online and off-line, or a hybrid operation that requires a combination of online and off-line aspects to complete a transaction. For example, a company offers items for sale online and requires that the customers pick up the items from a nearby store. (Aigbedo, 2005) 2: An e-commerce company that has both online presence and a physical store. (Wang, Ding, et al., 2006)

**Click-Through**
When a Web page visitor clicks on a link, such as an advertisement, for more information. (Owen, 2006a)

**Click-Through Rate (CTR)**
A ratio of the number of Web page visitors who clicked on an ad link vs. the number of visitors who were exposed to the ad, expressed as a percentage. (Owen, 2006a)

**Clickstream**
1: A sequence of mouse clicks. (Quah et al., 2006c) 2: In Web research, the sequence of Web pages visited by the experimental subject. A clickstream data record can be as simple as URL and sequence number, or a time stamp can be added. This latter approach allows for analysis of page viewing time. (Westin, 2005) 3: The sequence of mouse clicks executed by an individual during an online Internet session. (Agresti, 2005) 4: The sequence of movement as a person clicks on a Web site, then moves from page to page within that site, and then moves to another site. (Waterson, 2006) 5: Virtual trail left by a user's computer as the user surfs the Internet. The clickstream is a record of every Web site visited by a user, how long they spend

on each page, and in what order the pages are viewed. It is frequently recorded in Web server logs. (Nasraoui, 2005) 6: A sequential series of Web page view requests from an individual user. (Lee-Post & Jin, 2005b)

**Clickstream Data**
Web usage data. A virtual trail that a user leaves behind while surfing the Internet (e.g., every Web site and every page of every Web site that the user visits; how long the user was on a page or a site). (Dholakia, Bang, et al., 2005)

**Clickstream Tracking**
The use of software to monitor when people use the Internet and what sites they visit. (Szewczak, 2005)

**Clickwrap Agreement**
Applies to software acquired without any packaging (e.g., when it is copied to a computer ("downloaded") from a Web site or is pre-loaded on a computer). When the buyer installs the software, a dialogue box is displayed containing the license agreement. The user is instructed to select a button to accept the terms of the license agreement and complete the installation. (Sprague, 2005)

**Client**
1: A computer, other device, or application that receives services from a server. (Maris, 2005) 2: A computer that requests and receives data and services from servers on a computer network. Computer users work with clients to access information on the Internet and World Wide Web. (Dasgupta & Chandrashekaran, 2005) 3: A computer that downloads files or requests documents or services from a file server. (Hantula, 2005) 4: Customers who pay for good and services. (Guan, 2006b)

**Client Organization**
Public or private entity that uses international outsourcing workers to perform different tasks. (St.Amant, 2006b)

**Client-Centered Transaction Environment**
A service portal with available services that cross agency boundaries organized by their relevance to a client's situation. For citizens, these may be organized by "life events" such as marrying, employment, or health care. (Knepper & Chen, 2006)

**Client-Originated ERP Maintenance Request**
Originated from within a client organization. Intended to fix bugs, adapt internal and external changes to business

processes, make enhancements to the installed system to meet new user requirements, and provide helpdesk supports. (Ng, 2005)

## Client-Server Model

**1:** A model defining a basis for communication between two programs called respectively the client and the server. The requesting program is a client and the service-providing program is the server. (Karoui, 2005) **2:** A communication where one host has more functionality than the other. It differs from the P2P network. (Hosszú, 2006)

## Client/Server Architecture

**1:** Computer network model separating computers providing services (servers) from computers using these services (clients). (Framinan, 2005) **2:** A network architecture in which each computer or process on the network is either a client or a server. Servers are powerful computers or processes dedicated to managing disk drives (file servers), printers (print servers), or network traffic (network servers). Clients are PCs or workstations on which users run applications. Clients rely on servers for resources, such as files, devices, and even processing power. (Díez-Higuera & Díaz-Pernas, 2005) **3:** The architecture built on top of Remote Procedure Call (RPC) commonly used in business applications. (Fiege, 2005)

## Client-Side/Server-Side Scripting

**1:** In a Web environment, this term relates to the fact that scripted tasks can be handled by the browser software (client side) or by the Web server software (server side). A single Web page may contain both client-side and server-side scripts. The script host is determined by the RUNAT attribute of the SCRIPT tag. (Westin, 2005) **2:** Activities that occur on the user's computer which may interact with the server. (Note that "clients" may now include mobile devices, such as smart phones and PDAs.) (Moore et al., 2006)

## Clinical Audit

The assessment of professional clinical practices. General information routinely provided includes lengths of stay, deaths, and re-admissions. More specific information such as drugs administered and operative procedures performed are available via the appropriate feeder systems. The data allow aspects of case mix, clinical management, diagnostic accuracy, and patient outcomes to be compared. (Barnes, 2005)

## Clinical Coding

Categorizes diagnoses and procedures for patient episodes according to a detailed clinical standard index. The most common standard is the International Classification of Diseases (ICD), particularly for financial audit, but a UK standard Read is very popular with medical staff. These are grouped to provide aggregate information for audit. (Barnes, 2005)

## Clip

A set of segments having the same salient objects. (Kacimi et al., 2005)

## Cloaking

Another means of spamdexing in which sites provide a different page to the search engine spider than the one that will be seen by human users. (Kasi & Jain, 2006)

## Clock Synchronization

Physical clocks in a network are synchronized to within certain precision and accuracy. The precision refers to the difference between readings of clocks, and the accuracy refers to the difference between the clock reading and the universal standard time. (Yang et al., 2005b)

## CLOD

A virtual collaborative learning paradigm enabling a self-tutored, interactive, and cooperative learning process where a small group of remote students requests, watches, and controls the playback of an archived lecture by exchanging questions with each other. (Fortino, 2005)

## Closed Frequent Graph

A frequent graph pattern G is closed if there exists no proper super-pattern of G with the same support in the dataset. (Katsaros & Manolopoulos, 2005b)

## Closed Itemset

An itemset that is a maximal set of items common to a set of objects. An itemset is closed if it is equal to the intersection of all objects containing it. (Pasquier, 2005)

## Closed Loop

Transfer of value happens as with digital cash. For instance, when the user receives the issue from the issue subject, and the digital money is allotted to the money payment of the commodity or service, the seller will shut the settlement to the issue subject for the transfer of value. (Kurihara, 2006)

**C**

## Closed Sequential Pattern

A frequent sequential pattern that is not included in another frequent sequential pattern having exactly the same support. (Masseglia et al., 2005)

## Closed Shape

A shape is represented by the ordered set of points and the ordered set of lines connecting points. The start point and the end point are coincident in closed shapes. (Ferri & Grifoni, 2006)

## Closed (or Proprietary) Software

Software that is owned by an individual or a company (usually the one that develops it) and is protected from unauthorized use by patents, trademarks, or copyrights. Such software is often sold or leased to other individuals or organizations, usually with strict restrictions regarding its use, modification, and further distribution. In many cases the source code is kept secret. (Curti, 2005)

## Closed-Loop MRP

The combination of MRP functionality with planning and production execution modules, with the potential for feedback from the execution cycle to the planning cycle. (Carton & Adam, 2005)

## Closed-World Assumption

**1:** A principle that claims that every atom not entailed by the KDB is assumed to be false. This principle is sound on KDBs with simple syntax as logic programs. (Alonso-Jiménez et al., 2005) **2:** The assumption that any goal that is not provable is false. For example, if the knowledge base cannot prove that there is a flight from Taipei to New York, then you can assume that there is no such flight. This assumption is used by most knowledge bases. For class algebra, which is decidable (i.e., membership in a class expression is either true or false for a given object), the closed-world assumption corresponds to the "true-complement~" operator. A "pseudo-complement -" operator is used in proving that something has negative evidence, but the pseudo-complemented predicates are treated like positive literals in terms of Horn clauses. The maximum proofs of positive and negative evidence produce a fuzzy interval for any class algebra expression. (Buehrer, 2005) **3:** An assumption made in classical planning that all facts that are not implied by the knowledge base are false. Closed-world assumption rests on the assumption of completeness of knowledge. (Babaian, 2005)

## Closeness Centrality

A measurement of centrality indicating how close an actor is to all other actors in a network. The idea here is that actors are central if they can quickly interact with all other actors in a network. (Assimakopoulos & Yan, 2006)

## Closure Operator

Let S be a set and c: $\wp(S) \rightarrow \wp(S)$; c is a closure operator on S if $\forall$ X, Y$\subseteq$S, c satisfies the following properties: (1) extension, Xc$\subseteq$(X); (2) mononicity, if X$\subseteq$Y, then c(X)$\subseteq$c(Y); (3) idempotency, c(c(X)) = c(X). Note: s$^\circ$t and t$^\circ$s are closure operators, when s and t are the mappings in a Galois connection. (Dumitriu, 2005)

## Cluster

**1:** A group of content-similar multimedia objects. (Hurson & Yang, 2005) **2:** A group of elements that have some characteristics or attributes in common. (Antonio do Prado et al., 2005) **3:** A group of linked enterprises that share a common purpose of gaining competitive advantage and economies of scale. (Braun, 2006) **4:** A group of organizations that are linked together around a particular industry. (Mason et al., 2006) **5:** A set of entities that are similar between themselves and dissimilar to entities from other clusters. (Ma & Li, 2005) **6:** A group of objects of a dataset that are similar with respect to specific metrics (values of the attributes used to identify the similarity between the objects). (Santos et al., 2005) **7:** Parallel architecture that contains multiple "standard" computers connected via a high-performance network that work together to solve the problem. (Geisler & Kao, 2005) **8:** Subset of data records; the goal of clustering is to partition a database into clusters of similar records such that records that share a number of properties are considered to be homogeneous. (Hirji, 2005)

## Cluster Analysis

**1:** A data analysis technique involving the grouping of objects into sub-groups or clusters so that objects in the same cluster are more similar to one another than they are to objects in other clusters. (Voges, 2005) **2:** A multivariate statistical technique that assesses the similarities between individuals of a population. Clusters are groups or categories formed so members within a cluster are less different than members from different clusters. (Lee, Peterson, et al., 2005) **3:** Defining groups based on the "degree" to which an item belongs in a category. The degree may be determined by indicating a percentage amount. (Lenard & Alam, 2005) **4:** Dividing objects into groups using varying assumptions regarding the number of groups, and the deterministic and stochastic mechanisms that generate the observed values. (Burr, 2005a) **5:** Partitioning a given data set into clusters where data assigned to the same cluster should be similar, whereas data from different clusters should be dissimilar. (Klawonn & Georgevia, 2005) **6:** The process that includes the clustering method and the analysis of its results in order to discover and understand the contents of a set of elements, texts, or objects, and the relations among them. (Antonio do Prado et al., 2005)

## Cluster Center (Prototype)
A cluster in objective function-based clustering is represented by one or more prototypes that define how the distance of a data object to the corresponding cluster is computed. In the simplest case a single vector represents the cluster, and the distance to the cluster is the Euclidean distance between cluster center and data object. (Klawonn & Georgevia, 2005)

## Cluster Frequent Item
A global frequent item is cluster frequent in a cluster Ci if the item is contained in some minimum fraction of documents in Ci. (Fung et al., 2005)

## Cluster Sampling
The process in which a sample of clusters is selected and observations/measurements are made on the clusters. (Lutu, 2005)

## Cluster Validation
Evaluating the clustering results, and judging the cluster structures. (Ma & Li, 2005)

## Cluster-Support of Feature F in Cluster Ci
Percentage of objects in Ci possessing f. (Saquer, 2005)

## Clustering
**1:** A technique that uses features to find the linking pages of each other automatically. Usually, the Web pages with near features will be clustered together. (Chen, Tsai, et al., 2005) **2:** Two or more interconnected computers that create a solution to provide higher availability, higher scalability, or both. (Tong & Wong, 2005b) **3:** A form of unsupervised learning that divides a data set so that records with similar content are in the same group and groups are as different from each other as possible. (Lingras et al., 2005) **4:** A process of grouping instances into clusters so that instances are similar to one another within a cluster but dissimilar to instances in other clusters. (Liu & Yu,

2005) **5:** A process of mapping a data item into one of several clusters, where clusters are natural groupings for data items based on similarity metrics or probability density models. (Oh et al., 2005) **6:** A process to group, based on some defined criteria, two or more terms together to form a large collection. In the context of image segmentation, clustering is to gather several pixels or groups of pixels with similar property to form a region. (Y.-J. Zhang, 2005c) **7:** A task that segments objects into groups according to object similarity. (Chen & McLeod, 2006) **8:** A technique in data mining that attempts to identify the natural groupings of data, such as income groups that customers belong to. (Amaravadi, 2005) **9:** An algorithm that takes a dataset and groups the objects such that objects within the same cluster have a high similarity to each other, but are dissimilar to objects in other clusters.(Cunningham & Hu, 2005) **10:** An unsupervised process of dividing data into meaningful groups such that each identified cluster can explain the characteristics of underlying data distribution. Examples include characterization of different customer groups based on the customer's purchasing patterns, categorization of documents on the World Wide Web, or grouping of spatial locations of the earth where neighbor points in each region have similar short-term/long-term climate patterns.(Chung et al., 2005) **11:** Clustering algorithms discover similarities and differences among groups of items. They divide a dataset so that patients with similar content are in the same group, and groups are as different as possible from each other. (Kusiak & Shah, 2005) **12:** The process of identifying groups in data. In the classification, all groups are pre-defined in the classification system and products are arranged into the existing group structure. Contrary to this, the clustering process identifies groups based on the product data. This means that the groups change depending on the product data. (Abels & Hahn, 2006) **13:** Data-mining approach that partitions large sets of data objects into homogeneous groups. (Garrity et al., 2005) **14:** Data-mining task in which the system has to classify a set of objects without any information on the characteristics of the classes. (Jourdan et al., 2005)

## Clustering Algorithm
An algorithm that sorts data into groups of similar items, where the category boundaries are not known in advance. (Dixon, 2005)

## Clustering Data-Mining Task
The act of identifying items with similar characteristics, and thus creating a hierarchy of classes from the existing set of events. A data set is partitioned into segments of

**C**

elements (homogeneous) that share a number of properties. (Nayak, 2005c)

## Clustering Model
A pattern or set of patterns that allows examples to be separated into groups. All attributes are treated equally and no attribute is selected as "output." The goal is to find "clusters" such that elements in the same cluster are similar between them but are different to elements of other clusters. For instance, a model that groups employees according to several features is a clustering model. Clustering models can be learned by many different techniques: k-means, minimum spanning trees (dendrograms), neural networks, Bayesian, fuzzy, genetic techniques, and so forth. (Hernandez-Orallo, 2005b)

**CLV:** See *Customer Lifetime Value.*

**CMA:** See *Career Management Account.*

**CMC:** See *Computer-Mediated Communication.*

**CME:** See *Computer-Mediated Education.*

**CMI:** See *Computer-Managed Instruction; Computer-Mediated Interaction.*

**CMM:** See *Capability Maturity Model.*

## CMM I (CMM-I1; CMM-I2)
A model enhanced in two dimensions: scope dimension and evaluation dimension. The CMM-I1 incorporated both approaches: the traditional (called staged CMM) and the maturity profile (called continuous CMM). (Monteiro de Carvalho et al., 2005)

## CMM-KMKE
A capability maturity model, based on the CMM, for knowledge management and knowledge engineering. (Berztiss, 2006a)

**CMS:** See *Content Management System.*

**CMT:** See *Computer-Mediated Technology.*

## CNC Machine
Tool machine with a computer numeric control; a standard in the mechanical engineering field. (Röse, 2006a)

## Co-Clustering
Performing simultaneous clustering of both points and their attributes by way of utilizing the canonical duality contained in the point-by-attribute data representation. (Ma & Li, 2005)

## Co-Construction
Unlike the process of a lone researcher documenting a "construction" (whether this is a ritual, an identity, a discourse, and so forth) that preexists the research project, in this case, the researcher is engaged in the construction along with those that in conventional research would have simply been called "informants." Also called Co-Production. (Forte, 2005)

## Co-Located Team
A traditional team that shares a common goal and works toward that goal in a face-to-face, same-office environment. (Long et al., 2005)

## Co-Located Work
Collaborative work carried out by several persons at the same geographical location. (Wiberg, 2005)

## Co-Location
**1:** When members of a community work in the same physical space and time. (Raja et al., 2006) **2:** Team members sharing the same physical location, which allows for face-to-face interaction. (Wong-MingJi, 2005)

## Co-Partnership Managers
The course instructor on the university side and a senior manager of the client organization, who jointly manage a course partnership project. (Kock, 2005)

**Co-Production:** See *Co-Construction.*

## Co-Sourcing
Used instead of outsourcing to emphasize that the outsourcing arrangement is based on cooperation (or "partnering") between the parties. Partnering is often used to signify a highly cooperative arrangement, but Australian law only recognizes written contracts (not "a spirit of cooperation") and "de facto" relationships. (Beaumont, 2005)

**COAC:** See *Comparative Online Analysis of Cultures.*

## Coach

A user who helps other users participate in design work by coaching them. This is the fourth stage in the developmental theory of participatory-design relationships between users and designers. (Carroll, 2005)

## Coaching

The action of a trainer or coach in monitoring the performance of individuals and providing feedback for successful completion of a task. (Ally, 2005d)

## Coaction Field

A place where inhabitants, real or virtual, work or play together as if they were gathered at the same place. (Terashima, 2005)

## Coalesce

**1:** In the context of phylogenetic trees, two lineages coalesce at the time that they most recently share a common ancestor (and hence, "come together" in the tree). (Burr, 2005b) **2:** Combining tuples whose times are contiguous or overlapping into one tuple whose time reference includes the time of constituent tuples. (Tansel, 2005)

**COBIT:** See *Control Objectives for Information and Related Technologies.*

## Cocited

Web pages that have the same parent page or have the same child pages are said to be cocited. (Chen, Tsai, et al., 2005)

## Code Division Multiple Access (CDMA)

**1:** One of several protocols used in 2G (second-generation) and 3G (third-generation) wireless communications. It allows numerous signals to occupy a single transmission channel optimizing the use of available bandwidth. (Pease et al., 2005) **2:** Also known as CDMA-ONE or IS-95, this is a spread spectrum communication technology that allows many users to communicate simultaneously using the same frequency spectrum. Communication between users is differentiated by using a unique code for each user. This method allows more users to share the spectrum at the same time than alternative technologies. (Akhtar, 2005) **3:** A digital wireless technology, and a spread spectrum technology used in Uganda for wireless local loop. It supports data transmission effectively. (D. Stern, 2005) **4:** A technology that allows mobile phone and satellite signals from different users to share the available bandwidth by uniquely encoding each signal. (Dyson, 2005)

## Code Growth/Code Bloat

The proliferation of solution elements (e.g., nodes in a tree-based GP representation) that do not contribute toward the objective function. (Hsu, 2005b)

## Code of Ethics

**1:** A code of ethics can have a positive impact if it satisfies four criteria: (1) the code is distributed to every employee; (2) it is firmly supported by top management; (3) it refers to specific practices and ethical dilemmas likely to be encountered by target employees; and (4) it is evenly enforced with rewards for compliance and strict penalties for non-compliance. (Grieves, 2006a) **2:** A detailed set of principles, standards, and rules aimed at guiding the behavior of groups, usually of professionals in business, government, and the sciences. (Goodman, 2005)

## Codec

**1:** Short for compressor/decompressor. (Hutchinson, 2005) **2:** A computer application that compresses and decompresses the signal for transmission over the Internet. (Dudding, 2005) **3:** Compression and decompression algorithms provided by either a software application or a hardware device. (Vitolo et al., 2005)

## Codification

Putting knowledge into a form that makes it accessible to others, for example, writing down a formula. (Mitchell, 2005b)

## Coding

A manner in which a solution of a given problem can be represented. (Kacem, 2005)

## Coding Data

Analyzing data by assigning codes and categorizing information based on specified research constructs and patterns. (Neale et al., 2005)

**CoE:** See *Community of Experts.*

## Coefficient of Determination

A statistical measure of how well predictive variables did indeed predict the variable of interest. (Benrud, 2005)

## Coevolution

Describes the mutual influences among actors in a collective, as well as their environment; mutual influences can be desirable and undesirable, constructive or destructive. In the case of an organization, it can be envisaged as a set of multi-dimensional networks, themselves part of a larger set of networks to which they are linked. Nodes in the networks represent entities such as offices, factories, teams, and individuals. They are linked formally or informally to other nodes. Activities at any node send messages—and by implication, knowledge—to other nodes in the form of feedback, or feed-forward, thereby triggering activities in those nodes. The messages may use the formal or the informal links in the network. They may be sent intentionally or accidentally. (Land, Amjad, et al., 2006a)

## Cognition

**1:** The mental processes of an individual, including internal thoughts, perceptions, understanding, and reasoning. Includes the way we organize, store, and process information, as well as make sense of the environment. It can also include processes that involve knowledge and the act of knowing, and may be interpreted in a social or cultural sense to describe the development of knowledge. (Faiola, 2006) **2:** The psychological result of perception, learning, and reasoning. (Alkhalifa, 2005a) **3:** The collection of mental processes and activities used in perceiving, remembering, thinking, and understanding, and the act of using those processes. (Atkinson & Burstein, 2006)

## Cognition-Based Trust

A rational view of trust associated with competence, ability, responsibility, integrity, credibility, reliability, and dependability. (Huotari & Iivonen, 2005)

## Cognitive

Psychological phenomena relating to thinking processes as opposed to senses or movement. (N.C. Rowe, 2006b)

## Cognitive/Affective Aspects

The aspects of mental processes or behavior directed toward action or change and including impulse, desire, volition, and striving. (Raisinghani & Hohertz, 2005)

## Cognitive Appraisal Theory

The categorization of emotions through the evaluation of stimuli. (Byl & Toleman, 2005)

## Cognitive Apprenticeship

**1:** Originates from traditional apprenticeship, which has the following well-known features: modeling, coaching, scaffolding, and fading. When applied to educational and research situations, the new features of articulation, reflection, and exploration must be added to the ones above.

(Cartelli, 2006b) **2:** Students work in teams on projects or problems with close scaffolding of the instructor. Cognitive apprenticeships are representative of Vygotskian "zones of proximal development" in which student tasks are slightly more difficult than students can manage independently, requiring the aid of their peers and instructor to succeed. (Jennings et al., 2005)

## Cognitive Complexity

A function of the intensity of information exchanged and the multiplicity of views held. (Willis, 2005)

## Cognitive Conflict

Overt discrepancy among intervening parties about how a particular task or issue should be resolved and their subsequent engagement in action to redress the situation. (Fernández, 2005)

## Cognitive Constructivism

An approach to constructivism based on the work of the Swiss psychologist Jean Piaget, particularly his theory of cognitive development. According to Piaget, the knowledge of human beings is "constructed" through experience, but not from the information they are given. (Bodomo, 2005a)

## Cognitive Dissonance

The situation where a person simultaneously holds two contradictory models of the same subject matter (e.g., an ICT system). (Macefield, 2006)

## Cognitive Engineering

A field aiming at understanding the fundamental principles behind human activities that are relevant in context of designing a system that supports these activities. (Jaspers, 2006)

## Cognitive Flexibility Theory

**1:** Refers to the flexible way learners assemble and retrieve knowledge from their brains. This theory is best used in designing learning environments that support the use of interactive technology. (Sala, 2005b) **2:** The ability to spontaneously restructure one's knowledge, in many ways, in adaptive response to radically changing situational demands. (Burrage & Pelton, 2005)

## Cognitive Gap

The difference in cognitive problem-solving style between two people, especially two people who are obliged to interact as members of a group or team. (Mullany, 2005)

**C**

## Cognitive Graphical Walkthrough

A modification of the initial Cognitive Walkthrough interface evaluation method which materializes diagrams to enable the evaluators to assess the time variable as well as accelerating the evaluation procedure. (Karoulis et al., 2006)

## Cognitive Jogthrough

A modification of the initial Cognitive Walkthrough in order to speed up the procedure. A video camera now records the evaluation session. (Karoulis et al., 2006)

## Cognitive Learning

**1:** A consequence of the vision of the situation in light of a new aspect that enables the comprehension of logic relations or the perception of relations between means and aims. (Xodo, 2005) **2:** The degree of comprehension and retention of knowledge by a student in an educational experience. (Woods & Baker, 2005)

## Cognitive Learning Outcomes

Learning that is associated with knowledge of facts or processes. (Aworuwa & Owen, 2005)

## Cognitive Learning Theory

**1:** The branch of cognitive science that is concerned with cognition and includes parts of cognitive psychology, linguistics, computer science, cognitive neuroscience, and philosophy of mind. (Alkhalifa, 2006) **2:** Provides a framework to understand learning, suggesting that although learning is not directly observable, it occurs through active mental processes where knowledge is progressively assimilated, making a change in behavior possible. (Knight et al., 2005)

## Cognitive Level

The level of cognitive functions in the order of increasing complexity of cognitive processing. (Alkhalifa, 2005b)

## Cognitive Load

**1:** Amount of mental resources necessary for information processing. (Utsi & Lowyck, 2005) **2:** The limited capacities of the visual and auditory channels in working memory. Since these channels can easily become overloaded, one potential benefit of multimedia learning is being able to present complex information in a format that minimizes potential overloads. (M. Mitchell, 2005c) **3:** The degree of cognitive processes required to accomplish a specific task. (Alkhalifa, 2005a)

## Cognitive Load Theory

A theory asserting that the capacities and limitations of the human memory system must be taken into account during the process of instructional design in order to produce optimal learning materials and environments. (Boechler, 2006b)

## Cognitive Map

**1:** A collection of nodes linked by some edges (arcs). From a logical perspective, a node is a logical proposition, and a link is an implication. Thus, a cognitive map consists of causal and temporal relations between cognitive concepts. (von Wartburg, 2006) **2:** A structure representation of contributions, structured with links, to represent one person's knowledge of a topic. Often a map is built by oneself or by an interviewer during an interview. (Shaw, 2006) **3:** A structured representation of decision depicted in graphical format (variations of cognitive maps are cause maps, influence diagrams, or belief nets). Basic cognitive maps include nodes connected by arcs, where the nodes represent constructs (or states) and the arcs represent relationships. Cognitive maps have been used to understand decision situations, to analyze complex cause-effect representations, and to support communication. (Te'eni, 2006) **4:** Internal representation of the world and its spatial properties stored in memory (also called mental map). (Rambaldi, 2005)

## Cognitive Modeling

Using algorithms to represent and simulate the cognitive process, for example, to add intelligence to software agents. (Arya, 2005)

## Cognitive Node

Scalable access point for augmenting knowledge and facilitating communication in knowledge networks. Nodes manage virtue maps and data relevant to knowledge workers. (Croasdell & Wang, 2006)

## Cognitive Overhead

The amount of mental resources that need to be expended to complete a given task. (Boechler, 2006a)

## Cognitive Presence

The extent to which discussion participants are able to construct meaning through sustained communication. (Swan, 2005)

**C**

### Cognitive Problem-Solving Style
The position an individual occupies between two extremes of cognitive problem-solving style personality—namely, the adaptor and the innovator. (Mullany, 2005)

### Cognitive Process
**1:** The performance of some composite cognitive activity. **2:** A set of connected series of cognitive activities intended to reach a goal. Cognitive activities can be considered as a function of their embodied experience. (Plekhanova, 2005a)

### Cognitive Reasoning
Learning through the process of thinking about an issue; the student learns new ideas and relationships by relating an issue to previously learned material. (Owen & Aworuwa, 2005)

### Cognitive Science
**1:** The field of science concerned with cognition and including parts of cognitive psychology, linguistics, computer science, cognitive neuroscience, and philosophy of mind. (Alkhalifa, 2005a) **2:** The multidisciplinary study of intelligent systems (natural, artificial, and hybrid). The disciplines that currently comprise cognitive science are (in alphabetical order) anthropology, artificial intelligence, education, linguistics, neuroscience, philosophy, and psychology. (Gelepithis, 2005)

### Cognitive Style
**1:** A person's preferred way of gathering, processing, and evaluating information. (Kaluzniacky, 2006) **2:** An individual exhibits characteristic ways of processing information and hence solving problems, known as his or her "cognitive style." (Mullany, 2005) **3:** Refers to enduring patterns of an individual's cognitive functioning that remain stable across varied situations. (Crossland, 2005)

### Cognitive System
A complex system that learns and develops knowledge. It can be a human, a group, an organization, an agent, a computer, or some combination. It can provide computational representations of human cognitive processes to augment the cognitive capacities of human agents. (Plekhanova, 2005a)

### Cognitive Task Analysis
The study of the way people perform tasks cognitively. (Jaspers, 2006)

### Cognitive Task Model
A model representing the cognitive behavior of people performing a certain task. (Jaspers, 2006)

### Cognitive Theory
Learning as a sense-making activity and teaching as an attempt to foster appropriate cognitive processing in the learner. (Cirrincione, 2005)

### Cognitive Tool
A tool that reduces the cognitive load required by a specific task. (Alkhalifa, 2005a)

### Cognitive Trait
An ability a human possesses for cognition. Working memory is an example. (Lin & Kinshuk, 2005)

### Cognitive Trait Model
A model representing one or more cognitive traits of learners. (Lin & Kinshuk, 2005)

### Cognitive Trust
Judgments regarding a person's competence and reliability. (Sonnenwald, 2005)

### Cognitive Walkthrough
**1:** An expert-based interface evaluation method. Experts perform a walkthrough of the interface according to pre-specified tasks, trying to pinpoint shortcomings and deficiencies in it. Their remarks are recorded by a recorder and are elaborated by the design team. (Karoulis et al., 2006) **2:** A model-based technique for evaluation of interactive systems designs. It is particularly suited for "walk up and use" interfaces such as electronic kiosks or ATMs. Its aim is to analyze how well the interface will guide first-time or infrequent users in performing tasks. Analysis is performed by asking three questions at each stage of the interaction: Will the correct action be made sufficiently evident to users? Will users connect the correct action's description with what they are trying to achieve? Will users interpret the system's response to the chosen action correctly? (Campos & Harrison, 2006)

### Cognitivism
**1:** A scientific branch of social sciences; also known as being part of cognitive science. Cognitivism focuses on cognition and on cognitive processes by following a perspective that is centered on the individual, on the idea of the mind, and on the neuro-physiology of brain processes. The Cartesian dualism and the radical distinction between individual and

social processes, the rationalist and utilitarist perspectives that interpret the human subject as an independent and autonomous entity, and the results-oriented and objectives-centered approaches to human action may all come under the broad umbrella of cognitivism. Mainstream management theory is largely influenced by cognitivist approaches. Pos-cognitivism does not deny the positive contributions brought by cognitivist thinking, though it highlights the need for further developments and for the exploration of alternative approaches. Communities of practice theory may be understood as being part of the pos-cognitivism movement, which calls attention to the social embeddedness and embodiedness of all knowledge-creation processes. (Nobre, 2006c) **2:** Concerned with what the learner is thinking in terms of processing information for storage and retrieval. (Ally, 2005b)

## Cognos

Business intelligence software that enables organizations to monitor performance and develop strategic business solutions based on collected data. (Athappilly & Rea, 2005)

## Coherence Bandwidth

The bandwidth over which the channel affects transmitted signals in the same way. (Iossifides et al., 2005)

## Cohesion

**1:** The extent to which nodes form a group such that all members have mutual strong ties. (Dekker & Hendriks, 2006) **2:** The strength of connection between the members of a community or network, and thus a community or network can be densely knit or only loosely coupled; cohesion is a result of intensity, frequency, and type of the members' contacts. (Müeller-Prothmann, 2006a) **3:** The degree to which elements within a class are related to one another and work together to provide well-bounded behavior. (Polgar, 2005b)

## Cohort

A group of students who take the same courses together throughout their academic program. (Murray & Efendioglu, 2005)

**CoL:** See *Community of Learners.*

## Collaborative Environment

An environment for work and experience that is capable of supporting the construction of collective practices and knowledge. (Matta, 2005)

## CoLKEN

Coopetitive Learning and Knowledge Exchange Network—that is, a specific setting for inter-organizational knowledge management initiatives focusing on issues related to cooperation-competition-dilemmas and intentional/unintentional knowledge transfer. (Loebbecke & Angehrn, 2006)

## CoLKEN Construct

Structure of main CoLKEN components: at the base level are knowledge, knowledge agents, and knowledge networks; at the CoLKEN focus level, we find the balancing act between cooperation and competition, which should lead to value maximization on the top level. (Loebbecke & Angehrn, 2006)

## CoLKEN Taxonomy

Depicting groups of CoLKENs by differentiating the overall variety along at least two dimensions, for example, along the dimensions of 'ICMT usage' and 'governance focus'. (Loebbecke & Angehrn, 2006)

## Collaboration

**1:** A close, functionally interdependent relationship, in which organizational units strive to create mutually beneficial outcomes. Collaboration involves mutual trust, the sharing of information and knowledge at multiple levels, and includes a process of sharing benefits and risks. Effective collaboration cannot be mandated. (Peterson, 2005) **2:** A project between at least two partners. The partners show consideration for each other and do not try to selfishly fulfill their own needs. Each partner enters collaborations voluntarily. Because of the impossibility to clearly specify all activities and control collaborations exactly, trust plays a major role. (Hofer, 2006) **3:** Group effort characterized by members of a group working together to complete all aspects of a project, and all members of the group are jointly accountable for the finished product. (Ingram & Hathorn, 2005b) **4:** Human behavior that facilitates the sharing of meaning and completion of tasks with respect to a mutually shared goal; takes place in social or work settings. (Sonnenwald, 2005) **5:** Human behavior, sharing of meaning, and completion of activities with respect to a common goal and taking place in a particular social or work setting. (Sonnenwald & Pierce, 2000) **6:** A philosophy of interaction and personal lifestyle. (Sala, 2005b) **7:** Occurs when small groups of people work together toward a common goal in ways that produce new products and knowledge that are unlikely to be developed by individuals. Three essential elements of collaboration are

**C**

interdependence, synthesis, and independence. (Ingram, 2005) **8:** Sharing responsibility in tasks with common goal(s). (Han & Hill, 2006) **9:** The mutual engagement of participants in a coordinated effort to solve a problem. (Cagiltay et al., 2005) **10:** The process of communication among people with the goal of sharing information and knowledge. (Loh et al., 2005) **11:** To facilitate the process of shared creation involving two or more individuals interacting to create shared understanding where none had existed or could have existed on its own. (Vat, 2005b)

## Collaboration Script
A detailed and explicit contract between the instructor and the learners, often in a sequence of phases, each phase typically consisting of a set of instructions that prescribe the task, the group composition, the way the task is distributed within and among the groups, the nature of interaction, and the timing. A well-known example of a collaborative script is the "Jigsaw." (Pöysä & Lowyck, 2005)

## Collaboration Server
Helps users work together via the Web, supporting tasks, projects, communities, calendars, discussions, and document sharing with version control. (Wojtkowski, 2006)

## Collaboration Tools
Technologies designed to allow users to share knowledge with one another. The key features include shared spaces, calendaring, workflow management services, and synchronous and asynchronous communication. (Chua, 2006)

## Collaborative Browsing
Online navigation on the Internet by a group of individuals that assembles in the same physical setting and browses online using the same or adjacent interfaces in the attainment of task-oriented objectives. (Bagozzi & Dholakia, 2005)

## Collaborative Commerce
The processes, technologies, and supporting standards that allow continuous and automated exchange of information between trading partners and can be horizontal competitive cooperation or coopetition, as well as vertical collaboration along a supply chain. (Rowe et al., 2006)

## Collaborative Community
A group of people sharing common interests and acting together toward common goals. (Nabuco et al., 2006)

## Collaborative Culture
By their nature, virtual organizations foster camaraderie between members even in the absence of face-to-face communications. Since the built-in communications tools are so easy to access and use, relationships form between members who have not even met. A corporate culture forms out of friendship that produces a highly collaborative nature, unlike traditional organizations where such extensive communicating is not required. (J. Lee, 2005)

## Collaborative Filter
A form of Recommender System that uses implicit or explicit recommendations of others to provide advice. (Dron, 2005)

## Collaborative Filtering
**1:** A method for making automatic predictions (filtering) about the interests of a user by collecting ratings and interest information from many users (collaborating). (Nasraoui, 2005) **2:** A recommendation technique that uses k-nearest neighbor learning algorithm. Variations include user-based and item-based algorithms. (Sarwar et al., 2005) **3:** A technique that is used for making recommendations by computing the similarities among users. (Chen & Liu, 2005) **4:** A technique used to collect user opinions or preferences for items of interest. A CF algorithm employs a correlation method to predict and recommend items to new or returning users based on the similarity of their interests with those of other users. (Dasgupta et al., 2006) **5:** Aims at exploiting preference behavior and qualities of other persons in speculating about the preferences of a particular individual. (Parmar & Angelides, 2005) **6:** An approach to provide recommendations based on the preferences of similar users. (Chen & McLeod, 2006) **7:** An approach that collects user ratings on currently proposed products to infer the similarity between users. (Lorenzi & Ricci, 2005) **8:** Such methods combine personal preferences of a user with preferences of like-minded people to guide the user. (Seitz, 2005) **9:** Selecting content based on the preferences of people with similar interests. (Schafer, 2005) **10:** Unveiling general patterns through "sniffing" through user's past activities. (Quah et al., 2006c)

## Collaborative Forecasting and Replenishment
An inter-organizational system that enables retailers and manufacturers to forecast demand and schedule production jointly by exchanging complex decision support models and manufacturer/retailer strategies so that the two supply chain

parties can reduce demand uncertainty and coordinate their decisions. (Abraham & Leon, 2006)

## Collaborative Interface
Interface in which the interaction between the user and the system is guided by the principles of collaborative behavior. (Babaian, 2005)

## Collaborative Learning
**1:** A model of learning that involves groups of students working together on a project or assignment. In this model, communication between students is crucial to a successful outcome. (Shaw, 2005) **2:** A more radical departure from "cooperative learning." Involves learners working together in small groups to develop their own answer through interaction and reaching consensus, not necessarily a known answer. Monitoring the groups or correcting "wrong" impressions is not the role of the trainer, since there is no authority on what the answer should be. (Blackmore et al., 2006) **3:** A philosophy of interaction where individuals are responsible for their actions, including learning, and respect the abilities and contributions of their peers. (Berg, 2005f) **4:** A style of teaching and learning in which students work in teams toward a common goal. In some online courses, collaborative learning teams are used to encourage students to work cooperatively with each other. The idea is that students learn from each other while participating in teams. (Du Mont, 2005) **5:** An instruction method in which students work in groups toward a common academic goal. (Moreira & da Silva, 2005) **6:** An instructional approach in which students of varying abilities work together in small groups to solve a problem, complete a project, or achieve a common goal. It is a philosophy that involves a sharing of authority and responsibility among group members who strive to build consensus and group ownership for the learning. (Sala, 2005b) **7:** A personal philosophy, not just a classroom technique. In all situations where people come together in groups, it suggests a way of dealing with people that respects and highlights individual group members' abilities and contributions. There is a sharing of authority and acceptance of responsibility among group members for the groups' actions. The underlying premise of collaborative learning is based upon consensus building through cooperation by group members, in contrast to competition in which individuals beat other group members. (Donnelly, 2005) **8:** An approach that involves learners (and sometimes teachers) working together and learning from each other. (Agosti, 2005) **9:** Engagement in learning wherein students utilize and build upon their individual strengths and interests for greater good.

(Bonk et al., 2005) **10:** Learning is integrated in the life of communities that share values, beliefs, languages, and ways of doing things. What holds the learners together is a common sense of purpose and a real need to know what the other knows. The essence is the underlying process of shared creation, involving two or more individuals interacting to create shared understanding where none could have existed on its own. (Vat, 2005a) **11:** Learning situation in which a group of learners work together on a task, where each learner's input is critical to the learning of the others in the group. (Collis & Moonen, 2005a) **12:** Learning that occurs through the exchange of knowledge among learners. Collaborative learning is a form of social learning. (Klobas & Renzi, 2005b) **13:** Learning that requires joint activity in which two or more learners negotiate meaning and process, and contribute to the final outcome. (Bennett, 2005) **14:** Learning where emphasis is placed on student-to-student interaction in the learning process, and the instructor's role becomes that of a facilitator (a "guide-on-the-side"). (McInnerney & Roberts, 2005) **15:** A form of learning that involves collaborative learning processes. It is designed for coaches, helpers and faculty, and groups of learners to fulfill the learning objectives of groups and of each learner through sharing resources and interacting. (Kayama & Okamoto, 2005)

## Collaborative Learning and Teaching
Includes a process of creating a teaching and learning environment that focuses on the establishment of partnerships with which to approach learning tasks and achieve common goals. Key characteristics of collaborative learning and teaching include interactivity, interdependency, and shared learning goals. (McCracken, 2005)

## Collaborative Network
A network of services and the base infrastructure supporting distributed cooperative environments. (Unal et al., 2006)

## Collaborative Online Environment
Internet-based learning setting that facilitates collegial or collaborative relationships and attempts to maximize the efficiencies of virtual learning teams. (Bonk et al., 2005)

## Collaborative Planning, Forecasting, and Replenishment (CPFR)
**1:** A process where the entire extended supply chain, including manufacturers, distributors, and retailers, is

using the same information through collaborative process to improve sales and forecast accuracy, reduce inventory levels, and prevent stock outs due to promotions. (Khan et al., 2006) **2:** An industry-wide initiative that involves collaboration between trading (supply chain) partners in the retail industry in order to achieve lower costs, higher efficiency, and better customer satisfaction. (Saha, 2005) **3:** A global, open, and neutral business process standard for value chain partners to coordinate the various activities of purchasing, production planning, demand forecasting, and inventory replenishment, in order to reduce the variance between supply and demand, and to share the benefits of a more efficient and effective supply chain. (Archer, 2005)

## Collaborative Research

A type of research developed by individuals who belong to different academic or practical disciplines in which there is a variety of purposes, methods, and outcomes. (Córdoba & Robson, 2006)

## Collaborative Resources

An object representing a resource used/shared/exchanged by a pair of collaborating roles in order to perform certain simple tasks in collaboration with one another. (Daneshgar, 2005)

## Collaborative Technology (CT)

A technology that includes at a minimum a virtual workplace that provides a repository recording the process of the group, electronic information sharing (such as through file sharing, e-mail, electronic whiteboards, and electronic conference), meta-information on the entries in the repository (such as data, sequence, and author of each contribution), and ease access and retrieval from the repository. (Sun & Xiao, 2006)

## Collaborative Tele-Learning

The use of technology for distributed communication, collaboration, and problem solving among participants in a learning environment. (Wild, 2005)

## Collaborative Thinking

A strategic mindset where adjacent and even overlapping stages in the industry value chain are seen as potential partners rather than competitors. For example, Starbucks and Nestlé both produce coffee, but they nevertheless partnered up for the creation and distribution of chilled coffee-based soft drinks, thereby leveraging Starbucks'

premium brand name and Nestlé's manufacturing and distribution know-how. (Angehrn & Gibbert, 2005)

## Collaborative Tool

**1:** A tool or technique that facilitates distant collaboration geographically at different locations. (Nandavadekar, 2005) **2:** An electronic tool that supports communication and collaboration—people working together; essentially it takes the form of networked computer software. (Metaxiotis, 2006) **3:** E-mail, an intranets, a threaded discussions, or an online discussion room that allows learners to collaborate on projects. Such tools also allow moderated discussions to take place in an online environment. (Brown, 2006) **4:** Traditional chat, whiteboard, messaging, presentation, VoIP, or a conferencing system; a strong component of knowledge management in the military. (Maule, 2006)

## Collaborative Virtual Environment

**1:** An environment that actively supports human-human communication in addition to human-machine communication and which uses a virtual environment as the user interface. (Viktor & Paquet, 2005) **2:** An interactive space in cyberspace that allows communities to work, as opposed to communicate only, by interacting in defined virtual spaces, using specifically designed artifacts to mimic the physical environment in which they traditionally work. (Huq, 2006)

## Collaborative-Social-Filtering Recommender Systems

Technique based on the correlation between users' interest. This technique creates interest groups between users, based on the selection of the same. (Gil & García, 2006)

## Collaboratory

Provides groups with technologies and tools so that they can access each other, databases, and remote tools to better collaborate, coordinate activities, and enhance group processes. (Alavi et al., 2005)

## Collection Development

The portion of collection management activities that primarily deals with selection decisions. (Gregory, 2005)

## Collection Management

All the activities involved in information gathering, communication, coordination, policy formulation, evaluation, and planning that result in decisions about the acquisition, retention, and provision of access to information sources in support of the needs of a specific library community. (Gregory, 2005)

## Collection of Information

Comprises several (typically several thousand or several million) documents. (Trujillo, 2005)

## Collection Stage

Stage of the intelligence cycle in which sources regarding the required environmental data are located and accessed, and the data are retrieved from them. (Vriens, 2005b)

## Collection Type

A composite value comprising elements of some data types. SQL:1999 supports arrays, which are ordered and unbounded sets of elements. Another collection type not supported by the standard is a nested table. (Zendulka, 2005b)

## Collective Action

**1:** The voluntary cooperation of a group of individuals that typically involves the production of a public or semi-public good. (Teigland & Wasko, 2005) **2:** An initiative, undertaken by groups of owners, industry groups, government groups, and so forth, who audit the collective system operation and exchange information to detect patterns of distributed attacks. (Janczewski & Portougal, 2005)

## Collective Awareness

A common and shared vision of a whole team's context which allows members to coordinate implicitly their activities and behaviors through communication. (Daassi & Favier, 2006)

## Collective Dependence

A set V of variables is collectively dependent if V cannot be split into non-empty subsets X and Y such that X and Y are marginally independent, nor can V be partitioned into non-empty subsets X, Y, and Z, such that X and Y are conditionally independent given Z. (Xiang, 2005)

## Collective Human Knowledge

Shared human knowledge that has been linguistically represented. (Gelepithis, 2005)

## Collective Intentional Action

Mutual or joint behaviors performed by a group of persons, and explained by collective intentions (e.g., we-intentions)

and such social influence as compliance, group norms, and social identity and such personal mental states as anticipated emotions, desires, and value perceptions (e.g., purposive value, self-discovery, maintenance or personal connectivity, social enhancement, and entertainment value). (Bagozzi & Dholakia, 2005)

## Collective Knowledge

**1:** Knowledge produced and shared by a group of people. Virtual community is a source of collective knowledge with the contribution of its participants. (Wang, Wei, et al., 2006) **2:** The knowledge of the organization, including the knowledge of its employees, and customer/supplier and industry knowledge that can be actioned to bring about innovation. (Mitchell, 2005a)

## Collective Responsibility

The idea that a group is sanctioned with, and accepts responsibility for, creating change in the organization. Each member helps and supports other members to make progress on implementing actions. (Shaw et al., 2006)

## Collectivism

Concerned with group interest rather than individual interest (individualism). Collectivist societies support structures where people are born and live in extended families. The concept of collective strength includes sharing, nurturing, supporting, and empowering interdependent groups. (Peszynski, 2005)

## Collision

A usually destructive event resulting from the simultaneous access to the same bandwidth resource by multiple users. (Markhasin et al., 2005)

## Collusion Attack

**1:** An act of removing watermarks—a digital fingerprint that identifies the buyer(s) from the marked media. It is based on the idea that both the position and the content of the fingerprint embedded in every watermarked legal copy are different. If the attacker obtained plenty of legal copies, he or she could get sufficient knowledge about the positions of the fingerprints by comparing all the copies. Then he or she could arbitrarily modify the information on the positions so as to fool the fingerprint detector. (Si & Li, 2006) **2:** By averaging together the carriers of hidden information, the watermarks may be canceled out. (Lou et al., 2006)

**Color Feature**

Analyzing the color distribution of pixels in an image. (Chan & Chang, 2005)

**Color Histogram**

A method to represent the color feature of an image by counting how many values of each color occur in the image and then forming a representing histogram. (Farag, 2005a)

**Combination**

**1:** A knowledge transfer mode that involves new explicit knowledge being derived from existing explicit knowledge. (Wickramasinghe, 2005) **2:** One of four knowledge transmission mechanisms according to Nonaka. It is a tacit-to-explicit knowledge transfer taking place when individuals articulate their tacit knowledge base, converting it into explicit knowledge that can be shared with others. (Brock & Zhou, 2006)

**Combination of Forecasts**

Combining two or more individual forecasts to form a composite one. (C.K. Chan, 2005)

**Combinatorial Optimization**

Branch of optimization in applied mathematics and computer science related to algorithm theory and computational complexity theory. (Felici & Truemper, 2005)

**Commerce**

The selling of products from the manufacturing, distribution, and retail firms to customers. (Borders & Johnston, 2005)

**Commercial Groupware Packages**

Proprietary software that provides bundled software, including synchronous and asynchronous messaging, collaborative application development, information management through shared databases, data exchange, Web functions, and other tools. (Ferris & Minielli, 2005)

**Commercial Knowledge**

An important focus of practical knowledge transfer in business. It is exemplified by the implementation knowledge—sets of rules, tools, guidelines, and ways to effectively employ them—that is conveyed by a consultant who is aiding a client in implementing or customizing a complex information system. (King, 2006b)

**Commercial Off-the-Shelf (COTS)**

Software products that an organization acquires from a third party with no access to the source code and for which there are multiple customers using identical copies of the component. (Chroust, 2006)

**Commercial Off-the-Shelf Application**

**1:** An approach to software development where, instead of attempting to build an application from scratch, a generic standardized package is purchased that contains all the main functionality. This package is then configured and customized so as to meet the additional specific requirements. (M. Lang, 2005) **2:** The use of software components that are generic enough to be obtained and used in different applications; often well designed and well implemented to offer good performance. (Gaffar, 2005)

**Commit**

Activates all modifications performed by a transaction, makes them visible to the outside, and makes all modifications durable. (Meixner, 2005)

**Commitment**

A state of mind that holds people and organizations in the line of behavior. It encompasses psychological forces that bind an individual to an action. (Leonard, 2005)

**Commodity**

A generic and largely undifferentiated product that is usually bought or sold by itself without bundled value-added services or differentiated features. (Bahn, 2006)

**Commodity-Based Market**

A form of a market in which various suppliers and consumers participate to trade goods and services (i.e., commodities) of the same type. The market price is publicly agreed upon for each commodity, independent of any particular supplier. All consumers and suppliers decide whether and how much to buy or sell at each agreed-upon price. (Ghenniwa & Huhns, 2005)

**Common Carrier**

A company licensed, usually by a national government, to provide telecommunications services to the public, facilitating the transmission of voice and data messages. (Guah & Currie, 2005)

**Common Cost**

The cost of joint production of a set of services. (Hackbarth et al., 2005)

## Common Data Model (CDM)

The data to be shared across the scope of an integrated computing system in terms that are neutral with respect to the applications and technologies that make up that system. A CDM provides a vocabulary for talking meaningfully about the data that represent the information defined in the flow, transformation, and contents of data packages that are delivered from one application or technology to another. (Fulton, 2005)

## Common Gateway Interface (CGI)

**1:** A standard protocol for users to interact with applications on Web servers. (Goh & Kinshuk, 2005) **2:** A standard protocol used on the World Wide Web which allows Web pages and distributed applications to communicate with a Web server and request some services on the server side. (Gaffar & Seffah, 2005)

## Common Gateway Interface Program (CGI Program)

**1:** A small program that handles input and output from a Web server. Often used for handling forms input or database queries, it also can be used to generate dynamic Web content. Other options include JSP (Java server pages) and ASP (active server pages), and scripting languages allowing the insertion of server-executable scripts in HTML pages and PHP, a scripting language used to create dynamic Web pages. (Nasraoui, 2005) **2:** Any program designed to accept and return data that conforms to the CGI specification. CGI programs are the most common way for Web servers to interact dynamically with users. The program could be written in any programming language including C, Perl, Java, or Visual Basic. (Valenti, 2005)

## Common Ground

**1:** A form of self-awareness in the interaction between two people; the sum of their mutual, common, or joint knowledge, beliefs, and suppositions. (Ahmad & Al-Sayed, 2006) **2:** Shared knowledge and experience common to both sender and receiver. This "common ground" enables the references and context of the message to be deciphered successfully and meaning to be communicated. (Thomas & Roda, 2006b)

## Common Identity

A common ground/understanding to which many people/groups can subscribe; requires a shift from seeing oneself as separate to seeing oneself as connected to and part of an organizational unit. (Ali & Warne, 2005)

## Common Information Model (CIM)

A definition of the information to be shared across the scope of an integrated system. A CIM may span multiple domains, as long as the elements of each of the domains can be mapped uniquely to an element of the CIM. (Fulton, 2005)

## Common Interface Format (CIF)

A typical video or image resolution value with dimensions 352x288 pixels. (Koumaras et al., 2005)

## Common Knowledge

An organization's cumulative experiences in comprehending a category of knowledge and activities, and the organizing principles that support communication and coordination. (Becerra-Fernandez & Sabherwal, 2006)

## Common Law

The legal tradition that evolved in England from the 11th century onwards. Its principles appear for the most part in reported judgments, usually of the higher courts, in relation to specific fact situations arising in disputes that courts have adjudicated. (Zeleznikow, 2006)

## Common Log Format (CLF)

A W3C standard format for records in a server log. The main items in the CLF are IP address of the user, the date and time of the request, the URL of the page, the protocol, the return code of the server, and the size of the page if the request is successful. (Y. Fu, 2005)

## Common Object-Request Broker Architecture (CORBA)

**1:** An open-standards-based distributed computing solution. (Kasi & Young, 2006) **2:** A method to make heterogeneous systems interoperable by dealing with languages. It moves the language into the background through an interface definition language. Developers need to understand language bindings to use CORBA. More suitable for intra-enterprise environments. (Zhang, 2006) **3:** An object-oriented architecture that provides a standard mechanism for defining the interfaces between components, as well as tools to facilitate the implementation of interfaces using the developer's choice of languages, thus providing for language and platform independence. (Murthy & Krishnamurthy, 2005c)

## Common Vulnerabilities and Exposures (CVE)

A list of standardized names for vulnerabilities and other information security exposures. CVE aims to standardize the names for all publicly known vulnerabilities and security exposures. (Cardoso & Freire, 2005)

## Commonsense Knowledge

The knowledge expected of every individual in a society. It includes acquaintance with the physical world and the laws governing it, social behaviors, and procedures for everyday tasks, such as simple business transactions. It lies on the commonsense-expert knowledge dimension. (Ein-Dor, 2006)

## Communicating X-Machine

A set of stream X-machine components that are able to communicate with each other by exchanging messages. (Kefalas et al., 2005)

## Communication

**1:** The exchange of information between two or more people with the intent that the sender's message be understood and considered by the receiver. (Te'eni, 2006) **2:** H1 communicates with H2 on a topic T if and only if: H1 understands T (symbol: U(H1 T)), H2 understands T (symbol: U(H2 T)), U(H1 T) is presentable to and understood by H2, and U(H2 T) is presentable to and understood by H1. (Gelepithis, 2005) **3:** Human interaction to present, share, and build information and knowledge. (Han & Hill, 2006) **4:** The exchange of thoughts, messages, or information by speech, signals, writing, or behavior. Communication generally includes a sender, a receiver, a message, and a medium used to carry the message. (Croasdell & Wang, 2006)

## Communication Apprehension

Apprehension associated with real or anticipated communication with others. Traditional students with high communication apprehension tend to quietly sit in a large lecture room, having minimal interpersonal contact with the instructor or other students. (Adkins & Nitsch, 2005)

## Communication Channel

The medium used to convey the message. The channel could involve seeing, hearing, smelling, feeling, or tasting. Various media (e.g., e-mail, Web sites, telephone) may be more or less appropriate for various messages. (Jacobson, 2006)

## Communication Climate

**1:** Extent to which there is an open and free exchange of information, transparency of decision making, and how

constructively conflict is managed. (Ali & Warne, 2005) **2:** Or "atmosphere," can be defined as a set of conditions that transform cultural behavior and information into desired (or undesired) states of a given entity (person, group, organization, region, nation, globe) through the communication process. (Targowski & Metwalli, 2005)

## Communication Environment

In one sense, technology operates in a physical environment, but for computer-mediated communication, technology is the environment, that is, that through which communication occurs. (Whitworth, 2006b)

## Communication Infrastructure

"Glue" that links geographically dispersed users of a learning environment together and gives them the impression of being in the shared workspace of the virtual classroom. (Rugelj, 2005)

## Communication Media

The methods or tools in which information can be exchanged and communication can be facilitated. Examples include telephones, televisions, e-mail, Web sites, videoconferencing, and instant messaging, to name a few. (Y.D. Wang, 2005)

## Communication Norms

In the context of virtual teams, communication norms are typical routines and expectations for communicating within a virtual team using the communication media that the team has available to them (e.g., electronic communication such as e-mail or instant messaging, telephone, etc.). (Staples et al., 2005)

## Communication Preference

The selection of your own way in the art and technique of using words effectively to impart information or ideas. (Janvier & Ghaoui, 2006)

## Communication Strategies

The means by which communication goals can be fulfilled. (Willis, 2005)

## Communication Technology

The branch of technology concerned with the representation, transfer, interpretation, and processing of data among persons, places, and machines. (Melkonyan, 2005)

## Communications Center

A commercial venture that is reselling telephone services from a few number of telephone lines. (Frempong & Braimah, 2005)

## Communications Gap

Relates to that part of the knowledge gap that can be attributed to miscommunication between the parties involved (i.e., IT designers understand technology but not the realities of governance; officials and politicians understand the realities of governance but not the technology). (Velibeyoglu, 2005)

## Communications-Related Antecedent Factors

Source credibility and communications competence (in terms of both encoding and decoding capabilities) are communications-related antecedent factors for effective knowledge transfer. (King, 2006b)

## Community

**1:** Social network whose members are characterized by a common interest, similar behavior, and a sense of moral responsibility. (Flavián & Guinalíu, 2006) **2:** A destination within the portal used to deliver applications and group workspaces. For example, portal users can create communities to bring a team of people together to collaborate on a project or to deliver an employee services application to the entire company. Communities are assembled using portlets, and can be created from templates that control the community's functionality and appearance. (Wojtkowski, 2006)

## Community Access Center

A publicly funded computer center (also called Telecenter or Community Technology Center) providing community members with access to computer training and computer technology, including computers, printers, scanners, and the Internet. (Dyson, 2005)

## Community Broker

The leader of a community who provides the overall guidance and management to establish and/or maintain a community. He/she supports community activities, promotes the community within the organizations, and acts as the contact person for both community members and people interested in (joining) the community. (Zboralski & Gemünden, 2006)

## Community Building

All activities related to building and maintaining online communities. (Kindmüller et al., 2005)

## Community Building and Unpaid Work

Recognition that communities do not just happen. They are built and evolve, usually through the work of volunteers who are not paid, monetarily, for their work. (Crichton, 2005)

## Community Capacity Building

Investment in people, institutions, and practices that will, together, enable communities to achieve their goals. (Pease et al., 2005)

## Community College

A higher education institution supported by the government, emphasizing preparing students for transfer to four-year colleges and on providing skill education in specific vocations. (Berg, 2005b)

## Community Development

**1:** Activities that consider social and economic benefits, including self-determination. (Geiselhart & Jamieson, 2005) **2:** Concerned with the relationship between social and economic development, building a capacity for local cooperation, self-help, and the use of expertise and methods drawn from outside the local community. (Walker, 2006)

## Community Informatics

**1:** A multidisciplinary field for the investigation of the social and cultural factors shaping the development and diffusion of new ICT and its effects upon community development, regeneration, and sustainability. (Thompson, 2005) **2:** The process of using ICT, and ICT-related facilities, such as a telecenter, in social development programs to help the community develop economically, socially, and culturally. (Gnaniah, Songan, et al., 2005) **3:** The use of ICT and associated facilities in conjunction with the development and delivery of programs to aid community development—economically, culturally, and socially. (Pease et al., 2005) **4:** The use of information and computer technologies in communities in order to impact communities socially and economically. (Shea & Davis, 2005)

## Community Knowledge Building

Knowledge that derives from members' interaction in a community. (Lambropoulos, 2006b)

**C**

## Community Memory

Communities are made up of individuals, each of whom possesses unique memories. Community memory is the preservation, persistence, and sharing of individual memories and knowledge among a community through communicative means such as tradition, custom, language, writing, stories and myth, and various artifacts. (Leath, 2005)

## Community Mining

A Web graph mining algorithm to discover communities from the Web graph in order to provide a higher logical view and more precise insight of the nature of the Web. (Wen, 2005b)

## Community Model

A model in which all the partners in an interaction are able to communicate with one other on an equal basis. (Shan et al., 2006b)

## Community Moderators

Day-to-day leaders in virtual communities who control discussions in individual forums, point the community members in the right direction, and ensure that the social climate of the forum promotes participation and exchange among its members. (Ruhi, 2006)

## Community Network (Traditional)

A sociological concept that describes the rich Web of communications and relationships in a community. (Gibbs et al., 2005)

## Community Networking (Technology)

Computer-based ICT intended to support community relationships. (Gibbs et al., 2005)

## Community Normative State

Set of information about the community structure, regulating not only resource management but also policy enforcement. More precisely, the normative state contains community directions as well as policies regulating access to community resources. Additionally, it includes all those kinds of information that help the members to actively participate in community life. Such information concerns aspects such as the management of the community, sanctioning mechanisms, and violation punishments. (Bertino et al., 2006)

## Community of Circumstance

A community driven by position, circumstance, or life experiences. Such communities are distinguished from communities of practice in that they tend to be personally focused and are often built around "life stages," such as teenagehood, university, marriage, or parenthood. (Kimble & Hildreth, 2005)

## Community of Creation

**1:** A community of practice where members mainly focus on the sharing and generation of new knowledge for the purposes of creating new ideas, practices, and artifacts (or products). They can be legitimized through involvement in a company-sponsored product development effort, or they may be informal through various practitioners with similar experience and knowledge meeting where new innovations arise from this interaction. (Paquette, 2006a) **2:** The community that forms when companies organize their customers into groups holding similar expert knowledge and encouraging interaction in order to generate new knowledge. These groups are characterized by working together over a long period of time, sharing a common interest, and wanting to create and share valuable knowledge. Unlike traditional communities of practice, these groups span organizational boundaries and develop value for multiple organizations. (Paquette, 2006b)

## Community of Experts (CoE)

A collection of people who possess very high knowledge (expertise) in a particular field. They are subject-matter experts and provide intellectual leadership within an organization. A CoE can exist across company divisions and across organizational boundaries. (Sivakumar, 2006)

## Community of Implementation

A group whose purpose is to pool individual knowledge (including contacts and ways of getting things done) to stimulate collective enthusiasm in order to take more informed purposeful action, for which the members are responsible. (Shaw et al., 2006)

## Community of Interest

**1:** A group of people who share a common interest. Members exchange ideas and thoughts about the given interest, but may know little about each other outside of this area. Participation in a community of interest can be compelling and entertaining, but is not focused on learning in the same way as a community of practice. (Kimble & Hildreth, 2005) **2:** An online group that grows from common interest in a subject. They develop norms based on shared values and meanings. (Lambropoulos, 2006b)

## Community of Learners (CoL)

**1:** A community of students, teachers, tutors, and experts marked by the presence of the following elements: (1) multiple ZPDs (the ones of the subjects in the CoLs); (2) legitimated peripheral participation (the respect of the differences and peculiarities existing among the various subjects in the community); (3) distributed expertise; and (4) reciprocal teaching, peer tutoring, and various scaffoldings. In this community previous knowledge is analyzed, verified, and discussed, and new knowledge and theories are built. (Cartelli, 2006a) **2:** A community whose learning is fundamentally a social phenomenon. Namely, a CoL focuses on engagement in social practice as the fundamental process by which we learn and so become who we are. (Vat, 2005a)

## Community of Peers

A grouping of peers having something in common or considered grouped for a specific purpose, (e.g., having particular types of privacy policies as discussed above). (Yee & Korba, 2006)

## Community of Practice (CoP)

**1:** A community of individuals having the following elements in common: (1) a joint enterprise, as understood and continually renegotiated by its members; (2) a mutual engagement binding members together into a social entity; and (3) a shared repertoire of communal resources (routines, sensibilities, artifacts, vocabulary, etc.) that members developed over time. (Cartelli, 2006b) **2:** A group of people in an organization who are (somehow) held together by common interest in their work topic, purpose, and activities. (Disterer, 2005) **3:** A community of professional individuals who have the shared sense of purpose in a work situation (e.g., professionals at different institutions collaborating on best practice, or individuals that perform the same function in different parts of an organization). (Fleming, 2005c) **4:** A group of individuals that may be co-located or distributed, are motivated by a common set of interests, and are willing to develop and share tacit and explicit knowledge. (Coakes & Clarke, 2006a) **5:** A group of people who have work practices in common. (Elshaw, 2006a) **6:** A group of self-governing people with shared interests whose practice is aligned

with strategic imperatives, helping each other to solve problems, share and benefit from each other's expertise, and are committed to jointly developing better practice. (Ng & Pemberton, 2006) **7:** A relatively tightly knit, emergent social collective, in which individuals working on similar problems self-organize to help each other and share perspectives about their work practice, generally in face-to-face settings. (Wasko & Teigland, 2006a) **8:** An informal collective group of individuals bound by a common practice base engaged in knowledge-sharing activities to add value to work. (Huq, et al., 2006) **9:** An informal community of people bound by a common task or purpose (e.g., similar work activities). A CoP nurtures a critical skill set in an organization. It can exist across company divisions and sometimes across organizational boundaries. (Sivakumar, 2006) **10:** A group of people who share a set of concerns and sustain their collective actions through their participation and generation of new knowledge. (Córdoba & Robson, 2006) **11:** AHIMA's online networking and collaborating tool, created for the use of its members and launched in 2001. (Zender, 2006) **12:** The concept of a CoP was first introduced by Lave and Wenger in 1991 in relation to situated learning. Lave and Wenger saw the acquisition of knowledge as a social process in which people participated in communal learning at different levels depending on their authority in a group—that is, newcomers learn from old-timers by being allowed to participate in tasks relating to the practice of the community. Since 1991, the concept of CoPs has been extended and applied to areas such as knowledge management and virtual working. (Kimble & Li, 2006) **13:** A group of people who come together around common interests and expertise. They create, share, and apply knowledge within and across the boundaries of teams, business units, and even entire organizations—providing a concrete path toward creating a true knowledge organization. (Vat, 2006b) **14:** Although this term is common when referring to informal groups or networks of people who share similar interests and objectives, CoPs have been seen as an alternative to teamwork where a variety of problems may be better considered through knowledge shared by loose coalitions of people who develop their own tacit knowledge and methods for doing things. This is more common among certain professions such as lawyers, barristers, GPs, academics, and so forth whose conduct is regulated by professional associations and who share a similarity of attitudes and conventions. (Grieves, 2006b) **15:** Collaborative means to build and share knowledge and expertise, increase social capital and the economic value of relationships within the military, and lower the cost of training. (Maule, 2006) **16:** A community formed by people who engage in a process of collective learning in a shared domain of human endeavor. For a community of practice to function, it needs to generate and appropriate a shared repertoire of ideas, commitments, and memories. It also needs to develop various resources such as tools, documents, routines, vocabulary, and symbols that in some way carry the accumulated knowledge of the community. (Boersma & Kingma, 2006)

## Community of Practice Membership

In a community of practice, new members are included in tasks concerned with the practices of the group and they acquire knowledge from more expert members. Participation in a community of practice therefore involves movement from the periphery towards full participation in the group. (Ranguelov & Rodríguez, 2006)

## Community of Purpose

A community that forms around people who are to achieve a similar objective. Such a community only serves a functional purpose. Members of the community can assist each other by sharing experiences, suggesting strategies, and exchanging information on the process in hand. (Kimble & Hildreth, 2005)

## Community Place

Place inherent to the existence of a community, but not equivalent to it, with the following attributes: interactivity, sustainable membership, diversity of communicators, and a shared technology for group CMC. (Porto Bellini & Vargas, 2006)

## Community Portal

**1:** A portal designed and developed to provide access to community resources and serve community needs and interests. (Vrazalic & Hyland, 2005) **2:** A Web site tailored for the needs of a community. (Boateng & Boateng, 2006b) **3:** An online initiative often developed through participative processes which aims to achieve better coordination of relevant Web-based information and provide communication services for community members. (Thompson, 2005) **4:** Often set up by community groups or based around special group interests, a community portal attempts to foster the concept of a virtual community where all users share a common location or interest, and provide many different services. (Tatnall et al., 2006)

## Community Service Obligation

An obligation undertaken by particular levels of government to ensure the provision of certain services. (Cameron, 2005)

## Community Space

A space—real, virtual, or a combination of both—where a sense of community is created. (Walker, 2006)

## Community Telecenter

A public place that provides low-cost community access to ICTs such as computers, printers, telephones, faxes, e-mail, and the Internet. In many cases telecenters also have library resources, as well as audio, video, and documentation production facilities. They may also provide training in the use of ICTs, distance learning, and telemedicine, and also usually support the production of information resources relevant to the needs of local users. They are sometimes referred to as multipurpose community telecenters. (Mwesige, 2005)

## Community-Based Information Technology

The provision of training and information technology services to local communities to meet their communications needs. (Pease et al., 2005)

## Community-Building Activity

An online or off-line activity that promotes relational and social connection among participants. (Woods & Baker, 2005)

## Community-Oriented Policing

Contemporary policing approach that builds relationships between police officers and the citizens of a community on an ongoing basis. Crime prevention is stressed as a partnership approach before an actual emergency situation(s) develops. (Baim, 2005)

## Compact and Generalized Abstraction of the Training Set

A compact representation built by using the training set from which not only the original patterns, but also some new synthetic patterns can be derived. (Viswanath et al., 2005)

## Compact Disc Read-Only Memory (CD-ROM)

**1:** A type of optical disk capable of storing large amounts of data, up to 1 GB, although the most common size is 650 Mbytes. (Sala, 2005b) **2:** Optical data storage medium using the same physical format as audio compact discs, readable by a computer with a CD-ROM drive. (Kabene, Takhar, et al., 2005) **3:** A computer storage device offering a relatively high capacity. The full name denotes the fact that CD-ROMs are read-only devices; data cannot be written to a CD-ROM by a conventional player. (Duan, 2005)

## Comparative Online Analysis of Cultures (COAC)
A process in which individuals compare online media designed for two different cultural audiences in order to determine how cultures differ in their design expectations. (St.Amant, 2005e)

## Comparative Shopping Environment
Offers three features: customer reviews of a product, competitive prices of the product, and ratings of the merchant who sells the product. These features help customers select an appropriate product within a reasonable price range, and choose merchants they can trust and feel comfortable shopping with. (M. Wang, 2006)

## Comparison-Shopping Agent
A Web-based service that can collect product and service information, especially price-related information, from multiple online vendors, aggregate them, and then provide value-added service to online shoppers to assist with their online shopping. (Wan, 2006)

## Compatibility
**1:** The degree to which an innovation is seen to be compatible with existing values, beliefs, experiences, and needs of adopters. (Green et al., 2005) **2:** Describes the degree to which the new product is consistent with the adopter's existing values and product knowledge, past experiences, and current needs. (Owens et al., 2005) **3:** Designs that match our expectations in terms of characteristics, function, and operation. (Noyes, 2006) **4:** The ability to transmit data from one source to another without losses or modifications to the data or additional programming requirements. (Becker, 2006) **5:** Views $V_1$ and $V_2$ are compatible if functions $f_1$ and $f_2$ exist such that for all $x$, $f_1(x_1) = f_2(x_2) = f(x)$, where $f$ is the true target function. (Scheffer, 2005)

## Compatibility of Innovation
The degree of consistency of an innovation with the needs, expected values, and norms of potential adopters and their social systems. (Askarany, 2005)

## Compensating Transaction
A transaction that is executed to undo the effect of another committed transaction. Unlike ordinary transaction rollback or abort, both original and compensating transactions are visible in the committed projection of the execution history. (Leong, 2005a)

## Compensatory Strategy
An educational approach that focuses on providing structures that support and enhance learners' weaknesses rather than exploiting their strengths. (Boechler, 2006a)

## Competence
**1:** A description of the membership of a community of practice according to the degree of learning about practice in the community. (Córdoba, 2006b) **2:** One of the three preconditions for citizen participation in e-democracy (access-competence-motivation). Communications competence means that a person has the ability to use channels of communication, opportunity, access, and skills to use the devices involved and to formulate messages. (Keskinen & Kuosa, 2005)

## Competence Set
The nodes in a Bayesian Behavior Network are grouped into competence sets, where each competence set has an associated set of actions that must be performed by the Bayesian agencies depending on the states of the nodes in the competence set. (Potgieter et al., 2005)

## Competency
**1:** The recent focus on competency that comes from employers stands in contrast to previous ways of acknowledging learning, such as seat-based time or diplomas. To an increasing degree, graduates are being judged by what they can do, not by what they know. (Lindsay et al., 2005b) **2:** A combination of education and skills that qualify a professional for a certain task or field. (Kostopoulos, 2005) **3:** A statement that defines the qualification required to perform an activity or to complete a task. Faculty competencies for online distance education identify the qualifications needed to be successful in a job. (Sales, 2005) **4:** Demonstrated command of the knowledge, skills, and abilities required for effective performance in a particular degree area. (D.B. Johnstone, 2005)

## Competition
When two individuals or species are in competition with each other, they are each striving for the same thing. In

biological systems, this is typically for food, space, or some other physical need, but in IT, it can be any matter relating to IS curriculum. When the thing the competitors are striving for is not in adequate supply for both of them, the result is that both are hampered or adversely affected in some manner. (Tatnall & Davey, 2005)

## Competitive Advantage

**1:** A condition that enables companies to operate in a more efficient or higher quality manner than the companies it competes with, which results in financial benefits. (Braun, 2006) **2:** A positive, relative position held by a firm as compared with competitors within a market or industry. There are two types of competitive advantage: cost leadership and differentiation. (Cepeda-Carrión, 2006) **3:** Defines a place's or region's attribute(s) with the potential to place it in a leading position in any field (generally used with regard to commercial or economic activity), such as a natural or environmental icon that may give a region a competitive advantage in terms of tourism, or a mineral deposit in terms of mining. A region or place needs to identify and capitalize on distinctive assets and capacities to realize its competitive advantage. (Sutcliffe, 2005) **4:** Employing organizational resources in an advantageous manner that cannot be imitated readily by competitors. (Nissen, 2005) **5:** The ability to gain a disproportionately larger share of a market because of cost leadership, or product or service differentiation. (McManus & Carr, 2005) **6:** The head start a business has owing to its access to new or unique information and knowledge about the market in which it is operating. (Kroeze, 2005) **7:** Usually refers to characteristics that permit a firm to compete effectively with other firms due to low cost or superior technology, perhaps internationally. (Lubbe, 2005) **8:** A company is said to have a competitive advantage when, based on its strategic architecture and complementary resource combinations (CRCs), it is able to implement a strategy that generates returns and benefits in excess of those of its current competitors—who simultaneously are implementing strategies, similar or otherwise— because of the perceived value in the marketplace. The definition therefore also depends on what the company, its management, and its stakeholders define as what the required returns and benefits should be (because even though many would list it as financial, clearly this does not apply to all companies, i.e., an advantage could be something other than financial). One could reasonably expect, though, that companies within similar industries

would define similar variables as the required returns and benefits. A company is said to have a sustained competitive advantage when it is implementing a value-creating strategy, which generates returns and benefits at a level not enjoyed by current competitors and when these other companies are unable to reach an "equilibrium level" with the company enjoying the advantage. In this sense, the definition of sustained competitive advantage adopted here does not imply that it will "last forever," and does not depend upon the period of time during which a company enjoys a competitive advantage (rather, the equilibrium level is critical in this definition). (Potgieter et al., 2005)

## Competitive Intelligence

**1:** In IT literature, two definitions are used: a product definition and a process definition. In the product definition, competitive intelligence is defined as information about the environment, relevant for strategic purposes. The process definition highlights producing and processing this environmental information. Process definitions often refer to the intelligence cycle. (Achterbergh, 2005a) **2:** The set of interrelated measures that aim at systematically feeding the organizational decision process with information about the organizational environment in order to make it possible for people to learn about it, to anticipate its evolution, and to make better decisions in consequence. (de Carvalho & Ferreira, 2006)

## Competitive Neutrality

A principle that states that government agencies and businesses should not enjoy any competitive advantage over privately operated competitors in the delivery of services by virtue of being government owned. Competitive neutrality is achieved through transparent accounting and cost-reflexive charges for services. (Cameron, 2005)

## Complementarity

**1:** A product or service that provides more value as part of a group than individually. For example, hybrid e-retailers can leverage complementarities by providing off-line services to online shoppers. (I. Lee, 2005) **2:** Several activities are mutually complementary if doing more of any one activity increases (or at least does not decrease) the marginal profitability of each other activity in the group. Complementarities among activities imply mutual relationships and dependence among various activities whose exploration can lead to higher profitability. (Scupola, 2005)

## Complementary Core Competencies/Pooling of Resources

The ease with which two members of a virtual organization can communicate allows them to pool their resources, even with members not directly involved in a specific project. Separate entities can quickly be called upon to provide secondary service or consult on a project via virtual channels. (J. Lee, 2005)

## Complementary Resource Combination (CRC)

Not a factor input, but a complex combination of inter-related configurations, or a network of assets, people, and processes that companies use to transform inputs to outputs. Many of these configurations are a blend of "hard" tangible resources and "soft" intangible resources which simply cannot be recreated by another company. Finely honed CRCs can be a source of competitive advantage. (Potgieter et al., 2005)

## Complementary Similarity Measurement

An index developed experientially to recognize a poorly printed character by measuring the resemblance of the correct pattern of the character expressed in a vector. Referred to by some as a diversion index to identify the one-to-many relationship in the concurrence patterns of words in a large corpus or labels in a large database. (Ito, 2005)

## Complete Evaluation

To re-evaluate a CQ on the whole base data (i.e., the new result) and then find the symmetric difference with the previous result set. (Khan, 2005)

## Complete Test

Verifies that an update operation leads a consistent database state to either a consistent or inconsistent database state. (Ibrahim, 2005)

## Completion Rate

The most common measure for success in an online or distance learning course, frequently associated with program persistence and retention rates. No standardized algorithm currently exists for calculating completion rates; they are best used in comparing one cohort of the same course with another. (Howell & Wilcken, 2005)

## Complex Environment

In such an environment, complexity increases as the granularity increases, the frequency of changes increases, the time availability decreases, and the degree of judgment required increases. Decision making is ex-post, complex, and may require multiple steps. Initial monitoring uses a priori thresholds broader than in a simple environment—that is, more granular and produces exceptions that identify a Suspected Non-Compliant Event (SNCE). Evidence for decision making uses the results of the initial monitoring as well as important information related to the event, characterized by a need for judgmental expertise. (Goldschmidt, 2005)

## Complexity

**1:** Degree to which an innovation is seen by the potential adopter as being relatively difficult to use and understand. (Green et al., 2005) **2:** The degree to which the structure, behavior, and application of an organization is difficult to understand and validate due to its physical size, the intertwined relationships between its components, and the significant number of interactions required by its collaborating components to provide organizational capabilities. (Ng & Pemberton, 2006) **3:** The degree to which a system or component has a design or implementation that is difficult to understand and verify. The first and still classic measure of complexity is that introduced by Kolmogorov which is the shortest computer program capable of generating a given string. (Polgar, 2005b)

## Complexity of Innovation

The degree to which an innovation seems difficult to understand and use. (Askarany, 2005)

## Complex Situation

The current world state that the user needs to understand. The understanding in a complex situation extends beyond procedural information and requires understanding the dynamic interrelationships of large amounts of information. (Albers, 2006)

## Complex System

**1:** A collection of interrelated elements organized to accomplish a specific function or a set of functions. Complexity can be considered in terms of a number of elements and/or complexity of relationships. (Plekhanova, 2005a) **2:** From a mathematical perspective, a system described by differential or difference equations; from an informational perspective, a system for which information is the main resource and functioning in an information-rich environment. (Szczerbicki, 2005) **3:** A new field of science studying how parts of a complex system give rise to the collective behaviors of the system. Complexity (information-theoretical and computational) and emergence of collective behavior are the two main characteristics of such complex systems. Social systems formed (in part) out of people, the brain formed out of neurons, molecules formed out of atoms, and the weather formed out of air flows are all examples of complex systems. The field of complex systems cuts across all traditional disciplines of science, as well as engineering, management, and medicine. (Shahabi & Banaei-Kashani, 2005) **4:** Borrowed from Complexity Theory, a system that is neither rigidly ordered nor highly disordered. System complexity is defined as the number and variety of identifiable regularities in the structure and behavior of the group, given a description of that group at a fixed level of detail. (Farooq et al., 2006)

## Compliance

Social influence process whereby a person conforms to the expectations of others based upon the motivation of a need for approval. Also known as subjective norm. (Bagozzi & Dholakia, 2005)

## Compliance Verification

Ensuring the necessary and sufficient evidence supports the assertion of non-compliance. (Goldschmidt, 2005)

## Component

**1:** A term used to describe an information system and its composition for the purposes of this work. Specifically, the components in this work are: system quality, information quality, and service quality. (Wilkin, 2005) **2:** An encapsulated, autonomous, service-based software unit that delivers useful services through the well-specified interface to its environment. (Stojanovic & Dahanayake, 2005) **3:** Small pre-defined program snippets within Flash™ that allow reuse of elements. Examples are buttons, pull-down menus, text boxes, and text areas. (Barone, 2005)

## Component Interface

The behavior of a component along with constraints at a subset of component's interactions, data types used in exposing the behavior, configuration, and quality parameters of the behavior. (Stojanovic & Dahanayake, 2005)

## Component Middleware

A commercially available component technology and its associated connectivity capabilities; includes, for example,

CORBA components, EJB, and COM+/.NET. (Stojanovic & Dahanayake, 2005)

## Component Model

A model specifying the standards and conventions imposed on developers of components. Includes admissible ways of describing the functionality and other attributes of a component, admissible communication between components (protocols), and so forth. (Chroust, 2006)

## Component-Based Development

A software development approach where all aspects and phases of the development lifecycle are based on components. (Stojanovic & Dahanayake, 2005)

## Component-Based Solution

A set of smaller software components that link seamlessly to a wider framework through the adoption of standards. (Salter, 2005b)

## Component-Based Web Engineering

The application of systematic, disciplined, and quantifiable component-based and reuse-oriented approaches to the understanding, construction, operation, and evolution of Web-based applications and systems. (Gaedke et al., 2005)

## Composite Data

Data containing an ordered string of fields describing several attributes (parameters, properties, etc.) of an object. (Kulikowski, 2005)

## Composite Model

Model for collaboration between institutions where each institution is responsible for particular parts of certain courses or study programs; a cooperative method. (Haugen & Ask, 2005)

## Composition

**1:** A new class in an objected programming language that is composed of other classes. (D. Brandon, 2005a) **2:** A specific form of an aggregation. It is a relationship in which a composite object consists of non-shareable objects, and the latter are existence-dependent to the former. (Taniar et al., 2005)

## Compositional Design and Reuse

The design or composition of components from a collection of generic building-block components. (Gaedke et al., 2005)

# Comprehensibility

The understandability of a pattern to human beings; the ability of a data-mining algorithm to produce patterns understandable to human beings. (Zhou, 2005)

# Comprehension-Modeling Tool

A math representation tool that enables users to: (1) generate multiple representations of mathematical concepts and processes, (2) dynamically link the different representations, (3) communicate the mathematical ideas they have constructed, and (4) make movie-like sequences of animation slides that enable others to replay the process used to generate the solution. (Nason & Woodruff, 2005a)

# Comprehensive (Complete) Contracts

A contract specifying every possible contingency and paying attention to all different issues. (Khalfan et al., 2005)

# Compression

The act of reducing file size so an image can download more quickly on the Web. (Szabados & Sonwalkar, 2005)

# Compulsory Miss

Also called a cold-start miss, this occurs during the first access of a Web object. (Katsaros & Manolopoulos, 2005a)

# Computational Cardiology

Using mathematic and computer models to simulate the heart motion and its properties as a whole. (Liu et al., 2005)

# Computational Emergence

Assuming that computational interactions can generate different features or behaviors, this is one of the approaches in the field of artificial life. (Deb, 2005)

# Computational Experimentation

The use of validated, theory-driven computer models with experimental methods to assess systematic behaviors associated with alternate organizational designs. (Nissen & Levitt, 2006)

# Computational Problem

A relation between input and output data, where input data are known (and correspond to all possible different problem instances), and output data are to be identified, but predicates or assertions they must verify are given. (Calvo et al., 2005)

# Computationally Hard Problems

A mathematical problem is considered computationally hard if a slight increase in problem size dramatically increases the time for solving the problem. Typically, run-time is an exponential function of problem size for computationally hard problems. Many cryptographic applications are based on computationally hard problems like the Discrete Logarithm problem, the Discrete Square Root problem, and the problem of factoring large integers. (Stickel, 2005)

# Computed Radiography (CR)

A method of capturing and converting radiographic images into a digital form. The medium for capturing the X-ray radiation passing through the patient and generated by a standard X-ray system is a phosphor plate that is placed in a standard-size cassette, replacing the regular radiographic film. The X-ray exposure forms a latent image on a phosphor plate that is then scanned (read or developed) using a laser-beam CR reader. The CR unit displays the resultant digital image on a computer-monitor screen. By the end of the short process, the phosphor plate is erased and ready for another X-ray image exposure. (Tong & Wong, 2005b)

# Computed Tomography (CT)

A specialized radiology procedure that helps doctors see inside the body. CT uses X-rays and computers to create an image. The images show up as a cross-sectional image. (Tong & Wong, 2005b)

# Computer

A mechanical system composed of software and hardware designed to process data in support of various computing programs and applications. (Khosrow-Pour, 1990)

# Computer Algebra System

**1:** A software system that performs symbolic computations. (Farmer, 2006) **2:** A system using generic mathematical tools that allow users to perform complex calculations and algebraic manipulations of equations. (Burrage & Pelton, 2005)

# Computer Animation

Motion created by using a computer through a technique in which the illusion of movement is created by displaying on a screen or recording on a device a series of individual states of a dynamic scene. (Yong & Choo, 2005)

## Computer Anxiety

**1:** A diffuse, unpleasant, and vague sense of discomfort and apprehension when confronted by computer technology or people who talk about computers. (Blignaut et al., 2005) **2:** The degree to which an individual is nervous in his or her interaction with computers; the uneasiness some people feel when they have to use a microcomputer. Anxiety results from a danger or a danger threat. As a feeling, it has a clearly unpleasant character. (de Souza Dias, 2005) **3:** The tendency of a particular individual to experience a level of uneasiness over his or her impending use of a computer, which is disproportionate to the actual threat presented by the computer. (Kase & Ritter, 2005)

## Computer Attitude

A complex mental state that affects a human's choice of action or behavior toward computers and computer-related tasks. (Blignaut et al., 2005)

## Computer Comfort

The term used to describe when the user does not experience any suffering, anxiety, pain, and so forth when using a computer. (Blignaut et al., 2005)

## Computer Communication

A term often mistakenly used in relation to online education. Typically, the object of communication is another person, not a computer, and the term computer-mediated communication would be more accurate. (Salter, 2005c)

## Computer Conference

Communication between students, and between students and faculty, to share ideas and to comment on others' ideas. The information is seen as a threaded discourse so that individuals can track which comment belongs to which topic. (Ally, 2005d)

## Computer Conferencing

**1:** An effective electronic means of connecting learners who may or may not be separated by distance in a shared learning space using computers. (Wild, 2005) **2:** Exchanging information and ideas in a multi-user environment through computers (e.g., e-mail). (Nandavadekar, 2005)

## Computer Confidence

A term referring to when the user is confident that he or she would be able to master a required skill to solve a particular problem using a computer, for example, learning how to use a specific facility of an application program or learning a programming language. (Blignaut et al., 2005)

## Computer Engineering (CE)

The engineering of computer hardware. (Scime, 2005a)

## Computer Game

An interactive game played on a computer. (Ip & Jacobs, 2006)

## Computer Graphics (CG)

Field of science and technology concerned with methods and techniques for converting data to or from visual presentation using computers. (Andrés del Valle, 2005)

## Computer Hardware

Refers to computer equipment such as a CPU, disk drive, modem, printer, and so forth. (Magagula, 2005)

## Computer Information System (CIS)

An information system with an emphasis on information as an enterprise resource, and the design, development, implementation, and maintenance of an information system. (Scime, 2005a)

## Computer Interface

The way in which a person experiences the computer, its application programs, hardware components, output devices, and functionality. (Barolli & Koyama, 2005b)

## Computer Liking

The use of a computer to solve problems; considered enjoyable, stimulating, and even addictive. (Blignaut et al., 2005)

## Computer Literacy

**1:** The ability confidently and competently to make good or optimum use of the facilities that computers provide. (Vaast, 2005) **2:** The acquisition of basic knowledge and ability to operate or use a computer. (Magagula, 2005)

## Computer Reservation System

A computer system that manages the distribution of the tourist products to transportation, lodging, and entertainment companies. (Mendes-Filho & Ramos, 2005)

## Computer Science (CS)

**1:** A traditional IT curriculum whose focus is technical and theoretical rather than applied, with emphasis on software creation. (Beise et al., 2005) **2:** Hardware and software theory and design. (Scime, 2005a)

## Computer Self-Efficacy

**1:** A judgment of one's capability to use a computer. It incorporates judgments of an individual on his or her skills to perform tasks using a microcomputer. (de Souza Dias, 2005) **2:** Computer self-confidence or perceptions of ability. Beliefs about one's ability to perform a specific behavior or task on a computer. (Kase & Ritter, 2005)

## Computer Simulation

**1:** A simulation built using a computer language. (Pendegraft, 2005) **2:** The process of using authentic data in a computer program to simulate a real phenomenon. (Morphew, 2005)

## Computer Support Committee (CSC)

A committee formed around ICT Seva Kendra to work on specific community issues and consisting of village volunteers. (Shaligram, 2005)

## Computer Theorem Proving System

A software system that is used to discover, develop, or verify formal deductions. (Farmer, 2006)

## Computer Vision (CV)

**1:** A branch of artificial intelligence and image processing concerned with computer processing of images from the real world. Computer vision typically requires a combination of low-level image processing to enhance the image quality (e.g., remove noise, increase contrast), and higher-level pattern recognition and image understanding to recognize features present in the image. (Andrés del Valle, 2005) **2:** Using computers to analyze images and video streams and to extract meaningful information from them in a way similar to the human vision system. It is related to artificial intelligence and image processing, and is concerned with computer processing of images from the real world to recognize features present in the image. (Lovell & Chen, 2005)

## Computer Whiteboard

A whiteboard that supports graphical synchronous inputs from a group. (Morphew, 2005)

## Computer-Aided Design (CAD)

**1:** An interactive computer graphics system used for engineering design. (Mathieu & Levary, 2005) **2:** Software used in art, architecture, engineering, and manufacturing to assist in precision drawing. (Ferri & Grifoni, 2006) **3:** The use of computer programs and systems to design detailed two- or three-dimensional models of physical objects, such as mechanical parts, buildings, and molecules. (Cruz et al., 2005)

## Computer-Aided Instruction Interface

A point of communication between a human and a computer that is utilized with a system that is programmed to teach learners using a computer program. (Alkhalifa, 2005b)

## Computer-Aided Language Learning (CALL)

The use of computers in learning a language. (Zaphiris et al., 2005)

## Computer-Aided Learning (CAL)

Where the software teaches, trains, and also examines the students if required. (Whateley et al., 2005)

## Computer-Aided Manufacturing (CAM)

The use of computers to improve both the effectiveness and efficiency of manufacturing activities. (Mathieu & Levary, 2005)

## Computer-Aided Production Engineering (CAPE)

Using tools for creation that model the factory, production line, or work cell layout to simulate production processes and generate efficient operations plans. CAPE systems are appointed to help manufacturers fully computerize the industrial process and achieve a seamless transition from design to production. Advanced CAPE tools are able to create an integrated, computerized environment for planning, designing, simulating, and optimizing a complete factory at all levels of detail. (Modrák & Marcín, 2006)

## Computer-Aided Software Engineering (CASE)

**1:** This acronym refers to a set of tools dedicated to support various phases in the development process of software systems. Usually, they support modeling activities and the refinement of models toward implementation. (Bastide et

**C**

al., 2006) **2:** Software tools that provide computer-assisted support for some portion of the software or systems development process, especially on large and complex projects involving many software components and people. (Lee, Suh, et al., 2005) **3:** A tool to aid in the analysis and design of software systems. (Favre et al., 2005)

### Computer-Assisted Instruction (CAI)

**1:** A teaching process in which the learning environment is enhanced with the use of a computer. (Danenberg & Chen, 2005) **2:** An extension of the branching model of teaching machines in which a learner accesses computer-based lesson material (courseware) developed and programmed by teams of instructional designers and computer programmers. (Reisman, 2006) **3:** During the 1950s, CAI was first used in education, and training with early work was done by IBM. The mediation of instruction entered the computer age in the 1960s when Patrick Suppes and Richard Atkinson conducted their initial investigations into CAI in mathematics and reading. CAI grew rapidly in the 1960s, when federal funding for research and development in education and industrial laboratories was implemented. (I. Chen, 2005) **4:** The use of computers in educational settings—that is, tutorials, simulations, exercises. It usually refers either to stand-alone computer learning activities or to activities that reinforce educational material introduced and taught by teachers. (Magoulas, 2006)

### Computer-Assisted Language Learning (CALL)

The teaching practices and research related to the use of computers in the language classroom. (Liu & Chen, 2005)

### Computer-Assisted Language Testing (CALT)

An integrated procedure in which language performance is elicited and assessed with the help of a computer. (Laghos & Zaphiris, 2005b)

### Computer-Based Assessment

Addresses the use of computers for the entire process of assessment including production, delivery, grading, and provision of feedback. (Valenti, 2005)

### Computer-Based Information System (CBIS)

An information system that uses computer technology to perform input, processing, and output activities. A CBIS consists of people, procedures, data, hardware, and software. (Nightingale, 2005)

### Computer-Based Learning

Use of a computer to deliver instructions to students using a variety of instructional strategies to meet individual students' needs. (Ally, 2005a)

### Computer-Based Learning Resources

Instructional software and other computer, Internet, and Web-based learning resources encompassing activities such as tutorials, exercises, and low-stakes quizzes that provide frequent practice, feedback, and reinforcement of course concepts. Often synonymous with general Internet resources, including simulations, animations, games, and other resources supporting learning. (Twigg, 2005)

### Computer-Based Training (CBT)

**1:** Curriculum delivered primarily through the use of the computer, often linked with Internet technologies. (Rhoten, 2006b) **2:** Training delivered to employees or students on a computer, providing training on something like word processing or on a programming language such as Java. (Neville & Powell, 2005) **3:** Training material is delivered using hard support (CD ROM, films, and so on) or on site. (Cirrincione, 2005) **4:** Training and education delivered or enhanced using a computer-based system. (Duan, 2005) **5:** Training materials and programs usually delivered on a CD-ROM or via an organization's local area network. (Ng, 2006) **6:** A recent approach involving the use of microcomputer, optical disks such as compact disks, and/or the Internet to address an organization's training needs. (Pang, 2005b)

### Computer-Managed Instruction (CMI)

**1:** A form of computer-assisted instruction in which a computer serves the role of an instructional supervisor and media guide for learners, directing them to different curricular materials and/or media based on their performance in computer-administered pre- and post-tests. (Reisman, 2006) **2:** Teaching and tracking process in which the learning environment is enhanced with the use of a computer. (Danenberg & Chen, 2005)

### Computer-Mediated Communication (CMC)

**1:** The process of using computers to enhance communication between students, instructors, experts, and learning resources. Can include hypermedia, e-mail, conferencing, bulletin boards, listservs, the Internet or World Wide Web, and audio/videoconferencing. (Janes, 2005) **2:** A combination of telecommunication technologies and computer networks that enables users to transmit, receive, and store information via synchronous and asynchronous communication tools. (Erlich, 2005) **3:** A communication system that involves or is assisted by computers. Computer-mediated communication includes group support systems, e-mail, videoconferencing, chat rooms, and instant messaging. (Klein, 2005) **4:** CMC was made widely popular by the Internet, which allows people to communicate in a variety of modes such as e-mail or chat. CMC in turn is affecting translation practice as more and more people communicate in a CMC mode across languages and require language support. (O'Hagan, 2005) **5:** Communication between humans using the computer as a medium. (Link & Wagner, 2006) **6:** Communication that is facilitated by computer applications, for example, e-mail, bulletin boards, and newsgroups. (Kung-Ming & Khoon-Seng 2005) **7:** Communication that takes place through, or is facilitated by, computers. Examples include both asynchronous tools such as bulletin boards, e-mail, and threaded discussion, and synchronous tools such as chat and videoconferencing. (Swan, 2005) **8:** Human communication that takes place through or is facilitated by information technology, including networked telecommunications systems and computers. (Ridings, 2006a) **9:** Interactions in which all involved parties use computers as the primary or the only means of exchanging information. (St.Amant, 2006a) **10:** All media that are involved in the dynamic transfer and storage of data (analog and digital) across established networks. The technology includes the World Wide Web, e-mail, telephones, fiber optics, and satellites. (Zakaria & Yusof, 2005) **11:** Using technology-based tools such as e-mail, chat programs, or conferencing tools to communicate at a distance. (Schoenfeld & Berge, 2005) **12:** The use of information technology to support the interaction between people, directed to the resolution of a problem or activity in a task context. (Fleming, 2005c) **13:** CMC, like e-mail, is one-to-one, asynchronous communication mediated by electronic means. List e-mail seems to be many-to-many communication, but the transmission system simply duplicates one-to-one transmissions. In true one-to-many transmissions, like a bulletin board, one communication operation is transmitted to many people (e.g., posting a message). (Whitworth, 2006b) **14:** Communication between instructor and student or between students which discusses some aspect of course content, assignment, or student progress in an online course, utilizing the online computing environment for the communication. (Gold, 2005) **15:** Communication between two or more individuals that occurs via computer networks. Computer-mediated communication may be text, audio, graphics, or video based, and may occur synchronously (in "real time") or asynchronously (delayed). (Roberts et al., 2005) **16:** Communication that is facilitated using information technologies such as e-mail, videoconferencing, and teleconferencing. (Panteli, 2005)

## Computer-Mediated Communication System

Includes a wide range of telecommunication equipment such as phones, intranets, Internets, e-mail, group support systems, automated workflow, electronic voting, audio/video/data/desktop videoconferencing systems, bulletin boards, electronic whiteboards, wireless technologies, and so forth to connect, support, and facilitate work processes among team members. (Wong-MingJi, 2005)

## Computer-Mediated Education (CME)

Teaching using developed and still-evolving powerful and sophisticated hypermedia computer tools. (Danenberg & Chen, 2005)

## Computer-Mediated Information Technology

An effective means of storing and retrieving knowledge. IT tools such as Lotus Notes and intranets are designed to provide a means for retaining and accessing electronic archives. (Jasimuddin et al., 2006)

## Computer-Mediated Interaction (CMI)

Interaction mediated by electronic means, whether between people or computer agents. (Whitworth, 2006b)

## Computer-Mediated Technology (CMT)

The combination of technologies (e.g., hypermedia, handheld technologies, information networks, the Internet, and other multimedia devices) that are utilized for computer-mediated communication. (Kwok Lai-yin & Tan Yew-Gee, 2005)

## Computer-Supported Asynchronous Discourse Medium

An electronic medium for discussion where participants do not have to be communicating at the same time, as they do in an oral discussion. Participants make contributions to a community knowledge base accessible to everyone. The knowledge is represented by notes that are preserved in a database and are continually available for search, retrieval, comment, reference, and revision. (Woodruff & Nirula, 2005)

**C**

## Computer-Supported Collaborative/Cooperative Work (CSCW)

**1:** A research area that focuses on investigations and development of technologies that can be used for collaborative work in distributed settings. (Bélanger, 2005) **2:** Use of computer-based technology, including an Audience Response System (ARS), to support group processes. (Banks, 2005) **3:** Branch of computer science dedicated to the study of groupware technologies. (de Carvalho & Ferreira, 2006) **4:** A discipline of computer science dedicated to the use of computer tools to allow groups of participants to work together in the resolution of a problem domain. (Mohamedally et al., 2005) **5:** Provides tools for supporting people working together, for example, video and audio conferences, group calendar, e-mail, and text chat. Differs from workflow applications in having more flexibility and less coordination. (Pinheiro, 2005) **6:** Software tools and technology, as well as organizational structures, that support groups of people (typically from different sites) working together on a common project. (Kindmüller et al., 2005)

## Computer-Supported Collaborative Learning (CSCL)

**1:** Collaborative learning that occurs via the medium of computer-based communication networks such as the Internet. (Klobas & Renzi, 2005b) **2:** Learning facilitated through collaboration with fellow students (and tutors), supported by ICT networks. (Haugen & Ask, 2005) **3:** Occurs when students learn primarily by communicating amongst themselves via the Internet, and where student-to-student interaction plays a primary role in the learning process. (McInnerney & Roberts, 2005) **4:** A broad term combining both pedagogical and technological aspects. In CSCL, collaborative learning is supported by the use of different technological tools, from basic e-mail systems to more complex three-dimensional virtual learning environments. The term relies on various socially oriented theories of learning and has been applied from the primary school level to a higher education context within various domains. (Pöysä & Lowyck, 2005) **5:** Collaborative learning mediated by computers. (Nason & Woodruff, 2005a) **6:** The process in which multiple learners work together on tasks using computer tools that leads to learning of a subject matter by the learners. (Soh & Jiang, 2006) **7:** Combining communications and computer technologies to support various activities involving groups in collaborative problem-solving situations. (Donnelly, 2005) **8:** The acquisition by individuals of knowledge, skills, or attitudes occurring as the result of group interaction, or put more tersely, individual learning as a result of group purpose. (Sala, 2005b) **9:** Usually based on special tools (e.g., a knowledge forum) that can create electronic or virtual environments, improving collaborative learning by means of computer networks. Main ideas they are based on include: (1) intentional learning (based on motivation to learn), (2) involvement in a process of expertise development, and (3) looking at the group as a community building new knowledge. (Cartelli, 2006a) **10:** The field of study investigating the role of technology in the theory and practice of collaborative learning. (Woodruff & Nirula, 2005) **11:** A research area that uses software and hardware to provide an environment for collaborative learning. (Moreira & da Silva, 2005)

## Computer-Supported Cooperative Work (CSCW)

**1:** A computer-assisted coordinated activity, such as communication and problem solving, carried out by a group of collaborating individuals. Key issues of CSCW are group awareness, multi-user interfaces, concurrency control, communication and coordination within the group, shared information space, and the support of a heterogeneous open environment which integrates existing single-user applications. (Karacapilidis, 2005) **2:** A combination of an understanding of group process with the enabling technologies that support group work. CSCW systems focus on technologies and processes that support groups that work together in a cooperative, coordinated, and collaborative manner. CSCW systems are often categorized in terms of time and location, whether work is carried out at the same time (synchronously) or at different times (asynchronously), and whether work is done in the same place (face-to-face) or in different places (distributed). (Dara-Abrams, 2006) **3:** Research area that studies the design, evaluation, and deployment of computing technologies to support group and organizational activity. (Farooq et al., 2006)

## Computer-Supported Learning

Learning processes that take place in an environment that includes computer-based tools and/or electronically stored resources. (Nash et al., 2005b)

## Computerized Assisted Auditing Technique (CAAT)

A software application used to improve the efficiency of an audit. (Garrity et al., 2005)

## Computerized Criminal History (CCH)

A system containing offenders and their individual arrests, final disposition of those arrests, and custodial information for those arrests. (Holland, 2005)

## Computerized Language Labs

Foreign language instructional programs operated via computer disks, distributed to multiple computers by a file server, and accessed by an entire class of students. (Switala, 2005)

## Computerized School Information System

A specific information system for educational management, for example, an enrollment system or an assessment and reporting system. (Mackey, 2005)

## Computing Inspired by Nature

Embodies all approaches—mainly problem-solving techniques—developed using ideas from or inspired by natural phenomena and/or their corresponding theoretical models. It is also sometimes referred to as computing with biological metaphors. Instead of trying to create accurate (theoretical) models, it usually results in high-level abstractions of natural phenomena. (de Castro, 2005)

## Computing with Symbols

The interpretations of the symbols are not participating in the formal data processing or computing. (T.Y. Lin, 2005)

## Computing with Words

One form of formal data processing or computing in which the interpretations of the symbols do participate. L.A. Zadeh uses this term in a much deeper way. (T.Y. Lin, 2005)

## Concept

**1:** A mental structure derived from acquired information which, when applied to a problem, clarifies to the point of solving the problem. (Andrade, Ares, García, Rodríguez, & Silva, 2006) **2:** A pair (A, B) of a set A of objects and a set B of features such that B is the maximal set of features possessed by all the objects in A, and A is the maximal set of objects that possess every feature in B. (Saquer, 2005) **3:** Each category value of a categorical variable or a logical association of variables. For example, a concept can be simply a town or a type of unemployment, or in a more complex way, a socio-professional category (SPC) associated with an age category A, and a region R. (Murthy

& Diday, 2005) **4:** In the Galois connection of the (T, I, D) context, a concept is a pair (X, Y), $X \subseteq T$, $Y \subseteq I$, that satisfies $s(X)=Y$ and $t(Y)=X$. X is called the extent and Y the intent of the concept (X,Y). (Dumitriu, 2005) **5:** An abstract or generic idea, opinion, or thought generalized from particular instances by the selection of meaningful terms. The concept may be identified by the use of text-mining techniques, which are used to explore and examine the contents of talks, texts, documents, books, messages, and so forth. Concepts belong to the extra-linguistic knowledge about the world, representing real things in formal ways. (Antonio do Prado et al., 2005) **6:** A mental construct, unit of thought, or unit of knowledge created by a unique combination of characteristics. (Gillman, 2006) **7:** Simultaneously a result and an agent; concepts are formed within the discourse, however they lack meaning if isolated from it. It is the concepts that bring density and relief to a discourse's content. A concept is an accumulation of meaning, and this meaning is produced within a discourse, through a metaphorization process, constitutive of all natural language, and thus inherent to philosophy itself. The density and thickness of a text depends on the combination and hierarchization of concepts. Philosophy is not a sophistication or a purification of concepts; it is discourse and text, where concepts have a key role and can be searched for, never at the beginning but rather through the interpretation process itself. (Nobre, 2006b) **8:** A sort of scheme produced by repeated experiences. Concepts are essentially each little idea that we have in our heads about anything. This includes not only everything, but every attribute of everything. (Amoretti, 2005)

## Concept Abduction

Non-standard reasoning service provided by digital libraries. Abduction is a form of non-monotonic reasoning, modeling commonsense reasoning, usually aimed at finding an explanation for some given symptoms or manifestations. Concept abduction captures the reasoning mechanism—namely, making hypotheses—involved when some constraints required by a resource request R are not specified in a offered resource O—that obviously in later stages of the request/offer interaction might turn out to be fulfilled or not. (Colucci et al., 2006)

## Concept Contraction

Non-standard reasoning service provided by digital libraries. Contraction is the first step in belief revision. Concept contraction captures the possibility to relax some of the constraints of a requested resource R when they are in conflict with those of an offered resource O—that is, when O⊓R is an unsatisfiable concept. (Colucci et al., 2006)

## Concept Drift
A phenomenon in which the class labels of instances change over time. (Maloof, 2005)

## Concept Hierarchy
**1:** A directed graph in which the root node represents the set of all input instances and the terminal nodes represent individual instances. (Oh et al., 2005) **2:** The organization of a set of database attribute domains into different levels of abstraction according to a general-to-specific ordering. (Shen, 2005)

## Concept Map
**1:** A graphic outline that shows the main concepts in the information and the relationship between the concepts. (Ally, 2005c) **2:** A tool that assists learners in the understanding of the relationships of the main idea and its attributes; also used in brainstorming and planning. (Judd, 2005) **3:** A visual representation of knowledge of a domain consisting of nodes representing concepts, objects, events, or actions interconnected by directional links that define the semantic relationships between and among nodes. (Alpert, 2006)

## Concept-Based Image Retrieval
A term used to describe the classical approach to information management that focuses on the use of classification schemes and their indexing terms to retrieve images. (Venters et al., 2005)

## Concept-Based Search
Search over a corpus of documents or databases can proceed using a search that matches concepts rather than matching words. The value of concept-based search increases with the technical complexity of the domain of search. (Kapetanios, 2005)

## Concept-Based System
An information system that uses conceptual structures to organize and present the information content; typical systems are data intensive, retrieve content dynamically from a repository, and use hypermedia to present the output. (Houben et al., 2006)

## Conceptual Clustering
A type of learning by observations and a way of summarizing data in an understandable manner. (Oh et al., 2005)

## Conceptual Construction with Incomplete Data
A knowledge development process that reveals the patterns of the missing data as well as the potential impacts of these missing data on the mining results based only on the complete data. (H. Wang & S. Wang, 2005)

## Conceptual Data Modeling of Engineering Information
Using conceptual data models to implement the data modeling of engineering information. The conceptual data models for engineering data modeling include some special conceptual data models for industry such as EXPRESS/ STEP and IDEF1X, and some traditional conceptual data models such as ER/EER and UML. (Ma, 2005a)

## Conceptual Design of Fuzzy Databases
The conversion of fuzzy conceptual data models to fuzzy database models. The focus is on developing the rules of mapping fuzzy conceptual data models to fuzzy database models. (Ma, 2005b)

## Conceptual Diagrams
Schematic depictions of abstract ideas with the help of standardized shapes such as arrows, circles, pyramids, matrices, and so forth. (Eppler & Burkhard, 2006)

## Conceptual Framework
Structuring a portfolio around a specific idea, theme, or strategy. (Shaw & Slick, 2005)

## Conceptual Graph
Graph representation described by a precise semantics based on first-order logic. (Holder & Cook, 2005)

## Conceptual Maps
Semiotic representation (linguistic and visual) of the concepts (nodes) and their relationships (links); represent the organization process of the knowledge When people do a conceptual map, they usually privilege the level where the prototype is. They prefer to categorize at an intermediate level; this basic level is the first level learned, the most common level named, and the most general level where visual shape and attributes are maintained. (Amoretti, 2005)

## Conceptual Model

**1:** A model concerned with the real-world view and understanding of the data. It suppresses non-critical details in order to emphasize business rules and user objects. (Pardede et al., 2005) **2:** Abstraction of the real world/domain, and a mechanism for understanding and representing organizations and the information systems that support them. The most important types of models are: Object Model—Describes objects by data and operations on the data. The object's identity encapsulates its state (attributes and relationships with other objects) and its behavior (allowed operations on/with that object). Process Model—Describes (sub)processes by the activities they involve, the activity order, decision points, and pre-/post-conditions for the activity execution. Functional Model—Describes the information flow and transformation, as well as the constraints and functional dependencies among the activities in a process. Organizational Model—Describes the workflow (activities for the creation and movement of the documents) within an organization, the people's roles, and the communication among people for performing the activities. (Galatescu, 2005) **3:** An abstraction of the problem as well as a possible model of a possible conceptual solution to the problem. (Andrade et al., 2006a) **4:** Semi-formal framework (usually a language and a diagram notation) used to capture information about the structure and organization of things, properties, and relations in a fragment of the real world, called the domain, usually one of interest to a (software) system. The model represents the semantics of the domain to the system. (Mani & Badia, 2005) **5:** The abstraction of relevant aspects of a target—usually physical—system into a representation system consisting of symbols, logic, and mathematical constructs. (Vitolo & Coulston, 2005) **6:** A formal or semi-formal description of the actual world elements (objects, persons, organizations) to be included in the future software artifact. (Doorn, 2005) **7:** An action describing a domain with the help of some artificial or formalized language. (Fettke, 2005) **8:** High-level modeling; modeling at a high level of abstraction. (Barca et al., 2005) **9:** Process of forming and collecting conceptual knowledge about the Universe of Discourse, and documenting the results in the form of a Conceptual Schema. (Marjomaa, 2005) **10:** Starting point for database design that consists of producing a conceptual model. (Mani & Badia, 2005) **11:** The use of concepts and their relationships to deal with and solve a problem. (Andrade et al., 2006a) **12:** Tools to achieve a good design of information systems. These tools are used to express information system requirements specification, and their principal characteristic is easy and intuitive use. (Cuadra et al., 2005)

**Conceptual Modeling:** See *Conceptual Model.*

## Conceptual Modeling Language

A language used to represent conceptual models. (Andrade et al., 2006a)

## Conceptual Schema

**1:** A completely or partially time-independent description of a portion of the (real or postulated) world in the sense that a conceptual schema contains the definition of all concepts and all relationships between concepts allowed to be used in the description of that portion of the world. (Marjomaa, 2005) **2:** A structured technology-independent description of the information about an application domain such as a company or a library. By extension, it is also an abstract representation of the existing or project database that is made up of the data of this domain. (Hainaut et al., 2005) **3:** Specification of the structure of a business domain using language and terms easily understood by a non-technical domain expert. A conceptual schema typically declares the fact types and business rules that are relevant to the business domain. (Halpin, 2005)

## Conceptual Schema of a Database

A semi-formal, high-level description of the database, independent of its implementation. (De Antonellis et al., 2005)

## Conceptual/Functional Equivalence

Refers to whether a given construct has similar meaning across cultures. (Karahanna, Evaristo, & Srite, 2005)

## Conceptualism

An ontological position that entity classes exist only in the mind of the modeler. (Artz, 2005c)

## Conceptualization

**1:** A model of reality, a generalized abstraction of particular items. Example: A radio exists physically, but when conceptualized it exists symbolically as some form of knowledge representation: a word, picture, diagram, graph, or formula. (Buchholz, 2006) **2:** The process of constructing conceptual structures—that is, structures of concepts and their relationships that represent a subject domain. (Houben et al., 2006)

**C**

## Concern of Commercialization
A negative factor that the implantation and use of distance education may create. (B. Martz & V. Reddy, 2005)

## Concise Narrated Animation
A type of multimedia presentation that uses synchronized audio narration along with visual material, which is concise and uses a meaningful structure (such as a cause-and-effect chain). (M. Mitchell, 2005c)

## Concordancer
A text-manipulation tool originally used by lexicographers but nowadays popularly promoted among foreign-language teachers and learners. Such a program displays character strings before and after a key word or phrase based on the computer text corpus the program is fed. (Liou, 2005)

## Concurrency Control
**1:** A control method that secures that a transaction is executed as if it were executed in isolation (the "I" in the ACID properties) from other concurrent transactions. (Frank, 2005b) **2:** The task of the concurrency control is to coordinate the concurrent execution of several transactions so that the chosen consistency properties (e.g., ACID properties) are not violated. (Meixner, 2005)

## Concurrency Control Protocol
A protocol executed to ensure that the proper correctness criterion, usually serializability, is upheld for a set of concurrently executing transactions by controlling whether a certain operation can be performed, delayed, or rejected, and whether the transaction can be committed or has to be aborted. (Leong, 2005b)

## Concurrent Engineering
An integrated team approach (e.g., by design, production, and marketing departments) to produce and sell either a service or tangible good. (Jeffery & Bratton-Jeffery, 2005)

## Concurrent Models with an Object-Oriented Approach
Each object can potentially execute activities or procedures in parallel with all others. (Gurău, 2005)

## Condensed Representation
An alternative representation of the data that preserve crucial information for being able to answer some kind of queries. The most studied example concerns frequent sets and their frequencies. Their condensed representations can be several orders of magnitude smaller than the collection of the frequent itemsets. (Boulicaut, 2005)

## Condition
**1:** A predicate that evaluates a situation with respect to circumstances. (Ale & Espil, 2005) **2:** Part of a trigger that is evaluated when the event in the trigger takes place. It is usually a predicate in SQL that evaluates to true or false. (Badia, 2005b)

## Condition Number
Ratio between the largest and smallest condition number of a matrix, often employed to assess the degree of collinearity between variables associated to the columns of the matrix. (Galvão et al., 2005)

## Conditional
The formal algebraic term for a rule that need not be strict, but also can be based on plausibility, probability, and so forth. (Kern-Isberner, 2005)

## Conditional Access (CA) Service
Television services that allow only authorized users to select, receive, decrypt, and watch a particular programming package. (Hulicki, 2005)

## Conditional Distribution
Probability distribution of a parameter, given the values of other parameters and/or the data. (Rippon & Mengersen, 2005)

## Conditional Independence
**1:** A generalization of plain statistical independence that allows one to take a context into account. Conditional independence is often associated with causal effects. (Kern-Isberner, 2005) **2:** Consider two random variables X and Y. It will be said that X and Y are independent conditionally on a third random variable (or random vector) Z, if the joint probability distribution of X and Y, conditionally on Z, can be decomposed in the product of two factors, the conditional density of X given Z and the conditional density of Y given Z. In formal terms, X and Y are independent, conditionally on Z (in symbols: $X \perp Y | Z$) $f(x,y|Z=z) = f(x|Z=z) f(y|Z=z)$ (Giudici & Cerchiello, 2005) **3:** Let X, Y, and Z be three sets of random variables; then X and Y are said to be conditionally independent given Z, if and only if $p(x|z,y)=p(x|z)$ for all possible values x, y, and z of X, Y, and Z. (Ramoni & Sebastiani, 2005) **4:** Two sets X

and Y of variables are conditionally independent given a third set Z, if knowledge on Z (what value Z takes) makes knowledge on Y irrelevant to guessing the value of X. (Xiang, 2005)

## Conditional Probability

Probability of some event A, assuming event B, written mathematically as P(A|B). (Bashir et al., 2005)

## Conditional Structure

An algebraic expression that makes the effects of conditionals on possible worlds transparent and computable. (Kern-Isberner, 2005)

## Conditioning

Revision process of a belief by a fact accepted as true. (Smets, 2005)

## Condominium Fiber

A unit of dark fiber installed by a particular contractor (originating either from the private or the public sector) on behalf of a consortium of customers, with the customers to be owners of the individual fiber strands. Each customer-owner lights the fibers using his or her own technology, thereby deploying a private network to wherever the fiber reaches, that is, to any possible terminating location or endpoint. (Chochliouros et al., 2005a)

## Conduit Metaphor

A metaphor about communication which suggests that an addresser's ideas are objects contained in packages, known as words, that are directly sent to the addressee. (Zappavigna-Lee & Patrick, 2005)

## CONE

A new lifecycle in which development process occurs in iteration cycles, each one having many activities grouped together in phases. (Furtado, 2005)

## Conferencing System

A system specifically designed to facilitate synchronous virtual meetings by phone or computer. Teleconferencing utilizes computer-controlled audiovisual transmission. Computer conferencing uses computer-enabled conferencing to work together in real time using free proprietary software. (Ferris & Minielli, 2005)

## Confidence

**1:** A parameter used in the association-rules method for determining the percent of data cases that support the antecedent of the rule X that also support the consequent of the rule Y in the set of data cases D. (Swierzowicz, 2005) **2:** An asymmetric index that shows the percentage of records for which A occurred within the group of records and for which the other two, X and Y, actually occurred under the association rule of X, Y $\Rightarrow$ A. (Ito, 2005) **3:** Given an association rule X $\Rightarrow$ Y, the confidence of a rule is the number of transactions that satisfy X $\cup$ Y divided by the number of transactions that satisfy X. (Imberman & Tansel, 2006) **4:** The confidence of a rule is the support of the item set consisting of all items in the rule (A $\cup$ B) divided by the support of the antecedent. (Denton & Besemann, 2005) **5:** The confidence of a rule X $\rightarrow$ $I_j$, where X is a set of items and $I_j$ is a single item not in X, is the fraction of the transactions containing all items in set X that also contain item $I_j$. (Wong, & Fu, 2005) **6:** The proportion of records that belong to the target class from those that satisfy the antecedent of the rule. This is also often called the accuracy of the rule. An alternative definition is the proportion of records for which the rule makes the correct prediction of the target class. (Richards & de la Iglesia, 2005) **7:** The rule A=>B has confidence c, if c% of transactions that contain A also contain B. (Daly & Taniar, 2005a)

## Confidence in Vendor

Trust or faith in a vendor, especially trust or faith in the vendor's guarantees of a safe shopping environment. (Shan et al., 2006a)

## Confidence of a Rule

Percentage of the rows that contain the antecedent that also contain the consequent of the rule. The confidence of a rule gives us an idea of the strength of the influence that the antecedent has on the presence of the consequent of the rule. (Ale & Rossi, 2005)

## Confidence of Rule XY

The fraction of the database containing X that also contains Y, which is the ratio of the support of XY to the support of X. (Shen, 2005)

## Confidential Information

Sensitive organizational information that should be disclosed only to authorized users. Usually stored in the database or data warehouse, this information needs to kept secure from hackers and snoopers. (Wilson et al., 2006b)

**C**

## Confidentiality

**1:** A status accorded to information based on a decision, agreement, obligation, or duty. This status requires that the recipient of personal information must control disclosure. (Mullen, 2005) **2:** Assures that the exchange of messages between parties over wireless access networks or global networks is not being monitored by non-authorized parties. (Pierre, 2006b) **3:** Ensures that information is accessible only to those authorized to have access; typically ensured through encryption. (Mitrakas, 2006) **4:** Guarantees that shared information between parties is only seen by authorized people. (Lowry, Stephens, et al., 2005) **5:** Nonoccurrence of the unauthorized disclosure of information. The term confidentiality indicates aspects of secrecy and privacy. (Oermann & Dittmann, 2006) **6:** Prevention of unauthorized disclosure of information. (Tong & Wong, 2005a) **7:** The claim, right, or desire that personal information about individuals should be kept secret or not disclosed without permission or informed consent. (Goodman, 2005) **8:** The protection of information from exposure to others. (Buche & Vician, 2005)

## Configuration System

A software system in which the product components and the constraints existing between them are stored. A configuration system allows consistent and completely structured product variants that can be produced by the manufacturing system. (Blecker & Abdelkafi, 2006)

## Conflict

Refers to the conflicts between the addict and those around them (interpersonal conflict), conflicts with other activities (job, social life, hobbies, and interests), or from within the individual themselves (intrapsychic conflict) that are concerned with the particular activity. (Griffiths, 2005)

## Confluence

A rewrite system is confluent if, no matter in which order rules are applied, they lead to the same result. (Fischer, 2005)

## Conforming Learner

A complying learner who prefers to more passively accept knowledge, store it, and reproduce it to conform; follows simple steps to complete assigned tasks; and pleases others. (Raisinghani & Hohertz, 2005)

## Confusion Matrix

Contains information about actual and predicted classifications done by a classification system. (Yeo, 2005)

## Congestion Control

The algorithms used to detect and solve system-overload situations. (Iossifides et al., 2005)

## Conjoint Analysis

Decompositional method of preference measurement. On the basis of holistic preference statements, the part worth of object characteristics are derived. (Voeth & Liehr, 2005)

## Conjunctive Combination

The combination of the beliefs induced by several sources into an aggregated belief. (Smets, 2005)

## Connected Models with an Object-Oriented Approach

Each object can send messages to others through links. (Gurău, 2005)

## Connectedness

The feeling of being linked to or joined with an individual or group of individuals; this feeling is associated with the building of a relationship. (Gangeness, 2005)

## Connected Organization

An organization that serves the common good, serves constituents, creates a culture of service, collaborates, and engages in healthy internal communication. (Baer & Duin, 2005)

## Connection Theme

The central purpose of social communication consisting of links of closeness, understanding, or access. (Molinari, 2005)

## Connectionist Expert System

An expert system that uses an artificial neural network to develop its knowledge base and make inferences. A classical expert system is defined with IF-THEN rules, explicitly. In a connectionist expert system, training examples are used by employing the generalization capability of a neural network, in which the network is coded in the rules of an expert system. The neural network model depends on the processing elements that are connected through weighted connections. The knowledge in these systems is represented by these weights. The topology of the connections are explicit representations of the rules. (R., 2005)

### Connections in Planning
Refers to the degree of contact between HR and IT executives in their respective planning processes. (Dery & Samson, 2005)

### Connectivity
**1:** The ability to access various media via the necessary equipment and channels. (Reilly, 2005) **2:** The ability to link to the Internet via a computer. (Braun, 2005a) **3:** The interconnections that employees and users have through the use of the Internet or other knowledge management tools. (Borders & Johnston, 2005)

### Connectivity Phenomena
A term drawn from computational linguistics. In the presence of several logically linked elementary events, it denotes the existence of a global information content that goes beyond the simple addition of the information conveyed by the single events. The connectivity phenomena are linked with the presence of logico-semantic relationships like causality, goal, indirect speech, coordination, and subordination, as in a sequence like: "Company X has sold its subsidiary Y to Z because the profits of Y have fallen dangerously these last years due to a lack of investments." These phenomena cannot be managed by the usual ontological tools; in NKRL, they are dealt with using second-order tools based on reification. (Zarri, 2006c)

### Consensus Building
Also known as collaborative problem solving or collaboration, it includes techniques such as brainstorming, focus groups, techniques for managing meetings, negotiation techniques, Delphi, and NGT, and is used as a resolution process mainly to settle complex disputes or issues. (Janes, 2005)

### Consequent
A logical conclusion to an event. For example, in the relationship "When it is hot, Mary buys an ice cream," "buys an ice cream" is the consequent. (Beynon, 2005b)

### Consilience
The reconciliation of all knowledge with the historical and scientific observations of biology, chemistry, and physics

in the belief that the findings of those sciences offer a more robust foundation for the proper investigation of all phenomena. (Atkinson & Burstein 2006)

### Consistency
**1:** On Web sites, refers to keeping similar Web pages similar in their look and feel. Examples of ways to achieve consistency include using the same or similar colors, font, and layout throughout the site. (Chalmers, 2006) **2:** Similar to compatibility and sometimes used interchangeably; designs that match our expectations in terms of characteristics, function, and operation, and are applied in a constant manner within the design itself. (Noyes, 2006)

### Consistency of Warehouse Data and Web Documents
In order to introduce consistency among documents and data, the data warehouse library (DWL) must enjoy data warehouse features. Hence, documents are never removed from the DWL; all documents are properly described with metadata and linked to data warehouse objects. There are four levels of consistency between the DWL and DW that enable the eDW system to build retrieval queries: subject consistency, temporal consistency, semantic consistency, and personalization. These four levels together provide constraints for sub-setting the DWL and producing relatively small ranked lists of relevant documents associated with data warehouse reports. (Wecel et al., 2005)

### Consistent Answer
**1:** A set of tuples, derived from the database, satisfying all integrity constraints. (Flesca, Greco, et al., 2005) **2:** Data satisfying both the query and all integrity constraints defined on the given database. (Flesca, Furfaro, et al., 2005)

### Consistent Database
A database satisfying a set of integrity constraints. (Flesca, Furfaro, et al., 2005)

### Consolidation
Work models developed from individual observations are combined to identify both commonalities and uniquenesses. The third step in contextual design. (Notess, 2005)

### Consortia
An organization formed from several businesses or enterprises joining together as a group for a shared purpose. (Kung-Ming, 2005)

## Consortia-Type Distance Teaching Venture

A collaborating venture between several universities or between universities and other partners joining forces to offer distance teaching programs together. (Guri-Rosenblit, 2005a)

## Consortial Agreement

Allows students to access library resources at a library that is closer to their home, but one that is not affiliated with the college or university that they are attending. (Raisinghani & Hohertz, 2005)

## Consortium

A group of companies within a particular industry establishing an exchange connecting each of them and their suppliers. (Mockler et al., 2006)

## Consortium Exchange

A group formed by companies in the same industry, bringing their supply chains together for the purpose of facilitating transactions among themselves over the Internet. (Aigbedo, 2005)

## Constrained Movement

Movement (of a moving object) that is confined according to a set of spatial restrictions. (Vassilakopoulos & Corral, 2005)

## Constrained OLS Method

A method to estimate the "optimal" weights for combination of forecasts by minimizing the sum of squared errors as in a regression framework, and the weights are constrained to sum to one. (C.K. Chan, 2005)

## Constraint

1: As basic knowledge units, the constraints in engineering design are referred to the documents-related engineering design decision, which encompasses source, motivation, rationale, consequences, and a log of the various changes and updates they have undergone. (Ma, 2006) 2: Extensions to the semantics of a UML element. These allow the inclusion of rules that indicate permitted ranges or conditions on an element. (Gurău, 2005) 3: A way to restrict certain kinds of user interaction that can take place at a given moment. (Yong, 2005)

## Constraint-Based Data Mining

1: The active use of constraints that specify the interestingness of patterns. Technically, it needs strategies to push the constraints, or at least part of them, deeply into the data-mining algorithms. (Boulicaut, 2005) 2: Data mining obtained by means of evaluation of queries in a query language allowing predicates. (Meo & Psaila, 2005)

## Construct

1: A not directly observable hypothetical concept whose existence must be inferred by actions, behavior, or observable characteristics. (Real et al., 2006) 2: Constructs represent the research participant's interpretations of the elements. Further understanding of these interpretations may be gained by eliciting contrasts resulting in bi-polar labels. Using the same example, research participants may come up with bi-polar constructs such as "high user involvement–low user involvement" to differentiate the elements (i.e., IS projects). The labels represent the critical success factors of IS projects. (Tan & Hunter, 2005)

## Construct Bias

Occurs when a construct measured is not equivalent across cultures both at a conceptual level and at an operational level. (Karahanna et al., 2005)

## Constructed Data Type

The data type that is formed by a number of predefined data types. This data type is also provided by the software products. Examples are LIST and ARRAY. (Pardede et al., 2005)

## Construction Project Lifecycle

Analogous to comparing construction projects to real life. Thus projects may be assumed to evolve through the life phases of conception, development, implementation, and phase-out. Post-delivery involves the facilities operation/maintenance phase through to asset disposal. (Barima, 2006a)

## Constructionism

1: A pedagogy based on learners designing and creating some of their own learning materials and representations. (Collis & Moonen, 2005b) 2: A set of theories that defines the human beings as active constructors of their own learning and development. This learning and development of knowledge happens more effectively when individuals are involved in the construction of something external, something that can be shared, or both. (Ramos & Carvalho, 2005) 3: Asserts that (social) actors socially construct reality. (Carlsson, 2005) 4: An educational theory arguing that the student "constructs" his/her own knowledge on the domain, rather than "acquiring" certain behaviors on how to interact with it. (Athanasis & Andreas, 2005) **5:** Knowledge is constructed by the learner through experiential learning and interactions with the environment and the learner's personal workspace. (Ally, 2005b) **6:** A form of learning in which students construct their own unique understanding of a subject through a process that includes social interaction, so that the learner can explain understandings, receive feedback from teachers and other students, clarify meanings, and reach a group consensus. (Grasso & Leng, 2005) **7:** A learning theory based on the premise that students construct their own learning based on their own experiences. (Burrage & Pelton, 2005) **8:** A learning theory that knowledge is constructed by the learner through experience-based activities. (Judd, 2005) **9:** A learning theory that posits people construct knowledge by modifying their existing concepts in light of new evidence and experience. Development of knowledge is unique for each learner and is colored by the learner's background and experiences. (Stodel et al., 2005) **10:** A theory of learning and knowing that holds that learning is an active process of knowledge construction in which learners build on prior knowledge and experience to shape meaning and construct new knowledge. (Bieber et al., 2005) **11:** A theory of learning based on the idea that knowledge is constructed as learners attempt to make sense of their experiences. It is assumed that learners are not empty vessels waiting to be filled, but rather active organisms seeking meaning: regardless of what is being learned, learners form, elaborate, and test candidate mental structures until a satisfactory one emerges. (Vat, 2005a) **12:** A theory of learning that asserts that learning results from learners actively interacting with their learning environment rather than passively receiving information. (Pelton & Pelton, 2005) **13:** A very prominent learning theory that postulates that learning is a process essentially involving activity and involvement through which learners construct their own knowledge and skills. This naturally seems to imply that overhearers cannot learn from a learning dialogue. The theory of vicarious learning does not reject constructivism, but suggests that activity and involvement can arise cognitively through phenomena of empathy, and hence that "vicarious participation" in dialogue can also foster constructive processes. (J.R. Lee, 2005) **14:** An educational approach that takes the view that knowledge must be constructed within the cognitive structure of each individual. (Banks, 2005) **15:** An educational theory arguing that students construct their own knowledge on the domain, rather than acquiring

certain behaviors on how to interact with it. (Karoulis & Pombortsis, 2005a)

## Constructive Solid Geometry (CSG)

One of the most popular ways to describe a three-dimensional model. In CSG, a model is compiled from primitives and Boolean operators linking them. Data are stored in the tree structure, where the leaves are the primitives, and the nodes are the operations: intersection (AND), union (OR), and complement (NOT). (Cruz et al., 2005)

## Constructivist

Relating to a learning environment where the learner interacts with objects and events, thereby gaining an understanding of the features held of such objects or events. (Blicker, 2005)

## Constructivist Learning

**1:** A learning philosophy that contends that learning occurs in incremental steps, leveraging on the previous knowledge of the learner about the topic. (Hin & Subramaniam, 2005b) **2:** A model for learning based on the widely held notion that individuals construct their own knowledge of, and meaning for, the world around them. (Pritchard, 2005b)

## Constructivist Methodology

A teaching method based on the works of Jean Piaget and Lev Vygotsky by which the instructor helps the student construct meaning rather than simply lecturing. This method is learner centered and learner driven. (Trammell, 2005)

## Constructivist Perspective

A perspective on learning that places emphasis on learners as building their own internal and individual representation of knowledge. (Torrisi-Steele, 2005)

## Constructivist Theory

A theoretical framework developed by Jerome Bruner where learning is an active process in which learners construct new ideas or concepts based upon their current or past knowledge. The learner selects and transforms information, constructs hypotheses, and makes decisions, relying on a cognitive structure to do so. (Sala, 2005b)

## Consultancy

The process of helping organizations to better understand complex processes through their knowledge and experience, and provide solutions to achieve the objectives.

**C**

Consultants may help organizations in the whole ERP lifecycle. The usage of external consultants will depend on the internal know-how that the organization has at the moment. (Esteves & Pastor, 2005)

## Consumer

**1:** A person who buys goods/services and uses them personally instead of selling them. (Shan et al., 2006a) **2:** Of an e-service is a user of the service, possibly by paying a fee. (Yee & Korba, 2006) **3:** The consumer in the health care system is the patient. (Rada, 2006)

## Consumer Context

The setting in which certain consumer behavior occurs. It can be classified conceptually into "need context" and "supply context," and physically into "internal context," "proximate context," and "distal context." (Sun & Poole, 2005)

## Consumer Credit

A loan to an individual to purchase goods and services for personal, family, or household use. (de Carvalho et al., 2005)

## Consumer Experience

Such as increased customization, convenience in purchasing, responsiveness in product delivery, and so on. (Shih & Fang, 2006)

## Consumer Religio-Centrism

Individuals who are so strongly committed to their specific religious group (Christian, Muslim, etc.) that their buying preferences consist of purchases from companies owned or operated by individuals with their same religious beliefs. (Carstens, 2005)

## Consumer-to-Administration (C2A)

Data interchange between citizens and government bodies, typically using an Internet Web site; a component of e-government. (Whiteley, 2006)

## Consumer-to-Business

An e-commerce system that deals with the carrying out of commercial transactions with businesses or with individual customers by using the Internet as an electronic medium. Requires an extensive infrastructure of which the main features are a catalogue, online ordering facilities, and status checking facilities. See *Business-to-Consumer (B2C)*. (Møller, 2005)

## Consumer-to-Consumer (C2C)

Interactions between customers/consumers of a business's product/service are said to follow a C2C format. In common usage of the term C2C, the distinction between customers (purchasers of a product/service) and consumers (end users of a product/service) is not rigorously made. (Baim, 2006a)

## Consumption Mode

Determines which event instances are considered for firing rules. The two most common modes are recent and chronicle. (Cilia, 2005)

## Contact

The ability to exchange information directly with another individual. (St.Amant, 2005d)

## Contact Point

Used to describe a reference from one medium to another. (Uden, 2005)

## Container Model

Knowledge flows directly from the teacher to the learner, independently of the learner's environment. (Frank et al., 2005)

## Containment Query

A query based on the containment and proximity relationships among elements, attributes, and their contents. (Chen, 2005b)

## Content

**1:** An amount of well-presented subject information in text, graphics, or multimedia formats (portals, Web sites, e-mailings, news lines, etc.) built around a specific structure, based on established information standards, and targeted to a specific online audience. (Arkhypska et al., 2005) **2:** Corporate knowledge stored in any form (paper, data, reports, correspondence, e-mail, multimedia, etc.). (Sarmento, 2005) **3:** High-quality online content is considered to be comprehensive, authentic/industry-driven, and researched. (MacDonald et al., 2005) **4:** Online material or services that are relevant, useful, and timely for the community and that are made available in appropriate and affordable ways. (Williamson, 2005) **5:** The information, such as thoughts, ideas, and so forth, that someone wishes to communicate. Importantly, content is what is to be communicated but not how it is to be communicated. (Polovina & Pearson, 2006) **6:** The various genres of information available on the Internet. For instance, local content is information that is specific to a community, neighborhood, or area, such as businesses, housing, neighborhood services, and recreation activities. Community content is information about the neighborhood that promotes community development and facilitates community building. Examples include a listing of places where GED courses are offered, or a newsletter. Culturally relevant content is information that is significant to people with different cultural backgrounds. (Kvasny & Payton, 2005)

## Content Aggregation

A set of existing content units collected together for a specific use purpose. An aggregation may contain several versions of the same unit of content, and its creation may require human involvement. (Honkaranta & Tyrväinen, 2005)

## Content Aggregation Model

Specifies how to combine learning content labeled as a Sharable Content Object (SCO) in a standardized way for reusability and interoperability. Includes a metadata for describing content, XML binding to define how to code metadata tags using XML so they are machine readable, and an Instructional Management System (IMS) content specification that defines how to package a collection of SCOs and defines the design of the learning event. (Stavredes, 2005b)

## Content Aggregator

A business that transforms individuated content into specific and customer-tailored forms. (Rülke et al., 2005)

## Content Analysis

**1:** Identifying categories of statements and counting the number of items in the text that appear in the categories. (Ingram & Hathorn, 2005a) **2:** Objective, systematic, and quantitative analysis of communication content. The unit of measure can be the single words, sentences, or themes. In order to raise the reliability, two or more coders should apply. (Pace, 2005)

## Content Assembly

A collection of existing or new units of content which may be manipulated to produce content for a publication or for a specific target audience. May be produced (semi-)automatically or involve manual processing. A portion of

training content for specialists only may be an assembly. (Honkaranta & Tyrväinen, 2005)

## Content Compression

A term that describes approaches in which parts of a continuous media file are removed in order to speed up replay and data browsing or to automatically generate summaries or abstracts of the file. In relation to speech signals, content-compression techniques often shorten the signals by removing parts that have been identified as less relevant or unimportant based on pause detection and analysis of the emphasis used by the speakers. (Hürst & Lauer, 2006)

## Content Distribution Network (CDN)

**1:** The general term encompassing any technology for wide-area distribution of content. (Fiege, 2005) **2:** A network of cache servers owned by the same Internet service provider that delivers content to users on behalf of content providers. CDN servers are typically shared, delivering content belonging to multiple Web sites, though all servers may not be used for all sites. (Katsaros & Manolopoulos, 2005a)

## Content Gratification

Enjoyment of message specifics. Content can mean information, and often does, though it also includes entertainment in the form of medium-carried programming. (Stafford, 2005)

## Content Knowledge Resource

A knowledge resource that exists independently of an organization to which it belongs. (Holsapple & Joshi, 2006)

## Content Management

**1:** Implementation of a managed repository for digital assets such as documents, fragments of documents, images, and multimedia that are published to intranet and Internet WWW sites. (Asprey & Middleton, 2005) **2:** Management of Web pages as assisted by software; Web page bureaucracy. (N.C. Rowe, 2005a) **3:** Tools, methods, and processes to develop, implement, and evaluate the management of content intended mainly for human comprehension. Content has a lifecycle, and its management involves associated metadata. (Honkaranta & Tyrväinen, 2005)

## Content Management System (CMS)

**1:** Software used to manage the content of a Web site. Typically a CMS consists of two elements—the content management application and the content delivery application. Typical CMS features include Web-based publishing, format management, revision control, indexing, and search and retrieval. (Chapman, 2005a) **2:** Software that enables one to add and/or manipulate content on a Web site. (Du Mont, 2005) **3:** A system used to collect, manage, and publish the content of a Web site, storing the content either as components or as whole documents, while maintaining the links between components. (Arkhypska et al., 2005) **4:** Provides tools for organizing, delivering, and sharing documents and images. Usually used in conjunction with CSCW systems or workflow systems. (Pinheiro, 2005) See also *Document Management System*.

## Content Originator

A business that creates the highly specific types of content that is enhanced, combined, packaged, transmitted, and sold to customers. (Rülke et al., 2005)

## Content Repurposing

Reorganizing or modifying the content of a graphical display to fit effectively on a different device than its original target. (N.C. Rowe, 2005a)

## Content Scalability

The removal or alteration of certain subsets of the total coded bit stream to satisfy the usage environment, while providing a useful representation of the original content. (Knight & Angelides, 2005)

## Content Scrambling System (CSS)

A well-known technological protection measure for the access control and copy prevention of DVDs. It is based on encryption but was broken by the Norwegian teenager Jon Johansen (and two other individuals) in 1999. The decryption program, DeCSS, allows for the copying and playback of digital content on noncompliant machines. (Wang, Cheng, Cheng, & Huang, 2006)

## Content Seeding

Adding identifiers and metadata to content units or their parts to enable computerized assemblies and aggregations on the content. (Honkaranta & Tyrväinen, 2005)

## Content Server

Allows publication and management of Web content for portals and Web applications, with forms-based publishing, templates, and workflow. (Wojtkowski, 2006)

## Content Unit

The object with which the management metadata is associated. May be "a document," "a file," "a component," or "a section of a document," among others. (Honkaranta & Tyrväinen, 2005)

## Content-Addressable File Store (CAFS)

Specialized hardware from ICL (UK's International Computers Limited) used as a filter for database applications. (Thomasian, 2005a)

## Content-Based Access

A technique that enables searching multimedia databases based on the content of the medium itself and not based on a keyword description. (Farag, 2005a)

## Content-Based Filtering

**1:** A technique that involves a direct comparison between the content or attributes of a user's profile and the document to make recommendations. (Chen & Liu, 2005) **2:** An approach to provide recommendations based on the individual's preference. (Chen & McLeod, 2006) **3:** Approach where the user expresses needs and preferences on a set of attributes, and the system retrieves the items that match the description. (Lorenzi & Ricci, 2005) **4:** Organizes information based on properties of the object of preference and/or the carrier of information. (Parmar & Angelides, 2005)

## Content-Based Retrieval

**1:** An application that directly makes use of the contents of media rather than annotation inputted by the human to locate desired data in large databases. (Wei & Li, 2005) **2:** An important retrieval method for multimedia data which uses the low-level features (automatically) extracted from the data as the indexes to match with queries. Content-based image retrieval is a good example. The specific low-level features used depend on the data type: color, shape, and texture features are common features for images, while kinetic energy and motion vectors are used to describe video data. Correspondingly, a query also can be represented in terms of features so that it can be matched against the data. (Li, Yang, & Zhuang, 2005) **3:** Method for automatic multimedia content features extraction. (Hentea, 2005c) **4:** Retrieval based on image content. This includes retrieval based on image color, texture, shape and position of salient objects, dominant edges of image items, and regions. (Chang, 2005) **5:** The search for suitable objects in a database based on the content; often used to retrieve multimedia data. (Bretschneider & Kao, 2005)

## Content-Based-Filtering Recommender System

Technique based on the correlation between item contents by statistical studies about different characteristics. Such techniques compute user-purchase histories in order to identify association rules between items. (Gil & García, 2006)

## Content-Based Image Retrieval (CBIR)

**1:** A process framework for efficiently retrieving images from a collection by similarity. The retrieval relies on extracting the appropriate characteristic quantities describing the desired contents of images. In addition, suitable querying, matching, indexing, and searching techniques are required. (Y.J. Zhang, 2005a) **2:** The technique of image retrieval based on the features automatically extracted from the images themselves. (Y.-K. Chan et al., 2005) **3:** A general term used to describe the semiautomatic or automatic extraction, indexing, and retrieval of images by their visual attributes and characteristics. (Venters et al., 2005) **4:** In this kind of retrieval, symmetry between input image and images of database are established based on contents of the images under consideration. (Deb, 2005) **5:** Retrieval of images similar to a given image based only on features present in the image and not any external information. (Sural, Vadivel, & Majumdar, 2005) **6:** Search for suitable image in a database by comparing extracted features related to color, shape, layout, and other specific image characteristics. (Kao & Tendresse, 2005)

## Content-Centric Networks

A network where various functionalities such as naming, addressing, routing, storage, and so forth are designed based on the content. This is in contrast with classical networks that are node-centric. (Shahabi & Banaei-Kashani, 2005)

## Content-Driven Service

A television service to be provided depending on the content. (Hulicki, 2005)

## Context

**1:** An individual construct that emerges as an individual encounters a situation, including others and artifacts, as it is the individual's interpretation of a situation that results in context. (Shariq & Vendelø, 2006) **2:** Describes the working environment and atmosphere including policies, work hours, work climate, and work goals. (Schoenfeld & Berge, 2005) **3:** Everything—social, cultural, political, and historical factors—that surrounds a particular event. These are the forces of influence at play when the event actually occurs. Greater knowledge of the context of a thing leads to a deeper understanding of and a more balanced perspective on its nature. (Kasi & Jain, 2006) **4:** A mathematical model or group of mathematical models within which a piece of mathematical knowledge is understood. (Farmer, 2006) **5:** The information that characterizes the interaction between humans, applications, and the surrounding environment. Context can be decomposed into three categories: (1) computing context (e.g., network connectivity, communication cost); (2) user context (e.g., user profile, location, nearby people); and (3) physical context (e.g., lighting, noise levels). (Maamar, 2005) **6:** A triple (G, M, I) where G is a set of objects, M is a set of features, and I is a binary relation between G and M such that gIm, if and only if object g possesses the feature m. (Saquer, 2005) **7:** A triple (T, I, D) where T and I are sets and $D \subseteq T \subseteq I$. The elements of T are called objects, and the elements of I are called attributes. For any $t \in T$ and $i \in I$, note tDi when t is related to i, that is, $(t, i) \in D$. (Dumitriu, 2005) **8:** All information about the current user's situation. (Abramowicz, Banaśkiewicz, Wieloch, & Żebrowski, 2006)

## Context Lens

A visual classification scheme for a set of documents that can be dynamically updated. The classification scheme is arranged in a tree hierarchy to facilitate browsing. (Corral, LaBrie, & St. Louis, 2006)

## Context Query

Represents the short-term user information needs. It is created each time a business user launches a data warehouse report. The context query consists of three parts: subject constraints, time constraints, and semantic constraints. Subject constraints define the warehouse objects that are part of the report. Time constraints are represented by the actual time range grasped by the most current state of the report. Semantic constraints are represented as a set of CSL-based weighted keywords. The context query is executed on the data warehouse library, and personalized results are immediately returned to the user. (Wecel et al., 2005)

## Context-Aware Computing

A system that has information about the circumstances under which it is operating and can react/make assumptions accordingly. A Vehicular Telematics System (VTS) has a lot of information about its context, such as localization, user behaviors, vehicle operative state, and so forth. (Costagliola, Di Martino, & Ferrucci, 2006a)

## Context-Aware Technology

Technology that enables the collection, delivery, and utilization of user context information. As key enablers of a system-initiated wireless emergency service, context-aware technologies mainly include sensor-device and sensor-network technologies. (Sun, 2005)

## Context-Awareness

Makes applications aware of the dynamic changes in the execution environment. The execution context includes but is not limited to mobile user location, mobile device characteristics, network condition, and user activity. (Kunz & Gaddah, 2005)

## Context-Dependent Learning

The learning both of knowledge and of the way one behaves in specific scenarios in a realistic life context (preferably one that relates directly to past and future experiences of the learner). It allows the learning of terrain, procedures and processes, events, and almost anything else by doing rather than a priori. (Ariely, 2006b)

## Context-Mechanism-Outcome Pattern

Realist evaluation researchers orient their thinking to context-mechanism-outcome (CMO) pattern configurations. A CMO configuration is a proposition stating what it is about an IS initiative that works, for whom, and in what circumstances. A refined CMO configuration is the finding of IS evaluation research. (Carlsson, 2005)

## Context-Sensitive HCI

Human-computer interaction in which the computer's context with respect to nearby humans (i.e., who the current user is, where the user is, what the user's current task is, and how the user feels) is automatically sensed, interpreted, and used to enable the computer to act or respond appropriately. (Pantic, 2005a)

## Context-Specific Aspects

Covers the most important factors that shaped and become characteristics of organizational dynamics such as culture, business strategies, organization of work, management practices, current technology, workforce competency level, and working processes, among others. (Rentroia-Bonito, Jorge, & Ghaoui, 2006)

## Contextual Data Quality

A concept that data does not exist in a vacuum, but is driven by the circumstance in which data is used. Contextual dimensions include relevancy, timeliness, and appropriate amount of data. (Borchers, 2005)

## Contextual Design

A human-centered methodology for designing information systems from a rich understanding of customer work practice. (Notess, 2005)

## Contextual Information

Refers to several possible aspects of the core message: the situation in which the message was produced, the situation in which it is anticipated to be received, an explanation about a statement, an explanation of how to go about executing a request for action, or the underlying assumptions about an argument. (Te'eni, 2006)

## Contextual Inquiry

**1:** A field research method for observing real work practice in its natural environment and then co-interpreting the data with the person observed. The first step in contextual design. (Notess, 2005) **2:** Interviewing users in the context of their activities while they work and learn. (Neale et al., 2005) **3:** This interface design method employs an ethnographic approach such as observing user activities in a realistic context. (Chan & Fang, 2005)

## Contextual Knowledge

Knowledge of the contexts in which organizational tasks are performed. Depending on the task, this knowledge may be entirely internal to the organization or it may require acquaintance with many extra-organizational contexts—for example, markets, legal contexts, and legislative contexts. (Ein-Dor, 2006)

## Contextual Metadata

Information describing the context where the object of the contextual metadata is created. The contextual metadata can cover, for example, information about the producers and production processes of documents. (Lyytikäinen et al., 2005)

## Contextualism

Integrates process, content, and context to study organizational decision making. (Chou et al., 2005)

## Contextualizing Logic

Method to formally represent knowledge associated with a particular circumstance on which it has the intended meaning. (Alonso-Jiménez et al., 2005)

## Contingency Theoretic Software Development (CTSD)

A new model for MAS design using tenets from CT and Information Processing Theory (IPT). The CTSD design approach is focused on design for maintainability, a crucial requirement for complex, dynamic systems. (Durrett et al., 2005)

## Contingency Theory (CT)

**1:** A research branch of organizational theory that suggests that an organization's structure reflects its adaptation to the environment in which it operates. Hierarchical organizations operate best in stable, simple environments, while flat, team-based organizations are better adapted to dynamic, complex task environments. (Durrett et al., 2005) **2:** A meta-theory which argues that firm performance is defined by the environment-strategy-structure relationship, where the organization's strategy is contingent on the external environment and the organization structure is contingent on the firm's strategy. (Baker & Coltman, 2005) **3:** States that desired organizational outcomes—such as performance—are the consequence of "fit" or match between two or more factors (e.g., strategy, culture, structure, tasks, environment, and leadership style). The best way to organize depends upon the characteristics and the interplay between these factors. (Herschel, 2005)

## Continuation Pattern

A pattern in technical analysis that suggests, on the balance of probabilities, that price trend will continue in its current direction. (Vanstone & Tan, 2005)

## Continuing Education

**1:** Any form of learning provided for adults to supplement previous education or knowledge. (Ryan, 2005) **2:** The process of learning that continues beyond the formal years of education and/or outside the formal curriculum. (Hin & Subramaniam, 2005b) **3:** Education after professional education. A tool to support professional development in changing work life based on the principle of life-long learning. (Lammintakanen & Rissanen, 2005b)

## Continuous Animation

Animated objects deployed on a Web site to catch a visitor's attention to an advertising message or to attempt to entertain visitors. (Gao et al., 2006)

## Continuous Auditing

Type of auditing that produces audit results simultaneously, or a short period of time after, the occurrence of relevant events. (Garrity et al., 2005)

## Continuous Data

Data that can assume all values on the number line within their value range. The values are obtained by measuring. An example is temperature. (Yang & Webb, 2005)

## Continuous Quality Improvement (CQI)

A process that measures progress towards goals, using metrics and feedback from stakeholders for continuous improvement. (Moore et al., 2005)

## Continuous Query (CQ)

**1:** A query that is re-evaluated continuously. For example, the query "give me the most updated temperature" will return different readings depending on the current moment. Some continuous queries are also location dependent. For instance, the query "show me the nearest gas station" will continually execute a location-dependent query. An advanced query processing technique is needed in conjunction with moving object databases. (Leong, 2005a) **2:** The answer to a continuous query is produced over time, reflecting the stream data seen so far. Answers may be stored and updated as new data arrives or may be produced as data streams themselves. (Chatziantoniou & Doukidis, 2005)

## Continuous Query Language (CQL)

An expressive SQL-based declarative language developed by Stanford University's STREAM project for registering continuous queries against data streams. (Van Dyke et al., 2006)

## Continuous System

A system whose state variables show its behavior change continuously with respect to time. Hence, the behavior of the system is seen as changing continuously over time. Such systems are usually modeled using differential equations. (Vitolo & Coulston, 2005)

## Continuous Value Assumption (CVA)

A technique that allows the estimation of values inside a bucket by linear interpolation. (Buccafurri & Lax, 2005)

## Continuous-Time Signal

Defined along a continuum of time t and thus represented by continuous independent variables, for example xc(t). Continuous-time signals are often referred to as analog signals. (Jovanovic-Dolecek, 2005b)

## Contour Map

A line connecting points of equal elevation on topographic surface. The contour map depicts continuous distribution of the phenomena on earth surface. (Ali et al., 2005)

## Contract

A consistent and fault-tolerant execution of a program from one consistent state to another consistent state achieving the required precondition and ensuring that the post condition is met. (Murthy & Krishnamurthy, 2005b)

## Contract Right

The right that an individual has by reason of a valid contract that imposes duties on the other contracting party or parties. Enforceable under legal systems, but not the same as a citizen right. (Gilbert, 2005)

## Contract Theory

A theory dealing with aspects of negotiation and contracting between two or more parties. (Heucke et al., 2005)

## Contrast Set

Similar to an Emerging Pattern, it is also an itemset whose support differs across groups. The main difference is the method's application as an exploratory technique rather than as a classification one. (Butler & Webb, 2005)

## Contribution

A piece of knowledge about an issue. Represents a participant's view, idea, perspective, thought, or opinion. A contribution should be about 4-10 words in length, to ensure it is understandable when read, but not too wordy. (Shaw, 2006)

## Contribution-Oriented Pedagogy

**1:** An approach to learning in which students regularly contribute material they have found, created, or adapted to a common Web environment, where the contributions are assessed as part of the course requirements and where the contributions are further made use of by other students in further learning activities. (Collis & Moonen, 2005b) **2:** Learning scenario in which learners find or create products and make these available as learning resources to others. (Collis & Moonen, 2005a)

## Control Flow Graph

An abstract data structure used in compilers. It is an abstract representation of a procedure or program, maintained internally by a compiler. Each node in the graph represents a basic block. Directed edges are used to represent jumps in the control flow. (Tan & Zhao, 2005a)

## Control Group

**1:** A group of individuals who look like those in the treatment group but are not contacted. (Lo, 2005) **2:** The group in an experimental study that does not receive experimental treatment, but is similar to the group receiving the treatment in all relevant respects. (Fisher, 2005)

## Control Measure

A response taken by e-marketplace firms to manage, reduce, mitigate, and eliminate a risk. (Ratnasingam, 2005)

## Control Objectives for Information and Related Technology(ies) (COBIT)

**1:** Designed as an IT governance aid for understanding and managing the risks and benefits associated with information and related technology. It is intended that COBIT provide clear policy and good practice for IT governance throughout the organization. (Tassabehji, 2005b) **2:** An IT governance framework specified by the IT Governance Institute. The COBIT model describes the "control objectives" for 34 IT processes, as well as the management guidelines, implementation guidelines, and outcome measures for the processes. (Saha, 2006a)

## Control Packet

A control packet is sent in a separated channel and contains routing and scheduling information to be processed at the electronic level before the arrival of the corresponding data burst. Also called Burst Header Packet or Setup Message. (Rodrigues et al., 2005)

## Control Room

A special location in a plant where operators can monitor a process in great detail without having to physically be looking at it. This is particularly useful in dangerous environments. (Adam & Pomerol, 2005)

## Controlled Indexing

Objects may be indexed using controlled vocabularies, hierarchies, or classifications. (Gaedke et al., 2005)

## Controlled MA

A class of coordinated centralized or distributed collision-free multiple-access protocols. (Markhasin et al., 2005)

## Controlled Vocabulary

**1:** A limited menu of words from which metadata like captions must be constructed. (N.C. Rowe, 2005b) **2:** A set of standard terms that restricts synonyms to allow for maximum results when used with automated searching. (Leath, 2005)

## Controlling

Monitoring performance, comparing results to goals, and taking corrective action. Controlling is a process of gathering and interpreting performance feedback as a basis for constructive action and change. (Cragg & Suraweera, 2005)

## Controls

Countermeasures for vulnerabilities. (Tong & Wong, 2005a)

## Convenience

The quality of being suitable to one's comfort, purposes, or needs of shopping. (Shan et al., 2006a)

## Converged Network

A network that carries diverse types of traffic, such as real-time voice and video, Web browsing, traffic generated in grid computing, networked virtual environments, and so forth. (DaSilva, 2005)

## Convergence

**1:** In the ICT industry, convergence at the firm level means that firms cooperate to combine their different knowledge bases. Also industries, such as communications and media industries can be said to converge if focal actors leverage knowledge from two previously separated industries. (Blomqvist, 2005) **2:** The occurrence taking place with computing and telecommunications that emphasizes the preeminence of computer-based information and telecommunications networks. (Ochoa-Morales, 2005) **3:** The process of coming together or the state of having come together toward a common point. (M. Mitchell, 2005a) **4:** Uniting the functions of heterogeneous technologies with different features to form a homogeneous service bundle. (Blecker, 2006a)

## Convergence Factor

Measures the rate at which cross-platform populations increase as penetration of platforms increases. The convergence factor is derived from the penetrations of the three platforms multiplied by each other. (Pagani, 2005b)

## Convergence Index

An index representing the critical digital mass of consumers; it estimates the number of consumers likely to be present across all three platforms by the simple expedient of taking the population of each territory and multiplying it by the triple-platform penetration factor. (Pagani, 2005b)

## Converging/Diverging Gross Margin Analysis

A slope analysis tool used to plot actual sales and gross margin data for several periods in order to discern trends and likely outcomes. Measures operational efficiency or inefficiency. (Nugent, 2005)

## Converging Thinking Technique

One of several tools used during the convergent phases of Creative Problem Solving (CPS) to improve the evaluation and selection of the most relevant ideas, thoughts, or data. Pluses, potentials, and concerns; highlighting; and the evaluation matrix are some of the most common converging thinking techniques. (Torres-Coronas & Gascó-Hernández, 2005)

## Conversation Learning Community (CLC)

A kind of interactive and constructivist learning environment in which the instructor(s), learners, course materials, and links to remote experts and resources interact with each other. (Bodomo, 2005b)

## Conversational System

A system that can communicate with users through a conversational paradigm. (Lorenzi & Ricci, 2005)

**C**

## COO Cell/Origin

A positioning technique that determines a mobile user's location by identifying a cell in which the person's mobile device is registered. Also known as Cell Global Identity (CGI). (Fraunholz et al., 2005)

## Cookie

**1:** A message generated and sent by a Web server to a Web browser after a page has been requested from the server. The browser stores this cookie in a text file, and this cookie then is sent back to the server each time a Web page is requested from the server. (Nasraoui, 2005) **2:** A small amount of information that the Web site server requests the user's browser to save on the user's machine. (Sockel & Chen, 2005) **3:** A general mechanism that server-side connections (such as CGI scripts) can use to both store and retrieve information on the client side of the connection. The addition of a simple, persistent, client-side state significantly extends the capabilities of Web-based client/server applications. (Chim, 2006) **4:** Information, usually including a username, Internet address, and the current date and time, placed on the hard drive of a person using the World Wide Web by a Web site that one has visited. This information can be used to identify visitors who have registered or viewed the site, but also to report the visitor's unrelated Web activity, or worse, personal information stored by the user. (Friedman, 2005) **5:** A short string of text that is sent from a Web server to a Web browser when the browser accesses a Web page. The information stored in a cookie includes the cookie name, the unique identification number, the expiration date, and the domain. (Mullen, 2005) **6:** A string of text that a Web browser sends to you while you are visiting a Web page. It is saved on your hard drive, and it saves information about you or your computer. The next time you visit this Web site, the information saved in this cookie is sent back to the Web browser to identify you. (T. Stern, 2005) **7:** A text file created by a Web server and stored on a user's hard disk that contains data about a Web site that has been visited. (Szewczak, 2005)

## Cooperation

**1:** A group of people working on a common global task. (Villemur & Drira, 2006) **2:** Cooperative groups work together on group projects in ways that do not necessarily result in high-quality interaction, and new products and knowledge. A typical cooperative strategy is to divide up the work among the members and stitch the various contributions together at the end of the project. (Ingram, 2005) **3:** Group effort characterized by individuals in a group dividing the work so that each member of the group completes a portion of the project. (Ingram & Hathorn, 2005b) **4:** Acting together, in a coordinated way at work or in social relationships, in the pursuit of shared goals, the enjoyment of the joint activity, or simply furthering the relationship. (Sala, 2005b) **5:** Occurs when one species works with another in order to achieve an outcome beneficial to one or both. Proto-cooperation is the situation in which both benefit by the cooperation, but can survive without it. Mutualism occurs when each benefits and cannot otherwise survive. Commensalism occurs when two species habitually live together, one species being benefited by this arrangement and the other unharmed by it. (Tatnall & Davey, 2005)

## Cooperative Agent

Usually each agent participating in an agent system does not solve the whole problem by itself, but only a small subproblem for which it has the required competence. By means of cooperation with other agents, the whole problem is finished. While cooperating, an agent has to bid for solving some aspect of the problem or negotiates with other agents for the distribution of tasks. (Barolli & Koyama, 2005b)

## Cooperative Information System

A set of geographically distributed information systems that cooperate on the basis of shared objectives and goals. (Marchetti, Mecella, Scannapieco, & Virgillito, 2005)

## Cooperative Learning

**1:** A structure of interaction designed to facilitate the accomplishment of a specific end product or goal through people working together in groups. (Berg, 2005f) **2:** A learning situation in which students work together in small groups and receive rewards or recognition based on their group's performance. (Sala, 2005b) **3:** Learning where students are required to work in small groups, usually under the direct guidance of the instructor, who may set specific tasks and objectives for each session. (McInnerney & Roberts, 2005)

## Cooperative Marketing

The act of working together to conduct activities associated with buying and selling products or services. (Hornby, 2005)

## Coopetition

**1:** A situation where organizations, usually SMEs, are cooperating with each other and at the same time they are also competing against each other. (Mason et al., 2006) **2:** Simultaneous existence and relevance of cooperation and competition. (Loebbecke & Angehrn, 2006)

## Coopetive Network

A structured network of N organizations that are in simultaneous competition and cooperation (e.g., the VISA network). This network type is characterized by a decentralized structure, high competition, and a common scope of operations among members. (Priestley, 2006)

## Coordinate System

A reference system used to gauge horizontal and vertical distances on a planimetric map. It is usually defined by a map projection, a spheroid of reference, a datum, one or more standard parallels, a central meridian, and possible shifts in the x- and y-directions to locate x, y positions of point, line, and area features (e.g., in ARC/INFO GIS system, a system with units and characteristics defined by a map projection). A common coordinate system is used to spatially register geographic data for the same area. (Al-Hanbali & Sadoun, 2006)

## Coordination

**1:** Enabling and controlling the cooperation among members of a group of human or software-distributed agents. It can be considered as software glue for groupware tools, including architectural and behavioral issues. Coordination includes several synchronization and management services. (Villemur & Drira, 2006) **2:** The act of working together harmoniously. It consists of the protocols, tasks, and decision-making mechanisms designed to achieve concrete actions between interdependent units. (Daassi & Favier, 2006) **3:** The activity and effort associated with the information processing tasks of an organization. (Nissen & Levitt, 2006)

## Coordination of Commitments

The actions by humans leading to the completion of work. Coordination is described in terms of contracts and promises consisting of recurring loops of requesting, making, and fulfilling commitments. (Janssen, 2005)

## Coordination of Tasks

The management of dependencies between tasks. (Janssen, 2005)

## Coordination Theory

Assumes that the introduction and use of information technology will modify both the structure of the interaction between human agents and the overall organization of work. Organizations should understand the nature of coordination, establish what kinds of structures of organizations already exist, and discover the appropriate coordination processes. (Nichols & Chen, 2006)

## Coordination Within a Supply Chain

Occurs when the decisions made at different stages of the chain maximize the total supply chain's profitability. When a party makes a decision that maximizes its own local profitability, a lack of coordination can occur in the supply chain, as that decision may not be in the best interest of the entire chain. (Abraham & Leon, 2006)

**CoP:** See *Community of Practice.*

## Copper Line

The main transmission medium used in telephony networks to connect a telephone or other apparatus to the local exchange. Copper lines have relatively narrow bandwidth and limited ability to carry broadband services unless combined with an enabling technology such as ADSL. (Chochliouros et al., 2005c)

## Copresence

**1:** Copresence can only take place with a system where you have the sense of being in another place or environment other than the one you are physically in, and being there with another person. (Champion, 2006a) **2:** The coming together of people (face-to-face), people with objects (face-to-object), or people with places (face-to-place) in time and space. (Jain & Lyons, 2005)

## Copyleft

**1:** A non-exclusive, publicly accorded legal license backed by copyright law that permits derivative works from the copyright holder's licensed works, on the condition that licensees relicense their works to the public under a similarly liberal copyleft. (Okoli & Carillo, 2006) **2:** A term coined by Richard Stallman, leader of the free software movement and creator of the General Public License, or GPL. The key tenet of the GPL, which copyleft describes, is that software licensed under it can be freely copied, distributed, and modified. Hence, this software is copyleft, or the opposite of copyright. It insures that there are no protections or restrictions when copyright insures the opposite. (St.Amant & Still, 2005) **3:** Provision in the GNU General Public License that forces any derived work based on software covered by the GPL to be covered by the GPL; that is, the author of a derived work must make

**C**

all source code available and comply with the terms of the GPL. (Fleming, 2005b)

## Copyright

**1:** A legal term describing rights given to creators for their literary and artistic works. See World Intellectual Property Organization at www.wipo.int/about-ip/en/copyright.html. (Lowry, Grover, et al., 2005) **2:** The bundle of rights that control the copying and use of original works fixed in tangible form. The details of the exact rights granted, their duration, and their ownership all vary between different jurisdictions, but in its simplest form, copyright allows creators of original works control over whether or not their work is copied (either directly or through a derived work) and under what circumstances, including whether or not it is published or made available to the public. In most countries copyright comes into existence automatically when a work is fixed in some tangible form and is not conditional on any notice or formal process. The rights that are granted under copyright can be separated, licensed, sold, or waived entirely at the discretion of the owner (except moral rights in some countries). (Marshall, 2005) **3:** Protected right in many jurisdictions that controls ownership over any material of a creative nature originated by an individual or organization. (Fleming, 2005b) **4:** The exclusive right given to the creator of an intellectual work of text, audio, video, or software to restrict and control how their work and its derivatives are distributed or exploited for financial or other benefit. (Okoli & Carillo, 2006)

## Copyright Protection

A mechanism to ensure that no additional replication takes place if the entity/work is sold or licensed with a fixed number of copies. (Sattar & Yu, 2006)

## CORBA: See *Common Object-Request Broker Architecture.*

## Core

The main domain (focus) of a particular community pf practice. It is the common interest that is the driving force behind the formation of a Community of Practice. (Ray, 2006)

## Core Competency

Organizational capabilities or strengths—what an organization does best. (Petska & Berge, 2005)

## Core Group

The repository of knowledge, influence, and power in an organization. (Partow-Navid & Slusky, 2005)

## Core Knowledge

A highly structured, fact-based curriculum based on the work of E.D. Hirsch. (Glick, 2005b)

## Corporate Communications

The use by organizations of technology infrastructure and software solutions that empower them to create and deliver communication messages, both internally among employees and externally (outside the organization), to support their business needs and goals; operationally less costly. (Nandavadekar, 2005)

## Corporate E-Image

An overall impression held of an e-vendor by its customers at a particular point in time. This, in turn, is the net result of consumers' experiences with an organization, both online and off-line, and from the processing of information on the attributes that constitute functional indicators of image. (Yeo & Chiam, 2006)

## Corporate Information Factory (CIF)

A logical architecture with the purpose of delivering business intelligence and business management capabilities driven by data provided from business operations. (Yao et al., 2005)

## Corporate I.Q.

An enterprise's capability of connectivity (internal link and link with its partners), sharing (data and information shared among its personnel and its partners), and structuring (ability to extract knowledge from information and raw data). (Joia, 2005)

## Corporate Knowledge

The knowledge owned by an organization—its databases, technology, beliefs, culture, structure, processes, and procedures. The organization has access to, but does not own, the knowledge of employees, and through research acquires knowledge of the external environment. (Mitchell, 2005a)

## Corporate Memories and Narrative Documents

Knowledge is one of the most important assets of an enterprise, on the condition that it could be controlled, shared, and reused in an effective way. The core of any commercial/industrial organization can then be conceived under the form of a general and shared "corporate memory," that is, of an online, computer-based storehouse of expertise, experience, and documentation about all the strategic aspects of the organization. Given that this corporate knowledge is mainly represented under the form of narrative documents, the possibility of having at one's disposal tools for an effective management of these documents becomes an essential condition for the concrete setup and for the "intelligent" exploitation of non-trivial corporate memories. (Zarri, 2006c)

## Corporate Performance Management (CPM)

Enterprise Performance Management (EPM) is sometimes used as an umbrella term that describes the methodologies, metrics, processes, and systems used to monitor and manage an enterprise's business performance. CPM provides management with an overall perspective on the business. (Møller, 2005)

## Corporate Portal/Corportal

An online corporate Web site based on the model of an enterprise information portal. An enterprise information portal acts as a single gateway to a company's information and knowledge base for employees, and sometimes its customers and business partners as well. (Ruhi, 2006)

## Corporate Semantic Web or Organizational Semantic Web

Semantic Web at the scale of a limited organization (e.g., a company, an institution, a community). It is composed of resources, ontologies, and ontology-based semantic annotations. (Dieng-Kuntz, 2006)

## Corporate University

A university-style campus set up by a company to provide tailored learning, training, and development activities for its staff. Corporate universities typically offer qualifications at various levels. (Gordon & Lin, 2005)

## Corporeal Mobility

Bodily movement between places such as by car, rail, or foot. (Jain & Lyons, 2005)

## Corpus

Any systematic collection of speech or writing in a language or variety of a language. A corpus is often large and diverse, and can be classified according to contexts or styles tagged and indexed for specific features. (Ahmad & Al-Sayed, 2006)

## Correction Symbol

A symbol used to indicate a specific grammatical error. (Wu & Chen, 2005)

## Corrective Feedback

Visual, auditory, or tactile indications that the student stated the incorrect response. This type of feedback supplies the correct response, reteaches skills, and retests student learning. It also includes some type of encouragement, such as "Try again!" (Lazarus, 2005a)

## Correlation

**1:** Amount of relationship between two variables, how they change relative to each other, range: -1 to +1. (Morantz, 2005) **2:** Describes the strength or degree of linear relationship. That is, correlation lets us specify to what extent the two variables behave alike or vary together. Correlation analysis is used to assess the simultaneous variability of a collection of variables. For instance, suppose one wants to study the simultaneous changes with age of height and weight for a population. Correlation analysis describes how the change in height can influence the change in weight. (Katsaros & Manolopoulos, 2005b)

## Correlation Coefficient

A statistical method of measuring the strength of a linear relationship between two variables. (Benrud, 2005)

## Correspondence Course

**1:** A course in which instruction and assessment are conducted through the postal mail. (Lazarus, 2005b) **2:** Am education course typically offered via postal service. (Schifter, 2005)

## Correspondence Education

**1:** Delivery of class lessons by mail. (Witta, 2005) **2:** The form of distance education that is paper based; communication between teacher and students is by correspondence, not face-to-face. (Rogers & Howell, 2005)

## Corrupted Party

A party that participates in a protocol while under the control of the adversary. (Lindell, 2005)

## Cosine Measure

The vector angle between two documents that is used as a measure of similarity. (Chang, 2005)

## Cost Center

Administrative unit of an institution identified in terms of its responsibility for a given set of costs (rather than identified in terms of its functions per se). Cost center costing looks at aggregate charges to individual units rather than costs for particular activities which, per ABC costing, may be distributed across numerous cost centers. (Fisher, 2005)

## Cost Effectiveness

The quality principle that assures the institutional mission is conveyed online, affordably for the institution and for learners. (Moore et al., 2005)

## Cost-Benefit Study

A kind of policy study that aims to identify the ratio of costs to benefits for a given activity or set of activities, and so indicate whether the benefits merit the costs. (Fisher, 2005)

## Cost-Effectiveness Study

A kind of policy study that aims to identify the ratio of costs to effectiveness for a given set of alternative activities or interventions, and to indicate whether that ratio is more favorable for one alternative or another. (Fisher, 2005)

## Cost-Sensitive Classification

The error of a misclassification depends on the type of the misclassification. For example, the error of misclassifying Class 1 as Class 2 may not be the same as the error of misclassifying Class 1 as Class 3. (Zhou & Wang, 2005)

**COTS:** See *Commercial Off-the-Shelf.*

## Council for Higher Education Agency (CHEA)

A private, nonprofit national organization. It is the largest institutional higher education membership organization in the United States with approximately 3,000 colleges and universities. (Rhoten, 2006b)

## Council of Regional Organizations in the Pacific (CROP)

An organization comprising 10 regional inter-governmental agencies established to promote harmonization and collaboration between member programs, and to avoid duplication of effort and resources. Member agencies are the Pacific Community (formerly the South Pacific Commission), the Forum Fisheries Agency (FFA), the South Pacific Regional Environment Program (SPREP), the South Pacific Applied Geoscience Commission (SOPAC), the Pacific Island Development Program (PIDP), the South Pacific Tourism Organization (SPTO), the University of the South Pacific (USP), the Fiji School of Medicine (FSchM), the South Pacific Board for Educational Assessment (SPBEA), and the Forum Secretariat which acts as CROP's permanent chair. (Hassall, 2005)

## Country Code Top-Level Domain (ccTLD)

The TLD associated to a country and corresponding to its ISO3166 code. Differently from gTLD, these domains are exclusive of countries. (Maggioni & Uberti, 2005)

## Coupling

**1:** A measure of strength of association established by the communication link between two objects. (Polgar, 2005b) **2:** Used to measure the extent to which interdependencies exist between software modules: the higher the interdependencies, the higher the coupling. It implies that if you want to reuse one component, you will also have to import all the ones with which it is coupled. (Wan et al., 2006)

## Coupling Mode

The mode specifying the transactional relationship between a rule's triggering event, the evaluation of its condition, and the execution of its action. (Cilia, 2005)

## Course Applicability System (CAS)

A Web-based planning tool for academic programs and transfer. Developed and licensed by Miami University of Ohio. (Langer, 2005)

## Course Content

The main themes covered in a course. (Martz & Reddy, 2005)

## Course Design

Decisions regarding objectives and the most effective methods of ensuring that students accomplish the objectives. (C. Cavanaugh, 2005)

## Course Design and Development

Comprises all activities concerned with the planning, preparation, and production of student's study materials. (Naidu, 2005b)

## Course Development

The actual production of the software version of a course for online delivery and the supporting instructional materials. Faculty involved in the development of online courses are often required to have technology-specific knowledge and skills—digitizing, converting file formats, operation of specific software programs, and programming. (Sales, 2005)

## Course Development Tools

Software with high executive performance, good flexibility, easy utility, runtime softness, and so forth, suitable for the implementations of online Web courses. (Y.J. Zhang, 2005b)

## Course Management

Includes the ability to share materials and modules across course containers, the ability to edit comments and to track changes on learners' documents, and the ability to monitor and access learners' e-learning performance. In short, course management offers instructors the ability to electronically maintain and manage class rosters, distribute course materials, administer online exams, and communicate with learners. (Xu & Wang, 2006)

## Course Management Software

Instructional technology software packages created for educational use, primarily as course support or as a vehicle for online courses. Groupware features include messaging tools, conferencing tools, and information management and data resources. (Ferris & Minielli, 2005)

## Course Management System (CMS)

**1:** A server-based program that provides an easy-to-use tool for online course development, course delivery, and course management. Well-known providers such as WebCT and Blackboard offer these bundled, off-the-shelf online learning environment systems. (Cooper, 2005) **2:** Computer software system that provides a course shell with a number of integrated tools, which may include chat software, a threaded discussion board, online grade books, online testing, and other classroom functions. (Gregory, 2005) **3:** A software program that functions as an online classroom and can be used to deliver online instruction. Popular course management systems include Blackboard, Moodle, and WebCT. (Baker & Schihl, 2005) **4:** A software-based system for managing the development and delivery of online courses and programs, and managing student progress over the Internet. (Gold, 2005) **5:** Also known as "learning management software or system," this has proliferated in the last few years. There are both proprietary and open source CMSs now available to colleges and universities. Their goal is to integrate many of the functions associated with offering and managing an online course, so students and faculty members have only one program to use. (Johnstone, S.M., 2005) **6:** An integrated course environment (e.g., WebCT, Blackboard) that includes components such as e-mail, discussion group, chat, grade book for delivery, and management of instruction. (Hazari, 2006) **7:** An integrated learning tool or package that facilitates the tracking and monitoring of student online learning in a technology setting. (Bonk et al., 2005)

## Course Map

Graphical image that provides a pictorial representation of the course syllabus to allow for easy conversion from face-to-face to online delivery. (Etter & Byrnes, 2005)

## Course Partnership

Course-based industry-university partnerships, where a course is designed so that the concepts and theory discussed in class are applied in team course projects geared at solving immediate problems at the company partner. (Kock, 2005)

## Course Web Environment

A course management system or similar system offering integrated facilities for organization, contribution, collaboration, and communication for those associated with a particular course. (Collis & Moonen, 2005b)

## Course-Level Attrition vs. Program-Level Attrition

Attrition should be understood on two different levels—attrition on a course level and attrition on an entire degree program level. Course-level attrition includes no-shows, cancelled-outs, and course-withdrawals. Program-level attrition includes non-starters, failed-outs, transferred-outs, skip-outs, stop-outs, and drop-outs. Most 'drop-out' research studies reported in the literature deal with attrition on a course level. (Chyung, 2005)

## Course-Material Structure

As the course materials can be stored in XML (extensible markup language) format, which offers a tree-like or hierarchical structure, the prevailing relationships inside the course materials are of parent-to-child, which facilitates easier addition or removal of the course-material nodes or documents. Through techniques like Synchronized Media Integration Language (SMIL), multimedia data can not only be played on the Internet, but can also run in a synchronized manner. (Leung & Li, 2005)

**C**

**Course-Withdrawal**
The act of a student who withdraws from a course after the official drop-out deadline. (Chyung, 2005)

**Courseware**
Any type of instructional or educational course delivered via a software program or over the Internet. (Sánchez-Segura et al., 2005)

**Courseware Technology**
The set of tools and packages that facilitate student learning either as individuals or as members of groups. (Bonk et al., 2005)

**Covariance Matrix**
The square n x n of which the entries are the pairwise correlations of the variables of a random vector of length n; the (i,j)th entry is the correlation between the ith and the jth variables. (Zelasco et al., 2005)

**Cover Story**
A lie that is used to hide the existence of high classified data. (Gabillon, 2005)

**Cover Work**
The host media in which a message is to be inserted or embedded. (K. Chen, 2005)

**Cover-Medium**
A medium that does not contain any message. (Lou et al., 2006)

**Covering Constraint**
A constraint that states that the entity types that compose a category, taken together, contain all the elements of the category. (Mani & Badia, 2005)

**Covert Channel**
**1:** An unintended communications path that can be used to transfer information in a manner that violates the security policy. (Gabillon, 2005) **2:** A channel that is not meant to route information, but nevertheless does. (Haraty, 2005b)

**CPE:** See *Customer Premise Equipment.*

**CPFR:** See *Collaborative Planning, Forecasting, and Replenishment.*

**CPM:** See *Corporate Performance Management.*

**CPN:** See *Capacity Provisioning Network.*

**CPS:** See *Creative Problem Solving.*

**CQ:** See *Continuous Query.*

**CQI:** See *Continuous Quality Improvement.*

**CQL:** See *Continuous Query Language.*

**CR:** See *Computed Radiography.*

**Crackers**
Coined in the 1980s by hackers wanting to distinguish themselves from someone who intentionally breaches computer security for profit, malice, or because the challenge is there. Some breaking-and-entering has been done ostensibly to point out weaknesses in a security system. (Tassabehji, 2005a)

**Craft/Alchemy**
The intuitive and holistic grasp of a body of knowledge or skill relating to complex processes, often without the basis of rational explanation. (Nicholls, 2006)

**Crawler/Spider**
**1:** A program that automatically scans various Web sites and collects Web documents from them. It follows the links on a site to find other relevant pages and is usually used to feed pages to search engines. (Hu, Yang, Lee, et al., 2005) **2:** Program that downloads and stores Web pages. A crawler starts off with the Uniform Resource Locator (URL) for an initial page, extracts any URLs in it, and adds them to a queue to scan recursively. (Fernández & Layos, 2005)

**CRC:** See *Cyclic Redundancy Check, Complementary Resource Combination.*

**Creation**
**1:** An interaction between individuals that includes the exchange of tacit and explicit knowledge. (Lindsey, 2006) **2:** The ability and opportunity for communities to create and publish their own online content that actively reflects their own position and that is inherently counter-hegemonic. (Williamson, 2005)

## Creative Abrasion

The meeting of minds on common ground to explore and negotiate different opinions and, as a result, generate new ideas. (Chua, 2006)

## Creative Idea Generation

The production and development of original and useful ideas. Creative idea generation is a key activity in problem-solving groups. (Klein, 2005)

## Creative Learning

A type of learning that improves the ability to be creative and to develop original, diverse, or elaborate ideas. (Sala, 2005b)

## Creative Observation

A phenomenon that pertains to Field Creation. This form of observation involves conventional notions of participant observation, with one important difference: that which is being observed has, in fact, been created by the observer, either alone or in conjunction with collaborators. See *Co-Construction*. (Forte, 2005)

## Creative Performance

High level of capability in an idea or solution, applied to solve a problem in an imaginative way, resulting in effective action. Environmental factors such as autonomy and freedom, challenge, clear direction, diversity/flexibility/tension, support for creativity, trust, and participative safety directly affect the creative performance within work teams. (Torres-Coronas & Gascó-Hernández, 2005)

## Creative Problem Solving (CPS)

A systematic process model to solve problems and to harness creativity. Its six steps include objective-finding, data-finding, problem-finding, idea-finding, solution-finding, and acceptance-finding. Each step has a divergent and convergent phase. During the divergent phase, a free flow of ideas is elicited. Convergent phases involve the evaluation and selection of the ideas with the greatest potential or relevancy. The defer-judgment rule separates idea generation from idea evaluation. (Torres-Coronas & Gascó-Hernández, 2005)

## Creative Workflow

Workflow that is more discovery-oriented, hence more volatile and browse intensive. This workflow is characterized by the need to do many interactive searches and temporarily store candidate assets until a final decision can be made. (Subramanian, 2005)

## Creativity

**1:** The ability to generate or recognize ideas, alternatives, or possibilities that may be useful in solving problems, communicating with others, and entertaining ourselves and others. (Sala, 2005b) **2:** The production of something new or original that is useful; the act of creating recombining ideas or seeing new relationships among them. Creativity is usually defined in terms of either a process or a product and at times has also been defined in terms of a kind of personality or environmental press. These are four Ps of creativity: process, product, person, and press. (Torres-Coronas & Gascó-Hernández, 2005) **3:** In the context of discovery, creativity is the ability to generate or recognize ideas and alternatives that might be useful in solving problems. There are several aspects of creativity, including creative product or value, creative person/people, creative environment, creative symbols, and creative process. (Aurum, 2005)

## Creativity-Enhancing System

An information system designed to offer creative tools to help users formulate problems and perform other creative tasks in decision making. (Forgionne, 2005)

## Credibility

**1:** A characteristic of information sources that influences message persuasiveness, attitudes toward the information source, and behaviors relevant to message content, consisting of two primary attributes: expertise and trustworthiness. (Danielson, 2006c) **2:** The quality of being believable or trustworthy. (Wong, 2005)

## Credit

Delivery of a value in exchange of a promise that this value will be paid back in the future. (de Carvalho et al., 2005)

## Credit Scoring

A numerical method of determining an applicant's loan suitability based on various credit factors, such as types of established credit, credit ratings, residential and occupational stability, and ability to pay back loan. (de Carvalho et al., 2005)

**CRISP-DM:** See *Cross-Industry Standard Process for Data Mining*.

C

## Criteria

Each goal within the alternative assessment that ties into the instructional objectives of the lesson, unit, or course. (B.L. MacGregor, 2005)

## Criterion

The expressed characteristics of an interactive system. The criterion must be valuable, and it denies or supports options. (Lacaze et al., 2006)

## Criterion Path

**1:** A representation of an "ideal path" to go through a specific learning environment. It specifies for each possible step in the program what the most ideal subsequent steps are. (Clarebout et al., 2005b) **2:** A representation of an "ideal path" to go through a specific learning environment. It specifies for each possible step in the program the most ideal subsequent steps. (Clarebout et al., 2005a)

## Critical Business Process

An operation, or group of operations, within an organization that is key to its effectiveness. (Drake, 2006)

## Critical Digital-Mass Index

Measures the extent to which digital platforms (digital TV, PC, Internet access, and mobile phones) are present in a given territory. It is created for a territory by adding together the digital TV penetration, mobile phone penetration, and PC Internet penetration. (Pagani, 2005b)

## Critical Failure Factor (CFF)

The limited number of areas which, without careful monitoring of these areas, may lead to a failure of a system. (Peterson & Kim, 2005)

## Critical Incident

**1:** An observed or experienced episode in which things go surprisingly well or badly. (Carroll et al., 2005) **2:** Significant positive or negative incidents that can be used to evaluate behavioral data and system performance. (Neale et al., 2005)

## Critical Knowledge Area

A specific body of knowledge, or key resource-capability, that is unique to a firm and resides at the core of the business mission and value proposition to its customers. (Cepeda-Carrión, 2006)

## Critical Mass

**1:** A point at which a sufficient number of individuals have adopted an interactive communication technology to cause a rapid acceleration in its diffusion. (Chen & Lou, 2005) **2:** A subset of the collective that makes the majority of the contributions to the production and maintenance of the public good. (Wasko & Teigland, 2006b) **3:** A generative metaphor derived from the natural sciences (in particular nuclear physics) that describes a situation in which a chain reaction is self-sustaining. This metaphor acts as an aide, rather than a proximal cause, to assist the identification of contributing factors in humanities-based case studies. (Gibbs et al., 2005) **4:** The minimal number of adopters of an interactive innovation for the ongoing rate of adoption to be self-sustaining. (Gibbs et al., 2005)

## Critical Pedagogy

Focuses on political and economic issues of schooling such as the representation of texts and construction of subjective states of mind in the student; when applied to media education, it begins with an assessment of contemporary culture and the function of media within it. (Berg, 2005a)

## Critical Realism

**1:** Asserts that the study of the social world should be concerned with the identification of the structures and mechanisms through which events and discourses are generated. (Carlsson, 2005) **2:** One branch of social science that developed in the 1970s and which poses fertile intellectual challenges to current understanding of communities, organizations, and other social structures. It argues that without the concept of a social structure, we cannot make sense of persons as any predicate which applies to individuals, apart from a direct physical description, and presupposes a social structure behind it. Though we need the notion of a social structure, the only way to acknowledge it is through the social practices that it incarnates and reifies, which in turn are embedded in the actions of its members. A social structure is not visible or witnessable, only its social practices are. Though implicit and invisible, structures are enabling or constraining, as they open up or else severely restrict the actions of its members. However, structures are not simply a medium for social practices, as these practices also change and influence the structures themselves. This implies that structures are both a medium and a product of its practices. Social structures are reproduced and transformed by the practices of its members. Thus individuals have an agency capacity to interfere back, and thus promote social change—not isolated individuals, however, but units and collectivities of individuals. Individuals are persons, and their acts are situated in a world constituted by past and present human activity, thus a humanized natural and social world. Because social structures are incarnate in the practices of its members, this means that they do not exist independently of the conceptions of the persons whose activities constitute, and thus reproduce or transform them. It is because persons have beliefs, interests, goals, and practical and tacit knowledge, not necessarily cognitively available, acquired in their early stages as members of a society, that they do what they do and thus sustain, or transform, the structures to which they belong. Critical realism thus proposes a transformational model of social activity. It states that reality exists independently of our knowledge about it, and it takes science as a social practice, and scientific knowledge as a social product. Communities of practice theory implicitly incorporates a critical realism perspective. (Nobre, 2006a) **3:** The careful or critical application of the scientific approach to the social sciences. (Dobson, 2005)

## Critical Reflection

Questioning of moral, ethical, and equity issues that relate directly or indirectly to institutional and broader social and political contexts of schooling, and reflection oriented toward development of emancipatory strategies to resolve inequities identified; stems from a belief system that education can serve as an agent for social change, and teachers are professionals constantly engaged in the evaluation and resolution of a large number of competing variables using poorly understood processes (not a set of specific, identifiable technical skills). (Wieseman, 2005b)

## Critical Research

Critique of the status quo through the exposure of what are believed to be deep-seated, structural contradictions within social systems. (Trauth, 2005b)

## Critical Stance

Any approach to an accepted system that intentionally highlights issues of power structures supported by it, often emancipatory in nature and always political. (Kettley, 2006b)

## Critical Success Factor (CSF)

**1:** One of several factors that indicate the few key areas of activity in which favorable results are absolutely necessary for the manager to succeed. (Colmenares & Otieno, 2005) **2:** A methodology for managing projects and firms that concentrates on the areas where things must go right if the endeavor is to flourish. (Adam & Pomerol, 2005) **3:** One of a limited number of areas in which results, if they are satisfactory, will ensure successful competitive performance for the organization. (Peterson & Kim, 2005)

## Critical Theory

The branch of social theory, grounded on Kant and pursued by the Frankfurt School. The best known contemporary critical theorist is Jurgen Habermas (1929- ). (Clarke, 2006)

## Critical Thinking

**1:** Encompasses the belief that the function of the researcher is to provide warnings about the fallibility of current orthodoxies by pointing to the power and politics implicit in the process of knowledge creation and utilization. (Land, Nolas, et al., 2006) **2:** In academic contexts, this phrase usually refers to complex intellectual reasoning that questions assumptions, and seeks to assess evidence and examine claims made by others. More simply, it can also refer to logical thinking based on facts and evidence. (Kukulska-Hulme, 2005)

## Critical Value Activity

One of several value activities that an organization must execute satisfactorily to ensure successful performance. (Jeffcoate, 2005)

**CRM:** See *Customer Relationship Management.*

**CROP:** See *Council of Regional Organizations in the Pacific.*

## Cross and Edge Points

A cross point is an image pixel in the thinned image having at least three eight-neighbors, while an edge point has just one eight-neighbor in the thinned image. (Chakravarty et al., 2005a)

## Cross-Border Linkage

An active connection, relation, or association between two or more institutions separated by a geographic distance or boundary. (Poda & Brescia, 2005)

**C**

## Cross-Classification of Maps

A method that overlays two thematic maps of binary attributes to come up with an output theme containing attributes of both the themes. (Ali et al., 2005)

## Cross-Correlation

The sum of the chip-by-chip products of two different sequences (codes). A measure of the similarity and interference between the sequences (or their delayed replicas). Orthogonal codes have zero cross-correlation when synchronized. (Iossifides et al., 2005)

## Cross-Cultural

A situation where individuals from different cultures interact with or exchange information with one another; interchangeable with the term "intercultural." (St.Amant, 2005c)

## Cross-Cultural Environment

The coexistence of more than one cultural influence in different segments of a society, or the simultaneous adoption of different cultural practices at work, social events, and family life. (Law, 2005)

## Cross-Cultural IT Management

Managing the IT function and its personnel in a globally distributed setting. (Trauth, 2005a)

## Cross-Culture Communication

A process of communicating among different cultures. (Targowski & Metwalli, 2005)

## Cross-Disciplinary

The merging of disciplines in an effort to discover emergent and interconnected processes, models, and frameworks. Similar terms are multidisciplinary, interdisciplinary, and transdisciplinary, each with slightly different connotations. (Schaffer & Schmidt, 2006)

## Cross-Disciplinary Knowledge

The degree to which team members from different disciplines learn and share knowledge as a result of working together on a project. Ideally, team members evolve from a discipline-centric view of working to a cross-disciplinary view, in which team members use models and terminology from other disciplines. (Schaffer & Schmidt, 2006)

## Cross-Industry Standard Process for Data Mining (CRISP-DM)

1: An industry and tool-neutral data-mining process model developed by members from diverse industry sectors and research institutes. (Nemati & Barko, 2005) 2: An initiative for standardizing the knowledge-discovery and data-mining process. (Swierzowicz, 2005)

## Cross-Media Adaptation

Conversion of one multimedia format into another one, for example, video to image or image to text. (Knight & Angelides, 2005)

## Cross-Site Scripting (XSS)

An application to trick users into thinking they are dealing with a normal Internet situation, but the real purpose is to gather data from them. (Friedman, 2005)

## Cross-Validation

Resampling method in which elements of the modeling set itself are alternately removed and reinserted for validation purposes. (Galvão et al., 2005)

## Crossover

In genetic algorithms, it is the process of combining features of a chromosome with other chromosome(s). (Guan, 2005e)

## Crossover with Non-Internet Media

Target audiences' needs could be met by combining the interactive tools available online with some of the targeted off-line information delivery vectors, such as telephone conferencing, videoconferencing, direct mail, and other media. (Kardaras & Karakostas, 2006)

## Crossposting

Posting the same message on multiple threads of discussion, without taking into account the relevance of the message or every discussion thread. (Gurău, 2006a)

## Crosstalk

Interference present in a signal propagating through a communication produced by other signals present at an adjacent channel. (Perez-Meana & Nakano-Miyatake, 2005)

## Cryptographic Data-Mining Techniques

Methods that encrypt individual data before running data-mining algorithms so that the final result is also available in an encrypted form. (Jha & Sural, 2005)

## Cryptography

**1:** A study of making a message secure through encryption. Secret key and public key are the two major camps of cryptographic algorithms. In secret key cryptography, one key is used for both encryption and decryption; in public key cryptography, two keys (public and private) are used. (K. Chen, 2005) **2:** Protecting information by transforming it into an unreadable format using a number of different mathematical algorithms or techniques. (Tassabehji, 2005a) **3:** The art of protecting information by encrypting it into an unreadable format, called cipher text. Only those who possess a secret key can decipher (or decrypt) the message into plain text. (Guan, 2005a) **4:** The conversion of data into secret codes for transmission over a public network to prevent unauthorized use. (Wang, Cheng, & Cheng, 2006)

**CS:** See *Computer Science.*

**CSC:** See *Computer Support Committee.*

**CSCL:** See *Computer-Supported Collaborative Learning.*

**CSCW:** See *Computer-Supported Collaborative/ Cooperative Work; Computer-Supported Cooperative Work.*

**CSF:** See *Critical Success Factor.*

**CSG:** See *Constructive Solid Geometry.*

**CSLC:** See *Customer Services Life Cycle.*

**CSMA:** See *Carrier-Sense Multiple Access.*

**CSS:** See *Content Scrambling System.*

**CT:** See *Category Theory; Computed Tomography; Contingency Theory; Collaborative Technology.*

**CTR:** See *Click-Through Rate.*

**CTSD:** See *Contingency Theoretic Software Development.*

**C2A:** See *Consumer-to-Administration.*

**C2C:** See *Consumer-to-Consumer.*

## Cube

**1:** A collection of data aggregated at all possible levels over the dimensions. (Deshpande & Ramasamy, 2005) **2:** A data structure of aggregated values summarized for a combination of preselected categorical variables (e.g., number of items sold and their total cost for each time period, region, and product). This structure is required for high-speed analysis of the summaries done in online analytical processing (OLAP). Also called a Multi-Dimensional Database (MDDB). (Nigro & González Císaro, 2005b) **3:** A group of data cells arranged by the dimensions of the data. Assigning a value to each dimension of a cube, the measure is obtained by a mapping from this assignment. (Pourabbas, 2005b) **4:** A multi-dimensional representation of data that can be viewed from different perspectives. (Bellatreche & Mohania, 2005)

## Cube Cell

Represents an association of a measure m with a member of every dimension. (Abdulghani, 2005a)

## Cubegrade

A 5-tuple (source, target, measures, value, delta-value) where source and target are cells; measures is the set of measures that are evaluated both in the source as well as in the target; value is a function, value: measures→R, that evaluates measure m∈measures in the source; and delta-value is a function, delta-value: measures→R, that computes the ratio of the value of m∈measures in the target versus the source (Abdulghani, 2005b)

## Cuboid

A group-by of a subset of dimensions, obtained by aggregating all tuples on these dimensions. (Abdulghani, 2005a)

## Cue

A clue to a psychological phenomenon, often nonverbal. (N.C. Rowe, 2006b)

## Cultural Algorithm

Another kind of evolutionary algorithm that adds a belief space to the usual population space from the genetic algorithms in order to improve the search. It is inspired from human societies and cultural evolution. (Lazar, 2005)

## Cultural Cognition Theory

A theory that frames the concept that culture profoundly influences the contents of thought through shared knowledge structures and ultimately impacts the design and development of interactive systems, whether software or Web sites. (Faiola, 2006)

### Cultural Function of a Telecenter

Set of processes that a telecenter as an open social system carries out to strengthen grassroot values and identity. ICT should facilitate multi-culturalism instead of pursuing the standardization of society. (Santos, 2005)

### Cultural Metadata

Metadata obtained from the analysis of corpora of textual information, usually from the Internet or other public sources (radio programs, encyclopedias, etc.). (Pachet, 2006)

### Cultural Readiness

The preparedness of an organization's culture of its people and processes (past and present) to facilitate or inhibit change. (Ash & Burn, 2006)

### Culturally Appropriate Content

Information, documents, and programs delivered to users via the Internet, broadcasting, or CD-ROM which express and respect the users' culture and interests. (Dyson, 2005)

### Culture

1: A set of multi-layered characteristics, beliefs, and values shared by a group of people that are consistently held over time. (Petter et al., 2005) 2: A societal manifestation influenced by traditions, religion, history, acceptable behavior, and many other factors. (Mandal et al., 2005) 3: A value-guided, continuous process of developing patterned human behavior within and across cultures and civilizations. (Targowski & Metwalli, 2005) 4: Common meaning and values of a group. Members of such a group share and use the accorded signs and roles as a basis for communication, behavior, and technology usage. Mostly, a country is used as a compromise to refer or define rules and values, and is used often as a synonym for user's culture. (Röse, 2006b) 5: Covers the pattern of basic assumptions accepted and used about behaviors, norms, and values within an organization. (Disterer, 2005) 6: Expresses shared beliefs and ritualized habits of social agents toward each other and their environment via artifacts and language. (Champion, 2006b) 7: The background set of assumptions and values that structure our existence and orient us through the events of our lives.

(Cagiltay et al., 2005) 8: Integrated system of spiritual, material, intellectual, and emotional features of society or a social group that encompasses, among other things, art and literature, lifestyles, ways of living together, value systems, traditions and beliefs, and artifacts. (M. Mitchell, 2005a) 9: Multiple definitions exist, including essentialist models that focus on shared patterns of learned values, beliefs, and behaviors, and social constructivist views that emphasize culture as a shared system of problem solving or of making collective meaning. The key to the understanding of online cultures—where communication is as yet dominated by text—may be definitions of culture that emphasize the intimate and reciprocal relationship between culture and language. (Macfadyen, 2006b) 10: The collective programming of the mind, which distinguishes the members of one group or category of people from another. (Limayem, 2005) 11: The ideals, values, symbols, and behaviors of human societies that create a distinctive identification. (Sharma & Mishra, 2005)

### Culture Gap

A gap of misunderstanding in the sense of two different organizational cultures that coexist in most organizations. The two cultures under discussion in the IT context are the culture of the IT profession and the culture of the rest of the organization. (Leonard, 2005)

### Culture-Oriented Design

Specific kind of user-oriented design that focuses on the user as a central element of development and also takes into account the cultural diversity of different target user groups. (Röse, 2006b)

### Cumulative Annual Growth Rate (CAGR)

The percent of growth from one annual period to the next. (Nugent, 2005)

### Cumulative Proportion Surviving

The cumulative proportion of cases surviving up to the respective interval. Because the probabilities of survival are assumed to be independent across the intervals, this probability is computed by multiplying out the probabilities of survival across all previous intervals. The resulting function is also called the survivorship or survival function. Chen, Oppenheim, et al., 2005)

### Current Cost

The cost of the network investment over time, considering issues like amortization. (Hackbarth et al., 2005)

## Current Document Version

The most recent version of a temporal document. Note that a deleted document has no current version. (Nørvåg, 2005)

## Current Efficiency

The percentage of the electrical current (drawn into the reduction cell) that is utilized in the conversion of raw materials (essentially alumina and aluminum fluoride) into the end product, aluminum. The remaining percentage is lost due to complex reactions in the production process and the physical nature of reduction cells. (Nicholls, 2006)

## Curriculum

**1:** A comprehensive overview of what students should learn, how they will learn it, what role the instructor is playing, and the framework in which learning and teaching will take place. (Partow-Navid & Slusky, 2005) **2:** The content, structure, and format of an educational course or program. (Kung-Ming, 2005)

## Curse of Dimensionality

**1:** Phenomenon that refers to the fact that, in high-dimensional spaces, data become extremely sparse and are far apart from each other. As a result, the sample size required to perform an accurate prediction in problems with high dimensionality is usually beyond feasibility. (Domeniconi & Gunopulos, 2005) **2:** The problems associated with information overload, when the number of dimensions is too high to visualize. (Viktor & Paquet, 2005) **3:** The sharp dependency on the space dimension experimented by any search algorithm on vector or metric spaces. (Chávez & Navarro, 2005) **4:** This expression is due to Bellman; in statistics, it relates to the fact that the convergence of any estimator to the true value of a smooth function defined on a space of high dimension is very slow. It has been used in various scenarios to refer to the fact that the complexity of learning grows significantly with the dimensions. (Ma & Li, 2005) **5:** The original term refers to the exponential growth of hyper-volume as a function of dimensionality. In information retrieval, it refers to the phenomenon that the performance of an index structure for nearest-neighbor search and e-range search deteriorates rapidly due to the growth of hyper-volume. (X. Wang, 2005)

## Curse of Dimensionality Effect

When the number of samples needed to estimate a function (or model) grows exponentially with the dimensionality of the data. (Viswanath et al., 2005)

## Customer

Refers to the entity that procures goods and services. (Barima, 2006a)

## Customer Attraction

The ability to attract customers at the Web site. (Forgionne & Ingsriswang, 2005)

## Customer/Client Touchpoints Value Chain

A value chain that an organization establishes to meet its clients/customers in order to provide services or obtain feedback and allow them to share their experiences. (Chuang, 2006)

## Customer Confusion

The difficulties and uncertainties encountered by customers when they have to make an optimal choice out a product assortment with large product variety. (Blecker & Abdelkafi, 2006)

## Customer Conversion Rate (CCR)

The percentage of Web site visitors who engage in an ultimate target action such as making a purchase. (Owen, 2006a)

## Customer Data Integration (CDI)

The people, processes, and technologies required to create and maintain a unique, complete, and accurate customer profile and make it available to all operational systems. (Van Dyke et al., 2006)

## Customer Experience

The target customer's overall outcome, which includes both results and image factors, after using a product or visiting a retail store or a Web site. (Roberts & Schwaab, 2006)

## Customer Knowledge

Knowledge derived through relationships from consumers, suppliers, partners, joint ventures and alliances, and competitors. It is knowledge located externally to the firm and is not owned by the organization. It can be composed of a combination of consumer knowledge, supply chain knowledge, joint venture specific knowledge, and so forth. This knowledge is created within a two-way flow of knowledge which creates value for both parties. (Paquette, 2006b)

## Customer Knowledge Management

The collective processes that a firm employs to manage the identification, acquisition, and internal utilization of customer knowledge. It is within these processes that an organization and its customers work together to combine existing knowledge to create new knowledge. It differs from managing internal knowledge as it must facilitate the flow of knowledge across an external boundary. (Paquette, 2006b)

### Customer Lifetime Value (CLV)

Consists of taking into account the total financial contribution (i.e., revenues minus costs) of a customer over his or her entire life of a business relationship with the company. (Gurău, 2005)

### Customer Loyalty

**1:** Because there is no existing ownership to service products, suppliers have to make a special effort to get long-standing customers. (Seitz, 2005) **2:** The ability to develop and maintain long-term relationships with customers by creating superior customer value and satisfaction. (Forgionne & Ingsriswang, 2005)

### Customer Loyalty Plan

A strategy for improving financial performance through activities that increase stickiness. (Forgionne & Ingsriswang, 2005)

### Customer Management Software

Software application that allows a company to interact with multiple customer segments and to send them personalized offers. (Gurău, 2006b)

### Customer Premise Equipment (CPE)

End-user equipment. (Nugent, 2005)

### Customer Profiling

**1:** Selecting customers you want to find, going after them, and keeping them. (Borders & Johnston, 2005) **2:** Usage of the Web site to get information about the specific interests and characteristics of a customer. (Seitz, 2005)

### Customer Relationship Management (CRM)

**1:** A core business strategy that promotes interactions, and creates and delivers value to targeted customers to improve customer satisfaction and customer retention at a profit. It is grounded in high-quality customer data and enabled by information technology. (Dholakia et al., 2005a) **2:** Application system that allows a company to manage its relationship with a customer, including sales, marketing, customer service, and support. (Feuerlicht & Vorisek, 2006)

**3:** Methodologies, softwares, and capabilities that help an enterprise manage customer relationships in an organized way. (Morabito & Provera, 2005) **4:** Refers to retaining and using information about customers in databases to develop customer loyalty and increase sales. (Bridges et al., 2006) **5:** Systems with technological tools related to the implementation of relationship marketing strategies. (Flavián & Guinalíu, 2006) **6:** The methodologies, software, and Internet capabilities that help a company manage customer relationships in an efficient and organized manner. (Nemati & Barko, 2005) **7:** The technology, services, and processes that connect an organization with its customers in the most reliable, efficient, and cost-effective manner while striving to create long-term, profitable relationships. (Van Dyke et al., 2006) **8:** The process of attracting, retaining, and capitalizing on customers. CRM defines the space where the company interacts with the customers. At the heart of CRM lies the objective to deliver a consistently differentiated and personalized customer experience, regardless of the interaction channel. (Pagani, 2005b) **9:** A term describing how a company interacts with its customers, gathers information about them (needs, preferences, past transactions), and shares these data within marketing, sales, and service functions. (Burke et al., 2005) **10:** Management, understanding, and control of data on the customers of a company for the purposes of enhancing business and minimizing the customers' churn. (Meo & Psaila, 2005) **11:** An approach that manages in an integrated manner all business processes that directly involve customers, in an effort to build long-term and sustainable relationships with customers. A CRM system is a central repository of customer information that records information from all contact points with customers, and generates "customer profiles" available to everyone who wishes to "know the customer." (Tarafdar, 2005) **12:** An approach that recognizes that customers are the core of the business and that a company's success depends on effectively managing its relationship with them. CRM is about locating and attracting customers, and thereby building long-term and sustainable relationships with them. (Y.D. Wang, 2005) **13:** An enterprise-wide strategy enabling organizations to optimize customer satisfaction, revenue, and profits, while increasing shareholder value through better understanding of customers' needs. (Rahman, 2005e)

### Customer Retention

The ability to retain customers and their allegiance to the Web site. (Forgionne & Ingsriswang, 2005)

## Customer Satisfaction

**1:** Based on the consumption, a consumer would be satisfied if perceptions match expectations or if confirmations are reached. (Hsu & Kulviwat, 2006) **2:** Measure or determination that a product/service meets a customer's expectations, considering requirements of both quality and service. (Markellou et al., 2006)

## Customer Services Life Cycle (CSLC)

**1:** A framework that describes the stages (requirements, acquisition, ownership, and retirement) that a customer goes through when purchasing and using a product or service. (Porter, 2006) **2:** Serving customers based on a process of four stages: requirements, acquisition, ownership, and retirement. Many companies are using the approach to harness the Internet to serve the customers. (Chen, Zhang, et al., 2005a)

## Customer-Based/Customized Products

A virtual organization provides the unique opportunity to provide their customers with highly specialized products as per their specific needs. This can be accomplished through outsourcing work to a separate organization or through the use of a virtually connected interorganizational node located closer to the customer. Either way, it becomes simple to add a function based on the customer's request and seamlessly integrate that function into the existing framework. (J. Lee, 2005)

## Customer-Centric Approach

Organizational strategy that aims to explore and understand customers' needs and motivations, and to restructure all organizational processes to provide superior value to consumers. (Gurău, 2006b)

## Customer-Centric Value Chain

The seller tailors its products to meet fast-changing consumer needs. (Jeffcoate, 2005)

## Customer-Supplier Perspective

Refers to the linked interrelation between the requirements (needs, wants, etc.) of the customer to the provision of these by the supplier to their mutual benefit. (Barima, 2006a)

## Customer-to-Customer (C2C)

In this method, participants bid for products and services over the Internet, such as in an online auction. See Consumer-to-Consumer. (Shih & Fang, 2006)

## Customerization

The personalization of a Web site. (Samuel & Samson, 2006)

## Customization

**1:** Fundamental characteristic of a Web site regarding personalization of information or tailoring special requirements from a specific user. (Almazán & Gil-García, 2006) **2:** Customizable applications are those applications that can adapt themselves to the context in which they execute; applications (in particular, Web applications) can be adapted to the user profile, the location, the network connection, and so forth. Building applications that can adapt themselves to the current context involve many different software and information representation problems. In the context of Web applications, we can adapt the application behavior to the user profile, we can change the hypermedia topology for different users' tasks, or we can adapt the user interface for different appliances. (Rossi & Schwabe, 2005) **3:** The adjustment of products or services to individual needs. Basic characteristics are implemented in the product or service and may be controlled by parameters. (Seitz, 2005)

## Customized Protocol

A specific set of treatment parameters and their values that are unique for each individual. Customized protocols are derived from discovered knowledge patterns. (Kusiak & Shah, 2005)

## Customization and Mass Customization

Customization is consumer-centric strategy that produces goods and services to meet an individual's needs and preferences. Customization in general induces higher costs than mass production does. Mass customization means customized production with the cost of mass production. Virtual community fosters mass customization in that it helps identify needs and preferences of a group of consumers through interactive discussion without increasing cost. (Wang, Wei, et al., 2006)

## Cutoff Frequencies

The frequencies that determine the pass-band (the frequencies that are passed without attenuation) and the stop-band (the frequencies that are highly attenuated). (Jovanovic-Dolecek, 2005c)

## Cut-Point

A value that divides an attribute into intervals. A cut-point has to be included in the range of the continuous attribute to discretize. A discretization process can produce none or several cut-points. Also called a split-point. (Muhlenbach & Rakotomalala, 2005)

**CV:** See *Computer Vision.*

**CVA:** See *Continuous Value Assumption.*

**CVE:** See *Common Vulnerabilities and Exposures.*

**CWA:** See *Closed-World Assumption.*

**Cyber Elite**
A section of the population who has the disposable income, knowledge, and language for exploiting the many possibilities presented by ICTs. (Mwesige, 2005)

**Cyber Ethics**
A branch of ethics that focuses on behaviors that are specifically related to information technology. (Artz, 2005a)

**Cyber Gambling**
Gambling that takes place using an interactive technology such as the Internet or digital television. (Brindley, 2006)

**Cyber Security**
Techniques used to protect the computer and networks from threats. (Thuraisingham, 2005)

**Cyber-Identity Theft**
The online or electronic acquisition of personal information with the purpose of utilizing such information for deceitful activity either on the Internet or off-line. (Close et al., 2006)

**Cyber-Societies**
The set of natural, artificial, and virtual agents connected and interacting with each others through natural and artificial infrastructures within virtual institutions. (Falcone & Castelfranchi, 2005)

**Cybercafé**
A café that makes available a number of personal computers that are connected to the Internet for the use of the general public. (Ajiferuke & Olatokun, 2005)

**Cyberculture**
As a social space in which human beings interact and communicate, cyberspace can be assumed to possess an evolving culture or set of cultures ("cybercultures") that may encompass beliefs, practices, attitudes, modes of thought, behaviors, and values. (Macfadyen & Doff, 2006)

**Cyberlanguage**
The collection of communicative practices employed by communicators in cyberspace, and guided by norms of cyberculture(s). (Macfadyen & Doff, 2006)

**Cyberloafing**
Any voluntary act of employees using their organization's Internet access during office hours to surf non-work-related Web sites for non-work purposes and to access non-work-related e-mail. (Mahatanankoon, 2005)

**Cybermediary**
An online company specializing in electronic transactions and digital intermediation. (Scarso et al., 2006)

**Cybersex**
**1:** The act of computer-mediated sex either in an online or virtual environment. Examples include two consenting adults engaging in an e-mail or real-time chat sex session. The advantages to this are that two people who are at opposite ends of the globe can maintain a relationship. (Griffiths, 2005) **2:** Two or more individuals using the Internet as a medium to engage in discourses about sexual fantasies. (Whitty, 2005)

**Cyberslacking**
The process of using the Internet to waste time during a workday, similar to how an employee might spend time in a colleague's office or on the telephone. (Urbaczewski, 2005)

**Cyberspace**
**1:** The term used to describe the range of information resources available through computer networks. (Stodel et al., 2005) **2:** The boundaryless virtual world accessed through computer networks, whether one's access device is fixed or mobile. (Galloway, 2006) **3:** The default or mandatory space in which the members of a virtual community interact. (Signoret, 2006) **4:** While the "Internet" refers more explicitly to the technological infrastructure of networked computers that make

worldwide digital communications possible, "cyberspace" is understood as the virtual "places" in which human beings can communicate with each other and that are made possible by Internet technologies. (Macfadyen, 2006b)

## Cyberworld

An information world created in cyberspace either intentionally or spontaneously, with or without visual design. Cyberworlds are closely related to the real world and have a serious impact on it. (Sourin, 2006)

## Cyborg

Literally, a hybrid of cybernetics and organism. Generally it refers to humans as modified by technoscientific implants and drugs. (Srinivasan, 2006)

## Cycle

The time period required for each student to enter and complete all courses required for an academic degree; for example, MBA. (Murray & Efendioglu, 2005)

## Cyclic Graph

A directed graph that contains at least one cycle. (Y. Chen, 2005a)

## Cyclic Redundancy Check (CRC)

Block codes used for error detection. (Iossifides et al., 2005)

## Cyclical Process

An event or operation within a project that can occur and lead project teams back to areas that resemble the starting point of the project. (Nash et al., 2005b)

## Cyclomatic Complexity

A broad measure of soundness and confidence for a program. This measure was introduced by Thomas McCabe in 1976. (Polgar, 2005b)

# D

**DAC:** See *Discretionary Access Control.*

**DAG:** See *Directed Acyclic Graph.*

**DAI:** See *Digital Access Index; Distributed Artificial Intelligence.*

**DAISY:** See *Digital Accessible Information System.*

**DAM:** See *Digital Asset Management.*

**DAML:** See *DARPA Agent Markup Language.*

## Dark Fiber
Optical fiber for infrastructure (cabling and repeaters) that is currently in place but is not being used. Optical fiber conveys information in the form of light pulses, so dark means no light pulses are being sent. (Chochliouros et al., 2005a)

**DARM:** See *Distributed Association Rule Mining.*

## DARPA Agent Markup Language (DAML)
An extension of XML and the Resource Description Framework (RDF) providing constructs with which to create ontologies and to mark up information so that it is machine readable and understandable. (Jain & Ramesh, 2006)

**DARS™:** See *Degree Audit Reporting System™.*

## Dashboard
Specific display of information that presents key information about a process or device. A dashboard may or may not be computerized. (Adam & Pomerol, 2005)

## Data
**1:** A collection of attributes (numeric, alphanumeric, figures, pictures) about entities (things, events, activities). Spatial data represent tangible features (entities). Moreover, spatial data are usually an attribute (descriptor) of the spatial feature. (Al-Hanbali & Sadoun, 2006) **2:** A set of discrete and objective facts concerning events. (Joia, 2005) **3:** Binary (digital) representations of atomic facts, especially from financial transactions. Data may also be text, graphics, bit-mapped images, sound, or analog or digital live-video segments. Structured data are the raw material for analysis using a data-driven DSS. The data are supplied by data producers and are used by information consumers to create information. (Power, 2005) **4:** Combination of facts and meanings that are processed into information. (Yoon et al., 2005) **5:** Data are carriers of knowledge and information. They consist mostly of signs and are the raw material to be further processed. Data represent observations or facts out of context that are not directly meaningful. Both information and knowledge are communicated through data. (Haghirian, 2006) **6:** Highly explicit knowledge derived from the data in databases and data warehouses used for strategic decision making after summarizing, analyzing, mining, and so forth. (Kulkarni & Freeze, 2006) **7:** Something given or admitted as a fact on which an inference may be based. Simple observations of the world, which are often quantified, and easily structured, captured on machines, and transferred. The number of "baby boomers" born in a given year is data. (Mockler & Dologite, 2005) **8:** The generic term for signs, symbols, and pictures. Data can be saved, processed, printed, and so on. They are not bound to individuals. (Hofer, 2006) **9:** The raw material that feeds the process of information generation. (Hoxmeier, 2005) **10:** The set of samples, facts, or cases in a data repository. As an example of a sample, consider the field values of a particular credit application in a bank database. (de Carvalho et al., 2005) **11:** Often defined as the raw facts and information data. Knowledge is about the application of data and information for a given task so that the given task can be effectively performed. (R. Zhang, 2005)

## Data Accountability

The ability to trace back all the actions and changes made to information. (Wang, Cheng, & Cheng, 2006)

## Data Accuracy

An aspect of numerical ($\rightarrow$) data quality: a standard statistical error between a real parameter value and the corresponding value given by the data. Data accuracy is inversely proportional to this error. (Kulikowski, 2005)

## Data Actuality

An aspect of ($\rightarrow$) data quality consisting in its steadiness despite the natural process of data obsolescence increasing in time. (Kulikowski, 2005)

## Data Aggregation

The process in which information is gathered and expressed in a summary form. In case the aggregation operator is decomposable, partial aggregation schemes may be employed in which intermediate results are produced that contain sufficient information to compute the final results. If the aggregation operator is non-decomposable, then partial aggregation schemes can still be useful to provide approximate summaries. (Roussos & Zoumboulakis, 2005)

## Data Allocation

The process of determining what data to store at which servers in a distributed system. (Chin, 2005)

## Data and Model Assembly

A set of query functions that assemble the data and data visualization instruments for data mining. (S. Wang & H. Wang, 2005)

## Data Architecture

The underlying set of rules and descriptions of relationships that govern how the major kinds of data support the business processes defined in the business architecture. (Yoon et al., 2005)

## Data Assimilation

Statistical and other automated methods for parameter estimation, followed by prediction and tracking. (Ganguly et al., 2005)

## Data Auctioning

Process in which an individual uses data provided by multiple sources to create a profile of particular individuals; this profile is then auctioned off to the highest bidder(s). (St. Amant, 2006b)

## Data Availability

The ability to ensure the readiness of the information when needed. (Wang, Cheng, & Cheng, 2006)

## Data Center

A centralized repository for the storage and management of information, organized for a particular area or body of knowledge. (Ashrafi et al., 2005)

## Data Checking

Activity through which the correctness conditions of the data are verified. It also includes the specification of the type of the error or condition not met, and the qualification of the data and its division into the error-free and erroneous data. Data checking may be aimed at detecting error-free data or at detecting erroneous data. (Conversano & Siciliano, 2005)

## Data Cleaning (Cleansing)

**1:** The act of detecting and removing errors and inconsistencies in data to improve its quality. (Tzanis et al., 2005) **2:** The methodology of identifying duplicates in a single file or across a set of files by using a name, address, and other information. (Winkler, 2005) **3:** The elimination of anomalies or outright mistakes in data that will otherwise impede with its intended usage. These include the discovery and elimination of duplicates, homonyms, "fake" entries such as 999-99-9999 in a social security field, correcting names and addresses, and so on. (Malik, 2006)

## Data Cloud

Collection of data points in space. (Cottingham, 2005)

## Data Completeness

Containing by a composite data all components necessary to full description of the states of a considered object or process. (Kulikowski, 2005)

## Data Confidentiality

The ability to ensure the data is inaccessible to unauthorized users. (Wang, Cheng, & Cheng, 2006)

## Data Consistency

When the application state stored in the database remains consistent after a transaction commits. (Zhao et al., 2006)

**D**

## Data Content

The attributes (states, properties, etc.) of a real or of an assumed abstract world to which the given data record is referred. (Kulikowski, 2005)

## Data Conversion

A process involving moving existing data from legacy systems, performing an integrity check, and then transporting them to an ERP system that has been implemented. There are diverse tools available to reduce the effort of the conversion process. In some instances, there is the need to introduce manually the data into the system. Due to this effort, the conversion process must be planned at the beginning of the ERP project in order to avoid delays. (Esteves & Pastor, 2005)

## Data Credibility

An aspect of (→) data quality: a level of certitude that the (→) data content corresponds to a real object or has been obtained using a proper acquisition method. (Kulikowski, 2005)

## Data Cube

**1:** A collection of aggregate values classified according to several properties of interest (dimensions). Combinations of dimension values are used to identify the single aggregate values in the cube. (Tininini, 2005c) **2:** A data cube is a type of multi-dimensional matrix that lets users explore and analyze a collection of data from many different perspectives, usually considering three factors (dimensions) at a time. (Sethi & Sethi, 2006b) **3:** A data set is conceptually modeled as being embedded in a multi-dimensional hyper-rectangle, or data cube for short. The data cube is defined by its dimensions, and stores the values of measure attributes in its cells. (Riedewald et al., 2005) **4:** A preselection of aggregated data at several levels of detail according to several dimensions in a data mart. A data cube establishes the resolution and basic projection where selections can be made. The data cube aggregation detail can be modified through OLAP operators such as drill and roll, and their dimensions can be modified by slice & dice and pivot. (Hernandez-Orallo, 2005a)

## Data Cube Operator

Computes group-by, corresponding to all possible combinations of attributes in the cube-by clause. (Tan, 2005a)

## Data Definition

An elaborate statement of the representation of each piece of data, its source, storage method, and intended usage. (Law, 2005)

## Data Definition Language (DDL)

A language used by a database management system which allows users to define the database, specifying data types, structures, and constraints on the data. (Ramasamy & Deshpande, 2005)

## Data Dependency

One of the various ways that data attributes are related, for example, functional dependency, inclusion dependency, and so forth. (Tan & Zhao, 2005b)

## Data Dictionary

A part of a database that holds definitions of data elements, such as tables, columns, and views. (Sethi & Sethi, 2006b)

## Data Dissemination/Broadcasting

Periodical broadcast of database information to mobile clients through one or more wireless channels. (Waluyo et al., 2005)

## Data Driven

If the data drive the analysis without any prior expectations, the mining process is referred to as a data-driven approach. (Amaravadi, 2005)

## Data Editing

The activity aimed at detecting and correcting errors (logical inconsistencies) in data. (Conversano & Siciliano, 2005)

## Data Encryption

The process of "scrambling" the data for transmission to ensure that it is not intercepted along the way. (Wang, Cheng, & Cheng, 2006)

## Data Envelopment Analysis (DEA)

A data-oriented mathematical programming approach that allows multiple performance measures in a single model. (Chen, Motiwalla, et al., 2005)

## Data Exchange

The situation that the local source schemas, as well as the global schema, are given beforehand; the data integration problem then exists in establishing a suitable mapping between the given global schema and the given set of local schemas. (Balsters, 2005)

## Data Extraction

**1:** A process in which data is transferred from operational databases to a data warehouse. (Kontio, 2005) **2:** The process of creation of uniform representations of data in a database federation. (Balsters, 2005)

## Data Flow Diagram (DFD)

**1:** Used to model a system as a network of processes that transform and exchange data as a technique to provide a semantic bridge between users and system developers. The main components of DFDs are data process, actors, data flow, and data stores. (Tauber & Schwartz, 2006) **2:** A diagram used in functional analysis that specifies the functions of the system, the inputs/outputs from/to external (user) entities, and the data being retrieved from or updating data stores. There are well-defined rules for specifying correct DFDs as well as for creating hierarchies of interrelated DFDs. (Shoval & Kabeli, 2005) **3:** A graphical model describing data in a system and how the process transforms such data. A tool for modeling information flow and producing a functional analysis. (Ferri & Grifoni, 2006)

## Data Fragmentation

The technique used to split up the global database into logical units. These logical units are called fragment relations, or simply fragments. (Ibrahim, 2005)

## Data Fusion

**1:** Combining evidence for a conclusion from multiple sources of information. (N.C. Rowe, 2006b) **2:** The fully automated method of merging diverse data into a single, coherent representation of the tactical, operational, or strategic situation. (Ozer, Lv, & Wolf, 2005)

## Data Hiding

Important data being embedded into a host image. (Chen, Chen, & Cheng, 2005)

## Data Hijacking

Process in which an individual charged with a data processing activity demands more money for the task in exchange for not publicizing the data with which he or she is working. (St.Amant, 2006b)

## Data Imputation

**1:** Substitution of estimated values for missing or inconsistent data items (fields). The substituted values are intended to create a data record that does not fail edits. (Conversano & Siciliano, 2005) **2:** The process of estimating missing data of an observation based on the valid values of other variables. (Brown & Kros, 2005)

## Data Integration

**1:** A process providing a uniform integrated access to multiple heterogeneous information sources. (Flesca, Furfaro, et al., 2005) **2:** A process of unifying data that share some common semantics but originate from unrelated sources. (Buccella et al., 2005) **3:** The problem of combining data from multiple heterogeneous data sources and providing a unified view of these sources to the user. Such unified view is structured according to a global schema. Issues addressed by a data integration system include specifying the mapping between the global schema and the sources, and processing queries expressed on the global schema. (Aldana Montes et al., 2005) **4:** Unifying data models and databases so that all departments of an enterprise use the same data entities, with the same values. (Kurbel, 2005)

## Data Integration System

A system that presents data distributed over heterogeneous data sources according to a unified view. A data integration system allows processing of queries over such a unified view by gathering results from the various data sources. (Marchetti et al., 2005)

## Data Integrity

**1:** Guarantees that data in transmissions is not created, intercepted, modified, or deleted illicitly. (Lowry, Stephens, et al., 2005) **2:** Preventing forgeries, corruption, impairment, or modification of resources like information, services, or equipment. Data integrity is the quality or condition of being whole and unaltered, and it refers to the consistency, accuracy, and correctness of data. (Oermann & Dittmann, 2006) **3:** The ability to prevent information from being modified by unauthorized users. (Wang, Cheng, & Cheng, 2006)

## Data Interchange

The process of sending and receiving data in such a way that the information content or meaning assigned to the data is not altered during the transmission. (Vardaki, 2005)

**D**

## Data Irredundancy

The lack of data volume that by data recoding could be removed without information loss. (Kulikowski, 2005)

## Data Item

Database record or tuples. (Waluyo et al., 2005)

## Data Latency

An experienced time delay when a system or an agent sends data to a receiver. (Chen & McLeod, 2006)

## Data Laundering

Process in which international outsourcing is used to circumvent different national privacy laws when compiling personal data on individuals. (St.Amant, 2006b)

## Data Legibility

An aspect of (→) data quality: a level of data content ability to be interpreted correctly due to the known and well-defined attributes, units, abbreviations, codes, formal terms, and so forth used in the data record's expression. (Kulikowski, 2005)

## Data Management

The use of techniques to organize, structure, and manage data, including database management and data administration. (Thuraisingham, 2005)

## Data Management for Mobile Computing

Numerous database management issues exist in mobile computing environments, such as resource management and system support, representation/dissemination/management of information, location management, as well as others. Various new techniques for cache management, data replication, data broadcasting, transaction processing, failure recovery, as well as database security, have been developed. Applications of these techniques have been found in distributed mobile database systems, mobile information systems, advanced mobile computing applications, and on the Internet. Yet, many other related issues need to be addressed. (Parker & Chen, 2005)

## Data Manipulation Language (DML)

A language used by a database management system that allows users to manipulate data (querying, inserting, and updating of data). (Ramasamy & Deshpande, 2005)

## Data Manipulation Service

One of several computational services responsible by some functional facility that could exist in a hypermedia system. (Tobar et al., 2006)

## Data Mart

**1:** A data warehouse focused on a particular subject or department. Data warehouses may consist of several data marts. (Barca et al., 2005) **2:** A data warehouse designed for a particular line of business, such as sales, marketing, or finance. (Serrano et al., 2005) **3:** A data warehouse that is limited in scope and facility, but for a restricted domain. (Yao et al., 2005) **4:** A logical subset of the complete data warehouse. We often view the data mart as the restriction of the data warehouse to a single business process or to a group of related business processes targeted towards a particular business group. (Simitsis et al., 2005) **5:** A small database with data derived from a data warehouse. (Chen, Zhang, et al., 2005a) **6:** A database containing data extracted and often summarized from one or more operational systems or from a data warehouse, and optimized to support the business analysis needs of a particular unit. (Raisinghani & Nugent, 2005) **7:** Part of a data warehouse which gathers the information about a specific domain. Each data mart is usually viewed at the conceptual model as a multi-dimensional star or snowflake schema. Although each data mart is specialized on part of the organization information, some dimensions can be redundantly replicated in several data marts. For instance, time is usually a dimension shared by all data marts. (Hernandez-Orallo, 2005a) **8:** A scaled-down version of an enterprise-wide data warehouse that is created for the purpose of supporting the analytical requirements of a specific business segment or department. (Hirji, 2005)

**Data MCAR:** See *Data Missing Completely At Random.*

## Data Mining (DM)

**1:** Extraction of meaningful information from masses of data (e.g., data warehouse) usually employing algorithms to correlate among many variables faster than humanly possible. (Ribière & Román, 2006) **2:** Using powerful data collection methods to analyze a company's database or data stores and select information that supports a specific objective. (Lenard & Alam, 2005) **3:** A class of database applications or data processing that discovers hidden patterns and correlations in a group of data or large databases which can be used to predict future behavior. (Li et al., 2006) **4:** A component of the business intelligence decision-support process in which patterns of information in data are discovered through the use of a smart program that automatically searches the database, finds significant patterns and correlations through the use of statistical algorithms, and infers rules from them. (Raisinghani & Nugent, 2005) **5:** A database research area that aims at automated discovery of non-trivial, previously unknown, and interesting regularities, trends, and patterns in large data sets. (Manolopoulos et al., 2005) **6:** A discovering process aimed at the identification of patterns hidden in the analyzed dataset. (Santos et al., 2005) **7:** A form of information extraction activity whose goal is to discover hidden facts contained in databases; the process of using various techniques (i.e., a combination of machine learning, statistical analysis, modeling techniques, and database technology) to discover implicit relationships between data items and the construction of predictive models based on them. (Rahman, 2005e) **8:** A process by which information is extracted from a database or multiple databases using computer programs to match and merge data, and create more information. (T. Stern, 2005) **9:** A process by which previously unknown patterns, rules, and relationships are discovered from data. (Sadeghian et al., 2006) **10:** A process of seeking interesting and valuable information from a large database using a combination of methods. (Kumar, 2005) **11:** A research field that investigates the extraction of useful knowledge from large datasets. Clustering and Association Rule Mining are two examples of data-mining techniques. (Kontaki et al., 2005) **12:** A set of tools, techniques, and methods used to find new, hidden, or unexpected patterns from a large collection of data typically stored in a data warehouse. (Bala et al., 2005)

## Data Missing Completely At Random (Data MCAR)

When the observed values of a variable are truly a random sample of all values of that variable (i.e., the response exhibits independence from any variables). (Brown & Kros, 2005)

## Data Missing At Random

When given the variables X and Y, the probability of response depends on X but not on Y. (Brown & Kros, 2005)

## Data Model

**1:** A specification language where we can model and talk about models of a given class and their instances,

manipulations with instances, and models, queries, and constraints. A typical example of a well-developed data model is the relational model. The ER data model, though less formal, is another example. (Diskin & Kadish, 2005) **2:** Defines which information is to be stored in a database and how it is organized. (Bounif, 2005) **3:** Part of the run-time environment described in SCORM. The data model specification is needed to standardize what is communicated to the learning management system about the learner (i.e., score on quizzes, name, ID, time in content). (Stavredes, 2005b)

## Data Modeling

**1:** Implementing data management in engineering information systems with information technology and, in particular, database technology. The complex data semantics and semantic relationships are described in data modeling. (Ma, 2005a) **2:** The process of producing a model of a collection of data which encapsulates its semantics and hopefully its structure. (Delve, 2005)

## Data Multi-Dimensionality

The set of dimensions of a table or a data cube. (Rafanelli, 2005)

## Data Node

An entity containing virtue attributes used to describe and aggregate knowledge in a knowledge network. (Croasdell & Wang, 2006)

## Data Operability

An aspect of (→) data quality: a level of data record ability to be used directly, without additional processing (restructuring, conversion, etc.). (Kulikowski, 2005)

## Data Partitioning

A storage technique through which each data item is assigned to exactly one node. Data operations accessing different data partitions can be executed in parallel. However, if one operation needs to access more than one data partition, the execution is more complicated. (Pinheiro, 2005)

## Data Perturbation

**1:** Involves modifying confidential attributes using random statistical noise. The objective of data perturbation is to prevent disclosure of confidential attributes while maximizing access to both confidential and non-confidential attributes within a database. (Wilson et al.,

2006b) **2:** Modifying the data so that original confidential data values cannot be recovered. (Saygin, 2005)

## Data Planning

The projection of expected future needs for data, with specifications on data sources, data collection and storage, data processing and presentation, data distribution, and data security. (Law, 2005)

## Data Precision

An aspect of numerical (→) data quality: the maximum error between a real parameter and its value given by the data, caused by the data values' discretization. Data precision is inversely proportional to this error. (Kulikowski, 2005)

## Data Preprocessing

**1:** The application of several methods preceding the mining phase, done for improving the overall data-mining results. Usually, it consists of: (1) data cleaning—a method for fixing missing values, outliers, and possible inconsistent data; (2) data integration—the union of (possibly heterogeneous) data coming from different sources into a unique data store; and (3) data reduction—the application of any technique working on data representation capable of saving storage space without compromising the possibility of inquiring them. (Buccafurri & Lax, 2005) **2:** The data-mining phase that converts the usage, content, and structure information contained in various data sources into data abstractions necessary for pattern discovery. (Lee-Post & Jin, 2005b)

## Data Privacy

Current United States laws provide protection to student data, including performance data. Online distance education environments need to address privacy issues through design of courses and security features built into recordkeeping systems. (Sales, 2005)

## Data Processing

The operation performed on data in order to derive new information according to a given set of rules. (Vardaki, 2005)

## Data Quality

**1:** A dimension or measurement of data in reference to its accuracy, completeness, consistency, timeliness, uniqueness, and validity. Data are considered to be of high quality if they have all of the above attributes. (Yoon et al., 2005) **2:** A multi-faceted concept in information systems research that focuses on the fitness for use of data by consumers. Data quality can be viewed in four categories: intrinsic (accuracy, objectivity, believability, and reputation), contextual (relevancy, timeliness, and appropriate amount of data), representational (format of the data), and accessibility (ease of access). (Borchers, 2005) **3:** A set of data properties (features, parameters, etc.) describing their ability to satisfy the user's expectations or requirements concerning data using for information acquiring in a given area of interest, learning, decision making, and so forth. (Kulikowski, 2005) **4:** Data have good quality if they are fit for use. Data quality is measured in terms of many dimensions or characteristics, including accuracy, completeness, consistency, and currency of electronic data. (Marchetti et al., 2005) **5:** Ensuring that data supplied is fit for use by its consumer. Elements of data quality can extend to include the quality of the context in which that data is produced, the quality of the information architecture in which that data resides, the factual accuracy of the data item stored, and the level of completeness and lack of ambiguity. (Schwartz & Schreiber, 2005) **6:** Interchangeably used with information integrity, it can refer to an organizational data-quality program as well as quality of a data element. When applied to the latter, a data element's quality is measured against the dimensions of information integrity (accuracy, completeness, validity, uniqueness, precision, timeliness, accessibility, consistency, clarity, and sufficiency). (Malik, 2006) **7:** Most large databases have redundant and inconsistent data, missing data fields, and/or values, as well as data fields that are not logically related and that are stored in the same data relations. (Owrang O., 2006)

## Data Reconciliation

The process of resolving data inconsistencies in database federations (such as constraint conflicts). (Balsters, 2005)

## Data Reduction

A process of removing irrelevant information from data by reducing the number of features, instances, or values of the data. (Liu & Yu, 2005)

## Data Relevance

An aspect of (→) data quality: a level of consistency between the (→) data content and the area of interest of the user. (Kulikowski, 2005)

## Data Replication

A storage technique through which some nodes have copies of the same data. Replication of data is a common method to improve read performance, but is rather problematic if data are often updated. (Pinheiro, 2005)

## Data Repository

A complex catalog of a set of sources organizing both their description and all associated information at various abstraction levels. (De Meo & Ursino, 2005)

## Data Resource Management

The analysis, classification, and maintenance of an organization's data and data relationships. (Yoon et al., 2005)

## Data Retrieval

Denotes the standardized database methods of matching a set of records, given a particular query (e.g., use of the SQL SELECT command on a database). (Peter & Greenidge, 2005a)

## Data Schema

Collection of data types and relationships described according to a particular type language. (Marchetti et al., 2005)

## Data Schema Instance

Collection of data values that are valid (i.e., conform) with respect to a data schema. (Marchetti et al., 2005)

## Data Segment

A set of data items. (Waluyo et al., 2005)

## Data Semantics

A reflection of the real world that captures the relationship between data in a database, its use in applications, and its corresponding objects in the real world. Data semantics requires some form of agreement between the different agents (human and computer) that interact with and use the data. The field of data semantics deals with understanding and developing methodologies to find and determine data semantics, represent those semantics, and enable ways to use the representations of the semantics. (Schwartz & Schreiber, 2005)

## Data Sequence

The sequence of itemsets representing the behavior of a client over a specific period. The database involved in a sequential pattern mining process is a (usually large) set of data sequences. (Masseglia et al., 2005)

## Data Set

A set of instances of target concepts. (Maloof, 2005)

## Data Source

An external provider of information; the information is accessible either in a passive or active way. (Abramowicz et al., 2006)

## Data Staging Area (DSA)

An auxiliary area of volatile data employed for the purpose of data transformation, reconciliation, and cleaning before the final loading of the data warehouse. (Simitsis et al., 2005)

## Data Stream

**1:** A continuous flow of data. The most common use of a data stream is the transmission of digital data from one place to another. (Sayal, 2005) **2:** A data set distributed over time. (Maloof, 2005) **3:** Data items that arrive online from multiple sources in a continuous, rapid, time-varying, possibly unpredictable fashion. (Chatziantoniou & Doukidis, 2005) **4:** Opposite to the stationary view of a database, a data stream focuses on the continuous processing of newly arriving data (i.e., joining and comparing of streams). (Fiege, 2005)

## Data Stream Applications

The class of large receiver set, low-bandwidth, real-time data applications. (Hosszú, 2006)

## Data Stream Management System (DSMS)

**1:** A management system for efficient storage and querying of data streams. DSMS can be considered the Database Management System (DBMS) for data streams. The main difference between DSMS and DBMS is that DSMS has to handle a higher volume of data that is continuously flowing in, and the characteristics of data content may change over time. (Sayal, 2005) **2:** A data management system providing capabilities to query and process data streams and store a bounded part of it. (Chatziantoniou & Doukidis, 2005)

## Data Structure

Formal description of a ($\rightarrow$) composite data indicating the order, contents, lengths, and lists of attribute values of its fields. (Kulikowski, 2005)

**D**

### Data Tag

A quality indicator attached to a field, record, or table in a database to make decision makers aware of the level of data quality. (Chengalur-Smith et al., 2005)

### Data Tampering

The threats of data being altered in unauthorized ways, either accidentally or intentionally. (Butcher-Powell, 2005)

### Data Transformation/Translation

Transformation of data stored in one format (meta-model) to another format. (Diskin & Kadish, 2005)

### Data Type

The characteristic of a data element or a field that specifies what type of data it can hold. SQL classifies three main data types: predefined data type, constructed data type, and user-defined type. (Pardede et al., 2005)

### Data Validation

An activity aimed at verifying whether the value of a data item comes from the given (finite or infinite) set of acceptable values. (Conversano & Siciliano, 2005)

### Data Visualization

**1:** Presentation of data in human understandable graphics, images, or animation. (S. Wang & H. Wang, 2005) **2:** The method or end result of transforming numeric and textual information into a graphic format. Visualizations are used to explore large quantities of data holistically in order to understand trends or principles. (Kusiak & Shah, 2005) **3:** The visualization of the data set through the use of techniques such as scatter plots, 3D cubes, link graphs, and surface charts. (Viktor & Paquet, 2005) **4:** The transformation and analysis to aid in formation of a mental picture of symbolic data. Such a picture is simple, persistent, and complete. (Daassi et al., 2006)

### Data Warehouse

**1:** A database that is specifically elaborated to allow different analysis on data. Analysis exists generally to make aggregation operations (count, sum, average, etc.). A data warehouse is different from a transactional database since it accumulates data along time and other dimensions. Data of a warehouse are loaded and updated at regular intervals from the transactional databases of the company. (Schneider, 2005) **2:** A central repository for all or significant parts of the data that an enterprise's various business systems collect. (Mendes-Filho & Ramos, 2005) **3:** A database that is subject-oriented, integrated, time-variant, and non-volatile. (Chen, Zhang, et al., 2005a) **4:** A database, frequently very large, that can access all of a company's information. It contains data about how the warehouse is organized, where the information can be found, and any connections between existing data. (Bose, 2005) **5:** A form of data storage geared towards business intelligence. It integrates data from various parts of the company. The data in a data warehouse is read-only and tends to include historical as well as current data so that users can perform trend analysis. (Raisinghani & Nugent, 2005) **6:** A place where managed data are situated after they pass through the operational systems and outside the operational systems. (Jeong, Abraham, & Abraham, 2006) **7:** A platform consisting of a repository of selected information drawn from remote databases or other information sources which forms the infrastructural basis for supporting business decision making. (Hirji, 2005) **8:** A repository of information coming mainly from online transactional processing systems that provides data for analytical processing and decision support. (Barca et al., 2005) **9:** A repository of nonvolatile temporal data used in the analysis and tracking of key business processes. (Artz, 2005d) **10:** A subject-oriented, integrated, time-variant, non-volatile collection of data used to support the strategic decision-making process for the enterprise. It is the central point of data integration for business intelligence and the source of data for data marts, delivering a common view of enterprise data. (Simitsis & Theodoratos, 2005) **11:** A system for storing, retrieving, and managing large amounts of data using some sophisticated techniques of cleaning, filtering, hashing, and compression. (Pourabbas, 2005a) **12:** An instantiated view of integrated information sources to build mediators. In a spatial data warehouse, data can be combined from many heterogeneous sources to obtain decision support tools. These sources have to be adjusted because they contain data in different representations. Therefore, the construction of a data warehouse requires many operations such as integration, cleaning, and consolidation. (Faïz, 2005)

### Data Warehouse Library (DWL)

A repository of documents acquired from Web sources or located within the organizational intranet. Apart from the contents, the repository stores additional metadata about the documents, mainly temporal and semantic indices. Basically, DWL is an extensive Digital Library (DL) and enjoys all capabilities of a typical information retrieval system. However, there are three distinctive features that make a DWL something more than a typical DL: temporal indexing, CSL-based indices, and direct links to warehouse business metadata. All these features provide novel possibilities of sub-setting the collection of documents to be searched and establishing links among documents and data. (Wecel, Abramowicz, & Kalczynski, 2005)

## Data Warehousing

**1:** A compilation of data designed for decision support by executives, managers, analysts, and other key stakeholders in an organization. A data warehouse contains a consistent picture of business conditions at a single point in time. (Pang, 2005a) **2:** A form of data storage geared towards business intelligence. It integrates data from various parts of the company. The data in a data warehouse are read-only and tend to include historical as well as current data so that users can perform trend analysis. (Raisinghani, Klassen, et al., 2005) **3:** Refers to the process of extraction of data from different information sources (e.g., databases, files) and their integration in a single data warehouse. (Pourabbas, 2005b) **4:** The gathering and cleaning of data from disparate sources into a single database, optimized for exploration and reporting. The data warehouse holds a cleaned version of the data from operational systems, and data mining requires the type of cleaned data that lives in a data warehouse. (Nicholson & Stanton, 2005) **5:** The gathering and cleaning of data from disparate sources into a single database, which is optimized for exploration and reporting. The data warehouse holds a cleaned version of the data from operational systems, and data mining requires the type of cleaned data that live in a data warehouse. (Nicholson & Stanton, 2005)

## Data-Driven Decision Making

The practice of purposefully collecting, analyzing, and interpreting data according to accepted criteria, and using the outcomes to select and justify decisions. (Law, 2005)

## Data-Driven Design

A data warehouse design that begins with existing historical data and attempts to derive useful information regarding trends in the organization. (Artz, 2005b)

## Data-Driven Web Design

The data available in the organization are taken as the starting point for the design of the Web site. (De Troyer, 2005)

## Data-Mining Data Table

The flat file constructed from the relational database that is the actual table used by the data-mining software. (Breault, 2005)

## Data-Mining Group (DMG)

**1:** The process of searching and analyzing data in order to find latent but potentially valuable information, and to identify patterns and establish relationships from a huge database. (Dholakia, Bang, et al., 2005) **2:** A consortium of data-mining vendors for developing data-mining standards. They have developed a Predictive Model Markup Language (PMML). (Zendulka, 2005a)

## Data-Mining Guidelines

A set of standards by which medical data mining, in particular, might be conducted. This is a framework that adopts a forward-looking responsibility in the evaluation of methods and explanation of conclusions, especially in the context of heuristic methods (with outcomes that may be ill-defined). This extends not only to the methods of the data-mining procedure, the security and privacy aspects of data, but also to where and how the results of data mining are utilized, requiring that an ethical reference be made to the final purpose of the mining. (George, 2005a)

## Data-Mining Model

A high-level global description of a given set of data which is the result of a data-mining technique over the set of data. It can be descriptive or predictive. (Zendulka, 2005a)

## Data-Mining Technology (DMT)

**1:** Broadly defined, includes all types of data-dictated analytical tools and technologies that can detect generic and interesting patterns, scale (or can be made to scale) to large data volumes, and help in automated knowledge discovery or prediction tasks. These include determining associations and correlations, clustering, classifying, and regressing, as well as developing predictive or forecasting models. The specific tools used can range from traditional or emerging statistics and signal or image processing, to machine learning, artificial intelligence, and knowledge discovery from large databases, as well as econometrics, management science, and tools for modeling and predicting the evolutions of nonlinear dynamical and stochastic systems. (Ganguly, Gupta, Khan, 2005) **2:** Statistical, artificial intelligence, machine learning, or even database-query-based approaches that are capable of extracting meaningful insights or knowledge from large volumes of information. (Khan et al., 2006)

## Data-Mining Tool

A software application that extract predictive information from large databases, which can then be analyzed to enhance corporate data resources and generate predictions regarding business trends and customer behavior. (Gurău, 2006b)

## Database

**1:** A collection of facts, figures, and objects that is structured so that it can easily be accessed, organized, managed, and updated. (Pang, 2005a) **2:** A collection of related information. The information held in the database is stored in an organized way so that specific items can be selected and retrieved quickly. (Duan & Xu, 2005) **3:** A database (instance) is a set of finite relations over a fixed database schema. Each relation consists of a set of ground facts, that is, variable free facts. (Greco & Zumpano, 2005b) **4:** A self-describing collection of data that represents a model of an information domain. (Hoxmeier, 2005) **5:** An organized collection of data and information stored in a computer medium that can be easily accessed and manipulated. (Hornby, 2005)

## Database Administrator (DBA)

**1:** A person responsible for successfully maintaining a database system. (Chin, 2005) **2:** An IT professional who ensures the database is accessible when it is called upon, performs maintenance activities, and enforces security policies. (Slazinski, 2005)

## Database Benchmark

A benchmark specifically aimed at evaluating the performance of DBMSs or DBMS components. (Darmont, 2005)

## Database Clustering

The process of grouping similar databases together. (Zhang & Zhang, 2005)

## Database Computer

A specialized computer for database applications which usually works in conjunction with a host computer. (Thomasian, 2005a)

## Database Consistency

Means that the data contained in the database is both accurate and valid. (Ibrahim, 2005)

## Database Federation

Provides for tight coupling of a collection of heterogeneous legacy databases into a global integrated system. The main problem is achieving and maintaining consistency and a uniform representation of the data on the global level of the federation. (Balsters, 2005)

## Database Gap

Processing demand for database applications is twofold in 9-12 months, but it takes 18 months for the processor speed to increase that much according to Moore's Law. (Thomasian, 2005a)

## Database Index

An auxiliary physical database structure that is used to speed up the retrieval of data objects from the database in response to certain search conditions. Typically, indexes are based on ordered files or tree data structures. (Manolopoulos et al., 2005)

## Database Item

An item/entity occurring in the database. (Daly & Taniar, 2005b)

## Database Maintenance

The task of updating a database and enforcing constraints. (Schmidt et al., 2005)

## Database Management System (DBMS)

**1:** A collection of interrelated data that is called a database, and a variety of software tools for accessing those data. The three leading commercial DBMSs are: Oracle 9i, IBM DB2, and Microsoft SQL Server™. (Pallis et al., 2005) **2:** A set of programs used to define, administer, and process the database and its applications. (Yao et al., 2005) **3:** A software program (or group of programs) that manages and provides access to a database. (Chen, Holt, et al., 2005) **4:** Collection of software components to store data, access the data, define data elements, store data element definitions, build data storage structures, query the data, backup and secure the data, and provide reports of the data. (Vitolo et al., 2005) **5:** Software used to manage a database. It can be differentiated based on the data model such as Relational DBMS, Object-Oriented DBMS, Object-Relational DBMS, and so forth. (Pardede et al., 2005) **6:** A system that stores, organizes, retrieves, and manipulates databases. (Sadoun, 2006) **7:** A software system for organizing the information in a database in a way that permits data input, verification, storage, retrieval, and a combination of these. (Bozanis, 2006) **8:** A collection of programs that enables users to create and maintain a database. (Doorn, 2005)

## Database Marketing

A branch of marketing that applies database technology and analytics to understand customer behavior and improve effectiveness in marketing campaigns. (Lo, 2005)

## Database Model

Conceptual data models and logical database models. (Ma, 2005a)

## Database Modeling

The first step of database design, where the database designers define the data objects and their relationships to other data objects. Data modeling involves a progression from conceptual model to logical model to physical schema. (Pardede et al., 2005)

## Database Paradigm

The rational and theoretical framework or archetype used to formulate and support a database. (Doorn, 2005)

## Database Quality

Includes dimensions of data, process, model, information, and behavioral characteristics. (Hoxmeier, 2005)

## Database Repair

Minimal set of insert and delete operations which makes the database consistent. (Flesca, Furfaro, et al., 2005)

## Database Reverse Engineering

**1:** The process of analyzing an existing database to identify its components and their interrelationships, and to create representations of another data model. (Alhajj & Polat, 2005a) **2:** The process through which the logical and conceptual schemas of a legacy database or of a set of files are recovered or rebuilt from various information sources such as DDL code, data dictionary contents, database contents, or the source code of application programs that use the database. (Hainaut et al., 2005)

## Database Schema

**1:** A set of names and conditions that describe the structure of a database. For example, in a relational database, the schema includes elements such as table names, field names, field data types, primary key constraints, or foreign key constraints. (Koeller, 2005) **2:** The physical model or blueprint for a database. (Sethi & Sethi, 2006b)

## Database Schema Reengineering

The process of analyzing a subject database schema to recover its components and their relationships. It guides the reconstitution of such a system into an enhanced one, with a higher level of abstraction and semantically closer to the Universe of Discourse. (Rivero, 2005)

## Database Snapshot

A consistent collection of values of data items in a database that correspond to what a read-only transaction would collect. The snapshot can be used as a checkpoint for recovering a database upon. (Leong, 2005b)

## Database Status

The structure and content of a database at a given time stamp. It comprises the database object classes, their relationships, and their object instances. (Sindoni, 2005a)

## Database Synchronization

When a database is being synchronized, no new update transactions are allowed, and all open update transactions are finished. After that, all updated blocks are written to disk. (Bose et al. 2005)

## Database Trigger

A procedure that gets invoked by the database management system whenever a specific column gets updated or whenever a row gets deleted or inserted. (Millet, 2005)

## Datalog

A class of deductive databases that may contain various types of negation and disjunction. (Grant & Minker, 2006)

## DataMIME™

A prototype system designed and implemented on top of vertical database technology and a multi-layered software framework by the DataSURG group at North Dakota State University, USA. (Perrizo, Ding, Serazi, et al., 2005)

## Dataveillance

**1:** Monitoring people by digital representations in electronic databases created and managed by information technologies. (Dholakia, Zwick, et al., 2005) **2:** Surveillance by tracking shadows of data that are left behind as people undertake their electronic transactions. (Swierzowicz, 2005) **3:** Surveillance of data using automated data analysis to identify variances. These typically depend on data that identify source agents and their relationships, and is used to draw a compliance analyst's attention to a particular event or group of events that indicate possible anomalies. (Goldschmidt, 2005)

**DBA:** See *Database Administrator.*

**DB-MAIN**
An experimental CASE tool in development at the University of Namur since 1993. It supports most database engineering processes, among them: information analysis, database design, reverse engineering, federated database design, and database migration. Its generic structure model and method engineering environment allow users to build their own methodologies. (Hainaut et al., 2005)

**DBMS:** See *Database Management System.*

**DC:** See *Distributed Constructionism.*

**DCOM:** See *Distributed Component Object Model.*

**DCV:** See *Document Cut-Off Value.*

**DDI**
Digital Divide Index. (Tarnanas & Kikis, 2005)

**DDIR:** See *Duplicate Document Image Retrieval.*

**DDL:** See *Data Definition Language.*

**DDLM:** See *Demand-Driven Learning Model.*

**DDT:** See *Distributed Desktop Training.*

**DE:** See *Distance Education.*

**DEA:** See *Data Envelopment Analysis.*

**Dead Capital**
Assets owned by a nation or state that remain unrecognized and unaccounted for, thereby preventing their productive deployment. (De', 2005)

**Deadlink**
Text or a graphic that can be clicked on and then should lead to other information. When accessed, either an error message is returned or the link leads to an under-construction page. (Falk & Sockel, 2005)

**Deadlock**
A situation in which a transaction in a set of transactions is blocked while waiting for another transaction in the set, and therefore none will become unblocked (unless there is external intervention). (Haraty, 2005a)

**Decentralization**
Represents the move away from a tightly grouped core of administrators and personnel that facilitate distance education, to a system that is more integrated into the different units of an institution. (Lindsay, Williams, et al., 2005)

**Decentralized Decision Making**
In supply chains, it involves decisions where each entity (member of the supply chain) has control over decisions at their stage. However, the decisions not only have a local impact, but also impact the whole supply chain. (Abraham & Leon, 2006)

**Decentralized Model**
The dispersion of decision making in which different independent decisions are made simultaneously. (Peterson, 2005)

**Decentralized Peer-to-Peer Network**
In this network, there is no central directory server. Peers communicate with each other without any assistance or coordination of a third party (i.e., the server). A famous example is Gnutella. (Kwok, et al., 2006)

**Decentralized Strategy**
The structure of the information technology organization encompassing supporting units that are located at the school or college level. (Poda & Brescia, 2005)

**Decimation**
The process of decreasing the sampling rate. It consists of filtering and downsampling. (Jovanovic-Dolecek, 2005b)

**Decimation Filter**
The filter used in decimation to avoid aliasing caused by downsampling. (Jovanovic-Dolecek, 2005b)

**Decision Content**
**1:** Content refers to the particular decision under study; it explores the basic nature and scope of decisions. (Chou, Dyson, & Powell, 2005) **2:** The context includes the outer

context, which refers to the national economic, political, and social context for an organization, and the inner context that is the ongoing strategy, structure, culture, management, and political process of the organization. Context helps to shape the process of decision making. (Chou et al., 2005)

## Decision Explorer

Software often used in Journey Making events that supports the representation and analysis of maps. The Decision Explorer maps are projected onto a public screen for all participants to read and use to illustrate their opinion during the workshop. (Shaw, 2006)

## Decision Rule

**1:** An automatically generated standard that indicates the relationship between multimedia features and content information. (Hurson & Yang, 2005) **2:** In (U,A,d) is any expression of the form $\wedge\{a=v_a : a \in A$ and $v_a \in V_a\} \rightarrow$ d=v where d is the decision attribute and v is a decision value. This decision rule is true in (U,A,d) if for any object satisfying its left-hand side, it also satisfies the right-hand side; otherwise, the decision rule is true to a degree measured by some coefficients such as confidence. (Pawlak et al., 2005) **3:** Specification of the relationship between a collection of observations (conditions) and an outcome (a decision). (Grzymala-Busse & Ziarko, 2005) **4:** The result of an induction procedure providing the final assignment of a response class/value to a new object so that only the predictor measurements are known. Such a rule can be drawn in the form of a decision tree. (Siciliano & Conversano, 2005)

## Decision Set

Ordered or unordered set of decision rules; a common knowledge representation tool (utilized in the most expert systems). (Bruha, 2005)

## Decision Support

**1:** Evolutionary step in the 1990s with characteristics to review retrospective, dynamic data. OLAP is an example of an enabling technology in this area. (DeLorenzo, 2005) **2:** The tools, techniques, and information resources that can provide support to the decision maker in improving the efficiency and effectiveness of his/her decisions. Many of these decision support tools may employ ICTs and be part of the management information system itself. (Ritchie & Brindley, 2005)

## Decision Support System (DSS)

**1:** An interactive arrangement of computerized tools tailored to retrieve and display data regarding business problems and queries. (Peter & Greenidge, 2005a) **2:** An interactive computer-based system which helps decision makers utilize data and models to solve semi-structured or unstructured problems. (Duan & Xu, 2005) **3:** An interactive. computer-based system composed of a user-dialogue system, a model processor, and a data management system, which helps decision makers utilize data and quantitative models to solve semi-structured problems. (Forgionne et al., 2005) **4:** A computer-based system designed to assist in managing activities and information in organizations. (Mathieu & Levary, 2005) **5:** A computer system that enables managers to solve a given problem in their own personalized way. (Pomerol & Adam, 2005) **6:** A system designed, built, and used to support the decision-making process. Its components are the data management system, the model management system, the knowledge engine, the user interface, and the user or users. (Xodo & Nigro, 2005) **7:** A computer-based information system whose purpose is the support of (not replacement) decision-making activities. (Chen, Holt, et al., 2005) **8:** One of a specific class of computerized information systems that support decision-making activities. DSSs are interactive, computer-based systems and subsystems intended to help decision makers use communications technologies, data, documents, knowledge, and models to identify and solve problems and make decisions. Five more specific DSS types include communications-driven DSS, data-driven DSS, document-driven DSS, knowledge-driven DSS, and model-driven DSS. (Power, 2005) **9:** Broadly defined, includes technologies that facilitate decision making. Such systems can embed DMT and utilize these through automated batch processes and/or user-driven simulations or what-if scenario planning. The tools for decision support include analytical or automated approaches like data assimilation and operations research, as well as tools that help the human experts or decision makers manage by objectives or by exception, like OLAP or GIS. (Ganguly et al., 2005) **10:** In a broad sense, can be defined as a system/tools that affect the way people make decisions. In IT, could be defined as a system that increases the intelligence density of data. (Sundaram & Portougal, 2005b) **11:** A specific class of computerized information system that supports business and organizational decision-making activities. DSS is an interactive, software-based system that compiles useful information from raw data, documents, personal knowledge, and/or business models to identify and solve problems and make decisions. (Raisinghani et al., 2005) **12:** An information system that interactively supports the user's ability to evaluate decision alternatives and develop a recommended decision. (Forgionne, 2005) **13:** Typically, a business application that analyzes large amounts of data in warehouses, often for the purpose of strategic decision making. (Das, 2005) **14:** A system and tools that affect the way people make decisions. (Anke & Sundaram, 2006) **15:** Software designed to facilitate decision making, particularly group decision making. (Roibás, 2006b)

## Decision System

Is a tuple (U,A,d), where (U,A) is an information system with the set A of condition attributes and the decision (attribute) d: $U \rightarrow V_d$, where $d \notin A$. Informally, d is an attribute whose value is given by an external source (oracle, expert) in contradiction to conditional attributes in A whose values are determined by the user of the system. (Pawlak et al., 2005)

## Decision Technology System

An information system that is designed to support all phases of the decision-making process in a complete and integrated manner. See also Management Support System (MSS). (Forgionne, 2005)

## Decision Tree

**1:** A flow-chart-like tree structure, where each internal node denotes a test on an attribute, each branch represents an outcome of the test, and each leaf represents a class or class distribution. (Zhou, 2005) **2:** A model consisting of nodes that contain tests on a single attribute and branches representing the different outcomes of the test. A prediction is generated for a new example by performing the test described at the root node and then proceeding along the branch that corresponds to the outcome of the test. If the branch ends in a prediction, then that prediction is returned. If the branch ends in a node, then the test at that node is performed and the appropriate branch selected. This continues until a prediction is found and returned. (Oza, 2005) **3:** A tree-like way of representing a collection of hierarchical rules that lead to a class or value. (Beynon, 2005b) **4:** A tree-shaped structure that represents a set of decisions. These decisions generate rules for the classification of a dataset. (Hamdi, 2005a) **5:** Tree-structured data-mining model used for prediction, where internal nodes are labeled with predicates (decisions), and leaf nodes are labeled with data-mining

models. (Gehrke, 2005) **6:** A method of finding rules or rule induction which divides the data into subgroups that are as similar as possible with regard to a target variable. (Nigro & González Císaro, 2005c) **7:** Each decision-tree algorithm creates rules based on decision trees or sets of if-then statements to maximize interpretability. (Kusiak & Shah, 2005) **8:** A tree-shaped structure that represents sets of decisions. Different types of decisions trees, such as a Classification and Regression Tree (CART), allow experts to create validated decision models that can then be applied to new datasets. (Athappilly & Rea, 2005)

## Decision-Making Process

**1:** The process and act of making decisions. (Goldsmith & Pillai, 2006) **2:** The process whereby managers make decisions, including the stages described by Herbert Simon: intelligence, design, choice, and review. (Pomerol & Adam, 2005) **3:** The process of developing a general problem understanding, formulating the problem explicitly, evaluating alternatives systematically, and implementing the choice. (Forgionne, 2005) **4:** The actions, reactions, and interactions of the various interested parties as they seek to make a commitment to allocate corporate resources. Process incorporates both the formulation and evaluation processes. (Chou et al., 2005)

## Decision-Making Support System (DMSS)

An information system designed to support some, several, or all phases of the decision-making process. (Forgionne et al., 2005)

## Declarative Constraint

A schema object in the database that defines whether a state of the database is consistent or not. (Ale & Espil, 2005)

## Declarative Knowledge

**1:** Knowledge that is based on facts, is static, and is concerned with the properties of objects, persons, and events and their relationships. (Raisinghani, 2005) **2:** Knowledge of basic facts, generally referred to in computerized systems as data. Examples are the number of items in a storage bin, the balance of the account of a customer, or the date of birth of a person. It is one pole of the factual-procedural dimension. (Ein-Dor, 2006)

## Declarative Mode

Declaration oriented languages—such as Prolog—using declarative statements such as: x is greater than y. (Murthy & Krishnamurthy, 2005c)

## Declarative (Nonprocedural) Query Language

A general term for a query language, as opposed to an imperative query language. Imperative (or procedural) languages specify explicit sequences of steps to follow to produce a result, while declarative (non-procedural) languages describe relationships between variables in terms of functions or inference rules, and the language executor (interpreter or compiler) applies some fixed algorithm to these relations to produce a result. (Ferri & Rafanelli, 2005)

## Declarative vs. Procedural

Integrity constraints are declarative statements expressed in languages such as predicate logic, datalog, or SQL. Since their evaluation can be very costly, the potentially troublesome hand-coding of procedural triggers and stored procedures is recommended by most database manuals. The main thrust of this chapter is about reducing the cost of using declarative integrity constraints and avoiding hand-coded implementation. (Decker, 2005)

## DecNotes

An early bulletin board system providing threaded discussions. Developed inside Digital Equipment Corporation and eventually transformed into a product. (Isaak, 2006)

**Decoder:** See *Set-Top Box.*

## Deduction

Deductive knowledge is formal rationalism, mathematical knowledge, and logical reasoning. (Nobre, 2006a)

## Deductive Data Mining

A data-mining methodology that requires one to list explicitly the input data and background knowledge. Roughly it treats data mining as deductive science (axiomatic method). (T.Y. Lin, 2005)

## Deductive Database

An extension of relational database that allows relations to be implicitly defined by rules. (Grant & Minker, 2006)

## Deductive Verification

Technique that, based on models of systems defined as sets of axioms and rules, verifies them by mathematically proving propositions and theorems. (Fisteus & Kloos, 2006)

## Deep Discussion

Discourse that involves critical analysis and debate. (Lam et al., 2006)

## Deep Learning

**1:** Learning that goes beyond the bare minimum. Deep learners come to understand rather than simply know the subject matter and are able to make valid generalizations based upon it. (Pritchard, 2005a) **2:** An approach to learning that is contrasted with "surface" learning. Someone who adopts a deep learning approach may find the subject of study intrinsically motivating or very engaging. (Kukulska-Hulme, 2005)

## Deep Web Mining

Automatically discovering the structures of Web databases hidden in the deep Web and matching semantically related attributes between them. (Wen, 2005b)

## Deepest Inner Self

A psychological reality on a level deeper than (below) intellect, emotions, and body, where rejuvenating psychological energy that is always only positive is found. (Kaluzniacky, 2006)

## Defense in Depth

The multiple levels of security controls and safeguards that an intruder faces. (Mattord & Whitman, 2005)

## Defense Mechanisms

Freud used this term in 1894 to classify the set of manifestations through which the ego protects itself from internal as well as external aggressions. As different branches of psychoanalysis developed, there has been a significant distinction between approaches that interpreted psychoanalysis as the effort to reinforce the ego and the conscious through its adaptation to the external environment (e.g., ego psychology and self-psychology), and strong critics of this approach, considered to be 'hygienic' and 'social orthopedic' by Lacan, who develops a 'return to Freud' approach, and thus a focus and preponderance of the unconscious and of the id. Lacan investigated the conditions of possibility of psychoanalysis and studied Heidegger's ontology and questioning process, and Saussure's and Levy-Strauss' works on symbolism, which inspired his notion of the unconscious organized as a language. The epicenter of this polemic is located around the question of whether defense mechanisms may be manipulated and indoctrinated in order to adapt to the demands of society, versus defense mechanisms that witness the huge complexity of the unconscious life that may be explored in order to create fuller meaning and further development. Defense concepts include projection, introjection, deflection, idealization, splitting, and denial, and all have the common aim of overcoming anxiety. Groups and organizations develop their own defense mechanisms which may be explored through psychoanalytic-oriented consulting, aiming at social change. (Nobre, 2006b)

## Deferred Design Decision

The cornerstone of implementing tailorable information systems, the DDD mechanism through which decisions traditionally are taken during the design phase of an information system development project, as a result of a set of user requirements elicited during analysis, are now being deferred at run-time, until after the user decides about the required information system behavior. The information system can then follow the new design specifications without any maintenance or redevelopment action, and execute them to provide the user-defined behavior. (Stamoulis, Theotokis, & Martakos, 2005)

## Deferred Maintenance

The policy of not performing database maintenance operations when their need becomes evident, but postponing them to a later time. (Sindoni, 2005a)

## Deferred Option

The option to defer a project or an investment, giving a firm an opportunity to make an investment at a later point in time. (W. Li, 2005)

## Definable Set

A set that has a description precisely discriminating elements of the set from among all elements of the universe of interest. (Grzymala-Busse & Ziarko, 2005)

## Defrag

A disk defragmenter rearranges the files stored on hard disk drives so that they are not spread over the surface of the disk, and so access to the files is faster. (D. Stern, 2005)

## Degree

An index measured by the number of linkage incidents with an actor. (Assimakopoulos & Yan, 2006)

## Degree Audit Reporting System™ (DARS™)

This reporting system for electronic advising through a match of degree requirements with a student's completed courses includes transfer articulation of course equivalencies. (Langer, 2005)

## Degree of Abnormality

A probability that represents to what extent a segment is distant to the existing segments in relation with normal events. (Oh et al., 2005)

## Degree of Range

Type of transactions developed within the meta-business, and the way the companies are working together in order to set up a workgroup environment. (Joia, 2005)

## Degree of Reach

How the involved companies are linked within the meta-business in order to transmit data and information among themselves. (Joia, 2005)

## Degree of Structuring

The ability that the companies have to extract knowledge from the data, and information retrieved and shared by them. (Joia, 2005)

## Deixis

A linguistic expression whose understanding requires understanding something besides itself, as with a caption. (N.C. Rowe, 2005b)

## Delay Jitter

Variance of the network delay computed over two subsequent audio packets. (Roccetti & Ferretti, 2005)

## Delay Spike

Sudden, large increase in the end-to-end network delay, followed by a series of audio packets arriving almost simultaneously. (Roccetti & Ferretti, 2005)

## Deliberative Democracy

**1:** A form of democracy in which citizens share a commitment to the resolution of problems of collective choice through free public deliberation, and in which the basic democratic institutions provide a framework for this. (A.R. Edwards, 2005) **2:** Based on a decision-making consensus-oriented process, where parties can freely participate—the outcome of which is the result of reasoned and argumentative discussions. This model aims to achieve an impartial solution for political problems. (Magnani et al., 2006) **3:** Refers to citizen participation in the context of cultivating a public discourse regarding governmental issues, policies, and courses of action. (Holzer & Schweste, 2005)

## Deliberative Poll

Deliberative poll or TELEVOTE is a scientific public opinion poll with a deliberative element. Generally, a phone survey is conducted, then hundreds of respondents are invited, using statistical sampling technology, to come together at a single location, or they are asked to deliberate among themselves and with other interested people and form opinions. When they gather, they deliberate on the issue and have an opportunity to work in small groups (each like a citizens' jury or planning cell), also spending time in plenary sessions when experts are questioned. At the end of the gathering (usually conducted over two to three days), participants are surveyed again. There is no movement toward consensus, and responses are individual. (Keskinen & Kuosa, 2005)

## Deliberative Procedure

A discussion that is governed by the norms of equality and symmetry in participation, and the right of the participants to question the agenda and the discussion rules, as well as the way in which the agenda and rules are applied. (A.R. Edwards, 2005)

## Deliberative Process

A careful discussion, pondering, and weighing of facts. (O'Looney, 2006)

## Delivery

High-quality online delivery is defined as delivery that carefully considers usability, interactivity, and tools. (MacDonald et al., 2005)

## Delivery Mechanism

Process for delivering course material. (Hunter & Carr, 2005)

## Delivery Platform and Application

One of several communication tools including a handheld wireless device maker, a handheld computing device, a personal digital assistant, and a mobile handset. (Rülke et al., 2005)

## Delivery-vs.-Payment (DVP)

A securities-industry procedure in which the buyer's payment for securities is due at the time of delivery; that is, security delivery and payment are simultaneous. (Saha, 2006b)

## Delphi Method

**1:** A consensus technique used not only to obtain consensus but also to encourage visionary thinking. (Janes, 2005) **2:** The objective of most Delphi applications is the reliable and creative exploration of ideas or the production of suitable information for decision making. (Shih & Fang, 2006)

**DEM:** See *Digital Elevation Model.*

## DEM Geometric Quality

Geometric precision measured in terms of the difference between a digital elevation model (DEM) and a reference DEM (R-DEM). (Zelasco et al., 2005)

## Demand Forecasting

Projection of the estimated level of goods or service demand during the months or years covered by a marketing plan. (Cho, 2005)

## Demand-Driven Learning Model (DDLM)

Provides a framework to support and guide the design, delivery, and evaluation of quality e-learning. The DDLM has five main components: the quality standard of superior structure, three consumer demands (content, delivery, and service), and learner outcomes. Quality assurance in the DDLM is implied through ongoing program evaluation and continual adaptation and improvement. (MacDonald et al., 2005)

## Demand-Driven View of Knowledge

A view of knowledge stemming from the requirements of the organization—for example, what knowledge is needed to carry out a particular activity and how can it be applied? (J.S. Edwards, 2005)

## Demand-Side Stakeholder

A person or agency desirous of the services offered by any e-government system and who will have an impact on it in a practical sense. (De', 2005)

## Demat Form

The move from physical certificates to electronic bookkeeping. Actual stock certificates are slowly being removed and retired from circulation in exchange for electronic recording. (Saha, 2006b)

## Demographics

**1:** Involves the statistical study of characteristics within any population such as age, gender, marital status, address, occupation, mobility, health or disease rate, and so on. (De Weaver, 2005) **2:** Refers to the changing population profile of the United States, to its implications for higher education, to the reasons for the explosive growth of distance learning. (D.B. Johnstone, 2005)

## Dendrogram

**1:** A 'tree-like' diagram that summarizes the process of clustering. Similar cases are joined by links whose position in the diagram is determined by the level of similarity between the cases. (Oh  et al., 2005) **2:** A graphical procedure for representing the output of a hierarchical clustering method. It is strictly defined as a binary tree with a distinguished root that has all the data items at its leaves. (Chen & Liu, 2005)

## Denial-of-Service (DOS) Attack

A type of computer system security attack where an opponent prevents legitimate users from accessing a service or a resource, typically by overloading that resource with fabricated requests. (Knight & Labruyere, 2005)

## Denormalization

A step backward in the normalization process—for example, to improve performance. (Kontio, 2005)

## Denormalized Data Table

A database design that violates principles of a good (normalized) data model. Such a database design may lead to various problems such as data redundancy, reduced flexibility, and update anomalies. (Millet, 2005)

## Denotational Semantics

The meaning is given in terms of mathematical functions. (Dasso & Funes, 2005)

## Dense Data

Data that has metric values for a substantial percentage of all possible combinations of the dimension values. (Deshpande & Ramasamy, 2005)

## Dense Data Cube

A data cube is dense if a significant number of its cells (typically at least 1-10%) are not empty. (Riedewald et al., 2005)

## Dense-Wavelength Division Multiplexing (DWDM)

The operation of a passive optical component (multiplexer) that separates (and/or combines) two or more signals at different wavelengths from one (two) or more inputs into two (one) or more outputs. (Chochliouros et al., 2005a)

## Density

**1:** An index used to indicate how actors are closely or loosely connected in a network. It is measured by the proportion of possible lines that are actually present in a network. (Assimakopoulos & Yan, 2006) **2:** The ratio of realized to possible ties. In a network with a density of one, every member of a network is connected to every other. In a "sparse" network, there are few connections between people. The overall density of a network or a network's sub-region is closely related to every other network dimension. (Nelson & Hsu, 2006)

## Density-Biased Sampling

A database sampling method that combines clustering and stratified sampling. (Lutu, 2005)

## Deontic Effect

The establishment of an obligation or the fulfillment of an obligation. (Johannesson, 2005a)

## Dependability

A broader concept that includes availability, reliability, safety, integrity, and maintainability, but not confidentiality. A system is available if it is ready to perform a service; it is reliable if it continues providing a correct service. Safety refers to the absence of catastrophic consequences for users and the environment. A system's integrity guarantees no unauthorized modifications. When systems can be modified and repaired easily, they are maintainable. Confidentiality means that information is not disclosed to unauthorized subjects. (Weippl, 2006)

## Dependence Relation

Relates to data cube query, where some of the group-by queries could be answered using the results of other. (Tan, 2005a)

## Dependency

The relation between data items or fields, or occasionally, tables. Detecting dependencies is the key to putting tables in the various normal forms and, hence, is the key to avoiding anomalies. (Schultz, 2005)

## Dependent Variable

A value representing the presumed effect or consequence of various states of related independent variables. In other words, a dependent variable is the condition for which an explanation is sought. (McHaney, 2005)

## Deployment Cost

The IP-multicast requires additional knowledge in the routers to the basic unicast communication and extra work from the administrators of the routers; the ALM needs the traditional unicast IP infrastructure only. (Hosszú, 2005a)

## Depot

An intermediate server to choose a proxy server for a client request. (Tse, 2006)

## Depth of the Intervention

For Andrew Harrison, intervention strategies range from deep to surface level. Deep interventions are those which act on emotional involvement. These require a high level of behavioral knowledge and skill as well as a sensitivity to the client's needs. Furthermore, there are clearly ethical issues which require the willing participation of a client. (Grieves, 2006b)

## Depth-First

The method of generating candidates by adding specific items at the end of the sequences. See also *Generating-Pruning*. (Masseglia et al., 2005)

**DES:** See *Discrete Event Simulation.*

## Description Logic

**1:** A highly expressive formalism that allows users to specify concepts, properties of concepts, and relationships among concepts by writing independent logical propositions. (Kamthan & Pai, 2006) **2:** Also known as terminological logic, it is a family of logic formalisms for knowledge representation endowed of a syntax and a semantics, which is model theoretic. The basic syntax elements of description logics are: concept names standing for sets of objects, role names linking objects in different concepts, and individuals used for named elements belonging to objects. Basic elements can be combined using constructors to form concept and role expressions to be used in inclusion

assertions and definitions, which impose restrictions on possible interpretations according to the knowledge elicited for a given domain. Each description logic has its set of constructors. (Colucci et al., 2006) **3:** Considered to be the most important knowledge representation formalism unifying and giving a logical basis to the well-known traditions of frame-based systems, semantic networks and KL-ONE-like languages, object-oriented representations, semantic data models, and type systems. (Roldán-García et al., 2005) **4:** Logical formalism to represent structured concepts and the relationships among them. Formally, it is a subset of FOL dealing with concepts (monadic predicates) and roles (binary predicates) which are useful to relate concepts. Knowledge databases in description logic are composed of a Tbox (the intentional component) and an Abox (the box of asserts, the extensional component part). (Alonso-Jiménez et al., 2005)

## Descriptive Taxonomy

In educational theory and practice, an organizational scheme for classifying the structure of conditions for learning, describing the approaches, types, events, methods, and goals of instruction. While affective and psycho-motor capabilities are also important, classic instructional design theory has focused on the cognitive domain. (Lasnik, 2005)

## Deseasonalization

Sometimes also called seasonal adjustment, a process of removing seasonality from the time series. Most governmental statistics are seasonally adjusted to better reflect other components in a time series. (G.P. Zhang, 2005)

## Design

**1:** The intentional creation of objects. (Knight, 2006b) **2:** The structured composition of an object, process, or activity. (Murphy, 2005c)

## Design Framework

An open-ended design methodology that combines research and design activity. (Knight & Jefsioutine, 2006)

## Design Knowledge Comparison

The comparison of engineering design knowledge to identify and determine the relationships among design knowledge represented in the given knowledge model. (Ma, 2006)

**D**

### Design Method

A method, tool, or technique employed during research, design, and development. (Knight & Jefsioutine, 2006)

### Design Model

A model developed to represent the optimal technical solution of a specified user need (as represented in a requirements model). (Krogstie, 2005a)

### Design Perspective

A designer can abstract characteristic types of the modeling object and exploit only one characteristic type, such as behavior; and using that dimension she/he develops a model that represents that object. (Tobar et al., 2006)

### Design Rationale Environment for Argumentation and Modeling (DREAM)

A tool dedicated to design-rationale capture by the way of an extended QOC notation. (Lacaze et al., 2006)

### Design Recovery

Recreates design abstractions from a combination of code, existing design documentation (if available), personal experience, and general knowledge about problem and application domains. (Tan & Zhao, 2005b)

### Design Research

**1:** A methodology developed as a way to carry out formative research to test and refine educational designs based on principles derived from prior research. Design research is an approach of progressive refinements in design, with the design revisions based on experience, until all problems are worked out. It has dual goals of refining both theory and practice. (Woodruff & Nirula, 2005) **2:** Exploratory activity employed to understand the product, process of design, distribution and consumption, and stakeholders' values and influence. (Knight & Jefsioutine, 2006)

### Design, Specification, and Verification of Interactive Systems (DSV-IS)

An annual international workshop on user interfaces and software engineering. The first DSV-IS workshop was held in 1994 in Carrara, Italy. The focus of this workshop series ranges from the pure theoretical aspects to the techniques and tools for the design, development, and validation of interactive systems. (Campos & Harrison, 2006)

### Design Variables

Characteristics of an organization, its processes, control, and coordination structures that can be varied to produce a specific organization design. (Morris et al., 2005)

### Designation

Representation of a concept by a sign that denotes it. (Gillman, 2006)

### Designer

A user who collaborates with designers as domain experts, envisioning new work practices and tools. This is the third stage in the developmental theory of participatory-design relationships between users and designers. (Carroll, 2005)

### Design-for-All Principle

Design principle in which services are able to be used by all members of society. This includes multi-lingual and services for the disabled. (Knepper & Chen, 2006)

### Desirable/Undesirable Coevolution

A heuristic with which to talk about knowledge management as a process along a continuum. (Land, Amjad, et al., 2006)

### Desktop Delivery

Using electronic formats to send articles to users. (Burke et al., 2005)

### Desktop Publishing

Creating pages for print media using a standard home or office computer and commercial software, and then outputting them on a simple desktop printer. (Snyder, 2005)

### Desktop Search

The functionality to index and retrieve personal information that is stored in desktop computers, including files, e-mails, Web pages, and so on. (Hua et al., 2006)

### Desktop Video Conferencing (DVC)

The use of a desktop computer to send and receive video, audio, and text in real time via the Internet. (Wild, 2005)

### Destination Marketing Organization (DMO)

A public-sector organization charged with the promotion of a destination. It may operate at the local, regional, or national level, and often includes membership from private-sector organizations. (Carson, 2005)

## Destination Marketing System

A computerized information system used as a marketing tool, usually to distribute information on tourism attractions and tourism products for a particular geographical destination to potential visitors. (Hornby, 2005)

## Destination Marketing Web Site

Web site featuring information about individual products and generic information about a local, regional, or national destination. These sites may be purely for promotion, or may include e-commerce facilities for booking and purchasing a product. May be managed by DMOs, or by private firms or industry associations not affiliated with a DMO. (Carson, 2005)

## Detailed Project Plan

A plan(s) that specifies detailed schedules, milestones, humanpower, and equipment requirements necessary for complementing a project. (Peterson & Kim, 2005)

**DETC:** See *Distance Education and Training Council.*

## Deterministic Behavior

If a set of a shared application is started in an equivalent state, and the same set of events is presented to those instances, then if the same state transitions will happen for all instances, the application has deterministic behavior. It is important to note that this definition is more relaxed than other ones, in the sense that resources that an application might need are considered as part of the environment. Where other definitions might assume that an application is no longer behaving deterministically if, for example, the system time of the local machine is used, this definition regards the system time as a part of the environment. (Trossen & Molenaar, 2005)

## Deterrence-Based Trust

The first stage of trust is based on the consistency of behavior. It develops as team members simply comply as they fear sanctions and damage of the relationship. (Lettl et al., 2006)

## Detrending

A process of removing trend from the time series through either differencing of time series observations or subtracting fitted trends from actual observations. (G.P. Zhang, 2005)

## Developing Country

**1:** A country in which the average annual income is low, most of the population is usually engaged in agriculture, and the majority live near the subsistence level. In general, developing countries are not highly industrialized, dependent on foreign capital and development aid, whose economies are mostly dependent on agriculture and primary resources, and do not have a strong industrial base. (Rahman, 2005d) **2:** One of the group of countries generally accepted as containing the poorer nations of the world. It is often used interchangeably with the term "third world," i.e., belonging neither to the first world (developed countries) nor the second world (former countries with command economies). (Escalante, 2005) **3:** A country in the process of becoming industrialized, but having constrained resources with which to combat its economical problems. (Shareef & Kinshuk, 2005) **4:** A country with a relatively low per capital gross national product (GNP). (Ajiferuke & Olatokun, 2005) **5:** A country in the process of converting to a capitalist model in which the economy is founded mainly upon manufacturing and service vs. agricultural production. (St.Amant, 2005b) **6:** One of the nations, particularly in Asia and Latin America, that is are not as industrially developed as countries in Europe and North America. A developing country is are characterized by an underdeveloped and uneven infrastructure in the areas of telecommunications, roads, transportation, and electricity distribution. Other features of such societies include low-cost labor, and a large portion of the population living in rural areas and employed in the agriculture sector. (Tarafdar, 2005)

## Developing Project

Creation of a small group of people that work on an existing problematic theme and design solutions where information and communication technologies make sense. (Giorgi & Schürch, 2005)

## Development Awareness Project

Project aimed at promoted awareness and understanding of international development issues usually with people in high-income countries. (Pryor, 2005)

## Development Literature

Literature about impoverished countries of the world that are trying to modernize or to find different ways of supporting their populations. (McPherson, 2005)

**D**

### Development Process

The process for the improvement of society and community, through diversified means, creating demands and solutions at the appropriate dimension of necessity. (Rahman, 2006)

### Developmental Theory

Theory of learning that involves growth and other qualitative changes in skills, knowledge, and capacities. Developmental theory is contrasted to accretive theory in which learning is conceived of as a matter of quantitative improvement—more knowledge or faster performance. (Carroll, 2005)

### Deviance Information Criterion (DIC)

Measure introduced as a tool for comparing and selecting complex hierarchical models. DIC combines a measure of fit, the deviance statistic, and a measure of complexity—the number of free parameters in the model. Since increasing complexity is accompanied by a better fit, the DIC trades off these two quantities. (Vidal-Rodeiro et al., 2005)

### Deviation Analysis

Locates and analyzes deviations from normal statistical behavior. (Yeo, 2005)

### Device

**1:** A piece of equipment used in a network. Devices include, but are not limited to, workstations, servers, data storage equipment, printers, routers, switches, hubs, machinery or appliances with network adapters, and punch-down panels. (Maris, 2005) **2:** An entity that does not deal with information storage, retrieval, or transmission, but only deals with the exchange and transmission of data. (Benyon, 2006)

### Device Profile

A model of a device storing information about both its costs and capabilities. (De Meo, Quattrone, et al., 2005)

**DFD:** See *Data Flow Diagram.*

**DFT:** See *Discrete Fourier Transformation.*

**DHT:** See *Distributed Hash Table.*

**DHTML:** See *Dynamic Hypertext Markup Language.*

### Diagram Operation

An operation over objects and morphisms that takes a certain configuration of them as an input, input diagram, and augments it with a few new—derived—objects and morphisms matching the shape of the output diagram. (Diskin, 2005)

### Diagram Predicate

A property of a certain configuration, diagram, of objects and morphisms. (Diskin, 2005)

### Diagrammatic System

A computerized system that adopts different diagrammatic representation forms. Many different systems are currently used in a wide variety of contexts: logic teaching, automated reasoning, specifying computer programs, reasoning about situations in physics, graphical user interfaces to computer programs, and so on. (Ferri & Grifoni, 2006)

**Dial-Up Connection:** See *Modem.*

### Dial-Up Internet Connection

Method of using telephone lines to "call in" to a server that then allows the individual to access the Internet and the World Wide Web. (St.Amant, 2005e)

### Diaspora

**1:** A dispersion of a people from their original homeland, such as the Jewish Diaspora after WWII or the Vietnamese diaspora in the early 1970s. The Khmer diaspora was the result of the civil war and displacement of people due to the Khmer Rouge regime in the 1970s. Cambodian refugees mostly settled in the U.S., Canada, Australia, France, and Thailand. (Hutchinson, 2005) **2:** Immigrant communities that live in nation-states other than their original homelands. (Harris, 2005)

**DIC:** See *Deviance Information Criterion.*

### Dice

Selecting a range on multiple dimensions to select a sub-cube of the original space. (Deshpande & Ramasamy, 2005)

**DICOM:** See *Digital Imaging and Communications in Medicine.*

### Didactical Situation

A set of circumstances of a teaching situation that can be linked in a way that is coherent, regular, reproducible, and specific to the targeted knowledge. It is not a theory of learning but a process of guiding other people's learning (i.e., the dissemination and transposition of knowledge). (Pelton & Pelton, 2005)

## Differencing
Removes trend from a time series. This is an effective way to provide a clearer view of the true underlying behavior of the series. (Cho, 2005)

## Differential Correction
The effects of atmospheric and other GPS errors can be reduced using a procedure called differential correction. Differential correction uses a second GPS receiver at a known location to act as a static reference point. The accuracy of differentially corrected GPS positions can be from a few millimeters to about five meters, depending on the equipment, time of observation, and software processing techniques. (Olla, 2005b)

## Differential Time of Arrival (DTOA)
A positioning technology in which several transmitters (synchronized to a common time base) are used to measure time differences of arrival at the receiver and hence determine the receiver's geographical position. (Giaglis, 2005)

## Differential/Incremental Evaluation
To re-evaluate a CQ on the changes that have been made in the base data since its previous evaluation. (Khan, 2005)

## Differentiated Service (DiffServ)
**1:** Architecture for QoS differentiation in the Internet. It employs marking of IP datagrams to associate packets to predefined per-hop behaviors. The DiffServ architecture is described in the IETF RFC 2475. (DaSilva, 2005) **2:** Framework where network elements give preferential treatment to classifications identified as having more demanding requirements. DiffServ provides quality of services based on user group needs rather than traffic flows. (Gutiérrez & Ting, 2005)

## Differentiation
The state of segmentation or division of an organizational system into subsystems, each of which tends to develop particular attributes in relation to the requirements posed by the relevant environment. This includes both the formal division, as well as behavioral attributes of the members of organizational subsystems. (Peterson, 2005)

## Differentiation Agent
Comparison-shopping agent specializing in collecting price-related, impersonal information, for example, Pricewatch.com. (Wan, 2006)

**DiffServ:** See *Differentiated Service.*

## Diffusion
**1:** A model in which the uptake of an artifact is dependent on its intrinsic merit being easily recognized and passed on to other people. (Brady, 2005) **2:** A process by which an idea, product, practice, behavior, or object is communicated and circulated to those to whom it is relevant. (Askarany, 2005) **3:** The process of the spread of an innovation in a social system. (Voeth & Liehr, 2005) **4:** The act of a higher education institution using information, professional relationships, and structured methods to incorporate an innovation into learning, research, and administration, bringing about new integrated system-wide change. (Poda & Brescia, 2005) **5:** The process by which an innovation is communicated through certain channels over time among the members of a social system. (Askar & Halici, 2005) **6:** The process by which new behaviors, innovations, or practices spread through an organization as people learn about them from other employees and try them out. (Jones & Gupta, 2005) **7:** The spread of an innovation through a social system. (Green et al., 2005)

## Diffusion of Information Technology
Reflects the spreading of information technology concepts among the society of implementation, whether within an organization or within the community at large. (Kamel, 2005a)

## Diffusion of Innovation
**1:** The process by which an innovation is communicated through certain channels over time among the members of a social system. (Lertwongsatien & Wongpinunwatana, 2005) **2:** The spread of abstract ideas and concepts, technical information, and actual practices within a social system. In the context of small and medium enterprises (SMEs): flow or movement of innovation from a source to an adopter, typically via communication and influence. (Pease & Rowe, 2005)

D

## Digital

Information represented as discrete numeric values, for example in binary format (zeros or ones), as opposed to information in continuous or analog form. Binary digits (bits) are typically grouped into "words" of various lengths—8-bit words are called bytes. (Cosemans, 2005b)

## Digital Access Index (DAI)

An index developed, calculated, and published by the International Telecommunication Union that measures the overall ability of individuals in a country to access and use new information and communication technologies. Indicators used to calculate the index are fixed telephone subscribers per 100 inhabitants, mobile subscribers per 100 inhabitants, adult literacy, overall school enrollment (primary, secondary, and tertiary), Internet access price (20 hours per month) as a percent of per-capita income, broadband subscribers per 100 inhabitants, international Internet bandwidth per capita, and Internet users per 100 inhabitants. (Barrera, 2005)

## Digital Accessible Information Systems (DAISY)

A standard for digital talking books maintained by the DAISY Consortium. It was developed with the objective of making talking books more accessible and to facilitate navigation within the book. It allows the storage and retrieval of information in a multi-modal format in order to reach out to people with different disabilities. (Lahiri & Basu, 2005)

## Digital Asset

1: Any asset that exists in a digitized form and is of intrinsic or commercial value to an organization. (Subramanian, 2005) 2: An electronic media element that may be unstructured such as an image, audio, or video, or structured such as a document or presentation, usually with associated metadata. (Verhaart & Kinshuk 2006) 3: The information (in digital form) a company collects about its customers. Companies that create value with digital assets may be able to reharvest them through a potentially infinite number of transactions. (Lee et al., 2006)

## Digital Asset Management (DAM)

A set of processes that facilitate the search, retrieval, and storage of digital assets from an archive. (Subramanian, 2005)

## Digital Asset Store

A combination of file systems and databases. (Subramanian, 2005)

## Digital Audio

Digital representation of sound waveform, recorded as a sequence of discrete samples, representing the intensity of the sound pressure wave at a given time instant. Sampling frequency describes the number of samples recorded in each second, and bit resolution describes the number of bits used to represent the quantized (i.e., integer) value of each sample. (Wieczorkowska, 2005)

## Digital Camera

A camera that stores images in a digital format rather than recording them on light-sensitive film. Pictures then may be downloaded to a computer system as digital files, where they can be stored, displayed, printed, or further manipulated. (Garrett, 2006a)

## Digital Cash

Classified into electronic wallet (IC card) or online type (network). Note that both types of digital cash have appeared recently. The distinction between the two types has been disappearing. (Kurihara, 2006)

## Digital Certificate

1: An electronic "passport" that can be used to establish identity in an electronic environment. (Mundy & Otenko, 2005) 2: A unique digital ID used to identify individuals (personal certificates), software (software certificates), or Web servers (server certificates). They are based on a hierarchy of trust. (Sockel & Chen, 2005) 3: An electronic data file issued by a Certification Authority (CA) to a certificate holder. It contains the certificate holder's name, a serial number, the certificate holder's public key, expiration dates, and the digital signature of the CA. It can be used to establish the holder's credentials when doing transactions through the Internet. (Xu & Korba, 2005) 4: Used to authenticate both parties. CAs must issue these certificates. These are trusted third parties that have carried out identity checks on their certificate holders and are prepared to accept a degree of liability for any losses due to fraud. CAs also issue the public and private keys. (Lei et al., 2005b)

## Digital City

1: This concept encompasses a diversified number of approaches to the co-evolution spatial development and the diffusion ICT. (Moutinho & Heitor, 2005) **2:** Usually a Web site that is centered on a city, where public authorities, business, and citizens can communicate and exchange information. (Jaeger, 2005)

## Digital Community

A city, town, or community that actively applies interactive communication technologies to enhance all aspects of its culture, community, and commerce. (Geiselhart & Jamieson, 2005)

## Digital Darwinism

An ideology framing economic and social situations which argues that only the economically and socially fit will survive because of their ability to adapt to the digital world. (Skovira, 2005)

## Digital Deliberation

The process of thoughtful discussion regarding an issue or course of action through the use of ICTs. Digital deliberation in government is characterized by access to balanced information, an open agenda, time to consider issues expansively, freedom from manipulation or coercion, a rule-based framework for discussion, participation by an inclusive sample of citizens, broader and freer interaction between participants, and the recognition of differences between participants. (Holzer & Schweste, 2005)

## Digital Democracy

Encompasses the use of ICTs in the practice of democracy, whereby emphasis is placed on the processes and structures that define the relationships between government and citizens, between elected officials and appointed civil servants, and between the legislative and executive branches of government. (Holzer & Schweste, 2005)

## Digital Divide

**1:** Refers to individuals or members of communities and groups whose social, cultural, political, economic, or personal circumstances constrain access to electronic communications or limit benefit to their lives from contemporary electronic technologies. (Malina, 2005) **2:** A term used to describe the gap between the technology "haves" and "have-nots." It is a gap in opportunities experienced by those with limited accessibility to technology. (Rahman, 2005b) **3:** Unequal access and use of data, information, and communication. More specifically, digital divide means unequal access to ICT infrastructure or lacking skills in using it. (Heinonen, 2005) **4:** Gap existing between communities regarding their ability or the possibility to effectively access information and communication technologies. (Costagliola, Di Martino, Ferrucci, & Gravino, 2006) **5:** Refers to segments of the population lacking Internet access or Internet-related skills. (Holzer & Schweste, 2005) **6:** A term used to describe the disparity between persons who have access to information and computing technology, and those who do not. Often used to describe the lack of Internet accessibility to those living in rural or remote areas or who lack computing knowledge and skills. (Becker, 2005a) **7:** The discrepancy between people who have access to and the resources to use new information and communication tools, such as the Internet, and people who do not have the resources and access to the technology. It can exist between rural and urban areas, between the educated and uneducated, between economic classes, and between more and less developed nations. (Neumann, 2005) **8:** The disparity in access to technology that exists across certain demographic groups. Also, a term used to describe the discrepancy between those who have the skills, knowledge, and abilities to use technology and those who do not. (Sharma, 2006a) **9:** The gap between countries or communities with and without access to technology, usually because of a combination of economic, socio-political, and historical causes. The differences relate to ICT infrastructure and human resources and skills, although it is usually used in the context of the inadequate Internet connectivity in developing countries or in underdeveloped regions. (Arellano et al., 2005) **10:** The gap created between those using ICT and those who do not, for a range of reasons, including a lack of access to ICT as a result of social or economic factors, a lack of technical and keyboard skills to use ICT, and a lack of basic skills or computer literacy skills to understand the requirements and interpret the information of ICT. (Sutcliffe, 2005)

## Digital Economy

**1:** Accepts as its foundation ICT developments and represents the impact that these have had on the conduct of business and commercial activities. Changes in markets and supply chains as well as increasing global competition all represent what is encapsulated within the term the digital economy. (Ritchie & Brindley, 2005) **2:** The economy based more in the form of intangibles, information, innovation, and creativity, to expand economic potential; based on the exploitation of ideas rather than material things using digital infrastructure. (Sharma, 2006a) **3:** Economic system using Internet technology for business transactions. (Efendioglu, 2006) **4:** Economy based on digital technologies such as computer, software, and digital networks. (Tian & Stewart, 2006) **5:** The economy for the age of networked intelligence. The digital economy is also a knowledge economy. Information, in all forms digital, is the input of an organizational transformation or value-creation process. (Lee et al., 2006)

### Digital Elevation Model (DEM)

The set of points in a three-dimensional coordinate system modeling a real object's surface. (Zelasco et al., 2005)

### Digital Equity

The social-justice goal of ensuring that everyone in our society has equal access to technology tools, computers, and the Internet. Even more, it occurs when all individuals have the knowledge and skills to access and use technology tools, computers, and the Internet. (Schrum, 2005)

### Digital Ethos Condition

One of several factors individuals use to assess the credibility or the worth of an online presentation of information. (St.Amant, 2005c)

### Digital Filter

The digital system that performs digital signal processing, that is, transforms an input sequence into a desired output sequence. (Jovanovic-Dolecek, 2005a)

### Digital Filter Design

The process of deriving the transfer function of the filter. It is carried out in three steps: definition of filter specification, approximation of given specification, and implementation of digital filter in hardware or software. (Jovanovic-Dolecek & Díaz-Carmona, 2005)

### Digital Fingerprint

A larger document is not signed in its entirety. Generally a digital fingerprint of the larger document is computed and signed. For this purpose hash functions are used. They should be collision resistant and not invertible. Then two different meaningful messages have different fingerprints and it is not possible to construct a meaningful message, given a fingerprint. (Stickel, 2005)

### Digital Forensics

Techniques to determine the root causes of security violations that have occurred in a computer or a network. (Thuraisingham, 2005)

### Digital Gap

The disparity or breach among countries generated by the lack of communication infrastructure and computer-based power that contribute to accentuate socioeconomic differences. (Ochoa-Morales, 2005)

### Digital Government

**1:** Digital government has different possible definitions, from online services to any use of ICTs in the public. In general terms, digital government refers to the use of ICTs in government for at least three purposes: providing public services, improving managerial effectiveness, and promoting democracy. (Sharma, 2006b) **2:** The development, adoption, or use of ICT by government organizations and actors. (Hinnant & Sawyer, 2005) **3:** The use of information and communications technology to improve the relations between government and its employees, citizens, businesses, nonprofit partners, and other agencies by enhancing access to and delivery of government information and services. (Knepper & Chen, 2006)

### Digital Identity Management System

A system related to the definition and lifecycle of digital identities and profiles, as well as environments for exchanging and validating this information. (Cremonini et al., 2006)

### Digital Image

Image f(x,y) that has been discretized both in spatial coordinates and brightness, and consists of a set of elements, defined on an n-dimensional regular grid, that have the potential for display. It can be considered a matrix whose row and column indices identify a point in the image, and the corresponding matrix element values identify the grey level at that point. The elements of such a digital array are called image elements, picture elements, pixels, or pels. (Venters et al., 2005)

### Digital Imaging and Communications in Medicine (DICOM)

A medical image standard developed by the American College of Radiology and the National Electrical Manufacturers' Association. (Tong & Wong, 2005a)

### Digital Inclusion

**1:** The obverse of "digital divide"; seeks to proactively focus on including people in the use of ICT for local and personal benefit either directly or through distributed application of information, knowledge, practice, and process derived from such technologies. (Erwin & Taylor, 2005) **2:** Strategies and actions to assure more equal access to digital technologies and Web facilities, and to strengthen effective, meaningful, and beneficial use for all members of the public in their day-to-day lives. (Malina, 2005)

## Digital Interactivity

Despite the fact that interactivity as a blanket concept cannot be precisely defined, the quality of interactivity defined by the user generally depends on the amount of "common ground," the user's perceived ability to control and influence form and content of the mediated environment, to be "engaged" in mediated space (in terms of belief and/or in terms of sensory stimulation or displaced physical enactment or embodiment), and to participate in multi-dimensional feedback which offers choice in real time. (Thomas & Roda, 2006b)

## Digital Item Representation

Multimedia content related to the merchandise of the VR-mall, coupled with semantic information that describes and categorizes each item. (Lepouras & Vassilakis, 2006)

## Digital Library

**1:** An organized collection of digital information. (Gregory, 2005) **2:** A cultural infrastructure that collects and stores information in electronic format, and supports its users in accessing a large collection of information effectively through digital means. (Lai et al., 2005) **3:** A library that makes virtually all of its resources available to patrons via electronic channels. Individuals interested in using the library can access databases, catalogs, journals and other periodicals, some books, and a variety of other services over the Internet. (Baim, 2006b) **4:** A library that provides the resources to select, structure, offer, access, distribute, preserve, and maintain the integrity of the collections of digital works. (Wu & Lee, 2005) **5:** A set of electronic documents organized in collections, plus the system that provides access to them. The digital version of traditional libraries. (Martínez-González, 2005) **6:** A set of electronic resources (usually documents) combined with a software system that allows storing, organizing, and retrieving the resources. (Loh et al., 2005)

## Digital Literacy

A term used to describe the ability of users to perform in digital environments. (Eshet, 2005)

## Digital Map

**1:** A data set stored in a computer in digital form. It is not static, and the flexibility of digital maps is vastly greater than paper maps. Inherent in this concept is the point that data on which the map is based is available to examine or question. Digital maps can be manipulated easily in GIS package environments. (Al-Hanbali & Sadoun, 2006) **2:** Any form of geographic boundaries or spatially referenced drawings that have been captured, or "digitized," into an electronic form. Each element of the map is or may be linked to various descriptive or identifying types of information in a database. (Crossland, 2005)

## Digital Media Warehouse

A vast collection of digitized media objects from an unrestricted set of different domains. (Windhouwer & Kersten, 2005)

## Digital Multimedia

The bits that represent texts, images, audios, and videos, and are treated as data by computer programs. (Oh et al., 2005)

## Digital Reference Service

A human-mediated, Internet-based service in which users' queries are answered in real time. (Lewis, 2005)

## Digital Rights Expression (DRE)

The attachment of metadata to a work in order to describe the copyright status of that work. (Hassan & Hietanen, 2006)

## Digital Rights Management (DRM)

**1:** A set of technologies for content owners to protect their copyrights and stay in closer contact with their customers. In most instances, DRM is a system that encrypts digital media content and limits access to only those users who have acquired a proper license to play the content. That is, DRM is a technology that enables the secure distribution, promotion, and sale of digital media content on the Internet. (Kwok, 2005) **2:** Technology used to control or restrict the use of digital media content on electronic devices, in order to protect intellectual property and to combat piracy. (Ng, 2006) **3:** The protection and management of the intellectual property rights of digital content. It offers a means of setting up a contract between content consumers and providers. Specifically, it provides content creators or owners with a range of controls over their products or services. It also offers interoperability to consumers, including end users and any intermediaries such as dealers, distributors, and system administrators. (Wang, Cheng, Cheng, & Huang, 2006) **4:** A set of technologies whose purpose is to restrict access to, and the possible uses of, digital media objects, for example, by scrambling the data on a DVD to prevent unauthorized copying. (Hughes & Lang, 2005) **5:** The limitation of the access of users to information in a repository through the use of technical protection measures. (Hassan & Hietanen, 2006) **6:** A concept for managing and controlling the access and utilization of digital assets. (Karnouskos & Vilmos, 2006) **7:** Refers to methods and technologies designed to control access to or use of copyrighted data. (Gaedke et al., 2005) **8:** A platform to protect and securely deliver content on a computer. (Upadhyaya et al., 2006)

## Digital Satellite Image

A digital image sent by a satellite system that is usually launched in special orbits such as the geostationary orbit. The latter type of satellite system rotates at about 35,000 Km from the surface of the earth and is able to cover the same area of the earth 24 hours a day. (Al-Hanbali & Sadoun, 2006)

## Digital Signal

A discrete-time signal whose amplitude is also discrete. It is defined as a function of an independent, integer-valued variable n. Consequently, a digital signal represents a sequence of discrete values (some of which can be zeros) for each value of integer n. (Jovanovic-Dolecek, 2005a)

## Digital Signal Processing

Extracts useful information carried by the digital signals, and is concerned with the mathematical representation of the digital signals and algorithmic operations carried out on the signal to extract the information. (Jovanovic-Dolecek, 2005a)

## Digital Signature

**1:** An electronic signature can be deemed the digital equivalent of a handwritten signature. Electronic signatures can be used to authenticate the identity of the signer of the document and to also confirm the data integrity of the document. (Mundy & Otenko, 2005) **2:** Extra data appended to the message in order to authenticate the identity of the sender and to ensure that the original content of the message or document that has been sent is unchanged. (Guan, 2005c) **3:** A digital signature may be used to electronically sign a document. The signature

can be checked by anyone and, if properly used, assures integrity of the signed message, as well as the identity of the signer. (Stickel, 2005)

## Digital Subscriber Line (DSL)

**1:** Shortened from Asymmetric Digital Subscriber Line (ADSL). A family of digital telecommunications protocols designed to allow high-speed data communication over the existing copper telephone lines between end users and telephone companies. (Vician & Buche, 2005) **2:** A mechanism for transmitting online information through telephone lines, but at a faster speed than permitted by a normal telephone connection. (St.Amant, 2005e) **3:** A switched telephone service that provides high data rates, typically more than 1 Mbp. (Raisinghani & Ghanem, 2005) **4:** A technique for transferring data over regular phone lines by using a frequency different from traditional voice calls or analog modem traffic over the phone wires. DSL lines carry voice, video, and data. (Hentea, 2005a) **5:** Supports consolidation of data, video, and voice traffic for enabling broadband transmissions over ordinary twisted-copper-wire telephone lines between the telephone company central office and the subscriber's residence. (Littman, 2006) **6:** A method implementing a numerical coding technique for fast Internet access. It uses the ordinary telephone line and splits the signals of voice and data. It can offer speeds up to 8Mbps. (Kirlidog, 2005) **7:** A technique for transmitting large amounts of data rapidly on twisted pairs of copper wires, with the transmission rates for downstream access being much greater than for the upstream access. (Hin & Subramaniam, 2005a) **8:** A technology that provides high bandwidth digital data flows over existing ordinary copper telephone lines to homes and small businesses. (Pease et al., 2005)

## Digital Subscriber Loop (DSL)

The global term for a family of technologies that transform the copper local loop into a broadband line capable of delivering multiple video channels into the home. There are a variety of DSL technologies known as xDSL; each type has a unique set of characteristics in terms of performance (maximum broadband capacity), distance over maximum performance (measured from the switch), frequency of transmission, and cost. (Chochliouros et al., 2005c)

## Digital Television (DTV)

**1:** The term adopted by the FCC to describe its specification for the next generation of broadcast-television transmissions. DTV encompasses both HDTV and STV.

(Chochliouros et al., 2005b) **2:** The new generation of broadcast television transmissions. These are of better quality than the traditional analogical broadcasts and will presumably replace them. (Prata, 2005) **3:** Broadcasting of television signals by means of digital techniques, used for the provision of TV services. (Hulicki, 2005)

## Digital Thinking Skills

**1:** A refinement of the term Digital Literacy describing the variety of thinking skills that comprise digital literacy. (Eshet, 2005) **2:** Creation of a new mental model that is based on an asynchronous mental model and on the ability of linking, combining, and associating different, or even opposite ideas. (Joia, 2005)

## Digital Versatile Disc (DVD)

An optical disc technology expected to rapidly replace the CD-ROM (as well as the audio compact disc) over the next few years. The DVD holds 4.7 gigabytes of information on one of its two sides, or enough for a 133-minute movie. (Bochicchio & Fiore, 2005)

## Digital Video Broadcasting (DVB)

**1:** Originally meant television broadcasting using digital signals (as opposed to analog signals), but now refers to broadcasting all kinds of data as well as sound, often accompanied by auxiliary information and including bidirectional communications. (Chochliouros et al., 2005b) **2:** The European standard for the development of DTV. (Hulicki, 2005) **3:** A standard for sending and receiving digital information. It is used for transmitting television by satellite and for "broadcasting" Internet. (D. Stern, 2005) **4:** The European standard for digital TV. This standard provides a very high-speed, robust transmission chain capable of handling the many megabytes per second needed for hundreds of MPEG-2 digital TV channels. (Cosemans, 2005b)

## Digital Watermark(ing)

**1:** An image or a logo in digital format embedded in a host image. The embedded data can later be used to prove the rightful ownership. (Chen, Chen, Ma, et al., 2005) **2:** A process that secretly embeds a message, such as a logo or data about the authorship, into multimedia. The watermark information still can be detected or extracted after suffering from attacks. Its major intent is establishing an identity of multimedia to prevent unauthorized use. (Lou et al., 2006) **3:** A method of embedding secret information (watermark) into a host media—such as image, video,

and audio—for the purposes of copyright protection, authentication, content integrity verification, and so forth. (Si & Li, 2006) **4:** The practice of hiding a message in digital media, such as a digital image, audio, and/or video. Digital watermarking only gained enormous popularity as a research topic in the latter half of the 1990s. (Sattar & Yu, 2006) **5:** Sometimes also known as digital data hiding, a technique for inserting secret information into digital content in a seemingly innocuous and standards-compliant manner for applications of content authentication, covert communications, copyright control or protection, and so forth. In the case of covert communications, it is also called steganography. (Wang, Cheng, Cheng, & Huang, 2006) **6:** The act of inserting a message into a cover work. The resulting stego-object can be visible or invisible. (K. Chen, 2005)

## Digitality

The proportion of a company's business that is online. (Borders & Johnston, 2005)

## Digitation

The process of converting analog data to digital data where binary systems are usually used. Programmers find dealing with digital data is much easier than dealing with analog data. (Al-Hanbali & Sadoun, 2006)

## Digitization

Measures that automate processes. (Sundaram & Portougal, 2005a)

## Dilution of a Training Program

Short circuiting the full delivery of a program, or inaccurate presentation of material. (D. Wright, 2005)

## Dimension

**1:** A business perspective useful for analyzing data. A dimension usually contains one or more hierarchies that can be used to drill up or down to different levels of detail. (Bellatreche & Mohania, 2005) **2:** A category of information relevant to the decision-making purpose of the data warehouse (Scime, 2005b). **3:** A dimension attribute of an entity is a functional attribute that describes an aspect of the entity such as location or product. Dimension attributes can be hierarchical, for example, year-quarter-month-day for the time dimension. (Riedewald et al., 2005) **4:** A property of a fact that specifies or explains one aspect of said fact. Usually a dimension has information associated with it. (Badia, 2005c) **5:** A property of the data used to classify it and navigate the corresponding data cube. In multi-dimensional databases, dimensions are often organized into several hierarchical levels, for example, a time dimension may be organized into days, months, and years. (Tininini, 2005b) **6:** Corresponds to a perspective under which facts can be fruitfully analyzed. It is a structural attribute of a fact, that is, a list of members (variables), all of which are of a similar type in the user's perception of the data. (Rafanelli, 2005) **7:** Refers to the determinants of quality of each of the three components—namely, system quality, information quality, and service quality. (Wilkin, 2005) **8:** A set of members (criteria) allowing to drive the analysis (example for the Product dimension: product type, manufacturer type). Members are used to drive the aggregation operations. (Schneider, 2005) **9:** An axis along which the facts are recorded. (Deshpande & Ramasamy, 2005) **10:** Static, fact-oriented information used in decision support to drill down into measurements. (DeLorenzo, 2005)

## Dimension Dependency

Presents when there is an interaction of the different dimensions with one another. (Tan, 2005a)

## Dimension Table

**1:** A database table that stores the different possible values for a dimension, the attributes for those values, and the hierarchical values to which it maps. (Deshpande & Ramasamy, 2005) **2:** A table containing the data for one dimension within a star schema. The primary key is used to link to the fact table, and each level in the dimension has a corresponding field in the dimension table. (Bellatreche & Mohania, 2005) **3:** A dimension table contains the textual descriptors of the business process being modeled, and its depth and breadth define the analytical usefulness of the data warehouse. (Delve, 2005)

## Dimensional Attribute

One dimension of an m-dimensional context. (Feng & Dillon, 2005)

## Dimensional Model

**1:** A data model that represents measures of a key business process in the form of facts and the independent variables that affect those measurements. (Artz, 2005d) **2:** The data model used in data warehouses and data marts, the most common being the star schema, comprising a fact table surrounded by dimension tables. (Delve, 2005)

## Dimensionality Modeling

A logical design technique that aims to present data in a standard, intuitive form that allows for high-performance access. (Kontio, 2005)

## Dimensionality Reduction

**1:** A phase of classifier construction that reduces the number of dimensions of the vector space in which documents are represented for the purpose of classification. Dimensionality reduction beneficially affects the efficiency of both the learning process and the classification process. In fact, shorter vectors need to be handled by the learner and by the classifier, and often on the effectiveness of the classifier too, since shorter vectors tend to limit the tendency of the learner to "overfit" the training data. (Sebastiani, 2005) **2:** A technique used to lower the dimensionality of the original dataset. Each object is transformed to another object that is described by less information. It is very useful for indexing purposes, since it increases the speed of the filtering step. (Kontaki et al., 2005) **3:** Process of extracting a signature of low dimensionality from the original data while preserving some attributes of the original data, such as the Euclidean distance. (Sayal, 2005) **4:** The process of transformation of a large dimensional feature space into a space comprising a small number of (uncorrelated) components. Dimensionality reduction allows us to visualize, categorize, or simplify large datasets. (Aradhye & Dorai, 2005) **5:** The removal of irrelevant, weakly relevant, or redundant attributes or dimensions through the use of techniques such as principle component analysis or sensitivity analysis. (Viktor & Paquet, 2005)

## Diploma Mill

An organization that offers university diplomas that do not reflect learning. (Kostopoulos, 2005)

## Dipping Diffusion Pattern

A pattern of IT diffusion in which the late majority/minority of adopters never arrives, and disconnections from the Internet result in a reduction in overall numbers of adopters over time. (Griffin, 2005)

## Direct Audio Broadcasting

The possibility of listening to the transmission of radio broadcast programming directly from the Web. (Díaz-Andrade, 2005)

## Direct Impact

Information technology investments that can be evaluated as causally related to reduced cost or increased profits. For example, more effective management of inventory leads to reduced inventory carrying costs. (Dykman, 2005)

## Direct Instruction

A highly structured, often scripted lecture and recitation-based instructional method. (Glick, 2005b)

## Direct Manipulation User Interface

An interface that aims at making objects and actions in the systems visible by [graphical] representation. These were originally proposed as an alternative to command line interfaces. The system's objects and actions are often represented by metaphorical icons on screen (e.g., dragging a file to the recycle bin for deleting a file). Designers of direct manipulation user interface strive to provide incremental reversible operations and visible effects. (Thomas & Roda, 2006a)

## Direct Recommendation

This kind of recommendation is based on a simple user request mechanism in datasets. The user interacts directly with the system that helps him in the search of the item through a list, with the n-articles that are closest to his or her request in relation to a previously known profile. (Gil & García, 2006)

## Direct Recording Electronic (DRE) System

A new technique for collecting and counting ballots. This system utilizes, in most cases, some form of touchscreen and stores the vote results in a back-end database server. (Gibson & Brown, 2006)

## Direct Sale

The sale of a product or service made over a Web site and directly payable to the product/service provider (who is also the Web site owner). (Shan et al., 2006b)

## Direct Sequence Spread Spectrum (DSSS)

The data stream to be transmitted is divided into small pieces, each of which is allocated a frequency channel. Then the data signal is combined with a higher data-rate bit sequence known as a "chipping code" that divides the data according to a spreading ratio, thus allowing resistance from interference during transmission. (Akhtar, 2005)

## Direct-to-Customer

A ne-commerce business model that connects manufacturers with customers directly by bypassing intermediaries with Internet-related technology. (Wang, Ding, et al., 2006)

## Direct-to-Plate

Technology that enables digital layouts to be sent directly to a system that images plates appropriate to the printing process being used. (Snyder, 2005)

## Directed Acyclic Graph (DAG)

**1:** A graph with directed arcs containing no cycles; in this type of graph, for any node there is no directed path returning to it. (Ramoni & Sebastiani, 2005) **2:** A graph with one-way edges containing no cycles. (Pourabbas, 2005b) **3:** A graph in which each edge can be followed from one vertex to the next, and where no path starts and ends at the same vertex. (Lauría, 2005) **4:** A directed graph that does not contain a cycle. (Chen, 2005a)

## Directed Graphical Model

The graph in this model contains only directed links, which are used to model asymmetric relations among the variables. They give rise to recursive graphical models, also known as probabilistic expert systems. (Giudici & Cerchiello, 2005)

## Direction

**1:** Refers to specialists issuing rules, directives, and operating procedures to guide the behavior of non-specialists, less mature specialists, and specialists in other fields. Rules and directives can be interpreted as translations into a limited instruction of a wider body of explicit and tacit knowledge on a subject. (Berends et al., 2006) **2:** A stage of the intelligence cycle. In the direction stage, one determines the strategic (external) information requirements—that is, one determines what environmental data should be collected. (Achterbergh, 2005a)

## Directional Relation

The order between two salient objects according to a direction, or the localization of a salient object inside images. In the literature, 14 directional relations are considered: Strict: north, south, east, and west; Mixture: north-east, north-west, south-east, and south-west; and Positional: left, right, up, down, front, and behind. (Chbeir & Yetongnon, 2005)

## Directory

Other than search engines, directories provide another approach of Web searches. A directory is a subject guide, typically organized by major topics and subtopics, which is created based on the submissions from either Webmasters or editors who have reviewed the pages. (Hu, Yang, Yeh, et al., 2005)

## Directory of Expertise/Expert Locator

A directory with listings of individuals, their expertise, and contact information used to locate knowledgeable personnel within the enterprise. (Ribière & Román, 2006)

## Directory Resources

Individuals who can get you in touch with other immediately unknown knowledge stakeholders or experts. (Croasdell & Wang, 2006)

## Disability

**1:** There are two basic approaches. The medical model sees disability as a 'personal tragedy' or 'deficit' located within an individual. The social model argues that it is society that creates disability, with barriers to participation needing to be addressed systemically. (Newell & Debenham, 2005) **2:** Under the ADA, an individual with a disability is a person who: (1) has a physical or mental impairment that substantially limits one or more major life activities; (2) has a record of such an impairment; or (3) is regarded as having such an impairment. (Bursa, et al., 2005)

## Disabled Student

From the U.S. Federal Register: the child/student has been evaluated as having mental retardation, a hearing impairment including deafness, a speech or language impairment, a visual impairment including blindness, serious emotional disturbance (hereafter referred to as emotional disturbance), an orthopedic impairment, autism, traumatic brain injury, another health impairment, a specific learning disability, deaf-blindness, or multiple disabilities, and who, by reason thereof, needs special education and related services (IEP or 504). (T. Cavanaugh, 2005)

## Disablism

Similar to sexism and racism as a concept. (Newell & Debenham, 2005)

## Disambiguation in Iconic Interfaces

The process of context-sensitive, on-the-fly semantic interpretation of a sequence of icons. The process is difficult because of the huge world knowledge required for comprehending and reasoning about natural language. (Abhishek & Basu, 2006)

## Disaster Recovery

Recovery in a situation where both the current database and its log-files have been destroyed. (Frank, 2005a)

## Discount Usability Methods

A focused set of design and evaluation tools and methods aimed at improving usability with the minimum resources. (Knight & Jefsioutine, 2006)

## Discourse

**1:** Characterized by linguists as units of language longer than a single sentence, such that discourse analysis is defined as the study of cohesion and other relationships between sentences in written or spoken discourse. (Macfadyen & Doff, 2006) **2:** Closely associated with the notion of a text, discourse refers to meaning making. This meaning making may be of many forms such as written, spoken, written to be spoken, and spoken to be written. (Zappavigna, 2006)

## Discourse Analysis

Generally looks at aspects of texts above the clause or sentence level, and approaches them in their social contexts rather than as isolated aspects of grammar. (Zappavigna, 2006)

## Discourse Support System

A system of information and communication technologies providing a Web-based platform, a methodology, and appropriate tools for fruitful discussions. (A.R. Edwards, 2005)

## Discovery Informatics

**1:** Knowledge explored in databases with the form of association, classification, regression, summarization/generalization, and clustering. (Wu & Lee, 2005) **2:** The study and practice of employing the full spectrum of computing and analytical science and technology to the singular pursuit of discovering new information by identifying and validating patterns in data. (Agresti, 2005)

## Discovery Tool
A program that enables users to employ different discovery schemes, including classification, characteristics, association, and sequence for extracting knowledge from databases. (Owrang O., 2006)

## Discrepancy of a Model
Assume that f represents the unknown density of the population, and let g=p, be a family of density functions (indexed by a vector of I parameters $q$) that approximates it. Using, to exemplify, the Euclidean distance, the discrepancy of a model g, with respect to a target model f is:

$$\Delta(f, p_\vartheta) = \sum_{i=1}^{n} (f(x_i) - p_\vartheta(x_i))^2$$

(Giudici, 2005)

## Discrete Data
Assuming values that can be counted, the data cannot assume all values on the number line within their value range. An example is: number of children in a family. (Yang & Webb, 2005)

## Discrete Event Simulation (DES)
Use of a computer to mimic the behavior of a complicated system and thereby gain insight into the performance of that system under a variety of circumstances. Generally the system under investigation is viewed in terms of instantaneous changes due to certain sudden events or occurrences. (McHaney, 2005)

## Discrete Fourier Transformation (DFT)
A transformation from time domain into frequency domain that is widely used in signal-processing-related fields to analyze the frequencies contained in a sampled signal. (Sayal, 2005)

## Discrete Multitone Technology
A technique for subdividing a transmission channel into 256 subchannels of different frequencies through which traffic is overlaid. (Hin & Subramaniam, 2005a)

## Discrete System
A system where the state variables showing its behavior change only at isolated, discernible points of time. Hence, the behavior of the system is seen as changing in distinct, separate moments of time. Such systems can be modeled using difference equations or incremental event analysis. (Vitolo & Coulston, 2005)

## Discrete Wavelet Transformation (DWT)
An orthonormal decomposition that provides a multi-resolution (multi-scale) view of the "smooth" and "rough" elements of a signal. (Shahabi et al., 2005)

## Discrete/Continuous Attribute
An attribute is a quantity describing an example (or instance); its domain is defined by the attribute type, which denotes the values taken by an attribute. An attribute can be discrete (or categorical, indeed symbolic) when the number of values is finite. A continuous attribute corresponds to real numerical values (for instance, a measurement). The discretization process transforms an attribute from continuous to discrete. (Muhlenbach & Rakotomalala, 2005)

## Discrete-Event Simulation
Models a system by changing the system's state at discrete points in time. (Janssen, 2005)

## Discrete-Time Signal
Defined at discrete time values, and thus the independent variable has discrete values n, for example x(n). (Jovanovic-Dolecek, 2005b)

## Discretionary Access Control (DAC)
A model where the owner is responsible for defining policies in order to protect his/her resources, and (s)he can also define who is going to be assigned some access privileges. (Pallis et al., 2005)

## Discretionary Security
A form of security where access to data items is restricted at the discretion of the owner. (Haraty, 2005a)

## Discretization
**1:** A process that transforms quantitative data to qualitative data. (Yang & Webb, 2005) **2:** Conversion of a numeric variable into a categorical variable, usually though binning. The entire range of the numeric values is split into a pre-specified number of bins. The numeric value of the attributes is replaced by the identifier of the bin into which it falls. (Perlich & Provost, 2005)

## Discriminant Analysis
**1:** A multivariate statistical method that separates the data into categories. (Kumar, 2005) **2:** Statistical methodology used for classification that is based on the general regression model, and uses a nominal or ordinal dependent variable. (Garrity et al., 2005)

## Discriminant Function Algorithm

A term developed for Edward Altman in describing his Z Score analytical tool in determining the likelihood of an enterprise going into bankruptcy on a prospective basis. Used as a method for determining inflection points—changes in corporate health vs. for bankruptcy prediction. (Nugent, 2005)

## Discriminant Variable

One bit of information that really matters among the many apparently involved in the true core of a complex set of features. (Liberati et al., 2005)

## Discussion Board/Group

**1:** A Web site, or part of a Web site, that allows individuals to post messages, but does not have the capacity for interactive messaging. (Whitty, 2005) **2:** An intranet site where members can post their thoughts in writing. (Baugher et al., 2005) **3:** Also known as a 'message board', this term refers to a Web site component that enables users to participate in topics of discussion by posting and replying to comments electronically. (Riffee & Sessums, 2005) **4:** Many-to-many asynchronous communication in which a group of people exchanges messages and information on a specific topic. Members of the group send messages and reply to messages of other members. (Erlich, 2005)

## Discussion Thread

**1:** A series of posts related to a single topic in a discussion board. (Baugher et al., 2005) **2:** A set of sequential response messages to an original message in a discussion group. (Erlich, 2005) **3:** A string of messages that follow a common theme and consist of responses and replies to previous messages. (Ingram & Hathorn, 2005a)

## Discussion Tool

A Web-based tool that supports multimedia asynchronous communication among individuals in a learning community. (Morphew, 2005)

## Disease Mapping

The visual display of geographical patterns of disease in a map. The maps typically show standardized mortality or incidence ratios for geographic areas such as countries, counties, or districts. (Vidal-Rodeiro et al., 2005)

## Disease Rates

The level of disease in a given time period, population, and geographic area. It represents the proportion of disease cases in the exposed population or population-at-risk. (Garb & Wait, 2005a)

## Disembodied

Separated from or existing without the body. (Macfadyen, 2006c)

## Disinformation

False information repeatedly provided in a coordinated campaign. (N.C. Rowe, 2006d)

## Disintermediation

**1:** The reduction or elimination of the role of the middlemen in transactions between the producer and the customer, as in new electronic marketplaces, consumers interact directly with producers. (Sharma, Carson, et al., 2005) **2:** The removal of intermediaries from the supply chain. The possibility of disintermediation is said to occur when there is market transparency and the final buyers become aware of manufacturers' price intermediaries. (Fraser, 2005) **3:** Going around a player in a supply chain, as in rendering that player redundant. (Foley & Samson, 2006) **4:** The elimination of agents, like wholesale dealers or brokers, who built the former relationship between producer and consumer. Disintermediation allows the direct supply of the consumer. (Seitz, 2005) **5:** The process of eliminating intermediaries in the channels of distribution. (Borders & Johnston, 2005)

## Disjunctive Database

A database that allows indefinite information. (Grant & Minker, 2006)

## Disjunctive Datalog Program

**1:** A set of rules of the form: $A_1 \vee \ldots \vee A_k \leftarrow B_1, \ldots, B_m,$ not $B_{m+1}, \ldots,$ not Bn, k+m+n>0 where $A_p \ldots, A_k, B_p \ldots, B_n$ are atoms of the form $p(t_p \ldots, t_h)$, $p$ is a predicate symbol of arity $h$ and the terms $t_p \ldots, t_h$ are constants or variables. (Greco & Zumpano, 2005a) **2:** A set of rules $\underline{r}$ of the form: $A_1 \vee \ldots \vee A_k \bullet B_1, \ldots, B_m, \neg B_{m+1}, \ldots, \neg B_n,$ where $k+m+n>0$, $A_p \ldots, A_k, B_p \ldots, B_n$ are atoms of the form $p(t_p \ldots, t_h)$, $p$ is a predicate symbol of arity $h$, and the terms $t_p \ldots, t_h$ are constants or variables. The disjunction $A_1 \vee \ldots \vee A_k$ is called head of $r$ and is denoted by *Head(r)* while the conjunction $B_p \ldots, B_m, \neg B_{m+p} \ldots, \neg B_n$ is called body and is denoted by *Body(r)*. If $k=1$, then $r$ is normal (i.e., $\vee$-free); if $n=0$, then $r$ is positive (i.e., -free); if both $m=1$ and $n=0$, then $r$ is *normal and positive*; if $k=n=0$ then $r$ is a fact, whereas if $m=0$ then $r$ is a *constraint* or *denial rule*, that is, a rule which is satisfied only if *Body(r)* is false. (Greco & Zumpano, 2005b)

## Disjunctive Set of Conjunctive Rules

A conjunctive rule is a propositional rule whose antecedent consists of a conjunction of attribute-value pairs. A disjunctive set of conjunctive rules consists of a set of conjunctive rules with the same consequent. It is called disjunctive because the rules in the set can be combined into a single disjunctive rule whose antecedent consists of a disjunction of conjunctions. (An, 2005)

## Disorientation

The sensation of feeling lost in a hypermedia document, characterized by three categories of the user's experience: (1) the user does not know where to go next, (2) the user knows where to go but not how to get there, or (3) the user does not know where he or she is in relation to the overall structure of the document. (Boechler, 2006a)

## Disparity

The inequality or difference in access to media and technology. (Reilly, 2005)

## Disparity Map Generation

Solving the correspondence problem, that is, to find the corresponding points in the stereo images by finding the difference in spatial position of the points, namely, disparity. (Ozer et al., 2005)

## Dispersed/Distributed Team

A team separated by some degree of physical distance. (Connaughton, 2005)

## Displaying Pipeline

Collective term for the different stages which must be passed to show graphical content on screen. (Rosenbaum et al., 2006)

## Disposal

Even disconnected computers may lead to cyber-identity theft. Careless handling or disposal of discarded computers can lead to identity theft. Furthermore, disposed hardware and software may lead to cyber-identity theft. If a user fails to take precautions such as data deletion or physical destruction of a machine, the data are readily accessible for the next user—whoever may find it. (Close et al., 2006)

## Disruptive Innovation

An innovation that typically presents a different package of performance attributes—ones that, at least at the outset, are not valued by existing customers. (C.-S. Lee, 2005)

## Dissemination

**1:** Because information is not created equally, it must be codified and aggregated such that one producer of knowledge is not privileged over another. For example, a city portal where all community information is collated or republished. (Williamson, 2005) **2:** Stage of the intelligence cycle. In this stage, the intelligence produced in the analysis stage is presented and forwarded to strategic decision makers. (Achterbergh, 2005a)

## Distal Context

The physical scope of a consumer context that is outside the direct perception of the consumer. Most context-aware applications intend to help mobile consumers obtain useful and interesting information about their distal context. (Sun & Poole, 2005)

## Distance

A function from pairs of objects into non-negative real numbers. It can be zero only if the two arguments are the same. It must be symmetric and obey the triangle inequality. (Chávez & Navarro, 2005)

## Distance Communication

Communication under conditions of geographic separation that minimize the possibility of face-to-face and synchronous interactions. (Murphy, 2005c)

## Distance Education (DE)

**1:** Education in which there is a physical separation between the learner and the teacher, and is usually contrasted with on-campus education. (Taylor et al., 2005) **2:** A form of instruction in which a geographical separation exists between instructor and students; it may be same time/different place or different time/different place. Various types of technology may be used as part of this form of education, with more technology required for the same-time format. (Simon et al., 2005) **3:** A formal educational process in which instruction occurs when student and instructor are separated by geographic distance or by time. Instruction may be synchronous or asynchronous. Distance education may employ correspondence study or audio, video, or computer technologies. (Beck & Schornack,

**D**

2005) **4:** A teaching method in which students do not have to come to a specific location in order to hear lectures or study. The learning materials reach them either by mail, through the Internet, or through other means (satellite, cable). The main component of the method is usually written material together with additional components such as assignments, face-to-face (or computer-mediated) tutorials, and examinations. It involves learning outside of the traditional avenues of attendance at educational institutions. (Erlich & Gal-Ezer, 2005) **5:** Education that takes place when an instructor and student are separated by physical distance, and various technologies (e.g., the Internet, videoconferencing, etc.) are used to bridge the distance. These types of instructional delivery systems can provide non-traditional students with a second chance at a college education, and reach those disadvantaged by time constraints, physical disability, or remote geographical locations. It is sometimes called distance learning. (Paraskevi & Kollias, 2006) **6:** Also known as correspondence education, refers to the alternative approach to traditional classroom instruction, whereby learning packages are delivered to the learners via multiple channels. The term is used to designate any learning that takes place between a teacher and a learner when they are not in the same place at the same time. Distance learning has evolved into Web-based education due to information technology, especially the Internet. (Rahman, 2005f) **7:** Learners are connected with educational resources beyond the confines of a traditional classroom, and instructed via computer-mediated communication and different types of electronic technologies that can overcome the constraints of distance, time, physical presence, or location that separate instructors and students. Learning may be synchronous or asynchronous. (Malina, 2005)

## Distance Education and Training Council (DETC)

Established in 1926, the standard-setting agency for correspondence study and distance education institutions. (Rhoten, 2006b)

## Distance Education Course/Program

**1:** The curriculum offered through distance education. (Schifter, 2005) **2:** A course designed for students who are not present in person in class. (Novitzki, 2005)

## Distance Function

**1:** A function used to compute the similarity between two multimedia elements. In particular, it returns a number in the range [0,1], with values close to 0 for similar elements. (Chang et al., 2005) **2:** Used to express the similarity between two objects. It is usually normalized in the range between 0 to 1. Examples of distance functions used for time series data are the Euclidean Distance and the Time Warping Distance. (Kontaki et al., 2005)

## Distance Learner's Guide

Originally a consumer's guide to help prospective online students make intelligent decisions about their provider and the tools they will need to be successful. (S.M. Johnstone, 2005)

**Distance Learning:** See *Distance Education.*

## Distance Learning Library Service

Refers to one of several library services in support of college, university, or other post-secondary courses and programs offered away from a main campus or in the absence of a traditional campus, and regardless of where credit is given. These courses may be taught in traditional or non-traditional formats or media, may or may not require physical facilities, and may or may not involve live interaction of teachers and students. The phrase is inclusive of courses in all post-secondary programs designated as: extension, extended, off-campus, extended campus, distance, distributed, open, flexible, franchising, virtual, synchronous, or asynchronous. (Buchanan, 2005)

## Distance Learning Program

A program that typically does not meet or hold class sessions on campus. (Riffee & Sessums, 2005)

## Distance Learning Satellite Transmission

A learning program transmitted via television signal from a remote source and accessed locally by students through a receiver dish antenna. (Switala, 2005)

## Distance Measure

One of the calculation techniques to discover the relationship between two implicit words in a large corpus or labels in a large database from the viewpoint of similarity. (Ito, 2005)

## Distance Teaching University

**1:** A university that teaches students via a wide range of distance education methods and technologies. (Guri-Rosenblit, 2005a) **2:** A university in which instructors and students are separated by distance and interact mainly through communication technologies. It allows its students to study wherever convenient, and requires special methods of course and instructional design, as well as special organizational and administrative arrangements. (Erlich & Gal-Ezer, 2005)

### Distance Training and Education (DT&E)

The process of delivering instructional resources for the purposes of training and education to a location (or to locations) away from a classroom, building, or site to another classroom, building, or site by using video, audio, computer, multimedia communications, or some combination of these with other traditional delivery methods. (Brace & Berge, 2006)

### Distanced Leadership

Leadership of a team or organizational members that are separated by some degree of time and distance from their leader. (Connaughton, 2005)

### Distilled Statecharts

A statecharts-based formalism for lightweight mobile agents. (Fortino et al., 2006)

### Distributed Artificial Intelligence (DAI)

A subset of Artificial Intelligence that is concerned with the study of issues related to knowledge distribution and problem solving involving a society of decentralized but connected entities. (Tang & Sivaramakrishnan, 2005)

### Distributed Chase

A kind of recursive strategy applied to a database V, based on functional dependencies or rules extracted both from V and other autonomous databases, by which a null value or an incomplete value in V is replaced by a new, more complete value. Any differences in semantics among attributes in the involved databases have to be resolved first. (Ras & Dardzinska, 2005)

### Distributed Cognition

Cognition is understood as being derived from the environment. It is based on an assumption of equality between people and artifacts in structuring practice. (Munkvold, 2006)

### Distributed Component Object Model (DCOM)

**1:** A set of Microsoft concepts that provides a set of interfaces allowing clients and servers to communicate within the same platform. (Zhang, 2006) **2:** Sits on top

of the remote procedure-calling mechanism and allows calls to remote objects interacting with COM services. (Kasi & Young, 2006)

### Distributed Computing

The process of using a number of separate but networked computers to solve a single problem. (Zwitserloot & Pantic, 2005)

### Distributed Computing System

Computing distributed over networks instead of on single computers. (Kasi & Young, 2006)

### Distributed Constructionism (DC)

An extension of the Constructionism theory to knowledge-building communities, where the online learning community (instead of one student) collaboratively constructs knowledge artifacts. (Zaphiris et al., 2005)

### Distributed Data Mining

**1:** Mining information from a very large set of data spread across multiple locations without transferring the data to a central location. (Jha & Sural, 2005) **2:** Performing the data-mining task on data sources distributed in different sites. (Saygin, 2005)

### Distributed Database

A collection of multiple, logically interrelated databases distributed over a computer network. (Ibrahim, 2005)

### Distributed Delivery

A system whereby information or course content is delivered through several media, accessible to anyone regardless of their locations and platforms. (Aworuwa & Owen, 2005)

### Distributed Desktop Training (DDT)

Allows the student (employee) to avail of both audio and video applications to enhance training by providing interactive communication between the student and the trainer, without being limited by distance. (Neville & Powell, 2005)

### Distributed Environment

An environment in which different components and objects comprising an application can be located on different computers connected to a network. (Guan, 2005d)

**D**

## Distributed Expertise

Cognition and knowing are distributed over individuals, their tools, environments, and networks. (Muukkonen et al., 2005)

## Distributed Hash Table (DHT)

A distributed index structure with hash table-like functionality for information location in the Internet-scale distributed computing environment. Given a key from a pre-specified flat identifier space, the DHT computes (in a distributed fashion) and returns the location of the node that stores the key. (Shahabi & Banaei-Kashani, 2005)

## Distributed Knowledge Management Approach

A knowledge management approach based on the duality of perspective making and taking, the localization and centralization of knowledge, and the autonomy and coordination of organizational units. In this approach, subjectivity and sociality are considered as potential sources of value rather than as problems to overcome. (Cuel et al., 2006)

## Distributed Knowledge Management Model

The model that combines the interdependence of one partial product state model to others, with the idea of knowledge acquisition rather than just the operational exchange relationship. (Metaxiotis, 2006)

## Distributed Knowledge Management System

A knowledge management system that supports two qualitatively different processes: the autonomous management of knowledge locally produced within a single unit, and the coordination of the different units without centrally defined semantics. (Cuel et al., 2006)

## Distributed Learning

**1:** A student-centered approach to learning that incorporates the use of technology in the learning process and emphasizes four educational characteristics: (1) supports different learning styles by using mixed media, (2) builds on the learner's perspective through interactive educational experiences, (3) builds learning skills and social skills through collaboration among learners and with the community, and (4) integrates the learning into daily life by doing authentic tasks. (Rahman, 2005a) **2:** A type of learning made possible by technology that is dependent neither on place nor time. Distributed learning allows students and instructors to be at different locations at the same or different times. (Klein, 2005) **3:** Consists of learning situations in which the students and instructor are located in different localities. A bit broader than distance education, as it can be used to refer to both education and training. (Turoff et al., 2005b) **4:** A set of pedagogical strategies that integrate face-to-face with online methodologies. (Ketelhut et al., 2005) **5:** Using a wide range of information technologies to provide learning opportunities beyond the bounds of the traditional classroom. (Dixon et al., 2005)

## Distributed Learning Environment

A learning environment where participants are not co-located, and use computer-based technologies to access instruction and communicate with others. (Graham et al., 2005)

## Distributed Model with an Object-Oriented Approach

Each object maintains its own state and characteristics, distinct from all others. (Gurău, 2005)

## Distributed Open Ontology

Open ontology refers to the ontology that is represented in standard ways (knowledge representation language and structured documents) and can be accessed by standard interfaces. With the advent of 3W, encoding ontology definitions as distributed textual Web pages supported by Web description language and accessing methods is adopted. In e-learning systems, it is a sharing mechanism to provide commonly agreed understanding of multi-faceted knowledge for all stakeholders and services on the Web in e-learning applications. (Liu & Koppelaar, 2005)

## Distributed Organization

An organization that works across physical boundaries and time zones with multiple sites or offices. (Huq et al., 2006)

## Distributed System

A system made up of components that may be obtained from a number of different sources, which together work as a single distributed system providing the run-time infrastructure supporting today's networked computer applications. (Yow & Moertiyoso, 2005)

## Distributed Work

Collaborative work carried out by several persons at different geographical locations. (Wiberg, 2005)

## Distribution Channel

The sum of all organizations or parts of an organization that are involved in making a product or service available to a customer. Distribution channels can also apply media (e.g., the Internet or TV) in order to address customers. Also called Channel of Distribution. (Madlberger, 2006)

## Distribution Cycle Time

The span of time between the beginning of the shipment pickup and the end of the shipment delivery. (Tyan, 2006)

## Distribution List

An e-mail list of all participants in the virtual environment who can be contacted as a totality or divided into specified sub-groups. (Coakes & Willis, 2005)

## Distributive Function

An aggregate function F is called distributive if there exists a function g such that the value of F for an n-dimensional cuboid can be computed by applying g to the value of F in $(n + 1)$–dimensional cuboid. (Abdulghani, 2005a)

## Distributive Function of a Telecenter

Set of processes that a telecenter as an open social system carries out to foster the egalitarian distribution of its benefits and ICT growth and integration into the community's social dynamics. (Santos, 2005)

## Distributive Profile

A part of a user's profile that defines which documents (from the relevant ones) and how should be presented to him/her in a particular time moment. (Abramowicz et al., 2006)

## Distributor

A self-employed individual or a company engaged in network marketing on behalf of a manufacturer. (D. Wright, 2005)

## Divergent Thinking Technique

One of a number of tools used during the divergent phases of Creative Problem Solving to improve the generation of ideas, thoughts, or data without evaluation. These tools are classified according to their primary use of related or unrelated problem stimuli. Brainstorming, brainwriting, forced connections, analogies, and metaphors are some of the most used divergent thinking techniques. (Torres-Coronas & Gascó-Hernández, 2005)

## Diversity/Flexibility/Tension

Diversity, both in terms of the work assignments offered and the people one interacts with, and a tolerance of differences. In order to be tolerant of differences, flexibility is needed. Both diversity and flexibility can lead to creative tension. (Torres-Coronas & Gascó-Hernández, 2005)

## Divide-and-Conquer

A well-known algorithm design strategy where the dataset is partitioned into blocks and each block is processed independently. The resulting block-level (local) kernels are merged to realize the global output. It increases the efficiency of the algorithms in terms of both space and time requirements. (Murthy & Diday, 2005)

## Division of Knowledge

The way in which knowledge is dispersed over organization members, groups, and departments. The division of knowledge varies from a low degree of differentiation (a high degree of redundancy) to a high degree of differentiation (a low degree of redundancy). (Berends et al., 2006)

**DK/NF:** See *Domain Key/Normal Form.*

**DL:** See *Distance Learning.*

**DM:** See *Data Mining.*

**DMG:** See *Data-Mining Group.*

**DML:** See *Data Manipulation Language.*

**DMO:** See *Destination Marketing Organization.*

**DMSS:** See *Decision-Making Support System.*

**DMT:** See *Data-Mining Technology.*

## DNA

**1:** Deoxyribonucleic acid. DNA molecules carry the genetic information necessary for the organization and functioning of most living cells, and control the inheritance of characteristics. (Galitsky, 2005a) **2:** Nucleic acid, constituting the genes, codifying proteins. (Liberati et al., 2005) **3:** A specific sequence of deoxyribonucleotide units covalently joined through phosphodiester bonds. (Tsunoda et al., 2005)

**DNS:** See *Domain Name System.*

## Doctrine

A category endowed with a certain collection of diagram operations that allow one to perform certain logical manipulations with objects and morphisms. For example, in a category called logos, one can join and meet objects, take images and co-images of objects under given morphisms, and consider graphs (binary relations) of morphisms. In a transitive logos, one can, in addition, consider transitive closures of binary relations. Like relational algebra is an algebraic counterpart of some version of first-order predicate calculus, a categorical doctrine is a diagram-algebraic counterpart of some sort of logical calculus. Correspondingly, a hierarchy of logical calculi ranging from propositional to first-order predicate to higher-order predicate calculi gives rise to the corresponding hierarchy of categories—doctrines. (Diskin, 2005)

## Document

Any information-bearing message in electronically recorded form. Documents are the fundamental unit from which information collections are built, although they may have their own substructure and associated files. (Trujillo, 2005)

## Document Capture

Registration of an object into a document, image, or content repository. (Asprey et al., 2005)

## Document Categorization

A process that assigns one or more of the predefined categories (labels) to a document. (Mladenić, 2005)

## Document Clustering

**1:** A process that groups documents, based on their content similarity, using some predefined similarity measure. (Mladenić, 2005) **2:** An unsupervised learning technique that partitions a given set of documents into distinct groups of similar documents based on similarity or distance measures. (Kim, 2005) **3:** The automatic organization of documents into clusters or group so that documents within a cluster have high similarity in comparison to one another, but are very dissimilar to documents in other clusters. (Fung et al., 2005)

## Document Cut-Off Value (DCV)

The number of documents that the user is willing to see as a response to the query. (Fan & Pathak, 2005)

## Document Database

**1:** A collection of documents associated with a system to manage the documents and their content. (Lyytikäinen et al., 2005) **2:** A database designed for managing and manipulating XML documents or even more generic SGML documents. (Chen, 2005b) **3:** A collection of documents with a uniform user interface. (Schmidt et al., 2005)

## Document Frequency

The number of documents in the document collection that the term appears in. (Fan & Pathak, 2005)

## Document Imaging

Scanning and conversion of hard-copy documents to either analog (film) or digital image format. (Asprey et al., 2005)

## Document Management

**1:** Implements management controls over digital documents via integration with standard desktop authoring tools (word processing, spreadsheets, and other tools) and document library functionality. Registers and tracks physical documents. (Asprey & Middleton, 2005) **2:** Managing the content consisting of independent logical content units referred to or manipulated as documents. (Honkaranta & Tyrväinen, 2005)

## Document Management System

A set of information management tools that provide the storage, retrieval, tracking, and administration of documents within an organization. See also *Content Management System.* (Ribière & Román, 2006)

## Document Object Model (DOM)

An object-oriented model representing different components of a system and their interfaces. In XML, DOM allows working with language elements as interactive objects with data, methods, and events. (Arya, 2005)

## Document Ranking

A function that scores documents in a collection according to their relevance to a given query so that the more relevant a function is, the higher score it has. (Meng & Chen, 2005)

## Document Type Definition (DTD)

**1:** An XML DTD is a mechanism to define the structure of XML documents. It lists the various elements and attributes in a document and the context in which they are to be used. It can also list any elements a document cannot contain. (Passi et al., 2005) **2:** Provides guidelines about how specific elements in a document are represented or which segments of data may coexist or are mutually exclusive. (Hawk & Zheng, 2006) **3:** A formal description in XML declaration syntax of a particular type of document It begins with a <!DOCTYPE keyword and sets out what names are to be used for the different types of markup elements, where they may occur, the elements' possible attributes, and how they all fit together. For example, a DTD may specify that every person markup element must have a name attribute and that it can have an offspring element called id whose content must be text. There are many sorts of DTDs ready to be used in all kinds of areas that can be downloaded and used freely. (Zarri, 2005b) **4:** A set of rules defining the element types that are allowed within an XML document, and specifying the allowed content and attributes of each element type. Also defines all the external entities referenced within the documents and the notations that can be used. (Pallis, Stoupa, & Vakali, 2005) **5:** The capability of XML to specify constraints for a class of documents. A DTD defines element and attribute names and the hierarchic structure of the elements for the documents of a class. (Lyytikäinen et al., 2005)

## Document Vector

Each document is represented by a vector of frequencies of remaining items after preprocessing within the document. (Fung et al., 2005)

## Document Warehouse

A document database consisting of documents gathered from various independent sources. (Schmidt et al., 2005)

**DOM:** See *Document Object Model.*

## Domain

**1:** A scope of information definition. A domain defines a collection of information generally recognized as appropriate to a field of study, a business process or function, or mission. (Fulton, 2005) **2:** Combines several secondary structure elements and motifs; has a specific function. (Tsunoda et al., 2005) **3:** Scope or range of a subject or sphere of knowledge. (Coakes & Clarke, 2006a) **4:** The area of interest for which a data warehouse was created. (Scime, 2005b) **5:** The set of permitted values for a field in a database, defined during database design. The

actual data in a field are a subset of the field's domain. (Koeller, 2005)

## Domain Analysis Technique

Search for the larger units of cultural knowledge called domains, a synonym for person, place, or thing. Used to gain an understanding of the semantic relationships of terms and categories. (DeLorenzo, 2005)

## Domain Key/Normal Form (DK/NF)

Rather than functional dependencies, DK/NF is based on domain dependencies and key dependencies only. Although it is provable that a set of tables in DK/NF avoids all anomalies, it is also provable that there is no procedure for producing this normal form. (Schultz, 2005)

## Domain Knowledge

**1:** A set of small domain knowledge elements makes up domain knowledge. Domain knowledge represents all topics in teaching domain and forms a complete course structure. (Wu & Chen, 2005) **2:** Expertise in a given application area. (Hoxmeier, 2005)

## Domain Language

**1:** The language, including specific technical terms, phrases, and shortcuts/abbreviations of speech that are unique and specific to the sphere of knowledge. (Coakes & Clarke, 2006b) **2:** Used to learn about some specific subject domain, for example, in an academic discipline. This contrasts with more general learning of discussion strategies, metacognition, "learning to learn," and so forth. Vicarious learning has thus far been more effectively shown to work in the latter type of area than in domain learning, but this may be quite sensitive to the choice of domain. (J.R. Lee, 2005)

## Domain Model

**1:** A model that contains information about the course taught in a wireless emergency service. A usual representation is a concept network specifying concepts and their relationships. (Gaudioso & Montero, 2006) **2:** Codified information about an application domain, specifically a domain for which a business process is being developed. (Berztiss, 2006b) **3:** Representation of the subject domain at a conceptual level, often in terms of concepts and their relationships. (Houben et al., 2006)

**D**

**Domain Name**

Any name representing any record that exists within the domain name system (DNS), the system that attributes a domain name to an IP address and hence to an Internet host. Three main typologies of top-level domain (TLD) names exist that characterize the ending part of each WWW address: Generic Top-Level Domain (gTLD), Country Code Top-Level Domain (ccTLD), and infrastructure top-level domain. (Maggioni & Uberti, 2005)

**Domain of Rule**

The set of attributes listed in the IF part of a rule. (Ras, Tzacheva, & Tsay, 2005)

**Domain Ontology**

Either a domain-specific or an application-specific ontology. (Cristani & Cuel, 2006)

**Domain Restriction**

A condition, usually formulated in first-order logic, that defines the set of values that an attribute or variable may have. In database terminology, a domain restriction is a kind of integrity constraint. (Aldana Montes et al., 2005)

**Domain-Name Back Order**

A service provided by domain-name registrars that will watch for a domain name to be released upon expiration and will automatically register that name for the client when this happens. (Owen, 2006d)

**Domain-Name Grabbing**

Registering an abandoned or lapsed domain name immediately after it is released by a registrar. (Owen, 2006d)

**Domain-Name Hijacking**

Obtaining a domain-name transfer of ownership through fraud. (Owen, 2006d)

**Domain-Name Speculation**

Registering or purchasing a domain on the speculation that it could be used in the future to drive traffic or can be resold in the future at a higher amount. (Owen, 2006d)

**Domain-Name Squatting**

Registering a trademark, an organization's name, or a person's name as a domain name with the intention to profit from traffic to an unrelated Web site or by reselling

the domain name back to the person or organization. (Owen, 2006d)

**Domain-Name System (DNS)**

Because humans remember names more easily than long numbers, DNS allows names to be translated into IP addresses. DNS is used to translate the name information for URLs and e-mail addresses. (Leath, 2005)

**Domain-Specific Ontology**

An engineering object defining the model of knowledge in a specific domain. The level of specificity may be very deep, but the name is reserved for those ontologies that are not dependent on specific applications. (Cristani & Cuel, 2006)

**Domestic Product Design**

A process of producing a useful, usable, desirable, and attractive product in which the design process is grounded in the principles of human factors, engineering and manufacturing processes, marketing, and aesthetics. (Aurum & Demirbilek, 2006)

**Domestication of Technology**

Social learning through which users incorporate an introduced technology into their lives by a process of negotiation and translation, practical activity, and the utilization of local knowledge. (Gibbs et al., 2005)

**Door-to-Door Delivery**

Shipping service from shipper's door to receiver's door. (Tyan, 2006)

**Dot Map**

A map in which the geographic locations of events, people, or other entities are depicted as points or dots. (Garb & Wait, 2005b)

**Dot Product Queries**

A class of queries where the query answer can be seen as the inner product between a vector dependent only on the query and a vector dependent on the data. (Shahabi et al., 2005)

**Dot-Com**

1: A company with operations that are entirely or primarily Internet based or, more specifically, a company with a business model that would not be possible if the Internet did not exist. Dot-coms often deliver all their services over an Internet interface, but products might be delivered through traditional channels as well. Dot-coms are often divided into two categories: those that provide products and services for consumers (B2C) and those that provide products and services to other businesses (B2B). (Sharma & Wickramasinghe, 2005) **2:** An electronic retailer that operates exclusively through one distribution channel. By nature, dot-coms are non-store-based retailers. Also known as pure player. (Madlberger, 2006)

### Dot-Com Bubble

**1:** Refers to the late 1990s during which countless dot-com companies were booming with a frenzy of investment in Internet-related technical stocks and enterprises. (Hwang & Stewart, 2006) **2:** The exaggerated enthusiasm in Internet companies with the overvaluation of high-technology stocks in the late 1990s. (Tian & Stewart, 2006)

### Dot-Com Bust

Refers to the years 2000 to 2002, when dot-com industry collapsed and hundreds of dot-com companies went bankrupt due to the NASDAQ crash starting in March 2000. (Hwang & Stewart, 2006)

### Dot-Com Company

**1:** A company that conducts its primary business on the Internet. It is called dot-com company because the company's URL ends with ".com." (Tian & Stewart, 2006) **2:** A company using the Internet as its primary means to conduct business. The companies typically use the ".com" suffix in company name. (Hwang & Stewart, 2006)

### Dot-Com Crash

The stock market crash of Internet companies in 2000 and 2001, many of which failed during the crash. Those companies were overvalued before the crash. (Tian & Stewart, 2006)

### Double Talk

An interference produced when the speakers at both ends of a telephone line simultaneously speak. This phenomenon greatly disturbs the echo canceller performance. (Perez-Meana & Nakano-Miyatake, 2005)

### Double Taxation

When the same taxable item is taxed more than once by either the same or by different government agencies, there is said to be double taxation. The juridical type of double

taxation happens when comparable taxes are imposed by two or more taxing jurisdictions on the same taxpayer in respect of the same taxable income or capital. (Raisinghani & Petty, 2005)

### Double-Knit Organization

An organization where people work in teams for projects, but importantly also belong to a much more enduring and lasting community of practice in order to keep their skills sharp. (Ray, 2006)

### Double-Loop Learning

Together with single-loop learning, describes the way in which organizations may learn to respond appropriately to change. Single-loop learning requires adjustments to procedures and operations within the framework of customary, accepted assumptions, but fails to recognize or deal effectively with problems that may challenge fundamental aspects of organizational culture, norms, or objectives. Double-loop learning questions those assumptions from the vantage point of higher order, shared views, in order to solve problems. (Vat, 2005b)

### Down-Sampling

Discarding every M-1 sample (retaining every Mth sample). (Milić, 2005)

### Downlink

The communication link from a satellite to an Earth station. (Statica & Deek, 2006)

### Download

To move a digital file (such as a media file) from a server where it is stored to a local system for viewing or editing. (Cosemans, 2005a)

### Download Delay/Download Time

The amount of time needed for elements to appear on a Web page on the client computer after the page is accessed from the server. (Hantula, 2005)

### Drama Serial

An ongoing story told in dramatic form incorporating sound effects, music, dialogue, and/or narration. It may be broadcast once, twice, or several times in a week, and it is usually from 15 to 30 minutes in duration. Sometimes, it is referred to as a "soap opera." (Craddock & Duncan, 2005)

**D**

## Drama Series
A story told in dramatic form with a fixed number of episodes. (Craddock & Duncan, 2005)

## Drawing Management System
Implements repository management controls over digital drawings by integration with CAD authoring tools and using document library functionality. Registers and tracks physical drawings. (Asprey & Middleton, 2005)

## Drawing Program
A software program that creates digital images. (Judd, 2005)

**DRE:** See *Digital Rights Expression System.*

**DRE System:** See *Direct Recording Electronic System.*

**DREAM:** See *Design Rationale Environment for Argumentation and Modeling.*

## Drill Down/Roll Up
**1:** A method of exploring multi-dimensional data by moving from one level of detail to the next. (Sethi & Sethi, 2006b) **2:** The process of navigating from a top-level view of overall sales down through the sales territories, to the individual salesperson level. This is a more intuitive way to obtain information at the detail level. Drill-down levels depend on the granularity of the data in the data warehouse. Roll up is the opposite function. (Nigro & González Císaro, 2005b) **3:** User interface technique to navigate into lower levels of information in decision support systems. (DeLorenzo, 2005) **4:** Typical OLAP operation by which aggregate data are visualized at a finer (coarser) level of detail along one or more analysis dimensions. (Tininini, 2005c) **5:** A cube operation that allows users to navigate from summarized cells to more detailed cells. (Abdulghani, 2005b) **6:** Opposite operation of the previous one. (Schneider, 2005)

**DRM:** See *Digital Rights Management.*

## DRM Hook
Also known as an IPMP hook, this was developed in 1999 and standardized by MPEG-4 in 2000. It allows proprietary DRM systems to be used within an MPEG-4-compliant terminal by associating the IPIDS of an IPMP system with each audiovisual object. The IPIDS is unique for any

IPMP system and is assigned by a registration authority. (Wang, Cheng, Cheng, & Huang, 2006)

## Drug Discovery
A research process that identifies molecules with desired biological effects so to develop new therapeutic drugs. (Kusiak & Shah, 2005)

**DSA:** See *Data Staging Area.*

**DSL:** See *Digital Subscriber Line; Digital Subscriber Loop.*

**DSMS:** See *Data Stream Management System.*

**DSS:** See *Decision Support System.*

**DSSS:** See *Direct Sequence Spread Spectrum.*

**DSV-IS:** See *Design, Specification, and Verification of Interactive Systems.*

**DT&E:** See *Distance Training and Education.*

**DTD:** See *Document Type Definition.*

**DTOA:** See *Differential Time of Arrival.*

**DTV:** See *Digital Television.*

**DTW:** See *Dynamic Time Warping.*

## Dual-Channel Assumption
Based on the notion that working memory has two sensory channels, each responsible for processing different types of input. The auditory or verbal channel processes written and spoken language. The visual channel processes images. (Boechler, 2006b)

## Dual-Mode Distance Teaching University
A university that teaches concurrently on-campus and off-campus students. Usually, the same admission requirements and the same study materials apply to both categories of students. (Guri-Rosenblit, 2005a)

## Dual-Mode Institution
**1:** An organization that delivers some courses on-site and some courses off-site using distance delivery methods. (Ally, 2005d) **2:** An institution that simultaneously offers

on-campus courses and distance education courses. (Graham, Allen, et al., 2005)

## Dual-Task Study

A study in which two tasks are performed concurrently to observe changes in task interference. Usually the participant is expected to or asked to focus on the primary task so that interference is observed only in the secondary task, but this is not necessarily always the objective. Observations of task interference are taken to suggest that the limits of the processing system are being reached. (Owen, 2006c)

## Duality of Structure

The concept in structuration theory that structure is the medium and the outcome of the conduct it recursively organizes. (Saunders, 2006)

## Dublin Core

**1:** A set of 15 metadata fields, such as title and author, commonly used by library systems to manage digital assets. All fields are optional. (Verhaart & Kinshuk 2006) **2:** A widely accepted standard for metadata about electronic documents. Maintained by the Dublin Core Metadata Initiative. (Hänisch, 2005)

## Duplicate Document Detection

The technique to find the exact duplicates, which have exactly the same content, or partial duplicates, which have a large percentage of their text in common. (Chan, Ho, et al., 2005)

## Duplicate Document Image Retrieval (DDIR)

A system for finding the image-formatted duplicate of documents from a database. (Chan, Ho, et al., 2005)

## Dutch Auction

**1:** A descending-bid auction in which the price of an item is lowered until it gets the first bid, which is the highest price the customer is willing to pay. (Blecker & Abdelkafi, 2006) **2:** A popular kind of auction at many sites, commonly used when a seller has a number of the same items to sell, for example, 10 posters. The auctioneer starts with a high asking price. The seller then gradually decreases the offer price, and the first person to bid is the winner. (Lei et al., 2005b)

## Duties

The correlative of rights, since rights by their nature impose duties. (Gilbert, 2005)

**DVB:** See *Digital Video Broadcasting.*

**DVC:** See *Desktop Video Conferencing; Document Cut-Off Value.*

**DVD:** See *Digital Versatile Disc.*

**DVP:** See *Delivery-vs.-Payment.*

**DWL:** See *Data Warehouse Library.*

**DWT:** See *Discrete Wavelet Transformation.*

## Dyadic Communication

Refers to communication between two people: the source and the receiver. A dyadic approach to communication stresses the role of the relationship between the source and the receiver. (Jacobson, 2006)

## Dynamic Bandwidth Allocation

Using algorithms with the MPCP arbitration mechanism to determine the collision-free upstream transmission schedule of ONUs and generate GATE messages accordingly. (Freire et al., 2005)

## Dynamic Clustering

A scheme to discover simultaneous clusters and their representations in such a way that they fit together optimally. The cluster representation is called a Kernel. Mean is a special case of kernel, as in k-means. (Murthy & Diday, 2005)

## Dynamic Complexity

How much the communication process depends on time constraints, unclear or deficient feedback, and changes during the process. (Willis, 2005)

## Dynamic Conceptual Network

A hierarchical tree for developing the interrelations among learning concepts. Each learning concept is stored as a concept node in the dynamic conceptual network. A concept node includes contents, tasks, and attributes. The contents are represented by text, graphs, audio, and/or video, and these contents are stored in a knowledge base. (Leung & Li, 2005)

## Dynamic Digital Deliberation

Includes applications that are two-way or dialogical, such as digital town hall meetings and digital policy forums. (Holzer & Schweste, 2005)

**D**

## Dynamic E-Business

The next generation of e-business focusing on the integration and infrastructure complexities of B2B by leveraging the benefits of Internet standards and a common infrastructure to produce optimal efficiencies for intra- and interenterprise computing. (Jain & Ramesh, 2006)

## Dynamic Feature Extraction

Analysis and description of the media content at the time of querying the database. The information is computed on demand and discarded after the query is processed. (Geisler & Kao, 2005; Bretschneider & Kao, 2005)

## Dynamic Graph

Graph representing a constantly changing stream of data. (Holder & Cook, 2005)

## Dynamic Group Interaction Model

In this model elements of several theories with regard to group performance are brought together. Three levels of behavior are taken into account: individual goal-directed behavior, group processes, and a macro-social perspective. The various notions are brought together in a heuristic model concerning group processes. They are related to traditional input-process-output schemas. (Verburg et al., 2005)

## Dynamic Hypertext Markup Language (DHTML)

**1:** The new standard of HTML which adds scripting language and styling capabilities to HTML, hence allowing users more interactive sessions and layout changes of the Web pages. (Gaffar & Seffah, 2005) **2:** A collective term for a combination of new HTML tags and options, style sheets, and programming, which enable one to create Web pages that are more interactive and faster to download. (Díez-Higuera & Díaz-Pernas, 2005)

## Dynamic Model

A UML model describing dynamic behavior such as state changes, triggers, and object type operations. (D. Brandon, Jr., 2005a)

## Dynamic Model of a Relationship Between Paradigms

Following Kuhn's (1962) concepts of scientific paradigms, the model of the relationship between KM and IC is dynamic and entwined in other dominant paradigms in the correlating and overlapping scientific and practitioners' communities. (Ariely, 2006a)

## Dynamic Personalization

End-user tailoring that occurs during the regular use of the system within a context of a user task, as opposed to a specific context-free activity directed at the selection of customization options. (Babaian, 2005)

## Dynamic Perspective

The therapeutic approach based on a transference relationship between patient and therapist, and which includes psychoanalysis but also nineteenth-century approaches such as magnetism and hypnosis. Dynamic psychiatry is a term invented by historians in the early 1940s to describe the development of therapeutic methods interested in the psycho-genesis of mental illnesses. It takes from psychiatry its classifications and clinical approach; from psychology, the postulate of the dual reality of body and mind, and the proposal of the technique of observation of the subjects; and from the ancient tradition of witchcraft, the idea itself of transferential cure. Apart from the historiography context, in current use the term psychodynamic is directly linked to a psychoanalytical approach. The technical term of 'transference' belongs to psychoanalytical theory, as previously the term 'suggestion' was used. However, the historical interpretation of connecting psychoanalysis with anterior approaches risks reducing the rich and complex content of the specific use that 'transference' holds within psychoanalytic theory. Nevertheless, the full potential of psychoanalysis cannot be adequately understood without a reasonable understanding of its context and historical conditions for emergence. (Nobre, 2006b)

## Dynamic Planning System

A three-staged model identifying different approaches to planning at different stages of e-business growth. (Burn & Ash, 2006)

## Dynamic Programming

A method for deriving the optimal path through a mesh. For a Hidden Markov Model (HMM), it is also termed the Viterbi algorithm and involves a method for deriving the optimal state sequence, given a model and an observation sequence. (Caelli, 2005)

## Dynamic Sampling (Adaptive Sampling)

A method of sampling where sampling and processing of data proceed in tandem. After processing each incremental part of the sample, a decision is made whether to continue sampling or not. (Lutu, 2005)

## Dynamic Time Warping (DTW)

Sequences are allowed to be extended by repeating individual time series elements, such as replacing the sequence X={x1,x2,x3} by X={x1,x2,x2,x3}. The distance between two sequences under dynamic time warping is the minimum distance that can be achieved by extending both sequences independently. (Denton, 2005)

## Dynamic Topic Mining

A framework that supports the identification of meaningful patterns (e.g., events, topics, and topical relations) from news stream data. (Chung et al., 2005)

## Dynamic Topology

Due to the node mobility, the network topology of mobile multi-hop ad hoc networks are changing continuously in time. (Erbas, 2005)

## Dynamic Touch

An experience in cyberspace designed by a professional communicator to stimulate emotional responses that will help advance the interests of the communicator's client organization. (Galloway, 2006)

## Dynamic Virtual Enterprise

A set of business partners are linked dynamically on demand and according to customer requirements through the development of a virtual marketplace. (Tahinakis et al., 2006)

## Dynamic (Visual) Hierarchy

An alternative mechanism for presenting keywords that is based on a recognition paradigm and can be dynamically updated. Keywords are arranged in a tree hierarchy to facilitate links to keyword phrases and enable browsing. (Corral et al., 2006)

## Dynamic Web Page

**1:** A virtual page dynamically constructed after a client request. Usually, the request is managed by a specific program or is described using a specific query language whose statements are embedded into pages. (Sindoni, 2005b) **2:** A Web page whose content varies according to various events (e.g., the characteristics of users, the time the pages are accessed, preference settings, browser capabilities, etc.). An example would be the results of a search via search engine. (Falk & Sockel, 2005)

## Dynamic Weighting

Reassigning weights on the data points in each iteration of an iterative algorithm. (B. Zhang, 2005)

## Dynamics (of Organization)

Change in an organization's structure (see *Structural Dynamics*) or operation (see *Operational Dynamics*) along the time, when time as a parameter is indispensable for the organization, or some aspect of organization, description, and analysis. Otherwise, although the organization's state changes, if the time as a parameter can be disregarded, the organization, or some aspect of the organization, is considered static. The organization's state changes frequency, state change time, and intensity are examples of an organization's dynamics features and performance measures. (Cunha & Putnik, 2005)

## Dystopia

The converse of Utopia, a dystopia is any society considered to be undesirable. It is often used to refer to a fictional (often near-future) society where current social trends are taken to terrible and socially destructive extremes. (Macfadyen, 2006b)

# E

**E-**
Oftentimes used without the hyphen, the "e" originally stood for "electronic," as in "online." Today the term is used rather freely to describe any situation or solution that has made the migration from real world to the Internet. (Passi et al., 2005)

**E-Administration:** See *Electronic Administration.*

**E-Administrator:** See *Electronic Administrator.*

**E-ASEAN**
A concept capturing the essence of the intent to establish electronic links at all levels between ASEAN countries. (Sanzogni & Arthur-Gray, 2005)

**E-Assessment Project:** See *Electronic Assessment Project.*

**E-Auction:** See *Electronic Auction.*

**E-Bario Project**
A research initiative undertaken by the Universiti Malaysia Sarawak (UNIMAS) to demonstrate the many ways in which ICT can be used to help marginalized and remote communities in Malaysia to develop socially, culturally, and economically. (Gnaniah, Songan, et al., 2005)

**E-Bedian Project**
A research initiative by the Universiti Malaysia Sarawak (UNIMAS) modeled after the E-Bario research project. (Gnaniah, Songan, et al., 2005)

**E-Business:** See *Electronic Business.*

**E-Business Change:** See *Electronic Business Change.*

**E-Business Environment:** See *Electronic Business Environment.*

**E-Business Model:** See *Electronic Business Model.*

**E-Business Opportunity:** See *Electronic Business Opportunity.*

**E-Business Option:** See *Electronic Business Option.*

**E-Business Outcome:** See *Electronic Business Outcome.*

**E-Business Performance Gain:** See *Electronic Business Performance Gain.*

**E-Business Planning and Analysis Framework:** See *Electronic Business Planning and Analysis Framework.*

**E-Business Policy Group:** See *Electronic Business Policy Group.*

**E-Business Strategy:** See *Electronic Business Strategy.*

**E-Business System:** See *Electronic Business System.*

**E-Business Technology:** See *Electronic Business Technology.*

**E-Business Value Model:** See *Electronic Business Value Model.*

**E-Capability:** See *Electronic Capability.*

**E-Capability Maturity Level:** See *Electronic Capability Maturity Level.*

**E-Capacity:** See *Electronic Capacity.*

**E-Catalog:** See *Electronic Catalog.*

**E-Certificate:** See *Electronic Certificate.*

**E-Channel:** See *Electronic Channel.*

**E-Citizen:** See *Electronic Citizen.*

**E-Cluster:** See *Electronic Cluster.*

**E-Collaboration/Collaborative Commerce:** See *Electronic Collaboration/Collaborative Commerce.*

**E-Collaboration Technology:** See *Electronic Collaboration Technology.*

**E-Commerce:** See *Electronic Commerce.*

**E-Commerce Benefit:** See *Electronic Commerce Benefit.*

**E-Commerce Business Model:** See *Electronic Commerce Business Model.*

**E-Commerce Disadvantage:** See *Electronic Commerce Disadvantage.*

**E-Commerce Driving Force:** See *Electronic Commerce Driving Force.*

**E-Commerce Security Course:** See *Electronic Commerce Security Course.*

**E-Commerce Strategy:** See *Electronic Commerce Strategy.*

**E-Commerce Study:** See *Electronic Commerce Study.*

**E-Commerce System Simulation:** See *Electronic Commerce System Simulation.*

**E-Communication:** See *Electronic Communication.*

**E-Community:** See *Electronic Community.*

**E-Consultation:** See *Electronic Consultation.*

**E-Course:** See *Electronic Course.*

**E-Crime:** See *Electronic Crime.*

**E-CRM**
**1:** A subset of CRM that focuses on acquiring a thorough understanding of an organization's online (via the Internet) visitors and customers to create and maintain online loyalty. (Van Dyke et al., 2006) **2:** The fusion of a process, a strategy, and a technology to blend sales, marketing, and service information to identify, attract, and build partnerships with customers. (Borders & Johnston, 2005) **3:** A strategy that companies use to identify, manage, and improve relationships with their most profitable online customers to create long-term value for the firm when a company's customer service operations are on the Internet, using e-mail, fax, Internet call centers, FAQs, online chats, and Web-based forums. (Gupta & Iyer, 2005)

**E-CRM Analytics**
The process of analyzing and reporting online visitor and customer behavior patterns with the objective of acquiring and retaining customers. (Van Dyke et al., 2006)

**E-Deliberation:** See *Electronic Deliberation.*

**E-Democracy Technique:** See *Electronic Democracy Technique.*

**E-Democracy/Teledemocracy:** See *Electronic Democracy/Teledemocracy.*

**E-Discourse:** See *Electronic Discourse.*

**E-Document:** See *Electronic Document.*

**E-Dyad:** See *Electronic Dyad.*

**E-Education:** See *Electronic Education.*

**E-Enrollment:** See *Electronic Enrollment.*

**E-Fluentials:** See *Electronic Influentials.*

**E-Folio:** See *Electronic Portfolio.*

**E-Forum:** See *Electronic Forum.*

**E-Fulfillment:** See *Electronic Fulfillment.*

**E-Fulfillment Capability:** See *Electronic Fulfillment Capability.*

**E-Governance:** See *Electronic Governance.*

**E-Government:** See *Electronic Government.*

**E-Government Integration Stage:** See *Electronic Government Integration Stage.*

**E-Government Internet Security:** See *Electronic Government Internet Security.*

**E-Government Interoperability:** See *Electronic Government Interoperability.*

**E-Government Portal:** See *Electronic Government Portal.*

**E-Government Stage:** See *Electronic Government Stage.*

**E-Gradebook:** See *Electronic Gradebook.*

**E-Health:** See *Electronic Health.*

**E-Hierarchy:** See *Electronic Hierarchy.*

**E-HIM:** See *Electronic Health Information Management.*

**E-Hub:** See *Electronic Hub.*

**E-Innovation:** See *Electronic Innovation.*

**E-Journal:** See *Electronic Journal.*

**E-Journalism:** See *Electronic Journalism.*

**E-Knowledge:** See *Electronic Knowledge.*

**E-Knowledge Network:** See *Electronic Knowledge Network.*

**E-Lab:** See *Electronic Lab.*

**E-Learner:** See *Electronic Learner.*

**E-Learning:** See *Electronic Learning.*

**E-Learning Application:** See *Electronic Learning Application.*

**E-Learning Development Team:** See *Electronic Learning Development Team.*

**E-Learning Environment:** See *Electronic Learning Environment.*

**E-Learning Evaluation Framework:** See *Electronic Learning Evaluation Framework.*

**E-Learning Experience:** See *Electronic Learning Experience.*

**E-Learning Framework:** See *Electronic Learning Framework.*

**E-Learning Management System:** See *Electronic Learning Management System.*

**E-Learning Market:** See *Electronic Learning Market.*

**E-Learning Platform:** See *Electronic Learning Platform.*

**E-Learning Process:** See *Electronic Learning Process.*

**E-Learning Program:** See *Electronic Learning Program.*

**E-Learning Program Strategic Plan:** See *Electronic Learning Program Strategic Plan.*

**E-Learning Study Skill:** See *Electronic Learning Study Skill.*

**E-Learning Support and Development Team:** See *Electronic Learning Support and Development Team.*

**E-Learning System:** See *Electronic Learning System.*

**E-Learning Technology:** See *Electronic Learning Technology.*

**E-Lib:** See *Electronic Libraries Program.*

**E-Lifestyle:** See *Electronic Lifestyle.*

**E-Market:** See *Electronic Learning Management System.*

**E-Loyalty:** See *Electronic Loyalty.*

**E-Mail:** See *Electronic Mail.*

**E-Mail Aliasing:** See *Electronic Mail Aliasing.*

**E-Mail Bomb:** See *Electronic Mail Bomb.*

**E-Mail Management:** See *Electronic Mail Management.*

**E-Mail Newsletter:** See *Electronic Mail Newsletter.*

**E-Mail Protocol:** See *Electronic Mail Protocol.*

**E-Mall**
A number of e-shops that serve as a gateway through which a visitor can access other e-shops. (Tatnall et al., 2006)

**E-Market:** See *Electronic Market.*

**E-Marketing:** See *Electronic Marketing.*

**E-Marketplace:** See *Electronic Marketplace.*

**E-Marketplace Portal:** See *Electronic Marketplace Portal.*

**E-Marketplace Technology Course:** See *Electronic Marketplace Technology Course.*

**E-Meeting:** See *Electronic Meeting.*

**E-Mentor:** See *Electronic Mentor.*

**E-Model:** See *Electronic Model.*

**E-Negotiation:** See *Electronic Negotiation.*

**E-OTD:** See *Enhanced Observed-Time-Difference Method.*

**E-PAF:** See *E-Business Planning and Analysis Framework.*

**E-Participation:** See *Electronic Participation.*

**E-Partnership:** See *Electronic Partnership.*

**E-Petition:** See *Electronic Petition.*

**E-Policy:** See *Electronic Policy.*

**E-Politics:** See *Electronic Politics.*

**E-Portfolio:** See *Electronic Portfolio.*

**E-Press:** See *Electronic Press.*

**E-Procurement:** See *Electronic Procurement.*

**E-Questionnaire:** See *Electronic Questionnaire.*

**E-R Model:** See *Entity-Relationship Model.*

**E-Readiness:** See *Electronic Readiness.*

**E-Research:** See *Electronic Research.*

**E-Retailer:** See *Electronic Retailer.*

**E-Rollment:** See *Electronic Enrollment.*

**E-Sales Cycle:** See *Electronic Cycle.*

**E-Science:** See *Electronic Science.*

**E-Service:** See *Electronic Service.*

**E-Service Catalog:** See *Electronic Service Catalog.*

**E-Service Quality:** See *Electronic Service Quality.*

**E-Social Contract:** See *Electronic Social Contract.*

**E-Society:** See *Electronic Society.*

**E-Store:** See *Electronic Store.*

**E-Strategy:** See *Electronic Strategy.*

**E-Supply Chain:** See *Electronic Supply Chain.*

**E-Survey:** See *Electronic Survey.*

**E-Tailer:** See *Electronic Tailer.*

**E-Tailing:** See *Electronic Retailing.*

**E-Technology:** See *Electronic Technology.*

**E-Tendering:** See *Electronic Tendering.*

**E-Text:** See *Electronic Text.*

**E-Ticket:** See *Electronic Ticket.*

**E-Trust:** See *Electronic Trust.*

**E-Tutor:** See *Electronic Tutor.*

**E-Vite:** See *Electronic Invitation.*

**E-Voting:** See *Electronic Voting.*

**E-WOM:** See *Electronic Word-of-Mouth.*

**E-Work:** See *Electronic Work.*

**EAI:** See *Enterprise Application Integration.*

**EAI Technology**
Software systems that provide business-to-business integration functionality by sending and receiving messages, and retrieving and storing them in back-end application systems. (Bussler, 2005b)

**EAP:** See *Extensible Authentication Protocol.*

**Earcon**
Abstract, synthetic sounds used in structured combinations whereby the musical qualities of the sounds hold and convey information relative to application objects or activities. (Lumsden, 2005)

**Early Adopter**
One who embraces change and is the most likely to adopt technological innovations quickly. (Salter, 2005c)

**Easy PHP**
Software application written in the dynamic PHP language that combines an Apache Web server and a MySQL database to create flexible Web development tools. (Boateng & Boateng, 2006a)

**Eavesdropping**
The ability for one to access a call and, either in real time or after, reconstruct the conversation. (Wilsdon & Slay, 2005)

**EBBSC**
A balanced scorecard-based framework to formulate and evaluate e-business strategy consisting of four perspectives: business model, analytic e-CRM, process structure, and e-knowledge network. (Wang & Forgionne, 2006)

**EBPG:** See *E-Business Policy Group.*

**EBS:** See *Electronic Brainstorming System.*

**EBXML:** See *Electronic Business XML.*

**EC:** See *Electronic Commerce.*

**EC Techno-Structure:** See *Electronic Commerce Techno-Structure.*

**ECA Rule**
A (business) rule expressed by means of an event, a condition, and an action. (Cilia, 2005)

**ECMA:** See *European Computer Manufacturers Association.*

**ECMS:** See *Enterprise Content Management System.*

**ECN:** See *Electronic Communication Network.*

**Ecological Fallacy**
The relationship between geographical variation in disease incidence or mortality and explanatory covariates (e.g., environmental agents or lifestyle characteristics) measured on groups is often interpreted as a proxy of the relationship between disease and exposure in individuals. However, the association observed at the group or ecological level will not necessarily represent the association between the corresponding variables at the individual level. This type of bias is known as ecological fallacy. (Vidal-Rodeiro et al., 2005)

**Ecological Metaphor**
A way of describing a complex situation, such as IS curriculum development, by providing a way of allowing

for the inclusion of complexity, and a language and set of analytical and descriptive tools from the ecological sciences. (Tatnall & Davey, 2005)

### Ecological Niche

A place where a particular species that is well suited to this environment is able to thrive, where other species may not. (Tatnall & Davey, 2005)

### Ecological System

The organization and interactions of communities of living things, together with the chemical and physical factors in their environment. (O'Looney, 2006)

### Economic Evaluation

This approach to evaluation views IT/IS as an investment or a business facilitation project. Therefore, the focus of evaluation shifts from the performance of the IS per se to the quality of its outputs (e.g., information) and their utilization (e.g., customer satisfaction, creation of business value). Here the evaluation of IT investments is based on an organizational analysis that emphasizes the achievement of predetermined outcomes as a measure of effectiveness (e.g., critical success factors, business objectives/strategy). In other words the "worth" of an IS is sought in the system's performance and financial profitability. (Serafeimidis, 2005)

### Economic Order Quantity (EOQ)

An approach to defining the lot size for purchasing raw materials, the EOQ is a mathematical expression of the trade-off between ordering costs (for purchased items) or set-up costs (for manufactured items) and the cost of storing material as inventory. If set-up or ordering costs are high, it may make sense to deal in larger batches, with the inherent knock-on effect of increasing inventory costs. (Carton & Adam, 2005)

### Economic Risk

A risk derived from increased transaction costs that lead to reduced financial returns. (Ratnasingam, 2005)

### Economic Value Added (EVA)

An attempt to measure value over and above return of costs, and includes many of the intangibles. A typical approach would combine some form of ROI and QWL. (Burn & Ash, 2006)

### Economies of Scale

**1:** The achievement of lower average cost per unit through increased production, or the decrease in the marginal cost of production as a firm's extent of operations expands. (D. Kim, 2005) **2:** The notion of increased efficiency for the production and/or marketing of goods/products by pooling or sharing resources. (Braun, 2006) **3:** Supply-side economies of scale—reductions in unit costs resulting from increased size of operations. Demand-side economies of scale—the value of a technology or product increases exponentially as the number of users increase (network effects lead to demand-side economies of scale). (C.-S. Lee, 2005) **4:** The notion of increased efficiency for the production and/or marketing of goods/products by pooling or sharing resources. (Braun, 2005a)

### Economies of Scope

Supply-side economies of scope—cost of the joint production of two or more products can be less than the cost of producing them separately. Demand-side economies of scope—a single set of digital assets can provide value for customers across many different and disparate markets. (C.-S. Lee, 2005)

### Ecosystem

**1:** The ecosystem represented by the curriculum in a university information systems department contains (at least) the following "species": lecturers, researchers, students, professional bodies, university administrators, and representatives of the computer industry. (Tatnall & Davey, 2005) **2:** The entire ecological community composed of all living organisms interacting with the physical environment as one system. (Targowski, 2005)

**EDA:** See *Exploratory Data Analysis.*

**EDGE:** See *Enhanced Data Rates for GSM Evolution.*

**EDI:** See *Electronic Data Interchange.*

**EDIFACT:** See *Electronic Data Interchange for Administration, Commerce, and Transport.*

### Edit Distance

A measure of string similarity that counts the number of character insertions, deletions, and substitutions needed to convert one string into the other. (Navarro, 2005)

**Edit Restraint**
A logical restraint such as a set of business rules that assures that an employee's listed salary in a job category is not too high or too low, or that certain contradictory conditions, such as a male hysterectomy, do not occur. (Winkler, 2005)

**Edit Script**
A set of instructions that walk and update a document database node by node. (Schmidt et al., 2005)

**Editing Procedure**
The process of detecting and handling errors in data. It usually includes three phases: the definition of a consistent system of requirements, their verification on given data, and elimination or substitution of data that is in contradiction with the defined requirements. (Conversano & Siciliano, 2005)

**Editorial Metadata**
Metadata obtained manually, by a pool of experts. (Pachet, 2006)

**EDMS:** See *Enterprise Document Management System.*

**Education**
Formation or instruction process of an individual by means of the interiorization and assimilation of new assets of knowledge and capabilities. (Andrade, Ares, García, Rodríguez, Seoane, et al., 2006)

**Education Process**
The use of learning models and supporting learning technologies to deliver the learning experience and/or training with students. (LeRouge & Webb, 2005)

**Education Process Model**
A basic systems model that consists of resources and philosophy as inputs; an integrative process of objectives, methodology, audiences, and instructional technology; the outputs of outcomes and experiences; and assessment feedback. (Beck & Schornack, 2005)

**Educational Coordinator (Prison)**
A prison staff member who serves as an intermediary between a distance learning instructor and the prisoner. An educational coordinator aids prisoners in applying to programs, adding courses, and asking questions of the instructor. (Bagwell, 2005)

**Educational Evaluation**
Assessment of the educational value of a piece of educational software. (Karoulis & Pombortsis, 2005a)

**Educational Hypermedia**
A Web-based learning environment that offers learners browsing through the educational content supported by flexible user interfaces and communication abilities. (Magoulas, 2006)

**Educational Modeling Language (EML)**
Developed by the Open University of The Netherlands; since 1998, EML is a notational method for e-learning environments based on a pedagogical meta-model that considers that didactic design plays a main role. (García, Berlanga, & García, 2006)

**Educational Organization Structure**
The rules and resources offered by the internal educational institution that are derived from how it is organized, as well as program requirements, curriculum, and course objectives. (LeRouge & Webb, 2005)

**Educational Panacea**
The view that technology might be the cure-all or "holy grail" of education. (Salter, 2005a)

**Educational Software**
Software packages supporting specific goals in the education of target groups, for example, primary school tutees or impaired children. (Utsi & Lowyck, 2005)

**Educational Software Development Team**
A software development team in a university setting is multi-faceted and multi-skilled, requiring the skills of project managers, subject matter experts, educational designers, programmers, graphic designers, interface designers, IT support staff, editors, and evaluators. In many cases, one person can assume more than one role. (Williamson et al., 2006)

**Educational Task**
One of several tasks directly associated with the delivery of the educational component to students (e.g., lecturers, tutorials, assessment, and so forth). (Darbyshire & Burgess, 2005)

## Educational Technology

**1:** A field of study grounded in theories of learning and instructional design. Educational technology draws inspiration from other fields and disciplines, such as psychology, communications, management, and technology, and focuses on determining the most effective and efficient methods for positively impacting knowledge, learning, and human performance. (Schaffer et al., 2006) **2:** Application of one or more electronic or computer-based devices used in delivering education. (Hantula & DeRosa, 2005) **3:** Systematic identification, development, organization, or utilization of educational resources, and the management of these processes. The term is occasionally used in a more limited sense to describe the use of multimedia technologies or audiovisual aids as tools to enhance the teaching and learning process. (Kinuthia, 2005) **4:** Technology used in formal educational contexts, such as classrooms. Recent examples are television, personal computers, and the Internet. (Carroll, 2005) **5:** The use of technology to enhance individual learning and achieve widespread education. (Magoulas, 2006)

## Educational Television

Generally refers to a television program that has a broad cultural purpose, such as Sesame Street in America. (Berg, 2005d)

## EduPortal

A portal geared toward education that provides single sign-on access to academic and administrative resources for students, staff, and faculty. (Hazari, 2006)

**EEG:** See *Electroencephalogram.*

**EF:** See *Expedited Forwarding.*

## Effect

A change in the state of an object. (Dori, 2006)

## Effective Practice

An online practice that is replicable and produces positive outcomes in each of the pillar areas. (Moore et al., 2005)

## Effective Technical and Human Implementation of Computer-Based Systems (ETHICS)

A problem-solving methodology that has been developed to assist the introduction of organizational systems incorporating new technology. It has as its principal objective the successful integration of company objectives with the needs of employees and customers. (Singh & Kotzé, 2006)

## Effective Use

**1:** The capacity and opportunity to integrate information and communication technology into the accomplishment of self- or collaboratively identified goals. What is most important is not so much the physical availability of computers and the Internet, but rather people's ability to make use of those technologies to engage in meaningful social practices. (Kvasny & Payton, 2005) **2:** The use of communication technology that is fully adaptive and responsive to local needs and goals. Closely related to community development. (Geiselhart & Jamieson, 2005)

## Effectiveness

**1:** A measure of performance that specifies whether the system achieves its longer-term goals or not. (Abu-Samaha, 2005) **2:** A very general goal that refers to how good a system is at doing what it is supposed to do. (Yong, 2005) **3:** Explores whether it is an appropriate approach to assess the learning outcomes. (Diamadis & Polyzos, 2005) **4:** In the context of IT, this is the measurement of the capacity of the outputs of an information system or of an IT application to fulfill the requirements of the company and to achieve its goals, making this company more competitive. In a few words, effectiveness can be understood as the ability to "do the right thing." (Barbin Laurindo et al., 2005) **5:** The ability to accomplish a task with fewer errors. (Hunter, 2005)

## Effectiveness of Team Interaction

Effectiveness as linked to functional components such as: (1) interdependency in terms of the environment, (2) task interdependency of team members (skills development and consequences; sanctions based on results), and (3) the quality of transactions between team members (interpersonal relations, production energy, shared effectiveness, and group cohesion). (Tremblay, 2006b)

## Efficacy

A measure of performance that establishes whether the system works or not—if the transformation of an entity from an input stage to an output stage has been achieved. (Abu-Samaha, 2005)

## Efficiency

**1:** A measure of performance based on comparison of the value of the output of the system and the resources needed to achieve the output; in other words, is the system worthwhile? (Abu-Samaha, 2005) **2:** From an IT viewpoint, this usually relates to improvements within the business, so for a business it may mean IT systems that reduce costs or perform tasks more reliably or faster. (Darbyshire & Burgess, 2005) **3:** Related to the time spent for assessors to accomplish the assessment task. (Diamadis & Polyzos, 2005) **4:** The ability to accomplish a task with few resources. (Hunter, 2005) **5:** The way a system supports users in carrying out their tasks, and a measure of how quickly users can accomplish goals or finish their work when using the system. (Yong, 2005)

## Efficiency of Around-the-Clock Development

An index used to indicate a ratio between the time required to follow up the previous work and time spent to continue the work. (Lui & Chan, 2005)

## Efficient

Full efficiency is attained by any DMU if and only if none of its inputs or outputs can be improved without worsening some of its other inputs or outputs. (Chen, Mottiwalla, et al., 2005)

## Efficient Market

A market in which any relevant information is immediately impounded in asset or security prices. (Roofe, 2005)

## EFM Fiber

Defined by IEEE 802.3ah. It features a point-to-point fiber-to-the-home network, typically deployed as an active star, that uses active electronics and Ethernet as its transmission protocol. (Kelic, 2005)

## Egress Filtering

Process of checking whether outgoing packets contain valid source IP addresses before sending them out to the Internet. Packets with forged IP addresses are discarded on the router that connects to the Internet. (Syed et al., 2005)

## Eigenface

Another name for face recognition via principal components analysis. (Lovell & Chen, 2005)

## Eigenvalue

The quantity representing the variance of a set of variables included in a factor. (Lee, Peterson, et al., 2005)

**EIP:** See *Enhanced Instructional Presentation; Enterprise Information Portal; Enterprise Internal Portal.*

**EIP Model:** See *Enhanced Instructional Presentation Model.*

**EIS:** See *Executive Information System.*

**EISP:** See *Enterprise Information Security Policy.*

**EKM:** See *Enterprise Knowledge Management.*

## Elaboration

Issue- or message-relevant cognition. Elaboration is typically conceptualized as a continuum ranging from high elaboration to low elaboration. It is thought to be influenced by an individual's motivation and ability to cognitively process a message. (Duthler, 2005)

## Elaboration Likelihood Model (ELM)

An information processing theory of persuasion first proposed in 1981 by social psychologists Richard Petty and John Cacioppo. The model of persuasion proposes that individuals either think carefully about the acceptability of a persuasive appeal, or instead with little cognitive effort rely on cues in the persuasive situation to arrive at a conclusion of the advocacy. (Duthler, 2005)

## Elastic Application

A kind of network application that will always wait for data to arrive rather than proceed without it. (Yang et al., 2005a)

## Elastic Audio Slider

An interface design that enables the interactive manipulation of audio replay speed by incorporating the concept of elastic interfaces in common audio-progress bars. (Hürst & Lauer, 2006)

## Elastic Interface

An interface or widget that manipulates an object (e.g., a slider thumb), not by direct interaction, but instead by moving it along a straight line that connects the object with the current position of the cursor. Movements of the object are a function of the length of this connection, thus following the rubber-band metaphor. (Hürst & Lauer, 2006)

## Elastic Panning

An approach for navigation in visual data which has proven to be feasible not only for the visual browsing of static, time-independent data, but for continuous, time-dependent media streams as well. Similar to the FineSlider, it builds on the concept of elastic interfaces and therefore solves the scaling problem, which generally appears if a long document has to be mapped on a slider scale that is limited by window size and screen resolution. (Hürst, 2006)

## Elderly Time Bank

A virtual community applying the concept of time bank to support the active aging of elderly and that resorts to computer networks to facilitate the interactions among members. (Camarinha-Matos & Ferrada, 2006)

## Electricity Grid for E-Learning and Professional Development

A metaphor for a systemic environment in which e-learning and professional development resources and experiences flow to stakeholders throughout the system. Surplus is built into the system, and knowledge resources are "entered once and used anywhere." This model enables reduced marginal costs. (Norris, 2005)

## Electronic Administration

E-government initiatives that deal particularly with improving the internal workings of the public sector. (Olatokun, 2006)

## Electronic Administrator

Online course or program administrator. (Whateley et al., 2005)

## Electronic Assessment Project

A system-wide quality assurance project for Minnesota State Colleges and Universities' online programs. (Olson & Langer, 2005)

## Electronic Auction

**1:** A centralized protocol for redistributing resources among agents. Each agent attaches a value to each resource. The seller asks a price for a resource, the buyer offers a price, and they negotiate over the Internet to achieve a desired outcome satisfying to both, else the negotiation fails. (Murthy & Krishnamurthy, 2005a) **2:** The process of selling online, with the highest bidder winning the product. (Guan, 2006a)

## Electronic Auction Marketplace

A form of a virtual B2B community where goods, services, or information are offered for purchase and bid upon by various organizations under some pre-determined structured process. eBay would be an example of an electronic auction marketplace. (Turner, 2006)

## Electronic Board

A classic groupware tool that supports the functionalities of a traditional whiteboard (sharing sketches, pointing, annotating) through a set of distributed computers. (Villemur & Drira, 2006)

## Electronic Brainstorming System (EBS)

A computer-based system that facilitates brainstorming between group members. (Aurum, 2005)

## Electronic Bulletin Board

A Web site where students and instructors can post information for others to view at a later time. (Hawkins & Baker, 2005)

## Electronic Business (E-Business)

**1:** A comprehensive term used to describe the way an organization interacts with its key constituencies, including employees, managers, customers, suppliers, and partners through electronic technologies. It has a broader connotation than e-commerce because e-commerce is limited to business exchanges or transaction over the Internet only. (Zhao, 2005) **2:** The administration of conducting business via the Internet. This would include the buying and selling of goods and services, along with providing technical or customer support through the Internet. E-business is a term often used in conjunction with e-commerce, but it includes services in addition to the sale of goods. (Mockler et al., 2006) **3:** The conduct of business on the Internet. It is a more generic term than e-commerce because it refers to not only buying and selling, but also electronically back-end integration with other business processes such as servicing customers and collaborating with business partners. (Sharma, 2006c) **4:** A business made via the Internet, not only selling or buying, but also supporting customers and connecting the supply chain. (de Medeiros et al., 2006) **5:** A concept capturing the essence of conducting business by electronic means in addition to or as a substitute for a physical location (bricks and mortar). In its simplest form, the conduct of business on the Internet. It is a more generic term than e-commerce because it refers to not only buying and selling, but also servicing customers and collaborating with business partners. (Sanzogni & Arthur-Gray, 2005) **6:** Any financial or non-financial transaction involving an electronic process using the Internet or Internet technologies (O'Buyonge & Chen, 2006) **7:** Derived from such terms as e-mail and e-commerce, the conduct of business on the Internet or extranet, not only buying or selling, but also servicing customers and collaborating with business partners. (Malik, 2006) **8:** Business or business activities integrated with business processes and usually carried out online—for example, over the Internet. (Mizell & Sugarman, 2005) **9:** Refers to commerce that is conducted via the Internet. This also applies to e-finance, e-marketing, e-design, and e-management. (Reynolds, 2005)

## Electronic Business Change

The process surrounding the effective management of different stages of online business development and growth. (Ash & Burn, 2006)

## Electronic Business Environment

The business environment characterized by rapid time-to-market pressures, heterogeneous technical access, and quick IT strategic response requirements. (Steinbach & Knight, 2005)

## Electronic Business Model

**1:** That subset of the general business model that supports e-business. (Craig, 2005) **2:** The set of strategies that enable businesses to take advantage of the latest technologies to generate profits and customer satisfaction. (Boateng & Boateng, 2006a)

## Electronic Business Opportunity

An assessed and selected e-business option. (Boonstra & de Brock, 2006)

## Electronic Business Option

A possibility to use an electronic network for a business purpose. (Boonstra & de Brock, 2006)

## Electronic Business Outcome

E-business forces change to occur in three corporate domains—technology, process, and people—at strategic and operational levels. (Ash & Burn, 2006)

## Electronic Business Performance Gain

The improvement in corporate resourcing, employee work life, and customer satisfaction. (Ash & Burn, 2006)

## Electronic Business Planning and Analysis Framework (E-PAF)

A combination of QFD, VCA, and BSC that supports strategic e-business initiatives. (Clegg & Tan, 2006)

## Electronic Business Policy Group (EBPG)

A collaboration of representatives of the EU member states and the European Commission services. (Wiggins, 2006)

## Electronic Business Strategy

**1:** An elaborate and systematic plan of action intended to accomplish specific e-business goals which considers e-business multi-dimensional characteristics (Wang & Forgionne, 2006) **2:** Comprehensive set of planning approaches that reflect the stage of e-business growth within the organization. (Burn & Ash, 2006)

## Electronic Business System

An organized, structured whole that implements business activities that are based on electronic technologies, methodologies, and processes. (Trcek, 2005)

## Electronic Business Technology

Any technology that enables an organization to conduct business electronically, with the overall aim of improving firm performance. (Baker & Coltman, 2005)

## Electronic Business Value Model

A model that conveys to management where to focus organizational resources by highlighting specific areas of opportunity. (Boonstra & de Brock, 2006)

## Electronic Business XML (EBXML)

**1:** An EDI standard intended to supplant X12 and UN/EDIFACT. Based on eXtensible Markup Language (XML) and using standard Internet protocols, it is expected to lower the cost and difficulty of setting up and using EDI, thereby expanding its use to small and medium-sized enterprises. (Hawk & Zheng, 2006) **2:** An XML-based language and infrastructure that aims at enabling B2B interactions among companies of any size. (Fortino et al., 2006) **3:** An architecture and set of specifications designed to automate business-process interactions among trading partners. (Moser & Melliar-Smith, 2006) **4:** Any form of business or administrative transaction or information exchange that is executed using information and communications technology. This may be a transaction performed in a peer-to-peer fashion between companies or organizations, or with a customer. Electronic business impacts on the way business is perceived. (Richards et al., 2005)

## Electronic Capability

The abilities that an organization is able to leverage off in order to deliver online products and services. These are often described in terms of their "maturity levels." (Clegg & Tan, 2006)

## Electronic Capability Maturity Level

The conceptual model describing how advanced an organization is in the adoption of Internet-based solutions that support their strategy and operations. The levels range from "low" (little adoption) to "high" (sophisticated levels of adoption). (Clegg & Tan, 2006)

## Electronic Capacity

The limit of the e-business company's ability to produce or perform that is imposed by the equipment and/or available personnel, and the network technology and performance. (Wang & Forgionne, 2006)

## Electronic Catalog

**1:** A graphical user interface that presents product and/or service information to users, typically using the World Wide Web. (Gangopadhyay & Huang, 2005) **2:** Vendors' catalogs offered either on CD-ROM or on the Internet to advertise and promote products and services. (Singh, 2005)

## Electronic Channel

An online marketing channel where companies and customers conduct business, no matter where they are. Since the e-commerce revolution, many brick-and-mortar businesses have expanded their marketing channel to include e-channel. (I. Lee, 2005)

## Electronic Citizen

An e-government initiative that deals particularly with the relationship between government and citizens—either as voters/stakeholders from whom the public sector should derive its legitimacy, or as customers who consume public services. (Olatokun, 2006)

## Electronic Cluster

Digitally enabled communities of organizations that come together on a needs basis, in varying formations of virtual organizations, to meet a temporary business opportunity. (Mason et al., 2006)

## Electronic Collaboration/Collaborative Commerce

**1:** IT-enabled joint intellectual efforts between organizations for planning, design, development, production, and delivery of products and services. (Chuang et al., 2005) **2:** The use of ICT by citizens and business organizations to collaboratively plan, design, develop, manage, and research products and services and innovative ICT and e-commerce applications. Also called Virtual Collaboration. (Averweg, 2006) **3:** The process in which a set of individuals communicate through an intranet or Internet to coordinate their efforts towards the solution of a problem. (Karacapilidis, 2005) **4:** Collaboration among individuals engaged in a common task using electronic technologies. (Signoret, 2006)

## Electronic Collaboration Technology

Electronic technology that enables collaboration among individuals engaged in a common task. (Kock, 2006)

## Electronic Commerce (EC, E-Commerce)

**1:** Business transactions conducted by electronic means other than conventional telephone service, for example, facsimile or electronic mail (e-mail). (Melkonyan, 2005) **2:** The conduct of buying and selling products and services by businesses and consumers over the Internet. E- simply means anything done electronically, usually via the Internet. E-commerce is the means of selling goods and services on the Internet. (Sharma, 2006c) **3:** Involves a direct financial transaction in the electronic process using Internet technologies. E-commerce encompasses business-to-business or B2B, business-to-consumer or B2C (Amazon.com), and consumer-to-consumer or C2C. (O'Buyonge & Chen, 2006) **4:** The process of buying, selling, or exchanging products, services, and information using computer networks. (Pease & Rowe, 2005) **5:** The transaction of goods and services through electronic communications. E-commerce has two primary forms: B2B (business-to-business) and B2C (business-to-consumer). (Tian & Stewart, 2006) **6:** Usually refers to conducting business (electronically) with other businesses or consumers, but can be extended to include the inner workings within a business. (Peszynski, 2005) **7:** The buying and selling of information, products, and services via computer networks and especially the Internet. (Scupola, 2005) **8:** Selling and buying of products and services via the Internet. (de Medeiros et al., 2006) **9:** A concept capturing the essence of carrying out commerce by electronic means. E-commerce refers to the buying and selling of goods and services on the Internet, especially the World Wide Web. In practice, this term and a newer term, e-business, are often used interchangeably. (Sanzogni & Arthur-Gray, 2005) **10:** Any business done electronically. The electronic business where information technology is applied to all aspects of a company's operations. (Dholakia, Bang, et al., 2005) **11:** Commercial activities taking place over electronic networks (primarily the Internet); e-commerce is a subset of general commerce. (Craig, 2005) **12:** Conducting business and financial transactions online via electronic means. (T.S. Chan, 2005) **13:** Conducting commercial transactions on the Internet, where goods, information, or services are bought and then paid for. (Raisinghani & Petty, 2005) **14:** Connection, electronic data exchange, and transaction capability via the Internet. (Braun, 2005a) **15:** Consists of techniques and algorithms used to conduct business over the Internet. Trading processes such as supply-chain management, strategic purchase planning, and market mechanisms for trading commodities online are implemented using e-commerce. (Dasgupta et al., 2006) **16:** Doing business electronically, including buying and selling information, products, and services over a digital infrastructure via computer networks. (Rhodes, 2005) **17:** Using the Internet and related technologies and software to support business activities in general. It ranges from simple setup such as e-mail and file transfer to complex systems such as supply chain management and enterprise resources-planning systems. (Poon, 2005) **18:** The process of buying and selling goods and services online. (Gordon & Lin, 2005) **19:** Financial business transaction that occurs over an electronic network such as the Internet. (Liu & Tucker, 2005) **20:** Means selling items over the World Wide Web. Consequently, enterprises must incorporate new technology information and communication means. (Pires et al., 2006)

## Electronic Commerce Benefit

One of several tangible and intangible business advantages achieved by adopting e-commerce. (Vrazalic et al., 2005)

## Electronic Commerce Business Model

A structured description of an organization's activities in order to operate a business based on electronic commerce.

It consists of three main parts: the architecture for the flow of products, services, and information; the generation of value; and the source of revenue. (Madlberger, 2006)

## Electronic Commerce Disadvantage

One of the difficulties or problems experienced by a business following e-commerce adoption. (Vrazalic et al., 2005)

## Electronic Commerce Driving Force

A conditions and/or expectation that facilitates e-commerce adoption. (Vrazali et al., 2005)

## Electronic Commerce Security Course

Technologies, architectures, and infrastructure for securing electronic transactions over nonproprietary networks. Implementation and maintenance of mechanisms that secure electronic documents with confidentiality, authentication, integrity, and non-repudiation. Public key certificate. Digital signature. (Knight & Chan, 2005)

## Electronic Commerce Strategy

A subset of general business and information technology strategy, focusing on Web-based commercial opportunities. It may dominate general strategy in some firms. (Craig, 2005)

## Electronic Commerce Study

Contains elements of information systems, business processes, and communications technologies. (Tatnall & Burgess, 2005)

## Electronic Commerce System Simulation

An integrative procedure to run a business processes-oriented simulation program based on both internal and external business environmental factors to demonstrate the actual results of implementing an e-commerce business model by using computer-driven software toolkits. It is an effective, efficient, and economical approach, and can be used to experiment and evaluate different e-commerce business models or plans. (Chen, Li, et al., 2006)

## Electronic Commerce Techno-Structure

An e-commerce system dimension that is related to the formalized institutional procedures that govern online trade execution between e-market participants. (Wang, 2006)

## Electronic Communication

**1:** A vital concept to the virtual organization is the ability to communicate through purely electronic means, eliminating the need for physical contact and allowing the geographical dispersion of organization members. Online collaboration via e-mail, discussion boards, chat, and other methods, as well as telephone and facsimile communications, are primary contributors to the removal of time and space in this new organizational concept. (J. Lee, 2005) **2:** From a human perspective, it is the transfer of information—textual, graphic, oral, or visual—from one point/person to another via electric, electromagnetic, or photonic means. Machine-to-machine communications deals in bits and bytes only. (McManus & Carr, 2005)

## Electronic Communication Network (ECN)

An electronic system that brings buyers and sellers together for the electronic execution of trades. ECNs represent orders in NASDAQ stocks; they internally match buy and sell orders, or represent the highest bid prices and lowest ask prices on the open market. (Saha, 2006b)

## Electronic Community

**1:** A group of people sharing common interests, ideas, and feelings on the Internet or other collaborative networks. E-communities exist in discussion groups, chat rooms, newsgroups, and so forth. (Markellou et al., 2006) **2:** An online forum to discuss topics of mutual interest. (Coakes & Willis, 2005)

## Electronic Consultation

An e-democracy technique used for research of stakeholders' views, and evaluation of proposed rules' regulatory impact by ICT usage. (Pazyuk, 2005)

## Electronic Course

An online educational program that introduces and explains a specific educational subject (Paraskevi & Kollias, 2006)

## Electronic Crime

The illegal exploitation of computer technologies, such as the Internet. (Kyobe, 2006)

## Electronic Customer Relationship Management (E-CRM)

CRM comprises the methods, systems, and procedures that facilitate the interaction between the firm and its customers. The development of new technologies, especially the proliferation of self-service channels like the Web and WAP phones, has changed consumer buying behavior and forced companies to manage electronically the relationships with customers. The new CRM systems are using electronic devices and software applications that attempt to personalize and add value to customer-company interactions. (Gurău, 2005)

## Electronic Data Interchange (EDI)

**1:** A set of computer interchange standards developed in the 1960s for business documents such as invoices, bills, and purchase orders. It has evolved to use the Internet. (McManus & Standing, 2005) **2:** A standard, structured format for exchanging business data. (Hawk & Zheng, 2006) **3:** Exchange of business documents through computer networks in a standard format. It was the first generation of e-commerce, applied in B2B transactions before the availability of the Internet in its present form. (Tian & Stewart, 2006) **4:** A standard message layout used on computer-to-computer commercial data interchange. Traditional EDI uses an electronic method called Value-Added Network (VAN). However, it is increasingly adopting Internet protocol. (de Medeiros et al., 2006) **5:** A standard used by businesses to transmit documents such as invoices and purchase orders to each other electronically. The parties who exchange EDI messages (which can be encrypted and decrypted) are referred to as trading partners. (Duan, 2005) **6:** A standard used to govern the formatting and transfer of transaction data between different companies, using networks such as the Internet. As more companies are linking to the Internet, EDI is becoming increasingly important as an easy mechanism for companies to share transaction information on buying, selling, and trading. ANSI (American National Standards Institute) has approved a set of EDI standards known as the X12 standards. Although not yet a global standard, because of EDIFACT, a standard developed by the United Nations and used primarily in non-North American countries, negotiations are underway to combine the two into a worldwide standard. (Archer, 2005) **7:** A set of document-exchange standards used to implement interorganizational system exchanges to achieve automated computer-to-computer document exchange regardless of the communication technologies used. (Poon, 2005) **8:** Exchange between businesses of computer-readable data in a standard format. (Passi et al., 2005) **9:** Meta-term for a multitude of different electronic message standards that allow computerized and highly structured, low-error communication between computers. A "merge" between

EDI and Internet technology can be recently observed by the upcoming Web-based EDI solutions, where on EDI partner does not have to install EDI, but uses common Web browsers to communicate via EDI. (Kotzab, 2005) **10:** The computer-to-computer exchange of intercompany business documents and information through standard interfaces; requires hardware, software, and communications technology that permit those computers to transfer the data electronically (such as purchase orders, invoices, medical claims, and price lists). (Ratnasingam, 2006) **11:** The electronic exchange of business documents using standardized document formats. (Harris & Chen, 2006) **12:** The interchange of a data message structured under a certain format between business applications. (Mitrakas, 2005) **13:** The movement of specially formatted standard business documents, such as orders, bills, and confirmations sent between business partners. (Lertwongsatien & Wongpinunwatana, 2005)

## Electronic Data Interchange for Administration, Commerce, and Transport (EDIFACT)

**1:** An international standard for the electronic exchange of business documents widely used in Europe. (Harris & Chen, 2006) **2:** The worldwide EDI messaging standard, administered and maintained by the UN. (Whiteley, 2006)

## Electronic Deliberation

Online public engagement with emphasis on the deliberative element. (Kozeluh, 2005)

## Electronic Democracy Technique

One of the ways (methods) of citizen engagement in the process of decision making based on ICT usage. The main techniques are: e-consultation, e-petition, and e-voting. (Pazyuk, 2005)

## Electronic Democracy/Teledemocracy (E-Democracy)

**1:** The use of modern information and communications technologies as instruments to empower the people in a democracy to help set agendas, establish priorities, make important policies, and participate in decision making and implementation in an informed and deliberative way. (Keskinen & Kuosa, 2005) **2:** Interaction between public, private, and third sectors by ICT usage in democratic processes; the way in which citizens interact with government by ICT usage. (Pazyuk, 2005) **3:** A qualitative term to describe the use of ICT as a medium

in which to engage the community to participate in and contribute to the governance process generally, and to facilitate and enhance the capability of a citizen to have a say in the impact of governance on themselves and their communities. (Sutcliffe, 2005) **4:** Depending on what type of democracy it should support, ICT can be used for electronic voting, online referendums, or to support the political parties in their dialogue with the voters. It can also be used to support political debate in a local community or in other political processes. (Jaeger, 2005) **5:** A democracy in which e-government is involved in the development of direct forms of political deliberation and decision making through electronic referendums and similar devices. (Sharma, 2006b) **6:** A tool-oriented conception of democracy referring to new democratic practices in which ICTs and innovative institutional arrangements are utilized (cf. teledemocracy). (Anttiroiko, 2005a) **7:** Refers to relations of two-way and horizontal power—using technologies to enhance democratic practice. It is about: interconnecting citizens among themselves, participation, empowering those in the margins, inclusion, creating and maintaining responsiveness, accountability, maintaining universality, and openness. (Yigitcanlar & Baum, 2006a) **8:** The electronic process through which citizens engage with government and its agents (and vice versa), including consultation and voting. E-democracy is a two-way process that can be driven by either government or citizens. (Williamson, 2005) **9:** The use of electronic communications to support and increase democratic engagement, and deepen and widen citizen participation. (Malina, 2005) **10:** The use of electronic media such as the Internet to enhance democracy. (Boateng & Boateng, 2006b) **11:** The utilization of electronic communications technologies, such as the Internet, in enhancing democratic processes within a democratic republic or a representative democracy. It is a political development still in its infancy, as well as the subject of much debate and activity within government, civic-oriented groups, and societies around the world. E-democracy also includes within its scope electronic voting. (Chochliouros & Spiliopoulou-Chochliourou, 2006) **12:** The use of ICT, such as the Internet or WWW, to foster democratic processes such as citizen participation. (Hinnant & Sawyer, 2005)

## Electronic Discourse

Text-based conversation and discussion generated by computer-mediated communication asynchronously and synchronously. (Han & Hill, 2006)

## Electronic Document

A digital object that stores something of use to someone. More general than paper documents, electronic documents can take various forms, including word processing files, spreadsheet files, graphics, audio and video files, and so forth. (Corral et al., 2006)

## Electronic Dyad

Teacher/student and student/student interaction through electronic media. (Lerch et al., 2005)

## Electronic Education

A concept capturing the essence of carrying out education by electronic means. (Sanzogni & Arthur-Gray, 2005)

## Electronic Enrollment

Online student enrollment. (Whateley et al., 2005)

## Electronic Forum

Another name for a forum, which is an area on a Web site where you can read and post messages on a particular topic, allowing debate. (Coakes, 2006b)

## Electronic Fulfillment

**1:** A company meets the needs of its customers with whom it carries out some transactions through the Internet. It is most often associated with B2C e-commerce. (Aigbedo, 2005) **2:** The activities required to ensure that a product ordered through an online retailer is delivered to a consumer, and may also include reverse logistics (return of goods) activities. E-fulfillment providers provide services derived from those offered by traditional logistics, delivery and warehousing providers, as well as an emerging range of new capabilities. Such services may be provided by in-house departments or increasingly by third-party outsourcers who offer a wide range of supply chain services to online retailers. (Alexander & Burn, 2006)

## Electronic Fulfillment Capability

E-fulfillment providers may be identified from a well-defined set of capabilities they utilize in offering their services. These incorporate traditional logistical, delivery, and warehousing services, as well as picking and packing, kit delivery, and payment-taking systems. Increasingly, capabilities are incorporating knowledge-based skills and resources, and include such services as online retail Web site development or hosting, supplier management, and customer relationship management. These capabilities

are not uniformly adopted by provider organizations. (Alexander & Burn, 2006)

## Electronic Fund Transfer

Any transfer of funds that is initiated through an electronic terminal, telephone, computer, or magnetic tape for the purpose of ordering, instructing, or authorizing a financial institution to debit or credit an account. (Singh, 2005a)

## Electronic Governance (E-Governance)

**1:** A term to describe the delivery of the governance process using ICT rather than conventional and traditional means. (Sutcliffe, 2005) **2:** Communication by electronic means to place power in the hands of citizens to determine what laws need to be made and how these laws should be written. (Malina, 2005) **3:** Refers to a local government's inventiveness to electronically govern areas under its jurisdiction. (Averweg, 2006) **4:** Refers to a much broader range of issues and relationships around the impact of the Internet on political life at all levels, not just the level of states and their bureaucracies. E-governance is a broader concept, which includes the use of ICT by government and civil society to promote greater participation of citizens in the governance of political institutions. (Sharma, 2006b) **5:** Most commonly, the concept of governance is associated with "public governance," which refers to coordination, interaction, and institutional arrangements that are needed to pursue collective interest in policy-making, development, and service processes in the context of intersectoral stakeholder relations. Electronic governance is technologically mediated communication, coordination, and interaction in governance processes. (Anttiroiko, 2005a) **6:** The application of electronic means in the interaction between government and citizens and government and businesses, as well as in internal government operations to simplify and improve democratic, government, and business aspects of governance. (Joia, 2006) **7:** The delivery of government services in an electronic medium. It also includes the online interactions between government and citizens. (Boateng & Boateng, 2006b) **8:** The process of administration (elaboration and implementation of policy decisions and administration services delivery) based on full-scale ICT usage at all levels of decision making and all branches of public administration. (Pazyuk, 2005) **9:** The use of information and communication technologies to make public policy decisions. Examples include electronic voting to elect public officials (e-voting), electronic commenting on regulatory rules (e-rulemaking), and deliberating on public policy issues (deliberative e-democracy). (Knepper & Chen, 2006)

## Electronic Government (E-Government)

**1:** The ability of government to design and use ICTs to interact internally and externally with government bodies, citizens, and businesses in order to deliver integrated electronic public services. (Malina, 2005) **2:** A concept capturing the essence of carrying out the business of government by electronic means, including the delivery of public services and voting (in some instances). (Sanzogni & Arthur-Gray, 2005) **3:** A strategy for revolutionizing the business of government through the use of information technology (IT), particularly Web-based technologies, which improve internal and external processes, efficiencies, and service delivery. (Schelin, 2005) **4:** Based on ICT, taking place in public administration, concerns electronic ways to perform administrative tasks, and the communication between the public administration and the citizens. (Jaeger, 2005) **5:** Any government functions or processes that are carried out in digital form over the Internet. E-government refers to the use by government agencies of information technologies (such as wide area networks, the Internet, and mobile computing) that have the ability to transform relations with citizens, businesses, and other arms of government. (Sharma, 2006b) **6:** The use of technology to enhance the access to and delivery of government services to benefit citizens, business partners, and employees. (Averweg, 2006) **7:** Those aspects of government in which ICTs are or can be utilized, the basic functions being to increase efficiency in administrative processes (e-administration), to guarantee easy access to information for all, to provide quality e-services, and to enhance democracy with the help of new technological mediation tools (e-democracy). (Anttiroiko, 2005a) **8:** The use of information technologies to improve and facilitate citizens' relationships with government through democratic procedures, cost-effective transactions, and efficient regulations, all of which enhance these relationships. (Almazán & Gil-García, 2006) **9:** Government's use of information technology to introduce efficiency and transparency in its own functioning and in its service offerings to citizens. (De', 2005) **10:** A term used to describe several closely related topics, it introduces the notion and practicalities of 'electronic technology' into the various dimensions and ramifications of government. The most frequent use is related to the delivery of public services, where there is an online or Internet-based aspect to the delivery of the services (online government services are

sometimes called e-services); the conduct of government business where the activities are of those involved in the process of government itself (such as legislators and the legislative process), and where some electronic or online aspect is under consideration; voting where some technological aspect is under consideration. (Kozeluh, 2005) **11:** Reengineering the current way of doing business, by using collaborative transactions and processes required by government departments to function effectively and economically, thus improving the quality of life for citizens, and promoting competition and innovation. To put it simply, e-government is about empowering a country's citizens. (Singh, 2006) **12:** Public administration infrastructure of a government on the Internet; a range of services needed by citizens and businesses can be accessed here. (Hin & Subramaniam, 2005c) **13:** Refers to relations of top-down power—governing populations through use of online information and services. It is more about transforming government services to provide more effective and more efficient services, and also coming to the realization that those services have to be customer-centric. (Yigitcanlar & Baum, 2006a) **14:** Set of activities that aim to improve relationships between government institutions and citizens with the help of information systems and technologies. (Córdoba, 2006b) **15:** The application of information technology by public sector organizations to provide services and information to individuals and business organizations. (Toland, Purcell, et al., 2005)

## Electronic Government Integration Stage

Also partially referred to as Participation stage; it is the formation of networked governments and the integration of public services both internally (i.e., electronically interconnected, multi-tier-transaction-enabled business processes) and towards the customers, citizens, and businesses (i.e., offering of unified user access interfaces directly linked to integrated services). (Werth, 2005)

## Electronic Government Internet Security

Technological tools, standards, policies, and other decisions concerning the security of the information and systems used by government organizations or in public-sector settings. (Gil-García & Luna-Reyes, 2006)

## Electronic Government Interoperability

The ability of a public service to collaborate (i.e., to work together) with other public services without special effort on the part of the processing unit. This includes the collaboration of the service-executing business processes, as well as the interaction of the process-supporting application systems. (Werth, 2005)

## Electronic Government Portal

An inter-agency or inter-government Web site that integrates information and services at a single point of entrance and can be customized according to different constituencies. (Gil-García & Luna-Reyes, 2006)

## Electronic Government Stage

In an evolutionary approach, an e-government stage is one of the different steps in the development of e-government. Normally, the steps follow a logical progression of increased technological sophistication over time. (Gil-García & Luna-Reyes, 2006)

## Electronic Gradebook

Maintaining a record of a student's progress in a Web-based education class by posting grades on the course Web pages. General gradebooks show all enrollees; personalized gradebooks can only be viewed by the individual student. (Marold, 2005)

## Electronic Health

**1:** A concept in which Internet-based technologies are used to enhance access, delivery, quality, and effectiveness of health services, as well as information utilized by patients, physicians, health care organizations, and related partners such as pharmacies, vendors, and insurance providers. (Cannoy & Iyer, 2006) **2:** Refers to the market, companies, and initiatives for conducting health care-related transactions electronically using the Internet and/or wireless communications. (Wang, Cheng, & Cheng, 2006) **3:** The use of emerging technologies, especially the Internet, to improve or enable health and health care-related services. (O'Buyonge & Chen, 2006) **4:** Used to characterize not only "Internet medicine," but also virtually everything related to computers and medicine. (Kabene, Takhar, et al. 2005)

## Electronic Health Information Management (E-HIM)

The term created by AHIMA to represent the future reality of health information. (Zender, 2006)

## Electronic Hierarchy

A market that entails few suppliers as an intermediate step, from hierarchical, ownership strategies toward electronic markets. (Setzekorn et al., 2005)

## Electronic Hub

A virtual market among companies (B2B marketplaces or B2B information brokers). (de Medeiros et al., 2006)

## Electronic Influentials (E-Fluentials)

The 10% of Internet users who manifest the greatest influence on other Internet users' online behaviors. (Goldsmith, 2006)

## Electronic Innovation

An innovation encouraging users of new communications technologies to develop dependable and viable business plans or systems that can be used for an economic (business) or social (healthcare, education, etc.) enterprise. (Boateng & Boateng, 2006a)

## Electronic Invitation (E-Vite)

A party invitation online social networking application. (Mew, 2006)

## Electronic Journal

Electronic form with a series of questions (e.g., seven to eight) that help to document students' progress throughout a course, pertaining to the students' thought processes as they progress through the multimedia instructional material. (Bradley et al., 2005)

## Electronic Journalism

The use of every Internet resource to disseminate information on an ongoing, updating basis. (Díaz-Andrade, 2005)

## Electronic Knowledge

The fusion of perpetual, technology-assisted learning with access to vast knowledge resources that are continuously changing. E-knowledge is knowledge as it exists in a profoundly networked world. (Norris, 2005)

## Electronic Knowledge Network

A repository where new knowledge is created and collected, while existing knowledge archived in a data warehouse is renewed and updated. (Wang & Forgionne, 2006)

## Electronic Lab

The same as a virtual lab, but mainly delivered through the Web. (Chu & Lam, 2006)

E

## Electronic Learner

A student who takes advantage of learning that is usually Internet-based learning, but could be any electronically enhanced learning; e-learners are technology savvy, motivated, and self-directed. (Langer, 2005)

## Electronic Learning (E-Learning)

**1:** The application of computer and network technology in learning activities. (Handzic & Lin, 2005) **2:** A form of learning that involves "electronic" or technology-based delivery of learning; examples of forms of delivery include individual computer-based delivery, Internet/Web delivery, and virtual classroom delivery. Media can be in many forms, including videotape and DVD, CD-ROM, satellite transmissions, interactive television, and various Web-based media (Internet, intranet, extranet). (Simon et al., 2005) **3:** Technology-supported learning and delivery of content via all electronic media. These may include the Internet, intranets, computer-based technology, or interactive television. They may also include the use of e-technology to support traditional methods of learning, for example using electronic whiteboards or videoconferencing. This term covers a wide set of applications and processes, such as Web-based learning, computer-based learning, virtual classrooms, and digital collaboration. (Torres-Coronas, 2005) **4:** Term covering a wide set of applications and processes, such as Web-based learning, computer-based learning, virtual classrooms, and digital collaboration. It includes the delivery of content via the Internet, intranet/extranet (LAN/WAN), audiotape and videotape, satellite broadcast, interactive TV, CD-ROM, and more. (Blackmore et al., 2006) **5:** Learning using electronic media. (Janvier & Ghaoui, 2006) **6:** A special kind of technology-based learning. E-learning systems and tools bring geographically dispersed teams together for learning across great distances. It is now one of the fastest growing trends in computing and higher education. (Ishaya, 2005) **7:** A virtual environment in which the learner's interactions with learning materials, including readings, laboratories, software, assignments, exercises, peers, and instructors, is mediated through the Internet or intranets. E-learning includes the use of simulation systems used to enhance teaching activities and distance education supported by broadband multimedia communication and shared electronic work spaces. (Sivakumar, 2006) **8:** A way of fostering learning activity using electronic tools based on multimedia technologies. (Cirrincione, 2005) **9:** All teaching and learning processes and functions from course authoring, course management, examinations, content delivery, feedback, and course administration

developed, delivered, and monitored through synchronous or asynchronous communication. (Vitolo et al., 2005) **10:** An approach to facilitate and enhance learning through the use of devices based on information communication technologies and the Internet. (Ng, 2006) **11:** Any form of education or training that utilizes online media and remote connectivity for all or part of its curricula. This model includes both purely online courses and those in brick-and-mortar universities facilitated by e-mail, the Internet, newsgroups, or chat. (Durrett et al., 2005) **12:** Discipline that applies current information and communications technologies to the educational field. This discipline tries to facilitate the learning process, since its methods do not depend on physical location or timing circumstances of the pupil. (Andrade et al., 2006b) **13:** The delivery of a learning, training, or education activity by electronic means. E-learning covers a wide set of applications and processes such as Web-based learning; computer-based learning; virtual classrooms; and delivery of content via satellite, CD-ROM, audio, and videotape. In the last few years, e-learning tends to be limited to a network-enabled transfer of skills and knowledge. (Esmahi, 2005) **14:** Any online framework that brings education or training to an individual who may access this learning from the computer. (Iannarelli, 2005) See also *Distance Learning; Web-Based Learning; Online Learning.*

## Electronic Learning Application

An application that includes the development of teaching and learning materials, tools for managing the distant use of these materials by students, a platform for the delivery of courses, and standards and policies to be followed by users. (Rolland & Kaabi, 2006)

## Electronic Learning Development Team

The set of multidisciplinary professionals required to develop and evaluate an integrated e-learning evaluation. Each team should include designers, developers, instructors, process managers, social-science staff professionals (e.g., Psychology, Sociology, Human Resources practitioners, and managers, among others), and helpdesk staff, and eventually user representatives of target population. (Rentroia-Bonito et al., 2006)

## Electronic Learning Environment

ICT-based environment particularly aimed at facilitation of learning activities, for example by offering e-mail, conferencing, chat, FAQs, search engines, glossaries, and so forth. (Haugen & Ask, 2005)

## Electronic Learning Evaluation Framework

An integrated feedback based on people-, system-, and context-specific aspects. (Rentroia-Bonito et al., 2006)

## Electronic Learning Experience

A process by which people identify work-related learning needs, formulate related goals and the associated internal level-of-success criteria, search for feasible online options to achieve defined learning goals, select and acquire choices, and engage into and complete them successfully by achieving the related goals in a productive and satisfactory manner. (Rentroia-Bonito & Jorge, 2005)

## Electronic Learning Framework

A formal construct to diagnose and manage learning outcomes in terms of the operational dynamic of three basic entities: business process, information systems, and people. (Rentroia-Bonito & Jorge, 2005)

## Electronic Learning Management System (E-LMS)

A software program that is used to deliver and manage online instructional activities. (Aisami, 2005)

## Electronic Learning Market

The market for the provision, delivery, and administration of learning services through the use of new media and network technologies. (Gordon & Lin, 2005)

## Electronic Learning Platform

**1:** An information system that schools, universities, and institutions can use for teaching (only online or supporting traditional teaching) which can have the following features (altogether or individually): (1) be a content management system, guaranteeing the access to didactic materials for the students; (2) be a learning management system, where the use of learning objects makes easier the learning of a given topic; (3) be a computer-supported collaborative learning system, which makes easier the use of collaborative and situated teaching/learning strategies; and (4) build a virtual community of students, tutors, and professors using knowledge management strategies. (Cartelli, 2005a) **2:** A set of computer systems that enable the design, construction, and management of an educative environment for use on the Internet. These platforms treat learning aspects, materials, and communications between students and teachers, as well as tools for managing the courses. (Pedreira et al., 2005)

## Electronic Learning Process

A sequence of steps or activities performed for learning purposes and the use of technology to manage, design, deliver, select, transact, coach, support, and extend learning. (Sánchez-Segura et al., 2005)

## Electronic Learning Program

The entire organizational, technological, and administrative structure that enables students' learning via the Internet. (Levy & Ramim, 2005b)

## Electronic Learning Program Strategic Plan

The blueprint of the e-learning program implementation process that also includes foreseeable problems and solutions to such challenges. (Levy & Ramim, 2005a)

## Electronic Learning Study Skill

One of the unique study habits and learning strategies used by students in e-learning (i.e., online education) courses. (Watkins, 2005)

## Electronic Learning Support and Development Team

The team includes: a program director, a program coordinator or assistant, an instructional designer, system administrator(s), multiple developers/programmers, multiple support staff (for faculty and students), graphics and video production artist, and marketing coordinators. (Levy & Ramim, 2005a)

## Electronic Learning System

**1:** A distributed information system for supporting teaching and learning on the Internet (an intranet). (Liu & Koppelaar, 2005) **2:** The technological and management system that facilitates and enables student learning via the Internet. (Levy & Ramim, 2005a)

## Electronic Learning Technology

The technology used for e-learning. (Turoff, Howard, & Discenza, 2005a)

## Electronic Libraries Program

British digital library research and development program, 1995-2000. (McCarthy, 2005b)

## Electronic Lifestyle

An online environment in which citizens have equal access to information communication technology (ICT) regardless of age, language, social background, or ability. (Weber & Lim, 2005)

## Electronic Loyalty

**1:** A deeply held intention to repurchase a preferred product/service consistently from a particular e-vendor in the future, despite the presence of factors or circumstances that may induce switching behavior. (Yeo & Chiam, 2006) **2:** The degree to which online consumers are predisposed to stay with a specific e-shop and resist competitive offers. (Markellou et al., 2006)

## Electronic Mail (E-Mail)

**1:** The use of a computer for personal or business communications. An e-mail is an electronic document similar to a piece of mail that is sent from one person to another using an address, and contains information. Users leave short, written messages in each other's computer "mailboxes." E-mail commonly contains information such as sender name and computer address, list of recipient names and computer addresses, message subject, date and time composed, and message content. Sometimes an e-mail message can have attached computer files such as pictures, programs, and data files. (Magagula, 2005) **2:** Allows users to communicate electronically with other users as if two typewriters were connected by a channel. E-mail adds a new dimension to the office environment, replacing paper copies and reducing time of transmittal. E-mail is the transmission of messages, textual or graphic, over various communications networks. (McManus & Carr, 2005) **3:** An electronic means for communication in which text is usually transmitted; operations include sending, storing, processing, and receiving information; users are allowed to communicate under specified conditions; and messages are held in storage until called for by the addressee. (Melkonyan, 2005) **4:** A form of communication in which electronic mail is transmitted via communication networks. (Boateng & Boateng, 2006b) **5:** Messages sent and received electronically via telecommunication links. (Willis, 2005) **6:** The exchange of notes through electronic means, generally but not necessarily over the Internet. (El Louadi, 2005a)

## Electronic Mail Aliasing

Where an individual has more than one e-mail address; the practice allows the user to use different addresses for different tasks—for example, one address for Internet communications and another for business. (de Freitas & Levene, 2006a)

## Electronic Mail Bomb

An attempt to overwhelm a mail server by sending large numbers of e-mails to a particular account, consuming system resources and initiating a denial of legitimate access. (Horiuchi, 2005b)

## Electronic Mail Management

Implements management controls over e-mail and attachments. These controls may be implemented by direct capture (e-mail archiving software) or invoked by the end user in a document management application. (Asprey & Middleton, 2005)

## Electronic Mail Newsletter

A one-to-many communications device that allows people to update a large group of constituents quickly and cost effectively. Good e-mail newsletters rely on Web links for more extensive content, providing easy ways for the reader to judge if they are interested in something and quickly access the material. Newsletters are good for breaking news, keeping audiences posted about new Web site content, or for advocacy call to action. (Kardaras & Karakostas, 2006)

## Electronic Mail Protocol

Simple Mail-Transport Protocol (SMTP) is a set of commands for transport of ASCII-encoded e-mail messages. Post office protocol (POP3) retrieves new messages from a mailbox to a remote e-mail client. A remote e-mail client can simultaneously access several mailboxes on different mail servers with the Internet message access protocol (IMAP). (Pulkkis, Grahn, & Åström, 2005)

## Electronic Market (E-Market)

**1:** An Internet-based market with many traders (agents) popularly known as buyers and sellers. These agents negotiate over the Internet to sell or buy products in any market (e.g., shares or stocks in a stock market). (Murthy & Krishnamurthy, 2005a) **2:** An online environment where buyers and sellers use the Internet as a communication platform in order to exchange information, goods, and services, independent from time and space. (Iacob et al., 2005) **3:** a market characterized by infinite numbers of competing suppliers, selling completely specifiable products. (Setzekorn et al., 2005) **4:** The coordination of interdependent activities performed by autonomous organizations by exchanging data between information systems of buying, selling, and facilitating organizations, allowing them to agree on and fulfill commitments. (Janssen, 2005) **5:** An market free from inhibiting constraints and affordable for all businesses in any shape, form, or size, and to allow them to easily take part in e-business with beneficial returns. It is a market in which trust, security, and dependability apply, and in which regulatory and legal issues are unified. It is a market where buyers and sellers ubiquitously execute business transactions online. These may include searching and identifying competence; ability to identify the right product or service together with quality, price, and quantity; and virtual auctions. It is also based on an open, secure, and reliable collaborative platform for knowledge exchange, joint product design, production planning, and logistics in stable customer-supplier relationships. (Richards et al., 2005)

## Electronic Market System
An interorganizational information system that allows participating buyers and sellers to exchange information about prices and products. (Janssen, 2005)

## Electronic Marketing
**1:** Conducting marketing activities on any electronic device, including cell phones, PDAs, laptop computers, and fax machines. (Singh, 2006a) **2:** Using electronic means and the Internet to market products/services. (Markellou et al., 2006) **3:** Achieving marketing objectives through use of electronic communications technology. (Wang, 2006)

## Electronic Marketplace
**1:** An e-commerce environment that offers new channels and business models for buyers and sellers to trade goods and services over the Internet. (Fortino et al., 2006) **2:** A business model for a particular kind of e-business which aggregates potentially large numbers of business partners (including buyers, sellers, and intermediaries) and allows them to interact according to a variety of market structures, such as a commodity market, an auction, or an exchange. The result can be significant cost savings. (Ghenniwa & Huhns, 2005) **3:** An interorganizational system through which multiple buyers and sellers interact to accomplish one or more of the market-making activities. (Ratnasingam, 2005) **4:** An online marketplace where many buyers and sellers barter and conduct transactions. They are frequently owned and operated by a third party. (Toland, 2006) **5:** A Web-based system that enables automated transactions, trading, or collaboration between business partners. It is an interorganizational information system that allows the participating buyers and sellers to

exchange information about prices and product offerings. (Ratnasingam, 2006)

## Electronic Marketplace Portal
Extended enterprise portal that offers access to a company's extranet services. (Tatnall, 2006)

## Electronic Marketplace Technology Course
System development for online trading applications supporting complex interactions among a variety of users. Theoretical models of online information exchanges supporting negotiations, including auctions, brokerages, and exchanges. (Knight & Chan, 2005)

## Electronic Media
Interactive digital technologies used in business, publishing, entertainment, and arts. (Baralou & Stepherd, 2005)

## Electronic Meeting
An electronically facilitated meeting allowing participants to share and work on documents remotely. (Elshaw, 2006b)

## Electronic Mentor
A term for an online guide, system, or person that provides information, resources, assistance, and direction for learners. (Langer, 2005)

## Electronic Mentoring
Also called cyber-mentoring or telementoring, in which the traditional mentoring relationship between a mentor and a protégé occurs via an electronic format such as the Internet, videoconferencing, and so forth. (Day, 2005)

## Electronic Model
The designing of a prototype of electronic business or a system that illustrates how digital technology can be used in any enterprise. (Boateng & Boateng, 2006a)

## Electronic Negotiation
Standard practice in purchasing or sales consisting of using a networked environment to negotiate in order to reach an agreement (price, delivery, warranty, etc.) between a customer and a merchant. (Pierre, 2006a)

## Electronic Network of Practice (ENOP)
**1:** A self-organizing, open activity system that exists through computer-mediated communication and whose

members focus on a shared practice. (Teigland & Wasko, 2006) **2:** A relatively large, emergent social collective in which individuals working on similar problems self-organize to help each other and share perspectives about their work practice through text-based computer-mediated means, for example, listservs, discussion boards, and so forth. (Wasko & Teigland, 2006a) **3:** An emergent group of an unlimited number of dispersed individuals working on similar tasks using a similar competence whose communication channel is purely electronic. (Teigland & Wasko, 2005)

## Electronic Newsgroup

A collection of messages posted online by individuals on a specified subject matter. (Coakes & Willis, 2005)

## Electronic Participation

The engagement of an individual or a group in specific decision making and action by using ICT means. It aims to encourage those not normally involved in a particular process or decision-making system to be involved. (Yigitcanlar & Baum, 2006b)

## Electronic Partnership

A partnership relying on electronic (information) technologies to communicate and interact amongst partners. It is mostly associated with e-commerce or e-business partnerships. (Zhao, 2005)

## Electronic Patient Record

All health-related information related to a patient in electronic form, assembled as a single entity. (Suomi, 2005)

## Electronic Petition

An e-democracy technique used for citizens' appeal to public bodies by ICT usage (e-mail, online forums, public bodies online interface). (Pazyuk, 2005)

## Electronic Policy

The policy formulation and legal function of government. E-policy refers not only to the use of ICTs in government settings, but also to the leading role of government in promoting the information society through an adequate regulatory framework. (Sharma, 2006b)

## Electronic Politics

The use of ICT such as the Internet and WWW by political actors to inform and facilitate public participation in the political process. (Hinnant & Sawyer, 2005)

## Electronic Portfolio (E-Folio)

**1:** A Web-based collection of information and artifacts about an individual. (Wasko, 2005) **2:** Part of the brand name for the system developed by Avenet, LCC, and the Minnesota State Colleges and Universities: eFolioMinnesota. (Langer, 2005) **3:** A portfolio collected, saved, and stored in electronic format. (Wieseman, 2005a) **4:** An electronic (often Web-based) personal collection of selected evidence from coursework or work experience and reflective commentary related to those experiences. The e-portfolio is focused on personal (and often professional) learning and development, and may include artifacts from curricular and extra-curricular activities. (Garrett, 2006a) **5:** An electronic portfolio used by individuals to house personal information. An "e-folio" can be thought of as a specialized version of an e-portfolio. (Wasko, 2005)

## Electronic Prescription

A prescription created and handled in electronic form in an integrated information system. (Suomi, 2005)

## Electronic Press

A publishing service with a strong emphasis on the publishing of digital courseware. This does not mean that print and traditional media, such as film, are not used. However, the courseware packs are predominantly electronic. (Ching et al., 2005)

## Electronic Procurement (E-Procurement)

**1:** The use of ICT such as the Internet and WWW by government agencies to facilitate the purchasing of goods and services. (Hinnant & Sawyer, 2005) **2:** The business-to-business (B2B) or government-to-business (G2B) purchase and sale of supplies and services that is facilitated by the Internet and is sometimes referred to by other terms such as e-tendering or supplier exchange. (Demediuk, 2005) **3:** The business-to-business purchase and sale of supplies and services over the Internet. An important part of many B2B sites, e-procurement is also sometimes referred to by other terms, such as supplier exchange. Typically, e-procurement Web sites allow qualified and registered users to look for buyers or sellers of goods and services. Depending on the approach, buyers or sellers may specify prices or invite bids. Transactions can be initiated and completed. Ongoing purchases may qualify customers for volume discounts or special offers. E-procurement software may make it possible to automate some buying and selling. Companies participating expect to be able to control parts inventories more effectively, reduce purchasing agent overhead, and improve manufacturing cycles. E-procurement is expected to be integrated with the trend toward computerized supply-chain management. (Mockler et al., 2006) **4:** The means for the realization of online purchases, by using appropriate electronic communications services and infrastructures. (Chochliouros & Spiliopoulou-Chochliourou, 2006) **5:** The online provision of goods and services by government agencies. E-procurement includes online requests for proposal (RFPs), online requests for bids (RFBs), online bid acceptance, and online monitoring of contracts. (Schelin, 2005) **6:** The use of the Internet by government to procure or purchase goods and services, advertise their needs, select vendors, manage services, organize fulfillment of contracts, and effect payments. (Toland, 2006) **7:** Using the Internet and related technologies to facilitate procurement. (Foley & Samson, 2006)

## Electronic Procurement System

The process of electronically managing the procurement of goods. An e-procurement system cares about this process and offers interfaces to perform typical activities, such as ordering products or browsing a list of available products from product suppliers. (Abels & Hahn, 2006)

## Electronic Product Code (EPC)

**1:** Global coding scheme, administered by EPCglobal, identifying an item's manufacturer, product category, and unique serial number. The numerical code is stored on the RFID chip, which is comparable to a conventional bar code. (Loebbecke, 2006) **2:** Uniquely identifies each product and is normally a 128-bit code. It is embedded in the RFID tag of the product. (Owens et al., 2005)

## Electronic Questionnaire

A questionnaire in an electronic form that can be completed via the Internet. (Paraskevi & Kollias, 2006)

## Electronic Readiness (E-Readiness)

**1:** The aptitude of an economy to use Internet-based computers and information technologies to migrate traditional businesses into the new economy. (Lertwongsatien & Wongpinunwatana, 2005) **2:** The preparedness of an organization's technology, processes, and people to facilitate or inhibit e-business development. (Ash & Burn, 2006) **3:** A measurement of how ready a society is to benefit from recent developments in ICT.

An e-readiness assessment normally takes into account education levels, infrastructure, the accessibility of ICT, and legal and regulatory issues. (Toland et al., 2005b) **4:** Available technological, legal, institutional, and human resources infrastructures and political will to engage in online activities. (Misuraca, 2005) **5:** The capacity to participate in the global digital economy. (Finquelievich, 2005) **6:** The state of being prepared to operate and utilize electronic technology. (Poda & Brescia, 2005) **7:** E-readiness may be defined in terms of availability of ICT infrastructure, the accessibility of information and communication technologies (ICTs) to the general citizen and business organization population, and the effect of the legal and regulatory framework on ICT use. (Averweg, 2006)

## Electronic Research

Research that takes advantage of Internet-based tools and techniques. (Janes, 2005)

## Electronic Reserve

**1:** A digitized collection of reading materials, accessible via a Web browser. A common file format is .pdf, read through Adobe Acrobat Reader®. (Buchanan, 2005) **2:** The electronic storage and transmission of course-related information distributed by local area networks (LANs) or the Internet. Also known as e-reserves; in addition to displaying items on a screen, printing to paper and saving to disk are often allowed. (Burke et al., 2005)

## Electronic Retailer

A collective term applied to any Web site that sells a product or service, accepts payments, and fulfills orders; a retailer who has an online storefront. (Scarpi & Dall'Olmo-Riley, 2006)

## Electronic Retailing (E-Tailing)

The application of electronic networks, especially the Internet, as channels of distribution in order to address final consumers. Like traditional retailing, e-tailing is restricted to buying and selling physical or digital goods, but no services. (Madlberger, 2006)

## Electronic Sales Cycle

The time that elapses between the customer initiating the buying process online, and the point at which a decision is made on which product to buy. (Wang & Forgionne, 2006)

**E**

## Electronic Science

The large-scale science that will increasingly be carried out through distributed global collaborations enabled by the Internet. (Liu, 2005)

## Electronic Service

**1:** A collection of network-resident software programs that collaborate for supporting users in both accessing and selecting data and services of their interest handled by a provider site. Examples of e-services are e-commerce, e-learning, and e-government applications. (De Meo, Quattrone, et al., 2005) **2:** An electronic service accessed via a network such as the Internet. Example e-services include online banking, online stock broker, online tax information, and online learning. (Yee & Korba, 2006) **3:** The provision of a service using ICTs, especially the Internet and the World Wide Web. (Sharma, 2006b) **4:** The provision of government services via the Internet, including online information, online forms, online transactions, and online referral processes. (Schelin, 2005)

## Electronic Service Catalog

A mechanism enabling service consumers to locate the available e-services. Most often, these mechanisms are hierarchical classifications of the services under some categorization axis (offering organization, target group, etc). (Vassilakis & Lepouras, 2006)

## Electronic Service Delivery (ESD)

A method of delivering services and conducting business with customers, suppliers, and stakeholders to achieve local government developmental goals of improved customer service and business efficiency. (Averweg, 2006)

## Electronic Service Quality

Customers' overall perception and experience of the three levels of the service offered in e-business: foundation of service, customer-oriented services, and value-added services. (Wang & Forgionne, 2006)

## Electronic Shelf Label

A price tag that provides accurate pricing due to electronic linkage between the shelves and the checkout system. The technology is based on radio frequency, infrared, and/or WLAN linking a master checkout with the shelves. (Kotzab, 2005)

## Electronic Signature

**1:** The Electronic Signature Act that President Clinton signed into law on June 30, 2001, facilitates electronic contractual arrangements involving cryptography principles, resulting in a digital approval process, allowing for a handwritten signature or digital certification. (Inoue & Bell, 2005) **2:** This term refers to all electronic authentication technologies and methods of "signing" a digital document that serves the same purpose as manual signatures. (Escalante, 2005)

## Electronic Social Contract

Tacit set of conventions underlying the information society and any kind of digital interaction across the Internet and the World Wide Web. (Skovira, 2005)

## Electronic Society

E-government initiatives that deal particularly with the relationship between public agencies and other institutions—other public agencies, private sector companies, nonprofit and community organizations. (Olatokun, 2006)

## Electronic Space and Physical Space

These concepts have been coined to describe the role of geography in the information economy. Rather than marking the "end of geography" and the "death of distance," the rapid development of telecommunications networks, combined with the informatization of the economy and other activities, have enabled individuals and organizations to establish and maintain new forms of relations across time and space, often in ways impossible in the past. This essentially overlays a new electronic, virtual space on top of the physical space in which we live. (Kimble & Li, 2006)

## Electronic Store

A portal for purchasing and accessing Internet-delivered materials. (Ryan, 2005)

## Electronic Strategy

**1:** The overall framework for national ICT development. It has a social and an economic dimension. It consists of e-policies which concern the ICT environment, and ICT readiness and usage of three stakeholders in ICT: individuals, businesses, and governments. (Neumann, 2005) **2:** The use of the Internet and related technologies to add power to or reconfigure a business strategy. (Foley & Samson, 2006)

## Electronic Supply Chain

The physical dimension of e-business with the role of achieving a base level of operational performance in the physical sphere. (Zhao, 2005)

## Electronic Survey

A survey based on answers of an e-questionnaire. (Paraskevi & Kollias, 2006)

## Electronic Tailer

An online retail store. (Wang, Ding, et al., 2006)

## Electronic Technology

**1:** Encompasses information technology, but also includes any equipment or interconnected system or subsystem of equipment that is used in the creation, conversion, or duplication of data or information. Electronic technology includes telecommunications products such as telephones, and office equipment such as fax machines. (Burgstahler, 2005b) **2:** Technology including hardware and software, and their development using Internet, multimedia, mobile, wireless, and security technologies, and so forth. (Youn & McLeod, 2006)

## Electronic Tender System

A system to carry out a series of works from notification of order placement information on the homepage, application for tender participation, sending a tender document, and opening tender documents to the public announcement of the result. (Kitagaki, 2005)

## Electronic Tendering

Another term for e-procurement. (Demediuk, 2005)

## Electronic Text

An online electronic book. (Ryan, 2005)

## Electronic Ticket

A paperless electronic document used for ticketing passengers, particularly in the commercial airline industry. Virtually all major airlines now use this method of ticketing. (Mendes-Filho & Ramos, 2005)

## Electronic Town Meeting (ETM)

Includes discussion, deliberation among ordinary citizens, and a vote that determines the outcome. Electronic media are used to facilitate the process. Generally, a combination of several electronic means is used: interactive TV, interactive radio, scientific deliberative polling, telephone voting, mobile phones, plus a wide variety of face-to-face meetings. The focus of the process is on problem issues or on involved planning or envisioning processes. ETM can be conducted at local, regional, or national levels. (Keskinen & Kuosa, 2005)

## Electronic Trust

A set of specific beliefs dealing primarily with integrity (trustee honesty and promise keeping), benevolence (trustee caring and motivation to act in the truster's interest), competence (ability of trustee to do what truster needs), and predictability (trustee's behavioral consistency of a particular e-vendor). (Yeo & Chiam, 2006)

## Electronic Tutelage

Learning of new complex concepts (sometimes called scientific concepts), not with the intervention of a physical tutor, but via electronically delivered materials; the basic theory behind Web-based education. (Marold, 2005)

## Electronic Tutor

Off-campus, online academic tutor. (Whateley et al., 2005)

## Electronic Voting

**1:** A term used to describe any of several means of determining people's collective intent electronically. Electronic voting includes voting by kiosk, Internet, telephone, punch card, or optical scan ballot. (Kozeluh, 2005) **2:** An e-democracy technique used for direct expression of voters' will in collective decision making by ICT usage. (Pazyuk, 2005)

## Electronic Voting System

A system to vote electronically using an information terminal of a personal computer. Various technologies have been created to prevent illegal actions such as alteration of voting contents or the use of abstainers' votes. (Kitagaki, 2005)

## Electronic White Board

Interactive presentation tool that allows efficient preparation, integration, and display of lessons that might include Web-based materials, photographs, video/sound clips, and videoconferencing. Electronic white boards enable teachers to control the display from anywhere in a classroom and conduct a collaborative presentation with a student at the board. (Wild, 2005)

**E**

### Electronic Word-of-Mouth (E-WOM)
Social communication on the Internet. Web surfers either transmitting or receiving product-related information online. (Goldsmith, 2006)

### Electronic Work (E-Work)
Work carried out outside one's normal workplace—at home, tele-work center, or satellite office—by using ICT equipment and infrastructure. A previously common term for this concept is tele-work or tele-commuting (used especially in the United States). (Heinonen, 2005)

### Electronic Work Sample
A performance-based work sample collected, saved, and stored in electronic format. (Wieseman, 2005a)

### Elementary Entity
A data entity that semantically represents basic objects. (Hurson & Yang, 2005)

### Element
One object of attention within the domain of investigation. An element defines the entities upon which the administration of the RepGrid is based. For example, to explore the critical success factors of IS projects, IS researchers can use IS projects as elements in the RepGrid. (Tan & Hunter, 2005)

### Elementary Fact Type
In ORM, an elementary fact is an atomic proposition that applies a logical predicate to a sequence of one or more objects of a given type; it cannot be split into smaller facts without information loss. An elementary fact type is a kind of elementary fact. For example: Person smokes; Person was born in Country; Person introduced Person to Person. In UML, an elementary fact type is known as an elementary association or elementary relationship type. (Halpin, 2005)

**ELM:** See *Elaboration Likelihood Model; Employee Lifecycle Management.*

**ELMS:** See *Enterprise Learning Management System.*

### Elongated Diffusion Pattern
A pattern of IT diffusion in which, due to a reduction in the reputation effect, there is a hiatus prior to the arrival of a late minority of adopters. (Griffin, 2005)

### EM Algorithm
An iterative method for estimating maximum likelihood in problems with incomplete (or unlabeled) data. EM algorithm can be used for semi-supervised learning since it is a form of clustering algorithm that clusters the unlabeled data around the labeled data. (Kim, 2005)

### Emancipatory Learning
Learning under conditions that do not bind the learner to traditions, and provides a freedom to pursue learning needs and demands as determined or established by the learner. (Taylor et al., 2005)

### EMAS
Community Web site operated by Sabah State Library. (Gilbert, 2005a)

### Embedded Device
A full-featured computer integrated into a machine. (Blecker & Graf, 2006)

### Embedded PI Submodel
A full or partial PI model over a proper subset of domain variables. The most general PI models are those over large problem domains that contain embedded PI submodels. (Xiang, 2005)

### Embedded Subtree
Let $T(N,B)$ be a tree, where N represents the set of its nodes and B the set of its edges. We say that a tree $S(Ns,Bs)$ is an embedded subtree of T provided that: (1) $Ns \subseteq N$, and (2) $b=(n_x,n_y) \in Bs$ if and only if $n_x$ is an ancestor of $n_y$ in T. In other words, we require that a branch appear in S if and only if the two vertices are on the same path from the root to a leaf in T. (Katsaros & Manolopoulos, 2005b)

### Embedded Support Device
Support device integrated in the learning environment. Learners cannot but use these devices (e.g., structure in a text). (Clarebout et al., 2005b)

### Emergence
**1:** In the context of natural computing, an emergent phenomenon can be understood as the one whose global properties are neither possessed by, nor directly derivable from, any of its component parts. For instance, a single ant is a very simple insect with limited capabilities, but an ant colony is capable of performing complex tasks, such as nest building and organization. (de Castro, 2005) **2:**

The process by which often unexpected outcomes result from the interaction of different activities and occurrences within an organization. (Land, Amjad, et al., 2006)

## Emergence Index

Image retrieval where the hidden or emergence meanings of the images are studied and based on those hidden meanings as well as explicit meanings. Where there is no hidden meaning at all, an index of search is defined to retrieve images, called emergence index. (Deb, 2005)

## Emergent Behavior

The behavior that results from the interaction between a multitude of entities, where the observed behavior is not present in any single entity in the multitude comprising the system that shows emergent behavior. (Zwitserloot & Pantic, 2005)

## Emergent Forms of Educational Method

New methods and techniques that may be employed or used in the education process related to the deployment of Analytical Information Technology in academe. (LeRouge & Webb, 2005)

## Emergent Narrative

Aims at solving and/or providing an answer to the narrative paradox observed in graphically represented virtual worlds. Involves participating users in a highly flexible real-time environment, where authorial activities are minimized, and the distinction between authoring-time and presentation-time is substantially removed. (Hall & Woods, 2006)

## Emergent Properties

A systems concept from which it is proposed that a whole system contains properties which are not seen within any of its components or subsystems. It gives rise to the idea that a system is more than the sum of its parts. (Kimble & Hildreth, 2006)

## Emerging Pattern

An itemset that occurs significantly more frequently in one group than another. Utilized as a classification method by several algorithms. (Butler & Webb, 2005)

**EML:** See *Educational Modeling Language.*

## Emote

To express a physical emotion using the keyboard. (Griffiths et al., 2006)

## Emoticon

**1:** A text (ASCI) character used to indicate an emotional state in electronic correspondence. Emoticons or smileys, as they are also called, represent emotional shorthand. For example :-) represents a smile or happiness. (Garrett, 2006b) **2:** The word emoticon is probably derived from the words emotion and icon, suggesting that emoticons are icons—or images—expressing emotions. In written conversations, such as chats, IMs, or Post-It notes, the lack of visual and aural support often needs to be compensated. (Dunkels, 2005) **3:** A combination of punctuation marks and other special characters from the keyboard used to convey the tone of a computer-mediated communication message. (Link & Wagner, 2006) **4:** A graphical icon that represents one of various emotions in a chat-based environment. (Champion, 2006a) **5:** A graphic-like icon created using characters available on the standard keyboard. Emoticons are used to convey emotion or states of being, which are often communicated through facial expressions such as smiling, frowning, looking puzzled, and so forth. (Newberry, 2005) **6:** An icon created from ASCII text used to express an emotion. The most simple of these is the smiley, created using a colon and bracket :) (Roberts et al., 2006a)

## Emotion Icon

A combination of keyboard characters or small images meant to represent a facial expression. (Xu et al., 2006c)

## Emotion Synthesis

The process of representing emotions in computing devices using cognitive appraisal or other emotion classification theories. (Byl & Toleman, 2005)

## Emotion-Extraction Engine

A software system that can extract emotions embedded in textual messages. (Xu et al., 2006a)

## Emotional Intelligence

**1:** A facet of human intelligence that includes the ability to have, express, recognize, and regulate affective states; employ them for constructive purposes; and skillfully handle the affective arousal of others. The skills of emotional intelligence have been argued to be a better predictor than IQ for measuring aspects of success in life. (Pantic, 2005a) **2:** A set of competencies that derive from a neural circuitry emanating in the limbic system. Personal competencies related to outstanding leadership include self-awareness, self-confidence, self-management, adaptability, emotional self-control, initiative, achievement orientation, trustworthiness, and optimism. Social competencies include social awareness, empathy, service orientation, and organizational awareness. Relationship management competencies include inspirational leadership, development of others, change catalyst, conflict management, influence, teamwork, and collaboration. (Wong-MingJi, 2005)

## Empirical Evaluation

Evaluation methodology which employs users to interact with the system. (Athanasis & Andreas, 2005)

## Empirical Interface Evaluation

The empirical evaluation of an interface implies that users are involved. Known methods, among others, are "observational evaluation," "survey evaluation," and "thinking aloud protocol." (Karoulis et al., 2006)

## Empirical Method

Method in which a system is evaluated based on observed performance in actual use. (Danielson, 2006b)

## Employability

The extent to which employees have skills that the market and employers regard as attractive. (Scholarios et al., 2005)

## Employee Abuse

Employees, especially those employees who believe that they are treated unjustly, may provide the data necessary for cyber-identity theft. With e-mail and databases full of consumer information, an employee or other insider can pass spreadsheets along to thieves. Employees may divulge personal information unintentionally or intentionally. Also related to cyber-identity theft and the workplace is the possibility of phony job listings online in order to obtain consumer information. (Close et al., 2006)

## Employee Lifecycle Management (ELM)

The integration of all aspects of information and knowledge in relation to an employee, from the hiring to the retirement from the company. ELM enables enterprises to effectively manage their portfolio of competencies. (Møller, 2005)

## Emporium Model of Course Redesign

This model eliminates all regular class meetings, replacing classes with a learning resource center featuring online materials and on-demand personalized assistance. Additional features of the emporium model often include combining multiple sections of a course into one large section, and heavy reliance on computer-based learning resources and an instructional staff of varying levels of skills and expertise. (Twigg, 2005)

**EMS:** See *Enhanced Messaging Service.*

## Emulation

**1:** Actual software is written to execute something, instead of simulating it. (Janssen, 2005) **2:** The realization, sometimes also called emulation, of a system or organism corresponds to a literal, material model that implements functions; it is a substantive functiona l device. Roughly speaking, a realization is judged primarily by how well it can function as an implementation of a design specification. A system or function is used to emulate or realize another, when one performs in exactly the same way as another. A typical example in computer science is the emulation of one computer by (a program running on) another computer. (de Castro, 2005)

## Enabler

A factor that makes something possible, for example, alignment is an enabler for organizations to cut production costs by half. (Lubbe, 2005)

## Enabling Technology

A sphere of concern; consists of those technologies that are under development at a certain moment and that have potential to become part of the global infrastructure in the future. Currently, new 3G terminals and 4G network technologies are typical examples. (Veijalainen & Weske, 2005)

## Enactment

Knowledge only takes on meaning as it interacts with the learner's environment. (Frank et al., 2005)

## Encapsulation

**1:** Data and actions are packaged together in a class, with the details of the implementation hidden from other classes. (Lucas, 2005) **2:** The ability to insulate data in a class so that both data security and integrity is improved. (D. Brandon, Jr., 2005a) **3:** The addition of control information by a protocol entity to data obtained from a protocol user. (Ngoh & Shankar, 2005)

## Encoding

**1:** The process by which the content and meaning that is to be communicated is transformed into a physical form suitable for communication. It involves transforming thoughts and ideas into words, images, actions, and so forth, and then further transforming the words or images into their physical form. (Polovina & Pearson, 2006) **2:** The bit pattern to use for each symbol in a character set. (D. Brandon, Jr., 2005b) **3:** The process of using codecs to convert video files to different distribution file formats. The codecs used for encoding files for CD-ROM and DVD are MPEG-1 and MPEG-2, respectively. (Vitolo et al., 2005) **4:** To input or take into memory, to convert to a usable mental form, or to store into memory. (Atkinson & Burstein 2006)

## Encrypting

The process of scrambling data such that it appears meaningless to an average user. An authorized user can later restore the data back to its original. (Chen et al., 2005a)

## Encryption

**1:** A modification process that transforms data into a non-readable format to protect against unauthorized viewing. Encryption can be handled by special applications, but it is often included as a feature of a database system or as a utility application as part of the operating system. Depending on the encryption/decryption method, information transmitted in encrypted format may be decrypted routinely and without user intervention by e-mail software or commodity Web viewers, products such as Microsoft Internet Explorer™, Netscape Navigator™, or Mozilla™-compliant browsers. (Horiuchi, 2005a) **2:** A transformation of data from an original readily understandable version (plaintext) to a difficult-to-interpret format (ciphertext) as a way of protecting confidentiality until changed back to the original. Images can also be encrypted to prevent recognition. (Friedman, 2005) **3:** Concealing data by encoding it in a form that requires a secret "key" to decode. (N.C. Rowe, 2006c) **4:** Data coding schemes to protect information privacy. (Quah, Leow, & Ong, 2006) **5:** The transformation of plaintext into an apparently less readable form (called ciphertext) through a mathematical process. The ciphertext may be read by anyone who has the key that decrypts (undoes the encryption of) the ciphertext. (Mezgár, 2005) **6:** Scrambling of data into an unreadable format as a security measure. (Lawson-Body et al., 2005) **7:** The act of protecting information by transforming it. (Guan, 2006h)

## End

Results, consequences, impact, and payoffs. (Kaufman & Lick, 2005)

## End Result of Understanding

An entity E has understood something S, if and only if E can present S in terms of a system of its own primitives (i.e., self-explainable notions). (Gelepithis, 2005)

## End User

**1:** An individual who uses software packages or computer systems that do not require programming. (Jawahar, 2005) **2:** Tutee, working with dedicated educational software packages. (Utsi & Lowyck, 2005)

## End-User Computing (EUC)

**1:** Direct, hands-on use of information systems by end users whose jobs go beyond entering data into a computer or processing transactions. (Chen, Holt, et al., 2005) **2:** The optional development of computer applications and models by personnel (individuals or groups) outside the MIS department. (Shayo & Guthrie, 2005)

## End-User Computing Satisfaction

A widely accepted information systems success surrogate that measures the degree to which a technology provides the user with a sense of satisfaction that meaningful usage has been affected. (McHaney, 2005)

## End-User Development

The development of information systems by end users rather than information system specialists. (Chen, Holt, et al., 2005)

## End-User License Agreement (EULA)

Spells out the legal rights of both the purchaser and vendor of software. (Friedman, 2005)

## End-User Performance

Performance of end users. (Jawahar, 2005)

## End-User Training

Teaching end users to learn and use organizational computing technology. (Jawahar, 2005)

## Endemic

The usual level of disease in a geographic area in a given period of time. (Garb & Wait, 2005a)

**Enterprise Resource Planning (ERP)**
The set of processes of voluntary (conscious) control of attention. These processes are also referred to as top-down or goal-driven. An example of an endogenous attentional mechanism is the attention you are paying to this page as you are reading. Endogenous attention is voluntary; it requires explicit effort, and it is normally meant to last. (Thomas & Roda, 2006a)

**Energetic Engagement**
Active participation that refers to members' ability to suggest changes on the policies, the structure, and the environment/system. (N.C. Rowe, 2006d)

**Energy Management System**
The system used to efficiently manage power network operation, coordinate optimized power distribution, and manage costs of electricity production and distribution. (Jeong et al., 2006)

**Engagement**
Becoming involved with a topic at more than a simple and superficial level; a time when individuals come to know and understand the detailed content of what they are studying. (Pritchard, 2005b)

**Engagement-Supporting Technology**
One of a number of technologies that enable people to learn and communicate with fellow citizens about a specific policy-related event or challenge. (O'Looney, 2006)

**Engineering Design**
Encompasses a variety of activities aiming at generating and refining detailed product descriptions prior to their physical realization. (Ma, 2006)

**Engineering Design Knowledge**
All the standards, laws, and best practices that affect design decision are called engineering design knowledge. (Ma, 2006)

**Engineering Design Knowledge Management**
The management of engineering design knowledge generally entails its modeling (representation), maintenance, integration, and use. (Ma, 2006)

**Engineering Information System**
An information system used to manage the information in data and knowledge-intensive engineering applications, and to implement various engineering activities. (Ma, 2005a)

**Enhanced Data Mining with Incomplete Data**
Data mining that utilizes incomplete data through fuzzy transformation. (H. Wang & S. Wang, 2005)

**Enhanced Data Rates for GSM Evolution (EDGE)**
1: An enhanced version of GSM networks for higher data rates. The main difference is the adoption of 8 QPSK modulation in the air interface which increases the available bit rates. (Louvros et al., 2005b) 2: Gives GSM and TDMA the capability to handle 3G mobile phone services with speeds up to 384 kbps. Since it uses the TDMA infrastructure, a smooth transition from TDMA-based systems such as GSM to EDGE is expected. (Akhtar, 2005) 3: A faster version of the GSM wireless service, EDGE is designed to deliver data at rates up to 384 Kbps, and enable the delivery of multimedia and other broadband applications to mobile phone and computer users. (Olla, 2005a)

**Enhanced Instructional Presentation (EIP)**
A traditional linear presentation (e.g., text, video) supplemented with learner control features and hyperlinked material, providing answers to authentic learner questions and additional support information (e.g., enrichment, remedial). (Pelton & Pelton, 2005)

**Enhanced Instructional Presentation Model (EIP Model)**
A transformation model that guides the transformation of existing (or newly captured) linear content into hypermedia presentations (online or CD-ROM based). (Pelton & Pelton, 2005)

**Enhanced Messaging Service (EMS)**
An application-level extension to SMS for cellular phones available on GSM, TDMA, and CDMA networks. An EMS-enabled mobile phone can send and receive messages that have special text formatting (i.e., bold or italic), animation, pictures, icons, sound effects, and special ringtones. (Lalopoulos et al., 2005a)

**Enhanced Observed-Time-Difference Method (E-OTD)**
Similar to OTDOA, without the need for base stations to be synchronized (additional elements are used that measure

the real-time differences between base stations to correct the measurements). (Ververidis & Polyzos, 2006)

### Enhanced Television (Enhanced TV)
A television that provides subscribers with the means for bi-directional communication with real-time, end-to-end information transfer. (Hulicki, 2005)

### Enhanced TV: See *Enhanced Television.*

### Enneagram Personality System
Identifies nine personality types, each based on a specific compulsion and underlying emotion; the enneagram diagram shows a different growth path for each of the nine types. (Kaluzniacky, 2006)

### ENOP: See *Electronic Network of Practice.*

### Enriching Digital World
The process of embedding and encoding those clues or signs within an interface from which the user is enabled to exploit the functionalities of a certain product. (Magnani & Bardone, 2006)

### Enrollment
**1:** The initial acquisition and registration of biometric data for an individual. Dependent on the type of biometric system, this data may be registered in association with the identity of the user or against some pseudonym that preserves anonymity. (Fleming, 2005a) **2:** The initial process of collecting biometric data from a user and then storing it in a template for later comparison. There are two types: positive enrollment and negative enrollment. (Vatsa et al., 2005)

### Ensemble
**1:** A combination, typically weighted or unweighted aggregation, of single induction estimators able to improve the overall accuracy of any single induction method. (Siciliano & Conversano, 2005) **2:** A function that returns a combination of the predictions of multiple machine learning models. (Oza, 2005)

### Ensemble Learning
A machine learning paradigm using multiple learners to solve a problem. (Zhou, 2005)

### Ensemble-Based Method
A general technique that seeks to profit from the fact that multiple rule generation followed by prediction averaging reduces test error. (Muruzábal, 2005)

### Enterprise
A business organization. (Henry, 2006)

### Enterprise Application
Provides computer application support for the full lifecycle of business application development and system support. Involves in-depth understanding of business processes and workflow. (Yow & Moertiyoso, 2005)

### Enterprise Application Integration (EAI)
**1:** Extranets provide the ERP II system with a portal and a platform for integration with other systems inside or outside the corporation. EAI provides the support for automating processes across various IT platforms, systems, and organizations. (Møller, 2005) **2:** The process of coordinating the operations of various applications across an enterprise so they can perform as an integrated, enterprise-wide system. This term also refers to the set of commercial applications designed to facilitate this process. (Mockler et al., 2006) **3:** Application of aligned processes, software and hardware tools, methodologies, and technologies aimed at interconnecting and consolidating all computer applications, data, and business processes in order to achieve a friction-free network that allows real-time data exchange as well as easy management and (re)configuration activities. (Blecker, 2006a) **4:** Comprehensive middleware software suits that allow connection to an array of applications including Enterprise Resource Planning, Customer Relationship Management, and to various databases. (Hwang, 2005) **5:** The plans, methods, and tools aimed at modernizing, consolidating, and coordinating the computer applications in an enterprise. Typically, an enterprise has existing legacy applications and databases, and wants to continue to use them while adding or migrating to a new set of applications that exploit the Internet, e-commerce, extranet, and other new technologies. (Karakostas, 2005)

### Enterprise Architecture
A business and performance-based framework to support cross-agency collaboration, transformation, and organization-wide improvement. (Pang, 2005a)

**E**

## Enterprise Collaboration

Application of systems and communications technologies at the enterprise level to foster the collaboration of people and organizations to overcome varying levels of dispersion to accomplish a common goal. This term, when applied to the use of technologies, is also known as e-collaboration or distributed collaboration. (Morris-Jones & Carter, 2005)

## Enterprise Content Management System (ECMS)

An integrated approach to managing documents, Web content, and digital assets. It combines the capabilities of an Enterprise Document Management System (EDMS) and a Content Management System (CMS) with the ability to manage the full content lifecycle across a growing assortment of content types. (Sarmento, 2005)

## Enterprise Deployment

Term used in the computer industry to describe hardware and software configurations. These are aimed at addressing the corporation as a whole, as opposed to a single department. (Raisinghani & Nugent, 2005)

## Enterprise Document Management System (EDMS)

The set of programs, procedures, and/or software that manage, control, and provide access to electronic documents. (Sarmento, 2005)

## Education Multimedia

The use of multimedia for designing educational software. (Uden, 2005)

## Enterprise Function

Comprises the typical functions of a business such as human resources, marketing and sales, manufacturing, accounting, and finance. (Carstens, 2005)

## Enterprise Information Portal (EIP)

**1:** Single Web interface to corporate information. (de Carvalho, & Ferreira, 2006) **2:** A gateway to a corporate intranet used to manage knowledge within an organization. EIPs are designed primarily for business-to-employee (B2E) processes, and offer employees the means to access and share data and information within the enterprise. (Tatnall, 2006)

## Enterprise Information Security Policy (EISP)

A policy that sets the strategic direction, scope, and tone for all of an organization's security efforts. (Mattord & Whitman, 2005)

## Enterprise Integration

Refers to the plans, methods, and tools aimed at modernizing, consolidating, and coordinating software applications among a group of businesses or organizations that interact as consumers and suppliers. Enterprise integration might involve developing a total view of the organizations' businesses and applications, seeing how existing applications fit into the new model, and then devising ways to efficiently reuse what already exists, while adding new applications and data. Enterprise integration is done for the mutual benefit of all organizations involved. (Ghenniwa & Huhns, 2005)

## Enterprise Internal Portal (EIP)

A Web-based intranet that allows employees to access, store, and transfer knowledge within or outside the organization; it also provides a virtual community or forum for discussion. (Shen & Tsai, 2006)

## Enterprise Knowledge Management (EKM)

A process aimed at injecting knowledge into business processes and enabling reuse of human expertise through the creation of common data objects and definitions that can be used with equal ease and success by all employees in the enterprise. (Framinan, 2005)

## Enterprise Learning Management System (ELMS)

A full-featured learning management system that also includes some of the features and capabilities of a Web portal and content management system. An ELMS is designed for large-scale use and integration with other products and systems. It also includes multiple levels of administrative and user access. Content that is stored within the system is structured within a content hierarchy that does not need to be tied to a particular course. (Chapman, 2005a)

## Enterprise Miner

Data-mining software developed by SAS Corporation that is used to create predictive models to solve business challenges. (Athappilly & Rea, 2005)

## Enterprise Model

A diagrammatic representation of an enterprise or part of an enterprise. An enterprise usually focuses on certain aspects of the enterprise, such as its goals and strategies, its business processes, its organization structure, its information and knowledge, and so forth. (Opdahl, 2005)

## Enterprise Performance and Bottom-Line

Data critical for business success, such as employee productivity, customer satisfaction, and revenues. (Henry, 2006)

## Enterprise Performance Management (EPM)

A combination of planning, budgeting, financial consolidation, reporting, strategy planning, and scorecarding tools. Most vendors using the term do not offer the full set of components, so they adjust their version of the definition to suit their own product set. (Rahman, 2005e)

## Enterprise Resource Planning (ERP)

**1:** A business management system that can integrate all facets of the business, including planning, manufacturing, sales, and marketing, through a common database. As the ERP methodology has become more popular, software applications have been developed to help business managers implement ERP in business activities such as inventory control, order tracking, customer service, finance, and human resources. (Archer, 2005) **2:** A business management system that integrates all the back-office business functions of a business; for example, inventory, sales, marketing, planning, finance, manufacturing, purchase, and so forth. (Malik, 2006) **3:** ERP systems are integrated applications that satisfy the transaction processing requirements for a wide range of business activities, including purchasing, production planning, warehouse management, inventory control, sales order processing, distribution, finance, and human resources. (Carton & Adam, 2005) **4:** Set of activities supported by multi-module application software that helps a manufacturer or other business manage the important parts of its business, including product planning, parts purchasing, maintaining inventories, interacting with suppliers, providing customer service, and tracking orders. (Morabito & Provera, 2005) **5:** Packaged software to support corporate functions such as finance, human resources, material management, or sales and distribution. (Framinan, 2005) **6:** System designed to support and automate business processes for manufacturing, distribution, payroll, and finances for

an enterprise. (Feuerlicht & Vorisek, 2006) **7:** Typically, ERP systems are software packages composed of several modules, such as human resources, sales, finance, and production, and providing cross-organization integration of transaction-based data throughout imbedded business processes. These software packages can be customized to the specific needs of each organization. (Esteves & Pastor, 2005) **8:** An integrated information system that supports most of the business processes and information system requirements in an organization. (Sundaram & Portougal, 2005b) **9:** Configurable enterprise software that integrates business processes across functions. (Hwang, 2005) **10:** An off-the-shelf accounting-oriented information system that meets the information needs of most organizations. A complex and expensive information tool to meet the needs of an organization to procure, process, and deliver customer goods or services in a timely, predictable manner. (Bradley, 2005) **11:** An information system that spans organizational boundaries with various organizational functional modules and systems, integrated and managed by one system application. (Sarkis & Sundarraj, 2005) **12:** A business software package for running every aspect of a company, including managing orders, inventory, accounting, and logistics. Well-known ERP software providers include BAAN, Oracle, PeopleSoft, and SAP, collectively known to industry insiders as the "BOPS." (Colmenares & Otieno, 2005) **13:** An information technology tool with capacity to integrate a firm's business functions or facets (e.g., planning, manufacturing, marketing, human resources, finance, procurement, etc). (Barima, 2006b) **14:** An integrated system that supports a wide range of transaction processing functions common to most organizations. Applications are designed around modules, which are linked to a central database in such a manner that data entered once through one module are available to applications of all other modules. (Tarafdar, 2005) **15:** An integrated software system processing data from a variety of functional areas such as finance, operations, sales, human resources, and supply-chain management. (Troutt & Long, 2005) **16:** An enterprise-wide group of software applications centered on an integrated database designed to support a business process view of the organization, and to balance the supply and demand for its resources. This software has multiple modules that may include manufacturing, distribution, personnel, payroll, and financials, and is considered to provide the necessary infrastructure for electronic commerce. (Dunn & Grabski, 2005) **17:** Enables the company to integrate data used throughout the organizations in functions such as finance, operations, human resources, and sales. This system extends the pool of information for business intelligence. (Raisinghani & Nugent, 2005)

### Enterprise Resource Planning Community

A model defining the collective relationships and interactions between the three de facto actors (the ERP vendor, the ERP consultant, the implementing organization) within the ERP market. (Sammon & Adam, 2005)

### Enterprise Resource Planning Configuration

A tailoring option that involves setting or configuring a generic/industry-specific ERP system using the switches/tables provided by the vendor in order to personalize the ERP system to support an organization's business practices and requirements. (Ng, 2005)

### Enterprise Resource Planning Customization

Customization simply means that changes, modifications, or adaptations are needed in order to meet some user requirements. It can be carried out via configuration tables, adding extensions or making modifications to the standard code (but cannot be done by applying any patch provided by the vendor). (Ng, 2005)

### Enterprise Resource Planning Decision and Selection Stage

Stage at which the company decides to implement an ERP system and chooses the supplier. (de Souza & Zwicker, 2005)

### Enterprise Resource Planning Extension

A tailoring option that involves adding custom or third-party codes to user-exits, add-ons, reports, or user interfaces, without changing the vendor/standard code. (Ng, 2005)

### Enterprise Resource Planning Implementation Stage

Stage of an ERP project at which the ERP system's modules are put into operation. (de Souza & Zwicker, 2005)

### Enterprise Resource Planning Lifecycle

**1:** Consists of the several stages that an ERP system goes through during its whole life within the hosting organization. (Esteves & Pastor, 2005) **2:** The various stages through which a project of introducing an ERP system in a company passes through. (de Souza & Zwicker, 2005)

### Enterprise Resource Planning Modification

A tailoring option, which results in changes being made to the existing ERP (standard) code and custom objects being created. (Ng, 2005)

### Enterprise Resource Planning Patch-Option

A tailoring option, where vendor's patches are used to service a maintenance request. (Ng, 2005)

### Enterprise Resource Planning Stabilization Stage

The first weeks after the beginning of an ERP system operation in the company. (de Souza & Zwicker, 2005)

### Enterprise Resource Planning System

**1:** A comprehensive information system that collects, processes, and provides information about all parts of an enterprise, automating business processes and business rules within and across business functions, partly or completely. (Kurbel, 2005) **2:** An integrated information system purchased as a commercial software package with the aim of supporting most operations of a company. (de Souza & Zwicker, 2005)

### Enterprise Resource Planning Total Cost of Ownership

ERP software lifecycle cost covering the initial implementation and installation, continuous maintenance, and upgrades to the system until the software is retired from the production system. It includes all the software, hardware and equipment, annual maintenance fees, outsourcing, training, documentation, personnel, management, and service costs. (Ng, 2005)

### Enterprise Resource Planning II (ERP II)

**1:** A term that has been coined to denote the applications aimed at satisfying organizations that have already implemented ERP. This appears to include the realization of efficiency gains originally planned for ERP, the implementation of ERP solutions to more vertical market segments, and the further integration of key business processes (for example, to include PLM). (Carton & Adam, 2005) **2:** ERP II is understood to mean the re-implementation and expansion of ERP. It is an extended, open, vertical, and global approach to systems integration and can be understood as an application and deployment strategy for collaborative, operational, and financial processes within the enterprise, and between the enterprise and key external partners and markets in an effort to provide deep, vertical-specific functionality coupled with external connectivity. (Sammon & Adam, 2005) **3:** Opening up ERP systems beyond the enterprise level to exchange information with supply chain partners. ERP II extends beyond the four walls of the business to trading partners. (Bradley, 2005)

## Enterprise Resource Planning Utilization Stage
Stage of an ERP project at which the system starts to belong to the day-by-day operations of the company. (de Souza & Zwicker, 2005)

## Enterprise Resource Planning-Enabled Organization
An organization with a fully implemented enterprise resource planning system extending into B2B and/or B2C applications. (Burn & Ash, 2006)

## Enterprise Software Configuration
The process of implementing customized information flows, business logic, and database design in an ERP software. This requires activities such as designing forms, reports, and screen layouts; modifying existing programs; writing code for add-on applications; designing and implementing databases; and converting data from legacy systems. (Tarafdar, 2005)

## Enterprise-Wide Innovation
Includes leveraging successful innovations so they affect the entire enterprise; provides greater value toward competitive advantage than isolated, individual innovations. (Norris, 2005)

## Entertainment Service
Providing users recreational services (e.g., downloading hot pictures, music tunes, and games). (Lee & Pai, 2005)

## Entity
**1:** Anything that can be conceived as real and can be named. (Marjomaa, 2005) **2:** The basic element in a conceptual model that represents an abstraction with modeling purposes. (Cuadra et al., 2005)

## Entity Realism
An ontological position that entity classes exist in the world independent of their being perceived by the modeler. (Artz, 2005c)

## Entity Set
**1:** Similar entities or objects with common properties are summarized into entity sets or entity types; graphically represented in rectangles. (Bagui, 2005) **2:** An entity is a non-lexical object that in the real world is identified using a definite description that relates it to other things (e.g., the Country that has CountryCode 'US'). Typically, an entity may undergo changes over time. An entity type is a kind of entity, for example, Person, Country. In UML, an entity is called an object, and an entity type is called a class. (Halpin, 2005)

## Entity-Based Query
A probabilistic query that returns a set of objects. (Cheng & Prabhakar, 2005)

## Entity-Relationship (ER)
A conceptual data model that defines the domain in terms of entities, attributes, and relationships. ERD is an ER diagram in which entities are represented as rectangles, attributes as ellipses, and relationships between entities as diamonds. (Shoval & Kabeli, 2005)

## Entity-Relationship Diagram
**1:** A graphical representation of the entities and the relationships between them. Entity relationship diagrams are a useful medium to achieve a common understanding of data among users and application developers. (Alhajj & Polat, 2005a) **2:** The most widely used model to express the database conceptual schema. (De Antonellis et al., 2005)

## Entity-Relationship Model (E-R Model)
**1:** A model to represent real-world requirements through entities, their attributes, and a variety of relationships between them. E-R models can be mapped automatically to the relational model. (Denton & Besemann, 2005) **2:** One of the most well known and widely used conceptual models. The main concepts in the E-R model are entity types, relationships, and their attributes. (Mani & Badia, 2005)

## Entrepreneur
A business owner who makes all decisions and operates in uncertain environment. (Kyobe, 2006)

## Entrepreneurial Identity
There is a view that individuals 'become' entrepreneurs as they are reflexively constituted by the discourse of

enterprise—that is, they begin to characterize themselves as entrepreneurs as they adopt the norms, practices, and values of the entrepreneurial community with which they engage. (Warren, 2006)

## Entrepreneurial Management Style

An approach that supports interaction and shared decision making with employees and the early adoption of IT. Employees are encouraged to embrace ambiguity as a source of opportunity, present new ideas, and initiate action in new directions. (Winston & Dologite, 2005)

## Entrepreneurial Orientation

The practices and decision-making styles managers use to keep the firms competitive. (Kyobe, 2006)

## Entrepreneurial University

A wide-ranging term, used in IT to describe universities associated with high rates of knowledge transfer through the formation of spin-out companies, and the exploitation of intellectual property rights by faculty and students. (Warren, 2006)

## Entropic Distance

The entropic distance of a distribution g from a target distribution f, is:

$$_{E}d = \sum_{i} f_i \log \frac{f_i}{g_i}$$

(Giudici, 2005)

## Entropy

**1:** A measure of the degree of disorder or tendency toward the breakdown of any system. In physics this term is defined in the second law of thermodynamics, which states in part that "the entropy of the universe tends to a maximum." (Targowski, 2005) **2:** Measures the indeterminateness inherent to a probability distribution and is dual to information. (Kern-Isberner, 2005)

## Envelopes

Are calculated as upper and lower envelopes above and below the global baseline. These are the connected pixels that form the external points of the signature obtained by sampling the signature at regular intervals. (Chakravarty et al., 2005a)

## Environment Variable

One of a number of system variables whose value contains data about a user's system configuration and Web site last visited. (Szewczak, 2005)

## Environmental Constraint

A factors in the environment with potential to inhibit or constrain one's behavior and/or performance. (Jawahar, 2005)

## Environmental Factor

Reflects the pressure to adopt an innovation that is external to the organization. Such pressure may be exerted by competitors, clients, trading partners, government initiatives, and other characteristics of the marketplace. (Cragg & Mills, 2005)

## Environmental Influence

A factor external to an entity (i.e., in its environment) that affects its conduct of knowledge management. (Holsapple & Joshi, 2006)

## Environmental Scanning

The systematic gathering of information in order to reduce the randomness of the information flow into the organization, and to provide early warnings of changing conditions in both the external and internal environment. (Parker & Nitse, 2006)

## Environmental Variable

The context within which career decisions are made, such as the school and work environment. (Beise et al., 2005)

## E1

One of the links used for the physical interconnection between different networks. (Frempong & Braimah, 2005)

**EOQ:** See *Economic Order Quantity.*

**EPC:** See *Electronic Product Code.*

## EPCglobal

A joint venture between EAN International in Europe and the Uniform Code Council in the United States to administer the numbering and data standards for EPC. (Loebbecke, 2006)

## Ephemeris Data Parameter

A short section of the space vehicle or satellite orbit. New data are gathered by receivers each hour. However, the receiver is capable of using data gathered four hours before without significant error. Algorithms are used in conjunction with ephemeris parameters to compute the SV position for any time within the period of the orbit described by the ephemeris parameter set. (Freeman & Auld, 2005)

## Episodal Association Rule

A rule of the form $X \Rightarrow Y$, where $X$ is antecedent episode, $Y$ is the consequent episode, and $X \cap Y = \varnothing$. The confidence of an episodal association rule is the conditional probability that the consequent episode occurs, given the antecedent episode occurs under the time constraints specified. The support of the rule is the number of times it holds in the database. (Harms, 2005)

## Episode

**1:** A combination of events with a partially specified order. The episode ordering is parallel if no order is specified and serial if the events of the episode have a fixed order. (Harms, 2005) **2:** A subset or subsequence of a session composed of semantically or functionally related pageviews. (Mobasher, 2005b)

## Episodic Knowledge

Declarative memory consists of two types of knowledge— topic or semantic, and episodic. Episodic knowledge consists of one's experience with knowledge. These are learned through experience once the topic knowledge is obtained from textbooks, formal training, and education. (Raisinghani, 2005)

**EPM:** See *Enterprise Performance Management.*

**EPON:** See *Ethernet PON.*

## Equal Employment Opportunity Classification

A job classification system set forth by the Equal Employment Opportunity Commission (EEOC) for demographic reporting requirements. (Troutt & Long, 2005)

## Equal Error Rate

The error rate when the proportions of FAR and FRR are equal. The accuracy of the biometric system is inversely proportional to the value of EER. (Chakravarty et al., 2005b)

## Equal-Depth Discretization

A technique that divides the attribute value range into intervals of equal population (value density). (Shen & Horiguchi, 2005)

## Equal-Width Discretization

A technique that divides the attribute value range into intervals of equal width (length). (Shen & Horiguchi, 2005)

## Equivalence in Construct Operationalization

Refers to whether a construct is manifested and operationalized the same way across cultures. (Karahanna et al., 2005)

## Equivocality

An expression or term liable to more than one interpretation. Equivocality refers to ambiguity, confusion, a lack of understanding, or the existence of multiple and conflicting interpretations about a particular situation. Equivocality is addressed by the exchange of existing views among individuals to define problems and resolve conflicts through the enactment of shared interpretations that can direct future activities. It is used to decide which questions to ask to reach agreement and gain commitment. (Croasdell & Wang, 2006)

## ER

See *Entity-Relationship.*

**ER Diagram:** See *Entity-Relationship Diagram.*

## Ergonomy

The science of the interface between people and products. It is based on human factor considerations such as cognition, reasoning, memory, and language. In the context of a software product, it guides the design and constitutes a support for testing and evaluating user interfaces to facilitate the ease of use of the software system. (Daassi et al., 2006)

## Eriksson-Penker Process Diagram

UML extension created to support business modeling which adapts the basic UML activity diagram to represent business processes. (Gurău, 2005)

**ERP:** See *Enterprise Resource Planning.*

**ERP Community:** See *Enterprise Resource Planning Community.*

**ERP Configuration:** See *Enterprise Resource Planning Configuration.*

**ERP Customization:** See *Enterprise Resource Planning Customization.*

**ERP Decision and Selection Stage:** See *Enterprise Resource Planning Decision and Selection Stage.*

**ERP Extension:** See *Enterprise Resource Planning Extension.*

**ERP Implementation Stage:** See *Enterprise Resource Planning Implementation Stage.*

**ERP Lifecycle**: See *Enterprise Resource Planning Lifecycle.*

**ERP Modification:** See *Enterprise Resource Planning Modification.*

**ERP Patch-Option:** See *Enterprise Resource Planning Patch-Option.*

**ERP Stabilization Stage:** See *Enterprise Resource Planning Stabilization Stage.*

**ERP System:** See *Enterprise Resource Planning System.*

**ERP TCO:** See *Enterprise Resource Planning Total Cost of Ownership.*

**ERP II:** See *Enterprise Resource Planning II.*

**ERP Utilization Stage:** See *Enterprise Resource Planning Utilization Stage.*

**ERP-Enabled Organization:** See *Enterprise Resource Planning-Enabled Organization.*

## Error Control
Selection of a classification rule in such a way to obtain a desired proportion of false positive and false negative. (Felici & Truemper, 2005)

## Error Localization
The (automatic) identification of the fields to impute in an edit-failing record. In most cases, an optimization algorithm is used to determine the minimal set of fields to impute so that the final (corrected) record will not fail edits. (Conversano & Siciliano, 2005)

## Erudite Agent
Acts as a broker locating compatible candidates according to specific similarities found in their profiles. Erudite has two roles: one is upon the requesting of interface agents, it queries its knowledge base, searching for other candidates that seem to have the same interests; the other is to keep its knowledge base updated with the candidate's specific information provided by the resident interface agents. In doing so, it implements the processing part of the SHEIK system's architecture. (Nabuco et al., 2006)

**ES/KBS:** See *Expert System/Knowledge-Based System.*

**ESD:** See *Electronic Service Delivery.*

**ESS:** See *Extended Service Set.*

## Essentialism
The view that some properties are necessary properties of the object to which they belong. In the context of IT, essentialism implies a belief that an individual's cultural identity (nationality, ethnicity, race, class, etc.) determines and predicts that individual's values, communicative preferences, and behaviors. (Macfadyen, 2006a)

## Estimation-Maximization Algorithm
An algorithm for computing maximum likelihood estimates from incomplete data. In the case of fitting mixtures, the group labels are the missing data. (Burr, 2005b)

## Ethernet
**1:** A communications standard for a Local Area Network (LAN). When a device wishes to transmit, it waits until the link is empty and then transmits. In the event that two or more devices transmit simultaneously (collision), all devices stop transmitting and wait a random time period before attempting to retransmit. (Ruppel & Ruppel, 2005) **2:** A popular LAN technology that supports transmission rates at 10 Mbps and serves as the basis for the IEEE (Institute of Electrical and Electronics Engineers) 802.3 standard and its extensions. Newer and faster versions of Ethernet include Fast Ethernet (100 Mbps), Gigabit Ethernet (1 Gbps), and 10 Gigabit Ethernet (10 Gbps). (Littman, 2006)

## Ethernet Frame

A standardized set of bits, organized into several fields, used to carry data over an Ethernet system. Those fields include the preamble, a start frame delimiter, address fields, a length field, a variable size data field that carries from 46 to 1,500 bytes of data, and an error-checking field. (Freire et al., 2005)

## Ethernet PON (EPON)

As defined by IEEE 802.3ah, it features a passive optical network for fiber-to-the-home service that uses Ethernet as its transmission protocol. (Kelic, 2005)

## Ethical

Conforming to standards of professional or social behavior agreed to by all members of a virtual enterprise. (Wong, 2005)

## Ethical Behavior

Receives greater attention today, partly due to reported cases of questionable or potentially unethical behavior and the associated dysfunctions that emerge. Because ethics involves the study of moral issues and choices, it is concerned with moral implications springing from virtually every decision. As a result, managers are challenged to set the standards and act as role models for other employees. (Grieves, 2006a)

## Ethical Climate

Indicates whether an organization has a conscience. The more ethical the perceived culture of an organization, the less likely it is that unethical decision making will occur. (Grieves, 2006a)

## Ethical Design

Attempts to promote good through the creation of products that are made and consumed within a socially accepted moral framework. (Knight, 2006b)

## Ethical Local Governance

Refers to a government where members and staff recognize the importance of ethical standards in local governance, thus enabling the authority to construct and develop an ethical culture and values for the authority. (Yigitcanlar & Baum, 2006a)

## Ethics

**1:** A branch of moral philosophy that examines the standards for proper conduct. (Artz, 2005a) **2:** A set of principles of right conduct. The rules or standards governing the conduct of a person or the members of a profession. (Wang, Chen, et al., 2006) **3:** The branch of philosophy that concerns itself with the study of morality. (Goodman, 2005) **4:** The philosophy of morality. (Knight, 2006b) **5:** The study of social or interpersonal values and the rules of conduct that follow from them. (Gilbert, 2005) **6:** The study of the general nature of morals and values as well as specific moral choices; it also may refer to the rules or standards of conduct that are agreed upon by cultures and organizations that govern personal or professional conduct. (Cook, 2005)

**ETHICS:** See *Effective Technical & Human Implementation of Computer-Based Systems.*

## Ethics of Knowledge Management

The study of the impact of knowledge management on society, the organization, and the individual, with a particular emphasis on the damaging effects knowledge management can have. (Land et al., 2006b)

## Ethnocentric Content

Pieces of information provided by local journalists of particular interest for locals who find sufficient elements for understanding it. On the contrary, local and specific content could be strange to overseas readers. (Díaz-Andrade, 2005)

## Ethnography

**1:** An approach to research that involves in-depth study through observation, interviews, and artifact analysis in an attempt to gain a thorough understanding from many perspectives. (Roibás, 2006b) **2:** Research characterized by an extended period in the field and which involves the researcher being immersed in the community being studied. (Trauth, 2005b) **3:** The branch of anthropology that provides scientific description of individual human societies. (Zaphiris et al., 2005) **4:** The work of describing a culture. The essential core aims to understand another way of life from the native point of view. (DeLorenzo, 2005) **5:** While its Greek etymological origins mean "description of a people," ethnography has two separate meanings. One refers to the process of doing field research with a host community. The second refers to the writing of a documentary text based on that research. Ethnography has been the mainstay of qualitative research in anthropology. (Forte, 2005)

## Ethnomethodology

In the context of work, this is an approach to study how people actually order their working activities through mutual attentiveness to what has to be done. Ethnomethodology refuses any epistemological or ontological commitments, and limits its inquiry to what is directly observable and what can be plausibly inferred from observation. (Farooq et al., 2006)

## Ethos

The credibility, authority, or presence of an individual. (St.Amant, 2006a)

## Ethos Condition

One of several factors individuals use to asses the credibility or the worth of a presentation. (St.Amant, 2005c)

## Etic

**1:** A universal framework developed from universal constructs. (Hunter, 2006b) **2:** An outsider's (stranger's) view of a culture. More specifically, it is used to describe the anthropologist's method of describing cultures from his or her own external cultural perspective. (Champion, 2006a)

**ETL:** See *Extraction, Transformation, Load System.*

**ETM:** See *Electronic Town Meeting.*

**ETSI:** See *European Telecommunications Standards Institute.*

**EUC:** See *End-User Computing.*

## EUC Net Benefit

A measure that captures the balance of positive and negative impacts that result from EUC activities in an organization. (Shayo & Guthrie, 2005)

## EUC Satisfaction

An affective measure of an end user's opinion about the net benefits derived from EUC activities in an organization. (Shayo & Guthrie, 2005)

## EUC Success

The degree to which the organizational EUC strategy contributes to individual, group, and organizational computing success in an environment that includes applications developed by the information system department (ISD), application service providers, outsourcing parties, and off-the-shelf vendors. (Shayo & Guthrie, 2005)

**EULA:** See *End-User License Agreement.*

## Euclidean Distance

**1:** An index to measure structural similarity among actors of a network. The less two actors are structurally equivalent, the larger the Euclidean distance between them. (Assimakopoulos & Yan, 2006) **2:** Ordinary straight-line distance. (Chang, 2005) **3:** The distance between a vector of predicted values, $X_g$, and a vector of observed values, $X_f$, is expressed by the equation:

$$_2d\left(X_f, X_g\right) = \sqrt{\sum_{r=1}^{n}\left(X_{fr} - X_{gr}\right)^2}$$

(Giudici, 2005)

**4:** The straight-line distance between two points in a multi-dimensional space. It is calculated by summing up the squares of distances in individual dimensions and taking the square root of the sum. (Sayal, 2005)

## European Computer Manufacturers Association (ECMA)

Standardizes information and communication systems. (Barone, 2005)

## European Telecommunications Standards Institute (ETSI)

An organization promulgating engineering standards for telecommunications equipment. (Chochliouros et al., 2005b)

## Eustress

A change in biophysical or psychological variables that is considered good. (Molinari et al., 2005b)

**EVA:** See *Economic Value Added.*

## Evaluation

**1:** A process of finding the value of information services or products according to the needs of their consumers or users. (Córdoba, 2006b) **2:** A quality program has continual and ongoing evaluation. This includes a needs analysis (diagnostic); emergent data collected throughout the program/course/training allowing changes to be implemented even as the course/program/training is being delivered (formative); and end-of-the-course/program/ training surveys and interviews with learners, course facilitators, and programs to determine course/program/ training redesign (summative). (MacDonald et al., 2005) **3:** The gathering and observing of a broad range of evidence in order to gauge the impact and effectiveness of an object, program, or process. (Naidu, 2005a) **4:** The assessment of the effectiveness of service delivery and the identification of obstacles or barriers to service delivery. Some means of evaluation include understanding the perceptions of improvement in the organization in the manner in which it formalizes knowledge processes, knowledge structures, and underlying systems. These in turn will affect the operations, products, or services delivered. Another means of evaluation of the effectiveness of a KM strategy is through establishing increased awareness and participation in that strategy. (Zyngier, 2006) **5:** The systematic determination of the merit or worth of an object. (Nash et al., 2005a)

## Evaluation Agent

Comparison-shopping agent specializing in collecting product and service rating information. (Wan, 2006)

## Evaluation Management

Used to guide learners' e-learning and build their knowledge, and to verify if the information is successfully turned into knowledge. In order for e-learning to be proven effective, online learners need to verify that they have succeeded in gaining new knowledge or skills. During this phase, the relationship between information and knowledge becomes visible with respect to e-learning. (Xu & Wang, 2006)

## Evaluation Strategy

A process designed to guide the collection and reporting of evaluation results. (Waddington et al., 2005)

## Evaluative Judgment

An assessment based on characteristics of an information object, independent of assessments based on information prior to encountering the object (predictive judgments). (Danielson, 2006c)

## Event

**1:** An act performed by a whole or to the whole that is perceived by an observer directly or through its consequences on other wholes. (Gelman et al., 2005) **2:** An occurrence of an event type at a given timestamp. (Harms, 2005) **3:** An occurrence of a happening of interest (also known as primitive event). If the event involves correlation or aggregation of happenings, then it is called a complex or composite event. (Cilia, 2005) **4:** Part of a trigger that refers to the occurrence of a certain situation. When the event occurs, the rule is triggered (i.e., is scheduled so that its condition is evaluated). In most systems, the event can mention only basic database actions (e.g., insertions, deletions, updates). (Badia, 2005b) **5:** Something that happens at a point in time. (Ale & Espil, 2005) **6:** A phenomena that changes the application's state. (Trossen & Molenaar, 2005) **7:** In contrast to request/reply, producers send unsolicited notifications about events they observe. Instead of delivering notifications directed to consumers, they are first sent to an intermediary service. This service delivers the notifications according to the subscriptions consumers have issued. (Fiege, 2005)

## Event Algebra

Composite events are expressed using an event algebra. Such algebras require an order function between events to apply event operators (e.g., sequence) or to consume events. (Cilia, 2005)

## Event Handler

A procedure (subroutine) that executes in response to an event. The event may represent a specific user action (e.g., a mouse click) or may be a manifestation of a system process (e.g., page has finished loading). Details surrounding the event are provided as arguments of the procedure. (Westin, 2005)

## Event Instance

An event is an instance of an event type associated to a point in time that belongs to the validity interval of its type. (Vargas-Solar, 2005)

## Event Logger

A text file used to record the timestamps, attributes, and types of navigation events invoked by the teacher during the recording stage. The log is treated as synchronization information for dynamic presentation. (Liu & Chen, 2005)

## Event Management Model

Defines policies for detecting, producing, and notifying instances of event types. (Vargas-Solar, 2005)

## Event Management Software

Integrated software (desktop, network, or Web based) to assist a variety of functions for event managers. This may

**E**

include venue booking, delegate registrations, speaker requirements, transport, and accommodation management. (Carson, 2005)

## Event Sequence

A finite, time-ordered sequence of events. A sequence of events includes events from a single finite set of event types. (Harms, 2005)

## Event Study

Event studies have long been used in finance market research to assess how capital markets respond to the release of new information contained in company reports to the market. Information event analysis can be used to frame and interpret quantitative aspects of forum conversation by providing a study timeframe around some particular event such as stock ramping. (Campbell, 2006)

## Event Type

**1:** A discretized partition identifier that indicates a unique item of interest in the database. The domain of event types is a finite set of discrete values. (Harms, 2005) **2:** Represents a class of situations produced within an event producer and that is interesting for a consumer. In the context of active systems, an event type represents the class of significant situations that trigger an active rule. Such situations are produced within a validity interval, which is the time interval during which instances of the event type can be detected. (Vargas-Solar, 2005)

## Event-Based System

A system in which clients (subscribers) must express (subscribe) their interest in receiving particular events. Once clients have subscribed, servers (publishers) publish events, which will be sent to all interested subscribers. (Kunz & Gaddah, 2005)

## Event-Sharing Paradigm

Shared applications that are realized based on the event-sharing paradigm instantiate a copy of the application on each participating host, distribute an initial start state among all copies, and further distribute all future events among those copies that result in a state transition of the applications. (Trossen & Molenaar, 2005)

## Evidence-Based Medicine

Health care based on best practice which is encoded in the form of clinical guidelines and protocols. (Metaxiotis, 2006)

## Evolutionary Algorithm

An algorithm incorporating aspects of natural selection or survival of the fittest. (Guan, 2005e)

## Evolutionary Aligning Idea

A framing idea created over time in an evolutionary manner aimed to align a paradox or tension between paradigms toward a perception of unification. (Ariely, 2006a)

## Evolutionary Approach to E-Government

A way to study e-government that identifies different stages as the right path for e-government evolution. (Almazán & Gil-García, 2006)

## Evolutionary Computation

**1:** A solution approach based on simulation models of natural selection which begins with a set of potential solutions and then iteratively applies algorithms to generate new candidates and select the fittest from this set. The process leads toward a model that has a high proportion of fit individuals. (Hsu, 2005a) **2:** A solution approach guided by biological evolution that begins with potential solution models, then iteratively applies algorithms to find the fittest models from the set to serve as inputs to the next iteration, ultimately leading to a model that best represents the data. (Lingras et al., 2005) **3:** A computer-based problem-solving system that uses a computational model of evolutionary processes as the key element in design and implementation. (Lazar, 2005) **4:** The solution approach guided by artificial evolution; it begins with random populations (of solution models), then iteratively applies algorithms of various kinds to find the best or fittest models. (Muruzábal, 2005)

## Evolutionary Design

System development methodology where an ongoing approach is taken to analyzing the requirements of the application. (Adam & Pomerol, 2005)

## Evolutionary Game Theory

Study of equilibria of games played by a population of players where the "fitness" of the players derives from the success each player has in playing the game. It provides tools for describing situations where a number of agents interact. Evolutionary game theory improves upon traditional game theory by providing dynamics describing how the population will change over time. (Polgar, 2005a)

## Evolutionary Innovation

A type of innovation which contains narrow extensions or improvements of an existing product or process which is not substantially changed. The applied changes are rather small and incremental; the knowledge needed is inside the innovator's domain. (Paukert et al., 2006)

## Evolutionary Process

The process of change in a certain direction regardless of external planning exerted upon the process. Related to the notion that a project can "take on a life of its own." (Nash et al., 2005b)

## Evolutionary Strategy

An evolutionary algorithm devoted to the parametric optimization. (Lazar, 2005)

## Evolutionary System

Involves continuous adjustments of its functionalities and UI according to the user and/or technological changes. (Furtado, 2005)

## Ex Ante Predictor of Student Performance

One of several student characteristics prior to beginning a class which have been determined to help forecast the relative performance of the students. (Benrud, 2005)

## Exact Learning

The set of learning approaches that are capable of inducing exact rules. (Dai, 2005a)

## Exact Rule

A rule without uncertainty. (Dai, 2005a)

## Exception Rule

A rule with low support and high confidence. (Daly & Taniar, 2005a)

## Exceptional Pattern

A pattern that is strongly supported (voted for) by only a few of a group of data sources. (Zhang & Zhang, 2005)

## Exchange Interaction

Involves the interactive relationship between e-government and the construction industry for potential mutual gain. (Barima, 2006a)

## Exchange Trust

Customer confidence that the e-tailer: (1) will fulfill its transaction-specific obligations consistent with the terms of the purchase agreement or other internally held reference standards developed as a result of interaction with other e-tailers or non-store retailers (competence), and (2) will not engage in opportunistic behavior at any time in the process of product or service delivery (benevolence). (Yeo & Chiam, 2006)

## Executive Information System (EIS)

**1:** A computer-based information delivery and communication system designed to support the needs of senior managers and executives. (Duan & Xu, 2005) **2:** A computer-based system composed of a user-dialogue system, a graph system, a multi-dimensional database query system, and an external communication system—all which enable decision makers to access a common core of data covering key internal and external business variables by a variety of dimensions (such as time and business unit). (Forgionne et al., 2005) **3:** An IS that provides high-level information tailored to the needs of decision makers. Typically a graphics-oriented system, in the context of CMIS, the EIS aggregates and uses summary data to present information to clinicians, executives, and business managers in the form of graphs, histograms, pie charts, tables, and so on. (Barnes, 2005) **4:** An application designed for top executives that often features a dashboard interface, drill-down capabilities, and trend analysis. (Pang, 2005b) **5:** A computerized system intended to provide current and appropriate information to support decision making for senior managers using a networked workstation. The emphasis is on graphical displays, and there is an easy-to-use interface. (Power, 2005) **6:** An information system that accesses, reports, and helps users interpret problem-pertinent information. (Forgionne, 2005)

## Executive Judgment

A decision an executive makes when he or she does not have a full understanding of the decision problem, based on his or her mental model of the environment and vision for the organization. (Baker & Coltman, 2005)

## Existence Time

The time when an object exists in the reality. It can be seen as the valid time of the existence of an object—that is, the valid time of "object o exists." (Rodríguez-Tastets, 2005b)

## Existent Knowledge

All the knowledge that characterizes a certain situation, entity, organization, and so on. Because it characterizes all the circumstances of that universe, identified or not, it will not be known in all its extension. (Analide et al., 2006)

## Exogenous Attentional Process

Refers to one of the set of processes by which attention is captured by some external event. These processes are also referred to as bottom-up or stimulus-driven. An example of this mechanism would be the attention shift from your reading due to a sudden noise. Exogenous attention is triggered automatically, and it normally lasts a short time before it is either shifted or becomes controlled by endogenous processes. (Thomas & Roda, 2006a)

## Exosomatic System

A computerized system that operates as an extension to human memory; the information spaces of it will be consistent with the cognitive spaces of its human users. (Liu & Koppelaar, 2005)

## Expanded Filter

Expanded filter $G(z^M)$ is obtained by replacing each delay $z^{-1}$ in the filter $G(z)$ with M delays $z^M$. In the time domain this is equivalent to inserting M-1 zeros between two consecutive samples of the impulse response of $G(z)$. (Jovanovic-Dolecek & Díaz-Carmona, 2005)

## Expansive Questioning

A questioning technique that asks the learner to consider how a remark might be applied, to more fully explain a remark or to respond to a "what if" question. The technique has the capacity to invite re-engagement or processing at a deeper level. (Bedard-Voorhees, 2005)

## Expectance Theory

Expectation including two components: the probability of occurrence and an evaluation of the occurrence. The discrepancy of confirmation could be either positive or negative. (Hsu & Kulviwat, 2006)

## Expectancy Theory

**1:** An individual will act in a certain way based on the expectation that the act will be followed by a given outcome and on the attractiveness of that outcome to the individual. (Kankanhalli et al., 2006) **2:** Expectancy models are cognitive explanations of human behavior that cast a person as an active, thinking, predicting creature in his or her environment. He or she continuously evaluates the outcomes of his or her behavior and subjectively assesses the likelihood that each of his or her possible actions will lead to various outcomes. (Chen & Lou, 2005)

## Expectation Maximization

Process of updating model parameters from new data where the new parameter values constitute maximum posterior probability estimates. Typically used for mixture models. (Caelli, 2005)

## Expedited Forwarding (EF)

A per-hop behavior defined in DiffServ meant to provide a "virtual leased line" type of service with guarantees on delay and jitter. (DaSilva, 2005)

## Experience

**1:** A holistic account of a particular episode, which stretches over time, often with a definite beginning and ending. Examples of (positive) experiences are: visiting a theme park or consuming a bottle of wine. An experience consists of numerous elements (e.g., product, user's psychological states, beliefs, expectations, goals, other individuals, etc.) and their relation. It is assumed that humans constantly monitor their internal, psychological state. They are able to access their current state during an experience and to report it (i.e., experience sampling). Individuals are further able to form a summary, retrospective assessment of an experience. However, this retrospective assessment is not a one-to-one summary of everything that happened during the experience, but rather overemphasizes single outstanding moments and the end of the experience. (Hassenzahl, 2006) **2:** Experience is a subset of tacit knowledge, but not all experiences are tacit. It can be either obtained through repeatedly performing a task in a similar way or through experimentation with new approaches to complete a task. (Fong, 2006b)

## Experience Design

The intentional creation of a time-based activity that includes physical objects, agents, and situations. (Knight, 2006b)

## Experience Good

A good whose value can be estimated after acquisition and use. This raises the problem of pricing and other marketing issues. Generally speaking, digital goods (e.g., books, music, software, news, and, of course, information) are all experience goods. (Scarso et al., 2006)

## Experience-Based Learning

This learning model positions the learner and his or her experience in the center of all activities. This experience comprises all kinds of events in the life of the learner, including those that happened earlier, the current events, or those arising from the learner's participation in activities implemented by teachers and facilitators. The experience analysis by reflecting, evaluating, and reconstructing is a key element. It encompasses formal, informal, and nonformal learning, lifelong learning, incidental learning, and workplace learning. (Correia & Sarmento, 2005)

## Experienced Credibility

A credibility assessment based upon first-hand experience with a system. (Danielson, 2006c)

## Experiential Learning

**1:** A process through which a learner constructs knowledge, skill, and value from direct experiences. (Sala, 2005a) **2:** Learning achieved through the everyday practice of an activity, rather than in a formal classroom setting or other directed training program; experience as a source of learning and development. (Warren, 2006) **3:** Learning based on direct and unmediated instruction, or on physical interaction with people and materials. (Russell, 2005b) **4:** Learning based on experiences rather than listening or reading. (Pendegraft, 2005) **5:** Refers to knowledge generated from and situated in experience; for an experience to facilitate learning, the student must be able to identify and analyze specific goals, needs, and outcomes. (McCracken, 2005)

## Experiment

Research method in which the researcher manipulates some independent variables to measure the effects on a dependent variable. (Pace, 2005)

## Experimental Design

The process of defining dependent and independent variables of the underlying model and acceptable ranges for these variables. In terms of input, output, and model, the experimental design describes which input variables and parameters to manipulate, and according to what range of changes. As these elements are manipulated, specific output variables will be assessed. The connection between the input- and output-set pairings is embodied in the description of the model. Identifying what items to manipulate and which correspondence should reveal the effect of the manipulation describes the plan of the experiment. (Vitolo & Coulston, 2005)

## Expert Jury

A method based on forecasting and planning using the expertise of a panel of the firm's executives. (Pemberton & Stalker, 2006)

## Expert Knowledge

Possessed by individuals who have acquired deep knowledge in some particular field by training and experience. Examples are the specialized knowledge of physicians, vintners, or architects. Expert knowledge is opposite commonsense knowledge on their shared dimension. (Ein-Dor, 2006)

## Expert Reasoning

Implementing rules or procedures, often programmed to occur automatically, in order to make a decision. Background and heuristics that identify how to reach a conclusion are based on the knowledge of human experts in that field. (Lenard & Alam, 2005)

## Expert System

**1:** A special type of artificial intelligence system that contains a limited domain knowledge base, an inference mechanism to manipulate this base, and an interface to permit the input of new data and user dialogue. (de Carvalho, & Ferreira, 2006) **2:** A computer program that simulates the judgment and behavior of a human or an organization that has expert knowledge and experience in a particular field. Typically, such a system contains a knowledge base of accumulated experience and a set of rules for applying the knowledge base to each particular situation that is described in the program. (R., 2005) **3:** Computer program that uses coded knowledge to (help) solve problems of decision making of some complexity. (Svensson, 2005) **4:** A computer system that attempts to replicate what human experts normally do. Human experts make decisions and recommendations, such as what company strategy to follow or who to give a bank loan to, and do tasks, such as adjust temperature controls in a manufacturing plant. They also assist (or help) and train others to do tasks and to make decisions. So do expert systems. (Mockler & Dologite, 2005) **5:** A computer system that facilitates solving problems in a given field or application by drawing inference from a knowledge base developed from human expertise. Some expert systems are able to improve their knowledge base and develop new inference rules based on their experience with previous problems. (Raisinghani et al., 2005) **6:** A computer-based system that performs functions similar to those normally performed by a human expert. It has a knowledge base, an inference engine, and a user interface. (Duan & Xu, 2005) **7:** Approach designed to mimic human logic to solve complex problems. (Hentea, 2005b) **8:** An information system that contains and helps disseminate expert knowledge. (Kimble & Hildreth, 2006)

## Expert System/Knowledge-Based System (ES/KBS)

A computer-based system composed of a user-dialogue system, an inference engine, one or several intelligent modules, a knowledge base, and a work memory, which emulates the problem-solving capabilities of a human expert in a specific domain of knowledge. (Forgionne et al., 2005)

## Expert-Based Evaluation

Evaluation methodology which employs experts, mostly from different cognitive domain, to assess certain system aspects. (Athanasis & Andreas, 2005)

## Expert-Based Interface Evaluation

Evaluation methodology that employs experts from different cognitive domains to assess an interface. (Karoulis et al., 2006)

## Expertise

**1:** A source's perceived ability to provide information that is accurate and valid (based on attributes such as perceived knowledge and skill); with trustworthiness, it is one of two primary attributes of credibility. (Danielson, 2006c) **2:** Highly tacit, domain-specific knowledge gained through experience, formal education, and collaboration. (Kulkarni & Freeze, 2006)

## Explanation

A sequence of statements of the reasons for the behavior of the model of a system. (Kontos & Malagardi, 2006)

## Explanation-Oriented Data Mining

A general framework includes data pre-processing, data transformation, pattern discovery and evaluation, pattern explanation and explanation evaluation, and pattern presentation. This framework is consistent with the general model of scientific research processes. (Yao & Zhao, 2005)

## Explication

The act of making clear or removing obscurity from the meaning of a word, symbol, expression, and such. (Marjomaa, 2005)

## Explicit

This refers to the act of articulating our reasoning and the rationale for our teaching and learning theories. In effect we are attempting to articulate our tacit theories in order to make them more public and observable for other colleagues and pre-service teachers. (Keppell et al., 2005)

## Explicit Edit

An edit explicitly written by a subject matter specialist. (Conversano & Siciliano, 2005)

## Explicit Goal

Similar to meta-management, each member of the organization is charged with an explicit task to complete as it relates to the overall function of the organization. Often times, after this single goal is completed, the link between the organization and the entity is dissolved until a further need for it is realized. At this point, the link is reestablished. (J. Lee, 2005)

## Explicit Knowledge/Information

**1:** Knowledge that is external in the form of documents, graphs, tables, and so forth. (Woods et al., 2006) **2:** A type of knowledge that can be described, formalized, coded, and stored in documents, magazines, journals, and so forth. (Aurum & Demirbilek, 2006) **3:** Also known as information, this is knowledge that is adequately and properly represented by facts, figures, symbols, and data. (Ray, 2006) **4:** Can be expressed in words and numbers, and shared in the form of data, scientific formulae, specifications, manuals, and the like. This kind of knowledge can be readily transmitted between individuals formally and systematically. (Zeleznikow, 2006) **5:** Context-free knowledge that can be codified using formal and systematic language. Explicit knowledge can be expressed using words (language) or as mathematical formulae, procedures, or principles. Explicit knowledge is easy to codify and communicate. (Sivakumar, 2006) **6:** Formal knowledge—that is, "know-what" represents knowledge that is well established and documented. (Wickramasinghe, 2006) **7:** Information that has specific meaning and that can be easily and clearly understood. (Neville & Powell, 2005) **8:** Knowledge codified into a formal and systematized language. It may be transmitted, preserved, retrieved, and combined. (Falivene & Kaufman, 2006) **9:** Knowledge that can be codified in words, numbers, or rules and can take the shape of documents, or perhaps result in the production of some type of equipment. (Qayyum, 2005)

## Explicit Team Process

Openly articulated, overt communication and coordination behaviors. Example: Member A directly requests task-relevant information from Member B. (Cuevas et al., 2005)

## Exploit

**1:** A program that uses a vulnerability to attack the system's security mechanisms. Exploits usually compromise secrecy, integrity, or availability and often lead to elevation of privilege. (Weippl, 2006) **2:** Taking advantage of a software vulnerability to carry out an attack. To minimize the risk of exploits, security updates or software patches should be applied frequently. (Kayacik et al., 2005) **3:** Weakness in a system through which hackers can gain entry into the system. (Friedman, 2005)

## Exploratory Analysis

Part of the Data Analysis French School, developed between 1960 and 1980. The process of analysis takes as a target to discover new relations between the sets of the analyzed information. (Nigro & González Císaro, 2005c)

## Exploratory Data Analysis (EDA)

Comprises a set of techniques used to identify systematic relations between variables when there are no (or not complete) a priori expectations as to the nature of those relations. In a typical exploratory data analysis process, many variables are taken into account and compared, using a variety of techniques in the search for systematic patterns. (Katsaros & Manolopoulos, 2005b)

## Exploratory Factor Analysis

A process used to identify statistically significant constructs underlying a set of data. (Martz & Reddy, 2005)

## Exploratory Tree

An oriented tree graph formed by internal nodes and terminal nodes, the former allowing the description of the conditional interaction paths between the response variable and the predictors, whereas the latter are labeled by a response class/value. (Siciliano & Conversano, 2005)

## Exponentially Decaying

A quantity that decreases such that the momentary rate of decrease is directly proportional to the quantity. (Kushnir, 2006)

## Export/Import

Information systems may define atoma and roles and then export them to be used by other information systems. An information system may import any of the exported

atoma and roles and use it in its own context. (Lepouras et al., 2006)

## Export Restriction

A restriction on the type, quantity, or destination of goods that can be exported out of a country. (D. Brandon, Jr., 2005b)

## Export-Oriented Software

A unit is considered export oriented if at least 70% of its revenue comes from export. (Raisinghani & Rahman, 2005)

## Exposed Node

The problem where a transmitting or "exposed" node is within range of a sender, but is out of range of the intended destination. (Erbas, 2005)

## EXPRESS/STEP

To share and exchange product data, the Standard for the Exchange of Product Model Data (STEP) is being developed by the International Organization for Standardization (ISO). EXPRESS is the description method of STEP and can be used to model product design, manufacturing, and production data. (Ma, 2005a)

## Expression

The utterance through any language system of prelinguistic emotion or understanding toward the creation of consensual meaning between people. (Kettley, 2006b)

## Expressiveness

The ability of employees to use oral or facial expression and body language to clearly express what they know. (Chen, Duan, et al., 2006)

## Extended Enterprise

The seamless Internet-based integration of a group or network of trading partners along their supply chains. (Sammon & Adam, 2005)

## Extended ERP

Extends the foundation ERP system's functionalities such as finances, distribution, manufacturing, human resources, and payroll to customer relationship management, supply chain management, sales-force automation, and Internet-enabled integrated e-commerce and e-business. (Rashid, 2005)

**E**

## Extended Item

An item associated with the context where it happens. (Feng & Dillon, 2005)

## Extended Knowledge Management

KM methods and practices applied to inter-firm knowledge management. The adjective "extended" means activities that span the organizational boundaries, involving suppliers, customers, vendors, business partners, and institutions. (Scarso et al., 2006; Bolisani et al., 2006)

## Extended Model of Knowledge-Flow Dynamics

A four-dimensional model used to classify and visualize flows of knowledge in the organization. (Nissen, 2005)

## Extended Organization

A knowledge-based organization with links to customers and suppliers across an electronic supply chain. (Burn & Ash, 2006)

## Extended RDBMS Schema

A database schema specified according to the relational data model extended with new data types. RDBMSs allowing the extension of the basic Type System are those implementing the concept of Universal Server. Examples are Oracle, Informix, DB2, and Illustra. (Polese et al., 2005)

## Extended Service Provider (XSP)

An entity that provides total IT-related services from online applications through maintenance and reengineering of IT resources to business process consulting for its clients. Success of the XSP model should presume the rapid proliferation of the ASP services in an overly complex market. If the ASP service demand grows explosively in a short period of time, the XSP model will debut in the market earlier on, increasing the possibility of XSPs dominating the industry, as they have scale advantage in terms of cost. (D. Kim, 2005)

## Extended Service Set (ESS)

A WLAN architecture consisting of dedicated station computers and many dedicated wireless access points. (Pulkkis et al., 2005b)

## Extended Transaction

A transaction associated with the context where it happens. (Feng & Dillon, 2005)

## Extensible Authentication Protocol (EAP)

An authentication protocol used with the IEEE 802.1x Standard® to pass authentication-information messages between a suppliant and an authentication server. (Pulkkis et al., 2005b)

## Extensible Business Reporting Language (XBRL)

**1:** A markup language that allows for the tagging of data and is designed for performance reporting. It is a variant of XML. (Garrity et al., 2005) **2:** A general-purpose data representation language similar to the HyperText Markup Language (HTML) used in Web pages. (Arya, 2005) **3:** A language written in Standard Generalized Markup Language (SGML) that allows one to design markup tags for easy interchange of documents and data on the Internet. (Zhang, 2006) **4:** A simplified meta language, derived from SGML, emerging as the standard for self-describing data exchange in Internet applications. (Passi et al., 2005) **5:** A standard language for defining the syntax and structure of documents with the goals of interoperability, portability, and automatic processing of applications among different enterprises; the data in an XML document are tagged and thus are self-describing. (Moser & Melliar-Smith, 2006) **6:** Document type definitions that can be used to specify or describe various types of objects. When a set of these is used on the Web to describe product information, it is referred to as cXML or commerce XML. It works as a meta-language that defines necessary information about a product, and standards are being developed for cXML in a number of industries, performing a function similar to that of EDI for non-Web-based systems. It will help to standardize the exchange of Web catalog content and to define request/response processes for secure electronic transactions over the Internet. The processes include purchase orders, change orders, acknowledgments, status updates, ship notifications, and payment transactions. (Archer, 2005) **7:** Has been created to overcome some difficulties proper to HTML that—developed as a means for instructing the Web browsers how to display a given Web page—is a "presentation-oriented" markup tool. XML is called "extensible" because, contrary to HTML, it is not characterized by a fixed format, but lets the user design its own customized markup languages—a specific Document Type Description (DTD)—for limitless different types of documents; XML is then a "content-oriented" markup tool. (Zarri, 2006b) **8:** Markup language proposed by the World Wide Web Consortium (W3C) for data and documents interchange. (De Antonellis et al., 2005) **9:** The novel language, standardized by the World Wide Web Consortium, for representing, handling, and exchanging information on the Web. (De Meo et al., 2005a) **10:** A markup language for representing information as structured documents. Developed from an earlier language called SGML (Standard Generalized Markup Language) for the purposes of information management on the Internet. (Lyytikäinen et al., 2005)

## Extensible Markup Language (XML)

**1:** A standard with very flexible and simple syntax (a small set of rules in human-readable plaintext) used to describe and share commonly structured platform-independent information. Main components of its structure are elements (markups) and attributes of elements that are nested to create a hierarchical tree that easily can be validated. XML is extensible, because, unlike HTML, anyone can define new tags and attribute names to parameterize or semantically qualify content. It has been a formal recommendation from W3C since 1998, playing an increasingly important role in the exchange of a wide variety of data on the Web. (Pereira & Freire, 2005) **2:** A mechanism for encoding data into computer-understandable forms, useful for applications such as business-to-business electronic document interchange via the World Wide Web. (Lang, 2006) **3:** A specification developed by the World Wide Web Consortium (W3C). XML is a pared-down version of the Standard Generalized Markup Language (SGML), designed especially for Web documents. It allows designers to create their own customized tags, enabling the definition, transmission, validation, and interpretation of data between applications and between organizations. (Raisinghani & Sahoo, 2006) **4:** A subset of SGML, designed to describe data. It incorporates features of extensibility, structure, and validation, and is currently playing an increasingly important role in the exchange of a wide variety of data on the Web and elsewhere. (Dotsika, 2006) **5:** A text-based markup language that describes data in a document. Since XML is a platform-independent language, it is used as the standard format for transferring data over a network using Web services. (Sethi & Sethi, 2006a) **6:** An application-independent meta-language for defining markup languages. It serves as the basis for syntactic interoperability among information systems. (Antoniou et al., 2005) **7:** Created to overcome some difficulties proper to HTML, which—developed as a means for instructing Web browsers how to display a given Web page—is a "presentation-oriented" markup tool. XML is called "extensible" because, contrary to HTML, it is not

characterized by a fixed format but lets the user design his own customized markup languages—a specific Document Type Description (DTD)—for limitless different types of documents. XML is then a "content-oriented" markup tool. (Zarri, 2005b) **8:** A meta-language defining the syntax for presenting and exchanging data in Web environments. It overcomes the limit of fixed tags in HTML and allows users to define their document structures. W3C has designated XML as the standard for Web data. (Wang, Cheng, Cheng, et al., 2006) **9:** An open standard, developed by the W3C, that involves formal syntax for adding structure and/or content information in a Web-based document. This subset of SGML defines data elements in a neutral way for easy interchange of structured data, such as markup tags, definitions, transmission validation, and interpretations across applications and organizations. (Parikh & Parolia, 2005) **10:** A language for creating markup languages. There are two kinds of XML documents: well-formed and valid. The first respects the XML standard for the inclusion and the names of the tags. The second must be well formed and uses a grammar to define the structure and the types of data described by the document. (Nicolle et al., 2005) **11:** A meta-language directly derived from SGML but designed for Web documents. It allows the structuring of information and transmission between applications and between organizations. (de Campos et al., 2005) **12:** A sublanguage of SGML that provides a way to structure and format data, especially in textual form. The data is represented as XML documents; an XML document may have an optional schema associated with it. XML is considered a semistructured data model because a schema is not always necessary, and even if a schema is present, it could be quite flexible. (Mani & Badia, 2005) **13:** An easy-to-use dialect of SGML, this is a flexible technique for storage and interchange of data. One important aspect of XML is the combination of data and metadata in a single document. (Hänisch, 2005) **14:** A markup language that is quite different from HTML in that XML gives document authors the ability to create their own markup. XML is flexible in creating data formats and sharing both the format and the data with other applications or trading partners, compared with HTML. (Suh & Kim, 2005) **15:** A markup language for structured documents. Structure is represented with textual markup that intermixes with document content. XML is a recommendation from the World Wide Web Consortium. (Martínez-González, 2005) **16:** A W3C standard similar to HTML, but it allows creators to create their own tags. (Goh & Kinshuk, 2005) **17:** A specification for computer-readable documents. XML is actually a meta-language, a mechanism for representing other languages in a standardized way; therefore, XML provides a syntax to encode data. (Vardaki, 2005)

### Extensible Markup Language (XML) Content Analysis Mining

Concerned with analyzing texts within XML documents. (Nayak, 2005b)

### Extensible Markup Language Database (XMLDB)

A database that accepts XML documents for storage, and allows for retrieving them in their original XML format. XMLDB can physically store XML data in their original format or can transform them internally into relational tables, which are then reverted to their XML format upon retrieval. (Gaffar & Seffah, 2005)

### Extensible Markup Language (XML) Document

A document consisting of an (optional) XML declaration, followed by either an (optional) DTD or XML schema and then followed by document elements. (Chen, 2005b; Pallis et al., 2005)

### Extensible Markup Language (XML) Interstructure Mining

Concerned with the structure between XML documents. Knowledge is discovered about the relationship among subjects, organizations, and nodes on the Web. (Nayak, 2005b)

### Extensible Markup Language Metadata Interchange (XMI)

A widely used interchange format for sharing objects using XML. (Paiano, 2005)

### Extensible Markup Language (XML) Mining

Knowledge discovery from XML documents (heterogeneous and structural irregular). For example, clustering data-mining techniques can group a collection of XML documents together according to the similarity of their structures. Classification data-mining techniques can classify a number of heterogeneous XML documents into a set of predefined classifications of schemas to improve XML document handling and achieve efficient searches. (Nayak, 2005b)

### Extensible Markup Language (XML) Rewrite

A document that is not originally written in XML can be rewritten in XML format by adding the necessary syntax and semantics to it. (Gaffar & Seffah, 2005)

### Extensible Markup Language (XML) Schema

**1:** A database-inspired method for specifying constraints on XML documents using an XML-based language. Schemas address deficiencies in DTDs, such as the inability to put constraints on the kinds of data that can occur in a particular field (e.g., all numeric). Since schemas are founded on XML, they are hierarchical, so it is easier to create an unambiguous specification, and possible to determine the scope over which a comment is meant to apply. (Passi et al., 2005) **2:** A more complete way of specifying the semantics of a set of XML markup elements. XML schema supplies a complete grammar for specifying the structure of the elements, allowing one, for example, to define the cardinality of the offspring elements, default values, and so forth. (Zarri, 2005b) **3:** An alternative to DTDs, it is a schema language that assesses the validity of a well-formed element and attribute information items within an XML document. There are two major schema models: W3C XML Schema™ and Microsoft Schema™. (Chen, 2005b)

### Extensible Markup Language (XML) Structural Change

Not all changes to XML may cause structure changes the language when it is represented as a tree structure. In IT use, only insertion and deletion are called XML structural changes. (Zhao & Bhowmick, 2005)

### Extensible Markup Language (XML) Structural Clarification Mining

Concerned with distinguishing the similar structured documents based on content. (Nayak, 2005b)

### Extensible RDBMS

Relational DBMS implementing the concept of universal server. It allows the extension of the DBMS type system by enabling the definition of user-defined data types (UDTs), and the associated user-defined manipulation functions (UDFs). (Chang et al., 2005)

### Extensible Representation of Requirements

A way to represent easy requirements that were not necessarily identified nor truly considered in the requirements analysis. (Furtado, 2005)

### Extension

**1:** A Boolean function f that satisfies f(x)=1 for $x \in T$ and f(x)=0 for $x \in F$ for a given pdBf (T, F). (Boros et al., 2005) **2:** An extramural department or division that operates within a university and offer mainly continuing education and professional upgrade courses. Extensions are typical mainly to American universities. (Guri-Rosenblit, 2005a)

## Extension, Deep

Of a concept C, denotes the shallow extension of C union the deep extension of C's sons. (Sacco, 2006)

## Extension Mechanism

Specifies how model elements are customized and extended with new semantics. (Riesco et al., 2005)

## Extension, Shallow

Of a concept C, denotes the set of documents classified directly under C. (Sacco, 2006)

## Extensional Inference Rule

Two concepts A and B are related if there is at least one item d in the knowledge base which is classified at the same time under A (or under one of A's descendants) and under B (or under one of B's descendants). (Sacco, 2006)

## External Data

**1:** A broad term indicating data that is external to a particular company. Includes electronic and non-electronic formats. (Peter & Greenidge, 2005a) **2:** Data originating from other than the operational systems of a corporation. (Peter & Greenidge, 2005b) **3:** Traditionally, most of the data in a warehouse have come from internal operational systems such as order entry, inventory, or human resource data. However, external sources (i.e., demographic, economic, point-of-sale, market feeds, Internet) are becoming more and more prevalent and will soon be providing more content to the data warehouse than the internal sources. (Owrang O., 2006)

## External Environment

**1:** Comprises factors external to an organization—such as new technology, product developments, or changing rates of market growth—which an organization must respond to. (Baker & Coltman, 2005) **2:** Includes relevant work structure variables (e.g., task complexity) and other external forces (e.g., organizational climate) within the sociotechnical system that both act on and are acted upon by the organizational unit. (Cuevas et al., 2005) **3:** The set of conditions, trends, and forces essentially outside the control of organizational members. (Rowe et al., 2006)

## External Environmental Structure

The set of rules and resources offered by outside interests, including academic standards bodies, technology developers and vendors, industrial organizations, employers, and end users. (LeRouge & Webb, 2005)

## External Knowledge

The kind of knowledge that a firm needs in order to compete, but that is standard and available in an open market to any organization on the same conditions of price and functionality. Thus, it can be bought and sold, and therefore it is relatively easily integrated in a firm even if it is implicit and collective. (Andreu & Sieber, 2006)

## External Link

A URL address that connects to a site on an intranet or the Internet. (Baugher et al., 2005)

## External Metric

A metric used to measure attributes of the product that can be measured only with respect to how the product relates to its environment. (Xenos, 2006)

## External Stakeholder

Organizations exchange information and communicate with all external stakeholders, who can be divided into business partners and other stakeholders. (Boonstra & de Brock, 2006)

## External Support

Assistance from persons outside the firm. Some firms pay for such support by employing a consultant. Other common forms of external support include IS vendors and advice from peers—that is, managers in other firms. (Cragg & Suraweera, 2005)

## Externalization

A knowledge transfer mode that involves new explicit knowledge being derived from existing tacit knowledge. (Wickramasinghe, 2005)

## Extraction

To select the related fields from the Web logs. Traversal patterns typically require three fields: IP address, access time, and the page accessed. Other fields, such as referrer and user agent, can be used in cleansing and sessionization. (Yao & Xiao, 2005)

**E**

## Extraction Group Research Methodology (X-Group Methodology)

Refers to the combination of focus groups and forum messages discourse analysis. X-Group Methodology advances the identification of important actors in a community and the actual implementation of members' suggestions into their environment as an interaction within an immediate space of use. (Lambropoulos, 2006a)

## Extraction, Transformation, Load (ETL) System

**1:** A category of software that efficiently handles three essential components of the warehousing process. First, data must be extracted (removed from originating system), then transformed (reformatted and cleaned), and third, loaded (copied/appended) into the data warehouse database system. (Peter & Greenidge, 2005a) **2:** The system in charge of extracting data from internal transactional databases and other sources (e.g., external data), transforming it to accommodate the data warehouse schema, loading the data initially and refreshing the data periodically. The design of the ETL system is generally the most time-consuming task in the construction of a data warehouse. (Hernandez-Orallo, 2005a) **3:** Data warehousing functions that involve extracting data from outside sources, transforming it to fit business needs, and ultimately loading it into the data warehouse. ETL is an important part of data warehousing; it is the way data actually gets loaded into the warehouse. (Simitsis et al., 2005) **4:** A process by which the data warehouse is (re)populated from data in the data sources. During the process, relevant data is extracted from the source, adequately processed for integration, and loaded into the DW. (Badia, 2005c) **5:** A key transitional set of steps in migrating data from the source systems to the database housing the data warehouse. Extraction refers to drawing out the data from the source system, transformation concerns converting the data to the format of the warehouse, and loading involves storing the data in the warehouse. (Pang, 2005a) **6:** A set of database utilities used to extract information from one database, transform it, and load it into a second database. This represents processing overhead required to copy data from an external DBMS or file. (Rahman, 2005e) **7:** Describes the three essential steps in the process of data source integration: extracting data and schema from the sources, transforming it into a common format, and loading the data into an integration database. (Koeller, 2005)

## Extran

An external transaction that is requested by a mobile host to be performed in another external computing environment, using message communication. (Murthy & Krishnamurthy, 2005b)

## Extranet

**1:** A private network that uses Internet protocols and the public tele-communications system to share a business's information, data, or operations with external suppliers, vendors, or customers. (Vaast, 2005) **2:** Allowing an organization's external partners (i.e., pharmacies, insurance companies, vendors) to access a computer system via a username and password. (Cannoy & Iyer, 2006) **3:** A set of Internet-based applications that use standard protocols, middleware, and browser software that fulfill functional requirements to support supply-chain operations. (Ratnasingam, 2006)

## Extreme Programming

An agile system development methodology that decomposes very large projects into many small projects with minimal requirements and taking just a few weeks to complete, characterized by pair programming and refractoring. (Steinbach & Knight, 2005)

## Extrinsic Motivation

**1:** An external force that motivates a person. (Whitfield, 2005) **2:** Motivation that derives from what you obtain from engaging in an activity. An example of extrinsic motivation for using microcomputers is using it because you think it is useful for your job. (de Souza Dias, 2005) **3:** Motivation through factors external to the person being motivated. (Wishart, 2005) **4:** The motivation to engage in an activity as a means to an end, based on the belief that participation will result in desirable outcomes such as a reward or avoidance of punishment. (Hendriks & Sousa, 2006) **5:** Motivation that has a material or symbolic manifestation in the outside world, for example, a bonus, promotion, vacation, reputation, recognition, and so forth. (Ekbia & Hara, 2006)

## Eye Tracker

Device used to determine point-of-regard and to measure eye movements such as fixations, saccades, and regressions. Works by tracking the position of various distinguishing features of the eye, such as reflections of infrared light off the cornea, the boundary between the iris and sclera, or apparent pupil shape. (Poole & Ball, 2006)

## Eye Tracking

A technique whereby an individual's eye movements are measured so that the researcher knows where a person is looking at any given time and how the a person's eyes are moving from one location to another. (Poole & Ball, 2006)

## Eye-Mind Hypothesis

The principle at the origin of most eye-tracking research. Assumes that what a person is looking at indicates what the person currently is thinking about or attending to. Recording eye movements, therefore, can provide a dynamic trace of where a person's attention is being directed in relation to a visual display such as a system interface. (Poole & Ball, 2006)

# F

**F Value:** See *Fisher Value.*

**FA:** See *Facial Animation.*

### Face Detection
Given an arbitrary image, the goal of face detection is to determine whether or not there are any faces in the image, and if present, return the image location and extent of each face. (Tan & Zhang, 2006)

### Face Localization
Given a facial image, the goal of face localization is to determine the position of a single face. This is a simplified detection problem with the assumption that an input image contains only one face. (Tan & Zhang, 2006)

### Face Model
General information required for recreating faces in a computer graphics system, for example, geometrical parameters. (Arya, 2005)

### Face Model Feature
One of a set of features used to represent (model) the face or facial features, such as the width, height, and angle in a template of the eye, or all nodes and triangles in a 3D face mesh model. (Tan & Zhang, 2006)

### Face Recognition
A technique for identity verification or identification based on the users' facial features, such as positions of cheekbones, and positions and shapes of eyes, mouth, and nose. (Li, 2006)

### Face Space
The vector space spanned by the eigenfaces. (Lovell & Chen, 2005)

### Face Synthesis
A process of creating a talking head that is able to speak, display (appropriate) lip movements during speech, and display expressive facial movements. (Pantic, 2005b)

### Face-Based Interface
Regulating (at least partially) the command flow that streams between the user and the computer by means of facial signals. This means associating certain commands (e.g., mouse pointing, mouse clicking, etc.) with certain facial signals (e.g., gaze direction, winking, etc.). Face-based interface can be effectively used to free computer users from classic keyboard and mouse commands. (Pantic, 2005b)

### Face-to-Face (F2F)
**1:** Term used to describe the traditional classroom environment. (Blackmore et al., 2006) **2:** Communication occurring in the same physical domain. (Whateley et al., 2005) **3:** Communication requiring the synchronous presence of participants in space and time. (Beuschel et al., 2005)

### Face-to-Face Learning
Considered as a traditional environment in which the instructor and students meet in a classroom setting. (S.-K. Wang, 2005)

### Facet
One of several top-level (most general) concepts in a multi-dimensional taxonomy. In general, facets are independent and define a set of "orthogonal" conceptual coordinates. (Sacco, 2006)

### Facial Action Coding System (FACS)
**1:** A comprehensive system that can distinguish the most possible visually distinguishable facial movements. FACS

derives from an analysis of the anatomical basis of facial movement. Using FACS, it is possible to analyze any facial movement into anatomically based minimal action units (AUs). (Andrés del Valle, 2005) **2:** The most widely used and versatile method for measuring and describing facial behaviors which was developed in the 1970s by determining how the contraction of each facial muscle (singly and in combination with other muscles) changes the appearance of the face. (Tan & Zhang, 2006)

### Facial and Body Animation (FBA)

**1:** A part of the MPEG-4 specifications dealing with the definition and the animation at very low bit rate of an avatar represented as a segmented object. (Prêteux & Preda, 2005) **2:** This MPEG-4 system tool was designed for the compression and networked delivery of virtual human animation. The facial animation part is still in use, while the body animation part is being replaced by Bone-Based Animation (BBA) for the sake of genericity. (Di Giacomo et al., 2005)

### Facial Animation (FA)

The set of CG and CV techniques used to recreate facial motion and expression. We can classify animated characters in two groups: avatars and clones. An avatar is a general, standard representation of a human; a clone is the exact replication of an existing individual. (Andrés del Valle, 2005)

### Facial Animation Parameter (FAP)

The standard MPEG-4 defines 68 FAPs, each associated with the movement of specific vertices that compose a head mesh so to generate a different facial expression. (Andrés del Valle, 2005)

### Facial Deformation Model

Model that explains the non-rigid motions of human faces. The non-rigid motions are usually caused by speech and facial expressions. (Wen et al., 2005)

### Facial Expression Recognition

1: Classifying the facial expression to one facial action unit defined in FACS or a combination of action units, which is also called FACS encoding. (Tan & Zhang, 2006) 2: Classifying the facial expression to one basic emotional category or a combination of categories. Often, six basic emotions are used, including happiness, sadness, surprise, fear, anger, and disgust. (Tan & Zhang, 2006)

### Facial Feature

One of the prominent features of the face, which includes intransient facial features such as eyebrows, eyes, nose, mouth, chin, and so forth, and transient facial features such as the regions surrounding the mouth and the eyes. (Tan & Zhang, 2006)

### Facial Motion Analysis

Procedure of estimating facial motion parameters. It can also be called "face tracing" and can be used to extract human face motion information from video, which is useful input for intelligent video surveillance and human-computer interaction. (Wen et al., 2005)

### Facial Motion Synthesis

Procedure of creating synthetic face animations. Examples include text-driven face animation and speech-driven face animation. It can be used as an avatar-based visual interface for human-computer interaction. (Wen et al., 2005)

### Facilitated Meeting

A group of people getting together to explore the issues with the help of a facilitator. The facilitator brings a methodology of facilitation which provides process support and content management. Process support heightens the effectiveness of relational behaviors in the group (e.g., everyone getting airtime) and feeling free to share controversial ideas. Content support enables the mass of complexity shared during the meeting to be made sense of. (Shaw et al., 2006)

### Facilitation

**1:** A teaching style that is student centered. Encourages self-directed learning. The instructor is not a content transmitter, but rather a coach and partner in student learning. (Ordonez, 2005) **2:** The leadership contributions of structuring, enabling, and encouraging good group interaction and process, normally with low reliance on positional authority and content expertise, but high reliance on communication, and interpersonal skills and presence. (Cargill, 2006a)

### Facilitator

**1:** A faculty role that allows learners to take a more active role in learning and determining how they will learn. The role of a faculty member as a facilitator is to guide learners in connecting with the learner's knowledge and experience. (Stavredes, 2005a) **2:** A knowledgeable guide

**F**

for a discussion, activity, or course. In many cases, a course facilitator or faculty facilitator acts as a mentor for a course, providing guidance, assistance, or trusted advice to the student. (Riffee & Sessums, 2005) **3:** A person who acts in such a way as to allow others to take an active role in learning, especially in groups. Teachers in this role typically assist students by asking probing questions and by stimulating discussion. (Kukulska-Hulme, 2005) **4:** A community member who coordinates the activities within the community's place. (Porto Bellini & Vargas, 2006) **5:** An AHIMA member who volunteers to support and champion the success of a particular community. Such a volunteer monitors activity within the community, encourages member participation, organizes community events, posts resources, and reviews and approves all submitted resources. (Zender, 2006) **6:** Someone helping people self-discover new approaches and solutions to problems. (Whitfield, 2005) **7:** An instructor who utilizes the facilitative method for course delivery, is focused on a student-centered environment, is attentive to students needs, and assists students in achieving self-actualization. (Ordonez, 2005)

**FACS:** See *Facial Action Coding System.*

## Fact (Multi-Dimensional Datum)

**1:** A single elementary datum in an OLAP system, the properties of which correspond to dimensions and measures. (Tininini, 2005b) **2:** An entity of an application that is the subject of decision-oriented analysis. It is usually represented graphically by means of a table or, using a metaphor, by a data cube. (Rafanelli, 2005) **3:** Basic, irreducible data item that is stored in the data warehouse. It represents the basic unit of business analysis and therefore must represent the basic activity of the enterprise under consideration. (Badia, 2005c) **4:** Element recorded in a warehouse (e.g., each product sold in a shop) and whose characteristics (i.e., measures) are the object of the analysis (e.g., quantity of a product sold in a shop). (Schneider, 2005)

## Fact Table

**1:** A database table that stores the base facts that consist of values of different metrics for different combinations of dimension values. (Deshpande & Ramasamy, 2005) **2:** A member of the star schema data model which records data about a set of phenomena of interest. (Pourabbas, 2005b) **3:** A table of (integrated) elementary data grouped and aggregated in the multi-dimensional querying

process. (Tininini, 2005a) **4:** The central table in a star schema, containing the basic facts or measures of interest. Dimension fields are also included (as foreign keys) to link to each dimension table. (Bellatreche & Mohania, 2005)

## Faction

In the most basic form, faction is simply street creditability or worthiness in the eyes of NPCs, as it is inevitable that there will be enemies among the races. When players make friends with one particular race, this can consequently make you disliked or hated by another, so as your faction goes up with one race, it will go down with another. This effect is not an all or nothing, but a gradual process. (Griffiths et al., 2006)

## Factor

The expressed requirement of the customer. (Lacaze et al., 2006)

## Factor Analysis

**1:** A process used to identify statistically significant constructs underlying a set of data. (W.B. Martz, Jr. & V.K. Reddy, 2005) **2:** Any of several methods for reducing correlational data to a smaller number of dimensions or factors; beginning with a correlation matrix, a small number of components or factors are extracted that are regarded as the basic variables that account for the interrelations observed in the data. (Colmenares & Otieno, 2005) **3:** Method of grouping questions based on the correlation of each question to other questions. (Witta & Lee, 2005)

## Factor Score

A measure of a factor's relative weight to others; it is obtained using linear combinations of variables. (Lee, Peterson, et al., 2005)

## Factual Data

Data that include demographic information such as name, gender, and birth date. It also may contain information derived from transactional data such as someone's favorite beverage. (Cook, 2005)

## Factual Data Analysis

Another term for data mining, often used by government agencies. (Cook, 2005)

## Faculty

The collection of teachers at a school, college, or university. (Shaw, 2005)

## Faculty Development
A purposeful, institutionalized approach to doing that which helps faculty do their work better as individuals within an institution and within the collective enterprise of higher education. (Kinuthia, 2005)

## Faculty Function
Basic functions of faculty in a cost analysis generally include preparation, presentation, and assessment of student work. (Berg, 2005c)

## Faculty Satisfaction
The quality principle that recognizes faculty as central to quality learning. (Moore et al., 2005)

## Faded Information Field
A group of server machines connected in a topology that allows information documents to be distributed in a fashion that can improve retrieval efficiency, typically through some algorithmic computation to determine server locations. (Quah et al., 2006b)

## Failed Project
A projects that is cancelled before completion, never implemented, or scrapped following installation. (Dalcher, 2005)

## Failed-Out
A student who failed a course (or courses) and did not meet the academic standard. Therefore, he or she has been automatically removed from the program. Failed-outs are different from no-shows since the failing grade resulted from the lack of academic competence rather than abandoning behavior. (Chyung, 2005)

## Failure
The inability of a system or component to perform its required functions within specified performance requirements. (Schneidewind, 2005)

## Failure Analysis
Computing the time it takes for a manufactured component to fail. (Chen, Oppenheim, et al., 2005)

## Failure, Error, Fault
A failure is the event of a system generating a result that does not satisfy the system specification or of the system not generating a result that is required by the system specification. An error is incorrect information, or lack of information, within the system that will, unless detected and corrected, lead to failure of the system. A fault is the original cause of the error. (Zhao et al., 2005)

## Failure Recovery
Recovery in a situation where log-files and the current database or an old database copy are available. (Frank, 2005a)

## Failure to Enroll Rate
The condition that arises if the biometric sample captured is not of proper quality that a template can be generated from it. (Vatsa et al., 2005)

## Fair Use
**1:** A term defined in the U.S. Copyright Act. It states the exemption for schools to some copyright regulations. (This exemption pre-dates many current educational applications of technology and may be not address some online learning situations.) (Sales, 2005) **2:** The exception to the rights of the copyright owner set out under section 107 of the United States Copyright Act of 1976. This allows for a limited amount of personal copying in the context of activities such as criticism, teaching, scholarship, and research. The freedom to copy under this section is widely misunderstood, and it is important to note that the courts have quite tightly restricted the use of this exclusion. Generally, this exception will only hold if the use is non-commercial, relates to a factual work of a small amount, and is not done in a way that impacts on the commercial market for the original. Fair use only applies in the United States, and while some exceptions for similar uses exist in other jurisdictions, the details differ significantly. Despite this, the term is commonly used internationally to describe uses of copyright material that are considered defendable exceptions to the normal regime of protection. (Marshall, 2005)

## Fairness
**1:** A subjective term defining the level to which a student feels he or she was treated fairly by the professor with respect to the class, including but not limited to test questions, grading, schedule flexibility, and so forth. (Martz & Reddy, 2005) **2:** It is recognized that the greater the diversity in the methods of assessment, the fairer the assessment is to students. Therefore, assessment needs to embrace a variety of kinds of activity, so that candidates have a greater opportunity to demonstrate their skills on at least some of the assessment occasions they encounter. (Diamadis & Polyzos, 2005)

## Fairness and Justice

The philosophical view that the moral act is the one that treats similarly situated people in similar ways with regard to both process and outcome. (Gilbert, 2005)

## False Acceptance Rate

**1:** Rate of acceptance of a forged signature as a genuine signature by a handwritten signature verification system. (Chakravarty et al., 2005b) **2:** The probability of incorrectly identifying any impostor against a valid user's biometric template. (Vatsa et al., 2005) **3:** A case where an individual is authenticated when they were not the person that enrolled the original sample. (Fleming, 2005a)

## False Alarm

A case in which a candidate match is found during preprocessing step of a similarity analysis algorithm when a match does not really exist. Minimization of false alarms is important because extracting a large amount of false candidates in early steps of an algorithm causes performance degradation that will not improve the accuracy of the result. (Sayal, 2005)

## False Discovery Rate (FDR)

The expected proportion of false positives among the objects selected as relevant. (Mukherjee, 2005)

## False Dismissal

A case in which a candidate match is eliminated during the preprocessing step of a similarity analysis algorithm when a match does exist. Minimization of false dismissals is important because it reduces accuracy of the algorithm. (Sayal, 2005)

## False Drops

A property of signature files. Since signature files use hash to activate bits corresponding to the set elements, possibility exists for one or more set elements setting the same bits. When a query signature is evaluated using signatures in signature files, there is a probability that the signatures might match, but the actual sets might not match. These are called false drops. (Ramasamy & Deshpande, 2005)

## False Negative

**1:** A potential usability problem discovered in a usability inspection that upon analysis is incorrectly eliminated by the analyst as an improbable problem. The discovered problem is confirmed in real use as causing difficulties to users. (Woolrych & Hindmarch, 2006) **2:** The error committed when a truly relevant object is not selected.

More generally, a false negative occurs when the null hypothesis is erroneously accepted. Also called Type II error. (Mukherjee, 2005) **3:** A mail message that the filter tags as ham but is actually spam. (de Freitas & Levene, 2006a)

## False Positive

**1:** A filtering system can make two types of errors: false acceptance and false rejection. The latter is a false positive. A spam filter can wrongly let spam through, or wrongly filter real e-mail as spam. In false acceptance, it is not doing its job, while in false positives, it is doing it too well. Decreasing one type of error tends to increase the other, as with Type I and Type II errors in experimental design. As the spam-filter catch rate rises above 99.99%, the number of false positives also rises. (Whitworth, 2006b) **2:** A prediction of a usability problem reported in a usability inspection that in reality is not a problem to the real users. (Woolrych & Hindmarch, 2006) **3:** The error committed when an object is selected as relevant when it is in fact irrelevant. More generally, a false positive occurs when the null hypothesis is erroneously rejected. Also called Type I error. (Mukherjee, 2005) **4:** A mail message that the filter tags as spam but is actually ham. (de Freitas & Levene, 2006a)

## False Rejection

A case where an individual is not authenticated, although he or she has previously enrolled biometric data. (Fleming, 2005a)

## False Rejection Rate

**1:** Rate of rejection of a genuine signature as a forged signature by a handwritten signature verification system. (Chakravarty et al., 2005b) **2:** The probability of incorrectly rejecting the valid users or failing to verify the legitimate claimed identity of any user. (Vatsa et al., 2005) **3:** The probability that a biometric system will fail to identify an enrollee or verify the legitimate claimed identity of an enrollee. (Vatsa et al., 2005)

## Falsification Testing

A method for testing the accuracy of predictions made during usability inspections. (Woolrych & Hindmarch, 2006)

## Familiarity-Based Trust

Knowing what to expect of the trusted party based on previous interactions with it. (Paravastu & Gefen, 2006)

## Family PC Program

A program launched in Tunisia in April 2001 to help households acquire a PC and printer at a total cost of 1000 TD (US$700). (El Louadi, 2005a)

## Fantasy Role-Playing (FRP)

Like being and playing in an improvisational drama or free-form theatre, in which the participants (actors) adopt imaginary characters or parts that have personalities, motivations, and backgrounds different from their own. (Medeni & Medeni, 2006)

## Fantasy Role-Playing Game

A type of game that allows players to role-play imaginary characters in an imaginary setting. Usually, role-players engage in cooperatively creating a story, each restricting themselves to the character they themselves introduced to the story. (Medeni & Medeni, 2006)

## Fantasy-Based Virtual Community

A virtual environment where users create their own avatars and personalities, and interact with other users through role-playing fantasies. (Jong & Mahatanankoon, 2006)

**FAP:** See *Facial Animation Parameter.*

## FAQ

Frequently asked question. (Toland et al., 2005b)

## Farmers and Explorers

Two typologies of data warehouse users. Farmers are users of data warehouses and other analytical tools that generate periodical reports, such as sales by week, category, and department. Explorers are more ambitious users of data warehouses which try to better understand the data, to look for patterns in the data, or to generate new reports. (Hernandez-Orallo, 2005a)

**FAST:** See *Fast Algorithm for Splitting Trees.*

## Fast Algorithm for Splitting Trees (FAST)

A splitting procedure to grow a binary tree using a suitable mathematical property of the impurity proportional reduction measure to find out the optimal split at each node without trying out necessarily all candidate splits. (Siciliano & Conversano, 2005)

## Fat Client/Server Architecture

A client/server network architecture where the client (PCs or workstations on which users run applications) performs the bulk of the data-processing operations while the data itself is stored on the server. (Rashid, 2005)

## Fault (Crash, Timing, Omission, Commission, Byzantine)

A crash fault occurs when a component operates correctly up to some point in time, after which it produces no further results. A timing fault occurs when a component produces results at the wrong time. An omission fault occurs when a component produces some results but not others. A commission fault occurs when a component generates incorrect results. A Byzantine or malicious fault is a form of commission fault in which a component generates incorrect results intentionally to mislead the algorithms or components of the system. (Zhao et al., 2005)

## Fault Detector, Analyzer, Notifier

A fault detector monitors the occurrence of faults in a component. A fault analyzer subscribes to fault reports from a fault notifier and aggregates multiple related fault reports into a single fault report. A fault notifier receives fault reports from fault detectors and fault analyzers, and supplies fault reports to subscribers for those reports. (Zhao et al., 2005)

## Fault Tolerance

The ability to provide continuous service, even in the presence of faults. (Zhao et al., 2005)

**FBA:** See *Facial and Body Animation.*

**FCL:** See *Fostering Communities of Learners.*

**FD:** See *Field Dependence.*

**FDBS:** See *Federated Database Schema.*

**FDI:** See *Foreign Direct Investment.*

**FDLP:** See *Federal Depository Library Program.*

**FDR:** See *False Discovery Rate.*

## Feature

**1:** An attribute derived from transforming the original multimedia object by using an analysis algorithm; a feature is represented by a set of numbers (also called feature vector). (Hentea, 2005c) **2:** Quantity or quality describing an instance. (Jourdan et al., 2005) **3:** Information that can be gathered to describe a raw trace such as angles between sampled points, lengths, and the speed of the sketched trace. (Mohamed & Ottmann, 2006)

## Feature Extraction

**1:** A subject of multimedia processing that involves applying algorithms to calculate and extract some attributes for describing the media. (Wei & Li, 2005) **2:** The process to obtain a group of features with the characters we need from the original data set. It usually uses a transform (e.g., principal component analysis) to obtain a group of features at one time of computation. (Chu & Wang, 2005) **3:** Use of one or more transformations of the input features to produce more useful features. (Hentea, 2005c)

## Feature Reduction Method

The goal of a feature reduction method is to identify the minimum set of non-redundant features (e.g., SNPs, genes) that are useful in classification. (Kusiak & Shah, 2005)

## Feature Selection

**1:** A process of choosing an optimal subset of features from original features, according to a certain criterion. (Yu & Liu, 2005) **2:** The process of selecting some features we need from all the original features. It usually measures the character (e.g., t-test score) of each feature first, then chooses some features we need. (Chu & Wang, 2005) **3:** The process of identifying the most effective subset of the original features. (Hentea, 2005c) **4:** The task of identifying and selecting a useful subset of features from a large set of redundant, perhaps irrelevant features. (Jourdan et al., 2005) **5:** The process of identifying the most effective subset of the original features to use in data analysis such as clustering. (Huang, 2005) **6:** The process of identifying those input attributes that contribute significantly to building a predictive model for a specified output or target. (Mani et al., 2005)

## Feature Space

The higher dimensional space that results from mapping the input space, as opposed to the input space occupied by the training examples. (Awad & Khan, 2005)

## Feature Vector

**1:** A vector in which every dimension represents a property of a 3D structure. A good feature vector captures similarity and dissimilarity of 3D structures. (X. Wang, 2005) **2:** Data that describes the content of the corresponding multimedia object. The elements of the feature vector represent the extracted descriptive information with respect to the utilized analysis. (Bretschneider & Kao, 2005)

## Feature-Based Image Retrieval

Based on specific visual characteristics called "features" and considered at a low abstraction level. Features are commonly referred to perceptive attributes of images, such as color, texture, shape, and so forth, of images. (Y.-J. Zhang, 2005a)

## Feature-Level Architecture

In this type of architecture, modality fusion operates at a low level of modality processing. The recognition process in one modality can influence the recognition process in another modality. Feature-level architectures generally are considered appropriate for tightly related and synchronized modalities, such as speech and lip movements. (Bourguet, 2006)

**FEC:** See *Forwarding Equivalence Class.*

## Federal Depository Library Program (FDLP)

Federal program of disseminating government program information products in all media to participating libraries. (Inoue & Bell, 2005)

## Federal Model

A hybrid configuration of centralization and decentralization in which decision making is differentiated across divisional and corporate units. (Peterson, 2005)

## Federated Database

A type of multi-database in which component databases preserve their autonomy. (Unal et al., 2006)

## Federated Database Schema (FDBS)

Collection of autonomous cooperating database systems working in either a homogenous environment—that is, dealing with schemas of databases having the same data model and identical database management systems—or a heterogeneous environment. (Bounif, 2005)

## Federated Database System

**1:** A network of independent and autonomous databases cooperating in a loosely coupled manner to share and exchange information. (Leong, 2005a) **2:** A system that integrates a number of pre-existing autonomous database management systems (DBMSs) that can be homogeneous or heterogeneous. They can use different underlying data models, data definition and manipulation facilities, and transaction management and concurrency control mechanisms. A DBMS in the federation can be integrated by a mediator providing a unified view of data: a global schema, a global query language, a global catalog, and a global transaction manager. The underlying transaction model considers, in general, a set of transactions synchronized by a global transaction. Synchronization is achieved using protocols such as the Two-Phase Commit (2PC) Protocol. (Vargas-Solar, 2005)

## Federated Information System (FIS)

An information system is considered federated when it supports interoperation among several autonomous and possibly heterogeneous information systems, by means of a shared global data schema. (De Antonellis et al., 2005)

## Federated Representational Model

An approach for building representational models according to which each information system defines some aspects of an entity model, contributing thus to a "global" entity model. (Lepouras et al., 2006)

## Federated Web Service

Usually, problems like authorization are handled on a network-by-network basis—a given login may only be valid to a single network or site. Federation provides a means to transcend this limitation. In our example, groups could federate by declaring trust in each other, thus permitting authorization across multiple organizations. (Gaedke et al., 2005)

## Feedback

A process whereby an input variable is fed back by the output variable. For example, an increased (or decreased) customer base leads to an increase (or decrease) in sales from word of mouth, which then is fed back to the customer base, increasingly or decreasingly. (Qudrat-Ullah, 2006)

## Feedback Learning

Deals with learning based on the input-process-output-feedback process in which three laws shape the learning process: (1) exercise law: reiteration strengthens the connection between response and stimulus; (2) effect law: the succession of stimulus-response is not enough for learning, and reinforcement is needed; and (3) disposition law: achieving goals is a reinforcement particular to every action that has a clear aim. (Xodo, 2005)

## Feedback Loop

A self-perpetuating mechanism of change. (O'Looney, 2006)

## Feedback Technique

One of a number of methods such as questionnaires used to acquire information or data on the question under study. (Martz & Shepherd, 2005)

## Feedforward Neural Network

A special type of neural network where processing elements are arranged in layers and the information is one-directional from input layer to hidden layer(s) to output layer. (G.P. Zhang, 2005)

**FHSS:** See *Frequency Hopping Spread Spectrum.*

**FI:** See *Frequent Itemset.*

## Fiankoma Method

An approach to community, working with ICTs emphasizing active authorship. (Pryor, 2005)

## Fiber Optic

A technology that uses bundles of glass fiber to transmit data at high speed by rapid laser light signal pulses. It can carry a much greater amount of data than metal cable. (D. Stern, 2005)

## Fiber Optic Cable

**1:** A transmission medium that provides high data rates and low errors. Glass or plastic fibers are woven together to form the core of the cable. The core is surrounded by a glass or plastic layer, called the cladding. The cladding is covered with plastic or other material for protection. The cable requires a light source, most commonly laser or light-emitting diodes. (Raisinghani & Ghanem, 2005) **2:** Composed of one or more optical fibers, a fiber-optic cable transmits data as a lightwave over long distances at a high speed. (Harris, 2005)

## Fiber-to-the-Home (FTTH)

The use of fiber-optic cable, for the provisioning of narrowband and broadband services to the residential customer, rather than traditional copper wiring. (Kelic, 2005)

## Fibration

A basic construct of category theory. Roughly, it is a triple $(C, B, f)$ with $C$ a category (of, say, models), $B$ another category (say, meta-models) called base, and $f: C \rightarrow B$ a functor (mapping) between categories (that assigns to each model its meta-model). Given a base object (meta-

$M{\in}B$, $C$—objects (models, schemas) $S$ for which $S.f = M$ and $C$—arrows between them $s$: $S{\to}S'$ for which $s.f = \mathbf{id}_M$ (identity mapping of M), form a category (of models in the meta-model $M$), $C_M$. This category is called the fiber over M. Fibers are mutually connected in the following way. Let $m$: $M'{\to}M$ be a base arrow (meta-model interpretation) and $S$ be an object over $M$, $S.f = M$. Then there is an object $S^*$ over $M'$, $S^*.f = M'$, and an arrow $m^*$: $S^*{\to}S$ over $m$, $m^*.f = m$, having some remarkable properties (their formulation is too technical to be presented here). In the MMt context, object $S^*$ is the same model $S$, but its elements are renamed in terms of meta-model $M'$ as governed by the interpretation $m$, and $m^*$ is the renaming mapping. The technical properties just mentioned abstract this intuition in terms of morphisms in $C$ and $B$. (Diskin, 2005)

## Fidelity

The measure of how well the rules extracted from a complicated model mimic the behavior of that model. (Zhou, 2005)

## Field Creation

In traditional ethnographic field research (see ethnography, fieldwork), an anthropologist would spend time in a "field site" (i.e., a village belonging to a tribe) that logically predated the existence of a research project. Field creation involves this process, only in reverse. In this case, an anthropologist or other researcher constructs a particular "site" that then attracts interest and generates a network of social interaction around it—"informants" come to the "site" created by the researcher. The creation of a Web-based information resource that fosters a community of interacting interests, and then becomes a site of research about itself, is one example of field creation. (Forte, 2005)

## Field Dependence (FD)

Measures a person's ability to separate an item from an organized field or to overcome an embedded context. (Crossland, 2005)

## Field Learning

Derives rules by looking at the field of the values of each attribute in all the instances of the training data set. (Dai, 2005a)

## Field-Area Network

Real-time network on the field level (shop floor) of industrial firms' communication systems for the interconnection of automation devices, for example, assembly lines, production cells, or single machines. Depending on the nature of the business, different types of FANs are applied, which are either based on field buses or Internet technologies. Well-known FANs are, for example, Profibus, DeviceNet, CAN Open, and SERCOS. (Blecker, 2006a)

## Fieldwork

Often used interchangeably with ethnography (see definition), it is, in fact, less precise and much broader as a concept. Fieldwork may be ethnographic or not, qualitative or quantitative, short term or long term. What defines fieldwork is a situation of doing research outside of the confines of a laboratory or a library, gathering primary data in person, and locating oneself within a given social formation (e.g., a neighborhood, political party, social club, school, hospital, etc.). Fieldwork in the ethnographic mode typically involves an anthropologist relocating to a distant society to learn and document another culture, usually involving periods of continuous stay of a year or more, and relying heavily on Participant Observation as a research method. (Forte, 2005)

## Figuration

As defined in image theory, a complex construction comprising multiple images. Figurations are inherently less efficient for extracting information than images, according to image theory. (Crossland, 2005)

## File Format

The way a file stores information—the way in which a file is saved. The file format depends on the content that is being stored, the application that is being used, and the compression algorithm that is being used. (Prata, 2005)

## File Server

A piece of equipment that allows one to distribute a software program from a single source to a number of computers. (Switala, 2005)

## File Transfer Protocol (FTP)

**1:** An application and network protocol for transferring files between host computers. Such a protocol allows users to quickly transfer text and binary files to and from a distant or local PC. (Gillani, 2005b) **2:** A computer protocol used for accessing a remote computer over the Internet and retrieving files from it. (Kirlidog, 2005) **3:** A protocol used to transfer files over a TCP/IP network (Internet, UNIX, etc.). (Parikh & Parolia, 2005) **4:** A protocol to transfer files from one computer to another over the

Internet. (Moreira & da Silva, 2005) **5:** A convention for the transfer of files across computer networks. (Murphy, 2005a) **6:** Protocol that allows users to copy files between their local system and any system they can reach on the network. (Kontolemakis et al., 2005)

## Filter
A saved set of chosen criteria that specifies a subset of information in a data warehouse. (Nigro & González Císaro, 2005b)

## Filter Technique
Any technique for reducing the number of models, with the aim of avoiding overwhelming the user. (Butler & Webb, 2005)

## Filter-Based Information Access Approach
System responses are filtered on the basis of a rudimentary user profile storing long-term user interests. (Koutrika, 2005)

## Filter-Refinement Processing
A technique used in query processing composed of the filter step and the refinement step. The filter step discards parts of the database that cannot contribute to the final answer and determines a set of candidate objects, which are then processed by the refinement step. Filtering is usually enhanced by efficient indexing schemes for improved performance. (Kontaki et al., 2005)

## Filtering
**1:** A collective term for techniques that automatically select product attributes that meet customer profiles and preferences by applying predefined rules, similarities, or clustering. (Blecker, 2006b) **2:** A technique that selects specific things according to criteria of similarity with particular patterns. (Nabuco et al., 2006)

## Filtering Machine
Filtering is performed autonomously by a set of specialized source agents dispatched by the agent-based filter. We introduced a new automatic navigation technique: information ants. The ant-like agents carry the warehouse profiles. New documents are parsed, indexed, and matched with all profiles respectively. If a document matches the profile, it is downloaded and re-indexed in order to store it in a Data Warehouse Library (DWL). (Wecel et al., 2005)

## Financial Distress
A company is said to be under financial distress if it is unable to pay its debts as they become due, which is aggravated if the value of the firm's assets is lower than its liabilities. (Galvão et al., 2005)

## Financial Information Exchange (FIX)
A vendor-neutral standard-message-format protocol for describing real-time security transactions. FIX is a public-domain specification owned and maintained by FIX Protocol, Ltd. The protocol supports all electronic conversations between brokers and other financial institutions. (Saha, 2006b)

## Financial Intermediary
A bank, securities firm, or other financial institution that collects deposits and makes loans, manages the risk associated with the loan process, and/or facilitates the flow of capital between operating units and the economy. (Roofe, 2005)

## Financial Service
Providing users services of financial issue (e.g., mobile banking, mobile shopping, etc.). (Lee & Pai, 2005)

## Financial Virtual Community
A Virtual Community focusing on financial products and services from a consumer perspective. (Kardaras & Karakostas, 2006)

## Financing Models
A model that provides capital to the public sector. Exemplary financing models are factoring, lending, or borrowing (finance market models); leasing, renting, or contracting out (reward models); and marketing of one's own resources or sponsoring (fundraising). (Knust & Hagenhoff, 2005)

## Financing Round
One of a number of successive stages of financing received by a new venture (seed, first, second, etc.); also called tranch; may be an 'up round' or a 'down round' (in an up round, the value of the venture has increased since the previous round). (Craig, 2006b)

## Fingerprint
Also called a label, this is a feature of the carrier and is used to distinguish it from other carriers. Moreover, it

allows the copyrighted owner to trace pirates if the carrier is redisseminated illegally. The major difference between watermarking and fingerprinting is whether the identity of the transmitter or that of the recipient is embedded in the carrier. (Lou et al., 2006)

## Fingerprint Scanning
Enables the identification of an individual based on the analysis of unique patterns and ridges found in a fingerprint. (Scott et al., 2006)

## Fingerprinting
**1:** A technique for identity verification or identification based on the users' fingerprint features, such as location and orientation of bifurcations and endings of ridges, peaks, and valleys. (Li, 2006) **2:** A technique to associate a single—and small—representation of an audio signal that is robust to usual audio deformations. Used for identification. (Pachet, 2006) **3:** Used for calling the hidden serial numbers or anything else that should allow the copyright owner to identify which reseller broke the license agreement. It is used for multi-level document distribution. (Nesi & Spinu, 2005)

## Finite Element Method
**1:** Numerical method to solve the differential equations with boundary/initial conditions over a domain. (Kanapady & Lazarevic, 2005) **2:** A second approach to simulate soft bodies and deformations. It is also used to model fabrics by considering its surface as a continuum and not a fixed set of points. This method is more accurate but slower to compute. (Volino et al., 2005)

## Finite Impulse Response (FIR) Filter
**1:** A digital filter with a finite impulse response. FIR filters are always stable. FIR filters have only zeros (all poles are at the origin). (Jovanovic-Dolecek, 2005a) **2:** This digital filter can be designed to have linear phase; it filters with the symmetric impulse response. The main disadvantage is high complexity. (Jovanovic-Dolecek & Díaz-Carmona, 2005)

**FIPA:** See *Foundation for Intelligent Physical Agents.*

**FIPSE:** See *Fund for the Improvement of Post-Secondary Education.*

**FIR Filter:** See *Finite Impulse Response Filter.*

## Firewall
**1:** A combination of hardware and software that prevents unauthorized access to network resources—including information and applications. (Tassabehji, 2005a) **2:** A set of related programs that reside on a network gateway server that protects the resources of a private network from users from other networks. (Dudding, 2005) **3:** A system that implements a set of security rules to enforce access control to a network from outside intrusions. (Syed et al., 2005b) **4:** Special software used to prevent unauthorized access to a company's confidential data from the Internet through filtering all network packets entering the firewall at one or more levels of network protocols. (Wang, Cheng, & Cheng, 2006a) **5:** The set of related programs, located at a network gateway server, that protects the resources of a private network from users from other networks. Basically, a firewall, working closely with a router program, filters all network packets to determine whether to forward them toward their destination. A firewall is often installed away from the rest of the network so that no incoming request can get directly at private network resources. (Vaast, 2005) **6:** Hardware or software to prevent unauthorized users from gaining access to a computer or network. (Friedman, 2005)

## First Generation (1G)
**1:** A first-generation system is analog, circuit-based, narrowband, and suitable for voice communication only. (Lei et al., 2005a) **2:** An old-fashioned analog mobile phone system capable of handling very limited or no data at all. (Akhtar, 2005)

## First Story Detection
A Topic Detection and Tracking (TDT) component that identifies whether a new document belongs to an existing topic or a new topic. (Chung et al., 2005)

## First-Person Perspective
The visualization of the gaming environment through the eyes of the character. (Ip & Jacobs, 2006)

**FIS:** See *Federated Information System.*

## Fisher Exact Test
A statistical test that can distinguish differences in data sets with binary categories and small sizes. In our case, 19 total students with two choices (agree-disagree). (Martz & Shepherd, 2005)

## Fisher Value (F Value)

**1:** A statistical distribution, used here to indicate the probability that an ANOVA model is good. In the ANOVA calculations, it is the ratio of squared variances. A large number translates to confidence in the model. (Morantz, 2005) **2:** Combines recall and precision in a single efficiency measure (it is the harmonic mean of precision and recall): $F = 2 * (recall * precision) / (recall + precision)$. (Song, Song, Hu, & Han, 2005)

## Fit/Alignment

Terms used to explain the relationship between IT and strategy. The IT strategy should work in synergy with the organization's strategy. These terms have their roots in the meta-theory contingency theory. (Baker & Coltman, 2005)

## Fitness for Use

Describes the many variables that need to be considered when evaluating the quality of an information product. (Chengalur-Smith et al., 2005)

## Fitness Landscape

Optimization space due to the characteristics of the fitness measure used to define the evolutionary computation process. (Muruzábal, 2005)

## Five Forces Model

A theoretical framework proposed by Michael Porter that can be used to analyze the relative attractiveness of an industry from five different dimensions. (Wang, Ding, et al., 2006)

## Five Pillars

The Sloan-C quality elements of learning effectiveness, cost effectiveness, access, faculty satisfaction, and student satisfaction. (Moore et al., 2005)

**FIX:** See *Financial Information Exchange.*

## Fixation

The moment when the eyes are relatively stationary, taking in or encoding information. Fixations last for 218 milliseconds on average, with a typical range of 66 to 416 milliseconds. (Poole & Ball, 2006)

## Fixed Context of Use

Traditional user interface design and testing assumes a single domain, with the users always using the same computer to undertake tasks alone or in collaboration with others. (Chan & Fang, 2005)

## Fixed Cost

One of the set of one-time costs that must be incurred for an activity to occur. (Fisher, 2005)

## Fixed Weighting

"Optimal" weights are estimated and are used unchanged to combine forecasts for a number of periods. (C.K. Chan, 2005)

## Flame War

The repetitive exchange of offensive messages between members of a discussion forum which can eventually escalate and degenerate an exchange of injuries. (Gurău, 2006)

## Flaming

Posting a personally offensive message, as a response to an opinion expressed on a discussion forum. (Gurău, 2006)

## Flaming Episode

An inappropriate, rude, or hostile exchange that occurs in an asynchronous discussion group. (Shaw, 2005)

## Flash™

**1:** A multimedia authoring tool in which interactive learning objects may be created. (Kaur et al., 2005) **2:** A tool that is a registered trademark of Macromedia and was originally created to allow developers to create simple animations or movies that could be inserted into a Web page and displayed on any computer that had the appropriate browser plug-in. (Burrage & Pelton, 2005)

## Flash Crowd Problem

Occurs when the request load overwhelms some aspect of a Web site's infrastructure, such as the front-end Web server, network equipment or bandwidth, or the back-end transaction-processing infrastructure. The resulting overload can crash a site or cause unusually high response times. (Katsaros & Manolopoulos, 2005a)

## Flash Memory

A kind of non-volatile storage similar to EEPROM, but updating can only be done either in blocks or for the entire chip, making it easy to update. (Hu, Yeh, et al., 2006)

**F**

**Flash Player**
A multiple-platform client that Web users must download and install (a browser plug-in) in order to view and interact with Macromedia Flash™ content. (Barone, 2005)

**Flexibility**
**1:** The ease with which a system or component can be modified for use in applications or environments other than those for which it was originally designed. A flexible system may be transformed by IT professionals and customized by end users. (Vaast, 2005) **2:** The host- and the IP-multicast are flexible, and it is easy to change the topology of the multicast tree. (Hosszu, 2005a) **3:** Virtual organizations are, by their nature, flexible. Traditional organizational structures are rooted in the physical world and rely on structures, unalterable networks, and specific locations to function properly. Because of this, when it becomes necessary to introduce change into a specific organization, a barrier is reached where further alteration requires physical, costly modifications. A virtual organization is unhindered by these problems. These structures are designed so that they can operate regardless of time or place, independent of existing physical realities. (J. Lee, 2005)

**Flexible Attribute**
An attribute is called flexible if its value can be changed in time. (Ras et al., 2005)

**Flexible Calendar Option**
Typically, school districts are bound to a relatively fixed calendar, either by state or local policy. Flexible calendar option refers to one of a variety of programs that might include year-round schooling, alternate calendars, or alternate daily schedules. (Glick, 2005a)

**Flexible Job Shop**
A shop in which resources are flexible and can execute many types of tasks with variable performances according to the assignment choices. (Kacem, 2005)

**Flexible Learning**
**1:** A combination of varied teaching practices, including applied research and investigative projects within a flexible learning mode, that is aimed at maximizing learner engagement through action learning methodologies and advanced technologies. The key focus driving educational design is meeting the learners' needs. (Baskin et al., 2005) **2:** A systems in which students may choose to complete some of their learning on campus and some of their learning off campus. (Klobas & Renzi, 2005b)

**Flexible Mining of Association Rules**
Mining association rules in user-specified forms to suit different needs, such as on dimension, level of abstraction, and interestingness. (Shen, 2005)

**Flexible Workplace**
Organizational settings that can quickly take external and internal changes into account in their processes. (Oravec, 2005)

**Flexography**
A printing process that uses a raised or relief-type image on a flexible photoploymer or rubber plate. Commonly used for printing corrugated and flexible packaging, newsprint, and other media. (Snyder, 2005)

**Floating Catchment Area Method**
A Geographic Information System (GIS)-supported method for assessing the scarcity of supply vs. demand. For example, assuming a threshold travel distance of 15 miles for primary healthcare, a 15-mile circle is drawn around a residential location as its catchment area. The circle "floats" from one location to another throughout a study area, and the physician-to-population ratio within each catchment indicates whether an area is medically underserved. (Wang & Lou, 2005)

**Flooding-Based Broadcasting Mechanism**
The unconditional broadcasting mechanism utilized by Gnutella peers to forward their searching queries. Gnutella peers implement such a flooding-based searching mechanism in order to maximize their searching coverage on the networks. (Kwok et al., 2006)

**Floor Control**
Functionality that allows for resolving concurrent access to common resources, such as mouse pointers in shared applications. A floor is usually assigned to such a resource together with a policy for access authorization. (Trossen & Molenaar, 2005)

**FLOSS:** See *Free/Libre Open Source Software.*

**Flow**
**1:** The amount of change in a variable over time. Flow represents the change in the status or the quantity of a

variable over a specified time unit. (Maani, 2005) **2:** A psychological state experienced when there is a match between task requirements and a user's skills, a state that involves high attention and leads to feelings of control and enjoyment. (Sas, 2006) **3:** A psychological state in which one is so focused on an activity that one loses a sense of self and of the passage of time. (Bridges et al., 2006) **4:** A representation of the rate of change in the condition of a variable in a system dynamics model. (Casado, 2005) **5:** A set of packets associated with a single application and that share common requirements. (Gutiérrez & Ting, 2005) **6:** The holistic sensation that people feel when they act in total involvement. (Scarpi & Dall'Olmo-Riley, 2006)

**F/OSS:** See *Free/Open Source Software.*

## Focal Element
Subset of the frame of discernment with a positive mass value associated with it. (Beynon, 2005a)

## Focus Group
A small group interview, conducted by a moderator, which is used to discuss one or more issues. (McPherson, 2005)

## Focus+Context Technique
Allows one to interactively transfer the focus as desired while the context of the region in focus remains in view, with gradually degrading resolution to the rim. In contrast, allows the standard zoom+panning technique to select the magnification factor, trading detail, and overview, and involves harsh view cut-offs. (Walter, 2005)

## For-Profit Business
A business enterprise or organization that exists to provide products and/or services to customers in exchange for delivering a profit to the owners and/or investors of the business. (Baim, 2006a)

## Force Model
A model showing that a user's motivation to exert effort into using an application is the summation of the products of the attractiveness of the application and the probability that a certain level of effort will result in successfully using the application. (Chen & Lou, 2005)

## Forecasting Model
A computational and/or mathematical model that simulates time series behavior with the purpose of forecasting their future values. (Castro & Braga, 2006)

## Foreign Direct Investment (FDI)
An acquisition of an asset in a foreign country (host country) made by an investor in another country (home country) with the intention to manage this asset. (Brock & Zhou, 2006)

## Foreign Key
**1:** A key is a field or set of fields in a relational database table that has unique values—that is, no duplicates. A field or set of fields whose values form a subset of the values in the key of another table is called a foreign key. Foreign keys express relationships between fields of different tables. (Koeller, 2005) **2:** A set of one or more attributes that correspond to a primary key in order to simulate a relationship. It links two tables. (Alhajj & Polat, 2005a)

## Forensic Systems Engineering
Postmortem analysis and study of project failures and disasters aimed at uncovering causes and relationships. (Dalcher, 2005)

## Foresight Methodology
Provides tools and systematic approaches to integrate various partners and views in order to provide the necessary framework for, for example, measures to improve economic development. It is closely connected with the Triple-Helix Model. (Hofer, 2006)

## Forking
Source code is said to fork when another group of developers creates a derivative version of the source code that is separate, if not incompatible, with the current road the source code's development is following. The result is source code that takes a different fork in the road. (St. Amant & Still, 2005)

## Form Element
Any part of an HTML form, including input boxes, check boxes, pull-down menus, submit or reset buttons, or radio options. (Fagan, 2005)

## Form Factor
This platform or operating system runs on a handheld device. Major form factors include Palm, Pocket PC, and WAP. (Chan & Fang, 2005)

## Formal Communication
Communication that is institutionally planned and functionally defined. (Beuschel et al., 2005)

**F**

## Formal Concept Analysis

A mathematical framework that provides formal and mathematical treatment of the notion of a concept in a given universe. (Saquer, 2005)

## Formal Leader

One who is formally appointed or authorized by either the group or an external party to hold an officially designated leadership role for the group or team. Such a leader may or may not display strong leadership behavior. (Cargill, 2006a)

## Formal Learning System

A system specially designed to facilitate learning. This situation takes place at a given time in a particular physical environment equipped with dedicated furniture and technical facilities. (Blandin, 2005)

## Formal Mentoring

A deliberate pairing of a more skilled or experienced person with a lesser skilled or experienced one, with the agreed-upon goal of having the lesser skilled or experienced person grow and develop specific competencies. (Long et al., 2005)

## Formal Method

**1:** One of a set of rigorous techniques based on mathematical notation that can be used to specify and verify software models. (Kefalas et al., 2005) **2:** A set of tools and notations (based on formal semantics) used for unambiguously specifying the requirements of computing systems that allow one to prove properties of specifications and to prove the consistency of implementations with their specifications. (Fisteus & Kloos, 2006) **3:** The variety of mathematical modeling techniques that are applicable to computer system (software and hardware) design. Formal methods may be used to specify and model the behavior of a system, and to mathematically verify that the system design and implementation satisfy system functional and safety properties. These specifications, models, and verifications may be done using a variety of techniques and with various degrees of rigor. (Mauco & Riesco, 2005)

## Formal Network of Practice

A network of practice that has a membership controlled by fees and/or acceptance through some central authority that also assists in organizing, facilitating, and supporting member communications, events, and discussion topics. (Archer, 2006)

## Formal Ontology

A formal representation of a shared conceptualization. In the context of the Semantic Web, ontologies provide shared "vocabularies" for metadata descriptions. (Sicilia & García-Barriocanal, 2006)

## Formal Verification

Act of proving or disproving the correctness of a system with respect to a certain property (specification) using mathematical formalisms and methods. (Fisteus & Kloos, 2006)

## Formative Evaluation of Learning

**1:** Used when the intention is to give feedback to guide or improve practice. (Diamadis & Polyzos, 2005) **2:** An evaluation designed and used to improve a program, especially when it is still being developed. (Nelson, 2005) **3:** Evaluation performed throughout the design process conducted for the purpose of improving and changing whatever is evaluated. (Zaphiris & Zacharia, 2005) **4:** The collection of usability data during the development of a system in order to guide iterative design. (Danielson, 2006b) **5:** The elicitation of information that can be used to improve a program while it is in the development stage. (Nash et al., 2005a) **6:** The elicitation of information that can be used to improve a program while it is in the development stage. (Nash et al., 2005b) **7:** The gathering of data from stakeholders on an innovation during the process of its development. (Naidu, 2005a)

## Formulary

A list of drugs that are approved for use under a given health insurance program. (Rosson, 2006)

## Forum

The context or the setting in which information is presented to other individuals. (St. Amant, 2006a)

## Forward Engineering

The process of transforming a model into code through a mapping to a specific implementation language. (Favre et al., 2005)

## Forward Error Correction

A technique used in the receiving system for correcting errors in data transmission. (Hin & Subramaniam, 2005a)

## Forward-Looking Responsibility

Addresses the particular responsibilities of individuals, groups, and partners in advance of a product's use or a system's implementation; it defines guidelines for creating quality products, measures the quality of the products, and defines the method of evaluation, the limitations, and the scope of the operation in advance of harmful incidents. (George, 2005a)

## Forwarding Equivalence Class (FEC)

A group of network packets forwarded in the same manner (e.g., over the same path, with the same forwarding treatment). A forwarding equivalence class is therefore the set of packets that could safely be mapped to the same label. Note that there may be reasons that packets from a single forwarding equivalence class may be mapped to multiple labels (e.g., when stream merge is not used). (Gutiérrez & Ting, 2005)

## Fostering Communities of Learners (FCL)

Main features of FCL with respect to communities of learners are represented by reflection and discussion. The reflection is based on three main activities: research, sharing of information, and fair jobs. Discussions and speech have the main aim of stimulating auto-criticism and auto-reflective thinking in these communities. (Cartelli, 2006a)

## Foundation for Intelligent Physical Agents (FIPA)

An international non-profit association of companies promoting and developing specifications to support interoperability among agents and agent-based applications. (Cardoso & Freire, 2005)

**4C/ID-model**: See *Four-Component Instructional Design Model*.

## Four-Component Instructional Design Model (4C/ID-Model)

An instructional design model incorporating teaching of knowledge structures and algorithmic methods in supporting roles to mental models and heuristic problem-solving instruction. Its four components are: compilation (algorithmic learning and instruction), restricted encoding (includes facts, concepts, principles, and plans), elaboration (includes conceptual models, goal plan hierarchies, causal models, mental models), and induction (includes heuristics and systematic approaches to problem solving). (Pelton & Pelton, 2005)

**4G:** See *Fourth Generation*.

## Fourth Generation (4G)

Planned evolution of 3G technology expected to provide support for data rates up to 100 Mbps, allowing high-quality and smooth-video transmission. (Akhtar, 2005)

## Fourth-Generation Language

Includes business application languages and tools such as database and decision supports tools such as SQL, ACCESS, and EXCEL; ERP and other reporting tools; and Web development environments such as ColdFusion and FrontPage. (Beise et al., 2005)

## Fractal Geometry

The geometry of the irregular shapes found in nature; in general, fractals are characterized by infinite details, infinite length, self-similarity, fractal dimensions, and the absence of smoothness or derivative. (de Castro, 2005)

## Fractional Factorial

A subset of the full factorial design—that is, a subset of all possible combinations. (Lo, 2005)

## Fragile

After a message is embedded into a carrier, the hidden message is destroyed if the carrier is destroyed or modified. The scheme is not suitable to prove a legal copyright, but useful to detect a carrier that has been tampered with. (Lou et al., 2006)

## Fragile Watermarking

**1:** A method for embedding a secret message that is intended to be undetectable even after minor malicious or non-malicious manipulations on the host media in which it is embedded. (C.-T. Li, 2005) **2:** Another category of digital watermarking which requires the embedded watermark to be un-extractable after any manipulation on the host media. It is widely used in the applications of authentication and content integrity verification. (Si & Li, 2006) **3:** A technique that does not guarantee the watermark presence after few document manipulations. (Nesi & Spinu, 2005)

## Fragmentation

When the data packet is too large to transfer on a given network, it is divided into smaller packets. These smaller packets are reassembled on a destination host. Along with other methods, intruders can deliberately divide the data packets to evade IDSs. (Kayacik et al., 2005)

**F**

## Fragmented Value Chain
Neither the buyer-driven nor the seller-driven model of the value chain dominates. (Jeffcoate, 2005)

## Frame
A small piece of information or a statement to which the student is exposed, such as a page with a single question. In linear programmed instruction, a frame includes a stimulus, a response, and reinforcement (positive feedback). (Owen & Aworuwa, 2005)

## Frame of Discernment
A finite, non-empty set of hypotheses. (Beynon, 2005a)

## Frame Rate
The number of frames projected per second. (Vitolo et al., 2005)

## Frame Relay
A form of packet switching based on the use of variable-length link layer frames. (Butcher-Powell, 2005)

## Frame Size
The height and width of the video window according to the number of pixels. (Vitolo et al., 2005)

## Frame-Based Representation
A way of defining the "meaning" of a concept by using a set of properties ("frame") with associated classes of admitted values—this "frame" is linked with the node representing the concept. Associating a frame with the concept $c_i$ to be defined corresponds to establishing a relationship between $c_i$ and some of the other concepts of the ontology; this relationship indicates that the concepts $c_1, c_2 \ldots c_n$ used in the frame defining $c_i$ denote the "class of fillers" (specific concepts or instances) that can be associated with the "slots" (properties, attributes, qualities, etc.) of the frame for $c_i$. (Zarri, 2005a)

## Framework
**1:** A software foundation that specifies how a software system is to be built. It includes standards at all levels, both internal construction and external appearance and behavior. (D. Brandon, 2005a) **2:** The underlying structure supporting or containing something. (Solberg, Oldevik, & Jensvoll, 2005)

## Franchise Network
A structured network of N organizations sharing a common brand or public identity (e.g., Holiday Inn® hotels). This network type is characterized by a centralized structure, low competition, and a common scope of operations among members. (Priestley, 2006)

## Franchisee
The individual or business that receives the business rights and pays the royalties for using the rights. (Chen et al., 2005b)

## Franchisee Lifecycle
The stages a franchisee goes through in the franchise system: Courting, 'We', 'Me', Rebel, Renewal. (Chen et al., 2005a)

## Franchising
A business opportunity based on granting the business rights and collecting royalties in return. (Chen et al., 2005a)

## Franchisor
The individual or business who grants the business rights. (Chen et al., 2005a)

## Franchisor/Franchisee Learning Process
The stages of learning, including beginner, novice, advanced, master, and professional. (Chen et al., 2005b)

## Franchisor/Franchisee Relationship Management
The vital factor for the success of a franchise, including: Knowledge, Attitude, Motivation, Individual Behavior, and Group Behavior. (Chen et al., 2005b)

## Fraud
Criminal deception leading to unjust enrichment. (Rowe, 2006b)

## Fraudulent Financial Reporting
Intentional or reckless conduct, whether by act or omission, that results in materially misleading financial statements. (Lenard & Alam, 2005)

## Free (Random) MA
A class of non-coordinated distributed multiple-access protocols where collisions may occur. (Markhasin et al., 2005)

## Free Riding
**1:** Using person-to-person (P2P) file-sharing networks to acquire files by downloading without making any files

on one's own machine available to the network in return. (Hughes & Lang, 2005) **2:** The act of enjoying the public good without contributing anything to its creation or maintenance. (Teigland & Wasko, 2005) **3:** Consuming community resources without contributing, a well-known problem in peer-to-peer file-sharing systems (and in many other public good provisioning settings) where certain users only download files without sharing files themselves. (Efstathiou & Polyzos, 2006) **4:** The user behavior when a user contributes nothing or undesired content to the P2P network, while consuming the contributions of others. (Kwok et al., 2006)

## Free Software

**1:** An earlier name for open source software, emphasizing the liberties given to end users and developers of derivative works. There is no requirement that the software be distributed at no charge; thus, distinct from freeware. (Carillo & Okoli, 2006) **2:** Software that is distributed under the terms of a license agreement that makes it freely available in source code form. Strong advocates of free software insist that the ideas underlying a piece of software, once published, must always be freely available. (Fleming, 2005b)

## Free Software Foundation (FSF)

Founded by Richard Stallman in 1985 to promote free software, especially the Copyleft concept. Produced the GNU Manifesto (1985), the GNU General Public License (1989, 1991), the GNU Lesser General Public License (1991, 1999), and the GNU Free Documentation License (2000, 2001, 2002). (Okoli & Carillo, 2006)

## Free Tree

Let G be a connected acyclic labeled graph. Because of its acyclicity, each connected acyclic labeled graph has at least one node which is connected to the rest of the graph by only one edge—that is, a leaf. If we label the leaves with zero and the other nodes recursively with the minimal label of its neighbors plus one, then we get an unordered, unrooted tree-like structure, a so-called free tree. It is a well-known fact that every free tree has at most two nodes, which minimize the maximal distance to all other nodes in the tree, the so-called centers. (Katsaros & Manolopoulos, 2005b)

## Free/Libre Open Source Software (FLOSS)

Generically indicating non-proprietary software, combines the concepts of free software and open source software. It makes it easier to talk about one movement and not ignore the other, and as such, can be used as a compromise term palatable to adherents of either movement. It also emphasizes the libre meaning of the word "free" rather than the "free of charge" or gratis meaning, which those unfamiliar with the subject might assume. This all-inclusive acronym has the extra advantage of being non-anglo-centric: the F stands for Frei in German while the L stands for Libre in French and Spanish, Livre in Portuguese, and Libero in Italian, showing that the concepts and their implementation are not exclusive to the English-speaking world. (Y.-W. Lin, 2005)

## Free/Open Source Software (F/OSS)

**1:** Software whose source code, under certain license agreements, is freely available for modification, distribution, and innovation. (Sowe, Samoladas, & Stamelos, 2005) **2:** Software with an unrestrictive license whose source code is made available for modification, customization, and distribution by others. (Boateng & Boateng, 2006a)

## Freeblock Scheduling

A disk arm scheduling method that uses opportunistic accesses to disk blocks required for a low-priority activity. (Thomasian, 2005a)

## Freely Available

Wide distribution at no cost to the consumer. (Fleming, 2005b)

## Freeware

Software provided at no charge to the user. Might be open source or proprietary—that is, the developer only permits redistribution and use, with no modifications permitted. In fact, most open source software is freeware, but most freeware is not open source. (Carillo & Okoli, 2006)

## Freight Consolidation

The combining of small shipments into a composite truckload or other unit of volume that is sent to a destination point. (Tyan, 2006)

## Frequency

Rate of signal oscillation in Hertz. (Statica & Deek, 2006)

## Frequency Domain

The representation of a signal as a function of frequency, for example as the sum of sinusoidal waves of different amplitudes and frequencies. (Dixon, 2005)

**F**

### Frequency Hopping Spread Spectrum (FHSS)

When a broad slice of bandwidth spectrum is divided into many possible broadcast frequencies to be used by the transmitted signal. (Akhtar, 2005)

### Frequency Response

$H(e^{j\omega})$: The discrete-time Fourier transform of the impulse response of the system; it provides a frequency-domain description of the system. In general, it has a complex value. (Jovanovic-Dolecek, 2005c)

### Frequency Selective Filter

A digital filter which passes desired frequency components in a signal without distortion and attenuates other frequency components. A low-pass (LP) filter passes low-frequency components to the output while eliminating high-frequency components. Conversely, a high-pass (HP) filter passes all high-frequency components and rejects all low-frequency components. A band-pass (BP) filter blocks both low- and high-frequency components while passing the intermediate range. A bands-stop (BS) filter eliminates the intermediate band of frequencies while passing both low- and high-frequency components. (Jovanovic-Dolecek & Díaz-Carmona, 2005)

### Frequency-Division Multiplexing

The process of subdividing a telecommunications line into multiple channels, with each channel allocated a portion of the frequency of the line. (Hin & Subramaniam, 2005a)

### Frequent Itemset (FI)

**1:** An itemset whose support is greater than or equal to the minimal support. (Zou & Chu, 2005) **2:** The itemset with support greater than or equal to a certain threshold, called minsupport. (Wong, & Fu, 2005) **3:** A set of items (e.g., {A, B, C}) that simultaneously co-occur with high frequency in a set of transactions. This is a prerequisite to finding association rules of the form (e.g., {A, B}→C). When items are URLs or products (i.e., books, movies, etc.) sold or provided on a Web site, frequent itemsets can correspond to implicit collaborative user profiles. (Nasraoui, 2005) **4:** A set of itemsets that have the user-specified support threshold. (Ashrafi et al., 2005) **5:** An itemset contained in a number of objects at least equal to some user-defined threshold. (Pasquier, 2005) **6:** An itemset that has a support greater than user-specified minimum support. (Shen, 2005) **7:** An itemset with support higher than a predefined threshold, denoted minsup. (Dumitriu, 2005) **8:** The support of an itemset refers to as the percentage of transactions that contain all the items in the itemset. A frequent itemset is an itemset with support above a pre-specified threshold. (Zhou & Wang, 2005) **9:** An itemsets that has support at least equal to minsup. (Daly & Taniar, 2005a)

### Frequent Pattern

Pattern the support of which exceeds a user-specified threshold. (Kryszkiewicz, 2005)

### Frequent Subgraph

A subgraph that occurs in a certain percentage of all graphs in a database. (Fischer & Meinl, 2005)

### Frequent Subgraph Mining

Finding all subgraphs within a set of graph transactions whose frequency satisfies a user-specified level of minimum support. (Holder & Cook, 2005)

### Frictionless Capitalism

A view of economic/business relationships that suggests information and communication technologies can reduce or eradicate barriers to profit making, such as distance between businesses and markets, imperfect market knowledge, and low productivity. (Lepawsky & Park, 2006)

### Friendster®(.com)

The original and still most popular online social networking application. Claims to have more than five million registered users. (Mew, 2006)

### Front and Back Region

Front region is a setting that stays put, geographically speaking (e.g., an office, a class). Back region is a setting which cannot be easily intruded upon. (Baralou & Stepherd, 2005)

### Front-End Analysis

The process of collecting information before and in preparation for the design, development, and implementation of any innovation. This is also referred to as needs assessment. (Naidu, 2005a)

### Front-End Interoperability

User-centric integration approach that presents consolidated information retrieved from different sources and enables the access to multiple application systems in order to perform a set of coherent transactions at once. (Werth, 2005)

## Front-End Processing

Computing the raw data and managing the pre-computed aggregated data in either in 3D data cube or n-dimensional table. (Tan, 2005b)

**FRP:** See *Fantasy Role-Playing.*

**FSF:** See *Free Software Foundation.*

**FTE:** See *Full-Time Equivalent.*

**FTP:** See *File Transfer Protocol.*

**FTTH:** See *Fiber-to-the-Home.*

## FTTx

Fiber to the cabinet (Cab), curb (C), building (B), or home (H). (Chochliouros et al., 2005a)

**F2F:** See *Face-to-Face.*

## Fulfillment

The capability to deliver that which is transacted. (Samuel & Samson, 2006)

## Full PI Model

A PI model where every proper subset of variables is marginally independent. Full PI models are the most basic PI models. (Xiang, 2005)

## Full REALLOCATE

A heuristic algorithm for computing a new data allocation, given some number of servers and a system optimization parameter. This heuristic is iterative, searching for stepwise solution refinement. This heuristic evaluates the effect of independently moving each database relation to the new server joining the distributed database system. It then holds this relation at the new server and reiterates with a reevaluation of moving an additional relation. (Chin, 2005)

## Full-Text Index

An index supporting retrieval of identifiers from documents containing a particular word. (Nørvåg, 2005)

## Full-Time Equivalent (FTE)

An accumulation of work time that adds up to a "full-time" position. For example, two half-time positions equal one full-time equivalent; or 20 hours per week equals one-half of a full-time equivalent. (Calzonetti & deChambeau, 2006)

## Fully Interactive Video

Two-way interactive video. The interaction between two sites with audio and video. (Danenberg & Chen, 2005)

## Fully Online Model of Course Redesign

This model shares many of the features of the other course redesign models. For example, it shares the feature of online interactive learning activities of the Replacement model, heavy reliance on computer-based learning resources, and instructional staffing of the Emporium and Supplemental models. The most distinctive feature is that learners generally do not meet face to face on campus. (Twigg, 2005)

## Function

A programming construct where code that does a particular task is segregated from the main body of a program; the function may be sent arguments and may return arguments to the body of the program. (D. Brandon, Jr., 2005a)

## Functional Area

Companies that make products to sell have several functional areas of operations. Each functional area comprises a variety of business functions or business activities. (Sundaram & Portougal, 2005a)

## Functional Dependence

**1:** For attribute sets C, D, we say that D depends functionally on C, in symbols C→D, in case IND(C)⊆IND(D). Also non-exact (partial) functional dependencies to a degree are considered. (Pawlak et al., 2005) **2:** Intuitively, one attribute is functionally dependent on a second attribute when you need to know the value of the second in order to find out the value of the first. More precisely, each value of the second attribute has no more than one value of the first associated with it. (Schultz, 2005) **3:** For any record r in a record type, its sequence of values of the attributes in X is referred to as the X-value of r. Let R be a record type, and X and Y be sequences of attributes of R. We say that the functional dependency, X→Y of R, holds at time t, if at time t, for any two R records r and s, the X-values of r and s are identical, then the U-values of r and s are also identical. (Tan & Zhao, 2005a)

## Functional Genomics

The study of gene functions on a genomic scale, especially based on microarrays. (Fu, 2005)

**F**

## Functional Illiteracy

A person can read such things as menus or environmental print (signs, wrappers of food, labels, etc.), but cannot read a sentence or make meaning out of text. (Trammell, 2005)

## Functional Information

Information, based on engineering knowledge, that describes how components and subsystems of a tangible product interact, and how these interactions give rise to different product features and varying levels of product performance. (McIntosh & Siau, 2005)

## Functional Margin

Geometrically, the Euclidean distance of the closest point from the decision boundary to the input space. (Awad & Khan, 2005)

## Functional Model

A model concerned primarily with how to interact with a system, how it is operated. (Macefield, 2006)

## Functional Product

A product having stable and predictable demand, a long lifecycle, and well-developed competition that results in a low profit margin. (Abraham & Leon, 2006)

## Functional Use Quality

The quality of a product to deliver a beneficial value to the user. (Knight, 2006a)

## Functionality

**1:** The external quality factor that refers to a set of functions and specified properties that satisfy stated or implied needs. (Xenos, 2006) **2:** The task that the parties wish to jointly compute. (Lindell, 2005)

## Functionally or Culturally Diverse

The nature of global diversity and the ability to locate organizational functions across the globe creates a diverse environment for the entire organization. Since members are all in different locations and charged with different tasks, diversity exists that is only found in the very largest multi-national corporations. (J. Lee, 2005)

## Fund for the Improvement of Post-Secondary Education (FIPSE)

A granting group within the U.S. Department of Education. In the last 10 years it has been instrumental in supporting the development of new approaches to teaching and learning online. (S.M. Johnstone, 2005)

## Fundamental Analysis

The use of company-reported financial data to determine an intrinsic (or fair value) for a security. Used to identify cases where companies are undervalued, with a view to profiting from the future price movements. This style of analysis is generally long term. (Vanstone & Tan, 2005)

## Funding Organization

Organization, either corporate or academic, that funds an e-learning project to meet some need within the organization. (Kapp, 2005)

## Fusion System

A system based on an architecture that associates diverse sources of data, information, and knowledge. (Tauber & Schwartz, 2006)

## Fuzzy Association Rule

An implication rule showing the conditions of co-occurrence of itemsets that are defined by fuzzy sets whose elements have probabilistic values. (Shen & Horiguchi, 2005)

## Fuzzy Clustering

Cluster analysis where a data object can have membership degrees to different clusters. Usually it is assumed that the membership degrees of a data object to all clusters add up to one, so a membership degree can also be interpreted as the probability that the data object belongs to the corresponding cluster. (Klawonn & Rehm, 2005)

## Fuzzy Conceptual Data Model

The extension of traditional conceptual data models, such as ER/EER and UML fuzzy conceptual data models, which can model imperfect data and semantic relationships at a high level of data abstraction. (Ma, 2005b)

## Fuzzy C-Means Algorithm

A clustering algorithm that assigns a fuzzy membership in various clusters to an object instead of assigning the object precisely to a cluster. (Lingras et al., 2005)

## Fuzzy Database Model

A database model with the ability to store and handle fuzzy data, mainly including the fuzzy relational database model, fuzzy nested relational database model, and fuzzy object-oriented database model. (Ma, 2005b)

## Fuzzy Database Modeling

In addition to the issues of fuzzy database models, fuzzy conceptual data models, and conceptual design of fuzzy databases, fuzzy database modeling focuses on fuzzy database systems and discusses (fuzzy) query, (fuzzy) data handling, database theory (e.g., fuzzy data dependencies and formalization in fuzzy relational databases), database implementation, and so forth. (Ma, 2005b)

## Fuzzy Estimate

Generalized statistical estimation technique for the situation of non-precise data. (Viertl, 2005)

## Fuzzy Histogram

A generalized histogram based on non-precise data whose heights are fuzzy numbers. (Viertl, 2005)

## Fuzzy Information

Information not given in the form of precise numbers, precise vectors, or precisely defined terms. (Viertl, 2005)

## Fuzzy Logic

**1:** A mathematical technique that classifies subjective reasoning and assigns data to a particular group or cluster, based on the degree of possibility the data has of being in that group. (Lenard & Alam, 2005) **2:** A procedure for analyzing approximate reasoning, which uses its imprecision and settles borderline cases with the concept of precision. Human reasoning is imprecise, and the ability to make reasonable decisions in such a clear environment of uncertainty is a major aspect that depends on the possibilities to obtain an approximate answer to some questions based on the acquired knowledge, which is normally inexact and not always reliable. (Xodo & Nigro, 2005) **3:** A type of logic that does not rely on a binary yes or no. Instead, computer systems are able to rank responses on a scale of 0.0 to 1.0, with 0.0 being false to 1.0 being true. This allows computer systems to deal with probabilities rather than absolutes. (Athappilly & Rea, 2005) **4:** Fuzzy logic is applied to fuzzy sets where membership in a fuzzy set is a probability, not necessarily 0 or 1. (Xu et al., 2006a) **5:** Fuzzy logic provides an approach to approximate reasoning in which the rules of inference are approximate rather than exact. Fuzzy logic is useful in manipulating information that is incomplete, imprecise, or unreliable. (Hou, Sheng, et al., 2005) **6:** The concept of

fuzzy logic is that many classes in the natural environment are fuzzy rather than crisp. It deals with imprecise and uncertain data. (Begg, 2005)

## Fuzzy Membership

Instead of specifying whether an object precisely belongs to a set, fuzzy membership specifies a degree of membership between [0,1]. (Lingras et al., 2005)

## Fuzzy Number

Quantitative mathematical description of fuzzy information concerning a one-dimensional numerical quantity. (Viertl, 2005)

## Fuzzy Relation

In fuzzy relations, degrees of association between objects are represented not as crisp relations, but membership grade in the same manner as degrees of set membership are represented in a fuzzy set. (Kim, 2005)

## Fuzzy Set

**1:** A set that captures the different degrees of belongingness of different objects in the universe instead of a sharp demarcation between objects that belong to a set and those that do not. (Bala et al., 2005) **2:** The set in which elements are associated with membership degrees in (0,1) to indicate how they belong to the set. Fuzzy-set theory was originated by L. A. Zadeh in 1965 and can be used for imprecise information processing. (Ma, 2005b) **3:** Let $U$ be a set of objects so called universe of discourse. A fuzzy set $F$ in $U$ is characterized by a function of inclusion $m_F$ taking values in the interval [0,1], i.e., $\mu_F: U \rightarrow [0,1]$; where $\mu_F(u)$ represents the degree in which $u \in U$ belongs to fuzzy set $F$. (Nigro & González Císaro, 2005c)

## Fuzzy Set Theory

Replaces the two-valued set-membership function with a real-valued function—that is, membership is treated as a probability or as a degree of truthfulness. (Lazar, 2005)

## Fuzzy Statistics

Statistical analysis methods for the situation of fuzzy information. (Viertl, 2005)

## Fuzzy Transformation

The process of transforming an observation with missing values into fuzzy patterns that are equivalent to the observation based on fuzzy set theory. (H. Wang & S. Wang, 2005)

**F**

## Fuzzy Valued Function
Generalized real valued function whose value is a set of fuzzy numbers. (Viertl, 2005)

## Fuzzy Vector
Mathematical description of non-precise vector quantities. (Viertl, 2005)

# G

**GA:** See *Genetic Algorithm.*

**GAAP:** See *Generally Accepted Accounting Principles.*

**GADP:** See *General Additive Data Perturbation.*

**Gait Analysis**
Analysis of human walking patterns. It is used to analyze abnormality in lower limb problems and assess treatment or intervention outcomes. (Begg, 2005)

**Galaxy Structure**
Structure of a warehouse for which two different types of facts share a same dimension. (Schneider, 2005)

**Galois Lattice**
Provides some meanings to analyze and represent data. Refers to two-ordered set. An ordered set (I,#) is the set I, together with a partial ordering # on I. (Nigro & González Císaro, 2005c)

**Gambling**
A leisure activity in which money is staked with the anticipation of making a gain and/or winning a prize. (Brindley, 2006)

**Game**
A simulation in which people are part of the model and their decisions partially determine the outcome. (Pendegraft, 2005)

**Game Building**
Stage in Gaming and Simulation. During the building stage, game constructors make a model of the problem they want to incorporate into the game. Next, they transform the model into a specific game, and finally they define different scenarios that can be played during the game. (Achterbergh, 2005a)

**Game Theory**
Mathematical theory of rational behavior for situations involving conflicts of interest. (Heucke et al., 2005)

**Game User Interface**
Elements and devices through which the user interacts with the game. (Ip & Jacobs, 2006)

**Game Using**
Stage in Gaming and Simulation. During the using stage, game facilitators make preparations for playing the game, and participants actually play the game (given a certain scenario). (Achterbergh, 2005a)

**Gaming and Simulation**
The process of building and using simulation games as a means to deal with complex problems. See also *Simulation Game.* (Achterbergh, 2005a)

**Gantt Chart**
A chart displaying schedule information in a graphical form. It may display tasks, duration, start/finish dates for activities and milestones, dependencies, and allocated resources. (Asprey, 2005)

**Gap/Racial Gap**
Inequality of access to media and technology based on ethnicity. (Reilly, 2005)

**Gathering**
An event where participants share their knowledge with the group on a particular topic. A gathering focuses exclusively on occupational knowledge and encourages an evaluation of the legitimacy of other peoples' contributions. A gathering is unlike a brainstorm, which discourages evaluation and encourages 'wild and wacky' ideas. Following a gathering, facilitated group discussion is conducted on the contributions shared. (Shaw, 2006)

**G**

**Gaze**

An eye-tracking metric, usually the sum of all fixation durations within a prescribed area. Also called dwell, fixation cluster, or fixation cycle. (Poole & Ball, 2006)

**Gaze Tracking**

The set of mechanisms allowing the recording and analysis of human eye-gaze. Gaze tracking is normally motivated by the assumption that the locus of eye-gaze may, to some extent, correspond to the locus of attention, or it can help capture user interests. Several techniques exist for eye tracking varying in their level of intrusion (from requiring the user to wear special lenses to just having camera-like devices installed on the computer), their accuracy, and ease to use. Normally devices need to be calibrated before use (some systems allow memorized calibrations for specific users). (Thomas & Roda, 2006a)

**GCI:** See *Growth Competitiveness Index; Group Competitiveness Index.*

**GCSS:** See *Group Communication Support System.*

**GDB:** See *Geographic Database.*

**GDP:** See *Gross Domestic Product.*

**GDSS:** See *Group Decision Support System.*

**GDT:** See *Geographically Dispersed Team.*

**Gender Divide**

The term broadly used to indicate the difference between males and females that have ready accessibility to information and technology, and the skills to use information and technology, and those males and females who do not have the same or similar level of accessibility to information and technology, and the skills to use information and technology. (Arthur-Gray & Campbell, 2005)

**Gene**

**1:** A hereditary unit consisting of a sequence of DNA that contains all the information necessary to produce a molecule that performs some biological function. (Yu & Liu, 2005) **2:** The unit of heredity. A gene contains hereditary information encoded in the form of DNA and located at a specific position on a chromosome in a cell's nucleus. Genes determine many aspects of anatomy and physiology by controlling the production of proteins. Each individual has a unique sequence of genes, called genetic code. (Galitsky, 2005a)

**Gene Expression**

**1:** Describes how the information of transcription and translation encoded in a segment of DNA is converted into proteins in a cell. (Fung & Ng, 2005) **2:** Production of mRNA from DNA (a process known as transcription) and production of protein from mRNA (a process known as translation). Microarrays are used to measure the level of gene expression in a tissue or cell. (Fu, 2005) **3:** The proteins actually produced in a specific cell by an individual. (Liberati et al., 2005)

**Gene Expression Microarray**

One of a number of silicon chips that simultaneously measure the expression levels of thousands of genes. (Yu & Liu, 2005)

**Gene Expression Profile**

Through microarray chips, an image that describes to what extent genes are expressed can be obtained. It usually uses red to indicate the high expression level and uses green to indicate the low expression level. This image is also called a gene expression profile. (Chu & Wang, 2005)

**Gene Microarray Data**

Measurements of mRNA abundances derived from biochemical devices called microarrays. These are essentially measures of gene activity. (Mukherjee, 2005)

**General Additive Data Perturbation (GADP)**

A general form of Additive Data Perturbation techniques. This method is based on the idea that the relationships between the confidential and non-confidential attributes should be the same before and after perturbation of the confidential attributes has occurred. Designed both to eliminate all forms of statistical bias found in other additive methods and to provide for the highest level of security of all data perturbation techniques. (Wilson et al., 2006b)

**General Knowledge**

The contextual knowledge that goes across or is shared by particular individuals, groups, societies, times, and locations. General knowledge can be tacit or explicit. (Medeni, 2006a)

## General (or Mega) Portal
A portal that provides links to all sorts of different sites of the user's choosing, often from a menu of options. (Tatnall, 2006)

## General Packet Radio Service (GPRS)
**1:** A packet-linked technology that enables high-speed wireless Internet and other data communications. GPRS provides more than four times greater speed than conventional GSM systems. Using a packet data service, subscribers are always connected and always online, so services will be easy and quick to access. (Wong, 2006) **2:** A standard for wireless communications that operates at speeds up to 115 kilobits per second. It is designed for efficiently sending and receiving small packets of data. Therefore, it is suited for wireless Internet connectivity and such applications as e-mail and Web browsing. (Garrett, 2006a) **3:** An evolution of GSM networks that supports data services with higher bit rates than GSM. It uses the same air interface as GSM, but it supports IP signaling back to the core network. (Louvros, Karaboulas, et al., 2005) **4:** A wireless data protocol suited for data transmission, available to users of GSM mobile phones. Its theoretical bandwidth is 170 kbit/s, while the realistic one is 30-70 kbit/s. Sometimes it is referred as "2.5G" (i.e., a technology between the second generations of mobile systems) like GSM, and the third one (3G) like UMTS. (Costagliola, Di Martino, & Ferrucci, 2006) **5:** A packet-based wireless communication service that promises data rates from 56 up to 114 Kbps, and continuous connection to the Internet for mobile phone and computer users. The higher data rates will allow users to take part in videoconferences, and interact with multimedia Web sites and similar applications using mobile handheld devices as well as notebook computers. (Olla, 2005a) **6:** Provides data rates up to 115 kbps for wireless Internet and other types of data communications, using packet data services. (Akhtar, 2005) **7:** A standard for wireless communication that runs at speeds up to 115 kilobits per second, compared to current GSM (global system for mobile communications) systems' 9.6 kilobits. GPRS supports a wide range of bandwidths, is an efficient use of limited bandwidth, and is particularly suited for sending and receiving small bursts of data, such as e-mail and Web browsing, as well as large volumes of data. (Roibás, 2006b)

## General Public License (GPL)
**1:** License designed so that people can freely (or for a charge) distribute copies of free software, receive the source code, change the source code, and use portions of the source code to create new free programs. (Lowry et al., 2005a) **2:** Specifically links source code to legally protected freedom to publish, distribute, and make use of derived works. (Fleming, 2005b)

## General Purpose Methodology
Methodology that attempts to be applicable across domains and for different kinds of systems and purposes. (Solberg et al., 2005)

## General System Theory
Collection of tools, approaches, hypotheses, and models that can be used for scientific discovery. (Szczerbicki, 2005)

## Generalist E-Fulfillment (GO) Provider
Third party e-fulfillment providers may choose to offer a large range of e-fulfillment capabilities. These may be either Physco or Knowco in nature, though a greater proportion of GO providers are tending to concentrate on Knowco capabilities. GOs appear likely to compete in more open markets using innovation and cost-competition. Though these providers may have large customers, they are more likely to have a large range of customers. (Alexander & Burn, 2006)

## Generality
A measure that quantifies the coverage of an explanation in the whole data set. (Yao & Zhao, 2005)

## Generalization
**1:** The goal of neural network training is to develop a model that generalizes its knowledge to unseen data. Overtraining must be avoided for generalization to occur. (Smith, 2005) **2:** When entities have similar basic attributes, they can be classified into a generalized entity type. Generalization is the process of finding commonalities between entities to be able to abstract to a higher-level entity set. (Bagui, 2005) **3:** A cubegrade is a generalization if the set of descriptors of the target cell are a subset of the set of attribute-value pairs of the source cell. (Abdulghani, 2005b)

## Generalization-Specialization Hierarchy
A set of concepts organized by specialization and generalization relationships into an inverted tree-like structure, such that concepts higher in the tree are broader and encompass the concepts lower in the tree. (Woods et al., 2006)

**G**

## Generalized Disjunction-Free Pattern

Pattern the support of which is not determinable from the supports of its proper subsets. (Kryszkiewicz, 2005)

## Generalized Disjunctive Pattern

Pattern the support of which is determinable from the supports of its proper subsets. (Kryszkiewicz, 2005)

## Generalized Division

A generalized version of the binary relational algebra division operation where the tuples of the left table are grouped by an attribute and only those groups whose set of values for another specified attribute satisfies a desired set comparison (e.g., equality) with a set of similar values from the right table are passed to the output table. The generalized division operator can be expressed in terms of the five principal relational algebra operations. (Dadashzadeh, 2005)

## Generalized Icon

One of a set of icons used to describe multimedia objects such as images, sounds, texts, motions, and videos. It is a dual object with a logical part and a physical part. (Chang et al., 2005)

## Generalized Reciprocity

Cooperative interchange of favors or obligations between individuals in a group, where return is not expected from the same specific individual given to, but rather from anyone in the group or the group as a whole. (Ridings, 2006b)

## Generally Accepted Accounting Principles (GAAP)

A widely accepted set of rules, conventions, standards, and procedures for reporting financial information, as established by the Financial Accounting Standards Board. (J. Wang et al., 2006a)

## Generating-Pruning

The method of finding frequent sequential patterns by generating candidates' sequences (from size 2 to the maximal size) step by step. At each step a new generation of candidates having the same length is generated and tested over the databases. Only frequent sequences are kept (pruning) and used in the next step to create a new generation of (longer) candidate sequences. (Masseglia et al., 2005)

## Generation

The basic unit of progress in genetic and evolutionary computation, a step in which selection is applied over a population. Usually, crossover and mutation are applied once per generation, in strict order. (Hsu, 2005a)

## Generation 1 Portfolio

A paper-based portfolio. (Wasko, 2005)

## Generation 2 Portfolio

Refers to any form of electronic portfolio. eFolio Minnesota is a current example of a Generation 2 portfolio. (Wasko, 2005)

## Generation 3 Portfolio

A Generation 2 portfolio that includes tools to assist an individual in developing his or her individual education and/or career goals. (Wasko, 2005)

## Generative Knowledge Integration

Occurs when communication and exchange of knowledge within a group or a team evokes novel associations, connections, and hunches such that new meanings and insights are generated. (Newell, 2006)

## Generative Strategy

Encourages learners to construct their own learning experience by allowing them to develop their own structure for acquiring knowledge and skills. (Stavredes, 2005a)

## Generic Algorithm

An algorithm for optimizing a binary string based on an evolutionary mechanism that uses replication, deletion, and mutation operators carried out over many generations. (An, 2005)

## Generic Model Management (gMMt)

An MMt environment/system applicable to a wide range of MMt tasks across a wide range of meta-models. (Diskin & Kadish, 2005)

## Generic Top-Level Domain (gTLD)

TLD reserved regardless of the geographical position. At present, there are the following gTLDs: .aero, .biz, .com, .coop, .info, .int, .museum, .name, .net, .org, and .pro. Three peculiar gTLDs exist—.edu, .mil, and .gov—that are reserved to United States educational, military, and governmental institutions or organizations. (Maggioni & Uberti, 2005)

## Genetic Algorithm (GA)

**1:** A class of algorithms commonly used for training neural networks. The process is modeled after the methods by which biological DNA are combined or mutated to breed new individuals. The crossover technique, whereby DNA reproduces itself by joining portions of each parent's DNA, is used to simulate a form of genetic-like breeding of alternative solutions. Representing the biological chromosomes found in DNA, genetic algorithms use arrays of data, representing various model solutions. Genetic algorithms are useful for multi-dimensional optimization problems in which the chromosome can encode the values for connections found in the artificial neural network. (Kitchens, 2005) **2:** A field of algorithms inspired by the evolution of species and applying natural operators like selection, crossover, and mutation. (Kacem, 2005) **3:** A heuristic used to find approximate solutions to difficult-to-solve problems through application of the principles of evolutionary biology to computer science. (Guan, 2006f) **4:** An optimization algorithm based on the mechanisms of Darwinian evolution, which uses random mutation, crossover, and selection procedures to breed better models or solutions from an originally random starting population or sample. (Hou, Sheng, et al., 2005) **5:** A heuristic optimization algorithm based on the concept of biological evolution. (Caramia & Felici, 2005) **6:** A search and optimization technique that uses the concept of survival of genetic materials over various generations of populations much like the theory of natural evolution. (Bala et al., 2005) **7:** An iterative procedure that consists of a constant-size population of individuals, each represented by a finite string of symbols, known as the genome, encoding a possible solution in a given problem space. (Martí, 2005) **8:** Class of algorithms used to find approximate solutions to difficult-to-solve problems, inspired and named after biological processes of inheritance, mutation, natural selection, and generic crossover. Genetic algorithms are a particular class of evolutionary algorithms. (Polgar, 2005a) **9:** Evolutionary algorithm using a population and based on the Darwinian principle, the survival of the fittest. (Jourdan et al., 2005) **10:** Optimization technique inspired by the mechanisms of evolution by natural selection, in which the possible solutions are represented as the chromosomes of individuals competing for survival in a population. (Galvão et al., 2005) **11:** A large collection of rules that represents all possible solutions to a problem. Inspired by Darwin's theory of evolution, these rules are simultaneously applied to data using powerful software on high-speed computers. The best solutions are then used to solve the problem. (Athappilly & Rea, 2005) **12:** An evolutionary algorithm that generates each individual from some encoded form known as a "chromosome" or "genome." Chromosomes are combined or mutated to breed new individuals. "Crossover," the kind of recombination of chromosomes found in sexual reproduction in nature, is often also used in GAs. Here, an offspring's chromosome is created by joining segments chosen alternately from each of two parents' chromosomes, which are of fixed length. (Lazar, 2005)

## Genetic Operators, Crossover and Mutation

"Crossover" takes two selected chromosomes, the "parents," and cuts their gene (bit) strings at some randomly chosen position, producing two "head" and two "tail" substrings. The tail substrings are then switched, giving rise to two new individuals called "offsprings," which each inherit some genes from each of the parents. The offsprings are then created through the exchange of genetic material. "Mutation" consists of a random modification of the genes with a certain probability (normally a small one, e.g., 0.0001) called the "mutation rate." (Zarri, 2006a)

## Genetic Programming

**1:** A stochastic search algorithm based on evolutionary theory, with the aim to optimize structure or functional form. A tree structure is commonly used for representation of solutions. (Fan & Pathak, 2005) **2:** Search method inspired by natural selection. The basic idea is to evolve a population of "programs" candidates to the solution of a specific problem. (Yeo, 2005)

## Genetic Tree

A variety of dendrogram (diagram) in which organisms are shown arranged on branches that link them according to their relatedness and evolutionary descent. (Galitsky, 2005a)

## Genome

**1:** All the genetic information or hereditary material possessed by an organism. (Yu & Liu, 2005) **2:** All the genetic material in the chromosomes of a particular organism; its size is generally given as its total number of base pairs. (Galitsky, 2005a) **3:** The genetic information of an organism. (Tsunoda et al., 2005)

## Genomic Database

An organized collection of data pertaining to the genetic material of an organism. (Segall, 2005)

**G**

## Genomic Medicine

Integration of genomic and clinical data for medical decision. (Fu, 2005)

## Genotype

**1:** Anthony Dunne's alternative to the prototype—a non-working yet complete product specifically aimed at provoking fictive, social, and aesthetic considerations in an audience. (Kettley, 2006a) **2:** The exact genetic makeup of an organism. (Tzanis et al., 2005)

## Genuine Miss

A usability problem that causes user difficulties that remains undiscovered in usability inspection. (Woolrych & Hindmarch, 2006)

## Geo-Field

An object class used to represent objects and phenomena that are continuously distributed over the space. Examples of phenomena that are represented using geo-fields are temperature, rainfall, topography, and soil type. (Davis et al., 2005)

## Geo-Object

An object class that represents an individual, particular real-world geographic object. Such objects can usually be traced back to individually identifiable elements, such as houses, lakes, and trees. (Davis et al., 2005)

## Geo-Reference

The relationship between page-coordinates on a planar map and known, real-world coordinates. (Rambaldi, 2005)

## Geocoding

**1:** A function of the GIS through which the geographic location of an address is given a set of geographic coordinates by reference to a standard geographically referenced database. These coordinates are then used for mapping. (Garb & Wait, 2005b) **2:** A generic term used to describe the GIS function of providing a specific location to descriptive data. Geocoding applies to point data (e.g., alcohol outlet) as well as to area data (e.g., assaults in a census tract). (Lipton et al., 2005)

## Geographic Data

Characterized by the fact that they are constituted of two kinds of attributes: descriptive or non-spatial attributes, and positioning or spatial attributes. Non-spatial data are not specific of geographic applications, and they are usually handled by standard relational DBMSs. Spatial attributes need additional power in order to design, store, and manipulate the spatial part of geographic entities. (Faïz, 2005)

## Geographic Database (GDB)

A database integrated into the GIS, storing spatial and alphanumerical data. (Faïz & Mahmoudi, 2005)

## Geographic Information System (GIS)

**1:** A database of a region and software interfaces to view and manage the data. GIS implementation often begins with a digitized map of an area derived from original parcel maps or aerial photography. Multiple "layers" are created for the map to include different infrastructure systems such as roads, sewers, and telecommunications. (Horiuchi, 2005a) **2:** A marriage of accurately scaled digital maps with a database. The digital maps comprise spatially referenced details such as natural elements (lakes, rivers, topographic elevation contours, etc.), man-made objects (buildings, roads, pipelines, etc.), and political boundaries (city limits, state and county lines, international boundaries, etc.). These natural elements are typically referenced, with varying degrees of precision, to latitude/longitude coordinates on the Earth's surface. (Crossland, 2005) **3:** Tool for processing localized information. A GIS will model and locate the spatial data of a real phenomenon. (Zelasco et al., 2005) **4:** An organized collection of computer hardware, software, data, and personnel designed to capture, store and update, manipulate, analyze, and display geographically referenced information. (Rambaldi, 2005) **5:** A spatial data management system that allows the user to deal with (save, retrieve, extract, manipulate, and visualize) the information of physical entities. (Jeong et al., 2006) **6:** Map-based tools used to gather, transform, manipulate, analyze, and produce information related to the surface of the Earth. (Pang, 2005a) **7:** A computerized database system used for the capture, conversion, storage, retrieval, analysis, and display of spatial objects. (Ferri & Rafanelli, 2005) **8:** Computer system for acquiring, storing, processing, analyzing, and displaying combined spatial and non-spatial data for academic, societal, or organizational purposes. (Hendricks, 2005) **9:** Information system storing geographical data along with alphanumeric and spatial components. GIS systems also provide the data structures and algorithms to represent and efficiently query a collection of geographical data. (De Antonellis et al., 2005) **10:** An information system that stores and manipulates data for geographical entities such as streets, road junctions, railway, land-use, or even terrain. The data is associated with the location of the entities to allow fast geo-referencing. (Leong, 2005a) **11:** The geographic use of data to develop maps and statistical relationships that help describe processes like the relationship between alcohol outlets and violence or vehicle crashes and alcohol outlets. (Lipton et al., 2005) **12:** A set of tools that rely on data management technologies to manage, process, and present geospatial data, which in turn can vary with time. (Ganguly et al., 2005) **13:** A system composed of computer hardware, software, geographic data, and personnel designed to capture, store, update, manipulate, analyze, and display all forms of geographically referenced information. (Gilbert, 2005a) **14:** A system to provide tools to provision and administer base map data such as built structures (streets and buildings) and terrain (mountain, rivers, etc.). (Fraunholz et al., 2005) **15:** A computer system that permits the user to examine and handle numerous layers of spatial data. The system is intended to solve problems and investigate relationships. The data symbolize real-world entities, including spatial and quantitative attributes of these entities. (Sadoun, 2006) **16:** A computer system capable of capturing, storing, analyzing, and displaying geographically referenced information. (Faïz & Mahmoudi, 2005) **17:** An information system that manages geographic data—that is, data for which the geometric shape and spatial location are indispensable parts, which must be considered while working with them. (Davis et al., 2005)

## Geographic Position System (GPS)

A satellite-based system with applications for determining locations, navigating, and monitoring the movement of people and objects, including provision of accurate times and velocities. (Barima, 2006b)

## Geographical Analysis Model

A model to derive new spatial information by combining existing spatial and attribute data sources as appear useful for a given research goal (e.g., route selection, service area definition). (Hendricks, 2005)

## Geographical Database

A database in which geographical information is store by x-y coordinates of single points, or points that identify the boundaries of lines (or polylines, which sometimes represent the boundaries of polygons). Different attributes characterize the objects stored in these databases. In general, the storing structure consists of "classes" of

objects, each of them implemented by a layer. Often a geographical database includes raster, topological vector, image processing, and graphics production functionality. (Ferri & Rafanelli, 2005)

## Geographical Dispersion

The combination of virtual organization with IT allows groups of employees to make progress on one project while working in tandem with another group in a distant physical location. Because information can be shared and meetings can be held with the use of high-speed networks and computers, tasks can be carried out in the location that is most appropriate and germane to that function. (J. Lee, 2005)

## Geographically Dispersed Team (GDT)

A group of people who work together across boundaries of time, space, and organizations, usually supported by network and communication technologies. Team members generally have complementary skills, sharing an overall purpose and interdependent performance goals, along with an approach to work that the team adopts, by which members hold themselves mutually accountable. (Dara-Abrams, 2006)

## Geometric Hashing

The technique identifying an object in the scene, together with its position and orientation. (Chan & Chang, 2005)

## Geometric Texture

Geometric distortions and additions applied to the original geometric shapes (e.g., roughness, bristle, fur, etc.). (Sourin, 2006)

## Geoprocessing

Operations in GIS for integrating, analyzing, computing, and presenting geospatial data. (Karimi & Peachavanish, 2005)

## Georeferencing

Identifying the geographic location of features and their boundaries on the Earth's surface, for example, derived from GPS, remote sensing, mapping, and surveying technologies. (Hendricks, 2005)

## Geospatial Data

Data representing objects on or near the surface of the Earth. (Karimi & Peachavanish, 2005)

**G**

**Geospatial Information System (GIS)**

**1:** An information system capable of storing, managing, computing, and displaying geospatial data for solving geospatial problems. (Karimi & Peachavanish, 2005) **2:** A system that provides a common framework for jointly visualizing the world. (Morris-Jones & Carter, 2005)

**Geospatial Problem**

One of a number of problems involving geospatial data, objects, and phenomena. (Karimi & Peachavanish, 2005)

**Geostationary**

Refers to geosynchronous satellite angle with zero inclination—that is, the satellite appears to hover over one spot on the Earth's equator. (Statica & Deek, 2006)

**Geovisualization**

Data representation using more than one dimension to convey meaning, including animation and dynamic cartography, and spatialization (using geographic metaphors to generate georeferenced displays of non-spatial data such as text, image, or sound archives). (Hendricks, 2005)

**Gesture**

Refers in our case to digital-pen gestures, which are movements of the hands while writing onto digital screens that are interpreted as system commands. (Mohamed & Ottmann, 2006)

**Gesture/Activity Recognition**

Dynamic body configuration that involves spatiotemporal analysis. (Ozer et al., 2005)

**Gesture Tracking**

The set of mechanisms allowing one to record and analyze human motion. Gesture may be tracked either in 2D or 3D. Gesture tracking ranges from the recording and analysis of postures (e.g., head, body) to that of more detailed elements such as hand-fine movement or facial expression. The aims of gesture tracking in HCI span from recognizing the user's current activity (or lack of), to recognizing emotional states. Gesture tracking is often used in combination with gaze tracking. (Thomas & Roda, 2006a)

**GIF**

Internet graphics image file format. (Friedman, 2005)

**GIG:** See *Global Information Grid.*

**Gigabit PON (GPON)**

Defined by the ITU-T G.984 series of recommendations; features a passive optical network for fiber-to-the-home service that is capable of providing at least 1 Gbps service in the downstream direction. (Kelic, 2005)

**GIS:** See *Geographic Information System; Geospatial Information Systems; Global Information Society.*

**GIS Distance and Adjacency Function**

The distance between individual objects (e.g., bars and crashes) and whether areas are adjacent to one another. (Lipton et al., 2005)

**Gisting**

Using computing technologies to provide a rough or imperfect but understandable translation of a text. (St. Amant, 2005e)

**Global Baseline**

The median value of pixel distribution along the vertical projection. (Chakravarty et al., 2005a)

**Global Civil Society**

Consists of the myriad groups and networks of action and knowledge that can, but do not necessarily, extend across state borders. (Smith & Smythe, 2005)

**Global Culture**

The new emerging layer of cultures, triggered by the developments of the global economy. At this layer, partners from different cultures and civilizations deliberately apply the same patterns of behavior in order to achieve successful communication in business (political, social, and so forth) endeavors. (Targowski & Metwalli, 2005)

**Global Delivery Model**

A model built to distribute and manage software development across multiple global locations. GDM requires infrastructure, project management, cultural sensitivity, and process guidelines to support communication and coordination between locations. (Hawk & Kaiser, 2005)

**Global Digital Divide**

The gap established due to unequal capacity among countries to access, adapt, and create knowledge via the use of digital information and communication technologies. (Trujillo, 2005)

**Global Distribution System**

A type of system used by airlines, travel agencies, and other intermediaries to manage product inventory, and to sell tourism products and packages. In the past, these have been dedicated-line electronic services, but virtually all of the major GDSs (Amadeus, SABRE, Galileo, etc.) have migrated to online systems. (Carson, 2005)

**Global Economy**

Largely understood in terms of worldwide economic and political convergence around liberal market principles and the increasing real-time integration of business, technological, and financial systems. (Targowski & Metwalli, 2005)

**Global Electronic Commerce**

Commercial activities that take place over a computer network, usually the Internet and the Web, across national borders. (He, 2006)

**Global E-Market Segmentation**

Process leading to the identification of homogeneous consumer groups in global Internet markets. (Ortega Egea & Menéndez, 2006)

**Global E-Marketing**

Marketing efforts undertaken by companies outside their domestic market. (Ortega Egea & Menéndez, 2006)

**Global E-Marketing Mix**

Combination of elements (promotion, price, place, and product) used by online companies to market their products/services on a global scale. (Ortega Egea & Menéndez, 2006)

**Global Feature**

One of a set of features extracted using the complete signature image or signal as a single entity. (Chakravarty et al., 2005b)

**Global Frequent Itemset**

A set of words that occur together in some minimum fraction of the whole document set. (Fung et al., 2005)

**Global (General) Knowledge Interaction**

Knowledge interaction that occurs among entities that are relatively at the same global level, such as the development and use of international standards among nations and institutions. (Medeni, 2006a)

**Global Information Grid (GIG)**

The Department of Defense's next-generation network and future infrastructure for advanced data, information, and knowledge operations. Current GIG initiatives involve high-security systems. (Maule, 2006)

**Global Information Society (GIS)**

Refers to the linking of people using the Internet to share information for the benefit of all societies around the globe. (Singh, 2005)

**Global Infrastructure**

A sphere of concern; consists of the wireless access and backbone networks, as well as servers and terminals that are necessary for e-commerce in general and m-commerce in particular at a certain moment. Global infrastructure is shaped by the organizational entities within the regulatory framework sphere, and controlled and operated by companies and governments. Global infrastructure consists of heterogeneous components (WLANs, 2G and 3G telecom network, wireline telecom networks, Internet, proprietary IP networks, and a great variety of wireless terminals) and evolves over time as new technologies are adopted from the enabling technologies sphere, where they are developed. (Veijalainen & Weske, 2005)

**Global Outsourcing**

**1:** The trend towards directing outsourcing—contracting with other firms to perform non-critical functions for a business—toward countries with low workforce costs. (Trauth, 2005a) **2:** The sourcing of IT jobs to foreign countries and corporations (outsourcing) or employment of foreign nationals in foreign countries by U.S. corporations (insourcing). (Mendonca, 2005)

**Global Popularity**

Depends on the number of requests to the object. (Kacimi et al., 2005)

**Global Positioning Satellite (GPS)**

A format of presenting geospatial data for tracking purposes used often in location-based services. (Morris-Jones & Carter, 2005)

**Global Positioning System (GPS)**

**1:** A satellite-based system used for determining geographical positions, with a precision of 10 meters. It uses a constellation of 24 satellites and is controlled by the U.S. Department of Defense. (Costagliola et al., 2006) **2:**

A system of determining the absolute location of features by calculating x, y, z coordinates of ground locations from the signal of satellites orbiting the Earth. (Hendricks, 2005) **3:** The worldwide satellite-based radio navigation system. The system's satellites transmit messages that a receiver uses to determine its own geographical position. (Giaglis, 2005) **4:** Provides real-time, satellite-derived location information based on information received by an appropriate GPS receiver. GPS is funded by and controlled by the U.S. Department of Defense. While there are many thousands of civil users of GPS worldwide, the system was designed for and is operated by the U.S. military. A GPS may be employed in the original construction of the digital map information to be stored in a GIS. Or, if the GIS is already constructed, the GPS may be employed to accurately render the position of new elements to be added to the GIS or the current position of a mobile element to be referenced against the information stored in the GIS. A good example might be a freight truck moving on a highway. The GPS receiver on the truck can derive its current latitude and longitude, and then send that information to the GIS system in the truck cab, to a GIS in a central control center via radio, or to both for subsequent reporting and analysis. (Crossland, 2005) **5:** Worldwide radio-navigation system formed from a constellation of 24 satellites and their ground stations that provide reference points to calculate positions accurate to a matter of meters, and with advanced forms, to less than a centimeter. GPS receivers are so miniaturized that they are becoming accessible to virtually everyone. Used in cars, boats, aircraft, construction equipment, farm machinery, and even laptop computers, they are predicted to become almost as basic as the telephone. (Latchem & Maru, 2005) **6:** Satellite technology that locates people and objects on earth with high accuracy. (Szewczak, 2006) **7:** A self-positioning, wave-based positioning system consisting of 24 satellites revolving around the Earth in six orbits, which send continuous radio signals using triangulation to determine an exact location. (Fraunholz et al., 2005) **8:** A system developed by the U.S. Department of Defense to allow the military to accurately determine its precise location anywhere in the world. GPS uses a collection of 24 satellites positioned in orbit to allow a person who has the proper equipment to automatically have their position triangulated to determine their location. (Kontolemakis et al., 2005) **9:** Utilizes a wide-reaching radio broadcasting system, originally produced to aid navigation, consisting of a group of 24 satellites plus terrestrial receiving devices. (Friedman, 2005) **10:** A satellite-based, publicly available navigation system that can determine the position of a small

portable GPS receiver very accurately. (Strauss, 2005) **11:** An MEO (medium earth orbit) public satellite navigation system consisting of 24 satellites used for determining one's precise location and providing a highly accurate time reference almost anywhere on Earth. (Dhar, 2005)

## Global Schema

Schema obtained after integrating local schemas. (Passi et al., 2005)

## Global Semantics of Referential Actions

The whole effect interacting referential actions lead to under update operations on the database state. (Rivero, 2005)

## Global Serializability

The correctness criterion for concurrent execution of global transactions over many database systems. It is a stronger correctness criterion than serializability. (Leong, 2005b)

## Global Software Team

Software teams located in different countries collaborate as a single team for a clear objective project. (Lui & Chan, 2005)

## Global System for Mobile Communication (GSM)

**1:** The second generation of mobile technology in Europe. (Hackbarth et al., 2005) **2:** A digital cellular telephone system introduced in 1991 that is the major system in Europe and Asia, and is increasing in its use in North America. GSM uses Time Division Multiple Access (TDMA) technology, which allows up to eight simultaneous calls on the same radio frequency. (Garrett, 2006a) **3:** A world standard for digital cellular communications using narrowband TDMA. It is the standard most commonly used in Europe and Asia, but not in the United States. (Lei et al., 2005a) **4:** Industry standard for second-generation digital cellular communications networks, soon to be superseded by Third Generation (3G) networks. (Gilbert, 2005b) **5:** A mobile network that provides all services of fixed telephony to wireless subscribers. (Louvros, Karaboulas, et al., 2005) **6:** Industry standard for 2G digital cellular networks. (Gilbert, 2005c) **7:** For mobile telecommunications, a digital cellular communication network standard. (Fraunholz et al., 2005) **8:** A digital mobile telephone system that is widely used in Europe and other parts of the world. GSM uses a variation of TDMA and is the most widely used of the three digital wireless telephone technologies (TDMA, GSM, and CDMA). GSM digitizes and compresses data, then sends it down a channel with two other streams of user data, each in its own time slot. It operates at either the 900-MHz or 1,800-MHz frequency band. (Olla, 2005a) **9:** The dominant digital mobile phone standard that uses SIM cards that subscribers place inside their phones. It supports data transmission as well as voice. (D. Stern, 2005) **10:** In 1982, the European Conference of Postal and Telecommunications Administrations founded a consortium for the coordination and standardization of a future pan-European telephone network called "Group Spécial Mobile" that was later renamed "Global System for Mobile Communications." (Kaspar & Hagenhoff, 2005) **11:** A worldwide standard for digital wireless mobile phone systems. The standard was originated by the European Conference of Postal and Telecommunications Administrations, who was responsible for the creation of ETSI. Currently, ETSI is responsible for the development of the GSM standard. (Akhtar, 2005)

## Global Test

Verifies that an update operation violates an integrity constraint by accessing data at remote sites. (Ibrahim, 2005)

## Global Village

As computers all over the world become interconnected via the Internet, and the frequency of communication in and between organizations, countries, cultures, societies, and so forth has increased accordingly via these networks, we can now on a daily basis and quite easily maintain contact with anybody independent of time and space; that is, we are able to interact anytime, anywhere. (Wiberg, 2005)

## Global Virtual Team

A group that: (1) is identified by its organization(s) and members as a team; (2) is responsible for making and/or implementing decisions important to the organization's global strategy; (3) uses technology-supported communication substantially more than face-to-face communication; and (iv) works and lives in different countries. (Wei & Wang, 2006)

## Global-As-View

The situation in which the global schema is defined directly in terms of the source schemas. GAV systems typically arise in the context where the source schemas are given, and the global schema is to be derived from the local schemas. (Balsters, 2005)

## Globalization

**1:** The bypassing of traditional geographic borders using information technology to enable global orientation of business and remote curriculum delivery. (Russell, 2005a) **2:** Commonly refers to the process whereby the capitalist economy becomes increasingly integrated and organized on a global scale. (Smith & Smythe, 2005) **3:** International exchange or sharing of labor force, production, ideas, knowledge, cultures, products, and services across national borders. (He, 2006) **4:** The marketing and selling of a product outside a company's home country. (D. Brandon, Jr., 2005b) **5:** The process of planning and implementing products and services so that they can be adapted to different local languages and cultures. (O'Hagan, 2005) **6:** The trend towards thinking and acting globally, with multi-national corporations, partners, and competitors across the globe. (Marshall & Gregor, 2005) **7:** This term was first applied to the world economy, which under conditions of global information and communication network can basically operate as a unified system in the real-time mode. (Azarov, 2005) **8:** Business issues associated with taking a product global. It involves both internationalization and localization. (T.S. Chan, 2005)

## Globalized Education

Educational programs in which both students and educators may be globally distributed. (Grasso & Leng, 2005)

## Glocal

A portmanteau expression created from the combination of the expressions "global" and "local" to denote something that is simultaneously global and local. (Taylor et al., 2005)

## Glocal Knowledge Interaction

Knowledge interaction from the global knowledge level to that of local knowledge; for instance, tailoring the product of a multi-national company, or the development project of an international aid organization, with respect to the unique characteristics of a region or community. (Medeni, 2006a)

## Glocalization

Creation of products or services intended for the global market, but customized to suit the local culture. (He, 2006)

## Glossing

The telling or retelling of a story in a way that emphasizes or excludes particular points of view. (Connell, 2006)

**Glycemic Control**
Tells how well controlled are the sugars of a diabetic patient. Usually measured by HgbA1c. (Breault, 2005)

**gMMt:** See *Generic Model Management.*

**GNU**
A recursive acronym for "GNU's Not Unix." The GNU Project was launched in 1984 to develop a free Unix-like operating system. (Lowry, Grover, et al., 2005)

**GNU General Public License**
**1:** The first and still the most radical open source software license, created for the GNU Project. Requires that all derivative works be equally free (in the open source sense); that is, all derivative works must provide the full source code and must permit free use, modification, and redistribution. (Carillo & Okoli, 2006) **2:** The first and still the most radical open source software license, created for the GNU Project. Requires that all derivative works be equally free (in the open source sense); that is, all derivative works must provide the full source code and must permit free use, modification, and redistribution. (Okoli & Carillo, 2006)

**GNU Project**
**1:** Stands for "Gnu's Not Unix." Established by Richard Stallman in 1983 under the auspices of the Free Software Foundation. Its goal was, and still is, to create an open source Unix-based operating system. This goal was realized in 1991 by Linus Torvald's creation of Linux. (Carillo & Okoli, 2006) **2:** Project launched by Richard Stallman with the goal of creating a complete free operating system: the GNU system. GNU is a recursive acronym for "GNU's Not Unix." (Curti, 2005)

**Go-Live**
The actual operation of an information system. (Sarkis & Sundarraj, 2005)

**Goal**
**1:** A high-level representation of the purpose of a multi-agent system. (Sterling, 2006) **2:** A specification of the desired changes a work system attempts to achieve in an application domain. (Diaper, 2006)

**Goal Condition**
A condition underlying application descriptions and related to external concepts to be considered by an application realization, such as a requirement to contemplate collaboration. (Tobar et al., 2006)

**Goal Orientation**
The degree of orientation towards a defined target; low goal orientation means the common intention of a community or network is diffuse. (Müeller-Prothmann, 2006a)

**Goal Setting**
**1:** Ability to articulate steps within a strategy and to accomplish them. (Crichton, 2005) **2:** Defining goals, be they benign or corrupt; political processes are invoked. The goals themselves can be constructive or destructive, formally or informally arrived at, at the level of the organization or the individual, public or private. (Land, Amjad, et al., 2006)

**Goal-Directed Behavior**
The concept that individuals are motivated to expend time and energy to achieve some desired objective (the goal). A significant amount of online consumer behavior is goal directed. (Porter, 2006)

**Goal-Oriented Representation**
An application designed to solve rather than simply describe a problem or process. (O'Looney, 2006)

**Goal-Setting Theory**
This theory, developed by Locke and Latham, states that individuals make calculated decisions about their desired goals, and that these goals and intentions, once established, direct and motivate efforts to attain them. (Hendriks & Sousa, 2006)

**Goals of Scientific Research**
The purposes of science are to describe and predict, to improve or to manipulate the world around us, and to explain our world. One goal of scientific research is to discover new and useful knowledge for the purpose of science. As a specific research field, data mining shares this common goal, and may be considered as a research support system. (Yao & Zhao, 2005)

**Goals-Based Evaluation**
A type of evaluation used to determine the extent to which programs are achieving their overall, predetermined objectives. (Nelson, 2005)

## GOMS

A set of techniques for modeling human task performance. It stands for Goals, Operators, Methods, and Selection rules. GOMS has become an important model for human-computer interaction studies. (Chen, Sockel, et al., 2005)

## Good Governance

The exercise of the governance authority with the participation, interest, and livelihood of the governed as the driving force (UNDESA/DPADM). (Misuraca, 2005)

## Good Practice

Institutional practice or design of a project, geared towards solving a problem, achieving a goal, improving the process, better rendering a service, or upgrading productivity, quality, or organizational effectiveness. (Falivene & Kaufman, 2006)

## Goodwill

The amount of repeat business resulting from happy and loyal customers. (Forgionne & Ingsriswang, 2005)

## Google AdWords

A plain, text-based advertisement displayed prominently on Google.com. For a fee, advertisers sponsor search words/terms entered by users of the Google.com search engine. The sponsored search words are predicted by the sponsor to relate to a product or service offered. (Duthler, 2005)

## Governance

**1:** A multi-faceted compound situation of institutions, systems, structures, processes, procedures, practices, relationships, and leadership behavior in the exercise of social, political, economic, and managerial/administrative authority in the running of public or private affairs (UNDESA/DPADM). **2:** A process that is a framework of authority to ensure the delivery of anticipated or predicted benefits of a service or process. The operationalization of the particular organizational strategy is therefore executed in an authorized and regulated manner. Governance acts to manage risk, evaluate and review strategic goals and objectives, and exercise fiscal accountability to ensure the return on investment of those strategies. (Zyngier, 2006)

## Governance Archetype

Archetypes typically involve various stakeholder constituencies and their decision rights within the purview of IT governance. (Saha, 2006a)

## Governance Decision

Represents the most crucial domain of IT decisions that are key to good IT governance, and includes IT principles, IT architecture, IT infrastructure, business application needs, and IT investment management. (Saha, 2006a)

## Governance Mechanism

The set of approaches adopted by organizations to implement and institutionalize governance structures and practices. (Saha, 2006a)

## Government

The art of managing relationships between citizens to ensure their welfare and in general their personal, economic, and social development. (Córdoba, 2006b)

## Government-Led E-Democracy

Top-down change process. Governments create points of electronic interface in order to consult or capture opinion from citizens. This is most often a change process—a new way of recreating existing communication and consultation models, for example, consultation on policy issues or planning processes and clinics with politicians. (Williamson, 2005)

## Government-Private Sector Partnership

The teaming of different entities in the government and the private sector to realize a change and a transformation in the development of information technology at large and, more specifically, in the software industry. (Kamel, 2005a)

## Government-to-Business (G2B)

Refers to government contracts and other services available online for businesses to bid for. (Hin & Subramaniam, 2006)

## Government-to-Citizen (G2C)

**1:** Different citizen-centric services provided by the government for the benefits of the citizen. These include providing birth and death certificates, records of rights of land, information on government Schemes, and so on. (Borbora & Dutta, 2005) **2:** Refers to the various government services that citizens need access to. (Hin & Subramaniam, 2006) **3:** Governments offering services to citizens online. (Toland, 2006)

### Government-to-Government (G2G)

**1:** Online interactions between different government agencies. (Toland, 2006) **2:** The digital-enabled collaboration and cooperation perspective among distinct government agencies. (Joia, 2006)

### Government-to-Partners (G2P)

The type of relationship that exists in associative or network governance models between government and partners or stakeholders, and vice versa. (Kaufman, 2005)

### Governmental Agency

A branch, division, or department of a local, regional, or national government that carries out one or more duties or activities in support of the public good. Such duties often involve regulating aspects of commerce, public health, safety, and so forth. (Baim, 2006a)

**GPL:** See *General Public License.*

**GPON:** See *Gigabit PON.*

**GPRS:** See *General Packet Radio Service.*

**GPS:** See *Geographic Position System; Global Positioning System; Global Positioning Satellite.*

### Grammars

A set of formal rules that define how to perform inference over a dictionary of terms. (Caelli, 2005)

### Grant, Tied Grant

A grant is generally a sum of money that is either paid in full or installments over the life of a particular project, while a tied grant stipulates particular conditions. (De Weaver, 2005)

### Granular Data

Data representing the lowest level of detail that resides in the data warehouse. (Peter & Greenidge, 2005b)

### Granularity

**1:** The level of detail or complexity at which an information resource is described. (Lin et al., 2005) **2:** A hierarchical concept associated with the relative degree of complexity of a component part to its aggregate, subsuming structure. Fine silt is more granular than sand, which is more granular than rock, and so forth. In taxonomic development, the smaller the relative size to the taxons (units) of classification, the higher the degree of granularity. In instructional design, the concept of granularity is multi-faceted and can refer to the size of learning units or scope (e.g., degree or certificate curricula, courses, lessons, modules, activities); learning element prioritization or sequencing (e.g., logical order of lessons, concept formation, and skill acquisition to optimize scaffolding in new knowledge construction); content domains architecture (e.g., superordinate concepts, subordinate concepts, rules, principles); teaching strategy (e.g., individual vs. group learning, passive learner/expository vs. active leaner/discovery, inductive vs. deductive, tutorial vs. simulation, abstract vs. problem oriented, synchronous online chat vs. asynchronous threaded discussions, etc.); media design and utilization (e.g., relative size and complexity of single components or combined components; type of media element including text, graphics/visuals, audio, animation, degree of user control, etc.); and learner assessment (e.g., conventional declarative-convergent testing using multiple-choice, matching, and short-answer questions vs. holistic, constructivist-divergent portfolios with demonstration work-product artifacts from individual and group projects, internships, and service learning). (Lasnik, 2005) **3:** Refers to the size of a shareable learning object. The smaller the learning object, the greater the granularity it has. Smaller learning objects have a greater opportunity for reusability. (Stavredes, 2005b) **4:** The level of detail of the facts stored in a data warehouse, or a concept in the database. (Nigro & González Císaro, 2005b)

### Granularity of Time

A concept that denotes precision in a temporal database. An example of progressive time granularity includes a day, an hour, a second, or a nanosecond. (Raisinghani & Klassen, 2005)

### Granulation and Partition

Partition is a decomposition of a set into a collection of mutually disjoint subsets. Granulation is defined similarly, but allows the subsets to be generalized subsets, such as fuzzy sets, and permits the overlapping. (T.Y. Lin, 2005)

## Graph

**1:** A graph consists of vertices and edges. Each edge is connected to a source node and a target node. Vertices and edges can be labeled with numbers and symbols. (Fischer, 2005) **2:** A set of vertices (nodes) connected in various ways by edges. (Caelli, 2005) **3:** In mathematics, a set of vertices or nodes connected by links or edges. A pair of vertices that are connected by multiple edges yield a multi-graph; vertices that are connected to themselves via looping edge yield a pseudo-graph. (Banerjee et al., 2005)

## Graph Encoding

A method to assign the nodes of a directed graph a number or a bit string, which reflects some properties of that graph and can be used to facilitate computation. (Chen, 2005a)

## Graph Grammar

Grammar describing the construction of a set of graphs, where terminals and non-terminals represent vertices, edges, or entire subgraphs. (Holder & Cook, 2005)

## Graph Invariants

Quantities to characterize the topological structure of a graph. If two graphs are topologically identical, they have identical graph invariants. (Li, 2005)

## Graph Production

Similar to productions in general Chomsky grammars, a graph production consists of a left-hand side and a right-hand side. The left-hand side is embedded in a host graph. Then it is removed and, in the resulting hole, the right-hand side of the graph production is inserted. To specify how this right-hand side is attached into this hole, how edges are connected to the new nodes, some additional information is necessary. Different approaches exist of how to handle this problem. (Fischer, 2005)

## Graph Rewriting

The application of a graph production to a graph is also called graph rewriting. (Fischer, 2005)

## Graph Spectra

The plot of the eigenvalues of the graph adjacency matrix. (Caelli, 2005)

## Graph-Based Data Mining

**1:** A method of data mining used to find novel, useful, and understandable patterns in graph representations of data. (Banerjee et al., 2005) **2:** Finding novel, useful, and understandable graph-theoretic patterns in a graph representation of data. (Holder & Cook, 2005)

## Graphical Content

Information represented by an image, perceived via the human visual system. (Rosenbaum et al., 2006)

## Graphical Curiosity

Curious to see visually complex or multimedia effects. (Wishart, 2005)

## Graphical Model

A family of probability distributions incorporating the conditional independence assumptions represented by a graph. It is specified via a graph that depicts the local relations among the variables (that are represented with nodes). (Giudici & Cerchiello, 2005)

## Graphical Process Modeling Technique

A technique for representing models of processes with a graphical notation. (Rodríguez-Elias et al., 2006)

## Graphical User Interface (GUI)

**1:** A software interface based on the computer's graphics capabilities with pointing devices such as the mouse that frees the user from learning complex commands for using programs. (Rashid, 2005) **2:** A software interface that relies on icons, bars, buttons, boxes, and other images to initiate computer-based tasks for users. (Mathieu & Levary, 2005) **3:** A standardized way of presenting information and opportunities for interaction on the computer screen using the graphical capabilities of modern computers. GUIs use windows, icons, standard menu formats, and so forth, and most are used with a mouse as well as a keyboard. (Henley & Noyes, 2006) **4:** Specifically involves pull-down menus for keyboard and mouse inputs. (Mohamed & Ottmann, 2006) **5:** Most of the modern operating systems provide a GUI, which enables a user to use a pointing device, such as a computer mouse, to provide the computer with information about the user's intentions. (Sarkar, 2005)

## Grassroots ICT Intermediary

Person serving a community by adding human skills and knowledge to the presence of ICT, often operating in a telecenter. (Cecchini, 2005)

## Gravity Model

A model that measures the interaction between social/economic objects, similar to the gravity model in physics.

**G**

In the model, the intensity of interaction (e.g., trips, migration, or communication) is positively related to the sizes of objects (e.g., population), but inversely related to the distance or travel time between them. (Wang & Lou, 2005)

## Gray Marketing
Occurs when products are sold through non-authorized channels of distribution. (Rosson, 2006)

## Grayscale Image
Shades of gray or continuous-tone of gray representing an image. (Chen, Chen, Ma, et al., 2005)

## Greedy Algorithm
An algorithm that always takes the best immediate, or local, solution while finding an answer. Greedy algorithms find the overall, or globally, optimal solution for some optimization problems, but may find less-than-optimal solutions for some instances of other problems. (Chakraborty et al., 2005)

## Greenstone
Widely used open source software for digital libraries developed in New Zealand. (McCarthy, 2005b)

## Grey Market Informatics
Processes in which differences in national privacy laws are used to compile and distribute personal data on individuals. (St.Amant, 2006b)

## Grid Computing
**1:** A distributed computing setting which has the tendency to allow users to communicate and share resources without much worry about its origin. (Sowe et al., 2005) **2:** A form of distributed computing that involves coordinating and sharing computing, application, data, storage, or network resources across dynamic and geographically dispersed organizations. (Yen, 2005) **3:** Grid (network) of computing resources designed to provide computing and storage to applications in a scalable and reliable manner, ensuring high levels of utilization. (Feuerlicht & Vorisek, 2006) **4:** Linking computers from different locations to a computer network, which allows users to share applications, computer power, data, and other resources. (Luppicini, 2006)

## Gross Domestic Product (GDP)
The sum of the total value of consumption expenditure, total value of investment expenditure, and government purchases of goods and services. (Dholakia & Kshetri, 2005)

## Grounded Theory
**1:** A method used to systematically derive theories of human behavior from empirical data. (Trauth, 2005b) **2:** A qualitative research methodology. (Molinari, 2005) **3:** A mutual understanding about problems and tasks for groups of learners. (Berg, 2005f)

## Group
A number of individuals who interact for purposes of addressing some shared purpose or task. This differentiates human collectives from random clusters of people who happen to be co-located, or who have no purpose that requires interaction. (Cargill, 2006b)

## Group Authoring and Design Tool
One of a set of collaboration tools used by work groups to jointly create or edit common documents interactively, including design documents. The display is updated on each participant's computer as changes are made jointly and can be saved by each participant for future reference. (Wild, 2005)

## Group Communication Support System (GCSS)
An environment created to support the communication process and reduce communication barriers. (Signoret, 2006)

## Group Decision
A decision adopted by a group of people with complete interaction under majority or consensus conditions. (Xodo, 2005)

## Group Dynamics
Field of inquiry dedicated to advancing knowledge about the nature of groups. (Verburg et al., 2005)

## Group Decision Support System (GDSS)
**1:** A collection of hardware and software used to support decision makers. (Banks, 2005) **2:** An interactive computer-based system that facilitates solutions to unstructured problems by decision makers working as a group. Among other features, the software package includes idea organizers, electronic brainstorming tools, questionnaire tools, and group dictionaries. (Ruhi, 2006) **3:** An interactive, computer-based system that aids a set of decision makers working together as a group in solving ill-

structured problems. It enables decision makers to analyze problem situations and perform group decision-making tasks. (Karacapilidis, 2005) **4:** Information systems that support the work of groups (communication, decision making) generally working on unstructured or semi-structured problems. (Duan & Xu, 2005) **5:** A collective of computer-based technologies that are specifically designed to support the activities and processes related to multi-participant decision making. (Xodo, 2005)

## Group Explorer

Software used in a group which (in part) enables each participant to directly insert his/her knowledge (in the form of contributions and causal links) into a group map. Group Explorer works with Decision Explorer, which displays the group map on the public screen. (Shaw, 2006)

## Group Formation

The process of creating a suitable group of learners to increase the learning efficiency for both the individual peers and the group as a whole. (Devedžić, 2006)

## Group Map

A structured representation of the contributions of a range of people. The contributions are structured with links that are agreed by the group members during intensive, facilitated discussion of the issues that follow a gathering. (Shaw, 2006)

## Group Potency

A collective belief in the capability of the group to meet a task objective. (Wong & Staples, 2005)

## Group Query

It is representative of a group, and the result of grouped queries is computed from the group query. (Khan, 2005)

## Group Support System (GSS)

**1:** An integrated computer-based system composed of a communication subsystem and model-driven DMSS (DSS), to support problem formulation and potential solution of unstructured decision problems in a group meeting. (Forgionne et al., 2005) **2:** A set of technologies used to help groups in their decision-making processes. (Bélanger, 2005) **3:** A wide variety of technologies configured to support group interactions. GSS typically features software and hardware arrangements that facilitate. (Alavi et al., 2005) **4:** Any combination of hardware and software that enhances group work. (Limayem, 2005) **5:** Interactive

computer-based information systems that support and structure group interaction and facilitate group meetings. (Klein, 2005) **6:** A system providing computer-based support for group communication, decision making, and work activities of co-located (same time, same place) or dispersed (same time, different place; or different time, different place) members of a group. (Chen & Lou, 2005)

## Group Technology (GP)

The concept of grouping parts, resources, or data according to similar characteristics. (Mathieu & Levary, 2005)

## Groupware

**1:** A generic term for specialized computer aids designed for the user of collaborative work groups. Typically, these groups are small project-oriented teams that have important tasks and tight deadlines. Groupware can involve software, hardware, services, and/or group process support. (Daassi et al., 2006) **2:** Class of technologies that allow groups to communicate and coordinate activities. Typically network-driven software. (Green et al., 2005) **3:** Computer software allowing groups, teams, and people in different locations to work together and share information. (Mitchell, 2005b) **4:** ICT applications that support communication, coordination, cooperation, learning, and/or social encounters through facilities such as information exchange, shared repositories, discussion forums, and messaging. (Verburg et al., 2005) **5:** Multi-user software for carrying out communication and collaborative activities. (Neale et al., 2005) **6:** Software applications that help people work together virtually while being physically located at a distance from one another. Groupware applications and services include the sharing of work schedules, event calendars, electronic meetings, shared databases, and group e-mail accounts. (Ruhi, 2006) **7:** Software that supports teams of individuals working together via network technology, facilitating communication, coordination, and collaboration among team members. (Dara-Abrams, 2006) **8:** Software that supports the collaborative efforts of a team to communicate, cooperate, coordinate, solve problems, compete, or negotiate. Groupware technologies are typically categorized along two primary dimensions: time (synchronous or asynchronous) and place (collocated or face to face, or non-collocated or distant). (Wild, 2005) **9:** Specific software which allows groups of people to share information and to coordinate their activities over a computer network. (Metaxiotis, 2006) **10:** The multi-user software supporting CSCW. Sometimes this term is broadened to incorporate the styles and practices that

**G**

are essential for any collaborative activity to succeed, whether or not it is supported by computer. (Karacapilidis, 2005) **11:** The software and technological part of CSCW. It contains application studies and platforms adapted to groups and supporting group working. (Villemur & Drira, 2006 CSCW) **12:** This software can be used by a group of people who are working on the same information at separate workstations. It includes features such as e-mail, shared calendar, task list, and address book, and is used for project management, brainstorming, and action planning. (Nightingale, 2005) **13:** Type of software designed to help teams that are geographically dispersed who need to work together. (de Carvalho & Ferreira, 2006)

## Groupware Application
A class of computer technologies designed to support communication, collaboration, and cooperation among a group of knowledge workers. (Chen & Lou, 2005)

## Groupz
Online groups. 'z' indicates the easiness of language use in online communication. (Lambropoulos, 2006b)

## Groupz Management
The organization of an online community by the moderator. (Lambropoulos, 2006b)

## Groupz-Ware Technology
The groupz-ware needed depending on the nature and culture of each community. (Lambropoulos, 2006b)

## Groupz-Ware Theory
Refers to the multidisciplinary nature of virtual communities and the interaction between disciplines such as learning, psychology of the individual and the masses, sociology, linguistics, communication studies, management, human-computer interaction, and information systems. (Lambropoulos, 2006b)

## Growth Competitiveness Index (GCI)
An index that aims to measure the capacity of the national economy to achieve sustained economic growth over the medium term, controlling for the current level of development. (Neumann, 2005)

## Growth Rate
The ratio of the proportion of data covered by the emerging pattern in one group over the proportion of the data it covers in another group. (Butler & Webb, 2005)

**GSM:** See *Global System for Mobile Communication.*

**GSS:** See *Group Support System.*

## GSS Anonymity
A key feature usually available in most group support systems that allows group members to interact with each other while remaining unidentified to each other. GSS anonymity masks status and gender cues, and reduces inhibitions. (Klein, 2005)

**gTLD:** See *Generic Top-Level Domain.*

**G2B:** See *Government-to-Business.*

**G2C:** See *Government-to-Citizen.*

**G2G:** See *Government-to-Government.*

**G2P:** See *Government-to-Partners.*

**GUI:** See *Graphical User Interface.*

## GUI Sharing Paradigm
A shared application follows the GUI sharing paradigm if the output of a centralized application is shared among all participants of the conference. Feedback from the participants is sent to the centralized server to be incorporated in the control of the application, if desired. (Trossen & Molenaar, 2005)

## Guided Tour
**1:** Combination of links that "guides" a user along a collection of hypermedia nodes that have some topic or concept in common. In MESH, guided tours are generated dynamically at runtime, based on the type of previously followed links by a particular user. (Lemahieu, 2005) **2:** A navigation type that leads users to a predefined trail of nodes without freely explorative navigation, using, for example, previous and next anchors. (Suh & Kim, 2005)

## Guideline
Design and development principles that must be followed in order to achieve a good application. (Prata, 2005)

## Guild
A collection of players who share a common principle or outlook. A guild is a specialized group. Guilds are popular among the variety of MMORPGs available. Often, guilds will have a deity alignment (good, evil, neutral) and carry

out actions consistent with that alignment. However, any players caught behaving badly or against the policies of the guild will be dealt with appropriately, such as being expelled from the guild. (Griffiths et al., 2006)

## Gulf Cooperation Council

A union consisting of the following Arabian Gulf nations: Bahrain, Kuwait, Oman, Saudi Arabia, Qatar, and the United Arab Emirates, which share a common economic market and defense-planning structure. (Reynolds, 2005)

# H

## H.323

An ITU-T specification that defines network protocols, operations, and components for transporting real-time video, audio, and data over IP networks such as the Internet and I2. (Littman, 2005)

## H-Anim (Humanoid Animation)

**1:** Part of VRML specifications consisting of node prototypes allowing the definition of an avatar. (Prêteux & Preda, 2005) **2:** The VRML Consortium Charter for Humanoid Animation Working Group recently produced the International Standard, "Information Technology—Computer Graphics and Image Processing—Humanoid Animation (H-Anim)," an abstract representation for modeling three-dimensional human figures. (Sappa et al., 2005)

**HA:** See *High Availability.*

## Habermasian Logic

The learning process of the human species takes place through the accumulation of both technical and moral-practical knowledge within social interactions yielding a 'logic of growing insight'. (Pemberton & Stalker, 2006)

**HAC:** See *Hierarchical Agglomerative Clustering.*

## Hack

To get access to the contents of a network's database without permission. (Msiska, 2005)

## Hacker

**1:** A very knowledgeable computer user who uses his or her knowledge to invade other people's computers through the computer network. (Chen, Holt, et al., 2005) **2:** An entity outside of an organization that gains or attempts to gain access to a system or system resource without having authorization to do so. (Wilson et al., 2006b) **3:** Someone who breaks into a computer system for fun. (Rowe, 2006c) **4:** A slang term for a computer enthusiast or clever programmer, more commonly used to describe individuals who gain unauthorized access to computer systems for the purpose of stealing or corrupting information or data. Hackers see themselves as the "white hats" or the good guys who breach security for the greater good. The media at large makes no distinction between a hacker and a Cracker. (Tassabehji, 2005a) **5:** A computer expert who breaks into a network or computer system with (usually) malicious intent. (De', 2006)

## Hacking

Hacking, or entering another's computer, is a common method of the cyber-identity thief. (Close et al., 2006)

## Hacktivism

Clandestine use of hacking for the advance of political causes. (De', 2006)

## Half-Band Filters

A low-pass or high-pass filter that divides the basis band in two equal bands, and satisfies prescribed symmetry conditions. (Milić, 2005)

## Halftone

A method to reproduce photographic images in printed media by creating a pattern of dots that change in size to create the perception of lighter and darker tones. (Snyder, 2005)

## HAM

Legitimate e-mail communication. (Willis, 2005)

## Hamming Clustering

A fast binary rule generator and variable selector able to build understandable logical expressions by analyzing the hamming distance between samples. (Liberati, 2005)

## Hamming Distance

The distance between two binary strings (with the same length) given by the number of different bits. (Muselli, 2005)

**Handheld**

A computer small and light enough to be held in a user's hand. (Ketelhut et al., 2005)

**Handheld Computer**

Also called personal digital assistant (PDA); an electronic device small enough to hold in one hand and lightweight enough to carry in a pocket. (Woodruff & Nirula, 2005)

**Handheld Device**

Also known as pen-based computing. (Garrett, 2006b)

**Handheld PC:** See *Web Pad.*

**Handheld Service**

The use of a handheld device, such as a Personal Digital Assistant (PDA) or Pocket PC, as an extension of workstation resources through the use of client-/server-based software for access and synchronization in conjunction with wireless access service provider. Handheld services are used for electronic prescribing, real-time drug references, scheduling, charge capture, and so forth. (O'Buyonge & Chen, 2006)

**Handheld Technology**

A computing device that can be easily held in one hand while the other hand is used to operate it. (Parikh & Parolia, 2005)

**Handoff/Handover**

1: The process of changing some of the parameters of a channel (frequency, time slot, spreading code, or a combination of them) associated with the current connection in progress. Handoffs are initiated by a client's movement, by crossing a cell boundary, or by a deteriorated quality of signal received on a currently employed channel. (Katsaros et al., 2005) 2: Process that occurs after a cell change. The mobile host identifies itself at the Management Support System (MSS) of the cell into which it has moved. (Coratella, Felder, Hirsch, & Rodriguez, 2005) 3: In a cellular network, the radio and fixed voice connections are not permanently allocated for the duration of a call. Handover, or handoff as it is called in North America, means switching an ongoing call to a different channel or cell. This often results in loss of connection. (K.J. MacGregor, 2005)

**Hands-Free Operation**

Allows the user to interact with data and information without the use of hands. (de Freitas & Levene, 2006b)

**Haptic**

1: Relating to the sense of touch. (Murphy, 2005b) 2: The technology of touch which uses the tactile sense to send and receive data. (Ajiferuke & Markus, 2005)

**Haptic Device**

Involves physical contact between the computer and the user, usually through an input and output device, such as a joystick or data gloves, that senses the body's movements. (Yong & Choo, 2005)

**Haptic Output**

A device that produces a tactile or force output. Nearly all devices with tactile output have been developed for graphical or robotic applications. (Bourguet, 2006)

**Hard Case**

A case that cannot be solved by simply applying formal rules, either because: (1) the characteristics of the case are not easily matched to the formal rules, (2) the formal rules do not deliver clear conclusions, and/or (3) applying the formal legal rules leads to unacceptable results. (Svensson, 2005)

**Hard Clustering**

Cluster analysis where each data object is assigned to a unique cluster. (Klawonn & Georgevia, 2005)

**Hard Data**

Historical, usually accurate data, often from transaction processing systems. (Holstein & Crnkovic, 2005)

**Hard Knowledge**

Knowledge that is unambiguous and unequivocal, can be clearly and fully expressed, can be formalized and structured, can be "owned" without being used, and is both abstract and static: it is about, but not in, the world. (Kimble & Hildreth, 2005)

**Hard Skill**

One of several measurable capabilities and academic knowledge acquired through traditional tertiary study. Current MIS curriculum examples include communications and report writing, systems analysis and design, client/server applications, and business applications. (Lowry & Turner, 2005)

**Hard Technology**

Examples include: computer equipment, software, networks, and so forth. (Graham et al., 2005)

**H**

## Hardware and Software Watermark

A unique identifier (e.g., a serial number) embedded in computer equipment and programs. (Szewczak, 2006)

## Harmony

A pleasing combination of elements in a whole. The combination of elements intended to form a connected whole, as opposed to alignment where the elements remain separate. (Johnston, 2005)

## Harvard Case-Based Learning

Students are given a realistic case relevant to the course (information systems, accounting, management, etc.). Students work through the case, in or out of class, and decide what should be done. They then meet with the entire class or in groups, and discuss and resolve the case. (Jennings et al., 2005)

**HASP:** See *High-Altitude Stratosphere Platform.*

**HAVA:** See *Help America Vote Act.*

## Hazard Communication Standard (HCS)

The OSHA (Occupational Safety and Health Act) regulation on the Hazard Communication Standard states that "chemical manufacturers and importers must research the chemicals they produce and import. If a substance presents any of the physical and health hazards specified in the HCS, then the manufacturer or importer must communicate the hazards and cautions to their employees as well as to 'downstream' employers who purchase the hazardous chemicals." (Jeong et al., 2006)

## Hazard Function

A time-to-failure function that gives the instantaneous probability of the event (failure) given that it has not yet occurred. (Chen, Oppenheim, et al., 2005)

**HCI:** See *Human-Computer Interaction.*

## HCI Pattern

A pattern that focuses on how users interact with computers via the interface of the application. (Gaffar & Seffah, 2005)

**HCS:** See *Hazard Communication Standard.*

**HDM:** See *Hypermedia Design Methodology.*

**HDTV:** See *High-Definition Television.*

## Head Pose

Position of the head in 3D space including head tilt and rotation (Lovell & Chen, 2005)

## Head-Mounted Display (HMD)

A visual display unit that is worn on the head as in the use of a virtual reality system. (de Freitas & Levene, 2006b)

## Head-Up Display (HUP)

A display of data and information that is superimposed upon the user's field of view. (de Freitas & Levene, 2006b)

## Header

The beginning portion of a message. By design, it should contain the source and target address for the message. (Horiuchi, 2005b)

## Health Care Enterprise Memory

A knowledge management info-structure which supports the functionality to acquire, share, and operationalize the various modalities of knowledge existent in a health care enterprise. (Metaxiotis, 2006)

## Health Care Industry

The complex of entities engaged in delivering, financing, or monitoring health care. (Rada, 2005)

## Health Care Supply Chain

A managed set of activities related to the health care activity of a patient, organized so that all necessary information is available all the time, and the participants in the chain have a complete picture of the total process. (Suomi, 2005)

## Health Care System

A system composed of health care providers, health plans or insurance companies, and patients. (Rada, 2006)

## Health Information Management (HIM)

The practice of managing, analyzing, and utilizing data vital for patient care and making it accessible to health care providers when it is needed most. (Zender, 2006)

## Health Information System

The system, whether automated or manual, that comprises people, machines, and /or methods organized to collect, process, transmit, and disseminate data that represent user information in health care. (Häyrinen & Saranto, 2005)

## Health Insurance Portability and Accountability Act (HIPAA)

**1:** Standard guidelines and policies enforced by the U.S. federal government to protect confidential medical records. (Wang, Cheng, & Cheng, 2006) **2:** Requires the U.S. Secretary of Health and Human Services to publicize standards for the electronic exchange, privacy, and security of health information. (Cannoy & Salam, 2006) **3:** An American law that put certain restrictions on the way health information can be used and transmitted. As part of their jobs, many AHIMA members design policies and procedures to help their facilities implement the law. (Zender, 2006)

## Health Literacy

The capacity of an individual to obtain, interpret, and understand basic health information and services, and the competence to use such information and services in ways that are health enhancing. (Becker, 2005a)

## Health Plan Employer Data and Information Set

A quality assurance system established by the National Committee for Quality Assurance (NCQA). (Troutt & Long, 2005)

## Health Professional Shortage Area (HPSA)

A geographic area or population group designated by the U.S. Department of Health and Human Services (DHHS) that is underserved in health care. (Wang & Lou, 2005)

**HEDIS:** See *Health Plan Employer Data and Information Set.*

## Hedonic

Referring to the senses, feelings, and emotions. (Bridges et al., 2006)

## Hedonic/Recreational Consumer

A consumer who enjoys shopping for his or her own sake, not just for the items purchased; such consumers are driven by fun, pleasure, curiosity, and exploration. (Scarpi & Dall'Olmo-Riley, 2006)

## Hedonic Use Quality

The quality of a product to deliver pleasurable value to the user. (Knight, 2006a)

## Hegelian/Kantian Perspective of Knowledge Management

Refers to the subjective component of knowledge management; can be viewed as an ongoing phenomenon, being shaped by social practices of communities, and encouraging discourse and divergence of meaning, and the recognition of the existence of multiple approaches. (Wickramasinghe, 2006)

## Help America Vote Act (HAVA)

Provided funding to states to encourage the adoption of new electronic voting systems. It also provided voluntary federal guidelines to be followed in implementing these systems. (Gibson & Brown, 2006)

## Help Desk

A section that can respond to technical queries by users. (Demediuk, 2005)

## Hermeneutic

**1:** A medium that allows for interpretation of different cultural and social perspectives. (Champion, 2006b) **2:** A branch of philosophy which studies interpretation processes. Methodology is the choice of the adequate method for performing research or any scientific activity. Hermeneutics can be understood as a parallel and complementary process to a method. The method identifies, organizes, and orders the necessary steps to accomplish a certain activity and a fixed objective. And hermeneutics calls attention to the intrinsic necessity of constantly interpreting the laws and adapting the rules, norms, and indications given by the method to the idiosyncrasy of a concrete situation, the context, the situatedness, and the horizons of the interpreting community. Hermeneutics developed out of the interpretation of sacred texts. It started from relatively rigid and formalized procedures, and then developed to highly dynamic and flexible approaches. The idea behind modern hermeneutics—developed from the 1950s onwards, though with roots from the late-nineteenth century—is that all reality is a text analog so that it may be read and interpreted as a text. This interpretation process, again, is not rigid and static, but rather it has an ontological and epistemological dimension. Through interpretation, reality manifests itself ontologically, and through this process the resulting knowledge is organized in an epistemic way—that is, creating meaningful structures and conceptualized hierarchies. This approach to hermeneutics proposes a highly creative, constructive, and transformative process of dealing with human interpretation of reality, thus its potential for fertile change and development at the community and organizational levels. (Nobre, 2006a)

## Heterogeneity
Effects that unobserved variables can introduce in disease rates and that vary in an unstructured manner in either space or time. (Vidal-Rodeiro et al., 2005)

## Heterogeneous Agent
Agent of a multi-agent system that differs in the resources available to it in the problem-solving methods and expertise it uses, or in everything except in the interaction language it uses. (Zwitserloot & Pantic, 2005)

## Heterogeneous Information System
A set of information systems that differs in syntactical or logical aspects, such as hardware platforms, data models, or semantics. (Buccella et al., 2005)

## Heterogeneous Network
A network where network clients run a variety of operating systems. An example would be a network of machines running Windows, Unix, and Mac OS X. (Ruppel & Ruppel, 2005)

## Heuristic
**1:** One of a set of rules intended to increase probability of solving problem. (Guan, 2006c) **2:** An algorithm, particularly used to solve and achieve near-optimal solutions to intractable problems. (Chin, 2005) **3:** From the Greek "heuriskein," meaning "to discover." A heuristic aids discovery, particularly the search for solutions in domains that are difficult and poorly understood. It is commonly known as a "rule of thumb." Unlike algorithms, heuristics do not guarantee optimal or even feasible solutions and frequently do not have a theoretical guarantee. (George, 2005a) **4:** One of a set of rules or criteria which derive directly from practice. Usually, they are not "proven" in a scientific way, yet they are broadly acceptable. (Athanasis & Andreas, 2005; Karoulis & Pombortsis, 2005a) **5:** A rule of thumb, simplification, or educated guess that reduces or limits the search for solutions in domains that are difficult and poorly understood. Unlike algorithms, heuristics do not guarantee optimal, or even feasible, solutions and are often used with no theoretical guarantee. (Lazar, 2005) **6:** A set of rules derived from years of experience in solving problems. These rules can

be drawn from previous examples of business successes and failures. Artificial intelligence models rely on these rules to find relationships, patterns, or associations among variables. (Athappilly & Rea, 2005)

## Heuristic Algorithm
An optimization algorithm that does not guarantee to identify the optimal solution of the problem it is applied to, but which usually provides good quality solutions in an acceptable time. (Calvo et al., 2005)

## Heuristic Evaluation
A technique for early evaluation of interactive systems designs. Heuristic evaluation involves systematic inspection of the design by means of broad guidelines for good practice. Typically, three to five experts should perform the analysis independently, and afterwards combine and rank the results. A well-known set of heuristics is the one proposed by Nielsen: visibility of system status; match between the system and the real world; user control and freedom; consistency and standards; error prevention; recognition rather than recall; flexibility and efficiency of use; aesthetic and minimalist design; help users recognize, diagnose, and recover from errors; help and documentation. (Campos & Harrison, 2006)

## Heuristic Rule
A commonsense rule (or set of rules) intended to increase the probability of solving some problem. (Barolli & Koyama, 2005a)

## Heuristic Sketch
An ad-hoc drawing used to assist the group reflection and communication process by making unstable knowledge explicit and debatable. (Eppler & Burkhard, 2006)

## HF
High-frequency or shortwave radio operating in 3-22 MHz range. (Chand & Leeming, 2005)

## HF Radio Modem
A device for transmitting data between high-frequency (HF) radios. HF has the advantage of transmitting over thousands of kilometers. Although the data throughput is relatively low compared to other frequencies, it is "free to air." (D. Stern, 2005)

## Hidden Markov Model (HMM)
**1:** A statistical model where the system being modeled is assumed to be a Markov process with unknown parameters,

and the challenge is to determine the hidden parameters from the observable parameters, based on this assumption. (Song et al., 2005) **2:** A variant of a finite state machine having a set of states, an output alphabet, transition probabilities, output probabilities, and initial state probabilities. It is only the outcome, not the state visible to an external observer, and therefore states are hidden to the outside; hence, the name Hidden Markov Model. (Chang & Hsu, 2005) **3:** A statistical model of sequential data utilized in many machine learning applications (e.g., speech and gesture recognition). (Karpouzis et al., 2005)

### Hidden Markov Random Field (HMRF)
A Markov Random Field (MRF) with additional observation variables at each node, whose values are dependent on the node states. Additional pyramids of MRFs defined over the HMRF give rise to hierarchical HMRFs (HHMRFs). (Caelli, 2005)

### Hidden Neurons
The name given to the layer of neurons between the input variables and the output neuron. If too many hidden neurons are used, the neural network may be easily overtrained. If too few hidden neurons are used, the neural network may be unable to learn the training data. (Smith, 2005)

### Hidden Node
A node may be hidden or out of range from a sender, but within range of its intended receiver. (Erbas, 2005)

### Hierarchical Agglomerative Clustering (HAC)
A family of clustering algorithms, which start with each individual item in its own cluster and iteratively merge clusters until all items belong in one cluster. (Katsaros et al., 2005)

### Hierarchical Bayesian Model
The enterprise of specifying a model over several levels is called hierarchical modeling, with each new distribution forming a new level in hierarchy. Suppose that we have a collection of observations $y=(y_1,y_2,...,y_k)$ that are assumed to come from a distribution $p(y|\theta)$ where $\theta=(\theta_1,\theta_2,...,\theta_k)$. It can also be assumed that $\theta$ is a random quantity draw from the distribution $p(\theta|\lambda)$ where $\lambda$ is a vector of parameters. In principle, the parameter $\lambda$ can depend itself on a collection of other parameters. This sequence of parameters and distributions constitutes a hierarchical model. The hierarchy must stop at some point, with the remaining parameters known. (Vidal-Rodeiro et al., 2005)

### Hierarchical Clustering
**1:** A clustering method characterized by the successive aggregation (agglomerative hierarchical methods) or desegregation (divisive hierarchical methods) of objects in order to find clusters in a dataset. (Santos et al., 2005) **2:** A hierarchy of partitions is generated as output; it may be depicted as a tree of partitions or a pyramid of overlapping clusters. (Murthy & Diday, 2005)

### Hierarchical Conjoint Analysis
Variant of conjoint analysis that allows the integration of an extended amount of conjoint features. (Voeth & Liehr, 2005)

### Hierarchical Data File
A database system that is organized in the shape of a pyramid, with each row of objects linked to objects directly beneath it. This approach has generally been superceded by relationship database systems. (Pang, 2005a)

### Hierarchical Storage Management (HSM)
An extension of storage management to include tape media as "tertiary storage," thereby extending "primary storage" (main memory) and "secondary storage" (disks) by an additional hierarchy level. For management of spatio-temporal objects such as raster data, spatial clustering on tape is an issue to minimize data access and tape load cycles. (Baumann, 2005)

### Hierarchy
**1:** A hierarchy on a dimension represents the different levels at which data can be aggregated and viewed along that dimension. (Deshpande & Ramasamy, 2005) **2:** An ordered structure where the order is established between individuals or between classes of individuals; the ordering function may be any function defining a partial order. (Rafanelli, 2005) **3:** The members of a dimension are generally organized along levels into a hierarchy. (Schneider, 2005) **4:** The structures created by an abstraction process by which a selection of a set of attributes, objects, or actions from a much larger set of attributes, objects, or actions according to certain criteria is defined. (Pourabbas, 2005a)

### Hierarchy of Learning
The concept that learning can be sequentially ordered along a continuum from lower order to higher order. "Bloom's Taxonomy" is one of many that have been proposed. (Owen & Aworuwa, 2005)

## High-Altitude Stratosphere Platform (HASP)

A special platform to support overlay coverage in large geographical areas with the advantage of a closer distance than satellites. They operate in the stratosphere at altitudes of up to 22 km, exploiting the best features of both terrestrial and satellite systems. They are usually implemented though the use of unmanned aeronautical vehicles. (Louvros, Karaboulas, et al., 2005)

## High Availability (HA)

A measure of the uptime of a system; typically means five nines (99.999%) or better, which corresponds to 5.25 minutes of planned and unplanned downtime per year. (Zhao et al., 2006)

## High Tech

A colloquial phrase meaning more use of technology than human resources and people. (Laws et al., 2005)

## High Technology

Includes space and aviation, computers and office machinery, electronics and telecommunication equipment, pharmaceuticals, scientific instruments, electrical machines and equipment, chemicals, non-electrical machines, and weapons. (Watson, 2005)

## High Touch

A colloquial phrase meaning more use of human resources and people than technology. (Laws et al., 2005)

## High-Context Culture

This is when one looks for information in the physical context or internalized in the person, while very little is coded, explicit, or transmitted as part of the message. (Zakaria & Yusof, 2005)

## High-Definition Television (HDTV)

A new type of television that provides much better resolution than current televisions based on the NTSC standard. There is a number of competing HDTV standards, which is one reason why the new technology has not been widely implemented. All of the standards support a wider screen than NTSC and roughly twice the resolution. To pump this additional data through the narrow TV channels, images are digitalized and then compressed before they are transmitted, and then decompressed when they reach the TV. HDTV can offer bit rates within the range of 20 to 30 Mbit/s. (Chochliouros et al., 2005b)

## High-Dimensional Index Structure

The organization of indexes for storing the feature vectors of images where the number of their dimensions is large, at least over 10. (Chang, 2005)

## High-Pass Digital Filter

Digital filter that passes only high frequencies defined by the pass-band cutoff frequency and attenuates all frequencies from 0 to cutoff stop-band frequency. (Jovanovic-Dolecek, 2005c)

## High-Vote Pattern

A pattern supported (voted for) by most of a group of data sources. (Zhang & Zhang, 2005)

## Higher Education

**1:** Education opportunities offered post-K-12 public education. (Schifter, 2005) **2:** Education at degree level and above. Higher education courses are those leading to the award of a bachelor's degree, graduate certificate, graduate diploma, master's degree, or doctoral degree. Some courses leading to the award of a diploma or advanced diploma may also be accredited as higher education. In the Republic of Ireland, a majority of all higher education is offered by universities and colleges of technology. (Donnelly, 2005)

## Higher Education Program

The processes, learning materials, and associated procedures and facilities that lead to the completion of a degree or related qualification. (Grasso & Leng, 2005)

## Highest Weighting

Use the individual forecast procedure that is given the highest weight in the fixed weighting method. This is not a combination. This method is equivalent to choosing the forecasting technique, which is the best on the weight estimation period. (C.K. Chan, 2005)

**HIM:** See *Health Information Management.*

**HIPAA:** See *Health Insurance Portability and Accountability Act.*

## Histogram

**1:** A data structure that maintains one or more attributes or columns of a relational database management system to assist the query optimizer. (Thomasian, 2005b) **2:** A set of buckets implementing a partition of the overall domain of a relation attribute. (Buccafurri & Lax, 2005) **3:** A vector whose components represent similar colors in an image. The value of a component is the number of image pixels having that color. (Sural et al., 2005) **4:** Approximation, obtained by sampling, of a distribution (e.g., a distance distribution). (Chávez & Navarro, 2005) **5:** The original term refers to a bar graph that represents a distribution. In information retrieval, it also refers to a weighted vector that describes the properties of an object or the comparison of properties between two objects. Like a feature vector, a good histogram captures similarity and dissimilarity of the objects of interest. (X. Wang, 2005) **6:** Typically used for representing one-dimensional data, though multi-dimensional histograms are being researched in the database field. A histogram is a division of the domain of a one-dimensional ordered attribute into buckets, where each bucket is represented by a contiguous interval along the domain, along with the count of the number of tuples contained within this interval and other statistics. (Das, 2005)

## Historical Cost

This type of cost reflects the price of the network equipment at the time of acquisition. (Hackbarth et al., 2005)

## Historical Document Version

A non-current document version. This is a version that has later been updated, and the last version that existed before the document was deleted. (Nørvåg, 2005)

## Historical XML

A sequence of XML documents, which are different versions of the same XML document. It records the change history of the XML document. (Zhao & Bhowmick, 2005)

## Historically Underserved Group

Refers to those who lack access to computers and the Internet. Historically this has included Americans who have low incomes, live in rural communities, have limited education, and are members of racial or ethnic minorities. (Kvasny & Payton, 2005)

## History of Implementation Success

Describes the track record of IT projects in HR and the effectiveness of HR into IT people management issues. (Dery & Samson, 2005)

## History Retrieval

In Web browsing, it is the act of recalling Web sites that have been previously visited. (Guan, 2005b)

## Hit Rate

**1:** Any request for data from a Web page, a way to compare the popularity/traffic of a site. (Waterson, 2006) **2:** The ratio of requests served by the cache (hits) over the total number of requests made by the clients. (Danalis, 2005)

## Hit Ratio

The number of times an item is found in the cache divided by the number of times an item is being matched. (Tse, 2006)

## Hit Request

An HTTP request made by a Web client agent (e.g., a browser) for a particular Web resource. It can be explicit (user initiated) or implicit (Web client initiated). Explicit Web requests are sometimes called clickthroughs. (Mobasher, 2005b)

**HITS:** See *Hypertext-Induced Topic Selection.*

## HITS Algorithm

A Web search technique for ranking Web pages according to relevance to a particular search term or search phrase. Two concepts, "authority" and "hub," are proposed to characterize the importance of each Web page. (Li, 2005)

**HMD:** See *Head-Mounted Display.*

**HMDS:** See *Hyperbolic Multi-Dimensional Scaling.*

## HMI in Manufacturing

Relation between a human operator and one or more machines via an interface for embracing the functions of machine handling, programming, simulation, maintenance, diagnosis, and initialization. (Blecker & Graf, 2006)

**HMM:** See *Hidden Markov Model.*

**HMRF:** See *Hidden Markov Random Field.*

**HMS:** See *Human-Machine System.*

## HOBBit Distance

A computationally efficient distance metric. In one dimension, it is the number of digits by which the binary

**H**

representation of an integer has to be right-shifted to make two numbers equal. In another dimension, it is the maximum of the HOBBit distances in the individual dimensions. (Perrizo, Ding, Ding, et al., 2005)

## Holdout Technique

A filter technique that splits the data into exploratory and holdout sets. Rules discovered from the exploratory set then can be evaluated against the holdout set using statistical tests. (Butler & Webb, 2005)

## Holistic Function

An aggregate function F is called holistic if the value of F for an n-dimensional cell cannot be computed from a constant number of aggregates of the (n+1)-dimensional cell. (Abdulghani, 2005a)

## Holistic Nature of an IT/End-User Relationship

The important elements making up a relationship between an IT professional and its end user(s) at a given time should be organized together as a whole. If any of these elements are disturbed in a negative sense, the whole relationship between the IT professional and the end user(s) is undermined. In other words, the relationship as a whole is more than the sum of its elements. (Leonard, 2005)

## Homeostasis

The condition of stability that an organization can obtain by being cognizant of and responsive to environmental changes. Homeostasis is one of the most typical properties of highly complex open systems. Such a system reacts to every change in the environment, or to every random disturbance, through a series of modifications of equal size and opposite direction to those that created the disturbance. The goal of these modifications is to maintain the internal balances. (Hall & Croasdell, 2006)

## Homepage

A textual and graphical display that usually welcomes users to a Web site and provides a point of access to other static and dynamic Web pages. (Handzic & Lin, 2005)

## Homogeneity

The degree of similarity or uniformity among individuals of a population. (Lee, Peterson, et al., 2005)

## Homogeneous Agent

One of the set of agents of a multi-agent system that are designed in an identical way and have a priori of the same capabilities. (Zwitserloot & Pantic, 2005)

## Homogenous Temporal Relation

Attribute values in any tuple of a relation are all defined with the same period of time. In a heterogeneous relation, attribute values in a tuple may have different time periods of existence. (Tansel, 2005)

## Homologous Point

The point in the DEM and the point in the R-DEM modeling the same point in the real surface. Their distance is the error of the DEM point, assuming the point in the R-DEM is without error. (Zelasco et al., 2005)

## Homology

Relationship by evolutionary descent from a common ancestral precursor. (Tsunoda et al., 2005)

## Homonymy

A particular interschema property. An homonymy between two concepts A and B indicates that they have the same name but different meanings. (De Meo, Terracina, et al., 2005)

## Homoscedasticity

A statistical assumption for linear regression models. It requires that the variations around the regression line be constant for all values of input variables. (Lee, Peterson, et al., 2005)

## Honeypot

A deceptive computer system that entraps attackers into revealing their methods. (Rowe, 2006c)

## Hopfield Neural Network

A neural network with a single layer of nodes that have binary inputs and outputs. The output of each node is fed back to all other nodes simultaneously, and each of the node forms a weighted sum of inputs and passes the output result through a nonlinearity function. It applies a supervised learning algorithm, and the learning process continues until a stable state is reached. (H. Wang & S. Wang, 2005)

## Horizon of Observation

Based in distributed cognitive theory, it is the portion of the workspace that a participant can observe or monitor. It addresses how learning in a collaborative environment takes place, and how technologies expand the 4 by allowing for the identification of different knowledge sources that can contribute to learning within communities. (Paquette, 2006a)

## Horizontal and Vertical Projections

Horizontal projection is the projection of the binary image along the horizontal axis. Similarly, vertical projection is the projection of the binary image along the vertical axis. They can be calculated as follows:

$$P_h[y] = \sum_{x=1}^{n} black.pixel(x, y), \quad P_v[x] = \sum_{y=1}^{m} black.pixel(x, y),$$

where m = width of the image and n = height of the image. (Chakravarty et al., 2005a)

## Horizontal ASP

Horizontal ASPs provide online applications for a specific business function such as human resource management, procurement, customer relations, and so forth. (D. Kim, 2005)

## Horizontal Classification System

Classification systems can be divided into horizontal and vertical classification systems. Horizontal classification systems try to cover all areas of a certain domain. Well-known examples are the ECl@ss-system and UNSPSC, which try to provide classes for all manufactured products. (Abels & Hahn, 2006)

## Horizontal Fiscal Equalization

A series of intergovernmental grants that ensures that all Australians have access to "an average" level of services. First implemented in Australia in 1934, Horizontal Fiscal Equalization was seen to be a basic tenet of Australian Federalism. Horizontal Fiscal Equalization was designed to prevent independent economies developing in the different communities in different geographic locations in Australia, and to ensure that citizens were not significantly disadvantaged in the delivery of government services due to their geographic location. (Cameron, 2005)

## Horizontal Industry Application

A horizontal industry is one that aims to produce a wide range of goods and services. Horizontal industry applications are utilized across many different industries. While the core part of the application does not require changes, an organization needs customization at the front end or at the back end. Database access and service representative dispatch are typical examples of these applications. (Bose et al., 2005)

## Horizontal Industry Portal

A portal utilized by a broad base of users across a horizontal market. (Tatnall & Burgess, 2006)

## Horizontal Integration

In information management systems, traditionally addresses information sharing across systems, which often means across functions or departments. In the context of organizational structure, horizontal integration typically refers to cross-business-unit integration in pursuit of scope economies. (Gordon & Mulligan, 2005)

## Horizontal Partitioning

Distributing the rows of a table into several separate tables. (Bellatreche & Mohania, 2005)

## Horizontal Portal

A multi-functional space used for information, navigation, communication, and e-commerce that offers broad content to the mass market. (Vrazalic & Hyland, 2005)

## Horizontal vs. Vertical Dimension

The horizontal dimension is represented by the current community at the institutional level. It is the dimension of structuralism that focuses on the 'parts' that make up a 'whole'. Science searches for total autonomy of its object, being thus insensitive to any referential—that is, to the vertical dimension. The horizontal dimension in philosophy represents the content and the ontological consistency of the de-centering in the world. Structuralism raises attention to the meaning of the content and to its relative autonomy. The horizontal dimension represents the presence of differences and the signification power of the elements of the world as a globality. An empty world, void of differences, could never be a philosophical world. On the other hand, the vertical dimension is represented by the institutional memory. The vertical dimension is the attraction towards a referent. Philosophy is always facing a referent, never being closed within the game of its internal structures, though these are present and crucial in philosophy, where both vertical and horizontal dimensions are present. (Nobre, 2006b)

## Horizontally Partitioned Data

A distributed architecture in which the all the sites share the same database schema but have information about different entities. The union of all the rows across all the sites forms the complete database. (Jha & Sural, 2005)

## Horn Clause

One of a set of clauses in conjunctive normal form (i.e., a conjunction of disjunctions of literals) is a Horn set of clauses if each clause contains at most one positive predicate. That is, all literals are positive when written as Prolog clauses (Head:-Body), since the negated literals become a conjunction of positive predicates when put into the Body of the clause. When resolved with positive facts, such clauses can only result in new positive facts, and the complete set of such results is enumerable for Horn clauses and is a unique "initial" (i.e., smallest) model for the clauses. (Buehrer, 2005)

## Host

A computer connected directly into a network such as the Internet. Whenever one dials into the Internet, one makes a connection through a host computer. (Magagula, 2005)

## Host-Multicast

Application-layer multicast technology that does not require any additional protocol in the network routers, since it uses the traditional unicast IP transmission. (Hosszú, 2005b)

## Host-Multicast Routing Protocol

The members of the hosts construct a delivery tree using similar algorithms than the IP-multicast routing protocols. (Hosszú, 2005b)

## Hot-Chatting

Two or more individuals engaging in discourses that move beyond light-hearted flirting. (Whitty, 2005)

## Hotelling (Neighborhood Work Center)

Organizational facility for employees to work at, but where they do not have a permanently assigned desk. They must "check-in" every time they come to work there. (Bélanger, 2005)

## Hotspot

Traditionally, an area where people congregate that would be appropriate for setting up a Wi-Fi access point. Now synonymous with an area where a Wi-Fi access point already exists. (Efstathiou & Polyzos, 2006)

**HPSA:** See *Health Professional Shortage Area.*

**HPT:** See *Human Performance Technology.*

**HR:** See *Human Resources.*

## HSI Model

A color model in which a color is described by three characteristics: hue (H), saturation (S), and intensity (I). They form a 3D color space. The HSI model is quite coherent with human perception. A closely related model is HSV model, in which value (V) takes the place of intensity. (Zhang, 2005c)

**HSM:** See *Hierarchical Storage Management.*

## HSV Color Space

A color space consisting of hue, saturation, and intensity value. It is a popular way of representing color content of an image. (Sural et al., 2005)

**HTML:** See *Hypertext Markup Language.*

## HTML Document

A document embedded with HTML codes or tags that specify how the document will be displayed when viewed on the Internet. (Cooper, 2005)

**HTTP:** See *Hypertext Transfer Protocol.*

## HTTP Server

A program that listens on various TCP/IP ports (usually port 80), awaiting an HTTP request from a browser. Once a request is made, the server authenticates the request and serves up either a static HTML document or runs a CGI program to generate dynamic HTML content. Apache is an example of an HTTP Server software suite. (Chim, 2006)

## HTTP Session

A program executed upon accessing a Web page. This is a security risk, because users end up running programs they do not know and/or trust. (Chim, 2006)

## H2

Two-dimensional hyperbolic space (plane). (Walter, 2005)

## H2DV

The Hybrid Hyperbolic Data Viewer incorporates two-stage browsing and navigation using the HSOM for a coarse thematic mapping of large object collections and the HMDS for detailed inspection of smaller subsets in the object level. (Walter, 2005)

**HU:** See *Hypothetical Update.*

## Hub

**1:** A Web site that provides collections of links to authorities. (Hu et al., 2005b) **2:** A centralized location where activities or interactions take place. (St.Amant, 2005b) **3:** A term for Web pages in link analysis. In contrast to an authority page, a hub page does not contain high-quality content itself, but links to the authorities. A hub represents an excellent information provider and may be a clearinghouse or a link collection. The high quality of these pages is shown by the information sources they contain. (Mandl, 2006)

## Hub Company

A lead company in a supply chain or value network that organizes and manages the work for end products and/or services. This is, for example, an automotive manufacturer, an aircraft manufacturer, a clothing manufacturer, or major food supplier. These are usually large companies, but can be small if the end product is in building construction, for instance. Usually the manufacturing and services chain is complex and contains many sub-products that have to be drawn together with processes and services to meet design-to-manufacture targets and delivery excellence. In a value network the tier N suppliers are part of the collaborative network. It is to be noted that communication in the old economy was EDI and in the new economy will be fully open system interoperable ICT. (Richards et al., 2005)

## Hub Page

One of the pages that contain a large number of links to pages that contain information about the query topics. (Lee-Post & Jin, 2005a)

## Hubs and Authorities

Web pages defined by a mutually reinforcing relationship with respect to their hyperlink structure. Hubs are Web pages that link to many related authorities; authorities are those pages that are linked to by many good hubs. (Mobasher, 2005a)

## Human Body Modeling

Digital model generally describing the shape and motion of a human body. (Sappa et al., 2005)

## Human Capital

**1:** The combination of knowledge, skill, innovativeness, and ability of a company's individual employees to meet the task. It refers to the tacit knowledge embedded in the minds of employees. (Hsu & Mykytyn, 2006) **2:** Reflects a human potential in knowledge, skills, and attitude that can provide better solutions (meaning), efficiency (time), and effectiveness (money) of work. (Targowski, 2005) **3:** The attributes, competencies, and mindsets of the individuals that make up an organization. (Smith, 2006b) **4:** The knowledge and knowing that exists within a particular unit which could be a team, an organization, an industry, or even a society. (Newell, 2006) **5:** The knowledge, skills, abilities, and experiences of employees that provide value-added contributions for a competitive advantage in organizations. (Wong-MingJi, 2005) **6:** The unique capabilities and knowledge of individuals that aid productivity. (Ridings, 2006b) **7:** Individual skills and capabilities that allow actors to act in new and innovative ways, and to respond to new challenges with creative solutions. (von Wartburg et al., 2006)

## Human Capital Index

A measurable definition of human capital is defined by the product of "competence" and "commitment." While they align with business strategy, competencies need to be generated through more than one mechanism, such as buy, build, borrow, bounce, and bind. Commitment is concerned with how employees relate to each other and feel about a firm. (Hsu & Mykytyn, 2006)

## Human Ecology

In a holistic vision of the environment, human ecology is an approach to read changes and transformation in action; a way of integration of history, culture, and work in peripheral regions in a communicative and distance-exchange perspective; a tool for creating conditions for sustainable development. (Giorgi & Schürch, 2005)

## Human Factor

A user characteristic in terms of personality and cognitive factors that impact the task performance and the quality of interaction with any artifact. (Sas, 2006)

## Human Language Technology

Branch of information science that deals with natural language information. (He, 2006)

## Human Perceptual Model

A set of features, including the Human Visual System (HVS) and Human Auditory System (HAS), describing the physical characteristics of human eyes and ears. This model expatiates on the sensitivities of human senses, and thus allows more distortions introduced to the host media by watermarking without being perceived. (Si & Li, 2006)

## Human Performance Technology (HPT)

The systematic and systemic identification and removal of barriers to individual and organizational performance. (Banerji & Scales, 2005)

## Human Resource Information System

An integrated system used to gather and store information regarding an organization's employees. (Troutt & Long, 2005)

## Human Resources (HR)

All activities of planning, staffing, appraisal and remunerating, improving employees and the working environment, and establishing and maintaining working relationships. (Dery & Samson, 2005)

## Human Right

One of those rights that all humans have simply by reason of being human, without regard to an individual government unit's laws. (Gilbert, 2005)

## Human-Centered Design

**1:** An alternative name for user-centered design (UCD) used in ISO process standards. (Knight & Jefsioutine, 2006) **2:** The process of designing sociotechnical systems (people in interaction with technology) based on an analysis of how people think, learn, perceive, work, and interact. (Sharples, 2006)

## Human-Computer Interaction (HCI)

**1:** A discipline concerned with the design, evaluation, and implementation of interactive computing systems for human use and with the study of major phenomena surrounding them. (Debbabi & Baile, 2006) **2:** A field of research and development, methodology, theory and practice with the objective of designing, constructing, and evaluating computer-based interactive systems—including hardware, software, input/output devices, displays, training and documentation—so that people can use them efficiently, effectively, safely, and with satisfaction. (Singh, 2005b) **3:** Study of human behavior in interacting with any computer-based device. HCI is concerned with identifying ways to optimize, such as through the design of technology, the relationship between humans and computers. (Carstens, 2005) **4:** The command and information flow that streams between the user and the computer. It is usually characterized in terms of speed,

reliability, consistency, portability, naturalness, and users' subjective satisfaction. (Pantic, 2005a) **5:** The study of how humans interact with computers, and how to design computer systems that are usable, easy, quick, and productive for humans to use. (Janvier & Ghaoui, 2006) **6:** The study, planning, and design of what happens when humans and computers work together. (Laghos & Zaphiris, 2005a)

## Human-Computer Interface

**1:** A software application, a system that realizes human-computer interaction. (Pantic, 2005a) **2:** Integrated computing environment that allows the data miner to access the data visualization instruments, select data sets, invoke the query process, organize the screen, set colors and animation speed, and manage the intermediate data-mining results.(S. Wang & H. Wang, 2005)

## Human-Machine System (HMS)

Based on the acceptance of an interaction between human and machine, it is a summary of all elements of hardware, software, and useware. The term includes the micro (UI) and macro (organization) aspects of a human-machine system. (Röse, 2006b)

## Humanistic Value

OD promotes humanistic values through empowerment—that is, by articulating values designed to facilitate visioning, organizational learning, and problem solving in the interests of a collaborative management. Values are seen to be central to promoting trust, collaboration, and openness. (Grieves, 2006a)

## Human/Problem-Sensitivity

The proximity to the human-centered/problem-oriented concepts, as opposed to the computer-centered/software-oriented concepts (i.e., computer/software solution-sensitivity). (Andrade et al., 2006a)

## Humanoid

An automaton that resembles a human being. (Yong & Choo, 2005)

## Humanoid Animation (H-Anim)

**1:** Part of VRML specifications consisting of node prototypes allowing the definition of an avatar. (Prêteux & Preda, 2005) **2:** The VRML Consortium Charter for Humanoid Animation Working Group recently produced the International Standard, "Information Technology—Computer Graphics and Image Processing—Humanoid

Animation (H-Anim)," an abstract representation for modeling three-dimensional human figures. (Sappa et al., 2005)

## Humanware

With more information- and knowledge-intensive issues driving economies, people or "humanware" become invaluable for their contribution to society's development and growth. (Kamel, 2005b)

**HUP:** See *Head-Up Display.*

## Hybrid

The instructor and students meet both in the online learning environment and in the classroom. (S.-K. Wang, 2005)

## Hybrid Course

**1:** A course taught using a combination of online and in-class instruction. (Baugher et al., 2005) **2:** Another name for a blended course. Typically, a course that replaces some face-to-face instructional time with computer-mediated activities. (Graham et al., 2005) **3:** University or college classes that contain a reduced number of face-to-face class meetings between the instructor and students while concurrently offering significant learning activities though the Internet. (Bahn, 2006)

## Hybrid Data Analysis Method

A data analysis technique using methods from statistics and from fuzzy modeling. (Viertl, 2005)

## Hybrid Distance Learning

A distance learning program using both electronic delivery and local facilitators or mentors to coach, counsel, and support students. (Riffee & Sessums, 2005)

## Hybrid E-Retailer

A click-and-mortar company that conducts retailing through e-channel as well as physical stores and other distribution channels. Compared to its pure e-commerce competitors, a hybrid e-retailer can leverage existing physical stores, brand recognition, distribution network, existing customer base, and so forth. (I. Lee, 2005)

## Hybrid Fiber Coaxial Cable Modem

A technology that enables transmission of information at high rates over the cable television network's infrastructure comprising optical fibers and coaxial cables. (Hin & Subramaniam, 2005c)

## Hybrid Filtering

A combination of filtering techniques in which the disadvantages of one type of filtering are counteracted by the advantages of another. (Parmar & Angelides, 2005)

## Hybrid Knowledge Network

On one side, it groups together elements from the traditional virtual community of interest and from the more sophisticated communities of practice, and on the other side, promotes collaborative multidisciplinary research that produces high-quality research results and stimulates their transfer. (Ranguelov & Rodríguez, 2006)

## Hybrid Learning

Learning that involves both computer-mediated and face-to-face communication. (Ketelhut et al., 2005)

## Hybrid Learning Environment

A mix of traditional and Web-based instructional delivery methods in which the class meets for lectures, assignments, and tests, while a course management platform is used to deliver course materials, and conduct discussions and exams. A term sometimes used synonymously with blended model. (Aworuwa & Owen, 2005)

## Hybrid Learning Taxonomy

A comprehensive organizational scheme in applied learning and instructional design theory and practice that integrates both descriptive and prescriptive taxonomic domains. While a number of conceptually useful hybrid learning taxonomies have been proposed, there is to date no single, inclusive, unifying hybrid taxonomy that effectively synthesizes all of the design elements of instruction to sufficient practical levels of granularity and application. (Lasnik, 2005)

**Hybrid MA:** See *Hybrid Multiple-Access.*

## Hybrid Model

In distance learning, a hybrid model reflects the learning model that combines traditional with unconventional tools and techniques in delivering knowledge to the community of recipients. (Kamel, 2005b)

## Hybrid Model of Investment Privatization Funds

The hybrid model is not, in the context of investment privatization funds, simply a model that incorporates elements of two or more organizational forms. This hybrid model encompasses a more dynamic entity. Firms that adopt this structure typically maintain a general affinity towards a dominant form (e.g., unified), but they temporarily create contrasting organizational relationships (e.g., allied or portal) that do not "fit" with the current organizational design. Much like evolution, the transition between dominant forms occurs over an extended period of time and as the result of numerous "hybridizations." (Gordon & Mulligan, 2005)

## Hybrid Multiple-Access (Hybrid MA)

A class of multiple-access consisting of a combination of controlled multiple-access and free multiple-access. (Markhasin et al., 2005)

## Hybrid Organizational Memory

An organizational memory whose contents are expressed by means of languages presenting different levels of formality (formal, semi-formal, informal). Such memories contain textual resources (be they structured or not, and either mono- or multimedia) as well as formal semantic resources (annotations and ontologies). (Fortier & Kassel, 2006)

## Hybrid Peer-to-Peer Networks

In hybrid peer-to-peer networks, no fixed central server but dynamic supernodes are present to provide directory services, serving a group of peers and reflecting only a partial view of the whole network. (Kwok et al., 2006)

## Hybrid Replication

A replication technique using protocols that may either behave as eager or as lazy, depending on the given system configuration. (Muñoz-Escoí et al., 2005)

## Hybrid System

**1:** The integration of two or more artificial intelligence tools to improve efficiency or system performance. (Begg, 2005) **2:** This system's evolution in time is composed by both smooth dynamics and sudden jumps. (Liberati, 2005)

## Hybrid Technique

A combination of two or more soft computing techniques used for data mining. Examples are neuro-fuzzy and neuro-genetic. (Bala et al., 2005)

## Hybrid Transformer

Device used to connect two one-directional with one bi-directional channel, keeping uncoupled among them the two one-directional channels. (Perez-Meana & Nakano-Miyatake, 2005)

## Hybridization

The phenomenon occurring at universities where there is an increasing overlap of the boundaries of traditional on-campus courses and distance education courses. (Graham et al., 2005)

## Hyperbolic Multi-Dimensional Scaling (HMDS)

Laying out objects in the H2 such that the spatial arrangement resembles the dissimilarity structure of the data as close as possible. (Walter, 2005)

## Hyperbolic Tree Viewer

Visualizes tree-like graphs in the Poincaré mapping of the H2 or H3. (Walter, 2005)

## HyperClass 1

**1:** Classes, lectures, seminars, and tutorials that take place in a co-action field in HyperReality. This means an interaction between virtual teachers and students and objects, and physically real teachers and students and objects to learn how to apply a specific domain of knowledge. It allows for the use of artificially intelligent tutors. Such systems are currently experimental, but have the potential to be used on the Internet. (Rajasingham & Tiffin, 2005) **2:** Intermixing a real classroom and a virtual classroom where a real teacher and students and a virtual teacher and students come together and hold a class. (Terashima, 2005)

## Hyperlink

**1:** A structural unit that connects a Web page to a different location, either within the same Web page or to a different Web page. A hyperlink that connects to a different part of the same page is called an intra-document hyperlink, and a hyperlink that connects two different pages is called an inter-document hyperlink. (Mobasher, 2005a) **2:** A link in a document to information within the same document or another document. These links are usually represented by highlighted words or images. (Lee-Post & Jin, 2005a) **3:** A selectable connection from one word, phrase, picture, or information object to another. By clicking on a hyperlink, a Web user can move easily from one Web page to another page. The most common form of hyperlink is the highlighted word, phrase, or picture. (Hu, Yang, Yeh, et al., 2005) **4:** Text or graphics that can be clicked on to view other information. (Falk & Sockel, 2005)

## Hyperlink Analysis

Also called link analysis, this is the analysis of Web hyperlinks for the purpose of identifying communities underlying the Web pages or hyperlinking practices within Web communities. (Thelwall, 2006)

## Hypermedia

**1:** Often taken as synonymous with "hypertext," though some authors use "hypermedia" to refer to hypertext systems that contain not just text data, but also graphics, animation, video, audio, and other media. Principal defining features of a hypermedia system are a highly interactive, visual, media-rich user interface and flexible navigation mechanisms. Hypermedia is a specialized type of interactive digital multimedia. (M. Lang, 2005) **2:** A term used to describe the interlinking of textual information and other forms of media, such as audio, video, and photographic images. (Theng, 2005) **3:** A computer-based information retrieval system that enables a user to gain or provide access to texts, audio and video recordings, photographs, and computer graphics related to a particular subject. (Rahman, 2005c) **4:** An extension of hypertext that supports linking graphics, sound, and video elements, in addition to text elements. (Sala, 2005b) **5:** The style of building systems for information representation and management around the network of multimedia nodes connected together by typed links. (García et al., 2006) **6:** A way of organizing data as a network of nodes and links. (Lemahieu, 2005)

## Hypermedia Authoring Tool

Authoring tools for hypermedia systems are meant to provide environments where authors may create their own hypermedia systems in varying domains. (García et al., 2006)

## Hypermedia Design Methodology (HDM)

**1:** Developed by Polytechnic of Milan (Italy), it is a methodology to design hypermedia applications. (Paiano, 2005) **2:** The modeling language used by W2000 to describe the information, navigation, and presentation aspects of a hypermedia application. (Bochicchio & Fiore, 2005)

## Hypermedia-Based Learning

Learning in hypermedia environments, allowing nonlinear access to information through links provided within text, images, animation, audio, and video. It is considered flexible, where varied instructional needs can be addressed. (Chambel & Guimarães, 2005)

## HyperReality

Providing a communication environment where inhabitants, real or virtual, at different locations, are brought together through the communication networks, and work or play together as if they were at the same place. (Terashima, 2005)

## HyperSchool/HyperCollege/HyperUniversity

The term hyper means that these institutions could exist in HyperReality. HyperReality is where virtual reality and physical reality seamlessly intersect to allow interaction between their components, and where human and artificial intelligences can communicate. The technological capability for this is at an experimental stage, but could be made available with broadband Internet. (Rajasingham & Tiffin, 2005)

## Hyperspace

**1:** Information spaces interlinked together with hypermedia structures. Concerning the World Wide Web, the term 'cyberspace' is sometimes used instead of hyperspace. (Suh & Kim, 2005) **2:** Space with more than three dimensions. (Murphy, 2005b) **3:** Users' view of the Semantic Web environment, which provides information and action services mainly through hypermedia pages. (Liu & Koppelaar, 2005)

## Hypertext

**1:** Any text that contains links to other documents. (Lee-Post & Jin, 2005a) **2:** A collection of documents containing cross-references that, with the aid of a browser program, allow the reader to move easily from one document to another. (Vician & Buche, 2005) **3:** A collection of electronic texts connected through electronic links. In addition to text, the documents also may contain pictures, videos, demonstrations, or sound resources. With the addition of such media, hypertext often is referred to as hypermedia. (Shapiro, 2006) **4:** A term conceived and coined by Ted Nelson, who described it as interactive branching of text information structured into non-sequential format into nodes and links. The nonlinear nature of hypertext provides freedom to readers who enjoy associational thinking and reading. (Theng, 2005) **5:** An approach to information management in which data is stored as a network of inter-related nodes (also commonly known as "documents" or "pages") that may be purposefully navigated or casually browsed in a nonlinear sequence by means of various user-selected paths, following hyperlinks. These hyperlinks may be hardcoded into the system or dynamically generated at run-time. (Lang, M., 2005) **6:** The presentation of information as a linked network of nodes that readers are free to navigate in a nonlinear fashion. It allows for multiple authors, a blurring of the

**H**

author and reader functions, extended works with diffuse boundaries, and multiple reading paths. (Sala, 2005a) **7:** The organization of information units as a network of associations, which a user can choose to resolve. Hypertext links are the instances of such associations. (Martínez-González, 2005)

## Hypertext Markup Language (HTML)

**1:** A language used to organize and present content on Web pages. HTML uses tags such as <h1> and </h1> to structure text into headings, paragraphs, lists, hypertext links, and so forth. (Burgstahler, 2005b) **2:** A markup language used to structure text and multimedia objects, as well as set up links between documents. This language is used extensively on the Internet and can be viewed in a Web browser. (Nightingale, 2005) **3:** A set of tags used to structure text and multimedia documents, and to set up hypertext links between documents, most commonly on the World Wide Web. (Fagan, 2005) **4:** A standard language for representing text, formatting specifications and hyperlinks. (Yen, 2005) **5:** The authoring language used to create documents on the World Wide Web. HTML defines the structure and layout of a Web document by using a variety of tags and attributes. HTML is derived from SGML, although it is not a strict subset. (Valenti, 2005) **6:** HTML was originally developed for the use of plain text to hide HTTP links. (Clayton, 2006a) **7:** The language in which most pages on the World Wide Web are written. These pages can be read using a browser. (Dasgupta & Chandrashekaran, 2005) **8:** A hypertext document format used on the World Wide Web. HTML is an application of the Standard Generalized Markup Language (SGML). Tags embedded into the text describe certain properties of the text elements and can include other elements such as links to HTML pages or to other resources such as images. HTML is a recommendation of the W3C. (Chang, 2005) **9:** Markup language that uses tags in pairs of angle brackets, for identifying and representing the Web structure and layout through Web browsers; it is not a procedural programming language like C, Fortran, or Visual Basic. (Suh & Kim, 2005) **10:** The most often-used coding language used on the World Wide Web. It uses basic word processing tags to specify formatting, linking, and so forth during the creation of Web pages. HTML requires no special Web layout software. (Szabados & Sonwalkar, 2005) **11:** A language based on labels to describe the structure and layout of a hypertext. (Sindoni, 2005b)

## Hypertext Structure

Organization structure described by Nonaka, distinguishing a functionally organized, hierarchical, and bureaucratic business system layer for regular knowledge exploitation; a project layer for development work; and a knowledge base layer connecting the first two layers. (Hendriks, 2006)

## Hypertext Transfer Protocol (HTTP)

The underlying protocol used by the World Wide Web. HTTP defines how messages are formatted and transmitted between Web servers and browsers. (Cardoso, 2006)

## Hypertext-Induced Topic Selection (HITS)

A Web graph mining algorithm to compute authority scores and hub scores for Web pages. (Wen, 2005b)

## Hypervideo

**1:** Indexed video enriched with hypertextual and multimedia elements. It is a fast and effective way to "navigate" in long video clips and to find out the main content of the video. (Bochicchio & Fiore, 2005) **2:** Refers to the integration of video in truly hypermedia spaces, where it is not regarded as a mere illustration, but can also be structured through links defined in its spatial and temporal dimensions. Sometimes called video-based hypermedia. (Chambel & Guimarães, 2005)

## HyperWorld

Intermixing a real world and a virtual world seamlessly. (Terashima, 2005)

## Hyponymy/Hypernymy

A particular interschema property. Concept A is said to be a hyponym of a concept B (which, in turn, is a hypernym of A), if A has a more specific meaning than B. (De Meo et al., 2005b)

## Hypothesis

One of a particular set or class of candidate functions before you begin to learn the correct function. (Awad & Khan, 2005)

## Hypothesis Test(ing)

**1:** A formal statistical procedure by which an interesting hypothesis (the alternative hypothesis) is accepted or rejected on the basis of data. (Mukherjee, 2005) **2:** The process of using statistical analysis to determine if the observed differences between two or more samples are due to random chance (as stated in the 'null' hypothesis) or to true differences in the samples (as stated in the 'alternate' hypothesis). (Tan & Zhao, 2005a)

## Hypothetical Reasoning
The process of creating hypothetical scenarios based on hypotheses and hypothetical assertions, and of exploring the hypothesis space for results of given queries. (Dang & Embury, 2005)

## Hypothetical Update (HU)
A proposed update that will not be applied on the real database, but the hypothetical effect of which we wish to explore. (Dang & Embury, 2005)

## Hypothetico-Deductive Reasoning
In a particular situation, applying relevant knowledge of principles and constraints, and visualizing, in the abstract, the plausible outcomes that might result from various changes one can imagine to be imposed on the system. (Donnelly, 2005)

# I

## i-mate

A PDA device manufactured by Carrier Devices with an integrated GSM cellular phone and digital camera. The device also incorporates a built-in microphone and speaker, a secure digital expansion card slot, and Bluetooth wireless connectivity. (Garrett, 2006a)

## i-mode

**1:** A packet-switching wireless technology, used by NTT DoCoMo (Japan). A range of commercial and financial services are offered, including browsing the Web from a mobile phone. (Petrova, 2006) **2:** A wireless Internet service for mobile phones using HTTP, popular in Japan and increasingly elsewhere (i.e., the United States, Germany, Belgium, France, Spain, Italy, Greece, Taiwan, etc.). It was inspired by WAP, which was developed in the U.S., and it was launched in 1999 in Japan. It became a runaway success because of its well-designed services and business model. (Lalopoulos et al., 2005a) **3:** Brand name for voice plus a wide range of data services delivered by NTT DoCoMo in Japan. (Gilbert, 2005b) **4:** The full-color, always-on, packet-switched Internet service for cellular phone users offered by NTT DoCoMo. With i-mode, cellular phone users are able to access to tens of thousands of Internet sites, as well as specialized services such as e-mail, online shopping and banking, ticket reservations, and restaurant advice. (Hu, Yang, & Yeh, 2006) **5:** The packet-based service for mobile phones offered by Japan's leader in wireless technology, NTT DoCoMo. The i-mode protocol uses compact HTML (cHTML) as its markup language instead of WAP's wireless markup language (WML) to provide mobile phone voice service, Internet, and e-mail. (Lei, 2006)

**IAB:** See *Internet Architecture Board.*

**IB:** See *Integration Broker.*

**IBL:** See *Inquiry-Based Learning.*

**IBSS:** See *Independent Basic Service Set.*

**IBT:** See *Identification-Based Trust.*

**IC:** See *Integrated Circuit; Intellectual Capital; Interaction Channel.*

**ICA:** See *Independent Component Analysis.*

**ICALL:** See *Intelligent Computer-Assisted Language Learning.*

**ICAT:**
Internet Categorization of Attacks Toolkit. (Cardoso & Freire, 2005)

**ICD-10:** See *International Statistical Classification of Diseases and Related Health Problems, Tenth Revision.*

**ICDL:** See *International Computer Driving License.*

## Iceberg Cubes

The set of cells in a cube that satisfies an iceberg query. (Abdulghani, 2005b)

## Iceberg Distance Join

A spatial query involving two spatial datasets, a distance threshold d, and a cardinality threshold K (K≥1). The answer is a set of pairs of objects from the two input datasets that are within distance d from each other, provided that the first object appears at least K times in the join result. (Corral & Vassilakopoulos, 2005)

## Iceberg Query

A query on top of a cube that asks for aggregates above a certain threshold. (Abdulghani, 2005b)

**ICM:** See *Intellectual Capital Management.*

**ICMP Message:** See *Internet Control Message Protocol Message.*

**ICMS:** See *Intellectual Capital Management System.*

**Icon**
**1:** In computer science, the icon is a graphic symbol (usually a simple picture) that denotes a program, command, data file, or concept in a graphical user interface. (Sala, 2005b) **2:** A principal feature of GUIs, an icon is a small picture representing an object, file, program, user, and so forth. Clicking on the icon will open whatever is being represented. (Henley & Noyes, 2006)

**ICR:** See *Intelligent Call Routing.*

**ICT:** See *Information and Communication Technology.*

**ICT Alliance:** See *Information and Communication Technology Alliance.*

**ICT Architecture:** See *Information and Communication Technology Architecture.*

**ICT as a Cognitive Partner:** See *Information and Communication Technology as a Cognitive Partner.*

**ICT Diffusion:** See *Information and Communication Technology Diffusion.*

**ICT Infrastructure:** See *Information and Communication Technology Infrastructure.*

**ICT Integration:** See *Information and Communication Technology Integration.*

**ICT Level of Knowledge:** See *Information and Communication Technology Level of Knowledge.*

**ICT Planning in Schools:** See *Information and Communication Technology Planning in Schools.*

**ICT Sector:** See *Information and Communication Technology Sector.*

**ICT Selection:** See *Information and Communication Technology Selection.*

**ICT Seva Kendra:** See *Information and Communication Technology Seva Kendra.*

**ICT-Based Development Projects:** See *Information and Communication Technology-Based Development Projects.*

**ICT-Enabled Knowledge Management:** See *Information and Communication Technology-Enabled Knowledge Management.*

**ICT Indicator:** See *Information and Communication Technology Indicator.*

**ICT in E-Procurement:** See *Information and Communication Technology in E-Procurement.*

**ICT in Teaching:** See *Information and Communication Technology in Teaching.*

**ID:** See *Instructional Design.*

**Idea-Generation Tool**
A technology designed to stimulate thinking and association. Enables users to detect hidden patterns from mounds of data and discover relationships among entities. (Chua, 2006)

**Ideal Model**
A virtual setting where all parties interact with an incorruptible trusted party who carries out the joint computation for them. (Lindell, 2005)

**Ideal Type**
An abstraction from the particulars and the idiosyncrasies of the world which produce statements of general validity, and we know some part of the world because of its character as ideal typical knowledge. (Shariq & Vendelø, 2006)

**Ideal Vision**
A statement, in measurable terms, that describes where we are headed and how to tell when we have arrived in terms of societal value added. (Kaufman & Lick, 2005)

**IDEF0 Notation**
Boxes within a diagram depict the sub-activities of the activity named by the diagram. Arrows between boxes depict availability of work products to activities. Arrows entering the left side of a box are inputs to the activity. Arrows exiting the right side of a box are outputs from the activity. Arrows entering the top of a box are controls that regulate the activity, and those entering the bottom are mechanisms that support the activity. (Leung, 2005)

**IDEF1X**
One of the IDEF tools developed by Integrated Computer-Aided Manufacturing (ICAM), it is a formal framework for consistent modeling of the data necessary for the integration of various functional areas in computer-integrated manufacturing. (Ma, 2005a)

**Identification**
1: A one-to-many matching process for establishing the identity of the user if the submitted biometric sample matches one of the registered templates. (Li, 2006) 2: A user is not compelled to claim an identity first; instead, the biometric is scanned and then matched against all the templates in the database (also referred to as recognition). (Lowry, Stephens, et al., 2005) 3: A condition where the interests of the individual merge with the interests of the organization, resulting in the creation of an identity based on those interests. (Kankanhalli et al., 2006) 4: The process in which an individual comes to see an object (e.g., an individual, group, organization) as being definitive of oneself and forms a psychological connection with that object. Although scholars have offered a variety of conceptual definitions for identification, we view it as a communicative process, rooted in discourse and constituting a communicative expression of one's identity. (Connaughton, 2005)

**Identification-Based Trust (IBT)**
1: Trust that is grounded in mutual understanding and appreciation of each other's wants, desires, and intentions. (Wang & Gwebu, 2006) 2: The third stage of trust is built on empathy and shared values; team members can completely rely on each other. (Lettl et al., 2006)

**Identity**
1: A thing to represent or identify oneself to the other party or audience. (Park, 2006) 2: The degree of identification of the individual members with the community or network, and thus also an indicator for the identification of a community or network as such; strong or weak identity show the identification of the members as a group and their sense of community. (Müeller-Prothmann, 2006a)

**Identity Theft**
1: The act of a person who successfully pretends to be another person for the purpose of committing fraud. An identity thief discovers some bit of your personal information and appropriates it for him/herself without your knowledge to acquire a privilege (e.g., driving license), some property, or some service for which the victim is billed. (Friedman, 2005) 2: Pretending to be someone or some category of person that one is not. (Rowe, 2006d) 3: The act of using someone else's personal information such as name, PIN, or even biometric data without her/his knowledge for malicious purposes. (Li, 2006) 4: The stealing and use of a person's identity through the acquisition of personal information without that person's knowledge or permission. (Szewczak, 2005)

**Idiographic**
An approach focusing on the subjective experiences of the individual, and presenting results in expressions and terms used by the individual. The resulting RepGrid is considered unique in that there are no common elements or constructs employed in the elicitation process across the sample. (Tan & Hunter, 2005)

**Idiomatic Expression**
A phrase associated with a particular, non-literal meaning. (St.Amant, 2005d)

**I-DMSS:** See *Integrated Decision-Making Support System; Intelligent Decision-Making Support System.*

**IDS:** See *Internet Discussion Site; Intrusion-Detection System.*

**IEE:** See *Innovation Engineering Environment.*

**IEEE 802.11**
1: A family of specifications developed by the IEEE for wireless LAN technology. 802.11 specifies an over-the-air interface between a wireless client and a base station or between two wireless clients. The IEEE accepted the specification in 1997. (Bose et al., 2005) 2: A family of IEEE standards for wireless local area networks. (Hu, 2005)

**IEEE 802.11b/a/g**
Generally refers to wireless LAN standards. The IEEE 802.11b is the wireless LAN standard with a maximum bandwidth of 11Mbps operating at 2.4GHz. The IEEE 802.11a is the high-speed wireless LAN with a maximum bandwidth of 54Mbps operating at 5GHz. The IEEE 802.11g is backward compatible with the IEEE 802.11b, with a maximum bandwidth of 54Mbps operating at 2.4GHz. (Sarkar, 2005)

**IEEE 802.11b**
An established protocol or standard for wireless networking. (Wilsdon & Slay, 2005)

## IEEE 802.1x Standard

A standard that defines port-based network-access control. It is used to provide authenticated network access for local area networks and, using some extensions, for wireless networks. (Knight & Labruyere, 2005)

## IEEE Learning Technologies Standards Committee (LTSC)

The LTSC was set up by IEEE to develop standards, and to recommend practices and guides for anyone developing tools and content for the e-learning market. Standards developed under the auspices of IEEE-LTSC will be put forward to ISO for full standardization. The most significant contribution from the IEEE-LTSC has been the draft standard for Learning Object Metadata (LOM), the committee's implementation of the IMS metadata specification. This has emerged as the most mature of all the emerging standards. (Gordon & Lin, 2005)

## IEEE LOM

IEEE 1484.12.1 Standard for Learning Object Metadata. The standard "specifies the syntax and semantics of learning object metadata, defined as the attributes required to fully/adequately describe a learning object. Learning objects are defined here as any entity, digital or non-digital, which can be used, reused, or referenced during technology-supported learning." (Sicilia & Sánchez-Alonso, 2006)

**IEEE LTSC:** See *IEEE Learning Technologies Standards Committee.*

**IETF:** See *Internet Engineering Task Force.*

**IFADIS:** See *Integrated Framework for the Analysis of Dependable Interactive Systems.*

## IFIR Structure

The cascade of the expanded shaping or model filter G(zM) and the interpolator I(z). (Jovanovic-Dolecek, 2005c)

**IGMP:** See *Internet Group Management Protocol.*

**IIR Filter:** See *Infinite Impulse Response Filter.*

## Ill-Formed XML Document

A document lacking any fixed and rigid structure. (Nayak, 2005b)

## Ill-Structured Problem

A learning challenge of a complex nature with no one right answer. (Molinari, 2005)

## Illumination Model

A mathematical formula for calculating the amount of diffuse light, ambient light, and specular reflection that contributes to the color value that will represent a particular surface point on the screen. (Cottingham, 2005)

## Illusory Shape Emergence

In illusory shape emergence, contours defining a shape are perceived even though no contours are physically present. Here set theory procedures are not enough and more effective procedures have to be applied to find these hidden shapes. (Deb, 2005)

**ILE:** See *Interactive Learning Environment.*

**ILP:** See *Inductive Logic Programming.*

**IM:** See *Instant Message; Instant Messaging.*

## Image:

As defined in image theory, a meaningful visual form, perceptible in a minimum instant of vision. (Crossland, 2005)

## Image Analysis

An important layer of image engineering concerned with the extraction of information (by meaningful measurements with descriptive parameters) from an image (especially from interesting objects), with the goal of finding what objects (based on identification, recognition, and classification) are present in the image. (Zhang, 2005c)

## Image Classification

Classifying a new image, according to the image content, to one of the predefined classes of images (supervised classification). (Swierzowicz, 2005)

## Image Clustering

Classifying a new image into an image cluster according to the image content (e.g., color, texture, shape, or their combination) without a priori knowledge (unsupervised classification). (Swierzowicz, 2005)

## Image Copyright

The rightful ownership of an image. (Chen, Chen, Ma, et al., 2005)

## Image Data Mining

A process of finding unusual patterns, and making associations between different images from large image databases. One could mine for associations between images, cluster images, classify images, as well as detect unusual patterns. (Oh et al., 2005)

## Image Engineering

A general discipline that encompasses all techniques for treating images. It could be referred to as the collection of three related and partially overlapped categories of image techniques, that is, image processing (IP), image analysis (IA), and image understanding (IU). It is a broad subject encompassing studies of mathematics, physics, biology, physiology, psychology, electrical engineering, computer science, automation, and so forth. (Y.J. Zhang, 2005a)

## Image Feature

**1:** A structure in the image with interesting characteristics. Examples of features are single points, curves, edges, lines, surfaces. (Aifanti et al., 2005) **2:** One of a number of discrete properties of images that can be local or global. Examples of local features include edges, contours, textures, and regions. Examples of global features include color histograms and Fourier components. (Caelli, 2005)

## Image Format

Used to permanently store graphical content, based on the use of raster graphics or vector graphics. (Rosenbaum et al., 2006)

## Image Indexing

**1:** Assigning concise and significant descriptors to an image. Objects' shapes and positions are used in several indexing approaches where image is represented as a graph or tree (R-tree, B-tree, etc.). (Chbeir & Yetongnon, 2005) **2:** Fast and efficient mechanism based on dimension reduction and similarity measures. (Swierzowicz, 2005)

## Image Mining

Extracting image patterns not explicitly stored in images from a large collection of images. (Swierzowicz, 2005)

## Image Processing (IP)

**1:** Processing technique algorithms designed to enhance and manipulate an image. (Andrés del Valle, 2005) **2:** A research area detecting abnormal patterns that deviate from the norm, and retrieving images by content. (Oh et al., 2005) **3:** The first of the three layers of image engineering;

primarily includes the acquisition, representation, compression, enhancement, restoration, and reconstruction of images. All of these treatments are concerned with the manipulation of an image to produce another (improved) image. (Y.J. Zhang, 2005b)

## Image Processing Technique

A group of techniques concerned with the manipulation of an image to produce another (improved) image. It primarily includes the acquisition, representation, compression, enhancement, restoration, and reconstruction of images. (Y.J. Zhang, 2005a)

## Image Resolution

The degree of discernible details of an image. It strongly depends on the number of samples and gray levels used in the digitization stage and then used for the representation of this image. (Y.J. Zhang, 2005a)

## Image Retrieval

Retrieving an image according to some primitive (e.g., color, texture, shape of image elements) or compound specifications (e.g., objects, given type, abstract attributes). (Swierzowicz, 2005)

## Image Sampling and Quantization

To be suitable for computer processing, an analog image obtained from a scene must be digitized both spatially and in amplitude. Digitization of the spatial coordinates is called image sampling, and amplitude digitization is called gray-level quantization. (Y.J. Zhang, 2005a)

## Image Score

An image obtained from a page of music sheet, it can include a main score or a part. (Nesi & Spinu, 2005)

## Image Understanding

The process of interpreting images in terms of what is being sensed. (Caelli, 2005)

## Imagesetter

An output device used primarily to generate films for the production of printing plates. (Snyder, 2005)

**IMM:** See *Interactive Multimedia Method.*

## Immediate Maintenance

The policy of performing database maintenance operations as soon as their need becomes evident. (Sindoni, 2005a)

## Immersion

**1:** A quality of a system, usually a computer-generated world consisting of a set of technological factors that enable users to experience the virtual world vividly and exclusively. (Sas, 2006) **2:** Reflects the degree to which a community member's behavior is dominated by the state of flow caused by human-machine interaction. (Signoret, 2006)

## Immersion School

A language or culturally based school that allows students to study all or most subjects in a language other than their own. These are typically schools within a school district or programs within a particular school. (Glick, 2005b)

## Immersive IntraVascular UltraSound (IVUS) Image

The real-time cross-sectional image obtained from a pullback IntraVascular UltraSound transducer in human arteries. The dataset is usually a volume with artifacts caused by the complicated immersed environments. (Liu et al., 2005)

## Immersive IVUS Image: See *Immersive IntraVascular UltraSound Images.*

## Immersive System

A system that provides the graphical illusion of being in a three-dimensional space by displaying visual output in stereo and in a three-dimensional perspective according to head position, and by allowing navigation through the space. (Modrák & Marcín, 2006)

## Impacted Domain

The area affected by a change to the pivot domain. (Abou-Zeid, 2005a)

## Impaired Learner

A learners hampered by physical or psychological deficiencies. (Utsi & Lowyck, 2005)

## Imperative Mode

Command-oriented languages such as Fortran and Cobol that use the commands, DO, GO TO, and so forth. (Murthy & Krishnamurthy, 2005c)

## Imperative or State-Oriented Formal Specification Language

Allows the use of variables. (Dasso & Funes, 2005)

## Imperceptibility

After a message is hidden in a carrier, it is difficult for a viewer or listener to distinguish between the carrier that contains the hidden message and those that do not. (Lou et al., 2006)

## Imperceptible

Not easily detectable with the human visual system. (Chen, Chen, Ma, et al., 2005)

## Imperfect Knowledge

The imperfection of knowledge has to do with its incompleteness (absence of a value), with its imprecision (lack of precision in a value), and with its uncertainty (doubt on the truthfulness of a fact). (Analide et al., 2006)

## Implementation

**1:** The code placed inside of methods. For some languages, this code is pre-compiled or interpreted. (D. Brandon, Jr., 2005a) **2:** The implementation of information system includes different phases: user needs and requirements analysis (specification), system design, and initial system implementation and testing. The system requirements analysis includes workflow analysis; the initial system implementation includes technical installation of information system, integration of the information system to other information systems, and users' training. (Häyrinen & Saranto, 2005)

## Implementation of an Innovation

The process of mutually fitting innovation and organization to one another until the fit is so good that the (former) innovation is routine. (Klobas & Renzi, 2005a)

## Implementation Quality

The outcome of an IT installation in an organization, where operational success can be indicated by increased internal organizational performance and efficiency, better customer service, and higher quality working life within the organization, although other traditional indicators are increased profits, greater market share, and improved return on investment performance. (Winston & Dologite, 2005)

## Implementation Risk

A risk derived from poor business practices such as lack of training, lack of uniform standards, quality, and procedures that causes dissatisfaction among trading partners. (Ratnasingam, 2005)

**I**

## Implicit Edit
An unstated edit derived logically from explicit edits that were written by a subject matter specialist. (Conversano & Siciliano, 2005)

## Implicit Function
When used in 3D shape modeling, implicit functions $f(x, y, z)=0$ define a 3D surface of the shape. For example, an origin-centered sphere with radius 5 is defined with $5^2-x^2-y^2-z^2=0$. (Sourin, 2006)

## Implicit (Tacit) Knowledge
**1:** A type of knowledge that is stored in the minds of individuals in the form of memory, skills, experience, education, imagination, and creativity. (Aurum & Demirbilek, 2006) **2:** Knowledge not explicitly given in the knowledge base but derivable from it using various assumptions. (Grant & Minker, 2006) **3:** Knowledge acquired through experience and task execution, where it helps individuals in performing their work. (Qayyum, 2005) **4:** Knowledge that is uncodified and difficult to diffuse. It is hard to verbalize because it is expressed through action-based skills and cannot be reduced to rules and recipes. Implicit knowledge is the same as tacit knowledge. (Herschel, 2005)

## Implicit Team Process
A set of largely unverbalized, tacit communication and coordination behaviors, founded on shared understanding of members' roles/abilities and task/situational demands. Example: Member A provides Member B with backup assistance without being asked. (Cuevas et al., 2005)

## Import Restriction
One of a number of restrictions on the type, quantity, or origin of goods that can be imported into a country. (D. Brandon, Jr., 2005b)

## Impression Building
Portraying outcomes of endeavors as highly positive achievements to promote an image of competence and success. (Sipior, 2005)

## Impulse Response
The time domain characteristic of a filter; represents the output of the unit sample input sequence. (Jovanovic-Dolecek, 2005a)

## Impulse Response h(n)
The response of a digital filter to a unit sample sequence, which consists of a single sample at index $n = 0$ with unit amplitude. (Jovanovic-Dolecek, 2005c)

## Imputation
The method of filling in missing data that sometimes preserves statistical distributions and satisfies edit restraints. (Winkler, 2005)

**IMS:** See *Instructional Management System; Instructional Management Specification.*

**IMSI:** See *International Mobile Subscriber Identity.*

## In Degree
The number of Web pages that link to the current Web page. (Chen, Tsai, et al., 2005)

## In-Group Trust
Communities of people that have similar beliefs, values, and personality traits induced by cultural forces and are more willing to identify members inside their group as trustworthy. Individuals within these communities obtain role models and opinion leaders within their group that influence individuals' beliefs and behavior to include buying decision processes. (Carstens, 2005)

## In-Network Processing
A technique employed in sensor database systems whereby the data recorded is processed by the sensor nodes themselves. This is in contrast to the standard approach, which demands that data is routed to a so-called sink computer located outside the sensor network for processing. In-network processing is critical for sensor nodes because they are highly resource constrained, in particular in terms of battery power, and this approach can extend their useful life quite considerably. (Roussos & Zoumboulakis, 2005)

## In-Service
Brief and/or short-duration training for practicing teachers that tends to be informative (about new mandates, for example). Delivery tends to be traditional, and attendees must determine for themselves how the data relates to their situation(s) or discipline(s). Follow-up is rare, as is any effort to collect evidence of change practices. (Bober, 2005)

## Inapplicable Response

Respondents omit an answer due to doubts of applicability. (Brown & Kros, 2005)

## Incentive

**1:** An intrinsic or extrinsic motivational factor that impacts faculty decisions to participate in distance education. (Dooley et al., 2005) **2:** An attractive inducement offered to providers of services to be more efficient. (De', 2005) **3:** Any factor that influences action or behavior by its presence or absence. (Marcinkiewicz & McLean, 2005a)

## Incentive Regulation

Simply stated, it refers to a variety of regulatory approaches (starting with "price caps") that attempt to provide or enhance incentives for utilities to operate more efficiently. Incentive regulation is a response to the limits of the traditional "rate of return regulation," which set rates so as to cover operating expenses and ensure a "reasonable" return on invested capital. This was administratively cumbersome, detrimental to efficiency, and subject to the risk of overcapitalizations. (Arbore, 2005)

## Incentive Structure

The material or symbolic reward or punishment mechanism that organizations apply in order to encourage or discourage a certain organizational behavior, for example, the sharing of knowledge, skills, or insights with other members of the organization. (Ekbia & Hara, 2006)

## Incentives and Rewards

To encourage knowledge sharing, incentives and rewards are offered. Research has established that intrinsic rewards, such as being recognized and being encouraged to participate in decision making, are powerful motivators. On the other hand, it is argued that with internal competition, knowledge workers would be very cautious about openly sharing their knowledge with colleagues so not to give up individual advantages. (Fink & Disterer, 2006)

## Incidental Impact

Impact that is un-planned; by-product of a system's development process that had not, or could not, have been envisaged at the project's outset. (Doherty & King, 2005)

## Include

Some code stored separately from the main body of a program, so that this code can be used in many programs

(or multiple places in the same program). (D. Brandon, 2005a)

## Inclusion

A classroom design where all students should take part and attend "regular" classes. Generally, an ESE and regular education teacher work together with the same group of students, including students with disabilities and general education students. Both of the teachers share the responsibility for all of the students. (T. Cavanaugh, 2005)

## Inclusion Dependency

**1:** A pattern between two databases, stating that the values in a field (or set of fields) in one database form a subset of the values in some field (or set of fields) in another database. (Koeller, 2005) **2:** The existence of attributes in a table whose values must be a subset of the values of the corresponding attributes in another (or the same). Expressed as $R[X] \subseteq S[Z]$. R and S are relation names (possibly the same); R[X] and S[Z] are named the inclusion dependency's left and right sides respectively. X, Z are compatible attributes. (Rivero, 2005) **3:** Let R and S be two record types (not necessarily distinct) and X and Y be sequences of attributes of R and S, respectively, such that the numbers of attributes in X and Y are identical. We say that the inclusion dependency (IND), $R[X] í S[Y]$, holds at time t if at time t, for each R record r, an S record s exists such that $r[X] = s[Y]$. (Tan & Zhao, 2005b)

## Inclusive Design

The design of mainstream products and/or services that are accessible to and usable by as many people as reasonably possible on a global basis, in a wide variety of situations, and to the greatest extent possible without the need for special adaptation or specialized design. (Keates et al., 2006)

## Inclusiveness

Both a value and a design process—that is, inclusive environments are purposefully designed to address accessibility challenges and to make resources and services available to the broadest (and most diverse) possible audience. An approach based on inclusiveness is also known as universal instructional design and user-centered design. (Campbell, 2005)

## Incomplete Contract (Flexibility)

Most outsourcing contracts are incomplete since rapidly changing technology, uncertainty (i.e., complexity), and organizational environments make it so difficult to specify every contingency in the contract. (Khalfan et al., 2005)

## Incomplete Data

The data set for data mining contains some data entries with missing values. For instance, when surveys and questionnaires are partially completed by respondents, the entire response data becomes incomplete data. (H. Wang & S. Wang, 2005)

## Inconsistency

Database state that does not reflect a real-world state. (Rivero, 2005)

## Inconsistency Tolerance

The strategy that lets a system answer and process data despite the fact that databases are inconsistent. (Rodríguez-Tastets, 2005a)

## Inconsistent Database

A database violating some integrity constraint. (Flesca et al., 2005a)

## Incorporation by Reference

To make one document a part of another by identifying the document to be incorporated, with information that allows the recipient to access and obtain the incorporated message in its entirety, and by expressing the intention that it be part of the incorporating message. Such an incorporated message shall have the same effect as if it had been fully stated in the message. (Mitrakas, 2005)

## Incoterm

One of a standard set of international logistic acronyms. (D. Brandon Jr., 2005b)

## Incremental Cost

The cost of providing a specific service over a common network structure. (Hackbarth et al., 2005)

## Incremental Development

An approach to software development in which fully working versions of a system are successively delivered over time, each new increment (version) adding to and upgrading the functionality of the previous version. May be used in conjunction with "timeboxing," whereby a "wishlist" of requirements is prioritized and ordered into a staged plan of increments to be rolled out over time. (M. Lang, 2005)

## Incremental Growth Framework

A methodology for incrementally expanding a distributed database system. A new data allocation is computed with the introduction of each new server. (Chin, 2005)

## Incremental Innovation

The generation of new ideas (new knowledge) that leads to the incremental development of new products or services that build on existing practices. (Newell, 2006)

## Incremental Mining

In most real-life applications, the data are incrementally accumulated in the database, and not completely altered overnight. This makes it possible to use the previously mined rules for updates, rather than reforming new ones. (Nigro & González Císaro, 2005a)

## Incubator Program

A form of collaboration usually between the industry, corporations, and the business community and educational sector, aiming at identifying industry and market needs, catering for these needs, and creating employment opportunities for the society, especially young graduates. (Kamel, 2005a)

## Independence

**1:** The ability and willingness of a group to work with minimal input from an instructor. (Ingram & Hathorn, 2005a) **2:** The independence of a group from a central authority, such as an instructor or manager, ensures that the group can truly collaborate among themselves and produce results that are unique and new. (Ingram, 2005) **3:** Views $V_1$ and $V_2$ are conditionally independent given the class if for all $x = (x_1, x_2)$, $P(x_1, x_2 | y) = P(x_1 | y)P(x_2 | y)$. (Scheffer, 2005)

## Independent

Two random variables are independent when knowing something about the value of one of them does not yield any information about the value of the other. (Bashir et al., 2005)

## Independent Basic Service Set (IBSS)

A WLAN architecture (also called ad hoc) in which each network unit has both AP and station-computer functionality. (Pulkkis, Grahn, & Karlsson, 2005)

## Independent Business-to-Business Marketplace (or E-Marketplace)

An Internet destination where businesses from around the world can come together to buy and sell goods and services in an auction format. (Mockler et al., 2006)

## Independent Component Analysis (ICA)

A higher-order signal processing technique used for blind source separation, in which the objective is to extract source signals from their linear mixtures by using as little *a priori* information as possible. (Sattar & Yu, 2006)

## Independent Learner

Students who are independent learners and information literate pursue information related to personal interests, appreciate literature and other creative expressions of information, and strive for excellence in information seeking and knowledge generation. (Jesness, 2005)

## Independent Testing Authority (ITA)

One of a number of companies authorized by the government to test and certify proprietary DRE software and hardware systems. (Gibson & Brown, 2006)

## Independent Variable

A value representing a presumed cause of a particular outcome. (McHaney, 2005)

## Index

**1:** A data structure built on a database to speed up searches. (Chávez & Navarro, 2005) **2:** In the area of information retrieval, an "index" is the representation or summarization of a data item used for matching with queries to obtain the similarity between the data and the query, or matching with the indexes of other data items. For example, keywords are frequently used indexes of textual documents, and a color histogram is a common index of images. Indexes can be manually assigned or automatically extracted. The text description of an image is usually manually given, but its color histogram can be computed by programs. (Li et al., 2005) **3:** In data storage and retrieval, the creation and use of a list that inventories and cross-references data. In database operations, a method to find data more efficiently by indexing on primary key fields of the database tables. (Lin et al., 2005) **4:** Mechanism for sorting the multimedia data according to the features of interest to users to speed up retrieval of objects. (Hentea, 2005c) **5:** Used to create an external memory data structure in order to speed up search and retrieval of information. (Bozanis, 2006)

## Index Structure

An adapted data structure to accelerate retrieval. The *a priori* extracted features are organized in such a way that the comparisons can be focused to a certain area around the query. (Bretschneider & Kao, 2005)

## Index Tree

Partitions the space in a single dimension or multiple dimensions for efficient access to the subset of the data that is of interest. (Thomasian, 2005b)

## Indexed Searching

Searching with the help of an index, a data structure previously built on the text. (Navarro, 2005)

## Indexing Parser

Because of the heterogeneous nature of Web documents, we argue that indexing must also be performed at the stage of parsing Web documents. Hence, each source agent has a built-in indexing parser capable of building a document representation (index) based on the internal structure and the content of a given Web document. Typically the hierarchy of tags is taken into account while building the document index. Another important part of the process is taking into account source-specific lists of stop words, thesauri, and ontologies. Each resulting index consists of a weighted set of terms that occurred in the analyzed document. This format is a standard vector space model format that is commonly utilized in document filtering and retrieval. (Wecel et al., 2005)

## Indicator

**1:** A term used to refer to something that would point to quality or a lack thereof. (Wilkin, 2005) **2:** Generally quantitative expressions that relate variables to defined criteria. They can be statistics, numbers, values, reasons, or other ways of representing information. (Xodo & Nigro, 2005)

## Indirect Impact

Information technology that is not clearly related to measurable impact. For example, a new system helps executives make better decisions through providing access to better or more accurate information. (Dykman, 2005)

## Indiscernibility Relation

Objects x,y are indiscernible iff information about x is equal to (similar with) information about y. In the former case the indiscernibility relation is an equivalence relation; in the latter it is a similarity relation. Any object x defines an indiscernibility class (neighborhood) of objects indiscernible with this object. Also soft cases of indiscernibility relation are considered. Discernibility relation is a binary relation on objects defined as follows: Objects x,y are discernible iff information about x is discernible from information about y. In the simplest case, objects x,y are discernible iff it is not true that they are indiscernible. (Pawlak et al., 2005)

## Individual

A single candidate solution in genetic and evolutionary computation, typically represented using strings (often of fixed length) and permutations in genetic algorithms, or using problem-solver representations (programs, generative grammars, or circuits) in genetic programming. (Hsu, 2005a)

## Individual Critical Mass

Characteristic of the installed base that has to be surpassed in order to make an individual willing to adopt a communication product. (Voeth & Liehr, 2005)

## Individual Difference

**1:** In the context of Web-based instruction, this term is usually used to denote a number of important human factors, such as gender differences, learning styles, attitudes, abilities, personality factors, cultural backgrounds, prior knowledge, knowledge level, aptitudes and preferences for processing information, constructing meaning from information, and applying it to real-world situations. (Magoulas, 2006) **2:** Many of a learner's personal characteristics can affect how he or she learns. Individual differences are often explanations for differences in learning and performance among learners. The study of individual differences among learners' permits is done with the idea that results can help educators design instruction that better meets the needs of each learner's needs. (Campbell & Berge, 2005)

## Individual Knowledge

Knowledge possessed by persons rather than social entities. It is frequently tacit in nature, rendering it absolutely personal. When tacit knowledge is made explicit, it moves toward the other end of its dimension—social knowledge. (Ein-Dor, 2006)

## Individual Learning

An instruction method in which students work individually at their own level and rate toward an academic goal. (Moreira & da Silva, 2005)

## Individual Privacy

Freedom from excessive intrusion by those seeking personal information about the individual. Allows for the individual to choose the extent and circumstances under which personal information will be shared with others. (Mullen, 2005)

## Individual Style (Learning and Cognitive Style)

Relates to implicit main individual modes of acquiring information, organizing, and processing information in memory. Assessed by using questionnaire or psychometric test. (Rentroia-Bonito et al., 2006)

## Individual Variable

One of several characteristics of individuals, such as attitudes and preferences. (Beise et al., 2005)

## Individualism/Collectivism

**1:** An individualist society is one where each person is expected to be self-sufficient and look after themselves and their immediate family. A collectivist society is one where every person is a member of a group, and loyalty is to that group. Typically, in an individualist society, any money earned will be kept by the individual that earns it, whereas in a collectivist society, earnings will be shared among the group. (Frank et al., 2005) **2:** Concerned with individual interest as opposed to group interest (collectivism). That is, everyone grows up to look after himself/herself. The relationship between superiors and subordinates is based on mutual advantage. (Peszynski, 2005) **3:** Refers to a preference for a loose-knit social framework in society in which individuals are only supposed to take care of themselves and their immediate families. This is opposed to collectivism, which implies a preference for a tightly knit social framework in which individuals can expect their relatives and clan to protect them in exchange for loyalty. (Limayem, 2005)

## Individualized Instruction

Providing dynamic content and presentation based on individual preferences, attitudes, and knowledge. (Shareef & Kinshuk, 2005)

## Individualized Temperament Network

A neural-network-like structure representing a particular cognitive trait (e.g., working-memory capacity) of the learner. (Lin & Kinshuk, 2005)

## Individuation

The process by which the individual develops into a fully differentiated, balanced, and unified personality. A concept introduced by Carl Jung. (Chambel & Guimarães, 2005)

## Indoor Global Positioning System (Indoor GPS)

A variation of the Global Positioning System (GPS) for use in indoor environments, where the normal GPS signal does not typically work, because the signal strength is too low to penetrate a building. Indoor GPS navigation signals are generated by a number of pseudolites (pseudo-satellites) and are sent to pseudolite-compatible receivers that use the information to determine their own geographical positions. (Giaglis, 2005)

**Indoor GPS:** See *Indoor Global Positioning System.*

## Induced Subtree

Let T(N,B) be a tree, where N represents the set of its nodes and B the set of its edges. We say that a tree S(Ns,Bs) is an induced subtree of T provided that: (1) NsÍN, and (2) b=(nx,ny)ÎBs if and only if nx is a parent of ny in T. Thus, induced subtrees are a specialization of embedded subtrees. (Katsaros & Manolopoulos, 2005b)

## Induction

**1:** The process of deriving a concept from particular facts or instances. Inductive knowledge is empirical knowledge, of facts and information. (Nobre, 2006a) **2:** Process of learning, from cases or instances, resulting in a general hypothesis of hidden concept in data. (Lenič et al., 2005) **3:** A technique that infers generalizations from the information in the data. (Beynon, 2005b)

## Inductive Database

**1:** Database system integrating in the database source data and data-mining patterns defined as the result of data-mining queries on source data. (Meo & Psaila, 2005) **2:** An emerging research domain, where knowledge discovery processes are considered as querying processes. Inductive databases contain both data and patterns, or models, which hold in the data. They are queried by means of more or less ad-hoc query languages. (Boulicaut, 2005)

## Inductive Learning System

**1:** One of a set of data mining or knowledge discovery tools that learn relationships among a dataset by systematically analyzing cases. Output of these approaches is typically in decision tree (or rule) form. Popular algorithms of this genre include See5, CART, ID3, and C4.5. (Fuller & Wilson, 2006) **2:** Acquiring concept descriptions from labeled examples. (Muslea, 2005)

## Inductive Logic Programming (ILP)

**1:** A field of research at the intersection of logic programming and inductive machine learning, drawing ideas and methods from both disciplines. The objective of ILP methods is the inductive construction of first-order Horn clauses from a set of examples and background knowledge in relational form. (Perlich & Provost, 2005) **2:** A set of techniques for learning a first-order logic theory to describe a set of relational data. (Holder & Cook, 2005)

## Inductive Reasoning

The task of extracting intelligible information from a collection of examples pertaining to a physical system. (Muselli, 2005)

## Industrial Economy

A traditional economic perspective that presumes restricted expansion opportunities based on scarcity of physical resources, available labor, capital, and so forth. (Ng & Pemberton, 2006)

## Industrial Ethernet

Special type of Ethernet for field-area networks based on the relevant international standards (e.g., IEEE 802.3). It is adjusted to the specific environmental conditions in industrial production systems, for example, regarding electromagnetic compatibility, shaking, moisture, and chemical resistance. (Blecker, 2006a)

## Industrial Wave

A phase of civilization in which industries based on material processing and handling are dominant factors in the economy. (Targowski, 2005)

## Industrialized Nation

A country in which capitalism has long served as the model upon which business practices are based and the economy is founded mainly upon manufacturing and services. (St. Amant, 2005b)

## Industry Certification

Certification involves passing a recognized standardized test (or set of tests) within particular subject areas. It intends to establish a standard of competency in defined areas. ICT industry certifications are designed to provide targeted skills that have immediate applicability in the workplace. (McGill & Dixon, 2005)

## Industry-University Gap

Disconnect between the knowledge and skill needs of industry practitioners, and the knowledge and skills imparted on students by universities. (Kock, 2005)

## Industry Value Chain

Consists of the organizational value chain, together with the value chains of the organization's competitors, suppliers, and customers. It represents the movement of goods and services from the source of raw materials through to the final customer. (Jeffcoate, 2005)

## Industry-Based Knowledge

A general type of knowledge, widely available to individuals in their role-related organizational activities, across both firms and industry. It is not specific to either organizations or any individual organizational tasks as such; it is, however, highly industry specific. Examples of this type of knowledge are knowledge of the industry structure, of its current state of development, and of the key individuals, networks, and alliances in an industry. (Butler & Murphy, 2006)

## Industry-Wide Platform

Uses a mixture of information and communications technologies set up over the Internet to set up a multi-purpose platform that enables firms within a sector, along a supply chain, or as part of a consortium to exchange business information and transact. (Poon, 2005)

## Inexact Learning

The learning by which inexact rules are induced. (Dai, 2005a)

## Inexact Rules

Rules with uncertainty. (Dai, 2005a)

## Inexperienced Software Team

Most members of a software team are graduates or inexperienced in disciplined software development. (Lui & Chan, 2005)

## Inference

**1:** A logical conclusion derived by making implicit knowledge explicit. (Kamthan & Pai, 2006) **2:** Capability to deduce new knowledge from existing knowledge. (Dieng-Kuntz, 2006) **3:** Derivation using rules and assumptions. (Grant & Minker, 2006)

**INET:** See *International Networking.*

## Inference Channel

A particular case of a covert channel that exists when high-classified data can be deduced from low-classified data. (Gabillon, 2005)

## Inference to the Best Interaction

Any interface provides some clue from which the user is enabled to perform the correct action in order to accomplish tasks with a product. The process of inferring the correct action can be called inference to the best interaction. (Magnani & Bardone, 2006)

## Inflection Point

A significant change in corporate performance. (Nugent, 2005)

## Infinite Impulse Response Filter (IIR Filter)

**1:** A digital filter with an infinite impulse response. IIR filters always have poles and are stable if all poles are inside the unit circle. (Jovanovic-Dolecek, 2005a) **2:** Digital filter with infinite impulse response. This filter must be checked for the stability and does not have linear phase. This filter has lower complexity than its FIR counterpart. (Jovanovic-Dolecek & Díaz-Carmona, 2005)

## Influence

Making a difference in a virtual community. (Signoret, 2006)

## Info Pyramid

Multimedia data representation based on storing different versions of media objects with different modalities and fidelities. (Cavallaro, 2005)

## Infocracy

A form of organization in which information provides the underpinning of structure and the primary basis of individual power. In a more typical bureaucracy, hierarchical organizational structure dominates and is a primary driver of individual power. Information flows are then designed to support the structure and reinforce the power relationships. In an infocracy, information flows from point of origin to point of use, without regard to structure or pre-determined power relationships. As such, the organizational structure evolves to support required information flows. (Gordon & Mulligan, 2005)

## Infodesign

A broad term for the design tasks of deciding how to structure, select, and present information. (Roibás, 2006a)

## Infolink

The human resources department Web site on the intranet. (Al-Gharbi & Khalfan, 2005)

## Infomediary

A combination of the words 'information' and 'intermediary'. Infomediary refers to a vehicle (e.g., a Web site) that can collect and provide information. A virtual community provides the functions of an infomediary in several ways. It is an information source of product and service to consumers, and an information source of consumers' needs to the business. (Wang, Wei, et al., 2006)

## Informal Communication

Communication that is neither institutionally planned nor functionally defined, but opportunistic and spontaneous. (Beuschel et al., 2005)

## Informal Leader

One who demonstrates substantial leadership behavior even though not officially appointed or designated to hold such authority. Informal leaders often emerge tacitly from within a group. (Cargill, 2006a)

## Informal Learning

**1:** Learning anytime, everywhere in a non-organized way, where most of the time learning is unidentified and without recognition. (Lambropoulos, 2006b) **2:** Learning that takes place often in work settings without any formal structure; often considered to be a main way that people learn at work. (Berg, 2005h)

## Informal Mentoring

The non-assigned pairing of an experienced person who respects, guides, protects, sponsors, promotes, and teaches younger, less experienced personnel; it develops naturally

at the discretion of the mentor and protégé, and persists as long as the parties involved experience sufficient positive outcomes. (Long et al., 2005)

## Informatic

Term used in Latin America as an equivalent to computer based. (Barrera, 2005)

## Informatics Project

One of a number of projects that involve in any way possible the use, design, delivery, implementation, and management of information technology irrespective of the element involved, including software, hardware, and so forth. (Kamel, 2005a)

## Information

**1:** A process with data as input and knowledge as output. An individual is the subject who transforms the data into knowledge. Relations between two technical devices are data exchange processes. Relations between two or more individuals are communication processes. The reverse information process is called documentation process (e.g., writing an article). (Hofer, 2006) **2:** Data with context and utility. (Hoxmeier, 2005) **3:** A comparative unit of cognition that defines a change between the previous and present state of the natural, artificial, or semiotic systems. (Targowski, 2005) **4:** A message, or data, which makes a difference. Information has meaning, and becomes knowledge when a person internalizes it. (Huotari & Iivonen, 2005) **5:** Commonly known as a collection of facts or data. In Computer Science, it refers to processed, stored, or transmitted data. In Knowledge Management, it refers to codified knowledge. (Theng, 2005) **6:** Contextualized data that can be analyzed and applied to decision-making circumstances. (Taylor, 2005) **7:** Data that is associated with some system that enables meaning to be derived by some entity. (Benyon, 2006) **8:** Data with attributes of relevance and purpose. (Joia, 2005) **9:** In intelligence usage, unprocessed data of every description which may be used in the production of intelligence. (Melkonyan, 2005) **10:** Interpreted symbols and symbol structures that reduce both uncertainty and equivocality over a defined period of time. (Hirji, 2005) **11:** Knowledge acquired through experience or study. (Drake, 2006) **12:** Knowledge derived from reading, observation, or instruction, at times consisting of unorganized or unrelated facts or data. Data endowed with relevance and purpose, for example, a firm's balance sheet and income statement. (Mockler & Dologite, 2005) **13:** A term referring to details about an event or situation in the past or simply a scientific fact. Information can be regarded as a piece of knowledge of an objective kind. It results from placing data within some meaningful context, often in the form of a message. It is purely descriptive and explicit, does not enable decisions or actions, nor does it trigger new questions. (Haghirian, 2006)

## Information About Object

x in a given information system (U,A) is defined by $Inf_A(x)=\{(a,a(x)): a\in A\}$. (Pawlak et al., 2005)

## Information Age

A label given to the post-Cold War sociological and economic conditions of the world, which are driven by technology and information. (Reynolds, 2005)

## Information Agent

Program capable of retrieving information from a remote Web site by means of Internet protocols, storing it in a data repository and using it for executing specific tasks. (Castro & Braga, 2006)

## Information and Communication System of Local and Regional Development

A system that combines all the subjects on the basis of common principles to realize information and communication interaction for local and regional development. (Molodtsov, 2005)

## Information and Communication Technology (ICT)

**1:** The technological convergence between digital computing, telecommunications, and broadcasting. Whereas computers were largely focused on the processing of information, ICT undertakes both processing and communication of information. (Moodley, 2005) **2:** A generic term used to encapsulate the diverse range of technological developments (e.g., computer storage and retrieval, computing capacity, wired communications, wireless communications, portable technologies) that have enhanced the internal and external activities of organizations. Especially important is the manner in which these strands of technological development have been integrated to provide greater synergy. (Ritchie & Brindley, 2005) **3:** While often meaning different things in different timescales, places, and contexts, ICTs describe all media and a mix of converging technology tools involved in the dynamic transfer and storage of analog and digital data. In

addition to Internet-based technologies such as computers, telephones, and networks, ICTs in a broad sense include digital television, cable and satellite technologies, and music formats (e.g., MP3), DVDs, and CDs. ICTs may be used to facilitate remote human interaction for good and evil purposes. ICTs are used to increase human communication; broaden education, literacy, and knowledge; and enhance social, cultural, political, and economic capacity. It is hoped that this will help address problems attributed to the so-called digital divide. (Malina, 2005) **4:** A sector including a great variety of technologies such as desktop and laptop computers, software, peripherals, and connections to the Internet that are intended to fulfill information processing and communications functions. (Chochliouros & Spiliopoulou-Chochliourou, 2006) **5:** The amalgam of computing, telecommunications, and data networking technologies used to handle information and communication. It is the convergence of information technology, telecommunications, and data networking technologies into a single technology. It encompasses an array of hardware and software such as computers, digital cameras, CD-ROMs, radio, television, video and digital cameras, digital media, the Internet, e-mail, word processing, databases, the Internet, e-business, and e-commerce. (Magagula, 2005) **6:** Refers to the utilization of technology to process and access information, and to assist and facilitate communication. (Bodomo, 2005b) **7:** Includes ICT equipment (computer hardware, end-user communications equipment, office equipment and datacom, and network equipment) plus software products, IT service, and carrier services. (Damaskopoulos & Gatautis, 2006) **8:** A range of goods, applications, and services used for producing, distributing, processing, and transforming information, including telecommunications, television and radio broadcasting, computer hardware and software, computer services, the Internet, electronic mail, and electronic commerce. (Rhodes, 2005)

## Information and Communication Technology Alliance

A partnership between two or more nation states to share knowledge and resources in the area of ICT developments. (Toland, Purcell, et al., 2005)

## Information and Communication Technology Architecture

The ICT architecture provides a conceptual model, specifying (at a general level) the parts of an ICT infrastructure (applications, databases, technological ICT elements) and their relations. In this chapter we concentrate on the application and database parts. (Achterbergh, 2005b)

## Information and Communication Technology as a Cognitive Partner

Traditionally, ICT is used as a vehicle of information, but when used as a cognitive partner, it collaborates in the thinking processes of humans by performing actions such as changing a graph instantaneously or supporting a person to build his ideas when designing a concept map. (Santos, 2005)

## Information and Communication Technology Diffusion

Spread of ICT benefits to the majority of the population for using ICT to increase productivity and regional development. (Borbora & Dutta, 2005)

## Information and Communication Technology Indicator

One of a number of indicators that show the extent of the development of an information and communication infrastructure. Examples include fixed telephone density, mobile telephone density, personal computer density, Internet access, and host density, usually expressed as a ratio of inhabitants. (Díaz-Andrade, 2005)

## Information and Communication Technology Infrastructure

**1:** The deployment of telecom (both fixed and mobile), TVs, radio, computers, and Internet connections to enable the populace access to ICT services. (Frempong & Braimah, 2005) **2:** The underlying facilities, services, and installations needed for information communication technology to operate. (M. Rowe, 2005b)

## Information and Communication Technology in E-Procurement

Portals and electronic systems that facilitate registration of suppliers; notification of tenders; issue and downloading of tender documents; receiving and responding to enquiries; submission of tender offers; notification of contract award; and supply administration. (Demediuk, 2005)

## Information and Communication Technology in Teaching

Hardware, software, networks, and services related to the use and operation of equipment in the preparation and diffusion of courseware, and to communication between teachers and students, including communication between teachers and between students by electronic means. (El Louadi, 2005a)

## Information and Communication Technology Integration

The degree to which ICT is used to achieve organizational goals. In the educational context, integration means that ICT is used transparently to achieve curriculum objectives and is not taught for its own sake. (Mackey, 2005)

## Information and Communication Technology Level of Knowledge

The level of knowledge in the field of information and communication technologies that someone has. (Paraskevi & Kollias, 2006)

## Information and Communication Technology Planning in Schools

Specific school planning relating to the provision, acquisition, implementation, curriculum integration, maintenance, and replacement of ICT, and the professional development of staff relating to ICT. (Mackey, 2005)

## Information and Communication Technology Sector

A combination of manufacturing and services industries that capture, transmit, and display data and information electronically. (Moodley, 2005)

## Information and Communication Technology Selection

The process of selecting proper parts of the technological infrastructure and/or specific applications. In the context of CI, specific criteria are used: criteria regarding costs, appropriateness in supporting intelligence activities, and their fit or contribution to the CI infrastructure. (Vriens, 2005a)

## Information and Communication Technology Seva Kendra

A community-owned cooperative entity that nurtures learning and innovation in the community. (Shaligram, 2005)

## Information and Communication Technology-Based Development Project

A development project that employs information communication technologies as a strategic tool or approach for achieving desired outcomes. (M. Mitchell, 2005a)

## Information and Communication Technology-Enabled Knowledge Management

ICT facilitates both knowledge personalization and codification. Examples of the former are expert finder systems containing profiles of employees with special expertise, communities of practice where employees with similar professional interests can meet, and electronic blackboards. Examples of the latter are classification systems to retrieve objects by keywords, full-text search features, and topic maps. (Fink & Disterer, 2006)

## Information Architecture

**1:** How the Web site's Web pages are organized, labeled, and navigated to support user browsing. (Falk & Sockel, 2005) **2:** Mostly, the technological architecture that acts as an enabling mechanism to the information system. (Dykman, 2006)

## Information Artifact

Any artifact whose purpose is to allow information to be stored, retrieved, and possibly transformed. (Benyon, 2006)

## Information Asymmetry

**1:** A situation where one party to a transaction has more information than another party. In many cases it is the seller who has more and better information about the quality and underlying costs of a product than the buyer. (Fraser, 2005) **2:** Condition in which at least some relevant information is known to some, but not all parties involved. Information asymmetry causes markets to become inefficient, since all market participants do not have access to the information they need for their decision-making processes. (Wong, 2005)

## Information Broker

A key software component that supports intelligent portals. The information broker has the ability to coordinate between search engine, workflow engine, and portal management. Without an information broker, an individual user's profile would not be managed and consequently would not be serviced by context-sensitive portals. The information broker may work behind the Web server to provide the personalized services for Web users. It may also work directly with WWW for searching Web services online. (Li, 2005a)

## Information Channel

**1:** A term used to describe the various combinations of sources and formats of information. (McGill & Dixon, 2005) **2:** Refers to how members of the community receive information from various sources such as face-to-face, newspaper, telephone, mail/letters, notice boards, community meetings, church congregation, church newsletter, radio, and television. (Gnaniah, Songan et al., 2005)

## Information Closure

Boundary defined by information, and the sources necessary for autonomous (sub)systems functioning. (Szczerbicki, 2005)

## Information Content

Availability of information to compare across alternatives the completeness of information provided about a firm, product and service, and so on. (Shih & Fang, 2006)

## Information Delivery Theory

Teaching is just a delivery of information and students are just recipients of information. (Cirrincione, 2005)

## Information Design

A similar soft technology applied to information more broadly for the purpose of successful access to information. (Duchastel, 2005)

## Information Dissemination

Content of any book, paper, map, machine-readable material, audiovisual, or other documentary material, regardless of physical form or characteristics; making them available to the public is a form of information dissemination. Means of dissemination may be through information resource databases, information portals, the Internet, or other available media. (Rahman, 2006)

## Information Divide

The term broadly used to indicate the difference between groups, societies, or countries that have ready accessibility to information and those groups, societies, or countries that do not have the same or similar levels of access to this or similar information. (Arthur-Gray & Campbell, 2005)

## Information Economics

A scoring method that assesses the value of the information that results from the use of an information system. (Dykman, 2005)

## Information Economy

**1:** An economic system characterized by knowledge-based work and processing, and exchange of information and data as its primary activities. (Hantula & DeRosa, 2005) **2:** An economy dominated by information-related activities. (Ajiferuke & Olatokun, 2005) **3:** A concept created to illustrate a fundamental change in the business environment. The nature of the economy has changed as measured by the informational (intangible) elements of our products, services, and production processes, and the proportion of the workforce whose primary activities are informational. Information has become the most important resource upon which the efficiency and competitiveness of all organizations depend. This is true in not only services or high-tech industries, but also across the board in primary and manufacturing industries—and in both private and public sectors. (Kimble & Li, 2006)

## Information Engineering

Proper design of information flow, its management, its use, and its maintenance. (Szczerbicki, 2005)

## Information Exchange

Putting ideas and concepts in the correct formats and getting them circulated to other persons can be termed as information exchange. However, experiences and prior knowledge about the content are essential for making it become knowledge. (Rahman, 2006)

## Information Extraction

**1:** A process of extracting data from the text, commonly used to fill the data into fields of a database based on text documents. (Mladenić, 2005) **2:** An information extraction task is to extract or pull out user-defined and pertinent information from input documents. (Chang & Hsu, 2005) **3:** The process of pulling out or extracting relevant or predefined types of information from a set of documents. The extracted information can range from a list of entity names to a database of event descriptions. (Lee-Post & Jin, 2005a) **4:** The process of using a computer to automatically extract specific facts and rules from texts. (Kulyukin & Nicholson, 2005)

## Information Filtering

Filtering information from a dynamic information space based on a user's long-term information needs. (Parmar & Angelides, 2005)

## Information Filtering Agent

Intelligent agent that applies user-input preferences autonomously to screen passively and sort information. (Gates & Nissen, 2005a)

## Information Filtering System

A system whose goal is to deliver to a user only this information that is relevant to her/his profile; the system operates on large streams of unstructured data. (Abramowicz et al., 2006)

## Information Format

The arrangement and appearance of information. Format includes both the media used and the style of presentation. (McGill & Dixon, 2005)

## Information Gain

Given a set E of classified examples and a partition $P = \{E_1, ..., E_n\}$ of E, the information gain is defined as

$$entropy(E) - \sum_{i=1}^{n} entropy(E_i) * \frac{|E_i|}{|E|}$$

where |X| is the number of examples in X, and

$$entropy(X) = -\sum_{j=1}^{m} p_j \log_2(p_j)$$

(assuming there are m classes in X and $p_j$ denotes the probability of the jth class in X). Intuitively, the information gain measures the decrease of the weighted average impurity of the partitions $E_1, ..., E_n$, compared with the impurity of the complete set of examples E. (An, 2005)

## Information Gap

A gap that exists between the amount and types of information received and needed by members of the community. (Gnaniah, Songan, et al., 2005)

## Information Granularity

The data structure that can be classified. (Gabillon, 2005)

## Information Heterogeneity

The differences in syntax, structure, and semantics used in different information systems. (Karimi & Peachavanish, 2005)

## Information Hiding

The umbrella term referring to techniques of hiding various forms of messages into cover work. (K. Chen, 2005)

## Information Integration

The process of consolidating and managing customer information from all available sources. Also called customer data integration. (Moore et al., 2006)

## Information Integrity

Comprising data management, data quality, and data cleansing disciplines, information integrity refers to the state of data within an organization or IT system that adheres to the proper definition of data standardization per established business rules and is accurate, correct, and complete. (Malik, 2006)

## Information Literacy

**1:** An ability that has been acquired by training to locate, understand, evaluate, and use needed data efficiently and effectively. (Poda & Brescia, 2005) **2:** An integrated set of skills and the knowledge of information tools and resources that allow a person to recognize an information need and locate, evaluate, and use information effectively. (Gregory, 2005) **3:** Consists of computer literacy and information retrieval abilities and communication skills. Computer literacy means basic skills in computer use, for example, being able to read and write with computers. (Häyrinen & Saranto, 2005) **4:** Students who are information literate access information efficiently and effectively, evaluate information critically and competently, and use information accurately and creatively. (Jesness, 2005)

## Information Management

The management of all aspects of information in an organization, generally seen to encompass technical, human, and organizational information. (Kimble & Hildreth, 2006)

## Information Model

A rich central model of the business or of a domain within the business. A traditional data model or object model may serve as the basis for an information model, but ideally data models should be extended to a full ontology. (Schwartz & Schreiber, 2005)

## Information Needs

The information that contributes to solving a goal. This information should be properly integrated and focused on the goal. (Albers, 2006)

## Information Overload

**1:** A situation where an individual has access to so much information that it becomes impossible for him or her to function effectively, sometimes leading to a situation in which nothing gets done and the user gives the impression of being a rabbit caught in the glare of car headlights. (Pritchard, 2005a) **2:** Learners face the information overload problem when acquiring increasing amounts of information from a hypermedia system. It causes learners frustration with the technology and anxiety that inhibits the creative aspects of the learning experience. (Magoulas, 2006) **3:** The availability of excess information beyond that which is desired or needed by a user, requiring non-productive processing. (Kasi & Jain, 2006) **4:** Undesirable or irrelevant information that disturbs the user and distracts him or her from the main objective. This kind of problem usually occurs in contexts that offer excessive amounts of information, badly handled due to low-usability systems. (Gil & García, 2006)

## Information Paralysis

A condition where too much data causes difficulty in determining relevancy and extracting meaningful information and knowledge. (Nemati & Barko, 2005)

## Information Portal

Can also be viewed as part of a category in their own right as portals whose prime aim is to provide a specific type of information. (Tatnall, 2006)

## Information Privacy

The interest an individual has in controlling, or at least significantly influencing, the handling of data about themselves. (Sharma, 2006b)

## Information Privacy Trust

Unauthorized tracking and unauthorized information dissemination which refer to an e-tailer's privacy protection responsibilities. (Yeo & Chiam, 2006)

## Information Process

The process of information products' creation, collection, processing, accumulating, storage, search, dissemination, and use. (Molodtsov, 2005)

## Information Processing

Study of how humans interact within their environment while interpreting information to identify a decision. Humans are a unique form of a machine and must process information in order to formulate a decision. (Carstens, 2005)

## Information Processing Theory (IPT)

An explanation for the organization structure-environment relationship suggested by CT. IPT suggests that the information processing requirements dictated through interactions with the environment force certain structures in order to be efficient and effective. (Durrett et al., 2005)

## Information Product

**1:** A specific audience-targeted content combined with the accompanying service. Different information products may be based on the same service. As an example, products "Regional News" and "Press Conference Announcements" may base on one service such as "Newsline." Additional services (i.e., searches, e-mail lists) may serve to support each information product that owns its own marketing strategy and development standards. Consideration of user needs, requests, and possibilities are the key to establishing quality information products. (Arkhypska et al., 2005) **2:** The output of an information manufacturing system; it implies stages of development, such as information suppliers, manufacturers, consumers, and managers. (Chengalur-Smith et al., 2005)

## Information Pull

The process of user access to information stored in servers linked via the Internet or an intranet. (Quah et al., 2006b)

## Information Push

The process of a directory server relocating information files to active server machines within a faded information field based on the frequency of users' accesses. (Quah, Leow, & Soh, 2006)

## Information Quality

**1:** A global judgment of the degree to which these stakeholders are provided with information of excellent quality with regard to their defined needs, excluding user manuals and help screens (features of system quality). (Wilkin, 2005) **2:** The accuracy, completeness, timeliness, and utility of performance-related information that is used as the basis of management decision making. (Wright & Taylor, 2005) **3:** The degree to which information consistently meets the requirements and expectations of the knowledge workers in performing their jobs. (Chengalur-Smith et al., 2005) **4:** The success of the information being meaningful and useful to the receiver. (Shayo & Guthrie, 2005)

## Information Requirement Elicitation (IRE)

An interactive mode of context-aware application that helps consumers specify their information requirements with adaptive choice prompts in order to obtain desired supply context information. (Sun & Poole, 2005)

## Information Reservoir

A container of data, information, concepts, knowledge, and wisdom. (Targowski, 2005)

## Information Resource

**1:** A collection of valuable information generated by human activities. In a broader sense, it also includes related equipment, personnel, and capital. (Lai, Fu, & Zhang, 2005) **2:** One of the set of resources required to produce information, including hardware, software, technical support, users, facilities, data systems, and data. (Law, 2005)

## Information Resources Development

The process of collecting, processing, storing, disseminating, and utilizing information resources according to the need of the society. (Lai et al., 2005)

## Information Resources Management

The planning, organization, allocation, and utilization of information and related resources through legal, technological, and other methods to support institutional goals and missions. (Lai et al., 2005)

## Information Resources of Local and Regional Development

An organized entity of information products, which are created and disseminated for local and regional development needs. (Molodtsov, 2005)

## Information Retrieval (IR)

**1:** Interdisciplinary science of searching for information, given a user query, in document repositories. The emphasis is on the retrieval of information as opposed to the retrieval of data. (Fernández & Layos, 2005) **2:** The art and science of searching for information in documents, searching for documents themselves, searching for metadata that describe documents, or searching within databases, whether relational stand-alone databases or hypertext-networked databases such as the Internet or intranets for text, sound, images, or data. (Denoyer & Gallinari, 2005) **3:** The research area that deals with the storage, indexing, organization of, search, and access to information items, typically textual documents. Although its definition includes multimedia retrieval (since information items can be multimedia), the conventional IR refers to the work on textual documents, including retrieval, classification, clustering, filtering, visualization, summarization, and so forth. The research on IR started nearly half a century ago; it grew fast in the past 20 years with the efforts of librarians, information experts, researchers on artificial intelligence, and other areas. A system for the retrieval of textual data is an IR system, such as all the commercial Web search engines. (Li et al., 2005) **4:** The process of discovering and indexing the relevant documents from a collection of documents, based on a query presented by the user. (Lee-Post & Jin, 2005a) **5:** A discipline that deals with finding documents that meet a set of specific requirements. (Cunningham & Hu, 2005) **6:** A technology that can retrieve useful information effectively for some themes from the Internet by artificial or automatic method. (Chen, Tsai, et al., 2005) **7:** Denotes the attempt to match a set of related documents to a given query using semantic considerations (e.g., library catalog systems often employ information retrieval techniques). (Peter & Greenidge, 2005a) **8:** Concerned with the representation of knowledge and subsequent search for relevant information within these knowledge sources. Information retrieval provides the technology behind search engines. (Mandl, 2006)

## Information Retrieval Agent

An intelligent agent that searches for and collects information autonomously based on user-prescribed criteria. (Gates & Nissen, 2005a)

## Information Sector

A component of the information economy. The primary information sector includes those who develop hardware, software, and information systems. The secondary information sector includes those engaged in information processing activities in the course of doing work related to some other primary activity such as insurance claims processing. (Trauth, 2005a)

## Information Security

**1:** Domain of knowledge dealing with issues of preserving confidentiality, integrity, and availability of information. (Janczewski & Portougal, 2005) **2:** The protection of information systems against unauthorized access to or modification of information, whether in storage, processing, or transit, and against the denial of service to authorized users or the provision of service to unauthorized users,

including those measures necessary to detect, document, and counter such threats. (Mitrakas, 2006)

## Information Security Management

A framework for ensuring the effectiveness of information security controls over information resources; it addresses monitoring and control of security issues related to security policy compliance, technologies, and actions based on decisions made by humans. (Hentea, 2005b)

## Information Security Management System (ISMS)

A part of the overall management system, based on a business risk approach, to develop, implement, achieve, review, and maintain information security. The management system includes organizational structure, policies, the planning of activities, responsibilities, practices, procedures, processes, and resources. (Tong & Wong, 2005a)

## Information Security Policy

A document that outlines the basic rules of safe processing and dissemination of information. (Janczewski & Portougal, 2005)

## Information Service

**1:** Providing users up-to-date information (e.g., information of weather, news, sports, mapping, etc.). (Lee & Pai, 2005) **2:** The activity of providing information products and related services according to users' needs. In a broader sense, it refers to providing users with information through any form of product or service. (Lai et al., 2005)

## Information Shopping

The gathering of auction information, including the time and place of the auction and other related information. (Guan, 2006a)

## Information Society

**1:** A context in which people interact with technology as an important part of life and social organization to exchange information. (Demediuk, 2005) **2:** A societal transformation in which information is the key resource. (Trauth, 2005a) **3:** A society in which economic and cultural life is integrated by complex communication networks, and critically dependent on information and communications technologies. (Rahman, 2005b) **4:** A society in which information is used heavily in the everyday life of most citizens. (Ajiferuke & Olatokun, 2005) **5:**

A society that is very much affected by the innovations and advancements in information and communication technology management and applications, and is gaining more ground within the development and diffusion of the global digital economy. (Kamel, 2005b) **6:** Communal interaction based on the global informational systems of the Internet and the World Wide Web. Social relationships are informational flows, and people are informational entities or links. (Skovira, 2005)

## Information Source

**1:** An organization or person from which information is obtained. (McGill & Dixon, 2005) **2:** The source from where information is obtained by members of the community, such as relatives, friends, government officers, teachers, community leaders, outside visitors, and the grapevine. (Gnaniah et al., 2005a)

## Information Space

**1:** A collection of information artifacts and, optionally, agents and devices that enable information to be stored, retrieved, and possibly transformed. (Benyon, 2006) **2:** The aggregate of all determined objects and subjects, and information ties between them, which function and interact to provide for information needs of people and professional corporate communities, subject to local self-governance, region, society, and state. (Molodtsov, 2005)

## Information Stratification

The role distribution between the information interaction objects according to the amounts and types of information products, the creation of which is based on specialization in a specific activity sphere and on its scale. (Molodtsov, 2005)

## Information Superhighway

**1:** Encompasses those components that capture the visions of a nationwide, invisible, dynamic Web learner and the source of information. Includes, but is not limited to: private and public high-speed interactive, narrow, and broadband networks; satellite, terrestrial, and wireless technologies; databases; the written word; a film; a piece of music; a sound recording; a picture; or computer software. (G. Lang, 2005) **2:** A mixture of the full duplex (two-way), wired and wireless capabilities of telephones and networked computers with television, and radio's capacity to transmit hundreds of programs. (Msiska, 2005)

## Information System (IS)

**1:** A system that communicates, transforms, and preserves information for human users. An information system comprises one or more computerized data systems along with their human users, operators, and maintainers. (Opdahl, 2005) **2:** A system that uses IT to capture, transmit, store, retrieve, manipulate, or display data for business processes in an organization. (Aurum, 2005) **3:** A collection of organized procedures collecting, storing, processing, and retrieving data. It provides information to support the organization. (Szczerbicki, 2005) **4:** A collection of sources containing potential information. Information systems can be of variable structure and size, from small bibliographic catalogs to the Web itself. (Pharo & Järvelin, 2005) **5:** A system consisting of functions for input, processing, storing, output, and presentation of information. (Avdic, 2005) **6:** A pair (U,A) where U is the universe of objects and A is a set of attributes—that is, functions on U with values in respective value sets Va for a∈A. (Pawlak et al., 2005) **7:** The set of all human and mechanical resources needed for acquisition, storage, retrieval, and management of the vital data of a given system. With human resources are usually intended both the individuals involved in the use of the system and the procedures they have to carry out. With mechanical resources have to be intended both the hardware and software instruments to be used for the management of data. (Cartelli, 2005b, 2006b) **8:** A system for supporting communication within and between organizations. (Johannesson, 2005A) **9:** A computer-based system that helps people deal with the planning for, development, management, and use of information technology tools to help them perform all tasks related to their information needs. (Chen, Holt, et al., 2005) **10:** A curriculum that integrates technical skills and knowledge with applied business and organizational knowledge. Sometimes found in business schools, other times in schools of science, engineering, or in stand-alone IT academic units. Variations include the Business Information System (BIS), Computer Information System (CIS), and Management Information System (MIS). (Beise et al., 2005) **11:** Uses data to create information and knowledge to assist in operational, management, and strategic organizational decision making. It is also an umbrella term for computer information systems, management information systems, and information technology. (Scime, 2005a) **12:** First known as business data processing (BDP) and later as management information system (MIS). The operative word is "system," because it combines technology, people, processes, and organizational mechanisms for the purpose of improving organizational performance. (Singh & Dix, 2006) **13:** The means to transform data into information; used in planning and managing resources. (Sadoun, 2006) **14:** Interrelated components working together to collect, process, store, and disseminate information to support decision making, coordination, control, analysis, and visualization in an organization. (Hunter, 2005) **15:** Normally taken to include all elements of information, encompassing both the technical and human aspects. (Dykman, 2006) **16:** Refers to a set of people, procedures, and resources used to collect, process/transform, and disseminate information in an organization. (Singh, 2005)

## Information System Blueprint

An initial, functioning skeleton of a tailorable information system, built to reflect a problem-solving framework within a specific problem domain which, by means of an inherent deferred design decision mechanism, can be tailored by the end user to acquire or amend its existing behavior, in order to meet the specific needs of a particular business/organizational context. A blueprint of a tailorable information system can truly achieve flexibility. (Stamoulis et al., 2005)

## Information System Outsourcing

The transfer of an organization's IS function(s) to an external provider who takes the responsibility for managing these functions on behalf of the organization. (Gupta & Iyer, 2005)

## Information Systems Architecture

The set of information systems in an organization, the relationships between those information systems, and the relationships between the information systems and the rest of the organization. (Opdahl, 2005)

## Information Systems Development

Constitutes analysis, design, construction, and implementation of information systems. (Ericsson & Avdic, 2005)

## Information Systems Project Management

The process of managing the creation of an IS through the establishment of project goals; organizing, leading, co-coordinating the efforts of staff processes and tasks; and controlling other resources to achieve a set of agreed objectives. (McPherson, 2005)

## Information Systems Security

The protection of information and systems that use, store, and transmit information. (Kyobe, 2006)

## Information Systems Support

An IS function supporting people taking purposeful action. This is often done by indicating that the purposeful action can itself be expressed via activity models, a fundamental re-thinking of what is entailed in providing informational support to purposeful action. The idea is that in order to conceptualize and so create an IS support that serves, it is first necessary to conceptualize that which is served, since the way the latter is thought of will dictate what would be necessary to serve or support it. (Vat, 2005c)

## Information Technology (IT)

**1:** Computer and information-based systems that are mediated through electronic communication and integrated into the activities of individuals and groups. (Córdoba & Robson, 2006) **2:** An umbrella term that encompasses a range of professional positions requiring at least a baccalaureate degree in Computer Science, Information Systems, or closely related majors. (Beise et al., 2005) **3:** A major that focuses mainly on fourth-generation language application development and maintenance. (Beise et al., 2005) **4:** A computer-based tool (hardware and software) that people use to work with information and support the information-processing needs of an organization. (Chen, Holt, et al., 2005) **5:** All hardware, software, communications, telephones, facsimiles; all personnel and resources dedicated to the delivery of information and processes via computerized mediums. (Dery & Samson, 2005) **6:** Computer hardware and software, as well as the peripheral devices closely associated with computer-based systems that facilitate data processing tasks, such as capturing, transmitting, storing, retrieving, manipulating or displaying data. IT includes matters concerned with design, development, and implementation of information systems and applications. (Aurum, 2005) **7:** The use of hardware, software, services, and supporting infrastructure to handle and deliver information using voice, data, and video. (Partow-Navid & Slusky, 2005) **8:** The comprehensive and diversified set of technologies for information processing, such as software, hardware, and telecommunications. (de Medeiros et al., 2006) **9:** The physical equipment (hardware), software, and telecommunications technology, including data, image, and voice networks, employed to support business processes. (Narayanan, 2005) **10:** The main vehicle for creating, collecting, transmitting, displaying, and storing information. This includes hardware, software media, and networks. IT is a term that encompasses all forms of technology used to create, store, exchange, and use information in its various forms (business data, voice conversations, still images, motion pictures, multimedia presentations, and other forms, including those not yet conceived). It is a convenient term for including both telephony and computer technology in the same word. It is the technology that is driving what has often been called "the information revolution." (Rahman, 2005f) **11:** Uses existing commercial software applications to solve organizational problems. Sometimes referred to as information systems. It is also the umbrella term for all the disciplines involved with the computer. (Scime, 2005a) **12:** According to the World Bank, it consists of hardware, software, and media for collection, storage, processing, transmission, and presentation of information. (Finquelievich, 2005) **13:** Computer systems and applications that include the organization's hardware, software, networking, and telecommunications. (McManus & Carr, 2005) **14:** Computer-based methods for processing data into a useable form for users. (Hunter & Carr, 2005) **15:** Encompasses all forms of technology used in processing and disseminating information. (Ajiferuke & Olatokun, 2005) **16:** Hardware and software that constitute informational systems, as well as techniques for handling informational content and flows. (Skovira, 2005) **17:** Hardware, software, network, and services related to the use and operation of equipment with the aim of processing and communication of analog and digital data, information, and knowledge. These include computers and computer applications such as the Internet, intranets, extranets, Electronic Data Interchange, electronic commerce, mobile and fixed lines, and so forth. (El Louadi, 2005b) **18:** Encompasses all forms of technology used in the processing and disseminating information. (Olatokun & Ajiferuke, 2006) **19:** Refers to the physical components that are needed to create information products; normally refers to the hardware, such as computers, monitors, printers, and other computer components. (Singh, 2005) **20:** Information technology is the crucial component of a modern virtual organization. Without advances in technology, many of the realities of today's virtual companies would be merely science fiction. These components include the Internet, LANs (local area networks), and WANs (wide area networks) for business, e-mail and online chat and bulletin boards, and real-time videoconferencing. These technologies allow smaller workgroups as part of a larger company to operate independently of each other across a room or the globe. (J. Lee, 2005)

## Information Technology Alignment

**1:** How well a firm's information systems are linked to the needs of the business. One way of measuring alignment is to examine how well a firm's business strategy is linked to its IS strategy. (Cragg & Suraweera, 2005) **2:** The "fit" between the business and its IT; particularly, the fit between business strategy and IT strategy. (Cragg & Todorova, 2005)

## Information Technology Application

**1:** A local business-functional application embedded in business processes, activities, products, and/or services. (Peterson, 2005) **2:** Research and development work performed to create a situation-specific bridge between new or existing IT hardware and software technologies, and the information needs/wants of a customer. The combination of proper hardware, software, and tailored application delivers a well-rounded IT solution for the customer's problem. (Baim, 2005)

## Information Technology Architecture

A conceptual framework of IT in an organization that supports business processes. IT includes hardware, software, telecommunications, database management, and other information processing technologies used in computer-based information systems. (Mandal et al., 2005)

## Information Technology Competitive Advantage (ITCA)

The increased profitability and market share by a better positioning due to strategy and structure selection based on the alignment model. (Theodorou, 2005)

## Information Technology Enabled

Indicating that a design variable or team can only function through the use of information technologies. (Morris, Marshall, & Rainer, 2005)

## Information Technology End-User Relationship

A relationship between IT and the end user consists of two dimensions, namely a physical dimension and an abstract dimension. The physical dimension describes those elements that are necessary in order to enable contact between IT and its end users, whereas the abstract dimension describes the soft issues of a relationship. (Leonard, 2005)

## Information Technology Fit

The best relation that can be achieved in a strategic alignment model among information technology, business structure, and business strategy. (Theodorou, 2005)

## Information Technology Governance

(1) Locus of IT decision-making authority (narrow definition). (2) The distribution of IT decision-making rights and responsibilities among different stakeholders in the organization, and the rules and procedures for making and monitoring decisions on strategic IT concerns (comprehensive definition). (Peterson, 2005)

## Information Technology Governance Comprehensiveness

Degree to which IT decision-making/-monitoring activities are systematically and exhaustively addressed. (Peterson, 2005)

## Information Technology Governance Formalization

Degree to which IT decision-making/-monitoring follows specified rules and standard procedures. (Peterson, 2005)

## Information Technology Governance Integration

Degree to which business and IT decisions are integrated administratively, sequentially, or reciprocally. (Peterson, 2005)

## Information Technology Governance Maturity Model

This is part of the COBIT management guidelines, and is a five-stage maturity model of IT governance and a series of tool kits, audit guidelines, and implementation guidelines. The levels ranging from "non-existent" to "optimized" represent a progressively higher degree of effective governance practices and processes. (Saha, 2006a)

## Information Technology Hardware

Includes telecommunications equipment, computing hardware, and computing parts. Excludes embedded hardware in other products. (Watson, 2005)

## Information Technology Implementation Process

All the activities involved in initiating IT in an organization, from the original inception of an idea to innovate or install IT, to evaluating the success or failure of the IT in an organization. (Winston & Dologite, 2005)

## Information Technology Implementation Success

Often, when a new system has been introduced, there is either a formal or informal evaluation of whether the system has benefited the organization. This evaluation could include the degree to which a system has achieved its expectations or goals. (Cragg & Todorova, 2005)

## Information Technology Industry

The accumulation of all elements of information technology design, delivery, and management. (Kamel, 2005a)

## Information Technology Industry Development

Measured by gross IT sales, IT sales relative to GDP, firms in IT and their relative size, and IT industry employment relative to total employment. (Watson, 2005)

## Information Technology Industry Success

Measured by IT software and hardware exports, high-technology exports, and IT stock market listings. Includes the IT hardware and IT software industries; excludes embedded hardware and software in other products (e.g., washing machines). (Watson, 2005)

## Information Technology Infrastructure

1: Technological infrastructure that enables the transfer of information. (Fernando, 2005) 2: The base foundation of the IT portfolio, delivered as reliable shared services throughout the organization, and centrally directed, usually by corporate IT management. (Peterson, 2005)

## Information Technology Investment Intensity

A concept similar to, but also somewhat different from, the concept of information intensity. Information intensity is the degree to which information is present in the product/service of a business. The degree to which IT is present in an investment decision reflects the IT level of intensity of that decision. IT investment intensity is defined as the ratio of spending on IT to total investment. (Chou et al., 2005)

## Information Technology Literacy

A process by which people undertake skills-based training in how to use information and communication technology. (Weber & Lim, 2005)

## Information Technology Master Plan (ITMP)

Strategic document identifying links among goals, actions necessary to achieve them, resources, and constraints. (Gilbert, 2005a)

## Information Technology Outsourcing

The outsourcing of enterprise information systems and management to computer manufacturers or software companies (the term outsourcing stems from using an outside resource). Companies can save purchasing cost, maintenance cost, and labor cost by outsourcing and paying for those services. Outsourcing has become a common practice in the United States where companies are faced with uncertain returns of massive investment in IT resources. (D. Kim, 2005)

## Information Technology Outsourcing Partnership

The relationship between the service recipient and the service provider is defined in contracts describing the mutual obligations. The contract value of IT outsourcing partnerships is substantial, meaning over 10 million U.S. dollars or Euros. These contracts are also long-term contracts. The average duration of a contract is over 36 months. (Beulen, 2005)

## Information Technology Portfolio

Portfolio of investments and activities regarding IT operations and IT developments spanning IT infrastructure (technical and organizational components) and IT applications. (Peterson, 2005)

## Information Technology Professional

A term used to describe a person for whom development and support of IT systems and related activities is their primary employment. This includes people who design hardware, who develop and support information systems, and who train end users. It does not include people who use ICT in the course of pursuing other professions. (McGill & Dixon, 2005)

## Information Technology Skill

All IT professionals require some computer skills; these may include particular programming languages, or database or networking skills. (McGill & Dixon, 2005)

## Information Technology Software

Includes software applications, computer services, and training. Excludes embedded software in other products. (Watson, 2005)

## Information Technology Standard

One of a set of international standards that ensure compatibility of technologies produced throughout the world. (M. Rowe, 2005a)

## Information Technology Strategic Alliance

A broad agreement between business partners to operate cooperatively, usually facilitated by IT systems. (Mandal et al., 2005)

## Information Technology Strategy

**1:** A description of the plans, actions, or steps an organization intends to take in order to make the best use of IT within itself. (Johnston, 2005) **2:** Refers to applications, technology, and management—in particular, the IT applications an organization chooses to run, the IT technology it chooses to operate, and how the organization plans to manage the applications and the technology. (Cragg & Todorova, 2005)

## Information Technology Transfer (ITT)

The movement of information technology from creators to users. (Petter et al., 2005)

## Information Technology (IT) Worker

One who works in the primary or secondary information sector. (Trauth, 2005a)

## Information Theory

In this method, probability and ergodic theory are employed to study the statistical characteristics of data and communication systems and coding theory, which uses mainly algebraic and geometric tools to contrive efficient codes for various situations. Introduced by Claude Shannon in 1948, it was a revolutionary new probabilistic way of thinking about communication and the first truly mathematical theory of entropy. (Polgar, 2005b)

## Information Type

The description of necessary content in an application. (Uden, 2005)

## Information Visualization

**1:** A field of study aims to utilize a human's perceptual and cognitive abilities to enable and enhance our understanding of patterns and trends in complex and abstract information. Computer-generated two- and three-dimensional interactive graphical representations are among the most frequently used forms. (Chen, Toprani, et al., 2006) **2:**

Computer-supported interactive visual representations of abstract data which help improve understanding. (Metaxiotis, 2006) **3:** The use of computer-supported methods to interactively explore and derive new insights through the visualization of large sets of information. (Eppler & Burkhard, 2006) **4:** The visualization of data-mining models, focusing on the results of data mining and the data-mining process itself. Techniques include rule-based scatter plots, connectivity diagrams, multi-attribute generalization, and decision tree and association rule visualization. (Viktor & Paquet, 2005) **5:** Visualization of phenomena by means of appropriate representations. It is a field different from scientific visualization since information visualization emphasizes delivering visualizations that improve comprehension, whereas scientific visualization emphasizes delivering realistic visualizations. (Pareja-Flores & Iturbide, 2005)

## Information Wave

A phase of civilization in which industries based on information processing and handling are dominant factors in the economy. (Targowski, 2005)

## Information-Based Integration

Process in which, given informational inputs and outputs of autonomous (sub)systems, an analyst develops the overall system being designed that meets the desired functions and is interconnected through the flow of information. (Szczerbicki, 2005)

## Information-Efficient Market

Information and its dissemination are central elements in the traditional view of an efficient market. Internet finance forums have the potential to enhance the information efficiency of a market by creating an environment where information is continuously discussed and evaluated. (Campbell, 2006)

## Information-Gathering Strategy

The approaches and processes used by information seekers. Information-seeking behavior is influenced by previous experience, mental models, and preferences of information seekers. (McGill & Dixon, 2005)

## Information-Literate Knowledge Worker

A worker who knows what information is needed, knows how and where to obtain that information, understands the meaning of the information, and can act based on the information to help the organization achieve its greatest advantage. (Mandal et al., 2005)

## Information-Retrieval Mobile Agent

A small, portable program code that can migrate from server to server and execute its master's instructions for information retrieval. (Quah, Leow, & Soh, 2006)

## Information-Rich Web Site

A Web site designed to provide the user with information about a topic, such as a medical site. In general, it contains more information than a user can be expected to read and understand. (Albers, 2006)

## Informational Digital Skill

The ability of information consumers to critically assess digital information they are flooded with in cyberspace. (Eshet, 2005)

## Informational Privacy

The control over one's personal information in the form of text, pictures, recordings, and such. (Cook, 2005)

## Informationalization

The process of social advances in which human society transforms from industrial society to information society. (Lai et al., 2005)

## Informationbase

Set of reports and graphs, structured by means of chapters, updated automatically and/or manually. (Dragan, 2005)

## Informationbase Chapter

Part of informationbase, group of reports or graphs. (Dragan, 2005)

## Informationbase Entry

Part of an informationbase chapter, single report or graph. (Dragan, 2005)

## Informativeness

A Web site's ability to inform consumers of product alternatives for their greatest possible satisfaction. (Gao, 2005a)

## Informed Consent

**1:** The process by which people make decisions based on adequate information, voluntariness, and capacity to understand and appreciate the consequences of whatever is being consented to. Also called 'valid consent'. (Goodman, 2005) **2:** An individual's freely given consent to participate in research based on information provided by the researcher(s) about the research, possible risks associated with the research, and the voluntary nature of participation. Informed consent must be obtained without coercion or undue influence. (Roberts et al., 2005)

## Informed Embedding

A data embedding method that exploits the information about the host media available at the embedder side. (C.-T. Li, 2005)

## Infostructure

The complementary set of infrastructures, including an underlying electrical and telephonic grid, national core computing, and capacity access to online subscriptions and digital libraries. (Trujillo, 2005)

## Infotainment

Word formed from information and entertainment. In the automotive domain, it identifies a set of features provided by a VTS, such as audio module, Web browser, and so forth. (Costagliolam Di Martino, & Ferrucci, 2006)

## Infrared (IR)

A wireless technology that enables short-range communication between senders and receivers through beaming. The signal goes straight and will not go through walls. (Yang, 2005)

## Infrastructure

**1:** A class of wireless networking architectures in which mobile stations communicate with each other via access points, which are usually linked to a wired backbone. Such a network has a fixed infrastructure and has centralized control. (Sarkar, 2005) **2:** An emerging class of companies have opted to approach the Application Service Provider (ASP) market by providing infrastructure management and outsourcing services to ASPs, freeing up their resources to focus more directly on application management issues (telco, data center, networking). (Guah & Currie, 2005) **3:** An internal supportive framework. Among other things, infrastructure can refer to the computer networking technology found in an organization. (Baker & Schihl, 2005) **4:** The often unseen network of services provided within the institution that supports the daily operations. In this case, the distance teaching and learning infrastructure includes people working behind the scenes that support students, albeit in an invisible fashion. For example, the registrar's office, the office of student finances, the financial aid office, information technology system specialists, as well as distance learning administrators, deans, and

department chairs. (Riffee & Sessums, 2005) **5:** The underlying resources that provide the necessary capability for achieving outcomes. (Samuel & Samson, 2006)

## Infrastructure Interdependency

Denotes a bidirectional relationship between two or more infrastructures, through which the state of each infrastructure influences or is correlated to the state of the other infrastructure. (Jeong et al., 2006)

## Infrastructure TLD: See *Infrastructure Top-Level Domain.*

## Infrastructure Top-Level Domain (TLD)

The .arpa (address and routing parameter area) domain is reserved exclusively for those who implement the architecture and infrastructure of the Internet. (Maggioni & Uberti, 2005)

## Infrequent Itemset

Itemset with support smaller than a certain threshold, called minsupport. (Wong & Fu, 2005)

## Infrequent Pattern

An itemset that is not a frequent pattern. (Zou & Chu, 2005)

## Inheritance

**1:** A class inherits its state and behavior from its superclass. Inheritance provides a powerful and natural mechanism for organizing and structuring software programs. (Wong & Chan, 2006) **2:** A feature of object-oriented languages that allows a new class to be derived from another class (a more general class); derived classes (more specific classes) inherit the form and functionality of their base class. (D. Brandon, 2005a) **3:** A special relation between two classes of objects; class A inherits from class B when it is considered that A possesses all the characteristics of B (and possibly some more) simply because it is a subclass of class B. Models that support inheritance explicitly allow economical expression of facts, because declaring A as a subclass of B implies inheritance in such models. (Badia, 2005d) **4:** A subclass inherits all the attributes of a superclass and all the relationships that it (the superclass) participates in. (Bagui, 2005) **5:** A way of organizing classes so that properties can be defined once and applied to a whole collection of classes, with a general class defining those properties and specialized classes inheriting them. (Lucas, 2005) **6:** The ability of a superclass to pass its characteristics (methods and instance variables) onto its subclasses, allowing subclasses to reuse these characteristics. (Alhajj & Polat, 2005)

## Inheritance Hierarchy

Ontologies/taxonomies are structured as hierarchies of concepts ("inheritance hierarchies") by means of "IsA" links. A semantic interpretation of this relationship among concepts, when noted as (IsA $B$ $A$), means that concept $B$ is a specialization of the more general concept $A$. In other terms, A subsumes B. This assertion can be expressed in logical form as: ""$\forall x$ $(B(x){\rightarrow}A(x))$ (1)(1) says that, for example, if any elephant_ ($B$, a concept) IsA *mammal_* ($A$, a more general concept), and if clyde_ (an instance or individual) is an *elephant_*, then clyde_ is also a *mammal_*. (Zarri, 2005a)

## Inhibitor

A factor that can stop an activity. (Lubbe, 2005)

## Initial Model

The unique set of unit consequents of a set of Horn clauses. (Buehrer, 2005)

## Initial Public Offering

**1:** A company's first offering of its stock to the public. (Hwang & Stewart, 2006) **2:** First sale of a venture's common shares to the public; usually results in large profits for early stage venture investors. (Craig, 2006b)

## Initial Teacher Licensure or Teacher Credential

State certification document of an individual who has qualified for the first time to enter public school teaching, according to the state's requirements. (Wieseman, 2005a)

## Initial Trust

Trust in another person or organization before the trusting party gets to know them. (Paravastu & Gefen, 2006)

## Initiative

The characteristic of originating new ideas or methods. (Olatokun, 2006)

## Ink

A feature of tablet PCs that allows users to enter information using a pen. (Roldan, 2005)

## InkML

An Extensible Markup Language (XML) data format for representing digital-ink data. (Mohamed & Ottmann, 2006)

## Inlink

A link to a Web site from a different Web site. (Thelwall, 2006)

## Innovation

**1:** A new technology, idea, or process; (verb) the process of identifying, adopting, and implementing a new technology, idea, or process. (Klobas & Renzi, 2005a) **2:** A process in which organizations create and define problems, actively developing new knowledge to solve them, and generating new products, processes, or services. (Ng & Pemberton, 2006) **3:** An idea, practice, or object that is perceived as new by an individual or other unit of adoption. (Askar & Halici, 2005) **4:** Any idea, product, practice, behavior, or object that is apparent as new. (Askarany, 2005) **5:** Something new. It can be a product or a process and must provide benefit to the organization and to the advancement of society. An invention only becomes an innovation when it has become commercially successful. (Mitchell, 2005a) **6:** The application, in any organization, of ideas new to it, whether they are embodied in products, processes, or services. (Tatnall, 2005b) **7:** The creation of something new. This involves a radical step of making something different from before or creating something that has not existed before. (Fong, 2006a) **8:** The generation of new ideas (new knowledge) that leads to the development of new products or organizational practices. (Newell, 2006) **9:** The successful exploitation of a new idea. This may be in the industrial domain (products, processes, campaigns) or the scientific domain (theories, insights, methodologies). (Paukert et al., 2006) **10:** The term "innovation" involves the transformation of an idea into a marketable product or service, a new or improved manufacturing or distribution process, or a new method of social service. The term also encompasses social, institutional, and organizational innovation, including in the services sector. The concept of innovation is also used in connection with the analysis of processes of technological change. Traditionally, technological change was viewed as consisting of three stages: invention, innovation, and diffusion. Innovations can take place at any time in all areas of the economy. (Finquelievich, 2005)

## Innovation Capital

This innovation-oriented approach focuses on explicit knowledge that will eventually facilitate organizational learning. The learned organization will then have better capabilities to innovate and compete. (Hsu & Mykytyn, 2006)

## Innovation Diffusion

A theory of innovation in which the main elements are: characteristics of the innovation itself, the nature of the communication channels, the passage of time, and the social system through which the innovation diffuses. (Tatnall & Burgess, 2005)

## Innovation Engineering Environment (IEE)

A flexible and adaptable framework based on information and knowledge technology for systematic innovation support. It includes four core components: Innovation Process Management, Generic Innovation Support Components, Application-Specific Configuration Support, and Innovation Environment Configuration Support. (Paukert et al., 2006)

## Innovation Factor

One of the characteristics of a specific innovation that encourages an organization to adopt an innovation, including the perceived benefits of the innovation and the compatibility of the innovation to the organization. (Cragg & Mills, 2005)

## Innovation Hub

Designed to encourage the formation and growth of knowledge-based enterprises or high value-added tertiary firms. Innovation hubs generally aim at promoting and catalyzing innovation and entrepreneurship within an innovative milieu. (Moodley, 2005)

## Innovation Implementation Potential

The likelihood that a particular innovation will be adopted in the system it was intended for in a way similar to its intended purpose. (Taylor, 2005)

## Innovation Knowledge Lifecycle

Model of the knowledge-related activities in which the innovation process is embedded; this includes a problem cycle that feeds the innovation process and that can also be triggered by innovation, as well as a knowledge cycle that describes activities around knowledge objects within the innovation process on an abstract level. (Paukert et al., 2006)

## Innovation Network

A structured network of N organizations sharing common goals related to research and/or development of new products/technologies (e.g., The Human Genome Project). This network type is characterized by a decentralized structure, low-medium competition, and uncommon scope of operations among members. (Priestley, 2006)

## Innovation Translation

A theory of innovation in which, instead of using an innovation in the form it is proposed, potential adopters translate into a form that suits their needs. (Tatnall & Burgess, 2005)

## Innovation-Decision Process

The process through which an individual passes from having knowledge of an innovation, to the formation of an attitude toward the innovation, to a decision to adopt or reject it, to the implementation and use of the new idea, and then to the confirmation of this process (knowledge, persuasion, decision, implementation, and confirmation). (Askar & Kocak-Usluel, 2005)

## Innovative Cognition

A cognitive style that processes information, intuitively, integratively, and prefers to construct new paradigms. (Kaluzniacky, 2006)

## Innovative Culture

An organizational climate that fosters new ideas and reflection on learning from experiences. (Wright & Taylor, 2005)

## Innovative Product

A product having uncertain demand, a high profit margin, and a short lifecycle due to ensuing competition that forces companies to introduce newer innovations. (Abraham & Leon, 2006)

## Innovativeness

The degree to which an individual or other unit of adoption is relatively earlier in adopting new ideas than others. (Lertwongsatien & Wongpinunwatana, 2005)

## Input Acceleration

A technique for expanding user input, allowing a large volume of input to be provided with few user actions. (Trewin & Keates, 2006)

**Input Debugging**

A process performed on a router to determine from which adjacent router the packets matching a particular attack signature are coming from. (Syed, Nur, et al., 2005)

**Input/Output**

The performance measures used in DEA evaluation. Inputs usually refer to the resources used, and outputs refer to the outcomes achieved by an organization or DMU. (Chen, Motiwalla, et al., 2005)

**Inquiring Organization**

An organization founded on the principles of one or more inquiring systems that seeks to increase its learning potential. Inquiring organizations are learning-oriented organizations that strive to include both creation and management of knowledge in their cache of core competencies. The philosophical foundations of inquiring organizations come from Churchman's (1971) discourse of knowledge creation and inquiring systems from the viewpoints of selected Western philosophers. These perspectives are particularly well suited to knowledge management and serve to differentiate the inquiring organization from other learning organizations. (Hall & Croasdell, 2006)

**Inquiring System/Inquirer**

Any one of the systems developed by Churchman that supports inquiry and is founded on the philosophies of Leibniz, Locke, Kant, Hegel, or Singer. (Hall & Croasdell, 2006)

**Inquiring Theory**

The theory espoused by Churchman that systems should be designed to create new knowledge while incorporating ethics and aesthetics, culminating in knowledge that creates the greatest good for the greatest number. (Hall & Croasdell, 2006)

**Inquiry**

The process of being actively engaged in the pursuit of knowledge. (Hall & Croasdell, 2006)

**Inquiry Style**

An individual approach to learning based on dominant information acquisition, change, the relationship to others, and problem-solving behavior. (Handzic & Lin, 2005)

**Inquiry Training**

A structured teaching model that allows individuals to learn the way scientists learn. Such a model follows specific phases of instruction that include solving a real problem by making hypotheses, gathering and organizing data, and testing different hypotheses to come up with a possible solution to dealing with a problem. (Gillani, 2005b)

**Inquiry-Based Learning (IBL)**

A student-centered, active learning approach focusing on questioning, critical thinking, and problem solving. IBL is expressed by the idea "involve me and I understand." The IBL approach is more focused on using and learning content as a means to develop information-processing and problem-solving skills. The system is more student centered, with the teacher as a facilitator of learning. There is more emphasis on "how we come to know" and less on "what we know." Students are involved in the construction of knowledge through active involvement. The more interested and engaged students are by a subject or project, the easier it will be for them to construct in-depth knowledge of it. Learning becomes easier when it reflects their interests and goals, and piques their natural curiosity. (Lowry & Turner, 2005)

**Insourcing**

**1:** Formalization of the supply relationship between two departments of the same organization. (Beaumont, 2005) **2:** The internal IT division of service recipients executes the IT services to the departments of the service recipient. (Beulen, 2005)

**Inspirational Behavior**

Influences others by using emotional appeals, and vivid and persuasive images, to elevate their performance. (Sipior, 2005)

**Installed Base**

Number of current users of a certain communication product and compatible products. (Voeth & Liehr, 2005)

**Instance**

**1:** A set of attributes, their values, and a class label. Also called example, record, or case. (Maloof, 2005) **2:** A vector of attribute values in a multi-dimensional space defined by the attributes, also called a record, tuple, or data point. (Liu & Yu, 2005) **3:** Of a model: a set of data items structured according to the model. Data instantiate the model (or data schema in this context). (Diskin & Kadish, 2005) **4:** An example (or record) of the dataset; it is often a row of the data table. Instances of a dataset are usually seen as a sample of the whole population (the universe). An instance is described by its attribute values, which can be continuous or discrete. (Muhlenbach & Rakotomalala, 2005)

## Instance Selection

A process of choosing a subset of data to achieve the original purpose of a data-mining application as if the whole data is used. (Liu & Yu, 2005)

## Instant Message (IM)

A written message, synchronous or asynchronous, sent via an IM tool. The IM tool allows the user to see which pre-defined contacts are online and send synchronous messages, the conversation taking the character of a chat, or asynchronous, leaving the message until the contact goes online. Examples of IM tools are Icq and MSN. (Dunkels, 2005)

## Instant Messaging (IM)

**1:** A type of communications service that enables you to create a kind of private chat room with another individual in order to communicate in real time over the Internet. It is analogous to a telephone conversation but uses text-based, not voice-based, communication. Typically, the instant messaging system alerts you whenever somebody on your private list is online. You can then initiate a chat session with that particular individual. (Lalopoulos et al., 2005b) **2:** A method for real-time communication over a wired or wireless network. An evolution from IRC (inter-relay chat), an early Internet real-time communication protocol. (Horiuchi, 2005b) **3:** An application that provides immediate delivery of messages over fixed-line and mobile IP networks. (Gilbert, 2005b) **4:** Near-synchronous Internet-based one-to-one communication technology. IM allows two users to exchange short text messages in real time. (Hwang & Stewart, 2005) **5:** Communication service on the Internet that enables textual private chats with other individuals in real time. (Beuschel et al., 2005) **6:** A computer application that allows two or more users to communicate with each other in real time via typed messages. (Elshaw, 2006b) **7:** An application (such as ICQ, PowWow, and AOL's Instant Messenger) that allows members of a group to see who is online at any moment, send instant messages, and set up spontaneous small chats.

The applications are increasingly used to provide quick user help and feedback, build relationships, and easily share comments. (Kardaras & Karakostas, 2006) See Chat.

## Instant Messenger™

**1:** A program that hooks up to a service for conversation in real time. Involved parties see each line of text right after it is typed (line-by-line), thus making it more like a telephone conversation than exchanging letters. Popular instant messaging services on the public Internet include AOL® Instant Messenger, Yahoo!® Messenger, .NET Messenger Service, and ICQ. (Kao & Rerrer, 2006) **2:** An information technology that enables people to send real-time text messages. (Wang, J. et al., 2006b)

## Instantiation

Creation of an object, or class instance, from a class. (Lucas, 2005)

## Institution-Based Trust

**1:** Trust based on the guarantees of a third party. (Paravastu & Gefen, 2006) **2:** Trust formed when organizational members believe that their organization as a whole has their best interests at heart and acts accordingly. (Smith, 2006b)

## Institutional Connectivity

Refers to an organization or institution's ability to link with others' networks and the rate at which this connection is made. (Poda & Brescia, 2005)

## Institutional Dimension

Considering the need for integrated evaluation of business ideas/solutions enabled by IT, it is emergent that there are organizational dimensions (or institutions). They include the context where evaluation is integrated (e.g., the system's development lifecycle, the IS management practices and processes, the people's roles, the organizational culture) and furthermore, the understanding of stakeholders' behavior within this context. (Serafeimidis, 2005)

## Institutional Policy

A plan or course of action developed by an institution to guide actions. (Schifter, 2005)

## Institutional Strengthening

Awareness and effective use of human and technological available resources in all their scope to accomplish institutional goals. (Falivene & Kaufman, 2006)

## Instructional Conception

Conception about the functionalities of (elements of) a learning environment. Such conceptions can relate to the effectiveness or efficiency of specific features in a learning environment (e.g., tools) or to the environment as a whole (e.g., KABISA as a learning environment). (Clarebout et al., 2005b)

## Instructional Design (ID)

**1:** Conventionally, instructional design refers to linear and externally controlled design practices consisting of systematic choices and use of procedures, methods, prescriptions, and devices to bring about effective, efficient, and productive learning. However, in CSCL, "designing" often points to more iterative and cyclical design endeavors, where design activities and procedures integrate collaborative learning theories, technology-based learning environments, and diverse actors in a pedagogically relevant way. (Pöysä & Lowyck, 2005) **2:** A systematic approach for designing learning materials based on learning theories and research. (Ally, 2005b) **3:** Layout of an optimal integration of educational content and interface layout of end-user software. (Utsi & Lowyck, 2005) **4:** The process of analyzing the students, content, and intended context of an instructional program to provide detailed specifications for an instructional program or curriculum to achieve effective and efficient student learning within an affordable and accessible delivery format. (Boettcher, 2005a) **5:** A systematic approach for designing learning materials based on learning theories and research. (Ally, 2005a) **6:** A systematic process for responding to instructional problems, needs, and opportunities. (Shambaugh, 2005) **7:** An applied, cross-disciplinary professional (post-graduate) design discipline that integrates human learning theory and instructional practice to develop, produce, implement, and evaluate effective educational experiences and learning environments to improve human performance outcomes, knowledge construction, and the acquisition of robust transfer competencies. (Lasnik, 2005) **8:** The field of instructional design includes a range of professions from programmers and graphic artists to the instructional designer. Designers are able to analyze instruction, learners, environments, strategies, and media to develop effective instruction of training. Designers may or may not be subject matter experts. (Rogers, 2005a) **9:** The process of planning for the development and delivery of effective education and training materials. Instructional designers employ a systematic process that considers learner need, desired learning outcomes, delivery requirements and

constraints, motivation, psychology, and related issues. (Sales, 2005) **10:** The soft technology of organizing learning materials and events so that instruction will be most successful. (Duchastel, 2005) **11:** The systematic design of course materials. A common model called ADDIE includes Analysis, Design, Development, Implementation, and Evaluation. (Baker & Schihl, 2005) **12:** The systematic method of how to plan, develop, evaluate, and manage the instructional process effectively. (Askar et al., 2005) **13:** The systematic process of translating general principles of learning and instruction into plans for instruction and learning. (Askar & Halici, 2005)

## Instructional Design Model

**1:** A representation of how instructional design is conducted or how the analysis, design, development, implementation, and evaluation of an instructional design is conceptualized. (Shambaugh, 2005) **2:** Traditional design models are prescriptive step-by-step processes, usually associated with behaviorist instructional strategies. Phenomenological models incorporate constructivist philosophies and practices. In either aspect, design models guide the user in designing effective instruction that takes all aspects of design (see ADDIE) and reminds the user of critical elements and decisions in designing effective instruction. (Rogers, 2005a)

## Instructional Design Process

The process of analyzing the students, content, and intended context of an instructional program to provide detailed specifications for an instructional program or curriculum to achieve effective and efficient student learning within an affordable and accessible delivery format. (Boettcher, 2005b)

## Instructional Development

**1:** The development of learner, instructor, and management materials (both print and nonprint) that incorporates specifications for an effective, efficient, and relevant learner environment. Instructional development includes formative and summative evaluation of the instructional product. (Kinuthia, 2005) **2:** The process of implementing the design plans under instructional technology (instructional technology = instructional design + instructional development). Instructional development provides a process and framework for systematically planning, developing, and adapting instruction based on identifiable learner needs and content requirements. This process is essential in distance education, where the instructor and students may share limited common background and typically have minimal face-to-face contact. Although instructional development models and processes abound, the majority follow the same basic stages of design, development, evaluation, and revision. (Rahman, 2005a)

## Instructional Imperative

Any training or business requirement, such as strategies, delivery methods, or constraints, that accommodates the stakeholder requirement. (Jeffery & Bratton-Jeffery, 2005)

## Instructional Management System (IMS)

System and information technology tool that allows educators to create, organize, and manage online courses quickly and easily though the use of Web-based templates for online course delivery. Most IMS vendors advertise their product as a course management tool that allows individuals to create course content as easily as they create documents or presentations in software applications such as Word or PowerPoint. (Proctor, 2005)

## Instructional Management Specification (IMS)

IMS is originally an abbreviation for Instructional Management Specification, and is now also commonly used as the short form for the IMS Global Learning Consortium (www.imsproject.org), a group of interested parties (companies, academics, standards bodies, etc.). IMS is systematically trying to create workable specifications for all aspects of the learning process—aiming from enterprise issues through content creation and management to modeling learning styles. IMS has established working groups in every conceivable activity in the e-learning domain. The IMS Global Learning Consortium is specifically involved in development of specifications—leaving standards creation, accreditation paths, and so forth—to other bodies. (Gordon & Lin, 2005)

## Instructional Media

Modes of communication in which teaching takes place, such as instruction by face-to-face interaction, lessons by radio, deployment of curricula or interactive learning via the Internet, and so forth. (Fisher, 2005)

## Instructional Objective

A description of a performance you want learners to be able to exhibit before you consider them competent. An objective describes an intended result of instruction rather than the process of instruction itself. (I. Chen, 2005)

## Instructional Scaffolding

Refers to a developmental process of constructing sequential instruction components to achieve an original outcome. (McCracken, 2005)

## Instructional Strategy

A communication activity used to engage the learner in an educational experience and to assist the learner in acquiring the planned knowledge, skill, or attitude. Instructional strategies include lectures, discussions, reading assignments, panel presentations, study and media projects, problem analysis and solutions, field trips, and assessment activities. (Boettcher, 2005a)

## Instructional System Design (ISD)

A process that applies a systematic approach to design, develop, implement, and evaluate instruction. Such an approach is based on the target learners' needs and aims to achieve pre-defined learning outcomes. (Aisami, 2005)

## Instructional Technology

The systemic and systematic application of strategies and techniques derived from behavioral, cognitive, and constructivist theories to the solution of instructional problems. It is the systematic application of theory and other organized knowledge to the task of instructional design and development. (Rahman, 2005a)

## Instructional Television (ITV)

Typically used to describe whole videotaped academic courses; often set in a studio or classroom using a traditional lecture format. (Berg, 2005d)

## Instructional/Pedagogical Design/Approach

In the context of Web-based instruction, this usually relates to pedagogical decision making, which concerns two different aspects of the system design: planning the educational content (what concepts should be the focus of the course) and planning the delivery of instruction (how to present these concepts). (Magoulas, 2006)

## Instructivist Perspective

A perspective on learning that places emphasis on the teacher in the role of an instructor that is in control of what is to be learned and how it is to be learned. The learner is the passive recipient of knowledge. Often referred to as teacher-centered learning environment. (Torrisi-Steele, 2005)

## Instrumentality

The notion that action, including knowledge management, is carried out for a purpose, and that the purpose underlying the action can be maligning as well as beneficial. (Land, Nolas, et al., 2006)

## Insurance

Protection against future loss. In exchange for a dollar value (premium), insurance is a promise of reimbursement in the case of loss. Contractual arrangement of insurance may be voluntarily or by government mandate (such as minimum requirements for automobile insurance for licensed drivers). (Kitchens, 2005)

**Insurance Underwriter:** See *Underwriter.*

## Intangible Asset

**1:** Higher education institutions are traditionally based upon ideas, one form of intangible assets. However, the modern university frequently seeks to differentiate itself from its competition. Intangible assets include an investment or outcome enjoyed by the institution in knowledge-based resources and processes. Typically, these intangible assets are termed soft assets because they are not either infrastructure or equipment. Some examples are training programs, improvements to organizational communication flows, or new quality assurance systems. (Williamson et al., 2006) **2:** An organizational asset that does not have any physical manifestation, or that has physical measures with no bearing on its value. The following is a typical list of intangible assets that an organization may have: fragmented knowledge residing with individuals, or encapsulated in artifacts such as documentation and software code; codified and classified knowledge residing in repositories; unique systems, processes, methodologies, and frameworks that the organization follows; "formalized" intellectual property, such as patents, trademarks, and brands; and relationships and alliances that the organization may have shaped (Kochikar & Suresh, 2005)

## Intangible Cost

One of a number of costs that are difficult to be measured in a direct way, since they refer to vague concepts. (Esteves & Pastor, 2005)

## INTASC Principle

One of a set of core standards for what all beginning teachers should know, be like, and be able to do in order to practice responsibly, regardless of the subject matter or grade level being taught. (Shaw & Slick, 2005)

## Integrated Circuit (IC)

A small electronic device made out of a semiconductor material. Integrated circuits are used for a variety of devices, including microprocessors, audio and video equipment, and automobiles. (Lee & Warkentin, 2006)

## Integrated Decision-Making Support System (I-DMSS)

An information system that integrates the functions of one or more individual (standalone) decision-making support systems. (Forgionne, 2005) See also Management Support System (MSS).

## Integrated Framework for the Analysis of Dependable Interactive Systems (IFADIS)

A tool for the analysis of user interface models developed at the University of York (UK). (Campos & Harrison, 2006)

## Integrated ICT Planning

Planning that blends ICT planning or information systems planning with strategic planning. (Mackey, 2005)

## Integrated Learning Environment

Current and emerging learning management systems combine information management and productivity tools along with Group Support System (GSS) features for support and management of individual and collaborative learning. Document and multimedia information management (drop boxes and other tools for storage, retrieval, sharing, and organization of learning content and discussions), threaded discussions for asynchronous communication, instant messaging for synchronous communication, and advanced e-mail (spell check, multiple views allowing sorting of messages, and other extensive message editing capabilities) are important features in learning management systems. Testing, grading, student registration, and management of question-and-answer sessions also enable management of the learning process. (Alavi et al., 2005)

## Integrated Library System

The automation system for libraries that combines modules for cataloging, acquisition, circulation, end-user searching, database access, and other library functions through a common set of interfaces and databases. (Nicholson & Stanton, 2005)

## Integrated Personal Financial Service (IPFS)

The seamless integration of previously independent financial products and services. Prior independence of these financial products was a function of organizational, regulatory, and/or technological constraints imposed upon the providers. For example, in a true IPFS relationship, funds would flow seamlessly between insurance, banking, investment, and tax accounts. (Gordon & Mulligan, 2005)

## Integrated Services (IntServ)

Architecture where network resources are apportioned according to an application's Quality of Service (QoS) request, subject to bandwidth management policy and focused on individual flows. (Gutiérrez & Ting, 2005)

## Integrated Services Digital Network (ISDN)

**1:** A set of communications standards allowing a single wire or optical fiber to carry voice, digital network services, and video that may replace the plain, old telephone system. (Vician & Buche, 2005) **2:** A set of CCITT/ITU (Comité Consultatif International Téléphonique et Télégraphique/ International Telecommunications Union) standards for digital transmission over ordinary telephone copper wire as well as over other media. ISDN in concept is the integration of both analog or voice data, together with digital data over the same network. (Rahman, 2005c) **3:** A communication technology that allows the clear transmission of voice, data, image, and their combinations. ISDN users can have more than one call at a time. (Kirlidog, 2005) **4:** A telecommunication service that uses digital transmission and switching technology to support voice and digital communications. (Butcher-Powell, 2005) **5:** A digital telephone/telecommunications network which carries voice, data, and video over existing telephone network infrastructure. It is designed to provide a single interface for hooking up a phone, fax machine, PC, and so forth. (Cosemans, 2005a)

## Integration

**1:** The process of achieving unity of effort among various subsystems in the accomplishment of the organizational task (process focus); the quality of the state of collaboration that exists among departments which is required to achieve unity of effort by the demands of the environment (outcome focus). (Peterson, 2005) **2:** A system is integrated when it is sufficiently interconnected that a change to any element of the system by any component of the system is reflected appropriately—that is, according to the business rules of the system in every other component of the system. For example, if a Human Resources system is integrated, and an employee changes his or her address through any human interface that allows it, then the new address will be shown automatically every place else in the system. (Fulton, 2005) **3:** Refers to how work is performed. Knowledge entities cannot be merged but should be looked upon as a distributed system of cognitive elements whose integrative potential lies in the collective ability to perform. (Munkvold, 2006)

## Integration Adapter

Data and application adapters (also known as data interfaces or data drivers) are native software objects that allow integration tools to retrieve data efficiently from complex, sometimes proprietary stores of information. (Karakostas, 2005)

## Integration Broker (IB)

A middleware product that uses an internal (or virtual) representation of a Common Data Model (CDM) to mediate the exchange of data and data-related services among applications. An IB manages the physical, syntactic, and semantic translation of data from any application, the validation of rules of authorization and business processing, and the transport to each application and component required to preserve system-wide consistency of the virtual collection of data. (Fulton, 2005)

## Integration Hub

A hub is a messaging server that exchanges important information between different applications so that the applications can interact in a meaningful way. (Karakostas, 2005)

## Integration of Processes

The coordination and integration of processes seamlessly within and without the organization. (Sundaram & Portougal, 2005a)

## Integrity

**1:** Allows the system to verify whether modifications have occurred; it does not make sure that information was not altered. (Pierre, 2006b) **2:** In databases, 'integrity' is largely synonymous to 'semantic consistency'—that is, the correctness of stored data with regard to their intended meaning. Integrity, as expressed by integrity constraints, should not be confused with a namesake issue often associated with data security. (Decker, 2005)

**3:** The condition that exists when data is unchanged from its source and has not been modified, altered, or destroyed at any operation according to an expectation of data quality. (Mitrakas, 2006) **4:** Prevention of unauthorized modification of information. (Tong & Wong, 2005a) **5:** The belief the other party is honest and adheres to accepted modes of behavior. (Paravastu & Gefen, 2006) **6:** As defined by the American Institute of Certified Public Accountants, it includes the character traits of honesty, candor, and protection of confidentiality. (Wang, Chen, et al., 2006)

## Integrity Checking

Systematic tests ensuring that integrity remains satisfied (see Integrity Satisfaction). If integrity is violated (see Integrity Violation), then the update causing inconsistency must be rejected or some other action must be taken to enforce a consistent state, that is, one that satisfies integrity (see Integrity Enforcement). (Decker, 2005)

## Integrity Constraint

**1:** A rule that must be satisfied by the database or knowledge base if it is consistent. (Grant & Minker, 2006) **2:** A requirement on the consistency of the information stored. (Decker, 2005) **3:** One of a set of properties that the data of a database are required to satisfy; they are expected to be satisfied after each transaction performed on the database. Integrity constraints provide a way of ensuring that changes made to the database do not result in a loss of data consistency. Integrity constraints include key references and cardinality restrictions. (Aldana Montes et al., 2005) **4:** Set of constraints which must be satisfied by database instances. (Flesca, Furfaro, et al., 2005) **5:** A statement that specifies the set of valid values in a database. Integrity constraints must be satisfied to protect the database against inconsistencies. (Rivero, 2005)

## Integrity Control

Deals with the prevention of semantic errors made by the users due to their carelessness or lack of knowledge. (Ibrahim, 2005)

## Integrity Enforcement

Actions taken to ensure that integrity remains satisfied across database updates (see Integrity Satisfaction). Conservative integrity enforcement rejects updates that would violate integrity (see Integrity Violation). Progressive integrity enforcement attempts to satisfy the update while maintaining integrity by further data modifications, possibly consulting the user. (Decker, 2005)

## Integrity Satisfaction

A given database state satisfies integrity if each integrity constraint in the database schema, posed as a query, returns the required yes/no answer. An ostensibly equivalent, but in fact slightly weaker definition says that integrity is satisfied if it is not violated (see Integrity Violation). The difference between both definitions manifests itself in incomplete databases. (Decker, 2005)

## Integrity Violation

In a given database state, integrity is violated if any one of the integrity constraints, posed as a query, returns the opposite of the required yes/no answer. (Decker, 2005)

## Intellectual Alignment

Describes a state where the content of IT and HR business plans are consistent and externally valid. (Dery & Samson, 2005)

## Intellectual Capital (IC)

**1:** The aggregation of individual human capital in a sense that the aggregation is more than the sum of it parts, that is, encompassing organizational routines and capabilities. (von Wartburg et al., 2006) **2:** The sum of the individual imagination that, when aggregated, becomes everything everybody in an organization or team knows and which provides them with some advantage over their competitors. Organizational IC comes from the interplay of structural capital, which augments the value of human capital, leading to an increase in customer/supplier capital. (Williamson et al., 2006) **3:** Knowledge and know-how possessed by an individual or an organization that can be converted into value in markets. Roughly the same as the concept of intangible assets. (Anttiroiko, 2005b) **4:** Can be divided into three categories: human capital—that in the minds of individuals, including knowledge, competences, experience, know-how, and so forth; structural capital—that which is left after employees go home for the night, including processes, information systems, databases and so forth; and customer capital—customer relationships, brands, trademarks, and so forth (Herschel, 2005) **5:** Everything that is known within an organization as exemplified in knowledge itself, in ideas and competencies, and in systems and processes. (Archer, 2006) **6:** Refers to intellectual material—knowledge, information, intellectual property, and experience—that can be put to use for creating wealth. (Hsu & Mykytyn, 2006) **7:** Knowledge gathered by an organization and its employees that has value and would help the organization gain benefit when reused. (Elshaw, 2006a) **8:** Knowledge or information that is created through collaborative activity by a community. It can be difficult to ensure clear notions of ownership since knowledge is jointly held. The organization of communities must define codes of behavior to deal with ownership issues. (Fleming, 2005c) **9:** The human intelligence asset that belongs to a company. It consists of people, the skills, values, learning, and knowledge that they bring to the organization. (Ray, 2006) **10:** The set of intangible assets that enable a company to function. (Casado, 2005)

## Intellectual Capital Management (ICM)

A management of value creation through intangible assets. Close to the concept of knowledge management. (Anttiroiko, 2005b)

## Intellectual Capital Management System (ICMS)

A combination of communities, processes, and technology brought together to identify, value, categorize, and capture intellectual capital for reuse. (Elshaw, 2006a)

## Intellectual Creation

Any work of creation, such as authorship, visual arts, performing arts, or music. (Kieler & West, 2005)

## Intellectual Property (IP)

**1:** A product of the intellect (intangible property) that has commercial value such as patents, trademarks, copyrights, and so forth. (Zhao, 2005) **2:** Any product of the human intellect that is unique and has some value in the marketplace. It may be an idea, composition, invention, method, formula, computer software, or something similar. In practice, special attention is paid to such intellectual property that can be protected by the law (e.g., patent and copyright). (Anttiroiko, 2005b) **3:** A formal measurable subset of Intellectual Capital (IC); the tangible product that results from the idea, and is represented and recognized through patents, trademarks, designs, and copyright (which includes software and multimedia). IP can also be extended to cover a much broader and often more intangible grouping that extends to trade secrets, plant varieties, geographical indications, and performers' rights. (Williamson et al., 2006) **4:** The time-limited monopoly (a copyright or patent) given to one who has made a contribution to that progress. It is sufficient to define IP as the protection measure for IC once identified and defined. (Ariely, 2006a) **5:** Wider right to control ownership over any material of a conceptual nature (i.e., invention, idea, concept) as well as encompassing material originally covered by copyright.

(Fleming, 2005b) **6:** A comparatively recent description of the much older concept that intellectual effort can be treated as a form of property and controlled so as to circumscribe or limit the ways in which that intellectual effort is used by others. The concept of intellectual property encompasses copyright, patent, trademarks, moral rights, and other similar forms of legal protection. A contested implication of the use of the term is that intellectual work should attract the same level of legal protection that is given to physical property. (Marshall, 2005) **7:** A general term for intangible property rights that are a result of intellectual effort. (Pemberton & Stalker, 2006) **8:** Any product of the human intellect that is unique, novel, and unobvious (and has some value in the marketplace)—that is, an idea, invention, expression or literary creation, unique name, business method, industrial process, chemical formula, computer program process, or presentation. (Du Mont, 2005) **9:** Includes business designs, business process techniques, or patterns. Technology held proprietary through patents, copyrights, or trade secrets can deter new entrants and achieve a competitive advantage by exploiting economies of scale and scope or through differentiation. Five steps are suggested to establish intellectual property capital: conduct an intellectual property audit, incubate new ideas, reduce the ideas to practical form, protect the idea, and exploit the idea. (Hsu & Mykytyn, 2006) **10:** A concept allowing individuals or organizations to own their creativity and innovation in the same way that they can own physical property. The owners of IP can control its use and be rewarded for it; in principle, this encourages further innovation and creativity. (Warren, 2006)

## Intellectual Property Rights (IPRS)

**1:** Treating certain intangible products of the human mind as belonging to the creator or holder in legal form such as patents, trademarks, or copyright. (Demediuk, 2005) **2:** One of a set of copyright and connected rights that include, inter alia, the right of copying, modifying, and distributing the protected work. (Cevenini, 2005) **3:** Exclusive rights accorded by a state to legal persons based on intangible knowledge, permitting them to control how the knowledge is distributed or exploited for financial or other benefit. Consists of copyrights, patents, trademarks, and trade secrets. (Okoli & Carillo, 2006) **4:** Laws and enforcement mechanisms to afford the creator of an intellectual property (e.g., software) the means of controlling how their work is used, and ensuring that the creator is properly rewarded and recognized for his or her work. (Hawk & Kaiser, 2005)

## Intellectual Turning Point

Scientific work that has fundamentally changed the subsequence development in its field. Identifying intellectual turning points is one of the potentially beneficial areas of applications of trend detection techniques. (Chen, Toprani, et al., 2006)

## Intelligence

**1:** Ability of a given system to act appropriately (i.e., to increase the probability of the achievement of given aims) in an uncertain and changing environment. (Szczerbicki, 2005) **2:** Information, news, and advice. Brain power or cognitive skills. IBM uses the term "business intelligence systems" to describe its mixed integrated knowledge systems. (Mockler & Dologite, 2005)

## Intelligence Cycle

**1:** A complete process of intelligence data, divided into data collection, data processing and exploitation, data analysis, and production and dissemination. (Badia, 2006) **2:** Cycle of four stages (collections of intelligence activities). The stages are direction (also referred to as planning, in which the strategic information requirements are determined), collection (determining sources and retrieving data), analysis (assessing the strategic relevance of data), and dissemination (of the intelligence to strategic decision makers). (Vriens, 2005b)

## Intelligence Data Source

One of the origins of data captured in the data-collection phase; the term covers both people (HUMINT) and mechanical or technical means (SIGINT, IMINT, MASINT). (Badia, 2006)

## Intelligence Density

The useful "decision support information" that a decision maker gets from using a system for a certain amount of time, or alternately the amount of time taken to get the essence of the underlying data from the output. (Sundaram & Portougal, 2005b)

## Intelligence Infrastructure

**1:** Comprises all technological, human resources, and organizational means needed to manage, support, and perform the intelligence activities. It consists of three sub-infrastructures: the technological infrastructure, the human resources infrastructure, and the organizational infrastructure. (Vriens, 2005a) **2:** The organizational foundation that consists of information technology-based facilities, systems, and services that support holistic intelligent behaviors throughout an organization. (Tang & Sivaramakrishnan, 2005)

## Intelligence Need

One of the topics that an organization must monitor in order to stay competitive. (Parker & Nitse, 2006)

## Intelligent Agent

**1:** A proactive computer system capable of flexible autonomous action in order to meet its design objectives as set out by the designer. (Ally, 2005b) **2:** A piece of software, used extensively on the Web that performs tasks such as retrieving and delivering information, and automating repetitive tasks. It internally uses some form of knowledge representation based on logics. (Sicilia & García-Barriocanal, 2006) **3:** A proactive computer system that is capable of flexible autonomous action in order to meet its design objectives set out by the designer. (Ally, 2005a) **4:** A program that gathers information or performs some other service without your immediate presence and on some regular schedule. (Raisinghani et al., 2005) **5:** A program that makes use of Artificial Intelligence (AI) approaches to provide timely contextual help or instruction to a learner. (Askar et al., 2005) **6:** A software entity that performs a set of operations on behalf of a user or another program. Such entities are embedded in computer-based information systems to make them smarter. This is usually achieved with the employment of artificial intelligence techniques. (Karacapilidis, 2005) **7:** An agent that is capable of flexible behavior: responding to events timely, exhibiting goal-directed behavior and social behavior, and conducting machine learning to improve its own performance over time. (Soh & Jiang, 2006) **8:** An agent who acts in an intelligent way (autonomy, learning, reasoning, etc.). (Karoui, 2005) **9:** An autonomous software program that performs certain tasks delegated to it by its master. The program is able to learn and adapt to its environment in order to perform the tasks better. Task-specific intelligent agents are given different names based on their functionalities, such as interface agent, information agent, e-commerce agent, and personal assistant agent. (Tang & Sivaramakrishnan, 2005)

## Intelligent Agent Technology

Integration of network, Internet, and artificial intelligence techniques. (Hentea, 2005b)

## Intelligent Algorithm

A human-centered algorithm with the capacity for thought and reason, especially to a high degree. (Barolli & Koyama, 2005a)

## Intelligent Call Routing (ICR)

A communications service that provides companies with the ability to route inbound calls automatically to destinations such as a distributed network of employees, remote sites, or call-center agents. Call routing is typically based on criteria such as area code, ZIP code, caller ID, customer value, previous customer status, or other business rules. (Lalopoulos et al., 2005b)

## Intelligent Computer-Assisted Language Learning (ICALL)

The exploration of the use of artificial intelligence methods and techniques for language learning. (Laghos & Zaphiris, 2005a)

## Intelligent Data Analysis

An interdisciplinary study concerned with the effective analysis of data, which draws the techniques from diverse fields including artificial intelligence, databases, high-performance computing, pattern recognition, and statistics. (Liu, 2005)

## Intelligent Decision-Making Support System (I-DMSS)

Computer-based system composed of a user-dialogue subsystem, a multi-dimensional database and knowledge base subsystem, and a quantitative and qualitative processing subsystem enhanced with AI-based techniques, designed to support all phases of the decision-making process. (Forgionne et al., 2005)

## Intelligent Enterprise

**1:** An organization that is able to understand changing environments, and adapt with agility and resourcefulness in order to outperform competitors. (Jones & Gupta, 2005) **2:** An organization capable of acting effectively in the present and dealing effectively with the challenges of the future by being proactive, adaptable, knowledgeable, and well resourced. (Framinan, 2005)

## Intelligent Image Data

A data format that embeds pixel information of images as well as higher-level information, such as indices and semantic information. This format is self-descriptive in the sense that data could explain by themselves what contents are inside, and present and retrieve the related and interested portions for the users. (Y.-J. Zhang, 2005a)

## Intelligent Interface

A point of communication between a human and a computer that displays qualities that mimic traits observed in human communication such as the use of natural languages. (Alkhalifa, 2005b)

## Intelligent Key

Contains data that has a meaning beyond the unique identification of a database record. For example, a vehicle identification number (VIN) contains information about the manufacturer, model, and other attributes of the vehicle. (Millet, 2005)

## Intelligent Metabusiness

A metabusiness with a high degree of reach, range, and structuring. (Joia, 2005)

## Intelligent Organization

An organization is a living organism where all components and subsystems work coherently together to enable the organization to maximize its potential in its goal-driven endeavors. It is characterized by learning and adapting to the changing environment. (Tang & Sivaramakrishnan, 2005)

## Intelligent Portal

Portal designed for decision-making purposes. An intelligent portal is not an agent program, but a content-based information package that knows what it is used for and how it can achieve its goal. In practice, intelligent portals are supported by a software component, namely, an Information Broker running on application servers over the Internet. The intelligence comes from the mechanisms that support the portals to deliver information at the right time to the right place. (Li, 2005a)

## Intelligent Program

A program that is intelligent in some sense, using learning, adaptive, or evolutionary algorithms. (Guan, 2006d)

## Intelligent Query Answering

Enhancements of query answering systems into sort of intelligent systems (capable or being adapted or molded). Such systems should be able to interpret incorrectly posed questions and compose an answer not necessarily reflecting precisely what is directly referred to by the question, but rather reflecting what the intermediary understands to be the intention linked with the question. (Ras & Dardzinska, 2005)

## Intelligent Scale

A scale equipped with a special camera and identification software. Based on an object's structure, size, color, and thermal image, the scale automatically recognizes the item, weighs it, and prints out a price tag. (Kotzab, 2005)

## Intelligent (Smart) Querying

Querying that is driven by some kind of inference engine or mechanism for refining, formulating, or completing query construction. (Kapetanios, 2005)

## Intelligent Software Agent

**1:** A computer application software that is proactive and capable of flexible autonomous action in order to meet its design objectives set out by the designer. The software learns about the user, and adapts the interface and the information to the user's needs and style. (Ally, 2005c) **2:** A software agent that uses Artificial Intelligence (AI) in the pursuit of the goals of its clients. (Wan, 2006) **3:** An intelligent software agent acts at speed over the electronic communication channel on behalf of human individuals or companies as their proxy; it is a program acting on behalf of another person, entity, or process. An intelligent software agent is an autonomous program that is capable of perceiving and interpreting data sensed from its environment, reflecting events in its environment, and taking actions to achieve given goals without permanent guidance from its user. Agents have to have the intrinsic ability to communicate, cooperate, coordinate, negotiate, and learn, as well as the capability to evolve through their interactions with other agents. Agents can be stand-alone or be part of a multi-agent system. (Richards et al., 2005)

## Intelligent System

A conceptual system that learns during its existence and acts on the environment where it "lives," maybe modifying it. (Analide et al., 2006)

## Intelligent Tool

A tool that can adjust its responses based on learner needs and queries. (Bonk et al., 2005)

## Intelligent Tutoring System (ITS)

**1:** A software system capable of interacting with a student, providing guidance in the student's learning of a subject matter. (Soh, 2006) **2:** An automated tutor to help students achieve their learning goals by providing

content, pedagogical, and diagnostic expertise during the learning process. (Ally, 2005d) **3:** A computer-based instructional system using artificial intelligence modeling and reasoning techniques for providing a personalized learning experience. ITSs typically rely on three types of knowledge: expert model, student model, and instructor model. (Esmahi, 2005)

## Intelligent Web Search

A Web search system that learns a user's information preference. (Meng & Chen, 2005)

## Intention to Use

An attitude measure of an end user's goal to use a specific information system. (Shayo & Guthrie, 2005)

## Intentional Community of Practice

A community created by an organization rather than being an informal cluster or network of employees who share a passion, who share knowledge, or work together to solve problems. (Tremblay, 2006b)

## Intentional Online Learning Plan

Individualized written strategy developed between a student and facilitator that outlines needs and goals. (Crichton, 2005)

## Intentional Versioning

Automatic construction of versions based on configuration rules. (Martínez-González, 2005)

## Inter-Arrival Distribution

The probability density function that describes likely and unlikely inter-arrival times for packets. (Guster et al., 2005)

## Inter-Domain Routing Protocol

IP-level routing protocol in order to create paths through the border-routers of an Autonomous System (AS). (Hosszú, 2006)

## Inter-Organizational Information System (IOIS)

An automated information system, built around computer and communication technology, which is shared by two or more companies. It facilitates the creation, storage, transformation, and transmission of information across a company's organizational boundaries to its business partners. Sometimes referred to as an IOS. (Archer, 2005)

## Inter-Project Learning

**1:** A learning activity in which project-specific knowledge, templates, or designs are transferred from a source project to other projects. (Oshri, 2006) **2:** In project-based industries, people are organized around projects rather than on a functional basis. Learning rarely happens in a project, as people will disband upon its completion, and all the successes or failures are easily forgotten or not learned by those who are not involved. This concept involves trying to leverage knowledge and experience from other projects which may benefit the current one. (Fong, 2006a)

## Inter-Sectorial Cooperation

Cooperation that is represented by a more or less stable partnership between the private and the public sector. (Knust & Hagenhoff, 2005)

## Inter-University Cooperation

Cooperation between different universities or university institutes. Such universities must be state-run and not private-run, otherwise such cooperation would be considered an inter-sectorial one. (Knust & Hagenhoff, 2005)

## Interaction

**1:** Bidirectional information exchange between users and equipment (Bevan, 2006) **2:** Contact and communication between faculty and students, and between the students themselves, is one of the important determinants of completion and retention. (Lindsay, Howell, et al., 2005) **3:** How a user communicates, or interacts, with a computer. Interaction focuses on the flow of interaction, the dialogue between person and computer, how input relates to output, stimulus-response compatibility, and feedback mechanisms. (Singh, 2005) **4:** Interaction among members of a group is necessary to produce collaboration. It can be measured by examining the give-and-take nature of the discussion threads. (Ingram, 2005) **5:** Mediated communication between two or more individuals. (Woods & Baker, 2005) **6:** The mutual response and acknowledgment of members of the group to ideas and suggestions from other members of the group. It involves challenging, defending, and accepting those ideas. (Ingram & Hathorn, 2005a) **7:** Usually refers to reciprocal communication between two (or more) parties where there are feedback, comments, suggestions, and so forth. It can also be one way, for example, in learner-content interaction, where the interaction is reflective in nature. (Kung-Ming & Khoon-Seng 2005)

## Interaction Channel (IC)

A bidirectional channel established between the service provider and the user for interaction purposes. (Chochliouros et al., 2005b)

## Interaction Design

**1:** A similar soft technology focusing on the processes of interacting with information, particularly in high-impact or strongly emotive contexts. (Duchastel, 2005) **2:** The coordination of information exchange between the user and the system. (Ferre, Juristo, & Moreno, 2006) **3:** The process of designing interactive products to support people in their everyday and work lives. (Singh & Dix, 2006)

## Interaction Management

An entire system that monitors customer communications at every possible contact point, regardless of source—that is, Web, telephone, fax, e-mail, kiosks, or in person. (Borders & Johnston, 2005)

## Interaction Management System

An information system providing an environment for communications and coordination of work activities for virtual teams. (Dustdar, 2005)

## Interaction Method

The ways an e-shopper can manipulate items within the virtual mall. The interaction methods may vary, depending on the type of item representation (video, 3D model, photograph), the item semantics, and the preferences or expertise of the user. (Lepouras & Vassilakis, 2006)

## Interaction Process

The process customers go through in order to find or configure the product variations that meet their requirements via the online channel. (Blecker & Abdelkafi, 2006)

## Interaction Standard

One of a set of standards that are primarily used in business transactions. These standards address communication content and interfaces in e-business. (Hawk & Zheng, 2006)

## Interaction System

Comprehensive entity for optimal customer-supplier interaction in e-business consisting of two separate yet interconnected information systems: an advisory component and a product configurator. (Blecker, 2006b)

### Interaction with Classmates

Interaction among learners through debate, collaboration, discussion, and peer review, as well as informal and incidental learning among classmates. (Swan, 2005)

### Interaction with Content

The learners' interaction with the knowledge, skills, and attitudes being studied. (Swan, 2005)

### Interaction with Instructors

The myriad ways in which instructors teach, guide, correct, and support their students by interacting with them. (Swan, 2005)

### Interaction-Oriented Intervention

The appropriate presence of the teacher in an active learning and student-centered environment. (Bodomo, 2005a)

### Interactional Approach

An approach that acknowledges that both characteristics of the person and the environment influence behaviors and outcomes. (Jawahar, 2005)

### Interactive

**1:** A computer-delivered format allowing the user to control, combine, and manipulate different types of media, such as text, sound, video, computer graphics, and animation. (Ryan, 2005) **2:** A computer system that allows the person using it to affect the way in which it works or the outcome, such that the user is not playing a passive role. (Sieber & Andrew, 2005)

### Interactive Advertising

Advertising that simulates a one-on-one interaction to give consumers more control over their experience with product information than do traditional media ads. (Gao, 2005b)

### Interactive Classroom

A classroom that facilitates virtual and face-to-face conversations among teachers and learners. (Roldan, 2005)

### Interactive Data Mining

Human-computer collaboration knowledge discovery process through the interaction between the data miner and the computer to extract novel, plausible, useful, relevant, and interesting knowledge from the database. (S. Wang & H. Wang, 2005)

### Interactive Delivery Mode

Interaction between student and instructor in a synchronous mode. (Hunter & Carr, 2005)

### Interactive Digital Multimedia

A system enabling end users to customize and select the information they see and receive by actively engaging with the system (e.g., tourism kiosk, interactive television), as opposed to passive multimedia where the end user has no control over the timing, sequence, or content (e.g., videotape, linear presentation). (Lang, 2005)

### Interactive Learning

**1:** An environment where the student is actively involved in a reciprocal exchange of information with the teacher and other students. (Baxendale, 2005) **2:** The process of exchanging and sharing knowledge resources conducive to innovation between an innovator, its suppliers, and/or its clients. It may start with a resource-based argument, specified by introducing competing and complementary theoretical arguments, such as the complexity and structuring of innovative activities and cross-sectoral technological dynamics. (Rahman, 2005c) **3:** The process of exchanging and sharing knowledge resources conducive to innovation between an innovator, its suppliers, and/or its clients. It may start with a resource-based argument, which is specified by introducing competing and complementary theoretical arguments such as the complexity and structuring of innovative activities, and cross-sectoral technological dynamics. (Rahman, 2005a)

### Interactive Media

Media that allows for a two-way interaction or exchange of information via interactive tools. (Ketelhut et al., 2005)

### Interactive Learning Environment (ILE)

A software system that interacts with a learner and may immerse the learner in an environment conducive to learning; it does not necessarily provide tutoring for the learner. (Soh & Jiang, 2006)

### Interactive Multimedia Method (IMM)

A multimedia system in which related items of information are connected and can be presented together. This system combines different media for its communication purposes, such as text, graphics, sound, and so forth. (Rahman, 2005c)

## Interactive Multimedia Technique

One of several techniques that a multimedia system uses, and in which related items of information are connected and can be presented together. Multimedia can arguably be distinguished from traditional motion pictures or movies, both by the scale of the production (multimedia is usually smaller and less expensive) and by the possibility of audience interactivity or involvement (in which case it is usually called interactive multimedia). Interactive elements can include: voice command, mouse manipulation, text entry, touch screen, video capture of the user, or live participation (in live presentations). (Rahman, 2005d)

## Interactive Radio Counseling

Radio stations across the country broadcast interactive phone-in counseling every Sunday (4:00 to 5:00 p.m.). The students participate from their homes through toll-free telephone numbers to interact with the experts at various AIR studios. (Sharma, 2005)

## Interactive Service

A telecommunication service that provides users with the ability to control and influence the subjects of communication. (Hulicki, 2005)

## Interactive Session

A period of communication for the exchange of ideas by an assembly of people for a common purpose. (Mohamed & Ottmann, 2006)

## Interactive System

**1:** A system that supports communication in both directions, from user to computer and back again. A crucial property of any interactive system is its support for human activity. (Singh, 2005) **2:** A system that supports communication in both directions, from user to computer and back. A crucial property of any interactive system is its support for human activity. (Singh, 2005b)

## Interactive Television (ITV)

**1:** A course broadcast between two or more remote locations that allows instructor and students to interact in real time. (Dorniden, 2005) **2:** Domestic television boosted by interactive functions, made possible by the significant effects of digital technology on television transmission systems. It supports subscriber-initiated choices or actions that are related to one or more video programming streams. (Pagani, 2005a)

## Interactive Video

Presentation of class via video with student ability to respond to the instructor. (Witta, 2005)

## Interactive Voice Response (IVR)

An automated telephone answering system that responds with a voice menu, and allows the user to make choices and enter information via keypad. IVR systems are widely used in call centers and as a replacement for human switchboard operators. (Malik, 2006)

## Interactive Web Site

A Web site or page configured so as to invite correspondence between the user and the originator/sponsor of the site. Such sites go beyond passively providing information to those who browse the site. Customarily, there are options to complete online surveys, send e-mail to the sponsor, request specialized or personalized response(s), and so forth. (Baim, 2005)

## Interactivity

**1:** A characteristic of a medium in which the user can influence the form and content of the mediated presentation or experience. (Gao, 2005b) **2:** A reciprocal exchange between the technology and the learner, a process which is referred to as "feedback." (Askar et al., 2005) **3:** The set of functions and operations available to the learner that involve, engage, and motivate the learner to interact in a computer-based environment. (Kung-Ming & Khoon-Seng 2005) **4:** Concerned with the engagement between the medium itself, whereby people manipulate the medium to provide information or perform functions commanded by the user. (Weber & Lim, 2005) **5:** A process whereby students are systematically encouraged to be active participants in their own learning. It is achieved by teaching approaches that engage students in the construction of knowledge. (Sala, 2005a) **6:** Media or channels that permit two-way communication whether the format is one to one (telephone), one to many (interactive television), or many to many (the Internet). (Roberts & Schwaab, 2006) **7:** Occurs when a student works within a multimedia exercise in which the student and the program interchange information in order to complete the exercise. (Kaur et al., 2005) **8:** One of the main features of modern digital ICTs which refers to the interchange of responses and actions between humans and machines, or among human beings. (Bodomo, 2005b) **9:** The ability of a multimedia system to respond to user input. The interactivity element of multimedia is considered of central importance from the point of view that it facilitates the active knowledge construction by enabling learners to make decisions about pathways they will follow through content. (Torrisi-Steele, 2005) **10:** The level of interaction among communication partners. (Chan, Tan, et al., 2005) **11:** The relationship between the learner and the educational environment. (Russell, 2005b) **12:** Usually taken to mean the chance for interactive communication among subjects. Technically, interactivity implies the presence of a return channel in the communication system, going from the user to the source of information. The channel is a vehicle for the data bytes that represent the choices or reactions of the user (input). (Pagani, 2005a)

## Interactivity Dimension

The number of users that a single transducer, display system, or application software can support (by means of complete hardware or software simulations) during one particular interactive session. (Mohamed & Ottmann, 2006)

## Interactor

One of a number of elementary interactive components such as push buttons, text fields, list boxes, and so forth. (Bastide et al., 2006)

## Intercluster Similarity

**1:** A measurement of the similarity between the clusters identified in a particular clustering process. These clusters must be as dissimilar as possible. (Santos et al., 2005) **2:** The overall similarity among documents from two different clusters. (Fung et al., 2005)

## Intercultural

**1:** In contrast to multi-cultural (which simply describes the heterogeneous cultural identities of a group), cross-cultural (which implies some kind of opposition), or transcultural (which has been used to suggest a cultural transition), intercultural is used to describe the creative interactive interface that is constructed and shared by communicating individuals from different cultural backgrounds. (Macfadyen, 2006a) **2:** A situation where individuals from different cultures interact with or exchange information with one another; interchangeable with the term "cross-cultural." (St.Amant, 2005c)

## Intercultural Communication Competence

The ability to effectively and appropriately execute communication behaviors to elicit a desired response in a specific environment. (Zakaria & Yusof, 2005)

## Intercultural Human-Machine System

A system that takes into account the cultural diversity of human (different user requirements) and machine (variation of usage situations), in addition to a standard human-machine system. (Röse, 2006b)

## Interdependence

**1:** Interdependence among members of a small group is a necessary element of collaboration. It means that group members could not produce the results they did without one another. (Ingram, 2005) **2:** Mutual dependence between parties in an organizational setting. A situational factor proposed to contribute to the occurrence of LPB. (Moore & Burke, 2005) **3:** The level of dependence that one group member has on other group members in order to complete the learning tasks. (Graham & Misanchuk, 2005) **4:** The mutual sharing of information between members of a group to promote understanding in all members with the purpose of achieving the group goal. (Ingram & Hathorn, 2005a)

## Interestingness

**1:** An elusive concept that is very difficult to characterize and operationalize. A pattern is interesting if it arouses attention in the minds of the examiner. Interestingness has many facets like unexpectedness, actionability, prior knowledge, and knowledge goals, in addition to many unidentified domain-dependent features. Features of interestingness may be user dependent, domain dependent, or/and there might be a temporal aspect associated with it. (Natarajan & Shekar, 2006) **2:** The set of methods used to order and prune the set of rules produced by association rule algorithms. This facilitates their use and interpretation by the user. Metrics for interestingness include measures such as confidence, added value, mutual information. and conviction measures. (Imberman & Tansel, 2006)

## Interexchange Carrier (IXC)

Long-distance companies that transport inter Local Access Transport Area (LATA) traffic. (Nugent, 2005)

## Interface

**1:** A contract in the form of a collection of methods and constant declarations. When a class implements an interface, it promises to implement all of the methods declared in that interface. (Wong & Chan, 2006) **2:** A set of commands or menus through which a user communicates with a software program. (Proserpio & Magni, 2005) **3:** Portion of a computer application that is used by the user to communicate with the application. It is particularly important for a dashboard, because it may impinge on the ability of users to properly interpret the variations in the indicators shown to them. (Adam & Pomerol, 2005) **4:** The set of components of a computer program that allow the user to interact with the information. (Ally, 2005c) **5:** The design on the computer screen with which the user interacts. (Szabados & Sonwalkar, 2005) **6:** The point at which two systems connect, and the method by which communication is accomplished. The computer keyboard, mouse, printer, and video display exemplify interfaces between the machine's internal operations and the human user. (Horiuchi, 2005a) **7:** The specification for a method ("what" a method does); how that function is called from another program. Interfaces are provided in source form as opposed to implementations which are secure. This allows one to use a method without regard for "how" that method is coded. It also allows multiple implementations of the same interface. (D. Brandon, Jr., 2005a) **8:** The way a user interacts with a product, what he or she does, and how it responds. (Magnani & Bardone, 2006) **9:** In general, extraneous energy from natural or man-made sources that impedes the reception of desired signals. (Ragazzi, 2005)

## Interface Agent
A semi-autonomous agent that assists a user with, or partially automates, his or her tasks. (Mohamed & Ottmann, 2006)

## Interface Design
Design of the interactions between humans and computers. (Chan & Fang, 2005)

## Interface Evaluation
Interface evaluation of a software system is a procedure intended to identify and propose solutions for usability problems caused by the specific software design. (Karoulis et al., 2006)

## Intergalactic Client-Server Program
In the mobile computing environment, the traditional transaction model is replaced by a more realistic model called a "workflow model" between several clients and servers that interact, compete, and cooperate. This is called "an intergalactic client-server program." (Murthy & Krishnamurthy, 2005b)

## Interlibrary Loan
The process by which a library requests material from, or supplies material to, another library. (Raisinghani & Hohertz, 2005)

## Interlinking
Linking between two or more Web sites. (Thelwall, 2006)

## Intermedia Synchronization
Maintaining the requirements of the temporal relationships between two or more media. Lip synchronization between video and audio is an example of interstream synchronization where the display of video must synchronize with audio. (Yang et al., 2005b)

## Intermedia Transcoding
The process of converting the media input into another media format. (Cavallaro, 2005)

## Intermediary
**1:** In the tourism and travel sectors, intermediaries are those organizations that package or on-sell a product. These include travel agents, tour packagers, inbound tour operators, and destination marketing organizations. The Internet has led to the emergence of electronic intermediaries that offer their services entirely online. (Carson, 2005) **2:** A party that acts as an agent in transactions or markets. (Foley & Samson, 2006) **3:** A person or organization performing a (booking) role between consumers and business. (Braun, 2005b)

## Internal Audit
The first step to determining what is taught online via distance education, what is taught online onsite, and what is not taught online or uses limited technology. (Robinson, 2005)

## Internal Champion
Highly respected individual within an organization who possesses expertise in a specific area, specifically information systems. (Hunter, 2005)

## Internal Context
The physical scope of a consumer context comprised of sensible body conditions that may influence the consumer's physiological needs. Certain context-aware applications

can use bodily attached sensors to keep track of the internal context information of mobile consumers. (Sun & Poole, 2005)

## Internal Control

**1:** A system of people, technology, processes, and procedures designed to provide reasonable assurance that an organization achieves its business process goals. (Chengalur-Smith et al., 2005) **2:** A set of procedures applied by a business organization that ensures information is safeguarded, that it is accurate and reliable, and that it is processed efficiently and in accordance with management's prescribed policies. (Lenard & Alam, 2005)

## Internal Data

Previously cleaned warehouse data that originated from the daily information processing systems of a company. (Peter & Greenidge, 2005a)

## Internal Divide

The digital divide that exists between socioeconomic groups within a country. (Cecchini, 2005)

## Internal Knowledge

An organization-specific knowledge that gives idiosyncratic cohesiveness to the integration of external knowledge into a firm. Firm and context dependent, it is an indispensable complement to external knowledge in order to build up knowledge-based competitive advantages when it is appreciated by clients. It is more valuable inside the firm where it originates than in the open market. It is very difficult to be transmitted to a different context. (Andreu & Sieber, 2006)

## Internal Locus of Control

Characterized by the belief that personal achievement is due to ability and effort, as opposed to luck, fate, or situational factors. (Adkins & Nitsch, 2005)

## Internal Metric

A metric used to measure attributes of the product that can be measured directly by examining the product on its own, irrespective of its behavior. (Xenos, 2006)

## Internalization

**1:** A knowledge transfer mode that involves new tacit knowledge being derived from existing explicit knowledge. (Wickramasinghe, 2005) **2:** In international business and organization science literature, internalization means that an organization makes use of its organizational hierarchy to manage a specific business transaction, as opposed to buying it on the market. In knowledge management literature, internalization is one of four knowledge transmission mechanisms. It refers to the explicit-to-tacit process of knowledge transfer. This process takes place when individuals use explicit knowledge to extend their own tacit knowledge base. (Brock & Zhou, 2006) **3:** It is the process of making a Web site interoperable in a specific market or locale. In general, interoperability means that the functionality of the site is not dependent on a specific language or culture and is readily adaptable to others. (Becker, 2005b)

## International Computer Driving License (ICDL)

An international certification that serves as a benchmark for computer literacy. (Reynolds, 2005)

## International Divide

The digital divide that exists between countries. (Cecchini, 2005)

## International Division of Labor

The spatial location of production facilities in international networks resulting from capital investment by firms in countries or regions where wage rates and/or regulatory regimes offer cost savings in comparison to those in a firm's country of origin. The emergence of advanced telecommunications and the abilities they afford to coordinate industrial activity in different places and times are often cited as significant factors in organizing these divisions of labor. (Lepawsky & Park, 2006)

## International Instructor

In many regions of Asia and Africa, professional development programs rely on expertise from elsewhere in the world, and there is heavy use of experienced invited speakers. Increasingly, these invited speakers provide electronic resources and also teach online. They may even do all of their teaching in an online mode. These invited teachers, many of whom teach in English, are described as international instructors. (Ching et al., 2005)

## International Mobile Subscriber Identity (IMSI)

A specific number of subscriber, used exclusively in GSM network, according to international numbering standards referred to as E.212. (Louvros et al., 2006)

## International Networking (INET)

An annual meeting held by the ISOC. (Rhoten, 2006b)

## International Online Interaction (IOI)

Situation in which individuals from two or more cultures use an online medium to interact directly with one another. (St.Amant, 2005c)

## International Organization for Standardization (ISO)

A non-governmental organization consisting of standards institutes of 148 countries. ISO's central secretariat (located in Geneva, Switzerland) coordinates the system. (K. Chen et al., 2005)

## International Outsourcing

**1:** A production model in online media used to send work to employees located in a nation (generally, a developing nation). (St.Amant & Still, 2005) **2:** A production process in which work is sent to overseas employees for completion. (St.Amant, 2006b)

## International Statistical Classification of Diseases and Related Health Problems, Tenth Revision (ICD-10)

A medical classification system in which conditions have been grouped for general epidemiological purposes and the evaluation of health care. (Zender, 2006)

## International Telecommunications Union (ITU)

A body that closely works with all standards organizations to form an international uniform standards system for data communications over telephone networks. Before 1993, ITU was known as CCITT. (Rhoten, 2006a)

## International Virtual Office (IVO)

A work group composed of individuals who are situated in different nations and who use online media to collaborate on the same project. (St.Amant, 2005d)

## Internationalize

Generalizing a design so that it can handle multiple languages content. (T.S. Chan, 2005)

## Internet

**1:** The vast collection of interconnected networks that all use TCP/IP protocols. (Kabene, Takhar, et al., 2005) **2:** A worldwide system of computer servers from which users at any computer can extract information or knowledge. Intranets and extranets are Internet-like networks whose scope is to restrict access to internal personnel or external partners within an enterprise, with the goal of fostering information and knowledge sharing. (Ribière & Román, 2006) **3:** A decentralized, global network. The World Wide Web is only a part of this network. Other components of the Internet include e-mail, news servers, Gopher, and TELNET. (Cosemans, 2005a) **4:** A global network connecting millions of computers linking exchange of data, news, and opinions. The Internet is not synonymous with World Wide Web. (Sieber & Andrew, 2005) **5:** A global public network that utilizes TCP/IP protocols to transfer data from one computer to another. The Internet is often referred to as a 'network of networks', as it is made up of thousands of smaller privately owned networks. (Fraser, 2005) **6:** A global system of interconnected networks that allows for data transmission between myriad computers. The Internet can usually be accessed using Internet service providers. (Escalante, 2005) **7:** A large system of interconnected computer networks composed of backbone networks, mid-level networks, and local networks. This includes networks owned and managed by public, private, and nonprofit sector organizations. (Hinnant & Sawyer, 2005) **8:** A vast network of computers that connects millions of people worldwide. (Olatokun & Ajiferuke, 2006) **9:** A worldwide interconnection of individual networks operated by government, industry, academia, and private parties. (Phala, 2005) **10:** A worldwide information network connecting millions of computers. Also called the Net. (Burke et al., 2005) **11:** A worldwide network of computer networks that use the TCP/IP network protocols to facilitate data transmission. It provides access to a vast amount of information resources including multimedia (movies, sound, and images), software, text documents, news articles, electronic journals, travel information, and so forth. It also provides an environment for buying and selling products and services over a network. (Aurum, 2005) **12:** A worldwide system of networks that has transformed communications and methods of commerce by allowing various computer networks to interconnect. Sometimes referred to as a "network of networks," the Internet materialized in the United States in the 1970s, but did not become overtly visible until the early 1990s. (Nightingale, 2005) **13:** Global communications network consisting of thousands of interconnected networks. (Ortega Egea & Menéndez, 2006) **14:** A global network connecting millions of computers. The word is derived from interconnected network. (Sala, 2005a) **15:** The electronic system that links various computer networks around the world. It includes educational venues, databases, electronic mail, news agencies, and chat rooms. (Switala, 2005)

**Internet Abuse**

Any wrongful or improper use of the Internet in the workplace. (Mahatanankoon, 2005)

**Internet Addiction**

**1:** A term used to describe excessive Internet use; it has also been referred to as Internet addiction disorder, Internet addiction syndrome, and pathological Internet use. As with other addictions, Internet addiction features the core components of other addictive behaviors (salience, mood modification, tolerance, withdrawal, conflict, and relapse) and can be defined as a repetitive habit pattern that increases the risk of disease and/or associated personal and social problems. It is often experienced subjectively as "loss of control," and these habit patterns are typically characterized by immediate gratification (short-term rewards), often coupled with delayed, deleterious effects (long-term costs). Attempts to change an addictive behavior (via treatment or by self-initiation) are typically marked by high relapse rates (see also technological addictions). (Griffiths, 2005) **2:** Use of the Internet and network resources that undermines the fulfillment of some of an individual's basic human needs. (Oravec, 2005)

**Internet Adoption**

Occurs when a firm embraces an Internet application for the first time. Typical Internet applications include e-mail, Web browsing, Web site presence, and electronic transactions. Firms will often adopt Internet technology in stages (or levels) over time, beginning with one application and adding another and so on. Each new application can be regarded as an Internet adoption. (Cragg & Mills, 2005)

**Internet and Communication Technology (ICT)**

Technology that utilizes the Internet and networking capabilities. (Aggarwal, 2005)

**Internet Architecture Board (IAB)**

Chartered both as a committee of the Internet Engineering Task Force (IETF) and as an advisory body of the Internet Society (ISOC). (Rhoten, 2006b)

**Internet Browser Usage**

The set of Internet technologies and applications that center on the Internet browser and are generally involved in the presentation of Web sites to the viewer, in the undertaking of research and in open-forum communications. (Griffin, 2005)

**Internet Café**

**1:** A public place that offers access to computers, e-mail, and the Internet for a fee. In Uganda, as in many other parts of the world, cafés also offer other ICT-related services, such as printing and photocopying, as well as refreshments. (Mwesige, 2005) **2:** A cafeteria offering public-access online computers for Web surfing and e-mail transmission or service bureau, or offering other services such as online gaming and love matching. It sometimes also serves as an Internet service provider (ISP). (Hu et al., 2006a) **3:** Business units that resell Internet access to people. (Frempong & Braimah, 2005)

**Internet Cash**

Users are digitally signed but are not stored in the database. It is a kind of debit card. (Kurihara, 2006)

**Internet Control Message Protocol Message (ICMP Message)**

A message control and error-reporting protocol that operates between a host and a gateway to the Internet. (Syed, Nur, et al., 2005)

**Internet Credibility**

A multi-faceted concept in journalism research that consists of believability, accuracy, trustworthiness, and bias. (Borchers, 2005)

**Internet Data**

Data collected through the Internet by an organization. (Kumar, 2005)

**Internet Democracy**

A derivative term for electronic democracy, especially related to projects and concepts centered on using the Internet (and not other electronic communications technologies like short message services or teletext) for deliberative and participatory aims. Concrete implementations of Internet democracy projects include electronic town hall meetings or citizen consultations, the use of discussion boards on party or candidate Web sites, and the virtualization of traditional political institutions or mechanisms like party conventions, protest marches, or petitions. (Kozeluh, 2005)

**Internet Disconnection**

The event of firms becoming disenchanted with Internet applications and removing all Internet-based applications from their organization. (Griffin, 2005)

## Internet Discussion Site (IDS)

A text-based online forum where members can post a message or engage others in conversation on a range of financial topics usually in a bulletin board-style environment containing distinct topic threads. Forum participants include amateur investors, day traders, and professional brokers, all of whom, despite their diversity of expertise, share a common interest in stock market investment. (Campbell, 2006)

## Internet Economy

**1:** A large collection of global networks, applications, electronic markets, producers, consumers, and intermediaries. (Scupola, 2005) **2:** Economy with revenues from the Internet or Internet-related products or services. (Tian & Stewart, 2006) **3:** That part of the economy that deals with information goods such as software, online content, knowledge-based goods, the new media, and supporting technology industries using the Internet. (Sharma, 2006a)

## Internet EDI

The use of the Internet to exchange business documents using standardized document formats. (Harris & Chen, 2006)

## Internet Engineering Task Force (IETF)

**1:** A large, open, international community of network designers, operators, vendors, and researchers concerned with the evolution of the Internet architecture and the smooth operation of the Internet. (Rhoten, 2006b) **2:** An open international community engaged in Internet architecture evolution (IETF, 2003). Working Groups in several topical areas develop technical drafts and Internet standards. (Pulkkis, Grahn, & Åström, 2005) **3:** The collaboration of working groups in several topical areas that develop technical drafts and Internet standards. (Pulkkis et al., 2005a) **4:** A voluntary association for developing Internet standards. (Hosszu, 2005a)

## Internet Filtering and Monitoring Software

Software tools used for reducing occurrences of Internet abuse by blocking inappropriate Web sites and identifying frequently visited Web sites. (Mahatanankoon, 2005)

## Internet Group Management Protocol (IGMP)

Implemented within the IP module of a host and extends the host's IP implementation to support multi-casting. (Chakraborty et al., 2005)

## Internet Host

A domain name that has an Internet Protocol (IP) address record associated with it. This would be any computer system connected to the Internet (via full- or part-time, direct or dial-up connections). (Maggioni & Uberti, 2005)

## Internet Hyperlink (or Hypertext Link)

An active link placed in a Web page that allows the Net surfer to jump directly from this Web page to another and retrieve information. This dynamic and no-hierarchical idea of linking information was first introduced by Tim Barners Lee to manage information within a complex and continuously changing environment like CERN. The Internet hyperlinks are directional: outgoing links leaving a Web page and incoming links targeting a Web page. (Maggioni & Uberti, 2005)

## Internet Lag Time

The delay in transmitting the signals from users' terminals to the Internet server and back due to congestion of the Internet link connecting the two. (Kung-Ming & Khoon-Seng 2005)

## Internet Marketing

Conducting marketing activities on the Internet. (Singh, 2006a)

## Internet Native

Somebody who has never experienced life before the Internet. The term is sometimes used to distinguish the original Internet users, students, and researchers as examples, from those who want to exploit the Net for commercial or other reasons and who might be called Internet imperialists. (Dunkels, 2005)

## Internet Option

A possibility to use the Internet for a business purpose. (Boonstra & de Brock, 2006)

## Internet Pharmacy

A pharmacy that has no storefront presence and where the Internet is a key technology for serving customers. (Rosson, 2006)

## Internet Privacy

Concerns expressed by Internet users regarding the security and confidentiality of information transmitted electronically. Government agencies and business/industry professional groups share responsibility to address Internet privacy concerns. (Baim, 2005)

### Internet Protocol (IP)

**1:** Code numbers designating the computer attached to a network. (Rowe, 2006b) **2:** A network protocol that provides connectionless, best-effort delivery of datagrams (self-contained, independent set of data). IP and Transmission Control Protocol (TCP) are the networking protocols that the Internet is based on. (Papagiannidis et al., 2005) **3:** A protocol is a rule which guides how an activity should be performed. IP is used to define how devices can communicate across a packet-switched network of networks (including the public Internet). The umbrella suite of protocols to which IP is referred to is the TCP/IP suite, after two of the most important protocols in it: Transmission Control Protocol and the Internet Protocol. (Leath, 2005) **4:** Specifies the format of packets, also called datagrams, and the addressing scheme. IP by itself is something like the postal system. It allows you to address a package and drop it in the system, but there is no direct link between you and the recipient. (Singh, 2005a) **5:** The network layer protocol used on the Internet and many private networks. Different versions of IP include IPv4, IPv6, and IPng (next generation). (Raisinghani & Ghanem, 2005) **6:** The network-level protocol used in the Internet. (Hosszú, 2006) **7:** The protocol mechanism used in gateways to connect networks at the OSI Network Layer (Layer 3) and above. (Malik, 2006)

### Internet Protocol Backbone

XML is used to tag the data, SOAP is used to transfer the data, WSDL is used to describe the services available, and UDDI is used to list what services are available. Used primarily as a means for businesses to communicate with each other and with clients, Web services allow organizations to communicate data without intimate knowledge of each other's IT systems behind the firewall. (Blecker & Graf, 2006)

### Internet Protocol Security (IPSec)

Developed by an IETF Security Area Working Group. IPSec introduces a new TCP/IP stack layer below IP. IPSec adds authentication and optional encryption to transmitted data packets. Authentication ensures that packets are from the right sender and have not been altered. Encryption prevents unauthorized reading of packet contents. (Pulkkis, Grahn, Karlsson, 2005b)

### Internet Public Kiosk

A booth that provides Internet access in return for a payment on a time basis. (Díaz-Andrade, 2005)

### Internet Relay Chat (IRC)

**1:** A network of computer servers and client programs that provide a text-based virtual environment in which multiple users can engage in synchronous computer-mediated communication. (Roberts et al., 2006a) **2:** Internet-based chat technology that allows a group of people to exchange text messages in real time. To join group chatting, one needs an IRC program to connect to an IRC server. Examples include mIRC, Pirch, and Virc for Windows and Homer or Ircle for Macintosh. (Hwang & Stewart, 2005)

### Internet Remote Experimentation

The use of the Internet to carry out physical experimental work at a remote location. (Ko et al., 2005)

### Internet Security

The phenomenon by which a company assures that its data and entire Internet infrastructure are protected from damage caused by miscreants through activities such as hacking. (Aigbedo, 2005)

### Internet Service Provider (ISP)

**1:** Middleman between computer users and the Internet. Provides the local phone numbers a computer calls. At each of these, there is a bank of modems, sometimes ranging into the hundreds, connected to a router that allows all the data flowing through those modems to enter and exit the Internet. (Latchem, 2005) **2:** Refers to a company that provides access to the Internet and other related services (e.g., Web hosting) to the public and other companies. (Syed, Nur, et al., 2005) **3:** A company that provides other companies or individuals with access to, or presence on, the Internet. (Vician & Buche, 2005) **4:** An organization that provides Internet access to individuals or other organizations. (Escalante, 2005) **5:** A company such as a Netcom, UUNet, and SprintNet that sells to users Internet connectivity, either via a 24-hour dedicated line or a dial-up connection. This could either be on a dedicated connection (for example, a telephone connection that stays open 24 hours a day) or a dial-up connection. Usually users run software such as PPP or SLIP to allow Internet connectivity across the line. (Magagula, 2005) **6:** Provides access to the Internet via different communications channels such as traditional telephone lines or a high-speed fiber optics channel. (Guah & Currie, 2005) **7:** Provides the hardware that connects customers to content and applications providers, usually for a monthly fee. (Rülke et al., 2005) **8:** A company that provides Internet access to individuals, groups, or corporate organizations through normal telephones, satellites, or fiber optics. (Frempong & Braimah, 2005)

## Internet Society (ISOC)
Founded in 1992, a professional membership society with more than 150 organization and 16,000 individual members in over 180 countries. It provides leadership in addressing issues that confront the future of the Internet, and is the organization home for the groups responsible for Internet infrastructure standards, including the Internet Engineering Task Force (IETF) and the Internet Architecture Board (IAB). (Rhoten, 2006b)

## Internet Streaming
Video format that intermittently downloads sections of a media file to a client. (Vitolo et al., 2005)

## Internet Supply Chain Management Course
System architectures, technologies, and infrastructure requirements in the context of supply chain systems. Design, development, and implementation of systems that facilitate collaboration with customers and suppliers. Development of messaging-based collaborative frameworks using Web services. (Knight & Chan, 2005)

## Internet Technology
**1:** Family of technologies suitable for exchanging structured data through package-oriented transmissions on heterogeneous platforms, in particular, protocols, programming languages, hardware, and software. (Blecker, 2006a) **2:** The group of technologies that allow users to access information and communication over the World Wide Web (Web browsers, ftp, e-mail, associated hardware, Internet service providers, and so forth). (Darbyshire & Burgess, 2005)

## Internet Technology Cluster
The range of identifiably separate families of technologies involved in the e-business platform comprising e-mail, browser usages, and advanced Internet applications. (Griffin, 2005)

## Internet Usage Policy (IUP)
An organizational policy handed down to employees that governs the use of the Internet in a specific workplace. The goals of an IUP, if properly written and implemented, are

to help organizations communicate proper Internet usage behaviors, lessen employees' perceived expectation of privacy, and reduce costly litigation that may occur from the use of Internet monitoring and filtering software. (Mahatanankoon, 2005)

## Internet-Based EDI
An alternative to traditional Electronic Data Interchange (EDI) that uses proprietary systems in HTML format. (Ratnasingam, 2006)

## Internet-Based Learning
Learning delivered primarily by TCP/IP network technologies such as e-mail, newsgroups, proprietary applications, and so forth. Although the term is often used synonymously with Web-based training, Internet-based training is not necessarily delivered over the World Wide Web, and may not use the HTTP and HTML technologies that make Web-based training possible. (Torres-Coronas, 2005)

## Internet-Based Survey
A contemporary survey technique through which researchers may obtain respondents' opinions via online survey processes. Respondents may either be asked to go to a Web site to complete a survey (Web-based) or the survey questionnaire may be e-mailed to the respondents (e-mail-based) for them to complete and return electronically. (Baim, 2005)

## Internet-Mediated Community
Group of people sharing interests and making use for some time of the same class of Internet technologies to exchange information to each other regarding the shared interests. (Porto Bellini & Vargas, 2006)

## Internet-Scale Distributed Data Source
Autonomous data source connected through the Internet. (Khan, 2005)

## Interoperability
**1:** Ability to work together, sharing information, capabilities, or other specific goals, while being different at some technological level. (Ishaya, 2005) **2:** The ability of heterogeneous software and hardware to communicate and share information. (Nicolle et al., 2005) **3:** The ability of two or more heterogeneous systems to work together in a seamless manner. (Karimi & Peachavanish, 2005) **4:** The property of software applications that will enable

diverse applications to interact and share data seamlessly. (Yow & Moertiyoso, 2005)

## Interoperability Enterprise Architecture
A set of consistent methods to specify the interaction behavior of a network of public organizations. It includes organizational structures, public services, and business processes, as well as interaction interactions, protocols, and patterns. (Werth, 2005)

## Interoperability Framework
Not simply a purely technical issue concerned with linking up various systems, but the "wider" set of policies, measures, standards, practices, and guidelines describing the way in which various organizations have agreed, or should agree, to do business with each other. (Chochliouros & Spiliopoulou-Chochliourou, 2006)

## Interoperability Interface
An interface between XML documents and other software programs. The interoperability stems from the fact that the XML documents can be read and operated upon by any software application designed to use this interface. (Gaffar & Seffah, 2005)

## Interoperability Problem
Getting a collection of autonomous legacy systems to cooperate in a single federated system. (Balsters, 2005)

## Interorganization Cooperative Process
An abstraction of a complex business process involving different organizations that cooperate with one another to offer complex services. The interorganization cooperative process is supported by an application that helps in the coordination of services. (Rolland & Kaabi, 2006)

## Interorganizational Communication
Communication that includes entities that are legally external from the organization where legal recourse may occur due to the content of the message. (McManus & Carr, 2005)

## Interorganizational Information Technology (IOIT)
Consists of networking and software applications that enable business networks to share data and information with each other. Networks (public or private) are used to provide connectivity between the software applications located within each organization. The software applications are designed to share data and information without the need

for much human intervention. Examples of IOIT include Electronic Data Interchange (EDI) systems. (Abraham & Leon, 2006)

## Interorganizational Learning
The sharing of information and process knowledge across organizational boundaries. The information and knowledge pertain to tasks or processes that are carried out by the various organizations. By making use of the information and process knowledge, these organizations can change the way they carry out these tasks and processes to improve performance. (Abraham & Leon, 2006)

## Interorganizational Relationship
Cooperative interorganizational relationships include strategic alliances, partnerships, coalitions, joint ventures, franchises, and network organizations. (Rowe et al., 2006)

## Interorganizational System (IOS)
**1:** A computer and communication infrastructure that permits the sharing of an application across organizational boundaries. The aim of an IOS is to create and exploit interorganizational efficiencies. (Rowe et al., 2006) **2:** A system that provides information links between companies. (Harris & Chen, 2006)

## Interorganizational Trust
The confidence of one organization in the certainty of another organization's ability to perform an expected outcome, such as delivering promised goods, services, information, or payment. (Turner, 2006)

## Interpersonal Communication
This occurs in one-on-one situations or within a small group dynamic. (Weber & Lim, 2005)

## Interpolation
**1:** A family of mathematical functions to compute unknown states between two known states. For instance, it is possible to interpolate between two 3D models of a body to obtain an intermediate one. (Volino et al., 2005) **2:** The process of increasing the sampling rate. Interpolation consists of upsampling and filtering. (Jovanovic-Dolecek, 2005b)

## Interpolation Filter
The filter used in interpolation to remove the unwanted images in the spectra of the upsampled signal. (Jovanovic-Dolecek, 2005b)

## Interpolator

The filter I(z) which is used to eliminate the unwanted spectrum introduced by expansion of the model filter in an IFIR Structure. For the low-pass prototype filter design, this filter is a low-pass filter with lower complexity than the prototype filter. (Jovanovic-Dolecek & Díaz-Carmona, 2005)

## Interpretation

The process involved in converting the source speech in one natural language into the target speech in another language. (O'Hagan, 2005)

## Interpreter

The traditional definition in computer science is a program that translates and executes source language statements one line at a time. Also, a program that accesses the model to understand the requested navigation, one user action at a time. (Paiano, 2005)

## Interpretive Evaluation

Formal-rational approaches (technical and economic) emphasize the technology features at the expense of the organizational and social aspects. Also, a move towards the "interactionist" role of the technology with the organizational structures, culture, and stakeholders. IS evaluation focuses on the analysis and understanding of the social and subjective nature of the phenomenon. (Serafeimidis, 2005)

## Interpretive Research

Exploring the deeper structure of a phenomenon within its cultural context by examining the subjective meanings that people create. (Trauth, 2005b)

## Interpretivism

A research approach that attempts to reach an understanding of social action in order to arrive at a causal explanation of its course and effects. (McPherson, 2005)

## Interschema Property

Terminological and structural relationships involving concepts belonging to different sources. (De Meo, Terracina, et al., 2005)

## Interstitial

A page that is inserted in the normal flow of the editorial content structure on a Web site for the purpose of advertising or promoting. It is usually designed to move automatically to the page the user requested after allowing enough time for the message to register or the advertisement(s) to be read. (Lalopoulos et al., 2005b)

## Interstream Synchronization

Ensures that all receivers play the same segment of a medium at the same time. Interstream synchronization may be needed in collaborative environments. For example, in a collaborative session, the same media information may be reacted upon by several participants. (Yang et al., 2005b)

## Intertitle

One of the set of title cards used in silent films to describe settings, plot developments, or dialogue. (Berg, 2005e)

## Intertransactional Association

Correlations among items not only within the same transactions but also across different transactions. (Feng & Dillon, 2005)

## Interval Set

If a set cannot be precisely defined, one can describe it in terms of a lower bound and an upper bound. The set will contain its lower bound and will be contained in its upper bound. (Lingras et al., 2005)

## Interval Set Clustering Algorithm

A clustering algorithm that assigns objects to lower and upper bounds of a cluster, making it possible for an object to belong to more than one cluster. (Lingras et al., 2005)

## Interval Uncertainty

A model of sensor uncertainty where each stored data value is represented by a closed interval, called uncertain interval. (Cheng & Prabhakar, 2005)

## Interval-Based Model of Time

Temporality is specified using regular or irregular intervals or periods, which are durative temporal references. (Rodríguez-Tastets, 2005b)

## Intervention Strategy

Refers to specific approaches to developing the organization through its people. While obvious intervention strategies may include techniques such as team development, self-directed learning, training approaches to personal growth and empowerment, T-groups, force field analysis, and organizational learning, a more methodological approach is identified by Blake and Mouton. In their Strategies of Consultation, they identify five types of intervention—

acceptant, catalytic, confrontation, prescriptive, principles models and theories—that may be applied at five levels—individual, team, inter-group, organization, society. The important point about this schema is that it forces the consultant to think carefully about the purpose of the intervention. (Grieves, 2006b)

## Intonation

How the pitch pattern (the property of sound that varies with variation in the frequency of vibration) or fundamental frequency (F0) changes during speech. It refers to the rise and fall of the voice pitch. (Syed, Chakrobartty, et al., 2005)

## INTOPS-1

Requirements of the non-European market on machine design. This project was founded by the German Ministry of Education and Research (1996-1998). (Röse, 2006a)

## INTOPS-2

Requirements of the user in Mainland China for human-machine systems in the area of production automation. This project was founded by several companies from Germany and Switzerland (2000-2001). (Röse, 2006a)

## Intracluster Similarity

**1:** A measurement of the similarity between the objects inside a cluster. Objects in a cluster must be as similar as possible. (Santos et al., 2005) **2:** The overall similarity among documents within a cluster. (Fung et al., 2005)

## Intramedia Transcoding

A transcoding process that does not change the media nature of the input signal. (Cavallaro, 2005)

## Intran

A transaction that is executed within a mobile host as an internal transaction (for brevity, Intran) using its own internal operations and data. (Murthy & Krishnamurthy, 2005b)

## Intranet

**1:** A computer network that provides services within an organization. (Clayton, 2006a) **2:** A network-based Internet belonging to an organization or groups where information is accessed with authorization. (Inoue & Bell, 2005) **3:** A network based on TCP/IP belonging to an organization, usually a corporation, accessible only by the organization's members, employees, or others with

authorization. An intranet's Web sites look and act just like any other Web sites, but the firewall surrounding an intranet fends off unauthorized access. (Singh, 2005a) **4:** A network within the organization using Internet technologies. (Baugher et al., 2005) **5:** A private network inside a company or organization that is based on Web standards (i.e., TCP/IP) and offers various applications for members of a specified group. (Vaast, 2005) **6:** A restricted-access or internal network that works like the Internet. It enables employees, or those with access, to browse or share resources. Intranets are private computing networks, internal to an organization, used for sharing organizational information. (Boersma & Kingma, 2006) **7:** Allowing access to a hospital's computer system to internal users via a username and password. (Cannoy & Iyer, 2006) **8:** An intranet can be thought of as the Internet restricted to the confines of an organization in order for both the employer and employees to be able to share information within that organization. An intranet is based on a local area network. (Sarkar, 2005) **9:** A computer network contained entirely within an organization. (Ruppel & Ruppel, 2005)

## Intranet and Portal Course

Intranet development methodology, data warehousing, and online analytical processing. Enterprise information portals. Transforming information into knowledge. Decision support. Customer applications. Content personalization. (Knight & Chan, 2005)

## Intraorganizational Communication

Communication internal to the legal boundaries of an organization, though it may cross departmental or divisional boundaries. There is no legal recourse for the content of a message. (McManus & Carr, 2005)

## Intraorganizational Knowledge

Knowledge that is highly firm and industry specific, but is not specific to organizational activities or tasks. In effect, this component of social actors' knowledge is firm-specific meta-knowledge. Examples are knowledge about colleagues, knowledge about elements of the organizational culture, communication channels, informal networks, knowledge of the firm's strategy and goals, and so on. (Butler & Murphy, 2006)

## Intratransactional Association

Correlations among items within the same transactions. (Feng & Dillon, 2005)

## Intrinsic Difficulty

A numerical measure of how hard searching a given database is, independent of the index used. It grows with the Intrinsic Dimension. (Chávez & Navarro, 2005)

## Intrinsic Dimension

The minimum representational dimension in which the database could be represented without distorting its distances. (Chávez & Navarro, 2005)

## Intrinsic Motivation

**1:** Motivation that comes from within a person. (Whitfield, 2005) **2:** Motivation that derives from the activity itself. An example of intrinsic motivation for using microcomputers is using it because you enjoy it. (de Souza Dias, 2005) **3:** Motivation that stems from an internal desire for more satisfaction and challenge in one's career, rather than desires for enhanced salary and career mobility. (Adkins & Nitsch, 2005) **4:** Motivation through factors internal to the person being motivated. (Wishart, 2005) **5:** The motivation to engage in an activity for its own sake, because the activity is considered enjoyable, worthwhile, or important. (Hendriks & Sousa, 2006) **6:** Motivation that has no external manifestation in terms of rewards, but is psychologically effective in stimulating or driving people to seek self-satisfaction or self-consistency, for example, job satisfaction, commitment, and so forth. (Ekbia & Hara, 2006)

## Intrusion

Malicious, externally induced, operational fault in the computer system. (Lazarevic, 2005)

## Intrusion Prevention

Protecting networks against attacks by taking some preemptive action such as access control, preventing the transmission of invalid IP addresses, and so forth. (Syed, Nur, et al., 2005)

## Intrusion Tracking

The process of tracking an attack to its point of origin. (Syed, Nur, et al., 2005)

## Intrusion-Detection System (IDS)

**1:** A utility that continuously monitors for malicious packets or unusual activity (usually checks for matches with attack signatures extracted from earlier attack packets). (Syed, Chakrobartty, et al., 2005) **2:** A type of security management system for computers and networks in which the IDS gathers and analyzes information from various areas within a computer or a network in order to identify possible security breaches, which include both intrusions (attacks from outside the organization) and misuse (attacks from within the organization). (Cardoso & Freire, 2005) **3:** Software for detecting when suspicious behavior occurs on a computer or network. (Rowe, 2006b) **4:** Attempts to discover attacks while they are in progress, or at least discover them before much damage has been done. (Janczewski & Portougal, 2005) **5:** Detecting network attacks, usually by recognizing attack signatures extracted from earlier attack packets. (Syed, Nur, et al., 2005) **6:** Identifying a set of malicious actions that compromise the integrity, confidentiality, and availability of information resources. (Lazarevic, 2005) **7:** A set of techniques used to protect a computer system or network from a specific threat, which is unauthorized access. (Thuraisingham, 2005) **8:** Software for detecting when suspicious behavior occurs on a computer or network. (Rowe, 2006a)

**IntServ:** See *Integrated Services.*

## Intuitiveness

Knowing or understanding immediately how a product/system will work without reasoning or being taught. Intuitiveness is linked closely to naturalness (i.e., designs that are intuitive also will be perceived as being natural). (Noyes, 2006)

## Invalid Access Prevention Policy

A policy requiring that in order to manage multiple clients' concurrent read/write operations in the client/server architecture, no transactions that access stale multimedia data should be allowed to commit. In general, there are two different approaches to achieve this policy. The detection-based (lazy) policy ensures the validity of accessed multimedia data, and the avoidance-based (eager) policy ensures that invalid multimedia data is preemptively removed from the client caches. (Parker & Chen, 2005)

## Invention

The discovery or creation of new ideas. (Tatnall, 2005b)

## Inventory Carrying Cost

One of the costs associated with carrying the storage of supplies and final products. (Tyan, 2006)

## Inverse Transformation

Considering schema transformation $\Sigma$, the transformation $\Sigma'$ is the inverse of $\Sigma$ if its application undoes the result of the application of $\Sigma$. The instance mapping of $\Sigma'$ can be used to undo the effect of applying the instance mapping of $\Sigma$ on a set of data. (Hainaut, 2005)

## Investment

An item of value purchased for income or capital appreciation. (Lawson-Body, 2005)

## Investment Portfolio

A set of investments (sale and purchase of shares) in a determined period of time. The portfolio keeps a history of operations in the stock market. The construction of an optimal portfolio requires a priori estimates of asset returns and risk. (Castro & Braga, 2006)

## Invisible College

A group of researchers within the same branch of science who have personal relationships with one another. (Teigland & Wasko, 2006)

## Invisible Computer

A computer or computer interface that disappears cognitively either through user expertise or by direct mapping of the relationship between interface elements, and the actions afforded by them. Other current terms are transparency and seamlessness and their antonyms, reflection and seamfulness. (Kettley, 2006b)

## Invisible Web

Denotes those significant portions of the Internet where data is stored which are inaccessible to the major search engines. The invisible Web represents an often ignored/ neglected source of potential online information. (Peter & Greenidge, 2005a)

## Involuntary Attention

The idea that something can take a person's attention by being novel, contrasting, startling, and so forth. (Owen, 2006b)

## Inwards Projection

Estimating the expected number of customers that would sign on to a marketing promotion, based on customer characteristics and profiles. (Mani et al., 2005)

**IOI:** See *International Online Interaction.*

**IOIS:** See *Inter-Organizational Information System.*

**IOIT:** See *Interorganizational Information Technology.*

## Ionosphere

A band of particles 80-120 miles above the earth's surface. (Freeman & Auld, 2005)

**IOS:** See *Interorganizational System.*

**IP:** See *Image Processing; Intellectual Property; Internet Protocol.*

## IP Address

**1:** A unique number consisting of four parts separated by dots, such as 145.223.105.5. Every machine on the Internet has a unique IP address. (Nasraoui, 2005) **2:** A number assigned to a device for the purposes of identification by TCP/IP and associated protocols. It could be thought of as akin to a street address or telephone number that allows devices to communicate. (Leath, 2005)

## IP Asset Management

Involves management and enabling the trade of content, and includes accepting content from creators into an asset-management system. (Upadhyaya et al., 2006)

## IP Based

Network technologies based on Internet protocols. (Murphy, 2005c)

## IP Multicast

**1:** A set of IP packets transported via point-to-multipoint connections over a network to designated groups of multicast recipients. IP multicasts conserve bandwidth and network resources. (Littman, 2005) **2:** Network-level multicast technology that uses the special Class-D IP-address range. It requires multicast routing protocols in the network routers. (Hosszú, 2005b)

## IP Traceback

The process of tracking the attack packets back to their source along the route they traveled. (Syed, Nur, et al., 2005)

## IP-Multicast Routing Protocol

To forward the multicast packets, the routers must create multicast routing tables using multicast routing protocols. (Hosszú, 2005b)

## IP-Style Semantics

Similar to the traditional (unicast) IP communication, a source can send data at any time; for this it does not have to join the group of hosts. (Hosszu, 2005a)

**IPFS:** See *Integrated Personal Financial Service.*

**IPMA**
International Project Management Association. (D. Brandon, 2005b)

**IPO:** See *Initial Public Offering.*

**IPRS:** See *Intellectual Property Rights.*

**IPSec:** See *Internet Protocol Security.*

**IPT:** See *Information Processing Theory.*

**IPTV**
The result of large-scale adoption of broadband, as well as advances in networking technology and digital media, which together have made it possible for service providers to economically deliver high-quality live and on-demand movies and TV content over IP networks. (Papagiannidis et al., 2005)

**IR:** See *Information Retrieval; Infrared.*

**IRC:** See *Internet Relay Chat.*

**IRE:** See *Information Requirement Elicitation.*

**Iris Recognition**
A technique for identity verification or identification based on the users' encoded iris pattern. (Li, 2006)

**Iris Scanning**
Enables the identification of an individual based on the analysis of the colored tissue surrounding the pupil. (Scott et al., 2006)

**Irrational Commitment to Opportunities**
The tendency to seize opportunities without proper consideration given to potential implications. (Kyobe, 2006)

**Irrevocability**
The inability of an individual to be able to somehow cancel some credential. Biometric systems run a high risk of compromising irrevocability, if biometric data belonging to an individual is ever acquired and used to spoof a system. (Fleming, 2005a)

**IS:** See *Information System.*

**IS Success**
A global judgment of the degree to which stakeholders believe they are better off. The term is sometimes used interchangeably with IS effectiveness. (Wilkin, 2005)

**IS Support**
An information system (IS) function supporting people taking purposeful action. This is often done by indicating that the purposeful action can itself be expressed via activity models, through a fundamental re-thinking of what is entailed in providing informational support to purposeful action. The idea is that in order to create IS support that serves, it is first necessary to conceptualize the organizational system that is served, since this order of thinking should inform what relevant services would indeed be needed in the IS support. (Vat, 2006)

**IS/IT Benefits Realization Methodology**
An approach used to ensure that benefits expected in IS/IT investments by organizations are realized or delivered. (Lin & Pervan, 2005)

**IS/IT Evaluation**
The weighing up process to rationally assess the value of any acquisition of software or hardware that is expected to improve business value of an organization's information systems. (Lin & Pervan, 2005)

**IS/IT Investment Evaluation Methodology**
An approach used to evaluate organizations' IS/IT investments. (Lin & Pervan, 2005)

**IS/IT Outsourcing**
The process of transferring IS/IT assets, staff, and management responsibility for delivery of services from internal IS/IT functions to external contractors. (Lin & Pervan, 2005)

**IS-A Hierarchy**
A directed acyclic graph where each node is a class and each edge represents a "subclassOf" relationship from a class to one of its superclasses. In class algebra, the classes are labeled by normalized class algebra expressions. (Buehrer, 2005)

**IS-Architecture Alignment**
The process of selecting an IS-architecture vision that is strategically and operationally fit for the enterprise,

simple and well structured, well managed, and clearly and explicitly described. (Opdahl, 2005)

## IS-Architecture Model

An enterprise model that focuses on the enterprise's IS-architecture and that can be used to represent a current architecture or to illustrate a candidate or selected architecture vision. An IS-architecture sketch is a high-level model, whereas an architecture blueprint is more detailed. (Opdahl, 2005)

## IS-Architecture Principle

A high-level rule that can be used to make decisions about developing and/or evolving individual ICT systems. (Opdahl, 2005)

## IS-Architecture Vision

A coherent set of IS-architecture principles that together guide all the aspects of IS-architecture evolution that are considered important. (Opdahl, 2005)

**ISD:** See *Instructional System Design.*

**ISDN:** See *Integrated Services Digital Network.*

## ISEEK

An acronym for the Internet System for Education and Employment Knowledge system, a comprehensive online tool of information and resources on careers, jobs, education programs, and providers; developed by a collaboration of Minnesota agencies and institutions. (Langer, 2005)

**Ishikawa Diagram:** See *Root Cause Analysis.*

## Island Mode GP

A type of parallel GP, where multiple subpopulations (demes) are maintained and evolve independently, except during scheduled exchanges of individuals. (Hsu, 2005b)

**ISMS:** See *Information Security Management System.*

**ISO:** See *International Organization for Standardization.*

## ISO/IEC 17799

The British Standards Institute published a code of practice for managing information security following consultation with leading companies. BS7799 Part 1 incorporates a broad range of security practices and procedures that can be adopted by any organization of any size and in any industry sector. This is now international standard. (Tassabehji, 2005b)

## ISO 15504

An international standard that proposes the standard project SPICE, which establishes maturity levels for each individual process: Level 0—Incomplete; Level 1—Performed; Level 2—Managed; Level 3—Established; Level 4—Predictable; Level 5—Optimizing. (Monteiro de Carvalho et al., 2005)

## ISO 9001

An international standard that specifies the requirements of a quality management system. It is applicable to any organization regardless of product, service, organizational size, or whether it is a public or private company. (Leung, 2005)

## ISO 9001:2001

Provides standards used to assess an organization's ability to meet its customers' requirements and achieve customer satisfaction. Software firms use it as an alternative to CMM. (Hawk & Kaiser, 2005)

## ISO 9000-3

A guide to help ISO 9001 interpretation for the software field—that is, the development, supply, acquisition, and maintenance of software. (Monteiro de Carvalho et al., 2005)

## ISO 9241

A standard describing ergonomic requirements for office work with visual display terminals. It defines how to specify and measure the usability of products, and defines the factors that have an effect on usability. (Singh, 2005b)

## ISO 9241-11 1

**1:** A standard that describes ergonomic requirements for office work with visual display terminals. This standard defines how to specify and measure the usability of products and defines the factors that have an effect on usability. (Singh, 2006) **2:** The part of ISO 9241 that introduces the concept of usability but does not make specific recommendations in terms of product attributes. Instead, it defines usability as the "extent to which a product can be used by specified users to achieve specified goals with effectiveness, efficiency, and satisfaction in a specified context of use." (Singh & Dix, 2006)

### ISO 17799

International standard describing managing information security processes. (Janczewski & Portougal, 2005)

### ISO 13407

International standard providing guidance on human-centered design activities throughout the lifecycle of interactive computer-based systems. It is a tool for those managing design processes, and provides guidance on sources of information and standards relevant to the human-centered approach. It describes human-centered design as a multidisciplinary activity, which incorporates human factors and ergonomics knowledge and techniques with the objective of enhancing effectiveness and efficiency, improving human working conditions, and counteracting possible adverse effects of use on human health, safety, and performance. (Singh, 2006)

**ISOC:** See *Internet Society.*

### Isochronous

**1:** Processing that must occur at regular time intervals. (Swierzowicz, 2005) **2:** Time-dependent processes where data must be delivered within certain time constraints. For example, multimedia streams require an isochronous transport mechanism to ensure that data is delivered as fast as it is displayed, and to ensure that the audio is synchronized with the video. Isochronous processes can be contrasted with asynchronous processes, which refer to processes in which data streams can be broken by random intervals, and synchronous processes, in which data streams can be delivered only at specific intervals. Isochronous service is not as rigid as synchronous service, but not as lenient as asynchronous service. (Yang et al., 2005b)

### Isolation Anomaly

One of the set of inconsistencies that occur when transactions are executed without the isolation property. (Frank, 2005b)

### Isolation Level

One of the different degrees of isolation that use up to three different types of isolation anomalies, which are accepted when concurrent transactions are executed. (Frank, 2005b)

### Isoluminance Contour

Planar polygon that has a single constant color at all points it encloses. (Cottingham, 2005)

**ISP:** See *Internet Service Provider.*

### ISPS

Internet service providers provide access to the Internet via different communications channels such as traditional telephone lines or high-speed fiber optic channels. (Phala, 2005)

**ISSP:** See *Issue-Specific Security Policy.*

### Issue-Specific Security Policy (ISSP)

A policy that provides detailed, targeted guidance to instruct all members of the organization in the use of technology-based systems. (Mattord & Whitman, 2005)

**IT:** See *Information Technology.*

**IT Alignment:** See *Information Technology Alignment.*

**IT Application:** See *Information Technology Application.*

**IT Architecture:** See *Information Technology Architecture.*

**IT Enabled:** See *Information Technology Enabled.*

**IT End-User Relationship:** See *Information Technology End-User Relationship.*

**IT Governance:** See *Information Technology Governance.*

**IT Governance Comprehensiveness:** See *Information Technology Governance Comprehensiveness.*

**IT Governance Formalization:** See *Information Technology Governance Formalization.*

**IT Governance Integration:** See *Information Technology Governance Integration.*

**IT Governance Maturity Model:** See *Information Technology Governance Maturity Model.*

**I**

**IT Hardware:** See *Information Technology Hardware.*

**IT Implementation Process:** See *Information Technology Implementation Process.*

**IT Implementation Success:** See *Information Technology Implementation Success.*

**IT Industry:** See *Information Technology Industry.*

**IT Industry Development:** See *Information Technology Industry Development.*

**IT Industry Success:** See *Information Technology Industry Success.*

**IT Infrastructure:** See *Information Technology Infrastructure.*

**IT Investment Intensity:** See *Information Technology Investment Intensity.*

**IT Literacy:** See *Information Technology Literacy.*

**IT Outsourcing Partnership:** See *Information Technology Outsourcing Partnership.*

**IT Portfolio:** See *Information Technology Portfolio.*

**IT Software:** See *Information Technology Software.*

**IT Standard:** See *Information Technology Standard.*

**IT Strategy:** See *Information Technology Strategy.*

**ITA:** See *Independent Testing Authority.*

**ITCA:** See *Information Technology Competitive Advantage.*

**Item**
A sales product, or a feature or attribute. (Kryszkiewicz, 2005)

**Item Bias**
Refers to measurement artifacts. (Karahanna et al., 2005)

**Item Equivalence**
Refers to whether identical instruments are used to measure the constructs across cultures. (Karahanna et al., 2005)

**Item Presentation**
The set of WCDSS product display and promotion formats such as virtual catalogs, 3D picture display, and samples and trials. (F. Wang, 2006)

**Itemset**
**1:** A conjunction of items (attribute-value pairs) (e.g., *age = teen ∧ hair = brown*). (Butler & Webb, 2005) **2:** A set of binary attributes, each corresponding to an attribute value or an interval of attribute values. (Pasquier, 2005) **3:** A set of database items. (Daly & Taniar, 2005a) **4:** A set of one or more items that are purchased together in a single transaction. (Jha & Sural, 2005) **5:** An unordered set of unique items, which may be products or features. For computational efficiency, the items are often represented by integers. A frequent itemset is one with a support count that exceeds the support threshold, and a candidate itemset is a potential frequent itemset. A k-itemset is an itemset with exactly k items. (Woon et al., 2005) **6:** A set of items that occur together. (Masseglia et al., 2005)

**Itemset Support**
The ratio between the number of transactions in D comprising all the items in I and the total number of transactions in D (support(I) = $|\{T_i \in D| \ (\forall i_j \in I) \ i_j \in T_i \ \}| / |D|$). (Dumitriu, 2005)

**Iterative Development**
An approach to software development where the overall lifecycle is composed of several iterations in sequence. (Ferre et al., 2006)

**ITMP:** See *Information Technology Master Plan.*

**ITS:** See *Intelligent Tutoring System.*

**ITT:** See *Information Technology Transfer.*

**ITU:** See *International Telecommunications Union.*

**ITV:** See *Instructional Television; Interactive Television.*

**IUP:** See *Internet Usage Policy.*

**IVO:** See *International Virtual Office.*

**IVR:** See *Interactive Voice Response.*

**IVUS Data Reconciliation**
Mining in the IVUS individual dataset to compensate or decrease artifacts to get improved data usage for further cardiac calculation and medical knowledge discovery. (Liu et al., 2005)

**IXC:** See *Interexchange Carrier.*

# J

**JADE:** See *Java Agent Development Framework.*

## JalChitra

A village water resources mapping and water auditing software developed by Dr. Vikram Vyas. (Literal meaning of Jal is water and Chitra is picture.) (Shaligram, 2005)

## Java

**1:** A high-level programming language similar to C++ developed by SUN Microsystems. (Guan, 2005c) **2:** A platform-independent programming language, produced by Sun Microsystems. Java is built as a method to provide services over the WWW. With Java, a Web site provides a Java application (called an applet), which is downloaded by the client and executed on the client machine. Java is specifically built so that an application can be run on any kind of system, so a separate MAC, Windows, Sun, and so forth version is not needed. Java also has some security features built in, to make it more difficult for destructive applets to be written. (Díez-Higuera & Díaz-Pernas, 2005) **3:** An object-oriented language that is widely used for Internet or Web-based applications. It was designed specifically for distributed environments. (Dasgupta & Chandrashekaran, 2005) **4:** Programming language designed to be portable, used to create programs that will run on mobile phones and PDAs, as well as Macintosh, Windows, and Unix desktop computers. (Houser & Thornton, 2005)

## Java Agent Development Framework (JADE)

A middleware tool used in implementation of agent-based systems (http://jade.tilab.com). (Cardoso & Freire, 2005)

## Java Data Mining (JDM)

An emerging standard API for the programming language Java. An object-oriented interface that specifies a set of Java classes and interfaces supporting data-mining operations for building, testing, and applying a data-mining model. (Zendulka, 2005a)

## Java Media Framework (JMF)

A Java library for the development of stand-alone and networked multimedia systems. (Fortino, 2005)

## Java 2 Enterprise Edition (J2EE)

Designed to simplify complex problems with the development, deployment, and management of a multi-tier enterprise solution. J2EE is an industry standard that helps build Web services (e.g., used with IBM's WebSphere, HP's Web Services Platform, and Sun's Sun ONE). (Chen, 2006)

## Java Virtual Machine (JVM)

A platform-independent execution environment that converts Java byte-code into machine language and then executes it. (Lucas, 2005)

## Java/RMI

A Java application programming interface known as remote method invocation. (Yen, 2005)

## JavaScript

A scripting language developed to enable Web authors to add dynamic content to sites. Although it shares many of the features and structures of the Java language, it was developed independently. It is supported by recent browsers from Netscape and Microsoft. (Valenti, 2005)

**JAWS:** See *Job Access for Windows.*

**JDM:** See *Java Data Mining.*

## Jhai Foundation

A non-profit organization founded by American, Lee Thorn. The foundation is managed by an advisory board and includes many volunteers as well as paid contractors. Its aim is to assist the people of Laos in a collaborative manner in the areas of economic development, education, and information technology. (Anderson, 2005)

**JIT:** See *Just-In-Time Training.*

**JITAIT:** See *Just-In-Time Artificially Intelligent Tutor.*

**JMF:** See *Java Media Framework.*

### Job Access for Windows (JAWS)

A Windows screen reader from Henter-Joyce. JAWS works with PCs to provide access to software applications and the Internet. With its internal software speech synthesizer and the computer's sound card, information from the screen is read aloud for visually impaired and blind people. (Yu, 2005a)

### Job Characteristics Theory

**1:** Task attributes influence effectiveness through their impact on critical psychological states such as motivation and satisfaction with the work. (Wong & Staples, 2005) **2:** This motivation theory, which stems from Hackman and Oldham, identifies several characteristics of jobs, such as skill variety and autonomy, that influence the experienced meaningfulness of work, and therefore the internal motivation and job satisfaction of workers. (Hendriks & Sousa, 2006)

### Join Dependency

Any decomposition of tables must be able to be rejoined to recover the original table. Tables in 5NF are join dependent. (Schultz, 2005)

### Join Index

Built by translating restrictions on the column value of a dimension table to restrictions on a large fact table. The index is implemented using one of two representations, row id or bitmap, depending on the cardinality of the indexed column. (Bellatreche & Mohania, 2005)

### Joint Diagnostic Relationship

As a result of the methods used, the approach of OD is informed by a joint diagnostic relationship between the OD consultant or change agent and various stakeholders in the organization. This enables the problem to be understood from multiple perspectives. (Grieves, 2006b)

### Joint Enterprise

Allows the community to extend the boundaries and interpretations beyond those that were created. By sharing a common goal, members of the community negotiate their situations in their reactions to them. With joint enterprise it is more likely that the community will sustain its validity. (Louis, 2006)

### Joint Intellectual Property

The result of a company taking the view that it is owned by its customers and they have ownership in product development. This notion goes beyond normal customer relationships and co-creates new businesses based on customer education and co-development. It is probably the most intense form of cooperation between a company and its customers. (Paquette, 2006b)

### Joint Outcome

Part of the direct output and by-products of the education process including student learning, an employable workforce, AIT market exposure, and contributions to industrial and academic research. (LeRouge & Webb, 2005)

### Joint Probability

The probability of two events occurring in conjunction. (Bashir et al., 2005)

### Joint Probability Distribution

A function that encodes the probabilistic dependencies among a set of variables in a domain. (Vargas, 2005)

### Joint Venture Model

A model for collaboration between institutions where modules and courses are developed and offered through joint efforts; a jigsaw of different specialties and resources. (Haugen & Ask, 2005)

### Journey Making

Group mapping activities are often a central part of a group's JOint Understanding, Reflection, and NEgotiation of strategY. The methodology aims to support groups in their development of a feasible strategy that they are individually and collectively committed to implementing. (Shaw, 2006)

### Joypad

A palm-sized device designed for use with both hands to interact with the game. Its layout is typified by directional keys on the left, and buttons on the right and top sections of the pad. Modern pads incorporate additional analog sticks on the left or on both the left and right sides. (Ip & Jacobs, 2006)

**Joystick**

A 360-degree stick mounted on a sturdy platform of buttons used for interacting with the game; used predominantly in stand-alone arcade machines and early home consoles. (Ip & Jacobs, 2006)

**JPEG**

**1:** A standard file type for computerized images, determined by the Joint Photographic Experts Group. (M. Lang, 2005) **2:** Joint Photographic Experts Group specification for reproduction of digital images, widely used on the Internet. (McCarthy, 2005a)

**J2EE:** See *Java 2 Enterprise Edition.*

**Junction Tree**

A representation that captures the joint probability distribution of a set of variables in a very efficient data structure. A junction tree contains cliques, each of which is a set of variables from the domain. The junction tree is configured to maintain the probabilistic dependencies of the domain variables and provides a data structure over queries of the type "What is the most probable value of variable D given that the values of variables A, B, etc., are known?" (Vargas, 2005)

**Junction Tree Algorithm**

A two-pass method for updating probabilities in Bayesian networks. For triangulated networks the inference procedure is optimal. (Caelli, 2005)

**Junk Computing**

The use of organizational information technology that does not align with organizational goals. (Mahatanankoon, 2005)

**Just-in-Time**

An approach to learning where knowledge and skills are acquired when, how, and where needed by the learner, and using various technologies to deliver the learning event. (Stavredes, 2005a)

**Just-In-Time Artificially Intelligent Tutor (JITAIT)**

One of several expert systems available on demand in HyperReality environments to respond to frequently asked student questions about specific domains of knowledge. (Rajasingham & Tiffin, 2005)

**Just-In-Time Learning**

Strategic knowledge acquisition enmeshed in business activities to support employees in learning new skills when performing day-to-day tasks, while fostering the alignment between learning outcomes, and technological and strategic business issues. (Rentroia-Bonito & Jorge, 2005)

**Just-in-Time Material**

Material to supplement a traditional presentation available for the learner to access when it may be needed. (Pelton & Pelton, 2005)

**Just-In-Time Training (JIT)**

The philosophy of providing training at the exact point when one needs the knowledge/skills to perform a task or job function. (Hanson, 2005)

**JVM:** See *Java Virtual Machine.*

# References

Aarons, J. (2006). Epistemology and knowledge management. In D. Schwartz (Ed.), *Encyclopedia of knowledge management* (pp. 166-172). Hershey, PA: Idea Group Reference.

Abdulghani, A.A. (2005a). Computation of OLAP cubes. In J. Wang (Ed.), *Encyclopedia of data warehousing and mining* (pp. 196-201). Hershey, PA: Idea Group Reference.

Abdulghani, A.A. (2005b). Data mining with cubegrades. In J. Wang (Ed.), *Encyclopedia of data warehousing and mining* (pp. 288-292). Hershey, PA: Idea Group Reference.

Abels, S., & Hahn, A. (2006). Classification systems. In M. Khosrow-Pour (Ed.), *Encyclopedia of e-commerce, e-government, and mobile commerce* (pp. 95-102). Hershey, PA: Idea Group Reference.

Abhishek, & Basu, A. (2006). Iconic Interfaces for Assistive Communication. In C. Ghaoui (Ed.), *Encyclopedia of human computer interaction* (pp. 295-302). Hershey, PA: Idea Group Reference.

Abou-Zeid, E.-S. (2005a). Alignment of business and knowledge management strategies. In M. Khosrow-Pour (Ed.), *Encyclopedia of information science and technology* (pp. 98-103). Hershey, PA: Idea Group Reference.

Abou-Zeid, E.-S. (2005b). Autopoietic approach for information system development. In M. Khosrow-Pour (Ed.), *Encyclopedia of information science and technology* (pp. 200-204). Hershey, PA: Idea Group Reference.

Abraham, D.M., & Leon, L. (2006). Knowledge management in supply chain networks. In E. Coakes & S. Clarke (Eds.), *Encyclopedia of communities of practice in information and knowledge management* (pp. 293-300). Hershey, PA: Idea Group Reference.

Abramowicz, W., Banaśkiewicz, K., Wieloch, K., & Żebrowski, P. (2006). Mobile information filtering. In M. Khosrow-Pour (Ed.), *Encyclopedia of e-commerce, e-government, and mobile commerce* (pp. 799-804). Hershey, PA: Idea Group Reference.

Abu-Samaha, A. (2005). A systematic approach for information systems evaluation. In M. Khosrow-Pour (Ed.), *Encyclopedia of information science and technology* (pp. 22-28). Hershey, PA: Idea Group Reference.

Achterbergh, J. (2005a). ICT-supported gaming for competitive intelligence. In M. Khosrow-Pour (Ed.), *Encyclopedia of information science and technology* (pp. 1379-1384). Hershey, PA: Idea Group Reference.

Achterbergh, J. (2005b). IT supporting strategy formulation. In M. Khosrow-Pour (Ed.), *Encyclopedia of information science and technology* (pp. 1728-1734). Hershey, PA: Idea Group Reference.

Adam, F., & Pomerol, J.-C. (2005). Better executive information with the dashboard approach. In M.

Khosrow-Pour (Ed.), *Encyclopedia of information science and technology* (pp. 266-271). Hershey, PA: Idea Group Reference.

Adkins, M., & Nitsch, W.B. (2005). Student retention in online education. In C. Howard, J.V. Boettcher, L. Justice, K. Schenk, P.L. Rogers, & G.A. Berg (Eds.), *Encyclopedia of distance learning* (pp. 1680-1686). Hershey, PA: Idea Group Reference.

Aggarwal, A.K. (2005). Stakeholders in Web-based education. In C. Howard, J.V. Boettcher, L. Justice, K. Schenk, P.L. Rogers, & G.A. Berg (Eds.), *Encyclopedia of distance learning* (pp. 1660-1665). Hershey, PA: Idea Group Reference.

Agosti, G. (2005). Distance education in the era of Internet. In S. Marshall, W. Taylor, & X. Yu (Eds.), *Encyclopedia of developing regional communities with information and communication technology* (pp. 199-204). Hershey, PA: Idea Group Reference.

Agresti, W.W. (2005). Discovery informatics. In J. Wang (Ed.), *Encyclopedia of data warehousing and mining* (pp. 387-391). Hershey, PA: Idea Group Reference.

Ahmad, K., & Al-Sayed, R. (2006). Community of practice and the special language "ground". In E. Coakes & S. Clarke (Eds.), *Encyclopedia of communities of practice in information and knowledge management* (pp. 77-88). Hershey, PA: Idea Group Reference.

Aifanti, N., Sappa, A.D., Grammalidis, N., & Malassiotis, S. (2005). Human motion tracking and recognition. In M. Khosrow-Pour (Ed.), *Encyclopedia of information science and technology* (pp. 1355-1360). Hershey, PA: Idea Group Reference.

Aigbedo, H. (2005). Enhancing competitiveness of B2B and B2C e-commerce. In M. Khosrow-Pour (Ed.), *Encyclopedia of information science and technology* (pp. 1064-1070). Hershey, PA: Idea Group Reference.

Aisami, R.S. (2005). Teaching online courses. In C. Howard, J.V. Boettcher, L. Justice, K. Schenk, P.L. Rogers, & G.A. Berg (Eds.), *Encyclopedia of distance*

*learning* (pp. 1777-1786). Hershey, PA: Idea Group Reference.

Ajiferuke, I., & Markus, A. (2005). Potentials of information technology in building virtual communities. In M. Pagani (Ed.), *Encyclopedia of multimedia technology and networking* (pp. 836-841). Hershey, PA: Idea Group Reference.

Ajiferuke, I., & Olatokun, W. (2005). Information technology usage in Nigeria. In M. Khosrow-Pour (Ed.), *Encyclopedia of information science and technology* (pp. 1508-1512). Hershey, PA: Idea Group Reference.

Akhtar, S. (2005). 2G-4G networks. In M. Pagani (Ed.), *Encyclopedia of multimedia technology and networking* (pp. 964-973). Hershey, PA: Idea Group Reference.

Alavi, M., Dufner, D., & Howard, C. (2005). Collaborative learning technologies. In C. Howard, J.V. Boettcher, L. Justice, K. Schenk, P.L. Rogers, & G.A. Berg (Eds.), *Encyclopedia of distance learning* (pp. 284-289). Hershey, PA: Idea Group Reference.

Albers, M.J. (2006). Information Rich Systems and User's Goals and Information Needs. In C. Ghaoui (Ed.), *Encyclopedia of human computer interaction* (pp. 338-343). Hershey, PA: Idea Group Reference.

Aldana Montes, J.F., Gómez Lora, A.C., Vergara, N.M., Delgado, I.N., & García, M.M.R. (2005). Database technologies on the Web. In M. Khosrow-Pour (Ed.), *Encyclopedia of information science and technology* (pp. 745-749). Hershey, PA: Idea Group Reference.

Ale, J.M., & Espil, M.M. (2005). Triggers, rules and constraints in databases. In M. Khosrow-Pour (Ed.), *Encyclopedia of information science and technology* (pp. 2878-2881). Hershey, PA: Idea Group Reference.

Ale, J.M., & Rossi, G.H. (2005). Discovering association rules in temporal databases. In L. Rivero, J. Doorn, & V. Ferraggine (Eds.), *Encyclopedia of database technologies and applications* (pp. 195-200). Hershey, PA: Idea Group Reference.

Aleman-Meza, B., Halaschek-Wiener, C., & Arpinar, I.B. (2005). Collective knowledge composition in a P2P network. In L. Rivero, J. Doorn, & V. Ferraggine (Eds.), *Encyclopedia of database technologies and applications* (pp. 74-77). Hershey, PA: Idea Group Reference.

Alexander, P., & Burn, J. (2006). Transformation of e-fulfillment industry capabilities. In M. Khosrow-Pour (Ed.), *Encyclopedia of e-commerce, e-government, and mobile commerce* (pp. 1082-1088). Hershey, PA: Idea Group Reference.

Al-Gharbi, K., & Khalfan, A.M. (2005). Impacts of the Intranet on PDO. In M. Khosrow-Pour (Ed.), *Encyclopedia of information science and technology* (pp. 1385-1390). Hershey, PA: Idea Group Reference.

Alhajj, R., & Polat, F. (2005a). Converting a legacy database to object-oriented database. In L. Rivero, J. Doorn, & V. Ferraggine (Eds.), *Encyclopedia of database technologies and applications* (pp. 99-104). Hershey, PA: Idea Group Reference.

Alhajj, R., & Polat, F. (2005b). Proper placement of derived classes in the class hierarchy. In L. Rivero, J. Doorn, & V. Ferraggine (Eds.), *Encyclopedia of database technologies and applications* (pp. 486-492). Hershey, PA: Idea Group Reference.

Al-Hanbali, N., & Sadoun, B. (2006). A GIS-Based Interactive Database System for Planning Purposes. In C. Ghaoui (Ed.), *Encyclopedia of human computer interaction* (pp. 242-252). Hershey, PA: Idea Group Reference.

Ali, I., & Warne, L. (2005). Knowledge management and social learning. In M. Khosrow-Pour (Ed.), *Encyclopedia of information science and technology* (pp. 1764-1770). Hershey, PA: Idea Group Reference.

Ali, I., Warne, L., & Pascoe, C. (2006). Learning in organizations. In D. Schwartz (Ed.), *Encyclopedia of knowledge management* (pp. 561). Hershey, PA: Idea Group Reference.

Ali, M., Ashley, C., Huq, M.Z., & Streatfield, P.K. (2005). Spatial modeling of risk factors for gender-specific child mortality. In M. Khosrow-Pour (Ed.), *Encyclopedia of information science and technology* (pp. 2584-2590). Hershey, PA: Idea Group Reference.

Alippi, C., & Vanini, G. (2005). Perturbations, accuracy and robustness in neural networks. In M. Khosrow-Pour (Ed.), *Encyclopedia of information science and technology* (pp. 2282-2287). Hershey, PA: Idea Group Reference.

Alkhalifa, E.M. (2005a). Multimedia evaluations based on cognitive science findings. In M. Khosrow-Pour (Ed.), *Encyclopedia of information science and technology* (pp. 2058-2062). Hershey, PA: Idea Group Reference.

Alkhalifa, E.M. (2005b). Open student models. In C. Howard, J.V. Boettcher, L. Justice, K. Schenk, P.L. Rogers, & G.A. Berg (Eds.), *Encyclopedia of distance learning* (pp. 1417-1420). Hershey, PA: Idea Group Reference.

Alkhalifa, E.M. (2006). Cognitively Informed Multimedia Interface Design. In C. Ghaoui (Ed.), *Encyclopedia of human computer interaction* (pp. 79-84). Hershey, PA: Idea Group Reference.

Ally, M. (2005a). Designing effective computer-based learning materials. In C. Howard, J.V. Boettcher, L. Justice, K. Schenk, P.L. Rogers, & G.A. Berg (Eds.), *Encyclopedia of distance learning* (pp. 525-533). Hershey, PA: Idea Group Reference.

Ally, M. (2005b). Designing instruction for successful online learning. In C. Howard, J.V. Boettcher, L. Justice, K. Schenk, P.L. Rogers, & G.A. Berg (Eds.), *Encyclopedia of distance learning* (pp. 534-439). Hershey, PA: Idea Group Reference.

Ally, M. (2005c). Multimedia information design for mobile devices. In M. Pagani (Ed.), *Encyclopedia of multimedia technology and networking* (pp. 704-709). Hershey, PA: Idea Group Reference.

Ally, M. (2005d). Preparing faculty for distance learning teaching. In C. Howard, J.V. Boettcher, L. Justice, K. Schenk, P.L. Rogers, & G.A. Berg (Eds.), *Encyclopedia of distance learning* (pp. 1503-1507). Hershey, PA: Idea Group Reference.

Almazán, R.S., & Gil-García, J.R. (2006). E-government portals in Mexico. In M. Khosrow-Pour (Ed.), *Encyclopedia of e-commerce, e-government, and mobile commerce* (pp. 367-372). Hershey, PA: Idea Group Reference.

Alonso-Jiménez, J.A., Borrego-Díaz, J., & Chávez-González, A.M. (2005). Logic databases and inconsistency handling. In L. Rivero, J. Doorn, & V. Ferraggine (Eds.), *Encyclopedia of database technologies and applications* (pp. 336-340). Hershey, PA: Idea Group Reference.

Alpert, S.R. (2006). Computer-Based Concept Mapping. In C. Ghaoui (Ed.), *Encyclopedia of human computer interaction* (pp. 100-104). Hershey, PA: Idea Group Reference.

Al-Qirim, N.A.Y. (2005). Telemedicine in healthcare organisations. In M. Khosrow-Pour (Ed.), *Encyclopedia of information science and technology* (pp. 2784-2787). Hershey, PA: Idea Group Reference.

Al-Saggaf, Y., & Weckert, J. (2005). Political online communities in Saudi Arabia. In S. Marshall, W. Taylor, & X. Yu (Eds.), *Encyclopedia of developing regional communities with information and communication technology* (pp. 557-563). Hershey, PA: Idea Group Reference.

Amaravadi, C.S. (2005). Strategic utilization of data mining. In M. Khosrow-Pour (Ed.), *Encyclopedia of information science and technology* (pp. 2638-2642). Hershey, PA: Idea Group Reference.

Amoretti, M.S.M. (2005). Categorization process and data mining. In J. Wang (Ed.), *Encyclopedia of data warehousing and mining* (pp. 129-133). Hershey, PA: Idea Group Reference.

An, A. (2005). Classification methods. In J. Wang (Ed.), *Encyclopedia of data warehousing and mining* (pp. 144-149). Hershey, PA: Idea Group Reference.

Analide, C., Novais, P., Machado, J., & Neves, J. (2006). Quality of knowledge in virtual entities. In E. Coakes & S. Clarke (Eds.), *Encyclopedia of communities of practice in information and knowledge management* (pp. 436-442). Hershey, PA: Idea Group Reference.

Anderson, N. (2005). Pedal powered wireless Internet in the Laotion jungle. In S. Marshall, W. Taylor, & X. Yu (Eds.), *Encyclopedia of developing regional communities with information and communication technology* (pp. 544-549). Hershey, PA: Idea Group Reference.

Andrade, J., Ares, J., García, R., Rodríguez, S., & Silva, A. (2006). Human-centered conceptualization and natural language. In C. Ghaoui (Ed.), *Encyclopedia of human computer interaction* (pp. 280-286). Hershey, PA: Idea Group Reference.

Andrade, J., Ares, J., García, R., Rodríguez, S., Seoane, M., & Suárez, S. (2006). Knowledge management as an e-learning tool. In C. Ghaoui (Ed.), *Encyclopedia of human computer interaction* (pp. 381-388). Hershey, PA: Idea Group Reference.

Andrés del Valle, A.C. (2005). Face expression and motion analysis over monocular images. In M. Khosrow-Pour (Ed.), *Encyclopedia of information science and technology* (pp. 1174-1179). Hershey, PA: Idea Group Reference.

Andreu, R., & Sieber, S. (2006). External and internal knowledge in organizations. In D. Schwartz (Ed.), *Encyclopedia of knowledge management* (pp. 173-179). Hershey, PA: Idea Group Reference.

Angehrn, A.A., & Gibbert, M. (2005). Learning networks. In M. Pagani (Ed.), *Encyclopedia of multimedia technology and networking* (pp. 526-531). Hershey, PA: Idea Group Reference.

Anke, J., & Sundaram, D. (2006). Personalization techniques and their application. In M. Khosrow-Pour (Ed.), *Encyclopedia of e-commerce, e-government, and mobile commerce* (pp. 919-925). Hershey, PA: Idea Group Reference.

Antonio do Prado, H., Moreira de Oliveira, J.P., Ferneda, E., Wives, L.K., Silva, E.M., & Loh, S. (2005). Text mining in the context of business intelligence. In M. Khosrow-Pour (Ed.), *Encyclopedia of information*

*science and technology* (pp. 2793-2798). Hershey, PA: Idea Group Reference.

Antoniou, G., Christophides, V., Plexousakis, D., & Doerr, M. (2005). Semantic Web fundamentals. In M. Khosrow-Pour (Ed.), *Encyclopedia of information science and technology* (pp. 2464-2468). Hershey, PA: Idea Group Reference.

Anttiroiko, A.-V. (2005a). Democratic e-governance. In M. Khosrow-Pour (Ed.), *Encyclopedia of information science and technology* (pp. 791-796). Hershey, PA: Idea Group Reference.

Anttiroiko, A.-V. (2005b). Strategic knowledge management in public organizations. In M. Khosrow-Pour (Ed.), *Encyclopedia of information science and technology* (pp. 2632-2637). Hershey, PA: Idea Group Reference.

Aradhye, H.B., & Dorai, C. (2005). Multimodal analysis in multimedia using symbolic kernels. In J. Wang (Ed.), *Encyclopedia of data warehousing and mining* (pp. 842-847). Hershey, PA: Idea Group Reference.

Arbore, A. (2005). Local loop unbundling. In M. Pagani (Ed.), *Encyclopedia of multimedia technology and networking* (pp. 538-546). Hershey, PA: Idea Group Reference.

Archer, N. (2005). Management considerations for B2B online exchanges. In M. Khosrow-Pour (Ed.), *Encyclopedia of information science and technology* (pp. 1858-1863). Hershey, PA: Idea Group Reference.

Archer, N. (2006). A classification of communities of practice. In E. Coakes & S. Clarke (Eds.), *Encyclopedia of communities of practice in information and knowledge management* (pp. 21-29). Hershey, PA: Idea Group Reference.

Arellano, N., Chigona, W., Moore, J., & Van Belle, J.-P. (2005). ICT-based community development initiatives in South Africa. In S. Marshall, W. Taylor, & X. Yu (Eds.), *Encyclopedia of developing regional communities with information and communication technology* (pp. 399-404). Hershey, PA: Idea Group Reference.

Ariely, G. (2006a). Intellectual capital and knowledge management. In D. Schwartz (Ed.), *Encyclopedia of knowledge management* (pp. 281-288). Hershey, PA: Idea Group Reference.

Ariely, G. (2006b). Operational knowledge management in the military. In D. Schwartz (Ed.), *Encyclopedia of knowledge management* (pp. 713-720). Hershey, PA: Idea Group Reference.

Arkhypska, O., Bilous, S., & Yarinich, V. (2005). Civic space portal. In S. Marshall, W. Taylor, & X. Yu (Eds.), *Encyclopedia of developing regional communities with information and communication technology* (pp. 103-106). Hershey, PA: Idea Group Reference.

Arthur-Gray, H., & Campbell, J. (2005). Education trends in Thai businesses utilizing information technology. In S. Marshall, W. Taylor, & X. Yu (Eds.), *Encyclopedia of developing regional communities with information and communication technology* (pp. 256-262). Hershey, PA: Idea Group Reference.

Artz, J.M. (2005a). Addressing the central problem in cyber ethics through stories. In M. Khosrow-Pour (Ed.), *Encyclopedia of information science and technology* (pp. 58-61). Hershey, PA: Idea Group Reference.

Artz, J.M. (2005b). Data driven vs. metric driven data warehouse design. In J. Wang (Ed.), *Encyclopedia of data warehousing and mining* (pp. 223-227). Hershey, PA: Idea Group Reference.

Artz, J.M. (2005c). Ontological assumptions in information modeling. In L. Rivero, J. Doorn, & V. Ferraggine (Eds.), *Encyclopedia of database technologies and applications* (pp. 433-437). Hershey, PA: Idea Group Reference.

Artz, J.M. (2005d). Web technologies and data warehousing synergies. In M. Khosrow-Pour (Ed.), *Encyclopedia of information science and technology* (pp. 3065-3067). Hershey, PA: Idea Group Reference.

Arya, A. (2005). Content description for face animation. In M. Khosrow-Pour (Ed.), *Encyclopedia of information science and technology* (pp. 546-549). Hershey, PA: Idea Group Reference.

Ash, C.G., & Burn, J.M. (2006). Managing e-business change. In M. Khosrow-Pour (Ed.), *Encyclopedia of e-commerce, e-government, and mobile commerce* (pp. 729-735). Hershey, PA: Idea Group Reference.

Ashrafi, M.Z., Taniar, D., & Smith, K.A. (2005). Distributed association rule mining. In J. Wang (Ed.), *Encyclopedia of data warehousing and mining* (pp. 403-407). Hershey, PA: Idea Group Reference.

Askar, P., & Halici, U. (2005). Diffusion of e-learning as an educational innovation. In M. Khosrow-Pour (Ed.), *Encyclopedia of information science and technology* (pp. 849-852). Hershey, PA: Idea Group Reference.

Askar, P., & Kocak-Usluel, Y. (2005). Diffusion of computers in schools. In C. Howard, J.V. Boettcher, L. Justice, K. Schenk, P.L. Rogers, & G.A. Berg (Eds.), *Encyclopedia of distance learning* (pp. 568-572). Hershey, PA: Idea Group Reference.

Askar, P., Dönmez, O., Kizilkaya, G., Çevik, V., & Gültekin, K. (2005). Dimensions of student satisfaction on online programs. In C. Howard, J.V. Boettcher, L. Justice, K. Schenk, P.L. Rogers, & G.A. Berg (Eds.), *Encyclopedia of distance learning* (pp. 585-590). Hershey, PA: Idea Group Reference.

Askarany, D. (2005). Diffusion of innovations in organisations. In M. Khosrow-Pour (Ed.), *Encyclopedia of information science and technology* (pp. 853-857). Hershey, PA: Idea Group Reference.

Asprey, L. (2005). Project management for IT projects. In M. Khosrow-Pour (Ed.), *Encyclopedia of information science and technology* (pp. 2341-2347). Hershey, PA: Idea Group Reference.

Asprey, L., & Middleton, M. (2005). Integrative document and content management solutions. In M. Khosrow-Pour (Ed.), *Encyclopedia of information science and technology* (pp. 1573-1578). Hershey, PA: Idea Group Reference.

Asprey, L., Green, R., & Middleton, M. (2005). Integrative document and content management systems' architecture. In L. Rivero, J. Doorn, & V. Ferraggine (Eds.), *Encyclopedia of database technologies and applications* (pp. 291-297). Hershey, PA: Idea Group Reference.

Assimakopoulos, D., & Yan, J. (2006). Social network analysis and communities of practice. In E. Coakes & S. Clarke (Eds.), *Encyclopedia of communities of practice in information and knowledge management* (pp. 474-480). Hershey, PA: Idea Group Reference.

Athanasis, K., & Andreas, P. (2005). Usability and learnability evaluation of Web-based ODL programs. In M. Khosrow-Pour (Ed.), *Encyclopedia of information science and technology* (pp. 2929-2933). Hershey, PA: Idea Group Reference.

Athappilly, K., & Rea, A. (2005). Symbiotic data mining. In J. Wang (Ed.), *Encyclopedia of data warehousing and mining* (pp. 1083-1086). Hershey, PA: Idea Group Reference.

Atkinson, B.E., & Burstein, F. (2006). Biological and information systems approaches. In D. Schwartz (Ed.), *Encyclopedia of knowledge management* (pp. 17-23). Hershey, PA: Idea Group Reference.

Aurum, A. (2005). Innovative thinking in software development. In M. Khosrow-Pour (Ed.), *Encyclopedia of information science and technology* (pp. 1535-1539). Hershey, PA: Idea Group Reference.

Aurum, A., & Demirbilek, O. (2006). Virtual collaborative design. In S. Dasgupta (Ed.), *Encyclopedia of virtual communities and technologies* (pp. 482-486). Hershey, PA: Idea Group Reference.

Avdic, A. (2005). User spreadsheet systems development. In M. Khosrow-Pour (Ed.), *Encyclopedia of information science and technology* (pp. 2967-2972). Hershey, PA: Idea Group Reference.

Aversano, L., Canfora, G., & De Lucia, A. (2005). Migrating legacy systems to the Web. In M. Khosrow-Pour (Ed.), *Encyclopedia of information science and technology* (pp. 1949-1954). Hershey, PA: Idea Group Reference.

Averweg, U.R. (2006). Municipal information society in South Africa. In M. Khosrow-Pour (Ed.), *Encyclopedia of e-commerce, e-government, and mobile commerce* (pp. 836-841). Hershey, PA: Idea Group Reference.

Awad, M., & Khan, L. (2005). Support vector machines. In J. Wang (Ed.), *Encyclopedia of data warehousing and mining* (pp. 1064-1070). Hershey, PA: Idea Group Reference.

Aworuwa, B., & Owen, R. (2005). Instructional delivery and learning outcomes in distance learning. In C. Howard, J.V. Boettcher, L. Justice, K. Schenk, P.L. Rogers, & G.A. Berg (Eds.), *Encyclopedia of distance learning* (pp. 1117-1122). Hershey, PA: Idea Group Reference.

Azarov, S.S. (2005). The information society in Ukraine. In S. Marshall, W. Taylor, & X. Yu (Eds.), *Encyclopedia of developing regional communities with information and communication technology* (pp. 451-455). Hershey, PA: Idea Group Reference.

Babaian, T. (2005). Reasoning about user preferences. In M. Khosrow-Pour (Ed.), *Encyclopedia of information science and technology* (pp. 2403-2308). Hershey, PA: Idea Group Reference.

Badia, A. (2005a). Advanced query optimization. In L. Rivero, J. Doorn, & V. Ferraggine (Eds.), *Encyclopedia of database technologies and applications* (pp. 11-17). Hershey, PA: Idea Group Reference.

Badia, A. (2005b). Business rules in databases. In L. Rivero, J. Doorn, & V. Ferraggine (Eds.), *Encyclopedia of database technologies and applications* (pp. 47-53). Hershey, PA: Idea Group Reference.

Badia, A. (2005c). Data warehouses. In L. Rivero, J. Doorn, & V. Ferraggine (Eds.), *Encyclopedia of database technologies and applications* (pp. 121-126). Hershey, PA: Idea Group Reference.

Badia, A. (2005d). Relational, object-oriented and object-relational data models. In L. Rivero, J. Doorn, & V. Ferraggine (Eds.), *Encyclopedia of database technologies and applications* (pp. 530-535). Hershey, PA: Idea Group Reference.

Badia, A. (2006). Intelligence and counterterrorism tasks. In D. Schwartz (Ed.), *Encyclopedia of knowledge management* (pp. 289-296). Hershey, PA: Idea Group Reference.

Baer, L.L., & Duin, A.H. (2005). Partnerships. In C. Howard, J.V. Boettcher, L. Justice, K. Schenk, P.L. Rogers, & G.A. Berg (Eds.), *Encyclopedia of distance learning* (pp. 1473-1479). Hershey, PA: Idea Group Reference.

Bagozzi, R.P., & Dholakia, U.M. (2005). Collective intentional action in virtual communities. In M. Khosrow-Pour (Ed.), *Encyclopedia of information science and technology* (pp. 451-456). Hershey, PA: Idea Group Reference.

Bagui, S. (2005). Extended entity relationship modeling. In L. Rivero, J. Doorn, & V. Ferraggine (Eds.), *Encyclopedia of database technologies and applications* (pp. 233-239). Hershey, PA: Idea Group Reference.

Bagwell, C. (2005). Distance learning for incarcerated populations. In C. Howard, J.V. Boettcher, L. Justice, K. Schenk, P.L. Rogers, & G.A. Berg (Eds.), *Encyclopedia of distance learning* (pp. 656-661). Hershey, PA: Idea Group Reference.

Bahn, D.L. (2006). Clicks and mortar. In M. Khosrow-Pour (Ed.), *Encyclopedia of e-commerce, e-government, and mobile commerce* (pp. 103-105). Hershey, PA: Idea Group Reference.

Baim, S.A. (2005). Building police/community relations through virtual communities. In M. Khosrow-Pour (Ed.), *Encyclopedia of information science and technology* (pp. 318-324). Hershey, PA: Idea Group Reference.

Baim, S.A. (2006a). Business applications of virtual communities. In S. Dasgupta (Ed.), *Encyclopedia of virtual communities and technologies* (pp. 13-17). Hershey, PA: Idea Group Reference.

Baim, S.A. (2006b). Distance learning applications using virtual communities. In S. Dasgupta (Ed.), *Encyclopedia of virtual communities and technologies* (pp. 140-144). Hershey, PA: Idea Group Reference.

Baim, S.A. (2006c). Government applications of virtual communities. In S. Dasgupta (Ed.), *Encyclopedia of virtual communities and technologies* (pp. 218-222). Hershey, PA: Idea Group Reference.

Baim, S.A. (2006d). Understanding knowledge bases and building membership in virtual communities. In S. Dasgupta (Ed.), *Encyclopedia of virtual communities and technologies* (pp. 457-461). Hershey, PA: Idea Group Reference.

Baker, J.D., & Schihl, R.J. (2005). Faculty support systems. In C. Howard, J.V. Boettcher, L. Justice, K. Schenk, P.L. Rogers, & G.A. Berg (Eds.), *Encyclopedia of distance learning* (pp. 936-940). Hershey, PA: Idea Group Reference.

Baker, V., & Coltman, T. (2005). Executive judgement in e-business strategy. In M. Khosrow-Pour (Ed.), *Encyclopedia of information science and technology* (pp. 1149-1154). Hershey, PA: Idea Group Reference.

Bala, P.K., Sural, S., & Banerjee, R.N. (2005). Data mining in the soft computing paradigm. In J. Wang (Ed.), *Encyclopedia of data warehousing and mining* (pp. 272-277). Hershey, PA: Idea Group Reference.

Balsters, H. (2005). Integration of data semantics in heterogeneous database federations. In L. Rivero, J. Doorn, & V. Ferraggine (Eds.), *Encyclopedia of database technologies and applications* (pp. 286-290). Hershey, PA: Idea Group Reference.

Banerjee, P., Hu, X., & Yoo, I. (2005). Semantic data mining. In J. Wang (Ed.), *Encyclopedia of data warehousing and mining* (pp. 1010-1014). Hershey, PA: Idea Group Reference.

Banerji, A., & Basu, S. (2005). ICT aided education for people's empowerment. In S. Marshall, W. Taylor, & X. Yu (Eds.), *Encyclopedia of developing regional communities with information and communication technology* (pp. 331-336). Hershey, PA: Idea Group Reference.

Banerji, A., & Scales, G.R. (2005). Electronic performance support, e-learning and knowledge management. In C. Howard, J.V. Boettcher, L. Justice, K. Schenk, P.L. Rogers, & G.A. Berg (Eds.), *Encyclopedia of distance learning* (pp. 801-806). Hershey, PA: Idea Group Reference.

Banks, D.A. (2005). Audience response systems and face-to-face learning. In M. Khosrow-Pour (Ed.), *Encyclopedia of information science and technology* (pp. 178-183). Hershey, PA: Idea Group Reference.

Baralou, E., & Stepherd, J. (2005). Going virtual. In M. Pagani (Ed.), *Encyclopedia of multimedia technology and networking* (pp. 353-358). Hershey, PA: Idea Group Reference.

Barbin Laurindo, F.J., Monteiro de Carvalho, M., & Shimizu, T. (2005). Information technology strategic alignment. In M. Khosrow-Pour (Ed.), *Encyclopedia of information science and technology* (pp. 1503-1507). Hershey, PA: Idea Group Reference.

Barca, J.M.C., Martínez, E.M., Piattini Velthuis, M.G., & Sánchez de Miguel, A. (2005). Data warehouse development. In M. Khosrow-Pour (Ed.), *Encyclopedia of information science and technology* (pp. 729-733). Hershey, PA: Idea Group Reference.

Barima, O.K.B. (2006a). E-government and the construction industry. In M. Khosrow-Pour (Ed.), *Encyclopedia of e-commerce, e-government, and mobile commerce* (pp. 347-352). Hershey, PA: Idea Group Reference.

Barima, O.K.B. (2006b). Virtual concept use in the construction industry. In M. Khosrow-Pour (Ed.), *Encyclopedia of e-commerce, e-government, and mobile commerce* (pp. 1169-1174). Hershey, PA: Idea Group Reference.

Barnes, S.J. (2005). IS implementation in the UK health sector. In M. Khosrow-Pour (Ed.), *Encyclopedia of information science and technology* (pp. 1669-1672). Hershey, PA: Idea Group Reference.

Barolli, L., & Koyama, A. (2005a). Application of genetic algorithms for QoS routing in broadband networks. In M. Pagani (Ed.), *Encyclopedia of multimedia technology and networking* (pp. 22-30). Hershey, PA: Idea Group Reference.

Barolli, L., & Koyama, A. (2005b). Cooperative agents in Web-based distance learning. In C. Howard, J.V. Boettcher, L. Justice, K. Schenk, P.L. Rogers, & G.A. Berg (Eds.), *Encyclopedia of distance learning* (pp. 430-439). Hershey, PA: Idea Group Reference.

Barone, R. (2005). Macromedia flash on the client and the server. In M. Khosrow-Pour (Ed.), *Encyclopedia of information science and technology* (pp. 1854-1857). Hershey, PA: Idea Group Reference.

Barrera, L. (2005). Distance education in South America. In C. Howard, J.V. Boettcher, L. Justice, K. Schenk, P.L. Rogers, & G.A. Berg (Eds.), *Encyclopedia of distance learning* (pp. 628-634). Hershey, PA: Idea Group Reference.

Bashir, A., Khan, L., & Awad, M. (2005). Bayesian networks. In J. Wang (Ed.), *Encyclopedia of data warehousing and mining* (pp. 89-93). Hershey, PA: Idea Group Reference.

Baskin, C., Barker, M., & Woods, P. (2005). Industry-relevant smart community partnerships. In S. Marshall, W. Taylor, & X. Yu (Eds.), *Encyclopedia of developing regional communities with information and communication technology* (pp. 433-438). Hershey, PA: Idea Group Reference.

Bastide, R., Navarre, D., & Palanque, P. (2006). Tool Support for Interactive Prototyping of Safety-Critical Interactive Applications. In C. Ghaoui (Ed.), *Encyclopedia of human computer interaction* (pp. 603-608). Hershey, PA: Idea Group Reference.

Baugher, D., Varanelli, A., & Weisbord, E. (2005). Hybrid and traditional course formats. In C. Howard, J.V. Boettcher, L. Justice, K. Schenk, P.L. Rogers, & G.A. Berg (Eds.), *Encyclopedia of distance learning* (pp. 1012-1018). Hershey, PA: Idea Group Reference.

Baumann, P. (2005). Raster databases. In L. Rivero, J. Doorn, & V. Ferraggine (Eds.), *Encyclopedia of database technologies and applications* (pp. 517-523). Hershey, PA: Idea Group Reference.

Baxendale, S. (2005). Research-based distance learning services in the Northern Pacific. In C. Howard, J.V.

Boettcher, L. Justice, K. Schenk, P.L. Rogers, & G.A. Berg (Eds.), *Encyclopedia of distance learning* (pp. 1558-1563). Hershey, PA: Idea Group Reference.

Baylen, D.M., & Zhu, E. (2005). Going online-challenges and issues. In C. Howard, J.V. Boettcher, L. Justice, K. Schenk, P.L. Rogers, & G.A. Berg (Eds.), *Encyclopedia of distance learning* (pp. 969-974). Hershey, PA: Idea Group Reference.

Beaumont, N. (2005). Outsourcing information technology in Australia. In M. Khosrow-Pour (Ed.), *Encyclopedia of information science and technology* (pp. 2248-2254). Hershey, PA: Idea Group Reference.

Becerra-Fernandez, I., & Sabherwal, R. (2006). ICT and knowledge management systems. In D. Schwartz (Ed.), *Encyclopedia of knowledge management* (pp. 230-236). Hershey, PA: Idea Group Reference.

Beck, C.E., & Schornack, G.R. (2005). Systems model of educational processes. In C. Howard, J.V. Boettcher, L. Justice, K. Schenk, P.L. Rogers, & G.A. Berg (Eds.), *Encyclopedia of distance learning* (pp. 1732-1739). Hershey, PA: Idea Group Reference.

Becker, J., Algermissen, L., & Niehaves, B. (2006). Process-oriented reorganization projects in electronic government. In M. Khosrow-Pour (Ed.), *Encyclopedia of e-commerce, e-government, and mobile commerce* (pp. 926-932). Hershey, PA: Idea Group Reference.

Becker, S.A. (2005a). Web access by older adult users. In M. Khosrow-Pour (Ed.), *Encyclopedia of information science and technology* (pp. 3036-3041). Hershey, PA: Idea Group Reference.

Becker, S.A. (2005b). Web usability. In M. Khosrow-Pour (Ed.), *Encyclopedia of information science and technology* (pp. 3074-3078). Hershey, PA: Idea Group Reference.

Becker, S.A. (2006). PDA Usability for Telemedicine Support. In C. Ghaoui (Ed.), *Encyclopedia of human computer interaction* (pp. 457-462). Hershey, PA: Idea Group Reference.

Bedard-Voorhees, A. (2005). Facilitating asynchronous discussions. In C. Howard, J.V. Boettcher, L.

Justice, K. Schenk, P.L. Rogers, & G.A. Berg (Eds.), *Encyclopedia of distance learning* (pp. 912-917). Hershey, PA: Idea Group Reference.

Begg, R. (2005). Artificial intelligence techniques in medicine and health care. In M. Khosrow-Pour (Ed.), *Encyclopedia of information science and technology* (pp. 157-162). Hershey, PA: Idea Group Reference.

Beise, C., Moody, J., Myers, M., & Woszczynski, A. (2005). Women in the IT profession. In M. Khosrow-Pour (Ed.), *Encyclopedia of information science and technology* (pp. 3106-3110). Hershey, PA: Idea Group Reference.

Bélanger, F. (2005). Virtual work research agenda. In M. Khosrow-Pour (Ed.), *Encyclopedia of information science and technology* (pp. 3013-3017). Hershey, PA: Idea Group Reference.

Bellarby, L., & Orange, G. (2006). Knowledge sharing through communities of practice in the voluntary sector. In E. Coakes & S. Clarke (Eds.), *Encyclopedia of communities of practice in information and knowledge management* (pp. 301-306). Hershey, PA: Idea Group Reference.

Bellatreche, L., & Mohania, M. (2005). Physical data warehousing design. In J. Wang (Ed.), *Encyclopedia of data warehousing and mining* (pp. 906-911). Hershey, PA: Idea Group Reference.

Bennett, S. (2005). Online support for collaborative authentic activities. In C. Howard, J.V. Boettcher, L. Justice, K. Schenk, P.L. Rogers, & G.A. Berg (Eds.), *Encyclopedia of distance learning* (pp. 1412-1416). Hershey, PA: Idea Group Reference.

Benrud, E. (2005). The online discussion and student success in Web-based education. In M. Pagani (Ed.), *Encyclopedia of multimedia technology and networking* (pp. 778-784). Hershey, PA: Idea Group Reference.

Benyon, D. (2006). Information Space. In C. Ghaoui (Ed.), *Encyclopedia of human computer interaction* (pp. 344-347). Hershey, PA: Idea Group Reference.

Berends, H., van der Bij, H., & Weggeman, M. (2006). Knowledge integration. In D. Schwartz (Ed.), *Encyclopedia of knowledge management* (pp. 352-359). Hershey, PA: Idea Group Reference.

Berg, G.A. (2005a). Communication and media theory. In C. Howard, J.V. Boettcher, L. Justice, K. Schenk, P.L. Rogers, & G.A. Berg (Eds.), *Encyclopedia of distance learning* (pp. 299-301). Hershey, PA: Idea Group Reference.

Berg, G.A. (2005b). Community colleges in America and distance learning. In C. Howard, J.V. Boettcher, L. Justice, K. Schenk, P.L. Rogers, & G.A. Berg (Eds.), *Encyclopedia of distance learning* (pp. 302-303). Hershey, PA: Idea Group Reference.

Berg, G.A. (2005c). Economic models for distance learning. In C. Howard, J.V. Boettcher, L. Justice, K. Schenk, P.L. Rogers, & G.A. Berg (Eds.), *Encyclopedia of distance learning* (pp. 696-698). Hershey, PA: Idea Group Reference.

Berg, G.A. (2005d). Educational technology and learning theory. In C. Howard, J.V. Boettcher, L. Justice, K. Schenk, P.L. Rogers, & G.A. Berg (Eds.), *Encyclopedia of distance learning* (pp. 712-716). Hershey, PA: Idea Group Reference.

Berg, G.A. (2005e). Film narrative and computer-interface design. In C. Howard, J.V. Boettcher, L. Justice, K. Schenk, P.L. Rogers, & G.A. Berg (Eds.), *Encyclopedia of distance learning* (pp. 941-943). Hershey, PA: Idea Group Reference.

Berg, G.A. (2005f). Social or group learning theories. In C. Howard, J.V. Boettcher, L. Justice, K. Schenk, P.L. Rogers, & G.A. Berg (Eds.), *Encyclopedia of distance learning* (pp. 1630-1633). Hershey, PA: Idea Group Reference.

Berg, G.A. (2005g). The Open University, United Kingdom. In C. Howard, J.V. Boettcher, L. Justice, K. Schenk, P.L. Rogers, & G.A. Berg (Eds.), *Encyclopedia of distance learning* (pp. 1430-1432). Hershey, PA: Idea Group Reference.

Berg, G.A. (2005h). Workplace learning on the Internet. In C. Howard, J.V. Boettcher, L. Justice, K. Schenk, P.L. Rogers, & G.A. Berg (Eds.), *Encyclopedia of distance learning* (pp. 2064-2066). Hershey, PA: Idea Group Reference.

Bertino, E., Squicciarini, A.C., & Ferrari, E. (2006). Sanctioning mechanisms in virtual communities. In S. Dasgupta (Ed.), *Encyclopedia of virtual communities and technologies* (pp. 409-413). Hershey, PA: Idea Group Reference.

Berztiss, A.T. (2006a). Capability maturity. In D. Schwartz (Ed.), *Encyclopedia of knowledge management* (pp. 24-29). Hershey, PA: Idea Group Reference.

Berztiss, A.T. (2006b). Workflow systems and knowledge management. In D. Schwartz (Ed.), *Encyclopedia of knowledge management* (pp. 892-897). Hershey, PA: Idea Group Reference.

Beulen, E. (2005). Governance in IT outsourcing partnerships. In M. Khosrow-Pour (Ed.), *Encyclopedia of information science and technology* (pp. 1299-1304). Hershey, PA: Idea Group Reference.

Beuschel, W., Gaiser, B., & Draheim, S. (2005). Informal communication in virtual learning environments. In C. Howard, J.V. Boettcher, L. Justice, K. Schenk, P.L. Rogers, & G.A. Berg (Eds.), *Encyclopedia of distance learning* (pp. 1076-1081). Hershey, PA: Idea Group Reference.

Bevan, N. (2006). International Standards for HCI. In C. Ghaoui (Ed.), *Encyclopedia of human computer interaction* (pp. 362-372). Hershey, PA: Idea Group Reference.

Benyon, D. (2006). Information Space. In C. Ghaoui (Ed.), *Encyclopedia of human computer interaction* (pp. 344-347). Hershey, PA: Idea Group Reference

Beynon, M.J. (2005a). Using dempster-shafer theory in data mining. In J. Wang (Ed.), *Encyclopedia of data warehousing and mining* (pp. 1166-1170). Hershey, PA: Idea Group Reference.

Beynon, M.J. (2005b). Utilizing fuzzy decision trees in decision making. In J. Wang (Ed.), *Encyclopedia of data warehousing and mining* (pp. 1175-1180). Hershey, PA: Idea Group Reference.

Bickel, S., & Scheffer, T. (2005). Mining e-mail data. In J. Wang (Ed.), *Encyclopedia of data warehousing and mining* (pp. 768-772). Hershey, PA: Idea Group Reference.

Bieber, M., Shen, J., Wu, D., & Hiltz, S.R. (2005). Participatory learning approach. In C. Howard, J.V. Boettcher, L. Justice, K. Schenk, P.L. Rogers, & G.A. Berg (Eds.), *Encyclopedia of distance learning* (pp. 1467-1472). Hershey, PA: Idea Group Reference.

Blackmore, C., van Deurzen, E., & Tantam, D. (2006). E-learning vs. traditional teaching methods. In S. Dasgupta (Ed.), *Encyclopedia of virtual communities and technologies* (pp. 174-178). Hershey, PA: Idea Group Reference.

Blandin, B. (2005). Usability evaluation of online learning programs. In M. Khosrow-Pour (Ed.), *Encyclopedia of information science and technology* (pp. 2934-2938). Hershey, PA: Idea Group Reference.

Blecker, T. (2006a). Internet technologies in factory automation. In M. Khosrow-Pour (Ed.), *Encyclopedia of e-commerce, e-government, and mobile commerce* (pp. 678-683). Hershey, PA: Idea Group Reference.

Blecker, T. (2006b). Product configuration systems. In M. Khosrow-Pour (Ed.), *Encyclopedia of e-commerce, e-government, and mobile commerce* (pp. 941-947). Hershey, PA: Idea Group Reference.

Blecker, T., & Abdelkafi, N. (2006). Multi-agent system for Web-based customization. In M. Khosrow-Pour (Ed.), *Encyclopedia of e-commerce, e-government, and mobile commerce* (pp. 811-816). Hershey, PA: Idea Group Reference.

Blecker, T., & Graf, G. (2006). Web-Based Human Machine Interaction in Manufacturing. In C. Ghaoui (Ed.), *Encyclopedia of human computer interaction* (pp. 722-728). Hershey, PA: Idea Group Reference.

Blicker, L. (2005). Evaluating quality in the online classroom. In C. Howard, J.V. Boettcher, L. Justice, K. Schenk, P.L. Rogers, & G.A. Berg (Eds.), *Encyclopedia of distance learning* (pp. 882-890). Hershey, PA: Idea Group Reference.

Blignaut, P., Burger, A., McDonald, T., & Tolmie, J. (2005). Computer attitude and anxiety. In M. Khosrow-Pour (Ed.), *Encyclopedia of information science and technology* (pp. 495-501). Hershey, PA: Idea Group Reference.

Blomqvist, K. (2005). Trust in technology partnerships. In M. Khosrow-Pour (Ed.), *Encyclopedia of information science and technology* (pp. 2897-2901). Hershey, PA: Idea Group Reference.

Boateng, B.A., & Boateng, K. (2006a). Open source IMs for management and e-business applications. In M. Khosrow-Pour (Ed.), *Encyclopedia of e-commerce, e-government, and mobile commerce* (pp. 890-894). Hershey, PA: Idea Group Reference.

Boateng, K., & Boateng, B.A. (2006b). Open source community portals for e-government. In M. Khosrow-Pour (Ed.), *Encyclopedia of e-commerce, e-government, and mobile commerce* (pp. 884-889). Hershey, PA: Idea Group Reference.

Bober, M.J. (2005). Ensuring quality in technology-focused professional development. In C. Howard, J.V. Boettcher, L. Justice, K. Schenk, P.L. Rogers, & G.A. Berg (Eds.), *Encyclopedia of distance learning* (pp. 845-852). Hershey, PA: Idea Group Reference.

Bochicchio, M., & Fiore, N. (2005). Hyper video for distance learning. In M. Khosrow-Pour (Ed.), *Encyclopedia of information science and technology* (pp. 1361-1366). Hershey, PA: Idea Group Reference.

Bodomo, A. (2005a). Constructing knowledge through online bulletin board discussions. In C. Howard, J.V. Boettcher, L. Justice, K. Schenk, P.L. Rogers, & G.A. Berg (Eds.), *Encyclopedia of distance learning* (pp. 386-393). Hershey, PA: Idea Group Reference.

Bodomo, A. (2005b). Interaction in Web-based learning. In C. Howard, J.V. Boettcher, L. Justice, K.

Schenk, P.L. Rogers, & G.A. Berg (Eds.), *Encyclopedia of distance learning* (pp. 1130-1139). Hershey, PA: Idea Group Reference.

Boechler, P.M. (2006a). Supporting Navigation and Learning in Educational Hypermedia. In C. Ghaoui (Ed.), *Encyclopedia of human computer interaction* (pp. 574-578). Hershey, PA: Idea Group Reference.

Boechler, P.M. (2006b). Understanding Cognitive Processes in Educational Hypermedia. In C. Ghaoui (Ed.), *Encyclopedia of human computer interaction* (pp. 648-651). Hershey, PA: Idea Group Reference.

Boersma, K., & Kingma, S. (2006). Intranet and organizational learning. In D. Schwartz (Ed.), *Encyclopedia of knowledge management* (pp. 305-310). Hershey, PA: Idea Group Reference.

Boettcher, J.V. (2005a). Design levels for distance and online learning. In M. Khosrow-Pour (Ed.), *Encyclopedia of information science and technology* (pp. 802-809). Hershey, PA: Idea Group Reference.

Boettcher, J.V. (2005b). Online learning programs. In C. Howard, J.V. Boettcher, L. Justice, K. Schenk, P.L. Rogers, & G.A. Berg (Eds.), *Encyclopedia of distance learning* (pp. 1382-1389). Hershey, PA: Idea Group Reference.

Bolisani, E., Scarso, E., & Di Biagi, M. (2006). Economic issues of online professional communities. In E. Coakes & S. Clarke (Eds.), *Encyclopedia of communities of practice in information and knowledge management* (pp. 148-156). Hershey, PA: Idea Group Reference.

Bonk, C.J., Wisher, R.A., & Lee, J.-Y. (2005). Perspectives on e-learning. In C. Howard, J.V. Boettcher, L. Justice, K. Schenk, P.L. Rogers, & G.A. Berg (Eds.), *Encyclopedia of distance learning* (pp. 1488-1493). Hershey, PA: Idea Group Reference.

Boonstra, A., & de Brock, B. (2006). Identifying e-business options. In M. Khosrow-Pour (Ed.), *Encyclopedia of e-commerce, e-government, and mobile commerce* (pp. 580-586). Hershey, PA: Idea Group Reference.

Borbora, S., & Dutta, M.K. (2005). ICT in regional development. In S. Marshall, W. Taylor, & X. Yu (Eds.), *Encyclopedia of developing regional communities with information and communication technology* (pp. 387-392). Hershey, PA: Idea Group Reference.

Borchers, A. (2005). Media and personal involvement in the perceptions of data quality. In M. Khosrow-Pour (Ed.), *Encyclopedia of information science and technology* (pp. 1917-1921). Hershey, PA: Idea Group Reference.

Borders, A.L., & Johnston, W.J. (2005). eCRM in a manufacturing environment. In M. Khosrow-Pour (Ed.), *Encyclopedia of information science and technology* (pp. 966-971). Hershey, PA: Idea Group Reference.

Boros, E., Hammer, P.L., & Ibaraki, T. (2005). Logical analysis of data. In J. Wang (Ed.), *Encyclopedia of data warehousing and mining* (pp. 689-692). Hershey, PA: Idea Group Reference.

Bose, I. (2005). Data mining in diabetes diagnosis and detection. In J. Wang (Ed.), *Encyclopedia of data warehousing and mining* (pp. 257-261). Hershey, PA: Idea Group Reference.

Bose, I., Ping, W., Shan, M.W., Shing, W.K., Shing, Y.Y., Tin, C.L., et al. (2005). Databases for mobile applications. In L. Rivero, J. Doorn, & V. Ferraggine (Eds.), *Encyclopedia of database technologies and applications* (pp. 162-169). Hershey, PA: Idea Group Reference.

Boulicaut, J.-F. (2005). Condensed representations for data mining. In J. Wang (Ed.), *Encyclopedia of data warehousing and mining* (pp. 207-211). Hershey, PA: Idea Group Reference.

Bounif, H. (2005). Data model versioning and database evolution. In L. Rivero, J. Doorn, & V. Ferraggine (Eds.), *Encyclopedia of database technologies and applications* (pp. 110-115). Hershey, PA: Idea Group Reference.

Bourguet, M.-L. (2006). An Overview of Multimodal Interaction Techniques and Applications. In C. Ghaoui (Ed.), *Encyclopedia of human computer interaction* (pp. 451-456). Hershey, PA: Idea Group Reference.

Boyd, G.M., & Zhang, D. (2005). Re-enacted affiliative meanings and "branding" in open and distance education. In C. Howard, J.V. Boettcher, L. Justice, K. Schenk, P.L. Rogers, & G.A. Berg (Eds.), *Encyclopedia of distance learning* (pp. 1552-1556). Hershey, PA: Idea Group Reference.

Bozanis, P. (2006). Indexing mobile objects. In M. Khosrow-Pour (Ed.), *Encyclopedia of e-commerce, e-government, and mobile commerce* (pp. 594-599). Hershey, PA: Idea Group Reference.

Brabston, M.E. (2005). Strategic vision for information technology. In M. Khosrow-Pour (Ed.), *Encyclopedia of information science and technology* (pp. 2643-2647). Hershey, PA: Idea Group Reference.

Brace, T., & Berge, Z. (2006). Strategic planning for distance training. In M. Khosrow-Pour (Ed.), *Encyclopedia of e-commerce, e-government, and mobile commerce* (pp. 1053-1057). Hershey, PA: Idea Group Reference.

Bradley, J. (2005). Balancing risks and rewards of ERP. In M. Khosrow-Pour (Ed.), *Encyclopedia of information science and technology* (pp. 205-210). Hershey, PA: Idea Group Reference.

Bradley, R.V., Mbarika, V., Sankar, C.S., & Raju, P.K. (2005). Multimedia instructional materials in MIS classrooms. In M. Pagani (Ed.), *Encyclopedia of multimedia technology and networking* (pp. 717-723). Hershey, PA: Idea Group Reference.

Brady, F. (2005). Workarounds and security. In S. Marshall, W. Taylor, & X. Yu (Eds.), *Encyclopedia of developing regional communities with information and communication technology* (pp. 741-744). Hershey, PA: Idea Group Reference.

Brandon, D. (2005a). Object-oriented software reuse in business systems. In M. Khosrow-Pour (Ed.), *Encyclopedia of information science and technology* (pp. 2156-2160). Hershey, PA: Idea Group Reference.

Brandon, D. (2005b). Project management in graduate education. In M. Khosrow-Pour (Ed.), *Encyclopedia of information science and technology* (pp. 2348-2352). Hershey, PA: Idea Group Reference.

Brandon, D. Jr. (2005a). Business model application of UML stereotypes. In M. Khosrow-Pour (Ed.), *Encyclopedia of information science and technology* (pp. 325-330). Hershey, PA: Idea Group Reference.

Brandon, D. Jr. (2005b). Globalization of consumer e-commerce. In M. Khosrow-Pour (Ed.), *Encyclopedia of information science and technology* (pp. 1293-1298). Hershey, PA: Idea Group Reference.

Braun, P. (2005a). Action research methods. In S. Marshall, W. Taylor, & X. Yu (Eds.), *Encyclopedia of developing regional communities with information and communication technology* (pp. 1-5). Hershey, PA: Idea Group Reference.

Braun, P. (2005b). E-commerce and small tourism firms. In S. Marshall, W. Taylor, & X. Yu (Eds.), *Encyclopedia of developing regional communities with information and communication technology* (pp. 233-238). Hershey, PA: Idea Group Reference.

Braun, P. (2005c). Regional tourism and the Internet in Australia. In S. Marshall, W. Taylor, & X. Yu (Eds.), *Encyclopedia of developing regional communities with information and communication technology* (pp. 603-607). Hershey, PA: Idea Group Reference.

Braun, P. (2006). Linking small business networks with innovation. In E. Coakes & S. Clarke (Eds.), *Encyclopedia of communities of practice in information and knowledge management* (pp. 346-352). Hershey, PA: Idea Group Reference.

Breault, J.L. (2005). Diabetic data warehouses. In J. Wang (Ed.), *Encyclopedia of data warehousing and mining* (pp. 359-363). Hershey, PA: Idea Group Reference.

Bretschneider, T.R., & Kao, O. (2005). Content-based image retrieval. In J. Wang (Ed.), *Encyclopedia of data warehousing and mining* (pp. 212-216). Hershey, PA: Idea Group Reference.

Brewer, J.L. (2005). Project management best practices to increase success. In M. Khosrow-Pour (Ed.), *Encyclopedia of information science and technology* (pp. 2335-2340). Hershey, PA: Idea Group Reference.

Bridges, E., Goldsmith, R.E., & Hofacker, C.F. (2006). Businesses and consumers as online customers. In M. Khosrow-Pour (Ed.), *Encyclopedia of e-commerce, e-government, and mobile commerce* (pp. 83-88). Hershey, PA: Idea Group Reference.

Brindley, C. (2006). Gambling over the Internet. In M. Khosrow-Pour (Ed.), *Encyclopedia of e-commerce, e-government, and mobile commerce* (pp. 525-529). Hershey, PA: Idea Group Reference.

Brock, J.K.-U., & Zhou, Y.J. (2006). MNE knowledge management across borders and ICT. In D. Schwartz (Ed.), *Encyclopedia of knowledge management* (pp. 635). Hershey, PA: Idea Group Reference.

Brown, L.A. (2006). Technology-based models. In S. Dasgupta (Ed.), *Encyclopedia of virtual communities and technologies* (pp. 434-438). Hershey, PA: Idea Group Reference.

Brown, M.L., & Kros, J.F. (2005). Imprecise data and the data mining process. In J. Wang (Ed.), *Encyclopedia of data warehousing and mining* (pp. 593-598). Hershey, PA: Idea Group Reference.

Bruha, I. (2005). Rule qualities and knowledge combination for decision-making. In J. Wang (Ed.), *Encyclopedia of data warehousing and mining* (pp. 984-989). Hershey, PA: Idea Group Reference.

Bryde, D., & Petie, D. (2005). Sponsorship in IT project management. In M. Khosrow-Pour (Ed.), *Encyclopedia of information science and technology* (pp. 2597-2601). Hershey, PA: Idea Group Reference.

Buccafurri, F., & Lax, G. (2005). Approximate range queries by histograms in OLAP. In J. Wang (Ed.), *Encyclopedia of data warehousing and mining* (pp. 49-53). Hershey, PA: Idea Group Reference.

Buccella, A., Cechich, A., & Brisaboa, N.R. (2005). Ontology-based data integration. In L. Rivero, J.

Doorn, & V. Ferraggine (Eds.), *Encyclopedia of database technologies and applications* (pp. 450-456). Hershey, PA: Idea Group Reference.

Buchanan, E. (2005). Library services for distance education students in higher education. In C. Howard, J.V. Boettcher, L. Justice, K. Schenk, P.L. Rogers, & G.A. Berg (Eds.), *Encyclopedia of distance learning* (pp. 1261-1264). Hershey, PA: Idea Group Reference.

Buche, M.W., & Vician, C. (2005). A unified information security management plan. In M. Pagani (Ed.), *Encyclopedia of multimedia technology and networking* (pp. 993-1000). Hershey, PA: Idea Group Reference.

Buchholz, W. (2006). Ontology. In D. Schwartz (Ed.), *Encyclopedia of knowledge management* (pp. 694). Hershey, PA: Idea Group Reference.

Buehrer, D.J. (2005). Organizing multimedia objects by using class algebra. In M. Khosrow-Pour (Ed.), *Encyclopedia of information science and technology* (pp. 2243-2247). Hershey, PA: Idea Group Reference.

Burgess, S. (2005). Issues and challenges for IT in small business. In M. Khosrow-Pour (Ed.), *Encyclopedia of information science and technology* (pp. 1692-1696). Hershey, PA: Idea Group Reference.

Burgstahler, S. (2005a). Creating opportunities and barriers in distance learning courses. In C. Howard, J.V. Boettcher, L. Justice, K. Schenk, P.L. Rogers, & G.A. Berg (Eds.), *Encyclopedia of distance learning* (pp. 475-480). Hershey, PA: Idea Group Reference.

Burgstahler, S. (2005b). Web-based distance learning and the second digital divide. In M. Khosrow-Pour (Ed.), *Encyclopedia of information science and technology* (pp. 3079-3084). Hershey, PA: Idea Group Reference.

Burke, M., Levin, B.L., & Hanson, A. (2005). Online academic libraries and distance learning. In M. Khosrow-Pour (Ed.), *Encyclopedia of information science and technology* (pp. 2199-2202). Hershey, PA: Idea Group Reference.

Burn, J.M., & Ash, C.G. (2006). Dynamic planning models for e-business strategy. In M. Khosrow-Pour (Ed.), *Encyclopedia of e-commerce, e-government, and mobile commerce* (pp. 240-246). Hershey, PA: Idea Group Reference.

Burr, T. (2005a). Cluster analysis in fitting mixtures of curves. In J. Wang (Ed.), *Encyclopedia of data warehousing and mining* (pp. 154-158). Hershey, PA: Idea Group Reference.

Burr, T. (2005b). Methods for choosing clusters in phylogenetic trees. In J. Wang (Ed.), *Encyclopedia of data warehousing and mining* (pp. 722-727). Hershey, PA: Idea Group Reference.

Burrage, P., & Pelton, L.F. (2005). The Beam Analysis Tool (BAT). In C. Howard, J.V. Boettcher, L. Justice, K. Schenk, P.L. Rogers, & G.A. Berg (Eds.), *Encyclopedia of distance learning* (pp. 120-126). Hershey, PA: Idea Group Reference.

Bursa, D., Justice, L., & Kessler, M. (2005). U.S. disabilities legislation affecting electronic and information technology. In M. Khosrow-Pour (Ed.), *Encyclopedia of information science and technology* (pp. 2916-2920). Hershey, PA: Idea Group Reference.

Bussler, C. (2005a). Business-to-business integration. In L. Rivero, J. Doorn, & V. Ferraggine (Eds.), *Encyclopedia of database technologies and applications* (pp. 54-58). Hershey, PA: Idea Group Reference.

Bussler, C. (2005b). Enterprise application integration. In L. Rivero, J. Doorn, & V. Ferraggine (Eds.), *Encyclopedia of database technologies and applications* (pp. 229-232). Hershey, PA: Idea Group Reference.

Butcher-Powell, L.M. (2005). Telework information security. In M. Pagani (Ed.), *Encyclopedia of multimedia technology and networking* (pp. 951-956). Hershey, PA: Idea Group Reference.

Butler, S.M., & Webb, G.I. (2005). Mining group differences. In J. Wang (Ed.), *Encyclopedia of data warehousing and mining* (pp. 795-799). Hershey, PA: Idea Group Reference.

Butler, T., & Murphy, C. (2006). Work and knowledge. In D. Schwartz (Ed.), *Encyclopedia of knowledge management* (pp. 884-891). Hershey, PA: Idea Group Reference.

Byl, P.B., & Toleman, M. (2005). Engineering emotionally intelligent agents. In M. Khosrow-Pour (Ed.), *Encyclopedia of information science and technology* (pp. 1052-1056). Hershey, PA: Idea Group Reference.

Cadot, M., Maj, J.B., & Ziade, T. (2005). Association rules and statistics. In J. Wang (Ed.), *Encyclopedia of data warehousing and mining* (pp. 74-77). Hershey, PA: Idea Group Reference.

Caelli, T. (2005). Mining images for structure. In J. Wang (Ed.), *Encyclopedia of data warehousing and mining* (pp. 805-809). Hershey, PA: Idea Group Reference.

Cagiltay, K., Bichelmeyer, B.A., Evans, M.A., Paulus, T.M., & An, J.S. (2005). Collaboration among multicultural virtual teams. In C. Howard, J.V. Boettcher, L. Justice, K. Schenk, P.L. Rogers, & G.A. Berg (Eds.), *Encyclopedia of distance learning* (pp. 256-263). Hershey, PA: Idea Group Reference.

Calvo, R.W., de Luigi, F., Haastrup, P., & Maniezzo, V. (2005). Distributed data management of daily car pooling problems. In J. Wang (Ed.), *Encyclopedia of data warehousing and mining* (pp. 408-412). Hershey, PA: Idea Group Reference.

Calzonetti, J.A., & deChambeau, A. (2006). Telework and the academic librarian. In S. Dasgupta (Ed.), *Encyclopedia of virtual communities and technologies* (pp. 439-442). Hershey, PA: Idea Group Reference.

Camarinha-Matos, L.M., & Ferrada, F. (2006). Supporting a virtual community for the elderly. In S. Dasgupta (Ed.), *Encyclopedia of virtual communities and technologies* (pp. 428-433). Hershey, PA: Idea Group Reference.

Cameron, A. (2005). National competition policy and broadband provision in Australia. In S. Marshall, W. Taylor, & X. Yu (Eds.), *Encyclopedia of developing regional communities with information and communication technology* (pp. 506-511). Hershey, PA: Idea Group Reference.

Camolesi, L. Jr., & Vieira, M.T.P. (2005). Database engineering focusing on modern dynamism crises. In L. Rivero, J. Doorn, & V. Ferraggine (Eds.), *Encyclopedia of database technologies and applications* (pp. 140-146). Hershey, PA: Idea Group Reference.

Campbell, D., & Berge, Z. (2005). Teaching style in the online classroom. In C. Howard, J.V. Boettcher, L. Justice, K. Schenk, P.L. Rogers, & G.A. Berg (Eds.), *Encyclopedia of distance learning* (pp. 1787-1797). Hershey, PA: Idea Group Reference.

Campbell, J. (2006). Investor empowerment or market manipulation in financial virtual communities. In S. Dasgupta (Ed.), *Encyclopedia of virtual communities and technologies* (pp. 296-301). Hershey, PA: Idea Group Reference.

Campbell, K. (2005). Learning portals as new academic spaces. In M. Khosrow-Pour (Ed.), *Encyclopedia of information science and technology* (pp. 1815-1819). Hershey, PA: Idea Group Reference.

Campos, J.C., & Harrison, M.D. (2006). Automated Deduction and Usability Reasoning. In C. Ghaoui (Ed.), *Encyclopedia of human computer interaction* (pp. 45-52). Hershey, PA: Idea Group Reference.

Cannataro, M., Cluet, S., Tradigo, G., Veltri, P., & Vodislav, D. (2005). Using views to query XML documents. In L. Rivero, J. Doorn, & V. Ferraggine (Eds.), *Encyclopedia of database technologies and applications* (pp. 729-735). Hershey, PA: Idea Group Reference.

Cannoy, S.D., & Iyer, L. (2006). Using hospital Web sites to enhance communication. In M. Khosrow-Pour (Ed.), *Encyclopedia of e-commerce, e-government, and mobile commerce* (pp. 1139-1145). Hershey, PA: Idea Group Reference.

Cannoy, S.D., & Salam, A.F. (2006). Information assurance in e-healthcare. In M. Khosrow-Pour (Ed.), *Encyclopedia of e-commerce, e-government, and mobile commerce* (pp. 600-607). Hershey, PA: Idea Group Reference.

Caramia, M., & Felici, G. (2005). Web mining in thematic search engines. In J. Wang (Ed.), *Encyclopedia of data warehousing and mining* (pp. 1201-1205). Hershey, PA: Idea Group Reference.

Cardoso, J. (2006). Semantics for e-commerce applications. In M. Khosrow-Pour (Ed.), *Encyclopedia of e-commerce, e-government, and mobile commerce* (pp. 979-984). Hershey, PA: Idea Group Reference.

Cardoso, R.C., & Freire, M.M. (2005). Security vulnerabilities and exposures in Internet systems and services. In M. Pagani (Ed.), *Encyclopedia of multimedia technology and networking* (pp. 910-916). Hershey, PA: Idea Group Reference.

Cargill, B.J. (2006a). Leadership issues within a community of practice. In E. Coakes & S. Clarke (Eds.), *Encyclopedia of communities of practice in information and knowledge management* (pp. 320-322). Hershey, PA: Idea Group Reference.

Cargill, B.J. (2006b). Team-work issues in virtual teams. In E. Coakes & S. Clarke (Eds.), *Encyclopedia of communities of practice in information and knowledge management* (pp. 529-531). Hershey, PA: Idea Group Reference.

Carillo, K., & Okoli, C. (2006). Open source software communities. In S. Dasgupta (Ed.), *Encyclopedia of virtual communities and technologies* (pp. 363-367). Hershey, PA: Idea Group Reference.

Carlsson, S.A. (2005). Critical realism in IS research. In M. Khosrow-Pour (Ed.), *Encyclopedia of information science and technology* (pp. 611-616). Hershey, PA: Idea Group Reference.

Carroll, J.M. (2005). Building educational technology partnerships through participatory design. In M. Khosrow-Pour (Ed.), *Encyclopedia of information science and technology* (pp. 307-311). Hershey, PA: Idea Group Reference.

Carroll, J.M., Neale, D.C., & Isenhour, P.L. (2005). Classroom critical incidents. In C. Howard, J.V.

Boettcher, L. Justice, K. Schenk, P.L. Rogers, & G.A. Berg (Eds.), *Encyclopedia of distance learning* (pp. 233-239). Hershey, PA: Idea Group Reference.

Carson, D. (2005). Developing regional tourism using information communications technology. In S. Marshall, W. Taylor, & X. Yu (Eds.), *Encyclopedia of developing regional communities with information and communication technology* (pp. 176-181). Hershey, PA: Idea Group Reference.

Carstens, D.S. (2005). Cultural barriers of human-computer interaction. In S. Marshall, W. Taylor, & X. Yu (Eds.), *Encyclopedia of developing regional communities with information and communication technology* (pp. 146-151). Hershey, PA: Idea Group Reference.

Cartelli, A. (2005a). Between tradition and innovation in ICT and teaching. In C. Howard, J.V. Boettcher, L. Justice, K. Schenk, P.L. Rogers, & G.A. Berg (Eds.), *Encyclopedia of distance learning* (pp. 159-165). Hershey, PA: Idea Group Reference.

Cartelli, A. (2005b). Open source software and information systems on the Web. In L. Rivero, J. Doorn, & V. Ferraggine (Eds.), *Encyclopedia of database technologies and applications* (pp. 463-468). Hershey, PA: Idea Group Reference.

Cartelli, A. (2006a). Communities of learners in paleography and ICT. In E. Coakes & S. Clarke (Eds.), *Encyclopedia of communities of practice in information and knowledge management* (pp. 43-48). Hershey, PA: Idea Group Reference.

Cartelli, A. (2006b). ICT, CoLs, CoPs and virtual communities. In S. Dasgupta (Ed.), *Encyclopedia of virtual communities and technologies* (pp. 248-252). Hershey, PA: Idea Group Reference.

Carton, F., & Adam, F. (2005). Recursive nature of the market for enterprise applications. In M. Khosrow-Pour (Ed.), *Encyclopedia of information science and technology* (pp. 2309-2413). Hershey, PA: Idea Group Reference.

Casado, E. (2005). Expanding data mining power with system dynamics. In M. Khosrow-Pour (Ed.), *Ency-*

*clopedia of information science and technology* (pp. 1155-1161). Hershey, PA: Idea Group Reference.

Castro, C.L., & Braga, A.P. (2006). Forecasting the stock market with ANNs and autonomous agents. In M. Khosrow-Pour (Ed.), *Encyclopedia of e-commerce, e-government, and mobile commerce* (pp. 520-524). Hershey, PA: Idea Group Reference.

Cavallaro, A. (2005). Universal multimedia access. In M. Pagani (Ed.), *Encyclopedia of multimedia technology and networking* (pp. 1001-1007). Hershey, PA: Idea Group Reference.

Cavanaugh, C. (2005). Distance education success factors. In M. Khosrow-Pour (Ed.), *Encyclopedia of information science and technology* (pp. 897-901). Hershey, PA: Idea Group Reference.

Cavanaugh, T. (2005). Online learning as a form of accomodation. In M. Khosrow-Pour (Ed.), *Encyclopedia of information science and technology* (pp. 2209-2213). Hershey, PA: Idea Group Reference.

Cecchini, S. (2005). Poverty, inequality and new technologies in Latin America. In S. Marshall, W. Taylor, & X. Yu (Eds.), *Encyclopedia of developing regional communities with information and communication technology* (pp. 569-575). Hershey, PA: Idea Group Reference.

Cepeda-Carrión, G. (2006). Competitive advantage of knowledge management. In D. Schwartz (Ed.), *Encyclopedia of knowledge management* (pp. 34-43). Hershey, PA: Idea Group Reference.

Cevenini, C. (2005). Legal issues of virtual organizations. In M. Khosrow-Pour (Ed.), *Encyclopedia of information science and technology* (pp. 1831-1833). Hershey, PA: Idea Group Reference.

Chakraborty, D., Chakraborty, G., & Shiratori, N. (2005). Multicast routing protocols, algorithms and its QoS extensions. In M. Khosrow-Pour (Ed.), *Encyclopedia of information science and technology* (pp. 2036-2041). Hershey, PA: Idea Group Reference.

Chakravarty, I., Mishra, N., Vatsa, M., Singh, R., & Gupta, P. (2005a). Off-line signature recognition. In

J. Wang (Ed.), *Encyclopedia of data warehousing and mining* (pp. 870-875). Hershey, PA: Idea Group Reference.

Chakravarty, I., Mishra, N., Vatsa, M., Singh, R., & Gupta, P. (2005b). Online signature recognition. In J. Wang (Ed.), *Encyclopedia of data warehousing and mining* (pp. 885-890). Hershey, PA: Idea Group Reference.

Chalmers, P.A. (2006). The Effect of Usability Guidelines on Web Site User Emotions. In C. Ghaoui (Ed.), *Encyclopedia of human computer interaction* (pp. 179-186). Hershey, PA: Idea Group Reference.

Chambel, T., & Guimarães, N. (2005). Learning styles and multiple intelligences. In C. Howard, J.V. Boettcher, L. Justice, K. Schenk, P.L. Rogers, & G.A. Berg (Eds.), *Encyclopedia of distance learning* (pp. 1237-1247). Hershey, PA: Idea Group Reference.

Champion, E.M. (2006a). Cultural presence. In S. Dasgupta (Ed.), *Encyclopedia of virtual communities and technologies* (pp. 95-101). Hershey, PA: Idea Group Reference.

Champion, E.M. (2006b). Virtual places. In S. Dasgupta (Ed.), *Encyclopedia of virtual communities and technologies* (pp. 556-561). Hershey, PA: Idea Group Reference.

Chan, C.K. (2005). Data mining for combining forecasts in inventory management. In M. Khosrow-Pour (Ed.), *Encyclopedia of information science and technology* (pp. 703-707). Hershey, PA: Idea Group Reference.

Chan, H.C., Tan, B.C.Y., & Tan, W.-P. (2005). One-to-one video-conferencing education. In M. Khosrow-Pour (Ed.), *Encyclopedia of information science and technology* (pp. 2194-2198). Hershey, PA: Idea Group Reference.

Chan, S.S., & Fang, X. (2005). Interface design issues for mobile commerce. In M. Khosrow-Pour (Ed.), *Encyclopedia of information science and technology* (pp. 1612-1616). Hershey, PA: Idea Group Reference.

Chan, S.S., & Kellen, V. (2006). Web services and B2B collaboration. In M. Khosrow-Pour (Ed.), *Encyclopedia of e-commerce, e-government, and mobile commerce* (pp. 1230-1235). Hershey, PA: Idea Group Reference.

Chan, T.S. (2005). Constructing a globalized e-commerce site. In M. Pagani (Ed.), *Encyclopedia of multimedia technology and networking* (pp. 96-101). Hershey, PA: Idea Group Reference.

Chan, Y.-K., & Chang, C.-C. (2005). Content-based retrieval concept. In M. Khosrow-Pour (Ed.), *Encyclopedia of information science and technology* (pp. 564-568). Hershey, PA: Idea Group Reference.

Chan, Y.-K., Ho, Y.-A., Wu, H.-C., & Chu, Y.-P. (2005). A duplicate Chinese document image retrieval system. In M. Khosrow-Pour (Ed.), *Encyclopedia of information science and technology* (pp. 1-6). Hershey, PA: Idea Group Reference.

Chand, A., & Leeming, D. (2005). Impact of PFnet services on sustainable rural development. In S. Marshall, W. Taylor, & X. Yu (Eds.), *Encyclopedia of developing regional communities with information and communication technology* (pp. 412-419). Hershey, PA: Idea Group Reference.

Chang, C.-H., & Hsu, C.-N. (2005). Learning information extraction rules for Web data mining. In J. Wang (Ed.), *Encyclopedia of data warehousing and mining* (pp. 678-683). Hershey, PA: Idea Group Reference.

Chang, J.-W. (2005). Structure- and content-based retrieval for XML documents. In M. Khosrow-Pour (Ed.), *Encyclopedia of information science and technology* (pp. 2662-2664). Hershey, PA: Idea Group Reference.

Chang, S.K., Deufemia, V., & Polese, G. (2005). Normalizing multimedia databases. In L. Rivero, J. Doorn, & V. Ferraggine (Eds.), *Encyclopedia of database technologies and applications* (pp. 408-412). Hershey, PA: Idea Group Reference.

Chapman, D. (2005a). Introduction to learning management systems. In C. Howard, J.V. Boettcher, L. Justice, K. Schenk, P.L. Rogers, & G.A. Berg (Eds.), *Encyclopedia of distance learning* (pp. 1149-1155). Hershey, PA: Idea Group Reference.

Chapman, D. (2005b). Learning management systems. In C. Howard, J.V. Boettcher, L. Justice, K. Schenk, P.L. Rogers, & G.A. Berg (Eds.), *Encyclopedia of distance learning* (pp. 1223-1230). Hershey, PA: Idea Group Reference.

Chatziantoniou, D., & Doukidis, G. (2005). Incorporating data stream analysis into decision support systems. In M. Khosrow-Pour (Ed.), *Encyclopedia of information science and technology* (pp. 1431-1439). Hershey, PA: Idea Group Reference.

Chávez, E., & Navarro, G. (2005). Metric databases. In L. Rivero, J. Doorn, & V. Ferraggine (Eds.), *Encyclopedia of database technologies and applications* (pp. 367-372). Hershey, PA: Idea Group Reference.

Chbeir, R. (2005). Efficient method for image indexing in medical application. In M. Pagani (Ed.), *Encyclopedia of multimedia technology and networking* (pp. 257-264). Hershey, PA: Idea Group Reference.

Chbeir, R., & Yetongnon, K. (2005). Novel indexing method of relations between salient objects. In M. Khosrow-Pour (Ed.), *Encyclopedia of information science and technology* (pp. 2141-2145). Hershey, PA: Idea Group Reference.

Chen, A. (2006). Dot net and J2EE for Web services. In M. Khosrow-Pour (Ed.), *Encyclopedia of e-commerce, e-government, and mobile commerce* (pp. 223-227). Hershey, PA: Idea Group Reference.

Chen, A.Y.-U., & McLeod, D. (2006). Collaborative filtering for information recommendation systems. In M. Khosrow-Pour (Ed.), *Encyclopedia of e-commerce, e-government, and mobile commerce* (pp. 118-123). Hershey, PA: Idea Group Reference.

Chen, C., & Lobo, N. (2006). Analyzing and Visualizing the Dynamics of Scientific Frontiers and Knowledge Diffusion. In C. Ghaoui (Ed.), *Encyclopedia of human computer interaction* (pp. 24-30). Hershey, PA: Idea Group Reference.

Chen, C., Toprani, K., & Lobo, N. (2006). Human Factors in the Development of Trend Detection and Tracking Techniques. In C. Ghaoui (Ed.), *Encyclopedia of human computer interaction* (pp. 273-279). Hershey, PA: Idea Group Reference.

Chen, C.C., & Yang, S.C. (2006). E-commerce and mobile commerce applications adoption. In M. Khosrow-Pour (Ed.), *Encyclopedia of e-commerce, e-government, and mobile commerce* (pp. 284-290). Hershey, PA: Idea Group Reference.

Chen, I. (2005). Behaviorism. In C. Howard, J.V. Boettcher, L. Justice, K. Schenk, P.L. Rogers, & G.A. Berg (Eds.), *Encyclopedia of distance learning* (pp. 127-147). Hershey, PA: Idea Group Reference.

Chen, J., Chen, T.-S., & Cheng, M.-W. (2005). A new block data hiding method for the binary image. In M. Pagani (Ed.), *Encyclopedia of multimedia technology and networking* (pp. 762-769). Hershey, PA: Idea Group Reference.

Chen, J., Chen, T.-S., Ma, K.-J., & Wang, P.-H. (2005). Digital watermarking based on neural network technology for grayscale images. In M. Pagani (Ed.), *Encyclopedia of multimedia technology and networking* (pp. 204-212). Hershey, PA: Idea Group Reference.

Chen, J.C.H., Holt, R.W., & Sun, D.B. (2005). Organization and management issues of end user computing. In M. Khosrow-Pour (Ed.), *Encyclopedia of information science and technology* (pp. 2230-2235). Hershey, PA: Idea Group Reference.

Chen, K. (2005). Information hiding, digital watermarking and steganography. In M. Pagani (Ed.), *Encyclopedia of multimedia technology and networking* (pp. 382-389). Hershey, PA: Idea Group Reference.

Chen, K., Sockel, H., & Falk, L.K. (2005). Usability assessment in mobile computing and commerce. In M. Pagani (Ed.), *Encyclopedia of multimedia technology and networking* (pp. 1014-1020). Hershey, PA: Idea Group Reference.

Chen, Q., Oppenheim, A., & Wang, D. (2005). Survival analysis and data mining. In J. Wang (Ed.), *Encyclopedia of data warehousing and mining* (pp. 1077-1082). Hershey, PA: Idea Group Reference.

Chen, R.C., Tsai, M.Y., & Hsieh, C.H. (2005). Similarity Web pages retrieval technologies on the Internet. In M. Khosrow-Pour (Ed.), *Encyclopedia of information science and technology* (pp. 2486-2491). Hershey, PA: Idea Group Reference.

Chen, S., Duan, Y., & Edwards, J.S. (2006). Inter-organisational knowledge transfer process model. In E. Coakes & S. Clarke (Eds.), *Encyclopedia of communities of practice in information and knowledge management* (pp. 239-245). Hershey, PA: Idea Group Reference.

Chen, S.Y., & Liu, X. (2005). Data mining in practice. In M. Khosrow-Pour (Ed.), *Encyclopedia of information science and technology* (pp. 723-728). Hershey, PA: Idea Group Reference.

Chen, Y. (2005a). Graph encoding and recursion computation. In M. Khosrow-Pour (Ed.), *Encyclopedia of information science and technology* (pp. 1309-1316). Hershey, PA: Idea Group Reference.

Chen, Y. (2005b). Path-oriented queries and tree inclusion problems. In L. Rivero, J. Doorn, & V. Ferraggine (Eds.), *Encyclopedia of database technologies and applications* (pp. 472-479). Hershey, PA: Idea Group Reference.

Chen, Y., & Lou, H. (2005). Behavioral perspective of groupware adoption. In M. Khosrow-Pour (Ed.), *Encyclopedia of information science and technology* (pp. 248-252). Hershey, PA: Idea Group Reference.

Chen, Y., & Shi, Y. (2005). Signature files and signature file construction. In L. Rivero, J. Doorn, & V. Ferraggine (Eds.), *Encyclopedia of database technologies and applications* (pp. 638-645). Hershey, PA: Idea Group Reference.

Chen, Y., Motiwalla, L., & Khan, M.R. (2005). DEA evaluation of performance of e-business initiatives. In J. Wang (Ed.), *Encyclopedia of data warehousing and mining* (pp. 349-352). Hershey, PA: Idea Group Reference.

Chen, Y.-S., Zhang, B., & Justis, B. (2005a). Data mining in franchise organizations. In M. Khosrow-Pour (Ed.), *Encyclopedia of information science and technology* (pp. 714-722). Hershey, PA: Idea Group Reference.

Chen, Y.-S., Zhang, B., & Justis, B. (2005b). Franchising and information technology. In M. Khosrow-Pour (Ed.), *Encyclopedia of information science and technology* (pp. 1218-1225). Hershey, PA: Idea Group Reference.

Chen, Z., Li, H., Kong, S.C.W., Hong, J., & Xu, Q. (2006). Process simulation for e-commerce systems. In M. Khosrow-Pour (Ed.), *Encyclopedia of e-commerce, e-government, and mobile commerce* (pp. 933-940). Hershey, PA: Idea Group Reference.

Cheng, R., & Prabhakar, S. (2005). Sensors, uncertainty models, and probabilistic queries. In L. Rivero, J. Doorn, & V. Ferraggine (Eds.), *Encyclopedia of database technologies and applications* (pp. 613-618). Hershey, PA: Idea Group Reference.

Chengalur-Smith, I.-S., Neely, M.P., & Tribunella, T. (2005). The information quality of databases. In L. Rivero, J. Doorn, & V. Ferraggine (Eds.), *Encyclopedia of database technologies and applications* (pp. 281-285). Hershey, PA: Idea Group Reference.

Chim, H. (2006). User trust in the BBS communities. In S. Dasgupta (Ed.), *Encyclopedia of virtual communities and technologies* (pp. 474-477). Hershey, PA: Idea Group Reference.

Chin, A.G. (2005). Incremental expansion of a distributed database systems. In M. Khosrow-Pour (Ed.), *Encyclopedia of information science and technology* (pp. 1440-1445). Hershey, PA: Idea Group Reference.

Ching, H.S., McNaught, C., & Poon, P.W.T. (2005). Effective technology-mediated education for adult Chinese learners. In C. Howard, J.V. Boettcher, L. Justice, K. Schenk, P.L. Rogers, & G.A. Berg (Eds.), *Encyclopedia of distance learning* (pp. 724-731). Hershey, PA: Idea Group Reference.

Cho, V. (2005). Time series data forecasting. In J. Wang (Ed.), *Encyclopedia of data warehousing and mining* (pp. 1125-1129). Hershey, PA: Idea Group Reference.

Chochliouros, I.P., & Spiliopoulou-Chochliourou, A.S. (2006). Exploiting public sector information through innovative e-government policies. In M. Khosrow-Pour (Ed.), *Encyclopedia of e-commerce, e-government, and mobile commerce* (pp. 508-513). Hershey, PA: Idea Group Reference.

Chochliouros, I.P., Spiliopoulou-Chochliourou, A.S., & Lalopoulos, G.K. (2005a). Dark optical fibre as a modern solution for broadband networked cities. In M. Pagani (Ed.), *Encyclopedia of multimedia technology and networking* (pp. 158-164). Hershey, PA: Idea Group Reference.

Chochliouros, I.P., Spiliopoulou-Chochliourou, A.S., & Lalopoulos, G.K. (2005b). Digital video broadcasting (DVB) applications. In M. Pagani (Ed.), *Encyclopedia of multimedia technology and networking* (pp. 197-203). Hershey, PA: Idea Group Reference.

Chochliouros, I.P., Spiliopoulou-Chochliourou, A.S., & Lalopoulos, G.K. (2005c). Local loop unbundling measures and policies in the European Union. In M. Pagani (Ed.), *Encyclopedia of multimedia technology and networking* (pp. 547-554). Hershey, PA: Idea Group Reference.

Chou, T.-C., Dyson, R.G., & Powell, P.L. (2005). Managing strategic IT investment decisions. In M. Khosrow-Pour (Ed.), *Encyclopedia of information science and technology* (pp. 1875-1879). Hershey, PA: Idea Group Reference.

Choudhary, B. (2005). Effective learning through optimum distance among team members. In M. Khosrow-Pour (Ed.), *Encyclopedia of information science and technology* (pp. 976-979). Hershey, PA: Idea Group Reference.

Chroust, G. (2006). Motivation in Component-Based Software Development. In C. Ghaoui (Ed.), *Encyclopedia of human computer interaction* (pp. 414-421). Hershey, PA: Idea Group Reference.

Chu, F., & Wang, L. (2005). Biomedical data mining using RBF neural networks. In J. Wang (Ed.), *Encyclopedia of data warehousing and mining* (pp. 106-111). Hershey, PA: Idea Group Reference.

Chu, K.C. (2005). Interactive e-lab systems. In C. Howard, J.V. Boettcher, L. Justice, K. Schenk, P.L. Rogers, & G.A. Berg (Eds.), *Encyclopedia of distance learning* (pp. 1140-1144). Hershey, PA: Idea Group Reference.

Chu, K.C., & Lam, Q. (2006). Using an e-book for learning. In M. Khosrow-Pour (Ed.), *Encyclopedia of e-commerce, e-government, and mobile commerce* (pp. 1120-1125). Hershey, PA: Idea Group Reference.

Chua, A. (2006). The role of technology in supporting communities of practice. In E. Coakes & S. Clarke (Eds.), *Encyclopedia of communities of practice in information and knowledge management* (pp. 447-452). Hershey, PA: Idea Group Reference.

Chuang, T.-T. (2006). Virtual community sustainability. In S. Dasgupta (Ed.), *Encyclopedia of virtual communities and technologies* (pp. 533-538). Hershey, PA: Idea Group Reference.

Chuang, T.-T., Huang, W.W., & Zhang, Y.J. (2005). History and future development of group support systems. In M. Khosrow-Pour (Ed.), *Encyclopedia of information science and technology* (pp. 1338-1343). Hershey, PA: Idea Group Reference.

Chung, S., Jun, J., & McLeod, D. (2005). Incremental mining from news streams. In J. Wang (Ed.), *Encyclopedia of data warehousing and mining* (pp. 606-610). Hershey, PA: Idea Group Reference.

Chung, S.M., & Mangamuri, M. (2005). Mining association rules on a NCR teradata system. In J. Wang (Ed.), *Encyclopedia of data warehousing and mining* (pp. 746-751). Hershey, PA: Idea Group Reference.

Chyung, S.Y. (2005). Understanding different categories of attrition in distance education programs. In C. Howard, J.V. Boettcher, L. Justice, K. Schenk, P.L. Rogers, & G.A. Berg (Eds.), *Encyclopedia of distance learning* (pp. 1917-1925). Hershey, PA: Idea Group Reference.

Cilia, M.A. (2005). Active database management systems. In L. Rivero, J. Doorn, & V. Ferraggine (Eds.), *Encyclopedia of database technologies and applications* (pp. 1-4). Hershey, PA: Idea Group Reference.

Cirrincione, A. (2005). Multimedia technologies in education. In M. Pagani (Ed.), *Encyclopedia of multimedia technology and networking* (pp. 737-741). Hershey, PA: Idea Group Reference.

Clarebout, G., Elen, J., Lowyck, J., Van den Ende, J., & Van den Enden, E. (2005a). Tropical medicine open learning environment. In C. Howard, J.V. Boettcher, L. Justice, K. Schenk, P.L. Rogers, & G.A. Berg (Eds.), *Encyclopedia of distance learning* (pp. 1902-1906). Hershey, PA: Idea Group Reference.

Clarebout, G., Elen, J., Lowyck, J., Van den Ende, J., & Van den Enden, E. (2005b). Evaluation of an open learning environment. In M. Khosrow-Pour (Ed.), *Encyclopedia of information science and technology* (pp. 1134-1137). Hershey, PA: Idea Group Reference.

Clarke, I., III, & Flaherty, T. (2005). Portable portals for m-commerce. In M. Khosrow-Pour (Ed.), *Encyclopedia of information science and technology* (pp. 2293-2296). Hershey, PA: Idea Group Reference.

Clarke, S. (2006). Communities of practice and critical social theory. In E. Coakes & S. Clarke (Eds.), *Encyclopedia of communities of practice in information and knowledge management* (pp. 49-54). Hershey, PA: Idea Group Reference.

Clayton, J.F. (2006a). Education, the Internet, and the World Wide Web. In C. Ghaoui (Ed.), *Encyclopedia of human computer interaction* (pp. 175-178). Hershey, PA: Idea Group Reference.

Clayton, J.F. (2006b). Online Learning. In C. Ghaoui (Ed.), *Encyclopedia of human computer interaction* (pp. 435-440). Hershey, PA: Idea Group Reference.

Clegg, B., & Tan, B. (2006). E-business planning and analysis framework. In M. Khosrow-Pour (Ed.),

*Encyclopedia of e-commerce, e-government, and mobile commerce* (pp. 264-271). Hershey, PA: Idea Group Reference.

Close, A.G., Zinkhan, G.M., & Finney, R.Z. (2006). Cyber-identity theft. In M. Khosrow-Pour (Ed.), *Encyclopedia of e-commerce, e-government, and mobile commerce* (pp. 168-171). Hershey, PA: Idea Group Reference.

Coakes, E. (2006a). A comparison of the features of some CoP software. In E. Coakes & S. Clarke (Eds.), *Encyclopedia of communities of practice in information and knowledge management* (pp. 89-91). Hershey, PA: Idea Group Reference.

Coakes, E. (2006b). Communities of practice and technology support. In E. Coakes & S. Clarke (Eds.), *Encyclopedia of communities of practice in information and knowledge management* (pp. 63-65). Hershey, PA: Idea Group Reference.

Coakes, E., & Clarke, S. (2006a). Communities of practice. In D. Schwartz (Ed.), *Encyclopedia of knowledge management* (pp. 30-33). Hershey, PA: Idea Group Reference.

Coakes, E., & Clarke, S. (2006b). The concept of communities of practice. In E. Coakes & S. Clarke (Eds.), *Encyclopedia of communities of practice in information and knowledge management* (pp. 92-96). Hershey, PA: Idea Group Reference.

Coakes, E., & Willis, D. (2005). Communication management for large modules. In M. Khosrow-Pour (Ed.), *Encyclopedia of information science and technology* (pp. 464-471). Hershey, PA: Idea Group Reference.

Collis, B., & Moonen, J. (2005a). Collaborative learning in a contribution-oriented pedagogy. In C. Howard, J.V. Boettcher, L. Justice, K. Schenk, P.L. Rogers, & G.A. Berg (Eds.), *Encyclopedia of distance learning* (pp. 277-283). Hershey, PA: Idea Group Reference.

Collis, B., & Moonen, J. (2005b). Contribution-oriented pedagogy. In C. Howard, J.V. Boettcher, L. Justice, K. Schenk, P.L. Rogers, & G.A. Berg (Eds.),

*Encyclopedia of distance learning* (pp. 415-422). Hershey, PA: Idea Group Reference.

Colmenares, L.E., & Otieno, J.O. (2005). Critical success factors of ERP implementation. In M. Khosrow-Pour (Ed.), *Encyclopedia of information science and technology* (pp. 628-633). Hershey, PA: Idea Group Reference.

Colucci, S., Di Noia, T., Di Sciascio, E., Donini, F.M., & Mongiello, M. (2006). Description logic-based resource retrieval. In D. Schwartz (Ed.), *Encyclopedia of knowledge management* (pp. 105-114). Hershey, PA: Idea Group Reference.

Connaughton, S.L. (2005). Distanced leadership and multimedia. In M. Pagani (Ed.), *Encyclopedia of multimedia technology and networking* (pp. 226-232). Hershey, PA: Idea Group Reference.

Connell, N.A.D. (2006). Organisational storytelling. In D. Schwartz (Ed.), *Encyclopedia of knowledge management* (pp. 721-727). Hershey, PA: Idea Group Reference.

Conversano, C., & Siciliano, R. (2005). Statistical data editing. In J. Wang (Ed.), *Encyclopedia of data warehousing and mining* (pp. 1043-1047). Hershey, PA: Idea Group Reference.

Cook, J. (2005). Ethics of data mining. In J. Wang (Ed.), *Encyclopedia of data warehousing and mining* (pp. 454-458). Hershey, PA: Idea Group Reference.

Cooper, L.W. (2005). Successful strategies in online courses. In C. Howard, J.V. Boettcher, L. Justice, K. Schenk, P.L. Rogers, & G.A. Berg (Eds.), *Encyclopedia of distance learning* (pp. 1710-1715). Hershey, PA: Idea Group Reference.

Coratella, A., Felder, M., Hirsch, R., & Rodriguez, E. (2005). Mobile transaction models framework. In M. Khosrow-Pour (Ed.), *Encyclopedia of information science and technology* (pp. 1978-1983). Hershey, PA: Idea Group Reference.

Córdoba, J. (2006a). Boundaries in communities. In E. Coakes & S. Clarke (Eds.), *Encyclopedia of com-*

*munities of practice in information and knowledge management* (pp. 12-13). Hershey, PA: Idea Group Reference.

Córdoba, J. (2006b). Communities and evaluation of e-government services. In E. Coakes & S. Clarke (Eds.), *Encyclopedia of communities of practice in information and knowledge management* (pp. 32-34). Hershey, PA: Idea Group Reference.

Córdoba, J., & Robson, W. (2006). Understanding communities of practice to support collaborative research. In E. Coakes & S. Clarke (Eds.), *Encyclopedia of communities of practice in information and knowledge management* (pp. 558-564). Hershey, PA: Idea Group Reference.

Corral, A., & Vassilakopoulos, M. (2005). Query processing in spatial databases. In L. Rivero, J. Doorn, & V. Ferraggine (Eds.), *Encyclopedia of database technologies and applications* (pp. 511-516). Hershey, PA: Idea Group Reference.

Corral, K.L., LaBrie, R.C., & St. Louis, R.D. (2006). Document search practices. In D. Schwartz (Ed.), *Encyclopedia of knowledge management* (pp. 130-136). Hershey, PA: Idea Group Reference.

Correia, A.M.R., & Sarmento, A. (2005). Adult learners in higher education. In C. Howard, J.V. Boettcher, L. Justice, K. Schenk, P.L. Rogers, & G.A. Berg (Eds.), *Encyclopedia of distance learning* (pp. 72-78). Hershey, PA: Idea Group Reference.

Cosemans, A. (2005a). Connecting the unconnected in rural Ireland. In S. Marshall, W. Taylor, & X. Yu (Eds.), *Encyclopedia of developing regional communities with information and communication technology* (pp. 130-134). Hershey, PA: Idea Group Reference.

Cosemans, A. (2005b). Satellite technology in schools. In S. Marshall, W. Taylor, & X. Yu (Eds.), *Encyclopedia of developing regional communities with information and communication technology* (pp. 624-627). Hershey, PA: Idea Group Reference.

Costagliola, G., Di Martino, S., & Ferrucci, F. (2006). Vehicular telematics systems. In M. Khosrow-Pour (Ed.), *Encyclopedia of e-commerce, e-government, and mobile commerce* (pp. 1146-1151). Hershey, PA: Idea Group Reference.

Costagliola, G., Di Martino, S., Ferrucci, F., & Gravino, C. (2006). Web accessibility. In M. Khosrow-Pour (Ed.), *Encyclopedia of e-commerce, e-government, and mobile commerce* (pp. 1205-1210). Hershey, PA: Idea Group Reference.

Cottingham, M. (2005). Isoluminance contours for animated visualization. In M. Khosrow-Pour (Ed.), *Encyclopedia of information science and technology* (pp. 1685-1691). Hershey, PA: Idea Group Reference.

Craddock, P., & Duncan, P. (2005). Radio for social development. In S. Marshall, W. Taylor, & X. Yu (Eds.), *Encyclopedia of developing regional communities with information and communication technology* (pp. 598-602). Hershey, PA: Idea Group Reference.

Cragg, P.B., & Mills, A.M. (2005). Internet adoption by small firms. In M. Pagani (Ed.), *Encyclopedia of multimedia technology and networking* (pp. 467-474). Hershey, PA: Idea Group Reference.

Cragg, P.B., & Suraweera, T. (2005). IT management practices in small firms. In M. Pagani (Ed.), *Encyclopedia of multimedia technology and networking* (pp. 507-511). Hershey, PA: Idea Group Reference.

Cragg, P.B., & Todorova, N. (2005). Information systems strategic alignment in small firms. In M. Pagani (Ed.), *Encyclopedia of multimedia technology and networking* (pp. 411-416). Hershey, PA: Idea Group Reference.

Craig, R. (2005). Web initiatives and e-commerce strategy. In M. Khosrow-Pour (Ed.), *Encyclopedia of information science and technology* (pp. 3054-3069). Hershey, PA: Idea Group Reference.

Craig, R. (2006a). Developing a viable product for an emerging market. In M. Khosrow-Pour (Ed.), *Encyclopedia of e-commerce, e-government, and mobile commerce* (pp. 191-196). Hershey, PA: Idea Group Reference.

Craig, R. (2006b). Using failure to develop a successful business. In M. Khosrow-Pour (Ed.), *Encyclopedia of e-commerce, e-government, and mobile commerce* (pp. 1133-1138). Hershey, PA: Idea Group Reference.

Cremonini, M., Damiani, E., De Capitani di Vimercati, S., & Samarati, P. (2006). Security, privacy, and trust in mobile systems. In M. Khosrow-Pour (Ed.), *Encyclopedia of e-commerce, e-government, and mobile commerce* (pp. 973-978). Hershey, PA: Idea Group Reference.

Crichton, S. (2005). Intentional online learning plans. In S. Marshall, W. Taylor, & X. Yu (Eds.), *Encyclopedia of developing regional communities with information and communication technology* (pp. 463-467). Hershey, PA: Idea Group Reference.

Cristani, M., & Cuel, R. (2006). Domain ontologies. In D. Schwartz (Ed.), *Encyclopedia of knowledge management* (pp. 137-144). Hershey, PA: Idea Group Reference.

Croasdell, D.T., & Wang, Y.K. (2006). Virtue-Nets. In D. Schwartz (Ed.), *Encyclopedia of knowledge management* (pp. 876-883). Hershey, PA: Idea Group Reference.

Crossland, M.D. (2005). Geographic information systems as decision tools. In M. Khosrow-Pour (Ed.), *Encyclopedia of information science and technology* (pp. 1274-1277). Hershey, PA: Idea Group Reference.

Cruz, C., Nicolle, C., & Neveu, M. (2005). Using semantics to manage 3D scenes in Web platforms. In M. Pagani (Ed.), *Encyclopedia of multimedia technology and networking* (pp. 1027-1032). Hershey, PA: Idea Group Reference.

Cuadra, D., Martínez, P., & Castro, E. (2005). Relationship cardinality constraints in relational database design. In M. Khosrow-Pour (Ed.), *Encyclopedia of information science and technology* (pp. 2419-2424). Hershey, PA: Idea Group Reference.

Cuel, R., Bouquet, P., & Bonifacio, M. (2006). Distributed knowledge management. In D. Schwartz (Ed.), *Encyclopedia of knowledge management* (pp. 122-129). Hershey, PA: Idea Group Reference.

Cuevas, H.M., Fiore, S.M., Salas, E., & Bowers, C.A. (2005). Virtual teams as sociotechnical systems. In M. Khosrow-Pour (Ed.), *Encyclopedia of information science and technology* (pp. 3007-3012). Hershey, PA: Idea Group Reference.

Cumbie, B.A., Sankar, C.S., & Raju, P.K. (2006). Facilitating technology transfer among engineering community members. In E. Coakes & S. Clarke (Eds.), *Encyclopedia of communities of practice in information and knowledge management* (pp. 185-193). Hershey, PA: Idea Group Reference.

Cunha, M.M., & Putnik, G.D. (2005). Market of resources for agile/virtual enterprise integration. In M. Khosrow-Pour (Ed.), *Encyclopedia of information science and technology* (pp. 1891-1998). Hershey, PA: Idea Group Reference.

Cunningham, C., & Hu, X. (2005). Data mining medical digital libraries. In J. Wang (Ed.), *Encyclopedia of data warehousing and mining* (pp. 278-282). Hershey, PA: Idea Group Reference.

Curti, H.J. (2005). Free software and open source databases. In L. Rivero, J. Doorn, & V. Ferraggine (Eds.), *Encyclopedia of database technologies and applications* (pp. 246-249). Hershey, PA: Idea Group Reference.

Daassi, M., & Favier, M. (2006). Groupware and team aware. In S. Dasgupta (Ed.), *Encyclopedia of virtual communities and technologies* (pp. 228-231). Hershey, PA: Idea Group Reference.

Daassi, M., Daassi, C., & Favier, M. (2006). Integrating visualization techniques in groupware interfaces. In S. Dasgupta (Ed.), *Encyclopedia of virtual communities and technologies* (pp. 279-284). Hershey, PA: Idea Group Reference.

Dadashzadeh, M. (2005). Set comparison in relational query languages. In L. Rivero, J. Doorn, & V. Ferraggine (Eds.), *Encyclopedia of database technologies and applications* (pp. 624-631). Hershey, PA: Idea Group Reference.

Dai, H. (2005a). Inexact field learning approach for data mining. In J. Wang (Ed.), *Encyclopedia of data warehousing and mining* (pp. 611-614). Hershey, PA: Idea Group Reference.

Dai, H. (2005b). Software warehouse. In J. Wang (Ed.), *Encyclopedia of data warehousing and mining* (pp. 1033-1036). Hershey, PA: Idea Group Reference.

Dalcher, D. (2005). Methods for understanding IS failures. In M. Khosrow-Pour (Ed.), *Encyclopedia of information science and technology* (pp. 1931-1937). Hershey, PA: Idea Group Reference.

Daly, O., & Taniar, D. (2005a). Exception rules in data mining. In M. Khosrow-Pour (Ed.), *Encyclopedia of information science and technology* (pp. 1144-1148). Hershey, PA: Idea Group Reference.

Daly, O., & Taniar, D. (2005b). Negative association rules in data mining. In J. Wang (Ed.), *Encyclopedia of data warehousing and mining* (pp. 859-864). Hershey, PA: Idea Group Reference.

Damaskopoulos, P., & Gatautis, R. (2006). Developing virtual communities in transition economies. In S. Dasgupta (Ed.), *Encyclopedia of virtual communities and technologies* (pp. 125-130). Hershey, PA: Idea Group Reference.

Danalis, A. (2005). Web caching. In M. Khosrow-Pour (Ed.), *Encyclopedia of information science and technology* (pp. 3048-3053). Hershey, PA: Idea Group Reference.

Danenberg, J.O., & Chen, K. (2005). Web-based learning. In M. Pagani (Ed.), *Encyclopedia of multimedia technology and networking* (pp. 1084-1090). Hershey, PA: Idea Group Reference.

Daneshgar, F. (2005). Context-aware framework for ERP. In M. Khosrow-Pour (Ed.), *Encyclopedia of information science and technology* (pp. 569-572). Hershey, PA: Idea Group Reference.

Dang, L., & Embury, S.M. (2005). Hypothetical reasoning over databases. In M. Khosrow-Pour (Ed.), *Encyclopedia of information science and technology* (pp. 1367-1371). Hershey, PA: Idea Group Reference.

Danielson, D.R. (2006a). Usability Barriers. In C. Ghaoui (Ed.), *Encyclopedia of human computer interaction* (pp. 652-660). Hershey, PA: Idea Group Reference.

Danielson, D.R. (2006b). Usability Data Quality. In C. Ghaoui (Ed.), *Encyclopedia of human computer interaction* (pp. 661-667). Hershey, PA: Idea Group Reference.

Danielson, D.R. (2006c). Web Credibility. In C. Ghaoui (Ed.), *Encyclopedia of human computer interaction* (pp. 713-721). Hershey, PA: Idea Group Reference.

Dara-Abrams, B.P. (2006). Success of virtual environments. In S. Dasgupta (Ed.), *Encyclopedia of virtual communities and technologies* (pp. 424-427). Hershey, PA: Idea Group Reference.

Darbyshire, P., & Burgess, S. (2005). Tertiary education and the Internet. In M. Khosrow-Pour (Ed.), *Encyclopedia of information science and technology* (pp. 2788-2792). Hershey, PA: Idea Group Reference.

Darmont, J. (2005). Object database benchmarks. In M. Khosrow-Pour (Ed.), *Encyclopedia of information science and technology* (pp. 2146-2149). Hershey, PA: Idea Group Reference.

Das, G. (2005). Sampling methods in approximate query answering systems. In J. Wang (Ed.), *Encyclopedia of data warehousing and mining* (pp. 990-994). Hershey, PA: Idea Group Reference.

Dasgupta, P., Moser, L.E., & Melliar-Smith, P.M. (2006). Dynamic pricing for e-commerce. In M. Khosrow-Pour (Ed.), *Encyclopedia of e-commerce, e-government, and mobile commerce* (pp. 247-252). Hershey, PA: Idea Group Reference.

Dasgupta, S., & Chandrashekaran, R. (2005). Rotating banner advertisements on the World Wide Web. In M. Khosrow-Pour (Ed.), *Encyclopedia of information science and technology* (pp. 2438-2442). Hershey, PA: Idea Group Reference.

DaSilva, L.A. (2005). Challenges in quality of service for tomorrow's networks. In M. Khosrow-Pour (Ed.),

*Encyclopedia of information science and technology* (pp. 392-396). Hershey, PA: Idea Group Reference.

Dasso, A., & Funes, A. (2005). Formal methods in software engineering. In M. Khosrow-Pour (Ed.), *Encyclopedia of information science and technology* (pp. 1205-1211). Hershey, PA: Idea Group Reference.

David, M. (2005). Distance learning, telematics and rural social exclusion. In S. Marshall, W. Taylor, & X. Yu (Eds.), *Encyclopedia of developing regional communities with information and communication technology* (pp. 205-209). Hershey, PA: Idea Group Reference.

Davis, C.A., Jr., Borges, K.A.V., & Laender, A.H.F. (2005). Deriving spatial integrity constraints from geographic application schemas. In L. Rivero, J. Doorn, & V. Ferraggine (Eds.), *Encyclopedia of database technologies and applications* (pp. 176-183). Hershey, PA: Idea Group Reference.

Day, T. (2005). Online collaborative learning and learning styles. In C. Howard, J.V. Boettcher, L. Justice, K. Schenk, P.L. Rogers, & G.A. Berg (Eds.), *Encyclopedia of distance learning* (pp. 1339-1347). Hershey, PA: Idea Group Reference.

De Antonellis, V., Pozzi, G., Schreiber, F.A., Tanca, L., & Tosi, L. (2005). A Web-geographical information system to support territorial data integration. In M. Khosrow-Pour (Ed.), *Encyclopedia of information science and technology* (pp. 33-37). Hershey, PA: Idea Group Reference.

de Campos, L.M., Fernández-Luna, J.M., & Huete, J.F. (2005). Retrieving medical records using bayesian networks. In J. Wang (Ed.), *Encyclopedia of data warehousing and mining* (pp. 960-964). Hershey, PA: Idea Group Reference.

de Carvalho, A., Braga, A.P., & Ludermir, T. (2005). Credit card users' data mining. In M. Khosrow-Pour (Ed.), *Encyclopedia of information science and technology* (pp. 603-605). Hershey, PA: Idea Group Reference.

de Carvalho, R.B., & Ferreira, M.A.T. (2006). Knowledge management software. In D. Schwartz (Ed.),

*Encyclopedia of knowledge management* (pp. 410). Hershey, PA: Idea Group Reference.

de Castro, L.N. (2005). Natural computing. In M. Khosrow-Pour (Ed.), *Encyclopedia of information science and technology* (pp. 2080-2084). Hershey, PA: Idea Group Reference.

de Freitas, S., & Levene, M. (2006a). Spam. In C. Ghaoui (Ed.), *Encyclopedia of human computer interaction* (pp. 553-558). Hershey, PA: Idea Group Reference.

de Freitas, S., & Levene, M. (2006b). Wearable and Mobile Devices. In C. Ghaoui (Ed.), *Encyclopedia of human computer interaction* (pp. 706-712). Hershey, PA: Idea Group Reference.

De Lucia, A., Francese, R., & Scanniello, G. (2006). Distributed workflow management based on UML and Web services. In M. Khosrow-Pour (Ed.), *Encyclopedia of e-commerce, e-government, and mobile commerce* (pp. 271-222). Hershey, PA: Idea Group Reference.

de Medeiros Jr., A., Schneck de Paula Pessôa, M., & Barbin Laurindo, F.J. (2006). Evolution stages in Web applications. In M. Khosrow-Pour (Ed.), *Encyclopedia of e-commerce, e-government, and mobile commerce* (pp. 502-507). Hershey, PA: Idea Group Reference.

De Meo, P., Quattrone, G., Terracina, G., & Ursino, D. (2005). Agent-based mining of user profiles for e-services. In J. Wang (Ed.), *Encyclopedia of data warehousing and mining* (pp. 23-27). Hershey, PA: Idea Group Reference.

De Meo, P., Terracina, G., & Ursino, D. (2005). Interscheme properties' role in data warehouses. In J. Wang (Ed.), *Encyclopedia of data warehousing and mining* (pp. 647-652). Hershey, PA: Idea Group Reference.

de Souza Dias, D. (2005). Motivation for using microcomputers. In M. Khosrow-Pour (Ed.), *Encyclopedia of information science and technology* (pp. 2030-2035). Hershey, PA: Idea Group Reference.

de Souza, C.A., & Zwicker, R. (2005). Life cycle of ERP systems. In M. Khosrow-Pour (Ed.), *Encyclopedia of information science and technology* (pp. 1844-1849). Hershey, PA: Idea Group Reference.

De Troyer, O. (2005). Audience-driven Web site design. In M. Khosrow-Pour (Ed.), *Encyclopedia of information science and technology* (pp. 184-187). Hershey, PA: Idea Group Reference.

De Weaver, L.H. (2005). Applying for government grants for ICT in Australia. In S. Marshall, W. Taylor, & X. Yu (Eds.), *Encyclopedia of developing regional communities with information and communication technology* (pp. 16-20). Hershey, PA: Idea Group Reference.

De', R. (2005). Assessment of e-government projects. In S. Marshall, W. Taylor, & X. Yu (Eds.), *Encyclopedia of developing regional communities with information and communication technology* (pp. 35-39). Hershey, PA: Idea Group Reference.

De', R. (2006). Social resistance in virtual communities. In E. Coakes & S. Clarke (Eds.), *Encyclopedia of communities of practice in information and knowledge management* (pp. 487-493). Hershey, PA: Idea Group Reference.

Deb, S. (2005). Concepts of emergence index in image databases. In M. Khosrow-Pour (Ed.), *Encyclopedia of information science and technology* (pp. 519-522). Hershey, PA: Idea Group Reference.

Debbabi, S., & Baile, S. (2006). Creating telepresence in virtual mediated environments. In S. Dasgupta (Ed.), *Encyclopedia of virtual communities and technologies* (pp. 73-77). Hershey, PA: Idea Group Reference.

Decker, H. (2005). Principles of advanced database integrity checking. In M. Khosrow-Pour (Ed.), *Encyclopedia of information science and technology* (pp. 2297-2302). Hershey, PA: Idea Group Reference.

Dekker, D.J., & Hendriks, P.H.J. (2006). Social network analysis. In D. Schwartz (Ed.), *Encyclopedia of knowledge management* (pp. 818-825). Hershey, PA: Idea Group Reference.

Dell, L.A.B. (2005). Connecting K-12 schools in higher education. In C. Howard, J.V. Boettcher, L. Justice, K. Schenk, P.L. Rogers, & G.A. Berg (Eds.), *Encyclopedia of distance learning* (pp. 374-378). Hershey, PA: Idea Group Reference.

DeLorenzo, G.J. (2005). Ethnography to define requirements and data model. In J. Wang (Ed.), *Encyclopedia of data warehousing and mining* (pp. 459-463). Hershey, PA: Idea Group Reference.

Delve, J. (2005). Humanities data warehousing. In J. Wang (Ed.), *Encyclopedia of data warehousing and mining* (pp. 570-574). Hershey, PA: Idea Group Reference.

Demediuk, P. (2005). Government procurement ICT's impact on the sustainability of SMEs and regional communities. In S. Marshall, W. Taylor, & X. Yu (Eds.), *Encyclopedia of developing regional communities with information and communication technology* (pp. 321-324). Hershey, PA: Idea Group Reference.

den Braber, F., Lund, M.S., Stølen, K., & Vraalsen, F. (2005). Integrating security in the development process with UML. In M. Khosrow-Pour (Ed.), *Encyclopedia of information science and technology* (pp. 1560-1566). Hershey, PA: Idea Group Reference.

Denoyer, L., & Gallinari, P. (2005). Semi-structured document classification. In J. Wang (Ed.), *Encyclopedia of data warehousing and mining* (pp. 1015-1021). Hershey, PA: Idea Group Reference.

Denton, A. (2005). Clustering of time series data. In J. Wang (Ed.), *Encyclopedia of data warehousing and mining* (pp. 172-175). Hershey, PA: Idea Group Reference.

Denton, A., & Besemann, C. (2005). Association rule mining of relational data. In J. Wang (Ed.), *Encyclopedia of data warehousing and mining* (pp. 70-73). Hershey, PA: Idea Group Reference.

Derballa, V., & Pousttchi, K. (2006a). Mobile knowledge management. In D. Schwartz (Ed.), *Encyclopedia of knowledge management* (pp. 645). Hershey, PA: Idea Group Reference.

Derballa, V., & Pousttchi, K. (2006b). Mobile technology for knowledge management. In D. Schwartz (Ed.), *Encyclopedia of knowledge management* (pp. 651). Hershey, PA: Idea Group Reference.

Dery, K.F., & Samson, D.A. (2005). Alignment of information technology and human resources strategies. In M. Khosrow-Pour (Ed.), *Encyclopedia of information science and technology* (pp. 104-110). Hershey, PA: Idea Group Reference.

Deshpande, P.M., & Ramasamy, K. (2005). Data warehousing, multi-dimensional data models, and OLAP. In L. Rivero, J. Doorn, & V. Ferraggine (Eds.), *Encyclopedia of database technologies and applications* (pp. 134-139). Hershey, PA: Idea Group Reference.

Devedžić, V. (2006). Computer-Supported Collaborative Learning. In C. Ghaoui (Ed.), *Encyclopedia of human computer interaction* (pp. 105-111). Hershey, PA: Idea Group Reference.

Dexter, S. (2005). Principles to guide the integration and implementation of educational technology. In M. Khosrow-Pour (Ed.), *Encyclopedia of information science and technology* (pp. 2303-2307). Hershey, PA: Idea Group Reference.

Dhar, S. (2005). Mobile ad hoc network. In M. Pagani (Ed.), *Encyclopedia of multimedia technology and networking* (pp. 601-607). Hershey, PA: Idea Group Reference.

Dholakia, N., & Kshetri, N. (2005). From digital divide to digital dividend. In M. Khosrow-Pour (Ed.), *Encyclopedia of information science and technology* (pp. 1226-1230). Hershey, PA: Idea Group Reference.

Dholakia, N., Bang, J., Hamel, L., & Shin, S.-K. (2005). The CRM-KDD nexus. In M. Khosrow-Pour (Ed.), *Encyclopedia of information science and technology* (pp. 2803-2808). Hershey, PA: Idea Group Reference.

Dholakia, N., Zwick, D., & Pandya, A. (2005). Dataveillance and panoptic marketspaces. In L. Rivero, J. Doorn, & V. Ferraggine (Eds.), *Encyclopedia of database technologies and applications* (pp. 170-175). Hershey, PA: Idea Group Reference.

Di Giacomo, T., Joslin, C., & Magnenat-Thalmann, N. (2005). Production, delivery and playback of 3D graphics. In M. Pagani (Ed.), *Encyclopedia of multimedia technology and networking* (pp. 855-862). Hershey, PA: Idea Group Reference.

Diamadis, E.T., & Polyzos, G.C. (2005). Evaluating student learning in distance education. In C. Howard, J.V. Boettcher, L. Justice, K. Schenk, P.L. Rogers, & G.A. Berg (Eds.), *Encyclopedia of distance learning* (pp. 891-898). Hershey, PA: Idea Group Reference.

Diaper, D. (2006). Task Analysis at the Heart of Human-Computer Interaction. In C. Ghaoui (Ed.), *Encyclopedia of human computer interaction* (pp. 579-587). Hershey, PA: Idea Group Reference.

Díaz-Andrade, A. (2005). Journalism online in Peru. In M. Khosrow-Pour (Ed.), *Encyclopedia of information science and technology* (pp. 1742-1746). Hershey, PA: Idea Group Reference.

Dick, G.N. (2005). Academic workload in online courses. In C. Howard, J.V. Boettcher, L. Justice, K. Schenk, P.L. Rogers, & G.A. Berg (Eds.), *Encyclopedia of distance learning* (pp. 1-6). Hershey, PA: Idea Group Reference.

Dieng-Kuntz, R. (2006). Corporate semantic Webs. In D. Schwartz (Ed.), *Encyclopedia of knowledge management* (pp. 67-80). Hershey, PA: Idea Group Reference.

Díez-Higuera, J.-F., & Díaz-Pernas, F.-J. (2005). VRML-based system for a 3D virtual museum. In M. Khosrow-Pour (Ed.), *Encyclopedia of information science and technology* (pp. 3028-3035). Hershey, PA: Idea Group Reference.

Dingsøyr, T. (2006). Postmortem reviews. In D. Schwartz (Ed.), *Encyclopedia of knowledge management* (pp. 757-761). Hershey, PA: Idea Group Reference.

Diskin, Z. (2005a). Mathematics of generic specifications for model management, I. In L. Rivero, J. Doorn,

& V. Ferraggine (Eds.), *Encyclopedia of database technologies and applications* (pp. 351-358). Hershey, PA: Idea Group Reference.

Diskin, Z. (2005b). Mathematics of generic specifications for model management, II. In L. Rivero, J. Doorn, & V. Ferraggine (Eds.), *Encyclopedia of database technologies and applications* (pp. 359-366). Hershey, PA: Idea Group Reference.

Diskin, Z., & Kadish, B. (2005). Generic model management. In L. Rivero, J. Doorn, & V. Ferraggine (Eds.), *Encyclopedia of database technologies and applications* (pp. 258-265). Hershey, PA: Idea Group Reference.

Disterer, G. (2005). Impediments for knowledge sharing in professional service firms. In M. Khosrow-Pour (Ed.), *Encyclopedia of information science and technology* (pp. 1391-1396). Hershey, PA: Idea Group Reference.

Dixon, M.W., Karlsson, J.M., & McGill, T.J. (2005). Data communications and e-learning. In M. Khosrow-Pour (Ed.), *Encyclopedia of information science and technology* (pp. 685-690). Hershey, PA: Idea Group Reference.

Dixon, S. (2005). Audio analysis applications for music. In M. Khosrow-Pour (Ed.), *Encyclopedia of information science and technology* (pp. 188-196). Hershey, PA: Idea Group Reference.

Dobing, B., & Parsons, J. (2005). Use cases and the UML. In M. Khosrow-Pour (Ed.), *Encyclopedia of information science and technology* (pp. 2949-2953). Hershey, PA: Idea Group Reference.

Dobson, P.J. (2005). Critical realism as an underlying philosophy for IS research. In M. Khosrow-Pour (Ed.), *Encyclopedia of information science and technology* (pp. 606-610). Hershey, PA: Idea Group Reference.

Doherty, N.F., & King, M. (2005). Managing the organizational impacts of information systems. In M. Khosrow-Pour (Ed.), *Encyclopedia of information science and technology* (pp. 1880-1886). Hershey, PA: Idea Group Reference.

Domeniconi, C., & Gunopulos, D. (2005). Locally adaptive techniques for pattern classification. In J. Wang (Ed.), *Encyclopedia of data warehousing and mining* (pp. 684-688). Hershey, PA: Idea Group Reference.

Donnelly, R. (2005). Online problem-based learning approach in higher education. In C. Howard, J.V. Boettcher, L. Justice, K. Schenk, P.L. Rogers, & G.A. Berg (Eds.), *Encyclopedia of distance learning* (pp. 1402-1411). Hershey, PA: Idea Group Reference.

Dooley, K.E., Lindner, J.R., Elbert, C., Murphy, T.H., & Murghrey, T.P. (2005). Faculty perceptions and participation in distance education. In M. Khosrow-Pour (Ed.), *Encyclopedia of information science and technology* (pp. 1186-1189). Hershey, PA: Idea Group Reference.

Doorn, J.H. (2005). Database integrity. In M. Khosrow-Pour (Ed.), *Encyclopedia of information science and technology* (pp. 734-738). Hershey, PA: Idea Group Reference.

Dori, D. (2006). Object-process methodology. In D. Schwartz (Ed.), *Encyclopedia of knowledge management* (pp. 683). Hershey, PA: Idea Group Reference.

Dorniden, A. (2005). K-12 schools and online learning. In C. Howard, J.V. Boettcher, L. Justice, K. Schenk, P.L. Rogers, & G.A. Berg (Eds.), *Encyclopedia of distance learning* (pp. 1182-1188). Hershey, PA: Idea Group Reference.

Dotsika, F. (2006). An IT perspective on supporting communities of practice. In E. Coakes & S. Clarke (Eds.), *Encyclopedia of communities of practice in information and knowledge management* (pp. 257-263). Hershey, PA: Idea Group Reference.

Dragan, K.F. (2005). Informationbase - a new information system layer. In M. Khosrow-Pour (Ed.), *Encyclopedia of information science and technology* (pp. 1513-1517). Hershey, PA: Idea Group Reference.

Drake, P. (2006). Information security as a community of practice. In E. Coakes & S. Clarke (Eds.), *Ency-*

*clopedia of communities of practice in information and knowledge management* (pp. 224-225). Hershey, PA: Idea Group Reference.

Dron, J. (2005). Self-organizing networked learning environments. In M. Khosrow-Pour (Ed.), *Encyclopedia of information science and technology* (pp. 2459-2463). Hershey, PA: Idea Group Reference.

Du Mont, R. (2005). E-learning as organizational strategy. In C. Howard, J.V. Boettcher, L. Justice, K. Schenk, P.L. Rogers, & G.A. Berg (Eds.), *Encyclopedia of distance learning* (pp. 750-762). Hershey, PA: Idea Group Reference.

Duan, Y. (2005). E-commerce training for SMEs. In M. Khosrow-Pour (Ed.), *Encyclopedia of information science and technology* (pp. 962-965). Hershey, PA: Idea Group Reference.

Duan, Y., & Xu, M. (2005). Decision support systems in small businesses. In M. Khosrow-Pour (Ed.), *Encyclopedia of information science and technology* (pp. 754-758). Hershey, PA: Idea Group Reference.

Duchastel, P. (2005). Learnability. In M. Khosrow-Pour (Ed.), *Encyclopedia of information science and technology* (pp. 1803-1806). Hershey, PA: Idea Group Reference.

Duchastel, P. (2006). Information Interaction Beyond HCI. In C. Ghaoui (Ed.), *Encyclopedia of human computer interaction* (pp. 332-337). Hershey, PA: Idea Group Reference.

Dudding, C.C. (2005). Videoconferencing for supervision of graduate students. In C. Howard, J.V. Boettcher, L. Justice, K. Schenk, P.L. Rogers, & G.A. Berg (Eds.), *Encyclopedia of distance learning* (pp. 1965-1971). Hershey, PA: Idea Group Reference.

Dumitriu, L. (2005). Closed-itemset incremental-mining problem. In J. Wang (Ed.), *Encyclopedia of data warehousing and mining* (pp. 150-153). Hershey, PA: Idea Group Reference.

Dunkels, E. (2005). Young people's Net cultures. In C. Howard, J.V. Boettcher, L. Justice, K. Schenk, P.L. Rogers, & G.A. Berg (Eds.), *Encyclopedia of*

*distance learning* (pp. 2067-2074). Hershey, PA: Idea Group Reference.

Dunn, C.L., & Grabski, S.V. (2005). Semantically modeled enterprise databases. In L. Rivero, J. Doorn, & V. Ferraggine (Eds.), *Encyclopedia of database technologies and applications* (pp. 601-606). Hershey, PA: Idea Group Reference.

Durrett, J.R., Burnell, L., & Priest, J.W. (2005). Contingency theory, agent-based systems and a virtual advisor. In M. Khosrow-Pour (Ed.), *Encyclopedia of information science and technology* (pp. 577-583). Hershey, PA: Idea Group Reference.

Dustdar, S. (2005). Process-aware information systems for virtual teamwork. In M. Khosrow-Pour (Ed.), *Encyclopedia of information science and technology* (pp. 2314-2320). Hershey, PA: Idea Group Reference.

Duthler, K.W. (2005). The elaboration likelihood model and Web-based persuasion. In M. Pagani (Ed.), *Encyclopedia of multimedia technology and networking* (pp. 265-270). Hershey, PA: Idea Group Reference.

Dykman, C.A. (2005). Assessing the value of information systems investments. In M. Khosrow-Pour (Ed.), *Encyclopedia of information science and technology* (pp. 173-177). Hershey, PA: Idea Group Reference.

Dykman, C.A. (2006). Supporting communities of practice in the electronic commerce world. In E. Coakes & S. Clarke (Eds.), *Encyclopedia of communities of practice in information and knowledge management* (pp. 502-507). Hershey, PA: Idea Group Reference.

Dyson, L.E. (2005). Remote indigenous Australian communities and ICT. In S. Marshall, W. Taylor, & X. Yu (Eds.), *Encyclopedia of developing regional communities with information and communication technology* (pp. 608-613). Hershey, PA: Idea Group Reference.

Eberle, J., & Childress, M. (2005). Using heutagogy to address the needs of online learners. In C. Howard, J.V. Boettcher, L. Justice, K. Schenk, P.L. Rogers, & G.A.

Berg (Eds.), *Encyclopedia of distance learning* (pp. 1945-1951). Hershey, PA: Idea Group Reference.

Edwards, A.R. (2005). Moderator in government-initiated online discussions. In M. Khosrow-Pour (Ed.), *Encyclopedia of information science and technology* (pp. 2018-2023). Hershey, PA: Idea Group Reference.

Edwards, J.S. (2005). Business processes and knowledge management. In M. Khosrow-Pour (Ed.), *Encyclopedia of information science and technology* (pp. 350-355). Hershey, PA: Idea Group Reference.

Efendioglu, A.M. (2006). E-commerce use by Chinese consumers. In M. Khosrow-Pour (Ed.), *Encyclopedia of e-commerce, e-government, and mobile commerce* (pp. 327-333). Hershey, PA: Idea Group Reference.

Efstathiou, E.C., & Polyzos, G.C. (2006). Peer-to-peer wireless network confederation. In S. Dasgupta (Ed.), *Encyclopedia of virtual communities and technologies* (pp. 378-381). Hershey, PA: Idea Group Reference.

Ein-Dor, P. (2006). Taxonomies of knowledge. In D. Schwartz (Ed.), *Encyclopedia of knowledge management* (pp. 848-854). Hershey, PA: Idea Group Reference.

Ekbia, H.R., & Hara, N. (2006). Incentive structures in knowledge management. In D. Schwartz (Ed.), *Encyclopedia of knowledge management* (pp. 237-243). Hershey, PA: Idea Group Reference.

El Louadi, M. (2005a). E-mail as a teaching supplement in Tunisia. In S. Marshall, W. Taylor, & X. Yu (Eds.), *Encyclopedia of developing regional communities with information and communication technology* (pp. 275-281). Hershey, PA: Idea Group Reference.

El Louadi, M. (2005b). The Arab world, culture and information technology. In S. Marshall, W. Taylor, & X. Yu (Eds.), *Encyclopedia of developing regional communities with information and communication technology* (pp. 21-27). Hershey, PA: Idea Group Reference.

El-Gayar, O., Chen, K., & Tandekar, K. (2005). Multimedia interactivity on the Internet. In M. Pagani (Ed.), *Encyclopedia of multimedia technology and networking* (pp. 724-730). Hershey, PA: Idea Group Reference.

Elshaw, B. (2006a). Critical success factors for the successful introduction of an intellectual capital management system. In E. Coakes & S. Clarke (Eds.), *Encyclopedia of communities of practice in information and knowledge management* (pp. 124-128). Hershey, PA: Idea Group Reference.

Elshaw, B. (2006b). Virtual teaming. In E. Coakes & S. Clarke (Eds.), *Encyclopedia of communities of practice in information and knowledge management* (pp. 583-586). Hershey, PA: Idea Group Reference.

Eppler, M.J. (2006). Knowledge communication. In D. Schwartz (Ed.), *Encyclopedia of knowledge management* (pp. 317-325). Hershey, PA: Idea Group Reference.

Eppler, M.J., & Burkhard, R.A. (2006). Knowledge visualization. In D. Schwartz (Ed.), *Encyclopedia of knowledge management* (pp. 551). Hershey, PA: Idea Group Reference.

Erbas, F. (2005). Wireless ad hoc networking. In M. Khosrow-Pour (Ed.), *Encyclopedia of information science and technology* (pp. 3090-3094). Hershey, PA: Idea Group Reference.

Ericsson, F., & Avdic, A. (2005). Knowledge management systems acceptance. In M. Khosrow-Pour (Ed.), *Encyclopedia of information science and technology* (pp. 1778-1782). Hershey, PA: Idea Group Reference.

Erlich, Z. (2005). Computer-mediated communication. In C. Howard, J.V. Boettcher, L. Justice, K. Schenk, P.L. Rogers, & G.A. Berg (Eds.), *Encyclopedia of distance learning* (pp. 353-364). Hershey, PA: Idea Group Reference.

Erlich, Z., & Gal-Ezer, J. (2005). The Open University of Israel. In C. Howard, J.V. Boettcher, L. Justice, K.

Schenk, P.L. Rogers, & G.A. Berg (Eds.), *Encyclopedia of distance learning* (pp. 1421-1429). Hershey, PA: Idea Group Reference.

Erwin, G., Taylor, W. (2005). Assimilation by communities of Internet technologies. In S. Marshall, W. Taylor, & X. Yu (Eds.), *Encyclopedia of developing regional communities with information and communication technology* (pp. 40-46). Hershey, PA: Idea Group Reference.

Escalante, R.M. (2005). E-commerce challenges for Caribbean businesses. In S. Marshall, W. Taylor, & X. Yu (Eds.), *Encyclopedia of developing regional communities with information and communication technology* (pp. 239-245). Hershey, PA: Idea Group Reference.

Eshet, Y. (2005). Thinking skills in the digital era. In C. Howard, J.V. Boettcher, L. Justice, K. Schenk, P.L. Rogers, & G.A. Berg (Eds.), *Encyclopedia of distance learning* (pp. 1840-1845). Hershey, PA: Idea Group Reference.

Esmahi, L. (2005). Personalized web-based learning services. In M. Pagani (Ed.), *Encyclopedia of multimedia technology and networking* (pp. 814-820). Hershey, PA: Idea Group Reference.

Esteves, J., & Pastor, J. (2005). An ERP life-cycle costs model. In M. Khosrow-Pour (Ed.), *Encyclopedia of information science and technology* (pp. 111-116). Hershey, PA: Idea Group Reference.

Etter, S.J., & Byrnes, L.T. (2005). Using course maps for easy classroom to computer transition. In C. Howard, J.V. Boettcher, L. Justice, K. Schenk, P.L. Rogers, & G.A. Berg (Eds.), *Encyclopedia of distance learning* (pp. 1940-1944). Hershey, PA: Idea Group Reference.

Fagan, J.C. (2005). Text-only Web techniques. In C. Howard, J.V. Boettcher, L. Justice, K. Schenk, P.L. Rogers, & G.A. Berg (Eds.), *Encyclopedia of distance learning* (pp. 1833-1837). Hershey, PA: Idea Group Reference.

Faiola, A. (2006). Toward an HCI Theory of Cultural Cognition. In C. Ghaoui (Ed.), *Encyclopedia of human computer interaction* (pp. 609-614). Hershey, PA: Idea Group Reference.

Faïz, S. (2005). Knowledge discovery and geographical databases. In L. Rivero, J. Doorn, & V. Ferraggine (Eds.), *Encyclopedia of database technologies and applications* (pp. 308-312). Hershey, PA: Idea Group Reference.

Faïz, S., & Mahmoudi, K. (2005). Semantic enrichment of geographical databases. In L. Rivero, J. Doorn, & V. Ferraggine (Eds.), *Encyclopedia of database technologies and applications* (pp. 587-592). Hershey, PA: Idea Group Reference.

Falcone, R., & Castelfranchi, C. (2005). Socio-cognitive model of trust. In M. Khosrow-Pour (Ed.), *Encyclopedia of information science and technology* (pp. 2534-2538). Hershey, PA: Idea Group Reference.

Falivene, G.M., & Kaufman, E. (2006). Training and articulating public agencies in Argentina. In E. Coakes & S. Clarke (Eds.), *Encyclopedia of communities of practice in information and knowledge management* (pp. 537-543). Hershey, PA: Idea Group Reference.

Falk, L.K., & Sockel, H. (2005). Web site usability. In M. Pagani (Ed.), *Encyclopedia of multimedia technology and networking* (pp. 1078-1083). Hershey, PA: Idea Group Reference.

Fan, W., & Pathak, P. (2005). Discovering ranking functions for information retrieval. In J. Wang (Ed.), *Encyclopedia of data warehousing and mining* (pp. 377-381). Hershey, PA: Idea Group Reference.

Farag, W.E. (2005a). Assessing digital video data similarity. In M. Pagani (Ed.), *Encyclopedia of multimedia technology and networking* (pp. 36-41). Hershey, PA: Idea Group Reference.

Farag, W.E. (2005b). Video content-based retrieval techniques. In M. Khosrow-Pour (Ed.), *Encyclopedia of information science and technology* (pp. 2986-2990). Hershey, PA: Idea Group Reference.

Farmer, W.M. (2006). Mathematical knowledge management. In D. Schwartz (Ed.), *Encyclopedia of knowledge management* (pp. 599). Hershey, PA: Idea Group Reference.

Farooq, U., Fairweather, P.G., & Singley, M.K. (2006). Grounding CSCW in Social Psychology. In C. Ghaoui (Ed.), *Encyclopedia of human computer interaction* (pp. 257-260). Hershey, PA: Idea Group Reference.

Favre, L., Martinez, L., & Pereira, C. (2005). Forward engineering of UML static models. In M. Khosrow-Pour (Ed.), *Encyclopedia of information science and technology* (pp. 1212-1217). Hershey, PA: Idea Group Reference.

Felice, L., & Riesco, D. (2005). Reuse of formal specifications. In M. Khosrow-Pour (Ed.), *Encyclopedia of information science and technology* (pp. 2425-2430). Hershey, PA: Idea Group Reference.

Felici, G., & Truemper, K. (2005). The lsquare system for mining logic data. In J. Wang (Ed.), *Encyclopedia of data warehousing and mining* (pp. 693-697). Hershey, PA: Idea Group Reference.

Feng, L., & Dillon, T. (2005). Inter-transactional association analysis for prediction. In J. Wang (Ed.), *Encyclopedia of data warehousing and mining* (pp. 653-658). Hershey, PA: Idea Group Reference.

Fernández, V.F., & Layos, L.M. (2005). Text content approaches in Web content mining. In J. Wang (Ed.), *Encyclopedia of data warehousing and mining* (pp. 1103-1108). Hershey, PA: Idea Group Reference.

Fernández, W.D. (2005). Trust placement process in metateam projects. In M. Khosrow-Pour (Ed.), *Encyclopedia of information science and technology* (pp. 2910-2915). Hershey, PA: Idea Group Reference.

Fernando, S. (2005). Issues of e-learning in third world countries. In M. Khosrow-Pour (Ed.), *Encyclopedia of information science and technology* (pp. 1702-1707). Hershey, PA: Idea Group Reference.

Ferre, X., Juristo, N., & Moreno, A.M. (2006). Obstacles for the Integration of HCI Practices into Software Engineering Development Processes. In C. Ghaoui (Ed.), *Encyclopedia of human computer*

*interaction* (pp. 422-428). Hershey, PA: Idea Group Reference.

Ferri, F., & Grifoni, P. (2006). Sketching in knowledge creation and management. In D. Schwartz (Ed.), *Encyclopedia of knowledge management* (pp. 802-808). Hershey, PA: Idea Group Reference.

Ferri, F., & Rafanelli, M. (2005). Syntactical and semantical correctness of pictorial queries for GIS. In L. Rivero, J. Doorn, & V. Ferraggine (Eds.), *Encyclopedia of database technologies and applications* (pp. 671-676). Hershey, PA: Idea Group Reference.

Ferris, S.P., & Minielli, M.C. (2005). Teams and electronic technologies. In M. Khosrow-Pour (Ed.), *Encyclopedia of information science and technology* (pp. 2735-2741). Hershey, PA: Idea Group Reference.

Fettke, P. (2005). Unified modeling language. In M. Khosrow-Pour (Ed.), *Encyclopedia of information science and technology* (pp. 2921-2928). Hershey, PA: Idea Group Reference.

Feuerlicht, G., & Vorisek, J. (2006). Enterprise application service model. In M. Khosrow-Pour (Ed.), *Encyclopedia of e-commerce, e-government, and mobile commerce* (pp. 431-436). Hershey, PA: Idea Group Reference.

Fiege, L. (2005). Data dissemination. In L. Rivero, J. Doorn, & V. Ferraggine (Eds.), *Encyclopedia of database technologies and applications* (pp. 105-109). Hershey, PA: Idea Group Reference.

Fink, D., & Disterer, G. (2006). Knowledge management in professional service firms. In D. Schwartz (Ed.), *Encyclopedia of knowledge management* (pp. 381). Hershey, PA: Idea Group Reference.

Finquelievich, S. (2005). Civil society and the new economy. In S. Marshall, W. Taylor, & X. Yu (Eds.), *Encyclopedia of developing regional communities with information and communication technology* (pp. 107-112). Hershey, PA: Idea Group Reference.

Fischer, I. (2005). Graph transformations and neural networks. In J. Wang (Ed.), *Encyclopedia of data*

*warehousing and mining* (pp. 534-539). Hershey, PA: Idea Group Reference.

Fischer, I., & Meinl, T. (2005). Subgraph mining. In J. Wang (Ed.), *Encyclopedia of data warehousing and mining* (pp. 1059-1063). Hershey, PA: Idea Group Reference.

Fisher, S. (2005). Cost-effectiveness. In C. Howard, J.V. Boettcher, L. Justice, K. Schenk, P.L. Rogers, & G.A. Berg (Eds.), *Encyclopedia of distance learning* (pp. 455-461). Hershey, PA: Idea Group Reference.

Fisteus, J.A., & Kloos, C.D. (2006). Business process analysis. In M. Khosrow-Pour (Ed.), *Encyclopedia of e-commerce, e-government, and mobile commerce* (pp. 78-82). Hershey, PA: Idea Group Reference.

Flavián, C., & Guinalíu, M. (2006). Virtual communities and e-business management. In M. Khosrow-Pour (Ed.), *Encyclopedia of e-commerce, e-government, and mobile commerce* (pp. 1163-1168). Hershey, PA: Idea Group Reference.

Fleming, S.T. (2005a). Biometrics security. In M. Pagani (Ed.), *Encyclopedia of multimedia technology and networking* (pp. 63-68). Hershey, PA: Idea Group Reference.

Fleming, S.T. (2005b). Open source intellectual property rights. In M. Pagani (Ed.), *Encyclopedia of multimedia technology and networking* (pp. 785-790). Hershey, PA: Idea Group Reference.

Fleming, S.T. (2005c). Virtual learning communities. In M. Pagani (Ed.), *Encyclopedia of multimedia technology and networking* (pp. 1055-1063). Hershey, PA: Idea Group Reference.

Flesca, S., Furfaro, F., Greco, S., & Zumpano, E. (2005). Repairing inconsistent XML data with functional dependencies. In L. Rivero, J. Doorn, & V. Ferraggine (Eds.), *Encyclopedia of database technologies and applications* (pp. 542-547). Hershey, PA: Idea Group Reference.

Flesca, S., Greco, S., & Zumpano, E. (2005). Managing inconsistent databases using active integrity constraints. In L. Rivero, J. Doorn, & V. Ferraggine

(Eds.), *Encyclopedia of database technologies and applications* (pp. 345-350). Hershey, PA: Idea Group Reference.

Foley, P., & Samson, D. (2006). Internet in a commodity mining company. In M. Khosrow-Pour (Ed.), *Encyclopedia of e-commerce, e-government, and mobile commerce* (pp. 660-665). Hershey, PA: Idea Group Reference.

Fong, P.S.W. (2006a). Multidisciplinary project teams. In D. Schwartz (Ed.), *Encyclopedia of knowledge management* (pp. 665). Hershey, PA: Idea Group Reference.

Fong, P.S.W. (2006b). Working and learning in interdisciplinary project communities. In E. Coakes & S. Clarke (Eds.), *Encyclopedia of communities of practice in information and knowledge management* (pp. 594-601). Hershey, PA: Idea Group Reference.

Forgionne, G. (2005). Functional integration of decision making support. In M. Khosrow-Pour (Ed.), *Encyclopedia of information science and technology* (pp. 1236-1242). Hershey, PA: Idea Group Reference.

Forgionne, G., & Ingsriswang, S. (2005). Stickiness and Web-based customer loyalty. In M. Khosrow-Pour (Ed.), *Encyclopedia of information science and technology* (pp. 2610-2615). Hershey, PA: Idea Group Reference.

Forgionne, G., Mora, M., Gupta, J.N.D., & Gelman, O. (2005). Decision-making support systems. In M. Khosrow-Pour (Ed.), *Encyclopedia of information science and technology* (pp. 759-765). Hershey, PA: Idea Group Reference.

Forte, M.C. (2005). Web site development in action research. In S. Marshall, W. Taylor, & X. Yu (Eds.), *Encyclopedia of developing regional communities with information and communication technology* (pp. 729-734). Hershey, PA: Idea Group Reference.

Fortier, J.-Y., & Kassel, G. (2006). Organizational semantic Webs. In D. Schwartz (Ed.), *Encyclopedia of knowledge management* (pp. 741-748). Hershey, PA: Idea Group Reference.

Fortino, G. (2005). Collaborative learning on-demand. In M. Khosrow-Pour (Ed.), *Encyclopedia of information science and technology* (pp. 445-450). Hershey, PA: Idea Group Reference.

Fortino, G., Garro, A., & Russo, W. (2006). E-commerce services based on mobile agents. In M. Khosrow-Pour (Ed.), *Encyclopedia of e-commerce, e-government, and mobile commerce* (pp. 319-326). Hershey, PA: Idea Group Reference.

Foth, M. (2005). Sociocultural animation. In S. Marshall, W. Taylor, & X. Yu (Eds.), *Encyclopedia of developing regional communities with information and communication technology* (pp. 640-645). Hershey, PA: Idea Group Reference.

Framinan, J.M. (2005). Enterprise resource planning for intelligent enterprises. In M. Khosrow-Pour (Ed.), *Encyclopedia of information science and technology* (pp. 1089-1094). Hershey, PA: Idea Group Reference.

Frank, J., Toland, J., & Schenk, K.D. (2005). E-Mail usage in South Pacific distance education. In M. Khosrow-Pour (Ed.), *Encyclopedia of information science and technology* (pp. 1034-1039). Hershey, PA: Idea Group Reference.

Frank, L. (2005a). Replication methods and their properties. In L. Rivero, J. Doorn, & V. Ferraggine (Eds.), *Encyclopedia of database technologies and applications* (pp. 555-561). Hershey, PA: Idea Group Reference.

Frank, L. (2005b). Transaction concurrency methods. In L. Rivero, J. Doorn, & V. Ferraggine (Eds.), *Encyclopedia of database technologies and applications* (pp. 695-700). Hershey, PA: Idea Group Reference.

Fraser, S. (2005). Caribbean companies and the information superhighway. In S. Marshall, W. Taylor, & X. Yu (Eds.), *Encyclopedia of developing regional communities with information and communication technology* (pp. 79-84). Hershey, PA: Idea Group Reference.

Fraunholz, B., Jung, J., & Unnithan, C. (2005). Mobile location based services. In M. Pagani (Ed.), *Encyclo-*

*pedia of multimedia technology and networking* (pp. 629-637). Hershey, PA: Idea Group Reference.

Freeman, I., & Auld, J.M. (2005). Critical issues in global navigation satellite systems. In M. Pagani (Ed.), *Encyclopedia of multimedia technology and networking* (pp. 151-157). Hershey, PA: Idea Group Reference.

Freire, M.M., Monteiro, P.P., da Silva, H.J.A., & Ruela, J. (2005). Ethernet passive optical networks. In M. Pagani (Ed.), *Encyclopedia of multimedia technology and networking* (pp. 283-289). Hershey, PA: Idea Group Reference.

Frempong, G., & Braimah, I. (2005). Assessing universal access to ICT in Ghana. In S. Marshall, W. Taylor, & X. Yu (Eds.), *Encyclopedia of developing regional communities with information and communication technology* (pp. 28-34). Hershey, PA: Idea Group Reference.

Friedman, W.H. (2005). Privacy-dangers and protections. In M. Khosrow-Pour (Ed.), *Encyclopedia of information science and technology* (pp. 2308-2313). Hershey, PA: Idea Group Reference.

Fryer, D., & Turner, E. (2006). Virtual communities for development. In S. Dasgupta (Ed.), *Encyclopedia of virtual communities and technologies* (pp. 500-505). Hershey, PA: Idea Group Reference.

Fu, L.M. (2005). Microarray data mining. In J. Wang (Ed.), *Encyclopedia of data warehousing and mining* (pp. 728-733). Hershey, PA: Idea Group Reference.

Fu, Y. (2005). Web usage mining and its applications. In J. Wang (Ed.), *Encyclopedia of data warehousing and mining* (pp. 1221-1225). Hershey, PA: Idea Group Reference.

Fuller, C.M., & Wilson, R.L. (2006). Extracting knowledge from neural networks. In D. Schwartz (Ed.), *Encyclopedia of knowledge management* (pp. 188-196). Hershey, PA: Idea Group Reference.

Fulton, J.A. (2005). Common information model. In L. Rivero, J. Doorn, & V. Ferraggine (Eds.), *Encyclo-*

*pedia of database technologies and applications* (pp. 78-86). Hershey, PA: Idea Group Reference.

Fung, B.C.M., Wang, K., & Ester, M. (2005). Hierarchical document clustering. In J. Wang (Ed.), *Encyclopedia of data warehousing and mining* (pp. 555-559). Hershey, PA: Idea Group Reference.

Fung, B.Y.-M., & Ng, V.T.-Y. (2005). Heterogeneous gene data for classifying tumors. In J. Wang (Ed.), *Encyclopedia of data warehousing and mining* (pp. 550-554). Hershey, PA: Idea Group Reference.

Furtado, E. (2005). Usability of online learning systems and course materials. In M. Khosrow-Pour (Ed.), *Encyclopedia of information science and technology* (pp. 2939-2943). Hershey, PA: Idea Group Reference.

Gabillon, A. (2005). Multilevel databases. In L. Rivero, J. Doorn, & V. Ferraggine (Eds.), *Encyclopedia of database technologies and applications* (pp. 383-389). Hershey, PA: Idea Group Reference.

Gaedke, M., Nussbaumer, M., & Tonkin, E. (2005). Software contracts for component-based Web engineering. In M. Khosrow-Pour (Ed.), *Encyclopedia of information science and technology* (pp. 2557-2561). Hershey, PA: Idea Group Reference.

Gaffar, A. (2005). Component-based generalized database index model. In L. Rivero, J. Doorn, & V. Ferraggine (Eds.), *Encyclopedia of database technologies and applications* (pp. 87-92). Hershey, PA: Idea Group Reference.

Gaffar, A., & Seffah, A. (2005). An XML multi-tier pattern dissemination system. In L. Rivero, J. Doorn, & V. Ferraggine (Eds.), *Encyclopedia of database technologies and applications* (pp. 740-744). Hershey, PA: Idea Group Reference.

Galanxhi-Janaqi, H., & Nah, F.F.-H. (2005). Ubiquitous commerce. In M. Pagani (Ed.), *Encyclopedia of multimedia technology and networking* (pp. 980-984). Hershey, PA: Idea Group Reference.

Galatescu, A. (2005). Translation of natural language patterns to object and process modeling. In M. Khos-

row-Pour (Ed.), *Encyclopedia of information science and technology* (pp. 2851-2856). Hershey, PA: Idea Group Reference.

Galitsky, B. (2005a). Bioinformatics data management and data mining. In L. Rivero, J. Doorn, & V. Ferraggine (Eds.), *Encyclopedia of database technologies and applications* (pp. 29-34). Hershey, PA: Idea Group Reference.

Galitsky, B. (2005b). Distance learning rehabilitation of autistic reasoning. In C. Howard, J.V. Boettcher, L. Justice, K. Schenk, P.L. Rogers, & G.A. Berg (Eds.), *Encyclopedia of distance learning* (pp. 662-668). Hershey, PA: Idea Group Reference.

Galitsky, B. (2005c). Natural language front-end for a database. In L. Rivero, J. Doorn, & V. Ferraggine (Eds.), *Encyclopedia of database technologies and applications* (pp. 403-407). Hershey, PA: Idea Group Reference.

Galloway, C. (2006). Mobile public relations strategies. In M. Khosrow-Pour (Ed.), *Encyclopedia of e-commerce, e-government, and mobile commerce* (pp. 805-810). Hershey, PA: Idea Group Reference.

Galup, S.D., Dattero, R., & Hicks, R.C. (2005). Client/server and the knowledge directory. In M. Khosrow-Pour (Ed.), *Encyclopedia of information science and technology* (pp. 430-434). Hershey, PA: Idea Group Reference.

Galvão, R.K.H., Becerra, V.M., & Abou-Seada, M. (2005). Financial ratio selection for distress classification. In J. Wang (Ed.), *Encyclopedia of data warehousing and mining* (pp. 503-508). Hershey, PA: Idea Group Reference.

Gangeness, J.E. (2005). Online instruction as a caring endeavor. In C. Howard, J.V. Boettcher, L. Justice, K. Schenk, P.L. Rogers, & G.A. Berg (Eds.), *Encyclopedia of distance learning* (pp. 1361-1364). Hershey, PA: Idea Group Reference.

Gangopadhyay, A., & Huang, Z. (2005). Multilingual electronic commerce in a global economy. In M. Khosrow-Pour (Ed.), *Encyclopedia of information*

*science and technology* (pp. 2042-2044). Hershey, PA: Idea Group Reference.

Ganguly, A.R., Gupta, A., & Khan, S. (2005). Data mining and decision support for business and science. In J. Wang (Ed.), *Encyclopedia of data warehousing and mining* (pp. 233-238). Hershey, PA: Idea Group Reference.

Gao, Y. (2005a). Consumer attitude in electronic commerce. In M. Pagani (Ed.), *Encyclopedia of multimedia technology and networking* (pp. 102-109). Hershey, PA: Idea Group Reference.

Gao, Y. (2005b). Interactivity and amusement in electronic commerce. In M. Khosrow-Pour (Ed.), *Encyclopedia of information science and technology* (pp. 1607-1611). Hershey, PA: Idea Group Reference.

Gao, Y., Koufaris, M., & Ducoffe, R.H. (2006). Negative effects of advertising techniques in electronic commerce. In M. Khosrow-Pour (Ed.), *Encyclopedia of e-commerce, e-government, and mobile commerce* (pp. 842-847). Hershey, PA: Idea Group Reference.

Garb, J.L., & Wait, R.B. (2005a). Census data for health preparedness and response. In M. Khosrow-Pour (Ed.), *Encyclopedia of information science and technology* (pp. 373-380). Hershey, PA: Idea Group Reference.

Garb, J.L., & Wait, R.B. (2005b). Using geographic information systems to solve community problems. In M. Khosrow-Pour (Ed.), *Encyclopedia of information science and technology* (pp. 2978-2985). Hershey, PA: Idea Group Reference.

García, F.J., Berlanga, A.J., & García, J. (2006). A Semantic Learning Objects Authoring Tool. In C. Ghaoui (Ed.), *Encyclopedia of human computer interaction* (pp. 504-510). Hershey, PA: Idea Group Reference.

Garrett, B.M. (2006a). Mobile Clinical Learning Tools Using Networked Personal Digital Assistants (PDAs). In C. Ghaoui (Ed.), *Encyclopedia of human computer interaction* (pp. 404-407). Hershey, PA: Idea Group Reference.

Garrett, B.M. (2006b). The Development of the Personal Digital Assistant (PDA) Interface. In C. Ghaoui (Ed.), *Encyclopedia of human computer interaction* (pp. 160-164). Hershey, PA: Idea Group Reference.

Garrity, E.J., O'Donnell, J.B., & Sanders, G.L. (2005). Continuous auditing and data mining. In J. Wang (Ed.), *Encyclopedia of data warehousing and mining* (pp. 217-222). Hershey, PA: Idea Group Reference.

Garten, E.D. (2005). The birth of virtual libraries. In C. Howard, J.V. Boettcher, L. Justice, K. Schenk, P.L. Rogers, & G.A. Berg (Eds.), *Encyclopedia of distance learning* (pp. 166-171). Hershey, PA: Idea Group Reference.

Garten, E.D., & Thompson, T. (2005). Quality assurance and online higher education. In C. Howard, J.V. Boettcher, L. Justice, K. Schenk, P.L. Rogers, & G.A. Berg (Eds.), *Encyclopedia of distance learning* (pp. 1529-1537). Hershey, PA: Idea Group Reference.

Gates, W.R., & Nissen, M.E. (2005). Agent- and Web-based employment marketspaces in the U.S. Department of Defense. In M. Khosrow-Pour (Ed.), *Encyclopedia of information science and technology* (pp. 74-80). Hershey, PA: Idea Group Reference.

Gaudioso, E., & Montero, M. (2006). Adaptable and Adaptive Web-Based Educational Systems. In C. Ghaoui (Ed.), *Encyclopedia of human computer interaction* (pp. 8-11). Hershey, PA: Idea Group Reference.

Ge, N., & Liu, L. (2005). Mining microarray data. In J. Wang (Ed.), *Encyclopedia of data warehousing and mining* (pp. 810-814). Hershey, PA: Idea Group Reference.

Gehrke, J. (2005). Classification and regression trees. In J. Wang (Ed.), *Encyclopedia of data warehousing and mining* (pp. 141-143). Hershey, PA: Idea Group Reference.

Geiselhart, K., & Jamieson, P. (2005). Sustainability issues for Australian rural teleservice centres. In S. Marshall, W. Taylor, & X. Yu (Eds.), *Encyclopedia of developing regional communities with informa-*

*tion and communication technology* (pp. 659-664). Hershey, PA: Idea Group Reference.

Geisler, S., & Kao, O. (2005). Parallel and distributed multimedia databases. In M. Khosrow-Pour (Ed.), *Encyclopedia of information science and technology* (pp. 2265-2271). Hershey, PA: Idea Group Reference.

Gelepithis, P.A.M. (2005). Knowledge, IT, and the firm. In M. Khosrow-Pour (Ed.), *Encyclopedia of information science and technology* (pp. 1783-1787). Hershey, PA: Idea Group Reference.

Gelman, O., Mora, M., Forgionne, G., & Cervantes, F. (2005). Information systems and systems theory. In M. Khosrow-Pour (Ed.), *Encyclopedia of information science and technology* (pp. 1491-1496). Hershey, PA: Idea Group Reference.

George, S.E. (2005a). Heuristics in medical data mining. In M. Khosrow-Pour (Ed.), *Encyclopedia of information science and technology* (pp. 1322-1326). Hershey, PA: Idea Group Reference.

George, S.E. (2005b). Optical music recognition with wavelets. In M. Khosrow-Pour (Ed.), *Encyclopedia of information science and technology* (pp. 2225-2229). Hershey, PA: Idea Group Reference.

Ghenniwa, H.H., & Huhns, M.N. (2005). Marketplace architecture for enterprise integration. In M. Khosrow-Pour (Ed.), *Encyclopedia of information science and technology* (pp. 1899-1905). Hershey, PA: Idea Group Reference.

Giaglis, G.M. (2005). Mobile location services. In M. Khosrow-Pour (Ed.), *Encyclopedia of information science and technology* (pp. 1973-1977). Hershey, PA: Idea Group Reference.

Gibbs, M.R., Wright, P., & Arnold, M. (2005). Critical mass and self-sustaining activity. In S. Marshall, W. Taylor, & X. Yu (Eds.), *Encyclopedia of developing regional communities with information and communication technology* (pp. 138-143). Hershey, PA: Idea Group Reference.

Gibson, R. (2005). Software and systems engineering integration. In M. Khosrow-Pour (Ed.), *Encyclopedia*

*of information science and technology* (pp. 2551-2556). Hershey, PA: Idea Group Reference.

Gibson, R., & Brown, C. (2006). Electronic voting as the key to ballot reform. In M. Khosrow-Pour (Ed.), *Encyclopedia of e-commerce, e-government, and mobile commerce* (pp. 403-407). Hershey, PA: Idea Group Reference.

Gil, A.B., & García, F.J. (2006). Recommender Systems in E-Commerce. In C. Ghaoui (Ed.), *Encyclopedia of human computer interaction* (pp. 486-493). Hershey, PA: Idea Group Reference.

Gilbert, A.L. (2005a). Planning for electronic government in a remote Malaysian site. In S. Marshall, W. Taylor, & X. Yu (Eds.), *Encyclopedia of developing regional communities with information and communication technology* (pp. 550-556). Hershey, PA: Idea Group Reference.

Gilbert, A.L. (2005b). Understanding the out-of-the-box experience. In M. Pagani (Ed.), *Encyclopedia of multimedia technology and networking* (pp. 985-992). Hershey, PA: Idea Group Reference.

Gilbert, A.L. (2005c). Wireless in Vietnam. In S. Marshall, W. Taylor, & X. Yu (Eds.), *Encyclopedia of developing regional communities with information and communication technology* (pp. 735-740). Hershey, PA: Idea Group Reference.

Gilbert, J. (2005). Ethics of new technologies. In M. Khosrow-Pour (Ed.), *Encyclopedia of information science and technology* (pp. 1121-1124). Hershey, PA: Idea Group Reference.

Gil-García, J.R., & Luna-Reyes, L.F. (2006). Integrating conceptual approaches to e-government. In M. Khosrow-Pour (Ed.), *Encyclopedia of e-commerce, e-government, and mobile commerce* (pp. 636-643). Hershey, PA: Idea Group Reference.

Gillani, B.B. (2005a). Cognitive theories and the design of e-learning environments. In S. Marshall, W. Taylor, & X. Yu (Eds.), *Encyclopedia of developing regional communities with information and communication technology* (pp. 119-123). Hershey, PA: Idea Group Reference.

Gillani, B.B. (2005b). Problem-based learning and the design of e-learning environments. In S. Marshall, W. Taylor, & X. Yu (Eds.), *Encyclopedia of developing regional communities with information and communication technology* (pp. 581-586). Hershey, PA: Idea Group Reference.

Gillman, D.W. (2006). Data semantics. In D. Schwartz (Ed.), *Encyclopedia of knowledge management* (pp. 97-104). Hershey, PA: Idea Group Reference.

Giorgi, C., & Schürch, D. (2005). ICT, education, and regional development in Swiss peripheral areas. In S. Marshall, W. Taylor, & X. Yu (Eds.), *Encyclopedia of developing regional communities with information and communication technology* (pp. 393-398). Hershey, PA: Idea Group Reference.

Giudici, P. (2005). Evaluation of data mining methods. In J. Wang (Ed.), *Encyclopedia of data warehousing and mining* (pp. 464-468). Hershey, PA: Idea Group Reference.

Giudici, P., & Cerchiello, P. (2005). Web usage mining through associative models. In J. Wang (Ed.), *Encyclopedia of data warehousing and mining* (pp. 1231-1234). Hershey, PA: Idea Group Reference.

Glick, D.B. (2005a). K-12 online learning policy. In C. Howard, J.V. Boettcher, L. Justice, K. Schenk, P.L. Rogers, & G.A. Berg (Eds.), *Encyclopedia of distance learning* (pp. 1175-1181). Hershey, PA: Idea Group Reference.

Glick, D.B. (2005b). Online learning in the school reform movement. In C. Howard, J.V. Boettcher, L. Justice, K. Schenk, P.L. Rogers, & G.A. Berg (Eds.), *Encyclopedia of distance learning* (pp. 1375-1381). Hershey, PA: Idea Group Reference.

Gnaniah, J., Songan, P., Yeo, A.W., Zen, H., & Hamid, K.A. (2005). The need for community informatics in Malaysia. In S. Marshall, W. Taylor, & X. Yu (Eds.), *Encyclopedia of developing regional communities with information and communication technology* (pp. 512-517). Hershey, PA: Idea Group Reference.

Gnaniah, J., Yeo, A.W., Zen, H., Songan, P., & Hamid, K.A. (2005). E-bario and e-bedian project imple-mentation in Malaysia. In S. Marshall, W. Taylor, & X. Yu (Eds.), *Encyclopedia of developing regional communities with information and communication technology* (pp. 214-219). Hershey, PA: Idea Group Reference.

Goh, T.-T., & Kinshuk. (2005). Web content adaptation frameworks and techniques. In M. Pagani (Ed.), *Encyclopedia of multimedia technology and networking* (pp. 1070-1077). Hershey, PA: Idea Group Reference.

Gold, S.S. (2005). Effects of computer-mediated communication. In C. Howard, J.V. Boettcher, L. Justice, K. Schenk, P.L. Rogers, & G.A. Berg (Eds.), *Encyclopedia of distance learning* (pp. 732-736). Hershey, PA: Idea Group Reference.

Goldschmidt, P. (2005). Supporting assurance and compliance monitoring. In M. Khosrow-Pour (Ed.), *Encyclopedia of information science and technology* (pp. 2684-2689). Hershey, PA: Idea Group Reference.

Goldsmith, R.E. (2006). Electronic word-of-mouth. In M. Khosrow-Pour (Ed.), *Encyclopedia of e-commerce, e-government, and mobile commerce* (pp. 408-412). Hershey, PA: Idea Group Reference.

Goldsmith, R.E., & Pillai, K.G. (2006). Knowledge calibration. In D. Schwartz (Ed.), *Encyclopedia of knowledge management* (pp. 311-316). Hershey, PA: Idea Group Reference.

Goodman, K.W. (2005). Moral foundations of data mining. In J. Wang (Ed.), *Encyclopedia of data warehousing and mining* (pp. 832-836). Hershey, PA: Idea Group Reference.

Gordon, J., & Lin, Z. (2005). E-learning industry. In C. Howard, J.V. Boettcher, L. Justice, K. Schenk, P.L. Rogers, & G.A. Berg (Eds.), *Encyclopedia of distance learning* (pp. 786-793). Hershey, PA: Idea Group Reference.

Gordon, S., & Mulligan, P. (2005). Infocratic perspective on the delivery of personal financial services. In M. Khosrow-Pour (Ed.), *Encyclopedia of information*

*science and technology* (pp. 1452-1457). Hershey, PA: Idea Group Reference.

Graham, C.R., Allen, S., & Ure, D. (2005). Benefits and challenges of blended learning environments. In M. Khosrow-Pour (Ed.), *Encyclopedia of information science and technology* (pp. 253-259). Hershey, PA: Idea Group Reference.

Graham, C.R., & Misanchuk, M. (2005). Computer-mediated learning groups. In M. Khosrow-Pour (Ed.), *Encyclopedia of information science and technology* (pp. 502-597). Hershey, PA: Idea Group Reference.

Grant, J., & Minker, J. (2006). Logic and knowledge bases. In D. Schwartz (Ed.), *Encyclopedia of knowledge management* (pp. 583). Hershey, PA: Idea Group Reference.

Grasso, F., & Leng, P. (2005). Quality assurance issues for online universities. In M. Khosrow-Pour (Ed.), *Encyclopedia of information science and technology* (pp. 2382-2386). Hershey, PA: Idea Group Reference.

Greco, S., & Zumpano, E. (2005a). Consistent queries over databases with integrity constraints. In M. Khosrow-Pour (Ed.), *Encyclopedia of information science and technology* (pp. 529-534). Hershey, PA: Idea Group Reference.

Greco, S., & Zumpano, E. (2005b). Rewriting and efficient computation of bound disjunctive datalog queries. In L. Rivero, J. Doorn, & V. Ferraggine (Eds.), *Encyclopedia of database technologies and applications* (pp. 562-569). Hershey, PA: Idea Group Reference.

Greco, S., Sirangelo, C., Trubitsyna, I., & Zumpano, E. (2005). Preferred repairs for inconsistent databases. In L. Rivero, J. Doorn, & V. Ferraggine (Eds.), *Encyclopedia of database technologies and applications* (pp. 480-485). Hershey, PA: Idea Group Reference.

Green, C.W., & Hurley, T.A. (2006). Promoting participation in communities of practice. In E. Coakes & S. Clarke (Eds.), *Encyclopedia of communities of practice in information and knowledge management* (pp. 407-418). Hershey, PA: Idea Group Reference.

Green, G., Day, J., Lou, H., & Van Slyke, C. (2005). User perceptions and groupware use. In M. Khosrow-Pour (Ed.), *Encyclopedia of information science and technology* (pp. 2961-2966). Hershey, PA: Idea Group Reference.

Gregory, V.L. (2005). The changing library education curriculum. In M. Khosrow-Pour (Ed.), *Encyclopedia of information science and technology* (pp. 2799-2802). Hershey, PA: Idea Group Reference.

Grieves, J. (2006a). Communities of practice and organizational development for ethics and values. In E. Coakes & S. Clarke (Eds.), *Encyclopedia of communities of practice in information and knowledge management* (pp. 55-59). Hershey, PA: Idea Group Reference.

Grieves, J. (2006b). What organisational development theory can contribute to our understanding of communities of practice. In E. Coakes & S. Clarke (Eds.), *Encyclopedia of communities of practice in information and knowledge management* (pp. 589-593). Hershey, PA: Idea Group Reference.

Griffin, J. (2005). Diffusion patterns of the Internet technology cluster in Irish SMEs. In M. Khosrow-Pour (Ed.), *Encyclopedia of information science and technology* (pp. 858-863). Hershey, PA: Idea Group Reference.

Griffiths, M. (2005). Internet abuse and addiction in the workplace. In M. Khosrow-Pour (Ed.), *Encyclopedia of information science and technology* (pp. 1623-1628). Hershey, PA: Idea Group Reference.

Griffiths, M., Davies, M.N.O., & Chappell, D. (2006). Online gaming. In S. Dasgupta (Ed.), *Encyclopedia of virtual communities and technologies* (pp. 349-353). Hershey, PA: Idea Group Reference.

Grzymala-Busse, J., & Ziarko, W. (2005). Rough sets and data mining. In J. Wang (Ed.), *Encyclopedia of data warehousing and mining* (pp. 973-977). Hershey, PA: Idea Group Reference.

Guah, M.W., & Currie, W.L. (2005). Application service provision for intelligent enterprises. In M. Khosrow-Pour (Ed.), *Encyclopedia of information*

*science and technology* (pp. 140-145). Hershey, PA: Idea Group Reference.

Guan, S.-U. (2005a). Agents and payment systems in e-commerce. In M. Khosrow-Pour (Ed.), *Encyclopedia of information science and technology* (pp. 93-97). Hershey, PA: Idea Group Reference.

Guan, S.-U. (2005b). Interactive memex. In M. Pagani (Ed.), *Encyclopedia of multimedia technology and networking* (pp. 437-446). Hershey, PA: Idea Group Reference.

Guan, S.-U. (2005c). Mobile agent authentication and authorization in e-commerce. In M. Khosrow-Pour (Ed.), *Encyclopedia of information science and technology* (pp. 1960-1966). Hershey, PA: Idea Group Reference.

Guan, S.-U. (2005d). Modeling interactive distributed multimedia applications. In M. Pagani (Ed.), *Encyclopedia of multimedia technology and networking* (pp. 660-666). Hershey, PA: Idea Group Reference.

Guan, S.-U. (2005e). Ontology-based query formation and information retrieval. In M. Khosrow-Pour (Ed.), *Encyclopedia of information science and technology* (pp. 2214-2220). Hershey, PA: Idea Group Reference.

Guan, S.-U. (2006a). An electronic auction service framework based on mobile software agents. In S. Dasgupta (Ed.), *Encyclopedia of virtual communities and technologies* (pp. 179-187). Hershey, PA: Idea Group Reference.

Guan, S.-U. (2006b). E-commerce agents and payment systems. In M. Khosrow-Pour (Ed.), *Encyclopedia of e-commerce, e-government, and mobile commerce* (pp. 279-283). Hershey, PA: Idea Group Reference.

Guan, S.-U. (2006c). E-commerce product selection and evaluation services. In S. Dasgupta (Ed.), *Encyclopedia of virtual communities and technologies* (pp. 150-155). Hershey, PA: Idea Group Reference.

Guan, S.-U. (2006d). Intelligent product brokering and preference tracking services. In M. Khosrow-Pour (Ed.), *Encyclopedia of e-commerce, e-government,*

*and mobile commerce* (pp. 644-647). Hershey, PA: Idea Group Reference.

Guan, S.-U. (2006e). Mobile agent-based auction services. In M. Khosrow-Pour (Ed.), *Encyclopedia of e-commerce, e-government, and mobile commerce* (pp. 747-753). Hershey, PA: Idea Group Reference.

Guan, S.-U. (2006f). Ontology-based query formation and information retrieval. In M. Khosrow-Pour (Ed.), *Encyclopedia of e-commerce, e-government, and mobile commerce* (pp. 871-877). Hershey, PA: Idea Group Reference.

Guan, S.-U. (2006g). Secure agent for e-commerce applications. In M. Khosrow-Pour (Ed.), *Encyclopedia of e-commerce, e-government, and mobile commerce* (pp. 962-967). Hershey, PA: Idea Group Reference.

Guan, S.-U. (2006h). Virtual marketplace for agent-based electronic commerce. In S. Dasgupta (Ed.), *Encyclopedia of virtual communities and technologies* (pp. 539-546). Hershey, PA: Idea Group Reference.

Guidici, P. (2005). Evaluation of data mining methods. In J. Wang (Ed.), *Encyclopedia of data warehousing and mining* (pp. 464-468). Hershey, PA: Idea Group Reference.

Giudici, P., & Cerchiello, P. (2005). Web usage mining through associative models. In J. Wang (Ed.), *Encyclopedia of data warehousing and mining* (pp. 1231-1234). Hershey, PA: Idea Group Reference.

Gupta, B., & Iyer, L.S. (2005). Theoretical framework for CRM outsourcing. In M. Khosrow-Pour (Ed.), *Encyclopedia of information science and technology* (pp. 2841-2845). Hershey, PA: Idea Group Reference.

Gurău, C. (2005). Modelling eCRM systems with the unified modelling language. In M. Pagani (Ed.), *Encyclopedia of multimedia technology and networking* (pp. 667-677). Hershey, PA: Idea Group Reference.

Gurău, C. (2006a). Codes of ethics in virtual communities. In S. Dasgupta (Ed.), *Encyclopedia of virtual communities and technologies* (pp. 22-28). Hershey, PA: Idea Group Reference.

Gurău, C. (2006b). Implementing CRM systems in online enterprises. In M. Khosrow-Pour (Ed.), *Encyclopedia of e-commerce, e-government, and mobile commerce* (pp. 587-593). Hershey, PA: Idea Group Reference.

Gurău, C. (2006c). Managing advergames. In M. Khosrow-Pour (Ed.), *Encyclopedia of e-commerce, e-government, and mobile commerce* (pp. 722-728). Hershey, PA: Idea Group Reference.

Gurău, C. (2006d). Negotiating online privacy rights. In M. Khosrow-Pour (Ed.), *Encyclopedia of e-commerce, e-government, and mobile commerce* (pp. 848-852). Hershey, PA: Idea Group Reference.

Guri-Rosenblit, S. (2005a). Diverse models of distance teaching universities. In C. Howard, J.V. Boettcher, L. Justice, K. Schenk, P.L. Rogers, & G.A. Berg (Eds.), *Encyclopedia of distance learning* (pp. 674-680). Hershey, PA: Idea Group Reference.

Guri-Rosenblit, S. (2005b). Openness dimensions of distance teaching universities. In C. Howard, J.V. Boettcher, L. Justice, K. Schenk, P.L. Rogers, & G.A. Berg (Eds.), *Encyclopedia of distance learning* (pp. 1433-1439). Hershey, PA: Idea Group Reference.

Guster, D., Robinson, D., & Safonov, P. (2005). Packet inter-arrival distributions in computer network workloads. In M. Khosrow-Pour (Ed.), *Encyclopedia of information science and technology* (pp. 2260-2264). Hershey, PA: Idea Group Reference.

Gutiérrez, J.A., & Ting, W. (2005). Quality of service issues associated with Internet protocols. In M. Pagani (Ed.), *Encyclopedia of multimedia technology and networking* (pp. 869-874). Hershey, PA: Idea Group Reference.

Hackbarth, K.D., Portilla, J.A., & Díaz, C. (2005). Cost models for telecommunication networks and their application to GSM systems. In M. Pagani (Ed.), *Encyclopedia of multimedia technology and networking* (pp. 143-150). Hershey, PA: Idea Group Reference.

Hädrich, T., & Maier, R. (2006). Integrated modeling. In D. Schwartz (Ed.), *Encyclopedia of knowledge management* (pp. 251-258). Hershey, PA: Idea Group Reference.

Haghirian, P. (2006). International knowledge transfer as a challenge for communities of practice. In E. Coakes & S. Clarke (Eds.), *Encyclopedia of communities of practice in information and knowledge management* (pp. 234-238). Hershey, PA: Idea Group Reference.

Hainaut, J.-L. (2005). Transformation-based database engineering. In L. Rivero, J. Doorn, & V. Ferraggine (Eds.), *Encyclopedia of database technologies and applications* (pp. 707-713). Hershey, PA: Idea Group Reference.

Hainaut, J.-L., Henrard, J., Hick, J.-M., Roland, D., & Englebert, V. (2005). CASE tools for database engineering. In L. Rivero, J. Doorn, & V. Ferraggine (Eds.), *Encyclopedia of database technologies and applications* (pp. 59-65). Hershey, PA: Idea Group Reference.

Häkkilä, J., & Beekhuyzen, J. (2006). Using Mobile Communication Technology in Student Mentoring. In C. Ghaoui (Ed.), *Encyclopedia of human computer interaction* (pp. 680-685). Hershey, PA: Idea Group Reference.

Hall, D., & Croasdell, D. (2006). Inquiring organizations. In D. Schwartz (Ed.), *Encyclopedia of knowledge management* (pp. 244-250). Hershey, PA: Idea Group Reference.

Hall, L., & Woods, S. (2006). The Importance of Similarity in Empathic Interaction. In C. Ghaoui (Ed.), *Encyclopedia of human computer interaction* (pp. 303-310). Hershey, PA: Idea Group Reference.

Halpin, T. (2005). Information modeling in UML and ORM. In M. Khosrow-Pour (Ed.), *Encyclopedia of information science and technology* (pp. 1471-1475). Hershey, PA: Idea Group Reference.

Hamdi, M.S. (2005a). Employing neural networks in data mining. In J. Wang (Ed.), *Encyclopedia of data warehousing and mining* (pp. 433-437). Hershey, PA: Idea Group Reference.

Hamdi, M.S. (2005b). Support of online learning through intelligent programs. In C. Howard, J.V. Boettcher, L. Justice, K. Schenk, P.L. Rogers, & G.A. Berg (Eds.), *Encyclopedia of distance learning* (pp. 1716-1724). Hershey, PA: Idea Group Reference.

Han, S., & Hill, J.R. (2006). Collaboration, communication, and learning in a virtual community. In S. Dasgupta (Ed.), *Encyclopedia of virtual communities and technologies* (pp. 29-35). Hershey, PA: Idea Group Reference.

Handzic, M., & Lin, J.C.Y. (2005). Virtual knowledge space and learning. In M. Pagani (Ed.), *Encyclopedia of multimedia technology and networking* (pp. 1047-1054). Hershey, PA: Idea Group Reference.

Hanebeck, H.-C.L. (2005). Web-based supply chain strategy. In M. Khosrow-Pour (Ed.), *Encyclopedia of information science and technology* (pp. 3085-3089). Hershey, PA: Idea Group Reference.

Hänisch, T. (2005). Metadata for electronic documents using the Dublin core. In M. Khosrow-Pour (Ed.), *Encyclopedia of information science and technology* (pp. 1928-1930). Hershey, PA: Idea Group Reference.

Hanson, A. (2005). Overcoming barriers in the planning of a virtual library. In M. Khosrow-Pour (Ed.), *Encyclopedia of information science and technology* (pp. 2255-2259). Hershey, PA: Idea Group Reference.

Hanson, A., Ruscella, P., Arsenault, K., Pelland, J., Perez, D., & Shattuck, B. (2005). Library management and organizational change. In M. Khosrow-Pour (Ed.), *Encyclopedia of information science and technology* (pp. 1838-1843). Hershey, PA: Idea Group Reference.

Hantula, D.A. (2005). Download delay and its effects on online learning. In C. Howard, J.V. Boettcher, L. Justice, K. Schenk, P.L. Rogers, & G.A. Berg (Eds.), *Encyclopedia of distance learning* (pp. 683-686). Hershey, PA: Idea Group Reference.

Hantula, D.A., & DeRosa, D.M. (2005). Technology of formal education. In M. Khosrow-Pour (Ed.), *Encyclopedia of information science and technology* (pp. 2761-2764). Hershey, PA: Idea Group Reference.

Haraty, R.A. (2005a). Kernelized database systems security. In L. Rivero, J. Doorn, & V. Ferraggine (Eds.), *Encyclopedia of database technologies and applications* (pp. 304-307). Hershey, PA: Idea Group Reference.

Haraty, R.A. (2005b). Security issues in distributed transaction processing systems. In M. Khosrow-Pour (Ed.), *Encyclopedia of information science and technology* (pp. 2455-2458). Hershey, PA: Idea Group Reference.

Harms, S.K. (2005). Temporal association rule mining in event sequences. In J. Wang (Ed.), *Encyclopedia of data warehousing and mining* (pp. 1098-1102). Hershey, PA: Idea Group Reference.

Harris, A.L., & Chen, C. (2006). Traditional and Internet EDL adoption barriers. In M. Khosrow-Pour (Ed.), *Encyclopedia of e-commerce, e-government, and mobile commerce* (pp. 1075-1081). Hershey, PA: Idea Group Reference.

Harris, U.S. (2005). ICT for social and cultural capital in Pacific island communities. In S. Marshall, W. Taylor, & X. Yu (Eds.), *Encyclopedia of developing regional communities with information and communication technology* (pp. 377-381). Hershey, PA: Idea Group Reference.

Hartoonian, M., & Johnson, V. (2005). Opportunities and opportunity cost in preparing millennium teachers. In C. Howard, J.V. Boettcher, L. Justice, K. Schenk, P.L. Rogers, & G.A. Berg (Eds.), *Encyclopedia of distance learning* (pp. 1446-1447). Hershey, PA: Idea Group Reference.

Hassall, G. (2005). ITC policy and practice in the Fiji islands. In S. Marshall, W. Taylor, & X. Yu (Eds.), *Encyclopedia of developing regional communities with information and communication technology* (pp. 471-474). Hershey, PA: Idea Group Reference.

Hassan, A., & Hietanen, H. (2006). Open content distribution management in virtual organizations. In

M. Khosrow-Pour (Ed.), *Encyclopedia of e-commerce, e-government, and mobile commerce* (pp. 878-883). Hershey, PA: Idea Group Reference.

Hassan, A., Henttonen, K., & Blomqvist, K. (2006). The MENOS organization. In S. Dasgupta (Ed.), *Encyclopedia of virtual communities and technologies* (pp. 308-313). Hershey, PA: Idea Group Reference.

Hassenzahl, M. (2006). Hedonic, Emotional, and Experiential Perspectives on Product Quality. In C. Ghaoui (Ed.), *Encyclopedia of human computer interaction* (pp. 266-272). Hershey, PA: Idea Group Reference.

Haugen, H., & Ask, B. (2005). From R&D project to virtual universities. In C. Howard, J.V. Boettcher, L. Justice, K. Schenk, P.L. Rogers, & G.A. Berg (Eds.), *Encyclopedia of distance learning* (pp. 944-951). Hershey, PA: Idea Group Reference.

Hawk, S., & Kaiser, K. (2005). Offshore software development outsourcing. In M. Khosrow-Pour (Ed.), *Encyclopedia of information science and technology* (pp. 2174-2179). Hershey, PA: Idea Group Reference.

Hawk, S., & Zheng, W. (2006). Interaction standards in e-business. In M. Khosrow-Pour (Ed.), *Encyclopedia of e-commerce, e-government, and mobile commerce* (pp. 648-652). Hershey, PA: Idea Group Reference.

Hawkins, G.W., & Baker, J.D. (2005). Online learner expectations. In C. Howard, J.V. Boettcher, L. Justice, K. Schenk, P.L. Rogers, & G.A. Berg (Eds.), *Encyclopedia of distance learning* (pp. 1365-1369). Hershey, PA: Idea Group Reference.

Häyrinen, K.F., & Saranto, K. (2005). Successful health information system implementation. In M. Khosrow-Pour (Ed.), *Encyclopedia of information science and technology* (pp. 2678-2683). Hershey, PA: Idea Group Reference.

Hazari, S. (2006). Using emerging technologies for effective pedagogy in management education. In E. Coakes & S. Clarke (Eds.), *Encyclopedia of communities of practice in information and knowledge management* (pp. 575-579). Hershey, PA: Idea Group Reference.

He, S. (2006). Multilingual Web sites in global electronic commerce. In M. Khosrow-Pour (Ed.), *Encyclopedia of e-commerce, e-government, and mobile commerce* (pp. 823-828). Hershey, PA: Idea Group Reference.

Heavin, C., & Neville, K. (2006). Mentoring knowledge workers. In D. Schwartz (Ed.), *Encyclopedia of knowledge management* (pp. 621). Hershey, PA: Idea Group Reference.

Heinonen, S. (2005). Mobile e-work to support regional and rural communities. In S. Marshall, W. Taylor, & X. Yu (Eds.), *Encyclopedia of developing regional communities with information and communication technology* (pp. 497-500). Hershey, PA: Idea Group Reference.

Hendricks, P.H. (2005). Space opera-GIS basics. In M. Khosrow-Pour (Ed.), *Encyclopedia of information science and technology* (pp. 2571-2575). Hershey, PA: Idea Group Reference.

Hendriks, P.H.J. (2006). Organizational structure. In D. Schwartz (Ed.), *Encyclopedia of knowledge management* (pp. 749-756). Hershey, PA: Idea Group Reference.

Hendriks, P.H.J., & Sousa, C.A.A. (2006). Motivation for knowledge work. In D. Schwartz (Ed.), *Encyclopedia of knowledge management* (pp. 657). Hershey, PA: Idea Group Reference.

Henley, M., & Noyes, J. (2006). Traditional vs. Pull-Down Menus. In C. Ghaoui (Ed.), *Encyclopedia of human computer interaction* (pp. 622-625). Hershey, PA: Idea Group Reference.

Henry, P. (2006). Turning the Usability Fraternity into a Thriving Industry. In C. Ghaoui (Ed.), *Encyclopedia of human computer interaction* (pp. 626-629). Hershey, PA: Idea Group Reference.

Hentea, M. (2005a). Broadband solutions for residential customers. In M. Pagani (Ed.), *Encyclopedia of multimedia technology and networking* (pp. 76-81). Hershey, PA: Idea Group Reference.

Hentea, M. (2005b). Information security management. In M. Pagani (Ed.), *Encyclopedia of multimedia technology and networking* (pp. 390-395). Hershey, PA: Idea Group Reference.

Hentea, M. (2005c). Multimedia databases. In L. Rivero, J. Doorn, & V. Ferraggine (Eds.), *Encyclopedia of database technologies and applications* (pp. 390-394). Hershey, PA: Idea Group Reference.

Hernandez-Orallo, J. (2005a). Data warehousing and OLAP. In L. Rivero, J. Doorn, & V. Ferraggine (Eds.), *Encyclopedia of database technologies and applications* (pp. 127-133). Hershey, PA: Idea Group Reference.

Hernandez-Orallo, J. (2005b). Knowledge discovery from databases. In L. Rivero, J. Doorn, & V. Ferraggine (Eds.), *Encyclopedia of database technologies and applications* (pp. 313-318). Hershey, PA: Idea Group Reference.

Herschel, R.T. (2005). Chief knowledge officers. In M. Khosrow-Pour (Ed.), *Encyclopedia of information science and technology* (pp. 409-413). Hershey, PA: Idea Group Reference.

Heucke, A., Peters, G., & Tagg, R. (2005). Intelligent software agents. In M. Khosrow-Pour (Ed.), *Encyclopedia of information science and technology* (pp. 1598-1602). Hershey, PA: Idea Group Reference.

Hin, L.T.W., & Subramaniam, R. (2005a). Asymmetric digital subscriber line. In M. Pagani (Ed.), *Encyclopedia of multimedia technology and networking* (pp. 42-48). Hershey, PA: Idea Group Reference.

Hin, L.T.W., & Subramaniam, R. (2005b). Continuing science education of the global public. In C. Howard, J.V. Boettcher, L. Justice, K. Schenk, P.L. Rogers, & G.A. Berg (Eds.), *Encyclopedia of distance learning* (pp. 408-414). Hershey, PA: Idea Group Reference.

Hin, L.T.W., & Subramaniam, R. (2005c). Dot-comming SMEs in Singapore for a new economy. In M.

Khosrow-Pour (Ed.), *Encyclopedia of information science and technology* (pp. 912-917). Hershey, PA: Idea Group Reference.

Hin, L.T.W., & Subramaniam, R. (2006). Virtual government in Singapore. In M. Khosrow-Pour (Ed.), *Encyclopedia of e-commerce, e-government, and mobile commerce* (pp. 1191-1197). Hershey, PA: Idea Group Reference.

Hinnant, C.C., & Sawyer, S. (2005). Electronic government strategies and research in the U.S.. In M. Khosrow-Pour (Ed.), *Encyclopedia of information science and technology* (pp. 1012-1017). Hershey, PA: Idea Group Reference.

Hirji, K.K. (2005). Process-based data mining. In M. Khosrow-Pour (Ed.), *Encyclopedia of information science and technology* (pp. 2321-2325). Hershey, PA: Idea Group Reference.

Hofer, F. (2006). Knowledge transfer between academia and industry. In D. Schwartz (Ed.), *Encyclopedia of knowledge management* (pp. 544). Hershey, PA: Idea Group Reference.

Holder, L.B., & Cook, D.J. (2005). Graph-based data mining. In J. Wang (Ed.), *Encyclopedia of data warehousing and mining* (pp. 540-545). Hershey, PA: Idea Group Reference.

Holland, J.W. (2005). Automation of American criminal justice. In M. Khosrow-Pour (Ed.), *Encyclopedia of information science and technology* (pp. 197-199). Hershey, PA: Idea Group Reference.

Holsapple, C.W., & Jones, K. (2006). Knowledge management strategy formation. In D. Schwartz (Ed.), *Encyclopedia of knowledge management* (pp. 419). Hershey, PA: Idea Group Reference.

Holsapple, C.W., & Joshi, K.D. (2006). Knowledge management ontology. In D. Schwartz (Ed.), *Encyclopedia of knowledge management* (pp. 397). Hershey, PA: Idea Group Reference.

Holstein, W.K., & Crnkovic, J. (2005). Measurement issues in decision support systems. In M. Khosrow-

Pour (Ed.), *Encyclopedia of information science and technology* (pp. 1906-1911). Hershey, PA: Idea Group Reference.

Holzer, M., & Schweste, R. (2005). ICTs as participatory vehicles. In M. Khosrow-Pour (Ed.), *Encyclopedia of information science and technology* (pp. 1372-1378). Hershey, PA: Idea Group Reference.

Honkaranta, A., & Tyrväinen, P. (2005). Content management in organizations. In M. Khosrow-Pour (Ed.), *Encyclopedia of information science and technology* (pp. 550-555). Hershey, PA: Idea Group Reference.

Horiuchi, C. (2005a). E-government databases. In L. Rivero, J. Doorn, & V. Ferraggine (Eds.), *Encyclopedia of database technologies and applications* (pp. 206-210). Hershey, PA: Idea Group Reference.

Horiuchi, C. (2005b). E-mail data stores. In L. Rivero, J. Doorn, & V. Ferraggine (Eds.), *Encyclopedia of database technologies and applications* (pp. 211-215). Hershey, PA: Idea Group Reference.

Hornby, G. (2005). Developing regional destination marketing systems. In S. Marshall, W. Taylor, & X. Yu (Eds.), *Encyclopedia of developing regional communities with information and communication technology* (pp. 169-175). Hershey, PA: Idea Group Reference.

Hosszú, G. (2005a). Current multicast technology. In M. Khosrow-Pour (Ed.), *Encyclopedia of information science and technology* (pp. 660-667). Hershey, PA: Idea Group Reference.

Hosszú, G. (2005b). Reliability issues of the multicast-based mediacommunication. In M. Pagani (Ed.), *Encyclopedia of multimedia technology and networking* (pp. 875-881). Hershey, PA: Idea Group Reference.

Hosszú, G. (2006). Mediacommunication based on application-layer multicast. In S. Dasgupta (Ed.), *Encyclopedia of virtual communities and technologies* (pp. 302-307). Hershey, PA: Idea Group Reference.

Hou, W.-C., Guo, H., Yan, F., & Zhu, Q. (2005). Drawing representative samples from large databases. In J. Wang (Ed.), *Encyclopedia of data warehousing and mining* (pp. 413-420). Hershey, PA: Idea Group Reference.

Hou, W.-C., Sheng, Y.P., & Chen, Z. (2005). Mining for profitable patterns in the stock market. In J. Wang (Ed.), *Encyclopedia of data warehousing and mining* (pp. 779-784). Hershey, PA: Idea Group Reference.

Houben, G.-J., Aroyo, L., & Dicheva, D. (2006). Engineering adaptive concept-based systems for the Web. In M. Khosrow-Pour (Ed.), *Encyclopedia of e-commerce, e-government, and mobile commerce* (pp. 424-430). Hershey, PA: Idea Group Reference.

Houser, C., & Thornton, P. (2005). Mobile educational technology. In C. Howard, J.V. Boettcher, L. Justice, K. Schenk, P.L. Rogers, & G.A. Berg (Eds.), *Encyclopedia of distance learning* (pp. 1289-1296). Hershey, PA: Idea Group Reference.

Howell, S.L., & Wilcken, W. (2005). Student support services. In C. Howard, J.V. Boettcher, L. Justice, K. Schenk, P.L. Rogers, & G.A. Berg (Eds.), *Encyclopedia of distance learning* (pp. 1687-1692). Hershey, PA: Idea Group Reference.

Hoxmeier, J.A. (2005). Dimensions of database quality. In M. Khosrow-Pour (Ed.), *Encyclopedia of information science and technology* (pp. 886-891). Hershey, PA: Idea Group Reference.

Hsu, H.S., & Mykytyn, P.P., Jr. (2006). Intellectual capital. In D. Schwartz (Ed.), *Encyclopedia of knowledge management* (pp. 274-280). Hershey, PA: Idea Group Reference.

Hsu, H.Y.S., & Kulviwat, S. (2006). Personalization and customer satisfaction in mobile commerce. In M. Khosrow-Pour (Ed.), *Encyclopedia of e-commerce, e-government, and mobile commerce* (pp. 914-918). Hershey, PA: Idea Group Reference.

Hsu, W.H. (2005a). Evolutionary computation and genetic algorithms. In J. Wang (Ed.), *Encyclopedia of data warehousing and mining* (pp. 477-481). Hershey, PA: Idea Group Reference.

Hsu, W.H. (2005b). Genetic programming. In J. Wang (Ed.), *Encyclopedia of data warehousing and mining* (pp. 529-533). Hershey, PA: Idea Group Reference.

Hu, J. (2005). Mobile ad hoc networks. In S. Marshall, W. Taylor, & X. Yu (Eds.), *Encyclopedia of developing regional communities with information and communication technology* (pp. 494-496). Hershey, PA: Idea Group Reference.

Hu, W.-C., Yang, H.-J., Lee, C.-W., & Yeh, J.-H. (2005). World Wide Web usage mining. In J. Wang (Ed.), *Encyclopedia of data warehousing and mining* (pp. 1242-1248). Hershey, PA: Idea Group Reference.

Hu, W.-C., Yang, H.-J., Yeh, J.-H., & Lee, C.-W. (2005). World Wide Web search technologies. In M. Khosrow-Pour (Ed.), *Encyclopedia of information science and technology* (pp. 3111-3117). Hershey, PA: Idea Group Reference.

Hu, W.-C., Yang, H.-J., & Yeh, J. (2006). Mobile Internet and handheld devices for virtual communities. In S. Dasgupta (Ed.), *Encyclopedia of virtual communities and technologies* (pp. 314-320). Hershey, PA: Idea Group Reference.

Hu, W.-C., Yeh, J.-H., Yang, H.-J., & Lee, C.-W. (2006). Mobile handheld devices for mobile commerce. In M. Khosrow-Pour (Ed.), *Encyclopedia of e-commerce, e-government, and mobile commerce* (pp. 792-798). Hershey, PA: Idea Group Reference.

Hua, Z., Xie, X., Lu, H., & Ma, W.-Y. (2006). A Cooperative Framework for Information Browsing in Mobile Environment. In C. Ghaoui (Ed.), *Encyclopedia of human computer interaction* (pp. 120-127). Hershey, PA: Idea Group Reference.

Huang, W., Chen, Y., & Wang, K.L. (2006). E-government development and implementation. In M. Khosrow-Pour (Ed.), *Encyclopedia of e-commerce, e-government, and mobile commerce* (pp. 359-366). Hershey, PA: Idea Group Reference.

Huang, X. (2005). Clustering analysis and algorithms. In J. Wang (Ed.), *Encyclopedia of data warehousing and mining* (pp. 159-164). Hershey, PA: Idea Group Reference.

Hughes, J., & Lang, K.R. (2005). Peer-to-peer file-sharing systems for digital media. In M. Pagani (Ed.), *Encyclopedia of multimedia technology and networking* (pp. 807-813). Hershey, PA: Idea Group Reference.

Hulicki, Z. (2005). Multimedia communication services on digital TV platforms. In M. Pagani (Ed.), *Encyclopedia of multimedia technology and networking* (pp. 678-686). Hershey, PA: Idea Group Reference.

Hunter, M.G. (2005). Information systems and small business. In M. Khosrow-Pour (Ed.), *Encyclopedia of information science and technology* (pp. 1487-1490). Hershey, PA: Idea Group Reference.

Hunter, M.G. (2006a). Narrative inquiry and communities of practice. In E. Coakes & S. Clarke (Eds.), *Encyclopedia of communities of practice in information and knowledge management* (pp. 388-389). Hershey, PA: Idea Group Reference.

Hunter, M.G. (2006b). Virtual teams and communities of practice. In E. Coakes & S. Clarke (Eds.), *Encyclopedia of communities of practice in information and knowledge management* (pp. 587-588). Hershey, PA: Idea Group Reference.

Hunter, M.G., & Carr, P. (2005). IT to facilitate distance education. In C. Howard, J.V. Boettcher, L. Justice, K. Schenk, P.L. Rogers, & G.A. Berg (Eds.), *Encyclopedia of distance learning* (pp. 1156-1161). Hershey, PA: Idea Group Reference.

Huotari, M.-L., & Iivonen, M. (2005). Trust in knowledge-based organizations. In M. Khosrow-Pour (Ed.), *Encyclopedia of information science and technology* (pp. 2892-2896). Hershey, PA: Idea Group Reference.

Huq, A. (2006). Engaging organisational culture to overcome social barriers in virtual communities. In

S. Dasgupta (Ed.), *Encyclopedia of virtual communities and technologies* (pp. 193-197). Hershey, PA: Idea Group Reference.

Huq, A., Raja, J.Z., & Rosenberg, D. (2006). Linking organisational culture and communities of practice. In E. Coakes & S. Clarke (Eds.), *Encyclopedia of communities of practice in information and knowledge management* (pp. 340-345). Hershey, PA: Idea Group Reference.

Hurson, A.R., & Yang, B. (2005). Multimedia content representation technologies. In M. Pagani (Ed.), *Encyclopedia of multimedia technology and networking* (pp. 687-695). Hershey, PA: Idea Group Reference.

Hürst, W. (2006). Elastic Interfaces for Visual Data Browsing. In C. Ghaoui (Ed.), *Encyclopedia of human computer interaction* (pp. 187-195). Hershey, PA: Idea Group Reference.

Hürst, W., & Lauer, T. (2006). Interactive Speech Skimming via Time-Stretched Audio Replay. In C. Ghaoui (Ed.), *Encyclopedia of human computer interaction* (pp. 355-361). Hershey, PA: Idea Group Reference.

Hustad, E., & Munkvold, B.E. (2006). Communities of practice and other organizational groups. In E. Coakes & S. Clarke (Eds.), *Encyclopedia of communities of practice in information and knowledge management* (pp. 60-62). Hershey, PA: Idea Group Reference.

Hutchinson, K. (2005). Cambodian youth making connections. In S. Marshall, W. Taylor, & X. Yu (Eds.), *Encyclopedia of developing regional communities with information and communication technology* (pp. 66-71). Hershey, PA: Idea Group Reference.

Hvannberg, E.T., Gunnarsdóttir, S., & Atladóttir, G. (2006). From User Inquiries to Specification. In C. Ghaoui (Ed.), *Encyclopedia of human computer interaction* (pp. 220-226). Hershey, PA: Idea Group Reference.

Hwang, H.S., & Stewart, C. (2006). Lessons from dot-com boom and bust. In M. Khosrow-Pour (Ed.), *Encyclopedia of e-commerce, e-government, and mobile commerce* (pp. 698-702). Hershey, PA: Idea Group Reference.

Hwang, H.S., & Stewart, C.M. (2005). Instant messaging moves from the home to the office. In M. Khosrow-Pour (Ed.), *Encyclopedia of information science and technology* (pp. 1540-1544). Hershey, PA: Idea Group Reference.

Hwang, M.I. (2005). Enterprise resource planning and systems integration. In M. Khosrow-Pour (Ed.), *Encyclopedia of information science and technology* (pp. 1083-1088). Hershey, PA: Idea Group Reference.

Iacob, M.E., Boekhoudt, P., & Ebeling, F. (2005). Electronic commerce policies for Dutch SMEs. In M. Khosrow-Pour (Ed.), *Encyclopedia of information science and technology* (pp. 1006-1011). Hershey, PA: Idea Group Reference.

Iannarelli, B. (2005). Just-in-time training. In C. Howard, J.V. Boettcher, L. Justice, K. Schenk, P.L. Rogers, & G.A. Berg (Eds.), *Encyclopedia of distance learning* (pp. 1167-1174). Hershey, PA: Idea Group Reference.

Ibrahim, H. (2005). Checking integrity constraints in a distributed database. In L. Rivero, J. Doorn, & V. Ferraggine (Eds.), *Encyclopedia of database technologies and applications* (pp. 66-73). Hershey, PA: Idea Group Reference.

Imberman, S., & Tansel, A.U. (2006). Frequent itemset mining and association rules. In D. Schwartz (Ed.), *Encyclopedia of knowledge management* (pp. 197-203). Hershey, PA: Idea Group Reference.

Ingram, A.L. (2005). Measuring collaboration in online communications. In M. Khosrow-Pour (Ed.), *Encyclopedia of information science and technology* (pp. 1912-1916). Hershey, PA: Idea Group Reference.

Ingram, A.L., & Hathorn, L.G. (2005a). Analyzing collaboration in online communications. In C. Howard, J.V. Boettcher, L. Justice, K. Schenk, P.L. Rogers, & G.A. Berg (Eds.), *Encyclopedia of distance learning* (pp. 83-89). Hershey, PA: Idea Group Reference.

Ingram, A.L., & Hathorn, L.G. (2005b). Collaboration in online communications. In C. Howard, J.V. Boettcher, L. Justice, K. Schenk, P.L. Rogers, & G.A. Berg (Eds.), *Encyclopedia of distance learning* (pp. 264-268). Hershey, PA: Idea Group Reference.

Inoue, Y., & Bell, S.T. (2005). Electronic/digital government innovation, and publishing trends with IT. In M. Khosrow-Pour (Ed.), *Encyclopedia of information science and technology* (pp. 1018-1053). Hershey, PA: Idea Group Reference.

Iossifides, A.C., Louvros, S., & Kotsopoulos, S.A. (2005). FDD techniques towards the multimedia era. In M. Pagani (Ed.), *Encyclopedia of multimedia technology and networking* (pp. 315-323). Hershey, PA: Idea Group Reference.

Ip, B., & Jacobs, G. (2006). Visual and Physical Interfaces for Computer and Video Games. In C. Ghaoui (Ed.), *Encyclopedia of human computer interaction* (pp. 692-698). Hershey, PA: Idea Group Reference.

Isaak, J. (2006). Virtual communities wish list. In S. Dasgupta (Ed.), *Encyclopedia of virtual communities and technologies* (pp. 520-523). Hershey, PA: Idea Group Reference.

Ishaya, T. (2005). Interoperable learning objects management. In M. Pagani (Ed.), *Encyclopedia of multimedia technology and networking* (pp. 486-493). Hershey, PA: Idea Group Reference.

Ito, T. (2005). Discovering an effective measure in data mining. In J. Wang (Ed.), *Encyclopedia of data warehousing and mining* (pp. 364-371). Hershey, PA: Idea Group Reference.

Jacobson, C.M. (2006). Knowledge sharing between individuals. In D. Schwartz (Ed.), *Encyclopedia of knowledge management* (pp. 507). Hershey, PA: Idea Group Reference.

Jaeger, B. (2005). E-government, e-democracy and the politicians. In M. Khosrow-Pour (Ed.), *Encyclopedia of information science and technology* (pp. 990-994). Hershey, PA: Idea Group Reference.

Jain, J., & Lyons, G. (2005). Connecting dispersed communities on the move. In S. Marshall, W. Taylor, & X. Yu (Eds.), *Encyclopedia of developing regional communities with information and communication technology* (pp. 124-129). Hershey, PA: Idea Group Reference.

Jain, R., & Ramesh, B. (2006). Development and deployment of Web services. In M. Khosrow-Pour (Ed.), *Encyclopedia of e-commerce, e-government, and mobile commerce* (pp. 197-202). Hershey, PA: Idea Group Reference.

Janczewski, L.J., & Portougal, V. (2005). Road map to information security management. In M. Pagani (Ed.), *Encyclopedia of multimedia technology and networking* (pp. 895-902). Hershey, PA: Idea Group Reference.

Janes, D.P. (2005). Consensus building using e-research. In C. Howard, J.V. Boettcher, L. Justice, K. Schenk, P.L. Rogers, & G.A. Berg (Eds.), *Encyclopedia of distance learning* (pp. 379-385). Hershey, PA: Idea Group Reference.

Janssen, M. (2005). Simulation for business engineering of electronic markets. In M. Khosrow-Pour (Ed.), *Encyclopedia of information science and technology* (pp. 2503-2507). Hershey, PA: Idea Group Reference.

Janvier, W.A., & Ghaoui, C. (2006). Replicating Human Interaction to Support E-Learning. In C. Ghaoui (Ed.), *Encyclopedia of human computer interaction* (pp. 494-503). Hershey, PA: Idea Group Reference.

Jasimuddin, S.M., Connell, N.A.D., & Klein, J.H. (2006). Understanding organizational memory. In D. Schwartz (Ed.), *Encyclopedia of knowledge management* (pp. 870-875). Hershey, PA: Idea Group Reference.

Jaspers, M.W.M. (2006). The Think Aloud Method and User Interface Design. In C. Ghaoui (Ed.), *Encyclopedia of human computer interaction* (pp. 597-602). Hershey, PA: Idea Group Reference.

Jawahar, I.M. (2005). The past, present, and future of end-user performance. In M. Khosrow-Pour (Ed.), *Encyclopedia of information science and technology* (pp. 2826-2830). Hershey, PA: Idea Group Reference.

Jeanson, B., & Ingham, J. (2006). Consumer trust in e-commerce. In M. Khosrow-Pour (Ed.), *Encyclopedia of e-commerce, e-government, and mobile commerce* (pp. 141-150). Hershey, PA: Idea Group Reference.

Jeffcoate, J. (2005). Adoption of e-commerce in the value chain by SMEs. In M. Khosrow-Pour (Ed.), *Encyclopedia of information science and technology* (pp. 62-67). Hershey, PA: Idea Group Reference.

Jeffery, A.B., & Bratton-Jeffery, M.F. (2005). Quality function deployment in training design. In C. Howard, J.V. Boettcher, L. Justice, K. Schenk, P.L. Rogers, & G.A. Berg (Eds.), *Encyclopedia of distance learning* (pp. 1543-1551). Hershey, PA: Idea Group Reference.

Jennex, M.E. (2005). Internet support for knowledge management systems. In M. Khosrow-Pour (Ed.), *Encyclopedia of information science and technology* (pp. 1640-1644). Hershey, PA: Idea Group Reference.

Jennex, M.E. (2006a). Knowledge management success models. In D. Schwartz (Ed.), *Encyclopedia of knowledge management* (pp. 429). Hershey, PA: Idea Group Reference.

Jennex, M.E. (2006b). Knowledge management system success factors. In D. Schwartz (Ed.), *Encyclopedia of knowledge management* (pp. 436). Hershey, PA: Idea Group Reference.

Jennings, M., Mawhinney, C.H., & Fustos, J. (2005). Case-based learning in computer information systems. In M. Khosrow-Pour (Ed.), *Encyclopedia of information science and technology* (pp. 368-372). Hershey, PA: Idea Group Reference.

Jeong, H.S., Abraham, D.M., & Abraham, D.M. (2006). Knowledge management in civil infrastructure systems. In E. Coakes & S. Clarke (Eds.), *Encyclopedia of communities of practice in information and knowledge management* (pp. 286-292). Hershey, PA: Idea Group Reference.

Jesness, R. (2005). High school online learning. In C. Howard, J.V. Boettcher, L. Justice, K. Schenk, P.L. Rogers, & G.A. Berg (Eds.), *Encyclopedia of distance learning* (pp. 998-1005). Hershey, PA: Idea Group Reference.

Jha, N., & Sural, S. (2005). Privacy protection in association rule mining. In J. Wang (Ed.), *Encyclopedia of data warehousing and mining* (pp. 925-929). Hershey, PA: Idea Group Reference.

Johannesson, P. (2005). A language/action based approach to information modelling. In M. Khosrow-Pour (Ed.), *Encyclopedia of information science and technology* (pp. 7-10). Hershey, PA: Idea Group Reference.

Johnson, V. (2005). Infusion of technology into the P-16 environment. In C. Howard, J.V. Boettcher, L. Justice, K. Schenk, P.L. Rogers, & G.A. Berg (Eds.), *Encyclopedia of distance learning* (pp. 1099-1100). Hershey, PA: Idea Group Reference.

Johnston, K. (2005). Harmonizing IT and business strategies. In M. Khosrow-Pour (Ed.), *Encyclopedia of information science and technology* (pp. 1317-1321). Hershey, PA: Idea Group Reference.

Johnstone, D.B. (2005). Western Governors University and competency-based education. In C. Howard, J.V. Boettcher, L. Justice, K. Schenk, P.L. Rogers, & G.A. Berg (Eds.), *Encyclopedia of distance learning* (pp. 2029-2035). Hershey, PA: Idea Group Reference.

Johnstone, S.M. (2005). Advancing the effective use of technology in higher education. In C. Howard, J.V. Boettcher, L. Justice, K. Schenk, P.L. Rogers, & G.A. Berg (Eds.), *Encyclopedia of distance learning* (pp. 79-82). Hershey, PA: Idea Group Reference.

Joia, L.A. (2005). Intelligent metabusiness. In M. Khosrow-Pour (Ed.), *Encyclopedia of information science and technology* (pp. 1591-1597). Hershey, PA: Idea Group Reference.

Joia, L.A. (2006). Building government-to-government enterprises. In M. Khosrow-Pour (Ed.), *Encyclopedia of e-commerce, e-government, and mobile commerce* (pp. 72-77). Hershey, PA: Idea Group Reference.

Jones, N.B., & Gupta, J.N.D. (2005). Small business transformation through knowledge management. In M. Khosrow-Pour (Ed.), *Encyclopedia of information science and technology* (pp. 2514-2518). Hershey, PA: Idea Group Reference.

Jong, C., & Mahatanankoon, P. (2006). Extending online communities through virtual parallel systems. In S. Dasgupta (Ed.), *Encyclopedia of virtual communities and technologies* (pp. 213-217). Hershey, PA: Idea Group Reference.

Jourdan, L., Dhaenens, C., & Talbi, E.-G. (2005). Evolutionary data mining for genomics. In J. Wang (Ed.), *Encyclopedia of data warehousing and mining* (pp. 482-486). Hershey, PA: Idea Group Reference.

Jovanovic-Dolecek, G. (2005a). Digital filters. In M. Pagani (Ed.), *Encyclopedia of multimedia technology and networking* (pp. 180-196). Hershey, PA: Idea Group Reference.

Jovanovic-Dolecek, G. (2005b). Fundamentals of multirate systems. In M. Khosrow-Pour (Ed.), *Encyclopedia of information science and technology* (pp. 1249-1252). Hershey, PA: Idea Group Reference.

Jovanovic-Dolecek, G. (2005c). Simple methods for design of narrowband highpass FIR filters. In M. Khosrow-Pour (Ed.), *Encyclopedia of information science and technology* (pp. 2492-2498). Hershey, PA: Idea Group Reference.

Jovanovic-Dolecek, G., & Díaz-Carmona, J. (2005). One method for design of narrowband low-pass filters. In M. Khosrow-Pour (Ed.), *Encyclopedia of information science and technology* (pp. 2185-2193). Hershey, PA: Idea Group Reference.

Judd, D.L. (2005). Technology integrated activities in the elementary curriculum. In C. Howard, J.V. Boettcher, L. Justice, K. Schenk, P.L. Rogers, & G.A. Berg (Eds.), *Encyclopedia of distance learning* (pp. 1809-1814). Hershey, PA: Idea Group Reference.

Juszczyszyn, K. (2006). Virtual communities and the alignment of Web ontologies. In S. Dasgupta (Ed.), *Encyclopedia of virtual communities and technologies* (pp. 497-499). Hershey, PA: Idea Group Reference.

Kabene, S.M., Leduc, R., & Burjaw, R. (2005). Telework and the Canadian environment. In S. Marshall, W. Taylor, & X. Yu (Eds.), *Encyclopedia of developing regional communities with information and communication technology* (pp. 692-697). Hershey, PA: Idea Group Reference.

Kabene, S.M., Takhar, J., Leduc, R., & Burjaw, R. (2005). Medical education in the 21st century. In S. Marshall, W. Taylor, & X. Yu (Eds.), *Encyclopedia of developing regional communities with information and communication technology* (pp. 488-493). Hershey, PA: Idea Group Reference.

Kacem, I.M. (2005). Flexible job-shop scheduling problems. In M. Khosrow-Pour (Ed.), *Encyclopedia of information science and technology* (pp. 1197-1200). Hershey, PA: Idea Group Reference.

Kacimi, M., Chbeir, R., & Yetongnon, K. (2005). Multimedia proxy cache architectures. In M. Pagani (Ed.), *Encyclopedia of multimedia technology and networking* (pp. 731-736). Hershey, PA: Idea Group Reference.

Kaluzniacky, E. (2006). Psychologically aware IT workers. In E. Coakes & S. Clarke (Eds.), *Encyclopedia of communities of practice in information and knowledge management* (pp. 430-435). Hershey, PA: Idea Group Reference.

Kalvet, T. (2005). Digital divide and the ICT paradigm generally and in Estonia. In S. Marshall, W. Taylor, & X. Yu (Eds.), *Encyclopedia of developing regional communities with information and communication technology* (pp. 182-187). Hershey, PA: Idea Group Reference.

Kamel, S. (2005a). The software industry in Egypt. In M. Khosrow-Pour (Ed.), *Encyclopedia of information*

*science and technology* (pp. 2836-2840). Hershey, PA: Idea Group Reference.

Kamel, S. (2005b). Virtual organizations in postgraduate education in Egypt. In C. Howard, J.V. Boettcher, L. Justice, K. Schenk, P.L. Rogers, & G.A. Berg (Eds.), *Encyclopedia of distance learning* (pp. 1977-1983). Hershey, PA: Idea Group Reference.

Kamthan, P., & Pai, H.-I. (2006). Knowledge representation in pattern management. In D. Schwartz (Ed.), *Encyclopedia of knowledge management* (pp. 478). Hershey, PA: Idea Group Reference.

Kanapady, R., & Lazarevic, A. (2005). Data mining for damage detection in engineering structures. In J. Wang (Ed.), *Encyclopedia of data warehousing and mining* (pp. 245-250). Hershey, PA: Idea Group Reference.

Kang, K.W., Rosen, D.E., & Shin, S.K. (2006). Knowledge creation in online communities. In M. Khosrow-Pour (Ed.), *Encyclopedia of e-commerce, e-government, and mobile commerce* (pp. 691-697). Hershey, PA: Idea Group Reference.

Kankanhalli, A., Tan, B.C.Y., & Wei, K.-K. (2006). Knowledge producers and consumers. In D. Schwartz (Ed.), *Encyclopedia of knowledge management* (pp. 459). Hershey, PA: Idea Group Reference.

Kao, O., & Rerrer, U. (2006). Peer-to-peer-based collaboration for virtual communities. In S. Dasgupta (Ed.), *Encyclopedia of virtual communities and technologies* (pp. 382-386). Hershey, PA: Idea Group Reference.

Kao, O., & Tendresse, I.L. (2005). Mosaic-based relevance feedback for image retrieval. In J. Wang (Ed.), *Encyclopedia of data warehousing and mining* (pp. 837-841). Hershey, PA: Idea Group Reference.

Kapetanios, E. (2005). On the relativity of ontological domains and their specifications. In M. Khosrow-Pour (Ed.), *Encyclopedia of information science and technology* (pp. 2180-2184). Hershey, PA: Idea Group Reference.

Kapp, K.M. (2005). Winning an e-learning proposal or grant. In C. Howard, J.V. Boettcher, L. Justice, K. Schenk, P.L. Rogers, & G.A. Berg (Eds.), *Encyclopedia of distance learning* (pp. 2044-2050). Hershey, PA: Idea Group Reference.

Karacapilidis, N. (2005). E-collaboration support systems: issues to be addressed. In M. Khosrow-Pour (Ed.), *Encyclopedia of information science and technology* (pp. 939-945). Hershey, PA: Idea Group Reference.

Karahanna, E., Evaristo, R., & Srite, M. (2005). Cross-cultural research in MIS. In M. Khosrow-Pour (Ed.), *Encyclopedia of information science and technology* (pp. 640-644). Hershey, PA: Idea Group Reference.

Karakostas, B. (2005). Standards for Web-based integration adapters. In M. Khosrow-Pour (Ed.), *Encyclopedia of information science and technology* (pp. 2602-2604). Hershey, PA: Idea Group Reference.

Kardaras, D., & Karakostas, B. (2006). Virtual communities in banking customer retention. In S. Dasgupta (Ed.), *Encyclopedia of virtual communities and technologies* (pp. 515-519). Hershey, PA: Idea Group Reference.

Karimi, H.A., & Peachavanish, R. (2005). Interoperability in geospatial information systems. In M. Khosrow-Pour (Ed.), *Encyclopedia of information science and technology* (pp. 1645-1650). Hershey, PA: Idea Group Reference.

Karnouskos, S., & Vilmos, A. (2006). Universal approach to mobile payments. In M. Khosrow-Pour (Ed.), *Encyclopedia of e-commerce, e-government, and mobile commerce* (pp. 1114-1119). Hershey, PA: Idea Group Reference.

Karoui, K. (2005). Mobile agents. In M. Pagani (Ed.), *Encyclopedia of multimedia technology and networking* (pp. 608-614). Hershey, PA: Idea Group Reference.

Karoulis, A., & Pombortsis, A. (2005a). Heuristically evaluating Web-based ODL. In C. Howard, J.V. Boettcher, L. Justice, K. Schenk, P.L. Rogers, & G.A.

Berg (Eds.), *Encyclopedia of distance learning* (pp. 992-997). Hershey, PA: Idea Group Reference.

Karoulis, A., & Pombortsis, A. (2005b). Traditional education and distance learning. In C. Howard, J.V. Boettcher, L. Justice, K. Schenk, P.L. Rogers, & G.A. Berg (Eds.), *Encyclopedia of distance learning* (pp. 1880-1886). Hershey, PA: Idea Group Reference.

Karoulis, A., Demetriadis, S., & Pombortsis, A. (2006). Cognitive Graphical Walkthrough Interface Evaluation. In C. Ghaoui (Ed.), *Encyclopedia of human computer interaction* (pp. 73-78). Hershey, PA: Idea Group Reference.

Karpouzis, K., Drosopoulos, A., Ioannou, S., Raouzaiou, A., Tsapatsoulis, N., & Kollias, S. (2005). Facial and body feature extraction for emotionally-rich HCI. In M. Khosrow-Pour (Ed.), *Encyclopedia of information science and technology* (pp. 1180-1185). Hershey, PA: Idea Group Reference.

Kase, S.E., & Ritter, F.E. (2005). Gender and computer anxiety. In M. Khosrow-Pour (Ed.), *Encyclopedia of information science and technology* (pp. 1257-1265). Hershey, PA: Idea Group Reference.

Kasi, V., & Jain, R. (2006). Internet search engines. In M. Khosrow-Pour (Ed.), *Encyclopedia of e-commerce, e-government, and mobile commerce* (pp. 672-677). Hershey, PA: Idea Group Reference.

Kasi, V., & Young, B. (2006). Context and concept of Web services. In M. Khosrow-Pour (Ed.), *Encyclopedia of e-commerce, e-government, and mobile commerce* (pp. 151-156). Hershey, PA: Idea Group Reference.

Kaspar, C., & Hagenhoff, S. (2005). Mobile radio technologies. In M. Pagani (Ed.), *Encyclopedia of multimedia technology and networking* (pp. 645-651). Hershey, PA: Idea Group Reference.

Katsaros, D., & Manolopoulos, Y. (2005a). Cache management for Web-powered databases. In M. Khosrow-Pour (Ed.), *Encyclopedia of information science and technology* (pp. 362-367). Hershey, PA: Idea Group Reference.

Katsaros, D., & Manolopoulos, Y. (2005b). Tree and graph mining. In J. Wang (Ed.), *Encyclopedia of data warehousing and mining* (pp. 1140-1145). Hershey, PA: Idea Group Reference.

Katsaros, D., Yavaş, G., Nanopoulos, A., Karakaya, M., Ulusoy, O., & Manolopoulos, Y. (2005). Resource allocation in wireless networks. In J. Wang (Ed.), *Encyclopedia of data warehousing and mining* (pp. 955-959). Hershey, PA: Idea Group Reference.

Kaufman, E. (2005). E-government and e-democracy in Latin America. In S. Marshall, W. Taylor, & X. Yu (Eds.), *Encyclopedia of developing regional communities with information and communication technology* (pp. 263-268). Hershey, PA: Idea Group Reference.

Kaufman, R., & Lick, D.W. (2005). Mega-planning for online learning and technology change. In C. Howard, J.V. Boettcher, L. Justice, K. Schenk, P.L. Rogers, & G.A. Berg (Eds.), *Encyclopedia of distance learning* (pp. 1275-1282). Hershey, PA: Idea Group Reference.

Kaur, A., Dunning, J., Bhattacharya, S., & Ahmed, A. (2005). Re-purposeable learning objects based on teaching and learning styles. In M. Pagani (Ed.), *Encyclopedia of multimedia technology and networking* (pp. 882-886). Hershey, PA: Idea Group Reference.

Kayacik, H.G., Zincir-Heywood, A.N., & Heywood, M.I. (2005). Intrusion detection systems. In M. Pagani (Ed.), *Encyclopedia of multimedia technology and networking* (pp. 494-499). Hershey, PA: Idea Group Reference.

Kayama, M., & Okamoto, T. (2005). E-learning environment. In M. Khosrow-Pour (Ed.), *Encyclopedia of information science and technology* (pp. 1001-1005). Hershey, PA: Idea Group Reference.

Keates, S., Trewin, S., & Elliott, J.P. (2006). Including Users with Motor Impairments in Design. In C. Ghaoui (Ed.), *Encyclopedia of human computer interaction* (pp. 317-323). Hershey, PA: Idea Group Reference.

Kefalas, P., Holcombe, M., Eleftherakis, G., & Gheorghe, M. (2005). Formal development of reactive agent-based systems. In M. Khosrow-Pour (Ed.), *Encyclopedia of information science and technology* (pp. 1201-1204). Hershey, PA: Idea Group Reference.

Keinath, B.J. (2005). Evaluating online programs using a BSC approach. In C. Howard, J.V. Boettcher, L. Justice, K. Schenk, P.L. Rogers, & G.A. Berg (Eds.), *Encyclopedia of distance learning* (pp. 875-881). Hershey, PA: Idea Group Reference.

Kelic, A. (2005). Fiber-to-the-home technologies and standards. In M. Pagani (Ed.), *Encyclopedia of multimedia technology and networking* (pp. 329-335). Hershey, PA: Idea Group Reference.

Kenyon, S. (2005). Using virtual mobility to alleviate aspects of social exclusion. In S. Marshall, W. Taylor, & X. Yu (Eds.), *Encyclopedia of developing regional communities with information and communication technology* (pp. 715-722). Hershey, PA: Idea Group Reference.

Keppell, M., Au, E., Ma, A., & Chan, C. (2005). Curriculum development in technology-enhanced environments. In C. Howard, J.V. Boettcher, L. Justice, K. Schenk, P.L. Rogers, & G.A. Berg (Eds.), *Encyclopedia of distance learning* (pp. 492-504). Hershey, PA: Idea Group Reference.

Kern-Isberner, G. (2005). Mining data with group theoretical means. In J. Wang (Ed.), *Encyclopedia of data warehousing and mining* (pp. 763-767). Hershey, PA: Idea Group Reference.

Keskinen, A., & Kuosa, T. (2005). Citizen-oriented decision making. In S. Marshall, W. Taylor, & X. Yu (Eds.), *Encyclopedia of developing regional communities with information and communication technology* (pp. 96-102). Hershey, PA: Idea Group Reference.

Ketelhut, D.J., Whitehouse, P., Dede, C., & Brown-L'Bahy, T. (2005). Designing a distributed learning experience. In C. Howard, J.V. Boettcher, L. Justice, K. Schenk, P.L. Rogers, & G.A. Berg (Eds.), *Encyclopedia of distance learning* (pp. 518-524). Hershey, PA: Idea Group Reference.

Kettley, S. (2006a). Art as Methodology. In C. Ghaoui (Ed.), *Encyclopedia of human computer interaction* (pp. 31-37). Hershey, PA: Idea Group Reference.

Kettley, S. (2006b). On Not Designing Tools. In C. Ghaoui (Ed.), *Encyclopedia of human computer interaction* (pp. 429-434). Hershey, PA: Idea Group Reference.

Khalfan, A.M., Al-Hajery, M.Z., & Al-Gharbi, K. (2005). Contracting mechanisms in the IS/IT outsourcing phenomenon. In M. Khosrow-Pour (Ed.), *Encyclopedia of information science and technology* (pp. 590-595). Hershey, PA: Idea Group Reference.

Khan, S. (2005). Optimization of continual queries. In L. Rivero, J. Doorn, & V. Ferraggine (Eds.), *Encyclopedia of database technologies and applications* (pp. 469-471). Hershey, PA: Idea Group Reference.

Khan, S., Ganguly, A.R., & Gupta, A. (2006). Creating knowledge for business decision making. In D. Schwartz (Ed.), *Encyclopedia of knowledge management* (pp. 81-89). Hershey, PA: Idea Group Reference.

Khosrow-Pour, M. (1990). Microcomputer Systems Management and Applications. Boston: Boyd & Fraser Publishing Company.

Kieler, M., & West, M.J. (2005). Archival issues related to digital creations. In M. Khosrow-Pour (Ed.), *Encyclopedia of information science and technology* (pp. 152-156). Hershey, PA: Idea Group Reference.

Kim, D. (2005). Concepts and dynamics of the application service provider industry. In M. Khosrow-Pour (Ed.), *Encyclopedia of information science and technology* (pp. 514-518). Hershey, PA: Idea Group Reference.

Kim, H.-J. (2005). Text mining methods for hierarchical document indexing. In J. Wang (Ed.), *Encyclopedia of data warehousing and mining* (pp. 1113-1119). Hershey, PA: Idea Group Reference.

Kimble, C., & Hildreth, P. (2005). Virtual communities in practice. In M. Khosrow-Pour (Ed.), *Ency-

*clopedia of information science and technology* (pp. 2991-2995). Hershey, PA: Idea Group Reference.

Kimble, C., & Hildreth, P. (2006). The limits of communities of practice. In E. Coakes & S. Clarke (Eds.), *Encyclopedia of communities of practice in information and knowledge management* (pp. 327-334). Hershey, PA: Idea Group Reference.

Kimble, C., & Li, F. (2006). Effective virtual working through communities of practice. In S. Dasgupta (Ed.), *Encyclopedia of virtual communities and technologies* (pp. 156-160). Hershey, PA: Idea Group Reference.

Kindmüller, M.C., Leuchter, S., & Urbas, L. (2005). Online communities and community building. In M. Khosrow-Pour (Ed.), *Encyclopedia of information science and technology* (pp. 2203-2208). Hershey, PA: Idea Group Reference.

King, W.R. (2006a). Knowledge sharing. In D. Schwartz (Ed.), *Encyclopedia of knowledge management* (pp. 493). Hershey, PA: Idea Group Reference.

King, W.R. (2006b). Knowledge transfer. In D. Schwartz (Ed.), *Encyclopedia of knowledge management* (pp. 538). Hershey, PA: Idea Group Reference.

Kinuthia, W. (2005). Preparing African higher education faculty in technology. In S. Marshall, W. Taylor, & X. Yu (Eds.), *Encyclopedia of developing regional communities with information and communication technology* (pp. 576-580). Hershey, PA: Idea Group Reference.

Kirlidog, M. (2005). Developing regional communities in Turkey. In S. Marshall, W. Taylor, & X. Yu (Eds.), *Encyclopedia of developing regional communities with information and communication technology* (pp. 164-168). Hershey, PA: Idea Group Reference.

Kisielnicki, J. (2006). Transfer of information and knowledge in the project management. In E. Coakes & S. Clarke (Eds.), *Encyclopedia of communities of*

*practice in information and knowledge management* (pp. 544-551). Hershey, PA: Idea Group Reference.

Kitagaki, I. (2005). Promotion of e-government in Japan and its operation. In M. Khosrow-Pour (Ed.), *Encyclopedia of information science and technology* (pp. 2359-2363). Hershey, PA: Idea Group Reference.

Kitchens, F.L. (2005). Artificial neural networks used in automobile insurance underwriting. In M. Khosrow-Pour (Ed.), *Encyclopedia of information science and technology* (pp. 168-172). Hershey, PA: Idea Group Reference.

Klawonn, F., & Georgevia, O. (2005). Identifying single clusters in large data sets. In J. Wang (Ed.), *Encyclopedia of data warehousing and mining* (pp. 582-585). Hershey, PA: Idea Group Reference.

Klawonn, F., & Rehm, F. (2005). Clustering techniques for outlier detection. In J. Wang (Ed.), *Encyclopedia of data warehousing and mining* (pp. 180-183). Hershey, PA: Idea Group Reference.

Klein, E.E. (2005). Anonymity-featured group support systems and creativity. In C. Howard, J.V. Boettcher, L. Justice, K. Schenk, P.L. Rogers, & G.A. Berg (Eds.), *Encyclopedia of distance learning* (pp. 97-103). Hershey, PA: Idea Group Reference.

Klobas, J.E., & Renzi, S. (2005a). Innovation in Web-enhanced learning. In C. Howard, J.V. Boettcher, L. Justice, K. Schenk, P.L. Rogers, & G.A. Berg (Eds.), *Encyclopedia of distance learning* (pp. 1110-1116). Hershey, PA: Idea Group Reference.

Klobas, J.E., & Renzi, S. (2005b). Scenarios for Web-enhanced learning. In M. Khosrow-Pour (Ed.), *Encyclopedia of information science and technology* (pp. 2443-2449). Hershey, PA: Idea Group Reference.

Knepper, R., & Chen, Y.-C. (2006). Digital government development. In M. Khosrow-Pour (Ed.), *Encyclopedia of e-commerce, e-government, and mobile commerce* (pp. 203-209). Hershey, PA: Idea Group Reference.

Knight, D., & Angelides, M.C. (2005). Multimedia content adaption. In M. Khosrow-Pour (Ed.), *Encyclopedia of information science and technology* (pp. 2051-2057). Hershey, PA: Idea Group Reference.

Knight, J. (2006a). Engagability. In C. Ghaoui (Ed.), *Encyclopedia of human computer interaction* (pp. 196-198). Hershey, PA: Idea Group Reference.

Knight, J. (2006b). Ethics and HCI. In C. Ghaoui (Ed.), *Encyclopedia of human computer interaction* (pp. 199-204). Hershey, PA: Idea Group Reference.

Knight, J., & Jefsioutine, M. (2006). Design Frameworks. In C. Ghaoui (Ed.), *Encyclopedia of human computer interaction* (pp. 150-153). Hershey, PA: Idea Group Reference.

Knight, L.V., & Chan, S.S. (2005). E-commerce curriculum. In M. Khosrow-Pour (Ed.), *Encyclopedia of information science and technology* (pp. 951-956). Hershey, PA: Idea Group Reference.

Knight, L.V., & Labruyere, J.-P.P. (2005). Security laboratory design and implementation. In M. Pagani (Ed.), *Encyclopedia of multimedia technology and networking* (pp. 903-909). Hershey, PA: Idea Group Reference.

Knight, R., Whittington, K., Ford, W.C.L., & Jenkins, J.M. (2005). Teaching medical statistics over the Internet. In C. Howard, J.V. Boettcher, L. Justice, K. Schenk, P.L. Rogers, & G.A. Berg (Eds.), *Encyclopedia of distance learning* (pp. 1770-1776). Hershey, PA: Idea Group Reference.

Knust, M., & Hagenhoff, S. (2005). The cooperation solution for universities. In C. Howard, J.V. Boettcher, L. Justice, K. Schenk, P.L. Rogers, & G.A. Berg (Eds.), *Encyclopedia of distance learning* (pp. 423-429). Hershey, PA: Idea Group Reference.

Ko, C.C., Chen, B.M., & Cheng, C.D. (2005). Web-based remote laboratory. In C. Howard, J.V. Boettcher, L. Justice, K. Schenk, P.L. Rogers, & G.A. Berg (Eds.), *Encyclopedia of distance learning* (pp. 2009-2018). Hershey, PA: Idea Group Reference.

Kochikar, V.P., & Suresh, J.K. (2005). Experiential perspective on knowledge management. In M. Khosrow-Pour (Ed.), *Encyclopedia of information science and technology* (pp. 1162-1168). Hershey, PA: Idea Group Reference.

Kock, N. (2005). Bridging the industry-university gap through action research. In M. Khosrow-Pour (Ed.), *Encyclopedia of information science and technology* (pp. 292-297). Hershey, PA: Idea Group Reference.

Kock, N. (2006). Unexpected outcomes of lean e-collaboration. In M. Khosrow-Pour (Ed.), *Encyclopedia of e-commerce, e-government, and mobile commerce* (pp. 1109-1110). Hershey, PA: Idea Group Reference.

Koeller, A. (2005). Integration of data sources through data mining. In J. Wang (Ed.), *Encyclopedia of data warehousing and mining* (pp. 625-629). Hershey, PA: Idea Group Reference.

Kontaki, M., Papadopoulos, A.N., & Manolopoulos, Y. (2005). Similarity search in time series databases. In L. Rivero, J. Doorn, & V. Ferraggine (Eds.), *Encyclopedia of database technologies and applications* (pp. 646-651). Hershey, PA: Idea Group Reference.

Kontio, J. (2005). Data warehousing solutions for reporting problems. In J. Wang (Ed.), *Encyclopedia of data warehousing and mining* (pp. 334-338). Hershey, PA: Idea Group Reference.

Kontolemakis, G., Kanellis, P., & Martakos, D. (2005). Virtual communities. In M. Pagani (Ed.), *Encyclopedia of multimedia technology and networking* (pp. 1033-1039). Hershey, PA: Idea Group Reference.

Kontos, J., & Malagardi, I. (2006). Question Answering from Procedural Semantics to Model Discovery. In C. Ghaoui (Ed.), *Encyclopedia of human computer interaction* (pp. 479-485). Hershey, PA: Idea Group Reference.

Kostopoulos, G.K. (2005). Accreditation and recognition in distance learning. In C. Howard, J.V. Boettcher, L. Justice, K. Schenk, P.L. Rogers, & G.A.

Berg (Eds.), *Encyclopedia of distance learning* (pp. 29-33). Hershey, PA: Idea Group Reference.

Kotzab, H. (2005). Contemporary IT-assisted retail management. In M. Khosrow-Pour (Ed.), *Encyclopedia of information science and technology* (pp. 540-545). Hershey, PA: Idea Group Reference.

Koumaras, H., Martakos, D., & Kourtis, A. (2005). Objective measurement of perceived QoS for homogeneous MPEG-4 video content. In M. Pagani (Ed.), *Encyclopedia of multimedia technology and networking* (pp. 770-777). Hershey, PA: Idea Group Reference.

Koutrika, G. (2005). Database query personalization. In L. Rivero, J. Doorn, & V. Ferraggine (Eds.), *Encyclopedia of database technologies and applications* (pp. 147-152). Hershey, PA: Idea Group Reference.

Kozeluh, U. (2005). E-democracy as a contemporary framework for citizens' deliberation. In S. Marshall, W. Taylor, & X. Yu (Eds.), *Encyclopedia of developing regional communities with information and communication technology* (pp. 250-255). Hershey, PA: Idea Group Reference.

Kraaijenbrink, J., & Wijnhoven, F. (2006). External knowledge integration. In D. Schwartz (Ed.), *Encyclopedia of knowledge management* (pp. 180-187). Hershey, PA: Idea Group Reference.

Kroeze, J.H. (2005). Discovering unknown patterns in free text. In J. Wang (Ed.), *Encyclopedia of data warehousing and mining* (pp. 382-386). Hershey, PA: Idea Group Reference.

Krogstie, J. (2005a). Quality of UML. In M. Khosrow-Pour (Ed.), *Encyclopedia of information science and technology* (pp. 2397-2391). Hershey, PA: Idea Group Reference.

Krogstie, J. (2005b). Usable m-commerce systems. In M. Khosrow-Pour (Ed.), *Encyclopedia of information science and technology* (pp. 2944-2948). Hershey, PA: Idea Group Reference.

Kryszkiewicz, M. (2005). Reasoning about frequent patterns with negation. In J. Wang (Ed.), *Encyclope-* dia of data warehousing and mining (pp. 941-946). Hershey, PA: Idea Group Reference.

Kukulska-Hulme, A. (2005). Group leadership in online collaborative learning. In C. Howard, J.V. Boettcher, L. Justice, K. Schenk, P.L. Rogers, & G.A. Berg (Eds.), *Encyclopedia of distance learning* (pp. 975-983). Hershey, PA: Idea Group Reference.

Kulikowski, J.L. (2005). Data quality assessment. In L. Rivero, J. Doorn, & V. Ferraggine (Eds.), *Encyclopedia of database technologies and applications* (pp. 116-120). Hershey, PA: Idea Group Reference.

Kulkarni, U., & Freeze, R. (2006). Measuring knowledge management capabilities. In D. Schwartz (Ed.), *Encyclopedia of knowledge management* (pp. 605). Hershey, PA: Idea Group Reference.

Kulyukin, V.A., & Nicholson, J.A. (2005). Structural text mining. In M. Khosrow-Pour (Ed.), *Encyclopedia of information science and technology* (pp. 2658-2661). Hershey, PA: Idea Group Reference.

Kumar, K. (2005). Internet data mining using statistical techniques. In M. Khosrow-Pour (Ed.), *Encyclopedia of information science and technology* (pp. 1629-1634). Hershey, PA: Idea Group Reference.

Kung-Ming, T. (2005). Postgraduate degree by distance learning. In C. Howard, J.V. Boettcher, L. Justice, K. Schenk, P.L. Rogers, & G.A. Berg (Eds.), *Encyclopedia of distance learning* (pp. 1494-1502). Hershey, PA: Idea Group Reference.

Kung-Ming, T., & Khoon-Seng, S. (2005). Asynchronous vs. synchronous interaction. In C. Howard, J.V. Boettcher, L. Justice, K. Schenk, P.L. Rogers, & G.A. Berg (Eds.), *Encyclopedia of distance learning* (pp. 104-113). Hershey, PA: Idea Group Reference.

Kunz, T., & Gaddah, A. (2005). Adaptive mobile applications. In M. Khosrow-Pour (Ed.), *Encyclopedia of information science and technology* (pp. 47-52). Hershey, PA: Idea Group Reference.

Kurbel, K. (2005). Enterprise resource planning and integration. In M. Khosrow-Pour (Ed.), *Encyclopedia of information science and technology* (pp. 1076-1082). Hershey, PA: Idea Group Reference.

Kurihara, Y. (2006). Spreading use of digital cash. In M. Khosrow-Pour (Ed.), *Encyclopedia of e-commerce, e-government, and mobile commerce* (pp. 1041-1045). Hershey, PA: Idea Group Reference.

Kushnir, O.B. (2006). Predicting activity levels in virtual communities. In S. Dasgupta (Ed.), *Encyclopedia of virtual communities and technologies* (pp. 387-389). Hershey, PA: Idea Group Reference.

Kusiak, A., & Shah, S.C. (2005). Data mining and warehousing in pharma industry. In J. Wang (Ed.), *Encyclopedia of data warehousing and mining* (pp. 239-244). Hershey, PA: Idea Group Reference.

Kvasny, L., & Payton, F.C. (2005). Minorities and the digital divide. In M. Khosrow-Pour (Ed.), *Encyclopedia of information science and technology* (pp. 1955-1959). Hershey, PA: Idea Group Reference.

Kwok Lai-yin, P., & Tan Yew-Gee, C. (2005). Collaborative Web-based learning community. In M. Pagani (Ed.), *Encyclopedia of multimedia technology and networking* (pp. 89-95). Hershey, PA: Idea Group Reference.

Kwok, S.H. (2005). DRM technology for mobile multimedia. In M. Khosrow-Pour (Ed.), *Encyclopedia of information science and technology* (pp. 918-923). Hershey, PA: Idea Group Reference.

Kwok, S.H., Cheung, Y.M., & Chan, K.Y. (2006). Peer-to-peer technology for file sharing. In S. Dasgupta (Ed.), *Encyclopedia of virtual communities and technologies* (pp. 372-377). Hershey, PA: Idea Group Reference.

Kyobe, M. (2006). Entrepreneur behaviors on e-commerce security. In M. Khosrow-Pour (Ed.), *Encyclopedia of e-commerce, e-government, and mobile commerce* (pp. 437-444). Hershey, PA: Idea Group Reference.

Lacaze, X., Palanque, P., Barboni, E., & Navarre, D. (2006). Design Rationale for Increasing Profitability of Interactive Systems Development. In C. Ghaoui (Ed.), *Encyclopedia of human computer interaction* (pp. 154-159). Hershey, PA: Idea Group Reference.

Laghos, A., & Zaphiris, P. (2005a). Computer assisted/aided language learning. In C. Howard, J.V. Boettcher, L. Justice, K. Schenk, P.L. Rogers, & G.A. Berg (Eds.), *Encyclopedia of distance learning* (pp. 331-336). Hershey, PA: Idea Group Reference.

Laghos, A., & Zaphiris, P. (2005b). Computer-aided language learning. In C. Howard, J.V. Boettcher, L. Justice, K. Schenk, P.L. Rogers, & G.A. Berg (Eds.), *Encyclopedia of distance learning* (pp. 337-340). Hershey, PA: Idea Group Reference.

Lahiri, A., & Basu, A. (2005). Modern tools and technologies for the visually impaired. In S. Marshall, W. Taylor, & X. Yu (Eds.), *Encyclopedia of developing regional communities with information and communication technology* (pp. 501-505). Hershey, PA: Idea Group Reference.

Lai, M., Fu, X., & Zhang, L. (2005). Information resources development in China. In M. Khosrow-Pour (Ed.), *Encyclopedia of information science and technology* (pp. 1482-1486). Hershey, PA: Idea Group Reference.

Lajbcygier, P. (2005). Comparing conventional and non-parametric option pricing. In M. Khosrow-Pour (Ed.), *Encyclopedia of information science and technology* (pp. 472-474). Hershey, PA: Idea Group Reference.

Lalopoulos, G.K., Chochliouros, I.P., & Spiliopoulou-Chochliourou, A.S. (2005a). Evolution of mobile commerce applications. In M. Pagani (Ed.), *Encyclopedia of multimedia technology and networking* (pp. 295-301). Hershey, PA: Idea Group Reference.

Lalopoulos, G.K., Chochliouros, I.P., & Spiliopoulou-Chochliourou, A.S. (2005b). Challenges and perspectives for Web-based applications in organizations. In M. Pagani (Ed.), *Encyclopedia of multimedia technology and networking* (pp. 82-88). Hershey, PA: Idea Group Reference.

Lam, W., Chua, A., & Lee, C. (2006). Observed patterns of dysfunctional collaboration in virtual teams. In E. Coakes & S. Clarke (Eds.), *Encyclopedia of communities of practice in information and knowledge management* (pp. 392-396). Hershey, PA: Idea Group Reference.

Lambropoulos, N. (2006a). Human resources and knowledge management based on e-democracy. In S. Dasgupta (Ed.), *Encyclopedia of virtual communities and technologies* (pp. 238-242). Hershey, PA: Idea Group Reference.

Lambropoulos, N. (2006b). Sociability and usability for active participation. In S. Dasgupta (Ed.), *Encyclopedia of virtual communities and technologies* (pp. 414-416). Hershey, PA: Idea Group Reference.

Lammintakanen, J., & Rissanen, S. (2005a). Curriculum development in Web-based education. In M. Khosrow-Pour (Ed.), *Encyclopedia of information science and technology* (pp. 675-679). Hershey, PA: Idea Group Reference.

Lammintakanen, J., & Rissanen, S. (2005b). Online learning experiences of university students. In C. Howard, J.V. Boettcher, L. Justice, K. Schenk, P.L. Rogers, & G.A. Berg (Eds.), *Encyclopedia of distance learning* (pp. 1370-1374). Hershey, PA: Idea Group Reference.

Land, F., Amjad, U., & Nolas, S.-M. (2006). Knowledge management processes. In D. Schwartz (Ed.), *Encyclopedia of knowledge management* (pp. 403). Hershey, PA: Idea Group Reference.

Land, F., Nolas, S.-M., & Amjad, U. (2006). Theoretical and practical aspects of knowledge management. In D. Schwartz (Ed.), *Encyclopedia of knowledge management* (pp. 855-861). Hershey, PA: Idea Group Reference.

Lang, G. (2005). Virtual school administration. In C. Howard, J.V. Boettcher, L. Justice, K. Schenk, P.L. Rogers, & G.A. Berg (Eds.), *Encyclopedia of distance learning* (pp. 1984-1989). Hershey, PA: Idea Group Reference.

Lang, M. (2005). Designing Web-based hypermedia systems. In M. Pagani (Ed.), *Encyclopedia of multimedia technology and networking* (pp. 173-179). Hershey, PA: Idea Group Reference.

Lang, M. (2006). Hypermedia and associated concepts. In M. Khosrow-Pour (Ed.), *Encyclopedia of e-commerce, e-government, and mobile commerce* (pp. 565-572). Hershey, PA: Idea Group Reference.

Langer, G.R. (2005). 21st century e-student services. In C. Howard, J.V. Boettcher, L. Justice, K. Schenk, P.L. Rogers, & G.A. Berg (Eds.), *Encyclopedia of distance learning* (pp. 1907-1913). Hershey, PA: Idea Group Reference.

Lasnik, V.E. (2005). Developing prescriptive taxonomies for distance learning instructional design. In C. Howard, J.V. Boettcher, L. Justice, K. Schenk, P.L. Rogers, & G.A. Berg (Eds.), *Encyclopedia of distance learning* (pp. 554-567). Hershey, PA: Idea Group Reference.

Latchem, C.R. (2005). Telecentres in low-income nations. In S. Marshall, W. Taylor, & X. Yu (Eds.), *Encyclopedia of developing regional communities with information and communication technology* (pp. 677-682). Hershey, PA: Idea Group Reference.

Latchem, C.R., & Maru, A. (2005). ICT and distance learning for agricultural extension in low income countries. In S. Marshall, W. Taylor, & X. Yu (Eds.), *Encyclopedia of developing regional communities with information and communication technology* (pp. 342-347). Hershey, PA: Idea Group Reference.

Lateh, H., & Raman, A. (2005). Distance learning and educational technology in Malaysia. In C. Howard, J.V. Boettcher, L. Justice, K. Schenk, P.L. Rogers, & G.A. Berg (Eds.), *Encyclopedia of distance learning* (pp. 641-653). Hershey, PA: Idea Group Reference.

Lauría, E.J.M. (2005). Bayesian machine learning. In M. Khosrow-Pour (Ed.), *Encyclopedia of information science and technology* (pp. 229-235). Hershey, PA: Idea Group Reference.

Law, W.K. (2005). Information resources development challenges in a cross-cultural environment. In

M. Khosrow-Pour (Ed.), *Encyclopedia of information science and technology* (pp. 1476-1481). Hershey, PA: Idea Group Reference.

Laws, R.D., Howell, S.L., & Lindsay, N.K. (2005). Ten scalability factors in distance education. In C. Howard, J.V. Boettcher, L. Justice, K. Schenk, P.L. Rogers, & G.A. Berg (Eds.), *Encyclopedia of distance learning* (pp. 1825-1832). Hershey, PA: Idea Group Reference.

Lawson-Body, A. (2005). Investment strategy for integrating wireless technology into organizations. In M. Pagani (Ed.), *Encyclopedia of multimedia technology and networking* (pp. 500-506). Hershey, PA: Idea Group Reference.

Lawson-Body, A., Rotvold, G., & Rotvold, J. (2005). The decision making process of integrating wireless technology into organizations. In M. Pagani (Ed.), *Encyclopedia of multimedia technology and networking* (pp. 165-172). Hershey, PA: Idea Group Reference.

Lazar, A. (2005). Knowledge discovery using heuristics. In M. Khosrow-Pour (Ed.), *Encyclopedia of information science and technology* (pp. 1754-1758). Hershey, PA: Idea Group Reference.

Lazarevic, A. (2005). Data mining for intrusion detection. In J. Wang (Ed.), *Encyclopedia of data warehousing and mining* (pp. 251-256). Hershey, PA: Idea Group Reference.

Lazarus, B.D. (2005a). Programmed instruction overview. In C. Howard, J.V. Boettcher, L. Justice, K. Schenk, P.L. Rogers, & G.A. Berg (Eds.), *Encyclopedia of distance learning* (pp. 1522-1528). Hershey, PA: Idea Group Reference.

Lazarus, B.D. (2005b). Trends and issues of virtual K–12 schools. In C. Howard, J.V. Boettcher, L. Justice, K. Schenk, P.L. Rogers, & G.A. Berg (Eds.), *Encyclopedia of distance learning* (pp. 1898-1901). Hershey, PA: Idea Group Reference.

Leath, T. (2005). Capturing community memory with images. In S. Marshall, W. Taylor, & X. Yu (Eds.), *Encyclopedia of developing regional communities with information and communication technology* (pp. 72-78). Hershey, PA: Idea Group Reference.

Lee, C., Suh, W., & Lee, H. (2005). A development environment for customer-oriented Web business. In L. Rivero, J. Doorn, & V. Ferraggine (Eds.), *Encyclopedia of database technologies and applications* (pp. 184-190). Hershey, PA: Idea Group Reference.

Lee, C.-P., & Warkentin, M. (2006). Mobile banking systems and technologies. In M. Khosrow-Pour (Ed.), *Encyclopedia of e-commerce, e-government, and mobile commerce* (pp. 754-759). Hershey, PA: Idea Group Reference.

Lee, C.-S. (2005). Business model innovation in the digital economy. In M. Khosrow-Pour (Ed.), *Encyclopedia of information science and technology* (pp. 331-338). Hershey, PA: Idea Group Reference.

Lee, C.-S., Chen, Y.G., & Fan, Y.-H. (2006). Structure and components of e-commerce business model. In M. Khosrow-Pour (Ed.), *Encyclopedia of e-commerce, e-government, and mobile commerce* (pp. 1058-1063). Hershey, PA: Idea Group Reference.

Lee, C.-W., Kou, W., & Hu, W.-C. (2005). Mobile commerce security and payment. In M. Pagani (Ed.), *Encyclopedia of multimedia technology and networking* (pp. 615-621). Hershey, PA: Idea Group Reference.

Lee, C.-W., Hu, W.-C., & Yeh, J.-H. (2005). Mobile commerce Technology. In M. Khosrow-Pour (Ed.), *Encyclopedia of information science and technology, Vol. 4* (pp. 1967-1972). Hershey, PA: Idea Group Reference.

Lee, I. (2005). Triangular strategic analysis for hybrid e-retailers. In M. Khosrow-Pour (Ed.), *Encyclopedia of information science and technology* (pp. 2871-2877). Hershey, PA: Idea Group Reference.

Lee, J. (2005). Virtual organization in the human mind. In M. Khosrow-Pour (Ed.), *Encyclopedia of information science and technology* (pp. 2996-3001). Hershey, PA: Idea Group Reference.

Lee, J.R. (2005). Vicarious learning. In C. Howard, J.V. Boettcher, L. Justice, K. Schenk, P.L. Rogers, & G.A. Berg (Eds.), *Encyclopedia of distance learning* (pp. 1958-1964). Hershey, PA: Idea Group Reference.

Lee, M.R.-Y., & Pai, F.Y. (2005). Message-based service in Taiwan. In M. Pagani (Ed.), *Encyclopedia of multimedia technology and networking* (pp. 579-584). Hershey, PA: Idea Group Reference.

Lee, S.-W., Lin, H.-T., & Chen, H.-Y. (2005). Speech/text alignment in Web-based language learning. In C. Howard, J.V. Boettcher, L. Justice, K. Schenk, P.L. Rogers, & G.A. Berg (Eds.), *Encyclopedia of distance learning* (pp. 1643-1649). Hershey, PA: Idea Group Reference.

Lee, Z.-H., Peterson, R.L., Chien, C.-F., & Xing, R. (2005). Factor analysis in data mining. In J. Wang (Ed.), *Encyclopedia of data warehousing and mining* (pp. 498-502). Hershey, PA: Idea Group Reference.

Lee-Post, A., & Jin, H. (2005a). Trends in Web content and structure mining. In J. Wang (Ed.), *Encyclopedia of data warehousing and mining* (pp. 1146-1150). Hershey, PA: Idea Group Reference.

Lee-Post, A., & Jin, H. (2005b). Trends in Web usage mining. In J. Wang (Ed.), *Encyclopedia of data warehousing and mining* (pp. 1151-1154). Hershey, PA: Idea Group Reference.

Lei, P. (2006). M-commerce opportunities. In M. Khosrow-Pour (Ed.), *Encyclopedia of e-commerce, e-government, and mobile commerce* (pp. 736-739). Hershey, PA: Idea Group Reference.

Lei, P., Chatwin, C., & Young, R. (2005a). Challenges in m-commerce. In M. Khosrow-Pour (Ed.), *Encyclopedia of information science and technology* (pp. 387-391). Hershey, PA: Idea Group Reference.

Lei, P., Chatwin, C., & Young, R. (2005b). Security and trust of online auction systems. In M. Khosrow-Pour (Ed.), *Encyclopedia of information science and technology* (pp. 2450-2454). Hershey, PA: Idea Group Reference.

Lemahieu, W. (2005). MESH object-oriented hypermedia framework. In M. Khosrow-Pour (Ed.), *Encyclopedia of information science and technology* (pp. 1922-1927). Hershey, PA: Idea Group Reference.

Lenard, M.J., & Alam, P. (2005). Application of fuzzy to logic fraud detection. In M. Khosrow-Pour (Ed.), *Encyclopedia of information science and technology* (pp. 135-139). Hershey, PA: Idea Group Reference.

Lenič, M., Kokol, P., Povalej, P., & Zorman, M. (2005). Combining induction methods with the multimethod approach. In J. Wang (Ed.), *Encyclopedia of data warehousing and mining* (pp. 184-189). Hershey, PA: Idea Group Reference.

Leonard, A. (2005). The impact of sound relationships on achieving alignment. In M. Khosrow-Pour (Ed.), *Encyclopedia of information science and technology* (pp. 2815-2820). Hershey, PA: Idea Group Reference.

Leonardi, P.M. (2005). Technology and work in the virtual organization. In M. Khosrow-Pour (Ed.), *Encyclopedia of information science and technology* (pp. 2753-2756). Hershey, PA: Idea Group Reference.

Leong, H.V. (2005a). Database support for m-commerce. In M. Khosrow-Pour (Ed.), *Encyclopedia of information science and technology* (pp. 739-744). Hershey, PA: Idea Group Reference.

Leong, H.V. (2005b). Transactional support for mobile databases. In L. Rivero, J. Doorn, & V. Ferraggine (Eds.), *Encyclopedia of database technologies and applications* (pp. 701-706). Hershey, PA: Idea Group Reference.

Lepawsky, J., & Park, K. (2006). Cyberspace. In S. Dasgupta (Ed.), *Encyclopedia of virtual communities and technologies* (pp. 110-115). Hershey, PA: Idea Group Reference.

Lepouras, G., & Vassilakis, C. (2006). Adaptive virtual reality shopping malls. In M. Khosrow-Pour (Ed.), *Encyclopedia of e-commerce, e-government, and mobile commerce* (pp. 1-6). Hershey, PA: Idea Group Reference.

Lepouras, G., Sotiropoulou, A., Theotokis, D., & Vassilakis, C. (2006). Tailorable e-government information systems. In M. Khosrow-Pour (Ed.), *Encyclopedia of e-commerce, e-government, and mobile commerce* (pp. 1064-1069). Hershey, PA: Idea Group Reference.

Lerch, C.M., Bilics, A.R., & Colley, B. (2005). Zone of proximal development and scaffolding online. In C. Howard, J.V. Boettcher, L. Justice, K. Schenk, P.L. Rogers, & G.A. Berg (Eds.), *Encyclopedia of distance learning* (pp. 2075-2081). Hershey, PA: Idea Group Reference.

LeRouge, C., & Webb, H. (2005). Modeling ERP acedemic deployment via AST. In M. Khosrow-Pour (Ed.), *Encyclopedia of information science and technology* (pp. 1889-1995). Hershey, PA: Idea Group Reference.

Lertwongsatien, C., & Wongpinunwatana, N. (2005). Empirical study of e-commerce adoption SMEs in Thailand. In M. Khosrow-Pour (Ed.), *Encyclopedia of information science and technology* (pp. 1040-1044). Hershey, PA: Idea Group Reference.

Lettl, C., Zboralski, K., & Gemünden, H.G. (2006). Trust in virtual teams. In E. Coakes & S. Clarke (Eds.), *Encyclopedia of communities of practice in information and knowledge management* (pp. 552-557). Hershey, PA: Idea Group Reference.

Leung, E.W.C., & Li, Q. (2005). Towards a personalized e-learning system. In C. Howard, J.V. Boettcher, L. Justice, K. Schenk, P.L. Rogers, & G.A. Berg (Eds.), *Encyclopedia of distance learning* (pp. 1869-1879). Hershey, PA: Idea Group Reference.

Leung, H. (2005). Certifying software product and processes. In M. Khosrow-Pour (Ed.), *Encyclopedia of information science and technology* (pp. 381-386). Hershey, PA: Idea Group Reference.

Levy, Y., & Ramim, M.M. (2005a). Eight key elements of successful self-funding e-learning programs. In M. Khosrow-Pour (Ed.), *Encyclopedia of information science and technology* (pp. 995-1000). Hershey, PA: Idea Group Reference.

Levy, Y., & Ramim, M.M. (2005b). Successful self-funding e-learning programs. In C. Howard, J.V. Boettcher, L. Justice, K. Schenk, P.L. Rogers, & G.A. Berg (Eds.), *Encyclopedia of distance learning* (pp. 1703-1709). Hershey, PA: Idea Group Reference.

Lewis, M. (2005). ICT in medical education in Trinidad and Tobago. In S. Marshall, W. Taylor, & X. Yu (Eds.), *Encyclopedia of developing regional communities with information and communication technology* (pp. 382-386). Hershey, PA: Idea Group Reference.

Li, C.-T. (2005). Digital watermarking for multimedia security management. In M. Pagani (Ed.), *Encyclopedia of multimedia technology and networking* (pp. 213-218). Hershey, PA: Idea Group Reference.

Li, C.-T. (2006). Biometrics in virtual communities and digital governments. In S. Dasgupta (Ed.), *Encyclopedia of virtual communities and technologies* (pp. 1-3). Hershey, PA: Idea Group Reference.

Li, Q., Yang, J., & Zuang, Y. (2005). Multimedia information retrieval at a crossroad. In M. Pagani (Ed.), *Encyclopedia of multimedia technology and networking* (pp. 710-716). Hershey, PA: Idea Group Reference.

Li, W. (2005). Spectral methods for data clustering. In J. Wang (Ed.), *Encyclopedia of data warehousing and mining* (pp. 1037-1042). Hershey, PA: Idea Group Reference.

Li, W., Ng, W.-K., & Ong, K.-L. (2006). Information navigation and knowledge discovery in virtual communities. In S. Dasgupta (Ed.), *Encyclopedia of virtual communities and technologies* (pp. 273-278). Hershey, PA: Idea Group Reference.

Li, X. (2005a). Intelligent business portals. In M. Khosrow-Pour (Ed.), *Encyclopedia of information science and technology* (pp. 1584-1590). Hershey, PA: Idea Group Reference.

Li, X. (2005b). Real options analysis in strategic information technology adoption. In M. Khosrow-Pour (Ed.), *Encyclopedia of information science and technology* (pp. 2397-2402). Hershey, PA: Idea Group Reference.

Liberati, D. (2005). Model identification through data mining. In J. Wang (Ed.), *Encyclopedia of data warehousing and mining* (pp. 820-825). Hershey, PA: Idea Group Reference.

Liberati, D., Bittanti, S., & Garatti, S. (2005). Unsupervised mining of genes classifying Leukemia. In J. Wang (Ed.), *Encyclopedia of data warehousing and mining* (pp. 1155-1159). Hershey, PA: Idea Group Reference.

Lick, D.W., & Kaufman, R. (2005). Change creation for online learning and technology. In C. Howard, J.V. Boettcher, L. Justice, K. Schenk, P.L. Rogers, & G.A. Berg (Eds.), *Encyclopedia of distance learning* (pp. 211-217). Hershey, PA: Idea Group Reference.

Lightfoot, W.S. (2005). Implementing an online academic evaluation system. In M. Khosrow-Pour (Ed.), *Encyclopedia of information science and technology* (pp. 1402-1407). Hershey, PA: Idea Group Reference.

Limayem, M. (2005). Culture and anonymity in GSS meetings. In M. Khosrow-Pour (Ed.), *Encyclopedia of information science and technology* (pp. 655-659). Hershey, PA: Idea Group Reference.

Lin, B., Hong, Y., & Lee, Z.-H. (2005). Data warehouse performance. In J. Wang (Ed.), *Encyclopedia of data warehousing and mining* (pp. 318-322). Hershey, PA: Idea Group Reference.

Lin, C., & Pervan, G. (2005). Public sector case study on the benefits of IS/IT. In M. Khosrow-Pour (Ed.), *Encyclopedia of information science and technology* (pp. 2364-2367). Hershey, PA: Idea Group Reference.

Lin, H.-T., & Chen, H.-Y. (2005). Web-based multimedia children's art cultivation. In C. Howard, J.V. Boettcher, L. Justice, K. Schenk, P.L. Rogers, & G.A. Berg (Eds.), *Encyclopedia of distance learning* (pp. 2004-2008). Hershey, PA: Idea Group Reference.

Lin, T., & Kinshuk. (2005). Cognitive profiling in life-long learning. In C. Howard, J.V. Boettcher, L. Justice, K. Schenk, P.L. Rogers, & G.A. Berg (Eds.), *Encyclopedia of distance learning* (pp. 245-255). Hershey, PA: Idea Group Reference.

Lin, T.Y. (2005). High frequency patterns in data mining. In J. Wang (Ed.), *Encyclopedia of data warehousing and mining* (pp. 560-665). Hershey, PA: Idea Group Reference.

Lin, Y.-W. (2005). Free/libre open source software for bridging the digital divide. In S. Marshall, W. Taylor, & X. Yu (Eds.), *Encyclopedia of developing regional communities with information and communication technology* (pp. 316-320). Hershey, PA: Idea Group Reference.

Lindell, Y. (2005). Secure multiparty computation for privacy preserving data mining. In J. Wang (Ed.), *Encyclopedia of data warehousing and mining* (pp. 1005-1009). Hershey, PA: Idea Group Reference.

Lindsay, N.K., Howell, S.L., & Laws, R.D. (2005). Completion rates and distance learners. In C. Howard, J.V. Boettcher, L. Justice, K. Schenk, P.L. Rogers, & G.A. Berg (Eds.), *Encyclopedia of distance learning* (pp. 310-316). Hershey, PA: Idea Group Reference.

Lindsay, N.K., Williams, P.B., & Howell, S.L. (2005). Academic, economic, and technological trends affecting distance education. In C. Howard, J.V. Boettcher, L. Justice, K. Schenk, P.L. Rogers, & G.A. Berg (Eds.), *Encyclopedia of distance learning* (pp. 7-15). Hershey, PA: Idea Group Reference.

Lindsey, K.L. (2006). Knowledge sharing barriers. In D. Schwartz (Ed.), *Encyclopedia of knowledge management* (pp. 499). Hershey, PA: Idea Group Reference.

Lingras, P., Yan, R., Hogo, M., & West, C. (2005). Interval set representations of clusters. In J. Wang (Ed.), *Encyclopedia of data warehousing and mining* (pp. 659-663). Hershey, PA: Idea Group Reference.

Link, L., & Wagner, D. (2006). Computer-mediated communication in virtual learning communities. In

S. Dasgupta (Ed.), *Encyclopedia of virtual communities and technologies* (pp. 49-53). Hershey, PA: Idea Group Reference.

Liou, H.-C. (2005). Computer-assisted language learning in East Asia. In C. Howard, J.V. Boettcher, L. Justice, K. Schenk, P.L. Rogers, & G.A. Berg (Eds.), *Encyclopedia of distance learning* (pp. 341-352). Hershey, PA: Idea Group Reference.

Lipton, R., Gorman, D.M., Wieczorek, W.F., & Gruenewald, P. (2005). Spatial analysis in a public health setting. In M. Khosrow-Pour (Ed.), *Encyclopedia of information science and technology* (pp. 2576-2583). Hershey, PA: Idea Group Reference.

Littman, M.K. (2005). ATM technology and e-learning initiatives. In M. Pagani (Ed.), *Encyclopedia of multimedia technology and networking* (pp. 49-55). Hershey, PA: Idea Group Reference.

Littman, M.K. (2006). DWDM technology and e-government initiatives. In M. Khosrow-Pour (Ed.), *Encyclopedia of e-commerce, e-government, and mobile commerce* (pp. 234-239). Hershey, PA: Idea Group Reference.

Liu, H., & Yu, L. (2005). Instance selection. In J. Wang (Ed.), *Encyclopedia of data warehousing and mining* (pp. 621-624). Hershey, PA: Idea Group Reference.

Liu, K.-Y., & Chen, H.-Y. (2005). Web-based synchronized multimedia lecturing. In C. Howard, J.V. Boettcher, L. Justice, K. Schenk, P.L. Rogers, & G.A. Berg (Eds.), *Encyclopedia of distance learning* (pp. 2019-2028). Hershey, PA: Idea Group Reference.

Liu, S.-P., & Tucker, D. (2005). User experiences of the e-commerce site with the standard user interface. In M. Khosrow-Pour (Ed.), *Encyclopedia of information science and technology* (pp. 2954-2960). Hershey, PA: Idea Group Reference.

Liu, X. (2005). Intelligent data analysis. In J. Wang (Ed.), *Encyclopedia of data warehousing and mining* (pp. 634-638). Hershey, PA: Idea Group Reference.

Liu, X., & Koppelaar, H. (2005). Adaptive knowledge exosomatics for e-learning. In C. Howard, J.V.

Boettcher, L. Justice, K. Schenk, P.L. Rogers, & G.A. Berg (Eds.), *Encyclopedia of distance learning* (pp. 38-43). Hershey, PA: Idea Group Reference.

Liu, X., Koppelaar, H., Hamers, R., & Bruining, N. (2005). Immersive image mining in cardiology. In J. Wang (Ed.), *Encyclopedia of data warehousing and mining* (pp. 586-692). Hershey, PA: Idea Group Reference.

Lo, V.S.Y. (2005). Marketing data mining. In J. Wang (Ed.), *Encyclopedia of data warehousing and mining* (pp. 698-704). Hershey, PA: Idea Group Reference.

Lodhi, H. (2005). Kernel methods in chemoinformatics. In J. Wang (Ed.), *Encyclopedia of data warehousing and mining* (pp. 664-668). Hershey, PA: Idea Group Reference.

Loebbecke, C. (2006). RFID in the retail supply chain. In M. Khosrow-Pour (Ed.), *Encyclopedia of e-commerce, e-government, and mobile commerce* (pp. 948-953). Hershey, PA: Idea Group Reference.

Loebbecke, C., & Angehrn, A. (2006). Coopetition. In D. Schwartz (Ed.), *Encyclopedia of knowledge management* (pp. 58-66). Hershey, PA: Idea Group Reference.

Loh, S., Licthnow, D., Borges, T., Primo, T., Kickhöfel, R.B., Simões, G., Piltcher, G., & Saldaña, R. (2005). Mining chat discussions. In J. Wang (Ed.), *Encyclopedia of data warehousing and mining* (pp. 758-762). Hershey, PA: Idea Group Reference.

Long, S.D., Kohut, G.F., & Picherit-Duthler, G. (2005). Newcomer assimilation in virtual team socialization. In M. Khosrow-Pour (Ed.), *Encyclopedia of information science and technology* (pp. 2122-2128). Hershey, PA: Idea Group Reference.

Lorenzi, F., & Ricci, F. (2005). Case-based recommender systems. In J. Wang (Ed.), *Encyclopedia of data warehousing and mining* (pp. 124-128). Hershey, PA: Idea Group Reference.

Lou, D.-C., Liu, J.-L., & Tso, H.-K. (2006). Evolution of information-hiding technology. In M. Khosrow-Pour (Ed.), *Encyclopedia of e-commerce, e-government, and mobile commerce* (pp. 480-487). Hershey, PA: Idea Group Reference.

Louis, L.R. (2006). Technical issues facing work groups, teams, and knowledge networks. In E. Coakes & S. Clarke (Eds.), *Encyclopedia of communities of practice in information and knowledge management* (pp. 532-536). Hershey, PA: Idea Group Reference.

Louvros, S., Iossifides, A.C., Karaboulas, D., & Kotsopoulos, S.A. (2005). Plastic optical fiber applications. In M. Pagani (Ed.), *Encyclopedia of multimedia technology and networking* (pp. 829-835). Hershey, PA: Idea Group Reference.

Louvros, S., Karaboulas, D., Iossifides, A.C., & Kotsopoulos, S.A. (2005). Heterogeneous wireless networks using a wireless ATM platform. In M. Pagani (Ed.), *Encyclopedia of multimedia technology and networking* (pp. 359-367). Hershey, PA: Idea Group Reference.

Louvros, S., Pylarinos, G., & Kotsopoulos, S. (2006). Wireless LAN access technology. In M. Khosrow-Pour (Ed.), *Encyclopedia of e-commerce, e-government, and mobile commerce* (pp. 1254-1260). Hershey, PA: Idea Group Reference.

Lovell, B.C., & Chen, S. (2005). Robust face recognition for data mining. In J. Wang (Ed.), *Encyclopedia of data warehousing and mining* (pp. 965-972). Hershey, PA: Idea Group Reference.

Lowry, G., & Turner, R. (2005). Softening the MIS curriculum for a technology-based profession. In M. Khosrow-Pour (Ed.), *Encyclopedia of information science and technology* (pp. 2539-2545). Hershey, PA: Idea Group Reference.

Lowry, P.B., Grover, A., Madsen, C., Larkin, J., & Robins, W. (2005). Making money with open-source business initiatives. In M. Pagani (Ed.), *Encyclopedia of multimedia technology and networking* (pp. 555-561). Hershey, PA: Idea Group Reference.

Lowry, P.B., Stephens, J., Moyes, A., Wilson, S., & Mitchell, M. (2005). Biometrics, A critical consideration in information security management. In M.

Pagani (Ed.), *Encyclopedia of multimedia technology and networking* (pp. 69-75). Hershey, PA: Idea Group Reference.

Lu, X. (2005). Storage strategies in data warehouses. In J. Wang (Ed.), *Encyclopedia of data warehousing and mining* (pp. 1054-1058). Hershey, PA: Idea Group Reference.

Lubbe, S. (2005). Strategic alignment of organizational strategies. In M. Khosrow-Pour (Ed.), *Encyclopedia of information science and technology* (pp. 2622-2626). Hershey, PA: Idea Group Reference.

Lucas, W. (2005). Introducing Java to the IT master's curriculum. In M. Khosrow-Pour (Ed.), *Encyclopedia of information science and technology* (pp. 1662-1668). Hershey, PA: Idea Group Reference.

Lui, K.M., & Chan, K.C.C. (2005). Inexperienced and global software teams. In M. Khosrow-Pour (Ed.), *Encyclopedia of information science and technology* (pp. 1445-1451). Hershey, PA: Idea Group Reference.

Lumsden, J. (2005). The future of m-interaction. In M. Pagani (Ed.), *Encyclopedia of multimedia technology and networking* (pp. 342-347). Hershey, PA: Idea Group Reference.

Luo, X., & Warkentin, M. (2005). Malware and anti-virus procedures. In M. Pagani (Ed.), *Encyclopedia of multimedia technology and networking* (pp. 562-570). Hershey, PA: Idea Group Reference.

Luppicini, R.J. (2006). A Case Study on the Development of Broadband Technology in Canada. In C. Ghaoui (Ed.), *Encyclopedia of human computer interaction* (pp. 68-72). Hershey, PA: Idea Group Reference.

Lutu, P.E.N. (2005). Database sampling for data mining. In J. Wang (Ed.), *Encyclopedia of data warehousing and mining* (pp. 344-348). Hershey, PA: Idea Group Reference.

Lyytikäinen, V., Tiitinen, P., & Salminen, A. (2005). Contextual metadata for document databases. In M. Khosrow-Pour (Ed.), *Encyclopedia of information*

*science and technology* (pp. 573-576). Hershey, PA: Idea Group Reference.

Ma, S., & Li, T. (2005). Clustering techniques. In J. Wang (Ed.), *Encyclopedia of data warehousing and mining* (pp. 176-179). Hershey, PA: Idea Group Reference.

Ma, Z.M. (2005a). Engineering information modeling in databases. In L. Rivero, J. Doorn, & V. Ferraggine (Eds.), *Encyclopedia of database technologies and applications* (pp. 216-222). Hershey, PA: Idea Group Reference.

Ma, Z.M. (2005b). Fuzzy database modeling. In L. Rivero, J. Doorn, & V. Ferraggine (Eds.), *Encyclopedia of database technologies and applications* (pp. 250-257). Hershey, PA: Idea Group Reference.

Ma, Z.M. (2006). Engineering design knowledge management. In D. Schwartz (Ed.), *Encyclopedia of knowledge management* (pp. 161-165). Hershey, PA: Idea Group Reference.

Maamar, Z. (2005). Replication mechanisms over a set of distributed UDDI registries. In L. Rivero, J. Doorn, & V. Ferraggine (Eds.), *Encyclopedia of database technologies and applications* (pp. 548-554). Hershey, PA: Idea Group Reference.

Maani, K.E. (2005). Systems thinking and the Internet. In M. Khosrow-Pour (Ed.), *Encyclopedia of information science and technology* (pp. 2719-2723). Hershey, PA: Idea Group Reference.

MacDonald, C.J., Stodel, E.J., & Farres, L.G. (2005). The future of university and organizational learning. In C. Howard, J.V. Boettcher, L. Justice, K. Schenk, P.L. Rogers, & G.A. Berg (Eds.), *Encyclopedia of distance learning* (pp. 960-968). Hershey, PA: Idea Group Reference.

Macefield, R. (2006). Conceptual Models and Usability. In C. Ghaoui (Ed.), *Encyclopedia of human computer interaction* (pp. 112-119). Hershey, PA: Idea Group Reference.

Macfadyen, L.P. (2006a). Internet-Mediated Communication at the Cultural Interface. In C. Ghaoui (Ed.), *Encyclopedia of human computer interaction* (pp. 373-380). Hershey, PA: Idea Group Reference.

Macfadyen, L.P. (2006b). The Culture(s) of Cyberspace. In C. Ghaoui (Ed.), *Encyclopedia of human computer interaction* (pp. 143-149). Hershey, PA: Idea Group Reference.

Macfadyen, L.P. (2006c). The Prospects for Identity and Community in Cyberspace. In C. Ghaoui (Ed.), *Encyclopedia of human computer interaction* (pp. 471-478). Hershey, PA: Idea Group Reference.

Macfadyen, L.P., & Doff, S. (2006). The Language of Cyberspace. In C. Ghaoui (Ed.), *Encyclopedia of human computer interaction* (pp. 396-403). Hershey, PA: Idea Group Reference.

MacGregor, B.L. (2005). Rubrics as an assessment tool in distance education. In C. Howard, J.V. Boettcher, L. Justice, K. Schenk, P.L. Rogers, & G.A. Berg (Eds.), *Encyclopedia of distance learning* (pp. 1583-1588). Hershey, PA: Idea Group Reference.

MacGregor, K.J. (2005). Wireless middleware. In M. Khosrow-Pour (Ed.), *Encyclopedia of information science and technology* (pp. 3095-3100). Hershey, PA: Idea Group Reference.

Mackey, J. (2005). Technology planning in schools. In M. Khosrow-Pour (Ed.), *Encyclopedia of information science and technology* (pp. 2765-2770). Hershey, PA: Idea Group Reference.

Madlberger, M. (2006). Multi-channel retailing in B2C e-commerce. In M. Khosrow-Pour (Ed.), *Encyclopedia of e-commerce, e-government, and mobile commerce* (pp. 817-822). Hershey, PA: Idea Group Reference.

Magagula, C.M. (2005). Forging partnerships to provide computer literacy in Swaziland. In S. Marshall, W. Taylor, & X. Yu (Eds.), *Encyclopedia of developing regional communities with information and communication technology* (pp. 305-309). Hershey, PA: Idea Group Reference.

Maggioni, M.A., & Uberti, T.E. (2005). Webmetrics. In M. Pagani (Ed.), *Encyclopedia of multimedia technology and networking* (pp. 1091-1095). Hershey, PA: Idea Group Reference.

Magnani, L., & Bardone, E. (2006). Abduction and Web Interface Design. In C. Ghaoui (Ed.), *Encyclopedia of human computer interaction* (pp. 1-7). Hershey, PA: Idea Group Reference.

Magnani, L., Bardone, E., & Bocchiola, M. (2006). Moral Mediators in HCI. In C. Ghaoui (Ed.), *Encyclopedia of human computer interaction* (pp. 408-413). Hershey, PA: Idea Group Reference.

Magoulas, G.D. (2006). Web-Based Instructional Systems. In C. Ghaoui (Ed.), *Encyclopedia of human computer interaction* (pp. 729-738). Hershey, PA: Idea Group Reference.

Mahatanankoon, P. (2005). Personal Internet usage and quality of work life. In M. Khosrow-Pour (Ed.), *Encyclopedia of information science and technology* (pp. 2277-2281). Hershey, PA: Idea Group Reference.

Maier, R., & Hädrich, T. (2006). Knowledge management systems. In D. Schwartz (Ed.), *Encyclopedia of knowledge management* (pp. 442). Hershey, PA: Idea Group Reference.

Mäkinen, S. (2006). Document management, organizational memory, and mobile environment. In E. Coakes & S. Clarke (Eds.), *Encyclopedia of communities of practice in information and knowledge management* (pp. 141-147). Hershey, PA: Idea Group Reference.

Malik, P. (2006). Information integrity for CRM in a virtual world. In S. Dasgupta (Ed.), *Encyclopedia of virtual communities and technologies* (pp. 266-272). Hershey, PA: Idea Group Reference.

Malina, A. (2005). Bridging the digital divide in Scotland. In M. Khosrow-Pour (Ed.), *Encyclopedia of information science and technology* (pp. 278-283). Hershey, PA: Idea Group Reference.

Maloof, M.A. (2005). Concept drift. In J. Wang (Ed.), *Encyclopedia of data warehousing and mining* (pp. 202-206). Hershey, PA: Idea Group Reference.

Mandal, P., Shao, D.H., & Kim, C.W. (2005). Behavioral factors in strategic alliances. In M. Khosrow-Pour (Ed.), *Encyclopedia of information science and technology* (pp. 243-247). Hershey, PA: Idea Group Reference.

Mandl, T. (2006). Automatic Evaluation of Interfaces on the Internet. In C. Ghaoui (Ed.), *Encyclopedia of human computer interaction* (pp. 53-59). Hershey, PA: Idea Group Reference.

Mani, D.R., Betz, A.L., & Drew, J.H. (2005). Predicting resource usage for capital efficient marketing. In J. Wang (Ed.), *Encyclopedia of data warehousing and mining* (pp. 912-920). Hershey, PA: Idea Group Reference.

Mani, M., & Badia, A. (2005). Semistructured data and its conceptual models. In L. Rivero, J. Doorn, & V. Ferraggine (Eds.), *Encyclopedia of database technologies and applications* (pp. 607-612). Hershey, PA: Idea Group Reference.

Manolopoulos, Y., Nanopoulos, A., Morzy, M., Morzy, T., Wojciechowski, M., & Zakrzewicz, M. (2005). Signature-based indexing techniques for Web access logs. In M. Khosrow-Pour (Ed.), *Encyclopedia of information science and technology* (pp. 2481-2485). Hershey, PA: Idea Group Reference.Marchetti, C., Mecella, M., Scannapieco, M., & Virgillito, A. (2005). Data quality in cooperative information systems. In J. Wang (Ed.), *Encyclopedia of data warehousing and mining* (pp. 297-301). Hershey, PA: Idea Group Reference.

Marcinkiewicz, H., & McLean, J. (2005a). Administrative concerns for distance learning. In C. Howard, J.V. Boettcher, L. Justice, K. Schenk, P.L. Rogers, & G.A. Berg (Eds.), *Encyclopedia of distance learning* (pp. 53-55). Hershey, PA: Idea Group Reference.

Marcinkiewicz, H., & McLean, J. (2005b). Organizing faculty for distance learning. In C. Howard, J.V. Boettcher, L. Justice, K. Schenk, P.L. Rogers, & G.A. Berg (Eds.), *Encyclopedia of distance learning* (pp. 1448-1452). Hershey, PA: Idea Group Reference.

Maris, J.-M.B. (2005). Network-based information system model for research. In M. Pagani (Ed.), *En-

*cyclopedia of multimedia technology and networking* (pp. 756-761). Hershey, PA: Idea Group Reference.

Marjomaa, E. (2005). High quality conceptual schemes. In L. Rivero, J. Doorn, & V. Ferraggine (Eds.), *Encyclopedia of database technologies and applications* (pp. 276-280). Hershey, PA: Idea Group Reference.

Markellou, P., Rigou, M., & Sirmakessis, S. (2006). A closer look to the online consumer behavior. In M. Khosrow-Pour (Ed.), *Encyclopedia of e-commerce, e-government, and mobile commerce* (pp. 106-111). Hershey, PA: Idea Group Reference.

Markhasin, A., Olariu, S., & Todorova, P. (2005). Qos-oriented MAC protocols for future mobile applications. In M. Khosrow-Pour (Ed.), *Encyclopedia of information science and technology* (pp. 2373-2377). Hershey, PA: Idea Group Reference.

Marold, K.A. (2005). Delivering Web-based education. In M. Khosrow-Pour (Ed.), *Encyclopedia of information science and technology* (pp. 786-790). Hershey, PA: Idea Group Reference.

Marshall, S. (2005). Copyright with an international perspective for academics. In C. Howard, J.V. Boettcher, L. Justice, K. Schenk, P.L. Rogers, & G.A. Berg (Eds.), *Encyclopedia of distance learning* (pp. 440-454). Hershey, PA: Idea Group Reference.

Marshall, S., & Gregor, S. (2005). Transforming universities in the online world. In C. Howard, J.V. Boettcher, L. Justice, K. Schenk, P.L. Rogers, & G.A. Berg (Eds.), *Encyclopedia of distance learning* (pp. 1892-1897). Hershey, PA: Idea Group Reference.

Martí, R. (2005). Artificial neural networks for prediction. In J. Wang (Ed.), *Encyclopedia of data warehousing and mining* (pp. 54-58). Hershey, PA: Idea Group Reference.

Martínez-González, M. (2005). Document versioning in digital libraries. In L. Rivero, J. Doorn, & V. Ferraggine (Eds.), *Encyclopedia of database technologies and applications* (pp. 201-205). Hershey, PA: Idea Group Reference.

Martz, B., & Reddy, V. (2005). Critical success factors for distance education programs. In M. Khosrow-Pour (Ed.), *Encyclopedia of information science and technology* (pp. 622-627). Hershey, PA: Idea Group Reference.

Martz, W.B., Jr., & Reddy, V.K. (2005). Operational success in distance education. In C. Howard, J.V. Boettcher, L. Justice, K. Schenk, P.L. Rogers, & G.A. Berg (Eds.), *Encyclopedia of distance learning* (pp. 1440-1445). Hershey, PA: Idea Group Reference.

Martz, W.B., Jr., & Shepherd, M.M. (2005). Lower perceived performance in testing. In C. Howard, J.V. Boettcher, L. Justice, K. Schenk, P.L. Rogers, & G.A. Berg (Eds.), *Encyclopedia of distance learning* (pp. 1265-1271). Hershey, PA: Idea Group Reference.

Mason, C., Castleman, T., & Parker, C. (2006). Creating value with regional communities of SMEs. In E. Coakes & S. Clarke (Eds.), *Encyclopedia of communities of practice in information and knowledge management* (pp. 115-123). Hershey, PA: Idea Group Reference.

Masseglia, F., Teisseire, M., & Poncelet, P. (2005). Sequential pattern mining. In J. Wang (Ed.), *Encyclopedia of data warehousing and mining* (pp. 1028-1032). Hershey, PA: Idea Group Reference.

Mathieu, R., & Levary, R.R. (2005). Data warehousing and mining in supply chains. In J. Wang (Ed.), *Encyclopedia of data warehousing and mining* (pp. 323-327). Hershey, PA: Idea Group Reference.

Matta, A.E.R. (2005). Trans-urbanites and collaborative environments in computer networks. In S. Marshall, W. Taylor, & X. Yu (Eds.), *Encyclopedia of developing regional communities with information and communication technology* (pp. 704-708). Hershey, PA: Idea Group Reference.

Mattord, H.J., & Whitman, M.E. (2005). Infosec policy- the foundation for effective security programs. In M. Khosrow-Pour (Ed.), *Encyclopedia of information science and technology* (pp. 1518-1523). Hershey, PA: Idea Group Reference.

Mauco, M.V., & Riesco, D. (2005). Integrating requirements engineering techniques and formal methods. In M. Khosrow-Pour (Ed.), *Encyclopedia of information science and technology* (pp. 1555-1559). Hershey, PA: Idea Group Reference.

Maule, R.W. (2006). Military knowledge management. In D. Schwartz (Ed.), *Encyclopedia of knowledge management* (pp. 627). Hershey, PA: Idea Group Reference.

McCarthy, C. (2005a). Digital library structure and software. In S. Marshall, W. Taylor, & X. Yu (Eds.), *Encyclopedia of developing regional communities with information and communication technology* (pp. 193-198). Hershey, PA: Idea Group Reference.

McCarthy, C. (2005b). Promoting the culture and development of regional communities with digital libraries. In S. Marshall, W. Taylor, & X. Yu (Eds.), *Encyclopedia of developing regional communities with information and communication technology* (pp. 593-597). Hershey, PA: Idea Group Reference.

McCracken, H. (2005). Community in virtual learning environments. In C. Howard, J.V. Boettcher, L. Justice, K. Schenk, P.L. Rogers, & G.A. Berg (Eds.), *Encyclopedia of distance learning* (pp. 304-309). Hershey, PA: Idea Group Reference.

McGill, T., & Dixon, M. (2005). Staying up-to-date with changes in IT. In M. Khosrow-Pour (Ed.), *Encyclopedia of information science and technology* (pp. 2605-2609). Hershey, PA: Idea Group Reference.

McHaney, R. (2005). Success surrogates in representational decision support systems. In M. Khosrow-Pour (Ed.), *Encyclopedia of information science and technology* (pp. 2672-2677). Hershey, PA: Idea Group Reference.

McInnerney, J.M., & Roberts, T.S. (2005). Collaborative and cooperative learning. In C. Howard, J.V. Boettcher, L. Justice, K. Schenk, P.L. Rogers, & G.A. Berg (Eds.), *Encyclopedia of distance learning* (pp. 269-276). Hershey, PA: Idea Group Reference.

McIntosh, J.C., & Siau, K.L. (2005). Managing value-creation in the digital economy. In M. Khos-

row-Pour (Ed.), *Encyclopedia of information science and technology* (pp. 1887-1890). Hershey, PA: Idea Group Reference.

McManus, D.J., & Carr, H.H. (2005). E-mail as a strategic tool in organizations. In M. Khosrow-Pour (Ed.), *Encyclopedia of information science and technology* (pp. 1030-1033). Hershey, PA: Idea Group Reference.

McManus, P., & Standing, C. (2005). From communities to mobile communities of values. In M. Pagani (Ed.), *Encyclopedia of multimedia technology and networking* (pp. 336-341). Hershey, PA: Idea Group Reference.

McPherson, M. (2005). IS project management contemporary research challenges. In M. Khosrow-Pour (Ed.), *Encyclopedia of information science and technology* (pp. 1673-1678). Hershey, PA: Idea Group Reference.

Medeni, T. (2006a). Tacit-explicit and specific-general knowledge interactions in CoPs. In E. Coakes & S. Clarke (Eds.), *Encyclopedia of communities of practice in information and knowledge management* (pp. 514-522). Hershey, PA: Idea Group Reference.

Medeni, T. (2006b). The living tradition of "Yaren talks" as an indigenous community of practice in today's knowledge society. In E. Coakes & S. Clarke (Eds.), *Encyclopedia of communities of practice in information and knowledge management* (pp. 353-356). Hershey, PA: Idea Group Reference.

Medeni, T., & Medeni, T.I. (2006). Virtual role-playing communities, "wold" and world. In E. Coakes & S. Clarke (Eds.), *Encyclopedia of communities of practice in information and knowledge management* (pp. 580-582). Hershey, PA: Idea Group Reference.

Medlin, B.D., Cazier, J.A., & Dave, D.S. (2006). Password security issues on an e-commerce site. In M. Khosrow-Pour (Ed.), *Encyclopedia of e-commerce, e-government, and mobile commerce* (pp. 902-907). Hershey, PA: Idea Group Reference.

Meixner, M. (2005). Main memory databases. In L. Rivero, J. Doorn, & V. Ferraggine (Eds.), *Encyclo-*

*pedia of database technologies and applications* (pp. 341-344). Hershey, PA: Idea Group Reference.

Melkonyan, G. (2005). Telecommunication problems in rural areas of Armenia. In S. Marshall, W. Taylor, & X. Yu (Eds.), *Encyclopedia of developing regional communities with information and communication technology* (pp. 683-686). Hershey, PA: Idea Group Reference.

Melliar-Smith, P.M., & Moser, L.E. (2005). Mobile multimedia for commerce. In M. Pagani (Ed.), *Encyclopedia of multimedia technology and networking* (pp. 638-644). Hershey, PA: Idea Group Reference.

Mendes-Filho, L.A.M., & Ramos, A.S.M. (2005). Internet diffusion in the hospitality industry. In M. Khosrow-Pour (Ed.), *Encyclopedia of information science and technology* (pp. 1635-1639). Hershey, PA: Idea Group Reference.

Mendonca, J. (2005). Educating the business information technologist. In M. Khosrow-Pour (Ed.), *Encyclopedia of information science and technology* (pp. 972-975). Hershey, PA: Idea Group Reference.

Meng, X., & Chen, Z. (2005). Web search via learning from relevance feedback. In M. Khosrow-Pour (Ed.), *Encyclopedia of information science and technology* (pp. 3060-3064). Hershey, PA: Idea Group Reference.

Meo, R., & Psaila, G. (2005). Mine rule. In J. Wang (Ed.), *Encyclopedia of data warehousing and mining* (pp. 740-745). Hershey, PA: Idea Group Reference.

Metaxiotis, K. (2006). Healthcare knowledge management. In D. Schwartz (Ed.), *Encyclopedia of knowledge management* (pp. 204-210). Hershey, PA: Idea Group Reference.

Mew, L. (2006). Online social networking for new research opportunities. In S. Dasgupta (Ed.), *Encyclopedia of virtual communities and technologies* (pp. 359-362). Hershey, PA: Idea Group Reference.

Mezgár, I. (2005). Building and management of trust in information systems. In M. Khosrow-Pour (Ed.), *Encyclopedia of information science and technology* (pp. 298-306). Hershey, PA: Idea Group Reference.

Mezgár, I. (2006a). Building trust in virtual communities. In S. Dasgupta (Ed.), *Encyclopedia of virtual communities and technologies* (pp. 4-9). Hershey, PA: Idea Group Reference.

Mezgár, I. (2006b). Trust in e-government services. In M. Khosrow-Pour (Ed.), *Encyclopedia of e-commerce, e-government, and mobile commerce* (pp. 1094-1100). Hershey, PA: Idea Group Reference.

Mezgár, I. (2006c). Trust in virtual organizations. In S. Dasgupta (Ed.), *Encyclopedia of virtual communities and technologies* (pp. 452-456). Hershey, PA: Idea Group Reference.

Milić, L.D. (2005). Efficient multirate filtering. In M. Khosrow-Pour (Ed.), *Encyclopedia of information science and technology* (pp. 980-984). Hershey, PA: Idea Group Reference.

Millet, I. (2005). Managing hierarchies and taxonomies in relational databases. In M. Khosrow-Pour (Ed.), *Encyclopedia of information science and technology* (pp. 1870-1874). Hershey, PA: Idea Group Reference.

Misuraca, G. (2005). E-Africa initiative for good governance. In S. Marshall, W. Taylor, & X. Yu (Eds.), *Encyclopedia of developing regional communities with information and communication technology* (pp. 210-213). Hershey, PA: Idea Group Reference.

Mitchell, H. (2005a). Innovation link between organization knowledge and customer knowledge. In M. Khosrow-Pour (Ed.), *Encyclopedia of information science and technology* (pp. 1524-1528). Hershey, PA: Idea Group Reference.

Mitchell, H. (2005b). Technology and knowledge management. In M. Khosrow-Pour (Ed.), *Encyclopedia of information science and technology* (pp. 2748-2752). Hershey, PA: Idea Group Reference.

Mitchell, M. (2005a). Convergence of ICT and culture. In S. Marshall, W. Taylor, & X. Yu (Eds.),

*Encyclopedia of developing regional communities with information and communication technology* (pp. 135-137). Hershey, PA: Idea Group Reference.

Mitchell, M. (2005b). NetTel@Africa. In S. Marshall, W. Taylor, & X. Yu (Eds.), *Encyclopedia of developing regional communities with information and communication technology* (pp. 518-522). Hershey, PA: Idea Group Reference.

Mitchell, M. (2005c). Student-generated multimedia. In C. Howard, J.V. Boettcher, L. Justice, K. Schenk, P.L. Rogers, & G.A. Berg (Eds.), *Encyclopedia of distance learning* (pp. 1693-1702). Hershey, PA: Idea Group Reference.

Mitrakas, A. (2005). Policy frameworks for secure electronic business. In M. Khosrow-Pour (Ed.), *Encyclopedia of information science and technology* (pp. 2288-2292). Hershey, PA: Idea Group Reference.

Mitrakas, A. (2006). Information security for legal safety. In M. Khosrow-Pour (Ed.), *Encyclopedia of e-commerce, e-government, and mobile commerce* (pp. 620-625). Hershey, PA: Idea Group Reference.

Mizell, A.P., & Sugarman, C. (2005). Overcoming the digital divide. In C. Howard, J.V. Boettcher, L. Justice, K. Schenk, P.L. Rogers, & G.A. Berg (Eds.), *Encyclopedia of distance learning* (pp. 1453-1459). Hershey, PA: Idea Group Reference.

Mladenić, D. (2005). Text mining-machine learning on documents. In J. Wang (Ed.), *Encyclopedia of data warehousing and mining* (pp. 1109-1112). Hershey, PA: Idea Group Reference.

Mobasher, B. (2005a). Web mining overview. In J. Wang (Ed.), *Encyclopedia of data warehousing and mining* (pp. 1206-1210). Hershey, PA: Idea Group Reference.

Mobasher, B. (2005b). Web usage mining data preparation. In J. Wang (Ed.), *Encyclopedia of data warehousing and mining* (pp. 1226-1230). Hershey, PA: Idea Group Reference.

Mobasher, B. (2005c). Web usage mining. In J. Wang (Ed.), *Encyclopedia of data warehousing and*

*mining* (pp. 1216-1220). Hershey, PA: Idea Group Reference.

Mockler, R.J., & Dologite, D.G. (2005). Strategically-focused enterprise knowledge management. In M. Khosrow-Pour (Ed.), *Encyclopedia of information science and technology* (pp. 2648-2652). Hershey, PA: Idea Group Reference.

Mockler, R.J., Dologite, D.G., & Gartenfeld, M.E. (2006). B2B e-business. In M. Khosrow-Pour (Ed.), *Encyclopedia of e-commerce, e-government, and mobile commerce* (pp. 26-30). Hershey, PA: Idea Group Reference.

Modrák, V., & Marcín, J.N. (2006). Virtual reality technology in computer-aided production engineering. In S. Dasgupta (Ed.), *Encyclopedia of virtual communities and technologies* (pp. 562-565). Hershey, PA: Idea Group Reference.

Mohamed, K.A., & Ottmann, T. (2006). Pen-Based Digital Screen Interaction. In C. Ghaoui (Ed.), *Encyclopedia of human computer interaction* (pp. 463-470). Hershey, PA: Idea Group Reference.

Mohamedally, D., Zaphiris, P., & Petrie, H. (2005). User-centered mobile computing. In M. Pagani (Ed.), *Encyclopedia of multimedia technology and networking* (pp. 1021-1026). Hershey, PA: Idea Group Reference.

Molinari, D.L. (2005). Social comments and online problem-solving groups. In C. Howard, J.V. Boettcher, L. Justice, K. Schenk, P.L. Rogers, & G.A. Berg (Eds.), *Encyclopedia of distance learning* (pp. 1623-1629). Hershey, PA: Idea Group Reference.

Molinari, D.L., Anderberg, E., Dupler, A.E., & Lungstrom, N. (2005). Learning orientation and stress in an online experience. In C. Howard, J.V. Boettcher, L. Justice, K. Schenk, P.L. Rogers, & G.A. Berg (Eds.), *Encyclopedia of distance learning* (pp. 1231-1236). Hershey, PA: Idea Group Reference.

Molinari, D.L., Dupler, A.E., & Lungstrom, N. (2005a). Stress of nursing students studying online. In C. Howard, J.V. Boettcher, L. Justice, K. Schenk, P.L. Rogers, & G.A. Berg (Eds.), *Encyclopedia of distance learning* (pp. 1666-1673). Hershey, PA: Idea Group Reference.

Molinari, D.L., Dupler, A.E., & Lungstrom, N. (2005b). The stress of online learning. In C. Howard, J.V. Boettcher, L. Justice, K. Schenk, P.L. Rogers, & G.A. Berg (Eds.), *Encyclopedia of distance learning* (pp. 1674-1679). Hershey, PA: Idea Group Reference.

Møller, C. (2005). Next-generation ERP. In M. Khosrow-Pour (Ed.), *Encyclopedia of information science and technology* (pp. 2129-2134). Hershey, PA: Idea Group Reference.

Molodtsov, O. (2005). Establishing a "knowledge network" of local and regional development subjects. In S. Marshall, W. Taylor, & X. Yu (Eds.), *Encyclopedia of developing regional communities with information and communication technology* (pp. 289-294). Hershey, PA: Idea Group Reference.

Monteiro de Carvalho, M., Barbin Laurindo, F.J., & Schneck de Paula Pessôa, M. (2005). Project management models in IT. In M. Khosrow-Pour (Ed.), *Encyclopedia of information science and technology* (pp. 2353-2358). Hershey, PA: Idea Group Reference.

Moodley, S. (2005). Clustering dynamics of the ICT sector in South Africa. In S. Marshall, W. Taylor, & X. Yu (Eds.), *Encyclopedia of developing regional communities with information and communication technology* (pp. 113-118). Hershey, PA: Idea Group Reference.

Moore, J.C., Bourne, J.R., & Mayadas, A.F. (2005). The Sloan Consortium. In C. Howard, J.V. Boettcher, L. Justice, K. Schenk, P.L. Rogers, & G.A. Berg (Eds.), *Encyclopedia of distance learning* (pp. 1614-1622). Hershey, PA: Idea Group Reference.

Moore, J.E., & Burke, L.A. (2005). Limited-perspective bias in technology projects. In M. Khosrow-Pour (Ed.), *Encyclopedia of information science and technology* (pp. 1850-1853). Hershey, PA: Idea Group Reference.

Moore, R.S., Warkentin, M., & Moore, M. (2006). Information integration for relationship management. In M. Khosrow-Pour (Ed.), *Encyclopedia of e-commerce, e-government, and mobile commerce* (pp. 608-614). Hershey, PA: Idea Group Reference.

Morabito, V., & Provera, B. (2005). Application service providers. In M. Pagani (Ed.), *Encyclopedia of multimedia technology and networking* (pp. 31-35). Hershey, PA: Idea Group Reference.

Morantz, B. (2005). Automated anomaly detection. In J. Wang (Ed.), *Encyclopedia of data warehousing and mining* (pp. 78-82). Hershey, PA: Idea Group Reference.

Moreau, E.M.-F., Raymond, L., & Vermot-Desroches, B. (2005). E-business for SME development. In S. Marshall, W. Taylor, & X. Yu (Eds.), *Encyclopedia of developing regional communities with information and communication technology* (pp. 220-226). Hershey, PA: Idea Group Reference.

Moreira, D.D.A., & da Silva, E.Q. (2005). Improving student interaction with Internet and peer review. In M. Pagani (Ed.), *Encyclopedia of multimedia technology and networking* (pp. 375-381). Hershey, PA: Idea Group Reference.

Morphew, V.N. (2005). Constructivist teaching and learning in a Web-based environment. In C. Howard, J.V. Boettcher, L. Justice, K. Schenk, P.L. Rogers, & G.A. Berg (Eds.), *Encyclopedia of distance learning* (pp. 394-399). Hershey, PA: Idea Group Reference.

Morris, S.A., Marshall, T.E., & Rainer, R.K. (2005). Technological collaboration and trust in virtual teams. In M. Khosrow-Pour (Ed.), *Encyclopedia of information science and technology* (pp. 2742-2747). Hershey, PA: Idea Group Reference.

Morris-Jones, D.R., & Carter, D.A. (2005). Geospatial information systems and enterprise collaboration. In M. Khosrow-Pour (Ed.), *Encyclopedia of information science and technology* (pp. 1278-1283). Hershey, PA: Idea Group Reference.

Moser, L.E., & Melliar-Smith, P.M. (2006). Web services. In M. Khosrow-Pour (Ed.), *Encyclopedia of e-commerce, e-government, and mobile commerce* (pp. 1222-1229). Hershey, PA: Idea Group Reference.

Moustafa, K.S. (2006). Differences in the use of media across cultures. In S. Dasgupta (Ed.), *Encyclopedia of virtual communities and technologies* (pp. 131-132). Hershey, PA: Idea Group Reference.

Moutinho, J.L., & Heitor, M. (2005). Building human-centered systems. In S. Marshall, W. Taylor, & X. Yu (Eds.), *Encyclopedia of developing regional communities with information and communication technology* (pp. 53-65). Hershey, PA: Idea Group Reference.

Msiska, K. (2005). E-commerce in the Sub-Saharan Africa. In S. Marshall, W. Taylor, & X. Yu (Eds.), *Encyclopedia of developing regional communities with information and communication technology* (pp. 246-249). Hershey, PA: Idea Group Reference.

Müeller-Prothmann, T. (2006a). Knowledge communities, communities of practice, and knowledge networks. In E. Coakes & S. Clarke (Eds.), *Encyclopedia of communities of practice in information and knowledge management* (pp. 264-271). Hershey, PA: Idea Group Reference.

Müeller-Prothmann, T. (2006b). Use and methods of social network analysis in knowledge management. In E. Coakes & S. Clarke (Eds.), *Encyclopedia of communities of practice in information and knowledge management* (pp. 565-574). Hershey, PA: Idea Group Reference.

Muhlenbach, F., & Rakotomalala, R. (2005). Discretization of continuous attributes. In J. Wang (Ed.), *Encyclopedia of data warehousing and mining* (pp. 397-402). Hershey, PA: Idea Group Reference.

Mukherjee, S. (2005). Multiple hypothesis testing for data mining. In J. Wang (Ed.), *Encyclopedia of data warehousing and mining* (pp. 848-853). Hershey, PA: Idea Group Reference.

Mullany, M.J. (2005). Relating cognitive problem-solving style to user resistance. In M. Khosrow-Pour (Ed.), *Encyclopedia of information science and technology* (pp. 2414-2418). Hershey, PA: Idea Group Reference.

Mullen, P.R. (2005). Digital government and individual privacy. In M. Khosrow-Pour (Ed.), *Encyclopedia of information science and technology* (pp. 870-874). Hershey, PA: Idea Group Reference.

Mundy, D.P., & Otenko, O. (2005). Privilege management infrastructure. In M. Pagani (Ed.), *Encyclopedia of multimedia technology and networking* (pp. 849-854). Hershey, PA: Idea Group Reference.

Munkvold, G. (2006). Practice-based knowledge integration. In D. Schwartz (Ed.), *Encyclopedia of knowledge management* (pp. 762-768). Hershey, PA: Idea Group Reference.

Muñoz-Escoí, F.D., Irún-Briz, L., & Decker, H. (2005). Database replication protocols. In L. Rivero, J. Doorn, & V. Ferraggine (Eds.), *Encyclopedia of database technologies and applications* (pp. 153-157). Hershey, PA: Idea Group Reference.

Murphy, P. (2005a). Public opinion and the Internet. In M. Pagani (Ed.), *Encyclopedia of multimedia technology and networking* (pp. 863-868). Hershey, PA: Idea Group Reference.

Murphy, P. (2005b). The n-dimensional geometry and kinaesthetic space of the Internet. In M. Pagani (Ed.), *Encyclopedia of multimedia technology and networking* (pp. 742-747). Hershey, PA: Idea Group Reference.

Murphy, P. (2005c). Virtual work, trust and rationality. In M. Khosrow-Pour (Ed.), *Encyclopedia of information science and technology* (pp. 3018-3021). Hershey, PA: Idea Group Reference.

Murray, L.W., & Efendioglu, A.M. (2005). Delivering management education via tutored-video instruction. In C. Howard, J.V. Boettcher, L. Justice, K. Schenk, P.L. Rogers, & G.A. Berg (Eds.), *Encyclopedia of distance learning* (pp. 505-509). Hershey, PA: Idea Group Reference.

Murthy, M.N., & Diday, E. (2005). Symbolic data clustering. In J. Wang (Ed.), *Encyclopedia of data warehousing and mining* (pp. 1087-1091). Hershey, PA: Idea Group Reference.

Murthy, V.K., & Krishnamurthy, E.V. (2005a). Agent-based negotiation in e-marketing. In M. Khosrow-Pour (Ed.), *Encyclopedia of information science and technology* (pp. 88-92). Hershey, PA: Idea Group Reference.

Murthy, V.K., & Krishnamurthy, E.V. (2005b). Contract-based workflow design patterns in m-commerce. In M. Khosrow-Pour (Ed.), *Encyclopedia of information science and technology* (pp. 584-489). Hershey, PA: Idea Group Reference.

Murthy, V.K., & Krishnamurthy, E.V. (2005c). E-business transaction in Web integrated network environment. In M. Khosrow-Pour (Ed.), *Encyclopedia of information science and technology* (pp. 934-938). Hershey, PA: Idea Group Reference.

Murthy, V.K., & Krishnamurthy, E.V. (2005d). Multimedia computing environment for telemedical applications. In M. Khosrow-Pour (Ed.), *Encyclopedia of information science and technology* (pp. 2045-2050). Hershey, PA: Idea Group Reference.

Muruzábal, J. (2005). Evolutionary mining of rule ensembles. In J. Wang (Ed.), *Encyclopedia of data warehousing and mining* (pp. 487-491). Hershey, PA: Idea Group Reference.

Muselli, M. (2005). Rule generation methods based on logic synthesis. In J. Wang (Ed.), *Encyclopedia of data warehousing and mining* (pp. 978-983). Hershey, PA: Idea Group Reference.

Musicant, D.R. (2005). Support vector machines illuminated. In J. Wang (Ed.), *Encyclopedia of data warehousing and mining* (pp. 1071-1076). Hershey, PA: Idea Group Reference.

Muslea, I. (2005). Active learning with multiple views. In J. Wang (Ed.), *Encyclopedia of data warehousing and mining* (pp. 12-16). Hershey, PA: Idea Group Reference.

Muukkonen, H., Lakkala, M., & Hakkarainen, K. (2005). Technology-mediated progressive inquiry in higher education. In M. Khosrow-Pour (Ed.), *Encyclopedia of information science and technology* (pp. 2771-2776). Hershey, PA: Idea Group Reference.

Mwesige, P.G. (2005). The state of Internet access in Uganda. In S. Marshall, W. Taylor, & X. Yu (Eds.), *Encyclopedia of developing regional communities with information and communication technology* (pp. 655-658). Hershey, PA: Idea Group Reference.

Nabuco, O., Koyama, M.F., Pereira, E.D., & Drira, K. (2006). Agent-Based System for Discovering and Building Collaborative Communities. In C. Ghaoui (Ed.), *Encyclopedia of human computer interaction* (pp. 12-17). Hershey, PA: Idea Group Reference.

Naidu, S. (2005a). Evaluating distance education and e-learning. In C. Howard, J.V. Boettcher, L. Justice, K. Schenk, P.L. Rogers, & G.A. Berg (Eds.), *Encyclopedia of distance learning* (pp. 857-864). Hershey, PA: Idea Group Reference.

Naidu, S. (2005b). Researching distance education and e-learning. In C. Howard, J.V. Boettcher, L. Justice, K. Schenk, P.L. Rogers, & G.A. Berg (Eds.), *Encyclopedia of distance learning* (pp. 1564-1572). Hershey, PA: Idea Group Reference.

Nandavadekar, V.D. (2005). Corporate conferencing. In M. Pagani (Ed.), *Encyclopedia of multimedia technology and networking* (pp. 137-142). Hershey, PA: Idea Group Reference.

Nantz, K.S. (2005). Issues in delivering course material via the Web. In M. Khosrow-Pour (Ed.), *Encyclopedia of information science and technology* (pp. 1697-1701). Hershey, PA: Idea Group Reference.

Narayanan, V.K. (2005). Strategic experimentation and knowledge management. In M. Khosrow-Pour (Ed.), *Encyclopedia of information science and technology* (pp. 2627-2631). Hershey, PA: Idea Group Reference.

Nash, J.B., Richter, C., & Allert, H. (2005a). Evaluating computer-supported learning initiatives. In M. Khosrow-Pour (Ed.), *Encyclopedia of information science and technology* (pp. 1125-1129). Hershey, PA: Idea Group Reference.

Nash, J.B., Richter, C., & Allert, H. (2005b). Improving evaluations in computer-supported learning projects. In C. Howard, J.V. Boettcher, L. Justice, K. Schenk,

P.L. Rogers, & G.A. Berg (Eds.), *Encyclopedia of distance learning* (pp. 1048-1053). Hershey, PA: Idea Group Reference.

Nason, R., & Woodruff, E. (2005a). Innovations for online collaborative learning in mathematics. In M. Khosrow-Pour (Ed.), *Encyclopedia of information science and technology* (pp. 1529-1534). Hershey, PA: Idea Group Reference.

Nason, R., & Woodruff, E. (2005b). Supporting online collaborative learning in mathematics. In C. Howard, J.V. Boettcher, L. Justice, K. Schenk, P.L. Rogers, & G.A. Berg (Eds.), *Encyclopedia of distance learning* (pp. 1725-1731). Hershey, PA: Idea Group Reference.

Nasraoui, O. (2005). World Wide Web personalization. In J. Wang (Ed.), *Encyclopedia of data warehousing and mining* (pp. 1235-1241). Hershey, PA: Idea Group Reference.

Natarajan, R., & Shekar, B. (2006). Interesting knowledge patterns in databases. In D. Schwartz (Ed.), *Encyclopedia of knowledge management* (pp. 297-304). Hershey, PA: Idea Group Reference.

Naumenko, A. (2005). Basics of the triune continuum paradigm. In M. Khosrow-Pour (Ed.), *Encyclopedia of information science and technology* (pp. 217-221). Hershey, PA: Idea Group Reference.

Navarro, G. (2005). Text databases. In L. Rivero, J. Doorn, & V. Ferraggine (Eds.), *Encyclopedia of database technologies and applications* (pp. 688-694). Hershey, PA: Idea Group Reference.

Nayak, R. (2005a). Data mining and mobile business data. In M. Khosrow-Pour (Ed.), *Encyclopedia of information science and technology* (pp. 698-702). Hershey, PA: Idea Group Reference.

Nayak, R. (2005b). Discovering knowledge from XML documents. In J. Wang (Ed.), *Encyclopedia of data warehousing and mining* (pp. 372-376). Hershey, PA: Idea Group Reference.

Nayak, R. (2005c). Mining for Web-enabled e-business applications. In J. Wang (Ed.), *Encyclopedia of*
data warehousing and mining* (pp. 785-789). Hershey, PA: Idea Group Reference.

Nayak, R. (2005d). Wireless technologies to enable electronic business. In M. Khosrow-Pour (Ed.), *Encyclopedia of information science and technology* (pp. 3101-3105). Hershey, PA: Idea Group Reference.

Neale, D.C., Carroll, J.M., & Rosson, M.B. (2005). Evaluating distributed cooperative learning. In C. Howard, J.V. Boettcher, L. Justice, K. Schenk, P.L. Rogers, & G.A. Berg (Eds.), *Encyclopedia of distance learning* (pp. 865-871). Hershey, PA: Idea Group Reference.

Negash, S. (2005). ICT for Ethiopian community development. In S. Marshall, W. Taylor, & X. Yu (Eds.), *Encyclopedia of developing regional communities with information and communication technology* (pp. 370-376). Hershey, PA: Idea Group Reference.

Nelson, A.J. (2005). A model for evaluating online programs. In C. Howard, J.V. Boettcher, L. Justice, K. Schenk, P.L. Rogers, & G.A. Berg (Eds.), *Encyclopedia of distance learning* (pp. 1297-1306). Hershey, PA: Idea Group Reference.

Nelson, R.E., & Hsu, H.S. (2006). A social network perspective on knowledge management. In D. Schwartz (Ed.), *Encyclopedia of knowledge management* (pp. 826-832). Hershey, PA: Idea Group Reference.

Nemati, H.R., & Barko, C.D. (2005). Organizational data mining. In J. Wang (Ed.), *Encyclopedia of data warehousing and mining* (pp. 891-895). Hershey, PA: Idea Group Reference.

Nesi, P., & Spinu, M. (2005). Music score watermarking. In M. Khosrow-Pour (Ed.), *Encyclopedia of information science and technology* (pp. 2074-2079). Hershey, PA: Idea Group Reference.

Neumann, A. (2005). How the national e-strategy shapes competitiveness in the information economy. In S. Marshall, W. Taylor, & X. Yu (Eds.), *Encyclopedia of developing regional communities with information and communication technology* (pp. 325-330). Hershey, PA: Idea Group Reference.

Neville, K., & Powell, P. (2005). Knowledge-based support environment. In M. Khosrow-Pour (Ed.), *Encyclopedia of information science and technology* (pp. 1788-1792). Hershey, PA: Idea Group Reference.

Newberry, B. (2005). Social presence in distance learning. In C. Howard, J.V. Boettcher, L. Justice, K. Schenk, P.L. Rogers, & G.A. Berg (Eds.), *Encyclopedia of distance learning* (pp. 1634-1640). Hershey, PA: Idea Group Reference.

Newell, C., & Debenham, M. (2005). Disability, chronic illness and distance education. In C. Howard, J.V. Boettcher, L. Justice, K. Schenk, P.L. Rogers, & G.A. Berg (Eds.), *Encyclopedia of distance learning* (pp. 591-598). Hershey, PA: Idea Group Reference.

Newell, S. (2006). Understanding innovation processes. In D. Schwartz (Ed.), *Encyclopedia of knowledge management* (pp. 862-869). Hershey, PA: Idea Group Reference.

Ng, C.S. (2005). Enterprise resource planning maintenance concepts. In M. Khosrow-Pour (Ed.), *Encyclopedia of information science and technology* (pp. 1095-1101). Hershey, PA: Idea Group Reference.

Ng, F.F. (2006). E-learning concepts and development. In M. Khosrow-Pour (Ed.), *Encyclopedia of e-commerce, e-government, and mobile commerce* (pp. 391-396). Hershey, PA: Idea Group Reference.

Ng, L.L., & Pemberton, J. (2006). Managing complextiy via communities of practice. In E. Coakes & S. Clarke (Eds.), *Encyclopedia of communities of practice in information and knowledge management* (pp. 357-363). Hershey, PA: Idea Group Reference.

Ngoh, L.H., & Shankar P., J. (2005). Mobility over heterogeneous wireless networks. In M. Pagani (Ed.), *Encyclopedia of multimedia technology and networking* (pp. 652-659). Hershey, PA: Idea Group Reference.

Nicholls, M.G. (2006). Communities of practice and the development of best practices. In E. Coakes & S. Clarke (Eds.), *Encyclopedia of communities of practice in information and knowledge management* (pp. 66-67). Hershey, PA: Idea Group Reference.

Nichols, J., & Chen, A. (2006). Coordination of a service oriented architecture. In M. Khosrow-Pour (Ed.), *Encyclopedia of e-commerce, e-government, and mobile commerce* (pp. 157-162). Hershey, PA: Idea Group Reference.

Nicholson, S., & Stanton, J. (2005). Bibliomining for library decision-making. In M. Khosrow-Pour (Ed.), *Encyclopedia of information science and technology* (pp. 272-277). Hershey, PA: Idea Group Reference.

Nicolle, C., Simon, J.-C., & Yétongnon, K. (2005). Interoperability of information systems. In M. Khosrow-Pour (Ed.), *Encyclopedia of information science and technology* (pp. 1651-1656). Hershey, PA: Idea Group Reference.

Nightingale, J.P. (2005). Classroom communication on a different blackboard. In M. Khosrow-Pour (Ed.), *Encyclopedia of information science and technology* (pp. 425-429). Hershey, PA: Idea Group Reference.

Nigro, H.O., & González Císaro, S.E. (2005a). Intension mining. In L. Rivero, J. Doorn, & V. Ferraggine (Eds.), *Encyclopedia of database technologies and applications* (pp. 298-303). Hershey, PA: Idea Group Reference.

Nigro, H.O., & González Císaro, S.E. (2005b). Online data mining. In L. Rivero, J. Doorn, & V. Ferraggine (Eds.), *Encyclopedia of database technologies and applications* (pp. 427-432). Hershey, PA: Idea Group Reference.

Nigro, H.O., & González Císaro, S.E. (2005c). Symbolic objects and symbolic data analysis. In L. Rivero, J. Doorn, & V. Ferraggine (Eds.), *Encyclopedia of database technologies and applications* (pp. 665-670). Hershey, PA: Idea Group Reference.

Nissen, M.E. (2005). Delineating knowledge flows for enterprise agility. In M. Khosrow-Pour (Ed.), *Encyclopedia of information science and technology* (pp. 779-785). Hershey, PA: Idea Group Reference.

Nissen, M.E., & Levitt, R.E. (2006). Computational experimentation. In D. Schwartz (Ed.), *Encyclopedia of knowledge management* (pp. 51-57). Hershey, PA: Idea Group Reference.

Nobre, A.L. (2006a). Facilitating and improving organisational community life. In E. Coakes & S. Clarke (Eds.), *Encyclopedia of communities of practice in information and knowledge management* (pp. 177-184). Hershey, PA: Idea Group Reference.

Nobre, A.L. (2006b). Psychoanalysis, organisations, and communities. In E. Coakes & S. Clarke (Eds.), *Encyclopedia of communities of practice in information and knowledge management* (pp. 419-429). Hershey, PA: Idea Group Reference.

Nobre, A.L. (2006c). Social philosophy, communities, and the epistemic shifts. In E. Coakes & S. Clarke (Eds.), *Encyclopedia of communities of practice in information and knowledge management* (pp. 481-486). Hershey, PA: Idea Group Reference.

Norris, D.M. (2005). Driving systemic change with e-learning. In C. Howard, J.V. Boettcher, L. Justice, K. Schenk, P.L. Rogers, & G.A. Berg (Eds.), *Encyclopedia of distance learning* (pp. 687-695). Hershey, PA: Idea Group Reference.

Nørvåg, K. (2005). Query operators in temporal XML databases. In L. Rivero, J. Doorn, & V. Ferraggine (Eds.), *Encyclopedia of database technologies and applications* (pp. 500-505). Hershey, PA: Idea Group Reference.

Notess, M. (2005). Contextual design of online learning technologies. In C. Howard, J.V. Boettcher, L. Justice, K. Schenk, P.L. Rogers, & G.A. Berg (Eds.), *Encyclopedia of distance learning* (pp. 400-407). Hershey, PA: Idea Group Reference.

Novitzki, J.E. (2005). Necessities for effective asynchronous learning. In C. Howard, J.V. Boettcher, L. Justice, K. Schenk, P.L. Rogers, & G.A. Berg (Eds.), *Encyclopedia of distance learning* (pp. 1325-1331). Hershey, PA: Idea Group Reference.

Noyes, J. (2006). Expectations and Their Forgotten Role in HCI. In C. Ghaoui (Ed.), *Encyclopedia of human computer interaction* (pp. 205-210). Hershey, PA: Idea Group Reference.

Nugent, J.H. (2005). Critical trends in telecommunications. In M. Khosrow-Pour (Ed.), *Encyclopedia of information science and technology* (pp. 634-639). Hershey, PA: Idea Group Reference.

O'Buyonge, A.A., & Chen, L. (2006). E-health dotcoms' critical success factors. In M. Khosrow-Pour (Ed.), *Encyclopedia of e-commerce, e-government, and mobile commerce* (pp. 379-384). Hershey, PA: Idea Group Reference.

Ochoa-Morales, H.J. (2005). Social responsibility and the technology paradigm in Latin America. In M. Khosrow-Pour (Ed.), *Encyclopedia of information science and technology* (pp. 2529-2533). Hershey, PA: Idea Group Reference.

O'Dea, M. (2005). Educational technology standards. In M. Pagani (Ed.), *Encyclopedia of multimedia technology and networking* (pp. 247-256). Hershey, PA: Idea Group Reference.

Oermann, A., & Dittmann, J. (2006). Trust in e-technologies. In M. Khosrow-Pour (Ed.), *Encyclopedia of e-commerce, e-government, and mobile commerce* (pp. 1101-1108). Hershey, PA: Idea Group Reference.

Oh, J., Lee, J., & Hwang, S. (2005). Video data mining. In J. Wang (Ed.), *Encyclopedia of data warehousing and mining* (pp. 1185-1189). Hershey, PA: Idea Group Reference.

O'Hagan, M. (2005). Teletranslation. In M. Pagani (Ed.), *Encyclopedia of multimedia technology and networking* (pp. 945-950). Hershey, PA: Idea Group Reference.

Okoli, C., & Carillo, K. (2006). Intellectual property rights in open source software communities. In S. Dasgupta (Ed.), *Encyclopedia of virtual communities and technologies* (pp. 285-290). Hershey, PA: Idea Group Reference.

Olatokun, W.M. (2006). Challenges and policy imperatives for e-government in Africa. In M. Khosrow-Pour (Ed.), *Encyclopedia of e-commerce, e-government, and mobile commerce* (pp. 89-94). Hershey, PA: Idea Group Reference.

Olatokun, W.M., & Ajiferuke, I. (2006). E-commerce challenges and policy considerations in Nigeria. In M. Khosrow-Pour (Ed.), *Encyclopedia of e-commerce, e-government, and mobile commerce* (pp. 291-295). Hershey, PA: Idea Group Reference.

Olla, P. (2005a). Evolution of GSM network technology. In M. Pagani (Ed.), *Encyclopedia of multimedia technology and networking* (pp. 290-294). Hershey, PA: Idea Group Reference.

Olla, P. (2005b). Global navigation satellite systems. In M. Pagani (Ed.), *Encyclopedia of multimedia technology and networking* (pp. 348-352). Hershey, PA: Idea Group Reference.

O'Looney, J. (2006). Simulation technologies for enhancing citizen participation. In M. Khosrow-Pour (Ed.), *Encyclopedia of e-commerce, e-government, and mobile commerce* (pp. 1009-1015). Hershey, PA: Idea Group Reference.

Olson, L., & Langer, G.R. (2005). Building a system to deliver programs at a distance. In C. Howard, J.V. Boettcher, L. Justice, K. Schenk, P.L. Rogers, & G.A. Berg (Eds.), *Encyclopedia of distance learning* (pp. 187-191). Hershey, PA: Idea Group Reference.

Opdahl, A.L. (2005). Model-supported alignment of IS architecture. In M. Khosrow-Pour (Ed.), *Encyclopedia of information science and technology* (pp. 2012-2017). Hershey, PA: Idea Group Reference.

Oravec, J.A. (2005). Enhancing workplaces with constructive online recreation. In M. Khosrow-Pour (Ed.), *Encyclopedia of information science and technology* (pp. 1071-1075). Hershey, PA: Idea Group Reference.

Ordonez, B.M. (2005). Facilitation of Web-based courses designed for adult learners. In C. Howard, J.V. Boettcher, L. Justice, K. Schenk, P.L. Rogers, & G.A. Berg (Eds.), *Encyclopedia of distance learning* (pp. 918-921). Hershey, PA: Idea Group Reference.

Ortega Egea, J.M., & Menéndez, M.R. (2006). Global marketing on the Internet. In M. Khosrow-Pour (Ed.), *Encyclopedia of e-commerce, e-government, and mobile commerce* (pp. 530-536). Hershey, PA: Idea Group Reference.

Oshri, I. (2006). Knowledge reuse. In D. Schwartz (Ed.), *Encyclopedia of knowledge management* (pp. 487). Hershey, PA: Idea Group Reference.

Oulasvirta, A., & Salovaara, A. (2006). Ubiquitous Computing and the Concept of Context. In C. Ghaoui (Ed.), *Encyclopedia of human computer interaction* (pp. 630-633). Hershey, PA: Idea Group Reference.

Owen, R.S. (2006a). Online advertising fraud. In M. Khosrow-Pour (Ed.), *Encyclopedia of e-commerce, e-government, and mobile commerce* (pp. 853-857). Hershey, PA: Idea Group Reference.

Owen, R.S. (2006b). Tracking Attention through Browser Mouse Tracking. In C. Ghaoui (Ed.), *Encyclopedia of human computer interaction* (pp. 615-621). Hershey, PA: Idea Group Reference.

Owen, R.S. (2006c). Use of the Secondary Task Technique for Tracking User Attention. In C. Ghaoui (Ed.), *Encyclopedia of human computer interaction* (pp. 673-679). Hershey, PA: Idea Group Reference.

Owen, R.S. (2006d). Web traffic aggregation. In M. Khosrow-Pour (Ed.), *Encyclopedia of e-commerce, e-government, and mobile commerce* (pp. 1243-1247). Hershey, PA: Idea Group Reference.

Owen, R.S., & Aworuwa, B. (2005). Progammed instruction, programmed branching, and learning outtcomes. In M. Khosrow-Pour (Ed.), *Encyclopedia of information science and technology* (pp. 2326-2329). Hershey, PA: Idea Group Reference.

Owens, J., Chalasani, S., & Sounderpandian, J. (2005). Use of RFID in supply chain data processing. In J. Wang (Ed.), *Encyclopedia of data warehousing and mining* (pp. 1160-1165). Hershey, PA: Idea Group Reference.

Owrang O., M.M. (2006). Discovering implicit knowledge from data warehouses. In E. Coakes & S. Clarke (Eds.), *Encyclopedia of communities of practice in information and knowledge management* (pp. 131-137). Hershey, PA: Idea Group Reference.

Oza, N.C. (2005). Ensemble data mining methods. In J. Wang (Ed.), *Encyclopedia of data warehousing and mining* (pp. 448-453). Hershey, PA: Idea Group Reference.

Ozer, B., Lv, T., & Wolf, W. (2005). Human body part classification and activity recognition for real-time systems. In M. Khosrow-Pour (Ed.), *Encyclopedia of information science and technology* (pp. 1349-1354). Hershey, PA: Idea Group Reference.

Pace, S. (2005). Methods of research in virtual communities. In M. Pagani (Ed.), *Encyclopedia of multimedia technology and networking* (pp. 585-592). Hershey, PA: Idea Group Reference.

Pachet, F. (2006). Musical metadata and knowledge management. In D. Schwartz (Ed.), *Encyclopedia of knowledge management* (pp. 672). Hershey, PA: Idea Group Reference.

Pagani, M. (2005a). Interactive digital television. In M. Pagani (Ed.), *Encyclopedia of multimedia technology and networking* (pp. 428-436). Hershey, PA: Idea Group Reference.

Pagani, M. (2005b). Measuring the potential for IT convergence at macro level. In M. Pagani (Ed.), *Encyclopedia of multimedia technology and networking* (pp. 571-578). Hershey, PA: Idea Group Reference.

Paiano, R. (2005). Software reuse in hypermedia applications. In M. Khosrow-Pour (Ed.), *Encyclopedia of information science and technology* (pp. 2567-2570). Hershey, PA: Idea Group Reference.

Pallis, G., Stoupa, K., & Vakali, A. (2005). Storage and access control issues for XML documents. In M. Khosrow-Pour (Ed.), *Encyclopedia of information science and technology* (pp. 2616-2621). Hershey, PA: Idea Group Reference.

Pang, L. (2005a). Best practices in data warehousing from the federal perspective. In J. Wang (Ed.), *Encyclopedia of data warehousing and mining* (pp. 94-99). Hershey, PA: Idea Group Reference.

Pang, L. (2005b). Data mining in the federal government. In J. Wang (Ed.), *Encyclopedia of data warehousing and mining* (pp. 268-271). Hershey, PA: Idea Group Reference.

Panteli, N. (2005). Developing trust in virtual teams. In M. Khosrow-Pour (Ed.), *Encyclopedia of information science and technology* (pp. 844-848). Hershey, PA: Idea Group Reference.

Pantic, M. (2005a). Affective computing. In M. Pagani (Ed.), *Encyclopedia of multimedia technology and networking* (pp. 8-14). Hershey, PA: Idea Group Reference.

Pantic, M. (2005b). Face for interface. In M. Pagani (Ed.), *Encyclopedia of multimedia technology and networking* (pp. 308-314). Hershey, PA: Idea Group Reference.

Panton, M.M. (2005). Web conferencing in distance education. In C. Howard, J.V. Boettcher, L. Justice, K. Schenk, P.L. Rogers, & G.A. Berg (Eds.), *Encyclopedia of distance learning* (pp. 1997-2003). Hershey, PA: Idea Group Reference.

Paoletti, J.B. (2005). Creating and sustaining online learning communities. In C. Howard, J.V. Boettcher, L. Justice, K. Schenk, P.L. Rogers, & G.A. Berg (Eds.), *Encyclopedia of distance learning* (pp. 469-474). Hershey, PA: Idea Group Reference.

Papagiannidis, S., Berry, J., & Li, F. (2005). Potential implications of IPv6 for regional development. In S. Marshall, W. Taylor, & X. Yu (Eds.), *Encyclopedia of developing regional communities with information and communication technology* (pp. 564-568). Hershey, PA: Idea Group Reference.

Paquette, S. (2006a). Communities of practice as facilitators of knowledge exchange. In E. Coakes & S. Clarke (Eds.), *Encyclopedia of communities of practice in information and knowledge management* (pp. 68-73). Hershey, PA: Idea Group Reference.

Paquette, S. (2006b). Customer knowledge management. In D. Schwartz (Ed.), *Encyclopedia of knowledge management* (pp. 90-96). Hershey, PA: Idea Group Reference.

Paraskevi, T., & Kollias, S. (2006). E-questionnaire for innovative adaptive-learning scheme. In M. Khosrow-Pour (Ed.), *Encyclopedia of e-commerce, e-government, and mobile commerce* (pp. 445-450). Hershey, PA: Idea Group Reference.

Paravastu, N., & Gefen, D. (2006). Trust as an enabler of e-commerce. In M. Khosrow-Pour (Ed.), *Encyclopedia of e-commerce, e-government, and mobile commerce* (pp. 1089-1093). Hershey, PA: Idea Group Reference.

Pardede, E., Rahayu, J.W., & Taniar, D. (2005). New SQL standard in database modeling. In M. Khosrow-Pour (Ed.), *Encyclopedia of information science and technology* (pp. 2116-2121). Hershey, PA: Idea Group Reference.

Pareja-Flores, C., & Iturbide, J.Á.V. (2005). Program execution and visualization on the Web. In M. Khosrow-Pour (Ed.), *Encyclopedia of information science and technology* (pp. 2330-2334). Hershey, PA: Idea Group Reference.

Parikh, M.A., & Parolia, N. (2005). Multiple Internet technologies in in-class education. In M. Khosrow-Pour (Ed.), *Encyclopedia of information science and technology* (pp. 2069-2073). Hershey, PA: Idea Group Reference.

Park, E.G. (2006). Trust in virtual communities. In S. Dasgupta (Ed.), *Encyclopedia of virtual communities and technologies* (pp. 449-451). Hershey, PA: Idea Group Reference.

Park, K., & Lepawsky, J. (2006). Understanding virtual communities in online games. In S. Dasgupta (Ed.), *Encyclopedia of virtual communities and technologies* (pp. 462-467). Hershey, PA: Idea Group Reference.

Park, S. (2006). eBay's dominance in Internet auctions. In M. Khosrow-Pour (Ed.), *Encyclopedia of e-commerce, e-government, and mobile commerce* (pp. 259-263). Hershey, PA: Idea Group Reference.

Parker, K.R., & Nitse, P.S. (2006). Competitive intelligence gathering. In D. Schwartz (Ed.), *Encyclopedia of knowledge management* (pp. 44-50). Hershey, PA: Idea Group Reference.

Parker, S., & Chen, Z. (2005). Ensuring serializability for mobile-client data caching. In L. Rivero, J. Doorn, & V. Ferraggine (Eds.), *Encyclopedia of database technologies and applications* (pp. 223-228). Hershey, PA: Idea Group Reference.

Parmar, M.J., & Angelides, M.C. (2005). Multimedia information filtering. In M. Khosrow-Pour (Ed.), *Encyclopedia of information science and technology* (pp. 2063-2068). Hershey, PA: Idea Group Reference.

Parpinelli, R.S., Lopes, H.S., & Freitas, A.A. (2005). Classification-rule discovery with an ant colony algorithm. In M. Khosrow-Pour (Ed.), *Encyclopedia of information science and technology* (pp. 420-424). Hershey, PA: Idea Group Reference.

Partow-Navid, P., & Slusky, L. (2005). Change management and distance education. In C. Howard, J.V. Boettcher, L. Justice, K. Schenk, P.L. Rogers, & G.A. Berg (Eds.), *Encyclopedia of distance learning* (pp. 218-223). Hershey, PA: Idea Group Reference.

Pasquier, N. (2005). Mining association rules using frequent closed itemsets. In J. Wang (Ed.), *Encyclopedia of data warehousing and mining* (pp. 752-757). Hershey, PA: Idea Group Reference.

Passi, K., Lane, L., Madria, S., & Mohania, M. (2005). XML schema integration and e-commerce. In M. Khosrow-Pour (Ed.), *Encyclopedia of information science and technology* (pp. 3118-3121). Hershey, PA: Idea Group Reference.

Patrick, K., Cox, A., & Abdullah, R. (2006). Exploring the selection of technology for enabling communities. In E. Coakes & S. Clarke (Eds.), *Encyclopedia of communities of practice in information and knowledge management* (pp. 166-176). Hershey, PA: Idea Group Reference.

Paukert, M., Niederée, C., & Hemmje, M. (2006). Knowledge in innovation processes. In D. Schwartz (Ed.), *Encyclopedia of knowledge management* (pp. 344-351). Hershey, PA: Idea Group Reference.

Pauleen, D.J. (2005). Leader-facilitated relationship building in virtual teams. In M. Khosrow-Pour (Ed.), *Encyclopedia of information science and technology* (pp. 1793-1798). Hershey, PA: Idea Group Reference.

Pawlak, Z., Polkowski, L., & Skowron, A. (2005). Rough sets. In L. Rivero, J. Doorn, & V. Ferraggine (Eds.), *Encyclopedia of database technologies and applications* (pp. 575-580). Hershey, PA: Idea Group Reference.

Pazyuk, A. (2005). Extended democratic space for citizens' e-participation. In S. Marshall, W. Taylor, & X. Yu (Eds.), *Encyclopedia of developing regional communities with information and communication technology* (pp. 299-304). Hershey, PA: Idea Group Reference.

Pease, W., & Rowe, M. (2005). E-commerce and small business in regional Australia. In S. Marshall, W. Taylor, & X. Yu (Eds.), *Encyclopedia of developing regional communities with information and communication technology* (pp. 227-232). Hershey, PA: Idea Group Reference.

Pease, W., Rowe, M., & Wright, L. (2005). ICT and regional development in Australia. In S. Marshall, W. Taylor, & X. Yu (Eds.), *Encyclopedia of developing regional communities with information and communication technology* (pp. 348-352). Hershey, PA: Idea Group Reference.

Pedreira, N., Dorado, J., Rabuñal, J., & Pazos, A. (2005). Knowledge management as the future of e-learning. In C. Howard, J.V. Boettcher, L. Justice, K. Schenk, P.L. Rogers, & G.A. Berg (Eds.), *Encyclopedia of distance learning* (pp. 1189-1194). Hershey, PA: Idea Group Reference.

Pelton, L.F., & Pelton, T.W. (2005). Enhanced instructional presentation model. In C. Howard, J.V. Boettcher, L. Justice, K. Schenk, P.L. Rogers, & G.A. Berg (Eds.), *Encyclopedia of distance learning* (pp. 828-834). Hershey, PA: Idea Group Reference.

Pemberton, J., & Stalker, B. (2006). Aspects and issues of communities of (mal)practice. In E. Coakes & S. Clarke (Eds.), *Encyclopedia of communities of practice in information and knowledge management* (pp. 6-11). Hershey, PA: Idea Group Reference.

Pendegraft, N. (2005). Simulation and gaming in IT education. In M. Khosrow-Pour (Ed.), *Encyclopedia of information science and technology* (pp. 2499-2502). Hershey, PA: Idea Group Reference.

Pereira, R.G., & Freire, M.M. (2005). Semantic Web. In M. Pagani (Ed.), *Encyclopedia of multimedia technology and networking* (pp. 917-924). Hershey, PA: Idea Group Reference.

Perez-Meana, H., & Nakano-Miyatake, M. (2005). Speech and audio signal applications. In M. Khosrow-Pour (Ed.), *Encyclopedia of information science and technology* (pp. 2591-2596). Hershey, PA: Idea Group Reference.

Perlich, C., & Provost, F. (2005). Aggregation for predictive modeling with relational data. In J. Wang (Ed.), *Encyclopedia of data warehousing and mining* (pp. 33-38). Hershey, PA: Idea Group Reference.

Perrizo, W., Ding, Q., Ding, Q., & Abidin, T. (2005). Vertical data mining. In J. Wang (Ed.), *Encyclopedia of data warehousing and mining* (pp. 1181-1184). Hershey, PA: Idea Group Reference.

Perrizo, W., Ding, Q., Serazi, M., Abidin, T., & Wang, B. (2005). Vertical database design for scalable data mining. In L. Rivero, J. Doorn, & V. Ferraggine (Eds.), *Encyclopedia of database technologies and applications* (pp. 736-739). Hershey, PA: Idea Group Reference.

Peszynski, K.J. (2005). Trust in B2C e-commerce for the New Zealand Maori. In M. Khosrow-Pour (Ed.), *Encyclopedia of information science and technology* (pp. 2882-2886). Hershey, PA: Idea Group Reference.

Peter, H., & Greenidge, C. (2005a). Data warehousing search engine. In J. Wang (Ed.), *Encyclopedia of data warehousing and mining* (pp. 328-333). Hershey, PA: Idea Group Reference.

Peter, H., & Greenidge, C. (2005b). Modelling Web-based data in a data warehouse. In J. Wang (Ed.), *Encyclopedia of data warehousing and mining* (pp. 826-831). Hershey, PA: Idea Group Reference.

Peterson, D., & Kim, C.S. (2005). Critical strategies for IS projects. In M. Khosrow-Pour (Ed.), *Encyclopedia of information science and technology* (pp. 617-621). Hershey, PA: Idea Group Reference.

Peterson, R.R. (2005). Trends in information technology governance. In M. Khosrow-Pour (Ed.), *Encyclopedia of information science and technology* (pp. 2865-2870). Hershey, PA: Idea Group Reference.

Petrova, K. (2006). Mobile commerce applications and adoption. In M. Khosrow-Pour (Ed.), *Encyclopedia of e-commerce, e-government, and mobile commerce* (pp. 766-771). Hershey, PA: Idea Group Reference.

Petska, D., & Berge, Z. (2005). Leadership competency in virtual teams. In C. Howard, J.V. Boettcher, L. Justice, K. Schenk, P.L. Rogers, & G.A. Berg (Eds.), *Encyclopedia of distance learning* (pp. 1195-1202). Hershey, PA: Idea Group Reference.

Petter, S., Sevcik, G., & Straub, D. (2005). Transfering technology to the developing world. In M. Khosrow-Pour (Ed.), *Encyclopedia of information science and technology* (pp. 2846-2850). Hershey, PA: Idea Group Reference.

Phala, V. (2005). Telecommunications sector and Internet access in Africa. In S. Marshall, W. Taylor, & X. Yu (Eds.), *Encyclopedia of developing regional communities with information and communication technology* (pp. 687-691). Hershey, PA: Idea Group Reference.

Pharo, N., & Järvelin, K. (2005). Search situations and transitions. In J. Wang (Ed.), *Encyclopedia of data warehousing and mining* (pp. 1000-1004). Hershey, PA: Idea Group Reference.

Pierre, S. (2006a). Mobile electronic commerce. In M. Khosrow-Pour (Ed.), *Encyclopedia of e-commerce, e-government, and mobile commerce* (pp. 786-791). Hershey, PA: Idea Group Reference.

Pierre, S. (2006b). Security issues concerning mobile commerce. In M. Khosrow-Pour (Ed.), *Encyclopedia of e-commerce, e-government, and mobile commerce* (pp. 968-972). Hershey, PA: Idea Group Reference.

Pinheiro, F.A.C. (2005). Database support for workflow management systems. In L. Rivero, J. Doorn, & V. Ferraggine (Eds.), *Encyclopedia of database technologies and applications* (pp. 158-161). Hershey, PA: Idea Group Reference.

Pires, L.C.M., Carvalho, J.D.A., & Moreira, N.A. (2006). Virtual enterprise organization. In M. Khosrow-Pour (Ed.), *Encyclopedia of e-commerce, e-government, and mobile commerce* (pp. 1175-1184). Hershey, PA: Idea Group Reference.

Plekhanova, V. (2005a). Learning systems engineering. In M. Khosrow-Pour (Ed.), *Encyclopedia of information science and technology* (pp. 1820-1826). Hershey, PA: Idea Group Reference.

Plekhanova, V. (2005b). Respecting diverse talents and ways for learning. In C. Howard, J.V. Boettcher, L. Justice, K. Schenk, P.L. Rogers, & G.A. Berg (Eds.), *Encyclopedia of distance learning* (pp. 1573-1580). Hershey, PA: Idea Group Reference.

Poda, I., & Brescia, W.F. (2005). Improving electronic information literacy in West African higher education. In S. Marshall, W. Taylor, & X. Yu (Eds.), *Encyclopedia of developing regional communities with information and communication technology* (pp. 427-432). Hershey, PA: Idea Group Reference.

Polese, G., Deufemia, V., Costagliola, G., & Tortora, G. (2005). Object modeling of RDBMS based applications. In L. Rivero, J. Doorn, & V. Ferraggine (Eds.), *Encyclopedia of database technologies and applications* (pp. 413-420). Hershey, PA: Idea Group Reference.

Polgar, J. (2005a). Designing agents with negotiation capabilities. In M. Khosrow-Pour (Ed.), *Encyclopedia of information science and technology* (pp. 810-815). Hershey, PA: Idea Group Reference.

Polgar, J. (2005b). Object-oriented software metrics. In M. Khosrow-Pour (Ed.), *Encyclopedia of informa-*

*tion science and technology* (pp. 2150-2155). Hershey, PA: Idea Group Reference.

Polovina, S., & Pearson, W. (2006). Communication + Dynamic Interface = Better User Experience. In C. Ghaoui (Ed.), *Encyclopedia of human computer interaction* (pp. 85-91). Hershey, PA: Idea Group Reference.

Pomerol, J.-C., & Adam, F. (2005). Decision-making support systems and representation levels. In M. Khosrow-Pour (Ed.), *Encyclopedia of information science and technology* (pp. 766-771). Hershey, PA: Idea Group Reference.

Poole, A., & Ball, L.J. (2006). Eye Tracking in HCI and Usability Research. In C. Ghaoui (Ed.), *Encyclopedia of human computer interaction* (pp. 211-219). Hershey, PA: Idea Group Reference.

Poon, S. (2005). Future of small business e-commerce. In M. Khosrow-Pour (Ed.), *Encyclopedia of information science and technology* (pp. 1253-1256). Hershey, PA: Idea Group Reference.

Porter, T.W. (2006). Customer goals online. In M. Khosrow-Pour (Ed.), *Encyclopedia of e-commerce, e-government, and mobile commerce* (pp. 163-167). Hershey, PA: Idea Group Reference.

Porto Bellini, C.G., & Vargas, L.M. (2006). Internet-mediated communities. In S. Dasgupta (Ed.), *Encyclopedia of virtual communities and technologies* (pp. 291-295). Hershey, PA: Idea Group Reference.

Potgieter, A., April, K., & Bishop, J. (2005). Complex adaptive enterprises. In M. Khosrow-Pour (Ed.), *Encyclopedia of information science and technology* (pp. 475-480). Hershey, PA: Idea Group Reference.

Pourabbas, E. (2005a). Cooperation of geographic and multidimensional databases. In M. Khosrow-Pour (Ed.), *Encyclopedia of information science and technology* (pp. 596-602). Hershey, PA: Idea Group Reference.

Pourabbas, E. (2005b). Hierarchies in multidimensional databases. In M. Khosrow-Pour (Ed.), *Ency-*

*clopedia of information science and technology* (pp. 1327-1332). Hershey, PA: Idea Group Reference.

Power, D.J. (2005). Decision support systems concept. In M. Khosrow-Pour (Ed.), *Encyclopedia of information science and technology* (pp. 750-753). Hershey, PA: Idea Group Reference.

Pöysä, J., & Lowyck, J. (2005). Learning communities in virtual environments. In C. Howard, J.V. Boettcher, L. Justice, K. Schenk, P.L. Rogers, & G.A. Berg (Eds.), *Encyclopedia of distance learning* (pp. 1217-1222). Hershey, PA: Idea Group Reference.

Prat, N. (2006). A hierarchical model for knowledge management. In D. Schwartz (Ed.), *Encyclopedia of knowledge management* (pp. 211-220). Hershey, PA: Idea Group Reference.

Prata, A. (2005). iTV guidelines. In M. Pagani (Ed.), *Encyclopedia of multimedia technology and networking* (pp. 512-518). Hershey, PA: Idea Group Reference.

Prêteux, F., & Preda, M. (2005). Animated characters within the MPEG-4 standard. In M. Khosrow-Pour (Ed.), *Encyclopedia of information science and technology* (pp. 123-126). Hershey, PA: Idea Group Reference.

Priestley, J.L. (2006). Knowledge transfer within interorganizational networks. In E. Coakes & S. Clarke (Eds.), *Encyclopedia of communities of practice in information and knowledge management* (pp. 307-316). Hershey, PA: Idea Group Reference.

Pritchard, A. (2005a). Calling on constructivist theory to support Internet-based, information-rich learning. In C. Howard, J.V. Boettcher, L. Justice, K. Schenk, P.L. Rogers, & G.A. Berg (Eds.), *Encyclopedia of distance learning* (pp. 196-203). Hershey, PA: Idea Group Reference.

Pritchard, A. (2005b). Information-rich learning concepts. In C. Howard, J.V. Boettcher, L. Justice, K. Schenk, P.L. Rogers, & G.A. Berg (Eds.), *Encyclopedia of distance learning* (pp. 1093-1098). Hershey, PA: Idea Group Reference.

Proctor, D.W. (2005). Accessibility of technology in higher education. In C. Howard, J.V. Boettcher, L. Justice, K. Schenk, P.L. Rogers, & G.A. Berg (Eds.), *Encyclopedia of distance learning* (pp. 16-28). Hershey, PA: Idea Group Reference.

Proserpio, L., & Magni, M. (2005). Learning through business games. In M. Pagani (Ed.), *Encyclopedia of multimedia technology and networking* (pp. 532-537). Hershey, PA: Idea Group Reference.

Protogeros, N. (2006). Service-oriented architectures and virtual enterprises. In M. Khosrow-Pour (Ed.), *Encyclopedia of e-commerce, e-government, and mobile commerce* (pp. 1003-1008). Hershey, PA: Idea Group Reference.

Pryor, J. (2005). Analysing a rural community's reception of ICT in Ghana. In S. Marshall, W. Taylor, & X. Yu (Eds.), *Encyclopedia of developing regional communities with information and communication technology* (pp. 11-15). Hershey, PA: Idea Group Reference.

Pulkkis, G., Grahn, K., & Åström, P. (2005). Current network security systems. In M. Khosrow-Pour (Ed.), *Encyclopedia of information science and technology* (pp. 668-674). Hershey, PA: Idea Group Reference.

Pulkkis, G., Grahn, K.J., & Karlsson, J. (2005). WLAN security management. In M. Pagani (Ed.), *Encyclopedia of multimedia technology and networking* (pp. 1104-1113). Hershey, PA: Idea Group Reference.

Pyke, A. (2006). The reformation of communities of practice. In E. Coakes & S. Clarke (Eds.), *Encyclopedia of communities of practice in information and knowledge management* (pp. 443-446). Hershey, PA: Idea Group Reference.

Qayyum, M.A. (2005). Sharing organizational knowledge through knowledge repositories. In M. Khosrow-Pour (Ed.), *Encyclopedia of information science and technology* (pp. 2475-2480). Hershey, PA: Idea Group Reference.

Quah, J.T.S., & Seet, V.L.H. (2006). Auto-personalization WAP portal. In M. Khosrow-Pour (Ed.), *Encyclopedia of e-commerce, e-government, and mobile commerce* (pp. 13-19). Hershey, PA: Idea Group Reference.

Quah, J.T.S., Leow, W.C.H., & Ong, C.C. (2006). Payment mechanism of mobile agent-based restaurant ordering system. In M. Khosrow-Pour (Ed.), *Encyclopedia of e-commerce, e-government, and mobile commerce* (pp. 908-913). Hershey, PA: Idea Group Reference.

Quah, J.T.S., Leow, W.C.H., & Soh, Y.K. (2006). Mobile agent assisted e-learning system. In M. Khosrow-Pour (Ed.), *Encyclopedia of e-commerce, e-government, and mobile commerce* (pp. 740-746). Hershey, PA: Idea Group Reference.

Quah, J.T.S., Leow, W.C.H., & Yong, K.L. (2006). Auto-personalization Web pages. In M. Khosrow-Pour (Ed.), *Encyclopedia of e-commerce, e-government, and mobile commerce* (pp. 20-25). Hershey, PA: Idea Group Reference.

Qudrat-Ullah, H. (2006). Improving Dynamic Decision Making through HCI Principles. In C. Ghaoui (Ed.), *Encyclopedia of human computer interaction* (pp. 311-316). Hershey, PA: Idea Group Reference.

R., M. (2005). Hierarchical architecture of expert systems for database management. In L. Rivero, J. Doorn, & V. Ferraggine (Eds.), *Encyclopedia of database technologies and applications* (pp. 271-275). Hershey, PA: Idea Group Reference.

Rabuñal Dopico, J.R., Cebrián, D.R., Dorado de la Calle, J., & Souto, N.P. (2005). Knowledge discovery with artificial neural networks. In J. Wang (Ed.), *Encyclopedia of data warehousing and mining* (pp. 669-673). Hershey, PA: Idea Group Reference.

Rada, R. (2005). Online education and manufacturing mode. In C. Howard, J.V. Boettcher, L. Justice, K. Schenk, P.L. Rogers, & G.A. Berg (Eds.), *Encyclopedia of distance learning* (pp. 1357-1360). Hershey, PA: Idea Group Reference.

Rada, R. (2006). Cancer patient-to-patient online discussion groups. In S. Dasgupta (Ed.), *Encyclopedia of virtual communities and technologies* (pp. 18-21). Hershey, PA: Idea Group Reference.

Rafanelli, M. (2005). Basic notions on multidimensional aggregate data. In M. Khosrow-Pour (Ed.), *Encyclopedia of information science and technology* (pp. 211-216). Hershey, PA: Idea Group Reference.

Ragazzi, D. (2005). Innovation in wireless technologies. In S. Marshall, W. Taylor, & X. Yu (Eds.), *Encyclopedia of developing regional communities with information and communication technology* (pp. 458-562). Hershey, PA: Idea Group Reference.

Ragsdell, G. (2006). The contribution of communities of practice to project management. In E. Coakes & S. Clarke (Eds.), *Encyclopedia of communities of practice in information and knowledge management* (pp. 104-107). Hershey, PA: Idea Group Reference.

Rahman, H. (2005a). Distributed learning sequences for the future generation. In C. Howard, J.V. Boettcher, L. Justice, K. Schenk, P.L. Rogers, & G.A. Berg (Eds.), *Encyclopedia of distance learning* (pp. 669-673). Hershey, PA: Idea Group Reference.

Rahman, H. (2005b). Formation of a knowledge-based society through utilization of information networking. In S. Marshall, W. Taylor, & X. Yu (Eds.), *Encyclopedia of developing regional communities with information and communication technology* (pp. 310-315). Hershey, PA: Idea Group Reference.

Rahman, H. (2005c). Interactive multimedia technologies for distance education systems. In M. Pagani (Ed.), *Encyclopedia of multimedia technology and networking* (pp. 454-460). Hershey, PA: Idea Group Reference.

Rahman, H. (2005d). Interactive multimedia technologies for distance education in developing countries. In M. Pagani (Ed.), *Encyclopedia of multimedia technology and networking* (pp. 447-453). Hershey, PA: Idea Group Reference.

Rahman, H. (2005e). Synthesis with data warehouse applications and utilities. In J. Wang (Ed.), *Encyclopedia of data warehousing and mining* (pp. 1092-1097). Hershey, PA: Idea Group Reference.

Rahman, H. (2005f). Virtual networking as an essence of the future learners. In C. Howard, J.V. Boettcher, L. Justice, K. Schenk, P.L. Rogers, & G.A. Berg (Eds.), *Encyclopedia of distance learning* (pp. 1972-1976). Hershey, PA: Idea Group Reference.

Rahman, H. (2006). Social impact of virtual networking. In S. Dasgupta (Ed.), *Encyclopedia of virtual communities and technologies* (pp. 417-423). Hershey, PA: Idea Group Reference.

Raisinghani, M.S. (2005). Knowledge mining. In L. Rivero, J. Doorn, & V. Ferraggine (Eds.), *Encyclopedia of database technologies and applications* (pp. 330-335). Hershey, PA: Idea Group Reference.

Raisinghani, M.S., & Ghanem, H. (2005). Fiber to the premises. In M. Pagani (Ed.), *Encyclopedia of multimedia technology and networking* (pp. 324-328). Hershey, PA: Idea Group Reference.

Raisinghani, M.S., & Hohertz, C. (2005). Integrating library services into the Web-based learning curriculum. In C. Howard, J.V. Boettcher, L. Justice, K. Schenk, P.L. Rogers, & G.A. Berg (Eds.), *Encyclopedia of distance learning* (pp. 1124-1129). Hershey, PA: Idea Group Reference.

Raisinghani, M.S., & Klassen, C. (2005). Temporal databases. In L. Rivero, J. Doorn, & V. Ferraggine (Eds.), *Encyclopedia of database technologies and applications* (pp. 677-682). Hershey, PA: Idea Group Reference.

Raisinghani, M.S., Klassen, C., & Schkade, L.L. (2005). Intelligent software agents in e-commerce. In M. Khosrow-Pour (Ed.), *Encyclopedia of information science and technology* (pp. 1603-1606). Hershey, PA: Idea Group Reference.

Raisinghani, M.S., & Nugent, J.H. (2005). Intelligent agents for competitive advantage. In M. Khosrow-Pour (Ed.), *Encyclopedia of information science and technology* (pp. 1579-1583). Hershey, PA: Idea Group Reference.

Raisinghani, M.S., & Petty, D.S. (2005). E-commerce taxation issues. In M. Khosrow-Pour (Ed.), *Encyclo-*

*pedia of information science and technology* (pp. 957-961). Hershey, PA: Idea Group Reference.

Raisinghani, M.S., & Rahman, M.U. (2005). A socio-technical case study of Bangladesh. In M. Khosrow-Pour (Ed.), *Encyclopedia of information science and technology* (pp. 16-21). Hershey, PA: Idea Group Reference.

Raisinghani, M.S., & Sahoo, T.R. (2006). Emergent semantic Web. In M. Khosrow-Pour (Ed.), *Encyclopedia of e-commerce, e-government, and mobile commerce* (pp. 418-423). Hershey, PA: Idea Group Reference.

Raisinghani, M.S., & Singh, M.K. (2005). Data mining for supply chain management complex networks. In M. Khosrow-Pour (Ed.), *Encyclopedia of information science and technology* (pp. 708-713). Hershey, PA: Idea Group Reference.

Raja, H.Z., Huq, A., & Rosenberg, D. (2006). The role of trust in virtual and co-located communities of practice. In E. Coakes & S. Clarke (Eds.), *Encyclopedia of communities of practice in information and knowledge management* (pp. 453-458). Hershey, PA: Idea Group Reference.

Rajasingham, L., & Tiffin, J. (2005). Virtual reality and hyperreality technologies in universities. In M. Pagani (Ed.), *Encyclopedia of multimedia technology and networking* (pp. 1064-1069). Hershey, PA: Idea Group Reference.

Ramasamy, K., & Deshpande, P.M. (2005). Set valued attributes. In L. Rivero, J. Doorn, & V. Ferraggine (Eds.), *Encyclopedia of database technologies and applications* (pp. 632-637). Hershey, PA: Idea Group Reference.

Rambaldi, G. (2005). Participatory 3D modelling. In S. Marshall, W. Taylor, & X. Yu (Eds.), *Encyclopedia of developing regional communities with information and communication technology* (pp. 538-543). Hershey, PA: Idea Group Reference.

Ramoni, M.F., & Sebastiani, P. (2005). Learning bayesian networks. In J. Wang (Ed.), *Encyclopedia of*

*data warehousing and mining* (pp. 674-677). Hershey, PA: Idea Group Reference.

Ramos, I., & Carvalho, J.Á. (2005). Constructionist perspective of organizational data mining. In M. Khosrow-Pour (Ed.), *Encyclopedia of information science and technology* (pp. 535-539). Hershey, PA: Idea Group Reference.

Ranguelov, S., & Rodríguez, A. (2006). Hybrid knowledge networks supporting the collaborative multidisciplinary research. In E. Coakes & S. Clarke (Eds.), *Encyclopedia of communities of practice in information and knowledge management* (pp. 204-209). Hershey, PA: Idea Group Reference.

Ras, Z.W., & Dardzinska, A. (2005). Intelligent query answering. In J. Wang (Ed.), *Encyclopedia of data warehousing and mining* (pp. 639-643). Hershey, PA: Idea Group Reference.

Ras, Z.W., Tzacheva, A., & Tsay, L.-S. (2005). Action rules. In J. Wang (Ed.), *Encyclopedia of data warehousing and mining* (pp. 1-5). Hershey, PA: Idea Group Reference.

Rashid, M.A. (2005). Evolution of ERP systems. In M. Khosrow-Pour (Ed.), *Encyclopedia of information science and technology* (pp. 1138-1143). Hershey, PA: Idea Group Reference.

Ratnasingam, P. (2005). A risk-control framework for e-marketplace participation. In M. Pagani (Ed.), *Encyclopedia of multimedia technology and networking* (pp. 887-894). Hershey, PA: Idea Group Reference.

Ratnasingam, P. (2006). The evolution of trust in business-to-business e-commerce. In M. Khosrow-Pour (Ed.), *Encyclopedia of e-commerce, e-government, and mobile commerce* (pp. 495-501). Hershey, PA: Idea Group Reference.

Ray, D. (2006). Life cycle of communities of practice. In E. Coakes & S. Clarke (Eds.), *Encyclopedia of communities of practice in information and knowledge management* (pp. 323-326). Hershey, PA: Idea Group Reference.

Real, J.C., Leal, A., & Roldan, J.L. (2006). Measuring organizational learning as a multidimensional construct. In D. Schwartz (Ed.), *Encyclopedia of knowledge management* (pp. 614). Hershey, PA: Idea Group Reference.

Reilly, C. (2005). Digital divide. In C. Howard, J.V. Boettcher, L. Justice, K. Schenk, P.L. Rogers, & G.A. Berg (Eds.), *Encyclopedia of distance learning* (pp. 581-584). Hershey, PA: Idea Group Reference.

Reisman, S. (2006). Evolution of computer-based distance learning. In M. Khosrow-Pour (Ed.), *Encyclopedia of e-commerce, e-government, and mobile commerce* (pp. 472-479). Hershey, PA: Idea Group Reference.

Rennard, J.-P. (2005). Producing and sharing free advanced scientific and technological knowledge using the Internet. In S. Marshall, W. Taylor, & X. Yu (Eds.), *Encyclopedia of developing regional communities with information and communication technology* (pp. 587-592). Hershey, PA: Idea Group Reference.

Rennard, J.-P. (2006). Internet and access to scholarly publications. In M. Khosrow-Pour (Ed.), *Encyclopedia of e-commerce, e-government, and mobile commerce* (pp. 653-659). Hershey, PA: Idea Group Reference.

Rentroia-Bonito, M.A., & Jorge, J.A.P. (2005). Modeling for e-learning systems. In M. Khosrow-Pour (Ed.), *Encyclopedia of information science and technology* (pp. 1996-2000). Hershey, PA: Idea Group Reference.

Rentroia-Bonito, M.A., Jorge, J.A., & Ghaoui, C. (2006). An Overview of an Evaluation Framework for E-Learning. In C. Ghaoui (Ed.), *Encyclopedia of human computer interaction* (pp. 441-450). Hershey, PA: Idea Group Reference.

Reynolds, A.A. (2005). Educational technology in the Middle East. In C. Howard, J.V. Boettcher, L. Justice, K. Schenk, P.L. Rogers, & G.A. Berg (Eds.), *Encyclopedia of distance learning* (pp. 717-723). Hershey, PA: Idea Group Reference.

Rhodes, J. (2005). South African women's rural development and e-commerce. In S. Marshall, W. Taylor, & X. Yu (Eds.), *Encyclopedia of developing regional communities with information and communication technology* (pp. 646-652). Hershey, PA: Idea Group Reference.

Rhoten, E.S. (2006a). Cultural diversity and the digital divide. In S. Dasgupta (Ed.), *Encyclopedia of virtual communities and technologies* (pp. 87-94). Hershey, PA: Idea Group Reference.

Rhoten, E.S. (2006b). E-learning models. In S. Dasgupta (Ed.), *Encyclopedia of virtual communities and technologies* (pp. 166-173). Hershey, PA: Idea Group Reference.

Ribière, V.M., & Román, J.A. (2006). Knowledge flow. In D. Schwartz (Ed.), *Encyclopedia of knowledge management* (pp. 336-343). Hershey, PA: Idea Group Reference.

Richards, G., & de la Iglesia, B. (2005). Discovery of classification rules from databases. In M. Khosrow-Pour (Ed.), *Encyclopedia of information science and technology* (pp. 892-896). Hershey, PA: Idea Group Reference.

Richards, H.D., Makatsorsis, H.C., & Chang, Y.S. (2005). Change process drivers for e-business. In M. Khosrow-Pour (Ed.), *Encyclopedia of information science and technology* (pp. 397-403). Hershey, PA: Idea Group Reference.

Richter, K., & Roth, V. (2006). Human-Computer Interaction and Security. In C. Ghaoui (Ed.), *Encyclopedia of human computer interaction* (pp. 297-294). Hershey, PA: Idea Group Reference.

Ridings, C.M. (2006a). Defining "virtual community". In S. Dasgupta (Ed.), *Encyclopedia of virtual communities and technologies* (pp. 116-120). Hershey, PA: Idea Group Reference.

Ridings, C.M. (2006b). Virtual communities and social capital theory. In S. Dasgupta (Ed.), *Encyclopedia of virtual communities and technologies* (pp. 493-496). Hershey, PA: Idea Group Reference.

Ridings, C.M., & Gefen, D. (2005). Antecedents of trust in online communities. In M. Khosrow-Pour (Ed.), *Encyclopedia of information science and technology* (pp. 127-130). Hershey, PA: Idea Group Reference.

Riedewald, M., Agrawal, D., & El Abbadi, A. (2005). Dynamic multidimensional data cubes for interactive analysis of massive datasets. In M. Khosrow-Pour (Ed.), *Encyclopedia of information science and technology* (pp. 924-929). Hershey, PA: Idea Group Reference.

Riesco, D., Daniele, M., Romero, D., & Montejano, G. (2005). Extensions to UML using stereotypes. In M. Khosrow-Pour (Ed.), *Encyclopedia of information science and technology* (pp. 1169-1173). Hershey, PA: Idea Group Reference.

Riffee, W.H., & Sessums, C. (2005). Quality distance learning programs and processes. In C. Howard, J.V. Boettcher, L. Justice, K. Schenk, P.L. Rogers, & G.A. Berg (Eds.), *Encyclopedia of distance learning* (pp. 1538-1542). Hershey, PA: Idea Group Reference.

Ripamonti, L.A. (2005). Supporting online communities with technological infrastructures. In M. Pagani (Ed.), *Encyclopedia of multimedia technology and networking* (pp. 937-944). Hershey, PA: Idea Group Reference.

Rippon, P., & Mengersen, K. (2005). Bayesian modelling for machine learning. In M. Khosrow-Pour (Ed.), *Encyclopedia of information science and technology* (pp. 236-242). Hershey, PA: Idea Group Reference.

Ritchie, B., & Brindley, C. (2005). Risk management in the digital economy. In M. Khosrow-Pour (Ed.), *Encyclopedia of information science and technology* (pp. 2431-2437). Hershey, PA: Idea Group Reference.

Rittgen, P. (2005). Modeling information systems in UML. In M. Khosrow-Pour (Ed.), *Encyclopedia of information science and technology* (pp. 2001-2006). Hershey, PA: Idea Group Reference.

Rivero, L.C. (2005). Inclusion dependencies. In M. Khosrow-Pour (Ed.), *Encyclopedia of information*

*science and technology* (pp. 1425-1430). Hershey, PA: Idea Group Reference.

Roberts, L.D., Smith, L.M., & Pollock, C.M. (2005). Conducting ethical research in virtual environments. In M. Khosrow-Pour (Ed.), *Encyclopedia of information science and technology* (pp. 523-528). Hershey, PA: Idea Group Reference.

Roberts, L.D., Smith, L.M., & Pollock, C.M. (2006a). Communicating in synchronous text-based virtual communities. In S. Dasgupta (Ed.), *Encyclopedia of virtual communities and technologies* (pp. 42-48). Hershey, PA: Idea Group Reference.

Roberts, L.D., Smith, L.M., & Pollock, C.M. (2006b). Modelling stages of behaviour in social virtual communities. In S. Dasgupta (Ed.), *Encyclopedia of virtual communities and technologies* (pp. 321-328). Hershey, PA: Idea Group Reference.

Roberts, L.D., Smith, L.M., & Pollock, C.M. (2006c). Psychological sense of community in virtual communities. In S. Dasgupta (Ed.), *Encyclopedia of virtual communities and technologies* (pp. 390-396). Hershey, PA: Idea Group Reference.

Roberts, M.L., & Schwaab, E. (2006). Branding on the Internet. In M. Khosrow-Pour (Ed.), *Encyclopedia of e-commerce, e-government, and mobile commerce* (pp. 57-63). Hershey, PA: Idea Group Reference.

Robinson, E.T. (2005). Benefits of a content multi-purposing model. In C. Howard, J.V. Boettcher, L. Justice, K. Schenk, P.L. Rogers, & G.A. Berg (Eds.), *Encyclopedia of distance learning* (pp. 148-151). Hershey, PA: Idea Group Reference.

Robinson, L. (2006). Networks of people as an emerging business model. In E. Coakes & S. Clarke (Eds.), *Encyclopedia of communities of practice in information and knowledge management* (pp. 390-391). Hershey, PA: Idea Group Reference.

Roccetti, M., & Ferretti, S. (2005). Adaptive playout control schemes for speech over the Internet. In M. Khosrow-Pour (Ed.), *Encyclopedia of information*

*science and technology* (pp. 53-58). Hershey, PA: Idea Group Reference.

Rodrigues, J.J.P.C., Freire, M.M., Monteiro, P.P., & Lorenz, P. (2005). Optical burst switching. In M. Pagani (Ed.), *Encyclopedia of multimedia technology and networking* (pp. 799-806). Hershey, PA: Idea Group Reference.

Rodríguez-Elias, O.M., Martínez-García, A.I., Vizcaíno, A., Favela, J., & Piattini, M. (2006). Identifying knowledge flows in communities of practice. In E. Coakes & S. Clarke (Eds.), *Encyclopedia of communities of practice in information and knowledge management* (pp. 210-217). Hershey, PA: Idea Group Reference.

Rodríguez-Tastets, M.A. (2005a). Consistency in spatial databases. In L. Rivero, J. Doorn, & V. Ferraggine (Eds.), *Encyclopedia of database technologies and applications* (pp. 93-98). Hershey, PA: Idea Group Reference.

Rodríguez-Tastets, M.A. (2005b). Moving objects databases. In L. Rivero, J. Doorn, & V. Ferraggine (Eds.), *Encyclopedia of database technologies and applications* (pp. 378-382). Hershey, PA: Idea Group Reference.

Rogers, P.C., & Howell, S.L. (2005). Distance education from religions of the world. In C. Howard, J.V. Boettcher, L. Justice, K. Schenk, P.L. Rogers, & G.A. Berg (Eds.), *Encyclopedia of distance learning* (pp. 613-617). Hershey, PA: Idea Group Reference.

Rogers, P.L. (2005a). How teachers use instructional design in real classrooms. In M. Khosrow-Pour (Ed.), *Encyclopedia of information science and technology* (pp. 1344-1348). Hershey, PA: Idea Group Reference.

Rogers, P.L. (2005b). Interactivity as the key to online learning. In C. Howard, J.V. Boettcher, L. Justice, K. Schenk, P.L. Rogers, & G.A. Berg (Eds.), *Encyclopedia of distance learning* (pp. 1145-1148). Hershey, PA: Idea Group Reference.

Roibás, A.C. (2006a). Ubiquitous Internet Environments. In C. Ghaoui (Ed.), *Encyclopedia of human computer interaction* (pp. 634-640). Hershey, PA: Idea Group Reference.

Roibás, A.C. (2006b). WAP Applications in Ubiquitous Scenarios of Work. In C. Ghaoui (Ed.), *Encyclopedia of human computer interaction* (pp. 699-705). Hershey, PA: Idea Group Reference.

Roldan, M. (2005). Tablet PCs as online learning tools. In C. Howard, J.V. Boettcher, L. Justice, K. Schenk, P.L. Rogers, & G.A. Berg (Eds.), *Encyclopedia of distance learning* (pp. 1740-1745). Hershey, PA: Idea Group Reference.

Roldán-García, M.D.M., Navas-Delgado, I., & Aldana-Montes, J.F. (2005). Applying database techniques to the semantic Web. In L. Rivero, J. Doorn, & V. Ferraggine (Eds.), *Encyclopedia of database technologies and applications* (pp. 18-22). Hershey, PA: Idea Group Reference.

Rolland, C., & Kaabi, R.S. (2006). Designing service-based cooperative systems. In M. Khosrow-Pour (Ed.), *Encyclopedia of e-commerce, e-government, and mobile commerce* (pp. 183-190). Hershey, PA: Idea Group Reference.

Rollier, B., & Niederman, F. (2005). Trends and perspectives in online education. In M. Khosrow-Pour (Ed.), *Encyclopedia of information science and technology* (pp. 2861-2864). Hershey, PA: Idea Group Reference.

Roofe, A.J.A. (2005). ICT and the efficient markets hypothesis. In S. Marshall, W. Taylor, & X. Yu (Eds.), *Encyclopedia of developing regional communities with information and communication technology* (pp. 353-359). Hershey, PA: Idea Group Reference.

Röse, K. (2006a). Cultural Diversity and Aspects of Human Machine Systems in Mainland China. In C. Ghaoui (Ed.), *Encyclopedia of human computer interaction* (pp. 136-142). Hershey, PA: Idea Group Reference.

Röse, K. (2006b). Globalization, Culture, and Usability. In C. Ghaoui (Ed.), *Encyclopedia of human computer interaction* (pp. 253-256). Hershey, PA: Idea Group Reference.

Rosenbaum, R., Tominski, C., & Schumann, H. (2006). Graphical content on mobile devices. In M. Khosrow-Pour (Ed.), *Encyclopedia of e-commerce, e-government, and mobile commerce* (pp. 545-551). Hershey, PA: Idea Group Reference.

Rossi, G., & Schwabe, D. (2005). Designing Web applications. In M. Khosrow-Pour (Ed.), *Encyclopedia of information science and technology* (pp. 831-836). Hershey, PA: Idea Group Reference.

Rosson, P. (2006). Internet pharmacies. In M. Khosrow-Pour (Ed.), *Encyclopedia of e-commerce, e-government, and mobile commerce* (pp. 666-671). Hershey, PA: Idea Group Reference.

Roussos, G., & Zoumboulakis, M. (2005). Ubiquitous computing and databases. In L. Rivero, J. Doorn, & V. Ferraggine (Eds.), *Encyclopedia of database technologies and applications* (pp. 714-719). Hershey, PA: Idea Group Reference.

Rovai, A.P., & Gallien, L.B., Jr. (2006). Racial issues in the virtual classroom. In S. Dasgupta (Ed.), *Encyclopedia of virtual communities and technologies* (pp. 397-401). Hershey, PA: Idea Group Reference.

Rowe, M. (2005a). Information technology standards in China. In S. Marshall, W. Taylor, & X. Yu (Eds.), *Encyclopedia of developing regional communities with information and communication technology* (pp. 456-457). Hershey, PA: Idea Group Reference.

Rowe, M. (2005b). The role of multinationals in recent IT developments in China. In S. Marshall, W. Taylor, & X. Yu (Eds.), *Encyclopedia of developing regional communities with information and communication technology* (pp. 614-617). Hershey, PA: Idea Group Reference.

Rowe, M., Cripps, H., Burn, J., Standing, C., Walker, B., & Bode, S. (2006). Effective collaborative commerce adoptions. In M. Khosrow-Pour (Ed.), *Encyclopedia of e-commerce, e-government, and mobile commerce* (pp. 340-346). Hershey, PA: Idea Group Reference.

Rowe, N.C. (2005a). Content repurposing for small devices. In M. Pagani (Ed.), *Encyclopedia of multimedia technology and networking* (pp. 110-115). Hershey, PA: Idea Group Reference.

Rowe, N.C. (2005b). Exploiting captions for multimedia data mining. In M. Pagani (Ed.), *Encyclopedia of multimedia technology and networking* (pp. 302-307). Hershey, PA: Idea Group Reference.

Rowe, N.C. (2006a). Deception in electronic goods and services. In M. Khosrow-Pour (Ed.), *Encyclopedia of e-commerce, e-government, and mobile commerce* (pp. 177-182). Hershey, PA: Idea Group Reference.

Rowe, N.C. (2006b). Detecting and responding to online deception. In S. Dasgupta (Ed.), *Encyclopedia of virtual communities and technologies* (pp. 121-124). Hershey, PA: Idea Group Reference.

Rowe, N.C. (2006c). Ethics of deception in virtual communities. In S. Dasgupta (Ed.), *Encyclopedia of virtual communities and technologies* (pp. 204-206). Hershey, PA: Idea Group Reference.

Rowe, N.C. (2006d). Online deception types. In S. Dasgupta (Ed.), *Encyclopedia of virtual communities and technologies* (pp. 343-345). Hershey, PA: Idea Group Reference.

Roy, A. (2005). Virtual communities on the Internet. In M. Pagani (Ed.), *Encyclopedia of multimedia technology and networking* (pp. 1040-1046). Hershey, PA: Idea Group Reference.

Roy, A.G. (2005). Imagining APNA Punjab in cyberspace. In S. Marshall, W. Taylor, & X. Yu (Eds.), *Encyclopedia of developing regional communities with information and communication technology* (pp. 405-411). Hershey, PA: Idea Group Reference.

Rugelj, J. (2005). Workplace computer-supported network-based learning. In C. Howard, J.V. Boettcher, L. Justice, K. Schenk, P.L. Rogers, & G.A. Berg (Eds.), *Encyclopedia of distance learning* (pp. 2056-2063). Hershey, PA: Idea Group Reference.

Ruhi, U. (2006). A social informatics framework for sustaining virtual communities of practice. In E. Coakes & S. Clarke (Eds.), *Encyclopedia of communities of practice in information and knowledge management* (pp. 466-473). Hershey, PA: Idea Group Reference.

Rülke, A., Iyer, A., & Chiasson, G. (2005). Shaping the evolution of mobile commerce. In M. Khosrow-Pour (Ed.), *Encyclopedia of information science and technology* (pp. 2469-2474). Hershey, PA: Idea Group Reference.

Ruppel, D., & Ruppel, C. (2005). A university/community partnership to bridge the digital divide. In M. Khosrow-Pour (Ed.), *Encyclopedia of information science and technology* (pp. 29-32). Hershey, PA: Idea Group Reference.

Russell, G. (2005a). Problems and possibilities of virtual schools. In C. Howard, J.V. Boettcher, L. Justice, K. Schenk, P.L. Rogers, & G.A. Berg (Eds.), *Encyclopedia of distance learning* (pp. 1516-1521). Hershey, PA: Idea Group Reference.

Russell, G. (2005b). Virtual schools. In M. Khosrow-Pour (Ed.), *Encyclopedia of information science and technology* (pp. 3002-3006). Hershey, PA: Idea Group Reference.

Russell, G. (2006). Implications of virtual schooling for socialization and community. In S. Dasgupta (Ed.), *Encyclopedia of virtual communities and technologies* (pp. 253-257). Hershey, PA: Idea Group Reference.

Ryan, R.C. (2005). Increased benefits from using online class components. In C. Howard, J.V. Boettcher, L. Justice, K. Schenk, P.L. Rogers, & G.A. Berg (Eds.), *Encyclopedia of distance learning* (pp. 1064-1068). Hershey, PA: Idea Group Reference.

Sacco, G.M. (2006). Dynamic taxonomies. In D. Schwartz (Ed.), *Encyclopedia of knowledge management* (pp. 145-151). Hershey, PA: Idea Group Reference.

Sadeghian, P., Kantardzic, M., & Rashad, S. (2006). Knowledgeable Navigation in Virtual Environments. In C. Ghaoui (Ed.), *Encyclopedia of human computer interaction* (pp. 389-395). Hershey, PA: Idea Group Reference.

Sadoun, B. (2006). GIS Applications to City Planning Engineering. In C. Ghaoui (Ed.), *Encyclopedia of human computer interaction* (pp. 234-241). Hershey, PA: Idea Group Reference.

Saha, P. (2005). Developing dynamic balanced scorecards. In M. Khosrow-Pour (Ed.), *Encyclopedia of information science and technology* (pp. 837-843). Hershey, PA: Idea Group Reference.

Saha, P. (2006a). E-business process management and IT governance. In M. Khosrow-Pour (Ed.), *Encyclopedia of e-commerce, e-government, and mobile commerce* (pp. 272-278). Hershey, PA: Idea Group Reference.

Saha, P. (2006b). Straight-through processing adoption. In M. Khosrow-Pour (Ed.), *Encyclopedia of e-commerce, e-government, and mobile commerce* (pp. 1046-1052). Hershey, PA: Idea Group Reference.

Sahraoui, S. (2006). Open-source software issues. In S. Dasgupta (Ed.), *Encyclopedia of virtual communities and technologies* (pp. 368-371). Hershey, PA: Idea Group Reference.

Sala, N. (2005a). Hypermedia modules for distance education. In C. Howard, J.V. Boettcher, L. Justice, K. Schenk, P.L. Rogers, & G.A. Berg (Eds.), *Encyclopedia of distance learning* (pp. 1019-1024). Hershey, PA: Idea Group Reference.

Sala, N. (2005b). Learning-by-doing strategy using ITC. In C. Howard, J.V. Boettcher, L. Justice, K. Schenk, P.L. Rogers, & G.A. Berg (Eds.), *Encyclopedia of distance learning* (pp. 1205-1216). Hershey, PA: Idea Group Reference.

Sales, G.C. (2005). Developing online faculty competencies. In C. Howard, J.V. Boettcher, L. Justice, K. Schenk, P.L. Rogers, & G.A. Berg (Eds.), *Encyclopedia of distance learning* (pp. 547-553). Hershey, PA: Idea Group Reference.

Salo, J., & Tähtinen, J. (2006). Special features of mobile advertising and their utilization. In M. Khosrow-Pour (Ed.), *Encyclopedia of e-commerce, e-government, and mobile commerce* (pp. 1035-1040). Hershey, PA: Idea Group Reference.

Salter, G. (2005a). E-learning and m-learning problems. In C. Howard, J.V. Boettcher, L. Justice, K. Schenk, P.L. Rogers, & G.A. Berg (Eds.), *Encyclopedia of distance learning* (pp. 743-749). Hershey, PA: Idea Group Reference.

Salter, G. (2005b). Encouraging participation in voluntary, online staff development. In C. Howard, J.V. Boettcher, L. Justice, K. Schenk, P.L. Rogers, & G.A. Berg (Eds.), *Encyclopedia of distance learning* (pp. 821-827). Hershey, PA: Idea Group Reference.

Salter, G. (2005c). Factors affecting the adoption of educational technology. In C. Howard, J.V. Boettcher, L. Justice, K. Schenk, P.L. Rogers, & G.A. Berg (Eds.), *Encyclopedia of distance learning* (pp. 922-929). Hershey, PA: Idea Group Reference.

Sammon, D., & Adam, F. (2005). Defining and understanding ERP systems. In M. Khosrow-Pour (Ed.), *Encyclopedia of information science and technology* (pp. 772-778). Hershey, PA: Idea Group Reference.

Samuel, D., & Samson, D. (2006). B2C success at Wishlist.com. In M. Khosrow-Pour (Ed.), *Encyclopedia of e-commerce, e-government, and mobile commerce* (pp. 31-36). Hershey, PA: Idea Group Reference.

Sánchez-Segura, M.-I., de Amescua, A., García, L., & Esteban, L.A. (2005). Software ad hoc for e-learning. In M. Pagani (Ed.), *Encyclopedia of multimedia technology and networking* (pp. 925-936). Hershey, PA: Idea Group Reference.

Santos, A. (2005). Information literacy for telecenter users in low-income regional Mexican communities. In S. Marshall, W. Taylor, & X. Yu (Eds.), *Encyclopedia of developing regional communities with information and communication technology* (pp. 445-450). Hershey, PA: Idea Group Reference.

Santos, M.Y., Moreira, A., & Carneiro, S. (2005). Clustering in the identification of space models. In J. Wang (Ed.), *Encyclopedia of data warehousing and mining* (pp. 165-171). Hershey, PA: Idea Group Reference.

Sanzogni, L., & Arthur-Gray, H. (2005). Technology leapfrogging in Thailand. In S. Marshall, W. Taylor, & X. Yu (Eds.), *Encyclopedia of developing regional communities with information and communication technology* (pp. 671-676). Hershey, PA: Idea Group Reference.

Sappa, A.D., Aifanti, N., Malassiotis, S., & Grammalidis, N. (2005). Survey of 3D human body representations. In M. Khosrow-Pour (Ed.), *Encyclopedia of information science and technology* (pp. 2696-2701). Hershey, PA: Idea Group Reference.

Saquer, J.M. (2005). Formal concept analysis based clustering. In J. Wang (Ed.), *Encyclopedia of data warehousing and mining* (pp. 514-518). Hershey, PA: Idea Group Reference.

Sarkar, N.I. (2005). Enhancing learning and teaching wireless LAN design. In C. Howard, J.V. Boettcher, L. Justice, K. Schenk, P.L. Rogers, & G.A. Berg (Eds.), *Encyclopedia of distance learning* (pp. 835-844). Hershey, PA: Idea Group Reference.

Sarkis, J., & Sundarraj, R.P. (2005). Implementation management of an e-commerce-enabled enterprise information system. In M. Khosrow-Pour (Ed.), *Encyclopedia of information science and technology* (pp. 1397-1401). Hershey, PA: Idea Group Reference.

Sarmento, A. (2005). The organizational context in the use of a workflow system. In M. Khosrow-Pour (Ed.), *Encyclopedia of information science and technology* (pp. 2821-2825). Hershey, PA: Idea Group Reference.

Sarwar, B.M., Konstan, J.A., & Riedl, J.T. (2005). Distributed recommender systems for Internet commerce. In M. Khosrow-Pour (Ed.), *Encyclopedia of information science and technology* (pp. 907-911). Hershey, PA: Idea Group Reference.

Sas, C. (2006). Sense of Presence. In C. Ghaoui (Ed.), *Encyclopedia of human computer interaction* (pp. 511-517). Hershey, PA: Idea Group Reference.

Sattar, F., & Yu, D. (2006). Copyright protection through digital watermarking. In S. Dasgupta (Ed.), *Encyclopedia of virtual communities and technologies* (pp. 66-72). Hershey, PA: Idea Group Reference.

Saunders, C. (2006). Knowledge sharing in legal practice. In D. Schwartz (Ed.), *Encyclopedia of knowledge management* (pp. 515). Hershey, PA: Idea Group Reference.

Sayal, M. (2005). Time series analysis and mining techniques. In J. Wang (Ed.), *Encyclopedia of data warehousing and mining* (pp. 1120-1124). Hershey, PA: Idea Group Reference.

Saygin, Y. (2005). Privacy and confidentiality issues in data mining. In J. Wang (Ed.), *Encyclopedia of data warehousing and mining* (pp. 921-924). Hershey, PA: Idea Group Reference.

Scarpi, D., & Dall'Olmo-Riley, F. (2006). E-commerce consumer and product characteristics. In M. Khosrow-Pour (Ed.), *Encyclopedia of e-commerce, e-government, and mobile commerce* (pp. 296-301). Hershey, PA: Idea Group Reference.

Scarso, E., Bolisani, E., & Di Biagi, M. (2006). Knowledge intermediation. In D. Schwartz (Ed.), *Encyclopedia of knowledge management* (pp. 360-367). Hershey, PA: Idea Group Reference.

Schafer, J.B. (2005). The application of data mining to recommender systems. In J. Wang (Ed.), *Encyclopedia of data warehousing and mining* (pp. 44-48). Hershey, PA: Idea Group Reference.

Schaffer, S.P., & Schmidt, T.M. (2006). Cross-disciplinary learning in virtual teams. In S. Dasgupta (Ed.), *Encyclopedia of virtual communities and technologies* (pp. 78-81). Hershey, PA: Idea Group Reference.

Schaffer, S.P., Price, M.L., & Schmidt, T.M. (2006). Cross-disciplinary virtual design teams. In S. Dasgupta (Ed.), *Encyclopedia of virtual communities and technologies* (pp. 82-86). Hershey, PA: Idea Group Reference.

Scheffer, T. (2005). Semi-supervised learning. In J. Wang (Ed.), *Encyclopedia of data warehousing and mining* (pp. 1022-1027). Hershey, PA: Idea Group Reference.

Schelin, S.H. (2005). A primer on e-government. In M. Khosrow-Pour (Ed.), *Encyclopedia of information science and technology* (pp. 11-15). Hershey, PA: Idea Group Reference.

Schifter, C.C. (2005). Faculty participation in distance education programs. In C. Howard, J.V. Boettcher, L. Justice, K. Schenk, P.L. Rogers, & G.A. Berg (Eds.), *Encyclopedia of distance learning* (pp. 930-935). Hershey, PA: Idea Group Reference.

Schmetzke, A. (2005). Digitization of library information and its accessibilty for people with disabilities. In M. Khosrow-Pour (Ed.), *Encyclopedia of information science and technology* (pp. 880-885). Hershey, PA: Idea Group Reference.

Schmidt, A., Manegold, S., & Kersten, M. (2005). Storing XML documents in databases. In L. Rivero, J. Doorn, & V. Ferraggine (Eds.), *Encyclopedia of database technologies and applications* (pp. 658-664). Hershey, PA: Idea Group Reference.

Schneider, M. (2005). A general model for data warehouses. In J. Wang (Ed.), *Encyclopedia of data warehousing and mining* (pp. 523-528). Hershey, PA: Idea Group Reference.

Schneidewind, N.F. (2005). Software requirements risk and maintainability. In M. Khosrow-Pour (Ed.), *Encyclopedia of information science and technology* (pp. 2562-2566). Hershey, PA: Idea Group Reference.

Schoenfeld, J., & Berge, Z. (2005). Bringing out the best in virtual teams. In C. Howard, J.V. Boettcher, L. Justice, K. Schenk, P.L. Rogers, & G.A. Berg (Eds.), *Encyclopedia of distance learning* (pp. 180-186). Hershey, PA: Idea Group Reference.

Scholarios, D., van der Schoot, E., & van der Heijden, B. (2005). Employability management of ICT professionals. In S. Marshall, W. Taylor, & X. Yu (Eds.), *Encyclopedia of developing regional communities with information and communication technology* (pp. 282-288). Hershey, PA: Idea Group Reference.

Schrum, L. (2005). E-learning and K-12. In C. Howard, J.V. Boettcher, L. Justice, K. Schenk, P.L. Rogers, & G.A. Berg (Eds.), *Encyclopedia of distance learning* (pp. 737-742). Hershey, PA: Idea Group Reference.

Schultz, R.A. (2005). Functional dependency and other related dependancies. In M. Khosrow-Pour (Ed.), *Encyclopedia of information science and technology* (pp. 1231-1235). Hershey, PA: Idea Group Reference.

Schwartz, D.G. (2006). Aristotelian view of knowledge management. In D. Schwartz (Ed.), *Encyclopedia of knowledge management* (pp. 10-16). Hershey, PA: Idea Group Reference.

Schwartz, D.G., & Schreiber, Z. (2005). Semantic information management. In L. Rivero, J. Doorn, & V. Ferraggine (Eds.), *Encyclopedia of database technologies and applications* (pp. 593-600). Hershey, PA: Idea Group Reference.

Scime, A. (2005a). Computing curriculum analysis and development. In M. Khosrow-Pour (Ed.), *Encyclopedia of information science and technology* (pp. 598-513). Hershey, PA: Idea Group Reference.

Scime, A. (2005b). Web page extension of data warehouses. In J. Wang (Ed.), *Encyclopedia of data warehousing and mining* (pp. 1211-1215). Hershey, PA: Idea Group Reference.

Scott, M., Hill, S., Acton, T., & Hughes, M. (2006). Biometric identities and e-government services. In M. Khosrow-Pour (Ed.), *Encyclopedia of e-commerce, e-government, and mobile commerce* (pp. 50-56). Hershey, PA: Idea Group Reference.

Scupola, A. (2005). Strategies of e-commerce business value optimization. In M. Khosrow-Pour (Ed.), *Encyclopedia of information science and technology* (pp. 2653-2657). Hershey, PA: Idea Group Reference.

Sebastiani, F. (2005). Text categorization. In L. Rivero, J. Doorn, & V. Ferraggine (Eds.), *Encyclopedia of database technologies and applications* (pp. 683-687). Hershey, PA: Idea Group Reference.

Segall, R.S. (2005). Microarray databases for biotechnology. In J. Wang (Ed.), *Encyclopedia of data warehousing and mining* (pp. 734-739). Hershey, PA: Idea Group Reference.

Seitz, J. (2005). Software agents in e-commerce systems. In M. Khosrow-Pour (Ed.), *Encyclopedia of information science and technology* (pp. 2546-2550). Hershey, PA: Idea Group Reference.

Serafeimidis, V. (2005). Institutional dimensions of information systems evaluation. In M. Khosrow-Pour (Ed.), *Encyclopedia of information science and technology* (pp. 1545-1548). Hershey, PA: Idea Group Reference.

Serrano, M., Calero, C., & Piattini, M. (2005). Metrics for data warehouse quality. In M. Khosrow-Pour (Ed.), *Encyclopedia of information science and technology* (pp. 1938-1944). Hershey, PA: Idea Group Reference.

Seta, K. (2006). Task Ontology-Based Human-Computer Interaction. In C. Ghaoui (Ed.), *Encyclopedia of human computer interaction* (pp. 588-596). Hershey, PA: Idea Group Reference.

Sethi, N., & Sethi, V. (2006a). BigTrumpet.com. In M. Khosrow-Pour (Ed.), *Encyclopedia of e-commerce, e-government, and mobile commerce* (pp. 43-49). Hershey, PA: Idea Group Reference.

Sethi, N., & Sethi, V. (2006b). Data warehousing and data mining lessons for EC companies. In M. Khosrow-Pour (Ed.), *Encyclopedia of e-commerce, e-government, and mobile commerce* (pp. 172-176). Hershey, PA: Idea Group Reference.

Setzekorn, K., Rai, A., & Melcher, A.J. (2005). IT productivity impacts in manufacturing contexts. In M. Khosrow-Pour (Ed.), *Encyclopedia of information science and technology* (pp. 1721-1727). Hershey, PA: Idea Group Reference.

Shahabi, C., & Banaei-Kashani, F. (2005). Querical data networks. In L. Rivero, J. Doorn, & V. Ferraggine (Eds.), *Encyclopedia of database technologies and applications* (pp. 493-499). Hershey, PA: Idea Group Reference.

Shahabi, C., Sacharidis, D., & Jahangiri, M. (2005). Wavelets for querying multidimensional datasets. In J. Wang (Ed.), *Encyclopedia of data warehousing and mining* (pp. 1196-1200). Hershey, PA: Idea Group Reference.

Shaligram, A. (2005). One village one computer campaign in India. In S. Marshall, W. Taylor, & X. Yu (Eds.), *Encyclopedia of developing regional communities with information and communication technology* (pp. 528-532). Hershey, PA: Idea Group Reference.

Shambaugh, N. (2005). A scenario-based instructional design model. In C. Howard, J.V. Boettcher, L. Justice, K. Schenk, P.L. Rogers, & G.A. Berg (Eds.), *Encyclopedia of distance learning* (pp. 1589-1595). Hershey, PA: Idea Group Reference.

Shan, L.M., Sutanto, J., Kankanhalli, A., & Tan, B.C.Y. (2006a). Converting online community visitors into online consumers. In S. Dasgupta (Ed.), *Encyclopedia of virtual communities and technologies* (pp. 54-60). Hershey, PA: Idea Group Reference.

Shan, L.M., Sutanto, J., Kankanhalli, A., & Tan, B.C.Y. (2006b). Virtual community models in relation to e-business models. In S. Dasgupta (Ed.), *Encyclopedia of virtual communities and technologies* (pp. 527-532). Hershey, PA: Idea Group Reference.

Shapiro, A.M. (2006). Site Maps for Hypertext. In C. Ghaoui (Ed.), *Encyclopedia of human computer interaction* (pp. 518-522). Hershey, PA: Idea Group Reference.

Shareef, A.F., & Kinshuk. (2005). Distance education in small island nations. In C. Howard, J.V. Boettcher, L. Justice, K. Schenk, P.L. Rogers, & G.A. Berg (Eds.), *Encyclopedia of distance learning* (pp. 618-627). Hershey, PA: Idea Group Reference.

Shariq, S.Z., & Vendelø, M.T. (2006). Tacit knowledge sharing. In D. Schwartz (Ed.), *Encyclopedia of knowledge management* (pp. 833-839). Hershey, PA: Idea Group Reference.

Sharma, P., Carson, D., & Taylor, A. (2005). Adaptive use of ICT in response to disintermediation. In S. Marshall, W. Taylor, & X. Yu (Eds.), *Encyclopedia of developing regional communities with information and communication technology* (pp. 6-10). Hershey, PA: Idea Group Reference.

Sharma, R.C. (2005). Technology-based learning in open universities in India. In C. Howard, J.V. Boettcher, L. Justice, K. Schenk, P.L. Rogers, & G.A. Berg (Eds.), *Encyclopedia of distance learning* (pp. 1815-1824). Hershey, PA: Idea Group Reference.

Sharma, R.C., & Mishra, S. (2005). Multimedia as a cross-channel for cultures and languages. In C. Howard, J.V. Boettcher, L. Justice, K. Schenk, P.L. Rogers, & G.A. Berg (Eds.), *Encyclopedia of distance learning* (pp. 1310-1316). Hershey, PA: Idea Group Reference.

Sharma, S.K. (2006a). E-commerce in a digital economy. In M. Khosrow-Pour (Ed.), *Encyclopedia of e-commerce, e-government, and mobile commerce* (pp. 302-307). Hershey, PA: Idea Group Reference.

Sharma, S.K. (2006b). E-government services framework. In M. Khosrow-Pour (Ed.), *Encyclopedia of e-commerce, e-government, and mobile commerce* (pp. 373-378). Hershey, PA: Idea Group Reference.

Sharma, S.K. (2006c). Inherent e-commerce barriers for SMEs. In M. Khosrow-Pour (Ed.), *Encyclopedia of e-commerce, e-government, and mobile commerce* (pp. 626-630). Hershey, PA: Idea Group Reference.

Sharma, S.K., & Wickramasinghe, N. (2005). Obstacles for SMEs for e-adoption in the Asia Pacific region. In M. Khosrow-Pour (Ed.), *Encyclopedia of information science and technology* (pp. 2168-2173). Hershey, PA: Idea Group Reference.

Sharma, S.K., Wickramasinghe, N., & Gupta, J.N.D. (2005). SMEs in knowledge-based economies. In M. Khosrow-Pour (Ed.), *Encyclopedia of information science and technology* (pp. 2523-2528). Hershey, PA: Idea Group Reference.

Sharples, M. (2006). Socio-Cognitive Engineering. In C. Ghaoui (Ed.), *Encyclopedia of human computer interaction* (pp. 542-547). Hershey, PA: Idea Group Reference.

Shaw, D. (2006). Mapping group knowledge. In D. Schwartz (Ed.), *Encyclopedia of knowledge management* (pp. 591). Hershey, PA: Idea Group Reference.

Shaw, D., Baker, B., & Edwards, J.S. (2006). Communities of implementation. In E. Coakes & S. Clarke (Eds.), *Encyclopedia of communities of practice in information and knowledge management* (pp. 35-42). Hershey, PA: Idea Group Reference.

Shaw, G. (2005). The changing role of faculty. In C. Howard, J.V. Boettcher, L. Justice, K. Schenk, P.L. Rogers, & G.A. Berg (Eds.), *Encyclopedia of distance learning* (pp. 224-230). Hershey, PA: Idea Group Reference.

Shaw, P.A., & Slick, S. (2005). Creating an electronic student teaching portfolio. In C. Howard, J.V. Boettcher, L. Justice, K. Schenk, P.L. Rogers, & G.A. Berg (Eds.), *Encyclopedia of distance learning* (pp. 462-468). Hershey, PA: Idea Group Reference.

Shayo, C., & Guthrie, R.A. (2005). End-user computing success measurement. In M. Khosrow-Pour (Ed.), *Encyclopedia of information science and technology* (pp. 1045-1051). Hershey, PA: Idea Group Reference.

Shea, T., & Davis, C. (2005). Leveraging digital multimedia training for at-risk teens. In S. Marshall, W. Taylor, & X. Yu (Eds.), *Encyclopedia of developing regional communities with information and communication technology* (pp. 475-480). Hershey, PA: Idea Group Reference.

Shen, H. (2005). Flexible mining of association rules. In J. Wang (Ed.), *Encyclopedia of data warehousing and mining* (pp. 509-513). Hershey, PA: Idea Group Reference.

Shen, H., & Horiguchi, S. (2005). Mining quantitative and fuzzy association rules. In J. Wang (Ed.), *Encyclopedia of data warehousing and mining* (pp. 815-819). Hershey, PA: Idea Group Reference.

Shen, P.-D., & Tsai, C.-W. (2006). Web-based knowledge management model. In S. Dasgupta (Ed.), *Encyclopedia of virtual communities and technologies* (pp. 584-589). Hershey, PA: Idea Group Reference.

Shih, Y.-Y., & Fang, K. (2006). Overall satisfaction prediction. In M. Khosrow-Pour (Ed.), *Encyclopedia of e-commerce, e-government, and mobile commerce* (pp. 895-901). Hershey, PA: Idea Group Reference.

Shoval, P., & Kabeli, J. (2005). Essentials of functional and object-oriented methodology. In M. Khosrow-Pour (Ed.), *Encyclopedia of information science and technology* (pp. 1108-1115). Hershey, PA: Idea Group Reference.

Si, H., & Li, C.-T. (2006). Copyright protection in virtual communities through digital watermarking. In S. Dasgupta (Ed.), *Encyclopedia of virtual communities and technologies* (pp. 61-65). Hershey, PA: Idea Group Reference.

Sicilia, M.-A., & García-Barriocanal, E. (2006). Representing virtual communities for advanced services. In S. Dasgupta (Ed.), *Encyclopedia of virtual communities and technologies* (pp. 402-404). Hershey, PA: Idea Group Reference.

Sicilia, M.-A., & Sánchez-Alonso, S. (2006). Reusable learning resources for virtual learning environments. In S. Dasgupta (Ed.), *Encyclopedia of virtual communities and technologies* (pp. 405-408). Hershey, PA: Idea Group Reference.

Siciliano, R., & Conversano, C. (2005). Decision tree induction. In J. Wang (Ed.), *Encyclopedia of data warehousing and mining* (pp. 353-358). Hershey, PA: Idea Group Reference.

Sieber, V., & Andrew, D. (2005). Learning technologies and learning theories. In C. Howard, J.V. Boettcher, L. Justice, K. Schenk, P.L. Rogers, & G.A. Berg (Eds.), *Encyclopedia of distance learning* (pp. 1248-1256). Hershey, PA: Idea Group Reference.

Signoret, F.D. (2006a). Virtual communities in an MBA. In S. Dasgupta (Ed.), *Encyclopedia of virtual communities and technologies* (pp. 511-514). Hershey, PA: Idea Group Reference.

Signoret, F.D.B. (2006b). Virtual reality user acceptance. In S. Dasgupta (Ed.), *Encyclopedia of virtual communities and technologies* (pp. 566-569). Hershey, PA: Idea Group Reference.

Simitsis, A., & Theodoratos, D. (2005). Data warehouse back-end tools. In J. Wang (Ed.), *Encyclopedia of data warehousing and mining* (pp. 312-317). Hershey, PA: Idea Group Reference.

Simitsis, A., Vassiliadis, P., & Sellis, T. (2005). Extraction-transformation-loading processes. In L. Rivero, J. Doorn, & V. Ferraggine (Eds.), *Encyclopedia of database technologies and applications* (pp. 240-245). Hershey, PA: Idea Group Reference.

Simon, J.C., Brooks, L.D., & Wilkes, R.B. (2005). Students' perceptions of online courses. In M. Khosrow-Pour (Ed.), *Encyclopedia of information science and technology* (pp. 2665-2671). Hershey, PA: Idea Group Reference.

Sindoni, G. (2005a). Materialized hypertext view maintenance. In J. Wang (Ed.), *Encyclopedia of data warehousing and mining* (pp. 710-713). Hershey, PA: Idea Group Reference.

Sindoni, G. (2005b). Materialized hypertext views. In J. Wang (Ed.), *Encyclopedia of data warehousing and mining* (pp. 714-716). Hershey, PA: Idea Group Reference.

Singh, A.M. (2005). Information systems and technology in South Africa. In M. Khosrow-Pour (Ed.), *Encyclopedia of information science and technology* (pp. 1497-1502). Hershey, PA: Idea Group Reference.

Singh, A.M. (2006a). Evolution of marketing to e-marketing. In M. Khosrow-Pour (Ed.), *Encyclopedia of e-commerce, e-government, and mobile commerce* (pp. 488-494). Hershey, PA: Idea Group Reference.

Singh, A.M. (2006b). Mobile commerce in South Africa. In M. Khosrow-Pour (Ed.), *Encyclopedia of e-commerce, e-government, and mobile commerce* (pp. 772-778). Hershey, PA: Idea Group Reference.

Singh, S. (2005a). Electronic commerce technologies management. In M. Pagani (Ed.), *Encyclopedia of multimedia technology and networking* (pp. 278-282). Hershey, PA: Idea Group Reference.

Singh, S. (2005b). Usability. In M. Pagani (Ed.), *Encyclopedia of multimedia technology and networking* (pp. 1008-1013). Hershey, PA: Idea Group Reference.

Singh, S. (2006). HCI in South Africa. In C. Ghaoui (Ed.), *Encyclopedia of human computer interaction* (pp. 261-265). Hershey, PA: Idea Group Reference.

Singh, S., & Dix, A. (2006). Software Engineering and HCI. In C. Ghaoui (Ed.), *Encyclopedia of human computer interaction* (pp. 548-552). Hershey, PA: Idea Group Reference.

Singh, S., & Kotzé, P. (2006). Development Methodologies and Users. In C. Ghaoui (Ed.), *Encyclopedia of human computer interaction* (pp. 165-169). Hershey, PA: Idea Group Reference.

Sipior, J.C. (2005). Departure of the expert systems project champion. In M. Khosrow-Pour (Ed.), *Encyclopedia of information science and technology* (pp. 797-801). Hershey, PA: Idea Group Reference.

Sivakumar, S.C. (2006). E-learning for knowledge dissemination. In D. Schwartz (Ed.), *Encyclopedia of knowledge management* (pp. 152-160). Hershey, PA: Idea Group Reference.

Skovira, R.J. (2005). The social contract revised. In M. Khosrow-Pour (Ed.), *Encyclopedia of information science and technology* (pp. 2831-2835). Hershey, PA: Idea Group Reference.

Slazinski, E. (2005). Observations on implementing specializations within an IT program. In M. Khosrow-Pour (Ed.), *Encyclopedia of information science and technology* (pp. 2161-2167). Hershey, PA: Idea Group Reference.

Smatt, C., & Wasko, M. (2006). Discovering communities of practice through social network analysis. In E. Coakes & S. Clarke (Eds.), *Encyclopedia of communities of practice in information and knowledge management* (pp. 129-130). Hershey, PA: Idea Group Reference.

Smets, P. (2005). Transferable belief model. In J. Wang (Ed.), *Encyclopedia of data warehousing and mining* (pp. 1135-1139). Hershey, PA: Idea Group Reference.

Smith, K.A. (2005). Neural networks for prediction and classification. In J. Wang (Ed.), *Encyclopedia of data warehousing and mining* (pp. 865-869). Hershey, PA: Idea Group Reference.

Smith, P.A.C. (2006a). Collective learning within CoPs. In E. Coakes & S. Clarke (Eds.), *Encyclopedia of communities of practice in information and knowledge management* (pp. 30-31). Hershey, PA: Idea Group Reference.

Smith, P.A.C. (2006b). Organisational change elements of establishing, facilitating, and supporting CoPs. In E. Coakes & S. Clarke (Eds.), *Encyclopedia of communities of practice in information and knowledge management* (pp. 400-406). Hershey, PA: Idea Group Reference.

Smith, P.J., & Smythe, E. (2005). Citizenship and new technologies. In M. Khosrow-Pour (Ed.), *Encyclopedia of information science and technology* (pp. 414-419). Hershey, PA: Idea Group Reference.

Snowden, D. (2006). Narrative. In D. Schwartz (Ed.), *Encyclopedia of knowledge management* (pp. 678). Hershey, PA: Idea Group Reference.

Snyder, M. (2005). Changing trends in the preparation of print media. In M. Khosrow-Pour (Ed.), *Encyclopedia of information science and technology* (pp. 404-407). Hershey, PA: Idea Group Reference.

Sockel, H., & Chen, K. (2005). Internet privacy issues. In M. Pagani (Ed.), *Encyclopedia of multimedia technology and networking* (pp. 480-485). Hershey, PA: Idea Group Reference.

Sofokleous, A., Angelides, M.C., & Schizas, C. (2005). Mobile computing for m-commerce. In M. Pagani (Ed.), *Encyclopedia of multimedia technology and networking* (pp. 622-628). Hershey, PA: Idea Group Reference.

Soh, L.-K. (2006). Agent-Supported Interface for Online Tutoring. In C. Ghaoui (Ed.), *Encyclopedia of human computer interaction* (pp. 18-23). Hershey, PA: Idea Group Reference.

Soh, L.-K., & Jiang, H. (2006). Intelligent Multi-Agent Cooperative Learning System. In C. Ghaoui (Ed.), *Encyclopedia of human computer interaction* (pp. 348-354). Hershey, PA: Idea Group Reference.

Solberg, A., Oldevik, J., & Jensvoll, A. (2005). Generic framework for defining domain-specific models. In M. Khosrow-Pour (Ed.), *Encyclopedia of information science and technology* (pp. 1266-1273). Hershey, PA: Idea Group Reference.

Song, M., Song, I.-Y., Hu, X., & Han, H. (2005). Information extraction in biomedical literature. In J. Wang (Ed.), *Encyclopedia of data warehousing and mining* (pp. 615-620). Hershey, PA: Idea Group Reference.

Songan, P., Hamid, K.A., Yeo, A.W., Gnaniah, J., & Zen, H. (2005). Challenges to community informatics to bridging the digital divide. In S. Marshall, W. Taylor, & X. Yu (Eds.), *Encyclopedia of developing regional communities with information and communication technology* (pp. 85-89). Hershey, PA: Idea Group Reference.

Sonnenwald, D.H. (2005). Management of cognitive and affective trust to support collaboration. In M. Khosrow-Pour (Ed.), *Encyclopedia of information science and technology* (pp. 1864-1869). Hershey, PA: Idea Group Reference.

Sourin, A. (2006). Virtual campus of Nanyang Technological University. In S. Dasgupta (Ed.), *Encyclopedia of virtual communities and technologies* (pp. 478-481). Hershey, PA: Idea Group Reference.

Sowe, S.K., Samoladas, I., & Stamelos, I. (2005). Open source database management systems. In L. Rivero, J. Doorn, & V. Ferraggine (Eds.), *Encyclopedia of database technologies and applications* (pp. 457-462). Hershey, PA: Idea Group Reference.

Sprague, R.D. (2005). Liability for system and data quality. In M. Khosrow-Pour (Ed.), *Encyclopedia of information science and technology* (pp. 1834-1837). Hershey, PA: Idea Group Reference.

Srinivasan, V. (2006). Virtual communities' impact on politics. In S. Dasgupta (Ed.), *Encyclopedia of virtual communities and technologies* (pp. 506-510). Hershey, PA: Idea Group Reference.

St.Amant, K. (2005a). A rhetorical perspective on localization and international outsourcing. In L. Rivero, J. Doorn, & V. Ferraggine (Eds.), *Encyclopedia of database technologies and applications* (pp. 570-574). Hershey, PA: Idea Group Reference.

St.Amant, K. (2005b). Expanding e-commerce into e-ducation. In S. Marshall, W. Taylor, & X. Yu (Eds.), *Encyclopedia of developing regional communities with information and communication technology* (pp. 295-298). Hershey, PA: Idea Group Reference.

St.Amant, K. (2005c). International digital studies approach for examining international online interactions. In M. Khosrow-Pour (Ed.), *Encyclopedia of information science and technology* (pp. 1617-1622). Hershey, PA: Idea Group Reference.

St.Amant, K. (2005d). International virtual offices. In M. Pagani (Ed.), *Encyclopedia of multimedia technology and networking* (pp. 461-466). Hershey, PA: Idea Group Reference.

St.Amant, K. (2005e). Teaching culture and communication with online media. In C. Howard, J.V. Boettcher, L. Justice, K. Schenk, P.L. Rogers, & G.A. Berg (Eds.), *Encyclopedia of distance learning* (pp. 1761-1769). Hershey, PA: Idea Group Reference.

St.Amant, K. (2006a). Cyber rhetoric and online ethos. In S. Dasgupta (Ed.), *Encyclopedia of virtual communities and technologies* (pp. 105-109). Hershey, PA: Idea Group Reference.

St.Amant, K. (2006b). Grey market informatics. In S. Dasgupta (Ed.), *Encyclopedia of virtual communities and technologies* (pp. 223-227). Hershey, PA: Idea Group Reference.

St.Amant, K., & Still, B. (2005). Open source software and international outsourcing. In M. Pagani (Ed.), *Encyclopedia of multimedia technology and networking* (pp. 791-798). Hershey, PA: Idea Group Reference.

Stafford, T.F. (2005). Uses and gratifications for the World Wide Web. In M. Khosrow-Pour (Ed.), *Encyclopedia of information science and technology* (pp. 2973-2977). Hershey, PA: Idea Group Reference.

Stamoulis, D.S., Theotokis, D., & Martakos, D.I. (2005). Tailorable information systems. In M. Khosrow-Pour (Ed.), *Encyclopedia of information science and technology* (pp. 2730-2734). Hershey, PA: Idea Group Reference.

Staples, D.S., Wong, I.K., & Cameron, A.F. (2005). Best practices for effective virtual teams. In M. Khosrow-Pour (Ed.), *Encyclopedia of information science and technology* (pp. 260-265). Hershey, PA: Idea Group Reference.

Statica, R., & Deek, F.P. (2006). Topology for intelligent mobile computing. In M. Khosrow-Pour (Ed.), *Encyclopedia of e-commerce, e-government, and mobile commerce* (pp. 1070-1074). Hershey, PA: Idea Group Reference.

Stavredes, T. (2005a). Just-in-time learning. In C. Howard, J.V. Boettcher, L. Justice, K. Schenk, P.L. Rogers, & G.A. Berg (Eds.), *Encyclopedia of distance learning* (pp. 1162-1167). Hershey, PA: Idea Group Reference.

Stavredes, T. (2005b). Sharable learning objects. In C. Howard, J.V. Boettcher, L. Justice, K. Schenk, P.L. Rogers, & G.A. Berg (Eds.), *Encyclopedia of distance learning* (pp. 1607-1613). Hershey, PA: Idea Group Reference.

Steinbach, T.A., & Knight, L.V. (2005). System development for e-business. In M. Khosrow-Pour (Ed.), *Encyclopedia of information science and technology* (pp. 2712-2718). Hershey, PA: Idea Group Reference.

Sterling, L. (2006). Knowledge management agents. In D. Schwartz (Ed.), *Encyclopedia of knowledge management* (pp. 368). Hershey, PA: Idea Group Reference.

Stern, D. (2005). Schools-based community networking in Uganda. In S. Marshall, W. Taylor, & X. Yu (Eds.), *Encyclopedia of developing regional communities with information and communication technology* (pp. 628-634). Hershey, PA: Idea Group Reference.

Stern, T. (2005). Internet privacy from the individual and business perspectives. In M. Pagani (Ed.), *Encyclopedia of multimedia technology and networking* (pp. 475-479). Hershey, PA: Idea Group Reference.

Stickel, E. (2005). Public-key cryptography. In M. Khosrow-Pour (Ed.), *Encyclopedia of information science and technology* (pp. 2368-2372). Hershey, PA: Idea Group Reference.

Stodel, E.J., Farres, L.G., & MacDonald, C.J. (2005). Online mental training using WebExcellence. In C. Howard, J.V. Boettcher, L. Justice, K. Schenk, P.L. Rogers, & G.A. Berg (Eds.), *Encyclopedia of distance learning* (pp. 1390-1397). Hershey, PA: Idea Group Reference.

Stojanovic, Z., & Dahanayake, A. (2005). Component-oriented approach for designing enterprise architecture. In M. Khosrow-Pour (Ed.), *Encyclopedia of information science and technology* (pp. 481-487). Hershey, PA: Idea Group Reference.

Strauss, H. (2005). The future of teaching and learning technologies. In C. Howard, J.V. Boettcher, L. Justice, K. Schenk, P.L. Rogers, & G.A. Berg (Eds.), *Encyclopedia of distance learning* (pp. 954-959). Hershey, PA: Idea Group Reference.

Stuckenschmidt, H. (2005). Query processing for RDF data. In L. Rivero, J. Doorn, & V. Ferraggine (Eds.), *Encyclopedia of database technologies and applications* (pp. 506-510). Hershey, PA: Idea Group Reference.

Subramanian, R. (2005). Digital asset management concepts. In M. Khosrow-Pour (Ed.), *Encyclopedia of information science and technology* (pp. 864-869). Hershey, PA: Idea Group Reference.

Suh, W., & Kim, G.C. (2005). Organizational hypermedia document management through metadata. In M. Khosrow-Pour (Ed.), *Encyclopedia of information science and technology* (pp. 2236-2242). Hershey, PA: Idea Group Reference.

Sun, H., & Xiao, X. (2006). User acceptance of virtual technologies. In S. Dasgupta (Ed.), *Encyclopedia of virtual communities and technologies* (pp. 468-473). Hershey, PA: Idea Group Reference.

Sun, J. (2005). Wireless emergency services. In M. Pagani (Ed.), *Encyclopedia of multimedia technology and networking* (pp. 1096-1103). Hershey, PA: Idea Group Reference.

Sun, J., & Poole, M.S. (2005). Context-awareness in mobile commerce. In M. Pagani (Ed.), *Encyclopedia of multimedia technology and networking* (pp. 123-129). Hershey, PA: Idea Group Reference.

Sundaram, D., & Portougal, V. (2005a). Business processes. In J. Wang (Ed.), *Encyclopedia of data warehousing and mining* (pp. 118-123). Hershey, PA: Idea Group Reference.

Sundaram, D., & Portougal, V. (2005b). Intelligence density. In J. Wang (Ed.), *Encyclopedia of data warehousing and mining* (pp. 630-633). Hershey, PA: Idea Group Reference.

Suomi, R. (2005). Governance structures for IT in the health care industry. In M. Khosrow-Pour (Ed.), *Encyclopedia of information science and technology* (pp. 1305-1308). Hershey, PA: Idea Group Reference.

Suomi, R. (2006). Governing health care with IT. In M. Khosrow-Pour (Ed.), *Encyclopedia of e-commerce, e-government, and mobile commerce* (pp. 537-544). Hershey, PA: Idea Group Reference.

Sural, S., Vadivel, A., & Majumdar, A.K. (2005). Histogram generation from the HSV color space. In M. Khosrow-Pour (Ed.), *Encyclopedia of information science and technology* (pp. 1333-1337). Hershey, PA: Idea Group Reference.

Sutcliffe, K. (2005). ICT and developing social capital. In S. Marshall, W. Taylor, & X. Yu (Eds.),

*Encyclopedia of developing regional communities with information and communication technology* (pp. 337-341). Hershey, PA: Idea Group Reference.

Svensson, J.S. (2005). Legal expert systems in administrative organizations. In M. Khosrow-Pour (Ed.), *Encyclopedia of information science and technology* (pp. 1827-1830). Hershey, PA: Idea Group Reference.

Swan, K. (2005). Threaded discussion. In C. Howard, J.V. Boettcher, L. Justice, K. Schenk, P.L. Rogers, & G.A. Berg (Eds.), *Encyclopedia of distance learning* (pp. 1846-1855). Hershey, PA: Idea Group Reference.

Swierzowicz, J. (2005). Multimedia data mining concept. In M. Pagani (Ed.), *Encyclopedia of multimedia technology and networking* (pp. 696-703). Hershey, PA: Idea Group Reference.

Switala, W.J. (2005). Technology in the foreign language classroom. In M. Khosrow-Pour (Ed.), *Encyclopedia of information science and technology* (pp. 2757-2760). Hershey, PA: Idea Group Reference.

Switzer, J.S. (2005). Mentoring at a distance. In C. Howard, J.V. Boettcher, L. Justice, K. Schenk, P.L. Rogers, & G.A. Berg (Eds.), *Encyclopedia of distance learning* (pp. 1283-1287). Hershey, PA: Idea Group Reference.

Syed, M.R., Chakrobartty, S., & Bignall, R.J. (2005). Text-to-speech synthesis. In M. Pagani (Ed.), *Encyclopedia of multimedia technology and networking* (pp. 957-963). Hershey, PA: Idea Group Reference.

Syed, M.R., Nur, M.M., & Bignall, R.J. (2005). Network intrusion tracking for DoS attacks. In M. Pagani (Ed.), *Encyclopedia of multimedia technology and networking* (pp. 748-755). Hershey, PA: Idea Group Reference.

Szabados, A., & Sonwalkar, N. (2005). Type justified. In M. Pagani (Ed.), *Encyclopedia of multimedia technology and networking* (pp. 974-979). Hershey, PA: Idea Group Reference.

Szczerbicki, E. (2005). Integration framework for complex systems. In M. Khosrow-Pour (Ed.), *Encyclopedia of information science and technology* (pp. 1567-1572). Hershey, PA: Idea Group Reference.

Szewczak, E.J. (2005). Personal information privacy and Internet technology. In M. Khosrow-Pour (Ed.), *Encyclopedia of information science and technology* (pp. 2272-2276). Hershey, PA: Idea Group Reference.

Szewczak, E.J. (2006). Information privacy and e-technologies. In M. Khosrow-Pour (Ed.), *Encyclopedia of e-commerce, e-government, and mobile commerce* (pp. 615-619). Hershey, PA: Idea Group Reference.

Tahinakis, P., Mylonakis, J., Protogeros, N., & Ginoglou, D. (2006). Virtual enterprises' accounting difficulties. In M. Khosrow-Pour (Ed.), *Encyclopedia of e-commerce, e-government, and mobile commerce* (pp. 1185-1190). Hershey, PA: Idea Group Reference.

Tan, C.N.W., & Teo, T.-W. (2005). Mobile telecommunications and m-commerce applications. In M. Khosrow-Pour (Ed.), *Encyclopedia of information science and technology* (pp. 1984-1988). Hershey, PA: Idea Group Reference.

Tan, F.B., & Hunter, M.G. (2005). Cognitive research in information systems. In M. Khosrow-Pour (Ed.), *Encyclopedia of information science and technology* (pp. 439-444). Hershey, PA: Idea Group Reference.

Tan, H., & Zhang, Y. (2006). Automatic Facial Expression Analysis. In C. Ghaoui (Ed.), *Encyclopedia of human computer interaction* (pp. 60-67). Hershey, PA: Idea Group Reference.

Tan, H.B.K., & Zhao, Y. (2005a). Building empirical-based knowledge for design recovery. In J. Wang (Ed.), *Encyclopedia of data warehousing and mining* (pp. 112-117). Hershey, PA: Idea Group Reference.

Tan, H.B.K., & Zhao, Y. (2005b). Recovery of data dependencies. In J. Wang (Ed.), *Encyclopedia of data*

*warehousing and mining* (pp. 947-949). Hershey, PA: Idea Group Reference.

Tan, R.B.-N. (2005a). Evolution of data cube computational approaches. In J. Wang (Ed.), *Encyclopedia of data warehousing and mining* (pp. 469-476). Hershey, PA: Idea Group Reference.

Tan, R.B.-N. (2005b). Online analytical processing systems. In J. Wang (Ed.), *Encyclopedia of data warehousing and mining* (pp. 876-884). Hershey, PA: Idea Group Reference.

Tang, Z., & Sivaramakrishnan, S. (2005). Agent-based intelligence infrastructure. In M. Khosrow-Pour (Ed.), *Encyclopedia of information science and technology* (pp. 81-87). Hershey, PA: Idea Group Reference.

Taniar, D., Pardede, E., & Rahayu, J.W. (2005). Composition in object-relational database. In M. Khosrow-Pour (Ed.), *Encyclopedia of information science and technology* (pp. 488-494). Hershey, PA: Idea Group Reference.

Tansel, A.U. (2005). Modeling and querying temporal data. In L. Rivero, J. Doorn, & V. Ferraggine (Eds.), *Encyclopedia of database technologies and applications* (pp. 373-377). Hershey, PA: Idea Group Reference.

Tarafdar, M. (2005). ERP adoption in Indian organizations. In M. Khosrow-Pour (Ed.), *Encyclopedia of information science and technology* (pp. 1102-1107). Hershey, PA: Idea Group Reference.

Targowski, A., & Metwalli, A. (2005). Cross-culture communication. In M. Khosrow-Pour (Ed.), *Encyclopedia of information science and technology* (pp. 645-654). Hershey, PA: Idea Group Reference.

Targowski, A.S. (2005). Information laws. In M. Khosrow-Pour (Ed.), *Encyclopedia of information science and technology* (pp. 1464-1470). Hershey, PA: Idea Group Reference.

Tarnanas, I., & Kikis, V. (2005). Bridging the growing digital divide. In M. Khosrow-Pour (Ed.), *Encyclopedia of information science and technology* (pp. 284-291). Hershey, PA: Idea Group Reference.

Tassabehji, R. (2005a). Information security threats. In M. Pagani (Ed.), *Encyclopedia of multimedia technology and networking* (pp. 404-410). Hershey, PA: Idea Group Reference.

Tassabehji, R. (2005b). Principles for managing information security. In M. Pagani (Ed.), *Encyclopedia of multimedia technology and networking* (pp. 842-848). Hershey, PA: Idea Group Reference.

Tatnall, A. (2005a). Actor-network theory in information systems research. In M. Khosrow-Pour (Ed.), *Encyclopedia of information science and technology* (pp. 42-46). Hershey, PA: Idea Group Reference.

Tatnall, A. (2005b). Modelling technological change in small business. In M. Khosrow-Pour (Ed.), *Encyclopedia of information science and technology* (pp. 2007-2011). Hershey, PA: Idea Group Reference.

Tatnall, A. (2006). Web portal gateways. In M. Khosrow-Pour (Ed.), *Encyclopedia of e-commerce, e-government, and mobile commerce* (pp. 1217-1221). Hershey, PA: Idea Group Reference.

Tatnall, A., & Burgess, S. (2005). Actor-network theory and adoption of e-commerce in SMEs. In M. Khosrow-Pour (Ed.), *Encyclopedia of information science and technology* (pp. 38-41). Hershey, PA: Idea Group Reference.

Tatnall, A., & Burgess, S. (2006). Innovation translation and e-commerce in SMEs. In M. Khosrow-Pour (Ed.), *Encyclopedia of e-commerce, e-government, and mobile commerce* (pp. 631-635). Hershey, PA: Idea Group Reference.

Tatnall, A., Burgess, S., & Singh, M. (2006). Small business and regional portals in Australia. In M. Khosrow-Pour (Ed.), *Encyclopedia of e-commerce, e-government, and mobile commerce* (pp. 1016-1021). Hershey, PA: Idea Group Reference.

Tatnall, A., & Davey, B. (2005). Ecological models and information systems curriculum. In M. Khosrow-Pour (Ed.), *Encyclopedia of information science and technology* (pp. 946-950). Hershey, PA: Idea Group Reference.

Tauber, D., & Schwartz, D.G. (2006). Integrating knowledge management with the systems analysis process. In D. Schwartz (Ed.), *Encyclopedia of knowledge management* (pp. 259-266). Hershey, PA: Idea Group Reference.

Taylor, A. (2005). ICT and the tourism information marketplace in Australia. In S. Marshall, W. Taylor, & X. Yu (Eds.), *Encyclopedia of developing regional communities with information and communication technology* (pp. 360-366). Hershey, PA: Idea Group Reference.

Taylor, W., Dekkers, J., & Marshall, S. (2005). Using ICT to enable emancipatory learning. In C. Howard, J.V. Boettcher, L. Justice, K. Schenk, P.L. Rogers, & G.A. Berg (Eds.), *Encyclopedia of distance learning* (pp. 1952-1957). Hershey, PA: Idea Group Reference.

Te'eni, D. (2006). Organizational communication. In D. Schwartz (Ed.), *Encyclopedia of knowledge management* (pp. 734-740). Hershey, PA: Idea Group Reference.

Teghe, D., & Knight, B.A. (2005). Choosing online learning communities or collaborative learning. In S. Marshall, W. Taylor, & X. Yu (Eds.), *Encyclopedia of developing regional communities with information and communication technology* (pp. 90-95). Hershey, PA: Idea Group Reference.

Teigland, R., & Wasko, M. (2005). Knowledge exchange in electronic networks of practice. In M. Khosrow-Pour (Ed.), *Encyclopedia of information science and technology* (pp. 1759-1763). Hershey, PA: Idea Group Reference.

Teigland, R., & Wasko, M.M. (2006). Electronic networks of practice and communities of practice. In S. Dasgupta (Ed.), *Encyclopedia of virtual communities and technologies* (pp. 188-192). Hershey, PA: Idea Group Reference.

Terashima, N. (2005). Hyperreality. In M. Pagani (Ed.), *Encyclopedia of multimedia technology and networking* (pp. 368-374). Hershey, PA: Idea Group Reference.

Thelwall, M. (2005). Scientific Web intelligence. In J. Wang (Ed.), *Encyclopedia of data warehousing and mining* (pp. 995-999). Hershey, PA: Idea Group Reference.

Thelwall, M. (2006). Hyperlink analysis. In S. Dasgupta (Ed.), *Encyclopedia of virtual communities and technologies* (pp. 243-247). Hershey, PA: Idea Group Reference.

Theng, Y.-L. (2005). Designing hypertext and the Web. In M. Khosrow-Pour (Ed.), *Encyclopedia of information science and technology* (pp. 822-826). Hershey, PA: Idea Group Reference.

Theodoratos, D., & Simitsis, A. (2005). Materialized view selection for data warehouse design. In J. Wang (Ed.), *Encyclopedia of data warehousing and mining* (pp. 717-721). Hershey, PA: Idea Group Reference.

Theodorou, P. (2005). Business strategy, structure and IT alignment. In M. Khosrow-Pour (Ed.), *Encyclopedia of information science and technology* (pp. 356-361). Hershey, PA: Idea Group Reference.

Thomas, J., & Roda, C. (2006a). Attention Aware Systems. In C. Ghaoui (Ed.), *Encyclopedia of human computer interaction* (pp. 38-44). Hershey, PA: Idea Group Reference.

Thomas, J., & Roda, C. (2006b). Various Views on Digital Interactivity. In C. Ghaoui (Ed.), *Encyclopedia of human computer interaction* (pp. 686-691). Hershey, PA: Idea Group Reference.

Thomasian, A. (2005a). Active disks for data mining. In J. Wang (Ed.), *Encyclopedia of data warehousing and mining* (pp. 6-11). Hershey, PA: Idea Group Reference.

Thomasian, A. (2005b). Data reduction and compression in database systems. In J. Wang (Ed.), *Encyclopedia of data warehousing and mining* (pp. 307-311). Hershey, PA: Idea Group Reference.

Thompson, H. (2005). Building local capacity via scaleable Web-based services. In M. Khosrow-Pour (Ed.), *Encyclopedia of information science and technology* (pp. 312-317). Hershey, PA: Idea Group Reference.

Thuraisingham, B. (2005). Homeland security data mining and link analysis. In J. Wang (Ed.), *Encyclopedia of data warehousing and mining* (pp. 566-569). Hershey, PA: Idea Group Reference.

Tian, Y., & Stewart, C. (2006). History of e-commerce. In M. Khosrow-Pour (Ed.), *Encyclopedia of e-commerce, e-government, and mobile commerce* (pp. 559-564). Hershey, PA: Idea Group Reference.

Tininini, L. (2005a). Aggregate query rewriting in multidimensional databases. In J. Wang (Ed.), *Encyclopedia of data warehousing and mining* (pp. 28-32). Hershey, PA: Idea Group Reference.

Tininini, L. (2005b). Efficient computation of data cubes and aggregate views. In J. Wang (Ed.), *Encyclopedia of data warehousing and mining* (pp. 421-426). Hershey, PA: Idea Group Reference.

Tininini, L. (2005c). Querying multidimensional data. In M. Khosrow-Pour (Ed.), *Encyclopedia of information science and technology* (pp. 2392-2396). Hershey, PA: Idea Group Reference.

Tobar, C.M., Luís de Freitas, R., & Ricarte, I.L.M. (2006). Web design dimensions and adaptation. In M. Khosrow-Pour (Ed.), *Encyclopedia of e-commerce, e-government, and mobile commerce* (pp. 1211-1216). Hershey, PA: Idea Group Reference.

Toland, J. (2006). E-commerce in developing countries. In M. Khosrow-Pour (Ed.), *Encyclopedia of e-commerce, e-government, and mobile commerce* (pp. 308-313). Hershey, PA: Idea Group Reference.

Toland, J., Frank, J., & Schenk, K.D. (2005). Culture, interaction, and online learning. In C. Howard, J.V. Boettcher, L. Justice, K. Schenk, P.L. Rogers, & G.A. Berg (Eds.), *Encyclopedia of distance learning* (pp. 485-491). Hershey, PA: Idea Group Reference.

Toland, J., Purcell, F., & Huff, S. (2005). Electronic government in small island states. In S. Marshall, W. Taylor, & X. Yu (Eds.), *Encyclopedia of developing regional communities with information and communication technology* (pp. 269-274). Hershey, PA: Idea Group Reference.

Tong, C.K.S., & Wong, E.T.T. (2005a). Information security management in picture-archiving and communication systems for the healthcare industry. In M. Pagani (Ed.), *Encyclopedia of multimedia technology and networking* (pp. 396-403). Hershey, PA: Idea Group Reference.

Tong, C.K.S., & Wong, E.T.T. (2005b). Picture archiving and communication system in health care. In M. Pagani (Ed.), *Encyclopedia of multimedia technology and networking* (pp. 821-828). Hershey, PA: Idea Group Reference.

Torres-Coronas, T. (2005). Exploring the virtual learning environment. In C. Howard, J.V. Boettcher, L. Justice, K. Schenk, P.L. Rogers, & G.A. Berg (Eds.), *Encyclopedia of distance learning* (pp. 906-911). Hershey, PA: Idea Group Reference.

Torres-Coronas, T., & Gascó-Hernández, M. (2005). Improving virtual teams through creativity. In M. Khosrow-Pour (Ed.), *Encyclopedia of information science and technology* (pp. 1419-1424). Hershey, PA: Idea Group Reference.

Torrisi-Steele, G. (2005). Core principles of educational multimedia. In M. Pagani (Ed.), *Encyclopedia of multimedia technology and networking* (pp. 130-136). Hershey, PA: Idea Group Reference.

Trammell, A.-M. (2005). Adult illiteracy. In C. Howard, J.V. Boettcher, L. Justice, K. Schenk, P.L. Rogers, & G.A. Berg (Eds.), *Encyclopedia of distance learning* (pp. 64-71). Hershey, PA: Idea Group Reference.

Trauth, E.M. (2005a). Leapfrogging an IT sector. In M. Khosrow-Pour (Ed.), *Encyclopedia of information science and technology* (pp. 1799-1802). Hershey, PA: Idea Group Reference.

Trauth, E.M. (2005b). Qualitative methods in IS research. In M. Khosrow-Pour (Ed.), *Encyclopedia of information science and technology* (pp. 2378-2381). Hershey, PA: Idea Group Reference.

Trcek, D. (2005). E-business systems security for intelligent enterprise. In M. Khosrow-Pour (Ed.), *Encyclopedia of information science and technology* (pp. 930-933). Hershey, PA: Idea Group Reference.

Tremblay, D.-G. (2006a). Strategic objectives of CoPs and organizational learning. In E. Coakes & S. Clarke (Eds.), *Encyclopedia of communities of practice in information and knowledge management* (pp. 497-501). Hershey, PA: Idea Group Reference.

Tremblay, D.-G. (2006b). Teamwork issues in virtual teams. In E. Coakes & S. Clarke (Eds.), *Encyclopedia of communities of practice in information and knowledge management* (pp. 523-528). Hershey, PA: Idea Group Reference.

Trewin, S., & Keates, S. (2006). Computer Access for Motor-Impaired Users. In C. Ghaoui (Ed.), *Encyclopedia of human computer interaction* (pp. 92-99). Hershey, PA: Idea Group Reference.

Trossen, D., & Molenaar, E. (2005). Implementing the shared event paradigm. In M. Khosrow-Pour (Ed.), *Encyclopedia of information science and technology* (pp. 1408-1413). Hershey, PA: Idea Group Reference.

Troutt, M.D., & Long, L.K. (2005). Data mining in human resources. In J. Wang (Ed.), *Encyclopedia of data warehousing and mining* (pp. 262-267). Hershey, PA: Idea Group Reference.

Trujillo, M.F. (2005). Digital libraries and development for the illiterate. In S. Marshall, W. Taylor, & X. Yu (Eds.), *Encyclopedia of developing regional communities with information and communication technology* (pp. 188-192). Hershey, PA: Idea Group Reference.

Trusler, J., & Van Belle, J.-P. (2005). A rural multi-purpose community centre in South Africa. In S. Marshall, W. Taylor, & X. Yu (Eds.), *Encyclopedia of developing regional communities with information and communication technology* (pp. 618-623). Hershey, PA: Idea Group Reference.

Tse, P.K.C. (2006). Multimedia proxy servers. In M. Khosrow-Pour (Ed.), *Encyclopedia of e-commerce, e-government, and mobile commerce* (pp. 829-835). Hershey, PA: Idea Group Reference.

Tsekouras, G., & Roussos, G. (2006). Learning networks and service oriented architectures. In D. Schwartz (Ed.), *Encyclopedia of knowledge management* (pp. 569). Hershey, PA: Idea Group Reference.

Tsunoda, D.F., Lopes, H.S., & Vasconcelos, A.T. (2005). Web tools for molecular biological data analysis. In M. Khosrow-Pour (Ed.), *Encyclopedia of information science and technology* (pp. 3068-3073). Hershey, PA: Idea Group Reference.

Turner, E. (2006). Trust in B2B e-commerce virtual communities. In S. Dasgupta (Ed.), *Encyclopedia of virtual communities and technologies* (pp. 445-448). Hershey, PA: Idea Group Reference.

Turoff, M., Howard, C., & Discenza, R. (2005a). Innovation and technology for 21st century education. In C. Howard, J.V. Boettcher, L. Justice, K. Schenk, P.L. Rogers, & G.A. Berg (Eds.), *Encyclopedia of distance learning* (pp. 1101-1109). Hershey, PA: Idea Group Reference.

Turoff, M., Howard, C., & Discenza, R. (2005b). Technology's role in distance education. In M. Khosrow-Pour (Ed.), *Encyclopedia of information science and technology* (pp. 2777-2783). Hershey, PA: Idea Group Reference.

Twigg, C.A. (2005). Improving learning and reducing costs for online learning. In C. Howard, J.V. Boettcher, L. Justice, K. Schenk, P.L. Rogers, & G.A. Berg (Eds.), *Encyclopedia of distance learning* (pp. 1054-1060). Hershey, PA: Idea Group Reference.

Tyan, J.C. (2006). Using collaborative transportation management in global supply chain. In M. Khosrow-Pour (Ed.), *Encyclopedia of e-commerce, e-government, and mobile commerce* (pp. 1126-1132). Hershey, PA: Idea Group Reference.

Tzanis, G., Berberidis, C., & Vlahavas, I. (2005). Biological data mining. In L. Rivero, J. Doorn, & V. Ferraggine (Eds.), *Encyclopedia of database tech-*

*nologies and applications* (pp. 35-41). Hershey, PA: Idea Group Reference.

Tzouramanis, T. (2005). Benchmarking and data generation in moving objects databases. In L. Rivero, J. Doorn, & V. Ferraggine (Eds.), *Encyclopedia of database technologies and applications* (pp. 23-28). Hershey, PA: Idea Group Reference.

Udechukwu, A., Barker, K., & Alhajj, R. (2006). Knowledge extraction and sharing in external communities of practice. In E. Coakes & S. Clarke (Eds.), *Encyclopedia of communities of practice in information and knowledge management* (pp. 278-285). Hershey, PA: Idea Group Reference.

Uden, L. (2005). Multimedia instruction. In C. Howard, J.V. Boettcher, L. Justice, K. Schenk, P.L. Rogers, & G.A. Berg (Eds.), *Encyclopedia of distance learning* (pp. 1317-1324). Hershey, PA: Idea Group Reference.

Unal, O., Kaletas, E.C., Afsarmanesh, H., Yakali, H.H., & Hertzberger, L.O. (2006). Collaborative information management system for science domains. In S. Dasgupta (Ed.), *Encyclopedia of virtual communities and technologies* (pp. 36-41). Hershey, PA: Idea Group Reference.

Upadhyaya, S., Rao, H.R., & Padmanabhan, G. (2006). Secure knowledge management. In D. Schwartz (Ed.), *Encyclopedia of knowledge management* (pp. 795-801). Hershey, PA: Idea Group Reference.

Urbaczewski, A. (2005). Monitoring strategies for Internet technologies. In M. Khosrow-Pour (Ed.), *Encyclopedia of information science and technology* (pp. 2024-2029). Hershey, PA: Idea Group Reference.

Utsi, S., & Lowyck, J. (2005). Digital literacy and the position of the end-user. In M. Khosrow-Pour (Ed.), *Encyclopedia of information science and technology* (pp. 875-879). Hershey, PA: Idea Group Reference.

Vaast, E. (2005). Intranet use and the emergence of networks of practice. In M. Khosrow-Pour (Ed.), *Encyclopedia of information science and technology* (pp. 1657-1661). Hershey, PA: Idea Group Reference.

Valenti, S. (2005). Metrics for the evaluation of test delivery systems. In M. Khosrow-Pour (Ed.), *Encyclopedia of information science and technology* (pp. 1945-1948). Hershey, PA: Idea Group Reference.

Van Dyke, T.P., Nemati, H.R., & Barko, C.D. (2006). Leveraging customer data integration for effective e-CRM analytics. In M. Khosrow-Pour (Ed.), *Encyclopedia of e-commerce, e-government, and mobile commerce* (pp. 703-708). Hershey, PA: Idea Group Reference.

Vanstone, B., & Tan, C. (2005). Artificial neural networks in financial trading. In M. Khosrow-Pour (Ed.), *Encyclopedia of information science and technology* (pp. 163-167). Hershey, PA: Idea Group Reference.

Vardaki, M. (2005). Statistical metadata in data processing and interchange. In J. Wang (Ed.), *Encyclopedia of data warehousing and mining* (pp. 1048-1053). Hershey, PA: Idea Group Reference.

Vargas, J.E. (2005). Embedding bayesian networks in sensor grids. In J. Wang (Ed.), *Encyclopedia of data warehousing and mining* (pp. 427-432). Hershey, PA: Idea Group Reference.

Vargas-Solar, G. (2005). Active federated database systems. In L. Rivero, J. Doorn, & V. Ferraggine (Eds.), *Encyclopedia of database technologies and applications* (pp. 5-10). Hershey, PA: Idea Group Reference.

Vassilakis, C., & Lepouras, G. (2006). Ontology for e-government public services. In M. Khosrow-Pour (Ed.), *Encyclopedia of e-commerce, e-government, and mobile commerce* (pp. 865-870). Hershey, PA: Idea Group Reference.

Vassilakopoulos, M., & Corral, A. (2005). Spatio-temporal indexing techniques. In L. Rivero, J. Doorn, & V. Ferraggine (Eds.), *Encyclopedia of database technologies and applications* (pp. 652-657). Hershey, PA: Idea Group Reference.

Vat, K.H. (2005a). Conceiving a learning organization model for online education. In C. Howard, J.V. Boettcher, L. Justice, K. Schenk, P.L. Rogers, & G.A.

Berg (Eds.), *Encyclopedia of distance learning* (pp. 367-373). Hershey, PA: Idea Group Reference.

Vat, K.H. (2005b). Designing OMIS-based collaboration for learning organizations. In M. Khosrow-Pour (Ed.), *Encyclopedia of information science and technology* (pp. 827-830). Hershey, PA: Idea Group Reference.

Vat, K.H. (2005c). SSM-based IS support for online learning. In C. Howard, J.V. Boettcher, L. Justice, K. Schenk, P.L. Rogers, & G.A. Berg (Eds.), *Encyclopedia of distance learning* (pp. 1650-1659). Hershey, PA: Idea Group Reference.

Vat, K.H. (2006a). IS design for community of practice's knowledge challenge. In E. Coakes & S. Clarke (Eds.), *Encyclopedia of communities of practice in information and knowledge management* (pp. 246-256). Hershey, PA: Idea Group Reference.

Vat, K.H. (2006b). Virtual organizing online communities in support of knowledge synthesis. In S. Dasgupta (Ed.), *Encyclopedia of virtual communities and technologies* (pp. 547-555). Hershey, PA: Idea Group Reference.

Vatsa, M., Singh, R., Gupta, P., & Kaushik, A.K. (2005). Biometric databases. In L. Rivero, J. Doorn, & V. Ferraggine (Eds.), *Encyclopedia of database technologies and applications* (pp. 42-46). Hershey, PA: Idea Group Reference.

Veijalainen, J., & Weske, M. (2005). Surveying mobile commerce environments. In M. Khosrow-Pour (Ed.), *Encyclopedia of information science and technology* (pp. 2702-2711). Hershey, PA: Idea Group Reference.

Velibeyoglu, K. (2005). Urban information systems in Turkish local governments. In S. Marshall, W. Taylor, & X. Yu (Eds.), *Encyclopedia of developing regional communities with information and communication technology* (pp. 709-714). Hershey, PA: Idea Group Reference.

Venters, C.C., Hartley, R.J., & Hewitt, W.T. (2005). Content-based image retrieval query paradigms. In M. Khosrow-Pour (Ed.), *Encyclopedia of information*

*science and technology* (pp. 556-563). Hershey, PA: Idea Group Reference.

Verbraeck, A., Tewoldeberhan, T., & Janssen, M. (2006). E-supply chain orchestration. In M. Khosrow-Pour (Ed.), *Encyclopedia of e-commerce, e-government, and mobile commerce* (pp. 457-463). Hershey, PA: Idea Group Reference.

Verburg, R.M., Andriessen, J.H.E., & De Rooij, J.P.G. (2005). Analyzing the quality of virtual teams. In M. Khosrow-Pour (Ed.), *Encyclopedia of information science and technology* (pp. 117-122). Hershey, PA: Idea Group Reference.

Verhaart, M., & Kinshuk. (2006). A Dynamic Personal Portfolio Using Web Technologies. In C. Ghaoui (Ed.), *Encyclopedia of human computer interaction* (pp. 170-174). Hershey, PA: Idea Group Reference.

Ververidis, C., & Polyzos, G.C. (2006). Location-based services in the mobile communications industry. In M. Khosrow-Pour (Ed.), *Encyclopedia of e-commerce, e-government, and mobile commerce* (pp. 716-721). Hershey, PA: Idea Group Reference.

Vician, C., & Buche, M.W. (2005). Information technology and virtual communities. In M. Pagani (Ed.), *Encyclopedia of multimedia technology and networking* (pp. 417-423). Hershey, PA: Idea Group Reference.

Vidal-Rodeiro, C.L., Santiago-Pérez, M.I., Vázquez-Fernández, E., López-Vizcaíno, M.E., & Hervada-Vidal, X. (2005). Bayesian analysis of geographical variation in disease risk. In M. Khosrow-Pour (Ed.), *Encyclopedia of information science and technology* (pp. 222-228). Hershey, PA: Idea Group Reference.

Viertl, R. (2005). Fuzzy information and data analysis. In J. Wang (Ed.), *Encyclopedia of data warehousing and mining* (pp. 519-522). Hershey, PA: Idea Group Reference.

Viktor, H.L., & Paquet, E. (2005). Visualization techniques for data mining. In J. Wang (Ed.), *Encyclopedia of data warehousing and mining* (pp. 1190-1195). Hershey, PA: Idea Group Reference.

Villemur, T., & Drira, K. (2006). CSCW Experience for Distributed System Engineering. In C. Ghaoui (Ed.), *Encyclopedia of human computer interaction* (pp. 128-135). Hershey, PA: Idea Group Reference.

Viswanath, P., Murty, M.N., & Bhatnagar, S. (2005). Pattern synthesis for large-scale pattern recognition. In J. Wang (Ed.), *Encyclopedia of data warehousing and mining* (pp. 902-905). Hershey, PA: Idea Group Reference.

Vitolo, T.M., & Coulston, C. (2005). Simulation in information systems research. In M. Khosrow-Pour (Ed.), *Encyclopedia of information science and technology* (pp. 2508-2513). Hershey, PA: Idea Group Reference.

Vitolo, T.M., Panjala, S., & Cannell, J.C. (2005). E-learning and multimedia databases. In M. Pagani (Ed.), *Encyclopedia of multimedia technology and networking* (pp. 271-277). Hershey, PA: Idea Group Reference.

Voeth, M., & Liehr, M. (2005). Adoption of communication products and the individual critical mass. In M. Pagani (Ed.), *Encyclopedia of multimedia technology and networking* (pp. 1-7). Hershey, PA: Idea Group Reference.

Voges, K.E. (2005). Cluster analysis using rough clustering and k-means clustering. In M. Khosrow-Pour (Ed.), *Encyclopedia of information science and technology* (pp. 435-438). Hershey, PA: Idea Group Reference.

Volino, P., Di Giacomo, T., Dellas, F., & Magnenat-Thalmann, N. (2005). Integrated platform for networked and user-oriented virtual clothing. In M. Pagani (Ed.), *Encyclopedia of multimedia technology and networking* (pp. 424-427). Hershey, PA: Idea Group Reference.

von Wartburg, I. (2006). Metaphors as cognitive devices in communities of practice. In E. Coakes & S. Clarke (Eds.), *Encyclopedia of communities of practice in information and knowledge management* (pp. 386-387). Hershey, PA: Idea Group Reference.

von Wartburg, I., & Teichert, T. (2006). Leadership issues in communities of practice. In E. Coakes & S. Clarke (Eds.), *Encyclopedia of communities of practice in information and knowledge management* (pp. 317-319). Hershey, PA: Idea Group Reference.

von Wartburg, I., Teichert, T., & Rost, K. (2006). Shaping social structure in virtual communities of practice. In E. Coakes & S. Clarke (Eds.), *Encyclopedia of communities of practice in information and knowledge management* (pp. 459-465). Hershey, PA: Idea Group Reference.

Vrazalic, L., & Hyland, P.N. (2005). Measuring the maturity level of a community portal. In S. Marshall, W. Taylor, & X. Yu (Eds.), *Encyclopedia of developing regional communities with information and communication technology* (pp. 481-487). Hershey, PA: Idea Group Reference.

Vrazalic, L., MacGregor, R., & Bunker, D. (2005). Networks and electronic commerce adoption in small businesses. In M. Khosrow-Pour (Ed.), *Encyclopedia of information science and technology* (pp. 2085-2094). Hershey, PA: Idea Group Reference.

Vriens, D. (2005a). Information and communication technology tools for competitive intelligence. In M. Khosrow-Pour (Ed.), *Encyclopedia of information science and technology* (pp. 1458-1463). Hershey, PA: Idea Group Reference.

Vriens, D. (2005b). Supporting the evaluation of intelligent sources. In M. Khosrow-Pour (Ed.), *Encyclopedia of information science and technology* (pp. 2690-2695). Hershey, PA: Idea Group Reference.

Waddington, T., Aaron, B., & Sheldrick, R. (2005). Evaluation strategy for online courses. In C. Howard, J.V. Boettcher, L. Justice, K. Schenk, P.L. Rogers, & G.A. Berg (Eds.), *Encyclopedia of distance learning* (pp. 899-905). Hershey, PA: Idea Group Reference.

Walker, G.A. (2006). Building a dynamic model of community knowledge sharing. In E. Coakes & S. Clarke (Eds.), *Encyclopedia of communities of practice in information and knowledge management* (pp. 14-20). Hershey, PA: Idea Group Reference.

Walter, J.A. (2005). Hyperbolic space for interactive visualization. In J. Wang (Ed.), *Encyclopedia of data warehousing and mining* (pp. 575-581). Hershey, PA: Idea Group Reference.

Waluyo, A.B., Srinivasan, B., & Taniar, D. (2005). Data dissemination in mobile databases. In M. Khosrow-Pour (Ed.), *Encyclopedia of information science and technology* (pp. 691-697). Hershey, PA: Idea Group Reference.

Wan, K.-M., Lei, P., Chatwin, C., & Young, R. (2006). Service-oriented architecture. In M. Khosrow-Pour (Ed.), *Encyclopedia of e-commerce, e-government, and mobile commerce* (pp. 998-1002). Hershey, PA: Idea Group Reference.

Wan, Y. (2006). Comparison-shopping agents and online small business. In M. Khosrow-Pour (Ed.), *Encyclopedia of e-commerce, e-government, and mobile commerce* (pp. 129-134). Hershey, PA: Idea Group Reference.

Wang, C., Wei, K., & Kaarst-Brown, M.L. (2006). Virtual community as new marketing channel. In S. Dasgupta (Ed.), *Encyclopedia of virtual communities and technologies* (pp. 524-526). Hershey, PA: Idea Group Reference.

Wang, F. (2006). E-shoppers' perception of Web-based decision aid. In M. Khosrow-Pour (Ed.), *Encyclopedia of e-commerce, e-government, and mobile commerce* (pp. 451-456). Hershey, PA: Idea Group Reference.

Wang, F., & Forgionne, G. (2006). BSC-based framework for e-business strategy. In M. Khosrow-Pour (Ed.), *Encyclopedia of e-commerce, e-government, and mobile commerce* (pp. 64-71). Hershey, PA: Idea Group Reference.

Wang, F., & Lou, W. (2005). GIS-based accessibility measures and application. In M. Khosrow-Pour (Ed.), *Encyclopedia of information science and technology* (pp. 1284-1287). Hershey, PA: Idea Group Reference.

Wang, H., & Wang, S. (2005). Data mining with incomplete data. In J. Wang (Ed.), *Encyclopedia of data warehousing and mining* (pp. 293-296). Hershey, PA: Idea Group Reference.

Wang, J., Chen, Q., Yao, J., & Xing, R. (2006). E-commerce in Enron. In M. Khosrow-Pour (Ed.), *Encyclopedia of e-commerce, e-government, and mobile commerce* (pp. 314-318). Hershey, PA: Idea Group Reference.

Wang, J., Ding, Y., & Straub, D. (2006). Failure of Furniture.com. In M. Khosrow-Pour (Ed.), *Encyclopedia of e-commerce, e-government, and mobile commerce* (pp. 514-519). Hershey, PA: Idea Group Reference.

Wang, J., & Gwebu, K. (2006). Establishing and sustaining trust in virtual organizations. In S. Dasgupta (Ed.), *Encyclopedia of virtual communities and technologies* (pp. 198-203). Hershey, PA: Idea Group Reference.

Wang, M. (2006). Comparative shopping on agent Web sites. In M. Khosrow-Pour (Ed.), *Encyclopedia of e-commerce, e-government, and mobile commerce* (pp. 124-128). Hershey, PA: Idea Group Reference.

Wang, S., & Wang, H. (2005). Interactive visual data mining. In J. Wang (Ed.), *Encyclopedia of data warehousing and mining* (pp. 644-646). Hershey, PA: Idea Group Reference.

Wang, S.-K. (2005). Total online vs. hybrid. In C. Howard, J.V. Boettcher, L. Justice, K. Schenk, P.L. Rogers, & G.A. Berg (Eds.), *Encyclopedia of distance learning* (pp. 1856-1862). Hershey, PA: Idea Group Reference.

Wang, W. (2006). Location management and mobility modeling in wireless systems. In M. Khosrow-Pour (Ed.), *Encyclopedia of e-commerce, e-government, and mobile commerce* (pp. 709-715). Hershey, PA: Idea Group Reference.

Wang, X. (2005). Data management in three-dimensional structures. In J. Wang (Ed.), *Encyclopedia of data warehousing and mining* (pp. 228-232). Hershey, PA: Idea Group Reference.

Wang, Y., Cheng, Q., & Cheng, J. (2006). E-health security and privacy. In M. Khosrow-Pour (Ed.), *Encyclopedia of e-commerce, e-government, and mobile commerce* (pp. 385-390). Hershey, PA: Idea Group Reference.

Wang, Y., Cheng, Q., Cheng, J., & Huang, T.S. (2006). Digital rights management for e-content and e-technologies. In M. Khosrow-Pour (Ed.), *Encyclopedia of e-commerce, e-government, and mobile commerce* (pp. 210-216). Hershey, PA: Idea Group Reference.

Wang, Y.D. (2005). Trust in B2C e-commerce interface. In M. Khosrow-Pour (Ed.), *Encyclopedia of information science and technology* (pp. 2887-2891). Hershey, PA: Idea Group Reference.

Warren, L. (2006). Creating the entrepreneurial university. In E. Coakes & S. Clarke (Eds.), *Encyclopedia of communities of practice in information and knowledge management* (pp. 108-114). Hershey, PA: Idea Group Reference.

Wasko, M., & Teigland, R. (2006a). Distinguishing work groups, virtual teams, and electronic networks of practice. In E. Coakes & S. Clarke (Eds.), *Encyclopedia of communities of practice in information and knowledge management* (pp. 138-140). Hershey, PA: Idea Group Reference.

Wasko, M.M., & Teigland, R. (2006b). Examining social structure in an electronic network of practice. In S. Dasgupta (Ed.), *Encyclopedia of virtual communities and technologies* (pp. 207-212). Hershey, PA: Idea Group Reference.

Wasko, P. (2005). Implementing a statewide electronic portfolio infrastructure. In C. Howard, J.V. Boettcher, L. Justice, K. Schenk, P.L. Rogers, & G.A. Berg (Eds.), *Encyclopedia of distance learning* (pp. 1025-1032). Hershey, PA: Idea Group Reference.

Waterson, P. (2006). Motivation in online communities. In S. Dasgupta (Ed.), *Encyclopedia of virtual communities and technologies* (pp. 334-337). Hershey, PA: Idea Group Reference.

Watkins, R. (2005). E-learning study skills for online students. In C. Howard, J.V. Boettcher, L. Justice, K.

Schenk, P.L. Rogers, & G.A. Berg (Eds.), *Encyclopedia of distance learning* (pp. 794-800). Hershey, PA: Idea Group Reference.

Watson, R. (2005). IT industry success in Finland and New Zealand. In M. Khosrow-Pour (Ed.), *Encyclopedia of information science and technology* (pp. 1714-1720). Hershey, PA: Idea Group Reference.

Weber, I., & Lim, E.T.K. (2005). Selling Singapore's e-lifestyle initiative to late adopters. In S. Marshall, W. Taylor, & X. Yu (Eds.), *Encyclopedia of developing regional communities with information and communication technology* (pp. 635-639). Hershey, PA: Idea Group Reference.

Wecel, K., Abramowicz, W., & Kalczynski, P.J. (2005). Enhanced knowledge warehouse. In M. Khosrow-Pour (Ed.), *Encyclopedia of information science and technology* (pp. 1057-1063). Hershey, PA: Idea Group Reference.

Wei, C.-H., & Li, C.-T. (2005). Content-based multimedia retrieval. In M. Pagani (Ed.), *Encyclopedia of multimedia technology and networking* (pp. 116-122). Hershey, PA: Idea Group Reference.

Wei, K., & Wang, C. (2006). Virtual teams classification. In S. Dasgupta (Ed.), *Encyclopedia of virtual communities and technologies* (pp. 570-573). Hershey, PA: Idea Group Reference.

Weippl, E.R. (2006). Computer security in e-learning. In M. Khosrow-Pour (Ed.), *Encyclopedia of e-commerce, e-government, and mobile commerce* (pp. 135-140). Hershey, PA: Idea Group Reference.

Wen, J.-R. (2005a). Enhancing Web search through query log mining. In J. Wang (Ed.), *Encyclopedia of data warehousing and mining* (pp. 438-442). Hershey, PA: Idea Group Reference.

Wen, J.-R. (2005b). Enhancing Web search through Web structure mining. In J. Wang (Ed.), *Encyclopedia of data warehousing and mining* (pp. 443-447). Hershey, PA: Idea Group Reference.

Wen, Z., Hong, P., Tu, J., & Huang, T.S. (2005). Learning 3D face animation model. In M. Khosrow-

Pour (Ed.), *Encyclopedia of information science and technology* (pp. 1807-1814). Hershey, PA: Idea Group Reference.

Wenn, A. (2006a). Communities of practice for organisational learning. In E. Coakes & S. Clarke (Eds.), *Encyclopedia of communities of practice in information and knowledge management* (pp. 74-76). Hershey, PA: Idea Group Reference.

Wenn, A. (2006b). Sociotechnical theory and communities of practice. In E. Coakes & S. Clarke (Eds.), *Encyclopedia of communities of practice in information and knowledge management* (pp. 494-496). Hershey, PA: Idea Group Reference.

Werth, D. (2005). E-governement interoperability. In M. Khosrow-Pour (Ed.), *Encyclopedia of information science and technology* (pp. 985-989). Hershey, PA: Idea Group Reference.

Westin, S. (2005). Data collection methodologies for Web-based experiments. In M. Khosrow-Pour (Ed.), *Encyclopedia of information science and technology* (pp. 680-684). Hershey, PA: Idea Group Reference.

Whateley, G., Bofinger, I., & Calvo, P. (2005). New frontiers for the new Australian Institute of Music. In S. Marshall, W. Taylor, & X. Yu (Eds.), *Encyclopedia of developing regional communities with information and communication technology* (pp. 523-527). Hershey, PA: Idea Group Reference.

Wheeler, L., & Lewis-Fitzgerald, C. (2005). Building a framework for the development of RMIT learning networks. In S. Marshall, W. Taylor, & X. Yu (Eds.), *Encyclopedia of developing regional communities with information and communication technology* (pp. 47-52). Hershey, PA: Idea Group Reference.

Whiteley, D. (2006). Electronic data interchange. In M. Khosrow-Pour (Ed.), *Encyclopedia of e-commerce, e-government, and mobile commerce* (pp. 397-402). Hershey, PA: Idea Group Reference.

Whitfield, C. (2005). Andragogy. In C. Howard, J.V. Boettcher, L. Justice, K. Schenk, P.L. Rogers, & G.A. Berg (Eds.), *Encyclopedia of distance learning* (pp. 90-96). Hershey, PA: Idea Group Reference.

Whitty, M.T. (2005). Ethical implications of investigating Internet relationships. In M. Khosrow-Pour (Ed.), *Encyclopedia of information science and technology* (pp. 1116-1120). Hershey, PA: Idea Group Reference.

Whitworth, B. (2006a). Social-Technical Systems. In C. Ghaoui (Ed.), *Encyclopedia of human computer interaction* (pp. 533-541). Hershey, PA: Idea Group Reference.

Whitworth, B. (2006b). Spam as a Symptom of Electronic Communication Technologies that Ignore Social Requirements. In C. Ghaoui (Ed.), *Encyclopedia of human computer interaction* (pp. 559-566). Hershey, PA: Idea Group Reference.

Wiberg, M. (2005). "Anytime, anywhere" in the context of mobile work. In M. Khosrow-Pour (Ed.), *Encyclopedia of information science and technology* (pp. 131-134). Hershey, PA: Idea Group Reference.

Wickramasinghe, N. (2005). Incorporating the people perspective into data mining. In J. Wang (Ed.), *Encyclopedia of data warehousing and mining* (pp. 599-605). Hershey, PA: Idea Group Reference.

Wickramasinghe, N. (2006). Knowledge creation. In D. Schwartz (Ed.), *Encyclopedia of knowledge management* (pp. 326-335). Hershey, PA: Idea Group Reference.

Wickramasinghe, N., & Sharma, S.K. (2005). Knowledge discovery solutions for intelligent enterprises. In M. Khosrow-Pour (Ed.), *Encyclopedia of information science and technology* (pp. 1747-1753). Hershey, PA: Idea Group Reference.

Wieczorkowska, A.A. (2005). Automatic musical instrument sound classification. In J. Wang (Ed.), *Encyclopedia of data warehousing and mining* (pp. 83-88). Hershey, PA: Idea Group Reference.

Wieseman, K.C. (2005a). Electronic portfolios. In C. Howard, J.V. Boettcher, L. Justice, K. Schenk, P.L. Rogers, & G.A. Berg (Eds.), *Encyclopedia of distance learning* (pp. 807-813). Hershey, PA: Idea Group Reference.

Wieseman, K.C. (2005b). Preservice teachers creating electronic portfolios. In C. Howard, J.V. Boettcher, L. Justice, K. Schenk, P.L. Rogers, & G.A. Berg (Eds.), *Encyclopedia of distance learning* (pp. 1508-1515). Hershey, PA: Idea Group Reference.

Wiggins, A. (2006). EU SMEs and e-business innovation. In M. Khosrow-Pour (Ed.), *Encyclopedia of e-commerce, e-government, and mobile commerce* (pp. 464-471). Hershey, PA: Idea Group Reference.

Wijnhoven, F. (2006). Operational knowledge management. In D. Schwartz (Ed.), *Encyclopedia of knowledge management* (pp. 703-712). Hershey, PA: Idea Group Reference.

Wild, R.H. (2005). Collaborative tele-learning issues and observations. In C. Howard, J.V. Boettcher, L. Justice, K. Schenk, P.L. Rogers, & G.A. Berg (Eds.), *Encyclopedia of distance learning* (pp. 290-296). Hershey, PA: Idea Group Reference.

Wilkin, C. (2005). Evaluating IS quality as a measure of IS effectiveness. In M. Khosrow-Pour (Ed.), *Encyclopedia of information science and technology* (pp. 1130-1133). Hershey, PA: Idea Group Reference.

Williamson, A. (2005). Transforming democracy through ICT. In S. Marshall, W. Taylor, & X. Yu (Eds.), *Encyclopedia of developing regional communities with information and communication technology* (pp. 698-703). Hershey, PA: Idea Group Reference.

Williamson, A., Kennedy, D.M., DeSouza, R., & McNaught, C. (2006). Managing intellectual capital and intellectual property within software development communities of practice. In E. Coakes & S. Clarke (Eds.), *Encyclopedia of communities of practice in information and knowledge management* (pp. 364-374). Hershey, PA: Idea Group Reference.

Willis, D. (2005). E-mail and communication. In M. Khosrow-Pour (Ed.), *Encyclopedia of information science and technology* (pp. 1054-1029). Hershey, PA: Idea Group Reference.

Wilsdon, T., & Slay, J. (2005). Voice over IP for rural telecommunication provision. In S. Marshall, W. Taylor, & X. Yu (Eds.), *Encyclopedia of developing regional communities with information and communication technology* (pp. 723-728). Hershey, PA: Idea Group Reference.

Wilson, R.L., Rosen, P.A., & Al-Ahmadi, M.S. (2006a). Knowledge structure and data mining techniques. In D. Schwartz (Ed.), *Encyclopedia of knowledge management* (pp. 523). Hershey, PA: Idea Group Reference.

Wilson, R.L., Rosen, P.A., & Al-Ahmadi, M.S. (2006b). Secure knowledge discovery in databases. In D. Schwartz (Ed.), *Encyclopedia of knowledge management* (pp. 787-794). Hershey, PA: Idea Group Reference.

Windhouwer, M., & Kersten, M. (2005). Digital media warehouses. In L. Rivero, J. Doorn, & V. Ferraggine (Eds.), *Encyclopedia of database technologies and applications* (pp. 191-194). Hershey, PA: Idea Group Reference.

Winkler, W.E. (2005). Data quality in data warehouses. In J. Wang (Ed.), *Encyclopedia of data warehousing and mining* (pp. 302-306). Hershey, PA: Idea Group Reference.

Winston, E.R., & Dologite, D.G. (2005). IT implementation in small business. In M. Khosrow-Pour (Ed.), *Encyclopedia of information science and technology* (pp. 1708-1713). Hershey, PA: Idea Group Reference.

Wishart, J.M. (2005). Cognitive approaches to understanding the challenge of computer-based learning. In C. Howard, J.V. Boettcher, L. Justice, K. Schenk, P.L. Rogers, & G.A. Berg (Eds.), *Encyclopedia of distance learning* (pp. 240-244). Hershey, PA: Idea Group Reference.

Witta, E.L. (2005). Achievement in online vs. traditional classes. In C. Howard, J.V. Boettcher, L. Justice, K. Schenk, P.L. Rogers, & G.A. Berg (Eds.), *Encyclopedia of distance learning* (pp. 34-37). Hershey, PA: Idea Group Reference.

Witta, E.L., & Lee, C.-Y. (2005). Developing an online learning style instrument. In C. Howard, J.V. Boettcher, L. Justice, K. Schenk, P.L. Rogers, & G.A.

Berg (Eds.), *Encyclopedia of distance learning* (pp. 540-546). Hershey, PA: Idea Group Reference.

Wojtkowski, W. (2006). Web-enabled portals for e-business workplace. In M. Khosrow-Pour (Ed.), *Encyclopedia of e-commerce, e-government, and mobile commerce* (pp. 1248-1253). Hershey, PA: Idea Group Reference.

Wong, I.K., & Staples, D.S. (2005). Designing high performance virtual teams. In M. Khosrow-Pour (Ed.), *Encyclopedia of information science and technology* (pp. 816-821). Hershey, PA: Idea Group Reference.

Wong, R.C.-W., & Fu, A.W.-C. (2005). Association rule mining and application to MPIS. In J. Wang (Ed.), *Encyclopedia of data warehousing and mining* (pp. 65-69). Hershey, PA: Idea Group Reference.

Wong, T.T. (2005). Trust in virtual enterprises. In M. Khosrow-Pour (Ed.), *Encyclopedia of information science and technology* (pp. 2902-2909). Hershey, PA: Idea Group Reference.

Wong, T. T. (2006). ICT applications in aviation. In M. Khosrow-Pour (Ed.), *Encyclopedia of e-commerce, e-government, and mobile commerce* (pp. 573-579). Hershey, PA: Idea Group Reference.

Wong, T. T., & Chan, W.K. (2006). Internet-based marine maintenance information system. In M. Khosrow-Pour (Ed.), *Encyclopedia of e-commerce, e-government, and mobile commerce* (pp. 684-690). Hershey, PA: Idea Group Reference.

Wong-MingJi, D.J. (2005). Leadership competencies for managing global virtual teams. In M. Pagani (Ed.), *Encyclopedia of multimedia technology and networking* (pp. 519-525). Hershey, PA: Idea Group Reference.

Woodruff, E., & Nirula, L. (2005). Design research in the elementary school classroom. In C. Howard, J.V. Boettcher, L. Justice, K. Schenk, P.L. Rogers, & G.A. Berg (Eds.), *Encyclopedia of distance learning* (pp. 510-517). Hershey, PA: Idea Group Reference.

Woods, R.H., & Baker, J.D. (2005). The pedagogy of social development in online learning. In C.

Howard, J.V. Boettcher, L. Justice, K. Schenk, P.L. Rogers, & G.A. Berg (Eds.), *Encyclopedia of distance learning* (pp. 1480-1487). Hershey, PA: Idea Group Reference.

Woods, S., Poteet, S.R., Kao, A., & Quach, L. (2006). Dissemination in portals. In D. Schwartz (Ed.), *Encyclopedia of knowledge management* (pp. 115-121). Hershey, PA: Idea Group Reference.

Woolrych, A., & Hindmarch, M. (2006). Understanding and Improving Usability Inspection Methods. In C. Ghaoui (Ed.), *Encyclopedia of human computer interaction* (pp. 641-647). Hershey, PA: Idea Group Reference.

Woon, Y.-K., Ng, W.-K., & Lim, E.-P. (2005). Association rule mining. In J. Wang (Ed.), *Encyclopedia of data warehousing and mining* (pp. 59-64). Hershey, PA: Idea Group Reference.

Wright, C. (2005). Distance education delivery. In M. Pagani (Ed.), *Encyclopedia of multimedia technology and networking* (pp. 219-225). Hershey, PA: Idea Group Reference.

Wright, D. (2005). E-learning in the network marketing industry. In C. Howard, J.V. Boettcher, L. Justice, K. Schenk, P.L. Rogers, & G.A. Berg (Eds.), *Encyclopedia of distance learning* (pp. 779-785). Hershey, PA: Idea Group Reference.

Wright, G.H., & Taylor, W.A. (2005). Improving public sector service delivery through knowledge sharing. In M. Khosrow-Pour (Ed.), *Encyclopedia of information science and technology* (pp. 1414-1418). Hershey, PA: Idea Group Reference.

Wu, C.-H., & Lee, T.-Z. (2005). Material acquisitions using discovery informatics approach. In J. Wang (Ed.), *Encyclopedia of data warehousing and mining* (pp. 705-709). Hershey, PA: Idea Group Reference.

Wu, M.-H., & Chen, H.-Y. (2005). Adaptive Web-based learning framework. In C. Howard, J.V. Boettcher, L. Justice, K. Schenk, P.L. Rogers, & G.A. Berg (Eds.), *Encyclopedia of distance learning* (pp. 44-52). Hershey, PA: Idea Group Reference.

Xenos, M. (2006). Software metrics and measurements. In M. Khosrow-Pour (Ed.), *Encyclopedia of e-commerce, e-government, and mobile commerce* (pp. 1029-1034). Hershey, PA: Idea Group Reference.

Xiang, Y. (2005). Pseudo independent models. In J. Wang (Ed.), *Encyclopedia of data warehousing and mining* (pp. 935-940). Hershey, PA: Idea Group Reference.

Xodo, D. (2005). Multiparticipant decision making and balanced scorecard collaborative. In L. Rivero, J. Doorn, & V. Ferraggine (Eds.), *Encyclopedia of database technologies and applications* (pp. 395-402). Hershey, PA: Idea Group Reference.

Xodo, D., & Nigro, O. (2005). Knowledge management in tourism. In L. Rivero, J. Doorn, & V. Ferraggine (Eds.), *Encyclopedia of database technologies and applications* (pp. 319-329). Hershey, PA: Idea Group Reference.

Xu, D., & Wang, H. (2006). Integration of knowledge management and e-learning. In D. Schwartz (Ed.), *Encyclopedia of knowledge management* (pp. 267-273). Hershey, PA: Idea Group Reference.

Xu, J. (2006). Mobile caching for location-based services. In M. Khosrow-Pour (Ed.), *Encyclopedia of e-commerce, e-government, and mobile commerce* (pp. 760-765). Hershey, PA: Idea Group Reference.

Xu, Y., & Korba, L. (2005). Building trust for interactive e-learning. In C. Howard, J.V. Boettcher, L. Justice, K. Schenk, P.L. Rogers, & G.A. Berg (Eds.), *Encyclopedia of distance learning* (pp. 192-195). Hershey, PA: Idea Group Reference.

Xu, Z., John, D., & Boucouvalas, A.C. (2006a). Fuzzy Logic Usage in Emotion Communication of Human Machine Interaction. In C. Ghaoui (Ed.), *Encyclopedia of human computer interaction* (pp. 227-233). Hershey, PA: Idea Group Reference.

Xu, Z., John, D., & Boucouvalas, A.C. (2006b). Social Factors and Interface Design Guidelines. In C. Ghaoui (Ed.), *Encyclopedia of human computer interaction* (pp. 523-532). Hershey, PA: Idea Group Reference.

Xu, Z., John, D., & Boucouvalas, A.C. (2006c). The Influence of Expressive Images for Computer Interaction. In C. Ghaoui (Ed.), *Encyclopedia of human computer interaction* (pp. 324-331). Hershey, PA: Idea Group Reference.

Yamazaki, H. (2006). Open collectivism and knowledge communities in Japan. In E. Coakes & S. Clarke (Eds.), *Encyclopedia of communities of practice in information and knowledge management* (pp. 397-399). Hershey, PA: Idea Group Reference.

Yang, C.-c. (2005). Wireless technologies in education. In C. Howard, J.V. Boettcher, L. Justice, K. Schenk, P.L. Rogers, & G.A. Berg (Eds.), *Encyclopedia of distance learning* (pp. 2051-2055). Hershey, PA: Idea Group Reference.

Yang, H.-C., & Lee, C.-H. (2005). Topic maps generation by text mining. In J. Wang (Ed.), *Encyclopedia of data warehousing and mining* (pp. 1130-1134). Hershey, PA: Idea Group Reference.

Yang, Y., & Webb, G.I. (2005). Discretization for data mining. In J. Wang (Ed.), *Encyclopedia of data warehousing and mining* (pp. 392-396). Hershey, PA: Idea Group Reference.

Yang, Z., Yang, Y., Gu, Y., & Gay, R. (2005a). Integrated-services architecture for Internet multimedia applications. In M. Khosrow-Pour (Ed.), *Encyclopedia of information science and technology* (pp. 1549-1554). Hershey, PA: Idea Group Reference.

Yang, Z., Yang, Y., Gu, Y., & Gay, R. (2005b). Isochronous distributed multimedia synchronization. In M. Khosrow-Pour (Ed.), *Encyclopedia of information science and technology* (pp. 1679-1684). Hershey, PA: Idea Group Reference.

Yaniv, E., & Schwartz, D.G. (2006). Organizational attention. In D. Schwartz (Ed.), *Encyclopedia of knowledge management* (pp. 728-733). Hershey, PA: Idea Group Reference.

Yao, J.E., Liu, C., Chen, Q., & Lu, J. (2005). Administering and managing a data warehouse. In J. Wang

(Ed.), *Encyclopedia of data warehousing and mining* (pp. 17-22). Hershey, PA: Idea Group Reference.

Yao, J.-F., & Xiao, Y. (2005). Traversal pattern mining in Web usage data. In M. Khosrow-Pour (Ed.), *Encyclopedia of information science and technology* (pp. 2857-2860). Hershey, PA: Idea Group Reference.

Yao, Y., & Zhao, Y. (2005). Explanation-oriented data mining. In J. Wang (Ed.), *Encyclopedia of data warehousing and mining* (pp. 492-497). Hershey, PA: Idea Group Reference.

Yee, G., & Korba, L. (2006). Semi-automated seeding of personal privacy policies in e-services. In M. Khosrow-Pour (Ed.), *Encyclopedia of e-commerce, e-government, and mobile commerce* (pp. 985-992). Hershey, PA: Idea Group Reference.

Yen, V. (2005). Business process and workflow modeling in Web services. In M. Khosrow-Pour (Ed.), *Encyclopedia of information science and technology* (pp. 345-349). Hershey, PA: Idea Group Reference.

Yeo, A.C. (2005). Neural networks for automobile insurance customers. In M. Khosrow-Pour (Ed.), *Encyclopedia of information science and technology* (pp. 2095-2099). Hershey, PA: Idea Group Reference.

Yeo, A.Y.C., & Chiam, M.K.M. (2006). E-customer loyalty. In M. Khosrow-Pour (Ed.), *Encyclopedia of e-commerce, e-government, and mobile commerce* (pp. 334-339). Hershey, PA: Idea Group Reference.

Yigitcanlar, T., & Baum, S. (2006a). Benchmarking local e-government. In M. Khosrow-Pour (Ed.), *Encyclopedia of e-commerce, e-government, and mobile commerce* (pp. 37-42). Hershey, PA: Idea Group Reference.

Yigitcanlar, T., & Baum, S. (2006b). E-government and the digital divide. In M. Khosrow-Pour (Ed.), *Encyclopedia of e-commerce, e-government, and mobile commerce* (pp. 353-358). Hershey, PA: Idea Group Reference.

Yong, S.-T. (2005). Usability. In C. Howard, J.V. Boettcher, L. Justice, K. Schenk, P.L. Rogers, & G.A.

Berg (Eds.), *Encyclopedia of distance learning* (pp. 1931-1937). Hershey, PA: Idea Group Reference.

Yong, S.-T., & Choo, Y.-H. (2005). Computer animation. In C. Howard, J.V. Boettcher, L. Justice, K. Schenk, P.L. Rogers, & G.A. Berg (Eds.), *Encyclopedia of distance learning* (pp. 323-330). Hershey, PA: Idea Group Reference.

Yoon, V.Y., Aiken, P., & Guimaraes, T. (2005). Applying a metadata framework to improve data quality. In M. Khosrow-Pour (Ed.), *Encyclopedia of information science and technology* (pp. 146-151). Hershey, PA: Idea Group Reference.

Youn, S., & McLeod, D. (2006). Ontology development tools for ontology-based knowledge management. In M. Khosrow-Pour (Ed.), *Encyclopedia of e-commerce, e-government, and mobile commerce* (pp. 858-864). Hershey, PA: Idea Group Reference.

Yow, K.C., & Mittal, N. (2006). Mobile commerce multimedia messaging peer. In M. Khosrow-Pour (Ed.), *Encyclopedia of e-commerce, e-government, and mobile commerce* (pp. 779-785). Hershey, PA: Idea Group Reference.

Yow, K.C., & Moertiyoso, N.N. (2005). Java 2 micro edition for wireless enterprose. In M. Khosrow-Pour (Ed.), *Encyclopedia of information science and technology* (pp. 1735-1741). Hershey, PA: Idea Group Reference.

Yu, H. (2005a). Web accessibility and the law. In M. Khosrow-Pour (Ed.), *Encyclopedia of information science and technology* (pp. 3042-3047). Hershey, PA: Idea Group Reference.

Yu, H. (2005b). Web accessibility laws and issues. In C. Howard, J.V. Boettcher, L. Justice, K. Schenk, P.L. Rogers, & G.A. Berg (Eds.), *Encyclopedia of distance learning* (pp. 1990-1996). Hershey, PA: Idea Group Reference.

Yu, L., & Liu, H. (2005). Data mining methods for microarray data analysis. In J. Wang (Ed.), *Encyclopedia of data warehousing and mining* (pp. 283-287). Hershey, PA: Idea Group Reference.

Zaharias, P. (2005). E-learning design quality. In C. Howard, J.V. Boettcher, L. Justice, K. Schenk, P.L. Rogers, & G.A. Berg (Eds.), *Encyclopedia of distance learning* (pp. 763-771). Hershey, PA: Idea Group Reference.

Zakaria, N., & Yusof, S.A.M. (2005). The dynamics of virtual teams. In M. Pagani (Ed.), *Encyclopedia of multimedia technology and networking* (pp. 233-241). Hershey, PA: Idea Group Reference.

Zaphiris, P., & Kurniawan, S. (2005). Challenges and opportunities of computer-based learning for senior citizens. In C. Howard, J.V. Boettcher, L. Justice, K. Schenk, P.L. Rogers, & G.A. Berg (Eds.), *Encyclopedia of distance learning* (pp. 204-210). Hershey, PA: Idea Group Reference.

Zaphiris, P., Laghos, A., & Zacharia, G. (2005). Distributed construction through participatory design. In M. Khosrow-Pour (Ed.), *Encyclopedia of information science and technology* (pp. 902-906). Hershey, PA: Idea Group Reference.

Zaphiris, P., & Zacharia, G. (2005). Participatory design of interactive computer-based learning systems. In C. Howard, J.V. Boettcher, L. Justice, K. Schenk, P.L. Rogers, & G.A. Berg (Eds.), *Encyclopedia of distance learning* (pp. 1460-1466). Hershey, PA: Idea Group Reference.

Zappavigna, M.S. (2006). Tacit knowledge in communities of practice. In E. Coakes & S. Clarke (Eds.), *Encyclopedia of communities of practice in information and knowledge management* (pp. 508-513). Hershey, PA: Idea Group Reference.

Zappavigna-Lee, M., & Patrick, J. (2005). Tactic knowledge and discourse analysis. In M. Khosrow-Pour (Ed.), *Encyclopedia of information science and technology* (pp. 2724-2729). Hershey, PA: Idea Group Reference.

Zarri, G.P. (2005a). Ontologies and their practical implementation. In L. Rivero, J. Doorn, & V. Ferraggine (Eds.), *Encyclopedia of database technologies and applications* (pp. 438-449). Hershey, PA: Idea Group Reference.

Zarri, G.P. (2005b). Using semantic Web tools for ontologies construction. In L. Rivero, J. Doorn, & V. Ferraggine (Eds.), *Encyclopedia of database technologies and applications* (pp. 720-728). Hershey, PA: Idea Group Reference.

Zarri, G.P. (2006a). Knowledge representation. In D. Schwartz (Ed.), *Encyclopedia of knowledge management* (pp. 467). Hershey, PA: Idea Group Reference.

Zarri, G.P. (2006b). RDF and OWL. In D. Schwartz (Ed.), *Encyclopedia of knowledge management* (pp. 769-779). Hershey, PA: Idea Group Reference.

Zarri, G.P. (2006c). Representation languages for narrative documents. In D. Schwartz (Ed.), *Encyclopedia of knowledge management* (pp. 780-786). Hershey, PA: Idea Group Reference.

Zboralski, K., & Gemünden, H.G. (2006). The impact of communities of practice. In E. Coakes & S. Clarke (Eds.), *Encyclopedia of communities of practice in information and knowledge management* (pp. 218-223). Hershey, PA: Idea Group Reference.

Zelasco, J.F., Porta, G., & Ausinaga, J.L.F. (2005). Geometric quality in geographic information. In L. Rivero, J. Doorn, & V. Ferraggine (Eds.), *Encyclopedia of database technologies and applications* (pp. 266-270). Hershey, PA: Idea Group Reference.

Zeleznikow, J. (2006). Legal knowledge management. In D. Schwartz (Ed.), *Encyclopedia of knowledge management* (pp. 578). Hershey, PA: Idea Group Reference.

Zender, A. (2006). How an association evolved using communities of practice. In S. Dasgupta (Ed.), *Encyclopedia of virtual communities and technologies* (pp. 232-237). Hershey, PA: Idea Group Reference.

Zendulka, J. (2005a). API standardization efforts for data mining. In J. Wang (Ed.), *Encyclopedia of data warehousing and mining* (pp. 39-43). Hershey, PA: Idea Group Reference.

Zendulka, J. (2005b). Object-relational modeling in the UML. In L. Rivero, J. Doorn, & V. Ferraggine

(Eds.), *Encyclopedia of database technologies and applications* (pp. 421-426). Hershey, PA: Idea Group Reference.

Zendulka, J. (2005c). Using standard APIs for data mining in prediction. In J. Wang (Ed.), *Encyclopedia of data warehousing and mining* (pp. 1171-1174). Hershey, PA: Idea Group Reference.

Zhang, B. (2005). Center-based clustering and regression clustering. In J. Wang (Ed.), *Encyclopedia of data warehousing and mining* (pp. 134-140). Hershey, PA: Idea Group Reference.

Zhang, G.P. (2005). Neural networks for retail sales forecasting. In M. Khosrow-Pour (Ed.), *Encyclopedia of information science and technology* (pp. 2100-2104). Hershey, PA: Idea Group Reference.

Zhang, Q. (2006). Web services and virtual communities. In S. Dasgupta (Ed.), *Encyclopedia of virtual communities and technologies* (pp. 578-583). Hershey, PA: Idea Group Reference.

Zhang, R. (2005). Knowledge management on the Web. In M. Khosrow-Pour (Ed.), *Encyclopedia of information science and technology* (pp. 1771-1777). Hershey, PA: Idea Group Reference.

Zhang, S., & Zhang, C. (2005). Group pattern discovery systems for multiple data sources. In J. Wang (Ed.), *Encyclopedia of data warehousing and mining* (pp. 546-549). Hershey, PA: Idea Group Reference.

Zhang, Y., & Chen, Z. (2005). Service mechanism quality for enhanced mobile multimedia database query processing. In L. Rivero, J. Doorn, & V. Ferraggine (Eds.), *Encyclopedia of database technologies and applications* (pp. 619-623). Hershey, PA: Idea Group Reference.

Zhang, Y.J. (2005a). Better use of digital images in teaching and learning. In C. Howard, J.V. Boettcher, L. Justice, K. Schenk, P.L. Rogers, & G.A. Berg (Eds.), *Encyclopedia of distance learning* (pp. 152-158). Hershey, PA: Idea Group Reference.

Zhang, Y.J. (2005b). Important design considerations for online Web courses. In C. Howard, J.V. Boettcher,

L. Justice, K. Schenk, P.L. Rogers, & G.A. Berg (Eds.), *Encyclopedia of distance learning* (pp. 1042-1047). Hershey, PA: Idea Group Reference.

Zhang, Y.-J. (2005a). Advanced techniques for object-based image retrieval. In M. Khosrow-Pour (Ed.), *Encyclopedia of information science and technology* (pp. 68-73). Hershey, PA: Idea Group Reference.

Zhang, Y.-J. (2005b). Mining for image classification based on feature elements. In J. Wang (Ed.), *Encyclopedia of data warehousing and mining* (pp. 773-778). Hershey, PA: Idea Group Reference.

Zhang, Y.-J. (2005c). New advancements in image segmentation for CBIR. In M. Khosrow-Pour (Ed.), *Encyclopedia of information science and technology* (pp. 2105-2109). Hershey, PA: Idea Group Reference.

Zhao, F. (2005). The impact of IT on business partnerships and organizational structures. In M. Khosrow-Pour (Ed.), *Encyclopedia of information science and technology* (pp. 2809-2814). Hershey, PA: Idea Group Reference.

Zhao, L., & Deek, F.P. (2005). Open source software development model. In M. Khosrow-Pour (Ed.), *Encyclopedia of information science and technology* (pp. 2221-2224). Hershey, PA: Idea Group Reference.

Zhao, Q., & Bhowmick, S.S. (2005). Mining historical XML. In J. Wang (Ed.), *Encyclopedia of data warehousing and mining* (pp. 800-804). Hershey, PA: Idea Group Reference.

Zhao, W. Moser, L.E., & Melliar-Smith, P.M. (2006). High availability and data consistency for three-tier enterprise applications. In M. Khosrow-Pour (Ed.), *Encyclopedia of e-commerce, e-government, and mobile commerce* (pp. 552-558). Hershey, PA: Idea Group Reference.

Zhou, S., & Wang, K. (2005). Profit mining. In J. Wang (Ed.), *Encyclopedia of data warehousing and mining* (pp. 930-934). Hershey, PA: Idea Group Reference.

Zhou, Z.-H. (2005). Comprehensibility of data mining algorithms. In J. Wang (Ed.), *Encyclopedia of data*

*warehousing and mining* (pp. 190-195). Hershey, PA: Idea Group Reference.

Zhu, D. (2005). Reinforcing CRM with data mining. In J. Wang (Ed.), *Encyclopedia of data warehousing and mining* (pp. 950-954). Hershey, PA: Idea Group Reference.

Zou, Q., & Chu, W. (2005). Mining frequent patterns via pattern decomposition. In J. Wang (Ed.), *Encyclopedia of data warehousing and mining* (pp. 790-794). Hershey, PA: Idea Group Reference.

Zwitserloot, R., & Pantic, M. (2005). Agent frameworks. In M. Pagani (Ed.), *Encyclopedia of multimedia technology and networking* (pp. 15-21). Hershey, PA: Idea Group Reference.

Zyngier, S. (2006). Knowledge management governance. In D. Schwartz (Ed.), *Encyclopedia of knowledge management* (pp. 373). Hershey, PA: Idea Group Reference.